'This is a welcome and timely contribution to the interdisciplinary space that has long existed between the fields of Economic Geography and International Business. It brings together leading scholars from both disciplines in a wide-ranging volume that is sure to be essential reading for anyone interested in the many theoretical and empirical intersections that span these fields.'

—Professor Andrew Jones, Vice-President (Research and Enterprise), City, University of London, UK

'This comprehensive volume shows that International Business and Economic Geography are cognate, linked and complementary fields of endeavour. An outstanding list of authors provides a compelling guide to the synergies between these two research fields and the mutual benefits that cooperation across the subjects can bring. This results in a strong research agenda for the future.'

—Professor Peter J. Buckley OBE, FBA, Centre for International Business University of Leeds (CIBUL), UK

'This Companion decidedly shows how the disciplines of Economic Geography and International Business can and should engage with each other. An excellent collection of works by an array of authors, from household names to younger talent, from across the world.'

—Gabriel R.G. Benito, BI Norwegian Business School, Norway

To Juliette

THE ROUTLEDGE COMPANION TO THE GEOGRAPHY OF INTERNATIONAL BUSINESS

The fields of Economic Geography and International Business share an interest in the same phenomena, whilst each provides both a differing perspective and different research methods in attempting to understand those phenomena.

The Routledge Companion to the Geography of International Business explores the nature and scope of inter-disciplinary work between Economic Geography and International Business in explaining the central issues in the international economy. Contributions written by leading specialists in each field (including some chapters written by inter-disciplinary teams) focus on the nature of multinational firms and their strategies, where they choose to locate their activities, how they create and manage international networks and the key relationships between multinationals and the places where they place their operations. Topics covered include the internationalisation of service industries, the influence of location on the competitiveness of firms and the economic dynamism of regions and where economic activity takes place and how knowledge, goods and services flow between locations.

The book examines the areas for fruitful inter-disciplinary work between International Business and Economic Geography and sets out a road map for future joint research, and is an essential resource for students and practitioners of International Business and Economic Development.

Gary Cook is Professor of Economics and Head of School at the Hull University Business School. He gained his PhD in Industrial Economics from Manchester Business School. He has published many articles and book chapters in the area of clustering, innovation and multinational enterprise.

Jennifer Johns is a Senior Lecturer in International Business at the University of Liverpool Management School. She works on globalisation, the agglomeration of economic activities, entrepreneurship and innovation and global trade and production networks. Her latest project examines the impacts of additive manufacturing on global production networks.

Frank McDonald is Professor of International Business, University of Leeds Business School, and Author/Editor of 14 books and about 60 articles.

Jonathan Beaverstock is Professor of International Management at the University of Bristol, UK. Previously, he has held Professorships at the University of Nottingham and Loughborough University (both in the UK). He's published widely across the social sciences in leading international journals like the *Journal of Economic Geography*, *Environment and Planning A* and *Regional Studies*. He is a Fellow of the Academy of Social Sciences and Fellow of the Royal Society of Arts.

Naresh Pandit is Professor of International Business at Norwich Business School, University of East Anglia. His research focuses on the interface between International Business, Economic Geography and Economics. It has been funded by 12 grants and has produced 71 journal papers and book chapters.

ROUTLEDGE COMPANIONS IN BUSINESS, MANAGEMENT AND ACCOUNTING

Routledge Companions in Business, Management and Accounting are prestige reference works providing an overview of a whole subject area or sub-discipline. These books survey the state of the discipline including emerging and cutting edge areas. Providing a comprehensive, up to date, definitive work of reference, Routledge Companions can be cited as an authoritative source on the subject.

A key aspect of these Routledge Companions is their international scope and relevance. Edited by an array of highly regarded scholars, these volumes also benefit from teams of contributors which reflect an international range of perspectives.

Individually, Routledge Companions in Business, Management and Accounting provide an impactful one-stop-shop resource for each theme covered. Collectively, they represent a comprehensive learning and research resource for researchers, postgraduate students and practitioners.

Published titles in this series include:

THE ROUTLEDGE COMPANION TO TRUST
Edited by Rosalind Searle, Ann-Marie Nienaber and Sim Sitkin

THE ROUTLEDGE COMPANION TO TAX AVOIDANCE RESEARCH
Edited by Nigar Hashimzade and Yuliya Epifantseva

THE ROUTLEDGE COMPANION TO INTELLECTUAL CAPITAL
Edited by James Guthrie, John Dumay, Federica Ricceri and Christian Neilsen

THE ROUTLEDGE COMPANION TO BEHAVIOURAL ACCOUNTING RESEARCH
Edited by Theresa Libby and Linda Thorne

THE ROUTLEDGE COMPANION TO ACCOUNTING INFORMATION SYSTEMS
Edited by Martin Quinn and Erik Strauss

THE ROUTLEDGE COMPANION TO THE GEOGRAPHY OF INTERNATIONAL BUSINESS
Edited by Gary Cook, Jennifer Johns, Frank McDonald, Jonathan Beaverstock and Naresh Pandit

THE ROUTLEDGE COMPANION TO THE GEOGRAPHY OF INTERNATIONAL BUSINESS

Edited by Gary Cook, Jennifer Johns, Frank McDonald, Jonathan Beaverstock and Naresh Pandit

Routledge
Taylor & Francis Group
LONDON AND NEW YORK

First published 2018
by Routledge
2 Park Square, Milton Park, Abingdon, Oxon OX14 4RN

and by Routledge
711 Third Avenue, New York, NY 10017

Routledge is an imprint of the Taylor & Francis Group, an informa business

British Library Cataloguing-in-Publication Data
A catalogue record for this book is available from the British Library

Library of Congress Cataloging-in-Publication Data
Names: Beaverstock, Jonathan V., editor. | Cook, Gary, 1961- editor. | Johns, Jennifer (Economic geographer) editor.
Title: The Routledge companion to the geography of International Business / edited by Jonathan Beaverstock, Gary Cook, Jennifer Johns, Frank McDonald and Naresh Pandit.
Description: First Edition. | New York : Routledge, 2018. | Series: Routledge companions in business, management & accounting | Includes bibliographical references and index.
Identifiers: LCCN 2017046182| ISBN 9781138953345 (hardback) | ISBN 9781315667379 (ebook)
Subjects: LCSH: Economic geography. | International trade. | International economic relations.
Classification: LCC HF1025 .R678 2018 | DDC 338.88—dc23
LC record available at https://lccn.loc.gov/2017046182

ISBN: 978-1-138-95334-5 (hbk)
ISBN: 978-1-315-66737-9 (ebk)

Typeset in Bembo
by Swales & Willis Ltd, Exeter, Devon, UK

MIX
Paper from
responsible sources
FSC® C013056

Printed and bound in Great Britain by
TJ International Ltd, Padstow, Cornwall

CONTENTS

List of figures *xi*
List of tables *xiii*
Notes on contributors *xv*

1 Introduction to the Companion 1
Gary Cook, Frank McDonald, Jennifer Johns, Jonathan Beaverstock and Naresh Pandit

PART I
Some core material in International Business **25**

2 Space and International Business 27
Steven Brakman and Charles van Marrewijk

3 Networks and alliances 43
Keith W. Glaister

4 Outsourcing, offshoring and the global factory 60
Roger Strange and Giovanna Magnani

5 The regional MNE and coordination of MNE organizational structures 78
Quyen T.K. Nguyen

6 The dynamics of multinational enterprise subsidiary roles in an era of regionalization 94
Alain Verbeke and Wenlong Yuan

PART II
Some core material in Economic Geography **113**

7 The current research programme in Economic Geography 115
Trevor J. Barnes and Eric Sheppard

8 Evolutionary Economic Geography: an emerging field or framework? 129
David L. Rigby

9 Global production networks 147
Neil M. Coe

10 The relational turn in Economic Geography 161
James T. Murphy

PART III
The interface between Economic Geography and International Business **175**

11 Economic Geography and International Business 177
Henry Wai-chung Yeung

12 Toward a synthesis of micro and macro factors that influence foreign direct investment location choice 190
Bo Nielsen, Christian Asmussen and Anthony Goerzen

13 The region in International Business and Economic Geography 213
Crispian Fuller

14 Cities and International Business: insights from cross-disciplinary perspectives 227
Gary Cook and Naresh Pandit

15 Strategic cities within global urban networks 242
Ben Derudder, Peter J. Taylor, James Faulconbridge, Michael Hoyler and Pengfei Ni

16 The use of global value chain/global production network related literature in International Business research: investigating the nature and degree of integration 258
Noemi Sinkovics, Rudolf R. Sinkovics, Samia Ferdous Hoque and Matthew Alford

17 The firm as a differentiated network and Economic Geography 297
Jens Gammelgaard and Frank McDonald

PART IV
Key research at the interface of International Business and Economic Geography **315**

18 Corporate learning and knowledge flows: from glass pipelines to dark pools 317
Philip Cooke

19 International knowledge transfer 332
Yan Wu and Yong Yang

20 Capital projects and infrastructure in urban and economic development 345
Phillip O'Neill

21 Stepping out of the comfort zone? An examination of regional orientation in emerging-economy MNEs' cross-border M&As 358
Yoo Jung Ha, Yingqi Wei and Yaoan Wu

22 The effect of location on entrepreneurship 375
Tarun Kanti Bose, Pavlos Dimitratos and Frank McDonald

23 Language and the development of trade networks in Early Modern Europe: modern reflexes, unexpected consequences 394
Sierk Horn and Nigel Holden

24 Foreign direct investment motivated by institution shopping 410
Mike W. Peng and Young H. Jung

PART V
Location and competitiveness **425**

25 Multinational performance and the geography of FDI: issues of embeddedness, strategic fit and the dimensions of distance 427
Ioana R. Bedreaga, Raquel Ortega Argilés and Philip McCann

26 The competitiveness of location in International Business and Economic Geography 441
Philippe Gugler

27 The changing geography of innovation and the multinational enterprise 454
Davide Castellani

PART VI
Services, International Business and Economic Geography **475**

28 An Economic Geography of globalizing retail: emergence, characteristics, contribution 477
Neil Wrigley and Steve Wood

29 Innovation, market segmentation and entrepreneurship in services: the case of the hotel industry 493
Jeremy Howells and Michelle Lowe

30 The internationalization of producer services 509
Sharmistha Bagchi-Sen and Torsten Schunder

31 Designed here, re-designed there but made somewhere else: geography, translocal business and the exploitation of difference 529
John R. Bryson

32 The culture of finance 543
Gordon L. Clark

33 The internationalization and localization of professional services: the case of executive search firms in Australia 564
Jonathan Beaverstock and William S. Harvey

PART VII
Epilogue **579**

34 Epilogue 581
Gary Cook

Index *595*

FIGURES

2.1	Exporting activities in different sectors; USA, 2007	29
2.2	Exporter premia in percent; USA, 2007	30
2.3	Export distribution by product and country; USA, 2007	31
2.4	USA total and related party imports and exports, 2002–2014	32
2.5	Global trade flows and value-added over gross trade ratio, 1995–2009	33
2.6	Backward and forward linkages in value-added trade	35
2.7	Backward and forward linkages, 2011	36
2.8	Sum of backward and forward linkages in 1995 and 2011	37
2.9	Sustain points and break point (Tomahawk diagram)	39
2.10	Global intra- and inter-regional trade flows, percent of total	40
6.1	The impact of regional integration on the dynamics of subsidiary roles	96
6.2	Patterns of subsidiary dynamics in an era of regional integration	99
6.3	A Penrosean perspective of subsidiary evolution	107
10.1	The constitutive features of practices	169
12.1	Percentage of studies applying particular theoretical approaches	203
16.1	The nature of integration of IB and GVC/GPN literatures	285
16.2	Authors' number and disciplinary areas	290
17.1	Geographical factors and the development of competitive advantages	305
17.2	The evolution of net benefits from internationalization	307
24.1	FDI in tax havens	411
24.2	Conceptual framework of FDI	411
27.1	Number of regions with a least one patent, 1980–2011	460
27.2	Average number of patents per region, 1980–2011	460
27.3	Regional concentration of patents, 1980–1984	461
27.4	Regional concentration of patents, 2006–2011	461

27.5 Box-plot of number of patents per million inhabitants per region, 1980–2011 462
27.6 Kernel density of the regional distribution of patents per million inhabitants, 1980–2011 (five-year intervals) 463
27.7 Time varying coefficients of the persistence in regional patenting activity, OLS estimates (with country fixed effects) 465
27.8 Time varying coefficients of the persistence in regional patenting activity, within-group estimates 466
27.9 Box-plot of the propensity to co-patent, by location of the co-inventor, 1980–2011 (five-year periods) 467
27.10 Kernel density of the regional propensity to co-patent with foreign co-inventors, 1980–2011 (five-year intervals) 467
27.11 Concentration of cross-border investment projects by city, 2003–2014 470
28.1 Dimensions of the territorial embeddedness of retail MNCs 482
29.1 Innovation trajectory of differentiation and segmentation in the hotel industry 498
29.2 Innovation trajectories of UK boutique and shabby chic hotel diaspora 502
32.1 Contractual relationships between asset owners and asset managers 553
32.2 Competition for talent in the investment management industry 555

TABLES

2.1	World Bank regions – further subdivided	40
4.1	The global factory: location, ownership and governance issues	62
4.2	Empirical studies of the determinants of manufacturing outsourcing	67
9.1	An introduction to global chain/network approaches	149
9.2	Firm-specific strategies and organizational outcomes in global production networks	153
12.1	Macro-level determinants: industrial agglomeration and national institutions	192
12.2	Micro-level determinants: sub-national institutions and global cities	198
12.3	Firm-level determinants	202
12.4	Main findings: macro, micro and firm level	205
15.1	Intensive and extensive globalization	246
15.2	Global strategic firms	247
15.3	Strategic network connectivity	249
15.4	Residual from regressing strategic network connectivity against global network connectivity	250
16.1	Details of IB papers and the nature of their integration with GVC/GPN concepts	265
16.2	Breakdown of groups: degree of integration and perspectives	286
21.1	Correlation matrix and descriptive statistics	366
21.2	Empirical results (dependent variable: non-home region selection)	367
A21.A	The pattern of EMNEs' CBMAs in developed economies	369
A21.B	The number of EMNEs' CBMAs by acquirer countries and target countries, 2000–2010	369
A21.C	Countries by region	370
A21.D	Institutional dimensions	371
23.1	Summary of findings	406
23.2	Language as network enabler	407

24.1	List of tax havens	415
24.2	Recent five-year trend of FDI in tax havens (billion USD)	415
27.1	Basic information on the sample of regions	458
27.2	Transition matrix of regions, by quintiles of number of patents per million inhabitants, 1980–2011 (five-year periods)	463
27.3	Regressions of the number of patents by region, 1980–2011 (five-year periods)	464
27.4	Patenting activity, by groups of countries and five-year periods, 1980–2011	468
27.5	Cross-border investment projects and average distance, by main business activity, 2003–2014	470
28.1	Embeddedness in retail MNC expansion	481
29.1	New hotel formats, differentiation, segmentation and innovation	500
30.1	NAICS definitions	510
30.2	Definitions of knowledge-intensive business services (KIBS)	511
30.3	Global cities	515
33.1	Leading retained executive search firms in Australia, 2009–2013	565
33.2	The OLI paradigm applied to the internationalization of retained global executive search firms	568
33.3	World leading retained executive search firms in Australia, 1984/5	570
33.4	List of interviewees	571

CONTRIBUTORS

Matthew Alford is Lecturer in International Business and Management at Alliance Manchester Business School.

Raquel Ortega Argilés is Professor of Regional Economic Development in the Department of Strategy and International Business, Birmingham Business School, University of Birmingham.

Christian Asmussen is Professor with Special Responsibilities in the Department of Strategic Management and Globalisation, Copenhagen Business School.

Sharmistha Bagchi-Sen is Professor in the Department of Geography, State University of New York – Buffalo.

Trevor J. Barnes is Professor at the Department of Geography, University of British Columbia, and Fellow of the Royal Society of Canada and Fellow of the British Academy.

Jonathan Beaverstock is Professor of International Management at the School of Economics, Finance and Management at the University of Bristol.

Ioana R. Bedreaga is Junior Project Manager, Global Strategic Pricing at Credit Suisse.

Steven Brakman is Professor of International Economics at the University of Groningen.

Tarun Kanti Bose is Assistant Professor in Business Administration at Khulna University, Bangladesh, and a doctoral student at the Adam Smith Business School, University of Glasgow.

John R. Bryson is Professor of Enterprise and Economic Geography at Birmingham Business School, University of Birmingham.

Davide Castellani is Professor of International Business and Strategy at the Henley Business School, University of Reading.

Gordon L. Clark FBA is Professorial Fellow at St. Edmund Hall and Director of the Smith School of Enterprise and Environment, University of Oxford and Sir Louis Matheson Distinguished Visiting Professor at Monash University.

Neil M. Coe is Professor of Economic Geography and Head of the Department of Geography at the National University of Singapore.

Gary Cook is Professor of Economics and Head of School at the Hull University Business School.

Philip Cooke is Professor, Mohn Centre for Innovation and Regional Development at the West Norway University of Applied Sciences, Bergen, Norway.

Ben Derudder is Professor of Human Geography at the Department of Geography, Ghent University and Associate Director of the Globalization and World Cities research network.

Pavlos Dimitratos is Professorial Research Fellow at the Adam Smith School of Business, University of Glasgow.

James Faulconbridge is Professor and Head of the Department of Organisation, Work and Technology, Lancaster University Management School, Lancaster University.

Samia Ferdous Hoque is Postdoctoral Researcher in Responsible and International Business, Alliance Manchester Business School, The University of Manchester.

Crispian Fuller is Senior Lecturer in Human Geography in the School of Geography and Planning, Cardiff University.

Jens Gammelgaard is Professor of International Business and Head of the Department of International Economics and Management at Copenhagen Business School.

Keith W. Glaister is Professor of International Business, International Business Division, Leeds University Business School.

Anthony Goerzen is D.R. Sobey Professor of International Business at the Smith School of Business, Queen's University Canada.

Philippe Gugler of President of the Department of Economics, Faculty of Economics and Social Sciences and Director of the Centre for Competitiveness, University of Fribourg. He is also President and Fellow of the European International Business Academy.

Yoo Jung Ha is Lecturer in International Business at York Management School, University of York.

William S. Harvey is Professor of Management at the University of Exeter Business School.

Nigel Holden is Visiting Research Fellow at the University of Leeds.

Sierk Horn is Professor "Economy of Japan" in the Faculty for Cultural Studies, Ludwig Maximillians Universität – München.

Jeremy Howells is Visiting Fellow at Kellogg College, University of Oxford.

Michael Hoyler is Senior Lecturer in Human Geography at the Department of Geography, Loughborough University and Associate Director of the Globalization and World Cities research network.

Jennifer Johns is Senior Lecturer in International Business at the University of Liverpool Management School.

Young H. Jung is a doctoral student at the Jindal School of Management, University of Texas at Dallas, who will join California State University, Bakersfield, as Assistant Professor.

Michelle Lowe is Professor of Strategy and Innovation in the Faculty of Business & Law, University of Southampton and Fellow of the Academy of Social Sciences.

Giovanna Magnani is Postdoctoral Research Fellow in the Department of Economics and Management, University of Pavia.

Charles van Marrewijk is Professor of Economics and Head of Research, International Business School Suzhou, Xi'an Jiaotong-Liverpool University, China, and Professor of International Economics, Utrecht University, The Netherlands.

Philip McCann is Chair in Urban and Regional Economics at Sheffield University Management School.

Frank McDonald is Professor of International Business at the University of Leeds and past president of the Academy of International Business, UK & Ireland Chapter.

James T. Murphy is Associate Professor of Geography at Clark University and Editor-in-Chief of Economic Geography.

Phillip O'Neill is Professorial Research Fellow and Director, Centre for Western Sydney, University of Western Sydney.

Pengfei Ni is Professor of Economics at the Chinese Academy of Social Sciences, Beijing.

Bo Nielsen is Professor of Business Strategy at the University of Syndey Business School, University of Sydney.

Quyen T.K. Nguyen is Associate Professor of International Business and Strategy at Henley Business School, University of Reading.

Naresh Pandit is Professor of International Business at Norwich Business School, University of East Anglia.

Mike W. Peng is Jindal Chair of Global Strategy and Executive Director of the Centre for Global Business at the Jindal School of Management, University of Texas at Dallas.

David L. Rigby is Professor of Geography in the Department of Geography, University of California Los Angeles.

Torsten Schunder is a doctoral student in the Department of Geography, State University of New York – Buffalo.

Eric Sheppard is Humboldt Chair and Professor of Geography at the Department of Geography, University of California Los Angeles.

Noemi Sinkovics is Lecturer in International Business and Management at Alliance Manchester Business School, University of Manchester.

Rudolf R. Sinkovics is Professor of International Business at Alliance Manchester Business School, University of Manchester and Visiting Professor at Lappeenranta University of Technology, Finland.

Roger Strange is Professor of International Business at the School of Business, Management and Economics, University of Sussex.

Peter J. Taylor is Emeritus Professor of Human Geography at the School of Built and Natural Environment, Northumbria University, Emeritus Professor of Geography at Loughborough University, founder and Director of the Globalization and World Cities research network and Fellow of the British Academy.

Alain Verbeke is Professor of International Business and Strategy and holds the McCaig Research Chair in Management at the Haskayne School of Business, University of Calgary. He is also the Research Director of the Strategy and Organization Area at the Haskayne School of Business.

Yingqi Wei is Professor of International Business and Head of the International Business Division at the Leeds University Business School, University of Leeds.

Steve Wood is Professor of Retail Marketing and Management and Director of Research at Surrey Business School, University of Surrey.

Neil Wrigley is Professor of Human Geography in the School of Geography and Environment, University of Southampton, and a Fellow of the British Academy.

Yan Wu is a doctoral student at the School of Business, Management and Economics, University of Sussex

Yaoan Wu is R&D Manager at the Industrial and Commercial Bank of China.

Yong Yang is Reader in Strategy at the School of Business, Management and Economics, University of Sussex.

Henry Wai-chung Yeung is Professor of Economic Geography in the Department of Geography at the National University of Singapore.

Wenlong Yuan is the Stu Clark Chair in Entrepreneurship and Innovation at the Asper School of Business, University of Manitoba.

1

INTRODUCTION TO THE COMPANION

Gary Cook, Frank McDonald, Jennifer Johns,
Jonathan Beaverstock and Naresh Pandit

The genesis of the Companion

This edited collection was first proposed to Gary Cook in the autumn of 2014 by Routledge Commissioning Editor Terry Clague. Cook's own journey in exploring the interface between Economic Geography (EG) and International Business (IB) and the connections he has forged with the other editors of this volume (and many of the contributors) shed light on the many areas for fruitful interaction between the two disciplines and, more broadly, with economics and management. Cook and Pandit were contemporaries on the PhD programme at Manchester Business School and, indeed, shared the same PhD supervisor, Tony Cockerill, and have a common background in Industrial Economics. In 1996 they embarked on a stream of work, which continues to the current day into industrial clusters, in the first case in connection with a European Commission Funded project led by Peter Swann. Their initial work was a large scale econometric analysis of the links between cluster strength and firm growth rates and the prospects for surviving new firm start-ups, focusing on the Financial Services and Broadcasting industries. The positive correlations were strongly evident. The choice of sectors was not random. An important question – and one which finds some echoes in this Companion – is whether patterns evident in manufacturing industries would also be found in service industries. In broad outline, results were very consistent with those found in parallel projects on computing, biotechnology and aerospace.

Finding significant correlations and patterns which seemed to be mirrored across a range of industries was gratifying, but only to a limited degree. As the commonplace has it: correlation is not causation. The next project built on the "black box econometrics" through a comparative case study analysis of Financial Services and Broadcasting, based entirely on qualitative methods, which sought to identify whether there were real processes of "agglomeration economies" at work (the correlations could have been spurious for several reasons, including being just random or due to some third factor which did not involve spillovers between firms). Should there be real processes at work, then, of course, the key research question was: what were the processes driving the positive effects being picked up in the statistics? The design was to examine London, by far the dominant agglomeration in both industries and a leading example of a major node in a global network in the sense of Amin and Thrift (1992) and both undeniably meaningful clusters bearing comparison with the paradigmatic Silicon Valley (Saxenian, 1994).

London was to be compared with Bristol (dynamic in Broadcasting but not Financial Services) and Edinburgh-Glasgow (dynamic in Financial Services but much less so in Broadcasting). In order to make this comparison of differences in regional dynamism at sub-national scale, the literature in EG became essential, with its emphasis on variegation and the particularities of the historical and institutional context. By the same token, it was very heartening for two Industrial Economists to discover that the particularities of industry mattered too!

Cook met Jon Beaverstock when they both worked at Loughborough University. Beaverstock was in the Department of Geography and had spent many years crafting his research on the internationalisation of banking and professional services firms, and the competitiveness of the City of London and Singapore as global financial centres. In particular, Beaverstock's interest in IB was first stimulated by reading John Dunning and Peter Buckley's work in the late 1980s, and the theoretical foundation of his PhD in Economic Geography from the University of Bristol (1990) was heavily influenced by Dunning and others who used the OLI paradigm to explain the internationalisation of business services. Jon's work has always blended the softer and qualitative aspects of IB with EG and his latest research monograph on the internationalisation of executive search (Beaverstock et al., 2015) exemplifies neatly the contribution that EG and IB can make to explain the internationalisation of the firm. In a chat over coffee at Loughborough University in the early 2000s, Cook and Beaverstock soon discovered that they had areas of common interest. What followed was a substantial project on clustering in the City of London, jointly with Pandit and Peter J. Taylor (see Chapter 15 in this companion). This was instructive in several ways. First, it established that business scholars and economic and political geographers can work well together and that their differing perspectives are complementary. The world cities perspective and the relational turn were revelations to Cook and Pandit. It also showed that joint working is not always a simple matter, as each side makes taken-for-granted assumptions that can be impenetrable to the other. These are not insurmountable, but they can be subtle and rather baffling. The project brought into sharp relief the particular importance of multinationals in clusters and of clusters to multinationals. It also made very concrete the geographer's emphasis on processes taking place at a range of spatial scales. This started Cook and Pandit on a trajectory linking EG and IB, which is still going full steam ahead and along which this Companion is an important staging post. One of Cook's abiding memories of this immersion into the literature of EG is how difficult it was to build a conceptual map of the field. This was mainly due to the more heterodox nature of the field (see Chapter 7 by Barnes and Sheppard), which contrasts with the more structured coalescence around core models and assumptions in IB (and Economics). It was also, in part, due to a lack of appreciation of the core concerns of Economic Geographers and how they differ from those of IB scholars, not just in terms of the substantive issues addressed by research, but also doctrinal positions taken in terms of methodology and epistemology.

Cook met Jennifer Johns somewhat by accident at the University of Liverpool. Jennifer received her EG training at the University of Manchester. Jennifer was programme director for the Geography and Management degree and Cook needed to consult with her in preparing the annual programme review for undergraduate programmes in Management. Again, it quickly emerged that we had common interests, above all in clustering in the broadcasting industry. A joint research project on MediaCity quickly followed. It was also part of a process by which Jennifer made her move out of the Geography Department. Precipitated by University-wide restructuring, Jennifer moved into the Management School and continued to teach much the same material on the global economy, perpetuating sales of *Global Shift*. Having worked with Peter Dicken, Neil Coe, Henry Yeung and Martin Hess on Global Production Networks (GPNs) and completed a PhD on networks and agglomeration in creative industry, Jennifer's work has tended to take the firm as the initial unit of analysis. This made her work more understandable – at least at first glance – to her new colleagues in IB and management generally.

Beaverstock was, a little later, to make the same transition, moving to the Department of Management at Bristol University, from a Chair in Geography at the University of Nottingham. More comments on this exodus of Economic Geographers to Management Schools occur later in this introduction. Johns and Cook organised a special session on Geography and Management at the Royal Geographical Society – Institute of British Geographers conference in 2013, which attracted strong interest. One thing which sticks in Cook's mind about that session is the trepidation that several of the geographers expressed about possibly having to "sell their soul to the devil" if they dabbled in the management field, being constrained by the need to adopt a "managerialist" perspective. Johns remembers an air of cautious excitement about the potential scope for engagement between the disciplines and a strong sense of greater job security in more profitable, and expanding management and business schools where funding for research activities is often much greater than in geography departments.

Once the connections between clusters, EG and IB had been made, Cook became a regular attendee at the Academy of International Business conferences and made the acquaintance of Frank McDonald, the then President of the Academy of International Business UK & Ireland Chapter. Frank was then, and remains, highly interested in the links between EG and IB, and many of his thoughts are reflected in this introduction. The Chapter endorsed the University of Liverpool to organise the 2012 UK & Ireland Conference, and Frank made a particular request that it should be focused on the linkages between EG and IB. Accordingly, a special arrangement was made with the Economic Geography Research Group of the Royal Geographical Society and there was a good attendance by geographers at the conference, as well as a very well attended panel session and special paper sessions. An edited book captured the diverse contributions (Cook & Johns, 2013).

The Conference was fortunate to attract two excellent keynote speakers, who have spanned the two fields, Ram Mudambi from the IB side and Henry Yeung from the EG side. Both placed emphasis on the uneven and particular geographic distribution of economic activity. Henry Yeung spoke of the need to fuse the spatial perspective of EG with the agency of firms, which is central to the IB perspective. Putting it in a nutshell, he spoke of the geographic pattern of activity as being both a cause of and an outcome of International Business activity. He also offered a salutary reminder that the particular patterning of economic activity around the globe is also conditioned by physical, not just human geography. He also placed emphasis on the tendency in IB to downplay or ignore completely the interaction between firms and their particular locations. He contrasted the typical conception of space in IB, as a physical container (the region, the nation state) within which activity takes place, with the relational perspective in EG, where a key defining feature of what makes one spatial unit what it is, is its relationship to other spatial units. MNEs are important agents which link one physical space to another. It was clear from Yeung's presentation that the issues of power and embeddedness in the local context feature more prominently in Economic Geographical discourses and analysis than they do in IB, especially the nature and reality of power relationships. He also gave a rich analysis of how MNEs from emerging economies in South East Asia derive home-based advantages from the countries and the region in which they originate.

Yeung gave a very insightful analysis of how concepts from EG, enshrined in the theory of GPNs, enrich the analysis of firm strategies (see Chapters 9 and 16 in this Companion). A repeated phrase used by Yeung still resonates: IB, the phenomenon, is bigger than IB, the discipline. This crystallises the core rationale for this Companion, which seeks to identify how the boundaries of IB, the discipline, might be usefully extended by incorporating ideas from

EG, in order to better comprehend IB, the phenomenon. In summary, Yeung set out three challenges for the disciplines of IB and EG, answers to which are presented in the epilogue to this companion:

1. To explain the critical links between regions and the global economy, particularly through the lens of firms and their production networks.
2. To use a transdisciplinary perspective to understand flows and relations across space and their significance, moving beyond the agency(firm)-centric views of IB and Economics.
3. To transform knowledge in IB through engagement and connectivity.

Mudambi contrasted what he called the World of Yesterday, post-industrial revolution up to roughly the 1980s, with what he called the World of Today. The World of Yesterday was characterised by generally rising equality within nations and regions, but a growing disparity in income levels between the industrialised and developing and under-developed countries. The World of Today is witnessing a rapid rise in income equality as many emerging economies catch up quickly, but by rising inequality within countries. Mudambi attributes the foundation of this regime shift to a fall in spatial transaction costs, which have given rise to a geographic dispersal of higher-value-added activity and also a process of vertical disintegration of activities. He argues that Global Value Chains are a key theoretical lens through which to analyse the changes at work in the World of Today. The dispersal and disintegration of activities, as acts of strategy by MNEs, have contributed to the economic development of those countries and regions to which they have both made foreign direct investments (FDI) and to which they have subcontracted work. These positive spillovers have occurred through a variety of well-known channels such as training and turnover of labour, training of local suppliers, and imitation and unintended knowledge spillovers. This puts the spotlight on the abiding importance of the agency of firms, central to the concerns of IB the discipline, but recognising that the fortunes of firm and the spaces and places in which they act are inextricably linked. Acknowledging another key theme of EG, Mudambi also argued that the connections between key agglomerations was integral both to the success of those agglomerations and the functioning of the global economic system. He ended by claiming that the changes now being witnessed are every bit as profound as those ushered in by the Industrial Revolution, which shifted the basis of economic power from the control of land to the control of physical capital, and its control within certain privileged countries. The World of Today is seeing the shift towards the possession of human rather than physical capital, and the privileged locations are not confined to a small number of key countries but a more broadly dispersed set of agglomerations.

Summarising so far, the personal odyssey of the editorial team establishes some key propositions which variously represent key opportunities and challenges which interdisciplinary work between EG and also some key issues which this Companion seeks to address. The epilogue outlines how this Companion has addressed these propositions and challenges.

1. Both IB and EG scholars have developed powerful insights into IB, the phenomenon, both in terms of theory and conceptualisation and an empirical literature. An increasing number of scholars in each discipline are seeing the "elephant in the room", that each is seeing only part of the "elephant", albeit a significant part.
2. Each side needs to understand the key assumption the other is making, key frames of reference and the key questions each is interested in. Neither need agree with the substance of these things, or the importance placed on them, but there can be no proper engagement with the other field without understanding what they are. The conceptualisation of space is emblematic in this regard.

3 Engagement and debate are constructive and helpful. At the very least, they force scholars to reappraise the validity of their taken-for-granted assumptions. Few who heard Henry Yeung's analysis of the shortcomings of the agency-centric analysis of IB would deny that he made valuable and insightful observations and that they were helpful to IB scholars in improving their understanding. Yeung also exemplifies the importance of assembling careful argument and evidence to convince the uninitiated that the missing elements from another discipline really do matter for the questions they are researching and the phenomena they are studying.

4 There is much common cause between the two fields in seeking to understand the current (and current change in) the IB/economic system. The common broad research area has been defined as the aim to 'increase our understanding of the spatial and historical evolution of MNEs and current change dynamics in the global economic environment' (Johns et al., 2015, p. 78). Here there are a number of key substantive research questions of mutual interest around that broad theme:

   a What are the changes which firms are making in terms of their international strategies? This spans many issues such as: what activities are being outsourced, which offshored and which both outsourced and offshored; to where are overseas investments being directed and sub-contracts awarded; how do MNEs control their organisations?

   b How and why do MNEs from emerging economies succeed and what are the implications for global GDP and its distribution? What are the implications for the strategies of MNEs from developed economies?

5 There is a general fear about IB being too "managerialist" for Economic Geographers, who are more strongly wedded to a critical perspective. However, critical perspectives are not "off limits" in IB and the journal *Critical Perspectives on International Business*, founded in 2005, is alive and well and sponsors a prize at the Academy of International Business UK & Ireland Chapter Conference.

6 The common ground between IB and EG has been expanded by the acceptance of the institutional view into the mainstream of IB. As the dispersal of activity in production, consumption and R&D takes place, firms and academic observers are coming to a deeper understanding of the importance of institutions and culture in IB. The dominant frameworks, Scott's (2001) "three pillars" and the isomorphism framework of DiMaggio and Powell (1983) are both rooted in sociology, from which EG also draws its institutional underpinnings.

A framework for the Companion

Some reflections on IB and EG from the IB perspective

Foundational work in IB theory considers the influence of geographical factors for the location decisions of multinational corporations (MNCs). The geographical analysis centres on the competitive advantages arising from differences in the characteristics of national distributions of market, competition, resources and infrastructure conditions in different locations (Knickerbocker, 1973; Vernon, 1979). In one notable case this included city locations (Hymer, 1972). This work was not strongly influenced by research by Economic Geographers and it developed with a stress on firm-level drivers of FDI that focused on transaction costs and market and resource conditions in different national locations (Buckley & Casson, 1976, Dunning, 1979; Dunning & Rugman, 1985). Spatial factors played a minor role in this literature. IB theory developed therefore with a focus on strategic issues affecting location at firm level with geographical factors largely restricted to national differences in transaction costs, market characteristics and some consideration of the role of the geographical distribution of resource bundles. Interest in how spatial factors affected MNC strategy, however, increased due to a renewed focus on the location component in the Eclectic Paradigm and involved moves to better integrate spatial factors in consideration of the location strategies of MNCs (Buckley & Ghauri, 2004; McCann & Mudambi, 2005; Dunning, 2009; Cantwell & Mudambi, 2011; McCann, 2011). More recent developments in this area focus directly on how spatial factors influence the location decisions of MNCs. This work centres on exploring MNC strategies in the context of global value chain objectives that involve multiple crossing of national and sub-national frontiers embracing a multitude of interactions within and outside of the MNC in a host of different locations (Beugelsdijk, Mudambi & McCann, 2010; Beugelsdijk & Mudambi, 2013).

These developments in IB theory seek to incorporate contemporary understanding on spatial issues within and between locations with cutting edge research on the major business factors thought to drive MNC strategies. This work is influenced by contemporary research in Economy Geography that considers agglomeration benefits from resource and institutional factors and global connectivity in different locations (Dicken & Malmberg, 2001; Gertler, 2003; Coe et al., 2004; Boschma, 2005; Yeung, 2005). The evolution of IB theories appears to be returning to its origins by bringing spatial factors more clearly into consideration when considering MNC strategies and location issues. Most of the developments to more fully integrate spatial issues into IB theory are often directly linked to research from Economy Geography thereby offering potential for collaboration between these disciplines.

The increasing focus in contemporary IB research on spatial issues normal centre on strategic and managerial issues connected to creating and developing the global value chains (GVC) of MNCs. The unit of analysis in most of these studies is the MNC as a whole and/or at subsidiary level (see Chapters 4, 6, 12 and 21). This work connects to the work of Economic Geographers on GPNs that tend to have social networks and global connectivity as the core units of analysis (see Chapters 9 and 10). IB and EG scholars allude, sometimes explicitly but more often implicitly, to the importance of key GVC and GPN issues. What is currently lacking, however, is an integration of the major factors from GVC and GNP approaches (see Chapters 2, 11 and 16). In other words, what is needed is a better understanding on how the locational factors (including spatially influenced factors) affect the strategic and operational aspects of GVCs and vice-versa. In the context of GPN approaches, this involves how social networks and global connectivity in different locations can be woven together by MNCs in ways that enable them to achieve their GVC objectives.

Interest in integrating spatial factors into IB research extend to studies on sub-national locations (Meyer & Nguyen, 2005; Santangelo, 2009; Nguyen et al., 2013). Within this move to explore sub-national location issues is a literature on the role of cities (Nachum & Wymbs, 2005, 2007; Goerzen, Asmussen & Nielsen, 2013; Ma, Delios & Lau, 2013a, 2013b). The focus of this literature is normally on major world cities with little consideration of cities that are not major world cities. Many cities, however, have diverse resource and infrastructure bundles and global connectivity that can be attractive for national, regional or global niche roles rather than as important locations for globally important strategic activities (Taylor, 1997; Beaverstock, Smith & Taylor, 1999). An exception to the neglect of such "lesser" world cities in the IB literature is a study by Goerzen, Asmussen and Nielsen (2013), which considers a range of different types of city as locations for MNCs. The importance of location in cities will tend to be less for manufacturing operations requiring large amounts of land.

Studies on sub-national and city location have also considered the role of variations in liabilities of foreignness (Zaheer, 1995) and liabilities of outsidership (Vahlne, Schweizer & Johanson, 2012) in different locations. These studies examine the effects of institutional factors in sub-national locations that lead to lower liabilities in these areas and thereby provide attractive locations for MNCs (Goerzen, Asmussen & Nielsen, 2013; Ma, Delios & Lau, 2013a, 2013b; Nguyen et al., 2013). The role of these liabilities for location decisions of MNCs is central to much of contemporary research in IB, but is not prominent in the research on world cities by Economic Geographers. The diversity of institutional systems and their importance for location in world city locations is a strong feature in EG research (Beaverstock, Smith & Taylor, 1999; Dicken & Malmberg, 2001; Sim et al., 2003) but not explicitly in the context of mitigating for liabilities' foreignness and outsidership. This is therefore perhaps a fruitful area for collaborative research by IB and EG scholars.

How do foreign firms configure organisational systems to enable embedding in host locations whilst simultaneously linking with the other parts of their MNC centres on the configuration of inter- and intra-organisational network relationships (Frost, Birkinshaw & Ensign, 2002; Birkinshaw et al., 2005; Oehmichen & Puck, 2016) and autonomy (Young & Tavares, 2004; Kawai & Strange, 2014)? Using the resource-based view and network theory, studies find that complex interactions between autonomy and intra- and inter-network relationships are necessary to extract the benefits that stem from the resource bundles and connectivity available in host locations (Andersson, Björkman & Forsgren, 2005; Gammelgaard et al., 2012; Chiao & Ying, 2013). These studies only consider autonomy and network relationships configurations at national level, however. There are no studies on whether these configurations differ according to locations in world cities compared to other locations. Moreover, these studies are not strongly influenced by the work of Economic Geographers. The reverse is also true in that IB theories on the organisational systems of MNCs have little impact on the work of Economic Geographers. This relative neglect by both sets of scholars largely stems from the dominant view taken by the respective scholars about the nature of the firm. Many IB scholars view the firm from a transaction cost perspective with little consideration of the importance of relationship factors, particularly the spatial aspect affecting the impact of relationships on the organisational systems of firms (Yeung, 2005). There is, however, a growing understanding among IB scholars of the importance of social relationships for effective organisational systems for governing GVC (Mudambi & Swift, 2011). This is another potentially fruitful field for collaborative research between IB and EG researchers that would enable greater insight into how spatial factors affect the organisational configurations of MNCs. This would provide insight into the management of complex interactions involving multiple crossings of national and sub-national frontiers by many different parts of MNCs that are embedded into a diverse range of geographical locations.

Some reflections on EG and IB from the EG perspective

EG as a discipline started to engage with many aspects of IB from the 1960s, but that label wasn't recognised to describe geographical research on the internationalisation of firms and ensuing industrial restructuring. Instead the focus of attention was aim squarely on the "geography of" the multi-national firm or enterprise, interrogating patterns of industrial location and branch plants, subsidiaries and office networks, and FDI, particularly from the developed world to the developing, and the shift from primary and manufacturing to services. Notable interventions came from geographical authors like Peter Daniels, Peter Dicken, Peter Lloyd, Mike Taylor, Nigel Thrift, (for example, see Dicken & Lloyd, 1973, 1976; Dicken, 1976, 1977; Daniels, 1982; Taylor and Thrift, 1982, 1983). The publication of Peter Dicken's (1986) seminal book, *Global Shift: Industrial Change in a Turbulent World*, was the first major text which blended EG, both theoretically and empirically, with IB. The publication of *Global Shift* was a real game-changer in that it brought IB directly to the attention of EG and it is no coincidence that this book was crafted at the University of Manchester, the spiritual home of three of my co-editors in IB! Dicken's work has inspired economic geographers to engage in theoretical approaches outside of their backyard to analyse the internationalisation of firms and the emergence of multi- and transnational corporations. Such theoretical approaches have been informed by John Dunning and many other influential scholars in IB like Richard Whitley, for example (see Beaverstock, 2010). Fast forward to the present, there is now a multitude of scholars in EG who engage with IB as demonstrated by many papers published in the leading journals such as *Economic Geography* and *Journal of Economic Geography* and *Environment and Planning A*, and, of course, in this edited collection.

This edited collection signals several strands of interaction between EG and IB. First, the traditional communication through citation across the two disciplines which has slowly started to increase (for discussion in relation to Global Value Chains and GPNs in IB, see Chapter 16 by Sinkovics et al. in this Companion; Johns et al., 2015; Alford et al., 2017). Second, increased dialogue about complementary research areas through a series of initiatives including special conference and panel sessions (such as the panel session recorded by Johns et al., 2015). Third, the academic context in which the cross-fertilisation of IB and EG is taking place has also evolved. A study conducted by the Economic Geography Research Group of the Royal Geographical Society/Institute of British Geographers has identified 87 economic geographers who have moved from geography departments to Business and Management Schools, of which 95% moved between 2000 and 2015 (Bradshaw et al., 2016). This physical relocation of a relatively high percentage of scholars trained as Economic Geographers into Business and Management Schools is impactful to both disciplines. As more EG and IB scholars work together more closely, increased understanding can arise from formal mechanisms such as shared teaching programmes and courses and membership of research groups and informal mechanisms such as network building and corridor conversations. As all Economic Geographers (and increasingly IB scholars!) are aware, benefits can be derived from co-location. The chapters presented in this edited collection highlight some of the research outcomes arising from greater proximity between EG and IB scholars. This is therefore an opportunity for both EG and IB. The reality may be different. Some Economic Geographers in Business and Management Schools move well away from their original discipline. In other cases, they will continue, but with limited interaction or no impact on their management colleagues. Therefore, although the movement of Economic Geographers into Management Schools is resulting in closer geographical proximity of EG and IB colleagues, it is not necessarily leading to a closer integration of ideas and concepts (see Chapter 16 by Sinkovics et al. in this Companion).

However, this raises some important questions about the future of EG in general (the focus of the study by Bradshaw et al., 2016) and with regard to how the two sub-disciplines interact. Data presented by Alford et al. (2017) highlights the relatively small citation of the Global Production Network framework over that of the Global Commodity Chain, despite increased convergence between the two frameworks and their application. This is due in part to the relative sizes of IB and EG as sub-disciplines. The continuing future of EG is dependent on its ongoing vitality and through the meaningful and unique contribution of EG scholars. This does not appear to be diluting.

Economic Geographers have recognised the need to take firms seriously as economic actors. Now over 15 years old, Dicken and Malmberg (2001)'s 'firm-territory nexus' presented us with a framework to simultaneously conceptualise economic activities (including such phenomena as firms, industries and other types of systems of networked economic activity) on the one hand, and territorially defined economies, on the other. The firm-territory nexus represents the interconnections between economic activities and territories through an exploration of the mutually constitutive relationships between firms and territories (Dicken & Malmberg, 2001, p. 345). In many respects, this relationship between the firm and its environment underpins much of the shared intellectual space of EG and IB. As previously noted, Dicken's *Global Shift* is another key work which has taken firms seriously and, partly for this reason, has gained wide currency within IB.

Economic Geographers have had ambivalent attitudes towards Economics, which has been a foundational discipline, and remains so, for IB. Particular exception has been taken to the New Economic Geography, propounded by Krugman above all. One trenchant critique, Martin (1999), suggests that the models developed by Krugman and others are too stylised and abstract, and whilst they may shed some light on genuine influences on spatial concentration, they say nothing new and they leave out much that is important. Moreover, the New Economic Geography is seen as being cavalier in its approach to the different spatial scales at which forces promoting the spatial concentration of activity might operate and how these processes may interact (Martin & Sunley, 2001). The New Economic Geography, however, has had limited impact within IB.

Economic Geographers have likewise been very critical of Michael Porter's (1990) clusters concept. Martin and Sunley (2003) have provided a serious critique, exposing key areas where it makes questionable assumptions and appeals to vague concepts and empirical definitions. Despite the fact that Porter placed emphasis in *The Competitive Advantage of Nations* (1990) on the importance of clusters for promoting the international competitiveness of firms, Porter's diamond has found relatively limited appeal within the IB literature. Where IB scholars do examine the importance of sub-national scale, they are more likely to refer to the seminal ideas of Marshall (1927), Jacobs (1969) and work in EG.

Introduction to the chapters

The chapters have been arranged into broad sections, each of which is reasonably self-explanatory. A brief introduction is given here to each of the chapters, to allow readers to get a quick overview of the book and identify those chapters which will be of most interest to them. Chapters are introduced here in the order in which they appear in the book.

Some core material in IB

This section provides a guide to some of the key current areas of research in IB. The primary purpose is to give the non-expert an accessible guide to the field. Standard frameworks such as Dunning's Eclectic Paradigm, the Resource-Based View and the Institutional View are very widely known and there are very many quick sources of reference in standard textbooks.

Brakman and van Marrewijk take a close look at the changing spatial organisation of IB, both through the lens of trade flows and firm location strategies. The importance of comparative advantage in influencing the sectoral composition of trade flows continues to be apparent. They argue that falls in spatial transaction and transportation costs have created a more uneven, "spiky" pattern of economic activity and will continue to do so. They note that only a comparatively small proportion of firms engage in international trade and even fewer in direct foreign investment. Most firms that export do so only to a limited extent, whereas a small proportion of firms account for the vast majority of exports by value, and most of this group of firms are MNEs. They show that the participation of all countries in global supply chains has been rising, but that the extent of participation varies very widely across countries. Despite the criticism that has been made of the Uppsala model, the authors present evidence that most firms do build up their activity in an incremental way, serving "closer" markets first. Contrary again to some popular discourse, the authors identify that "global" supply chains are often based on proximity between advanced and middle income countries and that this proximity is important to deal with coordination and logistics challenges. The chapter shows that economic integration is positively associated with increasing agglomeration, framing the analysis within Krugman's core-periphery model.

Glaister provides a focused review of the literature on alliances and networks, paying particular attention to the literature in Business and Management and, to a somewhat lesser extent, EG. As Glaister points out, the past 30 years have seen a massive literature on networks and alliances emerge, from a wide range of disciplinary viewpoints, rendering it impossible to provide a comprehensive overview of everything that has been written about the phenomenon. This is testament to its importance in the current age, one which has been dubbed that of "alliance capitalism" by Dunning (1995). Definitions of the term alliance abound in the literature, some so elastic that almost any type of relationship would qualify. Glaister points out the importance of trust, a reliance on cooperation which is not guaranteed to be forthcoming. Much the same may be said of the term network and even where a particular definition is accepted, it can be very tricky to delineate particular networks empirically. There is a discussion of the key strategic consideration in forming alliances and alliance portfolios, which acknowledges that, in many cases, the panoply of alliances an MNE ends up with may not form a coherent whole. Glaister sets out clearly the contribution that geographers have made to understanding networks and alliances, most particularly within the literature on GPNs. As is acknowledged within the GPN literature itself, there is a current gap in that literature regarding opening up the black box of the firm, which is acknowledged to play a crucial role in coordinating such networks.

Strange and Magnani examine the phenomena of offshoring, outsourcing and the "global factory", whereby firms have created vertically disintegrated and geographically dispersed production operations. Offshoring does not imply outsourcing, nor the other way round. The choice of whether to produce in house and where to site or source production of a particular input are part of a set of strategic decisions about how best to produce and deliver to final consumers. The "global factory" literature has some correspondence with the EG concept of the GPN, although the two things are not equivalent. The chapter explores the different senses in which the term has been used. Several factors underlie this dispersal of activity, including the force of competition, improved ICT, logistics and transportation, greater openness to FDI and improved intellectual property protection in many countries and more open trade and financial flows. The chapter examines the literature on why disintegration and offshoring have been pursued, as a balance between competing advantages, such as lower costs and greater flexibility, and disadvantages such as greater complexity and risk. This balance may change over time and may be miscalculated by firms, leading to some reversals of decisions to either outsource, offshore or both. As the authors acknowledge, these decisions are not simple "technical" matters whereby the most efficient global arrangement is put in place, but power relationships are also influential to the creation and division of the gains. A special examination is made of so-called "factoryless goods producers", who outsource all of the physical production of their goods, although this literature is still in its infancy. The authors conclude with some excellent recommendations for future directions of research, noting the profound methodological difficulties that examining the relationship between "global factory" strategy and firm performance will pose.

Nguyen examines one of the hot topics in IB, which is the nature of the regional strategies of MNEs and the implications this has for the governance and coordination of subsidiaries.

The chapter gives an even-handed treatment of the fierce debate which has taken place in recent years regarding whether "globalisation is dead", with particular attention being paid to the definition of a region, which is crucial to what results follow regarding whether MNEs are globally or primarily regionally organised. This phrase was coined by the late Alan Rugman, who researched and wrote extensively on his thesis that almost all MNEs pursue regional strategies and that the number of truly global firms, in any meaningful sense of that term, can be counted on the fingers of two hands. This debate is an important one for any researchers with an interest in MNEs and the organisation of the world economy to be familiar with, as it offers a very important challenge to commonplace assumptions which abound not only in academic debate, but also in the wider political and policy discourse. Nguyen probes why it is that MNEs remain principally regional (in the triad region sense), and the answers indicate that there are still considerable frictions which impede the development of a truly integrated world economy, some due to cultural differences, some due to tariff and non-tariff barriers (both deliberate and accidental), and yet others due to the sheer complexity of coordinating dispersed and far-flung corporations. As Nguyen explains, the theory of the regional MNE rests on a crucial distinction between location-bound and non-location bound firm and subsidiary-specific assets. It is not necessarily easy to leverage all firm specific assets internationally, and intra-regional expansion is generally easier than extra-regional expansion. The particular balance between intra-regional and inter-regional sales also has important implications for the best structure for an MNE to adopt.

Verbeke and Yuan move away from a sole focus on the host country as the institutional environment relevant to internationalisation processes. They point out that MNEs have increasingly moved to integrate their activities on regional lines and go on to show how regional integration arrangements, such as the EU and NAFTA, can condition MNE strategies. As the authors point out, it is managers' perceptions of "distance" which are influential on their behaviours. The analysis is framed within Bartlett and Ghoshal's typology of subsidiary roles, itself based on the interplay between location-specific and firm-specific advantages. They show that, increasingly, regional integration schemes can reduce the impact of the national environment as the main external determinant of subsidiary roles. They develop a general framework to understand the influence of regional integration schemes on the dynamics of subsidiary roles and the evolution of subsidiary competencies. The more location-bound and location-specific are subsidiary competencies, the less impact closer regional integration will have. They also present eight patterns of subsidiary role evolution, based on changes in either subsidiaries' value chain activities or their geographic scope. Finally, at the subsidiary level, they provide a Penrosean analysis of the key, micro-level determinants of changes in subsidiary roles, and make a critical distinction between subsidiary capabilities to manage current operations efficiently, and entrepreneurial capabilities.

Some core material in EG

This section introduces some of the key schools of thought in EG, starting with a brief history of the development of thought in EG, which provides an excellent guide to the pluralism in EG and how it came to be.

Barnes and Sheppard identify four distinctive characteristics of EG: (1) understanding that geographies of economic activities co-evolve with the economy; (2) viewing economic processes as interrelated with political, cultural and biophysical processes; (3) that the predominance of capitalist economic activities should not be mistaken for their inevitability or desirability; and (4) valuing pluralism in theory and method. The chapter first provides a brief genealogical account of how EG came into being, including a discussion of its methods, before providing selected substantive examples from its research programme to illustrate the breadth of the field and its predilections. Eight substantive research clusters within EG are identified and summarised.

Rigby provides a brief overview of the emergence of evolutionary economics and the adoption of evolutionary arguments within EG. The aim of the chapter is to highlight recent theoretical and empirical research within Evolutionary Economic Geography and to foreground some key emerging debates. The chapter begins with a review of development of evolutionary economics and the competing strands of evolutionary thought that have been embraced by geographers. It then explores how those arguments have been deployed within EG with focus on the production and destruction of variety in EG, path dependence and lock-in as forms of retention in space, the silence of selection and self-organisation in networks. The chapter argues that there is relatively little research within EG that explicitly embraces notions of complexity and self-organisation. The conclusion links many of the themes explored by Evolutionary Economic Geography to related literature in IB. It suggests that deeper engagement of the two fields can yield mutual benefits and provides examples of areas of potential for such engagement.

Coe outlines the antecedents and development of the global production network approach and profiles recent developments in the field that collectively constitute an attempt to develop a 'GPN 2.0 iteration of the theory'. Here discussion is made of the delimiting, driving, developing and dependence of GPNs. The chapter outlines four interrelated themes that are considered ripe for the co-development of ideas across EG and IB: (1) the market imperative; (2) corporate strategy; (3) value capture; and (4) complex geographies. The conclusion reflects on these four areas of dialogue and argues that an enhanced two-way conversation between the fields of EG and IB seems to have considerable merit and has the potential to be a lively trading zone.

Murphy provides an overview of the relational turn in EG. Relational thinking is a core aspect of contemporary EG that has helped to reshape understandings of innovation processes, agglomeration economies, GPNs, markets, uneven development and the socio-spatial drivers of competitiveness. The first section of this chapter briefly outlines the origins and antecedents of relational thinking in human geography. The second section provides an overview of the contributions that relational approaches have made to extant debates and dialogues in EG, covering institutional and network embeddedness, micro-social agencies and the socio-material bases of economic order. Discussion is made of the "relational turn" in EG and how this has shaped its contemporary research agenda. The third section then discusses the value of relational concepts and approaches for the field of IB focusing on two ideas – relational proximity and socio-spatial practice – that are particularly relevant. The chapter concludes with a short summary discussion.

The interface between EG and IB

This section provides a selection of chapters which explore key themes that span the domains of IB and EG. Some integrate those two fields to a greater extent than others. Some are originated by IB scholars, others by Economic Geographers. The purpose of the section is to demonstrate the extent of mutual interest and the opportunities for and benefits of adopting an interdisciplinary perspective.

Yeung focuses on two key issues that speak well to the interface between EG and IB: (1) the geographical nature of IB and (2) the theorisation of spatiality in IB. Yeung examines the critical link between localities/regions and the global economy through examining key economic actors – business firms and their transnational production networks. The chapter argues for a relational framework for examining the geographical foundations of transnational corporations and for a new direction of research in IB studies that focuses on organisational space. The chapter concludes with reflections of the implications of a relational approach on both disciplines.

Nielsen, Asmussen and Goerzen provide a review of key theories and evidence regarding determinants of the location of MNEs. Specifically, the review probes micro-level influences which inform very particular location decisions at the sub-regional level. In so doing, they argue that IB needs to be informed by insights from EG and Urban Economics (see also the chapter by Cook and Pandit). By the same token, IB can inform EG by bringing into sharper focus the influence of firm strategies, resources and capabilities on their location decisions. The chapter reviews macro-level theories regarding location, rooted in theory regarding trade and international capital movement. The chapter argues that the Institutional View has been an important influence on the analysis of firm strategy, because it casts light on institutional factors which shape both opportunities and constraints of firms, as well as influencing the attractiveness of alternative locations. At the micro-level, they find empirical support for the particular attractiveness of global cities to MNEs, as well as other important attributes, such as costs, demand and the availability of agglomeration externalities. He also finds substantial evidence that there is a range of firm-specific characteristics which has a significant influence on firm location behaviour. There is some evidence that as firms become more experienced in FDI, they place less emphasis on generic benefits such as costs, demand and ease of doing business and more emphasis on the value of a specific location for augmenting the resources and capabilities of the firm. A key research agenda is identified to probe more carefully the micro-influences on firm location decisions and their interaction with first characteristics and firm strategies in influencing location choice. A second important research agenda is to increase our understanding of how the influence of these various elements changes over time and with the accumulated experience of the MNE. Third, little is known about how managers actually make location choices.

Fuller examines the sub-national region. It begins with an examination of EG's treatment of the region, starting with the relationship between the MNE and the region. The chapter then discusses more recent relational approaches in EG including the global production network framework that views the region as a site of territorialised firms, networks and assets. It then considers IB, and whilst IB is, by definition, concerned with geographical relations co-constituting particular forms of organisation, there has been no explicit conceptualisation of the region, nor geographical relations more broadly in the discipline. The section on the region in IB reviews literature in IB that engages with the notion of space in general, beginning with discussion of the 'L' (Location) in Dunning's (1979) OLI framework before outlining more recent research focusing on subsidiaries as causal agents. The chapter concludes with discussion of a future agenda for inter-disciplinary collaboration.

Cook and Pandit assess the importance of cities to key research questions in IB and the contributions which may be made to the research programme in IB from placing cities more centre stage and incorporating insights from two key related fields of enquiry on cities, EG and Urban Economics. They sound an appropriate note of caution about integrating the insights of these fields, which are focused on somewhat different questions to IB and which root their research within different methodological and epistemological assumptions. Cook and Pandit identify that all three fields share common reference to the important ideas of Marshallian (within industry) externalities and Jacobs (across industry) externalities, and note that these two distinct types of externality are apt to be present in differing degrees in different cities. They conclude that EG provides key insights regarding the relationship between cities of different prominence in the global economic system and the activities of MNEs. This presents a research agenda in probing how MNEs decide the scale and scope of activities in particular cities and how they actually operate both within cities and in coordinating their activities across cities and the full range of their global operations. Urban Economics opens up questions regarding the interconnections between MNEs, city dynamism, the operation of labour markets and innovation.

Derudder, Taylor, Faulconbridge, Hoyler and Ni explore the question of which cities can be considered as important strategic places in the world system. The focus is on the city network, rather than localised processes in cities, important though those are. Central to this treatment is the idea that strategic cities and firms are mutually constitutive. A city cannot be strategic unless firms have to be there. The analysis is built around key producer service industries, such as Law, Accountancy, Architecture, Advertising and Financial Services (see the Chapter 30 in this Companion by Bagchi-Sen and Schunder). Firms in these industries deliberately target certain cities in order to construct coordination capabilities for their international operations. Other literature has made the same point about manufacturing multinationals. The authors argue there is an important link between the strategic importance of a city and the propensity of firms to establish a presence through a wholly-owned subsidiary. Alliances are also used to offset risk. There are also important sector effects, with Accounting and Financial Services much more likely to follow a strategy of ubiquitous presence, whereas other sectors take a more strategic approach to which cities they will and will not set up operations in. The empirical evidence presented in the chapter is based on the office networks of 175 firms across 707 cities. The authors use principal components analysis to distil the essence of globalisation strategies to two key dimensions, the intensive and the extensive. The intensive strategy focuses on serving world markets through a very small number of key overseas cities and Brussels, Hong Kong and Beijing also emerge as the important globalisation arenas on this dimension. Home regions for the intensive strategy are dominated by nine US cities plus London. The extensive strategy is based on presence in a larger number of lower tier cities. Home regions for the extensive strategy are dominated by New York and London. Strategic firms are then defined as those scoring highly on both the intensive and extensive dimensions and key cities as cities that are home to ten or more of such firms. London and New York are identified as the only two cities which have a presence from all 25 strategic firms identified. The authors flesh out some of the broad statistical findings with a more in-depth interpretation based on what is known in the extant literature about the cities involved. For example, New York emerges as pre-eminent for financial innovations, London in adapting such innovations for global markets. This is reflected in New York's greater strategicness relative to London.

Sinkovics, Sinkovics, Hoque and Alford examine the linkages, actual and potential, between the GVC/GPN literatures in EG and the literature in IB. IB has traditionally placed the MNE centre stage, yet as MNEs have expanded their range of networks and have both dispersed and outsourced their value chains, so attention has become increasingly focused on their network relationships, both within and external to the firm. They argue that new questions have emerged within IB to which the GVC/GPN literature can provide a substantial contribution, including network governance, knowledge and power dynamics within networks and impacts on MNEs' network partners and wider society. The chapter presents the results of a systematic bibliographic analysis, which identified 79 key papers in the IB literature, published in core IB journals, and examined how the GVC/GPN literatures had been utilised in them. Six key uses are identified: (1) casual reference to the concepts; (2) use of the literatures to construct a theoretical framework; (3) use of the literatures to complement IB theories; (4) citation to support analysis of a particular industry; (5) making a critical review of GVC/GPN concepts; and (6) papers drawing primarily on other IB papers using GVC/GPN concepts, rather than the original sources. The literature in IB splits between those primarily focused on MNEs and those where the focus is on other actors in the system. The integration of GVC/GPN concepts has been most intensive in IB papers focused on emerging economy MNEs. Use of the frameworks tends to be lower in papers examining traditional MNE perspectives in IB. Finally, the chapter reveals that only a minority (40%) of the authors of the papers examined were mainstream IB scholars, which qualifies the extent to which ideas from Economics Geography have penetrated the IB mainstream.

Gammelgaard and McDonald examine the differing conceptions of space in IB and EG. As they argue, IB has had a long-standing interest in the reasons why MNEs place certain activities in certain places and how they then coordinate interactions between those dispersed activities. This is a rough correspondence in the analysis in EG between the space of places and the space of flows. Some key flows will be within firms, others between them. The chapter analyses Nohria and Ghoshal's concept of the differentiated network in the context of concepts related to EG contingencies. This framework places emphasis on the ability of firms to use their network to promote knowledge creation. In this endeavour, strongly centralised and top-down control is apt to be suboptimal. Differentiation arises, in part, due to the different (national) contexts in which subsidiaries operate. The internal system is regulated through the allocation of decision-making rights, formal controls and procedures and normative integration, imbuing organisation members with a common culture and sense of mission. In Nohria and Ghoshal's framework, they acknowledged that some key characteristics of the locations in which the firm operated would influence the desired balance between centralisation, formalisation and socialisation, e.g. the level of technological dynamism. As the authors note, elaboration of the framework over the last 20 years has placed more emphasis on the embedding of subsidiaries within external networks and the integration of subsidiaries with the strategic objectives of their corporate parent. Geographic factors play an influential role in the evolution of subsidiary mandates. They note that some of the country specific advantages are potentially amenable to government policy. They note that spatial coordination costs do tend to rise with physical distance. Firms also need to assess the risk of lock-in where they develop location-bound firm specific advantages which may become misaligned with corporate objectives. This risk rises with the degree of decentralisation. An additional risk is that firms may become too internationalised, under-estimating the effect on rising coordination costs. The authors identify a correspondence between the view of the firm as a differentiated network and the view of the firm taken in relational approaches to EG, albeit that there is less emphasis on the development of firm-specific advantages. The chapter concludes with an exploration of how the insights of the differentiated network approach and relational EG might be integrated to strengthen some of the weaknesses in each.

Key research at the interface of IB and EG

This section contains a series of chapters which show how the research in one field both draws on and can inform that in the other. The topics examined are also of interest in both disciplines.

Cooke focuses on the Economic Geography of corporate learning and knowledge flows. The chapter presents accounts of the sometimes convergent and sometimes divergent knowledge and learning pathways that informed the evolution of business knowledge and organisational learning in the corporate space economy until today. It concludes by referencing three major trends. First, the emergence of "postsocial" knowledge and learning that begins to supersede human cognition. Second, it traces the growth of the quaternary economy and its implications for economic growth, profitability and innovation. Here new models of "recombinant" or "crossover" exploitation of knowledge are explored. Third, the quaternary industries benefit from enormous wealth generation for a few (the "elites" of populist discourse) and emerge as a developmental model for rivalrous learner firms and countries.

Wu and Yang analyse a central theme which cuts across IB and EG: international knowledge transfer. Historically, knowledge has been recognised as the most important resource for the firm. MNCs are regarded as a repository for collecting and coordinating knowledge, and their ability to leverage dispersed knowledge and technology is crucial for maintaining their competitive advantages in the global market. Increasingly, MNCs have dispersed technology and innovation activities outside of the home market, and transferring knowledge from dispersed foreign subsidiaries to parent company, i.e. reverse knowledge transfer, has attracted attention in the literature of intra-MNC knowledge flows. It has been evidenced that the extent of knowledge flows is determined by the distance between parent company and the subsidiary. Notably, there is a growing literature that not only identifies the nature and extent of knowledge flows within the MNCs but also examines the effect of international knowledge transfer on firm productivity.

O'Neill examines the politics of infrastructure investment in the post-privatisation era. Infrastructure is fundamental to enabling efficient flows of people, goods, water, energy and information on which cities depend. It shows the tensions between the interests of private investors and the expectations of the citizenry for the assembly of a raft of capital assets that collectively underpin the operation of livable sustainable cities. The chapter traces the intrinsic role of infrastructure as a generator of urban economies and then of the state as a mediator of often conflicting demands in relation to economic outcomes, the availability and distribution of positive externalities and, crucially, of assignment of responsibility for infrastructure funding. Implications are drawn for urban planning and design. This brings a sharp perspective on the importance of infrastructure for enabling a city to generate the economic benefits which they are assumed to give rise to in several of the other chapters in this Companion. The success, or otherwise, of cities and the institutional arrangements which underpin them in providing infrastructure which is conducive to economic activity, including the reproduction of the labour supply, bears on central questions regarding the hierarchy of cities and the interplay between cities and MNEs. As O'Neill argues, infrastructure often has clear international articulation, such as transcontinental energy distribution systems and road and rail links. In the modern era, when the emphasis on provision has shifted away from the state to private providers, it also provides opportunities for MNEs in both carrying out and financing infrastructure projects. O'Neill's discussion touches on one of the grand challenges of the current age, the balance between the demands of "capital" for conditions which enhance its ability to generate profit and the demands of citizens for better "distributional" outcomes and amenity.

Ha, Wei and Wu explore the regional orientation of emerging economy MNEs. This chapter contributes to the debate about whether the rhetoric about globalisation and global strategy is overblown. This debate has been based primarily on evidence regarding developed country MNEs. Emerging economy MNEs, as the authors argue, differ from developed economies, as they often have a stronger incentive to venture abroad to develop, not just exploit, their competitive advantage. The chapter presents evidence based on 530 cross-order M&A deals made by 401 different emerging economy MNEs from 34 emerging economies into 22 OECD countries. Such cross-border M&As are associated with a desire for emerging economy MNEs to access strategic assets overseas, and the authors argue that they will venture outside their home region when the requisite strategic assets are not available there. Such an incentive is necessary given the institutional differences which arise between regions and which make M&As particularly difficult to integrate successfully. They argue that rather than looking for countries with similar institutions, emerging economy MNEs are more attracted to locations with high quality institutions. The authors find a positive and significant influence of the host region's institutions on the probability of an emerging economy MNE concluding a cross-border M&A there, although the effect of country institutions was not significant. There is no evidence of a significant simple mimetic effect, whereby an emerging economy MNE is more likely to be drawn to a country or regions where there already exist MNEs from the same home country; however, there is a significant mimetic effect where institutional quality is high.

Dimitratos and Bose examine the relationship between location and entrepreneurship, an important contribution given that the mainstream literature on international entrepreneurship has been largely aspatial, at odds with the evidence that international entrepreneurship has a specific and concentrated spatial distribution. The chapter briefly reviews key schools of thought on the sources of superior performance, namely the structure-conduct-performance paradigm, the relational view and the resource-based view. The chapter reviews theory and evidence regarding the links between location, performance and internationalisation. In line with the modern theory of the MNE, the chapter identifies that location may be key both in terms of access to strategic resources and the ability of firms to develop resources and capabilities. Building on this, it identifies that cities are privileged locations for accessing and developing resources. Key influences on strategy and performance that vary by location are identified to be: the degree of competition, networking opportunities, infrastructure, institutions, supplier networks, technologies and information. The chapter reviews some key theories regarding regional development, orthodox regional development theory and regional competitiveness theory. Running through the discussion is the importance of clustering and agglomeration externalities. The link with internationalisation is made chiefly through consideration of the Uppsala "stages model" and network theories of internationalisation. The chapter finishes by discussing a range of factors connecting location, performance and internationalisation, such as the benefits of staying in a familiar place, staying longer in the same place, obtaining regional embeddedness, overcoming the problem of foreignness, dealing with institutional frameworks, obtaining and mobilising resources, identifying and exploiting opportunities, and also gaining experience through value-chain operations.

Horn and Holden examine the relationship between language and the formation of business networks and their particular geographies. They do so through examination of German merchants in Early Modern Europe, between approximately 1500 and 1800. This period saw many important changes, including the development of modern industry and government. It also saw the development of trading empires and the use of European vernacular languages as the languages of business, trade and administration, even outside Europe. Horn and Holden place emphasis on cities as the crucibles of economic change and as important centres for assimilation of information, dissemination of knowledge, interchange of languages, and places where credit and payment were organised. Likewise, they identify merchants as key economic actors and ones who placed importance on acquiring foreign language skills. Horn and Holden contrast the flourishing of European vernacular languages along major European trade routes with the decline of the *lingua franca*, a patois used in commercial haggling in Mediterranean ports. The connection between cities and language was cemented by cities becoming important centres for professional language instruction and of culture and learning. In contrast with the modern era, language competence was seen as a pre-requisite for inter-cultural competence in IB. Language competence was essential to build up business networks, and these networks were in turn essential as pathways to information, resources and custom. Their concluding point, and an important one, is that geography plays an important role in the way in which language is used. This undermines the naïve view that geography has become less important because of the near ubiquitous use of English as the language of IB.

Taking an institutional perspective, Peng and Jung explore the question: why do MNEs undertake FDI? Conventional FDI research focuses on MNEs from developed economies that already hold competitive advantages with respect to their capabilities and exert such capabilities in foreign venues by seeking new markets or low-cost factors. The recent literature posits that MNEs from emerging economies (EMNEs) are leveraging FDI in order to obtain competitive advantages with respect to technology or innovation, and that EMNEs are mitigating competitive disadvantages. However, the literature has not sufficiently addressed the MNEs' motive of FDI for specific institutional attractiveness of FDI destinations. In consideration of the costs and benefits from institutions, the authors argue that MNEs "shop around world" for the institutions that enhance firms' overall net institutional benefits. They consider three arenas in which such window shopping takes place: tax avoidance, transfer pricing and capital round tripping. By focusing on such institution shopping, they advance contributions to the FDI literature by extending conventional asset-based motives to consider institution-based motives for FDI. They argue that both MNEs from advanced and emerging economies may have an incentive to invest overseas to avoid or mitigate the effect of "unhelpful" institutions in their home country. The authors argue that it is whether or not institutions are helpful or unhelpful to business which matters more than how "advanced" they are. The authors provide several case vignettes to illustrate their propositions. The authors call for more research on the influence of institutions on FDI and also on the ways in which MNEs act strategically to shape their institutional environment.

Location and competitiveness

This section presents three chapters which put the spotlight on the relationship between location and competitiveness. This acknowledges that firm location decisions will be related to the quest for competitive advantage. Some of these benefits will be static, such as access to lower production costs or better access to markets. Increasing importance is being attached, both by firms and within the IB literature, on dynamic advantages, whereby certain locations provide favourable environments for firms to increase their strategic resources, capabilities and knowledge.

Bedreaga, Arguilés and McCann examine the ideas and insights emerging from the EG and IB literatures on the strategic fit and embeddedness of multinationals, their subsidiaries and their affiliates in host economies. It offers analysis of three perspectives on this topic, first discussing concepts and definitions linking the multinational to its location and place. Second, the chapter reviews empirical research on embeddedness and strategic fit before focusing on multinational investment and the dimensions of distance. The chapter argues that in order to identify the strengths and weaknesses as well as the opportunities and challenges associated with embeddeness and strategic fit, it is important to develop a detailed understanding of the different dimensions of distance as they impact on multinationals.

Gugler examines the insights of IB and EG into the relationships between location and competitiveness. He considers four inter-related dimensions: (1) the factors which make a particular location attractive to MNEs; (2) the ways in which a favourable overseas location can enhance the competitive advantage of MNEs; (3) the ways in which the MNE's home location can enhance its competitive advantage; and (4) the ways in which spillovers from the MNE can enhance the competitiveness of its host location overseas. The factors which make a particular location attractive to MNEs can be condensed into two broad dimensions: resource endowments and institutional environment. Gugler argues that the location advantages of the home country will strongly influence the competitiveness (ownership advantages) of MNEs, as well as their international strategy. Gugler further argues that the specific advantages available in particular locations will have implications for the preferred entry mode of MNEs. In common with many contributions in this volume, Gugler singles out clusters are particularly privileged locations, above all for innovation. MNEs have the ability to create competitive advantage by combining the advantages offered by the range of locations at which they operate, both at firm and subsidiary level.

Castellani provides rich evidence on how the geographic pattern of innovation activity has changed over a 32-year period from 1980 to 2011, using OECD REGPAT data. He explores the role of MNEs in linking innovation hotspots through their corporate networks. He sets his analysis within a conceptual framework which recognises that the innovative dynamism of regions depends both on intense microprocesses at a very local scale and also extensive linkages to other innovation centres. MNEs are both the co-creators and beneficiaries of localised innovation and the global pipelines that link them. The analysis of MNE activity, with a particular focus on R&D, is based on data in 110,000 investment projects over the period 2003–2014, drawing on *fDi Markets* data. He identifies that one of the reasons why MNEs are able to act as conduits for knowledge flows from one location to another, apart from the obvious fact that they have operations in many locations, is that they can establish internal communities of practice, which are able to bridge the contextual gap between one location and another. This is akin to the idea that organisational proximity can substitute, to some degree, for physical proximity. It is also manifestly the case that MNEs have rapidly accelerated the international dispersion of their R&D efforts over the past 25 years or so. The evidence presented shows that the number of regions with at least one patent has increased threefold in the period 1980–2011, from fewer than 500 in 1980 to about 1,500 in 2010. The number of patents per region has simultaneously increased exponentially. Very strong geographic concentration of innovation, both across and within countries remains the dominant pattern. Regression analysis shows a high degree of persistence in patenting activity, controlling for other characteristics of the regions. Nevertheless, individual regions can significantly rise or decline as innovation hubs. Co-invention activities by MNEs across different regions are shown to have risen rapidly over time, and such collaboration has become increasingly focused on a small number of regions. Whilst there has been a degree of catch-up by emerging economies, there is still a very large gap between them and the most active countries in terms of patents per head of the population. There is also a higher degree of variation in the level of patenting activity across regions within emerging economies, compared to more advanced economies.

Services, IB and EG

This section takes a particular look at the internationalisation strategies and geographic patterning of service industries. These have been relatively neglected in the IB literature, but have been very important within the EG literature, which has, in particular, made them central in the analysis of the world cities network and has had a particular interest in the organisation and influence of Financial Services.

Wrigley and Wood focus on the internationalisation of retailing and specifically explore how EG has been able to make a distinct and strategically important impact despite its modest scale compared to the critical mass of IB studies. It begins with a review of IB's engagement with the globalisation of retailing, including discussion of Rugman's regionalisation thesis, Dunning's OLI framework and the Uppsala model. It notes a trend over recent years in IB towards increased richness in both uncovering the complexity of local geographies and appreciating the implications this can have for (retail) MNE development. The chapter then turns to EG's engagement with the globalisation of retailing. It frames the process of international retailing as embedded and networked, constrained by regulations across various spatial scales, affected by financial market relations and as exhibiting selective capability transfer and learning processes. The conclusion discusses the possibilities and potential for further engagement between IB and EG.

Although services are now the dominant form of economic activity and change in advanced economies, researchers are still grappling with the specificities of services. Howells and Lowe examine the hotel industry as a lens through which to examine three foci: (1) the services sector and the conceptualisation of innovation and entrepreneurial activity as a central concern within the "boundary space" between EG and IB; (2) to explore the emergence of new hotel forms in the sector, conceptualising those developments in terms of the disruptive and emergent forms of innovation; and (3) the connection of the creation of a new hotel form with wider social network relationships and trajectories associated with the emergence of a "diaspora" of entrepreneurial innovators. The chapter then relates the findings of this study to inform the theoretical development and conceptualisation of service innovation and internationalisation which covers the extant and overlapping realms of IB and EG.

Bagchi-Sen and Schunder review the literature on the internationalisation of producer services. Advanced producer services firms and their internationalisation strategies are of foremost importance, as they are key enablers for the internationalisation strategies of other MNEs. They are also critical for the constitution of world cities. The authors explore the defining features of producer services and the conceptual issues involved in defining what they are. As they point out, some services are tradable, like software; others have to be consumed at a fixed location, like hotels; and some services companies deal in services which combine tradable and non-tradable aspects in various proportions. Another important distinction is between capital intensity and knowledge intensity. These differences are reflected in differences in internationalisation strategy. As is the case for manufacturing firms, the lowering of trade barriers and improvements in ICT have allowed a degree of fine-slicing and offshoring in producer services, although they remain distinctly more local in general than manufacturing firms. Increased organisational complexity among manufacturing firms also drives demand for producer services. Akin to manufacturing firms, choice of entry mode turns on the balance between control (mitigating transaction costs) and the greater risk of higher-commitment entry modes. Moreover, firms may vary entry mode based on the specifics of particular overseas locations, with market size and potential and political risk being important moderating influences. The authors debate the extent to which the traditional Dunning eclectic paradigm explains service-based FDI. Internalisation is typically very important to preserve quality and protect reputation. Whilst they conclude that on the whole it does, the application of this framework needs to be modified by the key characteristics of services, namely intangibility, perishability, inseparability and heterogeneity. The authors also explain how capability perspectives, related to experiential learning, and network perspectives also have power in explaining the internationalisation strategies of producer service firms. The authors explore the strong rise in producer services and knowledge-intensive business services in emerging economies, due to both their economic development and their rapidly rising levels of human capital (with relatively modest labour costs).

Bryson examines how goods are designed and redesigned in order to meet consumer preferences in IB. Design is critical to competitiveness in IB and, with few exceptions, adaptation to local preferences is necessary. What is more, there is often a need to adapt to technical and regulatory standards in different countries. The need to do so varies by type of product. By the same token, firms have alternative ways in which they can foster local customisation, including the use of local independent designers and exposing their own in-house staff to education, training and work in overseas locations. In framing his analysis, Bryson makes appeal to the idea of the GPN, which, as he argues, tackles some of the complexities of operating IBs which are not centre stage, for example, in Dunning's eclectic paradigm. Bryson argues that macro perspectives on IB, such as the production network literature are important, as are micro- and meso-level perspectives. He is sceptical of the ability to develop a single integrated theory of IB and argues that multiple disciplinary perspectives are needed. Geography is central as cross-border business activities have very particular geographies. Bryson notes that there has been a sharp rise in the number of business and professional service firms in recent years, the vast majority of which are very small. He ascribes very little of this growth to simple outsourcing based on cost cutting of larger firms, but rather to a strong growth in demand for highly specialised technical services.

Clark examines Financial Services. Critics of the global Financial Services industry contend that it serves only the interests of traders and large institutions. Implied is a culture of finance embodying shared industry norms and conventions – a ruling ethic that trumps more desirable modes of behaviour. There is some truth to this claim: there is a set of norms and conventions that govern the relationships between the buy side and the sell side of the market. But the industry is not a homogeneous whole: it is characterised by functional, geographical and organisational diversity. These points are developed through a systematic mapping of the industry, focusing upon the ecology and morphology of finance. To the extent that there is a culture of finance, it reflects the lack of incentives on the buy side of the market to effectively govern relationships with service providers and employees. The chapter closes with a set of examples of innovation in industry norms and conventions.

Drawing on literatures from IB and EG, Beaverstock and Harvey examine global professional service firms in Australia in response to the contemporary gap in empirical examination of these firms outside North America and Europe. The discussion focuses specifically on the internationalisation of executive search. The chapter draws on primary and secondary data analysis to present research findings on the internationalisation and localisation of the executive search industry in the Asia-Pacific and Australia, respectively. Finally, the chapter reports several contributions from the research that raise many implications for future work. It also highlights the significant contribution of relevant work in organisation studies over IB.

References

Alford, M., Sinkovics, R., Sinkovics, N. & Hoque, S. (2017) 'Integrating global value chain/global production network analysis into International Business debates: A review and research agenda'. Paper presented at 44th Association of International Business UK/NI Chapter Annual Conference, Reading, 6–8 April.

Amin, A. & Thrift, N. (1992) 'Neo-Marshallian nodes in global networks', *International Journal of Urban and Regional Research*, 16(4), pp. 571–587.

Andersson, U., Björkman, I. & Forsgren, M. (2005) 'Managing subsidiary knowledge creation: The effect of control mechanisms on subsidiary local embeddedness', *International Business Review*, 14, pp. 521–538.

Beaverstock, J.V. (2010) 'Peter Dicken', in Hubbard, P., Kitchen, R. & Valentine, G. (Eds.), *Key Contemporary Thinkers on Space and Place*. 2nd Edition. London: Sage, pp. 108–112.

Beaverstock, J.V., Faulconbridge, J. & Hall, S.J.E. (2015) *The Globalization of Executive Search: Professional Services Strategy and Dynamics in a Contemporary World*. London: Routledge.

Beaverstock, J.V., Smith, R.G. & Taylor, P.J. (1999) 'A roster of world cities', *Cities*, 16, pp. 445–458.

Beugelsdijk, S. & Mudambi, R. (2013) 'MNCs as border-crossing multi-location enterprises: The role of discontinuities in geographic space', *Journal of International Business Studies*, 44, pp. 413–416.

Beugelsdijk, S., Mudambi, R. & McCann, P. (2010) 'Place, space and organization: Economic Geography and the multinational enterprise', *Journal of Economic Geography*, 10, pp. 485–493.

Birkinshaw, J., Young, S. & Hood, N. (2005) 'Subsidiary entrepreneurship, internal and external competitive forces and subsidiary performance', *International Business Review*, 14(2), pp. 227–248.

Boschma, R. (2005) 'Proximity and innovation: A critical assessment', *Regional Studies*, 39, pp. 61–74.

Bradshaw, M., Coe, N.M., Faulconbridge, J., James, A. & Souch, C. (2016) 'In the business of Economic Geography'. Panel Session. Royal Geographical Society/Institute of British Geographers Annual Conference, London, September 2016.

Buckley, P.J. & Casson, M.C. (1976) *The future of the multinational enterprise*. London: Homes & Meier.

Buckley, P.J. & Ghauri, P.N. (2004) 'Globalisation, Economic Geography and the strategy of multinational enterprises', *Journal of International Business Studies*, 35, pp. 81–98.

Cantwell, J.A. & Mudambi, R. (2011) 'Physical attraction and the geography of knowledge sourcing in multinational enterprises', *Global Strategy Journal*, 1, pp. 206–232.

Chiao, Y.C. & Ying, K.P. (2013) 'Network effect and subsidiary autonomy in multinational corporations: An investigation of Taiwanese subsidiaries', *International Business Review*, 22, pp. 652–662.

Coe, N.M., Hess, M., Yeung, H., Dicken, P. & Henderson, J. (2004) '"Globalizing" regional development: Global production networks perspective', *Transactions of the Institute of British Geographers*, 29, pp. 468–484.

Cook, G. & Johns, J. (2013) 'The transformation of broadcasting and film in Manchester and Liverpool: Changing cluster dynamics', In Karlsson, C. and Picard, R.G. (Eds.), *Media Clusters: Spatial Agglomeration and Content Capabilities*. London: Edward Elgar, pp. 161–198.

Daniels, P.W. (1982) *Service Industries: Growth and Location*. Cambridge, UK: Cambridge University Press.

Dicken, P. (1976) 'The multiplant enterprise and geographical space: Some issues in the study of external control and regional development', *Regional Studies*, 10, pp. 401–412.

Dicken, P. (1977) 'A note on location theory and the large business enterprise', *Area*, 9, pp. 138–143.

Dicken, P. (1986) *Global Shift: Industrial Change in a Turbulent World*. London: PCP.

Dicken, P. & Lloyd, P. (1973) *Location in Space*. London: Harper & Row.

Dicken, P. & Lloyd, P. (1976) 'Geographical perspectives on United States investment in the United Kingdom', *Environment and Planning A*, 8, pp. 685–705.

Dicken, P. & Malmberg, A. (2001) 'Firms in territories: A relational perspective', *Economic Geography*, 77, pp. 345–363.

DiMaggio, P. & Powell, W.W. (1983) 'The iron cage revisited: Institutional isomorphism and collective rationality in organizational fields', *American Sociological Review*, 48, pp. 147–160.

Dunning, J.H. (1979) 'Towards an eclectic theory of international production: Some empirical tests', *Journal of International Business Studies*, 11, pp. 9–31.

Dunning, J.H. (1995) 'Reappraising the Eclectic Paradigm in an age of alliance capital', *Journal of International Business Studies*, 26, pp. 461–491.

Dunning, J.H. (2009) 'Location and the multinational enterprise: John Dunning's thoughts on receiving the *Journal of International Business Studies* 2008 Decade Award', *Journal of International Business Studies*, 40, pp. 20–34.

Dunning, J.H. & Rugman, A.M. (1985) 'The influence of Hymer's dissertation on the theory of foreign direct investment', *The American Economic Review*, 75, pp. 228–232.

Frost, T., Birkinshaw, J. & Ensign, P. (2002) 'Centers of excellence in multinational corporations', *Strategic Management Journal*, 23, pp. 997–1018.

Gammelgaard, J., McDonald, F., Tüselmann, H.J., Dörrenbächer, C. & Stephan, A. (2012) 'The impact of changes in subsidiary autonomy and network relationships on performance', *International Business Review*, 20, pp. 1158–1172.

Gertler, M.S. (2003) 'Tacit knowledge and the Economic Geography of context, or the undefinable tacitness of being there', *Journal of Economic Geography*, 3, pp. 75–99.

Goerzen, A., Asmussen, C.G. & Nielsen, B.B. (2013) 'Global cities and multinational enterprise location strategy', *Journal of International Business Studies*, 44, pp. 427–450.

Hymer, S. (1972) 'The multinational corporation and the law of uneven development', in Bhagwati, J. (Ed.), *Economics and World Order from the 1970s to the 1990s*. London: Collier-Macmillan, pp. 113–140.

Jacobs, J. (1969). *The Economy of Cities*. Harmondsworth, UK: Penguin.

Johns, J. (2016) 'The future of Economic Geography'. Panel Presentation for 'In the business of Economic Geography'. Royal Geographical Society/Institute of British Geographers Annual Conference, London, September 2016.

Kawai, N. & Strange, R. (2014) 'Subsidiary autonomy and performance in Japanese multinationals in Europe', *International Business Review*, 23, pp. 504–515.

Knickerbocker, F.T. (1973) *Oligopolistic Reaction and the Multinational Enterprise*. Cambridge, MA: Harvard University Press.

Ma, X., Delios, A. & Lau, C.M. (2013a) 'Beijing or Shanghai? The strategic location choice of large MNEs' host-country headquarters in China', *Journal of International Business Studies*, 44, pp. 953–961.

Ma, X., Delios, A., & Lau, C.M. (2013b) 'A new tale of two cities: Japanese FDIs in Shanghai and Beijing, 1979–2003', *International Business Review*, 16, pp. 207–228.

Marshall, A. (1927) *Industry and Trade*. London: Macmillan.

Martin, R. (1999) 'The new "geographical turn" in economics: Some critical reflections', *Cambridge Journal of Economics*, 23, pp. 65–91.
Martin, R. & Sunley, P. (2001) 'Rethinking the "economic" in Economic Geography: Broadening our vision or losing our focus?' *Antipode*, 33, pp. 148–161.
Martin, R. & Sunley, P. (2003) 'Deconstructing clusters: Chaotic concept or policy panacea?' *Journal of Economic Geography*, 3, pp. 5–35.
McCann, P. (2011) 'International Business and Economic Geography: Knowledge, time and transaction costs', *Journal of Economic Geography*, 11, pp. 309–317.
McCann, P. & Mudambi, R. (2005) 'Analytical differences in the economics of geography: The case of the multinational firm', *Environment & Planning A*, 37(10), pp. 1857–1876.
Meyer, K.E. & Nguyen, H.V. (2005) 'Foreign investment strategies and sub-national institutions in emerging markets: Evidence from Vietnam', *Journal of Management Studies*, 42, pp. 63–93.
Mudambi, R. & Swift, T. (2011). 'Leveraging knowledge and competencies across space: The next frontier in International Business', *Journal of International Management*, 17(3), 186–189.
Nachum, L. & Wymbs, C. (2005) 'Product differentiation, external economies and MNE location choices: M&As in global cities', *Journal of International Business Studies*, 36, pp. 415–434.
Nachum, L. & Wymbs, C. (2007) 'The location and performance of foreign affiliates in global cities', in Rugman, A.M. (Ed.), *Regional Aspects of Multinationality and Performance: Research in Global Strategic Management, volume 13*. Bingley, UK: Emerald, pp. 221–259.
Oehmichen, J. & Puck, J. (2016) 'Embeddedness, ownership mode and dynamics, and the performance of MNE subsidiaries', *Journal of International Management*, 22, pp. 17–28.
Porter, M.E. (1990) *The Competitive Advantage of Nations*. London: MacMillan.
Santangelo, G.D. (2009) 'MNCs and linkages creation: Evidence from a peripheral area', *Journal of World Business*, 44, pp. 192–205.
Saxenian, A. (1994) *Regional Advantage: Culture and Competition in Silicon Valley and Route 128*. Cambridge, MA: Harvard University Press.
Scott, A.J. (Ed.) (2001) *Global City Regions: Trends, Theory, Policy*. Oxford, UK: Oxford University Press.
Sim, L.L., Ong, S.E., Agarwal, A., Parsa, A. & Keivani, R. (2003) 'Singapore's competitiveness as a global city: Development strategy, institutions and business environment', *Cities*, 20, pp. 115–127.
Taylor, M. & Thrift, N. (Eds.) (1982) *The Geography of Multinationals*. London: Croom Helm.
Taylor, M. & Thrift, M. (1983) 'Business organisations, segmentation and location', *Regional Studies*, 17, pp. 445–465.
Taylor, P.J. (1997) 'Hierarchical tendencies amongst world cities: A global research proposal', *Cities*, 14, pp. 323–332.
Vahlne, J.E., Schweizer, R. & Johanson, J. (2012) 'Overcoming the liability of outsidership: The challenge of HQ of the global firm', *Journal of International Management*, 18, pp. 224–232.
Vernon, R. (1979) 'The product cycle hypothesis in a new international environment', *Oxford Bulletin of Economics and Statistics*, 41, pp. 255–267.
Yeung, H. (2005) 'Rethinking relational Economic Geography', *Transactions of the Institute of British Geographers*, 30, pp. 37–51.
Young, S. & Tavares, A. (2004) 'Centralization and autonomy: Back to the future', *International Business Review*, 13, pp. 215–237.
Zaheer, S. (1995) 'Overcoming the liability of foreignness', *Academy of Management Journal*, 38, pp. 341–363.

PART I

Some core material in International Business

2
SPACE AND INTERNATIONAL BUSINESS

Steven Brakman and Charles van Marrewijk

Introduction

One of the most remarkable aspects of the global economic system is the unequal distribution of population and economic activity across the earth. Millions of people are living close together in New York, Moscow, and Beijing. At the same time, there are large, virtually empty spaces available in the USA, Russia, and China. This unequal distribution of economic activity also has consequences for firm interaction in an International Business environment.

One of the major actors in the present era of globalization is no doubt the multinational firm (multinationals for short). These firms are probably the most mobile among all firms, with sufficient 'international' knowledge to seize a profitable opportunity when it presents itself. Without specific cultural ties to individual nations, they can seemingly rapidly move in and out of countries, with only economic incentives to act upon. Traditionally, international trade theory focused on trade between countries and regions, with only limited attention for individual firms. The modern literature, however, has taken a strong micro-economic turn and the availability of micro-firm data has revealed many interesting stylized facts that eluded earlier research. These stylized facts are the main topic of this contribution (see also Beugelsdijk et al., 2013a, 2013b).

The footloose nature of multinationals is strengthened by the fact that such firms no longer produce 'under a single roof'. Richard Baldwin (2006) calls this process the *second unbundling.* The first unbundling was initiated by the transportation revolution of the industrial revolution (1750–1900) that made it possible to spatially separate production from consumption, thereby facilitating international specialization on an unprecedented scale. The second unbundling really took off after 1980 and spatially separates the different stages of the production process itself, where parts of the production process are organized in the most efficient location.

Recent advances in geographical economics argue that the continued decline of spatial interaction costs (falling transport costs, declining trade barriers, and new communication technology) are the primary causes of the unequal spatial distribution of economic activity, leading to a 'spiky' core-periphery world with large income differences between rich and poor countries (rather than a 'flat' world as some other people argue (Friedman, 2005)).

This chapter combines the above observations and illustrates its consequences in three sections.[1] The first section analyses recent characteristics of firm heterogeneity, trade, and multinational activity. The following section focuses on recent information regarding trade in value-added, trade links, and global supply chains. The final section reviews the geographical economics approach and the consequences for the distribution of economic activity and global trade flows. We first discuss the three main parts in more detail.

The first section starts by discussing firm heterogeneity and trade by showing that only a small fraction of all firms engage in trading activities, that this share varies per sector based on comparative advantage, and is firm-specific. We also note that trading firms are larger, more productive, use higher skilled workers, and pay higher wages. We then analyse trade and multinationals. First, by showing that the majority of trading firms only trade one or two goods with one or two other countries. Only a small fraction of (multinational) firms trade a range of different goods to a range of different countries. This small fraction of large firms is, however, responsible for the large majority of trade value. Second, we show that a large share of trade flows is 'related party' trade. Although we mainly use American data and mostly focus on exports, similar results hold for imports and other OECD countries.

The second section starts by introducing the new data on trade in value-added, which tries to estimate the extent to which a country's gross export flows incorporate domestically produced value-added and imported foreign value-added. As national production processes become increasingly intertwined with foreign production processes the share of value-added trade in gross trade flows has been steadily declining. It continues by analysing these trade linkages at the global level by identifying backward linkages (incorporated foreign value-added), forward linkages (domestic value-added used as foreign intermediate input), direct domestic content (created in the sector itself), and indirect domestic content (created in other sectors). It goes on to show the consequences for the participation in global supply chains. The extent to which countries participate in global supply chains varies substantially, but is rising for virtually all countries.[2]

The final section provides a brief overview of the 'core' model of geographical economics, which gives rise to a core-periphery structure of the world economy as spatial interaction costs fall. It concludes by illustrating the consequences of these developments for the structure of global regional trade flows.

Trade and firm heterogeneity

We start by providing some basic empirical information on firm heterogeneity and trade, largely based on data from Bernard et al. (2015).[3] Figure 2.1 shows on the horizontal axis that, on average, only 35 percent of the American manufacturing firms export their products. This differs widely for the 21 manufacturing sectors identified in the figure (bubbles proportional to the number of firms in the sector), ranging from 15 percent for Printing and Related Support to 75 percent for Computers and Electronic Products. We make four observations. First, on average it is relatively rare to be an exporting firm as only one in three firms engages in exporting activities. Second, the share of exporting firms differs per sector. Third, assuming that the USA has a 'traditional' (technology or factor-abundance based) comparative advantage in computers, the share of exporting firms is positively related to traditional sources of comparative advantage. Fourth, firm heterogeneity is substantial; even for the strongest sectors not *all* firms are exporting, while for the weak sectors there are still some firms that *do* export.

Figure 2.1 also indicates (on the vertical axis) the mean exports as a share of total shipments. The average export share is only 17 percent, considerably less than the 35 percent of firms that engage in exporting activities. The lowest share of export revenue is for Paper Manufacturing (6 percent) and the highest share for Electrical Equipment, Appliance (47 percent). Beverage

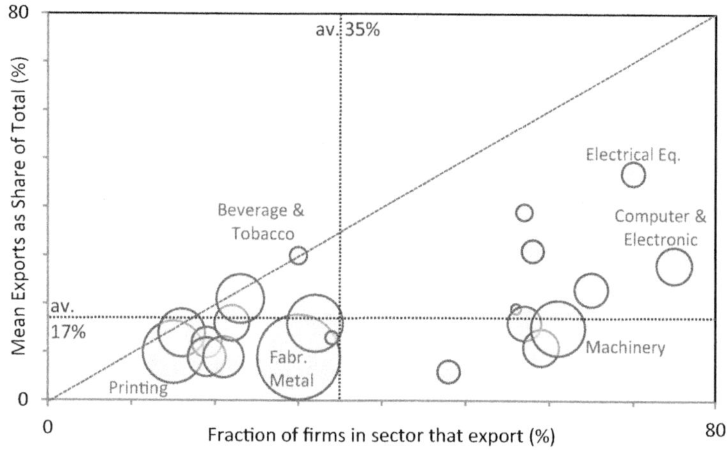

Figure 2.1 Exporting activities in different sectors; USA, 2007

Source: Authors' construction based on data in Bernard et al. (2015); 21 sectors; averages refer to Aggregate Manufacturing; bubble size proportional to the percent of firms in total manufacturing for that sector.

and Tobacco Products is the only sector where the mean exports as a share of total shipments (30 percent) is not less than the fraction of firms in the sector that exports (also 30 percent). For the majority of firms, the domestic market seems to be more important, but there is substantial variation among the different sectors.

Since not all firms engage in exporting activities it is worthwhile to investigate to what extent exporting firms differ from non-exporting firms. One way to do this is to analyse information for thousands of firms using regression analysis to estimate the size of the differences. This is done in Figure 2.2, which reports exporter premia over non-exporters in percent. Let's first focus on the simple regressions (the 'none' bars). Panel *b* of Figure 2.2 shows that exporting firms are larger than non-exporters; they employ about 128 percent more people and shipments are about 172 percent larger. Panel *a* shows that they have other characteristics as well; the skill per worker is about 6 percent higher, the capital per worker about 28 percent higher, the wages they pay about 21 percent higher, the value-added per worker about 33 percent higher, and the firm's total factor productivity is about 3 percent higher. Interestingly, the causality runs from productivity to exporting, and not the other way around (Melitz, 2003). This is remarkable, as it is often stated that international competition forces firms to become more competitive.

The simple regressions lump all firms in all sectors together. To control for differences between sectors we should look at the 'FE' bars, which allow for sector-specific fixed effects. In general, the estimated premia are a little bit lower (except for total factor productivity), but all are still strong and highly significant (except for skill per worker). Finally, we can also control for the size of the firm by looking at the 'FE+Empl' bars, which control for sector fixed effects and employment size. As expected, this reduces the estimated shipment premium (from 135 to 24 percent, see panel *b*). All other estimated firm characteristic premia in panel *a*, however, become larger and are highly significant (including skill per worker). Finally, we want to point out that there is overwhelming evidence of large differences in productivity between firms of similar type.

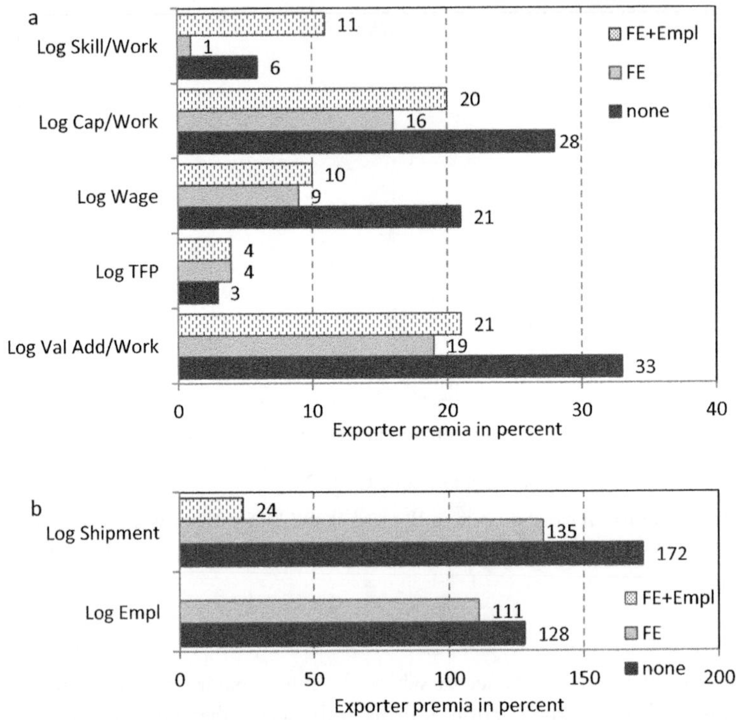

Figure 2.2 Exporter premia in percent; USA, 2007

Source: Authors' construction based on data in Bernard et al. (2015); legend identifies additional covariates in bivariate OLS regressions; FE = Industry Fixed Effects; FE+Empl = Industry Fixed Effects & Log Employment; Skill/Work = Skill per Worker; Cap/Work = Capital per Worker; TFP = Total Factor Productivity; Val Add/Work = Value Added per Worker; Empl = Employment; all significant at 1% except log skill/work FE.

Trade and multinationals

Recent research confirms that the linkage between firm productivity and internationalization also holds for multinationals; only the most productive firms can afford to become a multinational; investing abroad is expensive and only productive firms can afford this. Empirical research has confirmed this linkage between productivity and doing business abroad and detected a clear ranking between firms. Less productive firms are active domestically, more productive firms can afford to become exporters, and only the most productive firms become multinationals (Helpman, Melitz & Yeaple, 2004). But micro-data reveal more than only this linkage.

We now continue this discussion in two steps. First, we will analyse the extent to which trading firms differ regarding the number of products they trade and the number of countries they trade with, the so-called extensive margin of trade flows. Second, we analyse the extent to which trade involves within-firm transactions, so-called related party trade, where a firm in one country trades with a parent or affiliate in another country. We base our discussion on evidence for American firms, but similar observations hold for the structure of trade flows for other advanced countries. Recall that only about a third of all American manufacturing firms are active in exporting activities (see earlier). The differences between these exporting firms regarding the number of products they export, the number of countries they export to, and the value of these exports are enormous, as illustrated in Figure 2.3.

Panel *a* of Figure 2.3 shows the distribution of the share of exporting firms over the number of products and the number of countries. By far the largest number of exporting firms (35 percent of the total) export only one product to one other country, visualized in panel *a* by the high bar in the left corner. Fewer than 9 percent of the firms export one product to two countries, fewer than 4 percent of the firms export one product to three countries, and only about 1 percent of the firms export one product to 11 or more countries. In total, about 53 percent of the exporting firms export only one product. In the other dimension, about 2 percent of the firms export two products to one country and less than 1 percent of the firms export three products to one country, four products to one country, and so on. In total, about 38 percent of the exporting firms export only to one country. In the upper right corner of panel *a* we see the share of firms that export many products to many countries. About 16 percent of the firms export six or more products to six or more countries. We thus observe a clear distinction in this panel: the majority of firms (more than 51 percent) export one or two products to one or two countries (lower left corner), while only a small fraction of firms (less than 6 percent) export 11 or more products to 11 or more countries.

Panel *b* of Figure 2.3 shows the distribution of the export value over the number of products and the number of countries. This panel is clear: there are only four entries above 1 percent of export value and they are all in the top right corner for firms that export six or more products to six or more countries; taken together these 16 percent of firms account for more than 86 percent of all export value (about seven times higher than the average value for exporting firms). By far the highest bar in panel *b* is for the superstar firms that export more than 11 products to more than 11 countries; taken together these 5.5 percent of firms account for about 80 percent of all export value (about 15 times higher than the average value for exporting firms). A small fraction of very large firms is thus responsible for the large majority of export revenue. Most of these firms are multinationals, as we discuss later.

Firms start carefully when they decide to become international. Firms first become active in familiar markets and only then move to more 'foreign' markets, which are more expensive to

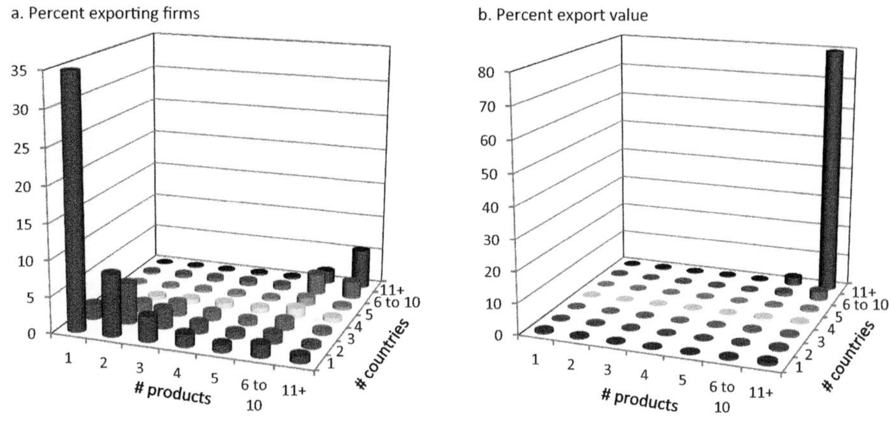

Figure 2.3 Export distribution by product and country; USA, 2007

Source: Authors' construction based on data in Bernard et al. (2015).

enter, because languages are unfamiliar, institutions are different, legal systems are different, and so on. Only if a multinational firm becomes productive/profitable enough does it become active in more 'distant' foreign markets. In general, this relation is confirmed by empirical research. A meta-study, however, also revealed that important differences exist between firms, sectors, and countries of origin. Based on an analysis of 359 studies across 32 countries between 1972 and 2012, Marano et al. (2016) conclude that the overall linkage between internationalization (multinationalization) and performance is positive but small and with large standard deviations.

Now that we have established that a few large firms are responsible for a large share of the value of international trade flows, we take the next step by analysing the extent to which multinational firms are involved in these trade flows. As an indication of their importance we show in Figure 2.4 the size of total trade (panel *a* for imports and panel *b* for exports) and the size of related party trade. Note that related party trade underestimates the importance of multinationals in total trade flows as it only records within-firm flows between parents and affiliates and not trade flows between multinationals and other firms.

In real terms (constant 2014 USD), total import value rose from $1,471 billion in 2002 to $2,314 billion in 2014 (an increase of 57 percent), with a substantial dip in 2009 (of more than $600 billion) as a result of the Great Recession, see panel *a* of Figure 2.4. The related party imports followed the same, but more pronounced pattern as they rose from $700 billion in 2002 to $1,179 billion in 2014 (an increase of 68 percent), also with a substantial dip (of more than $260 billion) in 2009 as a result of the Great Recession. We thus note that, as a consequence of these developments, the share of related party trade in total imports is substantial (about half of all imports) and rose from about 48 percent in 2002 to about 51 percent in 2014.

Panel *b* of Figure 2.4 depicts the same information for export value. Total export value rose from $802 billion in 2002 to $1,402 billion in 2014 (an increase of 75 percent), with a dip of more than $260 billion in 2009. Note that total exports are considerably less than total imports as the USA has a large trade deficit (in these data of about $670 billion in 2002 and more than $900 billion in 2014). The related party exports follow the same, but *less* pronounced pattern as they rose from $251 billion in 2002 to $408 billion in 2014 (an increase of 62 percent), with a dip of $74 billion in 2009. We thus note that, as a consequence of these developments, the

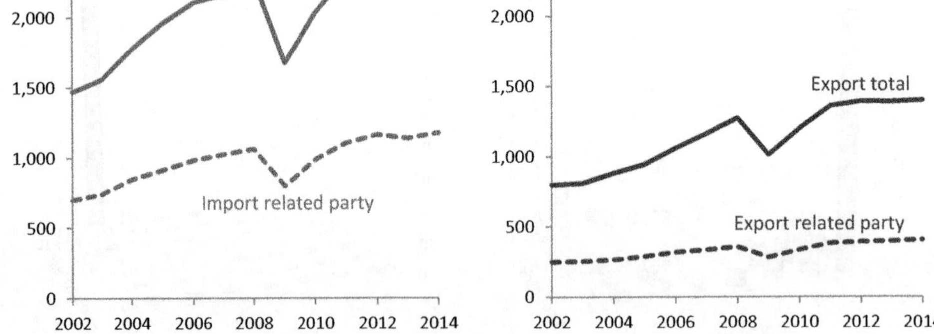

Figure 2.4 USA total and related party imports and exports, 2002–2014

Source: Authors' construction based on US Census Related Party Database; values in constant 2014 USD billion.

share of related party trade in total exports is substantial (around 30 percent of all exports), but considerably less than their share in total imports. Related party trade is thus particularly important for American imports. The share of related party exports in total exports declined slightly from about 31 percent in 2002 to about 29 percent in 2014.

Trade in value-added

Traditionally, international trade is analysed by using data on gross exports and imports. This is the trade that crosses national borders and is registered by customs officials (except for intra-EU trade, where it is estimated). The assumption is that gross trade flows provide sufficient information to analyse the structure of international trade and, for example, comparative advantage. As long as international fragmentation is limited gross trade flows indeed provide this information. This is, however, no longer the case. International fragmentation of the production process has become a salient characteristic of the world economy and international trade flows no longer, or to a lesser extent than they used to be, reflect what a country is producing and exporting (see Brakman, van Marrewijk & Partridge, 2015).

There have been several recent attempts to remedy this shortcoming by constructing estimates of value-added trade flows across countries rather than gross export flows, see Figure 2.5. We first focus on the EU-Groningen constructed World Input-Output Data (WIOD) database and then discuss the OECD-WTO trade in value-added database in the next section. The WIOD trade data identify 40 individual countries and a 'Rest of World' (RoW) group of countries to characterize global trade flows in the period 1995–2009. The countries are the 27 countries of the EU (as of January 1, 2007) combined with Australia, Brazil, Canada, China, India, Indonesia, Japan, Mexico, Russia, Taiwan, Turkey, and the USA. Together these countries represent about 85 percent of world GDP. Furthermore, the data cover 35 sectors and are constructed by combining national Input-Output tables with international trade data.

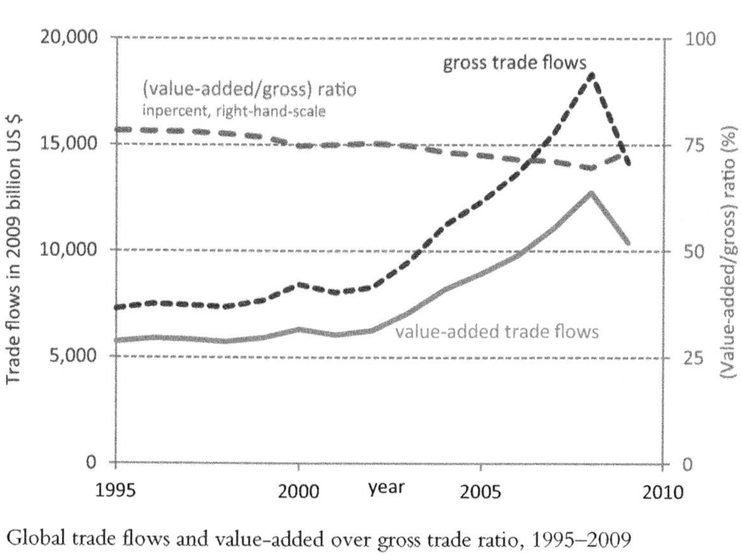

Figure 2.5 Global trade flows and value-added over gross trade ratio, 1995–2009

Source: Brakman and van Marrewijk (2017) (reproduced with permission from Wiley).

Expressed in constant 2009 USD, global gross trade flows increased by about 94 percent in this period (see Figure 2.5), from $7,305 billion in 1995 to $14,160 billion in 2009 (based on WIOD data; we converted current dollars to constant dollars using the American GDP deflator). Global gross trade flows peaked in 2008 at $18,315 billion (the drop in 2009 was almost 23 percent). Measured in value-added terms, global trade flows increased in the same period by about 82 percent, from $5,722 billion in 1995 to $10,397 billion in 2009. As illustrated in Figure 2.5, value-added trade and gross trade move up and down quite closely, although the gap between these flows is gradually increasing since value-added trade rises more slowly. As a consequence, the *ratio* of value-added trade to gross trade is gradually declining over time, from 78 percent in 1995 to 73 percent in 2009 (this ratio is depicted on the right-hand-scale of Figure 2.5).

Global trade linkages

The trade in value-added data is useful for identifying global supply chains, which usually involve the simultaneous importing and exporting of goods and components at different stages of the production process in the same broader sector involving locations in a range of different countries. The streams are usually co-ordinated at the firm level by multinational enterprises. The inter-dependencies are important, as are the logistics problems. As a consequence, supply chains tend to involve multiple countries at different stages of economic development (which allows for differences in comparative advantages between the countries), but these countries have to be relatively close together in space in order to manage the logistics and coordination problems (see e.g. Baldwin & Venables, 2013). Many large supply chains therefore involve advanced countries and nearby middle income countries, such as the USA and Mexico, Germany and the Czech Republic, or Japan and China. Indeed, it is not too far-fetched to argue that some middle income countries became precisely that (middle income countries) because they benefited from being at the right stage of economic development in the neighbourhood of advanced countries at the right time.

One way to identify supply chains is by looking at the value-added at each step of the production process. We do that in this section using the OECD-WTO trade in value-added database. The most recent version of this database identifies 61 different countries plus a RoW combination of other countries and provides information up to 2011. We start by discussing the main concepts involved. Suppose the American economy consists of three sectors, labelled 1, 2, and 3. For simplicity we assume that all American exports consist of sector 2 exports to China, which is taken to be the only other country in the world. The Chinese economy consists of two sectors, labelled 1 and 3. We focus attention on domestic value-added and so-called backward and forward international linkages in our discussion below. We use gross exports from America (equated to 100 percent) as our frame of reference; see Figure 2.6 for details.

Backward linkages. Not all value incorporated in America's gross exports is created in America since part of it is created in so-called upstream sectors that supply intermediate goods to sector 2. More specifically, both China sector 1 and China sector 3 supply intermediate products to the American producers in sector 2; we identify these flows by the arrows C_1A_2 and C_3A_2 in Figure 2.6. As a consequence, part of gross exports represents value-added imported from abroad. It is identified as FVA (foreign value-added) in Figure 2.6 and consists of the (international) backward linkages of global supply chains. The global average backward linkages were 24 percent of gross exports in 2011, as listed in the figure.

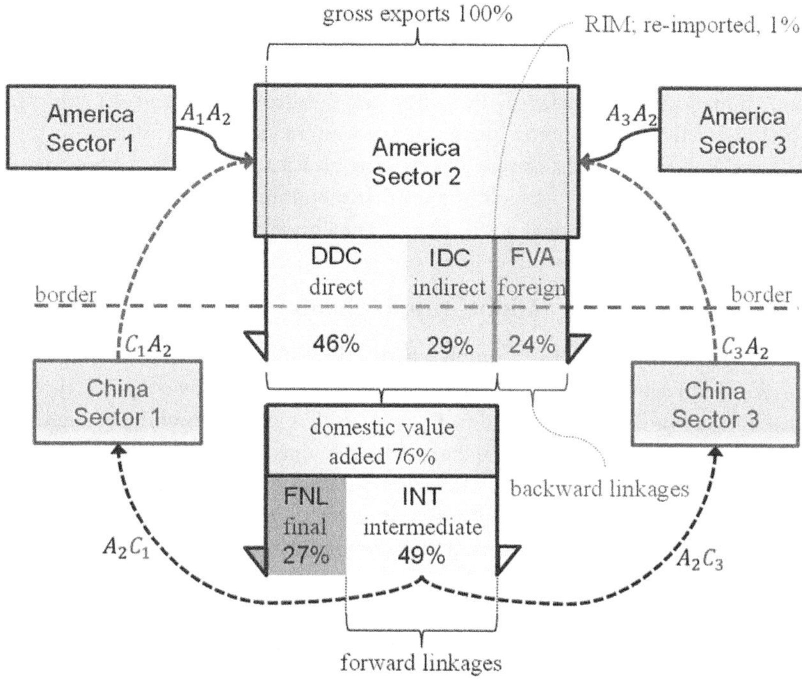

Figure 2.6 Backward and forward linkages in value-added trade

Source: Authors' construction. See main text for details; percentages are global averages for 2011 based on OECD-WTO database.

Domestic value-added. All value incorporated in America's gross exports that is not created abroad is domestic value-added. In view of the above, the global average domestic value-added share in 2011 was 76 percent, since the foreign value-added share was 24 percent. Not all of this value-added is created in sector 2, however, since both America sector 1 and America sector 3 supply intermediate products to the American producers in sector 2; we identify these flows by the arrows A_1A_2 and A_3A_2 in Figure 2.6. As a consequence, we can identify three different types of domestic value-added flows.

- *DDC – direct domestic contribution.* This is the value-added incorporated in the gross exports that is created in the exporting sector itself (in this case sector 2); the global average direct contribution was 46 percent of gross exports in 2011.
- *IDC – indirect domestic contribution.* This is the value-added incorporated in the gross exports that originates from domestic upstream sectors (in this case sectors 1 and 3). The global average indirect contribution was 29 percent of gross exports in 2011.
- *RIM – re-imported domestic value-added content of exports.* A small percentage of domestic value-added incorporated in the gross exports of a sector consist of value-added that was first exported from the country to be used as an intermediate input by foreign sectors (in this case China sectors 1 and 3), which is then subsequently re-imported into the country as an intermediate input in the production process. The global average re-imported domestic value-added share was about 1 percent of gross exports in 2011.

Forward linkages. The domestic value-added incorporated in gross exports can be used to satisfy the demand for final goods or it can be used as an intermediate input in the production process of a foreign sector. In this case, America sector 2 supplies intermediate goods to both China sector 1 and China sector 3; we identify these flows by the arrows A_2C_1 and A_2C_3 in Figure 2.6. These substantial deliveries of intermediate goods to international downstream sectors represent the forward linkages in global supply chains. The global average forward linkages were 49 percent of gross exports in 2011, which implies that the global average domestic value-added incorporated in the demand for final goods was 27 percent of gross exports in 2011.

Global supply chains

Regarding the participation in global supply chains, the OECD-WTO identifies two important international linkages, as explained in the previous section. An overview of the backward and forward linkages in 2011 is provided in Figure 2.7. The countries with the highest scoring forward linkages are the oil exporting nations Saudi Arabia and Brunei (87 percent of gross exports). This reflects the fact that most of the exported oil is subsequently used as an intermediate input in virtually all sectors of the importing countries. Other countries with high forward linkages are Russia and RoW (70 percent of gross exports). The global average forward linkage is 49 percent of gross exports, which is about equal to the value for the UK and close to the values for USA (51 percent) and Germany (46 percent).

The highest backward linkage by far is provided by Luxembourg (59 percent). This reflects the fact that many sectors in Luxembourg intensively use imported intermediate inputs in the production process. The backward linkages are, of course, equal to one minus the domestic value-added share, as analysed in Figure 2.7. This implies that the countries scoring high in

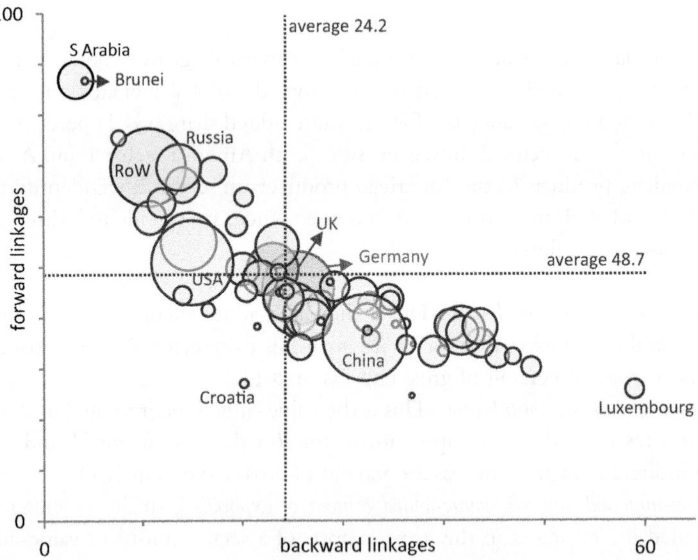

Figure 2.7 Backward and forward linkages, 2011

Source: Authors' construction based on data from OECD-WTO trade in value-added database (EXGR-DVASH); 61 countries plus RoW; EXGR-FVASH and EXGR-INTDVASH; bubble size proportional to gross exports.

domestic value-added, such as Saudi Arabia, Brunei, RoW, and Russia, score low in backward linkages. The global average backward linkage is 24 percent, which is close to the value for the UK, India, and Canada (the latter two are not identified separately in the figure). The USA has clearly lower backward linkages (15 percent), while Germany and China have higher backward linkages (26 and 32 percent, respectively), reflecting the fact that German and Chinese sectors more intensively use imported components from other countries in their production processes than UK and USA.

The sum of the backward and forward linkages is generally taken as an indication of the intensity with which a country participates in global value chains; see Koopman et al. (2010).[4] Figure 2.8 illustrates that for most countries there is a clear trade-off: higher backward linkages come at the expense of lower forward linkages. In fact, a simple regression of Figure 2.8 gives a slope of −0.95 and explains about 65 percent of the variance in forward linkages. There are, nonetheless, substantial differences between countries. The global average sum of backward and forward linkages is 73 percent, ranging from a low of 47 for Croatia to a high of 91 for Brunei.

To conclude our discussion of value-added measures of global supply chains, Figure 2.8 shows the sum of backward and forward linkages for both 1995 and 2011. This clearly shows that participation in global value chains is rising over time: the values for the 2011 score tend to be above those for the 1995 score. In fact, the global average sum of backward and forward linkages increased from 65 percent in 1995 to 73 percent in 2011. The values were higher for all individual countries except for Saudi Arabia (zero percent), Cambodia (minus 1 percent), and Croatia (minus 10 percent). The rise was above ten percentage points for 12 countries, with an increase of 15 percentage points for Hungary and Iceland and of 16 percentage points for India. The large drop for Croatia clearly puts it in a rather special (low) position in 2011 compared to the other countries. The ranking tends to be rather persistent over time, with Germany and RoW moving up a bit while USA and China are moving down. Also note the increase in bubble size for China and RoW, indicating their rapidly rising importance in global trade flows.

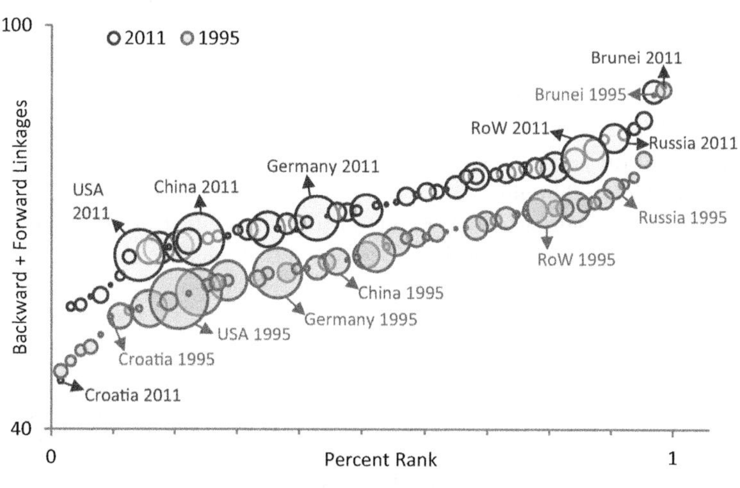

Figure 2.8 Sum of backward and forward linkages in 1995 and 2011

Source: Authors' construction based on data from OECD-WTO trade in value added database (sum of EXGR-FVASH and EXGR-INTDVASH); 61 countries plus RoW; bubbles proportional to percent of gross exports in the respective year.

Despite the difficulties of measuring supply chains because of data limitations, the evidence illustrates that global trade has changed over time from standard international trade in final products to trade in intermediate products. The second unbundling is visible whatever data source one uses. More and more international active firms specialize in smaller parts of the production chain. The increase in intermediate product trade is clear evidence of this phenomenon; it is increasing over time.

Geography and economics

It has long been evident that the unequal distribution of economic activity cannot be adequately explained using a neoclassical framework. In particular, economies of scale and imperfect competition, interacting with some form of local advantages, are essential. This implies that it is rather complicated to endogenously determine the size of economic activity in different locations in a general equilibrium framework. Such a framework was only fairly recently developed as it is based on tools that needed to be developed first in other fields of economics (tractable scale economies and monopolistic competition). The path-breaking contribution of the American economist Paul Krugman appeared in 1991. Since then many prominent researchers have published work on refinements, generalizations, and applications in this field now known as 'geographical economics' or 'new Economic Geography', which combines elements from international economics, industrial organization, Economic Geography, spatial economics, urban economics, and endogenous growth.

Krugman's original 'core' model focuses on the role of all sorts of spatial interaction costs (under the short-hand label *transport costs T*) for the endogenous determination of economic activity in a two-region setting where mobile manufacturing workers migrate to the location with the highest real wage rate. The main implications of this model hold quite generally (Fujita, Krugman & Venables, 1999; Neary, 2001) and can be summarized as follows.

- For all transport costs *below* a critical level, labelled the *sustain point*, complete agglomeration of manufacturing activity in one region is a stable long-run equilibrium. If the transport costs exceed the critical sustain point level, agglomeration is not 'sustainable', that is agglomeration is an unstable equilibrium.
- For all transport costs *above* another critical level, labelled the *break point*, spreading of manufacturing activity over the two regions is a stable equilibrium. If the transport costs are lower than the critical break point level, the spreading equilibrium 'breaks', that is spreading is an unstable equilibrium.
- The sustain point occurs at a higher level of transport costs than the break point. There is thus *always* an intermediate level of transport costs at which agglomeration of manufacturing activity is sustainable while simultaneously spreading of manufacturing activity is a stable equilibrium.

The analysis can be neatly summarized in the so-called Tomahawk diagram of Figure 2.9, where B is the break point, S_0 and S_1 are the sustain points, and the arrows indicate the direction of migration of mobile workers as a result of differences in the relative real wage. For each of the three stable equilibria the 'basin of attraction' is indicated, that is the area of initial parameter settings which will converge to this equilibrium; see the explanation below the figure. Under the plausible assumption that international interaction costs fall over time, the main implication of this work is economic activity will agglomerate in certain locations and a core-periphery pattern will emerge.

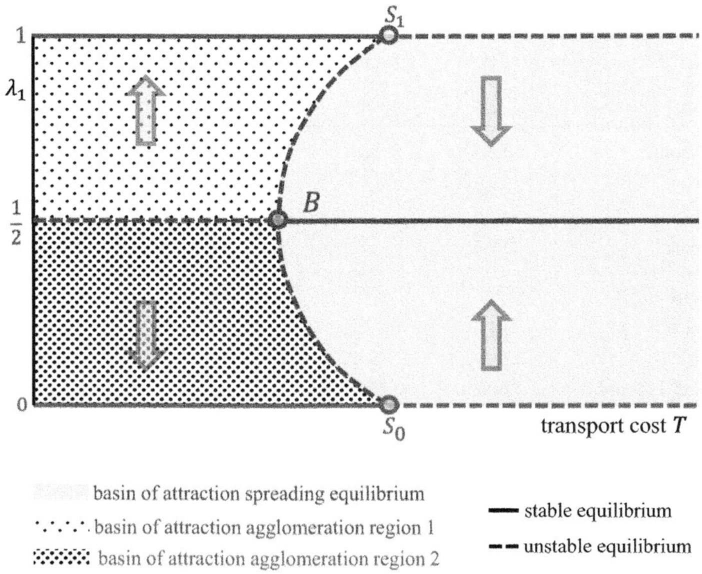

Figure 2.9 Sustain points and break point (Tomahawk diagram)
Source: van Marrewijk (2017).

The broad lesson of these models is that firms tend to agglomerate when economies integrate. Firms benefit from market access and local input-output linkages. Evidence indeed points out that especially international oriented firms tend to agglomerate more than domestic firms. Brakman et al. (2016), for example, show that since China joined the WTO in 2001, manufacturing firms show similar clustering patterns as firms in the USA, and Chinese firms are more localized than in the UK or Japan. Localization in China increases rapidly, even in the relatively short period between 2002 and 2008. Private Chinese firms, firms from Hong-Kong, Macao, and Taiwan, and foreign multinationals are more localized than state-owned firms. These findings are consistent with the notion that in liberalizing economies profit seeking manufacturing firms try to benefit from agglomeration economies and cluster together. This clustering has a not often recognized consequence for world trade, since trade is still localized.

Consequences for trade flows

For illustration purposes, we aggregate countries into global regions based on the World Bank classification after making two adjustments. First, we subdivide the large East Asia and Pacific region (31.3 percent of the world population) into three parts: East Asia (including China, Korea, and Japan), Southeast Asia (including Indonesia and the Philippines), and Pacific (including Australia and New Zealand). Second, we subdivide the Europe and Central Asia region into Europe and Central Asia (including Russia) separately. We thus have ten different global regions; see Table 2.1.

Total trade within a global region is the sum of all trade flows for the countries that are part of that global region. These flows can be sub-divided into *intra*-regional flows (within the same region; so from a country in the region to another country in the same region) and *inter*-regional

Table 2.1 World Bank regions – further subdivided

Region	*code*	*Population*				*# countries*	
		million	*%*	*million*	*%*		
East Asia and Pacific	EAP	2,225	31.3			36	
Pacific	PAC			31	0.4		17
East Asia	EAS			1,570	22.1		7
Southeast Asia	SEA			624	8.8		12
Europe and Central Asia	ECA	899	12.7			57	
Europe	EUR			542	7.6		45
Central Asia	CAS			357	5.0		12
Latin America and Caribbean	LAC	615	8.7			41	
Middle East and North Africa	MNA	403	5.7			21	
North America	NAM	351	4.9			3	
South Asia	SAS	1,671	23.5			8	
Sub-Sahara Africa	SSA	937	13.2			48	
Total		7,101	100			214	

Source: Authors construction based on World Bank Development Indicators classification, 2015.

flows (between regions; so from a country in the region to a country in some other region). The results of our calculations are visualized in Figure 2.10. The visualization in the figure uses a map for reference. Circles are located more or less at the geographic centre of a region on that map and proportional to the size of the region's total trade flows (average of exports and imports).

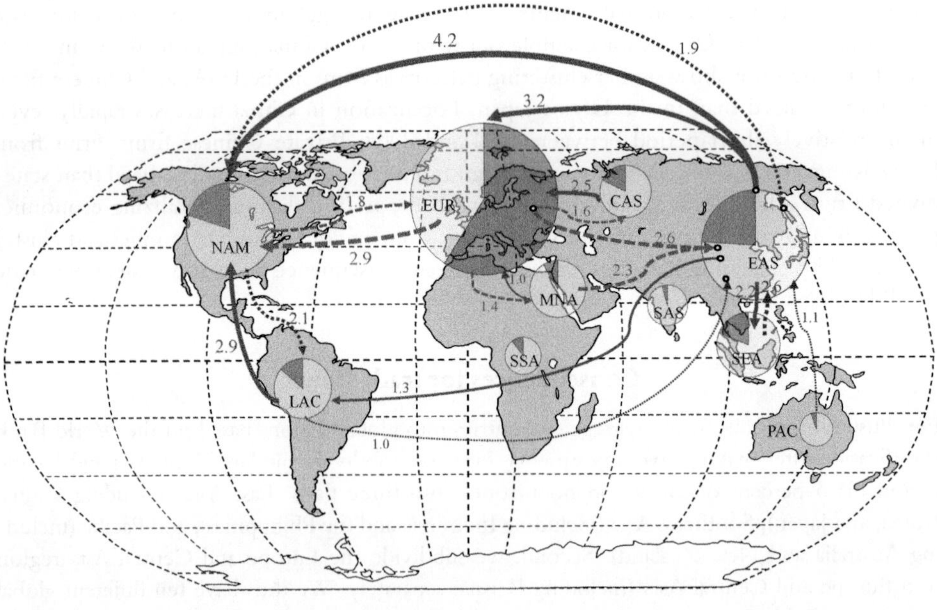

Figure 2.10 Global intra- and inter-regional trade flows, percent of total

Source: van Marrewijk (2017); bubbles proportional to size of trade flows in 2011; light-shaded area is extra-regional trade; dark-shaded area is intra-regional trade; weight of inter-regional trade flow is proportional to size (in percent); only flows of 1 percent or more are shown.

Arrows between the circles show trade flows from one region to another. In order not to clutter the diagram, only inter-regional flows of 1 percent or more are shown. To get an indication of the importance of these flows, the thickness of the line is proportional to the size of the flow. To get an indication of the size of the intra-regional versus the inter-regional trade flows, each circle is sub-divided into a light-shaded part and a dark-shaded part. The intra-regional flows are represented by the dark-shaded part.

A number of important observations can be made by looking at Figure 2.10.

- Europe is by far the most important region for international trade flows; it represents more than 37 percent of global trade. Other important regions are East Asia (China and Japan) with 20 percent of global trade and North America with 13.5 percent. Together these three regions account for 71 percent of all trade flows.
- There is only a limited number of sizeable inter-regional trade flows. Out of the 90 possible flows, only 18 exceed the 1 percent threshold.
- There are large flows between the three main centres; from East Asia to North America (4.2 percent), from East Asia to Europe (3.2), from Europe to North America (2.9), and so on.
- There are large flows from regions in the vicinity of the main centres to the main centre; from Latin America to North America (2.9 percent), from Southeast Asia to East Asia (2.6), from Central Asia to Europe (2.5), and so on.
- Two or three global regions are rather isolated with relatively little interaction with the rest of the world. This certainly holds for sub-Sahara Africa and South Asia (without any connecting arrow to any other region). To a somewhat smaller extent it also holds for Pacific (with one connecting arrow), which is geographically isolated, but in view of its relatively small population has a reasonable interaction with the world economy, particularly with East Asia (the destination of 59 percent of its export flows).
- A large share of international trade flows in the main economic centres (Europe, East Asia, and North America) is within the same region (intra-regional). These flows are related to the development of global supply chains, which requires intensive trade connections between nearby countries, preferably at different stages of economic development.

Conclusion

This chapter briefly discusses some stylized facts on internationally active firms. The increasing availability of micro-firm data has revealed some important stylized facts.

Internationalization is expensive. Only relatively productive firms are able to export, and only the most productive firms can become a multinational. Most firms are only active in a limited number of foreign markets with a limited range of products; only the largest multinationals are active in many markets, with a wide range of products. These broad conclusions hold in general, but differ between countries and sectors. These internationally oriented firms are larger, pay higher wages, have a higher value added per worker, and employ more people. Increasingly internationally active firms specialize in fragments of the international supply chain. This process has been dubbed the 'second-unbundling'. International active firms tend to cluster together, both within and between countries. The consequence of this agglomeration tendency is that most of world trade takes place within the EU, the American block, and an Asian block; trade between these blocks is relatively small compared to the within-block trade.

Notes

1 Our work is partially based on van Marrewijk (2017) and Brakman and van Marrewijk (2017).
2 Using an alternative measure, van Marrewijk (2017, ch. 15) shows that participation rises with income level and the least developed countries hardly participate in global supply chains at all.
3 See also Mayer and Ottaviano (2007, 2008), Bernard and Wagner (1997), and Aw and Hwang (1995). The relative recent availability of micro-firm data make this type of research possible. The theoretical basis for all this research was developed by Melitz (2003).
4 Taking log(1 + backward) + log(1 + forward) as an indicator does not affect our discussion below.

References

Aw, B.-Y. & Hwang, A.R. (1995) 'Productivity and the export market: A firm-level analysis', *Journal of Development Economics*, 47, pp. 313–332.
Baldwin, R. (2006) *Globalisation: The Great Unbundlings*. Helsinki: Prime Minister's Office, Economic Council of Finland.
Baldwin, R. & Venables, A.J. (2013) 'Spiders and snakes: Offshoring and agglomeration in the global economy', *Journal of International Economics*, 90, pp. 245–254.
Bernard, A.B., Jensen, J.B., Redding, S.J. & Schott, P.K. (2015) *Global Firms*. mimeo.
Bernard, A.B. & Wagner, J. (1997) 'Exports and success in German manufacturing', *Review of World Economics*, 133, pp. 134–157.
Beugelsdijk, S., Brakman, S., Garretsen, H. & van Marrewijk, C. (2013a) *International Economics and Business: Nations and Firms in the Global Economy*. Cambridge, MA: MIT Press.
Beugelsdijk, S., Brakman, S., van Ees, H. & Garretsen, H. (Eds.) (2013b) *Firms in the International Economy*. Cambridge, MA: MIT Press.
Brakman, S., Garretsen, H. & Zhao, Z. (2016) 'Spatial concentration of manufacturing firms in China', *Papers in Regional Science*, 96, S179–S205.
Brakman, S. & van Marrewijk, C. (2017) 'A closer look at revealed comparative advantage: Gross- versus value-added trade flows', *Papers in Regional Science*, 96, pp. 61–92.
Brakman, S., van Marrewijk, C. & Partridge, M. (2015) 'Local consequences of global production processes', *Journal of Regional Science*, 55, pp. 1–9.
Friedman, T. (2005) *The World is Flat*. London: Allen Lane.
Fujita, M., Krugman, P. & Venables, A. (1999) *The Spatial Economy: Cities, Regions, and International Trade*. Cambridge, MA: MIT Press.
Helpman, E., Melitz, M. & Yeaple, S. (2004) 'Export versus FDI with heterogeneous firms', *American Economic Review*, 94, pp. 300–316.
Koopman, R., Powers, W., Wang, Z. & Wei, S.J. (2010) *Give Credit Where Credit Is Due: Tracing Value Added in Global Production Chains*. NBER Working Paper No. 16426. Cambridge, MA: National Bureau of Economic Research.
Krugman, P.R. (1991) 'Increasing returns and Economic Geography', *Journal of Political Economy*, 99, pp. 483–499.
Marano, V., Arregle, J.-L., Hitt, M.A., Spadafora, E. & van Essen, M. (2016) 'Home country institutions and the internationalization-performance relationship: A meta-analytic review', *Journal of Management*, 42, pp. 1075–1110.
Marrewijk, C. van (2017) *International Trade*. Oxford, UK: Oxford University Press.
Mayer, T. & Ottaviano, G.I.P. (2007) *The Happy Few: The Internationalisation of European Firms*. Brussels: Bruegel Blueprint Series, Volume III.
Mayer, T. & Ottaviano, G.I.P. (2008) 'The happy few: The internationalisation of European firms', *Intereconomics*, 43, pp. 135–148.
Melitz, M. (2003) 'The impact of trade on intra-industry reallocations and aggregate industry productivity', *Econometrica*, 71, pp. 1695–1725.
Neary, J.P. (2001) 'Of hypes and hyperbolas: Introducing the new Economic Geography', *Journal of Economic Literature*, 39, pp. 536–561.

3
NETWORKS AND ALLIANCES

Keith W. Glaister

At the beginning of this century it is all but impossible to quickly review and categorize all of the relevant literature on alliances and networks

– *Hagedoorn and Osborn (2002, p. 518)*

Introduction

Since the mid-1980s the organization of firms and the underpinnings of competitive advantage have undergone a significant change with the flourishing of interfirm cooperation. For many firms, cooperation with other companies is now indispensable to strategic success (Contractor & Lorange, 2002b). More generally, Parkhe, Wasserman and Ralston (2006, p. 560) claim 'Of all the phenomena that have gripped the business world in recent years, few match the impact of networks'. Scholars from multiple fields have shown increasing interest in various aspects of networks and alliances (N&As), resulting in proliferation of research on N&As in the past several decades. There have been numerous books, journal papers and book chapters that have reported new work and reviewed extant work in the N&A area. For instance, there are collections of papers published by Contractor and Lorange (1988, 2002a), Reuer (2004) and Shenkar and Reuer (2006); review papers by Barringer and Harrison (2000), Borgatti and Foster (2003), Provan, Fish and Sydow (2007), Jack (2010), Kilduff and Brass (2010), Parmigiani and Rivera-Santos (2011), Di Guardo and Harrigan (2012), Beamish and Lupton (2016), Gomes, Barnes and Mahmood (2016); and book chapters summarizing key aspects, for example, Inkpen (2001a, 2001b) and Faulkner (2003).

Most alliance studies have focused on questions such as the motivation for alliance formation, the selection of partners, the management of alliances, the determinants of the governance structure or mode of alliance, learning and dynamics in alliances, and the performance of alliances (Lavie, 2006). In recent years the study of alliance networks has gained popularity. Although prior research has significantly improved understanding of N&A activity, it 'has led to a veritable jungle of work' (Parmigiani & Rivera-Santos, 2011, p. 1109) such that the sheer volume of research makes it extremely difficult to consolidate and integrate extant knowledge in the area with its collective impact difficult to appreciate (Shi, Sun & Prescott, 2011). Given this difficulty, this chapter does not attempt to provide a comprehensive review of the extant literature on N&A. Rather, there is a selective examination of research principally from the business/management literature and to an extent from the geography literature, given the increased interest in N&As by geography scholars and the focus of this book. With this in mind the chapter is set out as follows. After an attempt to set out the definitions of alliances, there follows a discussion on data availability and trends in alliances. The next section considers briefly the dominant theoretical perspectives adopted to investigate alliances. This serves as a background to a consideration of a recently growing interest in portfolio alliance management, which has become an important strategic issue (Hoffmann, 2007). Although considered critical to the management of the MNE, it remains underdeveloped in most firms (Goerzen, 2005). This is followed by an examination of global production networks, largely drawn from the geography literature. Conclusions are in the final section.

Definitions

Parmigiani and Rivera-Santos (2011, p. 116) note that definitions of alliances vary from narrow to so broad that almost any interorganizational relationship could be considered an 'alliance'. In the reviews they identified, definitions range from 'any agreement between two (or more) organizations to jointly carry out a task involving more interactions than a one-time arm's-length contract' (Rivera-Santos & Inkpen, 2009, p. 199) to 'any inter-firm cooperation that falls between the extremes of discrete, short-term contracts, and the complete merger of two or more organizations' (Contractor & Lorange, 2002b, p. 4). Essentially, an interfirm alliance is a voluntary arrangement between firms that exchange or share resources and that engage in the co-development or provision of products, services, or technologies (Gulati, 1998). Joint ventures, minority equity stake, coproduction, and joint research and development are just some forms of alliances. The distinguishing feature of joint ventures, as a subset of alliances, is that they involve the creation of a jointly owned separate entity by the partners (Contractor & Lorange, 2002b). Das and Teng (1998) note that the key features setting alliances apart from other single-firm strategies are the element of interfirm cooperation and the uncertainty about the presence of such desired cooperation, which has been termed 'relational risk'. Das and Teng (1998, p. 492) define partner cooperation as the willingness of a partner firm to pursue mutually compatible interests in the alliance rather than act opportunistically.

Although interorganizational networks are a commonly understood phenomenon, 'it is not always clear exactly what organizational scholars are talking about when they use the term' (Provan, Fish & Sydow, 2007, p. 480). In part this is because terms other than 'network' are often used, for example, partnerships, interorganizational relationships, coalitions, cooperative arrangements, or collaborative agreements. Borgatti & Foster (2003) provide some terminology, identifying a network as a set of actors (or 'nodes') connected by a set of ties, which connect pairs of actors. When attention is on a single focal actor, that actor is called 'ego'; the set of nodes that ego has ties with is called 'alters'. Together ego, alters, and all ties among them is called an ego-network. A network may therefore be defined as 'a set of nodes and the set of ties representing some relationship, or lack of relationship, between the nodes' (Brass, Galaskiewicz, Greve, & Tsai (2004, p. 795). Inkpen (2001a, p. 420) notes that although the ultimate definition of networks depends on arbitrary identification of boundaries, from an alliance perspective, networks can be defined as 'a set of organizations linked by a set of social and business relationships that create strategic interfirm opportunities for the organizations'. The key attribute of networks is 'the existence of multiple, intertwined partners with a many-to-many structure' (Parmigiani & Rivera-Santos, 2011, p. 1119). The essence is that the firm, from its perspective, lies at the centre of an extended network of organizations, bound by a variety of ties, from tight equity relationships to loose informal arrangements. Network models suggest that functional firm boundaries are 'fuzzy', or vague and somewhat uncertain (Tallman, 2003). Networks differ from alliances in that they generally involve a lower level of interdependence between the members, and the learning factor is rarely so important (Faulkner, 2003, p. 141).

Data availability and trends

Since the mid-1980s researchers have observed the proliferation and increasing importance of alliances (Hagedoorn, 1996, 2002; Gulati, 1998; Gulati, Nohria & Zaheer, 2000). However, a major problem with attempting to discern trends in alliance formation is that 'there is no omniscient database of alliances' (Schilling, 2009, p. 237). Firms are not required to report their alliances to any governing body, and although many firms make public announcements, whether and how these announcements are reported is highly variable. Also, the range of languages that may be used to announce an alliance means it is very difficult to search news retrieval sources to construct a comprehensive list of alliance announcements (Schilling, 2009). The implication is that the major databases used to analyse alliance formation cannot be considered to contain the population of alliances but are at best samples. Nevertheless, Schilling's examination of the available databases, including three replication studies, suggest that the databases are a valuable, and generally reliable, resource for the study of interorganizational relationships, providing the research design takes the sample limitations into account.

Several studies have examined the trend and distribution of alliances (for example, Hagedoorn, 2002; Moskalev & Swensen, 2007; Bojanowski, Corten & Westbrock, 2012), with all reporting an increase in alliance formation through the 1980s and early 1990s, but then observing a decline from the mid-1990s. Schilling (2009), for instance, in considering the extent to which the MERIT-CATI database, the CORE database, and the SDC database agree about alliance activity over the 1990–2005 time period, finds that all of the alliance databases report a steady increase in the number of alliances, reaching a significant peak in activity in 1995, followed by declines in activity from 1995 to 2000. The observed reduced propensity of MNEs to use Joint Ventures was investigated by Desai, Foley and Hines (2004) using the Bureau of Economic Analysis (BEA) annual survey of US direct investment abroad from 1982 through 1997. They maintain that the decline in the use of shared ownership is consistent with an increased preference for control by MNE parents that reflects growing differences between the costs of operating overseas operations as joint ventures and the costs of administering foreign activities as wholly owned subsidiaries. Desai et al. (2004) identify three sources of the rising coordination costs of shared ownership. First, tax-efficient structuring of worldwide operations is made more difficult by tensions between joint venture partners concerned with local profits and multinational parents concerned with global profits. Second, the ability to transfer intellectual property is limited by fear of its appropriation by local partners. Third, the desire to structure worldwide production in a decentralized way with greater intrafirm trade creates the room for more conflict with local partners who have competing goals. Desai et al. (2004) conclude that given MNEs increasingly rely on cost savings and market opportunities created by worldwide tax planning, technology transfer, and production decentralization, they face growing incentives to avoid sharing ownership of their foreign affiliates and to increase use of 100% ownership.

The suggestion that international alliances have been replaced by cross-border mergers and foreign direct investments is contested by Hagedoorn (2002), who proposes an alternative explanation. He argues that the share of international R&D partnerships has declined in the United States more as a result of domestic developments rather than changes in the international environment. Over the 1980s and 1990s there was a strong growth in the US biotech and information technology industries, associated with the establishment of many new businesses. According to Hagedoorn (2002), the diminishing importance of international collaboration is explained by the availability of attractive local partners, rather than a tendency to avoid foreign alliance partners.

Theoretical perspectives

Researchers have examined the alliance phenomenon through various theoretical perspectives, including, but not limited to, transaction cost economics (TCE) (Hennart, 1988), game theory (Parkhe, 1993), bargaining theory (Yan & Gray, 1994), resource dependence theory (Pfeffer & Salancik, 1978), resource-based view (Das & Teng, 2000), and strategic behaviour theory (Glaister & Buckley, 1996). As Hagedoorn and Osborn (2002, p. 529) observe, one perspective is not clearly dominant over another: 'They are all partially correct and incorrect'. The following sub-sections briefly outline some key theoretical perspectives.

Transaction cost economics

TCE suggests that firms act to minimize the sum of production and transaction costs. Alliances are formed as an efficient response to conditions where transactions cannot be easily conducted through market contracts, but the transaction costs of an alliance are not so high as to mandate internal organization (Williamson, 1991; Geyskens, Steenkamp & Kumar, 2006). Beamish and Lupton (2016) point out that in research on cooperative strategies TCE has been used in two general ways: in studying the choice between different modes of foreign direct investment, and in minimizing transaction costs within a particular agreement. Under conditions where transaction costs are high, firms tend to prefer a higher degree of control given by joint ventures, whereas market-based contractual agreements are more likely where transaction costs are low. Further, the minimization of transaction costs is an important consideration in partner selection. Partners' knowledge of local markets and institutional environments reduces the cost of market mechanisms, and hence impacts a foreign firm's choice of local partner. In summary, alliances are formed when it is more efficient for a firm to conduct an activity with a partner than either on its own or through the market. The focus is on creating an appropriate governance structure, obtaining complementary resources, and aligning incentives among partners (Parmigiani & Rivera-Santos, 2011).

Resource-based view

The resource-based view (RBV) of the firm argues that differential firm performance is fundamentally due to firm heterogeneity (Wernerfelt, 1984; Barney, 1991). Firms that are able to accumulate resources and capabilities that are rare, valuable, non-substitutable, and difficult to imitate will achieve a competitive advantage over competing firms (Rumelt, 1984; Dierickx & Cool, 1989; Barney, 1991). Thus, extant RBV theory views the firm as the primary unit of analysis. However, as noted by Dyer and Singh (1998), a firm's critical resources may span firm boundaries and may be embedded in interfirm routines and processes. Where partners bring distinctive resources to the alliance, they may be combined resulting in a synergistic effect, such that the combined resources are more valuable, rare, and difficult to imitate than they were before they were combined. Consequently, these alliances produce stronger competitive positions than those achievable by the firms operating individually. This indicates that firms who combine resources in unique ways may realize an advantage over competing firms who are unable or unwilling to do so (Dyer & Singh, 1998). Complementarity amongst resources is thus a significant driver of partner selection and alliance performance.

Learning

Firms form alliances with the specific intention of acquiring new knowledge and know-how. Various scholars have argued that interorganizational learning is critical to competitive success, noting that organizations often learn by collaborating with other organizations (Levinson & Asahi, 1996; Powell, Koput & Smith-Doerr, 1996). This implies that firms that are unable to create (or position themselves in) learning networks are at a competitive disadvantage (Powell et al., 1996). Consequently, a firm's alliance partners are, in many cases, the most important source of new ideas and information that result in performance-enhancing technology and innovations. Thus, alliance partners can generate rents by developing superior interfirm knowledge-sharing routines (Dyer & Singh, 1998). Alliance partners that are particularly effective at transferring know-how, especially tacit knowledge (which cannot be efficiently transferred in the marketplace, but its transfer between firms requires close cooperation in alliances), are likely to outperform competitors who are not. Jiang and Li (2008) show that collaborative forms of organization, such as international joint ventures, are superior knowledge transfer mechanisms compared to arm's-length (market) contracts, and that the associated learning translates into better financial performance. A partner's absorptive capacity (Cohen & Levinthal, 1990), that is the ability to recognize and assimilate valuable knowledge from a particular alliance partner, is crucial to interorganizational learning. This capacity necessitates employing a set of interorganizational processes that allows partner firms to identify valuable know-how and then transfer it across organizational boundaries.

Social network theories

Networks as a unit of analysis have become increasingly important in understanding the value creation and competitive advantage of firms. Maximizing the value of participating in alliances requires managers to assess not just each two-party alliance, but multiple ties in a network of innovation and learning (Ahuja, 2000). Social network theories cover a wide range of theoretical perspectives that focus on the analysis of patterns of relationships among interacting social actors. The fundamental unit of analysis is the network, which consists of the collection of actors and their connecting ties (Lavie, 2006). This literature is critical of perspectives that explain firm strategies and performance on the basis of independent profit-seeking behaviour in a resource-based or competition-oriented environment (Granovetter, 1985; Nohria, 1992; Gulati, 1995). Instead, social network researchers analyse interfirm relationship structures and examine the impact of network-level cooperation, communication, learning, and imitation on a firm's actions and performance (Lavie, 2006).

Agency theory

Reuer and Ragozzino (2006) offer a contrarian view of alliance formation. They argue that if joint ventures offer managers benefits which they value more than do shareholders, this encourages managers to develop joint venture portfolios. Consequently, part of the growth in firms' alliance portfolios may be accounted for by incentive misalignments owing to the separation of ownership and control in organizations. Further, the motivations usually given for inter-firm collaboration can be viewed from the perspective of the hazards emphasized by agency theory.

For example, learning views of alliances, as noted earlier, propose that collaboration provides rapid access to technologies or skills of other firms. However, Reuer and Ragozzino (2006) argue that they also can be undertaken for reasons of competitive avoidance or defensiveness, hence failing to generate competitive advantages for the firm. One argument for joint ventures is that they enable firms to reduce risk while facilitating growth opportunities. However, as Reuer and Ragozzino (2006) point out, the finance literature customarily emphasizes that shareholders are generally able to diversify their investment risks at lower transaction costs than the firm through portfolio investments. Reuer and Ragozzino (2006) also note several features of joint ventures and their resource allocation and monitoring processes which suggest that agency problems may have a bearing on firms' joint venture portfolios. For instance, joint ventures tend to be relatively small in size, so a firm with a given amount to invest can achieve a higher level of diversification and risk reduction through multiple joint venture investments than through a single acquisition. Further, joint ventures may not receive the due diligence and ongoing scrutiny expected with a large acquisition. While agency theory provides a contrarian view, this does not deny the possible benefits of alliances, however. Reuer and Ragozzino (2006) conclude that it does caution against imputing positive organizational payoffs or motives to alliance investments.

Alliance portfolios

Increasingly, researchers are recognizing that firms engage in multiple alliances, leading to alliance portfolios that can vary by number, type, and partners (Wassmer, 2010). Hagedoorn and Osborn (2002) make the point that with the vast number of partnerships, it would be difficult to assume that each one was 'strategic' or motivated by the firm's specific strategy. 'Instead of an alliance being strategic, it is the establishment of a portfolio of innovative alliances that is strategic' (Hagedoorn & Osborn, 2002, p. 532). Beamish and Lupton (2016) contend that researchers could gain a clearer understanding of the benefits, drawbacks, and uses of different cooperative arrangements by relaxing the common assumption that each represents a discrete investment choice. They argue it is likely that MNEs make multiple investments in a country or region as a suite. However, researchers tend to assume that the choice in locating a particular investment is discrete and do not consider the full spectrum of other investments the firm has made or is planning. Consequently, a subunit portfolio perspective could provide a more precise and accurate understanding of how managers make these decisions. Further, by examining the relationship between organizational, geographic, and 'spatial' diversity, a better understanding of how the MNE's (planned) portfolio of alliances and international joint ventures impacts location choice would be gained.

Contrasting with networks, the emphasis of alliance portfolios is on the focal organization and how it manages all of these one-to-one relationships simultaneously (Parmigiani & Rivera-Santos, 2011). Most previous alliance research has concentrated on the management problems associated with a dyadic relationship, neglecting the consequences where dyads are often embedded in an interorganizational network encompassing many different interorganizational relationships. Further, although numerous studies have explored the impact of strategic alliances on a firm's performance, the focus of prior research has been primarily limited to activity-based motivations, and there has been little research that addresses the impact of a firm's internal strategic orientation on its management of large numbers of external relationships (Vapola, Paukku & Gabrielsson, 2010).

Kale and Singh (2009, p. 57) observe that while each individual alliance is important, a firm can gain additional advantages by considering its entire set of alliances as one portfolio, and managing it as such. They contend that firms need to learn how to manage their alliance portfolio as a whole, which they term 'alliance portfolio capability'. This leads to a number of new issues. A firm needs to know how to configure its alliance portfolio along several dimensions (Hoffmann, 2007). First, it must assess the extent to which its portfolio is complete, such that collectively all of its alliances meet its strategic needs. Second, firms must guard against competition that might arise between individual alliances in the portfolio, which would be the case should a firm undertake more than one alliance for the same purpose. Where one alliance rivals another alliance in the portfolio, this can lead to significant adversities that might ultimately outweigh the benefits. Third, some alliances in a firm's portfolio may actually complement, rather than compete with each other, such that the benefits they offer are extra-additive in nature. Kale and Singh (2009) maintain that alliance portfolio capability comprises multiple dimensions, including the skills to configure an alliance portfolio (i.e. to create a set of complete, noncompetitive, and complementary alliances), to foster and maintain trust across different alliance partners, to resolve conflicts between alliances, to coordinate strategies and operations across alliances, to create routines to share operational know-how across individual alliances, to monitor the extra additive benefits (and costs) that arise due to interaction between different individual alliances in the portfolio, and so on.

Alliance portfolio configuration is about the content of alliance portfolios and its arrangement. Wassmer (2010) notes that alliance portfolio configuration is a complex concept comprising multiple dimensions including: (a) a size dimension determined by characteristics such as the number of alliances and partners; (b) a structural dimension constituted by characteristics such as breadth, density, and the level of redundancy (alliances are redundant if they provide access to the same information and resources) within the portfolio; (c) a relational dimension made up of characteristics such as the tie strength of individual alliances in the portfolio; and (d) a partner dimension focusing on certain partner-related characteristics. Additional complexity is added to the conceptualization of alliance portfolio configuration by the fact that these four configuration dimensions span across multiple levels of analysis. Although the size-related and structural characteristics of alliance portfolios are on the alliance portfolio level of analysis, the relational dimension is on the individual alliance level of analysis, and the partner dimension is on the partner firm level of analysis.

Hoffmann (2005) identified four tasks of multi-alliance management that are necessary for professional alliance portfolio management:

(1) Developing and implementing a portfolio strategy, i.e. a main strategic direction for all alliances in a particular business unit (alliance strategy) and general rules for managing all the alliances of the entire company (alliance policy).
(2) Portfolio monitoring, i.e. monitoring and controlling the contribution of the alliance portfolio to implement the business strategies (monitoring the alliance strategy) and the corporate strategy (monitoring the alliance policy).
(3) Portfolio co-ordination to utilize synergies and avoid conflicts among alliances.
(4) Institutionalizing multi-alliance management, i.e. establishing an alliance management system to support the other tasks of multi-alliance management.

In later work, Hoffmann (2007) examined portfolio strategy in detail. Empirical evidence shows that in a multi-business firm, the strategic alignment between company strategy and its alliance activities is mainly achieved at the business level, which leads Hoffmann (2007) to focus on business-level alliance portfolio strategy, whose purpose is to strategically align all alliances of a business unit with the business strategy. Alliance strategies, which are derived from the business strategy, thereby determine the goals of all alliances of the business unit and the configuration of the business alliance portfolio.

Hoffmann (2007) argues that alliances can act as buffers, which help the focal firm overcome the problem of environmental uncertainty. Consequently, strong inducement to form alliances comes from rapid and unpredictable change of the firm's environment and the accompanying high strategic uncertainty. Opportunities to establish new alliances depends on the firm's position in the interorganizational field and its prior interorganizational relationships as well as on its attractiveness to other firms because of its own resource endowment. The choice of an alliance strategy – and thus the configuration of the alliance portfolio – is therefore contingent on the shaping potential of the focal company, i.e. its resource strength, and on the strategic uncertainty it faces. For example, high strategic uncertainty fosters exploration strategies through alliances which can be used either to actively shape the environment according to the company's business strategy or to adapt the business development to the unfolding environmental changes. With less environmental uncertainty firms prefer exploitation strategies that deepen and exploit the resource base efficiently, which can be supported by alliances that stabilize the business environment and leverage the built-up resources (Hoffmann, 2007).

Hoffmann (2007) further argues that the characteristics of the particular alliance portfolio differ, such that when firms pursue an adapting strategy (reactively adapting to the changing environment), the alliance portfolio is characterized by a large number of alliances with high dispersion and weak linkage intensity as well as low redundancy. In contrast when firms pursue a shaping strategy (actively shaping the environmental development), the alliance portfolio is characterized by a small number of alliances with low dispersion and strong linkage intensity as well as high redundancy. Finally, when firms pursue a stabilizing strategy (stabilizing the environment in order to avoid organizational change), the alliance portfolio is characterized by a small number of alliances with low dispersion and strong linkage intensity as well as high redundancy. Hoffman's conjectures are supported by longitudinal data gathered to analyse the course of development of the Siemens alliance portfolios in two business units. Hoffmann (2007) stresses, however, that there is not a unidirectional relationship between shaping potential (resource strength) and strategic uncertainty as independent variables, and alliance strategy as a dependent variable. This is because the development of the resource endowment of a business unit and the strategic uncertainty it faces are also affected by the outcome of the firm's alliance activities. 'This interdependent relationship of contingency factors and alliance strategy represents how alliance portfolio, business strategy, resource endowment, and environmental changes coevolve' (Hoffmann, 2007, p. 834).

Wassmer (2010) argues that even though research such as that by Hoffmann (2007) has shown that alliance portfolio configuration is driven by business strategy and in many firms is not the outcome of a random process, the alliance portfolios of many firms are configured inefficiently and often represent nothing more than a random mix of strategic alliances with sometimes even conflicting demands. This may be explained by corporate governance issues such as agency hazards as discussed earlier (Reuer & Ragozzino, 2006).

Vapola et al. (2010) provide an international strategy perspective on alliance portfolio management. They note that while there is a wealth of literature both within the international strategy and the strategic alliance research streams, there is less research explicitly examining the link between the two. In order to address this gap, Vapola et al. (2010) consider how the MNE's choice of international strategy impacts its alliance portfolio management. Specifically, they extend the understanding of how the needs for local responsiveness and global integration, the Integration–Responsiveness (I–R) framework (Prahalad & Doz, 1987; Bartlett & Ghoshal, 1989), lead the MNE to choose different types of partners and different levels of partner integration. Their case firms represent three different types of international strategies: global, multi-domestic, and transnational. The empirical findings classify three different approaches to alliance portfolio management: alliance portfolios with a high level of integration, high level of heterogeneity, or a combination of both. Vapola et al. (2010) report a pattern and a relationship between the MNE's international strategy and the management characteristics of the partnerships within its alliance portfolios. A global strategy was associated with highly integrated global alliance portfolio management: in order to achieve a high level of integration internally, the MNE requires a similarly high need for integration of its partners as reflected in its alliance portfolio management. A multi-domestic strategy was associated with local demand oriented heterogeneous alliance portfolio management: in order to achieve a high level of local responsiveness the MNE requires high levels of customization in order to serve the local needs, which implies drawing on diverse partners best suited to a particular role or location. A transnational strategy was associated with dual-focused transnational alliance portfolio management: a transnational strategic orientation favouring both local responsiveness and global integration, requires both a greater partner heterogeneity and integration level of partners within the alliance portfolio.

Vapola et al. (2010) conclude that the alliance portfolio management approaches of the case MNEs vary according to their international strategies. Further, the observed pattern suggests that the I–R axes are a powerful explanatory paradigm by which to explain the alliance portfolio management of the case MNEs. Finally, it should be noted that Vapola et al.'s (2010) findings are not necessarily in contrast with Hoffmann (2007) because, as discussed, he focuses on the alliance portfolio in a given business unit, whereas they address the MNE as a whole.

Another dominant research strand examines if and how alliance network positions influence firm performance. Koka and Prescott (2008) note that research has emphasized two distinct yet interrelated approaches to the structural design of alliance networks. In the first, firms pursue a strategy that enables them to attain a position of prominence in the network. Benefits to network prominence result from access to crucial information in the network due to the formation of multiple ties with many partners. Network prominence also enables the firm to influence its partners so that it may follow its own strategic agenda, thereby enhancing its own performance. In the second, firms pursue a strategy that enables them to occupy an entrepreneurial position in the network. Benefits from such a position arise because of non-redundant information, information diversity, and control of information flow, which in turn enhance firm performance. There is, however, little consistent empirical evidence that either of these two different approaches positively affect firm performance. In their own work Koka and Prescott (2008) instead of asking if network positions affect firm performance, focus on a more nuanced question: under what conditions are the two different types of network positions effective in enhancing firm performance? Their findings indicate that when environmental change occurs in an industry, firms that have developed an entrepreneurial position perform better, while firms that were prominent in the network suffer performance decline. However, when there is more rather than less radical change, both network positions are negatively related to performance. Further, their results indicate that the effect of particular network positions on firm performance changes over time. 'This finding suggests that over time, managers need to assess their alliance portfolios and make structural adjustments based on environmental and strategic contingencies' (Koka & Prescott, 2008, p. 640). Koka and Prescott (2008) further note that their contingency findings support the call for a strategic approach to the design and management of strategic alliances, as such managers have multiple alliance design choices.

Sarkar, Aulakh and Madhok (2009) consider a process view of alliance capabilities, noting that literature on alliance capabilities is characterized by an emphasis on structure, with little regard for the processual aspects of this capability. Learning curves vary greatly between firms, which means that firms with similar accumulated experience can develop non-similar capabilities. Consequently, experience may be insufficient to guarantee superior collaborative performance without explicitly considering an organization's expertise with processes through which it designs and manages its alliance portfolio. Sarkar et al. (2009) identify a set of processes that constitute distinct dimensions of a firm's alliance portfolio management capability and relate these dimensions to value creation. Specifically, Sarkar et al. (2009, p. 586) delineate three organizational processes that constitute this capability: (1) partnering proactiveness: a proactive portfolio formation dimension reflecting organizational routines related to discovering and responding to promising partnering opportunities; (2) relational governance: a relational dimension related to the governance of the portfolio in a way that removes relational imperfections, such as feelings of mistrust and opportunism, and promote co-mingling of resources and capabilities across multiple partners; and (3) portfolio coordination: a coordination dimension which integrates strategies, activities, and knowledge flows across different alliance partners in the portfolio. Sarkar et al.'s (2009) findings suggest that each of the three constituent dimensions of this capability enhance the overall value of a firm's alliance portfolio. Moreover, after controlling for experiential (alliance experience), compositional (alliance diversity), and structural (dedicated alliance function) aspects, their results show that alliance portfolio capital uniquely contributes to the performance of a focal firm. Sarkar et al. (2009) further note that their study suggests that firms with similar structural positions in networks may accumulate heterogeneous levels of network capital due to variance in process capabilities, a finding that supports the work by Dyer and Hatch (2006).

Geographic perspectives on global production networks

Parkhe, Wasserman and Ralston (2006) note that network scholarship has a varied and impressive lineage, drawing on sociology, psychology, anthropology, and mathematics. Di Guardo and Harrigan (2012) also observe that several disciplines have contributed to the literature on alliances and alliance-related innovation processes, including economics, sociology, psychology, management, finance, accounting, law, and political science. Notably, this list of disciplines does not include geography and despite geographers' interest in networks and alliances, there is little recognition in the business/management literature on the contribution of geographers to research in this area. Nevertheless 'Global Production Networks (GPNs) have become a key focus of research in Economic Geography and related fields in recent years, focusing attention on the processes by which goods and services are produced, distributed and consumed' (MacKinnon, 2012, p. 227). Indeed, Glückler (2007, p. 620) notes, 'In Economic Geography, networks have celebrated an exceptional career over many years and they have coined terminology in theories of geographical clusters, global cities, international production systems and globalization'. Further, 'In Economic Geography the notion of the network has come to play a critical role in a range of debates' (Grabher, 2006, p. 163). It should be recognized, therefore, that geographers have made a significant contribution to the understanding of GPNs.

According to Coe, Dicken and Hess (2008a), the GPN framework was developed initially by researchers in Manchester and their collaborators (Henderson et al., 2002; Dicken & Henderson, 2003; Coe et al., 2004). They note that GPN analysis combines insights gained from global commodity chain (GCC) and global value chain (GVC) analysis with ideas derived from the actor-network theory (ANT) and the literature relating to varieties of capitalism/business systems. Hess and Yeung (2006) further note that the GPN framework in Economic Geography has a diverse set of historical precursors mostly from outside the discipline. They identify four influential antecedents: (1) the value chain framework in strategic management since the early

1980s; (2) the networks and embeddedness perspectives in economic and organizational sociology since the mid-1980s; (3) the actor-network analysis in science studies since the mid-1980s; and (4) the global commodity/value chain analysis in economic sociology and development studies since the mid-1990s.

Yeung (2009a) argues that the GPN approach seeks to provide a meso-level theorization of the geographical and organizational configuration of TNC activity:

> It does so, however, not by treating geography and location as an *exogenous* variable in the constitution of TNC activity. The GPN approach takes on board the TNC as the central orchestrator of GPNs and, yet, grounds it in complex geographies of cities, regions, and territories in today's global economy.
>
> *(Yeung, 2009a, p. 217)*

According to Glückler (2007) the relation between geography and networks can be theorized in (at least) two ways. First, proximity affects network formation. In Economic Geography the most widely used approach aims at assessing the latent effects of physical proximity/distance on economic processes. It should be recognized that geographical proximity is a matter of scale. Glückler (2007) points out that two firms may be co-located in the same office building but also in the same country. Second, place makes a difference, with place conceived of as a bundle of resources and opportunities with the additional characteristic of spatial contiguity. This localized resource profile comprises the structural aspects of relationships (e.g. social capital, structural holes) as well as the material, social, and institutional resources that these relationships access and transfer. Glückler (2007) stresses that the association between the region and the network is by no means unidirectional. Places not only constrain network formation but social interaction in networks also shapes its geography. For Glückler (2007, p. 622), 'Both views of geography matter in a concept of geographical network trajectory'.

Coe (2011, p. 389) considers that '[GPN] is perhaps best thought of as a heuristic framework for understanding the interconnectedness and uneven development of the global economy'. The GPN framework in Economic Geography thus deals with how actors in various GPNs are anchored in different places and multiple scales, from the national to the local scale (Hess & Yeung, 2006). The GPN 'aims to reveal the multi-actor and multi-scalar characteristics of transnational production systems through intersecting notions of power, value and embeddedness' (Coe et al., p. 267). 'By drawing distant actors both firms and non-firm institutions into a common analytical framework, the GPN analysis seeks to provide a dynamic conceptual apparatus that is sensitive to multiple scales and power relations' (Hess & Yeung, 2006, p. 1197). Coe, Dicken & Hess (2008b, p. 272) argue that there is a growing consensus that one of the most useful means to understanding the complexity of the global economy – especially its geographical complexity – is the concept of the network. For Coe et al. (2008b), GPNs incorporate all kinds of network configuration and attempt to encompass all relevant sets of actors and relationships. Moreover, production networks are a generic form of economic organization and are not a hybrid form between markets and hierarchies (as argued, for example, by Williamson, 1975, 1985).

For Coe et al. (2008b, p 274) a production network is:

> [t]he nexus of interconnected functions, operations and transactions through which a specific product or service is produced, distributed and consumed. A global production network is one whose interconnected nodes and links extend spatially across national boundaries and, in so doing, integrates parts of disparate national and subnational territories.

They go on to note that each stage of a production chain is embedded in a wide set of non-linear/horizontal relationships, such that the overall structure of a production network, may be viewed 'in terms of a series of intricate intersections between vertical and horizontal networks of varying degrees of size (length, width) and complexity' (Coe et al., 2008b, p. 275).

MacKinnon (2012, p. 228) notes that the GPN approach is based on three conceptual categories. First, value, i.e. the economic return or rent generated by the production of commodities for sale. 'Processes of value creation, enhancement and capture are central to GPN analysis' (Coe, 2011, p. 396). Second, power, defined primarily as a practice in terms of the capacity to exercise power. Third, embeddedness, of which three forms are identified: (1) societal embeddedness, emphasizing how actors are positioned within wider institutional and regulatory frameworks; (2) network embeddedness, which highlights the social and economic relationships in which a particular actor or firm participates; and (3) territorial embeddedness, which refers to the 'anchoring' of GPNs in different places. For instance, a GPN can become territorially embedded because of the lead firm's historic ties to a particular location, often its regions of origin, which may provide advantages such as government support, links with key suppliers, and access to labour skills.

For Coe et al. (2008b) a networked approach brings several advantages: it facilitates identification of a wide range of non-firm actors as constituent parts of the overall production system; it transcends the linear progression of the focal product/service to uncover the complex circulations of capital, knowledge and people that underlie the production of all goods and services; further, a multidimensional network perspective reveals the connections and synergies between processes of value creation in different production networks.

Coe et al. (2008b, p. 280) note, however, that GPNs are much more than economic phenomena, they are also fundamentally social, cultural, and political systems, which is why they argue that a critical cultural political economy of GPNs is needed. Although the economic processes of production, distribution, and consumption are at the core of a GPN, these processes are not simply driven by 'firms'. Rather, the operation and governance of GPNs involves, some or all of the other relevant actors – states, civil society organizations, labour and consumers – and these need to be incorporated into GPN analyses.

For instance, a criticism of the network approach is that it ignores consumption because it is overwhelmingly 'productionist'. Consequently, the consumer plays a marginal role – if any – with firms comprising the main unit of analysis. Coe et al. (2008b) point out that although it is really final consumption that has been neglected in much research, it is necessary to find ways of integrating the role of consumption more fully into GPN analysis. More broadly, they argue that GPNs are contested fields, made up of a diversity of actors and institutions, each with its own agenda. Achieving such agendas depends on the relative power configuration in specific situations. Importantly, Coe et al. (2008b) note that power relationships between GPN actors are not structurally determined and are not unidirectional, with each of the major sets of actors simultaneously involved in both cooperation/collaboration and in conflict/competition. MNEs in the same industry, for example, may be both fierce competitors and involved in a web of collaborative relationships.

In reviewing contemporary GPN research in Economic Geography, Hess and Yeung (2006) conclude that there is now a much better understanding of upgrading processes and their limits, with particular emphasis put on integrating local clusters into global value networks. An evolving literature is contextualizing global interfirm networks and value creation processes by incorporating the role of the state and other non-firm institutions as important agents of GPN in their analysis. Finally, more is now known about the embedded and path-dependent nature of GPN development and its spatialities.

A recent refinement of the GPN framework has made an analytical link between GPNs and regional development (a core issue for economic geographers since the 1980s) (Coe et al., 2004; Yeung, 2009a, 2009b). For Yeung (2009a) growth is no longer restricted to endogenous sources as previously stipulated in trade and growth theories, rather regions can plug into these global production systems that in turn sustain their growth efforts. The region is viewed as 'a porous territorial formation whose national boundaries are transcended by a broad range of network connections' (Coe et al., 2004, p. 469). While regional assets in the form of specific knowledge, skills, and expertise provide an important resource for regional development, they must be harnessed by regional institutions to 'complement the strategic needs of trans-local actors situated within global production networks' (Coe et al., 2004, p. 470). Coe et al. (2004, p. 469) conceptualize regional development 'as a dynamic outcome of the complex interaction between territorialized relational networks and global production networks within the context of changing regional governance structures'. From this perspective, regional development is a product of the strategic coupling (Yeung, 2009b) by which relational assets are matched to the strategic needs of lead firms in GPNs, with regional institutions playing a key role in this process. Coe et al. (2004) maintain that regional development will depend ultimately on the ability of this coupling to stimulate processes of value creation, enhancement, and capture. The strategic coupling process has three central characteristics: (i) it requires intentional and active intervention on the part of both institutions and inward investors to occur; (ii) it is a temporary coalition; and (iii) it transcends territorial boundaries (Yeung, 2009b; Coe, 2011, p. 391). MacKinnon (2012, p. 231) notes that recent contributions have started to examine the so-called 'dark side' of strategic coupling. This is associated with the tensions that arise from the differential strengths of key agents, particularly the often asymmetrical power relations between MNEs and local communities, associated with uneven value capture, labour exploitation, and social and class conflict. However, GPN research has tended to under-play these tensions.

Coe et al. (2008b) identify three gaps in virtually all studies of GPNs. The first relates to the circulation processes through which the nodes in the network are actually connected in a functional and physical sense. They argue that with the increased complexity and geographical extensiveness of production networks, and the need to coordinate and integrate operations as efficiently as possible, the logistics problem is central. However, the usual assumption is that the problem of moving materials, components, and finished products has been solved, so it is largely ignored.

The second gap concerns the treatment of the firm, which is usually treated as a black box. Virtually all of the attention in the GPN literature focuses upon interfirm relationships to the neglect of intra-firm relationships and of the ways in which the internal structures and relationships inside firms play a critical role in how GPNs operate and have an impact. For Coe et al. (2008b), opening up the black box of the firm would have important advantages. It would allow exploration of the way in which firms produce multiple responses to similar economic and competitive pressures, thereby avoiding the tendency for GPN analyses to assume that firms occupying similar positions in production networks will respond in a similar fashion. It would also help to explain how strategically proactive firms, despite the restraints prevailing in GPNs, can exploit the established power relationships and move into higher value-added activities.

The third gap concerns the failure of most of the GPN literature to connect the processes of production, distribution, and consumption to the natural environment. As is well known, all forms of production, distribution, and consumption place demands on the natural environment in terms of resource inputs to production and outputs in the form of pollution/waste. The result is the emergence of significant environmental stress. For Coe et al. (2008b), a GPN framework has the potential to be an insightful way of understanding such environmental issues, because it can integrate what are often seen as separate sets of processes dealt with by different academic interests. Moreover, they argue that making an attempt to incorporate materials flows and balances into GPN analyses will enrich the explanatory capacity of those analyses.

Coe (2011) also notes other lacunae. A persistent criticism of GPN research is that it has underplayed the role of financial capital and the financial sector in shaping the configuration of global production systems. A remaining research challenge is to examine in detail the impact of financialization at the sectoral and corporate level on GPN structures and dynamics. Also, the GPN literature has had little to say regarding labour as an active component of the global economy, as distinct from a passive casualty of restructuring processes. Coe (2011, p. 393) sees this as a substantial paradox, 'given both the centrality of labour to all elements of GPNs and the growing body of work under the labour geography banner that asserts the (always geographical and variable) agency of workers'.

Conclusion

It is clear that a wide variety of research approaches and topics make up the study of networks and alliances. This chapter has attempted to provide a flavour of recent work in this area, particularly that relating to alliance portfolios and the concept of GPNs in the context of the geography literature. There is a substantial literature on networks and alliances that has been produced on the back of a tremendous research effort since the mid-1980s; however, work in the area remains somewhat disparate, with a lack of synthesis among different perspectives. It is interesting to note that while geography scholars have taken much from the business/management literature relating to networks and alliances, there has been little reciprocal insight derived from the geography literature by business and management scholars. There is thus an opportunity for greater learning by the latter group of scholars from broadening their perspectives on the relevant and significant informing literature.

Despite the substantial contribution to knowledge on networks and alliances, clearly more remains to be done when it is recognized that researchers have only a marginal understanding of whole networks. This is especially the case in the relatively recently examined but under-researched areas relating to the strategic development and management of alliance portfolios and in particular network governance, where further work would be beneficial. Also, measuring alliance performance remains problematic. Research will need to move beyond examining performance of inter-firm dyadic alliances to considering value creation and appropriation at the network level, where little is known about performance and success. Research methods in this area also pose a challenge; however, many scholars have called for an increased use of longitudinal studies, in order to follow developmental patterns in detail over a longer time, for instance, in order to understand the evolution of alliance strategies and alliance management capability (Hoffmann, 2005).

Geographers recognize that fulfilling the potential of a GPN framework is some way off. Coe et al. (2008b) call for an integrative perspective that combines the insights from political economy and cultural economy approaches to describe and explain the complexities and emergent properties of GPNs. This is echoed by Hess and Yeung (2006) who argue that the ontological challenge that GPN research faces lies in integrating both the material and the socio-cultural dimensions of GPN development. Further, it is recognized that the GPN framework suffers from a relatively underdeveloped methodological foundation, i.e. 'there is no explicitly articulated methodology for doing GPN research' (Hess & Yeung, 2006, p. 1201).

References

Ahuja, G. (2000) 'The duality of collaboration: Inducements and opportunities in the formation of interfirm linkages', *Strategic Management Journal*, 21, pp. 317–343.

Barney, J.B. (1991) 'Firm resources and sustained competitive advantage', *Journal of Management*, 17, pp. 99–120.

Barringer, B.R. & Harrison, J.S. (2000) 'Walking a tightrope: Creating value through interorganizational relationships', *Journal of Management*, 26, pp. 367–403.

Bartlett, C A. & Ghoshal, S. (1989) *Managing Across Borders: The Transnational Solution*. Cambridge, MA: Harvard Business School Press.

Beamish, P.W. & Lupton, N.C. (2016) 'Cooperative strategies in International Business and management: Reflections on the past 50 years and future directions', *Journal of World Business*, 51, pp. 163–175.

Bojanowski, M., Corten, R. & Westbrock, B. (2012) 'The structure and dynamics of the global network of inter-firm R&D partnerships 1989–2002', *Journal of Technology Transfer*, 37, pp. 967–987.

Borgatti, S.P. & Foster, P.C. (2003) 'The network paradigm in organizational research: A review and typology', *Journal of Management*, 29, pp. 991–1013.

Brass, D.J., Galaskiewicz, J., Greve, H.R. & Tsai, W. (2004) 'Taking stock of networks and organizations: A multilevel perspective', *Academy of Management Journal*, 47, pp. 795–817.

Coe, N.M. (2011) 'Geographies of production II: A global production network A–Z', *Progress in Human Geography*, 36, pp. 389–402

Coe, N.M., Dicken, P. & Hess, M. (2008a) 'Introduction: Global production networks – debates and challenges', *Journal of Economic Geography*, 8, pp. 267–269.

Coe, N.M., Dicken, P. & Hess, M. (2008b) 'Global production networks: Realizing the potential', *Journal of Economic Geography*, 8, pp. 271–295.

Coe, N.M., Hess, M. Yeung, H.W.-C., Dicken, P. & Henderson, J. (2004) '"Globalizing" regional development: A global production networks perspective', *Transactions of the Institute of British Geographers*, 29, pp. 468–484.

Cohen, W.M. & Levinthal, D.A. (1990) 'Absorptive capacity: A new perspective on learning and innovation', *Administrative Science Quarterly*, 35, pp. 128–152.

Contractor, F.J. & Lorange, P. (Eds.) (1988) *Co-operative Strategies in International Business*. Lexington, MA: Lexington Books.

Contractor, F.J. & Lorange, P. (Eds.) (2002a) *Cooperative Strategies and Alliances*. Oxford, UK: Pergamon.

Contractor, F.J. & Lorange, P. (2002b) 'The growth of alliances in the knowledge-based economy', in Contractor, F.J. & Lorange, P. (Eds.) *Cooperative Strategies and Alliances*. Oxford, UK: Pergamon, pp. 3–22.

Das, T.K. & Teng, B.-S. (1998) 'Between trust and control: Developing confidence in partner co-operation in alliances', *Academy of Management Review*, 23, pp. 491–512.

Das, T.K. & Teng, B.-S. (2000) 'A resource-based theory of strategic alliances', *Journal of Management*, 26, pp. 31–61.

Desai, M.A., Foley, C.F. Jr. & Hines, J.R. (2004) 'The costs of shared ownership: Evidence from international joint ventures', *Journal of Financial Economics*, 73, pp. 323–374.

Dicken, P. & Henderson, J. (2003) 'Making the connections: Global production networks in Europe and East Asia', *ESRC Research Project R000238535*.

Dierickx, I., & Cool, K. (1989) 'Asset stock accumulation and sustainability of competitive advantage', *Management Science*, 35, pp. 1504–1511.

Di Guardo, M.C. & Harrigan, K.R. (2012) 'Mapping research on strategic alliances and innovation: A co-citation analysis', *The Journal of Technology Transfer*, 37, pp. 789–811.

Dyer, J.H. & Hatch, N.W. (2006) 'Relation-specific capabilities and barriers to knowledge transfers: Creating advantage through network relationships', *Strategic Management Journal*, 27, pp. 701–719.

Dyer, J.H. & Singh, H. (1998) 'The relational view: Cooperative strategy and sources of interorganizational competitive advantage', *Academy of Management Review*, 23, pp. 660–679.

Faulkner, D. (2003) 'Strategic alliances and networks', in Faulkner, D.O. & Campbell, A. (Eds.), *The Oxford Handbook of Strategy, volume II: Corporate Strategy*. Oxford, UK: Oxford University Press, pp. 118–156.

Geyskens, I., Steenkamp, J.-B.E.M. & Kumar, N. (2006) 'Make, buy, or ally: A transaction cost theory meta-analysis', *Academy of Management Journal*, 49, pp. 519–543.

Glaister, K.W. & Buckley, P.J. (1996) 'Strategic motives for international alliance formation', *Journal of Management Studies*, 3, pp. 301–332.

Glückler, J. (2007) 'Economic Geography and the evolution of networks', *Journal of Economic Geography*, 7, pp. 619–634.

Goerzen, A. (2005) 'Managing alliance networks: Emerging practices of multinational corporations', *Academy of Management Executive*, 19, pp. 94–107.

Gomes, E., Barnes, B.R. & Mahmood, T. (2016) 'A 22 year review of strategic alliance research in the leading management journals', *International Business Review*, 25, pp. 15–27.

Grabher, G. (2006) 'Trading routes, bypasses, and risky intersections: Mapping the travels of "networks" between economic sociology and Economic Geography', *Progress in Human Geography*, 30, pp. 163–189.

Granovetter, M. (1985) 'Economic action and social structure: The problem of embeddedness', *American Journal of Sociology*, 91, pp. 481–510.

Gulati, R. (1995) 'Social structure and alliance formation patterns: A longitudinal analysis', *Administrative Science Quarterly*, 40, pp. 619–652.

Gulati, R. (1998) 'Alliances and networks', *Strategic Management Journal*, 19, pp. 293–317.

Gulati, R., Nohria, N. & Zaheer, A. (2000) 'Strategic networks', *Strategic Management Journal*, 21, pp. 203–215.

Hagedoorn, J. (1996) 'Trends and patterns in strategic technology partnering since the early seventies', *Review of Industrial Organization*, 11, pp. 601–616.

Hagedoorn, J. (2002) 'Inter-firm R&D partnerships: An overview of major trends and patterns since 1960', *Research Policy*, 31, 477–492.

Hagedoorn, J. & Osborn, R.N. (2002) 'Interfirm R&D partnerships: Major theories and trends since 1960', in Contractor, F.J. & Lorange, P. (Eds.), *Cooperative Strategies and Alliances*. Oxford, UK: Pergamon, pp. 517–542.

Henderson, J., Dicken, P., Hess, M., Coe, N.M. & Yeung, H.W.-C. (2002) 'Global production networks and the analysis of economic development', *Review of International Political Economy*, 9, pp. 436–464.

Hennart, J.F. (1988) 'A transaction cost theory of equity joint ventures', *Strategic Management Journal*, 9, pp. 361–374.

Hess, M. & Yeung, H.W.-C. (2006) 'Whither global production networks in Economic Geography? Past, present and future', *Environment and Planning A*, 38, pp. 1193–1204.

Hoffmann, W.H. (2005) 'How to manage a portfolio of alliances', *Long Range Planning*, 38, pp. 121–143.

Hoffmann, W.H. (2007) 'Strategies for managing a portfolio of alliances', *Strategic Management Journal*, 28, pp. 827–856.

Inkpen, A.C. (2001a) 'Strategic alliances', in Rugman, A.M. & Brewer, T.L. (Eds.), *The Oxford Handbook of International Business*. Oxford, UK: Oxford University Press, pp. 402–427.

Inkpen, A.C. (2001b) 'Strategic alliances', in Hitt, M.A., Freeman, R.E. & Harrison, J.S. (Eds.), *The Blackwell Handbook of Strategic Management*. Oxford, UK: Blackwell, pp. 409–432.

Jack, S.L. (2010) 'Approaches to studying networks: Implications and outcomes', *Journal of Business Venturing*, 25, pp. 120–137.

Jiang, X. & Li, Y. (2008) 'The relationship between organizational learning and firms' financial performance in strategic alliances: A contingency approach', *Journal of World Business*, 43, pp. 365–379.

Kale, P. & Singh, H. (2009) 'Managing strategic alliances: What do we know now, and where do we go from here?' *Academy of Management Perspectives*, 23, pp. 45–62.

Kilduff, M. & Brass, D.J. (2010) 'Organizational social network research: Core ideas and key debates', *Academy of Management Annals*, 4, pp. 317–357.

Koka, B.R. & Prescott, J.E. (2008) 'Designing alliance networks: The influence of network position, environmental change, and strategy on firm performance', *Strategic Management Journal*, 29, pp. 639–661.

Lavie, D. (2006) 'The competitive advantage of interconnected firms: An extension of the resource-based view', *Academy of Management Review*, 31, pp. 638–658.

Levinson, N.S. & Asahi, M. (1996) 'Cross-national alliances and interorganizational learning', *Organizational Dynamics*, 24, pp. 51–63.

MacKinnon, D. (2012) 'Beyond strategic coupling: Reassessing the firm-region nexus in global production networks', *Journal of Economic Geography*, 12, pp. 227–245.

Moskalev, S.A. & Swensen, R.B. (2007) 'Joint ventures around the globe from 1990–2000: Forms, types, industries, countries and ownership patterns', *Review of Financial Economics*, 16, pp. 29–67.

Nohria, N. (1992) 'Introduction: Is a network perspective a useful way of studying organizations?' in Nohria, N. & Eccles, R.G. (Eds.), *Networks and Organizations: Structure, Form, and Action*. Boston, MA: Harvard Business School Press, pp. 1–22

Parkhe, A. (1993) 'Strategic alliance structuring: A game theoretic and transaction cost examination of interfirm co-operation', *Academy of Management Journal*, 16, pp. 794–839.

Parkhe, A., Wasserman, S. & Ralston, D.A. (2006) 'Introduction to special topic forum: New frontiers in network theory development', *Academy of Management Review*, 31, pp. 560–568.

Parmigiani, A. & Rivera-Santos, M. (2011) 'Clearing a path through the forest: A meta-review of interorganizational relationships', *Journal of Management*, 37, pp. 1108–1136.

Pfeffer, J. & Salancik, G. R. (1978) *The External Control of Organizations: A Resource Dependence Perspective*. New York: Harper & Row.

Powell, W.W., Koput, K.W. & Smith-Doerr, L. (1996) 'Interorganizational collaboration and the locus of innovation: Networks of learning in biotechnology', *Administrative Science Quarterly*, 41, 116–145.

Prahalad, C.K. & Doz, Y.L. (1987) *The Multinational Mission: Balancing Local Demands and Global Vision*. New York: Free Press.

Provan, K.G., Fish, A. & Sydow, J. (2007) 'Interorganizational networks at the network level: Empirical literature on whole networks', *Journal of Management*, 33, pp. 479–516.

Reuer, J.J. (Ed.) (2004) *Strategic Alliances: Theory and Evidence*. Oxford, UK: Oxford University Press.

Reuer, J.J. & Ragozzino, R. (2006) 'Agency hazards and alliance portfolios', *Strategic Management Journal*, 27, pp. 27–44.

Rivera-Santos, M. & Inkpen, A.C. (2009) 'Joint ventures and alliances', in Kotabe, M. & Helsen, K. (Eds.), *The Sage Handbook of International Marketing*. Thousand Oaks, CA: Sage, pp. 198–217.

Rumelt, R.P. (1984) 'Towards a strategic theory of the firm', in Lamb, R.B. (Ed.), *Competitive Strategic Management*. Englewood Cliffs, NJ: Prentice-Hall.

Sarkar, M.B., Aulakh, P.S. & Madhok, A. (2009). 'Process capabilities and value generation in alliance portfolios', *Organization Science*, 20, pp. 583–600.

Schilling, M.A. (2009) 'Understanding the alliance data', *Strategic Management Journal*, 30, pp. 233–260.

Shenkar, O. & Reuer, J.J. (Eds.) (2006) *Handbook of Strategic Alliances*. Thousand Oaks, CA: Sage.

Shi, W., Sun, J. & Prescott, J.E. (2011) 'A temporal perspective of merger and acquisition and strategic alliance initiatives: Review and future direction', *Journal of Management*, 38, 164–209.

Tallman, S. (2003) 'Dynamic capabilities', in Faulkner, D.O. & Campbell, A. (Eds.), *The Oxford Handbook of Strategy, Volume I: A Strategy Overview and Competitive Strategy*. Oxford, UK: Oxford University Press, pp. 372–403.

Vapola, T.J., Paukku, M. & Gabrielsson, M. (2010) 'Portfolio management of strategic alliances: An International Business perspective', *International Business Review*, 19, pp. 247–260.

Wassmer, U. (2010) 'Alliance portfolios: A review and research agenda', *Journal of Management*, 36, pp. 141–171.

Wernerfelt, B. (1984) 'A resource-based view of the firm', *Strategic Management Journal*, 5, pp. 171–180.

Williamson, O.E. (1975) *Markets and Hierarchies: Analysis and Antitrust Implications*. New York: Free Press.

Williamson, O.E. (1985) *The Economic Institutions of Capitalism: Firms, Markets, Relational Contracting*. New York: Free Press.

Williamson, O.E. (1991) 'Comparative economic organization: The analysis of discrete structural alternatives', *Administrative Science Quarterly*, 36, pp. 269–296.

Yan, A. & Gray, B. (1994) 'Bargaining power, management control, and performance in United States-China joint ventures: A comparative case study', *Academy of Management Journal*, 37, pp. 1478–1517.

Yeung, H.W.-C. (2009a) 'Transnational corporations, global production networks and urban and regional development: A geographer's perspective on "Multinational Enterprises and the Global Economy"', *Growth and Change*, 40, pp. 197–226.

Yeung, H.W.-C. (2009b) 'Regional development and the competitive dynamics of global production networks: An East Asian perspective', *Regional Studies*, 43, pp. 325–351.

4
OUTSOURCING, OFFSHORING AND THE GLOBAL FACTORY

Roger Strange and Giovanna Magnani

Introduction

Outsourcing and offshoring are terms that are often used interchangeably, yet they refer to different firm strategies and have different motivations. *Outsourcing*[1] refers to the procurement by lead firms[2] of goods and/or services from independent outside suppliers, when those goods and services had previously been provided internally within the firm. Outsourcing does not refer to one-off purchases, but involves the strategic decision to reject the vertical integration of an activity (Gilley & Rasheed, 2000; Grossman & Helpman, 2005). It is a process which involves the lead firm externalizing elements of its value chain,[3] i.e. there is an *organizational fragmentation of production*. For instance, an electronics goods manufacturer such as Sony might outsource the production of certain parts and components to local Japanese suppliers. Outsourcing thus involves a decision about ownership. In contrast, *offshoring*[4] refers to the relocation of the production of goods and/or services overseas and thus involves an *international fragmentation of production* and the creation of global value chains (GVCs). For instance, Sony has, through the establishment of factories overseas, offshored the manufacture of many of its electronic products to North America, Europe, and elsewhere. Offshoring thus involves a location decision.

Outsourcing and offshoring are different processes, but they can be combined.[5] Outsourced activities may be undertaken by suppliers located in the same country as the lead firm (domestic outsourcing), or may involve suppliers in foreign countries (offshore outsourcing). Thus when Apple contracts Foxconn to manufacture its iPads and iPhones in Asia, it is engaging in offshore outsourcing (Denicolai, Strange & Zucchella, 2015). Meanwhile, offshoring may be effected through offshore outsourcing, or when multinational enterprises (MNE) undertake foreign direct investment (FDI) and retain ownership of the offshored activities. As regards the temporal sequencing of the outsourcing and offshoring decisions, Mudambi and Venzin (2010) aver that there is no universal recommendation. When the lead firm's strategic objectives:

> [a]re not location-bound, as when the MNE leverages in-house knowledge to enter new markets, control is the primary decision (taken first) and the location (offshoring) decision is conditional on and subservient to it. Conversely when the MNEs' objectives are location-bound, as when it enters a technology cluster to access local knowledge (that is not available elsewhere), location becomes the primary decision.
>
> *(Mudambi & Venzin, 2010, p. 1515)*

Recent decades have witnessed a proliferation of activities taking place under (domestic and/or offshore) outsourcing contracts, increased offshoring through FDI by MNEs, and the growth of locally owned firms in many emerging economies: these developments have given rise to the concept of the *global factory* (Buckley & Strange, 2015), and have been driven in large part by a combination of technological advances (particularly in information and communication technologies and transportation), market liberalization and economic restructuring in many countries, international trade and investment liberalization, financial deregulation and the integration of global capital markets, and improved contract enforcement and protection of intellectual property rights in many jurisdictions (Maskus, 2000; Hillberry, 2011; Amador & Cabral, 2014).

There is a considerable literature on the outsourcing of support activities (e.g. IT and HR services),[6] but relatively little attention has been devoted to the outsourcing of primary activities such as manufacturing. Yet UNCTAD (2011, p. 135) report that the most active sectors for offshore outsourcing are garments ($200bn of cross-border outsourced sales and 7m employees), footwear ($50bn sales and 2m employees), toys ($15bn sales and 0.5m employees); electronics ($240bn sales and 1.7m employees), auto components ($220bn sales and 1.4m employees), and pharmaceuticals ($30bn sales and 0.2m employees). Increasing attention is being devoted to the growth of so-called *factoryless goods producers* (FGPs) in many advanced countries (Bernard & Fort, 2015; Morikawa, 2016), and the issue of whether firms that have outsourced their manufacturing activities should nevertheless be classified as part of the manufacturing sector.

In this chapter, we focus on the offshoring and outsourcing of manufacturing activities. We first briefly review the different conceptions of the global factory used in the literature. We then consider why firms choose to offshore manufacturing activities, what are the implications for the global distribution of the value-added in the resultant GVCs, and why some MNEs choose to reverse the offshoring process. We then address the issues of why firms may choose to vertically integrate their value-chain activities, why firms may instead decide to outsource manufacturing activities either offshore or within their domestic economies, the empirical evidence on the growth of FGPs, and what determines the extent of the outsourcing. The final section highlights some methodological problems encountered in empirical studies, suggests areas where further research is merited, and also considers the implications for the global factory of the latest wave of new manufacturing technologies including robotics and additive manufacturing (3D printing).

The global factory

Various authors (notably Grunwald & Flamm, 1985; Gereffi, 1989; Buckley & Ghauri, 2004) have used the term *global factory*, though each makes different assumptions about who maintains *control* over these geographically dispersed activities (Buckley & Strange, 2015). Thus Gereffi (1989, p. 97) envisages the *global factory* as 'a global manufacturing system in which production capacity is dispersed to an unprecedented number of developing as well as industrialized countries', and that a widening of corporate ownership on a global scale has been associated with this greater geographical dispersion of activity. In contrast, Grunwald and Flamm (1985) consider the *global factory* to be the result of offshore assembly operations being established by MNEs from the advanced economies to meet the competition of low-cost imports – echoing the work of Vernon (1966, 1979) on the product life cycle hypothesis of FDI. These MNEs had offshored many value chain activities to emerging economies, but these activities were still integrated (internalized) under common ownership notwithstanding their geographic dispersion. Finally, Buckley and Ghauri (2004) conceptualize the *global factory* as a complex strategy by MNEs from advanced economies, in which many value chain activities are offshored to emerging economies whilst also being outsourced (externalized) to independent suppliers.

Table 4.1 The global factory: location, ownership and governance issues

		Different conceptualizations of the global factory		
		Gereffi (1989)	*Grunwald and Flamm (1985)*	*Buckley and Ghauri (2004)*
Key issues	Location	Dispersion of manufacturing but national specialization in distinct industrial sectors and stages of the value chain	Relocation of assembly activities to developing countries	'Fine-slicing' and relocation of activities
	Ownership and control	Widening of corporate ownership	Largely internalized in MNEs	Increased externalization of control of operations; increased internalization of knowledge
	Governance	Growth of locally owned firms; more varied governance modes	Offshoring MNEs' control	Increased control of lead firm through internalization of knowledge and contractual control of operations

Source: Buckley and Strange (2015) (reproduced with the permission of the Academy of Management).

The MNEs are assumed to control the resultant geographically distributed networks of activities even though they have relinquished equity ownership. These different conceptions of the *global factory* thus make different assumptions regarding the location, ownership, and governance of the globally dispersed value chain activities.

These three conceptualizations of the global factory differ in terms of their assumptions about value chain governance, corporate ownership and control, and the (re)location of manufacturing activities – see Table 4.1. These differences in turn have important implications for the appropriation of the rents earned in GVCs and the global distribution of income (Buckley & Strange, 2015).

Why do firms offshore manufacturing activities?

Offshoring involves a location decision, independent of who actually undertakes the manufacturing activities. Lead firms can offshore manufacturing activities through FDI and thus maintain ownership, by contracting out production to foreign licencees, or by offshoring the activities to independent suppliers (offshore outsourcing). In all cases, the motivation is typically lower production costs in the foreign location, though less strict environmental regulations (Walter, 1982; List, McHone & Millimet, 2003; Copeland & Taylor, 2004), less stringent employment requirements (Levy, 2005; Olney, 2013), and greater contractual flexibility (Vivek, Richey Jr & Dalela, 2009) may also have an impact. The potential gains, however, may be mitigated by factors such as increased transportation and communication costs, enhanced exposure to systematic (political, social, and/or cross-cultural) risks, greater managerial complexity, and liabilities of foreignness.

The offshoring trend emerged in the early 1960s when US manufacturing companies began relocating manufacturing activities towards low-cost destinations to obtain cost-savings and increase financial performance (Nayyar, 1978; Maskell et al., 2007). Since the 1990s, thanks to the afore-mentioned developments in transportation and ICT developments, the offshoring phenomena has been growing intensively (Levy, 2005) enabling firms to increasingly locate activities and processes globally (Sidhu & Volberda, 2011). The current trend in advanced economies towards offshoring has been likened to a Third Industrial Revolution (Blinder, 2006; Blinder & Krueger, 2013), with similar potential to disrupt patterns of employment. Blinder and Krueger (2013: S117) measure the *offshorability* of various jobs, assessed in terms of whether the work can be moved overseas in principle even if that movement has not yet actually occurred: they estimate that about 24–25% of US jobs are potentially offshorable, but that this figure varies considerably across industrial sectors with their estimate for manufacturing as high as 50%.

Recent years, however, have witnessed moves by several manufacturing firms to bring back offshored production activities to their home countries (Albertoni et al., 2015), though the aggregate scale of the phenomenon is still limited (Oldenski, 2015).[7] This phenomenon has been termed *inshoring* (Liao, 2012), *reshoring* (Ellram, Tate & Petersen, 2013; Gray et al., 2013), or *backshoring* (Bals et al., 2015).[8] Various motives have been identified for reshoring. Albertoni et al. (2015) report that increased delivery times, poor production quality, and rising overseas labour costs were common motivations reported by reshoring firms. Other authors have added to the list of possible drivers. Kinkel (2014) suggests that many reshoring initiatives are operative corrections to previous managerial decisions, as firms understand that their offshoring strategies have not been compatible with meeting consumer needs (Gylling et al., 2015; Stentoft et al., 2015). Often firms need to be proximate to customers and to cut long supply chains (Albertoni et al., 2015), as customers require fast delivery and customized products (Arlbjørn & Mikkelsen, 2014; Bals et al., 2015). Martínez-Mora and Merino (2014) suggest that the imperative to reshore may depend upon the nature of market demand. They report that Spanish manufacturers of premium footwear have been reshoring all manufacturing so as to respond flexibly to customers' and distributors' needs, and to maintain quality standards. In contrast, manufacturers of lower-quality footwear continue to pursue offshoring strategies. Both Uluskan, Joines and Godfrey (2016) and Hikmet and Enderwick (2015) highlight reshoring as a response to concerns about the theft of intellectual property in the foreign locations.

Why do firms outsource manufacturing activities?

In this section, we first outline the potential advantages to firms from vertically integrating their value-chain activities before considering the possible benefits that might arise from outsourcing selected activities. We summarize the evidence on the rise of factoryless goods production, review the small empirical literature that aims to establish the firm-level determinants of manufacturing outsourcing, and the rather larger literature that looks at the implications of manufacturing outsourcing for the performance of the lead firms.

The rationale for vertical integration

Vertical integration is the counterpoint to outsourcing. Vertical integration involves lead firms internalizing value-chain activities under common ownership, and various authors have suggested that this may improve inter alia scheduling and coordination (Coase, 1937; Williamson, 1975; Chandler, 1977; Harrigan, 1984); eliminate imperfect competition in upstream markets

(Vernon & Graham, 1971; Westfield, 1981); facilitate investments in specialized assets, so protecting product quality and proprietary technology (Jones & Hill, 1988) and avoiding opportunistic recontracting (Monteverde & Teece, 1982); produce scope economies (Porter, 1987; D'Aveni & Ravenscraft, 1994); allow price discrimination (Perry, 1989); lead to positive externalities (Tirole, 1988; Perry, 1989); and increase bargaining power vis-à-vis buyers and suppliers (Porter, 1980). In the International Business context, the benefits of cross-border integration have typically been explored though the lens of internalization theory (Buckley & Casson, 1976; Rugman, 1981; Hennart, 1982), though attention has also been drawn to the associated information, coordination, and motivation costs (Buckley & Strange, 2011).

Indeed, Alfred Chandler (1977) in the *Visible Hand* testified how, in the late nineteenth and early twentieth centuries, the coordination requirements of high-throughput technologies, and the capabilities of contemporary markets and institutions to meet those requirements, led to the emergence of large vertically integrated firms. In turn, Richard Langlois (1993) commented that the managerial revolution chronicled by Chandler was an adaptation to a particular set of historical circumstances, during which the extant market-supporting institutions were inadequate for the profitable opportunities associated with the new technologies, and hence the costs of coordinating through markets were high. Langlois further suggested that managerial hierarchies were second-best solutions that emerged in the absence of better alternatives, but that, over time, markets 'catch up' and firms will find it cost-effective to delegate more and more activities. According to his *vanishing hand* hypothesis, Langlois asserted that market-supporting institutions had evolved in many countries by the late twentieth and early twenty-first centuries, and hence vertically integrated firms were increasingly succumbing to the forces of specialization, with the result being widespread vertical disintegration and outsourcing. This suggests that decisions regarding outsourcing (or vertical integration) may well depend not just upon firm-level characteristics, but also upon the institutional environments within which firms operate – and these institutional environments typically vary across countries and over time.

The rationale for outsourcing

Attention has thus shifted to the potential benefits of outsourcing as a performance-enhancing strategy. One common explanation is that lead firms are outsourcing activities so as to economize on their scarce financial and managerial resources, and focus on their *core competencies* (Prahalad & Hamel, 1990). Such core competencies form the basis of competitive advantage and represent the collective learning in the firm, especially how to coordinate diverse production skills and integrate multiple streams of technological and managerial competencies to enable individual firms to adapt quickly to changing opportunities (Coombs, 1996). Notwithstanding the intuitive plausibility of this argument, there are both conceptual and practical difficulties in actually defining what activities are core (and thus should be internalized) and which are non-core (and thus may be gainfully outsourced). A second common line of argument is provided by the *strategic outsourcing* literature (Quinn & Hilmer, 1994; Quinn, 1999; Shy & Stenbacka, 2003; Jacobides & Winter, 2005; Holcomb & Hitt, 2007) that highlights the exploitation of knowledge complementarities and learning opportunities thanks to the integration with independent agents in intermediate markets. The focus moves from the minimization of transaction costs to the maximization of value generated in the value chain. Lead firms not only pursue cost benefits but also explore alternative solutions thus obtaining higher value and innovative outcomes. Other suggested rationales for outsourcing include inter alia the lead firms being able to take advantage of specialized skills and/or economies of scale enjoyed by outside suppliers (Abraham & Taylor, 1996; Gilley & Rasheed, 2000); suppliers having lower labour and/or other production costs (Abraham & Taylor, 1996; Weil, 2014); greater flexibility in response to volatile output demand and/or technology changes (Abraham & Taylor, 1996; Díaz-Mora, 2008; Holl, 2008); reduced investment in plant and equipment (Gilley & Rasheed, 2000); and access to better quality inputs due to competition between outside suppliers (Gilley & Rasheed, 2000).

The above arguments all emphasize that outsourcing will be the preferred organizational arrangement because it is more *efficient*, as external suppliers are somehow able to provide the requisite intermediate goods and services at lower cost than the lead firms are able to do internally. A rather different explanation for outsourcing emphasizes the *asymmetric power* relationships between lead firms and their suppliers, which permit the lead firms to outsource even manufacturing activities whilst still retaining control over the disaggregated value chains (Hymer, 1972; Strange & Newton, 2006; Strange, 2011; Denicolai, Strange & Zucchella, 2015). This ability to leverage power asymmetries rests on the lead firms enjoying certain *isolating mechanisms* (Rumelt, 1984, 1987) that enable them to appropriate the rents from externalized value chains: such mechanisms may involve formal property rights (patents, trademarks, licences); firm-specific technical knowledge that is difficult to imitate; market-based firm-specific assets (marketing capabilities, distribution networks, corporate reputation, brand names); and/or first-mover advantages (Denicolai, Strange & Zucchella, 2015). Grossman and Helpman (2002) have provided a theoretical model in which the viability of outsourcing is determined by the distribution of bargaining power between the lead firms and their suppliers, the degree of competition in the market, and the number of potential partners in the market. They conclude that the benefits from outsourcing depend on the characteristics of the firm and industry in question. Denicolai, Strange and Zucchella (2015) further argue that the efficacy of isolating mechanisms – and hence the ability of lead firms to extract rents – will tend to dissipate over time as competitors emerge to imitate successful strategies and products (see further discussion later).

Notwithstanding these potential benefits, a strategy of outsourcing also brings potential disadvantages to lead firms including the creation of potential rivals (Prahalad & Hamel, 1990; Arrunada & Vásquez, 2006; Gilley & Rasheed, 2000); increased transaction costs (related to search, negotiation, contracts, coordination, etc.) especially in repeated transactions and/or over distance (Gilley & Rasheed, 2000; Díaz-Mora, 2008; Holl, 2008); and the erosion of capabilities in product and process innovation (Chesbrough & Teece, 2002; Pisano & Shih, 2012).

The evidence on factoryless goods production

The term *factoryless goods producers* (FGPs) has been applied to firms that add value to the production of goods through the provision of intellectual property, innovation, and marketing, yet which have outsourced all manufacturing activities and thus do not own any manufacturing facilities (Bernard & Fort, 2015). Well-known examples include Apple (Dedrick, Kraemer & Linden, 2010; Denicolai, Strange & Zucchella, 2015), Nike (Donaghu & Barff, 1990), Dyson (Loch, Chick & Huchzermeier, 2008), Nokia and Ericsson (Berggren & Bengtsson, 2004; Ali-Yrkkö et al., 2011). The FGPs provide substantial service inputs through product design, technology, and/or know-how, and control the interface with their final consumers, but do not supply (significant) material inputs to the production process.

The empirical evidence on the importance of FGPs is sparse (see also Bernard, Smeets & Warzynski, 2014). Bernard and Fort (2015) note that although such FGPs are involved in the production of manufactured goods, they are generally not recorded as part of the manufacturing sector in official government statistics.[9] This can be problematic in that the statistics on the manufacturing sector will under-estimate the activities, employment, and trade related to manufacturing, and may hinder a proper appreciation of the distribution of the gains within GVCs. They estimated (Bernard & Fort, 2015, p. 521) that the number of FGPs in the United States was 13,500 in 2007, and that these firms employed over 672,000 workers. The importance of FGPs had moreover risen steadily and substantially since 1992 when the corresponding figures were 4,900 firms and 285,000 workers. The US FGPs were particularly apparent in the electrical equipment, computers, pharmaceuticals, garment, and footwear sectors (see also Kamal, Moulton & Ribarsky, 2013). Furthermore, the US FGPs imported 38% of the value of their wholesale sales in 2007, suggesting that they had offshored a substantial proportion of their outsourced manufacturing activities. Bayard, Byrne and Smith (2015) focus on FGPs in US semiconductor manufacturing, and reported that semiconductor sales in 2007 would be 25% higher if FGPs were included. Morikawa (2016) reports that there were 2,688 FGPs in Japan in 2013, employing over 1.1 million workers. Most of these FGPs were active in domestic outsourcing rather than offshore outsourcing.

The literature and empirical analysis on FGPs is still in its infancy and, at the time of writing, there is still considerable debate as to how FGPs should be defined. Yet the fact that this debate is taking place in academic and government fora confirms that the scale of (domestic and offshore) manufacturing outsourcing in many countries is already substantial notwithstanding the lack of accurate aggregate data on the phenomenon.

The determinants of outsourcing

There has been a small empirical literature focusing on the firm-level determinants of manufacturing outsourcing – see Table 4.2.[10] These studies use either outsourcing propensity (operationalized as a dummy variable indicating whether or not the lead firm has outsourced some manufacturing activities) or outsourcing intensity (measured by the value of the outsourced activities as a proportion of sales) as the dependent variable in their analyses, and most rely on firm-level data collected in the course of broader enterprise surveys and reported in secondary sources.

Some studies use measures of outsourcing that do not correspond well to the theoretical constructs. Thus Kimura (2002) operationalizes outsourcing propensity by whether or not Japanese lead firms used subcontractors (using *shitauke*). The firm-level data were taken from surveys conducted by SMEA and METI, and it is not clear whether the subcontracting necessarily involves manufacturing activities. Girma and Görg (2004) proxied outsourcing intensity by the cost of industrial services received by the lead firms as a proportion of their wage bills. The firm-level data come from the UK Annual Respondents Database (ARD), and the industrial services include all purchases and not just those effected through outsourcing arrangements. Tomiura (2005) used firm-level data from the 1998 MITI[11] *Basic Survey of Commercial and Manufacturing Structure and Activity*, which reported the contracting out (*gaichu*) by lead firms in Japan of manufacturing or processing as a proportion of sales. But his study focused on the determinants of offshore outsourcing as opposed to domestic outsourcing.

Other studies have more appropriate measures of the dependent variable. Holl (2008) and Díaz-Mora and Triguero-Cano (2012) both model outsourcing propensity according to whether the lead firm reports that it has subcontracted production or not. Their firm-level data come from the Spanish Survey on Business Strategies carried out annually by the SEPI Foundation. Leiblein, Reuer and Dalsace (2002) modelled outsourcing propensity in a similar way, and concentrated on a very narrow group of products (integrated circuits). Bardhan, Whitaker and Mithas (2006) and Bardhan, Mithas and Lin (2007) considered processing, assembly, and packaging as separate activities, and constructed a composite measure of outsourcing propensity.

Table 4.2 Empirical studies of the determinants of manufacturing outsourcing

Article	*Data sample and source*	*Outsourcing measure*	*Explanatory variables and hypothesised impacts*	*Main findings*
Kimura (2002)	3,723 Japanese machinery (general, electric, transport, precision) manufacturing firms, 1994. MITI survey.	Outsourcing propensity.	⋆ Firm size (+) ⋆ Gross value added/sales (–) ⋆ Foreign sales ratio (+) ⋆ R&D intensity (+) ⋆ Advertising intensity (+) ⋆ Commissioning production dummy (+) ⋆ Working as subcontractor dummy ⋆ Foreign ownership (+)	Firms with high R&D intensity, high foreign sales ratios, and high foreign share ownership are more likely to engage in outsourcing. The outsourcing propensity is also associated with low value-added/sales ratios, and to whether the firms commission production and also work as subcontractors.
Leiblein, Reuer & Dalsace (2002)	714 production decisions by 176 integrated circuit manufacturers, 1996. Survey by Integrated Circuit Engineering Corporation (ICE).	Outsourcing propensity = (in-house production or not).	⋆ Firm size ⋆ Firm age/tenure ⋆ Ex ante number of suppliers (and squared term) ⋆ Demand uncertainty ⋆ Asset specificity ⋆ Demand uncertainty ⋆ Asset specificity	Outsourcing propensity is positively related to the ex ante number of suppliers, and negatively related to the squared term, suggesting an inverse U-shaped relationship. Outsourcing propensity is also positively related to asset specificity, demand uncertainty, and the interaction term, and negatively related to firm size and firm age.
Girma & Görg (2004)	43,024 UK establishments in three manufacturing (chemicals, mechanical and instrument engineering, electronics) sectors. Annual Respondents Database (ARD)	Outsourcing intensity = (cost of industrial services received/ total wage bill).	⋆ Firm size (+) ⋆ Wage rate for skilled workers (+) ⋆ Wage rate for unskilled workers (+) ⋆ Level of unionization (+) ⋆ Foreign ownership dummy (+) ⋆ Sector and time dummies	Outsourcing intensity is positively related to firm size, skilled wage rates, and foreign ownership. Current levels of outsourcing are heavily influenced by previous levels.

(continued)

Table 4.2 (continued)

Article	*Data sample and source*	*Outsourcing measure*	*Explanatory variables and hypothesised impacts*	*Main findings*
Taymaz & Kilicaslan (2005)	8,879 Turkish manufacturing (textiles and engineering) plants, 1993–2000. Annual Surveys of Manufacturing Industry.	Outsourcing intensity = (subcontracted inputs/total inputs).	⋆ Firm size (+) ⋆ Wage rate (+) ⋆ Capacity limits (+) ⋆ Regional clusters (+) ⋆ Product differentiation (+) ⋆ Advertising intensity (+) ⋆ Capital intensity (+) ⋆ Proportion of female personnel (–) ⋆ Proportion of admin personnel (+) ⋆ Proportion of skilled personnel (+) ⋆ Time dummies	Outsourcing intensity is positively related to firm size, wage rates, capacity constraints, advertising intensity, capital intensity, and high proportions of female, admin, and skilled personnel.
Tomiura (2005)	118,300 Japanese manufacturing firms, 1998. MITI survey.	Offshore outsourcing intensity = (value of contracted-out manufacturing/ firm sales)	⋆ Firm size (+) ⋆ Labour productivity (+) ⋆ IT usage (+) ⋆ Capital intensity (–) ⋆ Human skills (+) ⋆ R&D intensity (+) ⋆ Sector dummies	The intensity of offshore outsourcing is positively related to labour productivity, IT usage, labour-intensity, and R&D intensity.
Bardhan, Whitaker & Mithas (2006)	326 US manufacturing plants, 2004. Authors' own survey.	Outsourcing propensity = (index of three core processes).	⋆ Plant strategy (+) ⋆ IT spending/sales (+) ⋆ Supplier integration dummy (+) ⋆ Plant size (+) ⋆ Plant age (+) ⋆ High production volume dummy (–) ⋆ Large product mix dummy ⋆ Unionization dummy (+) ⋆ Discrete manufacturing process dummy (+)	Plants following high-quality strategies, and with high levels of IT spending and unionization are more likely to engage in outsourcing. Outsourcing propensity is also associated with low-volume plants using discrete manufacturing processes.
Bardhan, Mithas & Lin (2007)	964 US manufacturing plants, 2003. Authors' own survey.	Outsourcing propensity = (index of three core processes).	⋆ Operations management systems (+) ⋆ Enterprise management systems (+) ⋆ Plant strategy (+) ⋆ Plant size (+) ⋆ Plant age (+) ⋆ Sector dummies	Plants following low-cost or competency-focused strategies, and with high EMS implementation are more likely to engage in outsourcing.

Díaz-Mora (2008)	92 Spanish manufacturing sectors (NACE1 3-digit), 1993–2002. Industrial Companies Survey.	Outsourcing intensity = (production tasks contracted out to external suppliers /gross output).	* Outsourcing intensity in previous years (+) * Unit labour costs (+) * % of small firms in sector (–) * % of domestic firms in sector (–) * Export sales ratio in sector (+) * Skill requirements dummy (+) * Time dummies	Sector-level analysis. Outsourcing intensity is positively related to unit labour costs, high skill requirements, and the proportion of domestic firms in the sector. Current levels of outsourcing are heavily influenced by previous levels.
Holl (2008)	2735 Spanish manufacturing firms, 1990–1999. ESEE survey.	Outsourcing propensity (= answer to question in ESEE survey).	* Firm size (+/–) * Wage costs (+) * Firm age (+) * Foreign ownership (–) * Demand fluctuations (+) * Industry clusters (+) * Time and sector dummies	Larger and older firms with higher wage costs and which are located in industry clusters are more likely to engage in outsourcing. Some evidence that influence of firm-level characteristics depends upon location.
Díaz-Mora & Triguero-Cano (2012)	1550 Spanish manufacturing firms, 1991–2002. ESEE survey.	Outsourcing propensity (= answer to question in ESEE survey).	* Outsourcing propensity in previous years (+) * Firm size (+/–) * Labour costs (+) * Product differentiation (+) * Industry size (+) * Exporter (+) * Firm age (+) * Market volatility (+) * Innovator (+) * R&D intensity (+) * Market competition (+) * Foreign ownership (+/–) * Time and sector dummies	Larger firms with differentiated and innovative products, high labour costs, greater market volatility, R&D intensity, and which export are more likely to engage in outsourcing. Current propensity to outsource is heavily influenced by the propensity in previous years.
Holl, Pardo & Rama (2012)	1031 Spanish manufacturing firms, 2003. Authors' own survey.	Outsourcing propensity (= answer to question in own survey).	* Firm size (+) * Export sales ratio (+) * Capital reserves (+) * R&D intensity (+) * Product innovation (+) * Small batch production (+) * Foreign ownership (+) * Location dummies	Larger firms with small capital reserves, higher R&D intensity, and small batch production are more likely to engage in outsourcing. Some evidence that the influence of firm-level characteristics depends upon location.

Source: Authors' construction.

Taymaz and Kilicaslan (2005) proxied outsourcing intensity as the proportion of subcontracted inputs to total inputs, using data from annual Turkish surveys of manufacturing firms. Díaz-Mora (2008) had a similar measure of outsourcing intensity, but estimated her model using industry-level data taken from the Spanish Industrial Companies Survey. Finally, Holl, Pardo and Rama (2012) designed and administered their own survey of Spanish manufacturing firms, and measured outsourcing propensity according to the firms' responses as to whether they had outsourced production activities in the past three years.

The empirical results from this small literature suggest that manufacturing outsourcing (propensity, intensity) may be positively associated with the size of the lead firm, firm age, R&D intensity, export intensity, advertising intensity/product differentiation, foreign ownership, and industry – but the results are not consistent. This inconsistency may be due to the use of firm-level data – and, in the case of Díaz-Mora (2008), industry-level data – whereas it would be preferable to use product-level data, and to the fact that all studies – apart from Tomiura (2005) – fail to distinguish satisfactorily between domestic and offshore outsourcing. The range of empirical contexts is also narrow, and many of the studies do not specify whether the outsourced activities had previously been undertaken in-house by the lead firms.

Concluding remarks

In this chapter, we have reviewed the theoretical and empirical literature on the determinants of manufacturing outsourcing and offshoring, and drawn attention to the implications for the global distribution of income and for the nature of manufacturing organization as captured by the concepts of the *global factory* and *factoryless goods producers*.

A key strategic issue is whether firm performance will be improved or reduced by increased levels of manufacturing outsourcing. This is a difficult issue and beyond the scope of this chapter. A vertical integration strategy brings many potential benefits to lead firms but there are also costs, and firm performance will only be enhanced if increases in investment are not so high as to offset profit margins, firms have high levels of product innovation, assets are specific or complex, and upstream and downstream markets exhibit degrees of uncertainty (Buzzell, 1983; Lafontaine & Slade, 2007). Equally, an outsourcing strategy too has potential benefits and costs, and whether or not outsourcing enhances lead firm performance depends upon a range of factors including whether or not the benefits and costs have ex ante been properly assessed, whether or not the strategy has been implemented correctly, and whether or not the ex post outsourcing relationship(s) are managed effectively (Doig et al., 2001; Quélin & Duhamel, 2003).

We would also make the following observations. First, performance is a multi-dimensional concept, and different dimensions (e.g. profitability, sales growth, fixed asset investment, employment, wage levels, innovation) may be of importance to different stakeholders. The effects of manufacturing outsourcing on some of these dimensions may be positive, but the effects on others may be negative. A related issue is who benefits and who loses from outsourcing, as the lead firm shareholders may well welcome outsourcing whilst the labour force may be less enthusiastic. Second, there is the issue of the counterfactual. It may be difficult to establish a statistical association between outsourcing by the lead firm and any of the performance measures unless the firm's competitors refrain from new strategic initiatives during the period, and hence the competitive context can be assumed to be exogenous. This is, of course, highly unlikely in practice and it might be the case that all firms are implementing similar performance-enhancing outsourcing strategies but that the beneficial effects for the lead firms are cancelled out by competition. Third, there is the temporal issue. All corporate strategies take time to implement and to have an impact, and the lags may be both substantial (especially so in the case of the impact on innovation) and difficult to estimate. Fourth, it is important to consider the fit between the chosen governance arrangement, the underlying attributes of the transactions and the nature of the contracting environment: the so-called 'discriminating alignment' proposition (Leiblein, Reuer & Dalsace, 2002).

Lahiri (2016) provides an excellent overview of the empirical literature on outsourcing and performance, though he does not limit himself to consideration of manufacturing outsourcing. Much of the extant literature relies on firm-level (or even industry-level) data, but outsourcing (and offshoring) is a strategy that is typically applied by lead firms only to selected manufactured products. We would thus concur with the view of Gilley and Rasheed (2000, p. 787) that it would be useful 'to collect information on the product level, and then to aggregate the firm's various product-level outsourcing initiatives into a firm-level measure'. We would also endorse the view of Lahiri (2016, 493) that future research should devise:

> [a]ppropriate measures of outsourcing and firm performance . . . [as] . . . researchers use a wide variety of measures to operationalize these two variables. Scholars in future research need to devise *robust measures* [emphasis added] that tap the extent of value chain functions(s) given out for execution by third-party provider(s) who may be located in the same country or overseas.

As Ketchen, Ireland and Baker (2013) note, 'if a measure does not effectively capture the construct that it is purported to capture, any statistical tests involving the measure cannot be considered valid'. Our pessimistic assessment is that much of the extant empirical research on outsourcing fails to pass this test.

In terms of a future research agenda, we would suggest several promising lines of inquiry. First, various motivations for manufacturing outsourcing have been advanced in the literature, but as yet there has been none to test which are the most important in practice. Are lead firms outsourcing primarily to focus on core competencies, or to exploit knowledge complementarities and/or economies of scale enjoyed by suppliers, or to take advantage of lower production costs and/or greater flexibility, or to reduce fixed investments, or to secure better quality inputs, or to exploit power asymmetries? Do the motivations differ between domestic outsourcing (when the alternative is in-house production) and offshore outsourcing (when the alternative in FDI)? Second, outsourcing arrangements are inherently unstable, as the power asymmetries between lead firms and their suppliers will necessarily change over time as the efficacy of isolating mechanisms dissipate over time (Denicolai, Strange & Zucchella, 2015). In-depth case studies tracking the dynamics of outsourcing relationships would be valuable to understand the nature of the power asymmetries and how they evolve over time (Azmeh, Raj-Reichert & Nadvi, 2015). Third, Langlois (2003) advanced the proposition that contemporary outsourcing trends were a strategic reaction to the historical improvement in market-supporting institutions. This suggests that outsourcing will be more prevalent in countries with better market-supporting institutions (i.e. more advanced countries), and also that the extent of outsourcing should increase over time if such institutions adapt faster than the coordination requirements of new technologies. If this is indeed the case, it would point to the need to use multi-country samples and/or undertake longitudinal studies to capture the country and time effects. Fourth, much of the literature focuses on the motivations and performance outcomes of the lead firms, but what about the supplier firms? What motivates supplier firms to enter into outsourcing relationships, what are their performance outcomes, and how can supplier firms upgrade their positions within GVCs to capture a greater share of the rents (Navas-Aleman, 2011)? Fifth, small and medium-sized enterprises are increasingly important players in International Business

(Mohiuddin, 2011), yet too little attention has been given to their involvement in outsourcing relationships either as lead firms or as suppliers (Hätonen & Eriksson, 2009).

In the longer term, new manufacturing technologies (e.g. robotics, additive manufacturing) will alter the economics of production and make many production processes less labour intensive (*The Economist*, 2013). These technologies will reduce the share of labour costs in total costs, and will also facilitate remote control of many production processes. These developments in this so-called Fourth Industrial Revolution (Löffler & Tschiesner, 2013; Schwab, 2016) will clearly lessen the advantages of offshoring these processes to emerging/developing countries, and should herald the reshoring of many value chain activities to advanced countries. The effects of these technological advances on the outsourcing strategies of lead firms are less clear cut. Our assessment is that, as the technologies become more advanced and commercially viable, the Fourth Industrial Revolution may well herald a new phase of vertical integration as lead firms aim to protect and maximize the returns from their intellectual property.

Notes

1 Various synonyms for *outsourcing* are found in the literature, including externalization, subcontracting, and contracting out.

2 We use the term *lead firm* to refer to the firms which have outsourced significant activities within their value chains.

3 A *value chain* may be defined as the range of activities required in the production and distribution of a finished good or service, and may involve (Porter, 1985) both *primary* activities (i.e. design, procurement, production, marketing, distribution, after-sales service) and *support* activities (e.g. IT, HR, and other back-office services). These activities may all be located in one country, or may be dispersed in different countries within global value chains (Gereffi & Fernandez-Stark, 2011; Gereffi & Lee, 2012). Synonymous terms for value chain are commodity chain, supply chain, demand chain, production chain/network, and filière (Dicken, 2015).

4 Again various synonyms for *offshoring* are found in the literature, including global outsourcing, international sourcing, super-specialization, global production sharing, and co-production. Some authors (Fratocchi et al., 2014) refer to *nearshoring*, when activities are offshored to countries in the same region as the home country of the lead firm.

5 Unfortunately the literature is awash with other terms such as *captive offshoring*, which is simply foreign direct investment (FDI) under a new name.

6 See the reviews by Dibbern et al. (2004), Mahnke, Overby & Vang (2005), Gonzalez, Gasco & Llopis (2006), Chadee & Raman (2009), and Lacity, Khan & Willcocks (2009). More general reviews have been provided by Espino-Rodríguez & Padrón-Robaina (2006), Hätönen & Eriksson (2009), Mohiuddin (2011), Schmeisser (2013), and Lahiri (2016).

7 See also the January 2013 Special Report on 'Outsourcing and Offshoring' in The *Economist*.

8 We consider these three terms to be synonymous, and will refer in the rest of this paper to *reshoring*. As with offshoring, reshoring is a location decision independent of the ownership of the process. The reshored activities may be undertaken in-house by the lead firm, or the lead firm may simply choose to source from an independent domestic supplier. Other authors have coined additional terms (e.g. backsourcing, re-insourcing, near-reshoring, intelli-sourcing) and, in so doing, have often confounded the location choice with the issue of ownership.

9 A proposal by the US Office of Management and Budget (OMB) to expand the traditional definition of a manufacturing business, and create a 'factoryless goods producer' classification in the 2017 revision of the North America Industry Classification System (NAICS) was withdrawn in August 2015 after considerable opposition from various interested parties. See the formal notice in the *Federal Register*, 79(153): 46558-46559 published on 8 August 2015.

10 Other empirical studies (e.g. Abraham & Taylor, 1996) use samples of manufacturing lead firms, but focus on the outsourcing of support activities.

11 The Japanese Ministry of International Trade & Industry (MITI) was replaced by the Ministry of Economy, Trade & Industry (METI) in 2001.

References

Abraham, K.G. & Taylor, S.K. (1996) 'Firms' use of outside contractors: Theory and evidence', *Journal of Labor Economics*, 14, 394–424.

Albertoni, F., Elia, S., Fratocchi, L. & Piscitello, L. (2015) 'Returning from offshore: What do we know?', *AIB Insights*, 15, pp. 9–12.

Ali-Yrkkö, J., Rouvinen, P., Seppälä, T. & Ylä-Antilla, P. (2011) 'Who captures value in global supply chains? Case of Nokia N95 smartphone', *Journal of Industry, Competition, and Trade*, 11, pp. 263–278.

Amador, J. & Cabral, S. (2014) *Global Value Chains: Surveying Drivers and Measures*. European Central Bank, Working Paper no.1739.

Arlbjørn, J.S. & Mikkelsen, O.S. (2014) 'Backshoring manufacturing: Notes on an important but under-researched theme', *Journal of Purchasing and Supply Management*, 20, pp. 60–62.

Arrunada, B. & Vázquez, X.H. (2006) 'When your contract manufacturer becomes your competitor', *Harvard Business Review*, 84, pp. 135–140.

Azmeh, S., Raj-Reichert, G. & Nadvi, K. (2015) 'Who is running the show in global value chains? Rethinking the role of large trans-national first-tier suppliers in the garments and electronics industry'. Paper presented at the 2015 SASE Conference, LSE.

Bals, L., Daum, A. & Tate, W. (2015) 'From offshoring to rightshoring: Focus on the backshoring phenomenon', *AIB Insights*, 15, pp. 3–8.

Bardhan, I., Mithas, S. & Lin, S. (2007) 'Performance impacts of strategy, information technology applications, and business process outsourcing in US manufacturing plants', *Production and Operations Management*, 16, pp. 747–762.

Bardhan, P., Whitaker, J. & Mithas, S. (2006) 'Information technology, production process outsourcing, and manufacturing plant performance', *Journal of Management Information Systems*, 23, pp. 13–40.

Bayard, K., Byrne, D. & Smith, D. (2015) 'The scope of US "factoryless manufacturing"', in Houseman, S.N. & Mandel, M. (Eds.), *Measuring Globalization: Better Trade Statistics for Better Policy. Volume 2: Factoryless Manufacturing, Global Supply Chains, and Trade in Intangibles and Data*. Kalamazoo, MI: WE Upjohn Institute for Employment Research, pp. 81–117.

Berggren, C. & Bengtsson, L. (2004) 'Rethinking outsourcing in manufacturing: A tale of two telecom firms', *European Management Journal*, 22, pp. 211–223.

Bernard, A.B. & Fort, T.C. (2015) 'Factoryless goods producing firms', *American Economic Review*, 105, pp. 518–523.

Bernard, A.B., Smeets, V. & Warzynski, F. (2014) *Rethinking Deindustrialization*. University of Aarhus, School of Economics and Management, Working Paper 2014–14.

Blinder, A.S. (2006) 'Offshoring: The next industrial revolution', *Foreign Affairs*, 85, pp. 113–128.

Blinder, A.S. & Krueger, A.B. (2013) 'Alternative measures of offshorability: A survey approach', *Journal of Labor Economics*, 31, pp. S97–S128.

Buckley, P.J. & Casson, M. (1976) *The Future of the Multinational Enterprise*. London: Macmillan.

Buckley, P.J. & Ghauri, P.N. (2004) 'Globalisation, Economic Geography and the strategy of multinational enterprises', *Journal of International Business Studies*, 35, pp. 81–98.

Buckley, P.J. & Strange, R. (2011) 'The governance of the multinational enterprise: Insights from internalisation theory', *Journal of Management Studies*, 48, pp. 460–470.

Buckley, P.J. & Strange, R. (2015) 'The governance of the global factory: Location and control of world economic activity', *Academy of Management Perspectives*, 29, pp. 237–249.

Buzzell, R.D. (1983) 'Is vertical integration profitable?', *Harvard Business Review*, 61, pp. 92–102.

Chadee, D. & Raman, R. (2009) 'International outsourcing of information technology services: Review and future directions', *International Marketing Review*, 26, pp. 411–431.

Chandler, A.D., Jr. (1977) *The Visible Hand: The Managerial Revolution*. Cambridge, MA: Belknap Press.

Chesbrough, H.W. & Teece, D.J. (2002) 'Organizing for innovation: When is virtual virtuous?' *Harvard Business Review*, 80, pp. 127–135.

Coase, R.H. (1937) 'The nature of the firm', *Economica*, 4, pp. 386–405.

Coombs, R. (1996) 'Core competencies and the strategic management of R&D', in Belcher, A., Hassard, J. & Procter, S.J. (Eds.), *R&D Decisions: Strategy, Policy and Innovations*. London: Routledge, pp. 25–41.

Copeland, B.R. & Taylor, M.S. (2004) 'Trade, growth, and the environment', *Journal of Economic Literature*, 42, pp. 7–71.

D'Aveni, R.A. & Ravenscraft, D.J. (1994) 'Economies of integration versus bureaucracy costs: Does vertical integration improve performance?' *Academy of Management Journal*, 37, pp. 1167–1206.

Dedrick, J., Kraemer, K.L. & Linden, G. (2010) 'Who profits from innovation in global value chains? A study of the iPod and notebook PCs', *Industrial and Corporate Change*, 19, pp. 81–116.

Denicolai, S., Strange, R. & Zucchella, A. (2015) 'The dynamics of the outsourcing relationship', in Ven Tulder, R., Verbeke, A. & Drogendijk, R. (Eds.), *Multinational Enterprises and Their Organizational Challenges. Progress in International Business Research* (Vol. 10). Bingley, UK: Emerald, pp. 341–364.

Díaz-Mora, C. (2008) 'What factors determine the outsourcing intensity? A dynamic panel data approach for manufacturing industries', *Applied Economics*, 40, pp. 2509–2521.

Díaz-Mora, C. & Triguero-Cano, A. (2012) 'Why do some firms contract out production? Evidence from firm-level panel data', *Applied Economics*, 44, pp. 1631–1644.

Dibbern, J., Goles, T., Hirschheim, R. & Jayatalika, B. (2004) 'Information systems outsourcing: A survey and analysis of the literature', *Database for Advancements in Information Systems*, 35, pp. 6–102.

Dicken, P. (2015). *Global Shift: Measuring the Changing Contours of the World Economy*. 7th Edition. London: Sage.

Doig, S.J., Ritter, R.C., Speckhals, K. & Woolson, D. (2001) 'Has outsourcing gone too far?' *The McKinsey Quarterly*, 25, pp. 24–37.

Donaghu, M.T. & Barff, R. (1990) 'Nike just did it: International subcontracting and flexibility in athletic footwear production', *Regional Studies*, 24, pp. 537–552.

Ellram, L.M., Tate, W.L. & Petersen, K.J. (2013) 'Offshoring and reshoring: An update on the manufacturing location decision', *Journal of Supply Chain Management*, 49, 14–22.

Espino-Rodríguez, T.F. & Padrón-Robaina, V. (2006) 'A review of outsourcing from the resource-based view of the firm', *International Journal of Management Reviews*, 8, pp. 49–70.

Fratocchi, L., Di Mauro, C., Barbieri, P., Nassimbeni, G. & Zanoni, A. (2014) 'When manufacturing moves back: Concepts and questions', *Journal of Purchasing and Supply Management*, 20, pp. 54–59.

Gereffi, G. (1989) 'Development strategies and the global factory', *The Annals of the American Academy of Political and Social Science*, 505, pp. 92–104.

Gereffi, G. & Fernandez-Stark, K. (2011) *Global Value Chain Analysis: A Primer*. Duke University, NC: Center on Globalization, Governance & Competitiveness.

Gereffi, G. & Lee, J. (2012) 'Why the world suddenly cares about global supply chains', *Journal of Supply Chain Management*, 48, pp. 24–32.

Gilley, K.M. & Rasheed, A. (2000) 'Making more by doing less: An analysis of outsourcing and its effects on firm performance', *Journal of Management*, 26, pp. 763–790.

Girma, S. & Görg, H. (2004) 'Outsourcing, foreign ownership and productivity: Evidence from UK establishment level data', *Review of International Economics*, 12, pp. 817–832.

Gonzalez, R., Gasco, J. & Llopis, J. (2006) 'Information systems outsourcing: A literature analysis', *Information and Management*, 43, pp. 821–834.

Gray, J.V., Skowronski, K., Esenduran, G. & Rungtusanatham, J.M. (2013) 'The reshoring phenomenon: What supply chain academics ought to know and should do', *Journal of Supply Chain Management*, 49, pp. 27–33.

Grossman, G.M. & Helpman, E. (2002) 'Integration versus outsourcing in industry equilibrium', *Quarterly Journal of Economics*, 117, pp. 85–120.

Grossman, G.M. & Helpman, E. (2005) 'Outsourcing in a global economy', *The Review of Economic Studies*, 72, pp. 135–160.

Grunwald, J. & Flamm, K. (1985) *The Global Factory: Foreign Assembly in International Trade*. Washington, DC: Brookings Institution Press.

Gylling, M., Heikkilä, J., Jussila, K. & Saarinen, M. (2015) 'Making decisions on offshore outsourcing and backshoring: A case study in the bicycle industry', *International Journal of Production Economics*, 162, pp. 92–100.

Harrigan, K.R. (1984) 'Formulating vertical integration strategies', *Academy of Management Review*, 9, pp. 638–652.

Hätönen, J. & Eriksson, T. (2009) '30+ years of research and practice of outsourcing: Exploring the past and anticipating the future', *Journal of International Management*, 15, pp. 142–155.

Hennart, J.-F. (1982) *A Theory of Multinational Enterprise*. Ann Arbor, MI: University of Michigan Press.

Hikmet, T.K., & Enderwick, P. (2015) 'Offshore sourcing and reshoring: The impact of governance on cost and incentives', *AIB Insights*, 15, pp. 13–16.

Hillberry, R. (2011) 'Causes of international production fragmentation: Some evidence', in Sydor, A. (Ed.), *Global Value Chains: Impacts and Implications*. Toronto: Department of Foreign Affairs and International Trade, Canada, pp. 77–101.

Holcomb, T.R. & Hitt, M.A. (2007) 'Toward a model of strategic outsourcing', *Journal of Operations Management*, 25, pp. 464–481.

Holl, A. (2008) 'Production subcontracting and location', *Regional Science and Urban Economics*, 38, pp. 299–309.

Holl, A., Pardo, R. & Rama, R. (2012) 'Comparing outsourcing patterns in domestic and FDI manufacturing plants: Empirical evidence from Spain', *European Planning Studies*, 20, pp. 1335–1357.

Hymer, S.H. (1972) 'The United States multinational corporation and Japanese competition in the Pacific', *Chuokoron-sha* (Spring). Reprinted in Cohen, R.B., Felton, N., Nkosi, M. and van Liere, J. (Eds.), *The Multinational Corporation: A Radical Approach – Papers by Stephen Herbert Hymer*. Cambridge, UK: Cambridge University Press, pp. 239–255.

Jacobides, M.G. & Winter, S.G. (2005) 'The co-evolution of capabilities and transaction costs: Explaining the institutional structure of production', *Strategic Management Journal*, 26, pp. 395–413.

Jones, G.R. & Hill, C.W. (1988) 'Transaction cost analysis of strategy-structure choice', *Strategic Management Journal*, 9, pp. 159–172.

Kamal, F., Moulton, B.R. & Ribarsky, J. (2013) 'Measuring "factoryless" manufacturing: Evidence from US surveys'. Paper prepared for the conference on 'Measuring the Effects of Globalization', 28 February.

Ketchen, D.J. Jr., Ireland, R.D. & Baker, L.T. (2013) 'The use of archival proxies in strategic management studies: Castles made of sand?' *Organizational Research Methods*, 16, pp. 32–42.

Kimura, F. (2002) 'Subcontracting and the performance of small and medium firms from Japan', *Small Business Economics*, 18, pp. 163–175.

Kinkel, S. (2014) 'Future and impact of backshoring: Some conclusions from 15 years of research on German practices', *Journal of Purchasing and Supply Management*, 20, pp. 63– 65.

Lacity, M.C., Khan, S.A. & Willcocks, L.P. (2009) 'A review of the IT outsourcing literature: Insights for practice', *Journal of Strategic Information Systems*, 18, pp. 130–146.

Lafontaine, F. & Slade, M. (2007) 'Vertical integration and firm boundaries: The evidence', *Journal of Economic Literature*, 45, pp. 631–687.

Lahiri, S. (2016) 'Does outsourcing really improve firm performance? Empirical evidence and research agenda', *International Journal of Management Reviews*, 18, 464–497.

Langlois, R.N. (1993) 'The vanishing hand: The changing dynamics of industrial capitalism', *Industrial and Corporate Change*, 12, pp. 351–385.

Langlois, R.N. (2003) 'Strategy as economics versus economics as strategy', *Managerial and Decision Economics*, 24, pp. 283–290.

Leiblein, M., Reuer, J. & Dalsace, F. (2002) 'Do make or buy decisions matter? The influence of organisational governance on technological performance', *Strategic Management Journal*, 23, pp. 817–833.

Levy, D.L. (2005) 'Offshoring in the new global political economy', *Journal of Management Studies*, 42, pp. 685–693.

Liao, W.C. (2012) 'Inshoring: The geographic fragmentation of production and inequality', *Journal of Urban Economics*, 72, pp. 1–16.

List, J.A., McHone, W.W. & Millimet, D.L. (2003) 'Effects of air quality regulation on the destination choice of relocating plants', *Oxford Economic Papers*, 55, 657–678.

Loch, C.H., Chick, S. & Huchzermeier, A. (2008) 'Offshoring and jobs: Zyme, Dyson, and some general lessons', in Loch,, C.H., Chick, S. & Huchzermeier, A. (Eds.), *Managerial Quality and Competitiveness*. Berlin: Springer Verlag, pp. 111–128.

Löffler, M. & Tschiesner, A. (2013) *The Internet of Things and the Future of Manufacturing*. McKinsey & Company. Available at www.mckinsey.com.

Mahnke, V., Overby, M.L. & Vang, J. (2005) 'Strategic outsourcing of IT services: Theoretical stocktaking and empirical challenges', *Industry and Innovation*, 12, pp. 205–253.

Martínez-Mora, C. & Merino, F. (2014) 'Offshoring in the Spanish footwear industry: A return journey?' *Journal of Purchasing and Supply Management*, 20, pp. 225–237.

Maskell, P., Pedersen, T., Petersen, B. & Dick-Nielsen, J. (2007) 'Learning paths to offshore outsourcing: From cost reduction to knowledge seeking', *Industry and Innovation*, 14, pp. 239–257.

Maskus, K. (2000) *Intellectual Property Rights in the Global Economy*. Washington DC: Institute for International Economics.

Mohiuddin, M. (2011) 'Research on offshore outsourcing: A systematic literature review', *Journal of International Business Research*, 10, pp. 59–76.

Monteverde, K. & Teece, D.J. (1982) 'Supplier switching costs and vertical integration in the automobile industry', *Bell Journal of Economics*, 13, pp. 206–213.

Morikawa, M. (2016) 'Factoryless goods producers in Japan', RIETI Discussion Paper Series 16-E-065. Tokyo: Research Institute of Economy, Trade and Industry.

Mudambi, R. & Venzin, M. (2010) 'The strategic nexus of offshoring and outsourcing decisions', *Journal of Management Studies*, 47, pp. 1510–1533.

Navas-Aleman, L. (2011) 'The impact of operating in multiple value chains for upgrading: The case of the Brazilian furniture and footwear industries', *World Development*, 39, pp. 1386–1397.

Nayyar, D. (1978) 'Transnational corporations and manufactured exports from poor countries', *The Economic Journal*, 88, pp. 59–84.

Oldenski, L. (2015) *Reshoring by US firms: What Do the Data Say?* Peterson Institute for International Economics, Policy Brief PB15-14.

Olney, W.W. (2013) 'A race to the bottom? Employment protection and foreign direct investment', *Journal of International Economics*, 91, pp. 191–203.

Perry, M.K. (1989) 'Vertical integration', in Schmalensee, R. & Willig, R. (Eds.), *Handbook of Industrial Organization*. Amsterdam: North Holland, pp. 185–255.

Pisano, G.P. & Shih, W.C. (2012) 'Does America really need manufacturing?' *Harvard Business Review*, 90, pp. 94–102.

Porter, M.E. (1980) *Competitive Strategy*. New York: Free Press.

Porter, M.E. (1985) *Competitive Advantage: Creating and Sustaining Superior Performance*. London: Collier Macmillan.

Porter, M.E. (1987) 'From competitive advantage to corporate strategy', *Harvard Business Review*, 65, pp. 43–59.

Prahalad, C.K. & Hamel, G. (1990) 'The core competence of the corporation', *Harvard Business Review*, 68, pp. 79–93.

Quélin, B. & Duhamel, F. (2003) 'Bringing together strategic outsourcing and corporate strategy: Outsourcing motives and risks', *European Management Journal*, 21, pp. 647–661.

Quinn, J.B. (1999) 'Strategic outsourcing: Leveraging knowledge capabilities', *MIT Sloan Management Review*, 40, pp. 9–10.

Quinn, J.B. & Hilmer, F.G. (1994) 'Strategic outsourcing', *Sloan Management Review*, 35, pp. 43–56.

Rugman, A.M. (1981) *Inside the Multinationals: The Economics of the Multinational Enterprise*. New York: Columbia University Press.

Rumelt, R.P. (1984) 'Towards a strategic theory of the firm', *Competitive Strategic Management*, 26, 556–570.

Rumelt, R.P. (1987) 'Theory, strategy and entrepreneurship', in Teece, D.J. (Ed.), *The Competitive Challenge: Strategies for Industrial Innovation and Renewal*. Cambridge, MA: Ballinger, pp. 137–158.

Schmeisser, B. (2013) 'A systematic review of literature on offshoring of value chain activities', *Journal of International Management*, 19, pp. 390–406.

Schwab, K. (2016) *The Fourth Industrial Revolution*. Geneva: World Economic Forum.

Shy, O. & Stenbacka, R. (2003) 'Strategic outsourcing', *Journal of Economic Behaviour and Organization*, 50, pp. 203–224.

Sidhu, J.S. & Volberda, H.W. (2011) 'Coordination of globally distributed teams: A co-evolution perspective on offshoring', *International Business Review*, 20, pp. 278–290.

Stentoft, J., Olhager, J., Heikkilä, J. & Thoms, L. (2015) 'Moving manufacturing back: A content-based literature review'. Paper presented at the EurOMA Annual Conference, Neuchatel, Switzerland, 28–30 June.

Strange, R. (2011) 'The outsourcing of primary activities: Theoretical analysis and propositions', *Journal of Management & Governance*, 15, pp. 249–269.

Strange, R. & Newton, J. (2006) 'Stephen Hymer and the externalisation of production', *International Business Review*, 15, pp. 180–193.

Taymaz, E. & Kilicaslan, Y. (2005) 'Determinants of subcontracting and regional development: An empirical study on Turkish textile and engineering industries', *Regional Studies*, 39, pp. 633–645.

The Economist (2013) *Here, There and Everywhere: Special Report on Outsourcing and Offshoring*. Available at: www.economist.com/sites/default/files/20130119_offshoring_davos.pdf.

Tirole, J. (1988) *The Theory of Industrial Organization*. Cambridge, MA: MIT Press.

Tomiura, E. (2005) 'Foreign outsourcing and firm-level characteristics: Evidence from Japanese manufacturers', *Journal of the Japanese and International Economies*, 19, pp. 255–271.

Uluskan, M., Joines, J.A. & Godfrey, A.B. (2016) 'Comprehensive insight into supplier quality and the impact of quality strategies of suppliers on outsourcing decisions', *Supply Chain Management: An International Journal*, 21, pp. 92–102.

UNCTAD (2011) *World Investment Report 2011. Non-equity Modes of International Production and Development*. New York & Geneva: UNCTAD.

Vernon, J.M. & Graham, D.A. (1971) 'Profitability of monopolization by vertical integration', *Journal of Political Economy*, 79, 924–925.

Vernon, R. (1966) 'International investment and international trade in the product cycle', *Quarterly Journal of Economics*, 80, pp. 190–207.

Vernon, R. (1979) 'The product cycle hypothesis in a new international environment', *Oxford Bulletin of Economics and Statistics*, 41, pp. 255–267.

Vivek, S.D., Richey Jr, R.G. & Dalela, V. (2009) 'A longitudinal examination of partnership governance in offshoring: A moving target', *Journal of World Business*, 44, pp. 16–30.

Walter, I. (1982) 'Environmentally induced industrial relocation to developing countries', in Rubin, S.J. & Graham, T.R. (Eds.), *Environment and Trade: The Relation of International Trade and Environmental Policy*. Totowa, NJ: Allanheld. Osman & Co, pp. 67–101.

Weil, D. (2014) *The Fissured Workplace*. Cambridge, MA: Harvard University Press.

Westfield, F.M. (1981) 'Vertical integration: does product price rise or fall?' *American Economic Review*, 71, pp. 334–346.

Williamson, O.E. (1975) *Markets and Hierarchies: Analysis and Antitrust Implications*. New York: Free Press.

5

THE REGIONAL MNE AND COORDINATION OF MNE ORGANIZATIONAL STRUCTURES

Quyen T.K. Nguyen

Introduction

This chapter provides an overview of the key insights resulting from International Business (IB) research on the regional strategy of multinational enterprises (MNEs) and coordination of MNEs' organization structures. It consists of three main sections. The first section describes the debate of globalization and regionalization at the firm level with a focus on the actual behaviour of MNEs. It discusses the complex nature of regional strategy of MNEs, the definitions and measurements of regions, and the effects of regional strategy on the international expansion and performance of MNEs. The second section discusses the theory of regional MNE, which explains why MNEs concentrate their business activities within their home region. The liability of intra-regional expansion is lower than the liability of inter-regional expansion and there is unnoticed location-boundedness and region-boundedness of firm-specific advantages (FSAs). The third section discusses the regional organizational and management structures. The chapter concludes on the regional strategy and structure of MNEs.

The debate of regionalization versus globalization

Empirical evidence on the regional nature of MNEs and their foreign subsidiaries

Since the 2000s, the concept of globalization has attracted the attention of academics and managers alike. A number of scholars (Levitt, 1983; Prahalad & Doz, 1987; Bartlett & Ghoshal, 1989; Yip, 1992; Govindarajan & Gupta, 2001) presume the growth of globalization of markets, and advocate total global strategy. In 1992, George Yip published a book *Total Global Strategy: Managing for Worldwide Competitive Advantage*. Govindarajan and Gupta published a book in 2001, *The Quest for Global Dominance*. A few years later in 2005, Thomas Friedman published a popular book *The World is Flat: A History of the Twenty-First Century*. Such global strategy aims to yield economies of scale, a so-called integration strategy.

In contrast, Rugman (2000) challenges the globalization myth and presents regionalization theory in his thought-provoking book, *The End of Globalization: Why Global Strategy is a Myth and How to Profit from the Realities of Regional Markets*. Rugman and Collinson (2012, p. 7) argue that:

> [i]n its extreme form, globalization means the existence of a perfectly integrated world economic system. In such a global system, there would be perfect mobility of financial capital, goods and people. There would be a global commonality whereby identical values and tastes would occur. Yet, such a situation of perfect integration and globalization does not exist.

Rugman (2000) shows regionalization patterns of trade, foreign direct investment (FDI) flows, and regional strategy of individual MNEs through detailed analysis using case studies. Rugman (2000) provides analytical theoretical frameworks to explain this regionalization phenomenon.

Rugman and Verbeke (2004) and Rugman (2005a) further rebut the presumption of globalization of business by showing that the majority of the world's largest firms of the Fortune Global 500 are not global, but regional. Rugman (2005a) demonstrates that MNEs pursue regional rather than global strategies and that the regions are triad based of North America, Europe, and Asia Pacific. A firm which pursues a global strategy operates across these three broad triad regions of the world with equal distribution of sales and assets. However, Rugman and Verbeke (2004) find that there are only nine global firms.

Ten years after the publication of Rugman and Verbeke (2004), Oh and Rugman (2014) present ten-year longitudinal data and find that MNEs have a strong home-region concentration in their sales and assets. Specifically, these firms generate 70 percent of their total sales and have 72 percent of their total assets within the home region of the broad triad. The data on assets reflect investments in production, and/or distribution, and/or R&D of MNEs.

The literature has generated rich and abundant empirical evidence of the regional nature of MNEs. These include MNEs in the Fortune Global 500 (Rugman, 2000, 2005a, 2009; Rugman & Hodgetts, 2001; Rugman & Verbeke, 2004; Rugman & Oh, 2013; Oh & Rugman, 2014); European MNEs (Rugman & Collinson, 2005; Oh, 2009; Rugman & Oh, 2010); Japanese MNEs (Delios & Beamish, 2005; Collinson & Rugman, 2008); Asian MNEs (Collinson & Rugman, 2007; Rugman & Oh, 2008a); Korean MNEs (Rugman & Oh, 2008b); ASEAN MNEs (Sukpanich & Rugman, 2010); Chinese MNEs (Yin & Choi, 2005; Rugman & Li, 2007; Rugman, Nguyen & Wei, 2016), and emerging market MNEs (Rugman & Nguyen, 2014).

The regionalization patterns are empirically confirmed with evidence of MNEs operating in different industries. These include firms in the automobile industry (Rugman & Collinson, 2004); retail industry (Rugman & Girod, 2003; Mohr et al., 2014; Oh, Sohl & Rugman, 2015); pharmaceutical industry (Rugman & Brain, 2004); banking and financial services (Grosse, 2005); cosmetics industry (Oh & Rugman, 2006, 2007); food and beverage industry (Filippaios & Rama, 2008); merchandizing industry (Rugman & Sukpanich, 2007); and service industry (Rugman, 2003a; Li, 2005; Rugman & Verbeke, 2008b).

In a related manner, Nguyen (2014) and Nguyen and Rugman (2015) find that the foreign subsidiaries of MNEs operate regionally, not globally. These scholars conduct a survey with British multinational subsidiaries in six South East Asian countries and report that these subsidiaries generate 95 percent of their total sales in the broad Asia Pacific region (home region). Similarly, Nguyen (2015) uses an original dataset of publicly listed multinational subsidiaries in five South East Asia countries, with parent firms headquartered in the United States, the United Kingdom, France, Germany, the Netherlands, Switzerland, Japan, Hong Kong, Malaysia, Indonesia, the Philippines, Singapore, Thailand, China, India, Taiwan, South Africa, and Brazil. Nguyen (2015) finds that these subsidiaries generate 92 percent of their total sales in the Asia Pacific region (home region).

In summary, the research on regionalization has made a significant development with more theoretical and empirical contributions (for a comprehensive literature review, see Oh, 2009; Kolk, 2010; Banalieva & Dhanaraj, 2013; Nguyen, 2014; for a recent debate, see Mudambi & Puck, 2016; Verbeke & Asmussen, 2016). A large volume of literature shows that most MNEs and their foreign subsidiaries from various countries and industries pursue a home-regional strategy. There are very few firms (only nine firms) which pursue a global strategy (Rugman & Verbeke, 2004). There is a lack of evidence towards globalization of MNEs.

Definition of regions

The major debates in this literature are how to define and how to measure a region (Stevens & Bird, 2004; Aharoni, 2006; Westney, 2006; Aguilera, Flores & Vaaler, 2007; Asmussen, Pedersen & Petersen, 2007; Dunning, Fujita & Yakova, 2007; Osegowitsch & Sammartino, 2008; Asmussen, 2009; Seno-Alday, 2009; Wolf, Dunemann & Egelhoff, 2012; Verbeke & Kano, 2012; Banalieva & Dhanaraj, 2013; Flores, Aguilera, Mahdian & Vaaler, 2013). Rugman and his co-authors' original conceptualization of the triad region follows Ohmae's (1985) grouping of the core triad of North America, Western Europe, and Japan. With the increasing of regional economic integration, the core triad has been extended to the broad triad of North America, Europe, and Asia Pacific (Rugman, 2000; Rugman & Collinson, 2012). Rugman and Verbeke (2008a) maintain that the triad is relevant because it is the home of most large MNEs in the world, as well as the locus for the bulk of radical innovation in most industries (Rugman, 2006b).

Arregle, Beamish and Herbert (2009) use geographic criteria to define regions. Dunning et al. (2007) define regions by culture clusters. They confirm the broad regional patterns using macro FDI data. Aguilera et al. (2007) and Flores et al. (2013) suggest different definitions of regions, such as economic development, trade, investment flows, and income; socio-cultural and language; political, institutional proximity, including religion, political openness, and institutional systems; and the 25 UN geographic classifications. Ronen and Shenkar (2013) suggest 11 global/regional cultural clusters from their study of 96 countries.

It is important to highlight that Rugman and his co-authors use manually collected and carefully hand coded data from firms' annual reports in their empirical works on the regionalization of MNEs. However, they are often questioned by other scholars on the use of the broad triad regions instead of other conventions. Rugman (2003b, 2005a) argues that the triad regions are the appropriate regions for the simple reality that the MNEs publicly report the broad geographic regions of their sales, assets, profits, and employees in accordance with accounting standards.

Nguyen (2014) contributes to the regionalization debate by offering explanation for how firms define regions in compliance with international accounting standards. Specifically, the *US GAAP FASB 131 Disclosures about Segments of an Enterprise and Related Information* (issued in 1997 and effective for fiscal years beginning after December 15, 1997), and *IFRS8-Operating Segments* (issued in 2006 and applies to annual periods beginning on or after 1 January 2009) provide guidance on segment reporting and disclosures. Publicly listed entities are required to disclose information about operating geographic segments, business segments (products and services), and their major customers (see IFRS8, IFRS website).

Segment information is based on internal management reports, both in the identification of operating segments and measurement of disclosed segment information. Reportable segments are operating segments or aggregation of operating segments that meet specified criteria of either revenues, or profit/loss, or assets at 10 percent or more of the combined revenues, or profit/loss, or assets (for detailed information, see IFRS8, IFRS website). In practice, firms classify broad geographic regions on the basis of organizational structures and management reporting (Nguyen, 2014).

It would be highly impractical for firms to use the 25 UN geographic regions, or 11 global cultural clusters, or other criteria (as suggested by IB scholars) in their financial reporting and disclosures. Such an approach does not comply with accounting regulations, because the data for certain geographic regions or cultural clusters are likely below the threshold of 10 percent for disclosures. Furthermore, the costs of reporting and disclosures will exceed the benefits whereas the accounting rules emphasize the opposite.

Firms are not required to report geographic segments of sourcing and purchasing. However, a number of IB scholars use a global value chain perspective to argue for the globalization of MNE activities. In reality, firms may voluntarily disclose information of sourcing. For example, IKEA, a large privately owned furniture retailer founded in Sweden in 1943, published for the first time in 2010 some information about its financial data. It is clear that IKEA is a home-region-based MNE in terms of purchases, sales, and employees. For the year 2010, IKEA purchased 62 percent of goods from Europe, 34 percent from Asia and 4 percent from North America. IKEA generated 79 percent of its total sales in Europe, 15 percent from North America, and 6 percent from Asia and Australia. IKEA had 103,500 employees in Europe, 15,500 employees in North America, and 8,000 employees in Asia and Australia (IKEA Group, 2010).

Measures of regionalization

Rugman (2000, 2005a) and Rugman and Verbeke (2004) use the ratio of home-region sales divided by total sales as a measure of firms' degree of regionalization, in which home-region sales are defined as the home-country domestic sales plus rest of home-region sales. Foreign sales over total sales are sales in the rest of the home region plus sales in the rest of the world.

In the early period of implementing operating segment accounting standards, firms tended to report geographic segments of sales (the data which Rugman and Verbeke (2004) and Rugman (2005a) use in their studies). However, Rugman and Verbeke (2004) and Rugman (2005a) are criticized for using only sales data (Aharoni, 2006). Subsequently, firms have disclosed more information on geographic segments of sales, assets, and employees. Oh and Rugman (2014) present a ten-year longitudinal data of sales and assets of the world's largest firms in Fortune Global 500, in which the regionalization trend remains unchanged.

Rugman and Verbeke (2004) provide thresholds to classify firms into different categories, namely, home-regional, bi-regional, host-regional, and global firms. *Home-region-oriented firms* have at least 50 percent of their sales in their home region of the triad. *Bi-regional firms* have over 20 percent of their sales in at least two regions of the triad and less than 50 percent of their sales in their home region. *Host-region-oriented firms* have over 50 percent of their sales in a foreign region of the triad. *Global firms* mean firms that have at least 20 percent of their sales in each of the three regions of the triad, but not more than 50 percent in any one region. The same categories have been applied to assets in follow-up studies by Rugman and co-authors.

However, Osegowitsch and Sammartino (2008) challenge the regionalization measure in Rugman and Verbeke (2004), and criticize the thresholds as arbitrary because the thresholds can be manipulated by normalizing data. They also suggest that the regionalization pattern should be tested using longitudinal data. Similarly, Stevens and Bird (2004) question the specification of the threshold value and the categories. Other studies (Delios & Beamish, 2005; Li, 2005) argue that including home-country domestic sales in measuring regionalization overstates the degree of regionalization (Banalieva & Dhanaraj, 2013).

A number of scholars have developed two alternative measures of regionalization. The first measure is the ratio of rest of home-region sales to foreign sales, in which home-country domestic sales are excluded from home-region sales (Delios & Beamish, 2005; Li, 2005; Rugman & Verbeke, 2008a; Banalieva & Eddleston, 2011). They argue that the IB literature should focus on foreign sales only and disregard home-country domestic sales. However, this suggestion is problematic as domestic sales are highly important for firms from large economies, such as the United States, China, etc. The second measure is the ratio of rest of home-region sales to total sales (Elango, 2004; Rugman & Verbeke, 2008a). Asmussen (2009) suggests an alternative measure normalizing the ratios using GDP data; however, Banalieva and Dhanaraj (2013) argue that Asmussen's regionalization measure has little practical appeal.

The debate on the definition and measures of regionalization reveals that IB scholars have not taken into account developments in international accounting standards (IFRS8 and US GAAP FAS131) with which firms have to comply. The IB literature generally tends to use data from large databases but pays no attention to underlying accounting principles. Indeed, geographic regions are defined and measured by firms (Rugman, 2005a; Nguyen, 2014). Rugman and his co-authors use regional data as disclosed in firms' annual reports (see Rugman's responses (2005a) to comments by Stevens and Bird, 2004). This reflects Rugman's distinctive research methodology (Casson, 2016), and his philosophy in theory development which must be firmly grounded in data and empirical evidence of business reality and managerial insights.

Regionalization and international expansion

A number of studies have examined the relationship between regional strategy and entry modes (Oh & Rugman, 2007; Arregle et al., 2009; Arregle, Miller, Hitt & Beamish, 2013), international expansion (Rugman & Oh, 2013), international competitiveness (Rugman, Oh & Lim, 2012), and human resource management (Edwards, Jalette & Tregaskis, 2012). For example, Rugman and Oh (2013) use variance components to analyse the effects of home region, country, firm, and year on international expansion of firms. They find that the home-region effect outperforms the country effect. Together, the regional and industry effects explain most of the geographic expansion of MNEs, whereas country, firm, and year effects are very minor. The findings suggest the importance of large regions of the triad as the relevant unit of analysis for business strategy to supplement the conventional focus on the country.

The global versus regional strategy also attracts debate in the fields of marketing and strategic management. A number of studies find that firms focus on regional strategy due to differences in consumers' tastes and preferences, barriers to the implementation of global strategy and complexity of global operations (Morrison, Ricks & Roth, 1991; Roth & Morrison, 1992). Lewitt (1983) argues that MNEs should not worry much about customizing products and services to cultural preferences. Technology has largely homogenized consumer preferences, in which most consumers simply want quality, reliability, and low price. Therefore, MNEs should standardize their products and services worldwide in order to achieve economies of scale, and should implement global strategies across all markets.

Yet, Douglas and Wind (1987) critically examine the key assumptions underlying Levitt's global philosophy and the conditions under which it is likely to be effective. They highlight the barriers to its implementation. They conclude that global standardization is just one of many strategies in international markets. In reality, it is very challenging to sell the same products and services across borders as advocated by Levitt (1983). It has now widely recognized the benefits of integration resulting from global scale economies can only be reaped if accompanied by strategies of national responsiveness by both external pressures for local adaptation and internal pressures for requisite variation (Ghobadian, Rugman & Tung, 2014).

The concepts of global integration and national responsiveness have been developed by Bartlett and Ghoshal (1989) and Prahalad and Doz (1987). Global integration can be defined as the production and distribution of products and services of a homogenous type and quality on a worldwide basis. To a large extent, MNEs have homogenized tastes and help to spread international consumerism (Rugman & Collinson, 2012) as MNEs are the drivers of globalization. For example, there has been a growing acceptance of standardized consumer electronic goods and similar products. However, the goal of efficient economic performance through a universal globalization strategy has left MNEs open to the charge that they are overlooking the need to address national concerns (Rugman & Collinson, 2012). National responsiveness is the ability of MNEs to understand different consumer tastes in segmented regional markets and to respond to the different national standards and regulations imposed by autonomous governments and agencies. Multinationals will continually have to deal with the twin goals of economic integration and national responsiveness (Rugman & Collinson, 2012).

Nguyen (2014) finds that there is no evidence of the dominance of global products in the product and service offering portfolios of British multinational subsidiaries in manufacturing and services sectors. For manufacturing subsidiaries, regional product offerings account for 38 percent, local for 16 percent, and global for 46 percent. Service subsidiaries focus more on local and regional service offerings, of which regional service offerings account for 24 percent, local for 41 percent, and global for 35 percent.

Regionalization and performance of the firm

Rugman (2000, 2005a) and Rugman and Verbeke (2004) focus on the regional strategy of the MNE. Subsequent studies examine the implications of such regionalization strategy on performance of the parent-level MNE. However, the results are mixed. Studies by Rugman, Kudina and Yip, (2007), Rugman and Sukpanich (2007), and Qian et al. (2010) find a positive effect of regionalization on performance. On the contrary, studies by Elango (2004) and Delios and Beamish (2005) find a negative effect. Li (2005), Banalieva and Eddleston (2011), and Banalieva and Dhanaraj (2013) have adopted contingency perspectives to examine the simultaneous effects between home-region strategy and performance in an attempt to get a better understanding of the direction of causality between performance and home-region strategy. They find that performance significantly reduces home-region orientation, but home-region orientation does not have a significant effect on performance.

Gilbert and Heinecke (2014) argue that the relationship between regional strategies and MNE performance might be contingent upon conditions and developments within the firm and external environments (Bausch, Fritz & Boesecke, 2007; Heinecke, 2011; Banalieva & Dhanaraj, 2013). Gilbert and Heinecke (2014) examine success factors of regional strategies for MNEs by exploring the degree of regional management and product/service adaptations to regional market requirements and regional differences, which might lead to better regional performance. They find that low degrees of regional management autonomy and high levels of regional product/service adaptation are appropriate for MNEs to be regionally successful. The possible adverse effects of high degrees of regional management autonomy on regional success are mitigated by an MNE's inter-regional distance. The regional performance with high levels of regional product/service adaptation is positively influenced by both an MNE's regional orientation and its inter-regional distance. Their findings imply that MNEs should optimize the regional success by varying the regional management autonomy and regional product/service adaptation in light of the organizational and environmental context.

Nguyen (2015) examines the determinants of home-region strategy of the multinational subsidiary and the impact of such a strategy on its performance. Nguyen (2015) draws upon new internalization theory to develop a theory-driven model and empirically test the simultaneous relationships between home-region strategy and performance of the subsidiary. The findings are that subsidiary-level downstream knowledge (marketing advantages), and the geographic location of the subsidiary in the same home region as the parent firm are key antecedents of a subsidiary's home-region strategy. A subsidiary's profitability reduces home-region orientation; however, home-region strategy has an insignificant effect on performance. This study advances the existing literature on the regional nature of parent-level MNEs by demonstrating that their quasi-autonomous subsidiaries also operate mainly on a home-region basis.

Theory of regional multinationals

Rugman and Verbeke (2004, 2008a) and Rugman (2005a) develop the theory of regional MNEs in which their business activities are limited in the home region. Rugman and Verbeke (2003, 2005) focus on regional strategy as the substantive core of a strategic firm-level decision (Oh & Li, 2015). The regional strategy is a more refined alternative to a transnational solution which is built upon the concept of global integration and national responsiveness (Prahalad & Doz, 1987; Bartlett & Ghoshal, 1989).

Rugman and Verbeke (1992) develop the concepts of non-location-bound (NLB) firm-specific advantages and location-bound (LB) firm-specific advantages (FSAs), which they refer to as new internalization theory. Rugman and Verbeke (1992) argue that the benefits of integration, in the form of economies of sales and economies of scope and benefits of exploiting national differences, require NLB FSAs, i.e. strengths specific to the firm attributable to R&D knowledge, patented technology, and global brands which are internationally transferrable with low cost and without adaptation. This transfer can take place in the form of intermediate or final outputs. In contrast, the benefits of national responsiveness require LB FSA which are tied to a particular location, country, or a set of countries or a region, for example, the development of new knowledge and the access to complementary resources in the host countries by the foreign subsidiary. The LB FSAs and NLB FSAs can be generated by both parent firms and foreign subsidiaries and diffused in the home operation, host operation, and MNE networks (Rugman & Verbeke, 1992, 2001).

According to Rugman (2005a), the transnational solution requires a firm to effectively access and deploy the required dual knowledge bundles of NLB and LB FSAs. Each generic subsidiary type (strategic leaders, contributors, implementers, and black holes) has access to a set of FSAs bundles and resources.

The majority of MNEs operate on a home-region basis of the broad triad. Thus, there is a need to develop region-bound FSAs (Rugman, 2005a; Collinson & Rugman, 2008). Rugman and Sukpanich (2006) find that FSAs are region-bounded, i.e. they can be deployed across national borders, but only in a limited geographic region due to the tacit nature of knowledge and unnoticed location-boundedness (Nguyen, 2015).

Furthermore, Rugman (2005a) maintains that the required set of FSAs in upstream (back-end) activities to achieve broad geographic sourcing (R&D, raw materials and intermediate inputs, labour, and capital) and production may be very different from the FSAs required for downstream activities (customer-end) in the interface with customers (marketing, sales, and distribution). In this case, a new set of FSAs was developed by foreign subsidiaries, which are known as subsidiary-specific advantages (SSAs) (Rugman & Verbeke, 2001; Rugman, 2014). They are important to facilitate the access to customers in local and regional markets (for a comprehensive discussion on FSAs, see Rugman, Verbeke & Nguyen, 2011). Nguyen (2015) shows that SSAs in marketing created by foreign subsidiaries in the South East Asian region are more transferrable within the broad home region of the Asia Pacific than across regions.

According to Rugman and Verbeke (2004, 2007) and Rugman (2005a), an important explanation of the significant differences in geographic international expansion costs is that the liability of intra-regional expansion (i.e. expansion within a home region) is lower than the liability of inter-regional expansion (i.e. expansion across regions). In addition, Qian, Li and Rugman (2013) emphasize that the concepts of 'the liability of country foreignness (LCF)' and 'the liability of regional foreignness (LRF)' are different. Qian et al. (2013) argue that the costs of the LCF are directly associated with spatial distance, and the structural, relational, and institutional costs (Zaheer, 2002; Bell, Filatotchev & Rasheed, 2012). The LRF is the cost of doing business across different regions due to increasing complexities in internal coordination, the bounded rationality and bounded reliability problems (Verbeke & Greidanus, 2009; Verbeke, 2013), and differences in external environments across regions (for a detailed discussion, see Qian et al., 2013).

Rugman and Verbeke (2008a) demonstrate that intra-regional distance in the EU, North America, and Asia Pacific is decreasing thanks to regional economic integration, which results in a reduction of trade and investment barriers and more institutional convergence. Firms can take advantage of free trade agreements and regional integration schemes, e.g. The North America Free Trade Agreement (NAFTA), The European Union (EU), The Association of South East Asian Nations (ASEAN) Free Trade Agreement (AFT), and ASEAN free trade agreements with Japan, Korea, India, China, Australia, and New Zealand (ASEAN+6). Thus, expansion within the home region will often continue to be easier than equivalent growth elsewhere in the world, especially sales and profitability.

Regional organizational and management structures

Regional management structures represent an efficient intra-firm governance mechanism to support the regional strategy of MNEs (Rugman & Verbeke, 2008c). Rugman and Collinson (2005) argue that regional management structures are established to meet the needs of regional customers. Regional-level managerial support may include regional cash management (Venzin, Kumar & Kleine, 2008), the coordination of regional production (Rugman & Collinson, 2004), and regional product development (Verbeke & Asmussen, 2016). Rugman (2005a) observes that an HQ-based and centralized decision-making approach might lead to a lack of success in foreign markets because it may not always be appropriate to address region-specific challenges which may be better handled through region-based organizational structures.

Furthermore, regional management structures overcome the problems of bounded rationality and bounded reliability of managers at corporate headquarters (HQs) in managing a diverse network of foreign subsidiaries (Rugman & Verbeke, 2005; Verbeke & Kenworthy, 2008). According to Verbeke (2013), bounded rationality reflects the limitations of an intended rational human behaviour to absorb, process, and act upon complex and often insufficient information. Bounded rationality affects managers in the deployment and exploitation of FSAs (Verbeke & Kenworthy, 2008). Consequently, HQs delegate decision making to the regional headquarters (Rugman, 2005a) as the latter has better access to information of national and regional markets.

Bounded rationality creates the need for regional management structures when MNEs establish locally oriented subsidiaries in distant regions and when the number of different economies within a particular region increases (Enright, 2005a; Gilbert & Heinecke, 2014).

On the other hand, bounded reliability describes the limitations of individuals regarding their realization of a promised outcome (Verbeke & Kenworthy, 2008; Verbeke & Greidanus, 2009; Verbeke, 2013). Bounded reliability of foreign subsidiaries is influenced by the distance to corporate HQs, including immediate sanctions and reward systems, monitoring, and controlling mechanisms (Verbeke & Kenworthy, 2008; Verbeke & Greidanus, 2009; Verbeke, 2013). Bounded reliability explains how regional management structures might be influenced by the geographic proximity to HQs (Yeung, Poon & Perry, 2001).

Bartlett and Ghoshal (1989) advocate the adoption of the transnational solution, especially for MNEs with widely dispersed assets and sales. They argue that in order to evolve toward the transnational solution, managers should pursue an incremental, path-dependent trajectory of change. The selectivity required to manage the transformation towards a transnational company has three facets, namely, administrative heritage, extensive socialization, and the roles assigned to national subsidiaries, given the attractiveness of their location and their contribution to new NLB knowledge development (for detailed discussion, see Rugman & Verbeke, 2008c).

Rugman and Verbeke (2008c) make two important points. First, they argue that most large MNEs have not been successful in replicating the market performance achieved at home in other markets, especially distant host regions, which often require a completely different FSA-CSA configuration than the one that proves successful in the home market. Second, introducing a regional component in strategy and structure may address the managerial challenges expected for firms with a vastly different asset base and market position in various regions of the world. Rugman (2005a) argues that the strategic importance of each triad region, combined with the differences in market characteristics faced by MNEs in each of these regions, suggest the importance of geographic components in the MNEs' structure.

Indeed, there is a large body of literature on the need for a fit between strategy and structure in MNEs as a precondition for survival, profitability, and growth. Studies on the strategy and structure of MNEs can be attributed to Egelhoff (1982, 1988a) and Wolf and Egelhoff (2002). Egelhoff (1988b, 1991) uses an information processing theory to study the strategy-structure fit. Egelhoff (1982, p. 441) views the use of geographic divisions in MNEs as appropriate in cases whereby, 'operations within a region are relatively large, complex and sufficiently different from other regions that opportunities for specialization and economies of scale are greater within a region than they are along worldwide product lines'.

His empirical work shows that three variables which are critical to choose geographic divisions include size of foreign operations measured by percentage of a firm's sales occurring outside of the parent country (the ratio of foreign sales over total sales F/T), size of foreign manufacturing measured by the percentage of foreign sales accounted for by foreign manufacturing rather than exports from the parent country, and number of foreign subsidiaries measured by the number of foreign countries in which the company had either resident marketing or manufacturing operations. He identifies an area division structure which MNEs can use to divide the world into geographic areas, each with its own HQs, responsible for all products and business within that geographic area. Moreover, he finds that HQs organized into geographic area structures are more responsive than those organized into international divisions.

Rugman (2005a) makes two comments on the work of Egelhoff (1982). First, the mean foreign sales of the 34 Fortune 500 firms (17 US and 17 European firms) are 50 percent; however, no distinction has been made between intra-regional and inter-regional sales. Second,

Egelhoff (1982) assumes that one particular organizational structure always dominates the MNE (functional divisions, international divisions, geographical divisions, and a matrix structure) and can be readily identified based upon statements made by managers through interviews, and the analysis of publicly available information. However, the findings by Rugman and Verbeke (2004) and Rugman (2005a, p. 73) show that:

> [t]he geographic distribution of foreign sales does matter and that a strong discrepancy between intra-regional and inter-regional sales has important implications for MNE structure. More specifically, the differentiation between back-end and customer-end building upon different sets of FSAs should be reflected in the MNE's organizational structure, systems and perhaps even culture.

In a related manner, there is a growing literature on regional components in MNE organizational and management structures, such as regional headquarters (RHQs) (Heenan, 1979; Grosse, 1981; D'Cruz, 1986; Daniels, 1987; Dunning & Norman, 1987; Morrison et al., 1991; Lassere, 1996; Schuette, 1997; Picard, Boddenwyn & Grosse, 1998; Lehrer & Asakawa, 1999; Yeung et al., 2001; Mori, 2002; Ambos & Shlegelmilch, 2010); regional operating headquarters (Yin & Walsh, 2011); regional offices (Poon & Thompson, 2003; Yeung et al., 2001); regional management centres (Enright, 2005a, 2005b; Piekkari, Nell & Ghauri, 2010); and regional management structures (Mahnke, Ambos, Nell & Hobdari, 2012; Aman, Jaussaud & Schaaper, 2014). These studies emphasize the increasing importance of regions and regional organizational and management structures within MNEs.

Lasserre (1996) argues that Asian RHQs of Western MNEs serve entrepreneurship-enhancing roles (identifying new business opportunities, processing and distributing relevant information on the region, and signalling commitment to regional stakeholders) and integrative roles (exploitation of synergies across national subsidiaries, executing activities in areas where regional resource allocation should occur). However, there is little evidence that any of these roles improve the MNEs' effectiveness in bringing their products to the Asian customers (Rugman, 2005a).

Yeung et al. (2001) analyse RHQs in Singapore, building on Lasserre (1996). They define RHQs as business establishments which have control and management responsibilities for the operations of subsidiaries in the same region, while regional offices do not have decision-making authority on important strategic issues and mainly perform regional operating functions. They argue that the roles depend on three parameters. First, vast geographical distance requires Western MNEs (excepting Japanese and Taiwanese MNEs) to set up RHQs. Second, RHQs enables MNEs to better coordinate their international activities between HQs and Asian subsidiaries and thus the HQs can exercise greater control. Third, RHQs facilitate MNEs to be closer to host country markets and to make faster decisions in response to business opportunities. They find that MNEs establish RHQs in Asia as a part of regional strategy. This implicitly suggests the importance of using RHQs to complement in an idiosyncratic way each MNE's existing FSA bundles (Rugman, 2005a).

Picard et al. (1998) examine the 20-year period at the end of the twentieth century of European RHQs, which have been found to gain power and autonomy. Ambos and Schlegelmich (2010) examine the role of regional management of the US and Japanese MNEs in Europe and maintain that a key success factor in a host region is a strategy at regional level, not at the global level. They suggest that RHQs are important in managing global businesses. There are three important advantages of RHQs. First, RHQs play the parental role in organizing and coordinating economic activities of foreign subsidiaries within the region, which is the parenting advantage. Second, RHQs translate the global HQs' targets into successful strategies for local markets, which is the knowledge advantage. Third, RHQs may function as a safety valve to handle pressures from global integration and regional adaption to the corporate parent and pressures from regional integration and local adjustment to subsidiaries in the region, which is the organizational advantage.

On the other hand, Piekkari et al. (2010) use a single case study of Kone and find that the parent firm grants varying levels of responsibilities to the regional structures in different periods in the history of RHQs in the Asia-Pacific region. In the 1990s, Kone provides substantial resources to regions. By the late 1990s, Kone emphasizes more global integration and it stripped down the power of the regional structures and downsized regional management. In 2004, Kone reinforces the regional Asia-Pacific office as it has sought to find a balance between the regional and product dimensions in its organizational structures. These scholars find that the persistence of cultural, geographic, and language distances; the lack of social integration; and strong economic growth in the Asia Pacific region to strengthen the position of the regional organization.

Enright (2005b) examines the role of regional management centres (RMCs). He does not find any significant differences between the roles and the functions that North American and European MNEs assign to their RMCs in the Asia Pacific region. However, there are differences between Western and Japanese MNEs, in which the latter give less prominent roles to their Asia-Pacific regional structures. Japanese RHQs have little autonomy in decision-making, because important strategic decisions for the regions are made by the strategic business units (SBUs) in the HQs. The main roles of the Japanese regional structures are to execute the HQs' strategic decisions, to coordinate daily activities, and to support local subsidiaries (Lehrer & Asakawa, 1999; Mori, 2002; Paik & Sohn, 2004). The level of centralization for strategic decisions may be attributable to geographic, cultural and institutional differences of the home-country origins of the parent firms.

Li, Yu and Seetoo (2010) examine the sub-regional HQs of six Taiwanese MNEs in Asia. They identify four geographic decision-making levels: global HQs; RHQs; sub-regional HQs; and local subsidiaries for 22 upstream, downstream, and supporting activities. The R&D and technology transfer is centralized in the global HQs in Taiwan, whereas regional structures undertake upstream and supporting activities, such as regional supply chain management, production rationalization, regional human resource management, budgeting, and portfolio investments. National subsidiaries are mainly responsible for local sales, marketing, promotion, and advertising.

Hoenen, Nell and Ambos (2013) argue that RHQs have entrepreneurial capabilities and responsibilities, beyond the roles of coordination and control of national subsidiaries. RHQs might be involved in identifying new local business opportunities, initiating exploitation, and setting up new subsidiaries. They find that RHQs' entrepreneurial capabilities increase with external embeddedness and heterogeneous environments.

Aman, Jaussaud and Shaaper (2014) study the regional management structures of French MNEs in the Asia Pacific region. They find that MNEs organize the Asia Pacific region into clusters of countries, where they locate regional management centres (RHQs, regional offices, distribution centres, and local offices) with substantial functions and roles. The main drivers of a regional Asian strategy and organization are the overall size of the MNE and its sales in Asia; however, the presence of manufacturing activities does not exert any influence. The regional management structures overcome the distance challenge between global HQs and foreign subsidiaries.

Conclusion

MNEs dominate International Business and are the key drivers of globalization (Rugman, 2000). Yet, MNEs are regional, not global. The vast majority of MNEs undertake their business activities within their home region of the broad triad of North America, Europe, and Asia Pacific. There is no trend towards globalization since the pioneering works by Rugman (2000, 2005a), and Rugman and Verbeke (2004). Furthermore, MNEs emphasize the increasingly important roles of regional organizational and management structures which serve as efficient mechanisms to coordinate activities between the corporate HQs and foreign subsidiaries in distant host countries.

References

Aguilera, R.V., Flores, R. & Vaaler, P.M. (2007) 'Is it all a matter of grouping? Examining the regional effect in global strategy research', in Tallman, S.B. (Ed.), *International Strategic Management: A New Generation*. Cheltenham, UK: Edward Elgar, pp. 161–190.

Aharoni, Y. (2006) 'Book review: The regional multinationals MNEs and global strategic management', *International Business Review*, 15, pp. 439–446.

Aman, B., Jaussaud, J. & Schaaper, J. (2014) 'Clusters and regional management structures by Western MNCs in Asia: Overcoming the distance challenge', *Management International Review*, 54, pp. 879–906.

Ambos, B. & Schlegelmilch, B.B. (2010) *The New Role of Regional Management*. Basingstoke, UK: Palgrave Macmillan.

Arregle, J.-L., Beamish, P.W. & Hebert, L. (2009) 'The regional dimension of MNEs' foreign subsidiary localization', *Journal of International Business Studies*, 40, pp. 86–107.

Arregle, J.-L., Miller, T.L., Hitt, M.A. & Beamish, P.W. (2013) 'Do regions matter? An integrated institutional and semi-globalization perspective on the internationalization of MNEs', *Strategic Management Journal*, 34, pp. 910–934.

Asmussen, C.G. (2009) 'Local, regional, or global? Quantifying MNE geographic scope', *Journal of International Business Studies*, 40, pp. 1192–1250.

Asmussen, C.G., Pedersen, T. & Petersen, B. (2007) 'How do we capture "global specialization" when measuring firms' degree of globalization?' *Management International Review*, 47, pp. 1–23

Banalieva, E.R. & Dhanaraj, C. (2013) 'Home region orientation in international expansion strategies', *Journal of International Business Studies*, 44, pp. 89–116.

Banalieva, E.R. & Eddleston, K.A. (2011) 'Home-region focus and performance of family firms: The role of family and non-family leader', *Journal of International Business Studies*, 42, pp. 1060–1072.

Bartlett, C.A. & Ghoshal, S. (1989) *Managing Across Borders: The Transnational Solution*. Boston, MA: Harvard Business School Press.

Bausch, A., Fritz, T. & Boesecke, K. (2007) 'Performance effects of internationalization strategies: A meta-analysis', in Rugman, A.M (Ed.), *Regional Aspects of Multinationality and Performance*. Amsterdam: Elsevier, pp. 143–176.

Bell, G., Filatotchev, I. & Rasheed, A. (2012) 'The liability of foreignness in capital markets: Sources and remedies', *Journal of International Business Studies*, 43, pp. 107–122.

Casson, M. (2016) 'Alan Rugman's methodology', *International Business Review*, 25, 758–766.

Collinson, S. & Rugman, A.M. (2007) 'The regional focus of Asian multinational enterprises', *Asia Pacific Journal of Management*, 24, pp. 429–446.

Collinson, S. & Rugman, A.M. (2008) 'The regional nature of Japanese multinational business', *Journal of International Business Studies*, 39, pp. 215–230.

Daniels, J. (1987) 'Bridging national and global marketing strategies through regional operations', *International Marketing Review*, 4, pp. 29–44.

D'Cruz, J. (1986) 'Strategic management of subsidiaries', in Etemad, H. & Duledue, L.S. (Eds.), *Managing the Multinational Subsidiary*. London: Croom Helm, pp. 75–80.

Delios, A. & Beamish, P. W. (2005) 'Regional and global strategies of Japanese firms', *Management International Review*, 45, pp. 19–36.

Douglas, S.P. & Wind, Y. (1987) 'The myth of globalization', *Columbia Journal of World Business*, Winter, pp. 19–29.

Dunning, J.H., Fujita, M. & Yakova, N. (2007) 'Some macro-data on the regionalization/globalization debate: A comment on the Rugman/Verbeke analysis', *Journal of International Business Studies*, 38, pp. 177–199.

Dunning, J.H. & Norman, G. (1987) 'The location choices of offices of international companies', *Environmental Planning*, 19, pp. 613–631.

Edwards, T., Jalette, P. & Tregaskis, O. (2012) 'To what extent is there a regional logic in the management of labour in multinational companies? Evidence from Europe and North America', *International Journal of Human Resource Management*, 23, pp. 2468–2490.

Egelhoff, W.G. (1982) 'Strategy and structure in multinational corporations: An information processing approach', *Administrative Science Quarterly*, 27, pp. 435–458.

Egelhoff, W.G. (1988a) 'Strategy and structure in multinational corporations: A revision of the Stopford and Wells model', *Strategic Management Journal*, 9, pp. 1–14.

Egelhoff, W.G. (1988b) *Organizing the Multinational Enterprise: An Information-Processing Perspective*. Cambridge, MA: Ballinger.

Egelhoff, W.G. (1991) 'Information-processing theory and the multinational enterprise', *Journal of International Business Studies*, 22, pp. 341–358.

Elango, B. (2004) 'Geographic scope of operations by multinational companies: An exploratory study of regional and global strategies', *European Management Journal*, 22, pp. 431–441.

Enright, M.J. (2005a) 'Regional management centres in the Asia Pacific', *Management International Review*, 45, pp. 59–82.

Enright, M.J. (2005b) 'The role of regional management centres', *Management International Review*, 45, pp. 83–102.

Filippaios, F. & Rama, R. (2008) 'Globalisation or regionalisation? The strategies of the world's largest food and beverages MNEs', *European Management Journal*, 26, pp. 59–72

Flores, R., Aguilera, R.V., Mahdian, A. & Vaaler, P.M. (2013) 'How well do supra-national regional grouping schemes fit International Business research?' *Journal of International Business Studies*, 44, pp. 451–474.

Friedman, T. (2005) *The World Is Flat: A History of the Twenty-First Century*. New York: Farrar, Straus and Giroux.

Ghobadian, A., Rugman, A.M. & Tung, R. L. (2014) 'Strategies for firm globalization and regionalization', *British Journal of Management*, 25, pp. 1–5

Gilbert, D.U. & Heinecke, P. (2014) 'Success factors of regional strategies for multinational corporation: Exploring an appropriate degree of regional management autonomy and regional product/service adaptation', *Management International Review*, 54, pp. 615–651.

Govindarajan, V. & Gupta, A. (2001) *The Quest for Global Dominance*. San Francisco, CA: Josey-Bass/ Wiley.

Grosse, R. (1981) 'Regional offices of MNCs', *Management International Review*, 21, pp. 48–55.

Grosse, R. (2005) 'Are the largest financial institutions really "global"?' *Management International Review*, 45, (Special issue), pp. 129–144.

Heenan, D.A. (1979) 'The regional headquarters division: A comparative analysis', *Academy of Management Journal*, 22, pp. 410–415.

Heinecke, P. (2011) *Success Factors of Regional Strategies for Multinational Corporations*. Heidelberg, Germany: Springer.

Hoenen, A., Nell, P. & Ambos, B. (2013) 'MNE entrepreneurial capabilities at intermediate levels: The roles of external embeddedness and heterogeneous environments', *Long Range Planning*, 47, pp. 76–86.

IFRS website. (n.d.) IFRS8 Operating Segments. Available at http://eifrs.ifrs.org/eifrs/bnstandards/en/2012/ifrs8.pdf.

IKEA Group. (2010) *Welcome Inside*, Yearly Summary FY10, IKEA Group. www.ikea.com/ms/en_GB/pdf/yearly_summary/ys_welcome_inside_2010.pdf.

Kolk, A. (2010) 'Social and sustainability dimensions of regionalization and (semi)globalization', *Multinational Business Review*, 18, pp. 51–72.

Lassere, P. (1996) 'Regional headquarters: The spearhead for Asia Pacific markets', *Long Range Planning*, 29, pp. 30–37.

Lehrer, M. & Asakawa, K. (1999) 'Unbundling European operations: Regional management and corporate flexibility in American and Japanese MNCs', *Journal of World Business*, 34, pp. 267–286.

Levitt, T. (1983) 'The globalization of markets', *Harvard Business Review*, 61, pp. 92–102.

Li, G.H., Yu, C.M. & Seetoo, D.H. (2010) 'Towards a theory of regional organization: The emerging role of sub-regional headquarters and the impact on subsidiaries', *Management International Review*, 50, pp. 5–33.

Li, L. (2005) 'Is regional strategy more effective than global strategy in the US service industries?' *Management International Review*, 45, pp. 37–57.

Mahnke, V., Ambos, B., Nell, P. & Hobdari, B. (2012) 'How do regional headquarters influence corporate decisions in networked MNCs?' *Journal of International Management*, 18, pp. 293–301.

Mohr, A., Fastoso, F., Wang, C. & Shirodkar, V.C. (2014) 'Testing the regional performance of multinational enterprises in the retail sector: The moderating effects of timing, speed and experience', *British Journal of Management*, 25, S60–S76.

Mori, T. (2002) 'The role and function of European regional headquarters in Japanese MNCs', Working paper No. 141. Hirosaki University.

Morrison, A.J., Ricks, D.A. & Roth, K. (1991) 'Globalization versus regionalization: Which way for the multinational?' *Organizational Dynamics*, 19, pp. 17–29.

Mudambi, R. & Puck, J. (2016) 'A global value chain analysis of the "regional strategy" perspective', *Journal of Management Studies*, 53, pp. 1076–1093.

Nguyen, Q.T.K. (2014) 'The regional strategies of British multinational subsidiaries in South East Asia', *British Journal of Management*, 25, pp. 60–76.

Nguyen, Q.T.K. (2015) 'The subsidiaries of multinational enterprises operate regionally, not globally', *Multinational Business Review*, 23, pp. 328–354.

Nguyen, Q.T.K. & Rugman, A.M. (2015) 'Multinational subsidiary sales and performance in South East Asia', *International Business Review*, 24, pp. 115–123.

Oh, C.H. (2009) 'The international scale and scope of European multinationals', *European Management Journal*, 27, pp. 336–343.

Oh, C.H. & Li, J. (2015) 'Commentary: Alan Rugman and the theory of regional multinationals', *Journal of World Business*, 50, pp. 631–633.

Oh, C.H. & Rugman, A.M. (2006) 'Regional sales of multinationals in the world cosmetics industry', *European Management Journal*, 24, pp. 163–173.

Oh, C.H. & Rugman, A.M. (2007) 'Regional multinationals and the Korean cosmetics industry', *Asia Pacific Journal of Management*, 24, pp. 27–42

Oh, C.H. & Rugman, A.M. (2014) 'The dynamics of regional and global multinationals, 1999–2008', *Multinational Business Review*, 22, pp. 108–117.

Oh, C.H., Sohl, T. & Rugman, A.M. (2015) 'Regional and product diversification and the performance of retail multinationals', *Journal of International Management*, 21, pp. 220–234

Ohmae, K. (1985) *Triad Power: The Coming Shape of Global Competition*. New York: Free Press.

Osegowitsch, T. & Sammartino, A. (2008) 'Reassessing (home-)regionalisation', *Journal of International Business Studies*, 39, pp. 184–196.

Paik, Y. & Sohn, J.H.D. (2004) 'Striking a balance between global integration and local responsiveness: The case of Toshiba corporation in redefining RHQs' role', *Organization Analysis*, 12, pp. 347–359.

Picard, J., Boddenwyn, J.J. & Grosse, R. (1998) 'Centralization and autonomy in international marketing decision making: A longitudinal study', *Journal of Global Marketing*, 12, pp. 5–24.

Piekkari, R., Nell, P. & Ghauri, P.N. (2010) 'Regional management as a system: A longitudinal case study', *Management International Review*, 10, pp. 513–532.

Poon, J.P.H. & Thompson, E.R. (2003) 'Developmental and quiescent subsidiaries in the Asia Pacific: Evidence from Hong Kong, Singapore, Shanghai and Sydney', *Economic Geography*, 79, pp. 195–214.

Prahalad, C.K. & Doz, Y.L. (1987) *The Multinational Mission: Balancing Global Integration with Local Responsiveness*. New York: Free Press.

Qian, G., Khoury, T., Peng, M.W. & Qian, Z. (2010) 'The performance implications of intra- and inter-regional geographic diversification', *Strategic Management Journal*, 31, pp. 1018–1030.

Qian, G., Li, L. & Rugman, A.M. (2013) 'Liability of country foreignness and liability of regional foreignness: Their effects on geographic diversification and firm performance', *Journal of International Business Studies*, 44, pp. 635–647.

Ronen, S. & Shenkar, O. (2013) 'Mapping world cultures: Cluster formation, sources and implications', *Journal of International Business Studies*, 44, pp. 867–897.

Roth, K. & Morrison, A.J. (1992) 'Business-level competitive strategy: A contingency link to internationalization', *Journal of Management*, 18, pp. 473–487.

Rugman, A.M. (2000) *The End of Globalization: Why Global Strategy Is a Myth and How to Profit from the Realities of Regional Market*. London: Random House.

Rugman, A.M. (2003a) 'Regional strategies for service sector multinationals', *European Business Journal*, 15, pp. 1–9.

Rugman, A.M. (2003b) 'Regional strategy and the demise of globalization', *Journal of International Management*, 9, pp. 409–417.

Rugman, A.M. (2005a). *The Regional Multinationals: MNEs and 'Global' Strategic Management*. Cambridge, UK: Cambridge University Press.

Rugman, A.M. (2005b) 'A further comment on the myth of globalization', *Journal of International Management*, 11, pp. 441–445.

Rugman, A.M. (2009) 'Theoretical aspects of emerging market multinationals', in Ramamurti, R. & Singh, J.V. (Eds.), *Emerging Multinationals in Emerging Markets*. Cambridge, UK: Cambridge University Press, pp. 42–63.

Rugman, A.M. (2014) 'Subsidiary-specific advantages and multiple embeddedness in multinational enterprises', *The MNE Academy Journal*, 7, pp. 1–18.

Rugman, A.M. & Brain, C. (2004) 'Regional strategies of multinational pharmaceutical firms', *Management International Review*, 44, pp. 7–25.

Rugman, A.M. & Collinson, S. (2004) 'The regional nature of the world's automotive sector', *European Management Journal*, 22, pp. 471–482.

Rugman, A.M. & Collinson, S. (2005) 'Multinational enterprises in the new Europe: Are they really global?' *Organizational Dynamics*, 34, pp. 258–272.

Rugman, A.M. & Collinson, S. (2012) *International Business*, 6th Edition. Harlow, UK: Pearson.

Rugman, A.M. & Girod, S. (2003) 'Retail multinationals and globalization: The evidence is regional', *European Management Journal*, 21, pp. 24–37.

Rugman, A.M. & Hodgetts, R. (2001) 'The end of global strategy', *European Management Journal*, 19, pp. 333–343.

Rugman, A.M., Kudina, A. & Yip, G. (2007) 'The regional dimension of UK multinationals', in Rugman, A.M. (Ed.), *Regional Aspects of Multinationality and Performance: Research in Global Strategic Management*, Vol. 13. Greenwich, CT: JAI Press, pp. 297–315.

Rugman, A.M. & Li, J. (2007) 'Will China's multinationals succeed globally or regionally?' *European Management Journal*, 25, pp. 333–343.

Rugman, A.M. & Nguyen, Q.T.K. (2014) 'Modern International Business theory and emerging economy MNCs', in Cuervo-Cazurra, A. & Ramamurti, R. (Eds.), *Understanding Multinationals from Emerging Markets*. Cambridge, UK: Cambridge University Press, pp 53–80.

Rugman, A.M., Nguyen, Q.T.K. & Wei, Z. (2016) 'Rethinking the literature on the performance of Chinese multinational enterprises', *Management and Organization Review*, 12, pp. 269–302.

Rugman, A.M. & Oh, C.H. (2008a) 'The international competitiveness of Asian firms', *Journal of Strategy and Management*, 1, pp. 57–71.

Rugman, A.M. & Oh, C.H. (2008b) 'Korea's multinationals in a regional world', *Journal of World Business*, 43, pp. 5–15.

Rugman, A.M. & Oh, C.H. (2010) 'Does the regional nature of multinationals affect the multinationality and performance relationship?' *International Business Review*, 19, pp. 479–488.

Rugman, A.M. & Oh, C.H. (2013) 'Why the home region matters: Location and regional multinationals', *British Journal of Management*, 24, pp. 463–479.

Rugman, A.M, Oh, C.H. & Lim, D.S.K. (2012) 'The regional and global competitiveness of multinational firms', *Journal of the Academy of Marketing Science*, 40, 218–235.

Rugman, A.M. & Sukpanich, N. (2006) 'Firm specific advantages, intra-regional sales and performance of multinational enterprises', *The International Trade Journal*, 20, pp. 355–382.

Rugman, A.M. & Sukpanich, N. (2007) 'Intra-regional sales, product diversity, and the performance of merchandising multinationals', *Journal of International Management*, 13, pp. 131–146.

Rugman, A.M. & Verbeke, A. (1992) 'A note on the transnational solution and the transaction cost theory of multinational strategic management', *Journal of International Business Studies*, 23, pp. 761–772.

Rugman, A.M. & Verbeke, A. (2001) 'Subsidiary-specific advantages in multinational enterprises', *Strategic Management Journal*, 22, pp. 237–250.

Rugman, A.M. & Verbeke, A. (2003) 'Extending the theory of the multinational enterprise: Internalization and strategic management perspectives', *Journal of International Business Studies*, 34, pp. 125–137.

Rugman, A.M. & Verbeke, A. (2004) 'A perspective on regional and global strategies of multinational enterprises', *Journal of International Business Studies*, 35, pp. 3–18.

Rugman, A.M. & Verbeke, A. (2005) 'Towards a theory of regional multinationals: A transaction cost economics approach', *Management International Review*, 45, pp. 3–15.

Rugman, A. M. & Verbeke, A. (2007) 'Liabilities of regional foreignness and the use of firm-level versus country-level data: A response to Dunning et al.', *Journal of International Business Studies*, 38, pp. 200–205.

Rugman, A.M. & Verbeke, A. (2008a) 'The theory and practice of regional strategy: A response to Osegowitsch and Sammartino', *Journal of International Business Studies*, 39, pp. 326–332.

Rugman, A.M. & Verbeke, A. (2008b) 'A new perspective on the regional and global strategies of multinational service firms', *Management International Review*, 4, pp. 397–411.

Rugman, A.M. & Verbeke, A. (2008c) 'A regional solution to the strategy and structure of multinationals', *European Management Journal*, 26, pp. 305–313.

Rugman, A.M., Verbeke, A. & Nguyen, Q.T.K. (2011) 'Fifty years of International Business and beyond', *Management International Review*, 51, pp. 755–786.

Schuette, H. (1997) 'Strategy and organization: Challenges for European MNCs in Asia', *European Management Journal*, 15, pp. 436–445.

Seno-Alday, S. (2009) 'Market characteristics and regionalization patterns', *European Management Journal*, 27, pp. 366–376.

Stevens, M.J. & Bird, A. (2004) 'On the myth of believing that globalization is a myth: Or the effects of misdirected responses on obsolescing an emergent substantive discourse', *Journal of International Management*, 10, pp. 501–510.

Sukpanich, N. & Rugman, A.M. (2010) 'Multinationals and the international competitiveness of ASEAN firms', in Gugler, P. & Chaisse, J. (Eds.), *Competitiveness of the ASEAN Countries*. Cheltenham, UK: Edward Elgar, pp. 53–81.

Venzin, M., Kumar, V. & Kleine, J. (2008) 'Internationalization of retail banks: A micro-level study of the multinationality-performance relationship', *Management International Review*, 48, pp. 463–485.

Verbeke, A. (2013) *International Business Strategy*, 2nd Edition. Cambridge, UK: Cambridge University Press.

Verbeke, A. & Asmussen, C.G. (2016) 'Global, local, or regional? The locus of MNE strategies', *Journal of Management Studies*, 53, pp. 1051–1075.

Verbeke, A. & Greidanus, N.S. (2009) 'The end of the opportunism vs trust debate: Bounded reliability as a new envelope concept in research on MNE governance', *Journal of International Business Studies*, 40, pp. 135–152.

Verbeke, A. & Kano, L. (2012) 'An internalization theory for MNE regional strategy', *Multinational Business Review*, 20, pp. 135–152.

Verbeke, A. & Kenworthy, T.P. (2008) 'Multidividional vs. Metanational governance of the multinational enterprise', *Journal of International Business Studies*, 39, pp. 940–956.

US GAAP FAS 131 www.fasb.org/jsp/FASB/Document_C/DocumentPage?cid=1218220124541andacceptedDisclaimer=true.

Westney, D.E. (2006) 'Review of Alan M. Rugman, The regional multinationals: MNEs and "global" strategic management', *Journal of International Business Studies*, 37, pp. 445–449.

Wolf, J., Dunemann, T. & Egelhoff, W.G. (2012) 'Why MNCs tend to concentrate their activities in their home region', *Multinational Business Review*, 20, pp. 67–91.

Wolf, J. & Egelhoff, W.G. (2002) 'A reexamination and extension of international strategy-structure theory', *Strategic Management Journal*, 23, pp. 181–189.

Yeung, H.W., Poon, J. & Perry, M. (2001) 'Towards a regional strategy: The role of regional headquarters of foreign firms in Singapore', *Urban Studies*, 38, pp. 157–183.

Yin, E. & Choi, C.J. (2005) 'The globalization myth: The case of China', *Management International Review*, 45, pp. 103–120.

Yin, M.S. & Walsh, J. (2011) 'Analyzing the factors contributing to the establishment of Thailand as a hub for regional operating headquarters', *Journal of Economics and Behavioral Studies*, 2, pp. 275–287.

Yip, G.S. (1992) *Total Global Strategy: Managing for Worldwide Competitive Advantage*. Englewood Cliffs, NJ: Prentice Hall.

Zaheer, S. (2002) 'The liability of foreignness, redux: A commentary', *Journal of International Management*, 8, pp. 351–358.

6

THE DYNAMICS OF MULTINATIONAL ENTERPRISE SUBSIDIARY ROLES IN AN ERA OF REGIONALIZATION

Alain Verbeke and Wenlong Yuan

Introduction

Multinational enterprise (MNE) subsidiaries can take on various responsibilities and roles, due to corporate role assignment, subsidiary choice, and external environmental changes (Birkinshaw et al., 1998; Birkinshaw, 2000; Rugman & Verbeke, 2001). Internal changes or external environmental shifts may drive these roles to evolve over time. The literature on subsidiary dynamics has focused most of its attention on the impact of internal, organizational changes, while largely ignoring the influence of supranational, environmental changes (Rugman, Verbeke & Yuan, 2011; Verbeke & Yuan, 2013). Even when environmental characteristics are considered, researchers tend to limit themselves to parameters such as local competition at the level of single country (Birkinshaw et al., 1998). Meyer's co-authored study in 2009 called for the analysis of direct linkages between macro-level institutional environments and firm-level strategies; however, broader environmental factors, especially regional integration schemes, have been underemphasized and occupy only a minor position in most mainstream theoretical frameworks (Rugman, 2000, 2005).

Recently, a limited number of MNEs have implemented regional integration schemes to integrate their activities along regional lines, and to transform their locational strategic focus by adopting regional strategies (Hoenen, Nell & Ambos, 2014; Verbeke & Kano, 2016). This has resulted in increased internal competition among subsidiaries and business units, especially in cases whereby different subsidiaries command similar resource bundles. However, no general framework has yet been put forward to examine the effects of regional integration schemes, such as the EU and NAFTA, on subsidiary roles, in spite of regional agreements becoming increasingly instrumental to 'deep integration' (Buckley et al., 2001).

In this chapter, we analyze the impact of regional integration schemes on subsidiary role dynamics. We also present eight patterns of MNE subsidiary role dynamics, as a combination of changes in the subsidiary's scope of product offerings/value chain activities and geographic scope. Finally, we adopt a subsidiary perspective on region-based, organizational change by investigating subsidiaries' discretion, given their level of unused productive resources and management competences.

Regional integration as an economic determinant of subsidiary roles

The missing linkage between subsidiary roles and regional integration

Regional integration influences activities of MNEs both in terms of new investment into the region and the reorganization of existing activities in the region (Rugman & Verbeke, 2004). For example, Hogenbirk and van Kranenburg (2006) found that in the Dutch electronics and electrical appliances industry, regionally product-mandated hubs account for 25% of foreign-owned subsidiaries and export platforms account for another 24% (as regards to the remainder, 8% are miniature replicas and 43% are single activity satellites). The regional product hubs and export platforms were generally established after the implementation of the Single European Act, thus suggesting that regionalization leads to new types of subsidiary roles, with some subsidiaries taking on broader responsibilities at the European level.

Regarding existing activities, researchers have tended to focus on 'rationalization' or 'reorganization' as the major outcome of regionalization in MNEs (Rugman, Verbeke & Yuan, 2011). For example, the widely held prediction regarding free trade has been that lowering long-established tariffs would lead to an exodus of foreign investment and manufacturing jobs in some smaller countries in the region, e.g., Canada in the NAFTA area (Luxmore, Rugman & Verbeke, 1991). Since smaller miniature replica plants are less efficient than larger factories with greater economies of scale and lower labor costs per unit, MNEs would transfer production to lower-cost plants, in this case located in the United States. More generally, MNEs would reassess and consolidate their production network within the region as a consequence of trade creation effects, seeking to exploit the comparative advantages of countries or areas within the trading bloc and to maximize production efficiencies. This kind of reasoning suggests that MNEs would rationalize their production capabilities in the region with local plants manufacturing or assembling final products made primarily from core components produced in core locations for the entire region (Cohen & Zysman, 1987). Alternatively, the primary purpose of foreign-owned subsidiaries would be to market and sell products imported from abroad throughout the region (McFetridge, 1995).

The extant literature on the impact of regional integration on trade, FDI, and subsidiary roles misses the heterogeneous impact of regional integration on both markets and MNEs by assuming a homogeneous rationalization strategy adopted by MNEs as the sole response to regional integration. Many of the extant studies on MNE responses to regional integration have indeed assumed that MNEs adopt similar strategies, while missing the varied impacts of regional integration on perceived national market importance, on the evolution of subsidiary competences, and more generally on multinational managers' cognitive understanding of this macro-level phenomenon (Verbeke & Kano, 2016).

But in reality, strategic responses will be firm-specific. Krajewski noted in a 1992 Conference Board of Canada Report, that the substance of rationalization efforts, and related changes in subsidiary roles, were firm-specific. In a similar vein, Buckley and his co-authors argued in 2003 that "even if protectionism were the initial impetus to FDI, MNEs accrue intangible benefits from operating in host markets over time, which confer advantages on foreign-owned firms, fueling future competitiveness, and expansion of their operations in the host country" (Buckley et al., 2003, p. 855). The reality of persisting national non-tariff barriers together with the geographic size of niched submarkets within the overall NAFTA market, is likely to prevent most firms from effectively adopting a single regional strategy based on scale economies and exclusive of national considerations. The establishment of a regional free trade and investment area can lead MNEs to move from a multidomestic (or traditional "multinational") strategy towards a regional strategy, but this is likely to involve multidimensional reorganizing and rationalizing to exploit various location advantages through more specialized factories with larger production runs and less product diversification.

The impact of regional integration on subsidiary roles

We have developed a general framework (see Figure 6.1) to analyze the impact of regional integration on both the strategic importance of host country markets and subsidiary competences as compared to sister subsidiaries by relying on Bartlett and Ghoshal's (1986) typology of subsidiary roles. Among the many subsidiary role classifications published since the 1980s (White & Poynter, 1984; Bartlett & Ghoshal, 1986; Jarillo & Martinez, 1990; Gupta & Govindarajan, 1991; Birkinshaw & Morrison, 1995; Taggart, 1997a, 1997b, 1998; Homburg, Krohmer & Workman, 1999; Delany, 2000; Benito, Grogaard & Narula, 2003; Hogenbirk & van Kranenburg, 2006), the most influential classification has undoubtedly been the one developed by Bartlett and Ghoshal (1986). The Bartlett and Ghoshal (1986) typology is based on two dimensions, strategic importance of the local environment (location advantages) and the competences (firm-specific advantages or FSAs) held by the local organization. The strategic importance of the local environment depends on its significance to the MNE's overall strategy. Markets that are either large, particularly sophisticated, or technologically advanced, are the most likely to have high strategic importance to an MNE. As regards FSAs at the local level, these subsidiary competences can be in "technology, production, marketing, or any other area" (Bartlett & Ghoshal, 1986, p. 90).

We argue that the impact of regional integration on the strategic importance of host country markets depends on the extent of distance reduction engendered, and that the impact of regional integration on subsidiary competences is contingent upon the characteristics of these competences. Moreover, MNE managers' cognitive understanding of the two types of impact moderates the dynamics of subsidiary roles.

First, on the market side, as a result of regional integration, the regionally unified market becomes a new geographic level relevant to multinational strategic management, in addition to the global and national levels. In 2001, Ghemawat analyzed how distance can affect business and unbundled the concept into four dimensions, including cultural, geographic, economic, and administrative distance. Cultural distance represents differences in language, social norms, and religion; geographic distance refers to the physical distance and lack of communication links between countries;

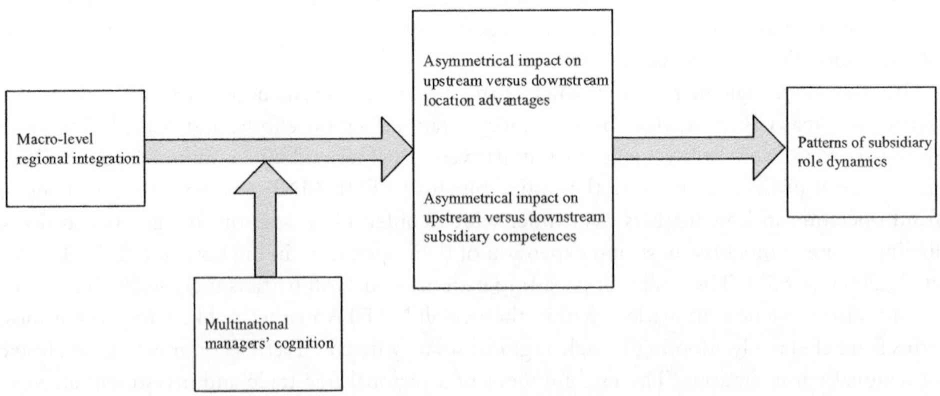

Figure 6.1 The impact of regional integration on the dynamics of subsidiary roles

economic distance includes differences in consumer income, and in costs and quality of natural resources, human resources, and infrastructure; and administrative distance includes not only differences in public policy, but also differences (or lack thereof) in preferential trade arrangements and political associations. The greater the overall distance between a potential host country and the home country, the less attractive that host country becomes.

Deep integration schemes, such as the EU and NAFTA, represent deliberate efforts to reduce one of these distance components, namely the administrative distance within the region, given that the other types of distance are not simply changeable through public policy. For example, in the case of NAFTA, tariff and non-tariff barriers have largely been removed to promote the free flow of goods, services, and capital; national treatment has been applied to foreign investors; and national tax policies have also been harmonized through bilateral tax treaties (Eden, 1996). For MNEs, the NAFTA region, as an integrated investment regime, allows them to pursue more integrated strategies through rationalized production plants and marketing strategies, see Rugman and Verbeke (2005). In the EU case, integration efforts have gone even further, as expressed in the single market and the widely applied principle of mutual recognition whereby rules of origin prevail, the creation of a single currency, and the harmonizing of fiscal and monetary policies (Malhotra, Agarwal & Baalbaki, 1998).

Although regional integration intends to overcome structural market distortions/imperfections (Dunning & Robson, 1987), it does not have an equal impact on all upstream/downstream markets. For example, Cantwell (1987) found that the British membership of the EC affected manufacturing and R&D activities in the pharmaceuticals sectors differently, with MNEs' European R&D programs becoming much more integrated than production. In case of a low impact, either regional market unification does not occur, or regional market unification already occurred before regional integration schemes. On the one hand, intrinsic differences among markets in the region may persist, even with regional integration, such as the heterogeneity in European food cultures (Askegaard & Madsen, 1998). On the other, the 1965 auto pact and tariff reductions under GATT created significant integration of auto trade and production in North America by the 1980s (UNCTAD, 1992). Therefore, the impact of NAFTA on comparative advantages for auto firms in the region was rather limited.

A high impact, however, reveals either the increasing overlap between the markets served by the subsidiaries or the location advantages recalibrated as a result of regional integration. On the downstream market side, removal of cross-border barriers may indicate the convergence of consumer behavior within the region and the expanded, similar downstream markets which were protected by barriers and which now morph into an integrated regional market. At the upstream market side, regional integration may also amplify location advantages, such as cheap labor, which previously was more difficult to access because of trade/FDI barriers. Put in other words, location advantages in the realm of factor endowments may become more accessible.

The above analysis suggests that there is no single, ubiquitous impact of regional integration on subsidiary dynamics. The impact depends on the comparison of the market conditions before and after regional integration, and on whether or not substantive changes in the market occur as a result of regional integration. Therefore, we propose the following:

Proposition 1. A stronger distance reduction because of regional integration, will amplify the impact of regional integration on subsidiary roles.

Second, regional integration also initiates changes in MNEs' strategies (Verbeke, Kano & Yuan, 2016). Many MNE strategies, expressed publicly by their senior executives or in their firms' official documentation, appear to include a regional factor. For example, Fujio Cho, Vice Chairman of Toyota, stated: "We intend to continue moving forward with globalization . . . by further enhancing the localization and independence of our operations in each region" (Ghemawat, 2005, p. 100). Furthermore, Nestlé's management often explicitly differentiates among global, regional, and local business components of corporate strategy and organization (Nestlé, 2006). The expanded regional market opens up new opportunities for MNEs to exploit new location advantages in the region (Hoenen, Nell & Ambos, 2014). Owing to the similarity of consumer needs, the expanded regional market allows MNEs to adopt an aggregation strategy so as to reap more scale and scope economies (Ghemawat, 2003), thereby exploiting the similarities across countries within the region. The expanded regional market also facilitates an arbitrage strategy (Ghemawat, 2003), namely to exploit different location advantages in the region, for example by concentrating labor-intensive activities in the cheaper labor economies within the region. The large economic differences between the United States and Mexico, together with the reduced administrative differences and the geographic proximity, have encouraged many U.S. firms to 'nearshore' production facilities to Mexico.

The potential to exploit the integrated market through aggregation or arbitrage has to be matched with appropriate subsidiary competences in the region. What matters here is subsidiary competences' similarity with those of other subsidiaries, the extent of subsidiary competences' fungibility, and the extent to which subsidiary competences are location-bound.

Similar competences refer to those competences that allow the subsidiary to undertake the same functional activities or fulfill the same mandates as other subsidiaries. For example, if several subsidiaries in the region perform similar activities, such as manufacturing quasi-identical products, they may enter into competition with each other and regional integration will facilitate parent-driven changes in subsidiary mandates to improve efficiency. Subsidiary competences can also be fungible (Birkinshaw & Lingblad, 2005), in the sense that they could be used to exploit new business opportunities. The fungibility of subsidiary competences may increase the subsidiary's ability to search for – and enter into – new markets, thereby allowing easy resource reallocation towards new business opportunities, when the corporate head office changes the subsidiary's formal mandate. Finally, subsidiary competences can be location-bound. Even with the integrated regional market, some subsidiary activities still have to be performed locally. For example, sales activities for some consumer goods often require proximity to the customers, and therefore may leave less room for regional integration at the firm level. Thus, the impact of regional integration on such subsidiaries is likely to be very small.

Proposition 2. More similarity and fungibility of the subsidiary's competences will increase the impact of regional integration schemes.

Proposition 3. More location-boundedness of the subsidiary's competences will reduce the impact of regional integration schemes

An often forgotten factor when discussing the impact of regionalization on subsidiary roles is the cognition of MNE managers, especially at the head office. As we argued earlier in this chapter, regional integration only reduces administrative distance, and other types of distance are likely to remain, even with regional integration. Thus, MNE managers' perceptions of the overall impact of regional integration may moderate the impact of market changes on subsidiary charter changes and dynamics.

For example, European appliances producers have exhibited a variety of behaviors to address regional integration (Stopford & Baden-Fuller, 1987). Italian managers believed that the European market was becoming more integrated and therefore increased efforts at UK market penetration, while most British producers believed that with non-tariff trade barriers and turbulence of demand, a lesser focus on exporting would better protect their market niches.

Such perceptions of market changes also affected investments by Japanese manufacturing firms in Europe (Hood & Young, 1987, p. 199). Due to the relatively recent nature of these firms' investments in Europe, they established operations with the prospect of serving the future integrated single European market. In this particular case, the Japanese MNEs applied a proactive strategy to address the expected impact of regional integration.

Therefore, we argue that cognition of MNE managers moderates the impact of regional integration on subsidiary role dynamics.

Proposition 4. MNE managers' cognition moderates the impact of regional integration on the dynamics of subsidiary roles.

Patterns of subsidiary role dynamics as responses to regional integration schemes

Eight patterns of subsidiary role dynamics

With the unbalanced impact of regional integration on the strategic importance of individual national markets and on the level of individual subsidiary competences, and the moderating effect of MNE executives' cognition of this impact, MNEs respond to regional integration in many different ways. In this section, we develop a framework (see Figure 6.2) to investigate

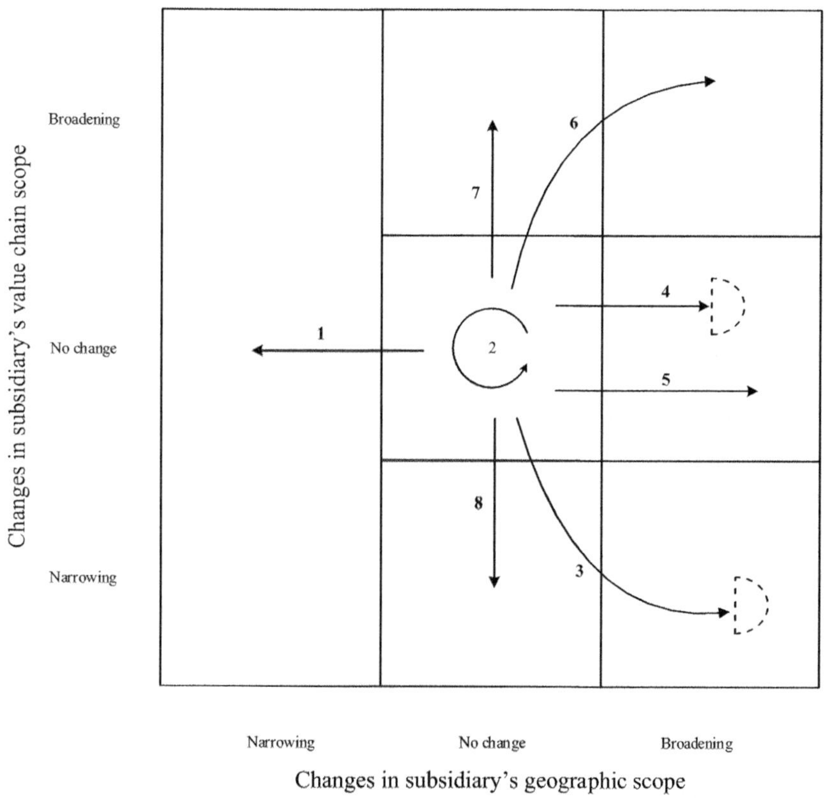

Figure 6.2 Patterns of subsidiary dynamics in an era of regional integration

the various alternative rationalization strategies available to MNEs. Further, we present eight patterns of subsidiary dynamics brought by regional integration schemes and describe the resulting effects on subsidiary competences, in line with Rugman, Verbeke and Yuan (2011).

We apply two observable parameters to describe the impact of regional integration on subsidiary dynamics: changes in the subsidiary's scope of product offerings/value chain activities, and changes in the subsidiary's geographic scope. These two visible parameters are related to subsidiary competences, which are more difficult to assess directly, but the two observable parameters do not necessarily match the 'invisible' subsidiary competences (Birkinshaw & Hood, 1998). Any change in the two observable parameters may reflect either actual subsidiary competences or the MNE headquarters' intention to develop new subsidiary competences, without these having yet materialized (Phelps & Fuller, 2015).

For example, historically, tariffs led MNEs to design each national subsidiary as a replica of the parent firm, so as to serve separate foreign markets. As a result, subsidiaries from different countries often bear high levels of similarity in their product scope and value chain functions, though sometimes they may differ in terms of resulting subsidiary competences. Once regional integration occurs, similar subsidiary resource bundles, dispersed across different subsidiaries in the same region, often become redundant and reduce the potential to earn scale economies. A rationalization program could be implemented, with some subsidiaries being closed down and others given extended charters, as recognition of their competences. Another rationalization program could entail reorganizing subsidiaries in the region towards more specialized product offerings, thereby developing some subsidiary competences in the associated product markets. Therefore, changing the two observable parameters may reflect either a formal way to recognize subsidiary competences that have been developed already, or the strategic intent to develop such subsidiary competences in the future.

Pattern 1. The first pattern implies a subsidiary shutdown: the strong reduction of distance among markets in the region, combined with a high resource similarity, fungibility, and non-location-boundedness of competences among competing MNE units in the region, makes the subsidiary unnecessary. The possibility of subsidiary closure usually represents a major source of uneasiness for small open economies, when contemplating whether or not to join a regional economic integration scheme. For example, two U.S. headquarters' respondents in the Blank and Haar's (1998) survey on the impact of regional integration had closed their operations in Canada.

However, the rationale for shutdowns of such plants may range "from poor performance . . . to adverse governmental action and inability to fulfill the expected benefits of diversification moves, acquisitions, and cooperative ventures" (Benito & Welch, 1997, p. 21). Internal competition or simple rationalization considerations themselves, without the presence of other factors, often do not lead to withdrawal. Little evidence supports the assertion that MNEs are likely to shut down their operations in a country, solely based on a free trade and investment agreement.

Pattern 2. The second pattern indicates that regional integration has no impact on subsidiary roles, generally as the outcome of only a limited reduction of distance among the markets in the region and the location-bound characteristics of extant subsidiary competences. For example, the UK's membership in the EC had a weak impact on MNE production networks in pharmaceuticals in the EC (Cantwell, 1987). In spite of the single EC market, various trade barriers, including government controls over prices and registration of new products, continued to divide the EC into distinct national markets. Therefore, regional integration did not really affect pharmaceutical production and MNEs were not incentivized to rationalize their regional production networks. Hood and Young (1987) also noted that the limited inter-plant product flows and subsidiaries' perceived level of corporate integration did not offer much evidence of integration across borders, though the large group of miniature-replica subsidiaries would suggest country-centered or region-centered strategies.

Pattern 3. Pattern 3 describes subsidiary specialization as the outcome of regional integration. For example, national plants, which manufactured similar products for the domestic market only, specialize in a narrower set of products or in distinct value-added activities for the regional market. Here, the plants typically need to augment extant competences to be successful in the regional market. In other words, expanded charters are granted before the full development of the relevant competences.

Subsidiary specialization cases have not been particularly well documented yet in the literature, but charter losses and gains at the product level provide some understanding of the processes at hand (Birkinshaw, 2000). One example is the investment in the London, Ontario, plant by 3M Canada that entailed a regional mandate for micro-encapsulation (Birkinshaw, 1995, pp. 295–260). This product line used to be manufactured in several plants. Although the London plant had not exhibited truly stronger competences than other, similar plants within the firm, the intent of the rationalization was to allocate the charter to a single subsidiary and subsequently to strengthen its competences in the relevant product domain.

Another example of this type of rationalization process is provided by Honeywell Home's, North American regional strategy formation. Among the overlapping product lines manufactured by both Canadian and U.S. plants, the Zone Valves line was moved to Canada, whereas regional mandates for other products were moved to the United States. Thus, each production site specialized in a narrower range of products, which resulted in improved efficiency of all sites (Birkinshaw, 1995, pp. 92–93).

Pattern 4. In Pattern 4, the focal subsidiary's extant product scope does not change, but its charter for the existing product lines is expanded to cover the entire regional market, with the expectation that the subsidiary will develop competences allowing it to be successful throughout this entire market. When MNEs apply Pattern 4, this reduces potential internal frictions related to internal competition, at least as compared to Pattern 3. At the same time, expanded mandates that cover the region can offer growth opportunities for all subsidiaries in the region.

For example, when the Asia/Oceania division of Nestlé sought growth through pursuing opportunities in the ASEAN (Association of Southeast Asian Nations) region, the non-dairy creamer operations of Nestlé in Thailand were allocated the charter to produce non-dairy creamer for the entire ASEAN region (Taucher & Toh, 2003). The Nestlé operation in Thailand not only needed to increase its production capacity, but also had to learn how to manufacture non-dairy creamer for other ASEAN countries with different preferences. In this case, the focal subsidiary was given the opportunity to expand its geographic scope, but had to develop new competences to meet this goal.

Pattern 5. Pattern 5 refers to the case of subsidiaries that are given an expanded regional geographic charter, covering extant product lines as was the case with Pattern 4, but with pre-existing competences to serve this regional market, largely as a result of the subsidiary's historical trajectory.

For example, many of the Japanese manufacturing investments in Europe were made close to the establishment of the single market. Japanese manufacturers set up their European operations with the prospect of serving the future, integrated single European market (Hood & Young, 1987,

p. 199). Regional integration simply meant the unfolding of the opportunity expected by these firms when making their initial investments. In this case, gains in scope of product offering and market domain at the subsidiary level were typically not associated with charter losses for other subsidiaries.

Pattern 6. Pattern 6 reflects the focal subsidiary expanding both its product scope/value chain activities and its geographic scope. The focal subsidiary still serves the initial national market, but adds additional products for the regional market. Similar to Pattern 4, the subsidiary must develop new competences to match its expanded charter.

This was the case with the regional project of Nestlé in ASEAN. Nestlé selected a few regional products and established new plants to cater to the broader regional market without closing down existing plants except one (Taucher & Toh, 2003). For example, Nestlé decided to add a production facility for soya source powder in Singapore. Functioning as the only soya source powder plant in ASEAN for Nestlé, the Singapore subsidiary expanded both its product offering and geographic scope.

Pattern 7. Pattern 7 and Pattern 8 represent the importance of location specificity and the strength of location-bound FSAs held by subsidiaries respectively. With Pattern 7, subsidiaries are not affected directly by regional integration. Moreover, these subsidiaries can even seek further growth opportunities in the national markets where they are located. For example, foreign subsidiaries in the food industry in the UK that were highly committed to this market (Pearce & Papanastassiou, 1997) implies that these subsidiaries could further expand their product offering in the UK market.

Pattern 8. In contrast to Pattern 7, Pattern 8 represents a 'pure loss' for the focal subsidiary, in the sense that mandates are removed from it and reallocated to another unit. Pattern 8 is often the mirror image of Pattern 3: the responsibility for some regional products having been allocated to another unit, the focal subsidiary ends up with a reduced product scope in its own national market. Unique location-bound competences may allow the focal subsidiary to continue serving the local market for some product lines.

A final note about the patterns of subsidiary dynamics is that such changes can be either competitive or cooperative, and either incremental or disruptive. First, subsidiary dynamics can be competitive or cooperative (Phelps & Fuller, 2000; Houston et al., 2001; Birkinshaw & Lingblad, 2005; Luo, 2005; Cerrato, 2006; Fong et al., 2007). Competitive subsidiary dynamics approximate a market mechanism, with any gain for one subsidiary meaning a loss for another unit. In contrast, cooperation-based subsidiary dynamics reflect the strategic intent to strengthen some subsidiaries without reallocating charters held by other units. Second, subsidiary dynamics can be incremental or disruptive. Incremental subsidiary dynamics are the outcome of subsidiary initiatives, through which subsidiaries gradually assume more responsibilities. In contrast, disruptive subsidiary dynamics typically entail reallocating major responsibilities, such as major production lines or value chain functions, from one subsidiary to another.

Major regional integration programs directed by corporate headquarters are likely to be competitive and disruptive. For example, with the restructuring of 3M in Europe (Ackenhusen, Muzyka & Churchill, 1996a, 1996b), spare parts management was reassigned to a single depot for the whole of Europe, from the initial 17 depots, thus leading to the closure of several units. As another example, regional customers may be similar to such an extent that a regionally designed marketing strategy may be justified. Such strategy entails concentrating several marketing activities in a single, regional centre, thereby helping the MNE to earn scope economies, in the sense that similar, local marketing planning activities at different subsidiaries become redundant and are taken over by the new, regional marketing centre. In contrast, subsidiary dynamics can be cooperative and incremental, as was the case with Nestlé's regionalization project in ASEAN (Taucher & Toh, 2003), whereby most national subsidiaries were not only allowed to retain their extant production lines, but were also selected as champions for producing specific new products for the entire region.

As another example, cooperative and disruptive subsidiary dynamics can be the result of an 'exchange of mandates' among competing subsidiaries, rather than the removal of mandates from one subsidiary, and the reallocation thereof to another unit. Here, all the affected subsidiaries become more specialized so as to achieve a comparatively more optimal scale of operations in a static sense, and a more effective accumulation of experience and know-how in a dynamic sense. With this pattern, all subsidiaries can strengthen their competences as compared with their initial position – there are no losers. The rationalization process at Honeywell Home's North American operations reflects precisely this phenomenon. Among the overlapping products by both the Canadian and U.S. plants, Zone Valves were moved to Canada, and the other products were moved to the United States. Thus, each production site concentrated on a narrower range of products, which resulted in improved efficiency of all sites (Birkinshaw, 1995, pp. 92–93).

Effects of regional integration on subsidiary competences

The above analysis of subsidiary dynamics has emphasized both scale economies and scope economies through which MNEs may attempt to improve their competitive position in an era of regional integration. However, the effect of regional integration on changes in subsidiary competences may be differentiated in terms of impacts on new competence creation and impacts on competence exploitation (Cantwell & Mudambi, 2005).

First, the MNE rationalization process may increase competence creation responsibility at the regional business unit level, as documented by the fact that 70% of respondents in a questionnaire survey administered with the headquarters of U.S.-based companies had adopted or considered adopting a North American focus in their corporate strategy and structure, as early as 1994 (Blank & Haar, 1998). Similar results for Europe were suggested by Bleackley and Williamson (1997), who surveyed 41 EU companies.

In these regionally organized companies such as 3M Europe (Ackenhusen et al., 1996a, 1996b), regional product line organizations (e.g., European business centers or North American business centers) are responsible for developing and implementing their own business plans. They also have extensive responsibilities in manufacturing, R&D, technical services, as well as profit and loss responsibilities. This organizational design thus allocates the competence creation, and often, entrepreneurial resources, to the regionally based subunits. Interestingly, the former national subsidiaries, if not functioning as regional business centers for specific product lines, will take a less important role in the search for – and pursuit of – new business opportunities, i.e., they will lose competence creation mandates.

Second, the efficiency focus, as a result of MNE rationalization at the regional level, will tend to increase national subsidiaries' responsibility for competence exploitation, even if they have lost some of their competence creation responsibility (including the loss of subsidiary autonomy and organizational slack at the subsidiary level). Indeed, on the competence creation side, national subsidiaries without region-wide responsibilities are likely to become more horizontally or vertically coordinated through a regional center, and will find themselves at the losing end of bundling (e.g., concentration) of some resources for the regional market. This implies a reduction in autonomy, for example in terms of the subsidiary's roles in product planning, as occurred in many Canadian operations after the implementation of NAFTA (Blank & Haar, 1998, pp. 50–51), and in international procurement as observed in many MNE subsidiaries in the EU (Tavares & Young, 2006). In addition, the increased operational efficiency is accompanied by a reduction of organizational slack at the subsidiary level, thereby constraining the pursuit of new business opportunities.

Third, there may be stronger effects of regional integration on upstream subsidiary competences than on downstream competences. On the one hand, there may be substantial potential to integrate upstream activities on a regional level, through concentrating production activities and sourcing inputs for the region as a whole. On the other, the need for localization is likely to prevail for downstream activities, as suggested by Bleackley and Williamson (1997). A somewhat extreme example is the case of Petrofina (now part of TotalFinaElf), an oil and chemicals company (Bleackley & Williamson, 1997), which "centralized the management of all those activities that were not directly 'seen' by customers and decentralized those that are" (Bleackley & Williamson, 1997, p. 492). Therefore, regional integration may bring more changes to the subsidiary upstream competences than the downstream competences.

A Penrosean perspective of subsidiary-driven evolution

Foundations of Penrosean analysis

Given the eight observed patterns of subsidiary role dynamics, what are the underlying parameters explaining whether and how subsidiaries will be able to influence their own development trajectories, especially in terms of expanding their activity scope and the geographic reach thereof? Below, we first discuss the underlying determinants of subsidiary trajectories in generic terms and subsequently apply this thinking to the regional integration context.

Birkinshaw and his co-authors (Birkinshaw, 1997; Birkinshaw & Hood, 1998; Birkinshaw, Hood & Jonsson, 1998) provide useful insights on subsidiary evolution and thus the dynamics of subsidiary roles. They make a stylized distinction between two phases of growth, and among three drivers of development and five subsidiary role trajectories. First, the two major phases of growth taken into account are: establishing viability and building sustainability. During the first phase, induced strategic behavior prevails. The subsidiary is mainly concerned with fulfilling its basic mandate and achieving satisfactory performance, through such activities as securing an expected market share (at the customer-end) and reducing production costs to a pre-specified standard (at the back-end). In the second stage, the subsidiary may pursue a mix of induced and autonomous activities to ensure its long-term sustainability, thereby attempting to earn a world product mandate or product specialist charter inside the MNE.

Second, three drivers of subsidiary development are recognized: host country characteristics, parent company management, and subsidiary management (Birkinshaw & Hood, 1998). All three factors affect the level of resources in the subsidiary, its mandate, and the scope of its functional activities.

Third, five subsidiary role trajectories are proposed, namely: parent-driven investment, subsidiary-driven charter extension, parent-driven divestment, atrophy through subsidiary neglect, and subsidiary-driven charter reinforcement. Of particular interest here is subsidiary-driven charter extension, meaning that subsidiary management engages in entrepreneurial activities and responds autonomously to new opportunities in its environment.

Interestingly, and perhaps surprisingly, the above work on subsidiary evolution refers to Penrose (1959) by drawing an analogy between subsidiary evolution and the growth of an independent firm (Birkinshaw & Hood, 1998), but without an in-depth analysis of the implications of Penrose's (1959) seminal work for the study of subsidiary evolution. Rather, the above work on subsidiary dynamics is grounded more in current International Business thinking, such as White and Poynter (1984), Bartlett and Ghoshal (1986), and Rugman and Verbeke (1992).

However, Birkinshaw argues that "[subsidiary] evolution and growth can be modeled in a way that is analogous to Edith Penrose's (1995) seminal treatise on the 'theory of the growth of the firm'" (Birkinshaw, 2000, p. 11). Furthermore, he states that "the evolution of the subsidiary can be modeled in a way that parallels Penrose's Theory of the Growth of the Firm (1959), and the dynamic capabilities perspective in general" (Birkinshaw, 2000, p. 96). Finally, Birkinshaw adds that "the subsidiary can be modeled as a semiautonomous entity whose development is analogous to that of an independent firm (cf. Penrose)" (Birkinshaw & Hood, 1998, p. 339).

In other places, Penrose is recognized for her association with the resource-based view, such as in the statement that "this literature can be traced back to Penrose's (1959) *Theory of the Growth of the Firm*" (Birkinshaw, 2000, p. 83).

Given the rather vague and non-specific nature of the above statements, the question could be raised as to what insights we can really infer from Penrose (1959), so as to understand better subsidiary evolution, especially against the backdrop of regional integration as described in this chapter. In the following, we examine Penrose's (1959) perspective on growth, with a focus on three elements: the 'enterprise of management' (entrepreneurial strength), the 'competence of management' (operational strength), and unused productive resources.

Assumptions in Penrosean analysis

Penrose carefully states that her theory explains the growth of successful firms only, as shown in the following statement:

> The firms with which we shall be concerned are enterprising and possess competent management; our analysis of the processes, possibilities, and direction of growth proceeds on the assumption that these qualities are present in the firm. (Penrose, 1959, p. 32)

In other words, the proposed relationships among the parameters described in the book are valid only when the above qualities are present in the firm. To put it differently, the framework is not generalizable to all firms, and any extensions of Penrose's theory should take this into account.

In this context, an important question needs to be raised as to the well-accepted linkage between slack and innovation (e.g., Bansal, 2003), or between what Penrose calls "unused productive resources" and innovation. Although the terms slack and unused productive resources are used interchangeably, there is actually a minor difference between them. At first sight, it would appear that Penrose suggests a causal relationship between slack and innovation, which may be inferred from statements, such as: "internal inducements to expansion arise largely from the existence of a pool of unused productive services, resources, and specialized knowledge" (Penrose, 1959, p. 66), and "so long as any resources are not used fully in current operations, there is an incentive for a firm to find a way of using them more fully" (Penrose, 1959, p. 67), and "Unused productive services are, for the enterprising firm, at the same time a challenge to innovate, an incentive to expand, and a source of competitive advantage" (Penrose, 1959, p. 85).

The last of the above references is used in Kor and Mahoney (2000) to support their argument that "unused productive services or resources can be a source of innovation" (Kor & Mahoney, 2000, p. 118). However, Penrose's last statement above hints at the importance of the "enterprising" characteristic, i.e., an entrepreneurial strength, as a pre-condition for the deployment of unused productive services. This begs the question what would happen with these unused services in an "un-enterprising firm". Penrose does not provide a clear answer to this question herself, but does emphasize that "failure to grow is often incorrectly attributed to demand conditions rather than to the limited nature of entrepreneurial resources" (Penrose, 1971, p. 38).

Penrose appears to focus on the importance of unused productive resources versus entrepreneurial services at different places in the book (1959), but her discussion of entrepreneurial services has, so far, attracted little attention. However, Penrose always made sure that readers of her work would understand the importance of entrepreneurial strengths, concluding her case study of the Hercules Powder Company by stating that "the entrepreneurship of a firm will largely determine how imaginatively and how rapidly it exploits its potentialities" (Penrose, 1971, p. 63). Penrose thus suggests it is the joint effect on innovation of an entrepreneurial strength and unused productive resources, rather than solely the impact of unused productive resources, that should be assessed.

Similar interactions have been suggested in the literature between slack and other organizational characteristics, when studying how firms respond to environmental parameters (e.g., Cheng & Kesner, 1997; Bansal, 2003). More specifically, slack has been proposed as a moderator of the relationship between organizational values and the scale of the firm's responses to new or important issues (Bansal, 2003). Cheng and Kesner (1997, p. 5) even suggest that:

> Organizational slack does not have an inherent positive or negative effect on the extent of an organization's response to changing environmental conditions . . . Rather, the exact nature of this effect depends on a firm's resource allocation pattern, as influenced by its strategic orientation.

Following Penrose (1959) and the above research on the interactions between slack and other parameters, it appears appropriate to assess unused productive resources in terms of their moderating effect on the relationship between the firm that possesses an entrepreneurial strength, and growth, rather than to view it as the key source of growth by itself. In the context of subsidiary-driven evolution, this approach suggests the need to consider the interactions between the volume of unused productive resources at the subsidiary level and the presence of a subsidiary entrepreneurial strength.

The enterprise of management and the competence of management

Penrose (1959) distinguishes between two specific management characteristics: the "competence of management" and the "enterprise of management". The former "refers to the way in which the managerial function is carried out" (Penrose, 1959, p. 32), e.g., to the firm's operational strengths, while the latter "refers to the entrepreneurial function" (Penrose, 1959, p. 32), e.g., to the firm's entrepreneurial strengths. The "enterprise of management" provides entrepreneurial services, such as those "which (are) related to the introduction and acceptance on behalf of the firm of new ideas, particularly with respect to products, location, and significant changes in technology" (Penrose, 1959, p. 31). In contrast, the "competence of management" relates to "the execution of entrepreneurial ideas and proposals and to the supervision of existing operations" (Penrose, 1959, p. 32). The same individuals may well provide both types of services, but each type is nevertheless conceptually distinct, as they have very different consequences. Penrose noted that "even if a firm is not very ambitious, it may nevertheless be competently managed" (Penrose, 1959, p. 34), and

> [s]uch men may have a high degree of managerial skill and imagination; they may be hard and efficient workers, but the ambition that would drive other men in the same circumstances to expand their operations in an unending search for more profit, and perhaps greater prestige, may be lacking. . . . a good businessman need not be a particularly ambitious one.
>
> *(Penrose, 1959, p. 35)*

The above distinction is also crucial for subsidiary evolution. Obviously, the operational strength of subsidiary management alone, even it is high, will not lead to a stream of subsidiary initiatives, if subsidiary managers do not have an entrepreneurial strength. They may be good implementers of corporate strategy, but an entrepreneurial strength suggests another growth route, namely subsidiary managers looking for new opportunities.

A Penrosean perspective of critical determinants of subsidiary-driven evolution

The analysis above has suggested that, from a Penrosean perspective, the level of unused productive resources, as well as the presence of two other parameters, namely the 'enterprise' (entrepreneurial strengths) and the 'competence' of management (operational strengths) at the subsidiary level, all affect the subsidiary's growth trajectory.

Figure 6.3 can now be constructed to illustrate the four alternative subsidiary evolution possibilities in a regional context.

Subsidiaries in quadrant 1 are those with a high potential for extensive subsidiary initiatives, as illustrated by Birkinshaw's case studies (2000). IBM Scotland can be viewed as a useful example. The management of the IBM Scotland factory successfully attracted the European production of PCs in the early 1980s, and thus grew rapidly. However, "the management were keen not to stop here" (Birkinshaw, 2000, p. 56). They sequentially and successfully proposed the transfer of monitor development to the plant, the consolidation of all order-fulfillment in Scotland, and the creation of a single European PC help center. The key point here is that entrepreneurial managers invest energy to search for new business opportunities, and that the presence of unused productive resources facilitates this search process, thereby supporting Patterns 3 to 6 from our framework described in Figure 6.2.

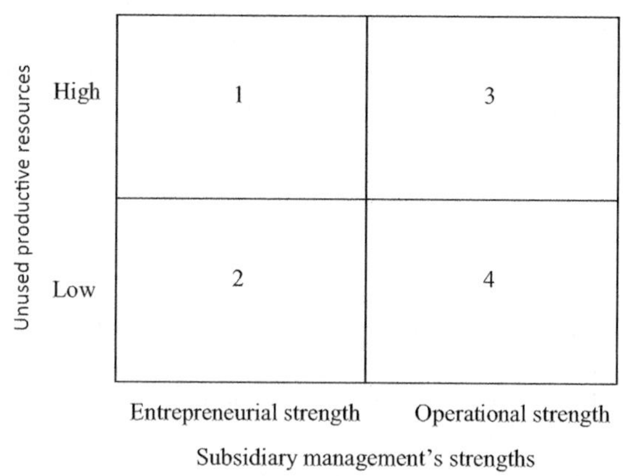

Figure 6.3 A Penrosean perspective of subsidiary evolution

In quadrant 2, the entrepreneurial managers at the subsidiary level do not have access to sufficient resources to implement their ideas. In some cases, they simply do not have enough time or energy to consider new opportunities, because of their participation in current operations, which absorb all of their services. In other cases, they may still be willing to embrace new ideas (e.g., act as entrepreneurs), but limited resources available to them hamper the actual application of these ideas, thus reinforcing Patterns 2 and 7 from our framework in Figure 6.2. In the best-case scenario, a broadening of the business in the subsidiary's country of location materializes, based on the entrepreneurial approach of the subsidiary's managers.

Quadrant 3 helps us to understand the importance of entrepreneurial strengths for subsidiary-driven evolution. Here the subsidiary is characterized by the presence of local management with operational strengths, but lacking in entrepreneurship, in the sense that subsidiary managers focus mainly on the current subsidiary operations. This quadrant will not lead to subsidiary initiatives and related subsidiary-driven charter extension. Rather, any changes in subsidiary roles will be assigned by corporate headquarters. An example documented in Phelps and Fuller (2000) is EngineCo's Welsh affiliate, in which "for the first five to six years, local managers were content with the initial investment" (Phelps & Fuller, 2000, p. 238). Only recently has the affiliate started to search for internal opportunities, as a result of local and parent company pressures. This passive attitude in the pursuit of internal opportunities in spite of the presence of unused productive resources indicates a relative lack of entrepreneurship.

The difference between quadrants 1 and 3 again highlights the interaction between unused productive resources and the "enterprise of management" on subsidiary-driven evolution. Subsidiaries characterized by entrepreneurial strengths will allocate unused productive resources in a proactive way, while those characterized by operational strengths only, will not, thus leading to pattern 2 and in the best case scenario, Pattern 8 in Figure 6.2, with an efficiency focus on expanding extant product lines domestically.

Quadrant 4 reflects efficiently operating subsidiaries with few unused productive resources. In the textbook design of transnational firms, this is the *expected* role of "implementers", as suggested by Bartlett and Ghoshal (1986), "without access to critical information, and having to control scarce resources, these national organizations lack the potential to become contributors to the company's strategic planning" (Bartlett & Ghoshal, 1986, p. 91). An example is the launching of Vizir by Procter & Gamble. Austria, Spain, Holland, and Belgium "took the refined strategy and made it work in their markets" (Bartlett & Ghoshal, 1986, p. 91). Unlike "strategic leaders" or "contributors", which are guided by entrepreneurial leaders, these subsidiary managers are expected only to generate funds for the parent company, following efficiency objectives. This type of organizational design precludes the emergence of subsidiary initiatives and thereby subsidiary-driven charter enhancement. They are especially vulnerable to regional integration, if other units command an equivalent resource base, which may lead to charter losses, as exemplified by Pattern 1 in Figure 6.2: the absence of both entrepreneurial skills of subsidiary management and slack resources in the subsidiary, creates the conditions for losing from regional integration.

Conclusion

In this chapter, we have developed a general framework to understand the influence of regional integration on the dynamics of subsidiary roles. We have also presented eight patterns of subsidiary role evolution, and have examined the key driving factors at the subsidiary level that may influence which subsidiary dynamics will prevail.

First, we highlighted regional integration as an important determinant of subsidiary role dynamics. Though we acknowledge the strategic importance of the local environment, we moved away from a sole focus on the host country and made clear that increasingly, regional integration schemes may make obsolete the concept of the national environment being the main external determinant of subsidiary roles. We emphasized the intraregional reconfiguration of subsidiary activities because of increased competition in similar value chain activities within the region. This regional scope of subsidiary roles corresponds to recent theorizing on internationalization decisions in a semi-globalized world, whereby subsidiaries engage mainly in exploiting and recombining knowledge at the intraregional level, and exploring new business opportunities at the interregional level (Kim & Aguilera, 2015).

Second, at the subsidiary level, we provided a Penrosean analysis of the key, micro-level determinants of changes in subsidiary roles. Here, we made a critical distinction between subsidiary capabilities to manage efficiently current operations and entrepreneurial capabilities. An important implication of linking subsidiary entrepreneurial capabilities with regional integration schemes is that subsidiaries may *assume* new responsibilities at the regional level, thereby becoming intermediate-level units located between the corporate headquarters and local subsidiaries. They may perform entrepreneurial tasks that are different from traditional corporate-level entrepreneurship and subsidiary-level initiatives (Hoenen, Nell & Ambos, 2014). Future research should examine under which conditions subsidiaries are more likely develop into such intermediate-level, region-based units.

References

Ackenhusen, M., Muzyka, D.F. & Churchill, N.C. (1996a) 'Restructuring 3M for an integrated Europe. Part one: Initiating the change', *European Management Journal*, 14, pp. 21–36.

Ackenhusen, M., Muzyka, D.F. & Churchill, N.C. (1996b) 'Restructuring 3M for an integrated Europe. Part Two: Implementing the change', *European Management Journal*, 14, pp. 151–159.

Askegaard, S. & Madsen, T.K. (1998) 'The local and the global: Exploring traits of homogeneity and heterogeneity in European food cultures', *International Business Review*, 7, pp. 549–568.

Bansal, P. (2003) 'From issues to actions: The importance of individual concerns and organizational values in responding to natural environmental issues', *Organization Science*, 14, pp. 510–527.

Bartlett, C.A. & Ghoshal, S. (1986) 'Tap your subsidiaries for global reach', *Harvard Business Review*, 64, pp. 87–94.

Benito, G.R.G., Grogaard, B. & Narula, R. (2003) 'Environmental influences on MNE subsidiary roles: Economic integration and the Nordic countries', *Journal of International Business Studies*, 34, pp. 443–456.

Benito, G.R.G. & Welch, L.S. (1997) 'De-internationalization', *Management International Review*, 37, pp. 7–25.

Birkinshaw, J. (1995) *Entrepreneurship in Multinational Corporations: The Initiative Process in Foreign Subsidiaries*. PhD thesis, University of Western Ontario, Canada.

Birkinshaw, J. (1997) 'Entrepreneurship in multinational corporations: The characteristics of subsidiary initiatives', *Strategic Management Journal*, 18, pp. 207–229.

Birkinshaw, J. (2000) *Entrepreneurship in Global Firms*. London: Sage Publications.

Birkinshaw, J. & Hood, N. (1998) 'Multinational subsidiary evolution: Capability and charter change in foreign-owned subsidiary companies', *Academy of Management Review*, 23, pp. 773–795.

Birkinshaw, J., Hood, N. & Jonsson, S. (1998) 'Building firm-specific advantages in multinational corporations: the role of subsidiary initiative', *Strategic Management Journal*, 19, pp. 221–241.

Birkinshaw, J. & Lingblad, M. (2005) 'Intrafirm competition and charter evolution in the multibusiness firm', *Organization Science*, 16, pp. 674–686.

Birkinshaw, J. & Morrison, A. J. (1995) 'Configurations of strategy and structure in subsidiaries of multinational corporations', *Journal of International Business Studies*, 26, pp. 729–754.

Blank, S. & Haar, J. (1998) *Making NAFTA Work: U.S. Firms and the New North American Business Environment*. Coral Gables, FL: The North-South Center Press at the University of Miami.

Bleackley, M. & Williamson, P. (1997) 'The nature and extent of corporate restructuring within Europe's single market: Cutting through the hype', *European Management Journal*, 15, pp. 484–497.

Buckley, P.J., Clegg, J., Forsans, N. & Reilly, K.T. (2001) 'Increasing the size of the "country": Regional in a economic integration and foreign direct investment globalised world economy', *Management International Review*, 41, pp. 251–274.
Buckley, P.J., Clegg, J., Forsans, N. & Reilly, K.T. (2003) 'Evolution of FDI in the United States in the context of trade liberalization and regionalization', *Journal of Business Research*, 56, pp. 853–857.
Cantwell, J.A. (1987) 'The reorganization of European industries after integration: Selected evidence of the role of multinational enterprise activities', *Journal of Common Market Studies*, 26, pp. 127–151.
Cantwell, J.A. & Mudambi, R. (2005) 'MNE competence-creating subsidiary mandates', *Strategic Management Journal*, 26, pp. 1109–1128.
Cerrato, D. (2006) 'The multinational enterprise as an internal market system', *International Business Review*, 15, pp. 253–277.
Cheng, J.L.C. & Kesner, I.F. (1997) 'Organizational slack and response to environmental shifts: The impact of resource allocation patterns', *Journal of Management*, 23, pp. 1–18.
Cohen, S. & Zysman, J. (1987) *Manufacturing Matters: The Myth of the Post-Industrial Society*. New York: Basic Books.
Delany, E. (2000) 'Strategic development of the multinational subsidiary through subsidiary initiative-taking', *Long Range Planning*, 33, pp. 220–244.
Dunning, J. & Robson, P. (1987) 'Multinational corporate integration and regional economic integration', *Journal of Common Market Studies*, 26, pp. 103–125.
Eden, L. (1996) 'The emerging North American investment regime', *Transnational Corporations*, 5, pp. 61–98.
Fong, C.-M., Ho, H.-L., Weng, L.-C. & Yang, K.-P. (2007) 'The intersubsidiary competition in an MNE: Evidence from the Greater China region', *Canadian Journal of Administrative Sciences*, 24, pp. 45–57.
Ghemawat, P. (2001) 'Distance still matters: The hard reality of global expansion', *Harvard Business Review*, 79, pp. 137–147.
Ghemawat, P. (2003) 'Semiglobalization and International Business strategy', *Journal of International Business Studies*, 34, pp. 138–152.
Ghemawat, P. (2005) 'Regional strategies for global leadership', *Harvard Business Review*, 83, pp. 98–108.
Gupta, A.K. & Govindarajan, V. (1991) 'Knowledge flows and the structure of control within multinational corporations', *Academy of Management Review*, 16, pp. 768–792.
Hoenen, A.K., Nell, P.C. & Ambos, B. (2014) 'MNE entrepreneurial capabilities at intermediate levels: The roles of external embeddedness and heterogeneous environments', *Long Range Planning*, 47, pp. 76–86.
Hogenbirk, A.E. & van Kranenburg, H.L. (2006) 'Roles of foreign owned subsidiaries in a small economy', *International Business Review*, 15, pp. 53–67.
Homburg, C., Krohmer, H. & Workman, J. (1999) 'Strategic consensus and performance: The role of strategy type and market-related dynamism', *Strategic Management Journal*, 20, pp. 339–357.
Hood, N. & Young, S. (1987) 'Inward investment and the EC: UK evidence on corporate integration strategies', *Journal of Common Market Studies*, 26, pp. 193–206.
Houston, M.B., Walker, B.A., Hutt, M.D. & Reingen, P.H. (2001) 'Cross-unit competition for a market charter: The enduring influence of structure', *Journal of Marketing*, 65, pp. 19–34.
Jarillo, J.C. & Martinez, J.I. (1990) 'Different roles for subsidiaries: The case of multinational corporations in Spain', *Strategic Management Journal*, 11, pp. 501–512.
Kim, J.U. & Aguilera, R.V. (2015) 'The world is spiky: An internationalization framework for a semi-globalized world', *Global Strategy Journal*, 5, pp. 113–132.
Kor, Y.Y. & Mahoney, J.T. (2000) 'Penrose's resource-based approach: The process and product of research creativity', *Journal of Management Studies*, 37, pp. 109–139.
Krajewski, S. (1992) *Multinational Firms across the Canada-U.S. Border: An Investigation of Intrafirm Trade and other Activities*. Ottawa: The Conference Board of Canada,
Luo, Y. (2005) 'Toward coopetition within a multinational enterprise: A perspective from foreign subsidiaries', *Journal of World Business*, 40, pp. 71–90.
Luxmore, S., Rugman, A. & Verbeke, A. (1991) 'Corporate strategy and the free trade agreement: Adjustment by Canadian multinational enterprises', *Canadian Journal of Regional Science*, 13, pp. 307–330.
Malhotra, N.K., Agarwal, J. & Baalbaki, I. (1998) 'Heterogeneity of regional trading blocs and global marketing strategies: A multicultural perspective', *International Marketing Review*, 15, pp. 476–506.

McFetridge, D.G. (1995) 'Knowledge, market failure and the multinational enterprise: A comment', *Journal of International Business Studies*, 26, pp. 409–416.

Meyer, K.E., Estrin, S., Bhaumik, S.K. & Peng, M.W. (2008) 'Institutions, resources, and entry strategies in emerging economies', *Strategic Management Journal*, 30, pp. 61–80.

Nestlé. (2006) Website. www.nestle.com.

Pearce, R. & Papanastassiou, M. (1997) 'European markets and the strategic roles of multinational enterprise subsidiaries in the UK', *Journal of Common Market Studies*, 35, pp. 243–266.

Penrose, E.T. (1959) *The Theory of the Growth of the Firm*. Oxford, UK: Oxford University Press.

Penrose, E.T. (1971) *The Growth of the Firm, Middle East Oil and Other Essays*. London: Frank Cass.

Phelps, N.A. & Fuller, C. (2000) 'Multinationals, intracorporate competition, and regional development', *Economic Geography*, 76, pp. 224–243.

Phelps, N.A. & Fuller, C. (2015) 'Inertia and change in multinational enterprise subsidiary capabilities: An evolutionary Economic Geography framework', *Journal of Economic Geography*, 16, pp. 109–130.

Rugman, A. (2000) *The End of Globalization*. London: Random House.

Rugman, A. (2005) *The Regional Multinationals: MNEs and 'Global' Strategic Management*. Cambridge, UK: Cambridge University Press.

Rugman, A.M. & Verbeke, A. (1992) 'A note on the transnational solution and the transaction cost theory of multinational strategic management', *Journal of International Business Studies*, 23, pp. 761–771.

Rugman, A.M. & Verbeke, A. (2001) 'Subsidiary-specific advantages in multinational enterprises', *Strategic Management Journal*, 22, pp. 237–250.

Rugman, A.M. & Verbeke, A. (2004) 'A perspective on regional and global strategies of multinational enterprises', *Journal of International Business Studies*, 35, pp. 3–18.

Rugman, A.M. & Verbeke, A. (2005) *Analysis of Multinational Strategic Management: The Selected Papers of Alan M. Rugman and Alain Verbeke*. Cheltenham, UK and Brookfield, WI: Edward Elgar Publishing.

Rugman, A.M., Verbeke, A. & Yuan, W. (2011) 'Re-conceptualizing Bartlett and Ghoshal's classification of national subsidiary roles in the multinational enterprise', *Journal of Management Studies*, 48, pp. 253–277.

Stopford, J.M. & Baden-Fuller, C. (1987) 'Regional-level competition in a mature industry: The case of European domestic appliances', *Journal of Common Market Studies*, 26, pp. 173–192.

Taggart, J.H. (1997a) 'Autonomy and procedural justice: A framework for evaluating subsidiary strategy', *Journal of International Business Studies*, 28, pp. 51–76.

Taggart, J.H. (1997b) 'An evaluation of the integration-responsiveness framework: MNC manufacturing subsidiaries in the UK', *Management International Review*, 37, pp. 295–318.

Taggart, J.H. (1998) 'Strategy shifts in MNC subsidiaries', *Strategic Management Journal*, 19, pp. 663–681.

Taucher, G. & Toh, T.S. (2003) 'Nestle in ASEAN', *mimeo*, IMD-3-0610 (GM 610), v.01.09.2003.

Tavares, A.T. & Young, S. (2006) 'Sourcing patterns of foreign-owned multinational subsidiaries in Europe', *Regional Studies*, 40, pp. 583–600.

UNCTAD (1992) *World Investment Report 1992: Transnational Corporations as Engines of Growth*. New York: United Nations,

Verbeke, A. & Kano, L. (2016) 'An internalization theory perspective on the global and regional strategies of multinational enterprises', *Journal of World Business*, 51, pp. 83–92.

Verbeke, A., Kano, L. & Yuan, W. (2016) 'Inside the regional multinationals: A new value chain perspective on subsidiary capabilities', *International Business Review*, 25, pp. 785–793.

Verbeke, A. & Yuan, W. (2013) 'The drivers of multinational enterprise subsidiary entrepreneurship in China: A new resource-based view perspective', *Journal of Management Studies*, 50, pp. 236–258.

White, R.E. & Poynter, T.A. (1984) 'Strategies for foreign-owned subsidiaries in Canada', *Business Weekly*, summer, pp. 59–69.

PART II

Some core material in Economic Geography

7

THE CURRENT RESEARCH PROGRAMME IN ECONOMIC GEOGRAPHY

Trevor J. Barnes and Eric Sheppard

Introduction

Economic Geography is a discipline concerned with examining the places and spaces in which economic activities are carried out and circulate. Originating in nineteenth-century Europe, Economic Geography is now a large international field of inquiry found in many countries, with a varied and dense research programme. Especially over the last sixty years, Economic Geography has become a lively, variegated and core sub-discipline within human geography. Moreover, economic geographers have also made a series of important substantive contributions to such topics as industrial districts, spatial labour markets, innovation milieus, global production networks and commodity chains that have received attention beyond the discipline.

Indeed, the term 'Economic Geography' is now widely used outside of human geography (e.g. World Bank, 2009). Stimulated by the work of Paul Krugman, economists especially have developed a rich body of research dubbed the 'new Economic Geography'. This work has close affinities with Economic Geography's location theory tradition influential during the 1960s. The economists' 'new' Economic Geography (new for them), and also labelled geographical economics (Overman, 2004), is closely aligned with contemporary mainstream economic theory; that is, it is grounded in the rational choice of individual self-interested economic agents whose actions are coordinated by the market and produce equilibrium outcomes.

While the external engagement between Economic Geography and geographical economics is important, in this chapter we are concerned principally with the internal research programme of Economic Geography (Barnes, Peck & Sheppard, 2012). We believe that there are four features that hold it together and make it distinctive. First, economic geographers conceptualize geographies of economic activities as co-evolving with the economy: economic processes produce emergent geographies that then shape how those processes unfold. Second, economic geographers examine how economic processes are intimately interrelated with political, cultural and biophysical processes. The economy cannot be hermetically sealed. Commodity production and market exchange are shaped by (even as they shape) political processes, discourses and cultural identities, as well as by the material world (which economic activities seek to transform into forms that humans can use). Third, economic geographers argue that the seeming contemporary predominance of capitalist economic activities should not be mistaken for their inevitability or desirability. More-than-capitalist economic processes – 'diverse economies' – coexist with capitalism, and may be necessary as well as preferable. Consequently, issues of politics, and even morals and ethics, are front and centre within Economic Geography. Finally, Economic Geography is theoretically and methodologically pluralist, receptive and encouraging of varied philosophical assumptions, scales of inquiry (from the globe to the body), conceptual frameworks and styles of empirical investigation (from qualitative to quantitative methods and everything in between).

The consequence of these four features is a research programme that is peculiarly open-ended, willing to study almost anything, especially as it undergoes change, and from any perspective. It is an anti-canonical project, continuously transgressing boundaries. We divide the chapter into two unequal parts. The first provides a brief genealogical account of how Economic Geography came into being, including a discussion of its methods. The second provides selected substantive examples from its research programme to illustrate the breadth of the field and its predilections.

A genealogy of Anglophone Economic Geography

Perhaps more than most social sciences, over its history Economic Geography has experienced a succession of varied approaches. None seem to stick for any prolonged period (unlike, for example, in economics which has stayed with a single general approach for more than a century – neoclassicism). Rather, Economic Geography's intellectual landscape is a palimpsest, with past versions of the discipline still partially visible in the present, not completely erased and continuing to contribute to the subject's vitality and present form. It is a messy discipline, with different approaches continually jostling and rubbing against one another, but along with that has gone energy and vigour. It is a discipline always living in 'interesting times'.

The beginning: commercial and regional geography

Like other academic disciplines originating in the nineteenth century, Economic Geography was tethered to European imperialism. Initially called commercial geography, the discipline's charge was to provide practical geographical knowledge to the agents of Empire: the military, the colonial bureaucracy and the business classes. Focused on the commodity, Economic Geography delivered meticulously detailed empirical information about where goods were produced and their patterns of spatial circulation. It may not have been intellectually riveting, but it provided the commercial scaffolding of Empire. The first-ever English language textbook in Economic Geography was George Chisholm's (1889) *Handbook of Commercial Geography* (even earlier texts existed in German). Jammed with maps, tables and economic geographical facts and figures, the *Handbook* was designed both to give Britain's business classes an applied education and a competitive edge, and its imperial civil servants knowledge of the globe that they administered.

If there was any larger conceptual framework, it was the idea that 'nature', the physical environment, made each place in the world uniquely fitted to undertaking a particular type of economic geographical activity. This view became extreme, however, coloured by racism, through the work of a number of environmental determinists working in Economic Geography at the beginning of the twentieth century. The Yale geographer Ellsworth Huntington (1915) was the most notorious, arguing that labour's "mental" and "physical efficiency" peaked in temperate climatic regimes found in Western Europe, parts of North America and white-settler colonies. In contrast, mental and physical efficiency fell disastrously to low levels in tropical regions, condemning them to "backwardness", making them "The White Man's Burden".

By the end of World War I, Economic Geography was well entrenched in both UK and US universities (Fellmann, 1986). Because of less rampant forms of colonialism and criticism of environmental determinism, there was also a turn away from the commodity as such, and its constitutive environmental conditions. Instead, the emphasis became the region, and conceived as the sum of its heterogeneous component elements. The task of the regional economic geographer was to classify those elements for every region using a common typological scheme, for example, "leading industries", "natural resources", "modes of transportation". Once the facts of each region were classified under a set of common categories, by reading along any given row of the typology it was immediately evident how one regional economy differed from another. For example, Vernor Finch's and Ray Whitbeck's (1924) *Economic Geography* used a fourfold classification scheme for each of the regions the book covered: agriculture; minerals; manufacture; and commercial trade, transportation and communications. That typology functioned as a grid into which regional facts, variously mapped, drawn, photographed and described, could be slotted. By typologically comparing the facts of different regions, economic geographical difference was transparent, and regional uniqueness shone by its own light.

The intellectual justification for this regional approach wasn't articulated until just before World War II. The American geographer Richard Hartshorne argued that by its very nature each region was a collection of exceptional features, describable only in their own terms. Consequently, no generalizing theories, no scientific laws, were possible. As Hartshorne (1939, p. 44) famously wrote, "Regional geography, we conclude, is literally what its title expresses . . . It is essentially a descriptive science concerned with the description and interpretation of unique cases".

Spatial science and the turn to theory

Hartshorne's (1939) book was published at exactly the wrong time. The regional descriptivism it proposed for geography, and Economic Geography in particular, was increasingly out of step with a number of contemporaneous social sciences and even humanities that were moving in completely the opposite direction. Those disciplines rather than embracing the type of descriptivism championed by Hartshorne instead emphasized scientific generalization and explanation, and designed to accomplish practical ends. In part because of Hartshorne's influence, Economic Geography initially resisted that impulse, but by the mid-1950s it began to join in too. The resulting shift to spatial science profoundly altered Economic Geography. It swept away talk of descriptive regionalism, replacing it with scientific forms of general spatial theorizing and statistical modelling and analysis.

Spatial science was defined by five features. First and foremost, there was its use of formal theories and explanatory models. Necessarily, these were imported from elsewhere: from economics (rational choice theory, general and partial equilibrium, and German location theory); and perhaps less likely, from physics (gravity and potential models, and later the entropy model). Second, there was utilization of an arsenal of sophisticated quantitative methods. At first they were off-the-peg, standard textbook statistical techniques, but later they were designed in-house to meet the peculiar features of the geographical case. Third, there was the deployment of the computer. At first it was crude and limited, but within a decade it performed hitherto unimaginable calculations at unimaginable speeds. Fourth, a philosophical justification was made for spatial science based on positivism, the idea that only the scientific approach guaranteed true knowledge (Harvey, 1969). Finally, there was a focus on abstract spatialities. Regions remained part of the economic geographical lexicon, but were now conceived utterly differently. Regions were explanatory, theoretical and instrumental, spatial units to achieve policy and planning objectives (and brilliantly realized in the parallel intellectual movement of regional science).

More than anything else, spatial science represented the introduction of theory, making Economic Geography for the first time a proper social science. While Economic Geography subsequently radically changed, the tie that bound all its subsequent versions was the concern with theory. Contemporary economic geographers might now reject spatial science, but through their continuing theoretical sensibility they are heirs to that earlier tradition.

Many flowers bloom: post-spatial science

The first signs of trouble for spatial science came in the early 1970s when former high-profile supporters became turncoats (Harvey, 1972). In retrospect, the problem was that the mathematically abstract and narrow conception of Economic Geography spatial science proffered was not true: to Economic Geography's variegated disciplinary history; to the historical moment of the early 1970s defined by social and political relevance; and to its own logic, as assorted contradictions, inconsistencies and *aporias* revealed. Consequently, since the 1970s, there has been a ceaseless proliferation of theoretical alternatives to spatial science. For the most part these alternative theories are couched not in terms of science as such. Nonetheless they are used to explain, and in some cases to intervene, within a robustly drawn and variegated empirical world.

In the early 1970s, Harvey introduced classical Marxism as his theoretical alternative to spatial science, and on which he continues to draw and find creative inspiration. Yet Marxist theory is only one component of a larger political economy tradition that more or less has dominated Economic Geography since that time. By political economy we mean the tradition that stems from Classical Economics that stresses economic processes cannot be understood without attention to politics and the state. As a larger approach, political economy has subsequently taken many different forms, some of which are in sharp disagreement with one another. In rough chronological order, following Harvey's classical Marxism, political economy was taken up in Economic Geography as Doreen Massey's (1984) spatial divisions of labour thesis; the locality approach (Cooke, 1989); as regulation theory, and taken primarily from French economists and influential in understanding both the decline of Fordism and the rise of post-Fordism (Scott & Storper, 1986); and an institutional approach concerned with identifying formative mechanisms of industrial districts, applied particularly to high-tech agglomerations (Amin & Thrift, 1992).

Yet this list takes us up only to the mid-1990s. Since then it has become only more complicated and variegated. Uneasily bolted onto political economy was a cultural approach ("the cultural turn"), one form of which was especially associated with examining issues of gender and drawing on poststructural feminist theory (McDowell, 1999). Gibson-Graham's (1996) *The End of Capitalism (As We Knew It)* was perhaps the most influential of those works, eclectically piecing together post-Marxism, feminism and post-structuralism into a critique of political economy that proposed a new substantive disciplinary agenda of research on alternative or 'diverse economies'. More recently, and remaining more or less within political economy have been: German geographers who drew on science studies to explore the geographical performativity of markets (Berndt & Boeckler, 2012); Dutch and other European geographers who added space to evolutionary economic models to examine firm dynamics, and the implications for the regions in which they are located (Boschma & Martin, 2010); and Asian and European economic geographers who developed network models (the Global Production Network is the most well-known) to understand contemporary globalization and regional economic development especially in Asia (Coe & Yeung, 2015).

Last but not least, European and North American scholars based at the London School of Economics have reconstructed a version of spatial science that is formal, resting on neoclassical micro-economic principles, deploying rigorous econometric testing and aspiring to influence government policy. Its intellectual basis was the 1990s work of the Nobel-prize winning economist Paul Krugman that turned on his innovative theorization of the relation between spatial growth, trade and agglomeration economies. That work catalysed a "new Economic Geography" or "geographical economics" (Brakman, Garretsen & von Marrewijk, 2009), leading to attempts to strike up a disciplinary conversation between geographers and economists, including a relatively new journal, *The Journal of Economic Geography* (launched in 2001).

In less than 150 years, Anglophone Economic Geography moved from a handmaiden of Empire to physics envy to an intellectually open, eclectic, pluralist and possibly chaotic discipline straddling the humanities and social sciences. Its seeming lack of a theoretical core can be disconcerting, however. Critics complain that the subject comes close to anarchy. Certainly, it has produced Balkanization, a discipline of many theoretical solitudes (Barnes & Sheppard, 2010). The counter response is that fragmented theorizing is necessary to understand the increasingly fragmented contemporary geographical economy. Another is that it makes for an exciting discipline, with no longer any chance, as a commentator once put it, of Economic Geography "boring its audience to death" (Thrift, 2000, p. 692). The unusual challenge for Economic Geography is less breaking new ground, which it seems now to do on a daily basis, than holding its existing ground.

Methodological diversity

Along with Economic Geography's theoretical diversity has also gone methodological diversity. Increasingly anything goes. Admittedly, economic geographers have not been very good in talking openly about their methods. The topic seems to be subject to a "don't ask, don't tell" policy. That said, economic geographers of all stripes have been concerned from the beginning of the discipline with the common end of empirical representation. Under commercial geography, that meant the assiduous collection of information that was as precise as possible, ideally numbers and statistics. Under spatial science the bar was raised to aspire to positivism; that is, the rigorous statistical testing of theory-driven hypotheses against the facts. Post-spatial science ushered in a qualitative revolution, a move to methods concerned with gathering and analysing non-numerical data. This was motivated in part by trenchant criticisms of the positivist philosophy underlying spatial science – criticisms that stressed the theory-laden nature of observation.

Economic Geography's qualitative revolution began with intensive case-study research pioneered by proponents of the methodology of critical realism in the early 1980s (Sayer, 1984). Since then those methods have multiplied and include now: in-depth interviews, focus groups, oral histories, ethnographies, participant observation, discourse and textual analysis, social network analysis, action research and much more besides. In this new methodological environment, nothing is proscribed, everything is permitted. Critics complain that the turn to qualitative methods in Economic Geography has induced slapdash and superficial research. In response, qualitative researchers stress that rigour means different things in different contexts. What is most important is that methods are appropriate to the data.

The qualitative revolution in methods has produced, as with the theoretical changes, disciplinary diversity and transformation. Most of the qualitative techniques listed earlier even in the 1990s would have been viewed as beyond the pale, or at best, suspiciously *avant garde*. Now they are run-of-the-mill. The downside of the qualitative revolution has been the derogation of quantitative analysis and loss of associated skills. Lacking the training, economic geographers are increasingly unable to undertake, or knowledgably critique, statistical and numerical analysis.

The current research programme

It is impossible to define the entire research programme of Economic Geography in a short chapter. Our approach is to identify and summarize briefly, research in eight active substantive clusters within the discipline.

Industry and services

From the beginning, economic geographers were interested in what was produced where, and how. Those questions continue to resonate, and within contemporary Economic Geography, three major areas of work stand out at the scale of the firm, the region and the globe.

At the firm level, emphasis is on understanding how firms make decisions, and the role that space plays. A useful recent body of literature is evolutionary Economic Geography. Drawing an analogy between a firm and a species, Darwin's theory of evolution is used in evolutionary Economic Geography to understand the effects of competition on the survivability and transformations of firms within a region. Unlike economics that focuses on a single rational agent, evolutionary Economic Geography begins with a population of firms varied in size, technology, strategy and labour relations. Hypothesizing that each firm has a production routine, and analogous to genes in organisms, evolutionary Economic Geography argues that the dynamics of a given regional population of firms depends on three processes: variation (between firms); selection (of firms through competition); and retention (the propagation of routines within and between firms). Given these processes, why do some regions experience lock-in, with their economic structures becoming stagnant, while others are dynamic, attracting emergent growth sectors? Evolutionary Economic Geography suggests it is a result of the variation within a region's population of firms. The more that firms are similar, the greater are localization economies and the more likelihood of innovation. When they are less similar (unrelated variety), there are fewer such advantages with the regions tending towards lock-in and economic sluggishness (Boschma & Iammarino, 2009; Boschma & Martin, 2010).

At the regional scale, economic geographers have tried to identify key factors in growth. The most important is agglomeration economies, the result of reduced transactions costs, tacit knowledge or local 'buzz', the socio-cultural milieu and the presence of a 'creative class'. Each of these agglomeration advantages enhances regional economic dynamism and flexibility under the right conditions, but equally they can produce regional decline under the wrong ones. Within this work the most important forms of regional economies are extended industrial districts, learning regions and city-regions (Scott, 2006; Storper, 2013).

At the global scale, economic geographers recognize that many economic activities are increasingly spatially decentralized, with different locations around the world playing different roles in the production and assembly of a commodity. Multinational corporations, surrounded by dense networks of sub-contractors and licensees, spread production around the world in a process that Richard Baldwin (2006) dubs "the great unbundling" of production. Those studying this unbundling examine not only the economic and power relations constituting the resulting production networks (global production networks) – some firms exert enormous influence while others are just bit players – but they also trace how the spatial strategies of states, labour unions and multilateral governance organizations each affect the resulting structures (Coe et al., 2004).

Worlds of consumption

Consumer markets were traditionally studied in terms of the location of retailers, consumer behaviour and the spatial price gradients. The use of central place theory from the 1950s led to a general theorization of the monopolistic nature of spatial market, which challenged conventional economics. Since the 1990s, geographers studying retailing have turned their attention to the spatial strategies of corporate retailers, including their roles within global production networks. This recent research aligns with how economic geographers characteristically begin with geographies of production, unlike mainstream economists who instead focus on markets and consumption (Coe & Wrigley, 2009).

With the advent of post-structural and feminist theory in Economic Geography, recent research has examined the relationship between retailers, consumption and consumer identity, with particular attention paid to issues of social difference; that is, identity formation formed at the intersection of gender, class, race, sexuality and geographical location (Jackson & Holbrook, 1995; Cook & Woodyear, 2012; Mansvelt, 2012). The work is especially concerned with how consumers' desires emerge from, and intersect with, their socio-spatial positionality, and how they also relate to marketing strategies (branding, store location and spatial organization).

More recently, economic geographers have taken up the question of marketization: how have spatial markets emerged and what are the implications? Here geographers have drawn on economic sociology rather than economics. They have examined how information networks unequally shape participants' ability to take advantage of markets ("the strength of weak ties"), how trading technologies shape market structure and performance, and how markets themselves are produced. In this work, market formations are regarded as emergent features, shaped by theoretical predispositions, ideology (e.g. neoliberalism), interests, technologies and geographies. If perfect markets emerge, it is because participants believe in their desirability and/or actively create them. Turning to the uneven geographies of marketization, economic geographers have examined the construction and elimination of boundaries, both those separating markets and those separating what is sold as a commodity and what is not (Grabher, 2006; Berndt & Boeckler, 2012; Gidwani, 2012; Parry, 2012).

Labour, work and bodies

From the beginnings of the discipline, labour was considered an important economic geographical factor influencing the location of firms and industry. But there was no analysis of labour markets as such, and nothing on either the conditions defining work, or especially the kinds of bodies doing the work. That changed in the 1970s when radical economic geographers began emphasizing the centrality of labour within production and the role of a distinct social and political class, the working class (Lier, 2007). The 1970s, though, was exactly the decade when old verities about labour, work, bodies and the working class changed. Hitherto labour in the Global North was conceived as expending brawn working in a factory (engaged in execution rather than conception). The bodies examined were predominantly male bodies, and the social class to which they belonged was the working class. That became less and less true, though, as the larger processes of deindustrialization, neoliberalism and globalization gained purchase during the 1980s, it became necessary to theorize labour geography. While elements of radical geography's approach were retained in that theorization, many new elements were added, drawn from poststructuralism, especially feminist and postcolonial theory, and emphasizing identity, embodiment and transnationalism.

From the 1970s, deindustrialization decimated traditional male Fordist industrial jobs in the Global North. It was the end of "Father Ford", provoking a crisis in masculine identity especially for young males (McDowell, 1991). Furthermore, with the roll-out of neoliberalism from 1980, traditional unions were also undermined. Manufacturing jobs in the Global North were moved offshore, often to the Global South, and within unfolding global production networks.

Operating from Free Trade Zones, large multinational corporations drew on abundant, very cheap labour, including pools of young women, who laboured excessive hours, and were subjected to extreme disciplinary measures both inside the factory and outside. They became the world's "disposable labour" (Wright, 2006).

Attention was also given to low-paid service workers in the Global North, especially women, international migrants and workers of colour. Their employment was increasingly precarious, creating a "precariat", and defined by part-timeism, short-term contracts and the absence of benefits (Theodore & Peck, 2013). That was not true at the opposite end of the labour market, and made up of highly paid knowledge workers (Richard Florida's 2002 "creative class"). They might also be on contract, carrying out project work, but they received high incomes, allowing them to choose in which country they lived, the city or the neighbourhood. The larger point is that labour and work are not neutral. Workers are always more than a technical input into production. The social, cultural and geographical contexts in which work is practised leaves its mark (sometimes literally), shaping social identity, bodily comportment and the life led, including where it is led geographically.

Governance and regulation

Since the 1980s, economic geographers have been concerned especially with state forms of economic regulation and governance. Regulation refers to rules enacted by state and quasi-state agencies at various scales to constrain the actions of both producers and consumers, while governance denotes forms of economic control executed by and through non-state institutions.

During the 1980s and 1990s, economic geographers drew extensively on so-called French regulation theory. That school argued that every economy was composed of two structural parts: a regime of accumulation (how commodity production was undertaken); and a mode of regulation (how the state controlled the market to manage the national balance between supply and demand) (Dunford, 1990). Originally developed to explain the emergence and problems of post-War Fordism as a national territorial economic system, economic geographers extended the theory to consider geographical scale and spatial variegation. They examined how regulatory regimes varied across space at the national scale, reflecting the persistence of national cultural and political traditions – variegated capitalisms (Peck & Theodore, 2007). They also argued that local governments within a national territory could develop regulatory norms that differed from those at the national level (Tickell & Peck, 1992).

Particularly at the sub-national scale, much attention was paid to how local states acted to foster investment in their territory. Urban entrepreneurial strategies included both inward investment tactics, e.g. subsidies and improvements to the local "business climate", designed to persuade firms (and knowledge workers) to move in (or stay), as well as incubator strategies to create conditions that fostered local innovation, dynamism and agglomeration economies (Hall & Hubbard, 1998).

Neoliberal forms of regulation and governance that first emerged during the 1980s have attracted much recent attention in the discipline (Larner, 2000; Harvey, 2006; Peck, 2010). There has been both an analysis of the diffusion of neoliberalism across space and time, as well as an examination of so-called policy mobilities; that is, the geographical spread of neoliberal "best practice" policy principles (Peck & Theodore, 2010). Important debates remain, however, about the ubiquity of neoliberalism and strategies of contestation (Leitner, Peck & Sheppard, 2007).

Finally, economic geographers have examined the various forms of institutional governance that bear on territorial economies. They have been particularly interested in the conditions under which institutions either facilitate or block regional and urban economic dynamism. Institutions can channel regional economic development along certain paths (path dependence), and while some paths are beneficial (cultivating regional assets), others result in stagnation (institutional lock-in). These alternatives have been discussed under the term "regional resilience" (Martin, 2000).

Finance

Until the 1990s, economic geographers paid scant attention to money and finance. Since then such inquiries have burgeoned massively. Sparking that research in part was the claim by some non-geographers that global financial markets, hooked together by leading-edge information technologies, were now beyond geography; place and distance no longer mattered. The counterclaim by economic geographers was that place and distance continued to be utterly essential. Certainly, face-to-face communication remained critical, and explaining why global financial markets were so concentrated in such a small number of sites, e.g. London, New York and Tokyo. Furthermore, digital networks have led to an extreme spatial concentration of high frequency trading servers to gain a millisecond advantage over competitors. In addition, economic geographers also examined spatially differentiated kinds of lending, uneven geographies of financial governance and the role of place-specific institutional actors such as pension funds and real estate investment trusts (Leyshon & Thrift, 1997; Clark & Wójcik, 2007).

There has also been much discussion about financialization and globalization. Echoing related scholarship in anthropology, economic geographers have argued that financialization is as much cultural as economic, and as a practice has seeped deeply into everyday life. There are now multiple ways, both real and discursive, in which financial investment and credit underwrite so many ordinary geographical activities (Pike & Pollard, 2010; Christophers, 2013).

Material worlds

The material worlds of nature and resources have been the focus of animated disciplinary discussions from the very start of the discipline, and for good reason. Currently around 50 trillion tonnes of the earth's material resources are annually appropriated for one human use or another, transformed into primary commodities by the "metabolic engine" of the economy (Bridge, 2009, p. 1222).

When Economic Geography was first institutionalized in the late nineteenth century, the discipline was primarily about material worlds and codified as meticulous lists of natural resources, their geographical distribution and corollary environmental conditions. Interest waned in the 1920s and 1930s, and under post-War spatial science the topic of "natural resources" became an intellectual backwater. Drawing upon Marx, David Harvey (1974) reinvigorated the subject. His was not nature "red-in-tooth-and-claw" but social-nature, the production of nature. One of capitalism's imperatives, Harvey argued, was to transform original "first" nature into a produced "second nature" (Smith, 1984). In the process, nature was commodified, subject to the market, becoming hybrid: nature and society joined forming "socio-nature" (Castree & Braun, 2001). But to become a commodity, conditions have to be just right. As Erich Zimmerman (1951, pp. 814–815) famously put it: "resources are not: they become". Coal is merely a rock that makes your hands dirty until capitalism invents the steam engine. Once capitalism emerges, pre-existing nature is transformed, however. Nature still exists, but how it is exploited, used, thought about and represented is irredeemably and sometimes cataclysmically altered.

When Harvey linked nature to political economy, Economic Geography began to overlap in interests with political ecology that similarly brought a political economic understanding to resource use and production within initially the Global South. Michael Watts' (2004) work in Nigeria was exemplary. It showed how social relationships, first under imperialism then under independence, made the country's natural resources neither natural nor even a resource, creating instead mal-development, inequality and social mayhem.

Another political economic approach, Immanuel Wallerstein's world systems theory, provided a complementary framework, the global commodity chain. By following the "thing" – a papaya, a cut flower, a barrel of oil – as it moved along the line from different producers in different places to the final consumer revealed: (i) the differential forms and effects of materiality; (ii) the diverse geographies inherent in all commodities; (iii) the asymmetrical socio-geographical relationships within the production process; and (iv) the uneven effects of state regulatory regimes (Cook & Woodyear, 2012).

The most recent body of work about resources elaborates precisely on this last point, focusing on how one regulatory regime in particular, neoliberalism, has stamped nature in its own likeness. As different as water, fish, trees, ores and CO_2 may seem, under neoliberalism they have all become privatized, commodified, priced and marketed. Geography, continues to remain vital, however. Each place does neoliberalism differently, creating not one seamless landscape of indistinguishable processes but a patchwork quilt of variegated resource regimes (Heynen et al., 2007).

Globalization and development

For many years, Anglophone economic geographers concentrated their effort on the parts of the world they inhabited, those of the first world – Europe, Japan and the white settler colonies of North America, Australia, South Africa and New Zealand. With the implosion of the Soviet sphere, attention turned to questions of 'transition' towards capitalism in the post-Soviet world. Yet the 'third world' – those countries whose inhabitants suffered from colonialism and still struggled to overcome the economic disadvantages and global peripheralization they inherited from colonialism – was largely left to what was styled 'development geography'. Since the late 2000s, recognizing that problems of under-development in the post-colonial world differ in scale rather than kind from those of impoverished regions in the first world, economic geographers increasingly turned to study the post-colonial, integrating development with Economic Geography (Slater, 2004; Lawson, 2007). In so doing, economic geographers focused on development at all geographical scales, tracing the inter-connections.

Globally, economic geographers have asked why uneven geographical development remains so persistent despite the increasing interconnectedness of the global economy. Does free trade and the unrestricted movement of direct and portfolio investment level the global playing field, or does it reinforce pre-existing inequalities? Challenging the tendency in development economics to attribute success or failure to local, place-based characteristics (culture, physical geography, governance institutions), economic geographers argue that the uneven relation connecting places – the flows and mobilities of commodities, finance, ideas and people – may be equally important in determining the wealth of territories (Sheppard, 2011). They examine not only how local possibilities are shaped by broader-scale processes, but also how local events trigger significant broader-scale consequences. Both disciplines have a strong current interest in development, although they have rather different interests and perspectives on the relationship between globalization and development. Economic geographers place more emphasis on uneven development and why some places fail to grow rapidly, whereas International Business scholars have more interest in why some places have developed rapidly, above all China, and the implications this has for MNE strategies, both MNEs from developed and emerging economies.

At the local scale, economic geographers have been interested in how to improve livelihood prospects. They have shown that traditional practices are often better adjusted to local circumstances than modern practices that were introduced to replace them. The focus has been on the diversity of economic practices, their relation to the biophysical environment and the role of power and constructed identities (race, age, class, caste, gender) in shaping these practices. Substantive topics have ranged from peasant farming and subsistence, to informal housing and economic practices, to formal employment in export processing zones, and connections between these places and practices (Rankin, 2004).

In addition, economic geographers have questioned the universality of development as an idea, as well as its crystallization in so-called 'improvement schemes' foisted on many post-colonial regions in the Global South. Specifically, they have turned to interrogating Northern definitions of development – as the product of globalizing capitalism – distinguishing between development, as the set of practices that arise in a particular geographical context that have enabled its residents to live well, and Development as a universal definition imposed on all people and places, and against which their progress should be judged (Hart, 2002).

Diverse economies

Dating back to commercial geography, economic geographers have long taken an interest in different economic practices found across the world. As ideas of development spread from the North Atlantic realm, non-capitalist practices were conceived as traditional and backward, as in need of replacement by integration into globalizing capitalism. Even economic geographers critical of capitalism tended to accept capitalist practices, and now globally hegemonic, as the only kind of economic activity worth examining.

This default position has been progressively questioned since the late 1990s, leading to proliferating research on non-capitalist, 'diverse economies'. Formative was *The End of Capitalism (As We Knew It)* by J. K. Gibson-Graham (1996) that forcefully argued that many non-capitalist economic practices continued to co-exist with capitalism. Connecting Marxism with feminist and post-structural theory, they argued that these diverse economies deserved far more attention from economic geographers than they have received given that they are a locus for potential alternatives to globalizing capitalism.

The result of Gibson-Graham's work has been the emergence of a branch of Anglophone Economic Geography devoted to the study of diverse economies. Beyond the study of such practices, economic geographers have worked with communities. They have brought both an awareness about such practices, and fostered and expanded them using novel forms of academic research. This work has been criticized for focusing on seemingly insignificant and marginal practices. Nevertheless, it has brought attention to the different forms that an economy can take, and more generally how it might be contested (Gibson-Graham, Cameron & Healy, 2013).

Conclusion

The on-going vitality and diversity of the Anglophone economic geographical research programme promises a bright future. Its practitioners, however, must be willing to engage constructively with one another and with scholars in cognate disciplines like economics and business studies. Economic geographers examine how economic processes shape, and are shaped by, geographical space (place, scale, connectivity, mobility); they examine how economic processes co-evolve with political, cultural and biophysical processes; they study how subject formation and identity at one end, and global political economic structures at the other, are interrelated; they take an interest in non-capitalist economic processes, and are critical of the proposition that regulated capitalist markets optimize societal wellbeing and ecological sustainability. Real-world oriented, economic geographers study some of the major challenges facing contemporary human society and its relation to political economic processes: global production networks, the politics and culture of consumption, work and labour, the role of state regulation and governance institutions, nature-economy relations, financialization, globalization and development, and diverse economic systems.

Of course, there are gaps in Economic Geography's research programme. For example, much more needs to be done on logistics, a key to globalization, as well as on the frightening and pressing environmental challenges that the world faces such as global climate change. It is our hope, though, that these and other issues will be taken up in the spirit of engaged pluralism across different approaches, national communities and related disciplines.

References

Amin, A. & Thrift, N.J. (1992) 'Neo-marshallian nodes in global networks', *International Journal of Urban and Regional Research*, 16, pp. 571–587.

Baldwin, R. (2006) *Globalisation: The Great Unbundling(s)*. Helsinki: Prime Minister's Office: Economic Council of Finland.

Barnes, T.J., Peck, J. & Sheppard, E. (Eds.) (2012) *The Wiley-Blackwell Companion to Economic Geography*. Oxford, UK: Wiley-Blackwell.

Barnes, T.J. & Sheppard, E. (2010) '"Nothing includes everything". Towards engaged pluralism in Anglophone Economic Geography', *Progress in Human Geography*, 34, pp. 193–214.

Berndt, C. & Boeckler, M. (2012) 'Geographies of marketization', in Barnes, T.J., Peck, J. & Sheppard, E. (Eds), *The Wiley-Blackwell Companion to Economic Geography*. Oxford, UK: Wiley-Blackwell, pp. 199–212.

Boschma, R.A. & Iammarino, S. (2009) 'Related variety, trade linkages, and regional growth in Italy', *Economic Geography*, 85, pp. 289–311.

Boschma, R.A. & Martin, R. (Eds.) (2010) *The Handbook of Evolutionary Economic Geography*. Cheltenham, UK: Edward Elgar.

Brakman, S., Garretsen, H. & von Marrewijk, C. (2009) *A New Introduction to Geographical Economics*. Cambridge, UK: Cambridge University Press.

Bridge, G. (2009) 'Material worlds: Natural resources, resource geography and the material economy', *Geography Compass*, 3, pp. 1217–1244.

Castree, N. & Braun, B. (Eds.) (2001) *Social Nature: Theory, Practice and Politics*. Oxford, UK: Blackwell Publishers.

Chisholm, G.G. (1889) *Handbook of Commercial Geography*. London and New York: Longman, Green, and Co.

Christophers, B. (2013) *Banking across Boundaries: Placing Finance in Capitalism*. New York: Wiley.

Clark, G.L. & Wójcik, D. (2007) *The Geography of Finance*. Oxford, UK: Oxford University Press.

Coe, N.M, Hess, M., Yeung, H. W.-C., Dicken, P. & Henderson, J. (2004) '"Globalizing" regional development: A global production networks perspective', *Transactions of the Insititute of British Geographers*, 29, pp. 468–484.

Coe, N.M. & Wrigley, N. (Eds.) (2009) *The Globalization of Retailing*. Cheltenham, UK: Edward Elgar.

Coe, N.M. & Yeung, H. W.-C. (2015) *Global Production Networks: Theorizing Economic Development in an Interconnected World*. Oxford, UK: Oxford University Press.

Cook, I. & Woodyear, T. (2012) 'Lives of things', in Barnes, T.J., Peck, J. & Sheppard, E. (Eds), *The Wiley-Blackwell Companion to Economic Geography*. Oxford, UK: Wiley-Blackwell, pp. 226–241.

Cooke, P. (Ed.) (1989) *Localities*. London: Unwin Hyman.

Dunford, M. (1990) 'Theories of regulation', *Environment and Planning D: Society and Space*, 8, pp. 297–322.

Fellmann, J.D. (1986) 'Myth and reality in the origin of American Economic Geography', *Annals of the Association of American Geographers*, 76, pp. 313–330.

Finch, V. & Whitbeck, R. (1924) *Economic Geography*. New York: McGraw Hill.

Florida, R. (2002) *The Rise of the Creative Class*. New York: Basic Books.

Gibson-Graham, J.K. (1996) *The End of Capitalism (As We Knew It): A Feminist Critique of Political Economy*. Oxford, UK: Blackwell.

Gibson-Graham, J.K., Cameron, J. & Healy, S. (2013) *Take Back the Economy, Any Time, Any Place*. Minneapolis, MN: University of Minnesota Press.

Gidwani, V. (2012) 'Waste/value', in T.J. Barnes, J. Peck and E. Sheppard (Eds.), *The Wiley-Blackwell Companion to Economic Geography*. Oxford, UK: Wiley-Blackwell, pp. 275–288.

Grabher, G. (2006) 'Trading routes, bypasses and risky intersections: Mapping the migration of "networks" between economic sociology and Economic Geography', *Progress in Human Geography*, 30, pp. 163–189.

Hall, T. & Hubbard, P. (Eds.) (1998) *The Entrepreneurial City*. London: John Wiley & Sons.

Hart, G. (2002) *Disabling Globalization: Places of Power in Post-Apartheid South Africa*. Berkeley, CA: University of California Press.

Hartshorne, R. (1939) *The Nature of Geography: A Critical Survey of Current Thought in Light of the Past*. Lancaster, PA: Association of American Geographers.

Harvey, D. (1969) *Explanation in Geography*. London: Edward Arnold.

Harvey, D. (1972) 'Revolutionary and counter revolutionary theory in geography and the problem of ghetto formation', *Antipode*, 4, pp. 1–13.

Harvey, D. (1974) 'Population, resources and the ideology of science', *Economic Geography*, 50, pp. 256–277.

Harvey, D. (2006) *A Brief History of Neoliberalism*. Oxford, UK: Oxford University Press.

Heynen, N.C., McCarthy, J., Prudham, S. & Robbins, P. (Eds.) (2007) *Neoliberal Environments: False Promises and Unnatural Consequences*. London: Routledge.

Huntington, E. (1915) *Civilization and Climate*. New Haven, CT: Yale University Press.

Jackson, P. & Holbrook, B. (1995) 'Multiple meanings: Shopping and the cultural politics of identity', *Environment and Planning A*, 27, pp. 1913–1930.

Larner, W. (2000) 'Neoliberalism: Policy, ideology, governmentality', *Studies in Political Economy*, 63, pp. 5–25.

Lawson, V. (2007) *Making Development Geography*. London: Routledge.

Leitner, H., Peck, J. & Sheppard, E. (Eds.) (2007) *Contesting Neoliberalism: Urban Frontiers*. New York: Guilford.

Leyshon, A. & Thrift, N. (1997) *Money/Space: Geographies of Monetary Transformation*. London: Routledge.

Lier, D. (2007) 'Places of work, scales of organising: A review of labour geography', *Geography Compass*, 1, pp. 814–833

Mansvelt, J. (2012) 'Making consumers and consumption', in Barnes, T.J., Peck, J. & Sheppard, E. (Eds.), *The Wiley-Blackwell Companion to Economic Geography*. Oxford, UK: Wiley-Blackwell, pp. 444–457.

Martin, R. (2000) 'Institutional approaches in Economic Geography', in Sheppard, E. & Barnes, T. (Eds.), *A Companion to Economic Geography*. Oxford, UK: Blackwell, pp. 77–94.

Massey, D. (1984) *Spatial Divisions of Labour*. London: MacMillan.

McDowell, L. (1991) 'Life without father and Ford: The new gender order of post-Fordism', *Transactions of the Insititute of British Geographers*, 16, pp. 400–419.

McDowell, L. (1999) *Gender, Identity, Place: Understanding Feminist Geographies*. Minneapolis, MN: University of Minnesota Press.

Overman, H. (2004) 'Can we learn anything from Economic Geography proper?' *Journal of Economic Geography*, 4, pp. 501–516.

Parry, B. (2012) 'Economies of bodily commodification', in Barnes, T.J., Peck, J. & Sheppard, E. (Eds.), *The Wiley-Blackwell Companion to Economic Geography*. Oxford, UK: Wiley-Blackwell, pp. 213–225.

Peck, J. (2010) *Constructions of Neoliberal Reason*. Oxford, UK: Oxford University Press.

Peck, J. & Theodore, N. (2007) 'Variegated capitalism', *Progress in Human Geography*, 31, pp. 731–772.

Peck, J. & Theodore, N. (2010) 'Mobilizing policy: Models, methods, and mutations', *Geoforum*, 41, pp. 169–174.

Pike, A. & Pollard, J. (2010) 'Economic geographies of financialization', *Economic Geography*, 86, pp. 29–51.

Rankin, K.N. (2004) *The Cultural Politics of Markets: Economic Liberalization and Social Change in Nepal*. Toronto: University of Toronto Press.

Sayer, A. (1984) *Method in Social Science: A Realist Approach*. London: Hutchinson.

Scott, A.J. (2006) *Global City-Regions*. Oxford, UK: Oxford University Press.
Scott, A.J. & Storper, M. (Eds.) (1986) *Production, Work, Territory: The Geographical Anatomy of Industrial Capitalism*. London: Allen & Unwin.
Sheppard, E. (2011) 'Geography, nature and the question of development', *Dialogues in Human Geography*, 1, pp. 3–22.
Slater, D. (2004) *Geopolitics and the Post-Colonial: Rethinking North-South Relations*. Oxford, UK: Blackwell.
Smith, N. (1984) *Uneven Development: Nature, Capital and the Production of Space*. Oxford, UK: Basil Blackwell.
Storper, M. (2013) *Keys to the City: How Economics, Institutions, Social Interaction, and Politics Shape Development*. Princeton, NJ: Princeton University Press.
Theodore, N. & Peck, J. (2013) 'Selling flexibility: Temporary staffing in a volatile economy', in Fudge, J. & Strauss, K. (Eds.), *Temporary Work Agencies and Unfree Labour: Insecurity in the New World of Work*. London: Routledge, pp. 26–47.
Thrift, N.J. (2000) 'Pandora's box? Cultural geographies of economics', in Clark, G.L., Feldman, M. &. Gertler, M.S. (Eds.), *The Oxford Handbook of Economic Geography*. Oxford, UK: Oxford University Press, pp. 689–701.
Tickell, A. & Peck, J. (1992) 'Accumulation, regulation and the geographies of post-Fordism: Missing links in regulationist research', *Progress in Human Geography*, 16, pp. 190–218.
Watts, M. (2004) 'Resource curse? Governmentality, oil and power in the Niger Delta, Nigeria', *Geopolitics*, 9, pp. 50–80.
World Bank (2009) *World Development Report 2009: Reshaping Economic Geography*. Washington, DC: The World Bank.
Wright, M. (2006) *Disposable Women and Other Myths of Global Capitalism*. London: Routledge.
Zimmerman, E. (1951) *World Resources and Industries*. 2nd edition. New York: Harper and Brothers.

8

EVOLUTIONARY ECONOMIC GEOGRAPHY

An emerging field or framework?

David L. Rigby

Introduction

At a very broad level Economic Geography seeks to understand spatial uneven development, how geographies of growth and decline are produced, how they change over time and what role the spatial distribution of economic activity plays in the processes that drive these dynamics. Since the 1980s, Economic Geography has been restless. For practitioners within this field, the research domain, theoretical cores and principal methodologies have been up for grabs, along with the preferred connections to other fields within geography and those further afar (Martin & Sunley, 1996; Amin & Thrift, 2000; Plummer & Sheppard, 2001; Bathelt & Glückler, 2003). There is little question that the pluralism introduced by various 'turns' has broadened Economic Geography. Whether such breadth deepens our leverage over substantive concerns remains to be seen. Against this changing backcloth, a shift to embrace evolutionary ideas, a variant of heterodox economics, stands as one of the most recent examples of the dynamism of the field. While the popularity of Evolutionary Economic Geography (EEG) has grown rapidly, precisely what it offers economic geographers, and whether and how it should be integrated with existing theoretical frameworks are important questions that are beginning to generate healthy debate (Boschma & Frenken, 2006; Grabher, 2009; Mackinnon et al., 2009; Boschma & Martin, 2010; Pike et al., 2016).

This chapter provides a brief overview of the emergence of evolutionary economics and the adoption of evolutionary arguments within Economic Geography. The aim of the chapter is to highlight recent theoretical and empirical research within EEG and to foreground some key emerging debates. The chapter is divided into three sections. The first section briefly reviews the development of Evolutionary Economics (EE) and the competing strands of evolutionary thought that have been embraced by geographers. The second section explores how those arguments have been deployed within Economic Geography. The final section offers a brief conclusion and links many of the themes explored by EEG to a related literature in International Business Studies.

Key perspectives in EE

Within economics, disagreement over the adoption of a mechanistic framework based on Newtonian physics versus the adoption of evolutionary claims resting on a Darwinian logic is longstanding (Mirowski, 1989; Hodgson, 1993). Parts of this 'debate' are well-known, from the biological mecca of Marshall (1920), that was stillborn in his concept of the representative agent, through Veblen's (1898) search for an evolutionary model of social structure based on the 'natural selection' of routines or habits of thought, on to Schumpeter's (1942) model of creative destruction, even though that explicitly eschews links to evolution in a biological sense. However, these concerns did little to slow the ascendancy of what is nowadays referred to as the orthodox model of Neoclassical Economics. The standard macro-form of this framework rests heavily on sets of homogeneous, utility-maximizing agents who are perfectly informed and adjust to exogenous price shocks instantaneously and at zero cost (Kirman, 1992; Hartley, 1997). The impact of such assumptions is well-known, from no real (or at best an undersocialized) interaction between agents, no purposeful decision-making or strategic behavior, no innovation and, in aggregate, no real dynamics.

Sustained interest in EE developed with the work of Nelson and Winter (1982) and an alternative framework for understanding economic dynamics in an explicitly historical sense. This framework was built around the strategic choices of heterogeneous profit-seeking firms operating under the constraints of bounded rationality in competitive markets (Simon, 1957). Nelson and Winter (1982) constructed models of technological search that were localized by experience and by routinized behaviors that changed slowly over time through learning. Firms, and their associated technologies and routines, were selected by market pressures thus reshaping the environment within which future competition was seen to unfold. In short, Nelson and Winter (1982) outlined a number of the core components of a Darwinian model of evolution within a socio-economic domain and thus laid the foundation for a resurgent EE.

Writing thirty years later, Dollimore and Hodgson (2014) claim that the field of EE has become so fragmented that no over-arching theoretical framework has developed out of the pioneering efforts of Nelson and Winter (1982). This, they contend, is a primary reason why EE has had so little traction within the broader discipline of economics. At least part of the explanation for this theoretical stasis has been internal battles over the core of the field (Hanappi, 1995). Two broad models of EE have been offered to understand the dynamics of processes that influence the behavior of economic agents and the environment within which they interact. The first of these is linked to arguments that we typically associate with modern biology and the evolutionary work of Darwin and Spencer. A second model for EE rests on the principles of self-organization in complex systems. These two models are briefly discussed next.

The Darwinian model of evolution in socio-economic systems rests on the concepts of variety, selection and retention. Variety refers to differences in the characteristics of individual agents, firms and workers that comprise the populations under study. Selection refers to processes through which economic agents with certain characteristics, for example technologies or behavioral routines, increase or decrease their (frequency) weight in the population (Hodgson & Knudsen, 2006). Retention refers to processes through which these characteristics are propagated over time. Within the socio-economic sphere, it is critical to add to these standard evolutionary claims a mechanism that generates novelty and so maintains the heterogeneity over which processes of selection can operate (Witt, 2003; Metcalfe, Foster & Ramlogan, 2006). Learning and experimentation with production technologies, with organizational routines or with institutions that shape individual and/or group behavior serve this purpose (Nelson & Winter, 1982; Arthur, 2014).

Attempts to build a social or economic Darwinism have themselves taken a number of forms (Witt, 2004). Early applications of neo-Darwinism, underpinning crude and dangerous forms of socio-biology (Wilson, 1975; Becker, 1976), looked for a genetic base to explain human behavior. An alternative vision relied on Darwin and Spencer for metaphorical inspiration, often constructing analogies between evolutionary processes in biology and economics (Vromen, 2001; Nelson, 2006). However, the most general model, proposed by Hodgson and Knudsen (2006) and defended by Aldrich et al. (2008), suggests that populations of heterogeneous agents in different domains (natural and social worlds) can be understood as 'evolving' through the mechanisms indicated earlier, though the precise form of those mechanisms, the actual processes involved, vary from domain to domain. This is the model of Generalized Darwinism that assumes a common evolutionary ontology across different populations of competing units, and explicitly rejects the notion that socio-economic dynamics should be explained using strictly biological terms. Metcalfe's (1998) important work is consistent with this view. Witt (2004, 2006) remains a prominent critic.

An alternative framework for EE is located in models of complex systems and self-organization (Arthur, 1989, 2014; Allen, 1992; Foster, 1997). At root, complex systems are dissipative structures that import energy used by interacting agents to fuel behaviors leading to the emergence of structures or higher-order patterns that, in turn, shape future interaction and behavior. Systems where order emerges export entropy to other systems outside their borders, and linkages between different systems can result in higher-order complexity (Foster, 2005). Complexity science explores these co-evolutionary patterns of self-organization in open systems that are far from equilibrium, where resources are distributed and where interactions are typically non-linear and adaptive (Byrne, 1998; Miller & Page, 2007). There is no single unified theoretical model at the heart of complexity science, research in this field tends to take the form of network models where non-deterministic relationships between agents and an environment are simulated via sets of algorithms, and where scientific discovery focuses on identification of emergent patterns and shifts in the nature of interactions over time. Complex systems are irreducible in that they cannot be understood by examining relationships between their sub-components, and they are evolutionary in the sense that phases of emergence and structural transformation have an explicit time dimension that is irreversible.

Economic systems have long been supposed to exhibit characteristics typical of complex systems. Adam Smith's (1776) notion of an 'invisible hand' and Friedrich Hayek's (1960) 'spontaneous order' that led groups of agents to unintentionally form socially beneficial higher-order structures are perhaps the most well-referenced examples, though whether such structures rest on unregulated self-interest is debated (Sugden, 1989). Thus, technologies, markets and other forms of networks, even patterns of uneven growth over space and time, represent emergent properties in complex systems of socio-economic behavior. Arthur (2014) and Beinhocker (2006) identify the core ideas of complexity economics, and Wilson and Kirman (2016) provide a recent overview. Evolutionary game theory is commonly regarded as distinct from EE proper (Hodgson & Huang, 2012). An excellent review of evolutionary economic modeling with a strong bias toward evolutionary game theory is provided by Safarzynska and van den Bergh (2010).

Evolutionary analysis within Economic Geography

Evolutionary strains within Economic Geography reach back at least as far as the embrace of political economy from the late-1970s and through much of the 1980s. Massey's (1984) geological metaphor of new rounds of investment, embodying new technologies and institutional forms, deposited on top of existing institutional arrangements interacting to revise forms of capital accumulation and rework economic landscapes, represents an early example. Harvey (1975, 1982) also provides a working out over space and time of the inherent intra- and inter-class dynamics that drive change within the capitalist mode of production. These dynamics are evolutionary in the sense that new structures of accumulation are formed out of existing constraints. Sheppard and Barnes (1990) and Webber and Rigby (1996) attempt to formalize these arguments in what might be considered an evolutionary geographical political economy. Mackinnon et al. (2009) and Pike et al. (2016) make a strong case to strengthen recent evolutionary analysis within Economic Geography by providing it with an explicit political economy motor.

In the following discussion, theoretical and empirical research within Economic Geography that has an evolutionary flavor is reviewed. To help structure the argument, the core evolutionary principles of variety, retention and selection are employed. This is not to claim that the materials examined speak directly to one or more of these issues, just that they provide a convenient framework to organize ideas. The discussion does not dwell on which of the two broad models of EE are followed by economic geographers. While some have endorsed Generalized Darwinism (Essletzbichler & Rigby, 2007, 2010) and others have experimented with complexity (Frenken, 2000; Plummer & Sheppard, 2006), most remain agnostic. In truth, there is much that is common between these viewpoints. Martin and Sunley (2006, 2007) provide detailed accounts of work in Economic Geography that is consistent with these models, and Boschma and Martin (2010) provide a highly readable overview.

The production and destruction of variety within Economic Geography

As noted in the last section, some form of variety, or heterogeneity, among decision-making agents is critical to evolutionary accounts of (regional) economic dynamics (Saviotti, 1996). That heterogeneity does not have to be assumed, it is likely to emerge in settings where economic agents interact and learn from one another over time in settings where information is incomplete, where rationality is imperfect and where actions are influenced by social structures that are themselves mutable. Those structures may emerge without direction from routinized behaviors at the individual level, in other cases they might be shaped by self-interested agents, or groups thereof, who have amassed the resources and thus the power to direct change (Martin, 2000; Gertler, 2010). Socio-economic spaces emerge through the interactions and choices of different sets of agents located in different places who both make and are subject to varying constraints and opportunities. Spaces are always in transformation, shaped by multi-scalar processes that are historical composites of the agency and the institutional arrangements, some more enduring than others, that they enmesh (Storper & Walker, 1989; Peck & Theodore, 2007).

While these simple arguments are broadly consistent with a vision of economic geographies that are evolving, it is certainly the case that economic geographers have not, until recently, thought carefully enough about the heterogeneity that underpins this vision. Important work in Economic Geography through the 1980s and 1990s, began to provide systematic evidence of regional differences in patterns of industrial specialization (Ellison & Glaeser, 1997), organizational forms (Scott, 1988; Saxenian, 1994), institutional practices (Storper, 1997; Peck & Theodore, 2007; Gertler, 2010), forms of labor organization (Herod, 1998) and technologies (Rigby & Essletzbichler, 1997, 2006). However, there have been relatively few attempts to identify the extent and the form of heterogeneity in any of these substantive fields, how different processes of selection may operate across that heterogeneity, how new forms of heterogeneity are developed and existing forms eliminated, and how variety in any single domain co-evolves with that in other domains (see also Potts, 2000). For some (Metcalfe, 1998), these issues are foundational to evolutionary accounts, guiding the structure of change in any space economy.

These claims motivated the early research of Essletzbichler and Rigby (2005) to map the nature of variety in production techniques across sectors of the U.S. economy. They used establishment level data for the population of U.S. manufacturing operations to examine how much heterogeneity existed within narrowly defined industries, and how that heterogeneity shifted over time and over space. The influence of selection (differential growth), plant entry and plant exit on aggregate shifts in industry technology were measured, and empirical support was provided for the work of Metcalfe and Gibbons (1986) who argue that the 'shape' of heterogeneity within industries directs the pace and direction of technological change. In similar work, Frenken, Saviotti and Trommetter (1999) develop product spaces as representations of variety across industrial sectors. They explore patterns of radical and incremental innovation within these sectors, the emergence of dominant designs and specialization that they relate to niche theory in evolutionary biology.

Frenken, van Oort and Verburg (2007) argue that different forms of variety are important to regional growth. Building on well-known debates around Marshall-Arrow-Romer externalities and Jacobs externalities in the agglomeration literature (Glaeser et al., 1992), Frenken, van Oort and Verburg (2007) developed the concept of related variety to indicate the extent to which different economic activities are related to one another in a technological or market sense. They argued that related forms of variety hold the possibility of dynamic economies of scope, of potential recombination of activities that are neither too close to one another to crowd the market, nor too distant from one another to impede useful interaction, not unlike Noteboom's (2000) claims about optimal cognitive distance. Unrelated variety, then, refers to activities that are so distant that viable recombination is unlikely. The concept of related variety, measurement issues and the meaning of specialization are discussed further by Essletzbichler (2015) and by Kemeny and Storper (2015).

Related variety as a way of thinking about the nature of heterogeneity and its influence on economic performance, has been given additional power through the work of Hidalgo et al. (2007) who measure the relatedness of products and how the structure of product variety within countries shapes development possibilities. In turn, these ideas have spawned a great deal of research within EEG that explores relatedness and related variety in different settings. For example, Boschma and Iammarino (2009) show that related variety in Italian exports has a positive and significant influence on regional growth and employment, and Quatraro (2010) reveals how knowledge coherence, another form of related variety, is a significant determinant of productivity growth within Italian regions. In other work, patterns of industrial diversification within regions, or regional branching, are explained by the relatedness of existing industrial capabilities to new sectoral growth paths (Neffke, Henning & Boschma, 2011; Boschma, Minondo & Navarro, 2013; Zhu, He & Zhou, 2015). Measures of skill relatedness and firm diversification are examined using Swedish micro-data by Neffke and Henning (2013), and Muneepeerakul et al. (2013) generate occupational relatedness measures for U.S. cities and address how occupational structure regulates the ability of urban labor markets to transform themselves. Within a different domain, and building on earlier work on technological coherence within firms (Jaffe, 1986; Teece et al., 1994) and regions (Graf, 2006), Kogler, Rigby and Tucker (2013), Balland, Boschma and Kogler (2015) and Rigby (2015) use patent data to estimate technological relatedness between knowledge classes and show how the knowledge architectures of different cities guide technological diversification. Kogler, Essletzbichler and Rigby (2016) trace the evolution of technological relatedness across European regions. Important extensions of this research are just beginning to tackle the question of relatedness among institutional structures and how these are distributed over space (Cortinovis et al., 2016).

Of course, there is a much larger literature on institutions that emphasizes the socio-cultural and political foundations of structured behaviors that help shape what we commonly understand as the economy. This work usually begins with the old institutionalism of Veblen (1898) and his 'settled habits of thought'. This provides a vision of institutions (rules and conventions) that limit agency and the power of actors to shape the systems within which they operate. In contrast, the new institutionalism of North (1990) and Williamson (1985) privileges a form of agency built around rationality and transaction cost theory from which organizations and institutions emerge. Here agency plays the dominant role. Sociological variants of institutional theory view the economy, a system of commodity production and exchange, as embedded within networks of social relationships through which trust, understanding and power are generated (Polanyi, 1957; Granovetter, 1985). Martin (2000) and Peck (2005) provide excellent overviews of these claims, both offering an understanding of capitalism as a socio-economic system in permanent flux, a complex interacting melange of forms of production and socio-cultural regulations, norms and values that periodically congeal in more or less durable socio-economic structures producing interlinked spaces and scales of economic activity within and across which agents of different kinds make choices that both reinforce and undermine existing socio-spatial arrangements. This vision of a dynamic and spatially variegated capitalism is more recently explored by Peck and Theodore (2007).

Within Economic Geography, models of evolutionary dynamics that stress the importance of institutions have largely been developed as part of the literature on national and regional systems of innovation, on learning regions and localized knowledge economies (Freeman, 1987; Morgan, 1997; Cooke, 2002; Asheim & Gertler, 2005). Across this literature there is broad agreement that the production of knowledge is highly uneven over space, especially that knowledge which is valuable as a result of its complex and tacit character (Maskell & Malmberg, 1999). With knowledge production increasingly imagined as a process of recombining existing ideas in new ways (Kauffman, 1993), that unevenness is explained by spatial variations in the volume and the quality of interaction (Lundvall & Johnson, 1994; Bathelt, Malmberg & Maskell, 2004; Storper & Venables, 2004), which, in turn, are thought to rest upon the development of localized communities of practice (Lawson & Lorenz, 1999), shared values, norms of behavior, and traded and untraded interdependencies that engender trust (Saxenian, 1994; Storper, 1997). The difficulty of replicating institutional formations over space only serves to exacerbate the critical role of geography in knowledge production. While Gertler (1995) reveals the importance of cultural, organizational and geographical proximity in technology adoption and use, Balland and Rigby (2017) show that complex forms of knowledge do not travel well. Boschma (2005) explores the linkages and tradeoffs between different forms of proximity.

This focus on the production of novelty, both in terms of institutions and technologies, is critical to the evolutionary framework, for it is the process by which variety is introduced to the socio-economic system. While the production of new forms of knowledge has been extensively studied within an evolutionary context, along with the links between technological and institutional systems (Freeman & Perez, 1988; Murman, 2003) and their co-evolution (Schamp, 2010), MacKinnon et al. (2009) charge that the production of new institutional forms has been somewhat neglected within EEG. To some extent this may reflect a rather narrow engagement with institutions in evolutionary economics whereby sets of rule-guided behaviors are sampled by economic agents, with profits influencing those practices to be maintained and discarded and thus prompting a search for alternatives (Nelson & Winter, 1982; Loasby, 2002; Hodgson, 2007; Wilson & Kirman, 2016). It is certainly the case that these arguments say relatively little about the processes through which institutions are created, copied and set into competition with one another, how hierarchies of institutions interact and shape behavior, how much variation in agency institutional formations allow and whether this heterogeneity is the source of new constraints on action. Though Boschma and Frenken (2009, 2011) dispute the broad charge of MacKinnon et al. (2009), they do agree that more work is required to understand how firm-level routines become institutionalized at various spatial scales. Research on this question demands that EEG broaden its methodological base, from quantitative analysis of secondary data, through case studies of regions and industries, toward ethnographies of firms and other agents as well as the 'lives' of institutions in spatial clusters that evolve over time.

Path dependence and lock-in as forms of retention in space

Individual agents within the market economy make choices that impact their survival. For example, firms choose products to produce and technologies, routines, organizational forms and locations that they hope will generate the returns to sustain their operations. Firms learn through production and through interacting with other agents. Processes of selection send frequent signals to firms indicating whether they should exploit current practices or whether they should explore new possibilities (March, 1991). However, limited information and steep increases in the cost of search around existing practices, as well as gains from learning and interaction, means that firms and other agents get locked into trajectories of action that are shaped by past decisions (Arthur, 1989, 1994; David, 1985). The concept of path dependence, of an historical inertia that reinforces logics of action over time, perhaps following random shocks or chance events, has exerted a significant influence on how economic geographers have imagined the historical dynamics of spatial uneven development (Grabher, 1993; Martin & Sunley, 2006; Hassink, 2007).

Path dependence is seen as positive, when firms and other agents coalesce around technologies, modes of organization and institutional forms that enhance mutual understanding, interaction, specialization and cost-sharing. The evolution of regional economies is not only path dependent, it is also place-dependent (Martin & Sunley, 2006). Thus, for Arthur (1994), when repeated choices of independent agents begin to favor one location over another, processes of cumulative and reinforcing advantage set in rapidly. Economies might develop around a dominant technological design (Clark, 1985; Anderson & Tushman, 1990), a more limited knowledge platform (Maskell, 2001; Iammarino & McCann, 2006), a shared organizational culture (Saxenian, 1994) or a common institutional or political configuration (Storper, 1997). For Maskell and Malmberg (1999), regional competitive advantage rests on a distinctive set of localized capabilities.

Boschma and Frenken (2011) examine the spatial clustering of economic activity as a path dependent, evolutionary process. They privilege Klepper's (2007) spinoff model of cluster formation, where successful firms birth spinoffs that also tend to be successful as they replicate the practices of their parents. When this process is concentrated in space, so clusters of related industrial activity emerge. A number of empirical studies provide support for this model (Boschma & Wenting, 2007; De Vaan, Boschma & Frenken, 2012). A more well-known model of cluster dynamics emerges from models of agglomeration. Thus, for Marshall (1920), localization economies are seen as emerging in particular places because of the formation of dense pools of skilled labor, spatially concentrated buyer-supplier networks and localized knowledge spillovers. For Jacobs (1969), urbanization economies are anticipated to flow from diverse industrial clusters that enhance possibilities for recombination. While these arguments are reasonably well-understood, empirical evidence on the relative strength of these two mechanisms remains inconclusive (Beaudry & Schiffauerova, 2009). For Potter and Watts (2011), the nature of agglomeration economies is argued to follow the life-cycle of industries. This claim is consistent with the nursery cities model of Duranton and Puga (2001), who also fit a geography to the life-cycle claims. Neffke, Henning and Boschma (2011) explore the dynamics of agglomeration economies along the life-cycle of industries, and Rigby and Brown (2015) show that new and old firms benefit from agglomeration in different ways.

Path dependence is negative when these same processes lock firms and other agents into forms of activity that are no longer profitable. For Grabher (1993), functional lock-in (inter-firm relations), cognitive lock-in (common worldview) and political lock-in generated a territorial-industrial trap that prevented the old industrial areas of the Ruhr from restructuring when decline was inevitable. Hassink (2010) investigates the circumstances under which different forms of lock-in have made it more or less difficult for new industrial capacity and growth paths to emerge in different regions. Martin (2010) extends our understanding of path dependency and raises questions that are taken up in accounts of path creation (Simmie, 2012; Dawley, 2014) and path destruction (Glückler, 2007).

While the concepts of path dependence and lock-in are undeniably important to EEG, they do not themselves comprise an independent framework of evolutionary dynamics. Nonetheless, exploration of these terms has forced us to think about the circumstances under which technological, institutional and industrial transformations occur, whether by design or historical accident, how such changes might be related, and what the dynamics of these changes mean for adaptation and the long-run resilience of regional economies (Christopherson, Michie & Tyler, 2010; Simmie & Martin, 2010; Balland, Rigby & Boschma, 2015). Central to much of this work on path dependence and resilience is the creation and destruction of variety, in all its forms, and of the management of that variety within and across regions.

The silence of selection

Though certain aspects of the evolutionary framework have enjoyed considerable attention within geography, selection is not one of them. Essletzbichler and Rigby (2007) offer a standard interpretation of individual selection in a heterogeneous population of competing firms where market choices reward some firms over others. They note that selection does not favor more efficient firms, rather that efficiency allows some firms to better translate revenues into profits and thus increase their weight in the market, along with the technologies and routines that such firms employ. In this way, markets themselves evolve through the actions of individual agents, altering the pressures of competition on remaining firms. Of course, some firms attempt to control the markets in which they operate through scale or product differentiation (Christophers, 2016). Processes of selection, insofar as they reference changes in the distribution of properties belonging to members of a population, are closely connected to the diffusion of those properties within and across populations and to processes of lock-in that periodically interrupt their operation (David, 1985). It is important to distinguish selection from other processes through which population characteristics change. Over the short-run, selection does not influence the characteristics of elements of a population, but it does impact the composition of the population (Hodgson & Knudsen, 2006).

Within socio-economic systems that are distributed over space, these simple observations on selection are significantly complicated, for agents interact in multiple ways and across different populations. Defining the boundaries of populations and how processes of selection work within and across those boundaries is difficult. In simple geographical settings where agents interact with one another over relatively small distances and where such interaction might help denote the boundaries of a region, then competition and selection might only need to be considered at one spatial scale. However, as soon as we admit the interaction of at least some agents across formerly independent regions, at what point do new regions and new markets form and how do processes of selection become established at new or multiple scales? These concerns raise the question of what are appropriate units of selection and whether the region might represent such a unit (MacKinnon et al., 2009). This issue forces us to think about non-market forms of selection that are, perhaps, of more relevance in the transformation of institutions over time and space. Glückler (2007) provides a quite different take on selection developed within a network perspective, but it is unclear how that might help us with some of the questions just raised. Questions of group and hierarchical selection further complicate the conceptual terrain (van den Bergh & Gowdy, 2009; Wilson, 2016).

Self-organization in networks

There is relatively little research within Economic Geography that explicitly embraces notions of complexity and self-organization. Plummer and Sheppard (2006) provide a prominent exception, adding an explicit socio-spatial dimension to the usual characterization of a complex system in order to examine how structure and agency co-evolve to produce complex, non-equilibrium trajectories of growth within a spatial-economic system. This work is extended by Fowler (2007) and Bergmann (2012) who both explore dynamics in spatial-economic systems that are not driven by equilibrium. Though not developed in explicitly spatial contexts, a series of complexity models has been deployed to understand innovation and the dynamics of technological change within evolutionary frameworks. Frenken (2006) offers a detailed review. Essletzbichler and Rigby (2007) echo Hodgson and Knudsen (2006) in calling for a synthesis of Generalized Darwinism and complexity approaches in EEG to help resolve how emergent structures are selected and how they may adapt within and across socio-economic landscapes. Beinhocker (2011) attempts this integration using information theory.

Within EEG, a rapidly growing corpus of research that embraces many of the concerns with self-organization and complexity theory focuses on networks and their evolution (Glückler, 2007; Ter Wal & Boschma, 2009; Glückler & Doreian, 2016). Following Grabher (2006), this new engagement with networks is less concerned with governance questions than it is with relationality and more formal social network analysis (Bathelt & Glückler, 2003). The vast bulk of this literature focuses on networks of firms and other agents engaged in knowledge production. Contrary to the assumptions of many writing on regional innovation systems, this new work makes clear that most agents within industrial districts or clusters are not 'linked-in' to local institutions in the same way. Indeed, the performance of individual firms and other agents is influenced by their centrality in networks and by the content of their network ties (Giuliani & Bell, 2005; Huggins & Prokop, 2017). Network size, structure and openness is shown to impact the production of knowledge within cities and regions (Fleming et al., 2007; Lobo & Strumsky, 2008), and the influence of different forms of proximity on network ties is explored by Broekel and Boschma (2012). Lengyel and Eriksson (2015) broaden this work in their analysis of co-worker networks and regional productivity growth. Morrison (2008) and Breschi and Lenzi (2015) illustrate how gatekeepers translate and regulate flows of knowledge between networks. An enduring theme in much of this research is the interaction between social networks and the spatial juxtaposition of economic activity. Thus, Breschi and Lissoni (2009) raise important questions about the relative strengths of social proximity and spatial proximity in their analysis of knowledge flows prompted by Jaffe et al. (1993).

Following Powell et al. (2005) and Cowan, Jonard and Zimmerman (2007), analysis of network evolution has developed rapidly over the last few years. For example, Cantner and Graf (2006) explore patterns of network entry and exit for innovators in Jena, Germany. Their work highlights the importance of social connections developed through job mobility for understanding collaboration. Balland (2012) investigates how different forms of proximity influence the changing structure of collaboration networks in the global navigation satellite industry, and Balland, De Vaan and Boschma (2012) use a stochastic actor-oriented model to estimate how different mechanisms of tie-formation shift along the industry life-cycle. At larger spatial scales, Cassi, Morrison and Ter Wal (2012) look at how patterns of globalization in wine trade and wine science co-evolve in Old World and New World settings, and Glückler and Panitz (2016) detail how countries shift positions within global value chain networks.

Conclusion

Those immersed in the wash-spin cycle that is Economic Geography might be forgiven for thinking that they inhabit a frenetic and fractured field that is far from disciplinary norms. A quick glance at the literature in International Business (IB) and management might provide some calming relief. Buckley (2003), for example, asks whether the IB research agenda has run out of steam, and Jack et al. (2008) seek an intervention within the field of International Management which they see as resistant to any examination of its ontological and epistemological foundations. Calls for a re-engagement with history (Jones & Khanna, 2006), with institutionalist logics (Peng, Wang & Jiang, 2008) and with a wider set of methodological approaches (Doz, 2011) in the IB field will sound all too familiar to economic geographers, along with appeals to evolutionary analysis as a framework for understanding firm organization, strategy and IB dynamics (see Kogut & Zander, 1993; Teece & Pisano, 1994; Cantwell, Dunning & Lundan, 2010).

While evolutionary ideas never gained much traction within mainstream economics departments, Dollimore and Hodgson (2014) note that the arguments of Nelson and Winter (1982) ushered in a remarkable period of creativity within the business and management literature. This creativity emerged, at least in part, around the work of Hannan and Freeman (1993) on organizational ecology and a recognition of the diversity of business operations. Attempts to understand that diversity build on the behavioral models of the firm of Cyert and March (1963). They were extended in the resource-based view of Barney (1991) and Wernerfelt (1984) as a platform for sustained competitive advantage, and developed further by Teece et al. (1997) in the form of strategy in dynamic contexts. As in EEG, knowledge production, management and absorption play central roles in the emergence of diversity and its strategic exploitation (Cohen & Levinthal, 1990; Kogut & Zander, 1992). These same concerns animate key research themes in the IB literature with its focus on activities that cross national borders (Kogut & Zander, 1993; Teece, 2014; Cano-Kollmann et al., 2016).

The linkages between recent work in (Evolutionary) Economic Geography and the IB literature should be clear. However, to date there has been relatively little interaction across these fields (though see Beugelsdijk, McCann & Mudambi, 2010), even in the work on globalization, global value chains and production networks (Dicken, 2004; McCann & Mudambi, 2005). This is surprising given shared substantive interests and, to some extent, shared methodologies. While it would be fair, perhaps, to say that research methods within Economic Geography are broader than those found across the IB literature, there is much more methodological correspondence between those working in EEG and in IB. A deeper engagement of these two fields is likely to yield mutual benefits. Let me provide a few brief examples.

First, mirroring Economic Geography, the adoption of an evolutionary approach within IB is increasingly seen as critical to understanding the co-evolution of firms, in this case multinational enterprises (MNEs), and the (multi-scalar) institutional environments that they help produce (Volberda & Lewin, 2003; Dunning & Lundan, 2008; Cantwell et al., 2010). For both IB and EEG, the interaction between economic agents, institutions and other features of the markets in which they operate are critical concerns. However, the creation of institutions, how they vary over space and whether the rise and fall of formal and informal institutional structures rest on processes of selection that resemble those in markets for goods and services are questions that remain not well understood (see Christophers, 2016). More detailed ethnographies of firm operations and decision making in particular local and national contexts would be especially useful to remedy these shortcomings. Furthermore, combining the traditional strengths of IB and EEG research at different spatial scales might lead to interesting findings regarding the geographical extent and the mobility of institutions.

Second, in both IB and in EEG, as well as in Economic Geography more generally, the analysis of how businesses organize, distribute and control or shape their networks of relationships over space requires improved data (Zander, 2002). This is most evident in IB where the use of gross import and export statistics, often at the national level, distorts our perception of the nature and the extent of economic activity distributed across sub-national spaces (Poon & Rigby, 2017). Value-added trade data and more enterprise-level business statistics are critical to unpack who does what and where. Within EEG too, value added trade data might issue significant correctives to the simple visions of national product spaces and sets of capabilities that are identified using gross trade flow data. How might our understanding of the dynamics of such spaces and the "development potential" of different countries shift as a result?

Finally, across IB and EEG literatures, knowledge production and its management are seen as playing an ever more critical role in the production of competitive advantage within a world economy that is increasingly flat across a number of important dimensions, yet stubbornly differentiated across others (Mudambi, 2008; Boschma & Frenken, 2011; Cano-Kollmann et al., 2016). For scholars of IB and EEG, how firms manipulate and connect the productive potential of economic agents, organizations and institutions across the fragmented knowledge landscapes that they are best adapted to exploit are key questions (Almeida, 1996; Cantwell & Vertova, 2004). Combining the literatures from both fields, we have made important progress in identifying the ways in which knowledge bases vary over space, about what kinds of knowledge are locked in place and those that are more mobile. We have begun to explore how firms source knowledge from different locations and how place is used to protect novelty. However, we know a lot less about the dynamics of knowledge cores at different spatial scales, about the value of different knowledge components and the characteristics of those places that are best able to recombine them in productive new ways. Further recombination of insights from IB and EEG scholars should help us with these questions too.

References

Aldrich, H., Hodgson, G., Hull, D., Knudsen, T., Mokyr, J. & Vanberg, V. (2008) 'In defense of generalized Darwinism', *Journal of Evolutionary Economics*, 18, pp. 577–596.

Allen, P. (1992) 'Modelling evolutionary and complex systems', *World Futures*, 34, pp. 105–123.

Almeida, P. (1996) 'Knowledge sourcing by foreign multinationals: Patent citation analysis in the US semiconductor industry', *Strategic Management Journal*, S2, pp. 155–165.

Amin, A. & Thrift, N. (2000) 'What kind of economic theory for what kind of Economic Geography?' *Antipode*, 32, pp. 4–9.

Anderson, P. & Tushman, M. (1990) 'Technological discontinuities and dominant designs: A cyclical model of technological change', *Administrative Science Quarterly*, 35, pp. 604–633.

Arthur, W. (1989) 'Competing technologies, increasing returns, and "lock-in" by historical events', *Economic Journal*, 99, pp. 116–131.

Arthur, W. (1994) *Increasing Returns and Path Dependence in the Economy*. Ann Arbor, MI: Michigan University Press.

Arthur, W. (2014) *Complexity and the Economy*. Oxford, UK: Oxford University Press.

Asheim, B. & Gertler. M. (2005) 'The geography of innovation: Regional innovation systems', in Fagerberg, J., Mowery, D. & Nelson, R. (Eds.), *The Oxford Handbook of Innovation*. Oxford, UK: Oxford University Press, pp. 291–317.

Balland, P. (2012) 'Proximity and the evolution of collaboration networks: Evidence from research and development projects within the global navigation satellite system (GNSS) industry', *Regional Studies*, 46, pp. 741–756.

Balland, P., Boschma, R. & Kogler, D. (2015) 'Relatedness and technological change in cities: The rise and fall of technological knowledge in U.S. metropolitan areas from 1981 to 2010', *Industrial and Corporate Change*, 24, pp. 223–250.

Balland, P., De Vaan, M. & Boschma, R. (2012) 'The dynamics of interfirm networks along the industry life-cycle: The case of the global video game industry, 1987–2007', *Journal of Economic Geography*, 13, pp. 741–765.

Balland, P. & Rigby, D. (2017) 'The geography of complex knowledge', *Economic Geography*, 93, pp. 1–23.

Balland, R., Rigby, D. & Boschma, R. (2015) 'The technological resilience of US cities', *Cambridge Journal of Regions, Economy and Society*, 8, pp. 167–184.

Barney, J. (1991) 'Firm resources and sustained competitive advantage', *Journal of Management*, 17, pp. 99–120.

Bathelt, H. & Glückler, J. (2003) 'Toward a relational Economic Geography', *Journal of Economic Geography*, 3, pp. 117–144.

Bathelt, H., Malmberg, A. & Maskell, P. (2004) 'Clusters and knowledge: Local buzz, global pipelines and the process of knowledge creation', *Progress in Human Geography*, 28, pp. 31–56.

Beaudry, C. & Schiffauerova, A. (2009) 'Who's right, Marshall or Jacobs? The localization versus urbanization debate', *Research Policy*, 38, pp. 318–337.

Becker, G. (1976) *The Economic Approach to Human Behavior*. Chicago, IL: Chicago University Press.

Beinhocker, E. (2006) *The Origin of Wealth: Evolution, Complexity and the Radical Remaking of Economics*. Boston, MA: Harvard Business School Press.

Beinhocker, E. (2011) 'Evolution as computation: Integrating self-organization with generalized Darwinism', *Journal of Institutional Economics*, 7, pp. 393–423.

Bergmann, L. (2012) 'A co-evolutionary approach to the capitalist space economy', *Environment and Planning A*, 44, pp. 518–537.

Beugelsdijk, S., McCann, P. & Mudambi, R. (2010) 'Introduction: Place, space and organization – Economic Geography and the multinational enterprise', *Journal of Economic Geography*, 10, pp. 485–493.

Boschma, R. (2005) 'Proximity and innovation: A critical assessment', *Regional Studies*, 39, pp. 61–74.

Boschma, R. & Frenken, K. (2006) 'Why is Economic Geography not an evolutionary science? Towards an evolutionary Economic Geography', *Journal of Economic Geography*, 6, pp. 273–302.

Boschma, R. & Frenken, K. (2009) 'Some notes on institutions in evolutionary Economic Geography', *Economic Geography*, 85, pp. 151–158.

Boschma, R. & Frenken, K. (2011) 'The emerging empirics of evolutionary Economic Geography', *Journal of Economic Geography*, 11, pp. 295–307.

Boschma, R. & Iammarino, S. (2009) 'Related variety, trade linkages, and regional growth in Italy', *Economic Geography*, 85, pp. 289–311.

Boschma, R. & Martin, R. (Eds.) (2010) *The Handbook of Evolutionary Economic Geography*. Cheltenham, UK: Edward Elgar.

Boschma, R., Minondo, A. & Navarro, M. (2013) 'The emergence of new industries at the regional level in Spain: A proximity approach based on product relatedness', *Economic Geography*, 89, pp. 29–51.

Boschma, R. & Wenting, R. (2007) 'The spatial evolution of the British automobile industry: Does location matter?' *Industrial and Corporate Change*, 16, pp. 213–238.

Breschi, S. & Lenzi, C. (2015) 'The role of external linkages and gatekeepers for the renewal and expansion of U.S. cities' knowledge base, 1990–2004', *Regional Studies*, 49, pp. 782–797.

Breschi, S. & Lissoni, F. (2009) 'Mobility of skilled workers and co-invention networks: An anatomy of localized knowledge flows', *Journal of Economic Geography*, 9, pp. 439–468.

Broekel, T. & Boschma, R. (2012) 'Knowledge networks in the Dutch aviation industry: The proximity paradox', *Journal of Economic Geography*, 12, pp. 409–433.

Buckley, P. (2003) 'Is the International Business research agenda running out of steam?' *Journal of International Business Studies*, 33, pp. 365–373.
Byrne, D. (1998) *Complexity Theory in the Social Sciences: An Introduction*. London: Routledge.
Cano-Kollmann, M., Cantwell, J., Hannigan, T., Mudambi, R. & Song, J. (2016) 'Knowledge connectivity: An agenda for innovation research in International Business', *Journal of International Business Studies*, 47, pp. 255–262.
Cantner, U. & Graf, H. (2006) 'The network of innovators in Jena: An application of social network analysis', *Research Policy*, 35, pp. 463–480.
Cantwell, J., Dunning, J. & Lundan, S. (2010) 'An evolutionary approach to understanding International Business activity: The co-evolution of MNEs and the institutional environment', *Journal of International Business Studies*, 41, pp. 567–586.
Cantwell, J. & Vertova, G. (2004) 'Historical evolution of technological diversification', *Research Policy*, 33, pp. 511–529.
Cassi, L., Morrison, A. & Ter Wal, A. (2012) 'The evolution of trade and scientific collaboration networks in the global wine sector: A longitudinal study using network analysis', *Economic Geography*, 88, pp. 311–334.
Christophers, B. (2016) *The Great Leveler: Capitalism and Competition in the Court of Law*. Cambridge, MA: Harvard University Press.
Christopherson, S., Michie, J. & Tyler, P. (2010) 'Regional resilience: Theoretical and empirical perspectives', *Cambridge Journal of Regions, Economy and Society*, 3, pp. 3–10.
Clark, K. (1985) 'The interaction of design hierarchies and market concepts in technological evolution', *Research Policy*, 14, pp. 235–251.
Cohen, W. & Levinthal, D. (1990) 'Absorptive capacity: A new perspective on learning and innovation', *Administrative Science Quarterly*, 35, pp. 128–152.
Cooke, P. (2002) *Knowledge economies: Clusters, Learning and Cooperative Advantage*. London: Routledge.
Cortinovis, N., Xiao, J., Boschma, R. & van Oort, F. (2016) 'Quality of government and social capital as drivers of regional diversification in Europe'. Papers in Evolutionary Economic Geography #16.10, Utrecht University, the Netherlands.
Cowan, R., Jonard, R. & Zimmerman, J. (2007) 'Bilateral collaboration and the emergence of innovation networks', *Management Science*, 53, pp. 1051–1067.
Cyert, R. & March, J. (1963) *A Behavioral Theory of the Firm*. Englewood Cliffs, NJ: Prentice-Hall.
David, P. (1985) 'Clio and the economics of QWERTY', *American Economic Review*, 75, pp. 332–337.
Dawley, S. (2014) 'Creating new paths? Offshore wind, policy activism, and peripheral region development', *Economic Geography*, 90, pp. 91–112.
De Vaan, M., Boschma, R. & Frenken, K. (2012) 'Clustering and firm performance in project-based industries: The case of the global video game industry, 1972–2007', *Journal of Economic Geography*, 13, pp. 965–991.
Dicken, P. (2004) 'Geographers and "globalization": (yet) another missed boat?' *Transactions of the Institute of British Geographers*, 29, pp. 5–26.
Dollimore, D. & Hodgson, G. (2014) 'Four essays on economic evolution: An introduction', *Journal of Evolutionary Economics*, 24, pp. 1–10.
Doz, Y. (2011) 'Qualitative research for International Business', *Journal of International Business Studies*, 42, pp. 582–590.
Dunning, J. & Lundan, S. (2008) 'Institutions and the OLI paradigm of the multinational enterprise', *Asia Pacific Journal of Management*, 25, pp. 573–593.
Duranton, G. & Puga, D. (2001) 'Nursery cities: Urban diversity, process innovation, and the life-cycle of products', *American Economic Review*, 91, pp. 1454–1477.
Ellison, G. & Glaeser, E. (1997) 'Geographic concentration in US manufacturing industries: A dartboard approach', *Journal of Political Economy*, 105, pp. 889–927.
Essletzbichler, J. (2015) 'Relatedness, industrial branching and technology cohesion in US metropolitan areas', *Regional Studies*, 49, pp. 752–766.
Essletzbichler, J. & Rigby, D. (2005) 'Technological evolution as creative destruction of process heterogeneity. Evidence from U.S. plant-level data', *Journal of Economic Systems Research*, 17, pp. 25–45.
Essletzbichler, J. & Rigby, D. (2007) 'Exploring evolutionary Economic Geography', *Journal of Economic Geography*, 7, pp. 537–548.

Essletzbichler, J. & Rigby, D. (2010) 'Generalized Darwinism and evolutionary Economic Geography', in Boschma, R. & R. Martin (Eds.), *The Handbook of Evolutionary Economic Geography*. Cheltenham, UK: Edward Elgar, pp. 43–61.

Fleming, L., King III, C. & Juda, A. (2007) 'Small worlds and regional innovation', *Organization Science*, 18, pp. 938–954.

Foster, J. (1997) 'The analytical foundations of evolutionary economics: From biological analogy to economic self-organization', *Structural Change and Economic Dynamics*, 8, pp. 427–451.

Foster, J. (2005) 'From simplistic to complex systems in economics', *Cambridge Journal of Economics*, 29, pp. 873–892.

Fowler, C. (2007) 'Taking geographical economics out of equilibrium: Implications for theory and policy', *Journal of Economic Geography*, 7, pp. 265–284.

Freeman, C. (1987) 'The "national system of innovation" in historical perspective', *Cambridge Journal of Economics*, 19, pp. 5–24.

Freeman, C. & Perez, C. (1988) 'Structural crises of adjustment: Business cycles and investment behavior', in Dosi, G., Freeman, C., Nelson, R., Silverberg, G. & Soete, L. (Eds.), *Technical Change and Economic Theory*. London: Pinter, pp. 38–66.

Frenken, K. (2000) 'A complexity approach to innovation networks. The case of the aircraft industry (1909–1997)', *Research Policy*, 29, pp. 257–272.

Frenken, K. (2006) 'Technological innovation and complexity theory', *Economics of Innovation and New Technology*, 15, pp. 137–155.

Frenken, K., Saviotti, P. & Trommetter, M. (1999) 'Variety and niche creation in aircraft, helicopters, motorcycles and microcomputers', *Research Policy*, 28, pp. 469–488.

Frenken, K., van Oort, F. & Verburg, T. (2007) 'Related variety, unrelated variety, and regional economic growth', *Regional Studies*, 41, pp. 685–697.

Gertler, M. (1995) '"Being there": Proximity, organization, and culture in the development and adoption of advanced manufacturing technologies', *Economic Geography*, 71, pp. 1–26.

Gertler, M. (2010) 'Rules of the game: The place of institutions in regional economic change', *Regional Studies*, 44, pp. 1–15.

Giuliani, E. & Bell, M. (2005) 'The micro-determinants of meso-level learning and innovation: Evidence from a Chilean wine cluster', *Research Policy*, 34, pp. 47–68.

Glaeser, E., Kallal, H., Scheinkman, J. & Shleifer, A. (1992) 'Growth in cities', *Journal of Political Economy*, 100, pp. 1126–1152.

Glückler, J. (2007) 'Economic Geography and the evolution of networks', *Journal of Economic Geography*, 7, pp. 619–634.

Glückler, J. & Doreian, P. (2016) 'Editorial: Social network analysis and Economic Geography – Positional, evolutionary and multi-level approaches', *Journal of Economic Geography*, 16, pp. 1123–1134.

Glückler, J. & Panitz, R. (2016) 'Relational upgrading in global value chains', *Journal of Economic Geography*, 16, pp. 1161–1185.

Grabher, G. (1993) 'The weakness of strong ties: The "lock-in" of regional development in the Ruhr area', in Grabher, G. (Ed.), *The Embedded Firm: On the Socio-Economics of Industrial Networks*. London: Routledge, pp. 255–277.

Grabher, G. (2006) 'Trading routes, bypasses, and risky intersections: Mapping the travels of networks between economic sociology and Economic Geography', *Progress in Human Geography*, 30, pp. 163–189.

Grabher, G. (2009) 'Yet another turn? The evolutionary project in Economic Geography', *Economic Geography*, 85, pp. 119–127.

Graf, H. (2006) *Networks in the Innovation Process: Local and Regional Interactions*. Cheltenham, UK: Edward Elgar.

Granovetter, M. (1985) 'Economic action and social structure: The problem of embeddedness', *American Journal of Sociology*, 91, pp. 481–510.

Hanappi, G. (1995) *Evolutionary Economics: The Evolutionary Revolution in the Social Sciences*. Aldershot, UK: Avebury.

Hannan, M. & Freeman, M. (1993) *Organizational Ecology*. Cambridge, MA: Harvard University Press.

Hartley, J. (1997) *The Representative Agent in Macroeconomics*. London: Routledge.

Harvey, D. (1975) 'The geography of capitalist accumulation: A reconstruction of Marxist theory', *Antipode*, 7, pp. 9–21.

Harvey, D. (1982) *The Limits to Capital*. Chicago, IL: Chicago University Press.

Hassink, R. (2007) 'The strength of weak lock-ins: the renewal of the Westmunsterland textile industry', *Environment and Planning A*, 39, pp. 1147–1165.

Hassink, R. (2010) 'Locked in decline? On the role of regional lock-ins in old industrial areas', in Boschma, R. and R. Martin (Eds.), *Handbook of Evolutionary Economic Geography*. Cheltenham, UK: Edward Elgar, pp. 450–468.

Hayek, F. (1960) *The Constitution of Liberty*. London: Routledge and Kegan-Paul.

Herod, A. (1998) *Organizing the Landscape: Geographical Perspectives on Labor Unionism*. Minneapolis, MN: University of Minnesota Press.

Hidalgo, C., Klinger, A., Barabasi, A. & Hausmann, R. (2007) 'The product space conditions the development of nations', *Science*, 317, pp. 482–487.

Hodgson, G. (1993) *Economics and Evolution: Bringing Life Back into Economics*. Ann Arbor, MI: University of Michigan Press.

Hodgson, G. (Ed.) (2007) *The Evolution of Economic Institutions: A Critical Reader*. Cheltenham, UK: Edward Elgar.

Hodgson, G. & Huang, K. (2012) 'Evolutionary game theory and evolutionary economics: Are they different species?' *Journal of Evolutionary Economics*, 22, pp. 345–366.

Hodgson, G. & Knudsen, T. (2006) 'Why we need a generalized Darwinism, and why generalized Darwinism is not enough', *Journal of Economic Behavior and Organization*, 61, pp. 1–19.

Huggins, R. & Prokop, D. (2017) 'Network structure and regional innovation: A study of university and industry ties', *Urban Studies*, 54, pp. 931–952.

Iammarino, S. & McCann, P. (2006) 'The structure and evolution of industrial clusters: Transactions, technology and knowledge spillovers', *Research Policy*, 35, pp. 1018–1036.

Jack, G., Calas, M., Nkomo, S. & Peltonen, T. (2008) 'Introduction to special topic forum: Critique and international management – An uneasy relationship?' *Academy of Management Review*, 33, pp. 870–884.

Jacobs, J. (1969) *The Economy of Cities*. New York: Penguin Books.

Jaffe, A. (1986) 'Technological opportunity and spillovers of R&D: Evidence from firms' patents, profits and market value', National Bureau of Economic Research Working Paper # 1815.

Jaffe, A., Trajtenberg, M. & Henderson, R. (1993) 'Geographic localization of knowledge spillovers as evidenced by patent citations', *Quarterly Journal of Economics*, 108, pp. 577–598.

Jones, G. & Khanna, T. (2006) 'Bringing history (back) into International Business', *Journal of International Business Studies*, 37, pp. 453–468.

Kauffman, S. (1993) *The Origins of Order: Self-organization and Selection in Evolution*. Oxford, UK: Oxford University Press.

Kemeny, T. & Storper, M. (2015) 'Is specialization good for regional economic development?' *Regional Studies*, 49, pp. 1003–1018.

Kirman, A. (1992) 'Whom or what does the representative individual represent?' *The Journal of Economic Perspectives*, 6, pp. 117–136.

Klepper, S. (2007) 'Disagreements, spinoffs, and the evolution of Detroit as the capital of the U.S. automobile industry', *Management Science*, 53, pp. 616–631.

Kogler, D., Essletzbichler, J. & Rigby, D. (2016) 'The evolution of specialization in the EU15 knowledge space', *Journal of Economic Geography*, 17, pp. 345–373.

Kogler, D., Rigby, D. & Tucker, I. (2013) 'Mapping knowledge space and technological relatedness in U.S. cities', *European Planning Studies*, 21, pp. 1374–1391.

Kogut, B. & Zander, U. (1992) 'Knowledge of the firm, combinative capabilities, and the replication of technology', *Organization Science*, 3, pp. 383–397.

Kogut, B. & Zander, U. (1993) 'Knowledge of the firm and the evolutionary theory of the multinational corporation', *Journal of International Business Studies*, 24, pp. 516–529.

Lawson, C. & Lorenz, E. (1999) 'Collective learning, tacit knowledge and regional innovative capacity', *Regional Studies*, 33, pp. 305–317.

Lengyel, B. & Eriksson, R. (2015) 'Co-worker networks and productivity growth in regions', Papers in Evolutionary Economic Geography # 15.13, Utrecht University.

Loasby, B. (2002) *Knowledge, Institutions and Evolution in Economics*. London: Routledge.

Lobo, J. & Strumsky, D. (2008) 'Metropolitan patenting, inventor agglomeration and social networks: A tale of two effects', *Journal of Urban Economics*, 63, pp. 871–884.

Lundvall, B. & Johnson, B. (1994) 'The learning economy', *Journal of Industry Studies*, 1, pp. 23–42.

MacKinnon, D., Cumbers, A., Pike, A., Birch, K. & McMaster, R. (2009) 'Evolution in Economic Geography: Institutions, political economy, and adaptation', *Economic Geography*, 85, pp. 129–150.

March, J. (1991) 'Exploitation and exploration in organizational learning', *Organization Science*, 2, pp. 71–87.

Marshall, A. (1920) *Principles of Economics*. 8th edition. London: Macmillan.

Martin, R. (2000) 'Institutional approaches to Economic Geography', in Sheppard, E. & Barnes, T. (Eds.), *Companion to Economic Geography*. Oxford, UK: Blackwell, pp. 77–97.

Martin, R. (2010) 'Roepke lecture in Economic Geography: Rethinking regional path dependence – Beyond lock-in to evolution', *Economic Geography*, 86, pp. 1–27.

Martin, R. & Sunley, P. (1996) 'Paul Krugman's geographical economics and its implications for regional development theory: A critical assessment', *Economic Geography*, 72, pp. 259–292.

Martin, R. & Sunley, P. (2006) 'Path dependence and regional economic evolution', *Journal of Economic Geography*, 6, pp. 395–437.

Martin, R. & Sunley, P. (2007) 'Complexity thinking and evolutionary Economic Geography', *Journal of Economic Geography*, 7, pp. 573–601.

Maskell, P. (2001) 'Towards a knowledge-based theory of the geographical cluster', *Industrial and Corporate Change*, 10, pp. 919–941.

Maskell, P. & Malmberg, A. (1999) 'The competitiveness of firms and regions: "Ubiquitification" and the importance of localized learning', *European Urban and Regional Studies*, 6, pp. 9–25.

Massey, D. (1984) *Spatial Divisions of Labour: Social Structures and the Geography of Production*. London: Macmillan.

McCann, P. & Mudambi, R. (2005) 'Analytical differences in the economics of geography: The case of the multinational firm', *Environment and Planning A*, 37, pp. 1857–1876.

Metcalfe, J. (1998) *Evolutionary Economics as Creative Destruction*. London: Routledge.

Metcalfe, J., Foster, J. & Ramlogan, R. (2006) 'Adaptive economic growth', *Cambridge Journal of Economics*, 30, pp. 7–32.

Metcalfe, J. & Gibbons, M. (1986) 'Technological variety and the process of competition', *Economie Appliquée*, 39, pp. 493–520.

Miller, J. & Page, S. (2007) *Complex Adaptive Systems*. Princeton, NJ: Princeton University Press.

Mirowski, P. (1989) *More Heat Than Light: Economics as Social Physics, Physics as Nature's Economics*. Cambridge, UK: Cambridge University Press.

Morgan, K. (1997) 'The learning region: Institutions, innovation and regional renewal', *Regional Studies*, 31, pp. S147–S159.

Morrison, A. (2008) 'Gatekeepers of knowledge within industrial districts: Who are they, how they interact', *Regional Studies*, 42, pp. 817–835.

Mudambi, R. (2008) 'Location, control and innovation in knowledge-intensive industries', *Journal of Economic Geography*, 8, pp. 699–725.

Muneepeerakul, R., Lobo, J., Shutters, S., Gomez-Lievano, A. & Qubbaj, M. (2013) 'Urban economies and occupation space: Can they get "there" from "here"?' *Plos One*, 8, pp. 1–8.

Murman, J. (2003) *Knowledge and Competitive Advantage: The Coevolution of Firms, Technology, and National Institutions*. Cambridge, MA: Cambridge University Press.

Neffke, F. & Henning, M. (2013) 'Skill relatedness and firm diversification', *Strategic Management Journal*, 34, pp. 297–316.

Neffke, F., Henning, M. & Boschma, R. (2011) 'How do regions diversify over time? Industry relatedness and the development of new growth paths in regions', *Economic Geography*, 87, pp. 237–265.

Nelson, R. (2006) 'Evolutionary social science and universal Darwinism', *Journal of Evolutionary Economics*, 16, pp. 491–510.

Nelson, R. & Winter, S. (1982) *An Evolutionary Theory of Economic Change*. Cambridge, MA: Belknap Press of Harvard University Press.

North, D. (1990) *Institutions, Institutional Change and Economic Performance*. New York: Cambridge University Press.

Noteboom, B. (2000) *Learning and Innovation in Organizations and Economies*. Oxford, UK: Oxford University Press.

Peck, J. (2005) 'Economic sociologies in space', *Economic Geography*, 81, pp. 129–176.

Peck, J. & Theodore, N. (2007) 'Variegated capitalism', *Progress in Human Geography*, 31, pp. 731–772.

Peng, M., Wang, D. & Jiang, Y. (2008) 'An institution-based view of International Business strategy: A focus on emerging economies', *Journal of International Business Studies*, 39, pp. 920–936.

Pike, A., MacKinnon, D., Cumbers, A., Dawley, S. & McMaster, R. (2016) 'Doing evolution in Economic Geography', *Economic Geography*, 92, pp. 123–144.

Plummer, P. & Sheppard, E. (2001) 'Must emancipatory Economic Geography be qualitative? A response to Amin and Thrift', *Antipode*, 30, pp. 758–763.
Plummer, P. & Sheppard, E. (2006) 'Geography matters: Agency, structures and dynamics at the intersection of economics and geography', *Journal of Economic Geography*, 6, pp. 619–638.
Polanyi, K. (1957) *The Great Transformation*. Boston: Beacon Press.
Poon, J. & Rigby, D.L. (2017) *International Trade: The Basics*. New York: Routledge.
Potter, A. & Watts, H. (2011) 'Evolutionary agglomeration theory: Increasing returns, diminishing returns, and the industry life-cycle', *Journal of Economic Geography*, 11, pp. 417–455.
Potts, J. (2000) *The New Evolutionary Microeconomics*. Cheltenham, UK: Edward Elgar.
Powell, W., White, D., Koput, K. & Owen-Smith, J. (2005) 'Network dynamics and field evolution: The growth of interorganizational collaboration in the life sciences', *American Journal of Sociology*, 110, pp. 1132–1205.
Quatraro, F. (2010) 'Knowledge coherence, variety and economic growth: Manufacturing evidence from Italian regions', *Research Policy*, 39, pp. 1289–1302.
Rigby, D. (2015) 'Technological relatedness and knowledge space: Entry and exit of U.S. cities from patent classes', *Regional Studies*, 49, pp. 1192–1937.
Rigby, D. & Brown, W. (2015) 'Who benefits from agglomeration?' *Regional Studies*, 49, pp. 28–43.
Rigby, D. & Essletzbichler, J. (1997) 'Evolution, process variety, and regional trajectories of technological change', *Economic Geography*, 73, pp. 269–284.
Rigby, D. & Essletzbichler, J. (2006) 'Technological variety, technological change and a geography of production techniques', *Journal of Economic Geography*, 6, pp. 45–70.
Safarzynska, K. & van den Bergh, J. (2010) 'Evolutionary models in economics: A survey of methods and building blocks', *Journal of Evolutionary Economics*, 20, pp. 329–373.
Saviotti, P. (1996) *Technological Evolution, Variety and the Economy*. Cheltenham, UK: Edward Elgar.
Saxenian, A. (1994) *Regional Advantage*. Cambridge, MA: Harvard University Press.
Schamp, E. (2010) 'On the notion of co-evolution in Economic Geography', in Boschma, R. & Martin, R. (Eds.), *The Handbook of Evolutionary Economic Geography*. Cheltenham, UK: Edward Elgar, pp. 432–449.
Schumpeter, J. (1942) *Capitalism, Socialism and Democracy*. New York: Harper and Row.
Scott, A. (1988) *New Industrial Spaces*. London: Pion.
Sheppard, E. & Barnes, T. (1990) *The Capitalist Space Economy*. London: Unwin Hyman.
Simmie, J. (2012) 'Path dependence and new technological path creation in the Danish wind power industry', *European Planning Studies*, 20, pp. 753–772.
Simmie, J. & Martin, R. (2010) 'The economic resilience of regions: Towards an evolutionary approach', *Cambridge Journal of Regions, Economy and Society*, 3, pp. 27–43.
Simon, H. (1957) *Models of Man*. New York: John Wiley.
Smith, A. (1776) *An Inquiry into the Nature and Causes of the Wealth of Nations*. London: Strahan and Cadell.
Storper, M. (1997) *The Regional World*. New York: Guilford Press.
Storper, M. & Venables, A. (2004) 'Buzz: Face-to-face contact and the urban economy', *Journal of Economic Geography*, 4, pp. 351–370.
Storper, M. & Walker, R. (1989) *The Capitalist Imperative: Territory, Technology and Industrial Growth*. New York: Basil Blackwell.
Sugden, R. (1989) 'Spontaneous order', *Journal of Economic Perspectives*, 3, pp. 85–97.
Teece, D. (2014) 'A dynamic capabilities-based entrepreneurial theory of the multinational enterprise', *Journal of International Business Studies*, 45, pp. 602–607.
Teece, D. & Pisano, G. (1994) 'The dynamic capabilities of firms: an introduction', *Industrial and Corporate Change*, 3, pp. 537–556.
Teece, D., Pisano, G. & A. Shuen (1997) 'Dynamic capabilities and strategic management', *Strategic Management Journal*, 18, pp. 509–533.
Teece, D., Rumelt, R., Dosi, G. & Winter, S. (1994) 'Understanding corporate coherence: Theory and evidence', *Journal of Economic Behavior and Organization*, 23, pp. 1–30.
Ter Wal, A. & Boschma, R. (2009) 'Applying social network analysis in Economic Geography: Framing some key analytic issues', *Annals of Regional Science*, 43, pp. 739–756.
Van den Bergh, J. & Gowdy, J. (2009) 'A group selection perspective on economic behavior, institutions and organization', *Journal of Economic Behavior and Organization*, 72, pp. 1–20.
Veblen, T. (1898) 'Why is economics not an evolutionary science?' *Quarterly Journal of Economics*, 12, pp. 373–397.

Volberda, H. & Lewin, A. (2003) 'Guest editors' introduction: Co-evolutionary dynamics within and between firms – From evolution to co-evolution', *Journal of Management Studies*, 40, pp. 2111–2136.
Vromen, J. (2001) 'The human agent in evolutionary economics', in Laurent, J. & Nightingale, J. (Eds.), *Darwinism and Evolutionary Economics*. Cheltenham, UK: Edward Elgar, pp. 184–208.
Webber, M. & Rigby, D. (1996) *The Golden Age Illusion: Rethinking Postwar Capitalism*. New York: Guilford.
Wernerfelt, B. (1984) 'A resource based view of the firm', *Strategic Management*, 5, pp. 171–180.
Williamson, O. (1985) *The Economic Institutions of Capitalism*. New York: The Free Press.
Wilson, D. (2016) 'Two meanings of complex adaptive systems', in Wilson, D. & Kirman, A. (Eds.), *Complexity and Evolution*. Cambridge, MA: MIT Press, pp. 31–46.
Wilson, D. & Kirman, A. (Eds.) (2016) *Complexity and Evolution*. Cambridge, MA: MIT Press.
Wilson, E. (1975) *Sociobiology: The New Synthesis*. Cambridge, MA: Belknap Press.
Witt, U. (2003) *The Evolving Economy: Essays on the Evolutionary Approach to Economics*. Cheltenham, UK: Edward Elgar.
Witt, U. (2004) 'On the proper interpretation of "evolution" in economics and its implications for production theory', *Journal of Economic Methodology*, 11, pp. 125–146.
Witt, U. (2006) 'Evolutionary concepts in economics and biology', *Journal of Evolutionary Economics*, 16, pp. 473–476.
Zander, I. (2002) 'The formation of international innovation networks in the multinational corporation: An evolutionary perspective', *Industrial and Corporate Change*, 11, pp. 327–353.
Zhu, S., He, C. & Zhou, Y. (2015) 'How to jump further? Path dependent and path breaking in an uneven industry space'. Papers in Evolutionary Economic Geography #15.24, Utrecht University, the Netherlands.

9
GLOBAL PRODUCTION NETWORKS

Neil M. Coe

Introduction

The world economy has changed profoundly in recent times. It is now widely accepted that organizationally fragmented and geographically dispersed production systems constitute the dominant 'architecture' of the contemporary global economy. These systems, which have risen to prominence since the 1990s, are tightly controlled and coordinated by lead firms that derive power from their dominant position in either intermediate or final consumer markets. In its *World Investment Report 2013*, for instance, UNCTAD estimated that some 80 per cent of international trade was now organized through so-called global value chains/production networks (UNCTAD, 2013). Their emergence has posed key challenges to theories from International Business (IB) that primarily focus on the transnational corporation (TNC) and its directly owned operations to understand the organizational and developmental dynamics of the global economy. Instead, theories are required that can accommodate the complex global webs of equity, non-equity and market relations through which the production and circulation of goods and services are increasingly controlled and coordinated. In this context, since the 1990s, significant progress has been made in developing global chain/network approaches for theorizing the organizational complexities of the contemporary global economy. Although first initiated in economic sociology, since the early 2000s economic geographers have made a notable series of contributions to this burgeoning field, primarily under the rubric of the *global production network* (GPN)[1] framework.

In general terms, GPN research seeks to develop a conceptual framework linking the processes of global production network formation and organization to differential developmental outcomes. A global production network can be defined as an organizational arrangement, comprising interconnected economic and non-economic actors, coordinated by a global lead firm, and producing goods or services across multiple geographical locations for worldwide markets (Coe & Yeung, 2015). This approach thus focuses squarely on the *actors* that constitute GPNs, with a lead firm, i.e. a powerful transnational corporation, being a necessary prerequisite, and on the *multiple locations* that are bound together by the economic relations between those various actors. In this sense, the idea of a global production network highlights the actor-specific coordination and cooperation strategies through which such networks are constructed, managed and sustained, and their on-the-ground developmental implications.

Against this general backdrop, this chapter seeks to do three things. First, it will very briefly map out the intellectual lineage and core elements of the GPN approach. Second, it will profile recent developments in the field that collectively constitute an attempt to develop a 'GPN 2.0' iteration of the theory.[2] Third, it will delimit several points of connection between contemporary GPN approaches and work in IB. These connections suggest the potential for a productive interchange of concepts and ideas between the two fields moving forward.

Context: from GCCs to GPNs

While several detailed accounts of the intellectual development of global chain/network approaches now exist (e.g. Bair, 2005; Sturgeon, 2009; Coe & Yeung, 2015), the bare bones are as follows (see also Table 9.1). The 1994 publication of Gereffi and Korceniewiecz's edited volume *Commodity Chains and Global Capitalism* launched a highly influential strand of global commodity chain (GCC) research. Building upon Immanuel Wallerstein's world-system framework, the analysis proposed GCCs as a new conceptual category for "understanding the changing spatial organization of production and consumption in the contemporary world-economy" (Gereffi, Korzeniewicz & Korzeniewicz, 1994, p. 2). Each global commodity chain was deemed to have four interrelated dimensions. First, the input–output structure identified the various economic activities that come together in a value-adding sequence to deliver a good or service. Second, the territoriality referred to the spatial configuration of the various actors involved, be that in terms of spatial concentration or dispersal, or more likely combinations of the two. Third, each global commodity chain embodied a governance regime reflecting the relations of power and authority within the chain and how they shaped the flows of materials, capital, technology and knowledge therein; in this regard, Gereffi's (1994) seminal distinction between 'producer-driven' and 'buyer-driven' commodity chains has subsequently been particularly influential. Fourth, GCCs are reflective of the wider institutional frameworks that surround them, and particularly state and supra-state policies and regulations in domains such as trade, investment and technology.

Although GCC work still continues today, in many ways it has been superseded by the emergence of the global value chains (GVC) perspective from the early 2000s onwards. Central to this initiative has been a concerted attempt to deepen the theorization of inter-firm governance. Most notably, by intersecting the three supply chain variables of complexity of transactions, the ability to codify transactions and the capabilities within the supply base, Gereffi, Humphrey and Sturgeon (2005) develop a five-fold typology of governance within GVCs. In addition to the pure forms of market and hierarchy, they identify modular, relational and captive forms of governance that rely on intermediate levels of coordination and control. More recent work has focused on the different modes and levels of governance operating within GVCs, distinguishing between overall drivenness (the GCC distinction between buyer or producer driven), different forms of coordination (the five types just noted), and the wider 'normalization' processes that operate along the chain (Ponte & Sturgeon, 2014). Two other important developments within the GVC literature relate to how sub-national spaces (e.g. clusters) 'plug-in' to global value chains (Humphrey & Schmitz, 2002), and how firms and localities can subsequently improve their position within such chains over time in a process commonly known as upgrading (Kaplinsky & Morris, 2001).

GCC research and early GVC work were clearly important inspirations for the development of the initial GPN framework in Economic Geography (here termed 'GPN 1.0') in the early 2000s (see Table 9.1). GPN 1.0 emphasizes the complex intra-, inter-, and extra-firm networks involved in any economic activity, and how these are structured both organizationally and

Table 9.1 An introduction to global chain/network approaches

	Global commodity chains (GCCs)	*Global value chains (GVCs)*	*Global production networks (GPNs) 1.0*	*Global production networks (GPNs) 2.0*
Disciplinary background	Economic Sociology	Economic Sociology Development Studies Industry Studies	Economic Geography International Political Economy	Economic Geography
Object of enquiry	Inter-firm networks in global industries	Sectoral logics of global industries	Global network configurations and regional development (heuristic)	Global network configurations and regional development (causal)
Orienting concepts	Industry structure Governance (producer-driven/ buyer-driven distinction) Industrial upgrading	Value-added chains Governance models (modular, relational, captive) Transaction costs Industrial upgrading and rents	Value creation, enhancement and capture Corporate, collective and institutional power Societal, network and territorial embeddedness Strategic coupling	Dynamic drivers Organizational strategies Value capture trajectories Modes and types of strategic coupling
Intellectual influences	World systems theory Organizational sociology	International Business literature Trade economics GCCs	Relational Economic Geography GCCs/GVCs, actor-network theory, varieties of capitalism	GVCs/GPN 1.0 Resource-based firm theory Financialization studies
Key texts	Gereffi and Korzeniewicz (1994); Gereffi (1999)	Humphrey and Schmitz (2002); Gereffi et al. (2005)	Henderson et al. (2002); Coe et al. (2004)	Coe and Yeung (2015); Yeung and Coe (2015)

Source: Inputs from Bair (2005) for first two columns.

geographically. In addition to similar impulses to those that were driving the shift from GCC to GVC analyses at that time – most notably the desire for more nuanced understandings of governance dynamics and more thorough incorporation of multiple scales of analysis beyond the global and the national – the GPN approach differs more profoundly in other aspects. Inspiration was drawn, for instance, from *actor-network theory* in terms of its conceptualization of social systems as complex networks of power relations with emergent properties, and the *varieties of capitalism* literature with respect to how different institutional configurations leave a distinctive imprint on firms that originate from, and/or are located in, particular national territories.

Hence, from the outset, GPN analysis sought to distinguish itself from GCC and GVC approaches in several key regards. First, through the explicit consideration of *extra-firm networks*, it necessarily brings into view the broad range of extra-firm institutions – for example, supranational organizations, government agencies, trade unions, employer associations, NGOs and consumer groups – that have the potential to shape firm activities in the locations that are connected by GPNs. In this way, it seeks to move beyond the prioritization of inter-firm networks in GCC/GVC accounts, and brings extra-firm actors into GPNs, rather than simply seeing them as part of the wider context. Second, GPN analysis is innately *multi-scalar*, and considers the interactions and mutual constitution of all spatial scales from the local to the global. Third, it is an avowedly *network* approach that seeks to move beyond the analytical limitations of the chain notion. Production systems are seen as networked and recursive meshes of intersecting vertical and horizontal connections in order to avoid deterministic linear interpretations of how production systems operate and how value is generated and distributed.

The mobilization of the GPN framework, in turn, depends on the operationalization of three interrelated variables. First, processes of *value creation, enhancement* and *capture* are scrutinized. Value is seen to derive from the rents of different kinds that firms can extract from their position within the wider GPN. Firms specialize in particular kinds of rents, and the nature of economic value will thus vary across the production network. While it is possible to think dynamically about the potential for value enhancement through firm-to-firm processes of knowledge and technology transfer, and industrial upgrading, ultimately it is important to consider which firms and which locations succeed in capturing value. Second, the distribution and operation of *power* of different forms within GPNs is considered. In GPN analysis, power is seen as relational, transaction specific and co-existing with relations of dependency. It can also be mobilized in GPNs not just by corporate actors, but by institutions such as the state and collective actors such as labour. Third, the *embeddedness* of GPNs – or how they constitute and are re-constituted by the ongoing economic, social and political arrangements of the places they inhabit – is investigated. Most notably a distinction between societal, network and territorial forms of embeddedness allows nuanced consideration of the importance of socio-cultural and institutional contexts to all GPN activities.

Another key contribution of GPN 1.0 analysis has been in the theorization of (subnational) regional economic development through the *strategic coupling* of GPNs with the localized assets of regional economies. GPN analysis suggests that economies of scale and scope embedded within specific regions are only advantageous to those regions, and bring about regional development, insofar as they can complement the strategic needs of lead firms in GPNs. The notion of strategic coupling has three important characteristics: it is strategic in that it needs active intervention on the part of both regional institutions and powerful GPN actors to occur, it is time-space contingent as it is subject to change and represents a temporary coalition between local and non-local actors, and it transcends territorial boundaries as actors from different spatial scales interact. This multi-scalarity also encompasses the activities of the institutional actors that seek to promote regional advantages and enhance a region's articulation into GPNs. These regional institutions include not only regionally specific institutions, but also local arms of national/supranational bodies (e.g. a trade union's local chapters), and extra-local institutions that affect activities within the region without necessarily having a presence (e.g. a national tax authority).

Currents: towards a GPN 2.0?

The original GPN 1.0 framework thus emphasizes the complex firm networks and territorial institutions involved in globalized economic activity, and how these are structured both organizationally and geographically. Indeed, it has proved relatively successful in offering a flexible, geographical *heuristic* framework for mapping the shifting arrangements of GPNs. Recently, however, there have been attempts to develop a new iteration – GPN 2.0 (see Table 9.1) – with enhanced capacity for *causal* explanation of the links between GPN configurations and uneven territorial development within the global economy (Coe & Yeung, 2015). This theoretical evolution is underpinned by four interlinked sets of conceptual developments which are considered in the following subsections.

Delimiting GPNs

Oddly, perhaps, given the relative maturity of the literature in this area, there are still challenges and inconsistencies relating to the definition and delimitation of GPNs. More specifically, the tendency to characterize GPN configurations at the industry level (a hallmark of GVC approaches) has important limitations. Instead, we need to understand individual GPNs as lead-firm based configurations. While they will exhibit industry traits, at the same time there will be considerable variation between GPNs even in the same industry or product category, depending on the lead firm's ownership mode, nationality, corporate culture and strategic disposition. Fuller attention also needs to be ascribed to how GPNs connect with their end users and markets, broadly defined. Many studies tend to identify a lead firm and then work 'backwards' or 'upstream' to explore inter-firm relationships with suppliers. We should perhaps give as much, if not more, consideration to forward or downstream linkages, first to reveal the networks of distributors, resellers, retailers, etc. that connect lead firms to their markets, and second, to enable consideration of the important recent literature highlighting recycling and the post-consumption 'after-lives' of products and services (e.g. Gregson et al., 2010).

Enhanced precision in delimiting these networks will in turn allow us to better conceptualize the intersections between different GPNs in different industries (e.g. the role of finance and logistics firms in the electronics industry or the role of ICT products and services in automobiles, aviation and banking). These cross-cutting connections are not peripheral to the operation of GPNs, but rather are fundamental to the value creation, enhancement and capture dynamics within all of the interconnecting industries. Finally, the complex spatiality of GPNs needs to be more effectively conceptualized. In addition to the often discussed 'vertical' dimension of GPNs (i.e. the links across the different nodes in the GPN), appreciation is required of the 'horizontal territorial interfaces' that co-constitute the GPN, i.e. the on-the-ground places and patterns of economic development that result from localities 'plugging in' to GPNs.

Driving GPNs

The second major imperative in GPN 2.0 is to theorize the underlying political-economic forces that shape the ongoing formation and reconfiguration of GPNs; so doing will help explain contemporary shifts in GPN organization (e.g. responding to the rise of Asia as a vitally important end-market). While there is often implicit or explicit acknowledgement of cost factors in the extant GVC/GPN literatures, there is less consideration of how costs are always traded off against firm capabilities, and of market development and financialization as further drivers of GPN dynamics. A productive way forward in this context is to think of how global lead firms and their suppliers are increasingly confronted with the competitive challenges of optimizing their cost-capability ratios, sustaining market development through, for example, shortening their time-to-market, and working with the immensely disciplining pressures of global finance. These three dynamic forces compel firms and extra-firm actors to develop active strategies in order to thrive in today's highly competitive global economy.

To sustain or further their competitive positions, lead firms and their network partners need to optimize cost-capability ratios in recursive ways that reduce costs over time and/or enhance firm-specific capabilities. These dynamics are at the forefront of globalizing industries such as apparel, electronics and automobiles. Over time, optimizing cost-capability ratios may allow lead firms to succeed only in existing markets. In delimiting the market development imperative, GPN 2.0 frames how, irrespective of their cost-capability ratios, global lead firms and their network partners must continually develop new markets for their products and services, whether in advanced economies or in newly emerging economies. This market-making highlights the causal importance of the intermediate and final consumption of goods and services in the geographical dispersion of their production and distribution. In so doing, it affords greater analytical weight to customers and their consumption in shaping how economic and non-economic actors orchestrate or participate in different GPNs.

As global financial integration takes place in tandem with global production, a third dynamic of financial discipline, often under-played in the existing literature (although see Milberg & Winkler, 2013), places great emphasis on short-term returns to shareholders and corporate restructuring and downsizing to increase shareholder value. This process of 'financializing' lead firms in manufacturing and non-financial service industries has profound impacts on the corporate organization and governance of GPNs. Coupled with the first two dynamic forces, financialization exerts enormous pressures on lead firms to optimize cost-capability ratios and to capture more value from new markets. More importantly, it incentivizes these lead firms to seek greater shareholder returns through investment not in new plants and equipment, but in financial assets that may not be related to these firms' core products or services. Investment decisions by lead firms are thus often trumped by short-term financial returns rather than longer-term synergies in production and market development arising from product and/or technological complementarities.

Bringing together these dynamics provides vital purchase on *why* GPNs emerge and evolve. But such analysis needs to be augmented with nuanced consideration of the diverse and substantial *risks* associated with global production. As global leading firms engage more in international outsourcing and as their foreign partners and suppliers actively develop their own firm-specific capabilities, all the firms are confronted with an operating environment that is much less certain and predictable than their home economies and domestic markets. Some of these uncertainties can be calculated and translated into different forms of risk specific to GPNs (e.g. economic, product, regulatory, labour and environmental risks). Mitigating these risks not only forces firms to develop specific strategies (see next subsection), but also necessitates the involvement of other non-economic actors in these GPNs.

Overall, deepening our understanding of these drivers can underpin development of an *evolutionary* approach to GPNs that foregrounds the factors underpinning (a) their initial formation and (b) their subsequent reconfigurations (both dimensions will vary considerably across firms, sectors, geographies and time periods). Oddly, many studies in the GVC/GPN genre seemingly take the initial formation of GPNs as a given, preferring to investigate their internal dynamics only in the post-establishment phase. The challenge here is to chart the shifting intersections of (or episodic shifts in) dynamics of technological change, market development, financialization and risk mitigation in shaping the formation and development of GPNs.

Developing GPNs

Third, GPN 2.0 advocates a clear focus on actor strategies. In short, strategy matters in analysing the diverse actor practices and network configurations that result from the intersecting drivers outlined earlier. Considering strategy reveals actor intentionality and agency, reducing the potential for simply 'reading off' firm actions in relation to their role and position in relation to wider sectoral or industrial organizational configurations. Actors tend to adopt multiple strategies to cope with different configurations of competitive dynamics and risk environments. By mapping the dynamics and risks of GPNs onto the strategic choices employed by different network actors, it is possible to demonstrate that not only are there diverse possible trajectories for competitive success in global industries, but also that this multiplicity of strategic choices and network configurations defies simple characterization (see Table 9.2).

More specifically it is possible to discern firm- and industry-specificities in the operationalization of four strategies in singular or combinatorial forms: intra-firm coordination, inter-firm control, inter-firm partnership and extra-firm bargaining. Intra-firm coordination tends to be deployed by firms subject to strong market imperatives and high levels of risk. Their network configurations are likely to be internalized through domestic expansion, FDI and M&As. On the contrary, firms under pressure from high cost-capability ratios and financial discipline are likely to engage in inter-firm control through production outsourcing and dependent integration of suppliers into their GPNs. In this mode of externalization, an inter-firm partnership relationship can be developed if firms enjoy significant complementarities and mutual dependency

Table 9.2 Firm-specific strategies and organizational outcomes in global production networks

Strategy as actor practice	*Competitive dynamics*			*Risks*	*GPN structure as organizational outcomes*
	Cost-capability ratio	*Market imperative*	*Financial discipline*		
Intra-firm coordination (e.g. pharmaceuticals and retail)	Low	High	Low	High	Domestic expansion and/ or FDI and M&As; high level of network integration
Inter-firm control (e.g. automobiles and IT services)	High	Low	High	Moderate	Outsourcing but dependent integration of suppliers
Inter-firm partnership (e.g. electronics and logistics)	High	High	High	High	Outsourcing, joint development with partners and platform leaders
Extra-firm bargaining (e.g. resources and agrofood)	Medium	High	High	High	Differentiated integration into global production systems

Source: Yeung and Coe, 2015, table 4.

in the context of highly competitive market dynamics and risky environments. Similar competitive and risk environments may also compel firms to enter into bargaining relationships with extra-firm actors in order to extract greater value from their GPNs.

While for analytical purposes it is useful to disentangle the four different types of strategy, the reality for many firms is that they are usually actively combining two or more such strategies across their various operations and activities. Global retailers, for instance, in different ways combine internalized store operations with strong control over myriad small- and medium-sized suppliers, partnership-style arrangements with large brand suppliers and logistics providers, and the ongoing management of multi-stranded extra-firm relations, for instance with planners and regulators in local and national government. Such an approach, then, is underpinned by recognition of the importance of variability in understanding how firms, originating from different home economies and endowed with different ownership structures and corporate cultures, might respond differently to competitive dynamics and risks, thereby pursuing contrasting firm-specific strategies in configuring their GPNs.

Depending on GPNs

Finally, GPN 2.0 seeks to further understand the development and dependency outcomes for the places that are connected into GPNs. Although highly productive in many ways, recent debates have revealed potential limitations within the prevailing upgrading approach (e.g. Tokatli, 2013). Instead it might be more productive to think in terms of the many different *value capture trajectories* that can result when a firm in a particular locality connects into a GPN (including instances of decoupling, recoupling and shifting between different networks). This approach allows consideration of the multiple possible outcomes – both positive and negative – in dynamic and evolutionary terms of such intersections, and reflects the multiple roles that a single firm may perform in a wider network. Regional economic development can then be thought of as powerfully shaped by the aggregation of these firm-level value capture trajectories.

In turn, the aforementioned notion of strategic coupling can be further developed to delimit the different ways in which regional economies intersect with GPNs. We can think in terms of different modes (e.g. indigenous, functional and structural coupling) and types (e.g. innovation hubs, logistics hubs, assembly platforms, etc.) of strategic coupling which reflect how certain kinds of value capture trajectories and couplings often come to dominate at the regional level. While individual regions may exhibit more than one type of coupling, straddling different modes is much less common. These different modes, in turn, underpin economic development due to their variable potential for value capture, their different configurations of control and dependency, and their different susceptibilities to decoupling. Importantly, strategic coupling must always be framed in dynamic terms (i.e. decoupling and recoupling) and as driving both positive and negative economic developmental outcomes.

This enhanced notion of strategic coupling also provides a way into thinking about the wider *political* contexts in which GPNs are incontrovertibly embedded – these are often obscured by the predominant focus on inter-firm relations in existing research. GPNs necessarily involve control of and struggle over power, resources and value on an ongoing basis (Levy, 2008). In other words, the 'extra-firm' or 'institutional' dimensions of GPNs need to be taken seriously. In addition to the multi-level state (e.g. international organizations and local authorities), the other key categories of non-firm actor are labour, civil society organizations, industry associations, consumers and standards-setting agencies (the latter may overlap with some or all of the former categories). By foregrounding notions of control, power, struggle, rivalry and contestation over value and its distribution, the constitutive role of such actors in GPNs can be revealed.

Such insights are vital for better theorization of the development implications of 'plugging in' to GPNs, for instance in terms of the distribution of value between production network participants, and beyond the network to other actors in the regional economy.

Connections: productive points of exchange

Thus far, the chapter has positioned GPN research and introduced current areas of debate and theoretical development within the field. This section moves on to discuss potential points of connection between the research agenda described earlier and contemporary concerns in IB. In making such an assessment, it is important to note that both fields are rapidly evolving, and static characterizations must be avoided. Nonetheless, it remains fair to say that *direct* engagements between the two literatures have hitherto been rather sparse (although see Beugelsdijk, Pedersen & Petersen, 2009; Narula & Dunning, 2010).[3] In general terms, as de Marchi, di Maria and Ponte (2014) note, GVC/GPN analysis poses several broad challenges to IB research with respect to: (1) appreciating the significance of the shift from individual firms to production networks as the key unit of analysis; (2) the rise of retailers and buyers as lead firms in addition to the well-studied manufacturing firms; (3) increasingly fine-grained analysis of modes of production network governance; and (4) the recognition that knowledge flows along production networks can be as important as those within TNCs. In short, as de Marchi, di Maria and Ponte (2014, p. 465) assert, "decisions on how to manage the value chain the MNC is embedded in are becoming as strategic as those concerning the internal configuration of the MNC, between HQ and subunits".

That being said, there has been increasing engagement with the idea of global production fragmentation in the IB literature, most notably through Buckley's notion of the 'world factory' created by the outsourcing of routine activities by advanced economy TNCs (e.g. Buckley & Ghauri, 2004; Buckley, 2009; Buckley & Strange, 2015). Buckley and Strange (2015), for instance, engage in direct dialogue with Gereffi's GVC work. Other studies have looked at the role of leading TNCs as network 'orchestrators' or 'coordinators' (Parkhe & Dhanaraj, 2003; Vahlne & Johanson, 2013). However, these approaches still tend to underestimate the degree of production fragmentation and the sophistication of the tasks that are coordinated through GPNs, and complex non-equity forms of control and coordination continue to be downplayed in relation to the internal hierarchies of TNCs. Other IB work has looked at the outsourcing/offshoring decision-making nexus in TNCs as a force driving the formation of GPNs, with routine tasks (including manufacturing) being identified as candidates for externalization and with knowledge-based activities being retained in-house (e.g. Mudambi, 2008; Mudambi & Venzin, 2010). In a nuanced analysis, for instance, Contractor et al. (2010) conceptualize how a firm's core competence lies in the ability to optimize its degree of value chain disaggregation, the mix of internal, alliance-based and contractual modes therein, the geographic spread of operations and the chronological coordination of distributed tasks. In a general sense, then, it is not hard to see how the concerns of the GPN and IB literatures can be brought together.

Beyond these general convergences, however, there are some more specific areas that offer potential for the co-development of ideas between GPN 2.0 analysis and IB. Four interrelated themes will be identified here, though the list is not meant to be exhaustive. First, as noted earlier, in GPN 2.0 the *market imperative* is seen as one of three under-studied dynamics driving processes of GPN formation and reconfiguration. In particular, the rise of new markets in emerging economies is proving transformative, and has implications both for lead firms from advanced economies looking to access these markets, and in the formation of new lead firms within emerging economies that may subsequently look to 'go global'. These ideas resonate clearly with recent work in IB by Brandt and Thun (2010, 2016), for instance. Through research on the automobile, construction and machine tool industries in China, they note how the 'low-end' of the large domestic market is dominated by domestic firms whose ability to operate cheaply insulates them from foreign competition, "allowing the more capable domestic firms to gain from scale, experience, and revenue vital to upgrading efforts and shifts to higher end segments" (Brandt & Thun, 2010, p. 1571). Emerging market firms that view their home territory as an important market may in turn engage with suppliers from developed economies in ways that challenge existing understandings of inter-firm governance modes (Sako & Zylberberg, 2015). At the same time, rapid growth in the 'low-end' segments is encouraging foreign lead firms to localize their design activities and sourcing patterns for both components and capital equipment. As Thun (2015, p. 2) aptly describes,

> [t]he growth of large emerging markets means that the endpoints of many GVCs are now in developing countries rather than developed, and as a result, different rules of the game apply. In buyer-driven chains, the emerging market firms will have the more nuanced understanding of what consumers want; in producer-driven chains, the technologies that are demanded are more likely to be within the range of emerging market firm's capabilities . . . the competitive dynamics of the "fight for the middle" are very different than traditional competition for the most technologically-demanding segments.

A second area of common interest relates to *corporate strategy*. Long a core concern in IB, GPN 2.0 attempts to enhance interest in the various corporate strategies that firms in GPNs pursue in response to competitive drivers. An obvious point here is that in re-opening the 'black-box' of the firm in order to understand these strategies, GPN research may learn from the IB literature in terms of characterizing different types of global strategic action. A perhaps more important insight, however, is that the different modes of governance identified in GVC analysis are as much an outcome of firm strategies as they are a shaper of those strategies. Such a view accords with work in IB suggesting that "firm-level strategy is not just about *positioning* the firm within an existing global value chain with a pre-determined governance mode, but also about *configuring* governance modes in line with the company's strategic goals" (Sako & Zylberberg, 2015, pp. 20–21, emphasis in original). Firms have considerable choice in terms of the governance forms they select, the markets they serve and their geographical configuration, and these choices need to be seen in the context of wider GPN structures, but as not necessarily driven by those structures (Thun, 2015). An area of common interest would thereby be to further explore the 'make or buy' decision, and the strategic considerations behind that, and how these decisions in turn create certain governance outcomes in GPNs, rather than the other way around. Importantly, this should apply not just to lead firms, but also other influential actors such as global suppliers (Azmeh & Nadvi, 2014), strategic partners and specialized service providers. Furthermore, as GPN 2.0 argues, the expectation should be of significant variation in, and complex combinations of, strategies across different firms, sectors and territories. As Sako and Zylberberg (2015, p. 23) note, firms "have a menu of strategic options to choose from, resulting in more than one potentially successful strategy in each sector for shifting governance mode and capturing more power".

Relatedly, a third area of potential symbiosis concerns the dynamics of *value capture*. In GPN 2.0, firm-level value capture dynamics are seen to be fundamental to processes of territorial economic development. Firms will strategize to maximize the level of capture, and their ability to do so effectively will depend on a number of broader influences: firm-level capabilities (e.g. managerial expertise, capacity to raise financial capital), GPN-level influences (e.g. the configuration of power relations between network members, the ease with which the role of the firm can be substituted), industry specificities (e.g. growing or stagnant market, level of cost competition), but also territorialized conditions (e.g. the extent to which activities are supported and facilitated by local policy and incentive structures) (Coe & Yeung, 2015). For de Marchi, di Maria and Ponte (2014), GVC/GPN analysis has the potential to reveal the importance of GPN dynamics in particular for shaping learning and value dynamics among suppliers, who may evolve autonomously or through lead firm investment. In this context, processes of value creation and enhancement need to be disentangled from those of value capture. Two points of connection with the IB literature are apparent here. While theoretically rich, GPN analysis has thus far struggled to actually quantify levels of value capture within GPNs. The seminal work of Dedrick, Kraemer and Linden (2010) on "who benefits from innovation" in consumer electronics is therefore instructive in this regard. In turn, Sako and Zylberberg (2015) suggest that Teece's (1986) "profiting from innovation" framework might usefully be brought to bear on GPN dynamics. With a focus on three sets of factors – the 'appropriability regime' (barriers to imitation, both technological and legal), the nature of technological evolution (whether cutting edge or standardized) and the nature of complementary assets (e.g. distribution channels and reverse logistics) – Teece provides ways of thinking about whether firm-level upgrading processes translate into value capture dynamics (see also Jacobides, Knudsen & Augier, 2006). When combined with the focus on firm strategy alluded to earlier, productive synergies with GPN approaches might be forged in this regard.

Finally, the *complex geographies* of GPNs would merit further examination from both perspectives. As one would expect from a framework emanating from geography, GPN theory currently has a more refined appreciation of those geographies – as noted earlier, GPN 2.0 makes a distinction between the vertical and horizontal dimensions to such networks, revealing not just the inter-place connections (vertical) but also the on-the-ground territorialities (horizontal) that constitute GPNs. These two dimensions, of course, are interdependent, with the lines of influence running in both directions at the network/territory interface. IB, by contrast, has hitherto tended to have a more impoverished spatial imagination in this context, with geography largely being interpreted as either 'locations' in Cartesian space or within contrasting national 'places' (e.g. Dunning, 1998; Beugelsdijk, McCann & Mudambi, 2010). The primacy of the national scale when accounting for spatial difference can also be seen in debates on the embeddedness of TNCs (e.g. Meyer, Mudambi & Narula, 2011). Two sets of refinements are required in this regard. First, IB approaches need to adopt a more nuanced spatial vocabulary which takes into account the full gamut of spatial scales. Taking the subnational regional scale seriously is particularly important. Beugelsdijk and Mudambi (2013, p. 421) have made a recent move in this direction within IB:

> [b]y defining a three-dimensional framework of place (localized agglomerations of economic activity), space (incorporating both smooth changes in variety as well as qualitative discontinuities) and organization (the activities of firms). Firms organize resources from places and integrate them across space in order to create value.

Key here is the recognition that what they term "subnational spatial heterogeneity" is a driver of firm strategy, and that TNCs choose to locate in particular agglomerations and not in a national territory in general. In turn, the urban and regional development implications of TNC activity can then be more effectively assessed, offering a clear point of connection to the work on strategic coupling in GPN analysis (see Yeung, 2009, for more). Second, geography needs to be incorporated in a more active sense in terms of territorial influences on firm strategies and governance modes in both home and host contexts. In other words, the inherent institutional diversity associated with GPNs needs to be brought to the fore. While Sako and Zylberberg's (2015) invocation of the causal properties of institutional distance is a step forward, it still equates institutional variation with the national scale (see also Peng, Wang & Jiang, 2008) rather than seeing institutions as multi-scalar and also potentially transnational in constitution.

Coda: deepening the dialogue

This chapter has served two main purposes. First, for readers less familiar with the field, it has sought to provide a cogent introduction to GPN research both by charting its intellectual lineage and by profiling current theoretical concerns and debates under the auspices of a move to a 'GPN 2.0' version. Second, it has identified potential contact points between contemporary GPN research and work in IB. Although meaningful dialogue has largely been noticeable by its absence thus far, this has the potential to be a lively trading zone, and an enhanced two-way conversation between the fields would seem to have considerable merit. From an IB perspective, the GPN literature offers a broad range of insights that will enable the contemporary TNC to be placed more effectively in its fragmented and multi-scalar organizational and institutional contexts. Importantly, a more sophisticated appreciation of the multiple geographies of GPNs (and their constituent actors) will need to be developed in this regard. From a GPN perspective, the IB literature offers ways of 'opening up' the black box of the many different kinds of TNCs enrolled into GPNs as strategic actors and for thinking about the processes underpinning value capture trajectories. As GPN research has shown, however, this must go beyond focusing on developed country lead firms to encompass lead firms from many different settings, and also to look at other segments of GPNs that are increasingly dominated by transnational capital (e.g. global suppliers).

Notes

1 In this chapter, for clarity I use the acronym "GPN" to denote theory or literature, and "global production networks" to refer to the empirical phenomenon. The same distinction applies to "GCC" and "global commodity chains", and "GVC" and "global value chains".
2 This second section draws on ideas and materials developed at greater length in Coe and Yeung (2015).
3 Sako and Zylberberg (2015) provide a bibliometric analysis that demonstrates this general lack of exchange, albeit framed in terms of a very narrowly defined GVC literature.

References

Azmeh, S. & Nadvi, K. (2014) 'Asian firms and the restructuring of global value chains', *International Business Review*, 23, pp. 708–717.

Bair, J. (2005) 'Global capitalism and commodity chains: Looking back, going forward', *Competition & Change*, 9, pp. 153–180.

Beugelsdijk, S., McCann, P. & Mudambi, R. (2010) 'Introduction: Place, space and organization – Economic Geography and the multinational enterprise', *Journal of Economic Geography*, 10, pp. 485–493.

Beugelsdijk, S. & Mudambi, R. (2013) 'MNEs as border-crossing multi-location enterprises: The role of discontinuities in geographic space', *Journal of International Business Studies*, 44, pp. 413–426.

Beugelsdijk, S., Pedersen, T. & Petersen, B. (2009) 'Is there a trend towards global value chain specialization? An examination of cross border sales of US foreign affiliates', *Journal of International Management*, 15, pp. 126–141.

Brandt, L. & Thun, E. (2010) 'The fight for the middle: Upgrading, competition, and industrial development in China', *World Development*, 38, pp. 1555–1574.

Brandt, L. & Thun, E. (2016) 'Constructing a ladder for growth: Policy, markets, and industrial upgrading in China', *World Development*, 80, pp. 78–95.

Buckley, P.J. (2009) 'The impact of the global factory on economic development', *Journal of World Business*, 44, pp. 131–143.

Buckley, P.J. & Ghauri, P.N. (2004) 'Globalization, Economic Geography and the strategy of multinational enterprises', *Journal of International Business Studies*, 35, pp. 81–98.

Buckley, P.J. & Strange, R. (2015) 'The governance of the global factory: Location and control of world economic activity', *Academy of Management Perspectives*, 29, pp. 237–249.

Coe, N.M., Hess, M., Yeung, H.W-C., Dicken, P. & Henderson, J. (2004) 'Globalizing regional development: A global production networks perspective', *Transactions of the Institute of British Geographers*, 29, pp. 468–484.

Coe, N.M. & Yeung, H. W-C. (2015) *Global Production Networks: Theorizing Economic Development in an Interconnected World*. Oxford, UK: Oxford University Press.

Contractor, F.J., Kumar, V., Kundu, S.K. & Pedersen, T. (2010) 'Reconceptualizing the firm in a world of outsourcing and offshoring: The organizational and geographical relocation of high-value company functions', *Journal of Management Studies*, 47, pp. 1417–1433.

Dedrick, J., Kraemer, K.L., & Linden, G. (2010) 'Who profits from innovation in global value chains? A study of the iPod and notebook PCs', *Industrial and Corporate Change*, 19, pp. 81–116.

De Marchi, V., Di Maria, E. & Ponte, S. (2014) 'Multinational firms and the management of global networks: insights from global value chain studies', in Pedersen, T., Venzin, T., Devinney, T.M. & Tihanyi, L. (Eds.), *Orchestration of the Global Network Organization (Advances in International Management, Volume 27)*. Bingley, UK: Emerald Group Publishing Limited, pp. 463–486.

Dunning, J.H. (1998) 'Location and the multinational enterprise: A neglected factor?' *Journal of International Business Studies*, 29, pp. 45–66.

Gereffi, G. (1994) 'The organization of buyer-driven global commodity chains: How US retailers shape overseas production networks', in Gereffi, G. & Korzeniewicz, M. (Eds.), *Commodity Chains and Global Capitalism*. Westport, CT: Praeger, pp. 95–122.

Gereffi, G. (1999) 'International trade and industrial upgrading in the apparel commodity chain', *Journal of International Economics*, 48, pp. 37–70.

Gereffi, G., Humphrey, J. & Sturgeon, T. (2005) 'The governance of global value chains', *Review of International Political Economy*, 12, pp. 78–104.

Gereffi, G. & Korzeniewicz, M. (1994) (Eds.) *Commodity Chains and Global Capitalism*. Westport, CT: Praeger.

Gereffi, G., Korzeniewicz, M. & Korzeniewicz, R.P. (1994) 'Introduction: Global commodity chains', in Gereffi, G. & Korzeniewicz, M. (Eds.), *Commodity Chains and Global Capitalism*. Westport, CT: Praeger, pp. 1–14.

Gregson, N., Crang, M., Ahamed, F., Akhter, N. & Ferdous, R. (2010) 'Following things of rubbish value: End-of-life ships, "chock-chocky" furniture and the Bangladeshi middle class consumer', *Geoforum*, 41, pp. 846–854.

Henderson, J., Dicken, P., Hess, M., Coe, N.M. & Yeung, H.W-C. (2002) 'Global production networks and the analysis of economic development', *Review of International Political Economy*, 9, pp. 436–464.

Humphrey, J. & Schmitz, H. (2002) 'How does insertion in global value chains affect upgrading in industrial clusters?' *Regional Studies*, 36, pp. 1017–1027.

Jacobides, M.G., Knudsen, T. & Augier, M. (2006) 'Benefiting from innovation: Value creation, value appropriation and the role of industry architectures', *Research Policy*, 35, pp. 1200–1221.

Kaplinsky, R. & Morris, M. (2001) *A Handbook for Value Chain Research*, available from: http://asiandrivers.open.ac.uk/documents/Value_chain_Handbook_RKMM_Nov_2001.pdf.

Levy, D.L. (2008) 'Political contestation in global production networks', *Academy of Management Review*, 33, pp. 943–963.

Meyer, K.E., Mudambi, R. & Narula, R. (2011) 'Multinational enterprises and local contexts: The opportunities and challenges of multiple embeddedness', *Journal of Management Studies*, 48, pp. 235–252.

Milberg, W. & Winkler, D. (2013) *Outsourcing Economics: Global Value Chains in Capitalist Development*. Cambridge, UK: Cambridge University Press.

Mudambi, R. (2008) 'Location, control and innovation in knowledge-intensive industries', *Journal of Economic Geography*, 8, pp. 699–725.

Mudambi, R. & Venzin, M. (2010) 'The strategic nexus of offshoring and outsourcing decisions', *Journal of Management Studies*, 47, pp. 1510–1533.

Narula, R. & Dunning, J.H. (2010) 'Multinational enterprises, development and globalisation: Some clarifications and a research agenda', *Oxford Development Studies*, 38, pp. 263–287.

Parkhe, A. & Dhanaraj, C. (2003) 'Orchestrating globally: Managing the multinational enterprise as a network', *Research in Global Strategic Management*, 8, pp. 197–214.

Peng, M.W., Wang, D.Y.L. & Jiang, Y. (2008) 'An institution-based view of International Business strategy: A focus on emerging economies', *Journal of International Business Studies*, 39, pp. 920–936.

Ponte, S. & Sturgeon, T. (2014) 'Explaining governance in global value chains: A modular theory-building effort', *Review of International Political Economy*, 21, pp. 195–223.

Sako, M. & Zylberberg, E. (2015) 'From governance to strategy: Injecting management studies into global value chains'. *Available at SSRN:* http://ssrn.com/abstract=2630066.

Sturgeon, T.J. (2009) 'From commodity chains to value chains: Interdisciplinary theory building in an age of globalization', in Bair, J. (Ed.), *Frontiers of Commodity Chains Research*. Stanford, CA: Stanford University Press, pp. 110–135.

Teece, D.J. (1986) 'Profiting from technological innovation: Implications for integration, collaboration, licensing and public policy', *Research Policy*, 15, pp. 285–305.

Thun, E. (2015) Concept Note for 'Global production and local outcomes: Challenges for governance', *Interdisciplinary Research Network and Policy Workshop*, University of Manchester, 30 June-1 July.

Tokatli, N. (2013) 'Toward a better understanding of the apparel industry: A critique of the upgrading literature', *Journal of Economic Geography*, 13, pp. 993–1011.

UNCTAD (2013) *World Investment Report 2013: Global Value Chains – Investment and Trade for Development*. New York: UN.

Vahlne, J-E. & Johanson, J. (2013) 'The Uppsala model on evolution of the multinational business enterprise: From internalization to coordination of networks', *International Marketing Review*, 30, pp. 189–210.

Yeung, H.W-C. (2009) 'Transnational corporations, global production networks, and urban and regional development: A geographer's perspective on multinational enterprises and the global economy', *Growth and Change*, 40, pp. 197–226.

Yeung, H.W-C. & Coe, N.M. (2015) 'Towards a dynamic theory of global production networks', *Economic Geography*, 91, pp. 29–58.

10
THE RELATIONAL TURN IN ECONOMIC GEOGRAPHY

James T. Murphy

Introduction

Relationality – the notion that socioeconomic phenomena are constituted, transformed, and embedded in relations between people, materials, places, institutions, firms, and states – has been a mainstay of concepts, theories, and methods in Economic Geography since the 1990s. Navigating between individualist and structuralist accounts of economic processes, relational thinkers strive to bridge the agency-structure divide through research that provides a geographically and socially situated understanding of economic action/agency, one where subjectivities, intersubjective processes, and structural factors shape business decisions and the pace and direction of industrial/economic change. Inspired initially by heterodox economics and economic sociology, principally, relational economic geographers examine the socio-spatial embeddedness of economic activities and the ways in which economic actors (e.g., firms, entrepreneurs, etc.) develop multi-scalar relationships that influence significantly the development of innovations, firms, industries, and regions. Economic geographers have advanced relational thinking through studies of industrial clusters, regional economies, innovation systems, global production networks (GPN), markets, and entrepreneurship. Such accounts are explicitly geographical in that the context specificity of economic activity is a central concern – manifest in territorial or place-specific settings, the social spaces where interactions occur, and multi-scalar factors that shape outcomes.

This chapter aims to explain what relational Economic Geography is and how it can be productively drawn upon by scholars of International Business. The first section briefly outlines the origins and antecedents of relational thinking in human geography. The second section provides an overview of the contributions that relational approaches have made to extant debates and dialogues in Economic Geography. The third section then discusses the value of relational concepts and approaches for the field of International Business focusing on two ideas – relational proximity and socio-spatial practice – that are particularly relevant. The chapter concludes with a short summary discussion.

Relational Economic Geography: origins and antecedents

The origins of relational thinking can be traced back to several theories and concepts, mainly from the fields of heterodox economics and economic sociology. Scholars in these areas sought to develop more robust conceptual and empirical understandings of the social bases and drivers of economic activities, broadly understood. Their contributions are manifold but can be summarized succinctly in relation to three themes – institutional and network embeddedness, microsocial agencies, and the socio-material bases of economic orders.

Institutional and network embeddedness

The concept of embeddedness has been a central theme associated with relational thinking from the outset, marked by institutionalist and networked accounts of how the economic is situated in the social (see Hess, 2004). Institutional accounts built significantly off Polanyi's (1944) seminal work, *The Great Transformation*, wherein he conceptualized economic activities as being embedded in social, cultural, and political structures (institutions) which sustain society-specific modes of economic integration – exchange, reciprocity, householding, and redistribution – leading to variegations in capitalism globally (Peck, 2013). This substantivist perspective demands careful attention to history, geography, political economy, and social formations in order to understand the context-specific drivers of economic development. Institutionalist perspectives also emerged through works in evolutionary economics (Nelson & Winter, 1982; Dosi & Nelson, 1994) that examined the role that structural context plays in shaping the trajectories of economic change. Economic actors – namely firms – are conceptualized as being embedded in historically derived institutional settings that create incentives and disincentives for particular actions that influence development outcomes. As Grabher (1993) argued, the institutional embeddedness of firms can encourage innovation or create "lock-ins" (cognitive, functional, political) that prevent progressive change.

While institutional perspectives on embeddedness remain influential (see Bathelt & Glückler, 2014), many relational economic geographers trace their work back to Mark Granovetter's (1985) seminal article on the embeddedness of economic action in social networks. Seeking a middle-ground between markets and hierarchies as explanations for industrial organization, Granovetter stressed the importance of the "networks of personal relations" that businesspeople are situated in. Network embeddedness fosters reciprocity, trust, and inter-dependence between actors and can make hierarchical (top-down, structural) or market-driven (i.e., individuated utility maximization) forms of economic organization unnecessary or inefficient given the sunk costs associated with established ties and relationships. This is particularly the case in industries, GPN, or markets where tacit knowledge, social interactions, and/or interpersonal trust play a key role in determining who participates, innovates, and performs better or worse (Powell, 1990). A relational focus thus demands that one attend to the ties or interconnections between actors – their strength, density, symmetry, and range – in order to understand how, why, and to whom/where resources and capital flow (e.g., Granovetter, 1973; Uzzi, 1996).

A core concept that emerged through studies of institutional and network embeddedness is social capital – understood succinctly as "norms and networks that enable people to act collectively" (Woolcock, 1998; Woolcock & Narayan, 2000, p. 226). Social capital shapes economic action and outcomes by providing access to resources (information, contacts, knowledge, finance) that can be mobilized by businesspeople (Coleman, 1988; Burt, 1997). Firms, industrial clusters, and regions able to create social capital through an institutionalized culture of cooperation, reciprocity, and collaboration, or a diversity of strong and weak network ties, are more innovative, responsive, and resilient to exogenous forces and events (Putnam, 1993; Cooke & Wills, 1999; Staber, 2007). Social capital is thus a key outcome of embeddedness and a core concept in relationally inspired research.

Micro-social agencies

While a focus on institutional and network embeddedness helped to contextualize economic processes and business activities, many scholars felt that it did not deal sufficiently with agency. Questions emerged regarding how business relationships, inter-firm networks, and social capital are established, created, and/or evolve over time. Some economic sociologists turned to the fields of social psychology and symbolic interactionism to address them, and Erving Goffman's work was particularly influential in this regard. Goffman (1959, 1974) provided a framework for conceptualizing the mechanics of social interactions, highlighting the key moments, meanings, roles, representations, and patterns that stabilize or make consistent the socioeconomic world. Actors assume "dramaturgical" roles or selves – performing theater as it were in accordance with the constraints imposed on them by social circumstances, their instrumental objectives, and the emotional energies that emerge in the course of an interaction (see Collins, 1981). Actors participate successfully in social exchanges when there is a shared "definition of the situation" and if/when they adhere adequately to the scripts and roles associated with it (e.g., in a business meeting or at a trade fair). This allows mutual understandings to emerge and resources (e.g., knowledge, capital, commodities, information) to flow or be exchanged effectively.

Building from this foundational work, relational sociologists developed a conceptualization of agency that incorporates a temporal dimension beyond that of in-the-moment performances. As detailed by Emirbayer and Mische (1998, p. 963), agency can be understood as:

> [a] temporally embedded process of social engagement, informed by the past (in its habitual aspect), but also oriented toward the future (as a capacity to imagine alternative possibilities) and toward the present (as a capacity to contextualize past habits and future projects within the contingencies of the moment). The agentic dimension of social action can only be captured in its full complexity, we argue, if it is analytically situated within the flow of time.

Viewed through this lens, the micro-social processes or agencies of economic actors are achieved through a continual tacking back-and-forth between past experiences, present interactions, and future trajectories – relationalities constituted through an individual's connections to others, materials, ideas, memories, experiences, meanings, rules, norms, and routines. When agency is understood in this manner, the simplistic notions of *homo economicus* (an autonomous utility-maximizing individual) or *homo sociologicus* (an actor who responds predictably to the structural environment) are supplanted by a richer, more contingent, and dynamic understanding of how individuals act in the world and why particular outcomes (innovation, entrepreneurship, exchange) become more or less possible.

A micro-social perspective on agency has been critical in enabling scholars to connect more directly the actions of individuals (and consequently firms) to the contexts, times, and spaces where they are situated. Moreover, as an epistemological maneuver, the focus on micro-social processes can reveal insights into the roles, meanings, identities, and power relations that hold larger order phenomena (firms, industrial clusters, regional economies, GPN) together and/or which embed these in particular spatial and geographical contexts. Empirically, this conceptualization of agency can only be operationalized through more intensive, qualitative studies of the social dynamics and dimensions of economic activities.

The socio-material bases of economic order

The third foundation in which relational Economic Geography is grounded is concepts and theories that seek to explain how social and economic orders (e.g., markets, GPN) or structures come into being through the interplay between agencies and structures. Although there is a very rich scholarship related to these themes, two perspectives stand out as particularly influential on relational Economic Geography – structuration theory and Actor-Network theory (ANT). Giddens' (1979, 1984) structuration theory was highly influential in sparking debates about the emergence, reproduction, and transformations of socioeconomic order and societal systems. For Giddens, enduring socioeconomic forms – like institutions, markets, and industries – come into being and evolve through an interplay between the everyday/practical life worlds of agents and the system worlds where structures are situated. Structures and agents co-constitute one another through their interrelationships thus creating what he calls a "duality of structure" in that structures mediate human agency while simultaneously being products of said agency (see Sewell, 1992). As such, structures are not "out there" per se but "in here" as well, constituted, reproduced, and transformed by the expected and sometimes unexpected actions of actors in the real world. The significance of structuration theory thus lies in its (albeit partial) attempt to understand socioeconomic order through a framework centered on the interdependencies and relationalities between agents and structures.

While Giddens' work was critical for sparking debate about how best to understand the emergence of structures, ANT – a post-structural approach developed initially by science and technology studies scholars – has been even more influential. At its core, ANT is not so much a theory but more an ontology and epistemology, or as Law (1992, p. 389) terms it, "a relational and process oriented sociology". ANT scholars view the world as being "flat" in that there are no structures "out there" but instead a continuous and constant unfolding of reality through the messy and power-laden interactions between humans, non-humans, materials, places, spaces, ideas, and meanings. Socioeconomic order comes about when there are (temporary) stabilizations of the relationships between these "things" as actor-networks – constellations of relations that can be extremely durable and/or impervious to change (e.g., hierarchies, rituals). In taking this ontological position, ANT scholars decenter structures and focus instead on the relationalities, materials, agencies, and power struggles through which the everyday world comes into being. Epistemologically, this ontology encourages scholars to "enter" into the actor-network that is a market, industry, value chain, or regional economy in alternative ways that can reveal novel/key insights into what holds the phenomenon together and enables or prevents progressive changes to it.

A central concept from ANT is translation (Callon, 1986; Law, 1992). As Callon (1986, p. 223) states: "to translate is . . . to express in one's own language what others say and want, why they act in the way they do and how they associate with each other: it is to establish oneself as a spokesman". In simpler terms, translation enables one actor (person, artifact, material, organization, or institution) to enroll another into the former's actor-network, that is to bring the other into alignment with the implicit or explicit aims and objectives of the former. As Murdoch (1995, pp. 747–748) states:

> In order for an actor successfully to enroll entities (human and non-human) within a network, their behavior must be stabilized and channeled in the direction desired by the enrolling actor. This will entail redefining the roles of the actors and entities as they come into alignment, such that they come to gain new identities or attributes within the network . . . Where the translation process has been weakly executed, the enrolling actors find their status continually in question and find it hard to mobilize other parts of the network.

For example, an efficiently run business might be understood as one where management (those in power) has created effective means to enroll employees into an actor-network – the firm – that functions without the need for micro-management. On a much larger scale, the same can be said for the diffusion of neoliberalism globally – facilitated in large part by so-called centers of translation such as the World Bank and the International Monetary Fund who have more or less effectively enrolled most countries on the planet into their ideological project.

Importantly, translation occurs not simply through spatially proximate interactions and exchanges but also when locations, agents, and materials are enrolled into actor-networks controlled from far-away places. For example, people all over the world participate daily in the global financial system even if they have never been to trading and investment centers such as London, Tokyo, or New York. In this case, money – particularly globalized currencies – acts as a powerful translation "device" that allows certain actors (e.g., financiers) to "act at a distance" through investments, currency exchanges, and equity trades. While there are clearly significant power imbalances between participants in a system like global finance, ANT scholars posit that all actors have (distributed) agency of some sort, and they suggest that even a powerful, hegemonic system can become destabilized in unexpected ways by seemingly peripheral actors. For example, in 2010 a "flash crash" occurred on Wall Street when a UK-based trader allegedly "spoofed" financial markets with false trade offers causing the Dow Jones Index to plunge 5% within minutes (Davies & Gayle, 2015). As this example illustrates, ANT scholars view translation, and consequently all forms of socioeconomic order, as inherently partial or incomplete, vulnerable to disruption or reordering at any time.

The relational "turn" in Economic Geography

During the 1990s, a diverse range of economic geographers began to engage with the concepts and approaches discussed earlier. Interest in institutional and network forms of embeddedness stemmed initially out of neo-Marshallian thinking as attention turned to understanding industrial restructuring in an age of flexible specialization and post-Fordism (Piore & Sabel, 1984; Amin & Thrift, 1992). Central to this work was the question of how small firms could persist and even thrive in an age of corporatized capitalism where economies-of-scale and oligopolistic competition dominated. The "rediscovery" of Marshall's (1919) idea of internal (intra-firm) and external (extra-firm) economies was central to early studies of industrial clusters, agglomeration economies, and Italianate industrial districts where production was organized through networks of smaller firms able to create economies of scope and specialization in particular commodities or services. From this came a plethora of studies linking innovation and growth in regional economies to the nature and quality of firms' embeddedness in institutions and networks (Amin & Thrift, 1993; Storper, 1995; Malecki, 1997; Oinas, 1997; Maskell & Malmberg, 1999).

By the early 2000s, the relational "turn" was gaining momentum spurred on by a Special Issue in the *Journal of Economic Geography* (Bathelt & Glückler, 2003; Boggs & Rantisi, 2003). Boggs and Rantisi's (2003) introduction argued that relational thinking emerged in part as a response to three central tensions facing economic geographers: agency versus structure; macro versus micro; and local versus global. Relational concepts, theories, and methodologies offered means to reconcile these binaries and to socialize and spatialize economic action in ways that reflected the contingency, heterogeneity, and dynamics of the real world. The subsequent integration of relational concepts into Economic Geography has had significant implications for our understanding of geographies of economic phenomena and processes. Relational thinking can be seen in many areas of contemporary research: evolutionary Economic Geography (Glückler, 2007; Hassink, Klaerding & Marques, 2014), innovation studies (Grabher, Ibert & Flohr, 2008; Fitjar & Huber, 2015), global production networks (Murphy, 2011; Coe & Yeung, 2015), feminist Economic Geography (Hanson & Blake, 2009; Werner, 2012), regional studies (Bathelt, 2006; Ter Wal, 2014), industrial clusters (Giuliani, 2007; Huber, 2009), financial geography (Hall, 2007; Lai, 2011), labor geography (Coe & Hess, 2013), and marketization studies (Berndt & Boeckler, 2010; Ouma, Boeckler & Lindner, 2013).

By-and-large, these works spatialize, scale, and territorialize socioeconomic relations in studies of the determinants and drivers of, among other things, learning, innovation, knowledge production, upgrading, global market integration, inequality, financialization, and uneven development. Moreover, relational economic geographers have reconceptualized core concepts such as embeddedness (Hess, 2004), institutions (Bathelt & Glückler, 2014), firms (Yeung, 2005), social capital (Huber, 2009), trust (Murphy, 2006), and communities of practice (Amin & Roberts, 2008). With respect to International Business studies, relational Economic Geography has much to contribute to research on the organization, management, and performance of firms, markets, and value chains. Two core concepts from the field strike as being particular useful in this regard: relational proximity and socio-spatial practice.

Rethinking proximity relationally

Spatial proximity has always been a core explanatory variable in Economic Geography, manifest principally as the physical or economic distance between individuals, firms, markets, and economies. It has long been established that co-location, physical proximity, or propinquity – i.e., "being there" (Gertler, 2003) – can play a central role in facilitating innovation, exchange, and the embedding of industries in geographical locations. Face-to-face interaction can reduce transaction costs and contribute to the "buzz" of ideas and information that is often associated with innovative clusters or industrial centers (Bathelt, Malmberg & Maskell, 2004). Proximity also makes certain forms of tacit knowledge "sticky" with respect to where they can be readily found, thus contributing to the externalities and "untraded interdependencies" that enable clusters and regions to sustain competitive advantages through learning and innovation (Storper, 1995; Gertler, 2003; Morgan, 2005). The co-location of firms in an industry also concentrates skilled labor in places and thus makes it less costly to staff businesses while helping to circulate knowledge locally when workers switch companies. Moreover, firms and businesspeople benefit from spatial proximity even when it is only temporarily achieved as in the case of trade fairs and business networking events; what some view as "temporary clusters" that can be vital for exchange and knowledge sharing in industries (Maskell, Bathelt & Malmberg, 2006).

On the contrary, however, co-location and spatial proximity can also work to stifle innovation and regional development especially when inter-firm or intra-firm networks become too restrictive, insular, and narrow in terms of who participates in them (Visser & Boschma, 2004; Broekel & Boschma, 2012). In such cases, proximity, and the social capital it helps to create, can work against innovation as it reinforces conformance and imitation among/by businesspeople such that firms are unable to disrupt preexisting hierarchies or ways of doing things. This has the effect of stifling innovation and creativity as it disincentivizes firms from upgrading their products, manufacturing processes, or marketing and management strategies. The net result is a lock-in of sorts, whereby firms' need to act reciprocally and sustain the network status quo prevents them from trying new things and innovating ahead of competitors based elsewhere.

As this research demonstrates, spatial proximity alone is insufficient for innovation and regional development as firms also need to develop distanciated or translocal relationships that can provide access to new ideas, markets, and GPN. As Bathelt, Malmberg and Maskell (2004) argued, the so-called "buzz" generated or facilitated through spatial proximity can be enhanced significantly when firms sustain "global pipelines" able to bring new ideas, investment, and other resources into businesses, clusters, or regional economies. Through these globalized ties, lock-in becomes less likely as the innovativeness, resilience, and responsiveness of the firm or region is enhanced. Creating successful pipelines requires an ability to build connections to actors from sometimes vastly different places, and to embed oneself or the firm into translocal networks through trust, reciprocity, and shared understandings with non-local businesspeople.

Given the limitations on spatial proximity as a means to develop translocal ties and global pipelines, businesspeople and firms must instead establish relational proximity with distant others. As Amin and Cohendet (2004, p. 74) and Murphy (2006, p. 430) note, relational proximity is "the degree to which individuals, firms, and communities are 'bound by relations of common interest, purpose, or passion, and held together by routines and varying degrees of mutuality'". Trust is thus a key indicator or determinant of relational proximity, one that is built through overlapping cognitive, social, and spatial factors and processes at three scales – the micro (subjective), meso (inter-subjective), and macro (structural) (Murphy, 2006). The subjective scale is shaped by an actor's disposition, her perceived capacity for action, and the risk-reward calculations made with respect to a particular relation. Inter-subjective processes – social interactions and performances through which businesspeople meet, exchange ideas, negotiate deals, and share information – are central to the creation of relational proximity as well; mediated in part through materials, artifacts, physical spaces, appearances, emotions, and expressions that influence their quality and significance. Importantly, these micro and meso-scales of trust are situated within structural and institutional settings (the macro) which may or may not be conducive to trust-building; particularly when actors are embedded in significantly different societal or territorial contexts and/or when external events (e.g., Volkswagen's emissions scandal) reduce the general climate for trust.

In taking a multi-scalar view on how trust or relational proximity are created, it is possible to account for the overlapping forms of embeddedness that shape who business actors can connect with, constrain the scale or scope of action in a given situational context, and determine if and how a more or less innovative or profitable pathway is chosen or possible. Moreover, thinking about proximity as a relational process is important for scholars striving to understand the ways in which business activities are coordinated over time and space, particularly in the case of transnational firms or corporations striving to develop markets internationally or to tap into centers of knowledge and innovation. Faulconbridge's (2007, 2008, 2010) contributions are highly relevant in this regard, particularly his call to think of TNCs as "embedded social communities" where relational processes are central to their organization, performance, innovativeness, and day-to-day management. As he states (Faulconbridge, 2010, p. 282), taking a relational-geographical perspective on International Business:

> [i]nvolves revealing the diversity of relations within TNCs and, rather than characterising relations within firms as universal and consistent, recognising that relations vary depending on: the types of negotiations, power games and compromises that play out in the firm, something related to the spatial dynamics of a relationship and variations in the societal embeddedness of situated actors. Hence, a transdisciplinary understanding of the TNC as an embedded community means asking questions about stretched relational spaces that involve interactions between managers and workers in different countries in a way that recognizes the insights economic geographers have provided into societal and network embeddedness.

Understanding proximity in a relational manner is an essential means through which one can examine and understand how such relational spaces are created, constituted, and transformed over time.

Socio-spatial practice: the everyday worlds of International Business

While a relational view on proximity provides a conceptual means to understand how inter- and intra-firm networks are held together or what enables businesspeople to gain access to resources near and far, economic geographers have also sought to develop concepts and methods to examine the everyday worlds of work and business. The goal is to advance further our understandings of socio-spatial embeddedness and the social dynamics that shape firms, industries, clusters, GPN, and local or regional economies. At the heart of this work are studies of where tacit and other forms of knowledge are held down in firms, how businesses and industrial activities evolve over time, and what social factors differentiate firms such that they are more or less competitive or innovative.

A key concept that has emerged in relation to this work is practice. Practice-oriented thinking emerged from several conceptual and philosophical foundations (see Jones & Murphy, 2011). Common to these is the belief or perspective that the everyday lifeworld can reveal key insights into the systems, structures, and processes governing economies and societies. In this view, agency is more than simply rule following or utility maximization. It is instead manifest through the performance of everyday activities; grounded in the contingent, material, and social contexts where desires and ideals must be reconciled with practical considerations and concerns such as profit making and wage earning. Performative agency is achieved through speech acts, conversations, and "mundane and repeated acts of delimitation" that reproduce or structure economic phenomena like markets, corporations, and GPN (Butler, 2010, p. 150).

Following Reckwitz (2002, p. 250), practices are "routinized way[s] in which bodies are moved, objects are handled, subjects are treated, things are described and the world is understood". They are thus foundational to socioeconomic orders in that they provide consistency, stability, and the ontological security that enables actors – such as businesspeople, entrepreneurs, and workers – to make sense of the world and attend to higher-order objectives such as quality, innovation, success, and livelihood fulfillment. As Schatzki (2005) observes, practices are sites for the social, and organizations or firms can be understood as being constituted by bundles of them that overlap with each other and distribute agency (e.g., accounting, supervising, reporting, etc.). Considered in (economic) geographical terms, practices can be understood as:

> [s]tabilized, routinized, or improvised social actions that constitute and reproduce economic space, and through and within which diverse actors (e.g., entrepreneurs, workers, caregivers, consumers, firms) and communities (e.g., industries, places,

> markets, cultural groups) organize materials, produce, consume, and/or derive meaning from the economic world. Although practices serve important instrumental purposes (e.g., production, consumption, learning), they are also significant analytically in that they can reveal the complexities, contingencies, identities, and meanings inherent in all forms of economic organization.
>
> (*Jones and Murphy, 2011, p. 367*)

Viewed as such, practices are epistemological objects whose study can enable us to develop more refined understandings of socio-spatialities wherein business activities and economic processes are embedded. Moreover, and following Wenger's (1998) work, firms and industries can be understood as communities of practice, held together relationally by networks, shared histories, tacit knowledge, heterogeneous materials, everyday routines, and socio-spatial interactions. As Figure 10.1 highlights, when carried out, practices set into motion an array of perceptions, patterns, performances, power relations, spatialities, and temporalities that get things done and regularize the business world in ways that make it more manageable. When practices fail or are undermined due to contingent circumstances (e.g., a rogue trader, labor unrest, an internet shutdown), economic orders can be destabilized in ways that reveal their fragility, precarity, and/or dependency on seemingly minor actions and artifacts. This, in turn, can initiate organizational changes, managerial responses, or new policies to restore order and avert future crises.

Considered in relation to International Business, a practice perspective calls attention to the everyday relationalities of firms, markets, and industries and the ways in which these

Perceptions	Patterns
• Intentionality, expectations • Situational definitions, interpretative contexts, or relational logics • Representations – symbols, identities, discourses, and meanings • Social selves, egos, and motivations	• Regulative and normative factors • Rules, norms, routines, conventions, and materials • Institutionalized and expected actions • Regularized forms of behavior
Performances	**Power relations**
• Social interaction and communication • Mutual recognition, reciprocity – intersubjectivity - "we" relationships • Situationally appropriate actions, bodies, language, materials, and emotions	• Structural (e.g., class, cultural, gender, etc.) positionalities of actors • Power embodied in, or expressed through, the strategies and tactics of actors seeking to control, align, or mobilize others

Perceptions, patterns, performances, and power relations are carried, or carried out by, agents (e.g., individuals, firms, organizations) within or in relation to particular time-space assemblages

- *Temporality*
  - When, why then?
  - Synchronicities, continuities, immediacies, generational characteristics, histories
- *Spatiality*
  - Where, why there?
  - Places, interactive spaces, scales, translocal connections

Figure 10.1 The constitutive features of practices

Source: Jones and Murphy (2011).

shape production, marketing, service provisioning, and innovation development activities (Jones, 2008, 2014; Faulconbridge & Muzio, 2009; Cranston, 2014). Although such an emphasis may seem micro-oriented, practices are fundamentally multi-scalar and multi-locational in their constitution, shaped by distanciated factors, trans-local relationships, and national or global scale conditions, institutions, regulations, and power asymmetries. For example, Horner and Murphy (in press), apply a practice-oriented approach to examine the emergence of India's pharmaceutical industry in the world economy, highlighting the discontinuities between South-North versus South-South GPNs and demonstrating why most firms in one GPN (South-South trade) face significant barriers – social, financial, technological, and professional – to achieving the kinds of value-creation, enhancement, and capture possible in the other (South-North GPN). Through a detailed unpacking of the constitutive features of core practices (e.g., production, exchange, finance), and comparing these across firms, industries, markets, and geographical settings, it is possible to understand how particular forms of territorial, network, and societal embeddedness (see Hess, 2004) shape the performance of firms and, subsequently, industrial and regional development dynamics. Practice thus provides an alternative epistemological and methodological strategy for understanding the world of International Business, a middle-ground of sorts between the parsimony of structured surveys and econometric variables, and the extensiveness/depth of ethnographic accounts.

Conclusion

Relational thinking is a core aspect of contemporary Economic Geography that has helped to reshape understandings of innovation processes, agglomeration economies, GPN, markets, uneven development, and the socio-spatial drivers of competitiveness. Building initially off the work of economic sociologists and heterodox economists, the "turn" toward relational ideas was driven in large part by a desire to better understand the spatial and territorial embeddedness of economic processes, and the multi-scalar relationships that influence significantly outcomes such as industrial development. Once considered a controversial shift in the field, the novelty of the "turn" toward relationality has long past and its legacy lives on in many areas of contemporary Economic Geography.

With respect to International Business studies, this chapter has sought to achieve two objectives. First, to explain what relational thinking is about, where it came from, and how it has been manifested in Economic Geography. Second, to argue for two specific ways that relational thinking can contribute to research in International Business through a rethinking of proximity relationally and an epistemological/empirical focus on socio-spatial practices. Conceptualizing proximity relationally is critical in order to understand how firms (e.g., TNCs) are able to coordinate their subsidiaries, suppliers, and other business dealings such that they can act at distance effectively without having to co-locate offices, be spatially proximate, or make significant capital and personnel investments everywhere they seek to do business. Building trust in these relationships is essential to achieving effective management and for facilitating flows of information and knowledge globally. As such, a more in-depth, context-sensitive, and socio-spatial understanding of how/why relational proximity or trust emerges, or why it does not, can reveal important insights into the relationalities enabling trade, investment, and knowledge flows worldwide.

Finally, the chapter has also argued for an attention to socio-spatial practices – understood here as the common everyday activities through which firms are organized internally, interfirm relations are created, sustained, and transformed, and larger-order economic phenomena (e.g., GPN, industrial clusters, innovation systems) are structured, reproduced, or governed consistently over time and space. Practices are, in effect, performative as it is through them that the business world comes into being on a daily basis and why it is geographically variegated. When businesses, industries, and inter-firm networks are viewed as phenomena constituted by bundles or arrangements of socio-spatial and socio-material (i.e., relational) practices, it is possible to develop a richer understanding of the ways in which businesses are embedded in territories, networks, and societies. In doing so, International Business researchers can reveal inductively novel understandings into what stabilizes firms, industries, markets, and economies and/or enables (or prevents) their progressive transformation. Moreover, such a perspective can identify the bases of geographical variations in business activities and lead to new insights regarding the relational challenges concomitant with economic globalization.

References

Amin, A. & Cohendet, P. (2004) *Architectures of Knowledge: Firms, Capabilities, and Communities*. Oxford, UK: Oxford University Press.

Amin, A. & Roberts, J. (2008) 'Knowing in action: Beyond communities of practice', *Research Policy*, 37, pp. 353–369.

Amin, A. & Thrift, N. (1992) 'Neo-Marshallian nodes in global networks', *International Journal of Urban and Regional Research*, 16, pp. 571–587.

Amin, A. & Thrift, N. (1993) 'Globalization, institutional thickness, and local prospects', *Revue d'Economie Regionale et Urbaine*, 3, pp. 405–427.

Bathelt, H. (2006) 'Geographies of production: Growth regimes in spatial perspective 3 – Toward a relational view of economic action and policy', *Progress in Human Geography*, 30, pp. 223–236.

Bathelt, H. & Glückler, J. (2003) 'Toward a relational Economic Geography', *Journal of Economic Geography*, 3, pp. 117–144.

Bathelt, H. & Glückler, J. (2014) 'Institutional change in Economic Geography', *Progress in Human Geography*, 38, pp. 340–363.

Bathelt, H., Malmberg, A. & Maskell, P. (2004) 'Clusters and knowledge: Local buzz, global pipelines and the process of knowledge creation', *Progress in Human Geography*, 28, pp. 31–56.

Berndt, C. & Boeckler, M. (2010) 'Geographies of markets: Materials, morals and monsters in motion', *Progress in Human Geography*, 35, pp. 559–567.

Boggs, J.S. & Rantisi, N.M. (2003) 'The "relational turn" in Economic Geography', *Journal of Economic Geography*, 3(2), pp. 109–116.

Broekel, T. & Boschma, R. (2012) 'Knowledge networks in the Dutch aviation industry: The proximity paradox', *Journal of Economic Geography*, 12, pp. 409–433.

Burt, R.S. (1997) 'The contingent value of social capital', *Administrative Science Quarterly*, 42, pp. 339–365.

Butler, J. (2010) 'Performative agency', *Journal of Cultural Economy*, 3, pp. 147–161.

Callon, M. (1986) 'Some elements of a sociology of translation: domestication of the scallops and the fishermen of St Brieuc Bay', in Law, J. (Ed.), *Power, Action and Belief: A New Sociology of Knowledge?* London: Routledge, pp. 196–223.

Cranston, S. (2014) 'Reflections on doing the expat show: Performing the global mobility industry', *Environment and Planning A*, 46, pp. 1124–1138.

Coe, N. & Hess, M. (2013) 'Global production networks, labour and development', *Geoforum*, 44, pp. 4–9.

Coe, N. & Yeung, H.W.-C. (2015) *Global Production Networks: Theorizing Economic Development in an Interconnected World*. Oxford, UK: Oxford University Press.

Coleman, J.S. (1988) 'Social capital in the creation of human capital', *American Journal of Sociology*, 94, pp. S95–S120.

Collins, R. (1981) 'On the microfoundations of macrosociology', *American Journal of Sociology*, 86, pp. 984–1014.

Cooke, P. & Wills, D. (1999) 'Small firms, social capital and the enhancement of business performance through innovation programmes', *Small Business Economics*, 13, pp. 219–234.

Davies, C. & Gayle, D. (2015) '"Flash crash" case: UK trader to fight extradition to US', *The Guardian*, 22 April. Available online at www.theguardian.com/business/2015/apr/22/flash-crash-case-uk-trader-to-fight-extradition-to-us.

Dosi, G. & Nelson, R.R. (1994) 'An introduction to evolutionary theories in economics', *Journal of Evolutionary Economics*, 4, pp. 153–172.

Emirbayer, M. & Mische, A. (1998) 'What is agency?' *American Journal of Sociology*, 103, pp. 962–1023.
Faulconbridge, J.R. (2007) 'London's and New York's advertising and law clusters and their networks of learning: Relational analyses with a politics of scale?' *Urban Studies*, 44, pp. 1635–1656.
Faulconbridge, J.R. (2008) 'Negotiating cultures of work in transnational law firms', *Journal of Economic Geography*, 8, pp. 497–517.
Faulconbridge, J.R. (2010) 'TNCs as embedded social communities: Transdisciplinary perspectives', *Critical Perspectives on International Business*, 6, pp. 273–290.
Faulconbridge, J.R. & Muzio, D. (2009) 'The financialization of large law firms: Situated discourses and practices of reorganization', *Journal of Economic Geography*, 9, pp. 641–661.
Fitjar, R.D. & Huber, F. (2015) 'Global pipelines for innovation: Insights from the case of Norway', *Journal of Economic Geography*, 15, pp. 561–583.
Gertler, M.S. (2003) 'Tacit knowledge and the Economic Geography of context, or the undefinable tacitness of being (there)', *Journal of Economic Geography*, 3, pp. 75–99.
Giddens, A. (1979) *Central Problems in Social Theory: Action, Structure and Contradiction in Social Analysis*. Berkeley, CA: University of California Press.
Giddens, A. (1984) *The Constitution of Society*. Berkeley, CA: University of California Press.
Giuliani, E. (2007) 'The selective nature of knowledge networks in clusters: Evidence from the wine industry', *Journal of Economic Geography*, 7, pp. 139–168.
Glückler, J. (2007) 'Economic Geography and the evolution of networks', *Journal of Economic Geography*, 7, pp. 619–634.
Goffman, E. (1959) *The Presentation of Self in Everyday Life*. Woodstock, UK: Overlook Press.
Goffman, E. (1974) *Frame Analysis: An Essay on the Organization of Experience*. Cambridge, MA: Harvard University Press.
Grabher, G. (1993) *The Embedded Firm: On the Socioeconomics of Industrial Networks*. London: Routledge.
Grabher, G., Ibert, O. & Flohr, S. (2008) 'The neglected king: The customer in the new knowledge ecology of innovation', *Economic Geography*, 84, pp. 253–280.
Granovetter, M.S. (1973) 'The strength of weak ties', *American Journal of Sociology*, 78, pp. 1360–1380.
Granovetter, M.S. (1985) 'Economic action and social structure: The problem of embeddedness', *American Journal of Sociology*, 91, pp. 481–510.
Hall, S. (2007) ''Relational marketplaces' and the rise of boutiques in London's corporate finance industry', *Environment and Planning A*, 39, pp. 1838–1854.
Hanson, S. & Blake, M. (2009) 'Gender and entrepreneurial networks', *Regional Studies*, 43, pp. 135–149.
Hassink, R., Klaerding, C. & Marques, P. (2014) 'Advancing evolutionary Economic Geography by engaged pluralism', *Regional Studies*, 48, pp. 1295–1307.
Hess, M. (2004) '"Spatial" relationships? Towards a reconceptualization of embeddedness', *Progress in Human Geography*, 28, pp. 165–186.
Horner, R. & Murphy, J.T. (in press) 'South-North and South-South production networks: Diverging socio-spatial practices of Indian pharmaceutical firms', *Global Networks*.
Huber, F. (2009) 'Social capital of economic clusters: Towards a network-based conception of social resources', *Tijdschrift Voor Economische en Sociale Geografie*, 100, pp. 160–170.
Jones, A. (2008) 'Beyond embeddedness: Economic practices and the invisible dimensions of transnational business activity', *Progress in Human Geography*, 32, pp. 71–88.
Jones, A. (2014) 'Geographies of production I: Relationality revisited and the "practice shift" in Economic Geography', *Progress in Human Geography*, 38, pp. 605–615.
Jones, A. & Murphy, J.T. (2011) 'Theorizing practice in Economic Geography: Foundations, challenges, and possibilities', *Progress in Human Geography*, 35, pp. 366–392.
Lai, K.P. (2011) 'Marketization through contestation: Reconfiguring China's financial markets through knowledge networks', *Journal of Economic Geography*, 11, pp. 87–117.
Law, J. (1992) 'Notes on the theory of the actor-network: Ordering, strategy and heterogeneity', *Systems Practice*, 5, pp. 379–393.
Malecki, E.J. (1997) 'Entrepreneurs, networks, and economic development: A review of recent research', *Advances in Entrepreneurship, Firm Emergence, and Growth*, 3, pp. 57–118.
Marshall, A. (1919) *Industry and Trade*. London: Macmillan.
Maskell, P., Bathelt, H. & Malmberg, A. (2006) 'Building global knowledge pipelines: The role of temporary clusters', *European Planning Studies*, 14, pp. 997–1013.
Maskell, P. & Malmberg, A. (1999) 'Localized learning and industrial competitiveness', *Cambridge Journal of Economics*, 23, pp. 167–185.

Morgan, K. (2005) 'The exaggerated death of geography: Learning, proximity and territorial innovation systems', *Journal of Economic Geography*, 4, pp. 3–21.

Murdoch, J. (1995) 'Actor-Networks and the evolution of economic forms: Combining description and explanation in theories of regulation, flexible specialization, and networks'. *Environment and Planning A*, 27, pp. 731–757.

Murphy, J.T. (2006) 'Building trust in economic space', *Progress in Human Geography*, 30, pp. 427–450.

Murphy, J.T. (2011) 'Global production networks, relational proximity, and the sociospatial dynamics of market internationalization in Bolivia's wood products sector', *Annals of the Association of American Geographers*, 102, pp. 208–233.

Nelson, R.R. & Winter, S.G. (1982) *An Evolutionary Theory of Economic Change*. Cambridge, UK: Belknap Press.

Oinas, P. (1997) 'On the socio-spatial embeddedness of business firms', *Erdkunde*, 51, pp. 23–32.

Ouma, S., Boeckler, M. & Lindner, P. (2013) 'Extending the margins of marketization: Frontier regions and the making of agro-export markets in northern Ghana', *Geoforum*, 48, pp. 225–235.

Peck, J. (2013) 'For Polanyian economic geographies', *Environment and Planning A*, 45, pp. 1545–1568.

Piore, M.J. & Sabel, C. (1984) *The Second Industrial Divide: Possibilities for Prosperity*. New York: Basic Books.

Polanyi, K. (1944) *The Great Transformation*. New York: Rinehart and Co.

Powell, W.W. (1990) 'Neither market or hierarchy: Network forms of organization', *Research in Organizational Behavior*, 12, pp. 295–336.

Putnam, R.D. (1993) *Making Democracy Work: Civic Traditions in Modern Italy*. Princeton, NJ: Princeton University Press.

Reckwitz, A. (2002) 'Toward a theory of social practices: A development in culturalist theorizing', *European Journal of Social Theory*, 5, pp. 243–263.

Schatzki, T.R. (2005) 'The sites of organizations', *Organization Studies*, 26, pp. 465–484.

Sewell, W.H. (1992) 'A theory of structure: Duality, agency, and transformation', *American Journal of Sociology*, 98, pp. 1–29.

Staber, U. (2007) 'Contextualizing research on social capital in regional clusters', *International Journal of Urban and Regional Research*, 31, pp. 505–521.

Storper, M. (1995) 'The resurgence of regional economics, ten years later: The region as a nexus of untraded interdependencies', *European Urban and Regional Studies*, 2, pp. 191–221.

Ter Wal, A.L. (2014) 'The dynamics of the inventor network in German biotechnology: Geographic proximity versus triadic closure', *Journal of Economic Geography*, 14, pp. 589–620.

Uzzi, B. (1996) 'The sources and consequences of embeddedness for the economic performance of organizations: The network effect', *American Sociological Review*, 61, pp. 674–698.

Visser, E.J. & Boschma, R. (2004) 'Learning in districts: Novelty and lock-in in a regional context', *European Planning Studies*, 12, pp. 793–808.

Wenger, E. (1998) *Communities of Practice: Learning, Meaning and Identity*. Cambridge, UK: Cambridge University Press.

Werner, M. (2012) 'Beyond upgrading: Gendered labor and the restructuring of firms in the Dominican Republic', *Economic Geography*, 88, pp. 403–422.

Woolcock, M. (1998) 'Social capital and economic development: Toward a theoretical synthesis and policy framework', *Theory and Society*, 27, pp. 151–208.

Woolcock, M. & Narayan, D. (2000) 'Social capital: Implications for development theory, research, and policy', *The World Bank Research Observer*, 15, pp. 225–249.

Yeung, H.W.-C. (2005) 'The firm as social networks: An organisational perspective', *Growth and Change*, 36, pp. 307–328.

PART III

The interface between Economic Geography and International Business

11
ECONOMIC GEOGRAPHY AND INTERNATIONAL BUSINESS

Henry Wai-chung Yeung

Introduction

The development and emergence of economic-geographical studies of International Business activities is an important topic. As these cross-border intra- and inter-firm activities are becoming more globally interconnected and interdependent today, their management and governance by firms, states and other institutions is much more challenging and complex. The geographical foundations and specificities of this phenomenon in a globalizing era has become a crucial research question for the academic fields of Economic Geography and International Business studies. Indeed, both fields are nested within the larger disciplines – respectively in human geography and in strategy and management studies. Both fields are primarily concerned with descriptions and explanations of real-world economic phenomena in the world. There is thus much commonality between Economic Geography and International Business studies.

In this chapter, I focus on two key issues that speak well to the interface between Economic Geography and International Business studies: (1) the geographical nature of International Business and (2) the theorization of spatiality in International Business studies. The first issue is fairly obvious in a global economy characterized by densely interconnected networks of firms and economies operating at different geographical scales. In short, there are clearly visible *geographical foundations* to International Business activities (Yeung, 2005a, 2009a). While the role of physical location and distance has been conceptualized in some leading theoretical perspectives in International Business studies (e.g. Dunning, 1998, 2009; Buckley & Ghauri, 2004), the nature of spatiality entails much more than location as a production factor, an agglomeration economy, or a competitive advantage. The next section offers a critical overview of these conceptions in International Business studies.

Second, geography matters to International Business in diverse ways beyond simply discrete locations as cost variables measured by their distance-decay effects (e.g. Beugelsdijk, McCann & Mudambi, 2010; McCann, 2011). A relational perspective on spatiality in International Business conceives location as only one dimension of the different spatial configurations of cross-border activities. Other critical spatial dimensions include the geographical scales of business organization, the territorial embeddedness of firms and their assets, the local and regional effects of firm activities, and so on. The second section seeks to rethink the importance of spatiality in International Business studies. In the concluding section, I draw together these discussions and examine some key research challenges for the two fields.

Geographical foundations: the Economic Geography of International Business

In its essence, International Business takes place through firms operating across national borders via different entry modes, such as wholly owned subsidiaries, joint ventures, strategic alliances and so on. These operations include activities along the entire value chain, from resource seeking (e.g. raw materials) to asset exploitation (e.g. R&D) and efficiency gain (e.g. production and distribution). In organizing their complex cross-border activities, these firms – commonly known as transnational corporations (TNCs) or multinational enterprises (MNEs) – develop different management strategies and exercise diverse control mechanisms in order to achieve specific corporate goals and competitive outcomes.

In this broad contour of International Business activities, there are tangible *geographical foundations* that underpin the competitive success of specific TNCs and the collective importance of economic globalization spearheaded by these movers and shapers of the global economy. At the most basic level, there must be geographical differences in resource endowments, assets, and production factors for cross-border activities to be profitable. Specific resources are only found in some places, but not others, and this uneven geographical distribution of physical resources often constitutes one of the *raisons d'être* of International Business, particularly in resource-seeking operations. Other forms of uneven geographical distribution of non-physical resources, such as labour and regulations, can also serve as an attractive reason for firms seeking international production for efficiency gains.

But why do firms take the trouble to establish and manage their operations in countries other than their home economies (notwithstanding substantial geographical unevenness even *within* these home economies)? Existing International Business theories tell us that there are significant transaction costs associated with exploiting the uneven geographical distribution of physical resources and human assets through non-equity forms of contractual arrangements, such as international trade prevalent in the 19th century and international outsourcing in the late 20th century and beyond. Domestic firms therefore seek to internalize these costs by taking direct ownership and control through establishing cross-border operations. In this process, these domestic firms are transformed into transnational corporations that fundamentally underpin the emergence of International Business as a late 20th-century phenomenon, dubbed "global shift" in Peter Dicken's (1986, 2015) treatise.

This transformation in the corporate arena raises a significant question – what are the geographical foundations of the behaviour and management of such TNCs? To me, at least three geographical dimensions are important considerations – origin, organization and outcome. First, *geographical origins* of TNCs matter in their global reach and business operations. Prior to their internationalization, domestic firms are often embedded strongly in the business systems of their home countries. These systems are defined in the varieties of capitalism literature as distinct labour relations, financial governance, management practices, state-firm relations and so on (Whitley, 1999; Hall & Soskice, 2001). When they eventually venture abroad to minimize transaction costs and/or seek new assets/efficiencies, these domestic firms carry with them distinctive business recipes and corporate cultures. This distinctive "home origin" has led to fairly divergent International Business practices among global lead firms (e.g. Coe & Lee, 2006, 2013). There is thus no doubt that many US TNCs operate quite differently from Japanese or Chinese TNCs in today's global economy.

Despite the advent of contemporary globalization, there is still no conclusive evidence that global corporations from different home countries are converging in their organizational behaviour and strategic management. Over two decades ago, Michael Porter (1990, pp. 614, 807 note 1) argued that:

> [t]he more competition becomes global, ironically, the more important the home base becomes . . . Yet my research on this book has made it clear that globalization does not eliminate a powerful role for the home nation. The role of location, particularly of the home base, is far greater than I once supposed.

This national difference in TNC origins constitutes one major geographical foundation in International Business activities. It makes sense theoretically to explain why persistent geographical differences in these corporations, presumably the key drivers of economic globalization that "even out" geographical differences in development, continue to exist.

Second, TNCs from even the same home country and/or sector may *organize* their cross-border operations in fundamentally different geographical ways. Some TNCs may prefer to concentrate on specific macro-regional economies and organize their operations on the basis of such regions as the Americas, Europe, Asia, Africa and so on, whereas other TNCs may seek global presence in every major macro-region. The former become TNCs with distinct regional presence and specialization, and the latter are known as global corporations. This geographical foundation in TNC organization reflects not just their difference in origins. More importantly, it demonstrates the critical role of market and production geographies in shaping strategy and organization of TNC activities (e.g. Wrigley, Coe & Currah, 2005; Wrigley & Lowe, 2007).

The nature of value chains also constrains this spatial organization of TNCs. In value chains characterized by spatially dispersed factors of production (e.g. mining and agro-food), TNCs tend to be more "regional-centric". The same regionalized pattern of TNC organization also occurs in industries dominated by highly specialized industrial clusters (see Enright, 2000; Rugman, 2005; Phelps, 2008). For example, while the electronics industry is fairly global in its market penetration, most leading electronics TNCs engage in vertical specialization to organize their International Business activities. In doing so, their value chain activities are highly concentrated in specific industrial clusters and regions (e.g. Silicon Valley for R&D and China's Yangtze River Delta for production). In short, TNCs intentionally build competitive advantages through different geographical organizations of their markets and production. These diverse organizational geographies of markets and production constitute the essential foundation of International Business activities (see also Jones, 2005, 2008; Faulconbridge, 2008).

Third, the cross-border activities of TNCs have undoubtedly led to much greater geographical interdependency and *heterogeneous outcomes* throughout the global economy. Ironically, these outcomes are not exclusively limited to the home and host countries of these TNCs. In fact, the advent of International Business activities has exacerbated the already existing uneven geographical development in the world. Through their spatially selective investments and operations, TNCs can make or break specific localities and regional economies that are over-dependent on a small number of such TNCs (Phelps & Fuller, 2000; Dawley, 2007, 2011). Other potential host localities not benefitting from TNC presence may lose out in terms of employment growth, new firm formation, local capability development and so on. The divestment and restructuring of TNC activities can also impact very significantly on their home countries. Taken together, uneven geographical outcomes of TNC activities at different spatial scales – from local and regional to national and macro-regional – have posed a fundamental challenge to the sustainable success of International Business and, more broadly, economic globalization as a new phenomenon since the late 20th century.

While the above geographical foundations underpin the Economic Geography of International Business, spatiality and the spatial relations of these origins, organization and outcomes remain largely under-theorized in mainstream studies of International Business. This is a reflection of the predominantly Anglo-American origins of management and organization theories. In their critical reflections on the field of organization theory, Ghoshal and Westney (1993, pp. 6, 11) observed that:

> [s]tudies focusing on organizations and environments in Europe or South-East Asia have been labelled "area studies", whereas research on organizations in California or Ohio has led to propositions that have been implicitly stated and accepted as universal . . . Organization theorists have ignored or underemphasized the case of diversified organizations whose various constituent units are located in different business or geographic contexts.

For decades, management and organization theorists have conceived organizations as ontological entities separate from two key dimensions of great social significance – time *and* space. As geographer Bob Sack (1980, p. 4) noted: "space is an essential framework of all modes of thought. From physics to aesthetics, from myth and magic to common everyday life, space, in conjunction with time, provides a fundamental ordering system interlacing every facet of thought". In short, space serves as a foundational organizing framework for virtually all dimensions of International Business. While time, as expressed in studies of organizational change and learning, has received some attention in management and organization theories, space remains largely outside the normal orbit of theory-development routines in management and organization studies.

Indeed, geographical dimensions – distance, location, space, territoriality, geographical scales and spatial relations – may exert such significant causal influences on the organization and behaviour of TNCs that they may fundamentally challenge our existing conceptions of the strategy, control and management, performance and impact of these corporations in society and communities. As the late John Dunning (1998, p. 46) reflected in relation to International Business studies: "the emphasis on the firm-specific determinants of international economic activity, while still driving much academic research by scholars in business schools, is now being complemented by a renewed interest in the spatial aspects of FDI [foreign direct investment]". In a reflection published a decade later, he further noted that:

> [w]hen asked to contribute to a JIBS symposium on the *Multinational Enterprise and Economic Analysis* in 1998, I chose as my subject "Location and the multinational enterprise: A neglected factor?" (Dunning, 1998). This was because, at the time, I did not consider mainstream IB theory had fully appreciated how the L component of the OLI [Ownership, Location, and Internalization] paradigm was influencing the extent, industrial and geographical pattern, and modality of MNE activity.
>
> *(Dunning, 2009, p. 23)*

Most recently, Peter Buckley (2016) noted in his reflection on the internalization theory in International Business studies that location theory remains a significant "unanswered question" that poses a challenge to the theory's analytical efficacy.

To a certain extent, this interest in the spatial aspects of international investments is related to the much wider geographical reach of TNCs in more recent decades. The late Raymond Vernon (1992, viii) observed sometime ago that "the enterprises of the 1990s routinely span distances with an ease that could not have been contemplated two or three decades ago, searching for opportunities and threats in distant places". This global reach of TNCs, however, has not diminished the role of geography as an important variable in analysing their ever-expanding tendencies. Instead, spatial differentiation inherent in today's global economy presents a significant challenge to the management, organization and success of all transnational corporations (see Dicken, 2015).

Despite the above critical observations, recent theoretical work in the "new Economic Geography" (NEG) (Combes, Mayer & Thisse, 2008; Iammarino & McCann, 2013), the geography of international production (Dunning, 2009; Beugelsdijk & Mudambi, 2013; Buckley & Strange, 2015), and the analysis of international strategy (Porter, 2000; Hitt, Li & Xu, 2016) has explicitly incorporated *location* in their analytical frameworks. Econometric studies in NEG have shown that geographical agglomeration produces external economies that lead to increasing returns to scale under conditions of imperfect competition and multiple equilibria. In their major review of the economics of agglomeration, Fujita and Thisse (1996, p. 347) footnoted that "the study of location problems in the international marketplace is still in [its] infancy and constitutes a very promising line of research". In the analysis of competitive strategy, location has been given theoretical prominence through the analytical coupling of the tight relationship between clusters and competitive strategy at the firm level. In this sense, Porter (2000, p. 272) argued that "geography and location must become one of the core disciplines in management. There is a compelling need to reorient our thinking about corporate strategy in a way that sees location and cluster participation as integral to a firm's success". Finally, location has also been incorporated into John Dunning's revised eclectic framework of international production (Dunning & Lundan, 2008). Spatial transaction costs are theorized to influence the *raison d'être* of transnational corporations.

These interrelated strands of theorization of the Economic Geography of International Business, nevertheless, remain partial and static in their consideration of the geographical foundations of International Business (see also Yeung, 2009b). First, space and location are incorporated into these theoretical frameworks as the backdrop or scaffolding on which economic and organizational processes operate. Although distance (both physical and cultural) and location are conceptualized as exerting some "friction" and influence, firms and organizations continue to be viewed as ontologically independent entities that operate according to some preordained and internalized economic logics and strategies. Even when "geography" is explicitly mentioned, it is conceived as a descriptor to put into context the location of TNC activities. As described by Dunning and Lundan (2008, p. 81) in *Multinational Enterprises and the Global Economy*:

> [t]he nature of FDI undertaken by MNEs is extremely varied. Because of this, both the motives for and the determinants of international production will differ. The parameters influencing a Finnish pulp and paper company investing in a mill in Indonesia are unlikely to be the same as those influencing the purchase of a French food processing company by a Canadian MNE. Similarly, those determining the pattern of rationalised production in the EU by a large and geographically diversified US motor vehicle MNE will be quite different from an investment by a Korean construction management company in Saudi Arabia, a Chinese state-owned oil company seeking new reserves in the [sic] Sudan, or a UK bank [opening] a call centre facility in India.

There is no doubt that the above nuanced understanding of differentiated TNC motives is important, particularly in light of the undifferentiated treatment of the firm as an actor in mainstream economics (see also Yeung, 2005b). Still, there is a missed opportunity to bring this firm-specific differentiation to bear on the dynamic processes of spatial differentiation in International

Business activities. To put it more bluntly, why do TNC motives matter if we are not yet told their connections with the geographical origin and host regions and/or countries? Are there specific contexts, institutional or otherwise, in these localities and/or nations that compel TNCs to act in particular ways and manners? How might these different geographical contexts interact with TNC behaviour to (re)constitute new opportunities for and/or threats to more spatially even development in these regional and national economies?

Second, important geographical dimensions, such as spatial scales and relations, are neglected in this more recent work in International Business studies. Geography is therefore essentially stripped down to "location", which in turn is translated into measurable distance between points in space (e.g. Baaij & Slangen, 2013; Blanc-Brude et al., 2014; Jiang, Holburn & Beamish, 2016). This is evident, for example, in Lomi's (1995, p. 111; my emphasis) observation that "the recurrence of patterns of organizational concentration in *space* across different industries and in a number of national contexts provides indirect evidence that *location* may be a general factor shaping the evolution of organizations". Even the latest thinking by Dunning (2009, p. 30; emphasis omitted), shortly before his death, continues to perpetuate this misplaced view of "the dynamics of the locational decisions of MNEs, which, to my mind, remains the central core of IB theory and that of the eclectic paradigm". These Euclidean conceptions of absolute distance and space as a "container" tend to dominate the emerging work on the geography of firms, economic development and international production. But they have neglected the critical importance of other dimensions in the geographical foundations of International Business. As argued critically by Beugelsdijk, McCann and Mudambi (2010, p. 488) in their introduction to a Special Issue of *Journal of Economic Geography* that aims to bridge Economic Geography and International Business studies:

> [n]one of these streams of research explicitly focuses on how the firm's organizational characteristics relate to the firm's fundamental geographical characteristics, both within and between countries, because the role of the firm in space is rarely the main object of study (Beugelsdijk, 2007). Notwithstanding the important contributions that NEG and firm heterogeneity studies have made to our understanding of multinational activity, MNEs are still basically portrayed in geographical space as independent units agglomerating in certain locations, leaving the nature of the interaction between places and space as a black box.

Third, the primary focus on the national scale in most work in International Business studies further exacerbates the problem of missing geographies at other geographical scales. This problem of "methodological nationalism" is common when economic processes, institutional structures and cultural practices are assumed to be homogenous and stable within national territories (e.g. Ma, Delios & Lau, 2013; Beugelsdijk et al., 2014). International Business studies remain firmly locked into the quest for understanding the location choice of TNCs at the national scale and the macro-economic dimensions of the changing international allocation of economic activity. This form of methodological nationalism not only leads to a fixed and uncritical notion of the national scale as the primary and natural unit of investigating into TNC activities, but also underestimates seriously the substantial heterogeneity of localities and regions within specific countries. Put simply, localities and regions differ significantly even within the same country; TNC activities at these spatial scales are also necessarily different. This spatially differentiated pattern of TNC activities and FDI behaviour poses one of the most significant lacunae in the existing research in International Business studies.

Rethinking spatiality in International Business studies: a relational economic-geographical perspective

Taking an economic-geographical perspective means rethinking spatiality in International Business studies. This section aims to draw upon the above conceptual work and the significantly larger body of theoretical literature in the discipline of Economic Geography to reassert the importance of space and geography in International Business studies. As argued by Schoenberger (2000, p. 329):

> Spatial form, however, is not merely a by-product of decisions taken according to the more compelling specifics of products, markets, and production processes. Firms produce and use and are shaped by spatial relations as a normal part of doing business and must continually create and seek to validate spatio-temporal processes and understandings as a condition of staying alive. Another way of saying this might be that spatial and temporal processes are very deeply part of the production function and the growth trajectory, not artifacts of them.

In attempting to answer the opening questions of this chapter, I argue for a relational framework for examining the geographical foundations of TNCs and for a new direction of research in International Business studies. Instead of taking space and location as the backdrop of organizational behaviour and change, we can theorize the complex relations and interactions between business firms and geography within the realm of *organizational space*. The conception of organizational space as relational is explained by the ways in which its geometry varies with specific relations constituted by different organizational units. Organizational space thus differs significantly from physical space in which location and distance can be directly observed and measured. Organizational space is also different from the concept of organizational fields in institutional theories that defines the *structural* or population characteristics of organizations as "the totality of relevant actors" (DiMaggio & Powell, 1983, p. 148; see also Fligstein & McAdam, 2012).

This theorization can potentially contribute to a *relational perspective* for understanding why and how business firms are fundamentally spatialized in their origin, organization, performance and impact (Yeung, 2005c, 2008). This relational approach aims to contribute to the development of more sophisticated theories in International Business studies that may not be directly operationalizable and measurable in quantitative terms. As Rousseau and Fried (2001, p. 3) cautioned, "the common demands for clean (read: simple) models do not always fit with the messy reality of contemporary work and organizational life". More specifically, my strategy of tackling these theoretical questions is to focus explicitly on one particular type of business organization – TNCs and their International Business activities. This specific choice reflects the greater likelihood of geography having a significant influence on the organization and behaviour of TNCs that operate across national boundaries in an integrated manner. For example, Frost (2001, p. 121) concluded that "the multinational firm may offer an ideal context for advancing our understanding of the firm-location nexus precisely because of the ability to study a single corporate entity in multiple institutional contexts".

To construct this relational perspective and to clear away "conventional notions to make room for artful and exciting insights" (DiMaggio, 1995, p. 391), an economic-geographical approach can offer several key insights to the field of International Business studies. First, we can conceive spatial differentiation and configurations as both cause and outcome of International Business activities. Geographical foundations serve as one of the major imperatives in explaining the competitive dynamics of TNCs and their cross-border activities. Second, uniting the two fields of Economic Geography and International Business studies means taking seriously both spatial structures and (international) business agency. The former are both inputs and outcomes of the strategic imperatives of the latter. It is through TNC activities that we can appreciate the critical role of geographical foundations. But these very activities further (re)produce and/or disrupt those geographical foundations to create conditions for future business reorganization and spatial restructuring. Third, linking home and host locations and impacts in transnational operations points to the analytical necessity of considering these issues at multiple spatial scales, such as local, regional, national and macro-regional scales. Taken together, these analytical insights help us go beyond the theorization of firm-specific drivers of International Business activities and put TNCs in their geographical contexts.

In the remainder of this chapter, I construct such a relational perspective on transnational activities by global firms. Here, spaces of TNCs can be defined as differentiated spatial configurations or areas constituted by ongoing relations and transactions controlled and coordinated by lead firms. The difference that space makes is in the co-evolution of International Business activity with these configurations. As a relational phenomenon subject to interactive effects among different firms and non-firm institutions, transnational activities reflect not only firm-specific locational decisions and the distance-effects of physical space. More importantly, these activities are driven by the organizational capabilities and global reach of TNCs and their competitors, customers and partners. Organizational decisions reflect these interactive relations among key actors in International Business, rather than abstract spatial variables such as physical or cultural distances.

When we take into account such constellations of intra-firm (parent-subsidiary), inter-firm (customer-supplier) and extra-firm (non-economic actors) relations, International Business activities can be better described and analysed as differentiated spatial configurations of *global production networks* (GPNs). These networks comprise both globalized and decentralized structures. The more globalized structures are often controlled and coordinated by TNCs as global lead firms (see Coe et al., 2004; Coe & Yeung, 2015; Yeung & Coe, 2015; Coe's Chapter 9 in this volume). These lead firms can exercise strong market or product definition and thus create and capture more value from such globalized structures of production and consumption. Some recent studies in International Business have considered how these geographical structures are determined by global lead firms or flagship firms (e.g. Buckley, 2011; Buckley & Strange, 2015; Buckley & Prashantham, 2016).

Not all GPNs, however, are highly globalized and centralized. Some networks are characterized by decentralized structures of multiple actors at various spatial scales. This phenomenon is particularly prevalent in new high-tech industries in which dominant lead firms are yet to emerge (e.g. 3D printing and artificial intelligence). In these decentralized networks, the role of large TNCs as global lead firms is less prominent and significant. Instead, localized and innovative firms embedded in strong social and institutional settings are likely to drive these networks. In such "webs without spiders", localities provide very critical geographical foundations to the emergence and evolution of multiple innovative firms. These localities are not simply "dots" on maps that are picked by global lead firms in their search for market domination. Analysing these decentralized structures requires us to go beyond the location-as-dots approach in strategic management and International Business studies (see also Faulconbridge, 2008; Jones, 2008, 2010).

Put together, TNC networks serve as a geographical constellation of unique configurations of GPNs. This approach extends beyond the aspatial strategy-structure-performance approach in most International Business studies of intra/inter-firm networks. As international production is becoming increasingly more prevalent in the global economy, TNC activities are organized on the basis of networks rather than arm's length transactions. Through such a heterarchical form of economic organization, the organizational boundary of each TNC continues to expand, and more firms and other institutions are enrolled into TNC networks (Ghoshal & Bartlett, 1990; Yeung, 2005b, 2008; Gulati, 2007; Levy, 2008).

In particular, the relational interaction between localities/places and TNCs in GPNs is determined by the mechanisms of *strategic coupling*, a process of multiple actors taking advantage of their mutual complementaries in networks. In Dicken's (2000) work, TNCs are seen as having their unique places because of their geographical embeddedness in regions of origin. But the same TNCs are also creating new "places" through their cross-border investment processes. As such, TNCs capitalize on existing local and regional assets and yet produce new "places" of assets. Strategic coupling serves as a set of dynamic mechanisms through which TNCs coordinate, mediate and arbitrage strategic interests between local actors and their counterparts in the global economy. To Dunning and Lundan (2008, p. 490):

> Such systems enable firms to structure and locate each part of their value chains more closely in line with the existing comparative resource and institution advantages of countries (e.g., in Asia and Latin America), while also allowing for the dynamic reconfiguration of these assets, depending on the role assigned to the affiliates, and their degree of integration with local firms.

This co-evolutionary place-TNC relation also leads to substantial spillover effects created by TNC activities. Buckley and Ghauri (2004, p. 91) thus argued that:

> The links between Economic Geography and development are also worthy of attention in the literature on "spillovers" from MNEs to the local economy. Many of these spillovers are enhanced by geographical proximity (in the formation of clusters of supporting industries, for instance) and this factor is not often explicitly included in the examination of spillovers.

In my earlier empirical work on East Asian economies (e.g. Yeung, 2009c, 2014, 2016), I have demonstrated that transnational corporations embody both local and non-local links in their emergence and evolution over time. Among East Asian TNCs, their organizational capabilities and global reach are crucially determined by the three mechanisms of strategic coupling with global lead firms based in North America, Western Europe and Japan: strategic partnership, industrial market specialization and (re)positioning as lead firms. These mechanisms of strategic coupling help draw different East Asian localities and regional economies into the diverse territorial configurations of GPNs in different industries, such as electronics, shipbuilding, semiconductors and automobiles. Mediated by TNC activities, this enrolment process of strategic coupling and its constitutive mechanisms inadvertently involve the localities and regions in which these other firms and institutions are embedded. As such, the globalization of TNC networks represents a powerful impetus to produce different kinds of economic specialization in these localities and regions (see also Yang, 2009; MacKinnon, 2012; Wei & Liao, 2013; Horner, 2014).

Conclusion: challenges for International Business studies and Economic Geography

This chapter has examined the critical link between localities/regions and the global economy through examining key economic actors – business firms and their transnational production networks. My arguments for closer intellectual interaction between Economic Geography and International Business studies points to the usefulness of making global connections through transdisciplinarity and the analytical relevance of understanding flows and relations across space. This geographical approach goes beyond agency-centric views common in International Business studies and moves towards a GPN of International Business studies through the engagement, connectivity and transformation of knowledge in the Economic Geography of International Business activities.

The implications of this approach for the analysis of the geography of International Business are manifold and complex. There are at least two explicit implications that should be laid out briefly here. First, instead of asking whether TNCs have a global strategy to compete for the future, International Business researchers can ask whether these global lead firms have a *spatial* strategy. Mundane as it might sound, this question can be fundamentally important to corporate performance and success because today's economic competition is not necessarily pitched at the global scale only. As discussed extensively in this chapter, corporate competition indeed operates at all spatial scales, and corporate success can only be secured through an understanding of these overlapping scales of competitive fields. By privileging the global scale, the competitive strategy literature in International Business studies might have misled us by placing too much emphasis on the centralization and implementation of corporate decisions on a global scale. This relentless pursuit of a global strategy is often championed at the expense of reaping potential geographical economies through more appropriate scalar (re)configurations and representations of organizational units in this "global" competition.

Second, International Business researchers can take stock of how geography is conceived by actors in business organizations – the idea of cognitive representations of space. Understanding and resolving the contradictions and tensions in these cognitive mindsets within an organization, such as a global lead firm, will help corporate managers to open better channels of communications within the organization and to strengthen intra-organizational cooperation and solidarity. For example, will it be effective for marketing executives in the parent company to champion a global branding approach if the R&D team takes a highly local orientation in their design of specific products? Alternatively, will a global corporation be efficient if its central purchasing department practises global sourcing and yet managers of its foreign manufacturing plants are so locally embedded as to source within the host countries? Ultimately, the success of business organizations depends critically on their willingness and ability to recognize complexity and differentiation in the global *space*-economy. Economic geographers and International Business researchers who are cognizant of the role of space and geography will not make this global economy less complex; but they can certainly enable it to be more comprehensible and, eventually, manageable.

References

Baaij, M.G. & Slangen, A.H.L. (2013) 'The role of headquarters: Subsidiary geographic distance in strategic decisions by spatially disaggregated headquarters', *Journal of International Business Studies*, 44, pp. 941–952.

Beugelsdijk, S. (2007) 'The regional environment and a firm's innovative performance: A plea for a multilevel interactionist approach', *Economic Geography*, 83, pp. 181–199.

Beugelsdijk, S., McCann, P. & Mudambi, R. (2010) 'Place, space, and organization: Economic Geography and the multinational enterprise', *Journal of Economic Geography*, 10, pp. 485–493.

Beugelsdijk, S. & Mudambi, R. (2013) 'MNEs as border-crossing multi-location enterprises: The role of discontinuities in geographic space', *Journal of International Business Studies*, 44, pp. 413–426.

Beugelsdijk, S., Slangen, A., Maseland, R. & Onrust, M. (2014) 'The impact of home–host cultural distance on foreign affiliate sales: The moderating role of cultural variation within host countries', *Journal of Business Research*, 67, pp. 1638–1646.

Blanc-Brude, F., Cookson, G., Piesse, J. & Strange, R. (2014) 'The FDI location decision: Distance and the effects of spatial dependence', *International Business Review*, 23, pp. 797–810.

Buckley, P.J. (2011) 'International integration and coordination in the global factory', *Management International Review*, 51, pp. 269–283.

Buckley, P.J. (2016) 'The contribution of internalisation theory to International Business: New realities and unanswered questions', *Journal of World Business*, 51, pp. 74–82.

Buckley, P.J. & Ghauri, P. (2004) 'Globalisation, Economic Geography and the strategy of multinational enterprises', *Journal of International Business Studies*, 35, pp. 81–98.

Buckley, P.J. & Prashantham, S. (2016) 'Global interfirm networks: The division of entrepreneurial labor between MNEs and SMEs', *Academy of Management Perspectives*, 30, pp. 40–58.

Buckley, P.J. & Strange, R. (2015) 'The governance of the global factory: Location and control of world economic activity', *Academy of Management Perspectives*, 29, pp. 237–249.

Coe, N.M., Hess, M., Yeung, H.W-C., Dicken, P. & Henderson, J. (2004) '"Globalizing" regional development: A global production networks perspective', *Transactions of the Institute of British Geographers*, 29, pp. 468–484.

Coe, N.M. & Lee, Y.-S. (2006) 'The strategic localization of transnational retailers: The case of Samsung-Tesco in South Korea', *Economic Geography*, 82, pp. 61–88.

Coe, N.M. & Lee, Y.-S. (2013) '"We've learnt how to be local": The deepening territorial embeddedness of Samsung–Tesco in South Korea', *Journal of Economic Geography*, 13, pp. 327–356.

Coe, N.M. & Yeung, H.W.-C. (2015) *Global Production Networks: Theorizing Economic Development in an Interconnected World*. Oxford, UK: Oxford University Press.

Combes, P-P., Mayer, T. & Thisse, J-F. (2008) *Economic Geography: The Integration of Regions and Nations*. Princeton, NJ: Princeton University Press.

Dawley, S. (2007) 'Fluctuating rounds of inward investment in peripheral regions: Semiconductors in the North East of England', *Economic Geography*, 83, pp. 51–74.

Dawley, S. (2011) 'Transnational corporations and local and regional development', in Pike, A., Rodríguez-Pose, A. & Tomaney, J. (Eds.), *Handbook of Local and Regional Development*. London: Routledge, pp. 394–412.

Dicken, P. (1986) *Global Shift: Industrial Change in a Turbulent World*. London: Harper & Row.

Dicken, P. (2000) 'Places and flows: Situating international investment', in Clark, G.L., Feldman, M.A. & Gertler, M.S. (Eds.), *The Oxford Handbook of Economic Geography*. Oxford, UK: Oxford University Press, pp. 275–291.

Dicken, P. (2015) *Global Shift: Mapping the Changing Contours of the World Economy*. 7th Edition. London: Sage.

DiMaggio, P.J. (1995) 'Comments on "What theory is not"', *Administrative Science Quarterly*, 40, pp. 391–397.

DiMaggio, P.J. & Powell, W.W. (1983) 'The iron cage revisited: Institutional isomorphism and collective rationality in organisational fields', *American Sociological Review*, 48, pp. 147–160.

Dunning, J.H. (1998) 'Location and the multinational enterprise: A neglected factor?' *Journal of International Business Studies*, 29, pp. 45–66.

Dunning, J.H. (2009) 'Location and the multinational enterprise: John Dunning's thoughts on receiving the *Journal of International Business Studies* 2008 Decade Award', *Journal of International Business Studies*, 40, pp. 20–34.

Dunning, J.H. & Lundan, S.M. (2008) *Multinational Enterprises and the Global Economy*. 2nd Edition. Cheltenham, UK: Edward Elgar.

Enright, M.J. (2000) 'Regional clusters and multinational enterprises', *International Studies of Management and Organization*, 30, pp. 114–139.

Faulconbridge, J.R. (2008) 'Managing the transnational law firm: A relational analysis of professional systems, embedded actors and time-space sensitive governance', *Economic Geography*, 84, pp. 185–210.

Fligstein, N. & McAdam, D. (2012) *A Theory of Fields*. New York: Oxford University Press.

Frost, T. (2001) 'The geographic sources of foreign subsidiaries' innovations', *Strategic Management Journal*, 22, pp. 101–123.

Fujita, M. & Thisse, J-F. (1996) 'Economics of agglomeration', *Journal of the Japanese and International Economies*, 10, pp. 339–378.

Ghoshal, S. & Bartlett, C.A. (1990) 'The multinational corporation as an interorganizational network', *Academy of Management Review*, 15, pp. 603–625.

Ghoshal, S. & Westney, D.E. (1993) 'Introduction and overview', in Ghoshal, S. & Westney, D.E. (Eds.), *Organization Theory and the Multinational Corporation*. New York: St. Martin's Press, pp. 1–23.

Gulati, R. (2007) *Managing Network Resources: Alliances, Affiliations, and Other Relational Assets*. Oxford, UK: Oxford University Press.

Hall, P.A. & Soskice, D. (Eds.) (2001) *Varieties of Capitalism: The Institutional Foundations of Comparative Advantage*. Oxford, UK: Oxford University Press.

Hitt, M.A., Li, D. & Xu, K. (2016) 'International strategy: From local to global and beyond', *Journal of World Business*, 51, pp. 58–73.

Horner, R. (2014) 'Strategic decoupling, recoupling and global production networks: India's pharmaceutical industry', *Journal of Economic Geography*, 14, pp. 1117–1140.

Iammarino, S. & McCann, P. (2013) *Multinationals and Economic Geography: Location, Technology and Innovation*. Cheltenham, UK: Edward Elgar.

Jiang, G.F., Holburn, G.L.F. & Beamish, P.W. (2016) 'The spatial structure of foreign subsidiaries and MNE expansion strategy', *Journal of World Business*, 51, pp. 438–450.

Jones, A. (2005) 'Truly global corporations? Theorizing "organizational globalization" in advanced business-services', *Journal of Economic Geography*, 5, pp. 177–200.

Jones, A. (2008) 'Beyond embeddedness: Economic practices and the invisible dimensions to transnational business activity', *Progress in Human Geography*, 32, pp. 71–88.

Jones, A. (2010) 'Theorizing global business spaces', *Geografiska Annaler*, 91B, pp. 203–218.

Levy, D.L. (2008) 'Political contestation in global production networks', *Academy of Management Review*, 33, pp. 943–963.

Lomi, A. (1995) 'The population ecology of organizational founding: Location dependence and unobserved heterogeneity', *Administrative Science Quarterly*, 40, pp. 111–144.

Ma, X., Delios, A. & Lau, C.-M. (2013) 'Beijing or Shanghai? The strategic location choice of large MNEs' host-country headquarters in China', *Journal of International Business Studies*, 44, pp. 953–961.

MacKinnon, D. (2012) 'Beyond strategic coupling: Reassessing the firm-region nexus in global production networks', *Journal of Economic Geography*, 12, pp. 227–245.

McCann, P. (2011) 'International Business and Economic Geography: Knowledge, time and transactions costs', *Journal of Economic Geography*, 11, pp. 309–317.

Phelps, N.A. (2008) 'Cluster or capture? Manufacturing foreign direct investment, external economies and agglomeration', *Regional Studies*, 42, pp. 457–473.

Phelps, N.A. & Fuller, C. (2000) 'Multinationals, intracorporate competition, and regional development', *Economic Geography*, 76, pp. 224–243.

Porter, M.E. (1990) *The Competitive Advantage of Nations*. London: Macmillan.

Porter, M.E. (2000) 'Locations, clusters, and company strategy', in Clark, G.L., Feldman, M.A. & Gertler, M.S. (Eds.), *The Oxford Handbook of Economic Geography*. Oxford, UK: Oxford University Press, pp. 253–274.

Rousseau, D.M. & Fried, Y. (2001) 'Location, location, location: Contextualizing organizational research', *Journal of Organizational Behavior*, 22, pp. 1–13.

Rugman, A.M. (2005) *The Regional Multinationals: MNEs and 'Global' Strategic Management*. Cambridge, UK: Cambridge University Press.

Sack, R.D. (1980) *Conceptions of Space in Social Thought*. London: Macmillan.

Schoenberger, E. (2000) 'The management of time and space', in Clark, G.L., Feldman, M.A. & Gertler, M.S. (Eds.), *The Oxford Handbook of Economic Geography*. Oxford, UK: Oxford University Press, pp. 317–332.

Vernon, R. (1992) 'Foreword', in Buckley, P.J. (Ed.), *Studies in International Business*. London: Macmillan, pp. viii–ix.

Wei, D.Y.H. & Liao, F.H.F. (2013) 'The embeddedness of transnational corporations in Chinese cities: Strategic coupling in global production networks?' *Habitat International*, 40, pp. 82–90.

Whitley, R. (1999) *Divergent Capitalisms: The Social Structuring and Change of Business Systems*. New York: Oxford University Press.

Wrigley, N., Coe, N.M. & Currah, A. (2005) 'Globalizing retail: Conceptualizing the distribution-based transnational corporation (TNC)', *Progress in Human Geography*, 29, pp. 437–457.

Wrigley, N. & Lowe, M. (Eds.) (2007) 'Special issue on transnational retail, supply networks, and the global economy', *Journal of Economic Geography*, 7, pp. 337–355.
Yang, C. (2009) 'Strategic coupling of regional development in global production networks: redistribution of Taiwan PC Investment from Pearl River Delta to Yangtze River Delta, China', *Regional Studies*, 43, pp. 385–408.
Yeung, H.W.-C. (2005a) 'Organizational space: a new frontier in International Business strategy?', *Critical Perspective on International Business*, 1, pp. 219–240.
Yeung, H.W.-C. (2005b) 'The firm as social networks: an organizational perspective', *Growth and Change*, 36, pp. 307–328.
Yeung, H.W.-C. (2005c) 'Rethinking relational Economic Geography', *Transactions of the Institute of British Geographers*, 30, pp. 37–51.
Yeung, H.W.-C. (2008) 'Perspectives on inter-organizational relations in Economic Geography' In Cropper, S., Ebers, M., Huxham, C. & Smith Ring, P. (Eds.) *The Oxford handbook of inter-organizational relations*. Oxford: Oxford University Press, pp. 473–501.
Yeung, H.W.-C. (2009a) 'Transnationalizing entrepreneurship: A critical agenda for Economic Geography', *Progress in Human Geography*, 33, pp. 210–235.
Yeung, H.W.-C. (2009b) 'Transnational corporations, global production networks, and urban and regional development', *Growth and Change*, 40, pp. 197–226.
Yeung, H.W.-C. (2009c) 'Regional development and the competitive dynamics of global production networks: An East Asian perspective', *Regional Studies*, 43, pp. 325–351.
Yeung, H.W.-C. (2014) 'Governing the market in a globalizing era: developmental states, global production networks, and inter-firm dynamics in East Asia', *Review of International Political Economy*, 21, pp. 70–101.
Yeung, H.W.-C. (2016) *Strategic coupling: East Asian industrial transformation in the new global economy*. Cornell Studies in Political Economy Series. Ithaca, NY: Cornell University Press.
Yeung, H.W.-C. & Coe, N.M. (2015) 'Toward a dynamic theory of global production networks', *Economic Geography*, 91, pp. 29–58.

12

TOWARD A SYNTHESIS OF MICRO AND MACRO FACTORS THAT INFLUENCE FOREIGN DIRECT INVESTMENT LOCATION CHOICE

Bo Nielsen, Christian Asmussen and Anthony Goerzen

Introduction

Recent evidence suggests that multinational corporations (MNCs) pay increasing attention to sub-national locational factors at the state, municipality, and city level when considering a suitable foreign direct investment (FDI) site (Cheng, 2007). While macro-level theories of economic agglomeration and institutions have provided insights into this phenomenon, additional guidance from Economic Geography and urban economics would provide a fuller picture of sub-national variation in FDI location attractiveness. Since MNCs look for specific geographic locations that enhance their ability to leverage firm-specific advantages, a synthesis of the interplay of national and sub-national, as well as firm-specific drivers of FDI location choice is needed in order to advance our understanding of MNC location strategy.

International Business (IB) theory has focused primarily on the economic organization of the geographically dispersed enterprise (Cantwell, 2009), specifically directing attention to the speed, means, and governance of international activities and, to a lesser extent, location choice. While location choice is an essential part of IB research (see, e.g., Dunning's Eclectic Framework (Dunning, 1998, 2009), IB scholars typically examine this factor at the national level. While more recent studies on location have begun to consider the sub-national level, these studies generally remain focused on large geographic areas such as states (e.g., within the US) or provinces (e.g., in China or Eastern Europe), without allowing for variability in micro-location specific attributes (for a recent review see Blanc-Brude et al., 2014).

Economic Geography and urban economic scholars, on the other hand, have long recognized the importance of sub-national (micro) spatial variation for economic activity (Krugman, 1991; Markusen et al., 1996; Lorenzen & Mudambi, 2013). Indeed, since Marshall (1920), researchers in these fields have examined different location unit types, ranging from regions, provinces, and states to clusters, industrial districts, and cities (e.g., Jacobs, 1969; Sassen, 1994, 2001, 2012; Head, Ries & Swenson, 1995; Belderbos & Carree, 2002).

Attracting FDI to a particular location is important, as countries, and the sub-national micro-locations within them, consider FDI inflows as pivotal for economic development and prosperity.

Hence, a rich literature within urban and developmental economics emphasizes the factors at the host country, regional, or micro-locational (e.g., state, municipality, or city) level that local policy can influence to attract FDI to a particular location (Zhou, Delios & Yang, 2002; Fung et al., 2005). These literatures have not been integrated to form a more complete understanding of how and why a particular firm chooses a specific location for a particular investment.

As noted recently by several scholars (e.g., Beugelsdijk, McCann & Mudambi, 2010; Beugelsdijk & Mudambi, 2013; Goerzen, Asmussen & Nielsen, 2013), IB research lacks a thorough understanding of the mechanisms that propel MNCs to favor one sub-national location over another, typically focusing on national level geographic and institutional distances, while under-appreciating the heterogeneity within countries. At the same time, the Economic Geography and urban economics literatures specify a number of factors that create spatial variation at sub-national levels, however, often with little or no attention to firm-specific characteristics and the match between motives, resources, capabilities, and location choice (Markusen et al., 1996; McCann, 2011).

The literature looking into FDI location choices includes a number of different theoretical perspectives that operate on different levels of aggregation. Some studies look at the push and pull of macro-location factors, defined as those factors that vary across countries, and thus may lead an MNC to place a given subsidiary in one country rather than another. Such factors include market size, entry barriers (tariffs and taxes), transportation costs, factor endowments, institutions, agglomeration economies, currencies, government incentives, political stability, labor costs, etc. that may give rise to imperfections in the markets for goods or factors. Other studies have examined micro-location factors, defined as those factors that might influence MNCs' decisions as to where to locate within a given country, e.g., in one state, municipality, or city rather than another. Such factors may include industrial clustering and city-specific attributes, in addition to the macro-location factors listed earlier.[1] In practice, however, location decisions entail a simultaneous (perhaps sequential) consideration of macro- and micro-location factors combined with firm-specific resources and characteristics, such as patents, technologies, know-how, production processes, or managerial talent (Nachum, Dunning & Jones, 2000; Galan, González-Benito & Zuñiga-Vincente, 2007).

We argue for the importance of disciplinary integration and attention to levels of analysis in future research, and we begin by reviewing the various theories that have been applied to FDI location choice. Our chapter, therefore, integrates insights from management and IB literatures with insights from urban economics and Economic Geography. Our objective is to identify and synthesize disparate studies of location choice to advance knowledge of the complex interplay in characteristics between firm and sub-national location that may determine why certain firms locate particular types of international activities in specific micro-locations. We contribute to IB and Economic Geography literatures by synthesizing the theoretical rationales and empirical evidence for MNC location choice beyond the national level to offer some potential new directions for FDI location research.

A review of theoretical approaches to FDI location choice

A wide variety of theories and models have been employed to explain FDI and its location. Rather than being exhaustive, the following brief review of the most salient theoretical approaches to FDI location choice is meant to provide guidance to the ensuring analysis of the empirical literature (see Table 12.1).

Neo-classical trade theory. According to neoclassical trade theory, firms will pursue profitable international markets by locating their investments in "attractive" host

Table 12.1 Macro-level determinants: industrial agglomeration and national institutions

Exemplary studies	*Context of study*	*Method*	*Dependent variable*	*Key findings*
Wheeler & Mody (1992)	US manufacturing FDI in 42 countries 1982–1988	Translog model	Country location choice of investment	Early example of agglomeration study: horizontal agglomeration & developed/emerging markets divide – US firms undertake FDI where other foreign and manufacturing firms are. However, this tendency is stronger in developed markets. In emerging markets, infrastructure and labor costs are stronger motivating factors
Guimaraes, Figueiredo, & Woodward (2000)	Location decisions of 758 foreign-owned manufacturing plants in the urban areas and outlying regions of Portugal 1985–1992	Conditional logit model and regression analysis	Probability that individual *I* locates in concelho *j*, based on expected profits from the concelho, relative to other concelhos	Industry-level and service agglomeration: both industry level and service agglomeration determine FDI inflows, with service agglomeration having a more significant pull over and above foreign firm agglomeration
Disdier & Mayer (2004)	1,843 location choices of French MNCs in 19 EU and Central Eastern European countries 1980–1999	Conditional and nested logit models	Probability of choosing country *j* conditional on the choice of region *i*	Agglomeration and institutionalism in emerging markets: both a larger market and a concentration of French firms from the same industry increase the likelihood of a country being chosen as an FDI destination. The countries with stronger institutions are overwhelmingly more likely to be chosen as FDI destinations
Pusterla & Resmini (2007)	4,103 foreign manufacturing investments in Poland, Hungary, Bulgaria, and Romania 1995–2001	Nested logit model	Probability that location *l* is selected by investor *i*, based on maximum profits	Location choice between countries: foreign firms prefer locations in Central Eastern Europe with access to an abundance of low cost labor, rather than a highly skilled population. Furthermore, foreign firms tend to agglomerate together and value access to growing markets, as well as connectivity to others, indicating the importance of infrastructure
Resmini (2000)	European FDI in the manufacturing sector of ten Central Eastern European countries 1991–1995	Three-way fixed effect panel data model	FDI flow for each sector, country, and year	Vertical agglomeration: manufacturing MNEs with large-scale economies that mass produce seek out larger markets where they are close to inputs and customers

Globerman & Shapiro (2003)	US FDI flows to 88 countries during 1994–1997	Regression analysis	Positive flows of FDI to a country and the logarithim of the value of US FDI received in a particular year	The role that institutional variables play in attracting FDI: a country's "governance infrastructure" (free and transparent markets, effective government, and, particularly, a well-functioning legal system that is based on English common law) attracts FDI from the US
Bevan, Estrin & Meyer (2004)	FDI flows to Bulgaria, Czech Republic, Estonia, Hungary, Latvia, Lithuania, Poland, Romania, Russia, Slovak Republic, Slovenia, and Ukraine 1994–1998	Regression analysis	Bilateral FDI flow from source country *i* to host country *j*	What type of institutions matter: FDI flows more freely to transition countries with private ownership, a developed banking sector, liberalized foreign exchange, and trade
Tahir & Larimo (2004)	Finnish manufacturing firms in ten South and Southeast Asian countries 1980–2000	Binomial logit model	Three dependent dummies: (1) market-seeking FDI, (2) efficiency-seeking FDI, and (3) risk-reduction-seeking FDI	Cultural distance: low cultural distance between the Finnish firm and the host country increases the likelihood of FDI
Majocchi & Strange (2007)	272 Italian FDIs in seven Eastern European countries (Poland, Hungary, Slovenia, the Czech Republic, the Slovak Republic, Romania, and Bulgaria)	Conditional logit model	Location of Italian affiliate *i* in country *j*	Location choice in transition economies: minimal state intervention, with liberal trade and market policies attracts FDI
Coeurderoy & Murray (2008)	241 British and 134 German "new technology-based" MNEs investing in 71 countries 1987–1995	Quantitative; binomial logit model	Three dependent variables: foreign entry, entry ranking, entry timing	Regulatory regimes, cultural distance: countries with strong IPR regimes attract more FDI; MNEs locate in countries that are in close geographic proximity, and with similar legal systems

Source: Authors' construction.

countries characterized by, for instance, high growth and low labor costs and exchange risks (Ohlin, 1933; MacDougall, 1960; Kemp, 1964). Broadly speaking, host country location-specific factors can be classified into two distinct types: (1) Ricardian type endowments of natural resources, labor, and consumer markets, and (2) macro environmental variables pertaining to political, institutional, economic, legal, and infrastructural factors. This traditional view of FDI location has identified a range of host country location factors that are theorized to influence an investment's profitability (Shaver, 1998), including (but not limited to) raw material and labor supply (Buckley and Casson, 1985; Dunning, 1988), economic growth and market size (Aharoni, 1966; Kobrin, 1976), agglomeration effects (Krugman, 1991), political and legal environment (Anderson & Gatignon, 1986; Agarwal, 1994), and host government policies (Davidson & McFetridge, 1985).

Market imperfections. A second theoretical approach focuses on how imperfections in the markets for goods or factors of production give rise to FDI (Kindleberger, 1969; Hymer, 1976). Linking FDI explicitly to the MNC, this theoretical stream emphasizes the importance of ownership advantages for monopolistic advantage. From this perspective, imperfect competition encourages horizontal FDI via for instance product differentiation (Caves, 1971). Other competition factors deemed important for location choice included increase in domestic competition, fear of loss of competitiveness, and a need to follow rivals into foreign markets (Aharoni, 1966). For instance, Knickerbocker (1973) asserted that FDI flows may be related to imitative behavior of strategic rivals in the global marketplace; firms may follow their competitors into specific market locations in order to avoid them gaining a strategic advantage.

Moreover, given higher information cost and the liability of foreignness (Hymer, 1976), together with general aversion to risk, foreign firms are likely to locate in stable, well-known, and accessible regions, characterized by large markets, developed infrastructure, and agglomeration economies (Vernon, 1974; Blackbourn, 1982). Vernon (1966) furthermore found the choice of FDI location to be a function of the product life cycle related to costs; in the growth stage, companies invest in developed markets in order to absorb local production, while in maturity and decline stages where products are less innovative production is shifted to developing markets to reduce costs.

Eclectic paradigm. Applying internalization theory (Coase, 1937) to the MNC, Buckley and Casson (1976) noted the imperfection of markets for intermediate goods, leading to information, enforcement, and bargaining transaction costs; in their model, the decision to internalize depended on country-, industry-, and firm-specific factors. Synthesizing the trade theoretical benefits of FDI with internalization theory's ideas regarding entry mode, Dunning (1976, 1979) developed the eclectic "Ownership Location Internalization" (OLI) paradigm which identifies the determinants of FDI and can be related to country-, industry-, and firm-level structural characteristics. Ownership advantages refer to both tangible and intangible resources, including machines, access to capital, skilled labor, production processes, patents, technology, knowledge, managerial skills, brand, corporate reputation, etc. Location advantages are typically associated with lower cost of production and transportation, favorable competitive conditions, access to protected markets. and favorable institutional and political environments. Compared to exporting or licensing, internalization of lower transaction costs minimizes risk of technological spillover and assures control and maintenance of firm reputation and product brands.

Within the OLI tradition, a separate theoretical strand asserts that MNC's FDI motives guide their location decisions (Dunning, 1988, 1998). According to Dunning (1998), MNCs are motivated by one or more of the four types of FDI motives: (1) resource-seeking, (2) market-seeking, (3) efficiency-seeking, and (4) strategic asset-seeking which may determine the nature and location of their investments. Accordingly, Dunning (1996) theorized that initial investments were typically resource-seeking and market-seeking investments, while efficiency-seeking and strategic asset-seeking investments were typically sequential investments.

Building on these insights, a number of scholars have argued that specific FDI motives lead firms to choose particular locations, such as resource- and market-seeking in developing markets and efficiency- and strategic asset-seeking in developed markets (e.g., Dunning & Narula, 1996; Makino, Lau & Yeh, 2002). Within strategic management, the resource-based view of the firm (Barney, 1991) helps explicate how ownership advantages may act as principal determinants of FDI location choice for value adding activities of the MNC. Specifically, to the extent the natural or immobile resources needed in conjunction with the firms' own competitive advantages favor a presence in a foreign location, the firm will likely choose to augment or exploit its ownership-specific advantages by engaging in FDI.

New trade theories. Explicitly focusing on knowledge capital as an ownership advantage and distinguishing between location advantages for horizontally versus vertically integrated firms, new trade theory has developed the "proximity-concentration hypothesis" to explain the existence of vertically integrated firms with geographically fragmented production and horizontally integrated firms with simultaneous activities in multiple similar countries (Helpman, 1984; Markusen, 1984). Empirical tests confirm the importance of country characteristics such as factor endowments, population, per capita income, land-labor ratio (i.e., density), average level of education (Eaton & Tamura, 1994) along with freight factors, average foreign import tariff, exchange rate appreciation, effective import tax rate, openness to trade, and FDI (Brainard, 1993). In a later "knowledge-capital model", scholars (e.g., Markusen et al., 1996; Markusen, 1997) combined horizontal and vertical motivations for FDI (i.e., the desire to place production close to customers and avoid trade costs versus the desire to carry out unskilled, labor-intensive production activities in locations with relative abundant and cheap unskilled labor). Later refinements of this model point to the importance of industry characteristics as co-determinants of FDI location.

Agglomeration. A conventional view suggests that factors such as production costs and infrastructure adequacy are among the main FDI determinants. Together with factors such as clustering of foreign firms from the same source country and/or industry, these are often categorized as agglomeration or cluster effects. Agglomeration, broadly speaking, consists of the network externalities pertaining to regional concentration of business operations (Krugman, 1991). According to Marshall (1920), knowledge is predominantly industry-specific, and knowledge spillovers may, therefore, arise between firms within the same industry and can be supported only by regional concentrations of a particular industry. These intra-industry spillovers are known as localization or "specialization" externalities. The positive externalities stemming from co-location, described by Arrow (1962) and Romer (1986), are complemented and intensified by several other interrelated elements, including the dense linkages among co-located buyers, suppliers, and customers (Porter, 1998). Hence, firms in a given industry tend to co-locate geographically so that they can exploit agglomeration effects in labor pooling, knowledge spillovers, and proximity to specialized suppliers.

The literature distinguishes between two types of (Marshallian) agglomeration: horizontal and vertical. Horizontal agglomeration refers to the clustering of FDI source country firms from the same industry in the same micro-location. According to the Economic Geography and urban economics literatures, such geographic co-location is thought to bring benefits due to knowledge spillovers, access to intermediate inputs, and specialized labor. More specifically, the positive network externalities associated with horizontal agglomeration pertains to: (1) scale economics in demand for specific input markets; (2) sharing of market and technology information; (3) pressure to innovate due to strong local rivals; and (4) improved access to infrastructure and, in particular, public goods (Krugman, 1991; Porter, 1998). Naturally, such close quarters also may bring negative externalities, and the literature points in particular to the risk of proprietary knowledge spillover when institutions are weak as well as intensified product and factor market competition resulting from local clustering (Du, Lu & Tao, 2008). Moreover, being located adjacent to similar firms within an industry may even lead to groupthink and innovative inertia (Chang & Park, 2005). The empirical evidence provides strong evidence of horizontal agglomeration being a significant pull factor toward specific locations for FDI, suggesting that firms perceive that the positive externalities outweigh the negative ones (Head, Ries & Swenson, 1995; Blanc-Brude et al., 2014). The vast majority of this empirical literature, however, is at the national level, examining the location choice in a blunt way.

Vertical agglomeration, on the other hand, refers to the clustering of domestic upstream and downstream firms in the same location. Co-locating with other upstream firms increases accessibility to local components suppliers, whereas the concentration of downstream firms provides access to local markets. Generally, producers of goods benefit from locating in close proximity to abundant suppliers and large markets for intermediate inputs because it will: (1) increase the availability and variety of inputs; (2) lower the average cost of purchasing; (3) mitigate any hold-up contracting problems between upstream and downstream firms; and (4) possibly generate learning and knowledge spillover (Krugman & Venables, 1996; Venables, 1996; Duranton & Puga, 2004).

Global cities. In contrast to Marshall (1920), Jacobs (1969) suggested that since ideas developed by one industry can be applied in other industries, knowledge may spill over between complementary rather than similar industries. The exchange of complementary knowledge across diverse firms and economic agents facilitates search and experimentation in innovation. Therefore, a diversified local production structure leads to increasing returns and gives rise to urbanization or "diversification" externalities.

Drawing on the agglomeration effects described by Jacobs (1969), global city theory (Beaverstock, Smith & Taylor, 1999; Sassen, 2001) posits that MNCs are attracted to global cities in that they are characterized by: (1) high degrees of interconnectedness to local and global markets; (2) cosmopolitan environment; and (3) high levels of advanced producer services (Goerzen, Asmussen & Nielsen, 2013) – all characteristics that help these MNCs overcome the liability of foreignness that they face as a consequence of internationalization (Zaheer, 1995). Thus, global cities "give rise to somewhat different sources of advantages and affect directly the existence and strength of the LOF" (Nachum, 2003, p. 1202). In contrast to the highly industry-specific clusters, global cities are relatively industry-agnostic since all firms supposedly benefit from these characteristics, but perhaps to different extents. At the same time, global cities also give rise to agglomeration diseconomies, as rent on property and wages is typically inflated by the competition for proximity to the global city center.

Institutions. Building on institutional economics (North, 1990) and sociology (Scott, 1995, 2001), the institutional perspective has been advanced as a powerful framework for analyzing business strategy in general (e.g., Oliver, 1997; Peng, 2003) and MNC international behavior in particular (e.g., Mudambi & Navarra, 2002; Ramamurti, 2003). There is general consensus that institutions (whether regional, national, or sub-national) shape the nature of business by providing the opportunities and constraints within which economic activity takes place. Hence, the nature and quality of host country institutions affects the location of FDI in a variety of ways.

The economics literature focuses predominantly on the risks and additional costs of doing business in environments characterized by poor institutions, often operationalized as the extent of red tape, bureaucracy, corruption, political instability, or the overall quality of the legal system (e.g., Wheeler & Mody, 1992; Wei, 1997; Daude & Stein, 2007). In contrast, the management literature has utilized institutional theory more broadly to: (1) identify country institutional profiles typically conceptualized as national environments in terms of regulatory, cognitive, and normative pillars (e.g., Kostova & Roth, 2002; Eden & Miller, 2004); (2) conceptualize processes of large-scale transformation of national systems through the notions of institutional transition, upheaval, and imperfection (e.g., Hoskisson et al., 2000; Wright et al., 2005); (3) explain comparative national business systems based on institutional embeddedness (e.g., Casper & Whitley, 2004; Hill, 1995); (4) study similarities in practices across organizations resulting from isomorphic pressures (e.g., Child & Tsai, 2005); (5) analyze constraints on the institutionalization of MNC practices across borders; and (6) investigate legitimacy and liability of foreignness issues related to the relationship between MNCs and their host environments (e.g., Kostova & Zaheer, 1999).

Whilst the great majority of studies utilizing institutional perspectives conceptualize institutions at national level, institutional variance of different locations within a country may also affect the attractiveness to foreign investors. Such local institutions may range from fiscal incentives such as tax holidays and subsidies to local bureaucratic practices (Oman, 2000). For instance, differences in corporate tax rates of individual states within the US has been found to affect FDI inflows (Hines, 1996) as has the institutional makeup of special economic zones in various Asian locations (Head & Ries, 1996; Meyer & Nguyen, 2005).

Micro-location factors as determinants of FDI location: empirical evidence

Sub-national institutions. The decision to locate foreign investment in a particular place may be influenced by institutional conditions that vary both between and within host countries (Wright et al., 2005) as investors adapt their strategies to prevailing formal and informal institutions at a particular location (Meyer and Nguyen, 2005). Yet, relatively little is known about the influence of intra-country institutions on FDI micro-locational choice (Zhou, Delios & Yang, 2002; Meyer & Nguyen, 2005; Kandogan, 2012). Given the abundant choice, businesses locate where the local environment is most conducive (or least restrictive) to their particular operations, putting a premium on research into micro-locational factors driving FDI location choice (Table 12.2).

The issue of sub-national institutional influences on location attractiveness is increasingly important for several reasons. First, clearly many countries exhibit great intra-country variation in institutions governing how foreign firms do business. Increasingly, many regulatory functions, such as import/export provisions, governance of land lease, and employment, have been delegated to local authorizes. Evidence from China and other countries clearly points to the importance of studying sub-national institutions, such as specific economic zones in Chinese cities (Head & Ries, 1996; Wei et al., 1999; Zhou, Delios & Yang, 2002), special economic zones in Poland (Cieślik & Ryan, 2004), corporate tax rates in US states (Coughlin, Terza & Arromdee, 1991; Hines, 1996), or market-supporting institutions in Vietnamese provinces (Meyer & Nguyen, 2005). Second, many centrally issued laws and regulations are purposely general in nature with interpretation and implementation left to local authorities. This may influence the formal and informal institutions of a particular sub-national locality and thus impact liability of foreignness for incoming FDI (Meyer & Nguyen, 2005).

To this end, Tenev et al. (2003) found significant variance between nine cities in Vietnam on the time senior management spent dealing with local laws and regulations. Ma and Delios (2007) found that the more business-oriented Shanghai attracted higher FDI inflows from Japanese MNCs compared to the politics-oriented Beijing, which was associated with higher levels of policy uncertainty and political hazards that could potentially affect firm operations. By the same token, in a recent study of inward FDI in China, Huang and Wei (2011) illustrated

Table 12.2 Micro-level determinants: sub-national institutions and global cities

Exemplary studies	*Context of study*	*Method*	*Dependent variable*	*Key findings*
Belderbos & Carree (2002)	229 Japanese electronics manufacturing plants in 29 Chinese regions 1990–1995	Conditional logit model	Choice of region	Horizontal agglomeration and keiretsu effects: smaller firms in the keiretsu tend to follow the leader's location choice, and are more responsive to Japanese investor agglomeration effects
Meyer & Nguyen (2005)	FDI in Vietnam's 61 provinces 2001–2002	Qualitative and quantitative: survey with 171 respondents; negative binomial regression model	The cumulative number of FDI projects registered up to the year 2000, and the number of new FDI projects in 2000	Sub-national institutions affect location choice and entry mode: joint ventures are the preferred entry mode; foreign firms will locate in special economic zones where access to resources is easier
Du, Lu & Tao (2012)	150,602 MNEs from Hong Kong, Japan, the EU, the USA, Taiwan, and Korea in China 1993–2001	Discrete choice model	Regional location choice	Cultural distance: MNEs from countries with greater cultural distance locate in cities where formal institutions are stronger
Zhou, Delios, & Yang (2002)	Japanese FDI flows into 190 Chinese cities 1980–1998	Tobit model	Extent of Japanese FDI in city *i* in year *t* (measured by the total number of Japanese subsidiaries located in the focal city)	Impact of political incentives on FDI: FDI investment incentives in the form of Special Economic Zones and Opening Coastal Cities in China had a time dependent influence on the location of Japanese investors
Coughlin, Terza & Arromdee (1991)	736 manufacturing companies in 50 US states 1981–1983	Conditional logit model	Location choice in USA	Taxes as deterrent of FDI: taxes are found to have a negative, but statistically insignificant effect on FDI. State spending targeted to attract FDI has a significant, positive effect

Goerzen, Asmussen & Nielsen (2013)	Data on location of 318 Japanese MNCs' subsidiaries 2001	Multilevel, multinomial logistic regression model	City class of subsidiary location	Global cities help overcome the liability of foreignness: so-called "global cities" attract FDI. Their international connectedness, advanced producer services and cosmopolitan environment help overcome the costs of doing business in a foreign location
Bathelt & Li (2013)	299 Canadian FDIs in China 2006–2010	Nested framework	Origin and destination of FDI-based cluster network from Canada to China	Global cluster networks and global city networks; Canadian FDIs that originate from clusters will seek out locations where Chinese clusters are located and try to build linkages within these. Cluster networks generate horizontal and vertical linkages between cities in different countries, which aids the development of global city networks
Wu & Radbone (2005)	Case study on Shanghai	Regression model	Totals of realized FDI, service FDI and manufacturing FDI from all sources in Shanghai's urban districts	Reducing uncertainty: MNCs investing in developing countries will choose cities as their location. They do this to take advantage of communication and transport infrastructure, large markets and labor pool, and other place-specific local advantages

Source: Authors' construction.

how the concentration of FDI moves from Guangdong toward the Pan-Yangtze River Delta and Bohai Rim Region, especially metropolitan areas such as Shanghai, Beijing, and Tianjin. Their results suggest that a combination of local institution, transportation, and agglomeration factors determines FDI micro location in China.

Agglomeration in global cities. Sub-national entities or agencies are increasingly (pro)active in seeking to attract FDI (Charlton, 2003; Markusen & Nesse, 2007). Indeed, given increased administrative decentralization, global competitiveness, and deregulation, sub-national localities compete for FDI by exploiting their location and structural attributes that interact with global capital (Wei et al., 2008). This inter-urban competition to attract FDI has led local policy makers and global agencies (e.g., AT Kearney) to pay attention to specific factors that may render a city or micro-locality specifically attractive to a segment of International Business activities. Whereas traditionally regions and states competed for FDI by offering a variety of economic incentives (Head, Ries & Swenson, 1999; Markusen & Nesse, 2007), increasingly the focus has shifted to cities competing on a range of global-city characteristics (Beaverstock, Smith & Taylor, 1999; Sassen, 2012; Goerzen, Asmussen & Nielsen, 2013).

Early studies primarily focused on local cost drivers as determinants of choice between cities. For instance, Black and Hoyt (1989) studied the bidding of cities for the location of plant and found that firms locate in the city with the best combination of wages, costs, and tax holidays. Other studies focused on the demand side and found local market size (i.e., inhabitants) to determine a city's attractiveness for FDI (e.g., Head & Ries, 1996; Takatsuka, 2011; Chen & Yeh, 2012). More recent evidence suggests that advanced infrastructure and the specialized managerial expertise are agglomerating in and around global cities and that these urban phenomena are becoming increasingly attractive to foreign investors (Sassen, 2001, 2012).

Investigating MNCs' location decisions, Goerzen, Asmussen and Nielsen (2013) demonstrated an overall high attractiveness of global cities for internationalizing firms in general, as well as showing the industry- and firm-specific contingencies for this attraction related to the ability to reduce liability of foreignness. This study is among the first to employ a multilevel approach that allows both firm (HQ) and subsidiary level influence on the location choice while distinguishing between various micro locations. Those authors found that the functional division between global metropolitan centers and their immediate hinterlands within a global city can be conceived as the spatial expression of FDI locality choice. Specifically, supply-driven investments (i.e., R&D and production) were more likely to be located outside global city centers while demand-driven (i.e., sales, marketing, and distribution) activities typically were located within the centers of global cities.

In a study of FDI inflow into China, Zhao and Zhang (2007) found evidence of micro-level factors attracting FDI to specific global cities and global city-regions. Their study showed how infrastructure such as ports and transportation systems, in addition to access to low cost labor, global connectedness, and government incentives, attract foreign investments to particular cities. Similar to Goerzen, Asmussen and Nielsen (2013), they also found evidence that FDI is not confined within the city proper, but rather diverged to the central business district or metropolitan areas of a particular global city depending on the nature of the investment (i.e., service versus manufacturing). Similar results have been reported by Wu and Radbone (2005) who found that, for Shanghai, service FDI tends to aggregate in the areas that already have a high density of service activities, while manufacturing FDI prefers to locate in the central government-designated areas where incentives and preferential treatment are available. This is consistent with statistical findings in Istanbul that 90 percent of service FDI is located in the business ring of the city (Berköz, 2000; Özdemir, 2002).

Li (2014) illustrated that cluster-based firms direct their FDIs to locations from which they can draw crucial knowledge inputs and agglomeration economies, whereas non-cluster-based FDIs seem to look for natural-resource locations, low-cost labor, and other advantages in their industry context. These results seem to be robust across different industries and point to MNCs as multilateral corporate networks that are embedded in – and linked with – various cluster networks. In turn, FDI linkages of cluster firms generate global city-region networks, within which city-regions are connected through horizontal and vertical linkages. In a similar vein, Bathelt and Li (2014) studied Canadian FDI flows to China over a four-year period and confirmed that FDI flows are increasingly taking place between global cities.

Firm-specific factors as determinants of FDI location: empirical evidence

Grounded primarily in macro-economic theories, the vast majority of empirical research on FDI location choice utilizes country- or industry-level data while ignoring firm characteristics. Yet, building on the idea of investing-firm heterogeneity, empirical studies have found strong evidence for relationships between various firm characteristics and FDI behavior, including location choice (see Table 12.3 below). For instance, Shi (2001) found a relationship between firm size and FDI location; smaller firms' location decisions were tied to access to cheap labor, whereas larger firms sought markets to exploit their technological advantages. Other studies have shown relationships between branch interdependence (or power) and location. For instance, Ó Huallacháin and Reid (1997) illustrated how wholly owned subsidiaries are more sensitive to site attributes than joint ventures. Hong (2007) included several firm characteristics in his model of FDI into China's logistics industry and found: (1) smaller firms to be more sensitive to labor costs, (2) branch companies to be less responsive to market and labor demands, and (3) wholly owned subsidiaries to be attracted to cities with cheap labor, whereas joint ventures put more emphasis on local market demand.

Nachum and Wymbs (2005) found significant association between product differentiation and the preferences of firms for proximity to other firms in their industry. These findings imply that the value of agglomeration varies for firms pursuing different product differentiation strategies. While Shaver and Flyer (2000) employ technological capability as the source of firm heterogeneity, their reasoning is similar to that of Nachum and Wymbs (2005); the more a firm differs from its competitors, the greater the likelihood that it will locate remotely. While Nachum and Wymbs (2005) argue that higher levels of product differentiation will increase the likelihood of a firm locating away from their competitors, Shaver and Flyer (2000) found empirical support for their claim that firms with superior technology, human capital, suppliers, etc. will have little incentive to agglomerate in an analysis of the location choice of greenfield investments in US manufacturing industries. Both studies illustrate how firm heterogeneity may affect the extent to which the negative aspects of agglomeration outweigh the potential benefits (such as the risk of spillovers and loss of proprietary information, or the high costs associated with locating in the same area).

Several other studies demonstrate that the attractiveness of a specific location varies among firms due to the unique characteristics of each organization. Not all locational attributes may be equally attractive for each individual firm. For example, Chung and Alcácer (2002) show that manufacturing firms with low technological capability will locate in areas within the USA where there is a high concentration of R&D, whereas firms with above average technological capabilities will locate away from these areas. Empirical evidence also suggests that MNCs prioritize different location attributes depending on their stage in the internationalization process. In the early stages, MNCs are often drawn to locations by virtue of market size, labor costs,

Table 12.3 Firm-level determinants

Exemplary studies	*Context of study*	*Method*	*Dependent variable*	*Key findings*
Hong (2007)	FDI in China's logistics industry 2001	Conditional logit model	Location choice of city *j* by firm *i* among N cities, only if city *j* offers the highest profit	Firm heterogeneity: different firm attributes such as size, ownership structure, home country, etc. affect the location choice. For example, small firms are more sensitive to labor costs than larger ones. Firms from countries in close geographic proximity to China tend to locate where they can access larger markets, whereas firms from farther afield choose locations based on labor costs and infrastructure
Nachum & Wymbs (2005)	Location choice of 573 MNCs via M&As in London and New York 1981–2001	Binary logistic regression	Geographic distance from all other firms in its own industry for firm *i*	Firm heterogeneity and agglomeration: the more differentiated the product offering, the less likely it is that it will seek out a location in close proximity to other firms from the same industry. This implies that location advantages vary across MNEs
Chung & Alcácer (2002)	Manufacturing FDI in 45 US states 1987–1993	Random parameter logistic regression model	State location for each inward FDI transaction	FDI as knowledge seeking exercise: firms with low technical capability locate in US states where there is a high concentration of PhD scientists and engineers and R&D. Location choice is determined by the availability of knowledge and skills
Chen & Yeh (2012)	731 Taiwanese firms' investments in China 1997–2007	Rank-ordered logit model	The rank of FDI cases in China for each Taiwanese firm based on date of approval	The attractiveness of location attributes is dependent on the stage of the internationalization process: in the early stages, firms attempt to exploit their existing competency and favor locations with advantages in infrastructure, labor cost, market size, and openness. In the later stages, as firms have familiarized themselves with the local business environment, locations with better production efficiency, labor quality, and R&D capability are more attractive. That is, locations that augment firm-specific advantages become more attractive

Source: Authors' construction.

quality of infrastructure, and the ease of doing business (i.e., low cultural distance or a relatively open political climate). However, as the frequency of FDI increases, the MNC is more drawn to specific location attributes that can contribute to and enhance firm-specific advantages, such as skilled labor or production efficiency (Coeurderoy & Murray, 2008; Chen & Yeh, 2012).

Research agenda: interaction of macro-locational, micro-locational, and firm-specific factors

Our review of the empirical literature has revealed a rather simplistic approach to determinant of FDI location. Most studies (76 percent) utilize a single theoretical approach only and the large majority (64 percent) employ either agglomeration or institutional theory, or both (14 percent). It is the rare study that integrates determinants at multiple levels; only about 10 percent of the studies reviewed allowed for interaction between firm characteristics and macro-level factors, and none integrated more than two perspectives in a single study. This is highly problematic since the decision to locate a specific investment in a given location is likely to be the result of the interplay between how well a particular firm's idiosyncratic resources can provide an advantage in a specific micro location, given the opportunities and/or constraints of agglomeration and institutional factors in that location (Zaheer & Nachum, 2011). Figure 12.1 shows the theoretical approaches used by the studies in our sample.

Goerzen, Asmussen and Nielsen (2013) provided evidence that the interplay between firm (both HQ and subsidiary-level) resources and the surrounding micro- and macro-competitive and institutional environment interact to determine where, how, and why (and perhaps when) a particular type of firm locates a particular value chain activity in a particular micro location (either city center, metropolitan area, or periphery of global cities). In a similar vein, Nachum and Wymbs (2005) investigated the interaction between firm heterogeneity and agglomeration. Their finding that the more differentiated the product offering, the less likely it is that a firm will seek out a location in close proximity to other firms from the same industry suggests that location advantages vary across MNCs. Other studies have provided insights into how local institutions may render certain firm characteristics, such as technical capabilities or financial resources, particularly valuable and thus drive location choice (e.g., Hong, 2007; Chen & Yeh, 2012).

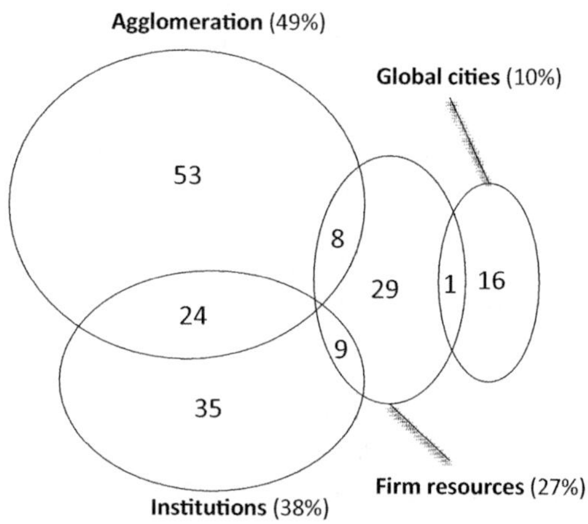

Figure 12.1 Percentage of studies applying particular theoretical approaches

Source: Authors' construction.

Notwithstanding these few studies, future research must strive to accurately identify the important drivers at each level and determine how combinations of factors interact to explain location choice of FDI. This suggests that careful attention must be paid to how firm specific characteristics may change according to the specific attributes of a particular micro location. To empirically study such interactions across analytical levels, future studies should employ multi-level research designs in order to adequately capture the sources of variation at each level and across levels (Klein, Dansereau & Hall, 1994; Andersson, Cuervo-Cazurra & Nielsen, 2014).

Moreover, most empirical studies assume each FDI location decision to be independent and thus neglect the fact that MNCs may adjust their criteria for choosing a particular FDI location based on their accrued FDI experience (Chen & Yeh, 2012). The experience of MNCs in international operations might affect their subsequent investment behavior (Lin & Yeh, 2004); especially for within-country FDI cases (Kogut & Chang, 1996). Hence, MNCs can show diverse location preferences during the FDI process, and the location advantages emphasized in early FDI cases might differ from those in later ones (Dunning, 1998). For instance, Coeurderoy and Murray (2008) found that as the number of FDIs an MNC undertakes increases, the probability that it will seek out culturally similar markets decreases. Instead, firms appear to base the FDI location decision on market possibilities in later stages of internationalization. At the micro location level, Chen and Yeh (2012) illustrate how the attractiveness of location attributes is dependent on the stage of the internationalization process. In the early stages, firms attempt to exploit their existing competency and favor locations with advantages in infrastructure, labor cost, market size, and openness (i.e., locations with favorable macro environments). In the later stages, as firms have familiarized themselves with the local business environment, locations with better production efficiency, labor quality, and R&D capability are more attractive (i.e., locations that augment firm-specific advantages). By the same token, Mudambi (1998) investigated the role of duration in a particular location for further investment in that location. His results that MNC investment is significantly duration dependent, i.e., firms with a longer tenure of operations are likely to invest more in that location in any period due to declining liability of foreignness, provide strong evidence for path dependency.

Among the few studies that examine both spatial and temporal variations in FDI location decisions, Flores and Aguilera (2007) found that MNCs also adjust the relative importance of location antecedents in their FDI trajectory. Analyzing FDI location decisions of the top 100 US MNCs in 1980 and 2000, they show a shift in their preferred location antecedents. Over time, US MNCs place greater emphasis on the population and infrastructure factors in their subsequent investments as opposed to gross domestic productivity. In a similar vein, Sun, Tong and Yu (2002) examine temporal variations in inward FDI into China by comparing the periods of 1986–1991 and 1992–1998. Their findings demonstrate how market factor becomes more important for MNCs when deciding where to locate, but labor wages significantly reverse that factor's effect on the location choice of MNCs, shifting from positive to negative. Seemingly, MNCs adjust their FDI strategy toward China from an export-oriented strategy to a local market-oriented one. While initially paying higher wages to their employees for high-quality products to export, over time MNCs take cost into consideration when the products target local consumers. Hence, the effects of, and changes in, specific location antecedents over time are thus of great importance for explaining FDI location choice. The few existing studies, albeit making great strides, fall somewhat short of capturing the complexity of interplay between spatial and temporal aspects of FDI location choice. For example, both Sun, Tong and Yu (2002) and Flores and Aguilera (2007) compare only two time periods. This puts a premium on studies that develop more nuanced models which simultaneously take into account evolutionary patterns of spatial and temporal variations in FDI location decisions.

Table 12.4 Main findings: macro, micro and firm level

Explanatory framework	*Market focus*	*Country focus*	*Key results*
Agglomeration – industrial clusters	Emerging and developed markets	Diverse	• Agglomeration effects dominate; this is confirmed by a number of studies; agglomeration draws more investment than short-term incentives such as tax concessions • MNEs, especially Japanese and Korean ones, express a preference for locating in the same area as other FDI source firms from their country or conglomerate • MNEs locate in areas where other MNEs are in order to gain access to knowledge spillovers, suppliers, and reduced information costs; these benefits are sufficiently strong to offset the impact that spatial clustering may have on firm profits • Agglomeration economies are less pronounced in the emerging European economies, while still strong in the more mature European economies
National-level institutional	Emerging markets	China, USA, Poland, Vietnam	• Taxation levels are less significant a deterrent of FDI than expected • Strong regulatory regimes and open market economies with minimal state intervention attract FDI • MNCs (especially from developed markets) avoid uncertainty when investing in emerging markets and will locate in cities where institutions are typically stronger • Distance matters; the greater the distance between the FDI source country and the host country, the less the probability of that country being chosen; this impact lessens as the firm conducts more FDI, although this seems to be receding over time • Evidence on fiscal incentives, e.g., Special Economic Zones is mixed; their impact appears to lessen over time, and other factors such as agglomeration are more significant, which suggests the ineffectuality of regional policies
Agglomeration – global cities	Emerging markets	Primarily Asian cities	• MNEs seek to offset the liability of foreignness; locating in global cities helps them overcome this, as they offer substantial benefits such as access to markets, skilled labor pools, good infrastructure, etc.
Firm-level characteristics	Emerging and developed markets	China, USA, Japan, Taiwan	• Individual firm characteristics impact upon the FDI location choice • FDI is not always conducted in order to exploit resources, sometimes it is to gain them (e.g., knowledge-seeking); therefore, rather than deterring FDI, high wages can actually attract it • The importance of cultural distance is a function of the number of FDIs a firm conducts – the more the firm internationalizes, the less important cultural (and geographic) distance becomes, therefore first-time FDIs tend to be in locations close to the home market, while later FDI is more based on market potential

Source: Authors' construction.

Finally, extant research is relatively silent about how managers make specific choices regarding FDI location. Recent studies have modeled decision-making as a sequence of choices based on a hierarchical choice process consisting of an initial choice of host country followed by a choice of regions or micro-locations within that country (e.g., Mucchielli & Puech, 2004; Mataloni, 2010, 2011). This sequential selection process based, presumably, on careful attention to first interaction between macro-location factors (e.g., national institutions and agglomerations) and firm characteristics followed by a new set of interactions between micro-location factors (e.g., local institutions and agglomerations) and firm characteristics, appears to match closely qualitative evidence (e.g., Haigh, 1990; Bingham & Eisenhardt, 2005). Very recently, Rasciute, Pentecost and Ferrett (2014) integrated macro-, micro-locational and firm characteristics into a framework for FDI location choice. Utilizing a decision-tree approach in which the choice between FDI and export has already been settled in favor of FDI, the question of location was modeled as a function of firm, industry, and country effects.

Yet, none of these studies has considered the role of managerial cognition or biases as a source of variation in the choice of FDI location. Research has shown that top management team characteristics, such as international experience, have a profound influence on the choice of foreign entry mode by influencing the risk propensity (Nielsen & Nielsen, 2011). Future research must integrate macro-, micro-, and firm-level antecedents of FDI location choice with careful consideration of temporal issues while keeping in mind the cognitive and behavioral aspects of strategy (Powell, Lovallo & Fox, 2011) embodied in the managers who make such decisions. Perhaps the best way to accomplish such an ambitious task is to apply mixed methods. Combining the strengths of both qualitative and quantitative methods, future researchers may seek to design studies that allow for deeper insights into both behaviors of individuals and teams, firm-level strategy processes, and large-scale temporal variations in antecedents of FDI location choice (as summarized below in Table 12.4).

Conclusion

Our examination of quantitative studies pertaining to FDI location choice spans more than six decades and integrates insights from hitherto disparate literatures, such as Economic Geography, urban and developmental economics, International Business, and management. Our findings suggest that our current understanding of the drivers of FDI location choice has developed as somewhat isolated in the various literatures. In the following we point to some of the areas that are most ripe for cross-fertilization in the hope of contributing to the building of a common stock of knowledge across disciplines of the drivers of location choice for FDI.

For IB scholars, our findings point to the increasing need to pay attention to within-country spatial (and temporal) variation among potential sites for FDI location. As suggested by recent research into global cities (e.g., Goerzen, Asmussen & Nielsen, 2013), the drivers that may propel or repel a particular type of firm from locating foreign activities in a particular micro-location must be understood in relation to the cost/benefits offered by that specific location. This warrants much closer scrutiny of sources of heterogeneity within sub-national locations, such as regions, clusters, or cities and may necessitate multilevel analyses to investigate the interplay between HQ, subsidiary, and locational factors in determining location choice.

By the same token, urban economics and geography scholars are encouraged to integrate insights about MNC strategy and firm-specific characteristics into their models of FDI distribution. Whilst, arguably, agglomeration factors matter a great deal for locational attractiveness, the ultimate decision to locate in a particular place is driven by managerial deliberations surrounding perceptions of cost/benefits of that location in relation to alternative locations. MNCs modularize their activities in order to gain returns on global flexibility and arbitrage (Ghemawat, 2007). Hence, MNCs often spread their activities geographically for a number of reasons and thus may seek labor economizing locations for certain activities (i.e., labor intensive manufacturing), but knowledge intensive locations (i.e., R&D) or attractive markets (e.g., sales and distribution) for others. Indeed, the competitiveness of MNCs rests on their ability to decompose their value-chains and locate specific elements in advantageous places as a function of firm- and location-specific characteristics (Dunning, 1998). Moreover, temporal aspects play an important role in location choice as firm-level experience, and the sequence of investments influences subsequent commitment to a particular location. MNCs prefer to increase their commitment to the host destination and switch FDI motives from asset exploitation to asset-exploration as a function of duration (Mudambi, 1998). In this regard, MNCs not only exploit their existing firm-specific advantages for short-term survival but also engage in developing sustainable competitiveness for long-term growth (Prange & Verdier, 2011).

Our chapter also offers important insights for both managers and policy makers. MNC managers involved in FDI location decisions may be informed by our review about some of the key micro-locational factors that serve to distinguish particular localities. For instance, our review reveals the importance of industry agglomeration effects at regional and city levels to attract, in particular, manufacturing FDI. By the same token, local policy makers may benefit from gaining a better understanding of the key determinants of FDI location from a managerial perspective; specifically, how firm-level characteristics such as strategic motives and resource/capability endowment may overpower seemingly "rational" agglomeration factors in the choice of micro-location. MNCs often manage their foreign subsidiaries as a portfolio of interconnected investments, and this interdependency may lead to specific attributes of a micro-location, such as a city center's access to services, being more attractive to certain types of investments (e.g., down-stream activities). Such insights may help local policy makers focus their initiatives for attracting particular types of firms or activities to their location.

Note

1 Note that while sub-national states and provinces potentially are subject to political, institutional, and natural resource influences, vast variability in location-specific attributes exist at lower geographical levels, such as municipalities or cities (Blanc-Brude et al., 2014).

References

Agarwal, S. (1994) 'Socio-cultural distance and the choice of joint ventures: A contingency perspective', *Journal of International Marketing*, 2, pp. 63–80

Aharoni, Y. (1966) 'The foreign investment decision process', *Thunderbird International Business Review*, 8, pp. 13–14.

Anderson, E. & Gatignon, H. (1986) 'Modes of foreign entry: A transaction cost analysis and propositions', *Journal of International Business Studies*, 17, pp. 1–26.

Andersson, U., Cuervo-Cazurra, A. & Nielsen, B.B. (2014) 'From the editors: Explaining interaction effects within and across levels of analysis', *Journal of International Business Studies*, 45, pp. 1063–1071.

Arrow, K. (1962) 'Economic welfare and the allocation of resources for invention', in National Bureau of Economic Research *The Rate and Direction of Inventive Activity: Economic and Social Factors*. Princeton, NJ: Princeton University Press, pp. 609–626.

Barney, J. (1991) 'Firm resources and sustained competitive advantage', *Journal of Management*, 17, pp. 99–120.

Bathelt, H. & Li, P. F. (2014) 'Global cluster networks: Foreign direct investment flows from Canada to China', *Journal of Economic Geography*, 14, pp. 45–71.

Beaverstock, J.V., Smith, R.G. & Taylor, P.J. (1999) 'A roster of world cities', *Cities*, 16, pp. 445–458.

Belderbos, R. & Carree, M. (2002) 'The location of Japanese investments in China: Agglomeration effects, keiretsu, and firm heterogeneity', *Journal of the Japanese and International Economies*, 16, pp. 194–211.

Berköz, L. (2000) 'Location of financial, insurance, and real estate firms in Istanbul', *Journal of Urban Planning and Development*, 126, pp. 75–88.

Beugelsdijk, S., McCann, P. & Mudambi, R. (2010) 'Introduction: Place, space and organization – Economic Geography and the multinational enterprise', *Journal of Economic Geography*, 10, 485–493.

Beugelsdijk, S. & Mudambi, R. (2013) 'MNEs as border-crossing multi-location enterprises: The role of discontinuities in geographic space', *Journal of International Business Studies*, 44, pp. 413–426.

Bevan, A., Estrin, S. & Meyer, K. (2004) 'Foreign investment location and institutional development in transition economies', *International Business Review*, 13, pp. 43–64.

Bingham, C.B. & Eisenhardt, K.M. (2005) *Learning from Heterogeneous Experience: The Internationalization of Entrepreneurial Firms*. Doctoral dissertation, Stanford University.

Black, D.A. & Hoyt, W.H. (1989) 'Bidding for firms', *American Economic Review*, 79, pp. 1249–1256.

Blackbourn, A. (1982) 'The impact of multinational corporations on the spatial organisation of developed nations: A review', in Taylor, M.J. & Thrift, N.J. (Eds.), *The Geography of Multinationals*. London: Croom Helm, pp. 147–157.

Blanc-Brude, F., Cookson, G., Piesse, J. & Strange, R. (2014) 'The FDI location decision: Distance and the effects of spatial dependence', *International Business Review*, 23, pp. 797–810.

Brainard, S.L. (1993) *An Empirical Assessment of the Proximity-Concentration Tradeoff between Multinational Sales and Trade* (No. 4580). National Bureau of Economic Research, Inc.

Buckley, P.J. & Casson, M. (1976) *The Future of the Multinational Enterprise* (Vol. 1). London: Macmillan.

Buckley, P.J. & Casson, M. (1985) *The Economic Theory of the Multinational Enterprise: Selected Papers*. London: Macmillan.

Cantwell, J. (2009) 'Location and the multinational enterprise', *Journal of International Business Studies*, 40, pp. 35–41.

Casper, S. & Whitley, R. (2004) 'Managing competences in entrepreneurial technology firms: A comparative institutional analysis of Germany, Sweden and the UK', *Research Policy*, 33, pp. 89–106.

Caves, R.E. (1971) 'International corporations: The industrial economics of foreign investment', *Economica*, 38, pp. 1–27.

Chang, S.J. & Park, S. (2005) 'Types of firms generating network externalities and MNCs' co-location decisions', *Strategic Management Journal*, 26, pp. 595–615.

Charlton, A. (2003) *Incentive Bidding for Mobile Investment: Economic Consequences and Potential Responses* (No. 203). Paris: OECD Publishing.

Child, J. & Tsai, T. (2005) 'The dynamic between firms' environmental strategies and institutional constraints in emerging economies: Evidence from China and Taiwan', *Journal of Management Studies*, 42, pp. 95–125.

Chen, C.I. & Yeh, C.H. (2012) 'Re-examining location antecedents and pace of foreign direct investment: Evidence from Taiwanese investments in China', *Journal of Business Research*, 65, pp. 1171–1178.

Cheng, S. (2007) 'Structure of firm location choices: An examination of Japanese greenfield investment in China', *Asian Economic Journal*, 21, pp. 47–73.

Chung, W. & Alcácer, J. (2002) 'Knowledge seeking and location choice of foreign direct investment in the United States', *Management Science*, 48, pp. 1534–1554.

Cieslik, Andrzej & Ryan, Michael (2004) 'Explaining Japanese direct investment flows into an enlarged Europe: A comparison of gravity and economic potential approaches', *Journal of the Japanese and International Economies*, 18, pp. 12–37.

Coase, R.H. (1937) 'The nature of the firm', Economica, 4, pp. 386–405.

Coeurderoy, R. & Murray, G. (2008) 'Regulatory environments and the location decision: Evidence from the early foreign market entries of new-technology-based firms', *Journal of International Business Studies*, 39, pp. 670–687.

Coughlin, C.C., Terza, J.V. & Arromdee, V. (1991) 'State characteristics and the location of foreign direct investment within the United States', *The Review of Economics and Statistics*, 73, pp. 675–683.

Daude, C. & Stein, E. (2007) 'The quality of institutions and foreign direct investment', *Economics & Politics*, 19, pp. 317–344.

Davidson, W.H. & McFetridge, D.G. (1985) 'Key characteristics in the choice of international technology transfer mode', *Journal of International Business Studies*, 16, pp. 5–21.

Disdier, A.C. & Mayer, T. (2004) 'How different is Eastern Europe? Structure and determinants of location choices by French firms in Eastern and Western Europe', *Journal of Comparative Economics*, 32, pp. 280–296.

Du, J., Lu, Y. & Tao, Z. (2008) 'FDI location choice: agglomeration vs institutions', *International Journal of Finance & Economics*, 13, pp. 92–107.

Du, J., Lu, Y. & Tao, Z. (2012) 'Institutions and FDI location choice: The role of cultural distances', *Journal of Asian Economics*, 23, pp. 210–223.

Dunning, J.H. (1976) *Trade, Location of Economic Activity and the MNE: A Search for an Eclectic Approach*. Reading, UK: University of Reading, Department of Economics.

Dunning, J.H. (1979) 'Explaining changing patterns of international production: In defence of the eclectic theory', *Oxford Bulletin of Economics and Statistics*, 41, pp. 269–295.

Dunning, J.H. (1988) 'The eclectic paradigm of international production: A restatement and some possible extensions', *Journal of International Business Studies*, 19, pp. 1–31.

Dunning, J.H. (1996) *The Geographical Sources of the Competitiveness of Firms: Some Results of a New Survey*. Reading, UK: University of Reading, Department of Economics.

Dunning, J.H. (1998) 'Location and the multinational enterprise: A neglected factor?', *Journal of International Business Studies*, 29, pp. 45–66.

Dunning, J.H. (2009) 'Location and the multinational enterprise: John Dunning's thoughts on receiving the *Journal of International Business Studies* 2008 Decade Award', *Journal of International Business Studies*, 40, pp. 20–34.

Dunning, J.H. & Narula, R. (1996) 'The investment development path revisited', in Dunning, J.H. & Narula, R. (Eds.), *Foreign Direct Investment and Governments: Catalysts for Economic Restructuring*. London: Routledge, pp. 1–41.

Duranton, G. & Puga, D. (2004) 'Micro-foundations of urban agglomeration economies', in Henderson, J.V. & Thisse, J.-F. (Eds.), *Handbook of Regional and Urban Economics*. Amsterdam: Elsevier, pp. 2063–2117.

Eaton, J. & Tamura, A. (1994) 'Bilateralism and regionalism in Japanese and US trade and direct foreign investment patterns', *Journal of the Japanese and International Economies*, 8, pp. 478–510.

Eden, L. & Miller, S.R. (2004) 'Distance matters: Liability of foreignness, institutional distance and ownership strategy', *Advances in International Management*, 16, pp. 187–221.

Flores, R.G. & Aguilera, R.V. (2007) 'Globalization and location choice: An analysis of US multinational firms in 1980 and 2000', *Journal of International Business Studies*, 38, pp. 1187–1210.

Fung, K.C., Garcia-Herrero, A., Iizaka, H. & Siu, A. (2005) 'Hard or soft? Institutional reforms and infrastructure spending as determinants of foreign direct investment in China', *Japanese Economic Review*, 56, pp. 408–416.

Galan, J.I., González-Benito, J. & Zuñiga-Vincente, J.A. (2007) 'Factors determining the location decisions of Spanish MNEs: An analysis based on the investment development path', *Journal of International Business Studies*, 38, pp. 975–997.

Ghemawat, P. (2007) *Redefining Global Strategy: Crossing Borders in a World Where Differences Still Matter*. Boston, MA: Harvard Business Publishing.

Globerman, S. & Shapiro, D. (2003) 'Governance infrastructure and US foreign direct investment', *Journal of International Business Studies*, 34, pp. 19–39.

Goerzen, A., Asmussen, C.G. & Nielsen, B.B. (2013) 'Global cities and multinational enterprise location strategy', *Journal of International Business Studies*, 44, pp. 427–450.

Guimaraes, P., Figueiredo, O. & Woodward, D. (2000) 'Agglomeration and the location of foreign direct investment in Portugal', *Journal of Urban Economics*, 47, pp. 115–135.

Haigh, R. (1990) 'Selecting a United States plant location: The management decision-process in foreign companies', *Columbia Journal of World Business*, 25, pp. 22–31.

Head, K. & Ries, J. (1996) 'Inter-city competition for foreign investment: Static and dynamic effects of China's incentive areas', *Journal of Urban Economics*, 40, 38–60.

Head, K., Ries, J. & Swenson, D. (1995) 'Agglomeration benefits and location choice: Evidence from Japanese manufacturing investments in the United States', *Journal of International Economics*, 38, pp. 223–247.

Head, K., Ries, J. & Swenson, D. (1999) 'Attracting foreign manufacturing: Investment promotion and agglomeration', *Regional Science and Urban Economics*, 29, pp. 197–218.

Helpman, E. (1984) 'A simple theory of international trade with multinational corporations', *The Journal of Political Economy*, 92, pp. 451–471.

Hill, C.W. (1995) 'National institutional structures, transaction cost economizing and competitive advantage: The case of Japan', *Organization Science*, 6, pp. 119–131.

Hines Jr, J.R. (1996) *Tax Policy and the Activities of Multinational Corporations* (No. w5589). National Bureau of Economic Research. Princenton, NJ: Princeton University Press.

Hong, J. (2007) 'Firm-specific effects on location decisions of foreign direct investment in China's logistics industry', *Regional Studies*, 41, pp. 673–683.

Hoskisson, R.E., Eden, L., Lau, C.M. & Wright, M. (2000) 'Strategy in emerging economies', *Academy of Management Journal*, 43, pp. 249–267.

Huang, H. & Wei, Y.D. (2011) 'Spatial-temporal patterns and determinants of foreign direct investment in China', *Erdkunde*, 65, pp. 7–23.

Hymer, S. (1976) *The International Operations of National Firms: A Study of Direct Foreign Investment.* Cambridge, MA: MIT Press.

Jacobs, J. (1969) *The Economy of Cities.* New York: Vintage.

Kandogan, Y. (2012) 'Regional foreign direct investment potential of the states within the US', *Journal of Economics and Business*, 64, pp. 306–322.

Kemp, M.C. (1964) *The Pure Theory of International Trade.* Englewood Cliffs, NJ: Prentice-Hall.

Kindleberger, C. (1969) *American Business Abroad.* New Haven, CT: Yale University Press.

Klein, K.J., Dansereau, F. & Hall, R.J. (1994) 'Levels issues in theory development, data collection, and analysis', *Academy of Management Review*, 19, pp. 195–229.

Knickerbocker, F.T. (1973) *Oligopolistic Reaction and Multinational Enterprise.* Boston, MA: Division of Research Graduate School of Business Administration Harvard University.

Kobrin, S.J. (1976) 'The environmental determinants of foreign direct manufacturing investment: An ex post empirical analysis', *Journal of International Business Studies*, 7, pp. 29–42.

Kogut, B. & Chang, S.J. (1996) 'Platform investments and volatility exchange rates: Direct investment in the US by Japanese electronic companies', *The Review of Economics and Statistics*, 78, pp. 221–231.

Kostova, T. & Roth, K. (2002) 'Adoption of an organizational practice by subsidiaries of multinational corporations: Institutional and relational effects', *Academy of Management Journal*, 45, pp. 215–233.

Kostova, T. & Zaheer, S. (1999) 'Organizational legitimacy under conditions of complexity: The case of the multinational enterprise', *Academy of Management Review*, 24, pp. 64–81.

Krugman, P. (1991) 'Increasing returns and Economic Geography', *The Journal of Political Economy*, 99, pp. 483–499.

Krugman, P. & Venables, A.J. (1996) 'Integration, specialization, and adjustment', *European Economic Review*, 40, pp. 959–967.

Li, P.F. (2014) 'Global temporary networks of clusters: Structures and dynamics of trade fairs in Asian economies', *Journal of Economic Geography*, 14, pp. 995–1021.

Lin, H. & Yeh, R.-S. (2004) 'To invest or not to invest in China', *Small Business Economics*, 22, pp. 19–31.

Lorenzen, M. & Mudambi, R. (2013) 'Clusters, connectivity and catch-up: Bollywood and Bangalore in the global economy', *Journal of Economic Geography*, 13, pp. 501–534.

Ma, X. & Delios, A. (2007) 'A new tale of two cities: Japanese FDIs in Shanghai and Beijing, 1979–2003', *International Business Review*, 16, pp. 207–228.

MacDougall, G.D.A. (1960) 'The benefits and costs of private investment from abroad: A theoretical approach', *Bulletin of the Oxford University Institute of Economics & Statistics*, 22, pp. 189–211.

Majocchi, A. & Strange, R. (2007) 'Trade and market liberalisation in Eastern Europe', *Journal of East-West Business*, 13, pp. 93–114.

Makino, S., Lau, C.M. & Yeh, R.S. (2002) 'Asset-exploitation versus asset-seeking: Implications for location choice of foreign direct investment from newly industrialized economies', *Journal of International Business Studies*, 33, pp. 403–421.

Markusen, A. & Nesse, K. (2007) 'Institutional and political determinants of incentive competition', in Markusen, A. (Ed.), *Reining in the Competition for Capital.* Kalamazoo, MI: Upjohn Institute Press, pp. 1–41.

Markusen, J.R. (1984) 'Multinationals, multi-plant economies, and the gains from trade', *Journal of International Economics*, 16, pp. 205–226.

Markusen, J.R. (1997) 'Foreign direct investment, country characteristics and lessons for policy', in *OECD Industrial Competitiveness in the Knowledge-Based Economy: The New Role of Governments.* Paris: OECD, pp. 83–89.

Markusen, J.R., Venables, A.J., Konan, D.E. & Zhang, K.H. (1996) *A Unified Treatment of Horizontal Direct Investment, Vertical Direct Investment, and the Pattern of Trade in Goods and Services* (No. w5696). National Bureau of Economic Research. Princeton, NJ: Princeton University Press.

Marshall, A. (1920) *Principles of Economics: An Introductory Volume*. London: Macmillan

Mataloni Jr, R.J. (2010) 'Do US multinationals engage in sequential choice? Evidence from new manufacturing operations in Europe', *Evidence from New Manufacturing Operations in Europe (November 14, 2007)*.

Mataloni Jr, R.J. (2011) 'The structure of location choice for new US manufacturing investments in Asia-Pacific', *Journal of World Business*, 46, pp. 154–165.

McCann, P. (2011) 'International Business and Economic Geography: Knowledge, time and transactions costs', *Journal of Economic Geography*, 11, pp. 309–317.

Meyer, K.E. & Nguyen, H.V. (2005) 'Foreign investment strategies and sub-national institutions in emerging markets: Evidence from Vietnam', *Journal of Management Studies*, 42, pp. 63–93.

Mucchielli, J.L. & Puech, F. (2004) 'Globalization, agglomeration and FDI location: The case of French firms in Europe', in Mucchielli, J.L. & Mayer, T. (Eds.), *Multinational Firms' Location and the New Economic Geography*. Cheltenham, UK: Edward Elgar, pp. 35–58.

Mudambi, R. (1998) 'The role of duration in multinational investment strategies', *Journal of International Business Studies*, 29, pp. 239–261.

Mudambi, R. & Navarra, P. (2002) 'Institutions and International Business: A theoretical overview', *International Business Review*, 11, pp. 635–646.

Nachum, L. (2003) 'Liability of foreignness in global competition? Financial service affiliates in the city of London', *Strategic Management Journal*, 24, pp. 1187–1208.

Nachum, L., Dunning, J.H. & Jones, G.G. (2000) 'UK FDI and the comparative advantage of the UK', *The World Economy*, 23, pp. 701–720.

Nachum, L. & Wymbs, C. (2005) 'Product differentiation, external economies and MNE location choices: M&As in global cities', *Journal of International Business Studies*, 36, pp. 415–434.

Nielsen, B.B. & Nielsen, S. (2011) 'The role of top management team international orientation in international strategic decision-making: The choice of foreign entry mode', *Journal of World Business*, 46, pp. 185–193.

North, D.C. (1990) *Institutions, Institutional Change and Economic Performance*. Cambridge, UK: Cambridge University Press.

Ohlin, B.G. (1933) *Interregional and International Trade*. Cambridge, MA: Harvard University Press.

Ó Huallacháin, B. & Reid, N. (1997) 'Acquisition versus greenfield investment: the location and growth of Japanese manufacturers in the United States', *Regional Studies*, 31, pp. 403–416.

Oliver, C. (1997) 'Sustainable competitive advantage: Combining institutional and resource-based views', *Strategic Management Journal*, 18, pp. 697–713.

Oman, C. & Organisation for Economic Co-operation and Development. Development Centre. (2000) *Policy Competition for Foreign Direct Investment: A Study of Competition among Governments to Attract FDI*. Development Centre of the Organisation for Economic Co-operation and Development. Paris: OECD.

Özdemir, D. (2002) 'The distribution of foreign direct investments in the service sector in Istanbul', *Cities*, 19, pp. 249–259.

Peng, M.W. (2003) 'Institutional transitions and strategic choices', *Academy of Management Review*, 28, pp. 275–296.

Porter, M.E. (1998) 'Clusters and the new economics of competition', *Harvard Business Review*, 76, 77–90.

Powell, T.C., Lovallo, D. & Fox, C.R. (2011) 'Behavioral strategy', *Strategic Management Journal*, 32, pp. 1369–1386.

Prange, C. & Verdier, S. (2011) 'Dynamic capabilities, internationalization processes and performance', *Journal of World Business*, 46, pp. 126–133.

Pusterla, F. & Resmini, L. (2007) 'Where do foreign firms locate in transition countries? An empirical investigation', *The Annals of Regional Science*, 41, pp. 835–856.

Ramamurti, R. (2003) 'Can governments make credible promises? Insights from infrastructure projects in emerging economies', *Journal of International Management*, 9, pp. 253–269.

Rasciute, S., Pentecost, E. & Ferrett, B. (2014) 'Firm heterogeneity in modelling foreign direct investment location decisions', *Applied Economics*, 46, pp. 1350–1360.

Resmini, L. (2000) 'The determinants of foreign direct investment in the CEECs: New evidence from sectoral patterns', *Economics of Transition*, 8, pp. 665–689.

Romer, P.M. (1986) 'Increasing returns and long-run growth', *The Journal of Political Economy*, 94, pp. 1002–1037.

Sassen, S. (1994) *Cities in a World Economy*. Thousand Oaks, CA: Pine Forge Press.

Sassen, S. (2001) *The Global City: New York, London, Tokyo*. Princeton, NJ: Princeton University Press.

Sassen, S. (2012) *Cities in a World Economy*. 4th Edition. Los Angeles, CA: Sage.

Scott, W.R. (1995) *Institutions and Organizations*. Thousand Oaks, CA: Sage.

Scott, W.R. (2001) *Institutions and Organizations*. 2nd Edition. Thousand Oaks, CA: Sage.

Shaver, J.M. (1998) 'Do foreign-owned and US-owned establishments exhibit the same location pattern in US manufacturing industries?' *Journal of International Business Studies*, 29, pp. 469–492.

Shaver, J.M. & Flyer, F. (2000) 'Agglomeration economies, firm heterogeneity, and foreign direct investment in the United States', *Strategic Management Journal*, 21, pp. 1175–1194.

Shi, Y. (2001) 'Technological capabilities and international production strategy of firms: The case of foreign direct investment in China', *Journal of World Business*, 36, pp. 184–204.

Sun, Q., Tong, W. & Yu, Q. (2002) 'Determinants of foreign direct investment across China', *Journal of International Money and Finance*, 21, pp. 79–113.

Tahir, R. & Larimo, J. (2004) 'Understanding the location strategies of the European firms in Asian countries', *Journal of American Academy of Business*, 5, pp. 102–109.

Takatsuka, H. (2011) 'Economic Geography of firms and skilled labor', *Journal of Regional Science*, 51, pp. 784–803.

Tenev, S., Carlier, A., Chaudry, O. & Nguyen, Q.T. (2003) *Informality and the Playing Field in Vietnam's Business Sector*. Washington, DC: World Bank and the International Finance Corporation.

Venables, A. (1996) 'Equilibrium locations of vertically linked industries', *International Economic Review*, 37, pp. 341–359.

Vernon, R. (1966) 'International investment and international trade in the product cycle', *The Quarterly Journal of Economics*, 80, pp. 190–207.

Vernon, R. (1974) 'The location of economic activity', in Dunning, J.H. (Ed.), *Economic Analysis and the Multinational Enterprise*. London: Routledge, pp. 89–114.

Wei, S.J. (1997) *Why Is Corruption so Much More Taxing Than Tax? Arbitrariness Kills* (No. w6255). National Bureau of Economic Research. Princeton, NJ: Princeton University Press.

Wei, Y., Liu, X., Parker, D. & Vaidya, K. (1999) 'The regional distribution of foreign direct investment in China', *Regional Studies*, 33, pp. 857–867.

Wei, Y., Liu, X. & Wang, C. (2008) 'Mutual productivity spillovers between foreign and local firms in China', *Cambridge Journal of Economics*, 32, pp. 609–631.

Wheeler, D. & Mody, A. (1992) 'International investment location decisions: The case of US firms', *Journal of International Economics*, 33, pp. 57–76.

Wright, M., Filatotchev, I., Hoskisson, R.E. & Peng, M.W. (2005) 'Strategy research in emerging economies: Challenging the conventional wisdom', *Journal of Management Studies*, 42, pp. 1–33.

Wu, J. & Radbone, I. (2005) 'Global integration and the intra-urban determinants of foreign direct investment in Shanghai', *Cities*, 22, pp. 275–286.

Zaheer, S. (1995) 'Overcoming the liability of foreignness', *Academy of Management Journal*, 38, pp. 341–363.

Zaheer, S. & Nachum, L. (2011) 'Sense of place: From location resources to MNE locational capital', *Global Strategy Journal*, 1, pp. 96–108.

Zhao, S.X. & Zhang, L. (2007) 'Foreign direct investment and the formation of global city-regions in China', *Regional Studies*, 41, pp. 979–994.

Zhou, C., Delios, A. & Yang, J.Y. (2002) 'Locational determinants of Japanese foreign direct investment in China', *Asia Pacific Journal of Management*, 19, pp. 63–86.

13
THE REGION IN INTERNATIONAL BUSINESS AND ECONOMIC GEOGRAPHY

Crispian Fuller

Introduction

The sub-national region has long been a central concern for economic geographers, from Marxist accounts of spatial divisions of labour in the 1970s and 1980s, to more recent explorations of their unbounded and fluid nature which has informed the global production networks perspective and related approaches to the corporation (Phelps & Fuller, 2016; Yeung & Coe, 2015). More recently in human geography the region has been understood to be an unbounded and emergent set of geographical relations, which are materialised through various economic, social and political processes, and involving differing temporal dimensions (see Hudson, 2005). This explicit focus on the region, which one would expect to be of critical concern for economic geographers, is markedly different to International Business (IB) studies that has tended to interpret geographical processes through particular conceptual lenses. Moreover, IB has tended to be more concerned with the 'macro region', typically focused on the triad areas of Europe, North America and Southeast Asia, rather than an explicit concern with the subnational region (see, for example, Rugman (2005) on 'regional multinationals'). IB has strong conceptual understandings of the black box of the MNE, including how and why it is organised in a particular way through strategic and operational means, whilst Economic Geography has knowledge of the spatial organisation of production networks in national and subnational geographical spaces. What is required is a bringing together of these two different approaches so that the black boxes are revealed in both disciplines, but where there is a progressive dialogue between the two. Indeed, for Beugelsdijk, McCann and Mudambi (2010), the cross fertilisation of ideas between IB and other social sciences, including Economic Geography, has not addressed a fundamental problem with these approaches, namely the insufficient consideration given to the relationship between the organisational and geographical attributes of MNEs.

Economic Geography and the region

In contrast to IB, mainstream Economic Geography has become more diverse since the 1960s, moving beyond positivist spatial science and assumptions around rational choice, to embrace a broader range of theoretical approaches. The infusion of critical realism and post-structural perspectives has been important in this process, with the MNE viewed as unbounded, embedded within the broader social, economic and political contexts in which it is situated. The corporate geography approach of the 1980s was concerned with how MNE decisions influence and were influenced by the geographies of economic activity, particularly within the context of political economic approaches concerned with structural accounts of external control and dependency (see Massey, 1984). This perspective did elucidate the relationship between the MNE and the region. The approach was concerned with the external control of regional economies by MNEs, and thus their dependence on these actors. The emphasis tended to be on large centralised MNEs, how they were seeking to organise across space through specific practices (e.g. cost-based vertical disintegration), rather than the influence and co-constitution of the latter with the MNE. A key element of this was a failure to develop and engage a suitable theoretical framework, and lacking consideration or ability to explain the impact of capitalist processes and their geographical relations (Walker, 1989).

Informed by critical realism and a 'network' perspective stemming from the works of Granovetter, the global production network (GPN) approach is now the prominent conceptual framework in which to examine MNEs, production networks and the region in Economic Geography. Influenced strongly by the economic geographer Peter Dicken, this approach explicates the increasingly unbounded and vertically and horizontally differentiated nature of MNEs. It moves beyond corporate geography by recognising that production functions through networks incorporating many different economic and non-economic actors. More importantly, it emphasises the critical role of a 'fluid' interpretation of the region and regional development following other approaches (see Hudson, 2008). This has involved critiquing 'new regionalism' and aligned perspectives that emphasise endogenous intra-regional underpinnings of regional economic development, to focus on various actors and practices operating through disparate geographical relations (Hess & Yeung, 2006). In this thinking the region is viewed as a site of territorialised firms (operating within GPNs), networks, and assets that can be unique or ubiquitous.

GPNs are defined as 'an organizational arrangement comprising interconnected economic and noneconomic actors coordinated by a global lead firm and producing goods or services across multiple geographic locations for worldwide markets' (Yeung & Coe, 2015, p. 32). This does not remove the importance of the MNE as these lead firms are a 'central and necessary prerequisite' (Yeung & Coe, 2015, p. 32), making the MNE a critical aspect of this account. Geographically, the network and region are foundational to GPNs. This reflects more recent thinking in geography around examining interwoven polymorphic geographical relations (see Jones & Jessop, 2010). As with the unbounded understanding of production networks, regions are believed to be bounded together through networked relations, thus recognising their fluid but interconnected nature. It is thus the articulation of regional actors and economies into GPNs through relational networks that is of central concern, and which places geographical relations at the centre of the approach, in contrast to IB studies.

Embeddedness of MNEs within geographical relations is central to the GPN approach, with its understanding of the importance of spatially configured contextual actors in interacting with and influencing the MNE, and manifest through various arenas of embeddedness (societal, network and territorial). GPN overlaps with what became known as 'new regionalism', including approaches concerned with 'learning regions', clusters and 'regional innovation systems', and more recently evolutionary thinking. Here, the region is viewed as a site of tangible and intangible territorialised assets that provide competitive advantages to MNEs through their embeddedness in network relations with regionally configured actors. We see the region therefore as a fluid space in which various forms of network embeddedness occurs (see Yang & Coe, 2009), as well as their disparate entrenchment within territorialised spaces of the region where this involves particular territorially specific assets.

A further important element of the GPN approach is the concept of 'coupling' between firms within regions and MNEs that are lead firms in GPNs. Various forms of coupling, ranging from the 'organic' co-evolution that characterises home regions of MNEs, and where there are often region-specific intangible assets; to 'strategic coupling' involving deliberate selection and efforts by regional institutions to attract and embed MNEs and GPN elements more broadly. The latter builds upon a long debate over the nature of deliberative relations and power relations between the firm and particular geographical relations, such as place and the region. Yeung (2009a, p. 332) defines strategic coupling as 'a mutually dependent and constitutive process involving shared interests and cooperation between two or more groups of actors who otherwise might not act in tandem for a common strategic objective'. The region is integral to strategic coupling, involving regional actors deliberating with other regional actors (e.g. firms) and more globally orientated actors, such as lead firms. It provides the basis for the key processes constituting strategic coupling, namely, intentional actors involved in deliberation; its time-space contingent nature which brings together the region and global relationally; and finally, broadranging relational networks that go beyond an endogenous region. In essence, strategic coupling captures the power relations between regional actors and GPNs, and particular lead firms and suppliers, with the qualitative and quantitative nature of relations producing particular types of regional development. Moreover, strategic coupling has become a further arena in which there is inter-regional competition for FDI and thus regional economic development (Yang, 2009).

Therefore, the region represents a negotiated space between GPN actors, and particularly lead firms, and regional actors seeking to provide or foster territorialised assets that can contribute to the value process central to a GPN. Where regions possess unique assets that provide value in the production process, they have higher degrees of bargaining power (Coe & Hess, 2011); however, this is typically not always the case. Indeed, there have been criticisms of the failure of the approach to fully elucidate the often asymmetrical power relations between MNEs and regional actors in processes of strategic coupling (Dawley, 2011).

MacKinnon (2011) has sought to expand the conceptual depth of strategic coupling by emphasising the critical role of evolutionary tendencies. Bargaining arrangements and spaces are partly contingent on historically constituted MNE investment strategies and activities, as well as regional institutional arrangements involving MNEs and regional actors. During phases of corporate selection of the region for investment, there are various potential forms of institutional change. Institutions, as dynamic and performative arrangements, evolve through gradual change involving additions (layering), reorientation of form and function (conversion), and redefining and recombining existing institutional elements to produce new forms (recombination) (see Martin, 2010). On the one hand, this does elucidate a dynamic framework for understanding coupling but, on the other, the region remains an under-theorised element, treated in a similar way to institutions as porous and unbounded, but where we have little understanding of how institutions and institutional change are related to particular geographical relations, and thus the 'region' as constituted by various socio-spatial relations.

Whilst GPN has advanced our understanding of networked production and geographical relations, and the relationship with the region, it has tended to lack consideration of the 'black box' of the firm (Hudson, 2008; Sunley, 2008). With prominence placed on actual 'relations', rather than how such relations are informed, influenced and directed by dynamics internal to the firm, this reduces the explanatory power of the approach in fully understanding the relationship with the actual region and broader geographical relations. This is particularly evident in accounts such as Yang and Coe (2009) which exam strategic coupling between Japanese and

Taiwanese corporations in Taiwan, but where there is little conceptualisation of the practices underpinning the corporate restructuring of Japanese corporations such as Fujitsu and their changing relations with the Chimei corporation.

In response to criticism of GPN lacking theoretical basis and rigour in which to identify and explain causality (see Sunley, 2008), Yeung and Coe (2015) develop an actor-centred conceptual framework. The purpose of this is to elucidate the causal capitalist drivers of GPNs, with the main causal factors being competitive dynamics and risk environments. The former includes cost-capability ratios, market imperatives and financial discipline, all of which influence and mediate decision-making by actors, which are expressed through firm strategies, and that shape networks and their organisational configurations. Various organisational strategies are identified as the consequence of these processes, including intrafirm coordination, interfirm control, interfirm partnership and extrafirm bargaining. So, for example, intrafirm coordination is often important for 'lead firms' with low costs and control of high proprietary capabilities, ensuring production is generally internalised. Regions have an important role in accommodating subsidiaries and affiliates, although recognising that cost-based units are vulnerable to disinvestment. Interfirm control is characterised by outsourcing of production to contractors to acquire cost-based advantages, and where extensive control of these actors is evident. Furthermore, there is recognition that there are intra-industry differences in lead firm assemblers arising from disparate corporate and national cultures, such as US firms focusing more on cost-based decisions, whilst Japanese firms are more engaged in regional business networks. In each case, strategic decisions have important implications for the role and importance of the region, whilst in the case of extrafirm bargaining it relates to strategic intentions and deliberations between firms and non-firm actors, and thus underpins processes of coupling.

These causal processes subsequently influence broader sectors and the actual regions in which the various actors involved in production networks operate or work through. The power of this approach is in terms of understanding various causal processes and, importantly, why actors are engaged in different strategies and networks even within the same sector and region. GPN 2.0 is therefore a conceptual framework that is concerned first and foremost with actors and capitalist dynamics, rather than the role of the region in such processes. The approach is presented as the precursor to GPN 1.0, as a way of understanding how actors influence the region, and which relies upon GPN 1.0 concepts around geographical networks, regions and their territorial assets, and embeddedness. This does, however, leave the region as a potentially reactive entity that is a consequence of the strategies and actions of actors, in response to capitalist dynamics.

An alternative perspective has continued to place the corporation and FDI at the forefront of analysis, and builds upon a historically constituted perspective stemming from corporate geography and, more importantly, Massey's (1984) spatial division of labour concept (e.g. Phelps, 1993). Such studies have been concerned with the continuation of the 'branch plant syndrome' and the locational dynamics arising from the reconfiguration of MNE activities (e.g. R&D investment abroad), and thus the impact of the MNE on regions is paramount (e.g. Phelps & Fuller, 2000). Such perspectives do not deny the vertically and horizontally disintegrated networked nature of production, but their concern is with understanding the locational preferences (e.g. McCann & Mudambi, 2004), impact (e.g. backward and forward linkages; see, e.g. Beugelsdijk, 2007), and power relations between MNEs and regions (e.g. Fuller, 2005). Many accounts are concerned with the subsidisation of the MNE, and thus market, by regional actors through various means. Moreover, this is a literature that has taken greater account of actual corporate actors, seeking to delve into the corporate practices leading to particular locational arrangements and impacts. This has included many studies examining the differential multiplier effects arising from actual tasks such as R&D and assembly operations (e.g. Dimitropoulou, Burke & McCann, 2008), employment (Jones & Wren, 2004), knowledge spillovers and linkages (e.g. Phelps, 2008) and supplier linkages (e.g. Phelps & Ozawa, 2003). Host locations in more economically peripheral regions have been found to lack positive multiplier effects from MNEs, with a continuing belief that more value added tasks continue to be attracted to the more prosperous regions (see MacCann & Iammarino, 2013), whilst less prosperous regions accommodate more cost-based corporate responsibilities, such as assemblage operations.

In this account, the conceptualisation of the actual region has not been at the forefront of analysis, with greater concern for a broadly defined 'location'. The actual boundaries of the 'location', which is often stated as the 'region', is often conceptually and empirically defined in terms of the activities of the firms and power relations with particular territorialised actors and practices (e.g. suppliers). Where there has been greater conceptualisation of the region, it has often been in terms of regional 'scalar' governing arrangements, and the interaction with MNEs that are seeking to invest or which are already located within the region (MacKinnon & Phelps, 2001; Fuller, 2005). Whilst this does at least conceptualise the manifestation of the 'region' through these social relations, it fails to connect this with the many other activities of MNEs beyond the political, and which produce particular geographical relations. More recently, Phelps and Fuller (2016) have sought to advance this agenda by way of a critical engagement with the recent evolutionary turn in Economic Geography. Focused primarily on the MNE, this account examines the various forms of change that occur through and by subsidiaries, and that co-constitute institutional arrangements within regions. Whilst not seeking to conceptualise the region, this perspective does emphasis the causal MNE actors and practices producing particular geographical relations, including that of the region. As with GPN 2.0, the emphasis is very much on the role of MNEs and production networks in the social construction of regions, but recognising the role of territorialised assets and scalar governing arrangements.

We can see therefore the increasing congruence between Economic Geography perspectives around unbounded and emergent understandings of the region. There is growing congruence with accounts of corporate practices and actors in the finance sector, which tend to adopt poststructuralist conceptual approaches (e.g. Faulconbridge, Hall & Beaverstock, 2008; Muzio et al., 2011). Such accounts view the MNE as a performative and unbounded entity, which is constantly being produced and assembled through practices, and that builds upon actor network theory and other elements of poststructuralism, such as Deleuze thinking. Such a perspective does advance a dynamic conception of regions, largely as one of many geographical relations, by recognising that such corporate practices and relations work through complex spatial arrangements which define such actions. So that in certain accounts there is a concern with the role of differing forms of proximity (e.g. virtual) in constructing particular geographical relations that convey power relations (Jones & Search, 2009); whilst in other accounts there is an explicit concern with nationally configured relations between the state and MNEs (e.g. Weller, 2009).

To conclude, what characterises these Economic Geography approaches is a concern with elucidating the multiple geographical relations that produce, constitute, work through and are produced through the 'region'. This has meant moving beyond scalar and territorial views of the region, to understanding their co-constitution and assembling with other geographical relations, including networks, topological 'folding' relations and place. Geographical accounts generally take a relational view of the region, but recognising the co-constitution with territoriality. So that whilst there is an understanding of an element of territorialised administration and cultural and societal elements, these are produced and constituted by relational socio-spatial relations that occur across space, and which are 'materialised in various forms, and representational narratives about them' (Hudson, 2005, p. 650).

International Business studies and the region

IB has traditionally been concerned with how the MNE goes about organising itself across spatial areas through quantitative analysis of spatial patterns. Whilst IB is by definition concerned with geographical relations co-constituting particular forms of organisation, there has been no explicit conceptualisation of the region, nor geographical relations more broadly in the discipline. As argued by McCann and Mudambi (2004, p. 494), 'The International Business literature has traditionally tended to treat locational issues in a manner which is very unspecific and rather non-analytical'. The conceptual basis of IB has been up to the present day the emphasis on examining Cartesian space and, more explicitly, how the MNE seeks to manage the different geographical locations in which it operates, but where there is an underdeveloped view of geographical relations (McCann & Mudambi, 2005). In itself this is a contradiction as the explicit focus is on spatial management of the organisation of the MNE, which thus involves socially constructed and performed 'relative space' (Schatzki, 2010).

The dominant conceptual framework in IB has been the ownership, location and internalisation (OLI) framework as developed by Dunning (1979). Recognised as a framework, rather than theory, the OLI framework builds upon internalisation theory, which takes a transaction cost economics approach to understanding how the MNE internalises market transactions across foreign borders where there is a lack of market provision, or costly provision by the market (Buckley & Casson, 1976). Internalised production within the MNE is manifest in FDI by way of foreign subsidiaries (Dunning, 1988). The 'ownership' element relates to the possession and organisation of different combinations of resources, transactions and patterns of governance that underpin competitive advantage. Location is viewed as a physical site of competitive advantages for the MNE, which makes FDI decisions based on the prevalence and importance of such location-specific advantages. More specifically, location is defined in terms of a set of factors to be managed by the MNE as it seeks to organise spatial relations and enact a corporate strategy. It was not viewed as a key factor influencing the actual MNE, with location advantages having been defined in terms of specific 'assets', ranging from cost considerations in many past accounts, to more recent considerations of location-specific high value added assets. The 'organisational' element is therefore conceptually separate from 'location', leaving the latter in an undefined manner (Fuller, 2002).

Taken together, OLI and internalisation theory have both had a considerable influence in IB studies, but the role of the region is largely absent in these perspectives. Of considerable concern is the difficulty of the OLI framework in fully explaining the complexities of intra-national location decisions, since it tends to focus on national circumstances rather than the relationship between different subnational spaces, MNE decision-making and the spatial nature of FDI behaviour (Sethi et al., 2003). Indeed, there has long been critique of the national focus of IB, even within more recent accounts such as Dunning and Lundan (2008) (see Yeung, 2009a). Location is viewed in the context of the nation with early studies concerned with the national-level data analysis of trade and investment flows. More recently, the emphasis has been on 'country-specific advantages' in the context of 'firm-specific advantages' (Rugman, 2005), and nation-based decision making by MNEs. The consequence of this is to dispel the considerable spatial heterogeneity of national territories, as well as the relational and topological networks of constituent spaces within nation spaces (Beugelsdijk, McCann & Mudambi, 2010).

Second, IB has traditionally drawn its conceptual and methodological foundations from positivism, seeking to align itself with economics, which has important implications for the understanding of geographical relations. In such thinking, IB views the rationale and external orientation of the MNE in terms of transaction cost economics, but this fails to address the social, cultural and institutional embeddedness of economic action and actors as propagated by the likes of Polanyi and Granovetter (see Yeung, 2009a; see, for example, Meyer & Nguyen, 2005). The 'internal' MNE has also been viewed in Weberian terms as largely bounded, with a relatively homogenous structure characterised by discrete units, but which largely adheres to a set of rules, regulations and procedures enacted by a corporate centre, and which is embedded within a corporate strategy.

IB has recently moved towards the analysis of MNEs as differentiated networks and federations, and with subsidiaries viewed as important causal agents (Andersson, Forsgren & Holm, 2007; Meyer, Mudambi & Narula, 2011). A key element of more networked MNEs is the creation of specialised subsidiaries and increasingly differentiated value chains, where parents possess and exercise disparate decision-making powers. It is within such MNE arrangements that there is an understanding of the greater role of subsidiaries as sites of strategic capabilities, assets, knowledge production and innovation, all of which contribute to the overall strategic competences of parent companies (Williams & Lee, 2011). Networked MNEs lead to greater sensitivity towards the regions which form part of these dispersed networked arrangements (see Dunning & Lundan, 2008), as well as recognition that IB has failed to take account of subsidiaries as embedded within greater regionally based relational networks. Indeed, this is congruent with the desire for IB to be more sensitive to the intricacies of 'location'; as Rugman, Verbeke and Yuan (2010, p. 9) argue, it is important to 'investigate separately the strategic importance of its [i.e. corporate] local environment in terms of location advantages for each value chain activity set, because these will vary with each activity'.

One key literature that has developed over the last twenty years is that on the nature, strategic positioning and evolutionary processes of subsidiaries, and thus the role of the location of subsidiaries (Papanastassiou & Pearce, 2009). Subsidiaries have become critical elements of MNEs in response to growing market segmentation and consumer sophistication, but also because of the increasing importance of location-specific knowledge and technology in the production process (Meyer et al., 2011). In particular, as value chains are being broken up through contracting, certain subsidiaries are acquiring individual responsibilities, whilst others form 'downstream' parts of complex 'global factories' (Buckley, 2009; Mudambi & Venzin, 2010). This takes place within an environment where the ownership advantages of MNEs are increasingly related to tangible and intangible knowledge-based capabilities and assets, which are embedded within particular spaces (Meyer et al., 2011). This includes the growing differentiation and importance of corporate subsidiaries, with many seeking to create unique competencies and bundles of local resources (Cantwell & Mudambi, 2005). Such issues are of particular importance with regard to geographical investment behaviour within networked and increasingly differentiated corporate networks that span a variety of geographical locations. MNEs work through integrated networks in which to produce ownership advantages critical to innovation and knowledge production, including local business networks, such as in the case of 'competence-creating' subsidiaries requiring highly innovative locations and thus a strong external focus (Cantwell & Mudambi, 2005).

An important element of this external focus is that of the nature of the network relations with customers, suppliers, distributors, competitors and complementary organisations such as universities, all of which are involved in the production of knowledge and technologies (Figueiredo, 2011). Subsidiary importance is related to embeddedness in networks of business relationships (Yamin & Andersson, 2011). The level of subsidiary involvement in external firms can influence the development of subsidiary roles (Andersson & Forsgren, 2000). Almeida and Phene (2004) found that differences in innovative capability were related to the locational knowledge sources available to subsidiaries. Knowledge from the host country had a significant impact on innovation, suggesting that physical proximity has a role in assimilation, particularly where a region is strong in knowledge creation (Phene & Almeida, 2008). Proximity is important in terms of being the basis for personal contact through social networks and reduced transaction costs. For Frost, Birkinshaw and Ensign (2002), advanced capabilities are typically located in subsidiaries, but that such capabilities are relatively heterogeneous within populations of subsidiaries, typically in relation to differing regional location advantages.

Recognising the limitations of the OLI framework through its focus on national locations and limited conceptualisation of spatial differentiation, various IB studies have focused on local 'business networks', local 'context' and Porterian clusters in understanding the main role of sub-national locational advantages (Forsgren, Holm & Johanson, 2005; Tavares & Teixeira, 2006; Andersson et al., 2007; Meyer et al., 2011). Subsidiaries are viewed as being embedded within local business networks and having to adapt to local 'contextual' institutions, particularly as a means in which to engage local actors (Figueiredo, 2011). This means knowledge and learning are widely dispersed and locally embedded, and with corporate HQs lacking knowledge of subsidiaries (Forsgren et al., 2005; Andersson et al., 2007). Ciabuschi, Dellestrand and Martín, (2011) argues that knowledge is intrinsically related to the local context in which subsidiaries' knowledge activities function; and that if knowledge is context-specific then corporate HQs can never possess perfect knowledge. This also builds upon the greater understanding of the increasing importance of location as a site of knowledge-based assets, often intangible in nature. Consequently, there has been greater sensitivity towards the critical role of explicit assets, often regionally embedded within clusters, in underpinning the global competitive advantage of MNEs (Dunning, 2009).

There have been calls for a greater focus on the region (see Dunning & Lundan, 2008), but these have typically been aligned to transaction cost-based perspectives on the benefits of business networks and clustering, particularly in relation to endogenous growth theory. IB has engaged with cluster theory, but not to advance it through critical conceptual engagement, but rather to expand accounts of local business networks (Andersson et al., 2007). In essence, many studies have tended to view the region as a competitive economic unit like a firm, whereby competitive advantages and transaction costs are the key determining factors (see Almeida & Phene, 2004). This is achieved through non-mobile and unique locational factors that produce a competitive advantage compared with other regions. Furthermore, McCann and Mudambi (2004) argue that such accounts fail to take account of the nature of MNEs and different types of clustering. There is a need for IB accounts to focus on the competitive advantage issue of when it is suitable for an MNE to locate in a cluster. Of critical importance is the failure to appreciate that MNEs exist because of the need to internalise knowledge transaction costs, whereas clusters denote working through inter-firm linkages of externalised knowledge. Similarly, knowledge spillovers from firms through networks are considered to be prevalent in clusters, yet MNEs are likely to want to keep such knowledge internal.

MNEs thus face opportunity-cost issues of whether to locate and work through clusters where they will lose propriety information, or being able to exploit public good information. Evidence suggests that MNEs do not tend to locate in areas where competitors function, neither do they tend to work through similar location-specific business networks where they are in the same locations (Cantwell & Santangelo, 2002; Alcácer & Chung, 2007). McCann and Mudambi (2004, p. 505) argue that it is therefore necessary to 'consider the firm's perception of the relationship between knowledge inflows and knowledge outflows'. This inevitably leads to the need to examine corporate decision-making concerning whether to internalise or externalise knowledge production through spatially concentrated activities; and through such an approach there is an examination of the inter-relationship between the MNEs' organisational arrangements and decision-making, and location behaviour.

A further element of this greater sensitivity towards the region is the appreciation of the role of institutions and an evolutionary understanding of MNE subsidiaries (Meyer et al., 2011). In the field of IB, this has been led by Dunning and Lundan's (2008) call for analysis of the role of institutional assets in the OLI framework, following the recognition of the institutional embeddedness of MNEs across space. This is based on Douglass North's understanding of institutions as rules within the MNEs, and particularly the way MNEs seek legitimacy in host locations. This does, however, present a rules-based understanding of institutions, which tends to undersocialise their basis, such as in their role as 'shared habits' (see Hodgson, 2006).

Complementarities, incompatibilities and a way forward

It would be quite easy to emphasise the incompatibilities between the two disciplines given their divergent focus over the last twenty years. However, such a perspective would ignore the complementarities between the two disciplines that have developed with the changing nature of capitalism and organisation of the MNE. A 'network' orientated perspective is now central to both IB and Economic Geography accounts. Indeed, in terms of complementarities, this is where the key area of learning and collaboration can occur, and with this an appreciation of a networked and relational viewpoint of the sub-national region. As the preceding discussion emphasises, each discipline lacks attention towards the academic focus and strengths of the other. In the case of Economic Geography, the dominant perspective of GPN has tended to provide an insufficient account of the internal dynamics of MNEs, thus leaving the 'black box' in place. This is despite efforts at developing a GPN 2.0 where only particular elements of the MNE are examined, and at a very broad level.

In contrast, IB has advanced our understanding of the internal dynamics of MNEs, but there is an even larger insufficient understanding of the role and intricacies of the region, which stems from a deficient understanding of the nature of geographical relations. Moreover, whereas Economic Geography emphasises the social and political institutions underpinning economic action, IB tends to place (spatial) transaction costs as central. In each case, therefore, there are opposing conceptual and empirical absences, but what now combines these perspectives is a greater emphasis on understanding externally configured production networks, such as 'global factories', and segmented value chains. It is within this realm of subsidiary specialisation, greater sensitivity towards geographical attributes and more networked production that collaboration can occur between the two disciplines.

A future agenda of inter-disciplinary collaboration

For Beugelsdijk et al. (2010) there needs to be an integrated discussion of the organisational arrangements of MNEs with the attributes of regions. This would first and foremost place geography at the centre of any discussion, working on the basis that the MNE is a geographical entity, since all actors and practices within the MNE, and acting beyond it, are in essence geographical in nature. However, whereas Beugelsdijk et al. (2010) call for an emphasis on 'place, space and organization', any consideration of the region has to work on the basis that it is socially constructed through various geographical relations, rather than simply a territory as is often the case in IB. Indeed, what is required is a collaborative effort that seeks to further develop a (society embedded) networked understanding of MNEs and regions. This does require a movement beyond existing approaches and, thus, the traditional approaches of both disciplines.

First, there is a need to comprehend the antecedents of the region through an understanding of geographical relations. Within geography, there have long been debates on the role of various geographical relations, but more recently there have been efforts to understand the 'polymorphic' socio-spatial relations constituting processes, events and sites. Most notably, Jones and Jessop (2010) call for a perspective that takes account of the interwoven social production of space through territories, places, scale and networks. These work in heterogeneous ways to causally produce 'compossible' socio-spatial relations, such as a particular 'region' (Jones & Jessop, 2010). This derives from contingently articulated processes of variation, selection, retention and institutionalisation of particular social relations. These produce and 'condense' emergent 'moments' of combined causal social mechanisms. Central to such a perspective is the role of actors and their strategies in the articulation and actualisation of socio-spatial relations, such as the region, through processes of condensation. From this position we can understand that the region is a socially produced moment of compossible socio-spatial relations enacted by actors, such as MNEs working through broader spatial networks, and regional political actors tied to legal-administrative scalar boundaries over a particular territory, but which also engage in network relations beyond their scalar operation. Through such a perspective it is possible to constantly question and ascribe (disparate) causality to the role of actors, including the internal organisational arrangements of MNEs, in the production of a socially constituted region.

Second, and building upon the above, as space and the region are socially constituted the issues of distance, including 'institutional distance', move beyond physical Cartesian distance. For instance, large physical distances are often superseded by closeness arising from similarities between MNEs and foreign regions in terms of institutional, social-cultural and political arrangements (Beugelsdijk & Frijns, 2010). On the one hand, this suggests greater sensitivity towards the role of different networked relations in MNEs, particularly as subsidiaries are embedded within spatially disparate compossible socio-spatial relations. On the other, the role of actors in (re)constructing, performing and rescinding socio-spatial relations is critical, forming part of the 'structuring principles' that come to produce compossible geographical arrangements.

One way in which to take this forward is to adopt a 'topological' approach that recognises the 'assembling' of 'particular' MNE-regional formations through various socio-spatial relations (see Ong & Collier, 2005; and Palmas (2013) on agribusiness). By 'assemblage' we mean the various historically constituted elements – human actors, practices and non-human objects working through different socio-spatial relations (from the proximate to the distant) – that constitute the creation of certain bounded notions, such as the 'region' (Allen & Cochrane, 2007). Actors construct assemblages with the purpose of aligning actors and objects with particular aims, courses of action and discursive spatial imaginaries (McFarlane & Anderson, 2011). These formations seek to temporarily stabilise 'discursive frames' or actual practices between different agents. 'Stability' is further defined as congruence between tactics, strategies and actual actions of human actors, but they are temporary formations that have to be constantly produced through their performance by actors. These are therefore formations characterised by deliberative practices between actors, such as in the case of 'strategic coupling', formation of regional institutional arrangements, actual relations between MNEs and their suppliers, and the relations between subsidiaries and corporate centres.

For example, Allen and Cochrane (2010) argue that the nation state can act in real time to participate in and influence regional actors, including MNEs and regional governing actors. This means the ability of the state to draw such actors within 'reach', through various actions, such as the use of national laws or intermediates such as management consultants. Thus, state power can act at both a distance and through proximity by means of being assembled within such spatialised political arrangements, and with actors and objects working through other socio-spatial relations, including those situated at lower governing scales, such as local government. One could argue that such real-time topological relations are the essence of the MNE, as an arena in which heterogeneous spatial assemblages are constantly produced with subsidiaries and the various external actors influencing the actions of MNEs, such as regional governments, suppliers and nation state regulatory bodies. As recognised by Yeung and Coe (2015), the latter for example are likely to directly interact with the MNE by way of subsidiaries, practices, objects (e.g. corporate strategies) and events in particular sub-national spaces. Similarly, the knowledge production activities of subsidiaries are likely to encompass both suppliers within close proximity, as well as those at a distance through 'global pipelines' (Morrison, Rabellotti & Zirulia, 2013).

Furthermore, such thinking does in fact build upon Yeung's (2009b) 'entrepreneurial spaces' perspective, encompassing spatialised networked relations that are created by actors through their strategic actions and negotiations with others. In so doing, they create particular spatial assemblage arrangements. Relations can therefore stretch beyond the physical market or operating region of a firm, with corporations therefore working through different geographies (Dicken & Malmberg, 2001). For Yeung (2009b), this suggests the need to reassess the role of agglomeration and clustering factors, since relations at a distance can have a stronger role in corporate entrepreneurship than relations with proximate locational advantages. This requires focusing on the particular actors that are of critical importance in processes of entrepreneurship, rather than focusing on 'entrepreneurial environments' (Zahra & Garvis, 2000). Through a relational approach on entrepreneurial spaces it is therefore possible to 'reveal that entrepreneurs may have divergent strategic objectives and heterogeneous resource repertoires' within the same geographical location (Zahra & Garvis, 2000, p. 215).

This presents a far more advanced understanding of the region, placing the topological practices of actors through various socio-spatial deliberative practices and networked relations at the forefront. In essence, this is to understand that individual geographical relations, such as territorial space, form part of the assembling of particular geographical formations that are social constructs. Such constantly produced regional assemblage formations are likely to be critical given that MNEs must balance internal networks' embeddedness and external embeddedness and responsiveness to host regions and markets (Narula & Dunning, 2010; Meyer et al., 2011). Similarly, subsidiaries seek to be a unique corporate site of knowledge and competences, and thus they have to constantly negotiate with various elements of the corporation to either protect such advantages or mitigate the impact of overspill (Almeida & Phene, 2004).

Conclusion

We have witnessed for some time the divergent development of IB studies and Economic Geography, most notably in terms of the understanding of spatial arenas such as the 'region'. Whilst it has been developed as a core conceptual element of Economic Geography, and particularly in GPN studies, it has remained poorly conceptualised in IB. Correspondingly, IB has significantly advanced our understanding of the changing organisation of the MNE, and the role of subsidiaries in such internal processes. However, they have each increasingly recognised the centrality of the 'network' as a basis of capitalism and the operation of International Business. It is at this point where both Economic Geography and IB can move forward in dialogue around examination of the role of regional assemblages that are produced through practices and deliberations of actors. This would form an important approach to understanding the relational and topological nature of MNEs and the production networks through which they work.

References

Alcácer, J. & Chung, W. (2007) 'Location strategies and knowledge spillovers', *Management Science*, 53, pp. 760–776.

Allen, J. & Cochrane, A. (2007) 'Beyond the territorial fix: Regional Assemblages, Politics and power', *Regional Studies*, 41, pp. 1161–1175.

Allen, J. & Cochrane, A. (2010) 'Assemblages of state power: Topological shifts in the organization of government and politics', *Antipode*, 42, pp. 1071–1089.

Almeida, P. & Phene, A. (2004) 'Subsidiaries and knowledge creation: The influence of the MNC and host country on innovation', *Strategic Management Journal*, 25, pp. 847–864.

Andersson, U. & Forsgren, M. (2000) 'In search of centres of excellence: Network embeddedness and subsidiary roles in multinational corporations', *Management International Review*, 40, pp. 329–350.

Andersson, U., Forsgren, M. & Holm, U. (2007) 'Balancing subsidiary influence in the federative MNC: A business network view' *Journal of International Business Studies*, 38, pp. 802–819.

Beugelsdijk, S. (2007) 'The regional environment and a firm's innovative performance: A plea for a multilevel interactionist approach', *Economic Geography*, 83, pp.181–199.

Beugelsdijk, S. & Frijns, B. (2010) 'A cultural explanation of the foreign bias in international asset allocation', *Journal of Banking and Finance*, 34, pp. 2121–2131.

Beugelsdijk, S., McCann, P. & Mudambi, R. (2010) 'Introduction: Place, space and organization – Economic Geography and the multinational enterprise', *Journal of Economic Geography*, 10, pp. 485–493.

Buckley, P.J. (2009) 'Internalisation thinking: From the multinational enterprise to the global factory', *International Business Review*, 18, pp. 224–235.

Buckley, P.J. & Casson, M. (1976) *The Future of the Multinational Enterprise*. London: Macmillan.

Cantwell, J.A. & Mudambi, R. (2005) 'MNE competence-creating subsidiary mandates', *Strategic Management Journal*, 26, pp. 1109–1128.

Cantwell, J.A. & Santangelo, G.D. (2002) 'M&As and the global strategies of TNCs', *Developing Economies*, 40, pp. 400–434.

Ciabuschi, F., Dellestrand, H. & Martín, O. (2011) 'Internal embeddedness, headquarters involvement, and innovation importance in multinational enterprises', *Journal of Management Studies*, 48, pp. 1612–1639.

Coe, N.M. & Hess, M. (2011) 'Local and regional development: A global production network approach', in Pike, A., Rodríguez-Pose, A. & Tomaney, J. (Eds.), *Handbook of Local and Regional Development*. London: Routledge, pp. 128–138.

Dawley, S. (2011) 'Transnational corporations and local and regional development', in Pike, A., Rodríguez-Pose, A. & Tomaney, J. (Eds.), *Handbook of Local and Regional Development*. London: Routledge, pp. 394–412.

Dicken, P. & Malmberg, A. (2001) 'Firms in territories: A relational perspective', *Economic Geography*, 77, pp. 345–363.

Dimitropoulou, D., Burke, S. & McCann, P. (2008) 'Multinational investment in UK regions', in Tamásy, C. & Taylor, M. (Eds.), *Globalising Worlds and New Economic Configurations*. Farnham, UK: Ashgate.

Dunning, J.H. (1979) 'Toward an eclectic theory of international production: Some empirical tests', *Journal of International Business Studies*, 11, pp. 9–31.

Dunning, J.H. (1988) 'The eclectic paradigm of international production: A restatement and some possible extensions', *Journal of International Business Studies*, 19, pp. 1–31.

Dunning, J.H. (2009) 'Location and the multinational enterprise: John Dunning's thoughts on receiving the *Journal of International Business Studies* 2008 Decade Award', *Journal of International Business Studies*, 40, pp. 20–34.

Dunning, J.H. & Lundan, S. (2008) *Multinational Enterprises and the Global Economy*. Cheltenham, UK: Edward Elgar.

Faulconbridge, J.R., Hall, S. & Beaverstock, J.V. (2008) 'New insights into the internationalization of producer services: Organizational strategies and spatial economies for global headhunting firms', *Environment and Planning A*, 40, pp. 210–234.

Figueiredo, P. (2011) 'The role of dual embeddedness in the innovative performance of MNE subsidiaries: Evidence from Brazil', *Journal of Management Studies*, 48, pp. 417–440.

Forsgren, M., Holm, U. & Johanson, J. (2005) *Managing the Embedded Multinational: A Business Network View*. Cheltenham, UK: Edward Elgar.

Frost, T.S., Birkinshaw, J.M. & Ensign, P.C. (2002) 'Centres of excellence in multinational corporations', *Strategic Management Journal*, 23, pp. 997–1018.

Fuller, C. (2002) After-care and the corporate investment process in Wales and Ireland. Unpublished PhD thesis. Cardiff University, UK.

Fuller, C. (2005) 'Corporate repeat investment and regional institutional capacity: The case of after-care services in Wales', *European Urban and Regional Development Studies*, 12, pp. 5–21.

Hess, M. & Yeung, H W.-C. (2006) 'Whither global production networks in Economic Geography? Past, present and future', *Environment and Planning A*, 38, pp. 1193–1204.

Hodgson, G. (2006) 'What are institutions?' *Journal of Economic Issues*, 40, pp. 1–25.

Hudson, R. (2005) 'Rethinking change in old industrial regions: Reflecting on the experiences of North East England', *Environment and Planning A*, 37, pp. 581–596.

Hudson, R. (2008) 'Cultural political economy meets global production networks: A productive meeting?' *Journal of Economic Geography*, 8, pp. 421–440.

Jones, A. & Search, P. (2009) 'Proximity and power within investment relationships: The case of the UK private equity industry', *Geoforum*, 40, pp. 809–819.

Jones, J. & Wren, C. (2004) 'Inward foreign direct investment and employment: a project-based analysis in North-East England', *Journal of Economic Geography*, 4, pp. 517–544.

Jones, M. & Jessop, B. (2010) 'Thinking state/space incompossibly', *Antipode*, 42, pp. 1119–1149.

MacCann, P. & Iammarino, S. (2013) *Multinationals and Economic Geography: Location and Technology, Innovation*. Cheltenham, UK: Edward Elgar.

MacKinnon, D. (2011) 'Beyond strategic coupling: Reassessing the firm-region nexus in global production networks', *Journal of Economic Geography*, 12, pp. 227–245.

MacKinnon, D. & Phelps, N.A. (2001) 'Regional governance and foreign direct investment: The dynamics of institutional change in Wales and North East England', *Geoforum*, 32, pp. 255–269.

Martin, R. (2010) 'Rethinking path dependence: Beyond lock-in to evolution', *Economic Geography*, 86, pp. 1–27.

Massey, D. (1984) *Spatial Divisions of Labour*. Basingstoke, UK: Macmillan.

McCann, P. & Mudambi, R. (2004) 'The location decision of the multinational enterprise: Some analytical issues', *Growth & Change*, 35, pp. 491–524.

McCann, P. & Mudambi, R. (2005) 'Analytical differences in the economics of geography: The case of the multinational firm', *Environment and Planning A*, 37, pp. 1857–1876.

McFarlane, C. & Anderson, B. (2011) 'Thinking with assemblage', *Area*, 43, pp. 162–164.

Meyer, K.E., Mudambi, R. & Narula, R. (2011) 'Multinational enterprises and local contexts: The opportunities and challenges of multiple embeddedness', *Journal of Management Studies*, 48, pp. 235–252.

Meyer, K.E. & Nguyen, H. (2005) 'Foreign investment strategies and sub-national institutions in emerging markets: Evidence from Vietnam', *Journal of Management Studies*, 42, pp. 63–93.

Morrison, A., Rabellotti, R. & Zirulia, L. (2013) 'When do global pipelines enhance the diffusion of knowledge in clusters?' *Economic Geography*, 89, pp. 77–96.

Mudambi, R. & Venzin, M. (2010) 'The strategic nexus of offshoring and outsourcing decisions', *Journal of Management Studies*, 47, pp. 1510–1533.

Muzio, D., Hodgson, D., Faulconbridge, J., Beaverstock, J. & Hall, S. (2011) 'Towards corporate professionalization: The case of project management, management consultancy and executive search', *Current Sociology*, 59, pp. 443–464.

Narula, R. & Dunning, J.H. (2010) 'Multinational enterprises, development and globalisation: Some clarifications and a research agenda', *Oxford Development Studies*, 38, pp. 263–287.

Ong, A. & Collier, S. (2005) *Global Assemblages: Technology, Politics, and Ethics as Anthropological Problems*. London: Wiley-Blackwell.

Palmas, K. (2013) 'The production of chemical worlds: Territory and field science in global agribusiness', *Culture and Organization*, 19, pp. 227–241.

Papanastassiou, M. & Pearce, R. (2009) *The Strategic Development of Multinationals*. London: Palgrave Macmillan.

Phelps, N.A. (1993) 'Branch plants and the evolving spatial division of labour: A study of material linkage change in the northern region of England', *Regional Studies*, 27, pp. 87–101.

Phelps, N.A. (2008) 'Cluster or capture? Manufacturing foreign direct investment, external economies and agglomeration, *Regional Studies*, 42, pp. 457–473.

Phelps, N.A. & Fuller, C. (2000) 'Multinationals, intracorporate competition, and regional development', *Economic Geography*, 76, pp. 224–243.

Phelps, N.A. & Fuller, C. (2016) 'Inertia and change in multinational enterprise subsidiary capabilities: An evolutionary Economic Geography framework', *Journal of Economic Geography*, 16, pp. 109–130.

Phelps, N.A. & Ozawa, T. (2003) 'Contrasts in agglomeration: Proto-industrial, industrial and post-industrial forms compared', *Progress in Human Geography*, 27, pp. 583–605.

Phene, A. & Almeida, P. (2008) 'Innovation in multinational subsidiaries: The role of knowledge assimilation and subsidiary capabilities', *Journal of International Business Studies*, 39, pp. 901–919.

Rugman, A. (2005). *The Regional Multinationals: MNEs and 'Global' Strategic Management*. Cambridge, UK: Cambridge University Press.

Rugman, A., Verbeke, A. & Yuan, W. (2010) 'Re-conceptualizing Bartlett and Ghoshal's classification of national subsidiary roles in the multinational enterprise', *Journal of Management Studies*, 48, pp. 253–277.

Schatzki, T. (2010) *The Timespace of Human Activity: On Performance, Society, and History as Indeterminate Teleological Events*. Lanham, MD: Lexington Books.

Sethi, D., Guisinger S.E., Phelan S.E. & Berg D.M. (2003) 'Trend in foreign direct investment flows: A theoretical and empirical analysis', *Journal of International Business Studies*, 34, pp. 315–326

Sunley, P. (2008) 'Relational Economic Geography: A partial understanding or a new paradigm?' *Economic Geography*, 84, pp. 1–26.

Tavares, A. & Teixeira, A. (2006) *Multinationals, Clusters and Innovation Does Public Policy Matter?* Basingstoke, UK: Macmillan.

Walker, R. (1989) 'A requiem for corporate geography: New directions in industrial organization, the production of place and uneven development', *Geografiska Annaler*, 71, pp. 43–68.

Weller, S.A. (2009) 'Shifting spatialities of power: The case of Australasian aviation', *Geoforum*, 40, pp. 790–799.

Williams, C. & Lee, S.H. (2011) 'Political heterarchy and dispersed entrepreneurship in the MNC', *Journal of Management Studies*, 48, pp. 1243–1268.

Yamin, M. & Andersson, U. (2011) 'Subsidiary importance in the MNC: What role does internal embeddedness play?' *International Business Review*, 20, pp. 151–162.

Yang, C. (2009) 'Strategic coupling of regional development in global production networks: Redistribution of Taiwanese personal computer investment from the Pearl River Delta to the Yangtze River Delta, China', *Regional Studies*, 43, pp. 385–408.

Yang, D.Y. & Coe, N. (2009) 'The governance of global production networks and regional development: A case study of Taiwanese PC production networks', *Growth and Change*, 40, pp. 30–53.

Yeung, H. (2009a) 'Regional development and the competitive dynamics of global production networks: An East Asian perspective', *Regional Studies*, 43, pp. 325–351.

Yeung, H. (2009b) 'Transnationalizing entrepreneurship: A critical agenda for Economic Geography', *Progress in Human Geography*, 33, pp. 210–235

Yeung, H. & Coe, N. (2015) 'Toward a dynamic theory of global production networks', *Economic Geography*, 91, pp. 29–58.

Zahra, S.A. & Garvis, D.M. (2000) 'Entrepreneurship and firm performance: The moderating effect of international environmental hostility', *Journal of Business Venturing*, 15, pp. 469–492.

14

CITIES AND INTERNATIONAL BUSINESS

Insights from cross-disciplinary perspectives

Gary Cook and Naresh Pandit

Introduction

Since the publication of Porter's *The Competitive Advantage of Nations* (1990) and the landmark article of John Dunning (1998), there has been a surge of interest in the sub-national geographic scale as a key unit of analysis when considering the geographic pattern of multinational activity. Likewise, the ideas of Economic Geographers, especially Dicken (2015), have also encouraged a more fine-grained analysis of where, exactly, firms will choose to locate particular activities. Cities as a spatial unit of analysis have not been absent in the field of International Business (IB), indeed Hymer (1976) wrote about cities; however, cities have not been prominent. This is changing, as it is being realised more broadly in IB that cities are distinctive places which play a vital role in the location of MNE activities and, indeed, in strategy formulation and implementation. Goerzen, Asmussen and Nielsen (2013) is a particularly important contribution, stating powerfully the case that cities matter. The issue is also gaining in importance, given the continuation of a process of urbanisation which already sees over half of the world's population living in cities (Scott, 2012). As Scott (2001, 2012) argues, cities are of huge economic significance as places generating disproportionate amounts of profit, wages and land rents.

The aim of this chapter is both to articulate why cities matter and to explore the ways in which approaches in IB can be informed by perspectives from Economic Geography (EG) and Urban Economics (UE). The insights of other fields are needed in order to get a better grip on how these highly complex phenomena work. The chapter is also an introductory guide to the literature, identifying key ideas and findings which need to be born in mind by IB researchers. It provides an entry route to those seeking to immerse themselves more fully in these complementary perspectives. The focus on EG and UE is not to gainsay the importance of insights from other fields, such as Urban Studies, Planning or Sociology; however, space constraints necessitate a partial view. There is no doubt that EG has become an influence on thinking in IB (Jones, 2016) and particular attention will be paid to this field. Due consideration will be given to some of the fundamental problems which ensue from trying to combine insights from separate fields, which have rather different research objectives, and which build on different epistemological assumptions. No attempt will be made to reconcile those differences; however, researchers need to be aware of them when spanning different fields. No chapter on cities would be complete without reference to the seminal work of Jane Jacobs, which will be treated as a standalone item.

Cities are inherently agglomerated. As a prelude to the discussion of cities, it is worth a quick recap on key theories about the benefits which exist in particular agglomerations or clusters. These benefits are recognised in all three of the IB, EG and UE literatures, and this provides a degree of overlap in the conceptual frameworks employed in each field. The classic Marshallian (1890) externalities are the formation of a large labour pool, which is associated with the development of highly specialised skills through the division of labour, the formation of a group of specialised suppliers, and knowledge spillovers which stimulate innovation and the dissemination of best practice. These are held to be specific to particular industries. Sometimes contrasted with these, although they are not mutually exclusive, are urbanisation economies, usually credited to Jacobs (1969), which are not exclusive to particular industries, but are instead based on the scale and variety of economic activity. Jacobs also places emphasis on exposure to imports, which can be conduits for competition and the diffusion of technology. Scale, variety and imports can constitute an environment which stimulates competition and innovation. It is important to note that, whilst elements of localisation and urbanisation economies may be present in particular cities, not all "clusters" are of the same type, and different cities may be based upon different mixes of these two factors, as well as other foundations such as an industrial complex (Gordon & McCann, 2000), or a strong state presence (Markusen, 1996).

Some key differences between IB, EG and UE

This section is being placed first in order to frame the presentation of the bulk of the material in this chapter. These differences are better borne in mind before delving into the various literatures, otherwise misunderstanding and, occasionally, bafflement are likely to ensue. There is no claim that this is an exhaustive treatment of the differences, just an attempt to flag up some very important and fundamental ones.

The basic purpose of IB is to explain how and why economic activity takes place across borders. Within IB, the central unit of analysis is the firm and the multinational enterprise has been a dominant focus of enquiry. Increasing focus has also been placed on relationships between firms as we have entered what Dunning (1995) termed the era of alliance capitalism. IB has a more sophisticated view of the firm than EG or UE, paying much greater attention in particular to the internal processes of firms. IB also has a greater interest in the particularity of specific firms than EG. This is not to say that firms are unimportant in EG, or that geographers are not interested in what goes on inside firms. Just as there has emerged a more fine-grained treatment of the firm, so there has emerged a more fine-grained treatment of space, with the focus on nation states being complemented with attention to the sub-national scale. Nevertheless, it remains the mainstream view in IB that national borders matter a lot (Beugelsdijk & Mudambi, 2013), a view from which this chapter does not dissent.

Just as IB has a stronger emphasis on the particularity of specific firms, so EG has a greater interest in the particularity of specific places, which is integral to a meaningful definition of space from an EG perspective. EG is concerned with the spatial patterning of economic activity and cross-border activity has been an important focus of research, though not as strongly as in IB. Space, defined at different scales from the local to the global, has been the central unit of analysis, rather than the firm, although firms do play an important role in EG and much has been written about MNEs. The black box of the firm has been opened up in different ways in EG (Taylor & Asheim, 2001), though in their view the task is not complete, even for the questions that are primarily for geographers. EG has placed far more importance on explaining why particular places are more "successful" than others, rather than why particular firms are more successful than others. Clearly, the two things are not entirely separate. This is reflected in a particular concern with regimes of uneven development, and its implications, such as creating an urban underclass, and informing regional and local development policy. EG has a greater interest in articulating what is unique and distinctive about particular places, whereas IB and UE are inclined to look for more general regularities. EG has a more sophisticated conception of space than does IB or UE (McCann & Mudambi, 2005) and recognises that in order to explain activity at a particular location, analysis must identify the simultaneous influence of processes operating at a range of spatial scales, which may vary from the highly localised to the global. In addition, space is not viewed as coming in discrete steps, such as local or regional, but as being continuous (Dicken & Malmberg, 2001) and not defined by administrative boundaries (Beugelsdijk & Mudambi, 2013). EG has taken a more critical perspective than IB and, partly for this reason, Marxist perspectives have been more influential than in IB.

Other important differences arise. Economics has had a much stronger influence in IB than it has in EG (and, clearly, it is central to UE). Early work in IB was strongly influenced by models in International Economics, particularly those concerned with international trade and international factor movements (McCann & Mudambi, 2005). Such formal models do not deal with space in a way which would be recognised by geographers (Brakman & Garretsen, 2003). The development of the internalisation approach in IB (Buckley & Casson, 1976) was strongly informed by transaction cost economics (Williamson, 1975). Ideas from industrial organisation have been influential in the analysis of competition between firms (Caves, 1982). More recently, the resource-based view (Wernerfelt, 1984; Barney, 1991), again strongly rooted in economics (Penrose, 1959), has come to be a standard workhorse for theorising and analysis in IB. EG has, for an extended period, been far more strongly rooted in sociology, having rejected economics, and the neoclassical paradigm in particular, for two key reasons. First, it was held to be poorly suited to the questions that economic geographers were interested in (Martin, 1999), with the role of institutions being a more prominent object of interest, being central both to the definition of space (e.g. what is local is defined by the degree of homogeneity of institutions) and the explanation of why some places are more economically vibrant than others. Second, it was rejected on fundamental epistemological grounds. Particular exception has been taken to: methodological individualism; "economic man", the hyper-rationality assumption and the optimisation approach; Popperian falsificationism; and instrumentalism (the view that the value of theories is related to their success in explaining and predicting, not in terms of whether they are true or false). It has rejected the idea that economics can be or ought to be a science, rather than a social science, as an intellectual dead end. In EG, economic activity and economic actors are viewed as being inherently rooted in particular social processes. Objects in natural science obey immutable laws of physics. There are no such laws governing human behaviour, which is contingent on social processes, and human actors can change and also have agency to change the social systems within which they operate in a way objects in natural science cannot (Sayer, 1992). Rather than falsificationism, EG is rooted in realism (Martin, 1999), an epistemological approach which has gained very limited traction in economics (Hausman, 1998) and, by extension, IB and UE.

UE is also distinct from both IB and EG. It is much more closely wedded to neoclassical economics and relies more on mathematical models and the rationality assumption in theorising. The central units of analysis are the city and the metropolitan region, and the key questions of interest are: why do cities exist and what explains the relative growth rates of cities (and by extension their absolute size at a point in time) (Glaeser, 2000)? At a fundamental level, a key explanation has been that cities economise on transaction and transportation costs. This has historically been centred on production and transportation costs and transaction costs in labour markets (where the efficiency of search and match are still key considerations). More recently, attention has focused on transaction costs as they affect the flow of ideas, and here there are direct links with endogenous growth theory in macroeconomics (Barro & Sala-i-Martin, 1995), with its emphasis on knowledge spillovers. UE operates at a much more aggregate level of analysis than either IB or EG and is concerned with processes that happen in broad systems of labour migration, residential settlement and markets for factors of production. Nevertheless, the broad factors which make a city relatively more or less successful will be influential on firm location decisions and are affected by those firm location decisions, and so questions that concern UE scholars are also of interest to IB (and EG) scholars.

It is important to note that there are many areas of overlap between EG and IB, which underlies the current interest in integrating the insights of both fields. There has been much less tendency for IB and UE to draw more closely together; however, the argument of this chapter is that IB scholars should be more cognisant of the UE literature. As already stated, these fields have an interest in the spatial organisation of international economic activity and make use of the same conceptual frameworks of Marshallian externalities and Jacobs' externalities when explaining the dynamism and attraction of particular agglomerations. IB and EG place emphasis on the importance of institutions for framing economic activity, and the importance of institutions is recognised in UE. All three recognise that industry matters. All three recognise that place matters and so reject the "world is flat"/"death of geography" thesis (Musil, 2013). All three have a particular interest in innovation and its spatial organisation. The widespread embrace of the institutional view in IB (Peng et al., 2009) goes some way to addressing what would be a fundamental epistemological divide between economic geographers and IB, that social processes are crucial to explaining what differentiates one place from another, both in terms of dynamic trajectories and comparisons at a single point in time (Martin, 1999).

Location in IB

The conception of location in IB remains strongly influenced by Dunning's Eclectic Paradigm (Dunning, 1980), which articulated the fundamental reasons which would induce firms to do business across borders. In a landmark article, Dunning (1998) identified that location had become a neglected factor in IB research and argued that more attention should be given to explaining location decisions at sub-national scale. The original motives of seeking markets, seeking natural resources, seeking efficiency (or low costs) was expanded by Dunning to include strategic asset seeking. All four of these can be related to agglomeration effects. Under the market-seeking motive, firms may or may not be drawn to a particular cluster. In some cases, the most pressing motive may be to jump over a tariff wall (very important in the run-up to the single European market) or to establish commitment to a particular national market. Here the imperative is to move across a national border, which may or may not be associated with a further motive to join a particular cluster. In other cases, location in a particular cluster may be key for winning customers. An example here may be getting a location in the City of London in financial services, which brings credibility to the firm and also gives more direct access to a huge focus of demand. Clusters may be associated with lower costs, although they are not necessarily, relating to the efficiency-seeking motive. It is a consistent finding that productivity is higher in clusters. There are three key dimensions to the strategic asset-seeking motive. One is access to technological know-how, and it has been recognised that there has been a marked shift whereby MNEs are dispersing their R&D efforts in order to tap into particular innovation hot-spots (Belderbos, Fukao & Iwasa, 2009). This is linked to a second important consideration, access to the most highly skilled labour, which in some cases may be scientists. The City of London is a classic example, as it has a labour market with truly global reach, and the sheer scale of the labour market means it is possible to find people with rare and highly specialised skills (Taylor et al., 2003). A third motive, and one which has not been as strongly emphasised as it might, is access to strategic thinking. As Amin and Thrift (1992) articulated, key metropolises, such as London, New York, Tokyo and Paris, are crucial arenas in which business elites make sense of the changing world and formulate strategy. Another important aspect is access to regulators, policy-makers and diplomats, who can provide expert information on crucial political factors shaping the environment in which strategy must be formulated and enacted. The ability to lobby politicians, civil servants and regulators is also very important.

There is comparatively little literature devoted centrally to cities in IB. An important recent contribution is Goerzen, Asmussen and Nielsen (2013), which sets out some important ideas regarding how and why city-regions are important to the research agenda in IB. The paper makes appeal to several key ideas in EG (see later for some further detail on these). It recognises the importance of the global hierarchy of cities and the concept of Global Cities at its apex. This will have a bearing on whether an MNE will see a strategic advantage in locating to a particular city and which activities will be sited there. Indeed, the paper points out the disproportionate tendency for MNEs to locate subsidiaries in global cities (see the following section on world cities). Laamanen, Simula and Torstila (2012) also demonstrate a clear tendency for the European HQs of MNEs to moved closer to national capitals. The key attraction of such global cities is their high level of connectivity in the international economy and the presence of key decision makers who are able to exert influence on the global economic system. Another key advantage of global cities for MNEs is argued to be the fact that MNEs are apt to be less burdened by the liability of foreignness in such sophisticated and cosmopolitan environments (Nachum & Wymbs, 2005; Castellani & Santangelo, 2016). Drawing on the ideas of Sassen (1991), the range and sophistication of business services are seen as important influences on MNE location decisions. A crucial feature of these high-level business services is that they often require mixes of skills to be assembled to deliver highly tailored projects to specific clients to very tight time deadlines (Scott et al., 2001; Taylor et al., 2003). Goerzen, Asmussen and Nielsen (2013) assert the high importance of access to highly skilled labour and the importance of city amenities in attracting such workers to the labour pool. They also add some qualifications to the attraction of global cities. They tend to be high cost locations and there is a danger of unwanted leakage of proprietary information in such densely networked places. Some activities may be better located outside the core of the city region, for example manufacturing, which has a large footprint. Location in the core is more strongly associated with market seeking and information seeking.

Jane Jacobs

A little more will be said about the work of Jane Jacobs (1961, 1969, 1985), which has informed work both on agglomeration in metropolitan areas and agglomeration more generally. For Jacobs it is cities, not nations, which are the "salient entities of economic life". The economic fortunes of nations (and indeed the global economy) turns on the dynamism or otherwise of its cities and, by extension, city regions. Cities are the wellspring of innovation and growth and exert an influence well beyond their administrative boundaries both within and between nations. Jacobs demonstrates that cities can come to enter either virtuous circles of self-sustaining growth and dynamism or alternatively enter cycles of decline, with trade and innovation providing what she terms the "master economic processes". Innovation, doing something new, is more important in explaining the success of cities than static efficiency (Florida et al., 2012). The key process by which cities enter into a cycle of dynamic growth is identified as the capacity of the city to develop the ability to produce for itself items it once imported and then, in turn, to export those goods. It is essential to recognise that imports in Jacobs' sense are goods which come from outside the city, whether from elsewhere within the national economy or from other countries. The process of import replacement feeds a virtuous circle in two ways. First, the emergence of new industries in the city creates skills and knowledge which can be applied in other lines of activity, many of which cannot be foreseen in advance of the innovation, which brings diverse knowledge and skills together in novel ways. Second, the new activity and especially its export activity provide the wherewithal to pay for a greater volume and variety of imports, which can themselves provide the opportunity for yet more indigenous firms to emerge to replace the new imports and so on. Looking a little more deeply behind the dynamic development of vibrant cities, Jacobs identifies a number of important processes:

1 The spin-off of and formation of new enterprises as entrepreneurs spot new market niches which they can fill.
2 As the city prospers, so it will draw in more labour.
3 As cities grow they develop economic diversity which makes it more likely that they will have the flexibility and versatility to develop new import-replacing and export industries.
4 Proximity in cities is associated with dense networks of symbiotic relationships.
5 Cities develop positive externalities on the demand side in terms of density and diversity of demand.

Jacobs does identify that one consequence of economic success is for land costs in the city to rise, but argues that successful firms are able to adapt to this.

The key literatures on cities and city regions in EG

There are several distinct literatures in EG, each giving an important perspective on what makes a city or city-region attractive as a location and, more specifically, the link between certain types of city and MNEs. Space constraints allow only a focus on key works and concepts.

World cities

The literature on world cities is highly important. World cities are of singular importance because of the international and strategic business activities which take place within them, and MNEs could not operate the strategies they do without such cities and the services they can call upon there (Knox & Taylor, 1995). By the same token, world cities could not be as they are without the presence of MNEs. World cities are endowed with complex and powerful economic, cultural and political attributes. The landmark contribution is Hall's (1966) *The World Cities*, which identified a set of cities in which a disproportionate amount of both political and economic work was done. In this account the emphasis was on the cities themselves, without importance being placed on the relationship between cities, which is emphasised in the more recent literature in EG. What Hall did identify was a number of key features which these cities shared. They were major political centres, transport hubs, centres for financial and professional services, and also centres for luxury consumption and entertainment. Hall also identified the preference of MNEs to locate activities in these cities. These remain important insights.

Another seminal contribution was Friedman's (1986) "The world cities hypothesis". There were two very important aspects of this paper, especially from the point of view of this chapter. Friedman emphasised the important interconnection between the status of these cities and their relationship with the strategies of MNEs. He also identified that cities were linked with other cities in a complex spatial hierarchy, therefore it would be misleading to try to consider cities in isolation. This view of cities as important nodes in a globalised capitalist system is an expression of a relational perspective, which is now central to the understanding of cities in EG (Scott et al., 2001). What is more, as Allen (2010) argues, cities at the top of the hierarchy do not simply exercise power as domination, they exercise the power to make things happen, which is to the advantage of other cities in their network and, important for the perspective of this chapter, to the advantage of firms that are located there. Key firms, major MNEs, are also important sources of the power of cities. In general cities are part of a division of labour in which cities are the location for higher-level management and service functions (Turok, 2004), particularly those with an international focus in world cities. These themes identified by Friedman have obvious relevance to central concerns in IB regarding the spatial organisation of MNEs and the nature of the governance relation between HQs and subsidiaries. In a later work, Friedman (2001) set out some of the key factors which would influence the importance of a city in the global economic system: high levels of "social capital", facilitating smooth coordination by promoting trust, cooperation and information flows; high levels of human capital in the labour force; a well-developed economic and social infrastructure; and directly productive physical capital. In some cases, these factors would be augmented by natural and environmental resource endowments. These internal factors promoting dynamism needed to be held in balance, he argued, with external connectivity.

Two other highly influential works are *The Rise of the Network Society* (Castells, 2000) and *The Global City* (Sassen, 1991), the latter being clearly influenced by the work of Hymer. Both emphasised the flow of money through major world cities in circuits of international finance. In Castells' work, this was used in conjunction with the idea of the city as a space of flows, i.e. that the importance of the city was determined not by the stock of assets there, but by the volume of economically significant flows that passed through it (clearly, the two things are related). These flows have three critical dimensions: transportation and communication infrastructure; what Castells terms social organisational, which relates to the work made possible by network connections between cities; and the behaviour of transnational elites and the services provided to them, particularly in the spheres of wealth management and luxury consumption. In this respect, Beugelsdijk and Mudambi (2013) suggest that cultural distance between cities may be less, due to a homogenisation among urban elites. Sassen, more than Castells, emphasised the importance of advanced producer services in global cities. Indeed, Sassen identifies global cities as being highly important command points for leading MNEs, and key strategic sites for the coordination of their widely dispersed corporate network and the planning of production, distribution, innovation and finance. The key producer services are argued to be law, accounting, finance, PR, consulting and advertising. She stresses that in global cities an essential feature is that these key services are all in close proximity (see Taylor et al., 2003 for an example of the City of London).

Building on this idea of the importance of flows of economic activity between cities, the "Globalisation and World Cities" (GaWC) studies produced a ranking of cities based on the analysis of such flows. Beaverstock, Taylor and Smith (1999) produced a ranking which quickly became a standard reference point, albeit that it is based on stocks rather than flows of services. This was based on a count of offices of differing status (prime, major or minor) in advertising, accounting, banking and law. The GaWC studies have been influential and have identified a number of important features which are associated with cities of greater importance in the world hierarchy. One was the importance of being connected to other cities, asserting the relational perspective. This challenges the notion that cities are in competition with each other. What is more, the connections between cities are, to some extent, the outcome of the location strategies of MNEs, with the location of HQ functions being particularly significant (Taylor et al., 2002). This external connectivity is especially forceful when combined with powerful agglomeration externalities within the city (Taylor, 2012). The studies argued that advanced producer services firms were the key sub-nodal actors and that their locational activities were decisive in influencing the status of cities within the global hierarchy.

The literature on world cities has clear relevance to the research agenda in IB. They are fundamental to the spatial organisation of MNEs, a point also emphasised in the literature on global city regions discussed in the following section (Scott, 2001). It bears on the issue of how large and geographically dispersed MNEs are governed. This is not simply a question of where and how HQ functions, which relate to global, regional or national HQs, are placed, or what type of relationship is established between those dispersed HQ functions and subsidiaries, but also recognises that those HQ functions need inputs from external specialist business services in order to fulfil their functions. The importance of the external network connections of cities is an area that has been underexplored generally (Taylor, 2012), and this is particularly true within the IB literature.

The regional world

The focus on regions has been long-standing in EG. The mid 1990s, however, saw a strong assertion of the primacy of regions over nation states. In some cases, cities are not centre stage in this literature; in others they are given more prominence (Scott & Storper, 2003). As Scott and Storper (2003, p. 581) state:

> The most striking forms of agglomeration in evidence today are the super-agglomerations or city-regions that have come into being all over the world in the last few decades . . . These city-regions are locomotives of the national economies within which they are situated, in that they are the sites of dense masses of interrelated economic activities that also typically have high levels of productivity by reason of their jointly-generated agglomeration economies and their innovative potentials.

One particularly influential work, which has prompted the title for this sub-section, was Storper's (1997) *The Regional World*. Storper argued that dynamic regions manifested a "holy trinity" of technology, organisation and territories. Innovation was argued to be key for dynamism, an idea also articulated by Florida (1995), who argued that high technology firms together with MNEs (these two often overlap) were the key economic actors in successful city regions. Storper argued that developments in information and communication technologies enabled MNEs to coordinate activities across wider space more efficiently and effectively, thus amplifying the attraction of particular city regions. Scott (1996) argued that the focus on privileged regions was particularly characteristic of high-technology manufacturing, design-intensive consumer goods and financial services. In addition, Storper (1997) stressed the importance of what he termed "relational assets", which were local norms and conventions that promoted smooth coordination and cooperation among locally embedded actors. Building on this, Storper developed the very influential concept of "untraded interdependencies", which refers to linkages between firms that are not based on market exchange. These are highly important in mediating the ability of firms to capitalise on the various externalities potentially available in dynamic city regions.

A strong theme in writing in the regional world literature is that much depends on the quality of the labour force. Cities are also important locations within which skills are developed and workers socialised (Scott, 2012). A strong connection was made somewhat later with the ability of particular types of city to attract very highly skilled labour, which is particularly important in innovative, knowledge-intensive and creative industries, by Florida (2002) in *The Creative Class* (see also Hall, 2000; Mommas, 2004). Nevertheless, as Scott (2012) points out, cities cannot prosper simply by being nice places to live, they have to provide employment opportunities.

Storper (2013) addresses the question of the dynamics of city development and why it is that some successful cities continue to be so, others decline (absolutely, as well as relatively in some cases), and yet others come to greater prominence through entering a process of unusually rapid growth. How such changes in trajectory come about remains a largely unanswered question, in the face of which Storper makes the case for an inter-disciplinary approach, including economics, EG, regional science, UE and economic sociology, but making no mention of IB. He further argues that the processes which underlie dynamic city regions are not easy to imitate, therefore there are no simplistic policy formulas.

The regional world literature links with IB research focuses on innovation and strategic asset seeking. It emphasises the importance of highly skilled labour pools and institutions which promote the circulation of knowledge and ideas, as well as sustaining cooperation among firms. It is also relevant to questions regarding the rising importance of emerging economies and the MNEs that have grown up in them. Scott (2012) argues that there is a particular tendency for cognitive-cultural work to gravitate to larger cities. As such, work becomes more important, not least within the attempts by firms to achieve competitive advantage, then there will be a further positive dynamic between city size, attractiveness to MNEs and city growth.

The relational and evolutionary turns

The importance of the relational perspective has already been pointed out, that one cannot understand the significance of particular places within the global economic system, or their degree of dynamism and innovation, without taking into account their connections to other places. These connections are forged through the agency of particular actors in each location, which can generate processes that reproduce those connections (Dicken & Malmberg, 2001). This has been strongly asserted by Boggs and Rantisi (2003), who argue that connectivity is more important than a particular spatial scale in explaining why some regions are more dynamic than others. MNEs are identified as particularly important conduits connecting locations by channelling flows of people, ideas and money (Bathelt, Malmberg & Maskell, 2004). Thus external connectivity and dense local processes of agglomeration *in cities* can be mutually reinforcing (Rozenblat, 2010). A relational perspective is also an important feature of the Global Production Network (GPN) perspective in EG and one which distinguishes it from the Global Commodity Chain and Global Value Chain perspectives, which have been influential in thinking in IB (Coe, Dicken & Hess, 2008). One important component of the GPN perspective is the importance of cities as locations where control and coordination of such networks takes place. Importantly, Coe et al. (2008) identify that little is really known about how, exactly, connections between nodes operate at the level of actors and how they actually solve the coordination problem faced by real-life MNEs.

The evolutionary turn (Boschma & Lambooy, 1999; Boschma, 2007) is another important perspective, albeit that it does not tend to place particular emphasis on cities as significant places. This literature is concerned with factors which influence the long-run prospects for particular places. Being rooted in evolutionary economics (Nelson & Winter, 1982), it places importance on random factors which may start a process of path-dependent cumulative causation that sets particular places on a trajectory of sustained growth. Like many other literatures referred to in this review, it also places particular importance on the accumulation of human capital over time.

This literature does not, in general, focus on the particular characteristics of cities as places, nevertheless it does acknowledge that the size of an agglomeration and the size of the businesses services sector are important components of dynamic regions (Boschma & Lambooy, 1999). This has some correspondence with what is argued in both the World Cities and UE literatures. The evolutionary turn literature relates to Vernon's (1966) idea about the importance of industry life cycles in the patterns of production and trade internationally. It is particularly pertinent in an era in which new locations for production are going through rapid phases of evolution. A good example would be China, which quickly established itself as a preferred site for production in a number of industries and, within a comparatively short space of time, has seen that advantage pass onto other economies such as Vietnam.

Key ideas from UE

Given the focus on cities as particular locations which contribute disproportionately to the creation of wealth and economic growth over time, and which can be highly attractive to MNEs, it is an obvious step to see what light UE can shed on the key characteristics and processes which explain the relative success of different cities. The central paradigm in the UE field is the spatial equilibrium concept (Glaeser & Gottlieb, 2009). A spatial equilibrium will only exist when there is equilibrium in the labour and housing markets and when there is "migration equilibrium" (i.e. no incentive for migration). This is simple and stylised, yet it is also rich and captures complex interdependencies which are absent from the other literatures reviewed in this chapter, which generally ignore the housing market altogether and have very little of substance to say about processes in labour markets and migration. This is a serious lacuna in the EG literature, given the importance placed on attracting labour to key cities. Another connection that the UE literature makes is that the presence of deep labour pools can serve to attract firms in a variety of different industries, which demand labour of the same particular type, e.g. knowledge workers or creatives. A simple example here would be the decision taken some years ago by Ford UK to relocate its design team from Dagenham to Soho, the latter being a cutting-edge hub in design and the creative industries, but insignificant as a cluster in the car industry. The UE literature makes a stronger connection between the formation of deep labour pools, with a finer division of labour and higher amounts of very specialised human capital, and the generation of ideas and innovation. It also traces feedback loops between innovativeness and the attraction of high quality labour (Black & Henderson, 1999).

The existence of both Jacobs' and Marshallian externalities feature prominently in this literature, although there has been an ongoing debate as to which is relatively the more important (Hoover, 1948; Glaeser et al., 1992; Henderson, 1996; Viladecans-Marsal, 2004). There is also importance placed on the quality of labour and human capital (Rauch, 1993; Glaeser et al., 1992). Dense urban environments ease the process of search and match and reduce transaction costs by raising competition and facilitating the formation of trust (Venables, 2011). Access to high levels of human capital both provides an incentive for firms to locate to a particular city and also increases the private incentive of individuals to invest further in their human capital (Black & Henderson, 1999). The ability of complex and tacit information to flow more easily in cities is compatible with the common observation that creative and ideas-based industries typically agglomerate in urban centres (Scott, 2000). These insights once more point towards a positive feedback loop which will propel city development.

This literature has identified a positive and persistent correlation between city size and city density and higher productivity (Sveikauskas, 1975; Rigby & Essletzbichler, 2002). Glaeser and Gottlieb (2009) suggest that the productivity advantages of cities are fundamental for their existence and are the basis on which labour can be attracted by the wage premium that they are paid in cities. This can itself be a source of positive feedback as more labour raises density, which raises productivity (Ciccone & Hall, 1990). Workers are also better able to learn from others in cities, and this has been associated with a permanent rise in their productivity (Lee & Rodriquez-Pose, 2013). There is also evidence of a selection effect, in that workers with higher levels of human capital will be disproportionately attracted to cities with higher average levels of human capital and hence productivity (Borjas, Bronars & Trejo, 1992). Rauch (1993) estimates that for each additional year of average education in US cities, total factor productivity rises by 2.8 per cent, consistent with other estimates. This shows that there is a direct connection between levels of human capital and productivity. Glaeser, Kolko and Saiz (2001) identify four critical urban amenities which will help attract people to live there: a wide variety of goods and services (particularly live performance venues and restaurants); a pleasing physical environment; good public services; and fast transportation links (which may be substituted for by high quality living space close to the central business district). Venables (2011) has also argued that cities, because they are typified by dense networks, also have particularly efficient labour markets, given that these networks generate important information about the quality of particular individuals, who will acquire particular reputations. High levels of labour mobility in dense labour markets, including the easier ability to found spin outs, is another source of advantage in cities (Wolfe & Gertler, 2004).

UE recognises the phenomenon of firms locating HQs in particular cities, which may be remote from their production facilities. The essential trade-off is between better access to information and the ability to outsource service functions against a reduced ability to directly monitor operations (Henderson & Ono, 2008). They note that where a firm has widely dispersed production facilities, then the strategic consideration will favour access to information and ability to outsource service functions, which concords with the viewpoint of the World Cities literature. In delivering services at a particular location, the service provider may draw on expertise at a range of its locations. Information seeking will create an incentive to be located close to the HQs of other firms, and this is particularly the case for larger firms. This literature contrasts with the World Cities and IB literature in that it squarely faces the question that firms need to decide the scale and scope of their HQ functions, not just their location. As Henderson and Ono (2008) point out, only 5 per cent of the firms in their sample had HQs entirely separate from their operations, but that these tended to be overwhelmingly large firms, and specifically large multinationals. The locational preference for large cities is explicitly linked to the strong need for coordination that such firms have.

One thing the UE literature brings out, which is not seen so sharply in either the IB or EG literatures, is the connection between the colocation of small numbers of inventors in cities and the propensity to foster major innovations. It also lays more emphasis on superior rates of entrepreneurship in cities (Di Giacinto et al., 2014). Related to this is the idea of the "nursery city", which reflects the observation that entirely new industries are often formed in metropolitan areas. The reasons why this may be so are easy to understand. Metropolitan areas do foster the generation of ideas, they have high levels of human capital and specialised labour skills, they are a focus for sophisticated demand and they have a rich array of specialised suppliers of inputs and specialised business services. Here there are echoes of Vernon (1966). As more firms are drawn into a particular location, however, centrifugal forces driven by congestion and land costs start to rise (Anas, 2004).

The UE literature contains insights for a variety of questions in IB related to choice of location, particularly strategic asset seeking, given the link between particular cities and deep pools of highly skilled and creative labour, and the association between key cities and innovation. The higher productivity in larger cities also speaks to the efficiency motive for FDI. It also provides a more compelling account of why large labour pools form and why large cities and higher population density in cities are associated with higher levels of productivity. One very important caveat regarding the usefulness of ideas and conceptual and analytical frameworks from UE, is that for IB they are too stylised to meaningfully represent large, complex, multilocational firms like MNEs (McCann & Mudambi, 2005). Firms in UE theory are not just black boxes, but highly stylised representations at a single point in space.

Conclusion

This brief survey indicates that there are good reasons for IB scholars to think carefully about cities and to bring them into centre stage as a unit of analysis. Two key lessons emerge from a consideration of the EG literature. First, dynamic regions are first and foremost *city regions* and that looking, for example, at the presence of Marshallian and Jacobs externalities, without considering the importance of the city context in which they arise is to give an incomplete and inaccurate picture. Second, city regions and their importance to, and interconnection with, MNEs needs to be understood within a relational perspective. Cities are not discrete entities, and an important part of what makes cities what they are is their relationship with other cities. Those relationships are intimately connected with networks formed by MNEs. This suggests an important research agenda for IB scholars and one which might fruitfully be undertaken as interdisciplinary work with economic geographers primarily, but to which UE can make some useful contributions. One obvious question is what is it that MNEs actually do in cities positioned differently in the global hierarchy of cities? How do MNEs decide which activities to perform in which cities, and how does this relate to corporate strategies? What is the relative importance of the city and the nation in deciding where MNE activities in cities are located? What are the key processes by which location in particular cities aids the formulation and execution of strategies by MNEs? How is the coordination of MNE activities across its geographic range of operations actually carried out, and how important are the coordination activities conducted from particular cities with particular positions in the global hierarchy? How do MNEs connect the cities in which they operate? What is the relationship between "production" MNEs and advanced business services in major cities? How important are MNEs relative to other factors in generating global cities and/or in intensifying cycles of decline in "failing" cities? What are the processes by which deep and highly skilled labour pools form in cities, and what role do MNEs play in those processes? What is the evolutionary path of emerging economy MNEs in terms of which cities they locate key functions in compared to MNEs from advanced economies? What explains the evolution of emerging economy cities to particular places within the global hierarchy of cities?

References

Allen, J. (2010) 'Powerful city networks: more than connections, less than domination and control', *Urban Studies*, 47, pp. 2895–2911.

Amin, A. & Thrift, N. (1992) 'Neo-Marshallian nodes in global networks', *International Journal of Urban and Regional Research*, 16, pp. 571–587.

Anas, A. (2004) 'Vanishing cities: What does the new Economic Geography imply about the efficiency of urbanization?' *Journal of Economic Geography*, 4, pp. 181–199.

Barney, J.B. (1991) 'Firm resources and sustained competitive advantage', *Journal of Management*, 17, pp. 99–120.

Barro, R.J. & Sala-i-Martin, X. (1995) *Economic Growth.* New York: McGraw-Hill.

Bathelt, H., Malmberg, A. & Maskell, P. (2004) 'Clusters and knowledge: Local buzz, global pipelines and the process of knowledge creation', *Progress in Human Geography*, 28, pp. 31–56.

Beaverstock, J.V., Taylor, P.J. & Smith, R.G. (1999) 'A roster of world cities', *Cities*, 16, pp. 445–458.

Belderbos, R., Fukao, K. & Iwasa, T. (2009) 'Foreign and domestic R&D investment', *Economics of Innovation and New Technology*, 18, pp. 369–380.

Beugelsdijk, S. & Mudambi, R. (2013) 'MNEs as border-crossing multi-locational enterprises: The role of discontinuities in geographic space', *Journal of International Business Studies*, 44, pp. 413–426.

Black, D. & Henderson, V. (1999) 'A theory of urban growth', *Journal of Political Economy*, 107, pp. 252–284.

Boggs, J.S. & Rantisi, N.M. (2003) 'The "relational turn" in Economic Geography', *Journal of Economic Geography*, 3, pp. 109–116.

Borjas, G.J., Bronars, S.G. & Trejo, S.J. (1992) 'Self-selection and internal migration in the United States', *Journal of Urban Economics*, 32, pp. 159–185.

Boschma, R.A. (2007) 'Editorial: Constructing an evolutionary Economic Geography', *Journal of Economic Geography*, 7, pp. 1–12.

Boschma, R.A. & Lambooy, J.G. (1999) 'Evolutionary economics and Economic Geography', *Journal of Evolutionary Economics*, 9, pp. 411–429.

Brakman, S. & Garretsen, H. (2003) 'Rethinking the "new" geographical economics', *Regional Studies*, 37, pp. 637–648.

Buckley, P.J. & Casson, M. (1976) *The Future of the Multinational Enterprise*. London: Macmillan.

Castellani, D. & Santangelo, G. (2016) 'Quo vadis? Cities and the location of cross-border activities', Paper presented at the European International Business Academy Conference, Vienna, 3–4 December.

Castells, M. (2000) *The Rise of the Network Society*. 2nd Edition. London: Wiley.

Caves, R.E. (1982) *The Economics of Multinational Enterprise*. Cambridge, UK: Cambridge University Press.

Ciccone, A. & Hall, R.E. (1990) 'Productivity and the density of economic activity', *American Economic Review*, 86, pp. 54–70.

Coe, N.M., Dicken, P. & Hess, M. (2008) 'Global production networks: Realizing the potential', *Journal of Economic Geography*, 8, pp. 271–295.

Dicken, P. (2015) *Global Shift*. 7th Edition. London: Sage.

Dicken, P. & Malmberg, A. (2001) 'Firms in territories: A relational perspective', *Economic Geography*, 77, pp. 345–363.

Di Giacinto, V., Gomellini, M., Micucci, G. & Pagnini, M. (2014) 'Mapping local productivity advantages in Italy: industrial districts, cities, or both?' *Journal of Economic Geography*, 14, pp. 365–394.

Dunning, J.H. (1980) 'Toward an eclectic theory in international production: Some empirical tests', *Journal of International Business Studies*, 11, pp. 9–31.

Dunning, J.H. (1995) 'Reappraising the eclectic paradigm in an age of alliance capital', *Journal of International Business Studies*, 25, pp. 461–491.

Dunning, J.H. (1998) 'Location and the multinational enterprise: A neglected factor?', *Journal of International Business Studies*, 29, pp. 45–66.

Florida, R. (1995) 'Toward the learning region', *Futures*, 27, pp. 527–536.

Florida, R. (2002) *The Rise of the Creative Class: And How It's Transforming Work, Leisure, Community and Everyday Life*. New York: Basic Books.

Florida, R., Mellander, C., Stolarick, K. & Ross, A. (2012) 'Cities, skills and wages', *Journal of Economic Geography*, 12, pp. 355–377.

Friedman, J. (1986) 'The world city hypothesis', *Development and Change*, 17, pp. 69–83.

Friedman, J. (2001) 'Intercity networks in a globalizing era', in Scott, A.J. (Ed.), *Global City Regions: Trends, Theory, Policy*. Oxford, UK: Oxford University Press, pp. 119–136.

Glaeser, E.L. (2000). 'The new economics of urban and regional growth', in Clark, G.L., Feldman, M.P. & Gertler, M.S. (Eds.), *The Oxford Handbook of Economic Geography*. Oxford, UK: Oxford University Press, pp. 83–98.

Glaeser, E.L. & Gottlieb, J.D. (2009) 'The wealth of cities: Agglomeration economies and spatial equilibrium in the United States', *Journal of Economic Literature*, 47, pp. 983–1028.

Glaeser, E.L., Kallal, H.D., Scheinkman, J.A. & Shleifer, A. (1992) 'Growth in cities', *Journal of Political Economy*, 100, pp. 1126–1152.

Glaeser, E.L., Kolko, J. & Saiz, A. (2001) 'Consumer city', *Journal of Economic Geography*, 1, pp. 27–50.

Goerzen, A., Asmussen, C.G. & Nielsen, B.B. (2013) 'Global cities and multinational enterprise location strategy', *Journal of International Business Studies*, 44, pp. 427–450.

Gordon, I.R. & McCann, P. (2000) 'Industrial clusters: Complexes, agglomeration and/or social networks', *Urban Studies*, 37, pp. 513–532.

Hall, P. (1966) *The World Cities*. London: Weidenfeld and Nicolson.
Hall, P. (2000) 'Creative cities and economic development', *Urban Studies*, 37, pp. 639–649.
Hausman, D.M. (1998) 'Problems with realism in economics', *Economics and Philosophy*, 14, pp. 185–213.
Henderson, J.V. (1996) 'Ways to think about urban concentration: Neoclassical urban systems versus the New Economic Geography', *International Regional Science Review*, 19, pp. 31–36.
Henderson, J.V. & Ono, Y. (2008) 'Where do manufacturing firms locate their headquarters?' *Journal of Urban Economics*, 63, pp. 431–450.
Hoover, E. (1948) *The Location of Economic Activity*. New York: McGraw-Hill.
Hymer, S.H. (1976) *The International Operations of National Firms*. Lexington, MA: Lexington Books.
Jacobs, J. (1961) *The Death and Life of Great American Cities*. New York: Random House.
Jacobs, J. (1969) *The Economy of Cities*. Harmondsworth, UK: Penguin.
Jacobs, J. (1985) *Cities and the Wealth of Nations. Principles of Economic Life*. Harmondsworth, UK: Penguin.
Jones, A. (2016) 'Geographies of production III: Economic geographies of management and International Business', *Progress in Human Geography*, 40, pp. 1–11.
Knox, P.L. & Taylor, P.J. (Eds.) (1995) *Word Cities in a World System*. Cambridge, UK: Cambridge University Press.
Laamanen, T., Simula, T. & Torstila, S. (2012) 'Cross-border relocations of headquarters in Europe', *Journal of International Business Studies*, 43, pp. 187–210.
Lee, N. & Rodriguez-Pose, A. (2013) 'Original innovation, learnt innovation and cities: Evidence from UK SMEs', *Urban Studies*, 50, pp. 1742–1759.
Markusen, A. (1996) 'Sticky places in slippery space: A typology of industrial districts', *Economic Geography*, 72, pp. 293–313.
Marshall, A. (1890) *Principles of Economics*. London: Macmillan.
Martin, R. (1999) 'The new "geographical turn" in economics: Some critical reflections', *Cambridge Journal of Economics*, 23, pp. 65–91.
McCann, P. & Mudambi, R. (2005) 'Analytical differences in the economics of geography: The case of the multinational firm', *Environment and Planning A*, 37, pp. 1857–1876.
Mommas, H. (2004) 'Cultural clusters and the post-industrial city: Towards the remapping of urban cultural policy', *Urban Studies*, 41, pp. 507–532.
Musil, R. (2013) 'World cities in a system of nation states', *GaWC Research Bulletin 426*. Loughborough, UK: GaWC.
Nachum, L. & Wymbs, C. (2005) 'Product differentiation, external economies and MNE location choices: M&As in global cities', *Journal of International Business Studies*, 36, pp. 415–434.
Nelson, R.R. & Winter, S.G. (1982) *An Evolutionary Theory of Economic Change*. Cambridge, MA: The Belknap Press.
Peng, M.W., Sunny, S.L., Pinkham, B. & Chen, H. (2009) 'The institution-based view as a third leg for a strategy tripod', *Academy of Management Perspectives*, 23, pp. 63–81.
Penrose, E.T. (1959) *The Theory of the Growth of the Firm*. New York: Oxford University Press.
Porter, M. E. (1990) *The Competitive Advantage of Nations*. London: Macmillan.
Rauch, J.E. (1993) 'Productivity gains from geographic concentration of human capital: Evidence from the cities', *Journal of Urban Economics*, 34, pp. 380–400.
Rigby, D.L. & Essletzbichler, J. (2002) 'Agglomeration economies and productivity differences in US cities', *Journal of Economic Geography*, 2, pp. 407–432.
Rozenblat, C. (2010) 'Opening the black box of agglomeration economies for measuring cities' competitiveness through international firm networks', *Urban Studies*, 47, pp. 2841–2865.
Sassen, S. (1991) *The Global City: Now York, London, Tokyo*. 2nd Edition. Princeton, NJ: Princeton University Press.
Sayer, A. (1992) *Method in Social Science. A Realist Approach*. London: Routledge.
Scott, A.J. (1996) 'Regional motors of the global economy', *Futures*, 28, pp. 391–411.
Scott, A.J. (2000) *The Cultural Economy of Cities*. London: Sage
Scott, A.J. (Ed.) (2001) *Global City Regions: Trends, Theory, Policy*. Oxford, UK: Oxford University Press.
Scott, A.J. (2012) *A World in Emergence. Cities and Regions in the 21st Century*. Cheltenham, UK: Edward Elgar.
Scott, A.J., Agnew, J., Soja, E.W. & Storper, M. (2001) 'Global city regions', in Scott, A.J. (Ed.), *Global City Regions: Trends, Theory, Policy*. Oxford, UK: Oxford University Press, pp. 11–30.
Scott, A.J. & Storper, M. (2003) 'Regions, globalization, development', *Regional Studies*, 37, pp. 579–593.

Storper, M. (1997) *The Regional World. Territorial Development in a Global Economy*. New York: The Guilford Press.
Storper, M. (2013) *Keys to the City: How Economics, Institutions, Social Interaction and Politics Shape Development*. Princeton, NJ: Princeton University Press.
Sveikauskas, L. (1975) 'The productivity of cities', *Quarterly Journal of Economics*, 89, pp. 392–413.
Taylor, M. & Asheim, B. (2001) 'The concept of the firm in Economic Geography', *Economic Geography*, 77, pp. 315–328.
Taylor, P.J. (2012) 'The challenge facing world city network analysis', *GaWC Bulletin 409*. Loughborough, UK: GaWC.
Taylor, P.J., Beaverstock, J., Cook, G., Pandit, N. & Pain, K. (2003) *Financial Services Clustering and Its Significance for London*. London: Corporation of London.
Taylor, P.J., Walker, D.R.F., Catalano, G. & Hoyler, M. (2002) 'Diversity and power in the world city network', *Cities*, 19, pp. 231–241.
Turok, I. (2004) 'Cities, regions and competitiveness', *Regional Studies*, 38, pp. 1069–1083.
Venables, A.J. (2011) 'Productivity in cities: Self-selection and sorting', *Journal of Economic Geography*, 11, pp. 241–251.
Vernon, R. (1966) 'International investment and international trade in the product cycle', *Quarterly Journal of Economics*, 80, pp. 190–07.
Viladecans-Marsal, E. (2004) 'Agglomeration economies and industrial location: City-level evidence', *Journal of Economic Geography*, 4, pp. 565–582.
Wernerfelt, B. (1984) 'A resource-based view of the firm', *Strategic Management Journal*, 5, pp. 171–180.
Williamson, O. (1975) *Markets and Hierarchies. Analysis and Antitrust Implications*. New York: Free Press.
Wolfe, D.A. & Gertler, M. (2004) 'Clusters from the inside and out: Local dynamics and global linkages', *Urban Studies*, 41, pp. 1071–1093.

15

STRATEGIC CITIES WITHIN GLOBAL URBAN NETWORKS[1]

Ben Derudder, Peter J. Taylor, James Faulconbridge, Michael Hoyler and Pengfei Ni

Introduction

The prime purpose of this chapter is to investigate cities as strategic places in contemporary globalization using the methodology developed as world city network analysis (Taylor, 2001; Taylor & Derudder, 2016). To this end, we draw on the work of Sassen (1991, pp. 3–4), who in her classic book *The Global City* identified processes of globalization that had 'created a new strategic role for major cities' resulting in a 'new type of city'. Our approach deals with many more cities than Sassen considers: here we ask the question, which of these numerous cities can be reasonably identified as strategic places? We deploy world city network analysis findings to answer this question quantitatively, so that amongst the cities thus identified we can measure degrees of 'strategic-ness'. From this we explore different ways in which cities are being strategic, drawing on the literature dealing with selected individual cities.

We treat the concept of strategic places from two directions. From the perspective of cities there are key firms that operate as strategic networks, which cities need to be part of; but equally, from the perspective of firms there are key cities that are strategic places, where firms have to be.

We build this analysis and interpretation on the foundations provided by literatures documenting the internationalization of advanced producer service firms such as accountancy, advertising, architecture, finance and law (Daniels, 1993; Bagchi-Sen & Sen, 1997; Jones, 2002; Bryson, Daniels & Warf, 2004; Faulconbridge, Hall & Beaverstock, 2008). This literature details the way firms' policies target particular city spaces (and thus render them strategic) as part of efforts to construct coordination capabilities that support both markets' exploitation/development and innovation priorities. We thus attempt to provide a distinct empirical contribution to the discussion based on the foundations of the literature on the internationalization policies of advanced producer service firms: a strongly evidenced, theoretically sound set of results that do add something new to understanding cities in globalization.

Our argument proceeds in seven parts: (i) we present the basic model that we use which specifies contemporary inter-city relations as an interlocking network; (ii) we outline the connections between the location policies of internationalizing advanced producer service firms and the production of strategic city places; (iii) we describe the data required to operationalize the model by creating a service values matrix showing how firms use cities, and initial forms of analyses from these data are described for both firms and cities; (iv) specific findings for 2016 data are presented describing city-dyad contrasts and globalization strategies of firms; (v) strategic networks are derived from the globalization strategies and these are employed to identify strategic places; (vi) the strategic-ness of cities is derived by relating strategic network positions to cities' encompassing global network positions; and (vii) we interpret our findings in relation to what the literature says about a number of specific cities we have found to be strategic places.

Advanced producer service internationalization through strategic cities

Since the seminal work on the role of advanced producer services (APS) in the global economy (Enderwick, 1989; Beyers, 1992; Daniels, 1993, 1995), questions about the strategic role of cities have been at the forefront of concerns. Originally centred around questions about why APS cluster in cities, and spurning extensive analysis of the way city economies function using agglomeration and localization logics and their explanations of markets and innovation processes respectively (Pryke, 1994; Grabher, 2001), this literature has developed since the late 2000s as questions about the way cities play varying roles in firms' strategies have come to the fore (Warf, 2001; Jones, 2002; Beaverstock, 2007; Faulconbridge et al., 2007, 2008, 2011; McNeill, 2008). In this regard, Bagchi-Sen and Sen (1997) were ahead of their time when they deployed Dunning and Norman's (1983) Eclectic Paradigm to analyse the location advantages for APS of different cities. In this work, the 'size and character of the market; regulation of markets . . . and the location of human (skilled labor) and physical assets' were identified as core factors influencing where internationalizing APS chose to establish foreign outposts (Bagchi-Sen & Sen, 1997, p. 1158). However, even at this early stage of research, it was noted that 'sector differentiation in terms of internationalization strategies' (p. 1171) was crucial, accounting and advertising being compared and contrasted by Bagchi-Sen and Sen (1997).

Further inspired by calls to open the black box used to represent firms and their strategies in studies of corporations driving economic globalization (Taylor & Asheim, 2001; Yeung, 2005), the most recent research on APS internationalization, therefore, seeks to identify (i) groups of firms that share common strategic objectives, and (ii) the differing roles of cities in fulfilling these objectives. In relation to issue (i), it is possible to distinguish between what might be called the ubiquitous presence versus the strategic presence approach. The former, most commonly adopted by the Big Four accountancy firms (Beaverstock, 1996), major financial institutions (Wójcik, 2013) and hybrid producer-consumer services such as temporary staffing agencies (Coe, Johns & Ward, 2007), involves maintaining a presence in as many cities as possible to allow revenue maximization through the servicing of local clients' needs. The latter, associated more with advertising (Faulconbridge et al., 2011), architecture (McNeill, 2008) and law firms (Faulconbridge, 2008), is driven by a desire to locate offices in the most strategically important places, strategic importance being defined in terms of both the global influence and connectedness of markets and the extent to which work in these places is cutting edge in terms of innovation and thus global profile.

Connected to questions about internationalization strategy and the more or less strategic role of different places, are also questions about the organizational form of APS. For instance, Faulconbridge et al. (2008) synthesize a range of research on APS and apply it to the case of executive search to reveal that depending on the strategic importance of a city, internationalization may involve: owned offices (traditional foreign direct investment); the establishment of networks (collaboration with local independent APS rather than direct investment); or a hybrid of the two former approaches (investment in already existing local APS that retain some autonomy but become tightly integrated into global corporate networks). Whilst there is some variability, owned strategies tend to be associated with *the* most strategically important sites, whilst networks are used to provide presence when needed in markets that are uncertain in terms of regulatory barriers, stability or strategic importance. Hybrids allowed mid-ranking city nodes that are integrated into global economic flows, but in less strategic ways, to be effectively served. The example of the executive search firm Korn/Ferry given by Faulconbridge et al. (2008) is illustrative of such connections between organizational form and the strategicness of a city. Owned offices dominate the firm's internationalization strategy, which involves presence in a total of over 70 cities. However, the owned approach is restricted to the most strategic locations, such as London, New York, Frankfurt, etc. Hybrid forms are used in locations that have less strategic importance, for instance in Mexico City and Monterey, whilst networks allow a flag to be planted in locations of potential future importance (e.g., Johannesburg) or where a token presence is required but markets are limited (e.g., Auckland).

The APS literature reveals, then, two important insights relevant to the analysis and interpretation of the way cities do or do not become strategic places in the world city network created by APS firms. First, it shows that not all APS have the same significance when presence or absence is being used as a proxy of strategicness. The ubiquitous presence strategy means that sectors such as accounting and finance potentially maintain a presence in both more and less strategic cities. Hence these sectors may not be good measures of strategicness. Meanwhile, other sectors that adopt a strategic presence approach may be better suited to analyses seeking proxies for city strategicness. Second, the APS literature also reveals that whilst a firm may have tens or hundreds of offices, not all of these offices share an equal level of strategic importance. Variations in strategicness may be reflected in the organizational form used to manage presence and also in other characteristics such as size and staffing. With these insights in mind, the remainder of the chapter considers how such understandings of variations in the strategic role of cities in APS internationalization might be both captured in world city network analysis methodologies and used to understand the urban spatial architecture of current day global capitalism.

Basic model: interlocking network specification

To deploy the insights gained from the APS literature, it is important to consider their implications for the assumptions in the interlocking network model used in world city network analysis (for an overview, see Taylor & Derudder, 2016). The choice of specifying advanced producer service firms as the economic agents making the world city network derives directly from Sassen's (1991) identification of this economic sector as key creator of her global cities. This occurs in two ways. First, global cities through their 'control and command functions' house corporate headquarters and agencies of government that provide the main market for advanced producer services. Second, it is these cities that are the production centers for advanced producer services, the places where product and process innovations keep growing this cutting edge economic sector. This consumption/production dual character of global cities will have a central role in interpreting the strategic places we identify below. However, we depart from Sassen's use of advanced producer services to identify a small subset of cities as 'global' and instead recognize that advanced producer services are much more widespread than her discussion implies. We define a world city network based upon the activities of advanced producer service firms that encompasses several hundred cities across the world. Thus we specify the world city network in terms of the worldwide office networks of leading advanced producer service firms.

The world city network is formally specified in Taylor (2001); here we provide the basic outline. The network is represented by a city-by-firm matrix $\mathbf{V}_{ij}$, where $v_{i,j}$ is the 'service value' of city i to firm j. This service value is a standardized measure of the importance of a city to a firm's office network, which depends on the size and functions of a firm's office(s) in a city.

The city-dyad connectivity between two cities a and i (CDC_{a-i}) is defined as:

$$CDC_{a-i} = \Sigma\, v_{a,j} \cdot v_{i,j} \text{ (where } a \neq i) \tag{15.1}$$

This provides a measure of the potential work flows, transfers of information and knowledge, between pairs of cities. The assumption behind conceiving the product of service values as a surrogate for actual flows between cities a and i for firm j is that the more important the office, the more links there will be with other offices in a firm's network. In other words, we are using a simple interaction relation as our measure of connectivity: two cities housing large offices will generate more inter-city work flows between them than two cities each with small offices.

Typically in world city network analysis these inter-city connectivities are aggregated for each city and the totals are interpreted as the global network connectivity of a city (GNC_a), indicating a city's overall importance within the network:

$$GNC_a = \Sigma\, CDC_{a-i} \text{ (where } a \neq i) \tag{15.2}$$

This has been the main measure derived from the model and can be interpreted as how well a city is integrated into the world city network, and hence its 'global status'.

Basic data: filling the service values matrix

To operationalize this model requires assessment of firms' office networks to empirically construct a city-by-firm matrix $\mathbf{V}_{ij}$ of service values. The data required for this exercise are readily available on firms' websites where they promote their 'global' status as a means of both impressing clients in a competitive services market and recruiting graduates in a competitive jobs market. However this source, plus supplementary information as available, produces different levels and types of information for every firm. Thus for each firm the data have to be converted by using a simple coding system to enable cross-firm comparison for analysis. We use a coding from 0 to 5, whereby the service values $v_{i,j}$: 0 indicates a city where firm j has no presence and 5 is firm j's headquarter city. Codes 1 to 4 are then allocated as follows: a typical office of firm j scores a city 2, there must be something deficient to lower the score to 1, and something extra for it to rise above 2. For the latter, an especially large office scores 3, an office with extra-city jurisdictions (e.g. regional HQ) scores 4. Each firm is assessed individually to decide on boundary decisions away from 2. With *n* firms and *m* cities, such data collection creates an *n* firms x *m* cities array of service values, the basic matrix for interlocking network analysis. Each column of the matrix shows a firm's location strategy as a string of integers from 0 to 5 across *m* cities; each row shows a city's service mix as a string from 0 to 5 across *n* firms.

In 2016 we assessed the office networks of 175 firms across 707 cities. The former consisted of 75 financial services firms and 25 each of accountancy, advertising, law and management consultancy firms. Firms were chosen using trade information ranking firms by size based upon the latest information available (e.g. on turnover). Cities were chosen on the basis of previous experience in this work (315 cities used in earlier data collections) plus all other cities with more than 2 million population, all other capital cities of countries with over one million population, and all other cities housing the headquarters of one of our 175 firms. These are arbitrary rules of inclusion but the aim was to include more cities than necessary so as not to exclude any potentially relevant cities in what is a very dynamic process of world city network formation. The end result is a 175 firms × 707 cities matrix for 2010 providing 123,725 service values for analysis.

Extensive and intensive globalization

Our identification of strategic cities is premised on an initial exploration of the location strategies of the advanced producer service firms. Their office networks constitute 175 specific location strategies, depending on idiosyncrasies, market analysis, historical trajectories, regulatory boundaries, etc. The outcome of these processes at any one point in time constitutes firms' specific location strategies. This particular geography is represented by a firm's column of integers in the service values matrix; for 2016 we have 175 such strategies. Although every strategy is different across our firms there are some clear similarities amongst them that can be teased out using a principal components analysis. This technique is a 'data reduction' method that converts x variables into y components where y is appreciably smaller than x. This is achieved by using the correlations between variables to combine them into groups of like variables, the 'principal components' of the data. The importance of each component is derived from its correlations (called 'loadings') with the original variables. In the analysis reported here the 175 individual firm location strategies (variables) are reduced to just two components that are interpreted as the most common dimensions of location strategies: between them, these two components account for almost one-third of the common variance found in the service values matrix. We concentrate on these two common location strategies here.

The characteristics of principal components can be discerned from their component scores on the objects of the analysis, in this case the cities. The scores for the two main components identified above, illustrating the two leading common location strategies from the 2010 service values matrix, are given in Table 15.1 for all cities scoring >0.50. These

Table 15.1 Intensive and extensive globalization

Intensive	*Scores*	*Extensive*	*Scores*
Home-region		**Home-region**	
Washington	7.50	New York	2.90
New York	4.75	London	2.75
Los Angeles	2.40		
Palo Alto	2.14	**Global outreach**	
London	1.99	Sao Paulo	1.82
Miami	1.25	Mexico City	1.55
Houston	1.16	Mumbai	1.49
San Francisco	1.01	Istanbul	1.47
Philadelphia	0.86	Bogota	1.44
Dallas	0.51	Buenos Aires	1.41
		Dubai	1.38
		Milan	1.18
Global outreach		Kuala Lumpur	1.09
Hong Kong	1.60	Johannesburg	1.09
Brussels	0.91	Madrid	1.09
Beijing	0.54	Santiago	1.07
		Barcelona	1.04
		New Delhi	0.98
		Moscow	0.97
		Paris	0.96
		Singapore	0.96

Jakarta	0.82
Lima	0.80
Warsaw	0.77
Caracas	0.77
Manila	0.77
Tokyo	0.76
Athens	0.73
Toronto	0.73
Vienna	0.66
Kiev	0.65
Tel Aviv	0.65
Prague	0.63
Cairo	0.60
Beijing	0.59
Seoul	0.59
Lisbon	0.57
Bangkok	0.56
Hong Kong	0.56
Montevideo	0.55
Bucharest	0.53
Beirut	0.53
Sofia	0.50

Table 15.2 Global strategic firms

APS firms	*Global strategic measure*	*Sector*	*Headquarters*
Cleary Gottlieb	0.182	Law	New York
Sullivan & Cromwell	0.158	Law	New York
White & Case	0.157	Law	New York
Citi	0.153	Finance	New York
Ogilvy & Mather	0.144	Advertising	New York
Simpson Thacher & Bartlett	0.125	Law	New York
Clifford Chance	0.120	Law	London
Baker & McKenzie	0.114	Law	Chicago
Skadden, Arps, Slate, Meagher & Flom	0.111	Law	New York
BKR International	0.110	Accountancy	New York
Mayer Brown	0.110	Law	Chicago
Morgan Stanley	0.108	Finance	New York
Goldman Sachs	0.104	Finance	New York
Publicis Healthcare Communications Group	0.099	Advertising	New York
Banco do Brasil	0.095	Finance	Brasilia
Allen & Overy	0.088	Law	London
HSBC	0.086	Finance	London
Nomura	0.084	Finance	Tokyo
Linklaters	0.084	Law	London
Moore Stephens International	0.083	Accountancy	London
Alvarez & Marsal	0.083	Management	New York
Bradesco	0.082	Finance	Sao Paulo
J.P. Morgan	0.082	Finance	New York
Jones Day	0.082	Law	Washington
Latham & Watkins	0.082	Law	Los Angeles

strategies are labelled intensive and extensive globalizations for reasons that will become apparent as we describe them. In each case we identify a 'home-region' on which the strategy is centered – most of the headquarters of the firms that constitute each component are to be found here (see Taylor et al., 2013) – and a 'global outreach' that identifies how the rest of the world is serviced through the location strategy. In both cases we find the home-region encompasses US cities plus London. However, although overlapping, the constitution of these two regions is quite distinctive: in the first list in Table 15.2 there are 9 US cities plus London, in the second just New York and London. With global outreach we find the obverse: just three cities in the first list but with 40 featuring in the second list. The reason for their specific labels is as follows. The intensive globalization strategy focuses on the prime locus through which economic globalization was initially constructed with the rest of the world serviced through just key cities in each of the two other major 'globalization arenas' – Brussels in Western Europe and Hong Kong and Beijing in Pacific Asia. In contrast the extensive globalization strategy emanates from just the two cities continuously found at the apex of the world city network combined with a very comprehensive servicing across the rest of the world.

Identifying strategic networks and strategic places

In our model it is the firms that are the agents of globalization, the transnational network makers, and therefore to comprehend strategy we start by identifying strategic firms, and then use them to find the strategic places that are our initial concern in this chapter.

Although the two components are orthogonal (i.e. not related, their correlation equals zero), there will be specific firms that use elements of both common strategies as reflected in their loadings on the two components. These are the firms we will identify as 'global strategic firms'. Specifically, we use firms' component loadings on (i.e. levels of correlations with) the intensive and extensive globalization strategies to define a 'global strategic measure' for all 175 firms in our data. We compute the product of the loadings on the two components for each firm to create this measure. Global strategic firms are then identified as the 25 firms with the largest component loading above. The basic reasoning behind this procedure is to find firms with relatively high positive loadings on both components. Thus firms with a negative loading on one of the components are immediately eliminated. Firms scoring high on one component but not the other are similarly discarded. The results of this exercise are shown in Table 15.2 where 25 global strategic firms are listed.

We can see from Table 15.2 that all five service sectors in our data are represented, albeit very unevenly so. Management consultancy, accountancy, and advertising only have one or two firms present. Financial services are somewhat more represented, but note that firms present here are above all US-headquartered investment banks and there were three times as much financial services firms compared to the other sectors. Thus the key sector represented is law with 12 firms, all of which are headquartered in either London or a leading US city.

We are now in a position to identify which cities are strategic places within the world city network: we define these as cities that house offices of 10 or more strategic firms. This produces a list of 49 cities shown in Table 15.3.[2] The cities are ranked by their strategic network connectivity derived from computing the network connectivity defined by equations (1) and (2) but only including the 25 strategic firms in the calculations. All 25 strategic firms are found in London and New York, the latter is ranked higher because its offices tend to be more important than London's (e.g. more headquarters): this is shown by the higher connectivity New York obtains from its strategic firms' offices.

Table 15.3 Strategic network connectivity

Rank	*City*	*Strategic network Connectivity*	*Number of offices*
1	New York	7124	25
2	London	6833	25
3	Hong Kong	5375	24
4	Washington	4383	23
5	Paris	4162	23
6	Dubai	4025	19
7	Frankfurt	3811	21
8	Tokyo	3799	22
9	Singapore	3763	18
10	Sao Paulo	3614	22
11	Beijing	3583	22
12	Chicago	3580	16
13	Moscow	3393	18
14	Milan	3337	20
15	Brussels	3334	18
16	Amsterdam	3243	16
17	Los Angeles	3223	17
18	Shanghai	3215	21
19	Madrid	3196	19
20	Sydney	3098	17
21	Mexico City	2873	14
22	Seoul	2682	19
23	Warsaw	2618	14
24	Istanbul	2597	13
25	Miami	2597	12
26	San Francisco	2552	14
27	Stockholm	2298	13
28	Luxembourg	2280	12
29	Taipei	2271	11
30	Jakarta	2228	14
31	Bangkok	2191	13
32	Mumbai	2164	10
33	Johannesburg	2137	12
34	Zurich	2123	11
35	Buenos Aires	2058	12
36	Munich	2043	12
37	Hanoi	2006	12
38	Riyadh	2003	14
39	Melbourne	1983	10
40	Doha	1982	11
41	Toronto	1938	11
42	Houston	1930	13
43	Abu Dhabi	1902	11
44	Boston	1873	11
45	Rome	1862	12
46	Düsseldorf	1737	11
47	Ho Chi Minh City	1733	10
48	Palo Alto	1560	10
49	Barcelona	1524	10

Relating strategic network connectivity to global network connectivity

We have regressed strategic network connectivity against global network connectivity and recorded the residuals. These are standardized (zero mean and a standard deviation of one) so that positive numbers indicate relative strategic over-connected-ness and negative numbers relative strategic under-connected-ness. In Table 15.4 cities are ranked by size of their residuals to show the importance of their strategic connectivity relative to overall connectivity.

Table 15.4 Residual from regressing strategic network connectivity against global network connectivity

Rank	*City*	*Residual*
1	Washington	3.054
2	Palo Alto	2.156
3	New York	2.087
4	Hong Kong	1.676
5	Frankfurt	1.123
6	London	1.084
7	Brussels	1.005
8	Los Angeles	0.847
9	Hanoi	0.815
10	Amsterdam	0.703
11	Miami	0.555
12	Doha	0.538
13	Abu Dhabi	0.491
14	Chicago	0.470
15	Madrid	0.408
16	San Francisco	0.349
17	Houston	0.346
18	Dubai	0.304
19	Moscow	0.282
20	Sao Paulo	0.280
21	Luxembourg	0.097
22	Munich	0.059
23	Paris	0.005
24	Rome	-0.001
25	Stockholm	-0.165
26	Milan	-0.176
27	Seoul	-0.328
28	Boston	-0.329
29	Taipei	-0.342
30	Riyadh	-0.371
31	Tokyo	-0.406
32	Düsseldorf	-0.492
33	Istanbul	-0.502
34	Bangkok	-0.516
35	Ho Chi Minh City	-0.580
36	Warsaw	-0.607
37	Zurich	-0.609
38	Buenos Aires	-0.668
39	Mexico City	-0.670

40	Sydney	-0.727
41	Beijing	-0.818
42	Jakarta	-1.030
43	Melbourne	-1.085
44	Barcelona	-1.105
45	Shanghai	-1.145
46	Singapore	-1.194
47	Johannesburg	-1.396
48	Toronto	-1.647
49	Mumbai	-1.824

The follow findings from this analysis are highlighted:

- Although both New York and London are strategically over-connected there is a clear difference between New York and London: the former is much more over-connected city relative to its global connectivity. In most of our analyses both cities are hard to separate in their connectivity profile, with London most commonly being somewhat more connected, but on this particular measure New York appears to be more central.
- Other leading US cities are also ranked high on this relative measure: Washington, DC, Los Angeles Chicago and San Francisco are also strategically over-connected, as are secondary cities such as Miami and Houston. Very few North American cities have a negative residual, with Toronto as leading Canadian city having a very large negative residual.
- Although there is much continuity with the initial study drawing on 2010 data (Taylor et al., 2014), the presence of Washington, DC represents a major change. The really interesting continuity is the presence of Palo Alto. Ranked a lowly 283rd in global network connectivity, which is even lower than in 2010, it has the second most strategic connectivity, which obviously reflects its special positionality in Silicon Valley.
- Although Mainland Chinese cities are increasingly important in terms of global network connectivity (especially Shanghai and Beijing) this is not being reflected in strategicness.
- Cities from other erstwhile 'third world' countries are generally under-connected: Buenos Aires, Jakarta, Kuala Lumpur, Mexico City, Ho Chi Minh City, Bangkok, and Mumbai all have large negative residuals have large negative residuals.
- Dubai, Abu Dhabi and Doha have posted major connectivity gains over the past years (see Derudder and Taylor, 2016), but this does not translate into major strategic positions: residuals are positive, but relatively small.

This strategic network geography that we have uncovered within the world city network forms the basis of our specific interpretations of strategic places and their differences below.

Interpretation of positionalities

The quantitative findings shown in Table 15.4 require interpretation based upon both theoretical extensions of the model employed and empirical knowledge of the cities as advanced producer service centres. In practice these two needs cannot be separated (and this is particularly the case when we try and comprehend our results on New York and London). However, in terms of the empirics, clearly we cannot deal with all 48 cities and therefore we proceed as follows. We begin with consideration of London and New York, surely the world's most studied cities, and focus on writings that have discussed their differences. We then deploy what we have learned from this prime city-dyad comparison to other specific cases. These are chosen from a mixture of intrinsic interest and availability of relevant literature to meet our needs. Thus we deal with Mainland Chinese cities, Palo Alto (the highly strategic but weakly connected city), Mexico City (an emerging market city).

London and New York

London and New York define the only city-dyad that actually has a name: NY-LON. It is part of a tradition that sees these cities at the forefront of fashion and which has been enhanced by economic globalization whereby leading world movers and shakers are said to work through three offices, one in each city and another in transit over the Atlantic. Smith (2012, p. 421) describes how these two cities have come to be viewed as a single city: 'a transatlantic metropolis that is the heart-beat of the global economy'. The key point that Smith makes is that the cities operate in conjunction for the benefit of a small rich minority. But the conflation of the two cities hides the differences that we are seeking. Their complementarities are based upon dissimilarity and this has been the subject of a careful comparison as global financial centers by Sassen (1999) and Wójcik (2013).

According to Sassen (1999, p. 81) New York and London constitute 'a cooperative division of labor' that operates as follows:

(i) 'London is the preeminent city for global finance today, in good part due to numerous international firms that have located key operations and resources in the City [so that] London's unique denationalized platform for global operations gives it its competitive advantage' (pp. 83–4);
(ii) But 'what London lacks is Wall Street's brilliant financial engineering' and therefore 'New York dominates in another way by offering market innovations and new financial products. Wall Street – still the Silicon Valley of finance – has made U.S. investment firms leaders in the global market' (pp. 83–4).

More than a decade later it seems that this differentiation is still very much in place; Wójcik (2013, pp. 6–7), partly drawing on Strange (1997) and Michie (2006), describes it this way:

> While New York commands access to the largest and most liquid domestic financial market in the world, London's physical, political and historical geography implies access to a different time zone, European markets, and global connections . . . Taking advantage of its sheer liquid domestic market, and the deepest pool of financial engineering talent, New York leads financial innovation . . . Hedge funds come from the USA, and so do venture capital and private equity. Most new products and methods of trading in the global securities markets emanated from New York. . . . London, in turn, has specialized as a centre, where financial firms (with US banks in the lead) adapt financial innovation from the USA to foreign and international markets.

The message is clear: London is particularly good for global financial business, New York is particularly good for global financial innovations.

London thus appears to be better integrating business while New York is more speciliazed in building new functions, the latter interpreted as being more strategic. Further, there is a sense in which London is 'used' with New York firms as key 'users', indicating a hierarchical element in the cities' complementarities that Sassen (1999, p. 81) recognized. And returning to her essential 'global city' process (Sassen, 1991) where the city is both a market for and a producer of APS, we can view the relationship between these two functions as variable across cities: high levels of new production relative to market (exchange) is a distinctive strategic place process, more focus on market service than production is a general network process. Indeed, we can see just such a distinction in the strategies of internationalizing US law firms. In the initial years at least, these firms primarily practiced US (and New York specifically) law in London as part of a strategy designed to exploit the demand for advice about the structuring of financial transactions using New York law (Warf, 2001; Cullen-Mandikos & MacPherson, 2002). Such an interpretation provides both an explanation for our results showing New York exhibiting more 'strategic-ness' than London, and also suggests a general means of comparing cities in the world city network in terms of their relative strategic-ness.

Beijing, Hong Kong and Shanghai

To illustrate the latter we can turn briefly to the China cities in our analysis using Lai's (2012) study of the mutualities between Beijing, Hong Kong and Shanghai as financial centers. She describes a 'dual headquarter strategy' for Beijing-Shanghai relations and 'parallel markets' for Hong Kong-Shanghai relations. She equates Hong Kong's role with that of New York (p. 1275), and this does indeed emerge in our findings with Hong Kong being the most strategic connected outside of the US.

The roles of the three China cities are quite distinctive. Beijing is the political center, 'responsible for policy-making and macro planning' (Lai 2012, p. 1283), in other words the locus of command and control. Shanghai, on the other hand, 'is tasked with testing new products, developing new markets and financial innovation' (p. 1283). The result is that Shanghai has 'the highest concentration of foreign banks' and hosts 'new financial markets in futures, derivatives and foreign exchange' (p. 1283). In contrast Hong Kong has grown as a strategic conduit 'connecting global capital and China' (p. 1275) and continues in the role of China's 'offshore financial centre' (p. 1275).

It takes very little imagination to equate this structural logic to similar relations between Washington as political centre, New York as innovative centre, and London as offshore centre. In the latter case both London and Hong Kong have exploited a political autonomy by being outside the direct sovereign/administrative control of the USA and China respectively. In other words these are necessary global platforms where you can do things that are not possible in the cities of the USA and mainland China.

Palo Alto

As the main city in Silicon Valley, Palo Alto is a very special strategic place, as reflected in our analysis through its unusual combination of very low general integration into the world city network with very high strategic-ness. How does the production of high tech innovations that Silicon Valley is famous for transfer into APS innovation as our results imply? This special place has distinctive servicing needs that have led to specialization in deal making, advising new firm start-ups and university spin-offs, arranging access to venture capital, taking successful firms public, plus mergers and acquisitions activity (Lashinsky, 2002; Reiffenstein, 2009). The main service sector providing these services is law and law firms, working as 'patent attorneys' in particular, illustrate servicing the business of innovation (Reiffenstein, 2009).

According to Reiffenstein (2009, p. 572) law firms 'by mediating between the private interests of firms and the public concerns of the patent office, perform a critical role that is not merely ancillary but instrumental to the workings of the knowledge economy'. In other words, these law firms are part of the technology community (2009, p. 579). In terms similar to those used to describe New York's role in finance, Reiffenstein quotes Friedman et al. (1989) as saying that 'the Silicon Valley lawyer not only works with engineers, he thinks of himself as a kind of engineer – a legal engineer' (2009, p. 578). Thus

> Silicon Valley occupies a special place in this [patent] system. Its attorneys are the 'engineers' of business and legal precedent particularly as it relates to the translation of science to industry. Firms located there enjoy a locational advantage from a proximity to milieus of basic and applied research: buyers and sellers of technology.
>
> *(p. 580)*

This special place is a strategic place because 'every one of the major Silicon Valley law offices is a component of a much larger branch network' (p. 579) enabling the firm 'to link buyers and sellers of technology and to lubricate the innovative process by linking places' (p. 580), now necessarily including 'international transactions' (Lashinsky, 2002). Thus Palo Alto is only a small city but it is a big player in the strategy of law firms and therefore the world city network as our strategic-ness analyses have shown.

Mexico City

Mexico City is strongly integrated into the world city network (ranked 14th in terms of GNC) but according to our analyses it is relatively under-connected strategically (Table 15.4). We use Parnreiter's (2010) study of how APS firms in Mexico City operate in global commodity chains to interpret our findings in this case.

Parnreiter (2010, pp. 36–7) begins by asking the crucial question, does the APS sector in Mexico City function as merely enabling agent of economic globalization or do these firms help shape the nature of the production networks they are servicing? To answer the question he finds he has to break with Sassen's (1991) 'equating the management of the world economy with its control' (p. 43). These are two separate mechanisms that are 'frequently conflated' despite the fact that

> ... it is questionable whether all high-wage, high-tech and high-profit services necessary for running global production processes are actually related to decision-making. This question is particularly relevant to global cities in non-core countries, which have a sizeable producer service sector but are normally not considered to host decision-making capacities.
>
> *(p. 44)*

Thus although many of the practitioners he interviewed emphasize the importance of their local office within the world city network, Parnreiter is able to show that this is largely necessary work but not strategic work. He concludes

> Though at first glance it seems that the networks of producer service firms are rather flat, their organizational model implies that there is the chain of command. Despite the fact that the local cooperation is . . . seen as . . . essential to do business, the 'big' strategies are made by the lead partners [and] the number of lead partners an office of a global service provider can have depends . . . by and large on the geography of headquarters of TNCs. Since there are far fewer companies with origins in Mexico that compete

> successfully in the world market than foreign firms in Mexico, the Mexico City offices of accountancy, legal or real estate firms will not often be in command.
>
> *(p. 47)*

This is entirely consistent with our finding on the differences between Mexico City's global network connectivity and its strategic network connectivity. It also directly corresponds with the example presented above in our review of the APS literature in which the executive search firm Korn/Ferry uses a hybrid strategy to service Mexico City rather than the owned form used in the most strategic places.

Since Parnreiter frames his argument in world-systems terms, we are invited to extrapolate this interpretation to other important cities from 'non-core countries': this would include Jakarta, Buenos Aires, Kuala Lumpur, and Mumbai. But there a complementary take is also possible: Mexico is not only non-core, it is also located in NAFTA. The fact that Toronto, the only Canadian city to be included in our 48 strategic places, is ranked bottom in Table 15.4 clearly suggests that NAFTA has tended to work for the benefit of APS firms in leading US cities at the expense of their Canadian and Mexican counterparts.

Concluding remarks

This chapter has added to our knowledge of the contemporary world city network by going beyond the basic measurement of global network connectivities to show a distinctive pattern of strategic network connectivities. Our findings appear credible and have been shown to link with literatures on selected individual cities and with work on APS and their strategic city location decisions and organizational forms. There are, of course, caveats to bear in mind when assessing these results overall.

- We have not produced definitive strategic places but rather specific strategic places relating to one economic sector, advanced producer services. We do argue the particular importance of this sector for economic globalization but there will be other strategic places for global commodity chains defined by other criteria.
- We have provided a cross-sectional analysis for 2016 to define city positionalities but, of course, these are inherently historical; information on city trajectories is a necessary addition to make better sense of our results.
- The latter point is very relevant to the fact we have used two USA-based (with London) location strategies of firms as the basis of the analysis. This choice was justified by their being both the most important strategies identified and because they are from the world region that largely generated economic globalization. However it is their recent history and present that are being designated 'most important'; but this designation may be less relevant for the future in a dynamic world economy: Pacific Asian, especially China, location strategies will have their own emerging strategic places that our methodology is not designed to find.

What we have been able to do is provide some order in an increasingly complex economy through excavating strategic places within world city network structures. In this way we present an extensive picture in which to view the mechanisms of contemporary economic globalization.

We began with Sassen's 'global cities' as new strategic places that have solved the problem of providing operational capacity in a new global economy. Although restricting ourselves to 'spatial' identification of the strategic, this concept has still emerged as a multifarious mix of processes. In particular, our strategic places appear to have various combinations of command capacity and generation of innovations with APS firms that develop strategic presence, internationalization policies choosing to operate in these but not other cities to access such qualities. In contrast APS firms with ubiquitous strategies maintain a presence in both strategic cities and less strategic cities that act as local market nodes.

Notes

1 This chapter presents an empirical and interpretational update of a paper published in *Economic Geography* as Taylor, P.J., Derudder, B., Faulconbridge, J., Hoyler, M. & Ni, P. (2014) 'Advanced producer service firms as strategic networks, global cities as strategic places', *Economic Geography*, 90, pp. 267–291. Data used in this chapter are for 2016 instead of 2010, and contents have been revised and updated accordingly. Operational details and discussion of results have been shortened and amended respectively, and in this chapter, we have included a more thorough discussion of related research, some of which has been published since the writing-up of the initial paper.

2 It should be noted that although this methodology includes arbitrary threshold decisions for defining strategic firms and strategic places, these were not the only ones tested in the research. The key point is that the different choices had very little effect on subsequent analysis. In other words, the results we present here are quite robust with minor differences having no relevance to the broader conclusions drawn.

References

Bagchi-Sen, S. & Sen, J. (1997) 'The current state of knowledge in International Business in producer services', *Environment and Planning A*, 29, pp. 1153–1174.

Beaverstock, J.V. (1996) 'Subcontracting the accountant! Professional labour markets, migration, and organisational networks in the global accountancy industry', *Environment and Planning A*, 28, pp. 303–326.

Beaverstock, J.V. (2007) 'Transnational work: Global professional labour markets in professional service accounting firms' In Bryson, J.R. (Ed.), *The Handbook of Service Industries*. Cheltenham, UK: Edward Elgar, pp. 409–432.

Beyers, W. (1992) 'Producer services and metropolitan growth and development', in Mills, E.S., Mcdonald, J.F. & Mclean, M.L. (Eds.), *Sources of Metropolitan Growth*. New Brunswick, NJ: Transaction Publishers, pp. 125–146.

Bryson, J.R., Daniels, P.W. & Warf, B. (2004) *Service Worlds: People, Technology, Organizations*. London: Routledge.

Coe, N.M., Johns, J. & Ward, K. (2007) 'Mapping the globalization of the temporary staffing industry', *The Professional Geographer*, 59, pp. 503–520.

Cullen-Mandikos, B. & MacPherson, A. (2002) 'US foreign direct investment in the London legal market: An empirical analysis', *The Professional Geographer*, 54, pp. 491–499.

Daniels, P.W. (1993) *Service Industries in the World Economy*. Oxford, UK: Blackwell.

Daniels, P.W. (1995) 'The internationalisation of advertising', *Service Industries Journal*, 15, pp. 276–294.

Derudder, B. & Taylor, P.J. (2016) 'Change in the world city network, 2000–2012', *The Professional Geographer*, 68, pp. 624–637.

Dunning, J.H. & Norman, G. (1983) 'The theory of the multinational enterprise: An application to multinational office location', *Environment and Planning A*, 15, pp. 675–692.

Enderwick, P. (1989) *Multinational Service Firms*. London: Routledge.

Faulconbridge, J.R. (2008) 'Managing the transnational law firm: A relational analysis of professional systems, embedded actors, and time-space-sensitive governance', *Economic Geography*, 84, pp. 185–210.

Faulconbridge, J.R., Beaverstock, J.V., Nativel, C. & Taylor, P.J. (2011) *The Globalization of Advertising: Agencies, Cities and Spaces of Creativity*. London: Routledge.

Faulconbridge, J.R., Engelen, E., Hoyler, M. & Beaverstock, J.V. (2007) 'Analysing the changing landscape of European financial centres: The role of financial products and the case of Amsterdam', *Growth and Change*, 38, pp. 279–303.

Faulconbridge, J.R., Hall, S.J. & Beaverstock, J.V. (2008) 'New insights into the internationalization of producer services: Organizational strategies and spatial economies for global headhunting firms', *Environment and Planning A*, 40, pp. 210–234.

Grabher, G. (2001) 'Ecologies of creativity: The village, the group, and the heterarchic organisation of the British advertising industry', *Environment and Planning A*, 33, 351–374.

Jones, A. (2002) 'The global city misconceived: The myth of global management in transnational service firms', *Geoforum*, 33, pp. 335–350.

Lai, K. (2012) 'Differentiated markets: Shanghai, Beijing and Hong Kong in China's financial centre network', *Urban Studies*, 49, pp. 1275–1296.

Lashinsky, A. (2002) 'Silicon Valley: The lawyers got screwed too', *Fortune*, 145, pp. 133–137.

Mcneill, D. (2008) *The Global Architect: Firms, Fame and Urban Form*. London & New York: Routledge.

Michie, R.C. (2006) *The Global Securities Market: A History*. Oxford, UK: Oxford University Press.

Parnreiter, C. (2010) 'Global cities in global commodity chains: Exploring the role of Mexico City in the geography of global economic governance', *Global Networks*, 10, pp. 35–53.

Pryke, M. (1994) 'Looking back on the space of a boom: (Re)developing spatial matrices in the City of London', *Environment and Planning A*, 26, pp. 235–264.

Reiffenstein, T. (2009) 'Specialization, centralization, and the distribution of patent intermediaries in the USA and Japan', *Regional Studies*, 43, pp. 571–588.

Sassen, S. (1991) *The Global City*. Princeton, NJ: Princeton University Press.

Sassen, S. (1999) 'Global financial centers', *Foreign Affairs*, January/February, pp. 75–87.

Smith, R.G. (2012) 'NY-LON', in Derudder, B., Hoyler, M., Taylor, P. J. & Witlox, F. (Eds.), *International Handbook of Globalization and World Cities*. Cheltenham, UK: Edward Elgar, pp. 421–428.

Strange, S. (1997) *Casino Capitalism*. Manchester, UK: Manchester University Press.

Taylor, M. & Asheim, B. (2001) 'The concept of the firm in Economic Geography', *Economic Geography*, 77, pp. 315–328.

Taylor, P.J. (2001) 'Specification of the world city network', *Geographical Analysis*, 33, pp. 181–194.

Taylor, P.J. & Derudder, B. (2016) *World City Network: A Global Urban Analysis*. 2nd Edition. London: Routledge.

Taylor, P.J., Derudder, B., Hoyler, M. & Ni, P. (2013) 'New regional geographies of the world as practised by leading advanced producer service firms in 2010', *Transactions of the Institute of British Geographers*, 38, pp. 497–511.

Taylor, P.J., Hoyler, M., Pain, K. & Vinciguerra, S. (2014) 'Extensive and intensive globalizations: Explicating the low connectivity puzzle of US cities using a city-dyad analysis', *Journal of Urban Affairs*, 36, pp. 876–890.

Warf, B. (2001) 'Global dimensions of US legal services', *The Professional Geographer*, 53, pp. 398–406.

Wójcik, D. (2013) 'The dark side of NY–LON: Financial centres and the global financial crisis', *Urban Studies*, 50, pp. 2736–2752.

Yeung, H.W.-C. (2005) 'Organizational space: A new frontier in International Business strategy?' *Critical Perspectives on International Business*, 1, pp. 219–240.

16

THE USE OF GLOBAL VALUE CHAIN/GLOBAL PRODUCTION NETWORK RELATED LITERATURE IN INTERNATIONAL BUSINESS RESEARCH

Investigating the nature and degree of integration

Noemi Sinkovics, Rudolf R. Sinkovics, Samia Ferdous Hoque and Matthew Alford

Introduction

We live in a world in which the production, distribution and consumption of goods and services are becoming progressively more complex, with increasing geographical spread and functional integration between economic activities (Dicken, 2015). These economic activities are undertaken within complex and geographically dispersed webs of production circuits and networks, conceptualised by a body of scholars as global production networks (GPNs) (Ernst & Kim, 2002; Coe, Dicken & Hess, 2008; Dicken, 2015). Dicken (2015, p. 54) defines a GPN as 'the circuit of interconnected functions, operations and transactions through which a specific commodity, good or service is produced, distributed and consumed'.

The GPN framework has close linkages with global commodity chain (GCC) analysis, proposed by Gereffi (1994), which subsequently evolved into the global value chain (GVC) framework (Gereffi, 1999; Gereffi, Humphrey & Sturgeon, 2005). Whilst GCC analysis focused on a 'set of inter-organisational networks clustered around one commodity or product' (Gereffi & Korzeniewicz, 1994, p. 2), GVC exploration concentrated on value-generating activities not only for 'commodities' but throughout the entire production process for goods and services. In this way, GVC scholars have analysed the characteristics of value chain transactions by proposing five distinct forms of inter-firm governance based on the complexity of transactions, supply base capabilities and codifiability of production (Gereffi, Humphrey & Sturgeon, 2005). Parallel to GCC/GVC analysis, GPN scholars study the networked nature of economic activities (Dicken et al., 2001; Coe, Dicken & Hess, 2008). They emphasise that, within the changing contours of the world economy, such networks integrate firms, industries and national economies (Coe, Dicken & Hess, 2008). Therefore, GPN analysis adopts the network rather than the chain as the central unit of analysis, positing that firms are part of wider networks of globalised production (Dicken et al., 2001). In this chapter, we refer to these two bodies of literature combined as the GVC/GPN literature.

Whilst the GVC/GPN literature places the chain or network at the heart of the analysis, International Business (IB) scholars have traditionally been interested in firms, and particularly multinational enterprises (MNEs) (Gui, 2010). The fragmentation of economic activities and functional integration have deeply transformed the way MNEs structure and manage productive and commercial activities on a global scale (de Marchi, di Maria & Ponte, 2014). In contrast to traditional forms of vertical integration associated with internationalisation, MNEs have more recently opted to extend their organisational boundaries to form equity and non-equity based relationships with other actors operating along the value chain, such as suppliers, distributors, agents and partners (Buckley, 2016). Therefore, in order to keep pace with the rapidly shifting world economy, de Marchi, di Maria and Ponte (2014) urge for continual insights on MNEs' changing organisational forms, internationalisation paths between outsourcing and offshoring, and approaches to knowledge management within organisations and networks. The emergence of these networked multinationals has also changed the process of value creation, and power and knowledge dynamics between MNEs and other actors in value chains (Johns et al., 2015). For this reason, a broader range of GVC/GPN actors beyond MNEs have started to gain analytical and empirical importance.

The increasing interdependencies between MNEs and other actors have set the groundwork for analysing inter-firm and non-firm relationships, governance and power dynamics and the distribution of gains throughout GPNs. However, such foci of analysis have so far received insufficient attention in IB and, we would argue, can no longer be overlooked (cf. Cairns & Sliwa, 2008). Not surprisingly then, a number of IB scholars have noted potential incoherence between theoretical progress made in IB and the practical impact of recent processes of economic globalisation (Storper, 1997; Dicken et al., 2001; Dicken, 2015). Whilst IB studies are increasingly adopting network-based perspectives to study MNEs (e.g. Parkhe & Dhanaraj, 2003; Mathews, 2006) along with other actors in the network (McDermott & Corredoira, 2010; Li, Kong & Zhang, 2016), the emphasis on internationalisation aspects combined with an analytical preoccupation with Western MNEs is still predominant in IB (Cairns & Sliwa, 2008; de Marchi, di Maria & Ponte, 2014).

More recently, a number of IB scholars, including Giuliani and Macchi (2013), de Marchi, di Maria and Ponte (2014), and Johns et al. (2015), have called for interdisciplinary research to integrate broader dimensions of analysis into IB scholarship. In particular, they urge for the integration of GVC/GPN-related ideas. Johns et al. (2015) have pointed out numerous commonalities between the IB and GVC/GPN literatures, noting that GVC/GPN concepts can contribute to key debates and unanswered questions in IB. Based on a bibliographic analysis of IB papers published from 2005 to 2014, they furthermore recognise that IB studies have very slowly been taking up references from the GVC/GPN literature. The authors identify 75 papers published in IB journals that have either cited or mentioned the term GVC/GPN. However, a more in-depth, qualitative examination of these papers was beyond the scope of their study. The purpose of this chapter is to build on and extend Johns et al.'s (2015) work by examining the *nature* and *degree* of integration of GVC/GPN-related articles cited in IB research. The focus is on the analysis of papers published since the mid-2000s in IB journals.

We also examine the disciplinary origin of the authors as this is an important factor in the discussion of idea migration and integration.

To undertake this analysis, we adopt Cairns and Sliwa's (2008) perspective on the boundaries of IB. They suggest that, in order to critically engage with the nature of contemporary IB, it is necessary to study IB processes as a network of power relations. They furthermore warn against viewing IB as a 'value-free activity of a purely economic nature' (p. 162), urging scholars to understand the power dynamics of different forms of networked relationships and the impact of MNEs' economic activity on other GVC/GPN actors. Subsequently, they call for broadening the boundaries of IB beyond the analysis of MNEs alone, by drawing upon neighbouring disciplines to solve key debates in IB whilst opening up possibilities for alternative structures and forms of IB. In view of that, Cairns and Sliwa (2008, p. 5) adopt a broader 'stakeholder-based approach' in order 'to take account of the different actors involved in and affected by IB'. Rather than (Western) MNEs alone, they consider all stakeholders within the boundaries of IB, such as suppliers, linkage firms, industries, employees, consumers, broader society and the natural environment. In this chapter, we utilise Cairns and Sliwa's (2008) stakeholder-based perspective of IB to identify the degree to which the GVC/GPN literature is adopted in IB studies.

The contents of this chapter are structured as follows. The first section presents a brief literature review on how the IB literature has evolved and taken shape over the ten-year period since the mid-2000s, along with how GVC/GPN studies can contribute to contemporary IB. The second section outlines the methodology of the systematic bibliographic analysis performed here. The third section discusses the findings regarding the nature of GVC/GPN integration into IB studies. This section also investigates the relationship between the authors' disciplinary backgrounds and the level of integration. The final section concludes with a summary of key findings along with recommendations for future research.

Literature review

Contemporary IB and its evolution

Up to and during the 1980s, IB scholars studied how the internal mechanisms of MNEs shaped their modes of foreign investment, location choices, hierarchical dimensions of coordination (Buckley & Casson, 1976; Porter, 1986; Bartlett & Ghoshal, 1987) and investment motives (Dunning, 1979, 1980). Internalisation thinking has therefore historically dominated the IB discipline in explaining internationalisation activities of MNEs (Buckley, 2014). Since the 1990s, the IB environment has become increasingly volatile, with the rise of Asian multinationals and associated emergence of cost-based competition (Buckley & Casson, 1998). Within this dynamic context, the survival and prosperity of Western MNEs has been thought to depend upon their flexibility and cost-efficiency, prompting them to extend their organisational boundaries in order to access wider information sources, information management systems and knowledge creation abilities (Buckley, 2016). This new trend of flexible MNEs was captured in internalisation thinking by Buckley and Casson (1998), who explained how MNEs adopted a hub-and-spoke structure by which they internally undertook activities (such as R&D and marketing) in which their competitiveness lay, whilst outsourcing activities such as production in which their focus was mainly on cost reduction. During the 2000s, internalisation thinking was further revived by the 'Global Factory' perspective (Buckley & Ghauri, 2004; Buckley, 2009b), which proposed a more networked approach to gaining efficiency. MNEs became the 'orchestrators' of their Global Factories, in which they 'fine sliced' their value chain tasks, pursued those in optimal, low-cost locations, and controlled each task by deciding on the level of internalisation of the firms that participated in their GPNs (Buckley, 2011; Buckley & Strange, 2011).

An alternative view to internalisation thinking was proposed by Stephen Hymer. In a rarely quoted paper, Hymer introduced his 'law of increasing firm size', which offered prescient insights regarding the externalisation of production by MNEs (Hymer, 1972). Drawing upon Hymer (1972), Strange and Newton (2006) proposed the theory of externalisation, commonly referred to as the subcontracting activities of MNEs. A key feature of externalisation is MNEs' unilateral control over their supplier firms in which MNEs have no equity ownership. To summarise the discussion thus far, since the mid-2000s MNEs have been conceptualised as 'networked multinationals' or 'integrated multinationals' (Buckley, 2016, p. 6) by numerous IB scholars (Parkhe & Dhanaraj, 2003; Strange & Newton, 2006; Buckley, 2009b).

From 2008 till 2013, foreign direct investment (FDI) outflows from developing economies have increased by 36%, whilst those from developed economies have declined by 46% (UNCTAD, 2014). Following these shifts in global trading dynamics and the emergence of network-based perspectives in IB, a number of scholars have begun studying internationalisation patterns of multinationals from emerging economies (EMNEs) (e.g. Mathews, 2006; Pananond, 2013). Mathews (2006) suggests that latecomer and newcomer multinationals (specifically from East Asia) internationalise by developing multiple connections with external firms, particularly from advanced economies, in order to accumulate learning and access resources. More recent IB literature perceives these EMNEs as 'rising power' MNEs (RP MNEs), with the potential to significantly challenge the 'rules of the competitive game' and 'hegemony' of Western MNEs in global markets (Yamin & Sinkovics, 2015). Contrary to Mathew's EMNEs that are interested in developing linkages with firms from advanced economies, RP firms have extensive and growing operations in developing countries and play an active role in global and regional value chains. This trend has encouraged a group of scholars to study the nature of south-south FDI and other non-equity-based economic activities (e.g. Azmeh & Nadvi, 2014).

With the rise of the networked MNEs and their increasing attention to economic efficiency, a limited number of IB scholars have questioned the developmental impact of MNEs' economic activities on other actors within their global networks (Meyer, 2004; Ramamurti, 2004; Ghauri & Buckley, 2006). In his commentary on the Global Factory, Yamin (2011b) points to the possible vulnerabilities of MNEs' new organisational forms, governance structures and role as powerful network orchestrators.

Overall, within the changing contours of the world economy, we argue that network-based thinking deserves to be at the heart of contemporary IB (Dicken, 2015). The emergence of a networked perspective has left a rich set of unanswered questions related to governance, location theory, knowledge and power dynamics, risk and uncertainty (Buckley, 2016), and the developmental impact on MNEs' networked partners and the wider society (Cairns & Sliwa, 2008; Dicken, 2015). These questions have set the groundwork for idea migration from GVC/GPN analysis to IB scholarship and opened the door for a possible integration of synergistic concepts and theory (Johns et al., 2015).

What can contemporary IB bring in from GVC/GPN research?

Based on the previous discussion, we argue that the notions of GVC/GPN can potentially contribute to a number of areas in contemporary IB research (de Marchi, di Maria & Ponte, 2014). First, GVC/GPN analysis facilitates the mapping of cross-border linkages and insights into the power dynamics that exist between firm and non-firm actors in the global production process. The GVC approach focuses on the inter-firm dynamics between actors operating along the value chain, using the term 'fragmentation' to describe the physical separation of different parts of the production process (Gereffi, Humphrey & Sturgeon, 2005). GVC scholars give analytical attention to the role of inter-relationships between firms that undertake different functional activities (e.g. R&D, production, sales, marketing, consumption and recycling) to bring a specific product from its conception to its end and beyond (Gereffi & Fernandez-Stark, 2011). Parallel to the GVC analysis, GPN scholars perceive fragmentation from a network perspective, in which they account for the role of both firm and non-firm actors in shaping cross-border value chain activities and influencing production outcomes in different countries (Coe, Dicken & Hess, 2008). In relation to IB scholarship, the organisation of GVC/GPN can provide insights in regard to mapping the structure and the process of value generation, enhancement and capture by different firm and non-firm actors involved in the GPNs of MNEs. Such mapping can serve as the basis for identifying the process of financialisation, and the distribution of profits and gains between MNEs and other actors in GPNs (Johns et al., 2015).

The GVC approach provides a holistic view of global industries from two vantage points: top-down and bottom-up (Gereffi & Lee, 2012). The top-down view focuses on the modes of governance coordinating the value chain (Gereffi, Humphrey & Sturgeon, 2005); whilst the bottom-up view focuses on upgrading by suppliers and other local actors (Giuliani, Pietrobelli & Rabellotti, 2005; Barrientos, Gereffi & Rossi, 2011; Pavlínek & Ženka, 2011). The top-down approach views the global economy as a complex network that is coordinated by lead-firm buyers, and connects them to a geographically dispersed supplier base (Lee & Gereffi, 2015). A core focus of GVC analysis is on the 'governance' of these cross-border relationships (Gereffi, Humphrey & Sturgeon, 2005), defined by Gereffi (1994) as 'authority and power relationships that determine how financial, material and human resources are allocated and flow within a chain'. Gereffi, Humphrey and Sturgeon (2005) identify five principal types of governance (market, modular, relational, captive, hierarchy) to conceptualise the coordination between lead firms and suppliers. These differing governance types are based on the varying complexity of information and knowledge in the buyer-supplier relationship; opportunities for codifying and transmitting information; and supply-base capabilities. The hierarchical mode refers to vertical integration and equity investment, whilst the market mode refers to arms-length relationships involving no equity investment. In between the hierarchical and the market modes exist network modes of governance that include different types of non-equity-based relational forms (i.e. modular, captive and relational networks).

This focus on external network linkages has led some to describe the GVC/GPN approach as a 'theory of externalisation in a global context' (de Marchi, di Maria & Ponte, 2014, p. 5), which we argue constitutes another area of contribution to current IB debates. Another insight comes from GVC/GPN scholars' research on a range of non-equity-based relational forms, providing an understanding of the ongoing network-based processes during internationalisation (cf. Strange & Newton, 2006). This is all the more important as the predominant focus of IB scholarship has continued to be put on internalised entry modes, rendering forms of externalisation underexplored. The framework of GVC governance furthermore facilitates the analysis of power dynamics and inter-firm linkages in MNE-driven GPNs (Johns et al., 2015). GVC/GPN studies also offer a more complex picture of non-firm actors that can act as network orchestrators. Whilst IB studies have mainly been concerned with the internationalisation of Western manufacturing MNEs, GVC research has extended the analysis to multinational retailers in the form of 'buyers' or 'brand vendors', through Gereffi's (1994) framework of buyer-driven versus producer-driven chains (de Marchi et al., 2014). The study of RP firms and EMNEs as network orchestrators further broadens the analytical horizon, beyond Western MNEs (Yamin & Sinkovics, 2015).

The bottom-up approach in the GVC literature focuses exclusively on how the organisation of GVC activities has created upgrading opportunities for SMEs from least developed and developing economies (Gereffi, 1999; Morrison, Pietrobelli & Rabellotti, 2008). Upgrading is defined as the 'capacity of a firm to innovate in order to increase the value added' (Giuliani, Pietrobelli & Rabellotti, 2005). The more specific concept of economic upgrading refers to 'a process of improving the ability of a firm to move to more profitable and/or technologically sophisticated capital and skill-intensive economic niches' (Gereffi, 1999, p. 38). A relatively recent interest within the GVC landscape is in social upgrading (Gereffi & Lee, 2012), which refers to the process of improving the rights and entitlement of workers as social actors, thereby enhancing the quality of their employment (Barrientos, Gereffi & Rossi, 2011). One strand of GVC research has advanced this agenda by examining the link between modes of governance and forms of upgrading (i.e. process, product, functional and chain upgrading) (Humphrey & Schmitz, 2002). In this sense, the GVC/GPN literature offers a distinct conceptualisation of upgrading and clear frameworks for studying social and economic upgrading in IB. It also facilitates the analysis of the impact that different forms of network governance mechanisms have on suppliers' and other linkage firms' upgrading success – an aspect that is still under-researched in IB (Gereffi & Lee, 2012). Additionally, GVC studies tend to accord more attention than IB studies do to the role of suppliers' capability building and their proactive investment in generating success in upgrading (Kadarusman & Nadvi, 2012).

Another stream of GVC research takes workers as a central unit of analysis and explores the extent of their gains from GVC participation (e.g. Barrientos & Kritzinger, 2004; Rossi, 2011; Lund-Thomsen et al., 2012; Lund-Thomsen & Coe, 2013; Lund-Thomsen & Lindgreen, 2013). This body of literature highlights a number of structural inequalities inherent in value chain organisation that restrict social gains, such as a lack of code harmonisation, the exclusion of workers' voice (Lund-Thomsen & Coe, 2013), a failure to account for the broader social context at local production sites (Lindgreen et al., 2010) and a stratified impact of governance mechanisms on workers (Barrientos & Kritzinger, 2004; Rossi, 2011). Insights from these studies can aid the understanding of the developmental impact of MNEs on other actors within their GPN, which again constitutes a black box in IB research (Cairns & Sliwa, 2008). Consequently, Lee and Gereffi (2015) rightly state that the 'GVC literature is uniquely positioned to provide a bridge between IB and development literatures' (p. 330).

As discussed in the previous section, a network-based perspective can potentially shape the contours of contemporary and future IB research (Cairns & Sliwa, 2008). To this end, the GVC/GPN literature can provide key insights into four under-researched areas in IB: (i) the process of value creation in MNEs' GPNs and the distribution of gains; (ii) the power and governance structure between MNEs (including buyers, RP firms and EMNEs) and other actors in GPNs, especially understanding the non-equity-based relational forms; (iii) the drivers and consequences of upgrading by suppliers and other linkage firms; and (iv) the developmental impact of MNEs' economic activities on other actors within their GPNs. Whilst it is clear (at least in theory) that IB research can significantly benefit from the integration of ideas from the GVC/GPN literature, it is currently unclear to what degree such integration has taken place so far. Therefore, in the coming sections, we pursue this agenda based on systematic bibliographic analysis.

Methodology

Search and selection strategy

To examine the nature and degree of GVC/GPN integration in IB research since the mid-2000s, we performed a systematic bibliographic analysis in three steps. First, we undertook an advanced search in Web of Science using the keywords 'global value chain', 'global production network', 'upgrading/upgrade', 'value chain' and 'global supply chain'. This search yielded 764 articles published during the years 2005 to 2015 in various journals in the field of GVC/GPN, Economic Geography, IB and general management. These articles had, in the abstract or title, at least some notion of GVCs or GPNs.

The next step involved identifying papers that had been used and cited in IB. From the initial 764 articles, those published in IB journals were selected for further analysis. The following 16 IB journals were considered: *Journal of International Business Studies, Journal of World Business, Management and Organisational Review, International Business Review, Management International Review, Journal of International Management, Asia Pacific Journal of Management, European Journal of International Management, Asia Pacific Business Review, Thunderbird International Business Review, Critical Perspectives on International Business, Transnational Corporations, Multinational Business Review, Journal of Asia Pacific Business, Global Strategy Journal* and *Journal of East West Business*. Further to this, a keyword search using the same keywords was also performed individually in each of the 16 listed journals for cross-checking purposes. Moving beyond these listed journals, the titles and abstract of the initial 764 articles were carefully studied, revealing additional relevant book chapters and papers published in journals not included in the original search, such as *European Planning Studies* and *Global Networks*. Through this filtering process, a total of 79 papers were identified for in-depth analysis.

The process of analysis

The final step involved the in-depth analysis of these 79 articles to try to understand how the concept of GVC/GPN had been used within each paper and with what effect in terms of contribution to the IB literature. The analysis was conducted by drawing on a template consisting of dimensions such as author/s, focus, theoretical background, GVC/GPN usage and application, and contribution to IB. The template facilitated the categorisation of papers according to the extent to which the concept of GVC/GPN was used. Furthermore, it aided the identification of domains in IB research most receptive to ideas from that body of literature.

The papers were divided according to two perspectives: (i) papers that focused on conventional (Western) MNEs and (ii) papers that concentrated on other GVC/GPN actors including suppliers, RP firms, EMNEs, workers, consumers, emerging markets, industries and clusters. This categorisation rests on Cairns' and Sliwa's (2008) stakeholder-based view of IB, in which both MNEs and the other GVC/GPN actors are considered. As stated in the introduction, a number of scholars (e.g. Cairns & Sliwa, 2008; Johns et al., 2015) suggest that in order to create synergies between the IB and GVC/GPN literatures, it is imperative to not only consider focal-firm (i.e. MNE) perspectives, but also those of other GVC/GPN actors positioned to shape and influence processes of governance and upgrading. Categorising papers in this way allows for the analysis and comparison of the degree of conceptual integration of GVC/GPN thinking in IB studies across these two main sets of papers. Additionally, this enables the identification of areas in IB research where the most extensive integration of ideas from the GVC/GPN literature has occurred.

We furthermore controlled for the disciplinary origins of the authors. This is important because, with increasing interdisciplinarity, scholars not only work with colleagues from different areas, but also often publish in outlets outside of their specific disciplinary boundaries. Authors' disciplinary origins were determined from their web profiles. This exercise yielded 16 disciplinary areas (see Table 16.1): IB, developmental studies, strategic management, management, marketing, accounting and finance, human resource management, corporate social responsibility, organisational studies, production and operations, innovation, economics, science and technology, information and communication, sociology and Economic Geography.

Table 16.1 Details of IB papers and the nature of their integration with GVC/GPN concepts

IB paper details					*Integration of GVC literature in the paper*	
Author/year	*Authors' area*	*Focus*	*Theoretical background*	*Methodology*	*How used*	*Contribution to IB literature*
Alvarez & Marin (2013)	a Economics b Economics	How the integration of firms from developing countries in sophisticated high-tech markets can be defined by the combined action of the MNE and the ability for technology absorption and creation.	Industrial competitiveness Catch-up/upgrading	Quantitative: secondary data	**Parallel citation** (cited papers, Mudambi, 2008; Kumaraswamy et al., 2012)	N/A
Azmeh & Nadvi (2014)	a Environment, education and development b International development	Illustrate how such firms manage complex international production linkages, and ensure the incorporation of Jordan into the global garment industry.	GVC governance GVC organisation structure	Qualitative: case study	**Core theoretical framework** Understanding the role of RP firms in GVC network	Integration of IB and GVC; understanding the role of firms in organisation of GVC network
Baaij & Slangen (2013)	a Strategic management and entrepreneurship b Strategic management and entrepreneurship	Examines how such HQ disaggregation changes the role that HQ–subsidiary geographic distance plays in HQ's decisions about subsidiaries.	Disintegration of HQ–subsidiary Ex post communication	Conceptual paper	**Citation only** (cited paper, Gereffi, Humphrey & Sturgeon, 2005)	N/A
Banalieva & Sarathy (2011)	a International Business and strategy b International Business and strategy	Analyses how the EMs' trade liberalisation can amplify or reduce the performance from foreign market penetration in the context of electronics vs. non-electronics EM MNEs.	Transaction cost economies Multi-stage general theory of internationalisation New trade theory (triangular manufacturing)	Quantitative: secondary data	**Complementing IB theory** Internationalisation performance in the context of trade liberalisation and triad firm	How trade linearisation benefits internationalisation performance

(continued)

Table 16.1 (continued)

IB paper details					*Integration of GVC literature in the paper*	
Author/year	*Authors' area*	*Focus*	*Theoretical background*	*Methodology*	*How used*	*Contribution to IB literature*
Beugelsdijk, Pedersen & Petersen (2009)	a International Business and management b International Business and management c Strategic management and globalisation	Discuss and empirically test whether MNEs' configuration of value-adding activities has shifted from a sparse and simple (host–home) international division of labour among the foreign affiliates to a more specialised and 'advanced' GVC configuration in which MNEs locate fine-sliced parts of the value chain at the most efficient locations.	GVC configuration and specialisation of labour	Quantitative: secondary data	**Citation only** (cited papers, Gereffi, 1999; Humphrey & Schmitz, 2002) **Parallel citation** Underlying structure of cross-border sales within MNE (i.e. the specific GVC configuration of the MNE)	N/A
Buckley (2009a)	a International Business	Paper advances four propositions on the impact of the Global Factory on the world economy.	Coasean framework Internalisation theory	Conceptual paper	**Citation only** (cited paper, Gereffi, Humphrey & Sturgeon, 2005)	N/A
Buckley (2014)	a International Business	The purpose of this paper is to review the key analytical principles of internalisation theory as a general theory of the MNE.	Coasean framework Internalisation theory	Conceptual paper	**Parallel citation** (cited papers, Mudambi, 2008; UNCTAD, 2013)	N/A
Buckley, Forsans & Munjal (2012)	a International Business b International Business c International Business	Examines the complementarity of country-specific linkages with country-specific advantages in explaining foreign acquisitions by Indian MNEs, by testing and further extending the Eclectic Paradigm.	Eclectic Paradigm, role of networks and linkages	Quantitative: secondary data	**Parallel citation** (cited paper, Mathews, 2006) Understanding the network and linkage strategies EMNEs are integrating into GVCs	N/A

Cairns (2014)	a Management	This paper aims to critically engage with the premise of development at the 'bottom of the pyramid' through consideration of the current and potential future status of the workers who dismantle end-of-life ships in the breaking yards of less developed countries.	Bottom of the pyramid	Qualitative: critical scenario analysis	**Contextual description** (cited paper, Nadvi, 2008; Lund-Thomsen et al., 2012) How standard compliance is a sin qua non in GVCs	Understanding the context of compliance and impact on bottom of the pyramid workers
Contractor, Kumar & Dhanaraj (2015)	a Management and global business b International Business c Strategy and global leadership	This paper reviews India's place in the international economy by identifying its areas of comparative advantage.	N/A	Qualitative: case study	**Citation only** (cited paper, Gereffi, Humphrey & Sturgeon, 2005)	N/A
Corredoira & McDermott (2014)	a Management and organisation b International Business	Drawing on insights from economic sociology and comparative capitalism, the paper posits that in these contexts of scarce resources and inferior technology, upgrading depends on the ways in which organisational and institutional networks enable firms to integrate imported advanced knowledge with local applied knowledge.	Economic sociology and comparative capitalism literatures Organisational and institutional network-based view Upgrading	Quantitative: survey data	**Complementing IB theory** Conceptualisation: defining and understanding upgrading	Linking upgrading with a comparative institutional perspective

(continued)

Table 16.1 (continued)

IB paper details					*Integration of GVC literature in the paper*	
Author/year	*Authors' area*	*Focus*	*Theoretical background*	*Methodology*	*How used*	*Contribution to IB literature*
Cuervo-Cazurra (2007)	a International Business	Studies multinationalisation – the decision to establish FDI – of developing country firms, in particular Latin American ones or 'multilatinas'.	Eclectic Paradigm Uppsala model	Qualitative: case study	**Mention only** (use of the term 'upgrade')	N/A
D'Agostino & Santangelo (2012)	a Science, politics and society b Science, politics and society	Drawing on the view that multinationals act as a link between home and host (the double diamond framework), the paper extends this framework and investigates the indirect impact of host on home location with reference to R&D internationalisation in emerging economies.	Eclectic Paradigm Double diamond model	Quantitative: secondary data	**Parallel citation** (cited paper, Mudambi, 2008)	N/A
Donzéa (2015)	a Economics	How the evolution of GVCs resulted in lost competitiveness for the Japanese watch industry.	Buyer-driven vs. producer-driven GVC	Qualitative: case study	**Core theoretical framework** How Seiko lost competitiveness due to its producer-driven chain at the global level	The link between GVC governance and competitiveness (authors do not explicitly point out)
Duanmu & Fai (2007)	a Management b Management	This paper investigates vertical knowledge transfers from inward-invested MNEs to indigenous Chinese suppliers in the electrical and electronics industry.	Intra-firm and inter-firm knowledge transfer	Qualitative: case study	**Citation only** (cited paper, Ernst & Kim, 2002)	N/A

Eapen (2012)	a International Business	Argues that a domestic firm's ability to absorb spillovers depends on the social structure in which it is embedded.	FDI spillover Network ties	Conceptual paper	**Citation only** (cited paper, Giuliani, Pietrobelli & Rabellotti, 2005)	N/A
Eapen (2013)	a International Business	Argues that identifying FDI spillover effects in such incomplete datasets is problematic, owing to measurement error and selection problems.	Spillover effect Productivity	Quantitative: secondary data	**Mention only** (use of the term 'upgrading')	N/A
Edwards et al. (2010)	a Management b Industrial relations and organisational behaviour c Human resource management	This paper analyses the issue of variation between multinational companies in the extent to which they use their foreign operating units as the origin of employment practices that are subsequently transferred across the firm.	Configuration of MNEs and diffusion of knowledge	Quantitative: survey	**Citation only** (cited paper, Gereffi, Humphrey & Sturgeon, 2005)	N/A
Eng & Spickett-Jones (2009)	a Digital marketing b Marketing	Examines eight different marketing capabilities to assess influence on manufacture upgrade performance.	Types of upgrading Capabilities-based view	Quantitative: survey	**Core theoretical framework** Understanding different phases or steps of upgrading	Linking marketing capabilities with upgrading performance
Fitzgerald & Rowley (2015)	a Business history and international management b Human resource management	How the strategies and capabilities of Japanese MNCs and their subsidiaries complicate or inhibit adaptation to the demands of global competition.	Historical perspectives used to reveal how the international competitive landscape has changed	Qualitative: case study, secondary data	**Mention only** (use of the phrase 'buyer-driven value chain')	N/A

(continued)

Table 16.1 (continued)

IB paper details					*Integration of GVC literature in the paper*	
Author/year	*Authors' area*	*Focus*	*Theoretical background*	*Methodology*	*How used*	*Contribution to IB literature*
Fleury, Fleury & Borini (2013)	a Production engineering b International management c Marketing	Examines whether internationalisation process relies on the firm's innovative capability.	Resource-based view Innovation capabilities	Quantitative: secondary data	**Mention only** (use of the term 'global value chain')	N/A
Fong, Lee & Dub (2013)	a Business management b Finance and economics	This study examines the effects of consumer animosity and reputation transferability of local targets on cross-border acquisitions.	Corporate reputation Consumer animosity Local target reputation transferability	Quantitative: survey	**Mention only** (use of the term 'global value chain')	N/A
Funk et al. (2010)	a Management b Management and operation c International Business d Marketing	Examine whether consumers' willingness to purchase a complex hybrid product is negatively affected by partial production shifts to an animosity-evoking country.	Consumer animosity	Quantitative: survey	**Contextual description** Consumer animosity in the changing context of GVC integration	N/A
Giroud & Mirza (2015)	a International Business b International Business	To show how the nature of the activities conducted by MNEs globally and the governance modes are changing.	GVC segments/stages GVC governance	Conceptual paper	**Core theoretical framework** Conceptualisation: how consideration of GVC segment and governance mode influence FDI decisions	Understanding FDI motives through the lens of GVC
Gooris & Peeters (2014)	a Econometrics b International Business	This paper studies the effect of home–host country distance on the choice of governance mode in service offshoring.	Transaction cost economies	Quantitative: secondary data	**Parallel citation** (cited paper, Buckley & Ghauri, 2004; Mudambi, 2008)	N/A

Gupta & Subramanian (2008)	a b	Global management Organisational studies	The paper identifies relevant generic strategies and bases of competitive advantage in regional clusters.	Krugman's geography, Porter's Diamond, and European regional innovation system perspectives, as well as three extensions of those perspectives	Qualitative: case study	**Complementing IB theory** How the strategies for competitive advantage changed over the period, explained through the lens of the GVC along with other theories	Competitive advantage of regional clusters through the lens of the GVC along with other relevant theories
Hansen, Pedersen & Petersen (2009)	a b c	Communication and management Communication and management Communication and management	The study addresses the implications MNC strategies have for linkage effects in developing countries.	FDI motives: integration-responsiveness framework Value chain configuration Intra-MNC coordination Upgrading	Quantitative: survey	**Complementing IB theory** How MNEs' integration-responsiveness strategy influences value chain configuration and upgrading	The effect of MNEs' local linkages on upgrading, through the lens of GVC configuration
Hatani (2009)	a	International Business	Drawing on the GVC analysis and institutional views, this paper explains the mechanism of 'spillover interception', a structural obstacle to technology spillovers in emerging economies.	GVC analysis Institutional view Technology spillover	Qualitative: case study	**Core theoretical framework** To understand the cross-border production linkages	Propose the concept of 'spillover interception', drawing upon GVC perspective
Hatani & McGaughey (2013)	a b	International Business International Business	How does global expansion, in particular entry into emerging markets, affect the cohesion of a large interfirm network and with what consequences?	Evolutionary perspective Global supply network	Qualitative: longitudinal case study	**Parallel citation** (Cited paper, Chen, 2004)	N/A

(continued)

Table 16.1 (continued)

IB paper details					*Integration of GVC literature in the paper*	
Author/year	*Authors' area*	*Focus*	*Theoretical background*	*Methodology*	*How used*	*Contribution to IB literature*
Haworth (2013)	a International Business	This paper provides a first analysis of the human resource development dimensions of the compressed development approach via GVC considerations, using an APEC case study.	GVC framework Compressed development approach Human resource development	Qualitative: case study	**Core theoretical framework** Developing HR for facilitating development through consideration of upgrading in specific GVCs	Understanding human resource development policies through the lenses of the GVC
Hill & Mudambi (2010)	a International Business b International Business	This paper describes three distinct but interrelated processes – spillover and catch up, brokering and bottom-up – that link globalisation to entrepreneurship in emerging economies.	Entrepreneurship (Kirznerian or Schumpeterian)	Conceptual paper	**Citation only** (cited paper, Giuliani & Macchi, 2013) **Parallel citation** (cited paper, Mudambi, 2008)	N/A
Jensen (2009)	a Strategic management and globalisation	Explores organisational learning that occurs over time in both home and host firms and uses learning as a measure of the firm impact of advanced services offshoring.	Services offshoring Organisational change	Qualitative: case study	**Citation only** (cited paper, Gereffi, Humphrey & Sturgeon, 2005)	N/A
Jensen (2012)	a Strategic management and globalisation	Investigates how determinants of the offshore outsourcing process contribute to the resource stocks of client firms.	Offshore outsourcing Resource-based view IB network theory	Conceptual paper	**Parallel citation** (Cited papers, Porter, 1986; Mudambi, 2008; Buckley, 2009b)	N/A

Jensen & Petersen (2013)	a Strategic management and globalisation b Strategic management and globalisation	This paper investigates under which circumstances a build-operate-transfer (BOT) outsourcing contract (i.e. a contract where the client firm exercises its call option) is beneficial, or the opposite, to the emerging market vendor firm.	BOT outsourcing Linkage, learning and leverage model	Qualitative: case study	**Contextual description** (cited paper, Gereffi, Humphrey & Sturgeon, 2005) **Parallel citation** (cited paper, Mudambi, 2008)	Understanding the distribution of power in relational ties in a BOT contract context
Jensen, Larsen & Pedersen (2013)	a Strategic management and globalisation b Strategic management and globalisation c Strategic management and globalisation	Argues that an organisational design perspective on offshoring can benefit research and practice in understanding how firms can coordinate and integrate offshoring activities.	Organisational design perspective of offshoring	Conceptual paper	**Citation only** (cited paper, Gereffi, Humphrey & Sturgeon, 2005)	N/A
de Jong & van Houten (2014)	a Strategy b Geoscience	Argues that the impact of the degree of internationalisation on MNE performance is contingent on MNE cultural diversity.	Internationalisation MNE cultural diversity	Quantitative: secondary data	**Citation only** (cited paper, Gereffi, Humphrey & Sturgeon, 2005)	N/A
Kenney, Massini & Murtha (2009)	a Human ecology b Economics and management of innovation c Management	Introduces the *Journal of International Business Studies* Special Issue on Offshoring Administrative and Technical Services (ATS).	N/A	Conceptual paper	**Citation only** (cited paper, Gereffi, Humphrey & Sturgeon, 2005)	N/A

(continued)

Table 16.1 (continued)

IB paper details					*Integration of GVC literature in the paper*	
Author/year	*Authors' area*	*Focus*	*Theoretical background*	*Methodology*	*How used*	*Contribution to IB literature*
Khan, Lew & Sinkovics (2015)	a Strategy and International Business b International Business c International Business	Explores inter-organisational linkages and the extent of technology transfer and develops propositions related to the linkages, technology transfer and upgrading of local suppliers in developing economies.	Upgrading in GVCs	Qualitative: interviews	**Core theoretical framework** Understanding inter-organisational linkages and forms of upgrading	The extent of technology transfer and effect on form of upgrading in specific inter-firm relational contexts
Kong, Zhang & Ramu (2016)	a Science and technology for development b Developmental studies c Economics	This paper examines how GPNs have benefited technological upgrading in the semiconductor industry in China.	Evolutionary economics Institutional support Upgrading	Quantitative: secondary data	**Core theoretical framework** Use of 'upgrading' as the key framework	The role of local institutions in upgrading in GPNs
Kothari, Kotabe & Murphy (2013)	a Management and human resources b Management	Examine the various strategies that EMNEs devise to circumvent the resource challenges faced in their home markets and develop routines and key capabilities that lead to their competitive advantage in developed nations.	Innovation 'Moving up' in value chain	Qualitative: historical analysis of four industries from India and China, secondary data	**Parallel citation** (cited paper, Mudambi, 2008)	N/A
Kumar, Mudambi & Gray (2013)	a International Business and strategy b International Business and strategy c International Business and strategy	Develops the structure of the 3 I's view (i.e. internationalisation, innovation and institutional change), drawing on examples that highlight the dynamic interaction between those factors.	Develop theory	Conceptual paper	**Citation only** (cited paper, Ernst & Kim, 2002)	N/A

Kumaraswamy et al. (2012)	a International Business and strategy b International Business and strategy c Production and operations d Accounting	How domestic supplier firms may adapt and continue to perform as market liberalisation progresses, through catch-up strategies aimed at integrating with the industry's GVC.	Catching up Smile of value creation	Quantitative: secondary data on Indian auto component firms	**Parallel citation** (cited paper, Mudambi, 2008)	N/A
Lamin & Livanis (2013)	a International Business and strategy b International Business and strategy	Examine the location choices of domestic and foreign firms in an emerging economy after market liberalisation.	Catch up strategies	Quantitative: secondary data	**Parallel citation** (cited paper, Mudambi, 2008)	N/A
Lee & Gereffi (2015)	a Organisational studies b Sociology	The purpose of this paper is to introduce the GVC approach so as to understand the relationship between MNEs and the changing patterns of global trade, investment and production, and their impact on economic and social upgrading.	GVC governance and upgrading RP firms	Conceptual paper	**Core theoretical framework** How GVCs can advance our understanding about MNEs and RP firms and their impact on economic and social upgrading in fragmented and dispersed global production systems	Understanding the RP firms and their impact on social and economic development through the lens of GVC
Lee & Rugman (2012)	a Organisational studies b International Business	Examines the impact that their firm-specific advantages have on performance as and when they receive inward direct investment from foreign countries.	Firm-specific advantages and country-specific advantages Resource-based view	Quantitative: secondary data	**Mention only** (Use of the term 'upgrading')	N/A

(continued)

Table 16.1 (continued)

IB paper details					*Integration of GVC literature in the paper*	
Author/year	*Authors' area*	*Focus*	*Theoretical background*	*Methodology*	*How used*	*Contribution to IB literature*
Lei & Chen (2011)	a Management b Management	Investigates the location choice behaviour of firms originating in newly industrialised economies (Taiwanese firms) investing in emerging countries (China and Vietnam).	Ownership advantages Motives of FDI Network relationship	Quantitative: survey	**Mention only** (Use of the term 'original equipment manufacturer (OEM)')	N/A
Li (2010)	a Chinese business studies	Proposes a learning-based view of internationalisation for MNEs, especially for MNE latecomers as the new species of MNEs from the emerging economies.	Transaction value Unilateral and bilateral learning Alliance and cross-border learning	Conceptual paper	**Parallel citation** (Cited paper, Chen, 2004)	N/A
Li, Kong & Zhang (2016)	a Management b Developmental studies c Chinese studies	Examines how integration in GPNs has stimulated upgrading of technological capabilities among automotive firms in China.	GVC Upgrading	Quantitative: secondary data	**Core theory** Use of the notion of upgrading as key framework	How integration into GVCs facilitates upgrading
Lo & Hung (2015)	a Management b Management and global business	Analyse how the structuring of offshoring disaggregation and geographical dispersion affects firm performance.	Dynamic capabilities perspective	Quantitative: secondary data	**Parallel citation** (cited paper, Mudambi, 2008)	N/A

Manning et al. (2010)	a Management b Economics and strategic management c Strategic management d Strategic management	This paper explores local and global dynamics underlying the development of knowledge services clusters.	Co-evolutionary perspective	Qualitative: case study analysis	**Citation only** (cited papers, Humphrey & Schmitz, 2002; Morrison, Pietrobelli & Rabellotti, 2008)	N/A
Martinez-Noya, Garcia-Canal & Guillen (2012)	a Economics b Economics c International management	Investigates (i) whether choosing an R&D offshore outsourcing strategy is advisable for technological firms, and (ii) where firms are likely to outsource R&D services.	Literatures on offshoring and outsourcing	Quantitative: survey data	**Parallel citation** (cited paper, Mudambi, 2008)	N/A
Mauri & de Figueiredo (2012)	a International Business b Business economics	This paper examines how the performance variability of an MNC is affected by the strategic patterns it has used to expand abroad.	Local responsiveness and global integration Strategies for internationalisation Outsourcing of value chain	Quantitative: US patent data	**Parallel citation** (cited paper, Mudambi, 2008)	N/A
McDermott & Corredoira (2010)	a International Business b Management and organisation	Analyses the Argentine auto parts sector to distinguish the relative impact of different types of network relationships on a firm's process and product upgrading.	Network theory Upgrading	Quantitative: secondary data	**Core theory** Understanding the role of network embeddedness in upgrading	Domestic suppliers at the lower end of the tier may encounter an upgrading 'glass ceiling'

(continued)

Table 16.1 (continued)

IB paper details					*Integration of GVC literature in the paper*	
Author/year	*Authors' area*	*Focus*	*Theoretical background*	*Methodology*	*How used*	*Contribution to IB literature*
Miozzo & Grimshaw (2008)	a Economics and management innovation b Employment studies	This paper draws on exploratory data to investigate the conditions that shape the nature of forward linkages between multinational services firms and their client firms in (middle-income) less developed countries.	Absorptive capacity GVC/GPN	Qualitative: case study of three large IT MNEs' outsourcing contracts in Argentina and Brazil	**Complementing IB theory** Understanding the relationships and distribution of power between MNEs and their forward linkages	The role of absorptive capacity and global strategy in a forward linkage relational context
Moghaddam et al. (2014)	a Management b International Business c History d Management	Evaluate the adequacy of the Dunning typology of MNE internationalisation motivations in classifying the international investment motives of EMNEs and developed country MNEs.	Dunning's Eclectic Paradigm Smile of value creation	Qualitative: case study of 766 M&As undertaken by emerging country MNEs and 766 M&As by developed country MNEs, secondary data	**Parallel citation** (cited paper, Mudambi, 2008)	N/A
Mudambi (2008)	a International Business	Examines extent to which firm should implement vertical integration and geographical dispersion with respect to its value chain activities.	Coasian approach (organisation and control) Smile of value creation	Qualitative: case study	**Citation only** (cited papers, Gereffi, 1999; Ernst & Kim, 2002) **Parallel citation** (cited paper, Mudambi, 2008)	N/A

Pananond (2013)	a	International Business	Why and how MNEs' local subsidiaries in developing economies undertake international expansion.	Governance and upgrading in GVCs Smile of value creation	Qualitative: case study Interviews Publicly available secondary sources	**Core theoretical framework** Linking international expansion (outward FDI) with upgrading	Subsidiary internationalisation through the lens of upgrading in GVCs
Pananond (2015)	a	International Business	Whether the weak position of emerging market firms and their interdependent relationship with lead firms in GVCs modifies the selection of internationalisation motives.	FDI motives	Conceptual paper	**Complementing IB theory** Understanding the position on EMNEs in GVCs and their relationships with lead firms/ MNEs (i.e. function, power) and upgrading by suppliers	FDI motives (or motives for internationalisation) of EMNEs through the lens of GVC
Pinkse & Kolk (2012)	a b	Strategy, innovation and entrepreneurship Corporate social responsibility	How climate change affects MNEs, focusing on the challenges they face in overcoming liabilities and filling institutional voids related to the issue.	Institutional failure Institutional embeddedness	Conceptual paper	**Citation only** (cited paper, Gereffi, Humphrey & Sturgeon, 2005)	N/A
Rasiah, Kimura & Oum (2016a)	a b c	Developmental studies Economics Economics	The role of host-site institutional support vis-à-vis GVC/GPN linkage experiences in driving technological upgrading in China and Southeast Asia.	Institutional change GVC governance GPN	Quantitative: questionnaire survey	**Critical lens on GVC/GPN** Opportunities arising from participation in GVC/GPN for emerging country firms vis-à-vis institutional support/change	The role of host-country institutional change compared to GVC participation in upgrading

(continued)

Table 16.1 (continued)

IB paper details					*Integration of GVC literature in the paper*	
Author/year	*Authors' area*	*Focus*	*Theoretical background*	*Methodology*	*How used*	*Contribution to IB literature*
Rasiah, Kimura & Oum (2016b)	a Developmental studies b Economics c Economics	Literature review to crucially examine the role of host-site institutional support vis-à-vis GVC/GPN linkage experiences in driving technological upgrading in China and Southeast Asia.	Industrial policy Regional production specialisation Global production sharing GVCs GPN	Conceptual paper	**Critical lens on GVC/GPN** Opportunities arising from participation in GVC/GPN for emerging country firms vis-à-vis institutional support/change	The role of host-country institutional change compared to GVC participation in upgrading
Rasiah, Kong & Vinanchiarachi (2011)	a Developmental studies b Science and technology for development c Economics	This study traces the transformation of Qiaotou city from a button distribution centre to a composite and advanced button manufacturing cluster accounting for 65% of world button production in 2006.	Theory of industrial clusters	Qualitative: secondary data	**Mention only**	N/A
Schmeisser (2013)	a Innovation and international management	This study maps and assesses the existing literature on offshoring of value chain activities and develops a framework that links offshoring with its antecedents and consequences.	Offshoring Offshoring organisation Consequences of offshoring	Conceptual: literature review of 63 articles	**Mention only** Use of the term 'Offshoring of value chain' instead of 'global value chain'	Presenting offshoring as a dynamic/strategic action

Schmitt & van Biesebroeck (2013)	a Economics b Economics	Evaluate the relative importance of three dimensions: geographical, cultural and relational proximity in sourcing strategy.	Geographical, relational and cultural proximity	Quantitative: secondary data on 235 model-component supplier contracts in Europe	**Contextual description** Context: the European auto industry	Mapping the location of suppliers
Sinkovics et al. (2015)	a International Business b International Business c International Business d Comparative analysis	Provides a reconceptualisation of social value creation as social constraint alleviation by producing synergies between bodies of literature.	Internalisation and externalisation GVC/GPN governance and social upgrading Bottom of the pyramid Corporate social responsibility and human rights	Conceptual paper	**Critical lens on GVC/GPN** Critical lens on social upgrading	Exploring the social impact of International Business that has received more attention in GVCs
Slangen & Beugelsdijk (2010)	a International Business b International Business	Examine whether the strength of negative relationships between institutional hazards and informal cultural distance and multinational activity varies systematically with the type of foreign activity (horizontal or vertical) and the type of institutional hazard (governance or cultural).	Horizontal and vertical value-creating foreign activities Exogenous vs. endogenous hazards	Quantitative: panel data analysis, secondary data	**Mention only**	N/A

(continued)

Table 16.1 *(continued)*

IB paper details					*Integration of GVC literature in the paper*	
Author/year	*Authors' area*	*Focus*	*Theoretical background*	*Methodology*	*How used*	*Contribution to IB literature*
Sonderegger & Täube (2010)	a Economic Geography b Innovation and entrepreneurship	Extends the local view of clusters and emphasises the complementary role of non-local linkages, in particular diasporas, illustrating our model employing the case of the evolution of the Bangalore IT cluster.	Cluster and local networks Cluster lifecycle Non-local inter-cluster networks Diaspora-mediated bridges	Qualitative: case study analysis Interview Historical accounts	**Complementing IB theory** How the GPN links non-local networks for tacit knowledge sharing among clusters	Understanding the role of non-local clusters linked through a GPN in knowledge transmission
Strange & Newton (2006)	a International Business b International Business	Illustrate the applicability of insights from the theory of externalisation and the GCC using the example of the global garment industry.	Externalisation of production Global Commodity Chain	Conceptual paper	**Complementing IB theory** Comparing and contrasting Hymer's externalisation of production with Gereffi's GCC analysis	Complementing Hymer's perspective on externalisation
Suder et al. (2015)	a International relations b International Business c Developmental studies d International Business e Developmental studies	What are the locational patterns of trade in value-added in East Asia and how are these patterns changing over time?	Internationalisation Economic Geography and GVC	Quantitative: secondary data on input-output from Asian international input-output table 1990–2005 IDE-JETRO	**Core theoretical framework** An interdisciplinary approach (use of IB and GVC perspectives) to the formulation of a hypothesis on locational patterns of trade in value-added and regional integration	Understanding the interdependencies in the East Asian region by analysing the location patterns of value chains

Swoboda et al. (2012)	a Marketing and retail b Accounting c Marketing and retailing d International management	Provides insights into how manufacturers adopt their Global Account Management (GAM) activities in response to the increasing expansion of retailers.	GAM coordination	Quantitative: survey of 172 manufacturers	**Citation only** (cited paper, Coe & Hess, 2005)	N/A
Taplin (2014)	a Sociology	Examine the various actors responsible for the recent tragedy at a clothing factory in Bangladesh.		Case study	**Citation only** (cited paper, Gereffi, 1994)	N/A
Teece (2014)	a Strategic management	This paper develops a dynamic capabilities-based theory of the MNE.	Internalisation Externalisation Dynamic capabilities-based theory	Conceptual paper	**Citation only** (cited paper, Gereffi, Humphrey & Sturgeon, 2005)	N/A
Vahlne & Ivarsson (2014)	a Management and organisation b International Business	By developing a Globalisation Process Model, the paper theoretically argues, in contrast to much of the existing literature, that globalisation may evolve into a more general phenomenon.	Globalisation/ internationalisation	Quantitative: MNEs annual report	**Mention only** (use of the term. MNEs' value chain)	N/A
Vahlne, Ivarsson & Johanson (2011)	a Management and organisation b International Business c International Business	Develops the Uppsala internationalisation model to focus on two aspects of the globalisation process: the configuration of the firm and its coordination processes. The paper argues the globalisation process is more difficult than often supposed, due to the need to manage complexities and uncertainties	Uppsala model of internationalisation	Qualitative: case study on Volvo's heavy truck business	**Citation only** (cited paper, Gereffi, Humphrey & Sturgeon, 2005)	N/A

(continued)

Table 16.1 (continued)

IB paper details					*Integration of GVC literature in the paper*	
Author/year	*Authors' area*	*Focus*	*Theoretical background*	*Methodology*	*How used*	*Contribution to IB literature*
Wang et al. (2012)	a Strategy and International Business b Management c International Business d Information and telecommunication	Investigates the impact of external technology acquisition, in particular technology licensing, on licensees' export performance.	External technology acquisition Technology licensing	Quantitative: secondary data on 141 Chinese indigenous manufacturing firms	**Mention only** (use of the term 'global value chain')	N/A
Williamson (2015)	a International management	Re-assess both the nature and sources of the competitive advantages which multinationals expanding from home bases in emerging economies may enjoy in the global market.	Value chain configuration Competitive advantage Cross-border M&A Innovation	Conceptual paper	**Parallel citation** (cited paper, Ramamurti & Singh, 2009)	N/A
Yamin (2011a)	a International Business	The commentary points to the possible vulnerabilities of the global factory as an organisational form and links these vulnerabilities to features of the governance regime that supports the Global Factory.	Global Factory GVC Externalisation	Conceptual paper	**Complementing IB theory** How social efficiency is better conceptualised in GVC literatures	The importance of social efficiency in International Business that has been ignored in the Global Factory

Source: Authors' construction.

Findings

Degree of integration

In-depth analysis of the selected papers revealed that the notion of GVC/GPN had been used in six different ways in IB research, with varying levels of intensity. The majority of papers had either simply cited papers from the GVC/GPN domain or merely mentioned the terms GVC/GPN or upgrading without any citations. Another category of articles had used the GVC/GPN literature to construct their core theoretical background. The third approach to integration was identified as drawing on GVC/GPN studies to complement IB theories and frameworks. A small set of articles in our sample had performed a critical analysis of GVC/GPN concepts from different perspectives, whilst another category of papers had used the GVC/GPN frameworks to describe the context of the industry under investigation. Lastly, a number of studies had employed concepts similar to those used in the GVC/GPN literature. However, instead of referring to articles from the original body of GVC/GPN literature, they had cited IB papers offering parallel views or direct citations of original GVC/GPN publications. In the following sub-sections, we elaborate on these six broad groupings.

We have presented the nature of GVC/GPN integration into the IB literature in a two by two matrix (Figure 16.1). Four groups of IB papers have been identified based on the two dimensions discussed earlier: (i) the degree of integration (high vs. low) and (ii) the perspectives/domains in IB (MNEs vs. other actors). In addition, details regarding the number of papers in the respective groups are presented in Table 16.2.

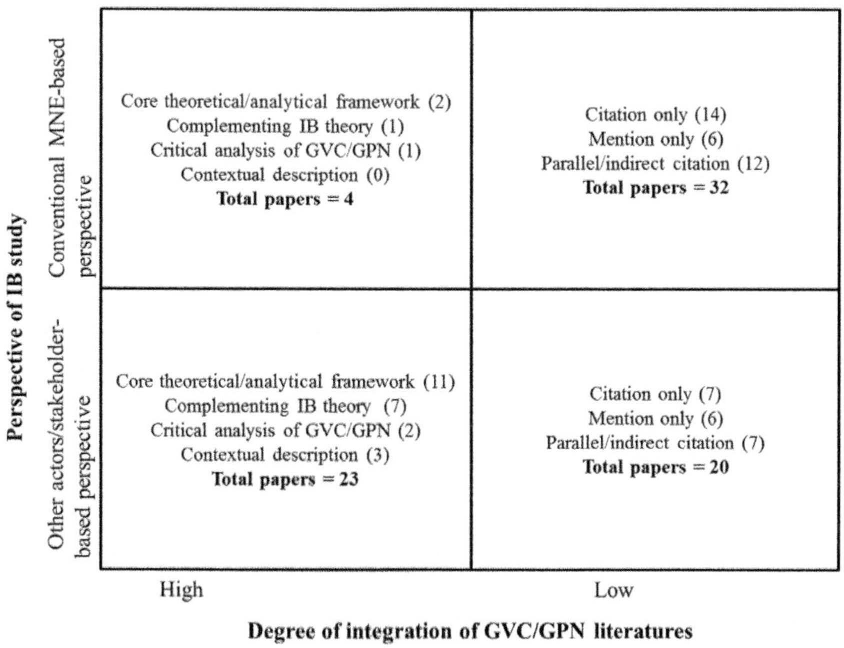

Figure 16.1 The nature of integration of IB and GVC/GPN literatures

Source: Authors' construction.

Table 16.2 Breakdown of groups: degree of integration and perspectives

Degree of integration/ perspective of IB studies	*Core theoretical framework*	*Complementary theory*	*Critical lens*	*Contextual description*	*Citation only*	*Mention only*	*Parallel citation*
Conventional MNEs	2	1	1	0	14	6	12
EMNEs	1	2	0	0	1	2	3
RP firms	2	0	0	0	0	0	0
Suppliers and linkage firms	5	3	2	0	5	2	4
Industry/cluster/emerging markets	3	2	0	1	1	0	0
Workers and consumers	0	0	0	2	0	2	0

Source: Authors' construction.

Core theoretical/analytical framework

Our analysis reveals that 13 papers use the GVC/GPN literature to build their core theoretical framework and so guide their empirical research, conceptualisation and data analysis. The degree of integration of concepts from the GVC/GPN literature is therefore the highest in this group of papers.

For instance, the notion of upgrading has been used to study emerging country firm or supplier capabilities at firm (Eng & Spickett-Jones, 2009; Khan, Lew & Sinkovics, 2015), cluster (McDermott & Corredoira, 2010), industry (Kong, Zhang & Ramu, 2016; Li, Kong & Zhang, 2016), and country level (Suder et al., 2015). Kong, Zhang and Ramu (2016) and Li, Kong and Zhang (2016) study how GVC integration has facilitated technological upgrading in the Chinese semiconductor and automotive industries respectively. Khan, Lew and Sinkovics (2015) analyse the upgrading of Pakistani automobile suppliers by exploring the extent of technology transfer received from their MNE partners within a specific relational context and governance structure. The link between different marketing capabilities and the progressive phases of upgrading has also been explored by Gereffi and Frederick (2010) and Eng and Spickett-Jones (2009). The data analysis further shows that Giuliani, Pietrobelli and Rabellotti (2005) and Humphrey and Schmitz (2002) are the two most widely cited GVC papers in IB with regards to upgrading.

The governance structure and the organisation of the value chain activities of EMNEs (Pananond, 2013) and RP firms (Azmeh & Nadvi, 2014; Lee & Gereffi, 2015; Yamin & Sinkovics, 2015) are other areas where the GVC literature has been utilised. For instance, drawing upon the concepts of GVC governance (Gereffi, Humphrey & Sturgeon, 2005) and GVC structural organisation (Bair & Gereffi, 2003), Azmeh and Nadvi (2014) explore how RP firms manage complex international production linkages and ensure Jordanian firms' incorporation into the global garment industry. Relatedly, Pananond (2013) studies the internationalisation strategies of EMNEs through a GVC lens, using Gereffi et al.'s (2005) governance and Humphrey and Schmitz's (2002) upgrading frameworks.

Whilst theoretical integration of GVC/GPN concepts has mostly occurred via the study of suppliers, EMNEs or RP EMNEs, Giroud and Mirza (2015) provide an exception to this trend. In a recent paper, they analyse the nature of internationalisation activities carried out by traditional Western MNEs, and highlight observable shifts in their modes of governance. Another exception is Haworth (2013), who examines the human resource development strategies of a Western MNE through the lens of GVC organisation.

Complementing IB theory

Eight papers use ideas from the GVC/GPN literature in conjunction with theories from IB or other management disciplines. In different ways, these papers adopt GVC/GPN concepts to complement other theories and strengthen their overarching research framework.

Internationalisation motives and EMNE performance have been studied in the context of GVCs whilst drawing upon traditional IB theories on internationalisation (Banalieva & Sarathy, 2011; Pananond, 2015). For example, Banalieva and Sarathy (2011) build on Williamson's (1985) transaction cost economies and Contractor's (2007) multistage general theory of internationalisation to examine the internationalisation performance of electronic versus non-electronic EMNEs. At the same time, the authors utilise Gereffi's (1999) work to locate their analysis in the context of new trade liberalisation and triangular manufacturing, thereby strengthening their overall research framework. The internationalisation motives of EMNEs are also explored by Pananond (2015) through the lens of Dunning's (1993) FDI motives framework, taking into account the position of those EMNEs in the wider GVC, and particularly their relationship with the lead firms.

Similarly, the notion of upgrading has been used by a number of studies in conjunction with other theories such as network-based perspectives, institutional theory and comparative institutional analysis. For instance, McDermott and Corredoira (2010) adopt a network-based perspective to highlight the relative impacts of different types of network relationships on upgrading in the Argentine auto parts cluster. Corredoira and McDermott (2014) examine upgrading in the same sector, adopting an organisational and institutional network-based perspective. The authors find that local firms' upgrading depends largely on support received from their host institutional networks, particularly for firms suffering from resource scarcity and lacking technological capabilities.

The GVC/GPN framework, in conjunction with other relevant concepts/theories (e.g. absorptive capacity, the diasporas effect and Porter's Diamond model), has been used to explain the nature of knowledge sharing among local and non-local linkage partners in GPNs (Miozzo & Grimshaw, 2008; Sonderegger & Täube, 2010), and to explore linkages between the competitive advantage of clusters and their regional integration (Gupta & Subramanian, 2008). For instance, Sonderegger and Täube (2010) study the evolution of the Bangalore IT industry using cluster life-cycle theory and the mediating effect of diasporas. The paper explores how the IT industry has linked with other foreign resourceful firms via GVCs/GPNs, and how these linkages have facilitated knowledge transfer within local IT clusters. Gupta and Subramanian (2008) draw upon Porter's Diamond, Krugman's Economic Geography and European regional innovation system perspectives to identify generic strategies and bases for competitive advantage in regional clusters. Significantly, the authors connect their findings with GVC/GPN trends to explain changes in competitive advantage over the period under study.

Critical analysis of GVC/GPN

In our sample, three papers critically analyse the GVC/GPN frameworks. By identifying gaps in the GVC/GPN literature, the articles highlight how IB research can contribute to addressing those gaps through theory development and alternative perspectives. At the same time, they make explicit recommendations of how GVC/GPN studies can benefit from integrating IB perspectives.

In two recent papers, Rasiah, Kimura and Oum (2016a, 2016b) examine the literature on industrial policy, regional production specialisation, global production sharing, GVCs and

GPNs. In doing so, they argue that the GVC/GPN literature undermines the role of host-site institutional support in facilitating industrial upgrading, which has proved to be vital for the technological capability development of the Chinese and South East Asian automotive, clothing and semiconductor industries. In fact, the authors assert that only sites with effective industrial policies and support systems have successfully moved up the value chain.

Similarly, Sinkovics et al. (2015) provide a review of GVC/GPN and other relevant literatures situated at the business-society interface. On the one hand, they highlight the GVC/GPN framework's ability to simultaneously focus on a wider range of issues than IB theories do. For example, social/economic upgrading and multiple actors such as corporations, governments, civil society organisations, labour unions and consumers who interactively shape the business society interface are all dimensions incorporated within the GVC/GPN frameworks. On the other hand, the authors emphasise the necessity of according attention to a wider range of human rights and development issues that exist beyond employment relationships, as identified in other bodies of literature such as that on corporate social responsibility.

Contextual description

Three papers use GVC/GPN frameworks to describe production arrangements and interrelationships between lead firms, suppliers and other network partners. However, these papers have not directly adopted GVC/GPN concepts to construct their research frameworks, meaning the integration has occurred primarily at a descriptive rather than theoretical level. For instance, Cairns (2014) critically analyses the developmental potential for workers at the bottom of the pyramid and describes the changing context for compliance by referring to the GVC literature (e.g. Nadvi, 2008; Lund-Thomsen et al., 2012;). Funk et al.'s (2010) study of consumer animosity uses GVC concepts to map out partial production shifts following GVC integration. Schmitt and van Biesebroeck (2013) draw on GVC mapping to describe the organisation of different value chain actors comprising the European auto industry, before analysing the relative importance of geographical, cultural and relational proximity in sourcing strategies.

Citation and/or mention only

The analysis identified 21 papers that only cite GVC/GPN papers, without integrating concepts at a theoretical or analytical level (Beugelsdijk, Pedersen & Petersen, 2009; Jensen, 2009; Manning et al., 2010; Vahlne, Ivarsson & Johanson, 2011; Eapen, 2012; Baaij & Slangen, 2013; Contractor, Kumar & Dhanaraj, 2015). The use of GVC/GPN concepts in these papers is unsystematic and there is no attempt to make a theoretical contribution to the IB literature. In addition to these 21 papers, we identified 12 papers that only mentioned the terms GVC, GPN or upgrading, without actually citing any papers from the original GVC/GPN literature.

Further, in line with Johns et al. (2015), we found that Gereffi, Humphrey and Sturgeon's (2005) paper on GVC governance in the *Review of International Political Economy* was the most widely cited GVC publication. IB papers studying upgrading in firm, industry or cluster contexts mostly cited and referred to Humphrey and Schmitz (2002) and Giuliani, Pietrobelli and Rabellotti (2005). With regards to GPN papers, Ernst and Kim's (2002) paper mostly received attention within studies focusing on knowledge sharing and/or transfer among network or linkage partners. Coe, Dicken and Hess (2008) and Coe and Hess (2005) were also cited in two papers.

Parallel/indirect citation

The analysis furthermore yielded 20 papers that used notions of GVC/GPN for research framing and core theory, but without directly citing any GVC/GPN-related articles. Instead, these papers cited IB publications offering parallel theories/concepts, in particular the work of Ram Mudambi. For instance, Mudambi's (2008) 'smile of value creation' has been widely used to conceptualise structural GVC organisation in IB research. More broadly, Mudambi's (2008) work has influenced IB papers examining internationalisation strategies (e.g. Beugelsdijk, Pedersen & Petersen, 2009; D'Agostino & Santangelo, 2012; Buckley, 2014), entry modes and governance strategies (e.g. Martinez-Noya, Garcia-Canal & Guillen, 2012), and FDI motives of traditional MNEs (e.g. Moghaddam et al., 2014). These topics have also been studied by means of drawing upon another influential IB scholar, Peter Buckley. His conceptualisation of the 'Global Factory' and ideas around fine slicing of value chains, which contain considerable parallels with GVC/GPN research (e.g. Buckley, 2014; Gooris & Peeters, 2014), have been widely received. Furthermore, the internalisation strategies of EMNEs have been studied by means of drawing upon Mathew's (2006) "Linkage, Learning and Leverage" model, albeit with some reference to the broader GPN context (e.g. Buckley, Forsans & Munjal, 2012).

In several other papers, supplier or EMNE upgrading has been studied by referral to Mudambi (2008) and Kumaraswamy et al. (2012). The terms 'catching up' (e.g. Lamin & Livanis, 2013) or 'moving up' (e.g. Kothari, Kotabe & Murphy, 2013) stand for something similar to or the same as 'upgrading' in GVC/GPN studies. In a number of papers, the term 'upgrading' appears without any reference to the original GVC/GPN literature. Lastly, the OEM-ODM-OBM differentiation is adopted by Li (2010) and Hatani and McGaughey (2013). Interestingly, those authors do not directly cite original GVC sources. Instead, they refer to Chen (2004) who, on the other hand, incorporates direct references to the GVC literature in his work.

The IB domains most receptive to GVC/GPN integration

Our analysis further reveals that the degree of conceptual GVC/GPN integration into the IB literature has been higher in studies incorporating a broader range of GVC/GPN actors into their analysis, compared to those focused predominantly on conventional MNEs. In total, 23 papers focusing on a broader range of actors adopt GVC/GPN concepts at a theoretical level or for analytical purposes. More specifically, 3 of those papers focus on internationalisation strategies and motives of EMNEs, 2 on the role of RP firms in network governance, 16 on firm/industry/cluster upgrading, and 2 on other stakeholders such as workers and consumers.

Contrastingly, only four papers studying conventional MNEs use the notions of GVC/GPN at a theoretical or analytical level. It can therefore be assumed that the degree of GVC/GPN conceptual integration into IB studies has been significantly lower during the examination of conventional MNEs than other GVC/GPN actors. At the same time, parallel/indirect citations were found to be a more common practice in studies focusing on conventional MNEs.

These findings demonstrate that IB studies adopting traditional MNE-focused perspectives tend to limit their theoretical/analytical lenses to the boundaries of IB and are less receptive to inter-disciplinary insights. Although the number of GVC/GPN citations and terminological references were higher in this group of papers, this was primarily strategic or descriptive exercise, as opposed to deeper theoretical integration or for analytical purposes.

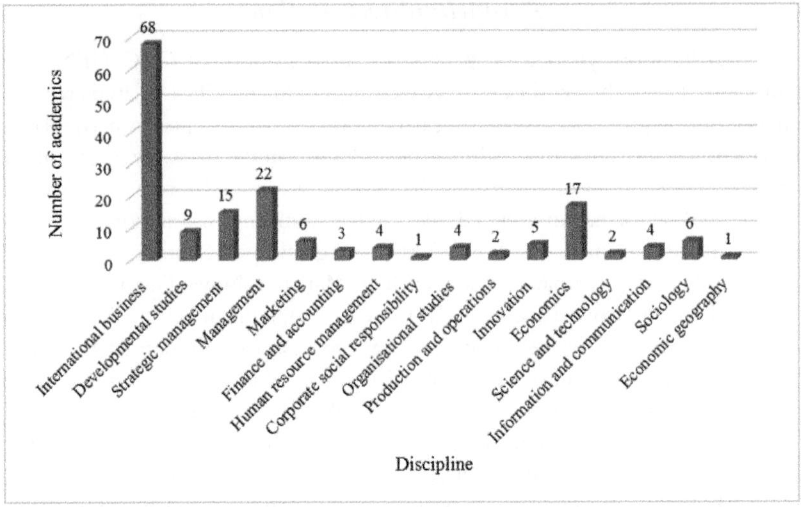

Figure 16.2 Authors' number and disciplinary areas

Source: Authors' construction.

The role of authors' disciplinary origin in the integration process

The analysis of author profiles revealed that the majority (60%) of papers in our sample had been written by non-IB scholars with the following disciplinary backgrounds: development studies (5%), strategic management (9%), management (13%), marketing (4%), finance and accounting (2%), human resource management (2%), corporate social responsibility (1%), organisational studies (2%), production and operations (1%), innovation (3%), economics (10%), science and technology (1%), information and communication (2%), sociology (4%) and Economic Geography (1%). Only 68 out of the 169 authors are IB scholars (40%) (Figure 16.2). The results, therefore, show that the integration of GVC/GPN thinking into papers published in IB journals is to a large extent driven by non-IB scholars, particularly those from the fields of strategic management, general management, economics and development.

Conclusion

The present chapter set out to analyse the nature and degree of GVC/GPN conceptual integration into IB research based on a systematic bibliographic analysis of papers published since the mid-2000s in IB-related journals. This endeavour contributes to a better understanding of which particular perspective in IB research (MNE-based vs. stakeholder-based) has been most receptive to ideas from the GVC/GPN literature so far, and to what extent.

Overall, the analysis shows a relatively low degree of GVC/GPN integration at a theoretical or analytical level, with the majority of IB papers restricting usage to citation or mention only. More specifically, the level of integration has been minimal in papers studying conventional MNEs, with a relatively higher degree of GVC/GPN conceptual integration for studies incorporating a broader range of GVC/GPN actors. Another notable trend is the tendency towards parallel citations in studies focusing on conventional MNEs, reflecting conservatism among this group of studies in welcoming ideas from other disciplines.

The relatively greater degree of GVC/GPN integration in IB studies adopting a stakeholder-based perspective underlines the potential theoretical contribution of GVC/GPN research to the study of stakeholders involved in and affected by, MNE-driven GPNs (Dicken et al., 2001; de Marchi, di Maria & Ponte, 2014). This finding also reflects a growing orientation in IB research towards studying a broader range of GVC/GPN actors beyond Western MNEs, actors that have been relatively under researched so far (cf. Cairns & Sliwa, 2008). As we have demonstrated, in some cases this emerging IB agenda has been undertaken by drawing upon the notion of GVCs/GPNs. Whilst it is important to continue integrating GVC/GPN concepts in stakeholder-based IB studies, future IB research can benefit significantly from integrating elements from GVC/GPN analysis into the study of conventional MNEs. In particular, the GVC/GPN frameworks can contribute to the study of MNEs' internationalisation paths in a networked economy, MNEs' strategies for governing their production networks, and an increased understanding of power and knowledge dynamics between MNEs and other GVC/GPN actors (de Marchi, di Maria & Ponte, 2014).

The finding that the majority of GVC/GPN-related papers published in IB journals have been written by non-IB scholars raises the question of how receptive IB scholars really are to ideas from the GVC/GPN literature. Moreover, the results show that only a small percentage (11%) of IB academics have collaborated with authors from other areas. This triggers a further question about the barriers to the integration of GVC/GPN thinking. Future empirical research may wish to investigate these two questions. Furthermore, the specific identification of those IB theories most accommodating of GVC/GPN concepts was beyond the scope of this chapter. Building on our investigation, future studies may therefore wish to categorise IB papers based on their theoretical backgrounds, and analyse the degree of GVC/GPN integration along these lines.

References

Alvarez, I. & Marin, R. (2013) 'FDI and technology as levering factors of competitiveness in developing countries', *Journal of International Management*, 19, pp. 232–246.

Azmeh, S. & Nadvi, K. (2014) 'Asian firms and the restructuring of global value chains', *International Business Review*, 23, pp. 708–717.

Baaij, M.G. & Slangen, A.H.L. (2013) 'The role of headquarters-subsidiary geographic distance in strategic decisions by spatially disaggregated headquarters', *Journal of International Business Studies*, 44, pp. 941–952.

Bair, J. & Gereffi, G. (2003) 'Upgrading, uneven development, and jobs in the north American apparel industry', *Global Networks*, 3, pp. 143–169.

Banalieva, E.R. & Sarathy, R. (2011) 'A contingency theory of internationalization performance for emerging market multinational enterprises', *Management International Review*, 51, pp. 593–634.

Barrientos, S., Gereffi, G. & Rossi, A. (2011) 'Economic and social upgrading in global production networks: A new paradigm for a changing world', *International Labour Review*, 150, pp. 319–340.

Barrientos, S. & Kritzinger, A. (2004) 'Squaring the circle: Global production and the informalization of work in south African fruit exports', *Journal of International Development*, 16, pp. 81–92.

Bartlett, C.A. & Ghoshal, S. (1987) 'Managing across borders: New organizational responses', *Sloan Management Review*, 29, pp. 43–53.

Beugelsdijk, S., Pedersen, T. & Petersen, B. (2009) 'Is there a trend towards global value chain specialization? An examination of cross border sales of US foreign affiliates', *Journal of International Management*, 15, pp. 126–141.

Buckley, P.J. (2009a) 'The impact of the global factory on economic development', *Journal of World Business*, 44, pp. 131–143.

Buckley, P.J. (2009b) 'Internalisation thinking: From the multinational enterprise to the global factory', *International Business Review*, 18, pp. 224–235.

Buckley, P.J. (2011) 'International integration and coordination in the global factory', *Management International Review*, 51, pp. 269–283.

Buckley, P.J. (2014) 'Forty years of internalisation theory and the multinational enterprise', *Multinational Business Review*, 22, pp. 227–245.

Buckley, P.J. (2016) 'The contribution of internalisation theory to International Business: New realities and unanswered questions', *Journal of World Business*, 51, pp. 74–82.

Buckley, P.J. & Casson, M. (1976) *The Future of the Multinational Enterprise*. London: Macmillan.

Buckley, P.J. & Casson, M. (1998) 'Models of the multinational enterprise', *Journal of International Business Studies*, 29, pp. 21–44.

Buckley, P.J., Forsans, N. & Munjal, S. (2012) 'Host-home country linkages and host-home country specific advantages as determinants of foreign acquisitions by Indian firms', *International Business Review*, 21, pp. 878–890.

Buckley, P.J. & Ghauri, P.N. (2004) 'Globalisation, Economic Geography and the strategy of multinational enterprises', *Journal of International Business Studies*, 35, pp. 81–98.

Buckley, P.J. & Strange, R. (2011) 'The governance of the multinational enterprise: Insights from internalization theory', *Journal of Management Studies*, 48, pp. 460–470.

Cairns, G. (2014) 'A critical scenario analysis of end-of-life ship disposal', *Critical Perspectives on International Business*, 10, pp. 172–189.

Cairns, G. & Sliwa, M. (2008) *A Very Short, Fairly Interesting and Reasonably Cheap Book About International Business*. Los Angeles, CA: Sage.

Chen, S. (2004) 'Extending internalization theory: A new perspective on international technology transfer and its generalization', *Journal of International Business Studies*, 36, pp. 231–245.

Coe, N.M., Dicken, P. & Hess, M. (2008) 'Global production networks: Realizing the potential', *Journal of Economic Geography*, 8, pp. 271–295.

Coe, N.M. & Hess, M. (2005) 'The internationalization of retailing: Implications for supply network restructuring in East Asia and eastern Europe', *Journal of Economic Geography*, 5, pp. 449–473.

Contractor, F.J. (2007) 'Is International Business good for companies? The evolutionary or multi-stage theory of internationalization vs. the transaction cost perspective', *Management International Review*, 47, pp. 453–475.

Contractor, F.J., Kumar, V. & Dhanaraj, C. (2015) 'Leveraging India: Global interconnectedness and locational competitive advantage', *Management International Review*, 55, pp. 159–179.

Corredoira, R.A. & McDermott, G.A. (2014) 'Adaptation, bridging and firm upgrading: How non-market institutions and MNCs facilitate knowledge recombination in emerging markets', *Journal of International Business Studies*, 45, pp. 699–722.

Cuervo-Cazurra, A. (2007) 'Sequence of value-added activities in the multinationalization of developing country firms', *Journal of International Management*, 13, pp. 258–277.

D'Agostino, L.M. & Santangelo, G.D. (2012) 'Do overseas R&D laboratories in emerging markets contribute to home knowledge creation? An extension of the double diamond model', *Management International Review*, 52, pp. 251–273.

Dicken, P. (2015) *Global Shift: Mapping the Changing Contours of the World Economy*. 7th Edition. Los Angeles, CA: Sage.

Dicken, P., Kelly, P.F., Olds, K. & Yeung, H.W-C. (2001) 'Chains and networks, territories and scales: Towards a relational framework for analysing the global economy', *Global Networks*, 1, pp. 89–112.

Donzéa, P-Y. (2015) 'Global value chains and the lost competitiveness of the Japanese watch industry: An applied business history of Seiko since 1990', *Asia Pacific Business Review*, 21, 295–310.

Duanmu, J-L. & Fai, F.M. (2007) 'A processual analysis of knowledge transfer: From foreign MNEs to Chinese suppliers', *International Business Review*, 16, pp. 449–473.

Dunning, J.H. (1979) 'Explaining changing patterns of international production: In defence of the eclectic theory', *Oxford Bulletin of Economics and Statistics*, 41, pp. 269–295.

Dunning, J.H. (1980) 'Toward an eclectic theory of international production', *The International Executive*, 22, pp. 1–3.

Dunning, J.H. (1993) *Multinational Enterprises and the Global Economy*. Wokingham, UK and Reading, MA: Addison Wesley.

Eapen, A. (2012) 'Social structure and technology spillovers from foreign to domestic firms', *Journal of International Business Studies*, 43, pp. 244–263.

Eapen, A. (2013) 'FDI spillover effects in incomplete datasets', *Journal of International Business Studies*, 44, pp. 719–744.

Edwards, T., Edwards, P., Ferner, A., Marginson, P. & Tregaskis, O. (2010) 'Multinational companies and the diffusion of employment practices from outside the country of origin explaining variation across firms', *Management International Review*, 50, pp. 613–634.
Eng, T.-Y. & Spickett-Jones, J.G. (2009) 'An investigation of marketing capabilities and upgrading performance of manufacturers in mainland China and Hong Kong', *Journal of World Business*, 44, pp. 463–475.
Ernst, D. & Kim, L. (2002) 'Global production networks, knowledge diffusion, and local capability formation', *Research Policy*, 31, pp. 1417–1429.
Fitzgerald, R. & Rowley, C. (2015) 'How have Japanese multinational companies changed? Competitiveness, management and subsidiaries', *Asia Pacific Business Review*, 21, pp. 449–456.
Fleury, A., Fleury, M.T.L. & Borini, F.M. (2013) 'The Brazilian multinationals' approaches to innovation', *Journal of International Management*, 19, pp. 260–275.
Fong, C.-M., Lee, C.-L. & Dub, Y. (2013) 'Target reputation transferability, consumer animosity, and cross-border acquisition success: A comparison between China and Taiwan', *International Business Review*, 22, pp. 174–186.
Funk, C.A., Arthurs, J.D., Treviño, L.J. & Joireman, J. (2010) 'Consumer animosity in the global value chain: The effect of international production shifts on willingness to purchase hybrid products', *Journal of International Business Studies*, 41, pp. 639–651.
Gereffi, G. (1994) 'The organisation of buyer-driven global commodity chains: How US retailers shape overseas production networks', in Gereffi, G. & Korzeniewicz, M. (Eds.), *Commodity Chains and Global Capitalism*. Westport, CT: Greenwood Press, pp. 95–122.
Gereffi, G. (1999) 'International trade and industrial upgrading in the apparel commodity chain', *Journal of International Economics*, 48, pp. 37–70.
Gereffi, G. & Fernandez-Stark, K. (2011) *Global Value Chain Analysis: A Primer*. Duke University, NC: Center on Globalization, Governance & Competitiveness (CGGC).
Gereffi, G. & Frederick, S. (2010) 'The global apparel value chain, trade and the crisis: Challenges and opportunities for developing countries', in Cattaneo, O., Gereffi, G. & Staritz, C. (Eds.), *Global Value Chains in a Postcrisis World: A Development Perspective*. Washington, DC: World Bank, pp. 157–208.
Gereffi, G., Humphrey, J. & Sturgeon, T. (2005) 'The governance of global value chains', *Review of International Political Economy*, 12, pp. 78–104.
Gereffi, G. & Korzeniewicz, M. (Eds.) (1994) *Commodity Chains and Global Capitalism*. Westport, CT: ABC-CLIO.
Gereffi, G. & Lee, J. (2012) 'Why the world suddenly cares about global supply chains', *Journal of Supply Chain Management*, 48, pp. 24–32.
Ghauri, P.N. & Buckley, P.J. (2006) 'Globalization, multinational enterprises and world poverty', in Jain, S.C. & Vachani, S. (Eds.), *Multinational Corporations and Global Poverty Reduction*. Cheltenham, UK: Edward Elgar Publishing, pp. 204–232.
Giroud, A. & Mirza, H. (2015) 'Refining of FDI motivations by integrating global value chains' considerations', *Multinational Business Review*, 23, pp. 67–76.
Giuliani, E. & Macchi, C. (2013) 'Multinational corporations' economic and human rights impacts on developing countries: A review and research agenda', *Cambridge Journal of Economics*, 38, pp. 479–517.
Giuliani, E., Pietrobelli, C. & Rabellotti, R. (2005) 'Upgrading in global value chains: Lessons from Latin American clusters', *World Development*, 33, pp. 549–573.
Gooris, J. & Peeters, C. (2014) 'Home-host country distance in offshore governance choices', *Journal of International Management*, 20, pp. 73–86.
Gui, L. (2010) 'Reshaping the boundaries of the firm: Global value chains and lead firm strategies', in Pla-Barber, J. & Alegre, J. (Eds.), *Reshaping the Boundaries of the Firm in an Era of Global Interdependence*. Progress in *International Business Research* Vol. 5. Bingley, UK: The Emerald Group Publishing Limited, pp. 29–55.
Gupta, V. & Subramanian, R. (2008) 'Seven perspectives on regional clusters and the case of Grand Rapids Office Furniture City', *International Business Review*, 17, pp. 371–384.
Hansen, M.W., Pedersen, T. & Petersen, B. (2009) 'MNC strategies and linkage effects in developing countries', *Journal of World Business*, 44, pp. 121–130.
Hatani, F. (2009) 'The logic of spillover interception: The impact of global supply chains in China', *Journal of World Business*, 44, pp. 158–166.
Hatani, F. & McGaughey, S.L. (2013) 'Network cohesion in global expansion: An evolutionary view', *Journal of World Business*, 48, pp. 455–465.

Haworth, N. (2013) 'Compressed development: Global value chains, multinational enterprises and human resource development in 21st century Asia', *Journal of World Business*, 48, pp. 251–259.

Hill, T.L. & Mudambi, R. (2010) 'Far from Silicon Valley: How emerging economies are re-shaping our understanding of global entrepreneurship', *Journal of International Management*, 16, pp. 321–327.

Humphrey, J. & Schmitz, H. (2002) 'How does insertion in global value chains affect upgrading in industrial clusters?' *Regional Studies*, 36, pp. 1017–1027.

Hymer, S.H. (1972) *The Multinational Corporation and the Law of Uneven Development*. New Haven, CT: Yale University, Economic Growth Center.

Jensen, P.D.Ø. (2009) 'A learning perspective on the offshoring of advanced services', *Journal of International Management*, 15, pp. 181–193.

Jensen, P.D.Ø. (2012) 'A passage to India: A dual case study of activities, processes and resources in offshore outsourcing of advanced services', *Journal of World Business*, 47, pp. 311–326.

Jensen, P.D.Ø., Larsen, M.M. & Pedersen, T. (2013) 'The organizational design of offshoring: Taking stock and moving forward', *Journal of International Management*, 19, pp. 315–323.

Jensen, P.D.Ø. & Petersen, B. (2013) 'Build-operate-transfer outsourcing contracts in services: Boon or bane to emerging market vendor firms?' *Journal of International Management*, 19, pp. 220–231.

Johns, J., Buckley, P., Campling, L., Cook, G., Hess, M. & Sinkovics, R.R. (2015) 'Geography and history matter: International Business and Economic Geography perspectives on the spatial and historical development of multinational enterprises', in Ha, Y.J., Konara, P., McDonald, F. & Wei, Y. (Eds.), *The Rise of Multinationals from Emerging Economies: Achieving a New Balance*. Basingstoke, UK: Palgrave Macmillan, pp. 51–80.

Jong, G. de & van Houten, J. (2014) 'The impact of MNE cultural diversity on the internationalization-performance relationship theory and evidence from European multinational enterprises', *International Business Review*, 23, pp. 313–326.

Kadarusman, Y. & Nadvi, K. (2012) 'Competitiveness and technological upgrading in global value chains: Evidence from the Indonesian electronics and garment sectors', *European Planning Studies*, 21, pp. 1007–1028.

Kenney, M., Massini, S. & Murtha, T.P. (2009) 'Offshoring administrative and technical work: New fields for understanding the global enterprise introduction', *Journal of International Business Studies*, 40, pp. 887–900.

Khan, Z., Lew, Y.K. & Sinkovics, R.R. (2015) 'The mirage of upgrading local automotive parts suppliers through the creation of vertical linkages with MNEs in developing economies', *Critical Perspectives on International Business*, 11, pp. 301–318.

Kong, X.X., Zhang, M. & Ramu, S.C. (2016) 'China's semiconductor industry in global value chains', *Asia Pacific Business Review*, 22, 150–164.

Kothari, T., Kotabe, M. & Murphy, P. (2013) 'Rules of the game for emerging market multinational companies from China and India', *Journal of International Management*, 19, pp. 276–299.

Kumar, V., Mudambi, R. & Gray, S. (2013) 'Internationalization, innovation and institutions: The 3 i's underpinning the competitiveness of emerging market firms', *Journal of International Management*, 19, pp. 203–206.

Kumaraswamy, A., Mudambi, R., Saranga, H. & Tripathy, A. (2012) 'Catch-up strategies in the Indian auto components industry: Domestic firms' responses to market liberalization', *Journal of International Business Studies*, 43, pp. 368–395.

Lamin, A. & Livanis, G. (2013) 'Agglomeration, catch-up and the liability of foreignness in emerging economies', *Journal of International Business Studies*, 44, pp. 579–606.

Lee, H. & Rugman, A.M. (2012) 'Firm-specific advantages, inward FDI origins, and performance of multinational enterprises', *Journal of International Management*, 18, pp. 132–146.

Lee, J. & Gereffi, G. (2015) 'Global value chains, rising power firms and economic and social upgrading', *Critical Perspectives on International Business*, 11, pp. 319–339.

Lei, H-S. & Chen, Y-S. (2011) 'The right tree for the right bird: Location choice decision of Taiwanese firms' FDI in China and Vietnam', *International Business Review*, 20, pp. 338–352.

Li, P.P. (2010) 'Toward a learning-based view of internationalization: The accelerated trajectories of cross-border learning for latecomers', *Journal of International Management*, 16, pp. 43–59.

Li, Y.S., Kong, X.X. & Zhang, M. (2016) 'Industrial upgrading in global production networks: The case of the Chinese automotive industry', *Asia Pacific Business Review*, 22, pp. 21–37.

Lindgreen, A., Córdoba, J.-R., Maon, F. & Mendoza, J.M. (2010) 'Corporate social responsibility in colombia: Making sense of social strategies', *Journal of Business Ethics*, 91, pp. 229–242.

Lo, Y.-J. & Hung, T.M. (2015) 'Structure offshoring and returns on offshoring', *Asia Pacific Journal of Management*, 32, pp. 443–479.

Lund-Thomsen, P. & Coe, N.M. (2013) 'Corporate social responsibility and labour agency: The case of Nike in Pakistan', *Journal of Economic Geography*, 15, pp. 1–22.

Lund-Thomsen, P. & Lindgreen, A. (2013) 'Corporate social responsibility in global value chains: Where are we now and where are we going?' *Journal of Business Ethics*, 123, pp. 1–12.

Lund-Thomsen, P., Nadvi, K., Chan, A., Khara, N. & Xue, H. (2012) 'Labour in global value chains: Work conditions in football manufacturing in China, India and Pakistan', *Development and Change*, 43, pp. 1211–1237.

Manning, S., Ricart, J.E., Rique, M.S.R. & Lewin, A.Y. (2010) 'From blind spots to hotspots: How knowledge services clusters develop and attract foreign investment', *Journal of International Management*, 16, pp. 369–382.

Marchi, V. de, Maria, E. di & Ponte, S. (2014) 'Multinational firms and the management of global networks: Insights from global value chain studies', in Pedersen, T., Venzin, M., Devinney, T.M. & Tihanyi, L. (Eds.), *Orchestration of the Global Network Organization. Advances in International Management*, 27. Bingley: Emerald Group Publishing Limited, pp. 463–486.

Martinez-Noya, A., Garcia-Canal, E. & Guillen, M.F. (2012) 'International R&D service outsourcing by technology-intensive firms: Whether and where?' *Journal of International Management*, 18, pp. 18–37.

Mathews, J.A. (2006) 'Dragon multinationals: New players in 21st century globalization', *Asia Pacific Journal of Management*, 23, pp. 5–27.

Mauri, A.J. & de Figueiredo, J.N. (2012) 'Strategic patterns of internationalization and performance variability: Effects of US-based MNC cross-border dispersion, integration, and outsourcing', *Journal of International Management*, 18, pp. 38–51.

McDermott, G.A. & Corredoira, R.A. (2010) 'Network composition, collaborative ties, and upgrading in emerging-market firms: Lessons from the Argentine autoparts sector', *Journal of International Business Studies*, 41, pp. 308–329.

Meyer, K.E. (2004) 'Perspectives on multinational enterprises in emerging economies', *Journal of International Business Studies*, 35, pp. 259–276.

Miozzo, M. & Grimshaw, D. (2008) 'Service multinationals and forward linkages with client firms: The case of it outsourcing in Argentina and Brazil', *International Business Review*, 17, pp. 8–27.

Moghaddam, K., Sethi, D., Weber, T. & Wu, J. (2014) 'The smirk of emerging market firms: A modification of the Dunning's typology of internationalization motivations', *Journal of International Management*, 20, pp. 359–374.

Morrison, A., Pietrobelli, C. & Rabellotti, R. (2008) 'Global value chains and technological capabilities: A framework to study learning and innovation in developing countries', *Oxford Development Studies*, 36, pp. 39–58.

Mudambi, R. (2008) 'Location, control and innovation in knowledge-intensive industries', *Journal of Economic Geography*, 8, 699–725.

Nadvi, K. (2008) 'Global standards, global governance and the organization of global value chains', *Journal of Economic Geography*, 8, pp. 323–343.

Pananond, P. (2013) Where do we go from here? Globalizing subsidiaries moving up the value chain', *Journal of International Management*, 19 (3), 207–219.

Pananond, P. (2015) 'Motives for foreign direct investment: A view from emerging market multinationals', *Multinational Business Review*, 23, pp. 77–86.

Parkhe, A. & Dhanaraj, C. (2003) 'Orchestrating globally: Managing the multinational enterprise as a network', in Rugman, A.M. (Ed.), *Leadership in International Business Education and Research in Global Strategic Management Volume 8*. Bingley, UK: Emerald Publishing Group Limited, pp. 197–214.

Pavlínek, P. & Ženka, J. (2011) 'Upgrading in the automotive industry: Firm-level evidence from Central Europe', *Journal of Economic Geography*, 11, pp. 559–586.

Pinkse, J. & Kolk, A. (2012) 'Multinational enterprises and climate change: Exploring institutional failures and embeddedness', *Journal of International Business Studies*, 43, pp. 332–341.

Porter, M.E. (1986) *Competition in Global Industries*. Boston, MA: Harvard Business Press.

Ramamurti, R. (2004) 'Developing countries and MNEs: Extending and enriching the research agenda', *Journal of International Business Studies*, 35, pp. 277–283.

Ramamurti, R. & Singh, J.V. (2009) *Emerging Multinationals in Emerging Markets*. Cambridge, UK: Cambridge University Press.

Rasiah, R., Kimura, F. & Oum, S. (2016a) 'Epilogue: Implications for promoting firm-level technological capabilities', *Asia Pacific Business Review*, 22, pp. 193–200.
Rasiah, R., Kimura, F. & Oum, S. (2016b) 'Host-site institutions, production networks and technological capabilities', *Asia Pacific Business Review*, 22, pp. 3–20.
Rasiah, R., Kong, X.X. & Vinanchiarachi, J. (2011) 'Moving up in the global value chain in button manufacturing in China', *Asia Pacific Business Review*, 17, pp. 161–174.
Rossi, A. (2011) 'Economic and social upgrading in global production networks: The case of the garment industry in Morocco'. Unpublished PhD thesis, University of Sussex, UK.
Schmeisser, B. (2013) 'A systematic review of literature on offshoring of value chain activities', *Journal of International Management*, 19, pp. 390–406.
Schmitt, A. & van Biesebroeck, J. (2013) 'Proximity strategies in outsourcing relations: The role of geographical, cultural and relational proximity in the European automotive industry', *Journal of International Business Studies*, 44, pp. 475–503.
Sinkovics, N., Sinkovics, R.R., Hoque, S.F. & Czaban, L. (2015) 'A reconceptualisation of social value creation as social constraint alleviation', *Critical Perspectives on International Business*, 11, pp. 340–363.
Slangen, A.H.L. & Beugelsdijk, S. (2010) 'The impact of institutional hazards on foreign multinational activity: A contingency perspective', *Journal of International Business Studies*, 41, pp. 980–995.
Sonderegger, P. & Täube, F. (2010) 'Cluster life cycle and diaspora effects: Evidence from the Indian IT cluster in Bangalore', *Journal of International Management*, 16, pp. 383–397.
Storper, M. (1997) 'Territories, flows, and hierarchies in the global economy', in Cox, K.R. (Ed.), *Spaces of Globalization: Reasserting the Power of the Local*. New York: Guilford, pp. 137–166.
Strange, R. & Newton, J. (2006) 'Stephen Hymer and the externalization of production', *International Business Review*, 15, pp. 180–193.
Suder, G., Liesch, P.W., Inomata, S., Mihailova, I. & Meng, B. (2015) 'The evolving geography of production hubs and regional value chains across East Asia: Trade in value-added', *Journal of World Business*, 50, pp. 404–416.
Swoboda, B., Schlüter, A., Olejnik, E. & Morschett, D. (2012) 'Does centralising global account management activities in response to international retailers pay off?' *Management International Review*, 52, pp. 727–756.
Taplin, I.M. (2014) 'Who is to blame? A re-examination of fast fashion after the 2013 factory disaster in Bangladesh', *Critical Perspectives on International Business*, 10, pp. 72–83.
Teece, D.J. (2014) 'A dynamic capabilities-based entrepreneurial theory of the multinational enterprise', *Journal of International Business Studies*, 45, pp. 8–37.
UNCTAD (2013) *The Least Developed Countries Report 2013*. New York and Geneva: United Nations Conference on Trade and Development.
UNCTAD (2014) *World Investment Report: Investigating in the SDGs – An action plan*. New York and Geneva: United Nations Conference on Trade and Development.
Vahlne, J.-E. & Ivarsson, I. (2014) 'The globalization of Swedish MNEs: Empirical evidence and theoretical explanations', *Journal of International Business Studies*, 45, pp. 227–247.
Vahlne, J.-E., Ivarsson, I. & Johanson, J. (2011) 'The tortuous road to globalization for Volvo's heavy truck business: Extending the scope of the Uppsala model', *International Business Review*, 20, pp. 1–14.
Wang, C., Deng, Z., Kafouros, M.I. & Chen, Y. (2012) 'Reconceptualizing the spillover effects of foreign direct investment: A process-dependent approach', *International Business Review*, 21, pp. 452–464.
Williamson, O.E. (1985) *The Economic Institutions of Capitalism*. New York: Free Press.
Williamson, P.J. (2015) 'The competitive advantages of emerging market multinationals: A re-assessment', *Critical Perspectives on International Business*, 11, pp. 216–235.
Yamin, M. (2011a) 'A commentary on Peter Buckley's writings on the global factory', *Management International Review*, 51, pp. 285–293.
Yamin, M. (2011b) 'International integration and coordination in the global factory: A commentary on Peter Buckley's writings on the global factory', *Management International Review*, 51, pp. 269–283.
Yamin, M. and Sinkovics, R.R. (2015) 'Rising power firms: The developmental promises and challenges – An introduction', *Critical Perspectives on International Business*, 11, pp. 210–215.

17

THE FIRM AS A DIFFERENTIATED NETWORK AND ECONOMIC GEOGRAPHY

Jens Gammelgaard and Frank McDonald

Introduction

Economic Geography deals with spatial analysis and focuses on the placement or localization of objects in the 'landscape' and how they relate to each other. There is a long tradition in International Business of considering issues connected to the spatial distribution of assets, markets and interaction between these distributions by cross-frontier transactions including foreign trade and foreign direct investment (FDI). Early studies in International Business considered cross-frontier transactions, analysing the importance of access to raw materials, costs of transport, trade and investment obstacles, market conditions, and developments in labour forces that make locations attractive (Hymer, 1972; Knickerbocker, 1973; Vernon, 1979). Recent studies of multinational corporations (MNC) by International Business scholars focus on the distribution and interaction across space of economic activity in nations, regions and cities. Such studies consider the spatially determined factors that make location in developed urban areas and in more peripheral places attractive for MNCs (Buckley & Ghauri, 2004; McCann & Mudambi, 2004; Beugelsdijk, Mudambi & McCann, 2010). Spatial factors are integral although often not explicitly in International Business research.

Important distinctions in Economic Geography are the concepts of *place* (physical and political locations), *space* (interaction between places) and *scale* (size of agencies involved in interacting in space – local, regional, national and global). In the International Business literature, specific attributes of place such as resource endowments, and economic, social and institutional environments are normally investigated in relation to the location choices of MNCs. These issues are normally examined by consideration of the impact of geographical, economic, political, institutional and cultural distance between home and host country (Beugelsdijk, Mudambi & McCann, 2010; Dau, 2013). The focus on space in International Business centres on how MNCs deal with issues arising from geographical distance that creates spatially related costs of the control and coordination of activities to achieve global value chain objectives (Jiang, Holburn & Beamish, 2016). These costs relate to additional expenditures arising from the need to obtain information on business environments in distant locations, costs of transport and complying with tariff and non-tariff barriers. In the International Business literature, scale normally relates to the organizational strategy of MNCs for control and coordination at local, regional, national and global levels.

In a perfect setting, MNCs manage place and space factors by designing organization systems that facilitate the optimal control and coordination over place and space, thereby arriving at effective decisions on when, where and how to internationalize (Dau, 2013). Alternative approaches examine the organizational means of effectively crossing the various spatial boundaries in ways that permit MNCs to develop and sustain effective global objectives (Beugelsdijk, Pedersen & Petersen, 2009; Meyer, Mudambi & Narula, 2011; Buckley & Strange, 2015). International Business theory therefore considers the three fundamental aspects of place, space and scale, but predominately uses political boundaries based on nation states, although there are some studies on sub-national locations (Meyer & Nguyen, 2005; Goerzen, Asmussen & Nielsen, 2013). Most International Business theory focuses on strategic issues connected to location, make or buy and entry mode decisions and often does not explicitly examine the nature of the organizational forms used by MNCs to secure these strategic objectives. The issue investigated in this chapter is therefore the relationship between a particular organization form, the 'Differentiated Network' (Nohria & Ghoshal, 1997) and Economic Geography factors.

The common held conceptualization of firms by business and management scholars is often somewhat different from how economic geographers regard firms. The relationship school among economic geographers view the firm as a type of network (Taylor & Asheim, 2001). In this view, firms are primarily networks with relationships between economic actors over space that are reciprocal, interdependent and often characterized by unequal distribution of power. Locations (place) have different social, political and institutional structures, and the firm is a type of a network system managing these differences across space by organizational systems that relate to a variety of scale factors (global, national, sub-national and local) in global value chains. Other economic geographers that take a relationship view of interactions across global space highlight the importance of the external and internal networks of firms as having a crucial role in how global value chains develop. Some of this literature includes reference to network views of the MNC (Morgan, 2001; Beaverstock, 2004; Jones, 2005; Yeung, 2005). These Economic Geography views of firms as networks have similarities to the MNCs as a differentiated network, but do not explicitly consider how firms use these networks to create and develop their global value chains.

This chapter analyses Nohria and Ghoshal's (1997) concept of the differentiated network in the context of concepts related to Economic Geography contingences. The differentiated network approach does not explicitly consider Economic Geography factors, but they are implicit in the concept of the MNC as a differentiated network. The chapter starts by outlining the key characteristics of the differentiated network paradigm. The chapter then examines the relationship of the MNC as a differentiated network in the context of key Economic Geography factors. The concluding part of the chapter suggests how Economic Geography perspectives might be further integrated into differentiated network analysis.

The differentiated network paradigm

In Nohria and Ghoshal's (1997) view, MNCs organize their activities so they can secure the benefits of innovations in multiple locations. In their description of such an organization, Nohria and Ghoshal position themselves away from transaction cost theory, because they regard this as a negative theory and prefer to focus on the organization's ability to promote knowledge creation. The competitive landscape they draw upon is MNCs competing against a few other MNCs, comparable in size, international resource access and worldwide market position. In this competitive scenario, some host country markets and resource bases tend to have different attractions as means to achieve global value chain objectives. In locations with features that are compatible with key global value chain objectives, subsidiaries become more important and therefore become more focal in the pursuit of strategic objectives. From this view, Nohria and Ghoshal hypothesize that the organizational form of a traditional hierarchy will be inferior because strong vertical control and coordination systems hinder the potential of subsidiaries to make important contributions to the overall strategic objectives of the MNC. The solution to obtaining competitive advantages are organizational systems based on differentiated networks to achieve effective control and coordination that is superior to hierarchical systems.

The differentiated network approach departs from an Economic Geography notion that differences arising from nation-states are of little importance in the interactions across space. In the differentiated network approach, an MNC consists of diverse subsidiaries that operate in distinct national environments that have different economic conditions, formal and informal institutional systems, cultures and time zones. Therefore, it is advantageous to have different relationships in the various national locations of MNCs. Thus, network relationships differ between headquarters and subsidiaries, between different subsidiaries and in the external linkages of subsidiaries. The differentiation within the MNC's network relationships is an outcome therefore of variation in business environmental conditions of the subsidiary. This leads to a constellation of three elements being relevant to define the network relationship for each subsidiary within the MNC:

1 Centralization (allocation of decision-making rights between headquarters and subsidiaries – autonomy)
2 Formalization (rules and procedures to control and coordinate subsidiaries)
3 Normative integration (creation of shared values among key agents in the MNC achieved through socialization processes)

Global linkages across the diverse national locations of companies and customers are based on linking centres of expertise and desirable resources to areas with high volume and/or priced market demand. This leads to a need for a differentiated organizational form that can draw effectively on competencies across the geographical dispersal of subsidiaries of the MNC to utilize effectively the geographically dispersed resource pools and market demands. This has similarities to the combinative capacity across national space suggested by Kogut and Zander (1992). Local innovation processes where subsidiaries use indigenous-based innovations, however, are prominent in Nohria and Ghoshal's analysis. They use the case of Unilever to highlight these host-based innovation effects. Unilever could not utilize its homegrown expertise in laundry detergents because washing in streams rather than using washing machines prevailed in India. The development of a solid tablet using a detergent derived from vegetable oil rather than clarified butter created a superior alternative to the traditional soap bar. This example of locally based innovation emphasizes the usefulness of network relationships within organizational systems that effectively weaves together local knowledge with the MNC-wide advantages to help satisfy strategic objectives.

Organizational complexity may arise in differentiated networks because of the interactions between diverse business environments. The importance for an MNC to access and exploit local knowledge may call for higher local autonomy of subsidiaries, but this can lead to a need for organizational forms that ensure the weaving together of locally obtained knowledge with the overall objectives of the MNC (Gammelgaard et al., 2012). Increased formalization of the organization system is often necessary when reducing centralization by granting local autonomy to subsidiaries. Formalization provides rules and procedures to ensure that subsidiaries embed into the overall strategic objectives of the MNC. Normative integration processes may further encourage the sharing of organizational goals by key players in the MNC thereby helping to fulfil strategic objective. As MNCs operate in many different business environments, diversity in organizational systems is often necessary to ensure satisfaction of strategic objectives. In principle, business environment conditions that require greater autonomy for subsidiaries lead to reduced centralization and an enhanced need for formalization and normative integration. Nohria and Ghoshal, however, depart from this simple framework by using the notion of contingency theory from Drazin and van de Ven (1985). This views the required type of organizational forms as being contingent on the key characteristics in the various business environments in which MNCs operate.

As the complexity of business environments increases, there is a need for a variety of constellations of centralization/formalization/socialization to manage effectively the operations of MNCs. Nohria and Ghoshal measure environmental complexity by two major factors: (a) technological dynamism, and (b) competition. The major driver of the development of complex organizational forms is technological dynamism that involves fast-changing technologies requiring access to intangible assets that enable the gathering of information and the development of knowledge to use effectively evolving technologies. High technological dynamism combined with strong competition based primarily on the qualities of products leads to complex business environments requiring a careful balance of the three key elements in the differentiated network of MNCs. In cases of a high level of business environment complexity, centralization is likely to be low to permit innovative behaviour by subsidiaries to cater for local conditions. With subsidiaries with low quality local resources, moderate relaxation of centralization is required to reduce the risk of futile innovation by subsidiaries that lack the necessary resources to provide innovations useful to the overall objectives of the MNC. Subsidiaries with limited valuable resource will, therefore, have little autonomy especially in cases where environmental complexity is low, but will have higher levels of autonomy if they possess valuable resources. Strong formalization is required in cases where subsidiaries control valuable resources and is strongest in cases of low environmental complexity. In cases of high complexity business environments moderation of formalization is necessary to prevent delay in innovation processes due to bureaucratic procedures that limited innovative behaviour. Normative integration is in principle always a good idea. The costs of engaging in such integration, however, renders this approach most useful in cases of highly complex business environments where there is a need to encourage innovation and entrepreneurship while harnessing subsidiaries to the overall objectives of the MNC.

Using the seminal work by Bartlett and Ghoshal (1989) on transnational companies, Nohria and Ghoshal (1997) divided large West European MNCs into categories. They found significant numbers of companies strong in only one of the key elements in the differentiated network (either centralization or formalization or socialization), other companies strong in two, and a few in all three (e.g. Digital Equipment, Siemens and Honeywell). Some companies are not strong in any of the categories. An MNC, however, does not necessarily need to be strong in all categories. Only in cases with high environmental complexity and valuable local resources in subsidiaries are the network connections of MNCs likely to make significant use of all three elements. In other words, differentiated networks (with integration of key components necessary for structural integration) are only necessary where business environments in host locations are complex and local resources are valuable.

Nohria and Ghoshal (1997) address the importance of some Economic Geography contingencies, as environmental complexity and value of resources in host locations relate to place characteristics. The geographical location of fast-changing, technological, market conditions and of valuable (often intangible) resources pay an important role in the requirement for differentiated networks. The differentiated network approach views headquarters as primarily an information processing unit that involves space characteristics associated with interconnections between places and scale issues in deciding at what level – global, national or local (Forsgren, 2004). Egelhoff (2010) finds that the differentiated network structure is helpful for bringing knowledge from different places together. The success in these circumstances depends on headquarters' ability to understand diffuse pieces of information from a variety of places, and translate them into meaningful evaluations in terms of strategy making. Further, Egelhoff highlights that Nohria and Ghoshal's conceptualization of differentiated networks focuses on the internal – or intra-organizational – relationships leading to a neglect of subsidiary relationships to external or inter-organizational relationships. Arvidsson and Birkinshaw (2004) address this gap in the Nohria and Ghoshal model and acknowledge that the basis of variation of capabilities across subsidiaries is a function of characteristics of how subsidiaries embed in local networks. In contrast to Nohria and Ghoshal, they argue that stickiness and complexities of transferring knowledge and managerial capabilities within the organization by formalization and/or normalization causes subsidiaries to remain 'different' instead of aligned. Rugman and Verbeke (2001) develop this idea in their work on location bound and non-location bound resources. The ideal of an MNC with a high presence of 'shared values' was moreover not confirmed in a survey by Forsgren, Holm and Johanson (2007), that found only 7 per cent of the cases of 97 subsidiaries of Swedish MNCs had a high degree of shared values. This study also found that issues of power and resource dependencies do not integrate well into the differentiated network framework. These studies indicate problems with control and coordination activities in differentiated networks connected to issues involving space (effectively interacting between different places) and with scale (finding the correct type of agents in locations for decision-making and to develop innovations, etc.).

In the final section of their book, Nohria and Ghoshal (1997) indicate the importance of issues connected to external networks and the high degree of connectedness between various stakeholders. This includes issues related to the development of clusters and global value chains. Here, Nohria and Ghoshal hint at the need to better integrate Economic Geography elements connected to communication and transportation infrastructures by referring to Chandler's work (1986). An industry like telecommunications, for instance, departed in many countries from being a national regulated industry with the need of local knowledge creation and implementation, but due to deregulation it evolved to become an industry of growing technological standardization and cross-national integration. Consequently, the MNC organizational systems for managing these kinds of industry contingencies were significant different according to place, requiring organizational systems of MNCs to be amenable to managing effectively across space and at differing scales. This often requires reallocation of mandates and decision-making rights among subsidiaries within the MNC (Dörrenbächer & Gammelgaard, 2010). The importance of place, space and scale in connection to the MNC as a differentiated network is therefore apparent, but not normally explicitly considered in the literature.

Much of the elaboration on the differentiated network paradigm of Nohria and Ghoshal, and later scholars referring to their work, has addressed the need of further investigating of the effects of host location networks and the effective embedding of subsidiaries into the strategic objectives of MNCs. The spatial effects have however been less emphasized. The next section outlines these attempts to better incorporate spatial issues into the concept of the MNC as a differentiated network.

Economic Geography and the differentiated network

International Business literature that considers spatial issues focuses on the importance of place (location) as a major driver of foreign direct investment (FDI), including the attractiveness of clusters (McCann, Arita & Gordon, 2002; Majocchi & Presutti, 2009). This literature tends to focus on the attractiveness of locations for FDI and the effect of such investment on host location productivity, and on how transfers of knowledge are affected by location (Teece, 1977; Biggiero, 2002; De Propris & Driffield, 2005; Dunning, 2009). Issues connected to securing strategic objectives involving cross-border transactions are examined, but normally in the context of entry modes and the need for learning strategies to obtain and process information over space to enable the fulfilment of strategic objectives (Buckley & Ghauri, 2004; Dunning, 2009; Beugelsdijk, Mudambi & McCann, 2010). The space issues involved with securing strategic objectives from internationalization are normally linked to costs associated with liabilities of foreignness and outsidership. These liabilities stem from additional costs in foreign operations arising from economic distance (including market and technology differences) and institutional distance (embracing both formal and informal institutional factors) between home and host locations (Eden & Miller, 2004; Johanson & Vahlne, 2009). The nature of the problems caused by space between places is therefore seen as being largely due to activities rather than cross-national borders, leading to the need to manage costs and risks associated with differences in economic and institutional systems from those that prevail in the home base. Most studies are conducted at national level, with a few studies examining cross-border issues from the perspective of sub-national or city location (Nachum, 2000; Goerzen, Asmussen & Nielsen, 2013). The organization structures (involving space and scale issues) that MNCs need to be able secure advantages in their various host location are often not explicitly examined in this literature.

Costs associated with space between locations (geographical distance) affect organizational forms such as differentiated networks. These costs include acquisition and transfer of information about host environments, transport/distribution costs and compliance with tariffs, non-tariff barriers and regulatory requirements. These spatially associated costs can be significant if a high degree of interaction between subsidiaries arises due to the complexity of business environments (Jiang, Holburn & Beamish, 2016). These spatially driven costs normally increase as proximity declines. This is obvious for transport and distribution costs, but there is also often a high degree of correlation between geographical distance and economic and institutional distance. The additional costs associated with distance provide incentives to reduce these costs by locating subsidiaries in close geographical proximity. This proximity incentive is also seen as encouraging location in specific region areas such as Europe or South Asia. The tendency for a regional area focus of subsidiary location is reinforced by economic factors connected to competition and consumer preferences (Rugman, 2005). These costs affect not only incentives for proximity between headquarters and subsidiaries but also between subsidiaries (Adler & Hashai, 2015). Tests of the effect of geographical distance on innovation transfers between subsidiaries find the further away headquarters are from subsidiaries, the lower are such transfers. The internal embeddedness of subsidiaries within their MNC structures, however, appears to mitigate the space-related costs (Dellestrand & Kappen, 2012). This also holds, albeit with lower influence, for subsidiary embeddedness in its host location. This literature on the effects of geographical distance therefore provides explanations of why linkages between headquarters and subsidiaries (including external network connections) in host locations alleviates the spatial costs that affect innovation-related FDI.

The role of headquarter relationships with subsidiaries affects subsidiary strategy (Pearce, 2001). This study does not investigate the differentiated network as such, but analyses the long-term effects of new FDI on the development of subsidiary roles. These factors include geographical factors that can lead to changes in subsidiary mandates. Pearce uses three types of subsidiary mandates:

1 The truncated miniature replicate (TMR) that pursues a market-seeking strategy which primarily acts as a sale subsidiary that may also adapt the MNC's product to local market conditions.
2 The rationalized product subsidiary (RPS) that is an efficiency-seeking unit often based on lower cost inputs such as labour.
3 The world/regional product mandate subsidiaries (PM), which have strategic mandates that go beyond supplying national markets and/or providing assembly facilities for exporting products; they have mandates to design and/or develop products and to product, distribute and provide after sales services globally or in regional areas.

The PM mandate types have the widest strategic responsibilities and are likely to be more common in complex business environments requiring a differentiated network approach to enable MNCs to achieve their strategic objectives, especially in cases with high spatial costs due to geographic distance. Given the increasing differences in specialized technological capabilities in countries and the heterogeneity of consumer demands, Pearce (2001) argues that many, often geographically distant countries, are prime candidates for subsidiaries with PM mandates. Subsidiaries of this type are likely to be best managed using some type of differentiated network.

The contribution of Pearce improves understanding of the links between differentiated network and Economic Geography factors. Pearce connects the development of subsidiaries and the embedding of them in overall MNC objectives to Economic Geography contingencies connected to economic, market and institutional developments in the places where PM type subsidiaries may be located. The importance of the relationship between the scope of what subsidiaries do and spatial factors includes aspects of regional bloc integration (Benito, Grøgaard & Narula, 2003). This study found that subsidiary development differs in the otherwise comparable countries of Denmark, Norway and Finland, because Denmark and Finland are EU members, whereas Norway is more peripherally connected to the EU. This study also found that 'country size' is important with subsidiaries in small countries being more marginal in the organizational systems of MNC organization.

The evolution of subsidiaries from TMR to PM is also considered by Pearce, and geographical factors play an important role in such developments. Trade agreements and market-based reforms in countries reduce place-related tariff and non-tariff barriers, making it easier to locate product manufacturing where it is most efficient. Location of production facilities in new places can lead to labour specialization and improved skills to address the technological demands of these RPS type subsidiaries. In host countries that develop highly skilled specialized labour forces with the necessary supporting infrastructures and institutional systems, the potential exists for the development of PM subsidiaries. Places that do not develop specialized labour forces face competition from other places for the location of TMR type subsidiaries. What is needed for a subsidiary development into a PM type, is that the host country supports and invest in its human capital and supporting infrastructures and institutional systems to provide places conducive to subsidiaries of the PM type. Buckley and Ghauri (2004) elaborate on this aspect of how MNC subsidiary policies connected to spatial factors have led to a deepening of the spatial division of labour. Changes in the attractiveness of places and costs associated with space between home and host locations can therefore lead to the alteration of the geographical proximity and characteristics of subsidiary development in differentiated networks.

The role of country specific assets (CSA) for subsidiary development (Rugman & Verbeke, 2003) provides other insights into differentiated network organizational structures as the outcome of the resource bases of the host countries. The sources of CSA arise from the resource base of countries and aspects of the economic, social and institutional systems that confer cost advantages and/or access to scarce and valuable assets (often intangible assets) that are not available or are only available at higher cost and risk in other countries. Access to CSA is not necessarily available (or is equally available) in all parts of a country, therefore selection of best sub-national locations is often an important factor in acquiring CSA (Meyer & Nguyen, 2005; Goerzen, Asmussen & Nielsen, 2013). The value of the resources normally increases with spatial proximity (due to reduced spatial associated costs) and the subsidiary's ability to embed into host country innovation systems to provide access to local innovations. This tends to increase the location bound nature of CSA. This may, however, create strong embeddedness into host locations that can lock in MNCs' global value chains into host locations. This can be counterproductive if subsidiaries pursue policies and practices that do not fit well with global value chain objectives. This risk provides incentives for the MNC to seek to make activities that are crucial for fulfilling the global value chain objectives less location bound. A differentiated network system may therefore encourage locations with desirable CSA and with low spatial associated costs due to geographical proximity, but which result in undesirable embedding into host locations. This leads to 'isolating mechanisms' arising from 'routines' shared by cluster participants that are difficult to replicate, imitate or otherwise acquire by outsiders' that leads to 'diseconomies, inter-organizational asset stock inter-connectedness, partner scarcity, resource indivisibility, and a specific institutional environment' (Rugman & Verbeke, 2003, p. 132). Strong embeddedness in host locations may therefore hinder MNCs from utilizing economies of scale and scope. This risk may be mitigated by careful balance of the decision on the centralization/formalization/normative nexus that lessens the chances of locking into activities by subsidiaries that are harmful for achieving the strategic objectives of MNCs.

The acquisition of CSA by location strategies is desirable if this leads to the enhancing of firm specific advantages (FSA) that give rise to competitive advantages (Rugman, 1981). The tendency for MNCs to concentrate their major activities in specific regional areas in the world leads Rugman to set his CSA-FSA model in a regional area context. This adds a regional specific advantage (RSA) component to the CSA-FSA model (Rugman, 2005). Trade and FDI flows appear to be strongly influenced by geographical distance, with proximity and size exercising a strong influence on these flows (Disdier & Head, 2008; Brun et al., 2005). The control and coordination costs across space also favour geographical proximity because market and institutional systems are often more similar in countries that are geographically close (Eden & Miller, 2004; Berry, Guillén & Zhou, 2010). Regional integration bodies and regional trade agreements can also reduce institutional obstacles to trade and FDI by reducing trading costs through reducing or eliminating tariffs/quotas and harmonizing regulatory frameworks. Membership of such bodies reinforces the proximity and size effects of trade and FDI flows. A major part of the attractiveness of CSA is often therefore the trade relationships of countries with their regional areas, especially membership of regional trade bodies and regionally based trade agreements (Rugman, 2014).

These geographically driven considerations may lead, in differentiated network structures, to low centralization to promote the ability to innovate in complex business environments, but with strong formalization and normative integration to limit unhelpful development from location bound assets. In this type of scenario, difficult spatially connected trade-offs can arise to balance securing innovations to help to prosper in complex business environments, but which have low spatially associated control and coordination costs. Trade-offs emerge from three key issues: (1) place issues connected to decisions about the location and relocation and types of mandates given to subsidiaries to obtain resources and innovations to enhance FSA; (2) space issues relating to choices about control and coordination of geographically dispersed activities that minimize spatially related costs; and (3) scale issues linked to the adoption of organizational structures that link different types of agents in network systems that weave the geographically scattered subsidiaries to enable the creation and sustaining of FSA. Locations may provide attractive features that would be helpful for achieving global value chain objectives, but they may be associated with high control and coordination costs due to large geographical distances. Linking subsidiaries across space with minimum interference by headquarters can promote innovations, but may lead to undesirable outcomes by, for example, promoting the locking-in to host locations that leads to higher costs or qualities of products that do not fit with global value chain objectives. In differentiated networks the decisions on the centralization/formalization/normative nexus are crucial in the search for trade-offs between such conflicting outcomes from choices about place, space and scale in global value chains.

Locations with desirable CSA and RSA are attractive, but these must be examined in the context of spatially associated costs (often favouring geographical proximity) and the dangers of the development of location bound assets that are not amenable to fulfilling the strategic objectives of the MNC. The overall objective is to develop organizational structures that enable MNCs to create and sustain firm FSA that lead to competitive advantages (Rugman, 1981; Rugman & Verbeke, 2001). This requires securing CSA and RSA and weaving them over space into FSA that have low spatially associated costs and with little prospects of lock-in to host locations that do not contribute to FSA at a global level. The addition of an evolutionary process for subsidiary strategy, as proposed by Pearce (2001), to the Rugman and Verbeke concept of obtaining FSA from CSA and RSA indicates that differentiated networks are likely to be involved in dynamic processes involving consideration of all three of the key elements of place, space and scale. This process is illustrated in Figure 17.1.

Place factors – location decisions including entry mode relating to CSA and RSA to secure desired assets and innovations to create and sustain FSA, relocation decisions as business environment changes to ensure locations continue to provide desired assets and innovations.

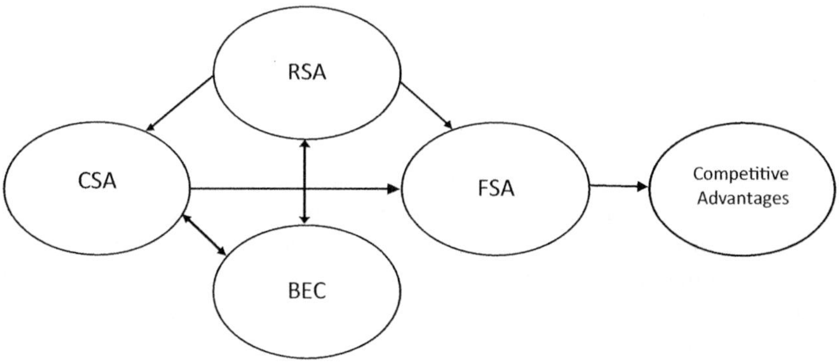

CSA – country specific advantages (including sub-national specific advantages)

RSA – regional specific advantages

BEC – business environment complexity

FSA – firm specific advantages

Figure 17.1 Geographical factors and the development of competitive advantages

Space factors – selecting headquarters to subsidiaries and subsidiaries to subsidiaries network relationships (and developing them as business environment complexity changes) to minimize spatially associated costs of control and coordination while also securing desired assets and innovations.

Scale factors – selecting mandates for subsidiaries and their development as business environments change, and creating and developing networks (both internal and external) between headquarters and subsidiaries (and between subsidiaries) that weave together the various parts of the MNC to secure the necessary resources and innovations to create and sustain FSA.

Complicated decisions need to be made in selecting locations and the network relationships between these locations to create and sustain FSA. Attributes of CSA and RSA may encourage location in countries (or sub-national locations within countries) to secure resources and capacities for developing innovations. Proximity and size effects as well as spatially associated control and coordination costs may also encourage locations with low geographical distance. In these circumstances, concentration of large parts of global value chains may be found in regional areas such as Europe or South East Asia, with operations outside of these vicinities being restricted to the availability of scarce and valuable resources that are not available in the main region of operations. Major changes to these regional area locations would arise in cases of major changes in business environments, for example the rise of the emerging economies that provide resource benefits that outweigh the costs associated with geographical distance. These types of complicated outcomes in location and network relationships accord with the views that regard proximity and size benefits and spatially associated costs as major drivers of MNC operations (Ghemawat, 2001; Rugman & Verbeke, 2003; Jiang, Holburn & Beamish, 2016).

The benefit-cost outcomes of weaving together these geographically dispersed parts of the MNC may lead to difficult trade-offs in network relationships. The availability of desirable markets, resources and innovation capacity in countries in certain regional areas may call for reduced centralization, but with increased formalization and/or normative integration to offset undesirable actions by subsidiaries that may lock in the MNC to these locations. In fast-changing and complex business environments, these locking-in effects may be harmful to the sustainability of FSA, further increasing the need for formalization and/or normative integration to mitigate these harmful outcomes of decreasing centralization. Securing innovations may encourage subsidiaries to embed in their host locations and to share valuable assets and knowledge via a host of complicated intra and inter-organizational networks. These networks may, however, encourage the development of routines and practices that are counterproductive to the overall development of FSA that accord with the strategy of the MNC. To mitigate these kinds of potentially harmful effects requires carefully balancing and rebalancing of the centralization, formalization and normative nexus in the differentiated network. The dynamic nature of complex business environments further increases the need for careful development of these balances in network relationships as major changes in technologies and the determinants of competitive environments change.

Increasing internationalization by firms leads to views that MNCs may become too internationally diversified. These concerns arise because the costs of operating complex global operations in a wide range of geographically dispersed locations may exceed the benefits of developing global value chains. Differing views on the issue of the possibilities of over internationalization are evident in the literature. These include u-shaped relationships that indicate initial performance losses until the firm learns how to operate in many diverse locations (Gaur & Kumar, 2009) and an inverted u-shaped relationship indicating rising performance as learning takes place, but which eventually declines as control and coordination costs of increasing internationalization exceed the performance benefits (Contractor et al., 2003). A more sophisticated view

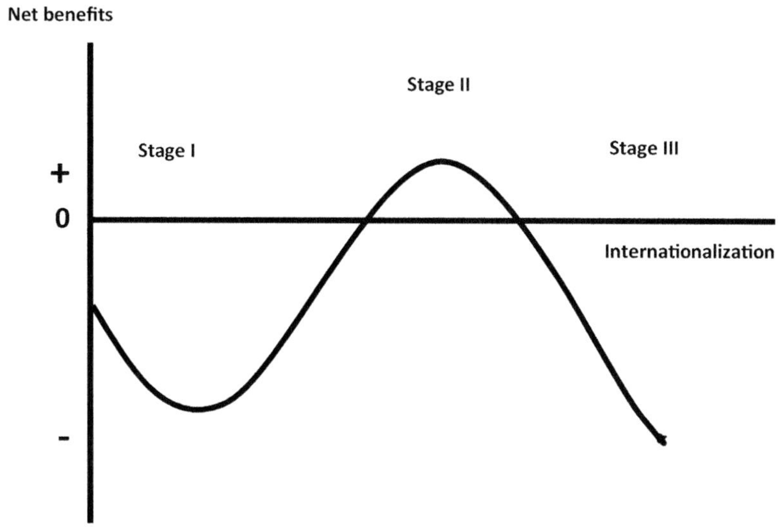

Figure 17.2 The evolution of net benefits from internationalization

is of a horizontal s-shaped relationship (Lu & Beamish, 2004) where firms initially face negative performance that moves into performance gains as firms learn how to engage effectively in internationalization processes, but where eventually diminishing performance returns. These issues are illustrated in Figure 17.2.

The net benefits of internationalization are the gross benefits (improvements in FSA) minus the costs of internationalization. These costs arise from geographical, economic, social and institutional distance (leading to liabilities of foreignness and outsidership), tariff/non-tariff costs, and transport and distribution costs. In addition, there are costs of control and coordination connected to managing interactions over the space between the different locations of the MNC. These are primarily the costs of achieving and managing balance in differentiated networks composed of geographically dispersed subsidiaries. These costs are associated with the selection and maintenance of an appropriate centralization/formalization/normative nexus that permits MNCs to weave together geographically dispersed subsidiaries to enhance FSA. Costs of internationalization rise as business environment complexity increases and as proximity declines. Increasing business complexity induces a need to secure additional resources and innovations, often requiring an escalating number of locations and deeper involvement in host locations. This tends to increase control and coordination costs. Decreasing proximity between the different parts of the MNC has a propensity to increase costs due to problems of communication and, in many cases, from increased institutional and cultural distance between home and host locations that hinders understanding of what headquarters require from subsidiaries.

Stage I

Early period of differentiated network – the benefits of internationalization minus the costs initially lead to negative net benefits. Learning how to mitigate costs of liabilities of foreignness and outsidership, however, leads to movement towards positive net benefits. Transport and distribution costs are unlikely to be significantly reduced as internationalization proceeds unless there are significant improvements in transport and distribution infrastructures and technologies. Reductions in tariff and non-tariff barriers will only transpire if there are bilateral and/or multilateral trade agreements, or from membership of effective regional integration bodies. In most cases, it is likely therefore that the move towards positive net benefits will mainly come from learning how to mitigate liabilities of foreignness and outsidership.

Stage II

Mature phase – the net benefits are positive as the networks of MNCs attain high-level effectiveness in weaving the various parts of the global value chains to enhance FSA. The net benefits, however, begin to decline as internationalization processes become wider and deeper, leading to new liabilities of foreignness and outsidership as new locations come online, and from rising control and coordination costs from increases in geographical dispersion and the multifaceted nature of global value chains.

Stage III

Declining net benefits phase – continuing internationalization leads to negative net benefits as the costs of widening and deepening internationalization exceed the benefits of enhanced FSA.

It is likely that an MNC in the downward part of Stage II and certainly by Stage III would revise its internationalization strategy. This could involve a radical reassessment of locations that involves divestment, relocation, abandoning of low return operations in some locations and changes to control processes, for example reducing ownership stake in subsidiaries. The centralization/formative/normative nexus of network relationships could also be simplified, or radically overhauled, to reduce control and coordination costs. These changes to control and coordination of network relationships would also follow from any reduction in the scale and scope of internationalization processes. In some cases, especially if Stage III is reached, MNCs may withdraw altogether from all or part of the places it operates in, or from some of the markets that it supplies. This would involve a move towards greater proximity in the important networks of the MNC. In some locations subsidiary mandates may move to simpler functions such as TMR or RPS. The overall effect would be to rationalize to a simpler and less costly internationalization process, often involving reduced geographical dispersion of subsidiaries and a moving away from deep internationalization in areas with high spatially associated costs. In other words, a relentless march to ever wider and deeper internationalization is not inevitable, even for what are MNCs with highly developed differentiated networks.

Many MNC that find themselves in the downward section of Stage II, or are in Stage III, may seek to introduce new products and/or develop existing products, create radical new technologies and change regional area focus to boost the benefits from developing FSA by use of internationalization processes. This would, if successful, reverse the downward section in Stage II and perhaps even lead to an upturn in Stage III. Investment in innovative centralization policies and/or greatly improved formalization and normative integration elements in the control and coordination of networks may also prevent costs from exceeding the benefits of internationalization. Changes that are external to the MNC in the complexity of business environments by improvements in technology and/or alterations in competitive conditions could also alter the shape of the relationship between net benefits and internationalization processes. Similarly, external developments in infrastructures, technologies and government policies associated with locational costs and benefits could affect the relationship. New or extended trade agreements and developments within regional integration blocs would have similar effects. The nature of the relationships between net benefits and internationalization processes are therefore likely to be dynamic and influenced by many internal and external factors. The development of the internationalization processes of the differentiated networks of MNCs is therefore likely to be a complex process of evolution that is driven in large part by issues connected to developments in geographical factors.

The firm in Economic Geography

Economic geographers that take a relationship view on the link between territory and firms in global production networks regard the nature of the firm in ways that have similarities to the transnational MNC and the differentiated network view (Nohria & Ghoshal, 1997; Bartlett & Ghoshal, 1989). The firm is viewed as a type of social network not as a production function, as in neo-classical economics, or as a transaction cost minimizing entity (Yeung, 2005). These studies examine control and coordination processes across space by use of expatriates (Beaverstock, 2004) and the use of formal and informal systems to manage interactions in network relationships (Morgan, 2001). These approaches to how firms manage network relationships in global production networks echo the formative and normative integration analyses of the differentiated network view of the MNC. In an interesting study the relationship between firms and territorial spaces is viewed as being controlled and coordinated by social networks that due to complex and dynamic economic and institutional environments lead to non-scalar outcomes (Jones, 2005). This view of firms in global production networks sees the association between the network relationships of firms and internationalization as being dynamic and with a variety of possible outcomes. Changes in business environments, economic and institutional conditions can therefore generate several possible paths for the internationalization processes of firms that are embedded in global production networks. This approach has similarities to the view of the development of differentiated networks outlined in Figure 17.2 above.

There are two major differences between how relationship economic geographers view MNCs in global production networks and the approach of the MNC as a differentiated network. First, the global production network approach tends to focus on firms in territories and in interactions with other territories. These territories are often sub-national (city regions, industrial clusters, free trade zones, etc). The relationships between regional area, national and sub-national locations as drivers of the location decisions of MNCs (as outlined above in Figure 17.1) tend therefore to be underplayed. This leads to a tendency to understate the influence of national and regional area aspects of locations for the nature of the network relationships of MNCs. The importance of these national and regional area aspects for location and therefore for the role of headquarters and subsidiaries in MNC networks is illustrated by the debate on location and relocation decisions of MNCs because of the UK exiting from the EU. The withdrawal of the UK could lead to the significant relocation of some headquarters and all or some of the activities of subsidiaries. Changes at national and regional level can therefore have profound effects on the nature of the networks of MNCs. The differentiated network view places these national and regional area influences at the heart of the analysis of network relationships. In the relational Economic Geography approach these drivers of network development are often not centre stage in the analysis. Second, analysis using the differentiated network approach places the securing of competitive advantages by developing FSA as the core of what drives MNCs. The use of network relationships to achieve this aim is therefore fundamental in the analysis. In other words, the focus is on how networks are created and sustained over space to develop FSA. In relationship Economic Geography approaches, analysis tends to emphasize the nature of social networks and how they are influenced primarily by changes in social, economic, political and institutional factors. In short, analysis in relationship Economic Geography is on how global production networks affect the development of territories and the interactions between territories. In the differentiated network the focus is on how the characteristics of national (including sub-national) and regional areas affect the network relationships of MNCs in the context of the overarching strategic aim of enhancing FSA.

These differences tend to lead to relationship Economic Geography analysis underemphasizing the role of the driving strategic force behind the decisions of MNCs, i.e. the securing of FSA, and the role of country and regional area characteristics. Analysis based on the differentiated network approach on the other hand normally has a poor understanding of the complexities of place, space and scale that often results in naïve views that may mean little more than that, somehow or other, proximity matters. This leads to a rather simplistic reliance on institutional, cultural and economic distance measures to capture what are complex issues connected to place, space and scale. The strengths and weaknesses of the relationship Economic Geography and differentiated network approaches call for greater integration of the strengths of each approach to reduce the weakness in these approaches to understanding the links between global value chains of MNCs and global production networks. The concluding part of this chapter therefore considers how integrating key issues from Economic Geography's analysis of global production networks may provide a better understanding of how the network relationships of MNCs help to manage global value chains in ways that enhance FSA.

Economic Geography and networks for managing global value chains

In the differentiated network approach, the purpose of creating and developing global value chains is to enhance FSA to obtain competitive advantages. In complex business environments, this requires designing and sustaining network relationships that facilitate this overriding strategic objective. This requires establishing in places that provide the resources and innovations that can help to achieve this objective and to link these sites over space and in the different scale dimension of these locations in an effective differentiated set of network relationships. This requires careful balance of the centralization/formalization/socialization nexus that provides at low cost, effective control and coordination and that can effectively manage the evolution of locations and interaction over space of these networks in the face of factors that alter the benefits and costs from internationalization. How Economic Geography contingencies affect the managing of global value chains is currently not well incorporated into studies using a differentiated network approach. These contingencies, however, exercise significant influence on the benefits and costs arising from the selection of places to locate, network relationships to manage interaction over the space between locations and the scale at which the components of the global value chain engage with these networks.

Currently, most research in International Business (including research using a differentiated network approach) assesses the costs arising from space between locations using national measures of economic, geographic, cultural and institutional distance. There are some studies that examine sub-national locations (Nachum, 2000; Meyer & Nguyen, 2005; Goerzen, Asmussen & Nielsen, 2013). There are also theoretical pieces on costs and benefits of crossing various national and sub-national borders (Beugelsdijk & Mudambi, 2013). These studies highlight the importance of geographical contingencies, but the means to measure these spatially related factors are few and often of poor quality. Consideration of differences in the costs of control and coordination of the various locations, spaces and scale in which cross-border transactions take place are necessary in global value chains. Improved knowledge in these areas would help to improve the choices made in the centralization/formalization/socialization nexus to enable global value chains to deliver FSA in the face of dynamic environments. Improved methods for evaluating the benefits associated with the place, space and scale of locations would also help to arrive at the net benefits of weaving together the various locations of the different parts of the MNC's global value chain. These costs and benefits need to be analysed in dynamic and evolutionary ways to assess how internationalization may develop in ways that prevent the costs of internationalization exceeding the benefits. Consideration should be given to how changes in factors that are internal and external to MNCs affect the internationalization processes of firms. Assessing the benefits and costs of altering proximity in network relationships is required. This involves the examination of location and relocation decisions (including subsidiary mandate changes) and the developing of the centralization/formalization/socialization nexus for creating and sustaining effective network relationships. This requires consideration of place, space and scale relationships and their associated costs and benefits in the face of complex business environments for MNCs and changing economic, political, technological, social and institutional environments in the various places in which the MNC's global value chain is located. Relationship Economic Geography approaches provide good insights into the environmental conditions and connections between locations in global production networks. This knowledge needs to be incorporated more fully into the core of the differentiated network approach to provide greater understanding of how internationalization processes of differentiated networks work and evolve.

References

Adler, N. & Hashai, N. (2015) 'The impact of competition and consumer preferences on the location choices of multinational enterprises', *Global Strategy Journal*, 5, pp. 278–302.

Arvidsson, N. & Birkinshaw, J. (2004) 'Identifying leading-edge market knowledge in multinational corporations', in Mahnke, V. & Pedersen, T. (Eds.), *Knowledge Flows, Governance and the Multinational Enterprise: Frontiers in International Management Research*. Basingstoke, UK: Palgrave Macmillan, pp. 161–176.

Bartlett, C.A. & Ghoshal, S. (1989) *Managing Across Borders: The Transnational Solution*. Boston, MA: Harvard Business School Press.

Beaverstock, J.V. (2004) '"Managing across borders": Knowledge management and expatriation in professional service legal firms', *Journal of Economic Geography*, 4, pp. 157–179.

Benito, G.R.G., Grøgaard, B. & Narula, R. (2003) 'Environmental influence on MNE subsidiary roles: Economic integration and the Nordic countries', *Journal of International Business Studies*, 34, pp. 443–456.

Berry, H., Guillén, M.F. & Zhou, N. (2010) 'An institutional approach to cross-national distance', *Journal of International Business Studies*, 41, pp. 1460–1480.

Beugelsdijk, S. & Mudambi, R. (2013) 'MNCs as border-crossing multi-location enterprises: The role of discontinuities in geographic space', *Journal of International Business Studies*, 44, pp. 413–416.

Beugelsdijk, S., Mudambi, R. & McCann, P. (2010) 'Place, space and organization: Economic Geography and the multinational enterprise', *Journal of Economic Geography*, 10, 485–493.

Beugelsdijk, S., Pedersen, T. & Petersen, B. (2009) 'Is there a trend towards global value chain specialization? An examination of cross border sales of US foreign affiliates', *Journal of International Management*, 15, pp. 126–141.

Biggiero, L. (2002) 'The location of multinationals in industrial districts: Knowledge transfer in biomedicals', *Journal of Technology Transfer*, 27, pp. 111–122.

Brun, J.F., Carrère, C., Guillaumont, P. & De Melo, J. (2005) 'Has distance died? Evidence from a panel gravity model', *The World Bank Economic Review*, 19, pp. 99–120.

Buckley, P.J. & Ghauri, P.N (2004) 'Globalisation, Economic Geography and the strategy of multinational enterprises', *Journal of International Business Studies*, 35, pp. 81–98.

Buckley, P.J. & Strange, R. (2015) 'The governance of the global factory: Location and control of world economic activity', *The Academy of Management Perspectives*, 29, pp. 237–249.

Chandler, A.D. (1986) 'The evolution of modern global competition', in Porter, M.E. (Ed.), *Competition in Global Industries*. Boston, MA: Harvard Business School Press, pp. 405–448.

Contractor, F.J., Kundu, S.K. & Hsu, C.C. (2003) 'A three-stage theory of international expansion: The link between multinationality and performance in the service sector', *Journal of International Business Studies*, 34, pp. 5–18.

Dau, L.A. (2013) 'Learning across geographic space: Pro-market reforms, multinationalization strategy, and profitability', *Journal of International Business Studies*, 44, pp. 235–262.

Dellestrand, H. & Kappen, P. (2012) 'The effect of spatial and contextual factors on headquarters resource allocation to MNE subsidiaries', *Journal of International Business Studies*, 43, pp. 219–243.

De Propris, L. & Driffield, N. (2005) 'The importance of clusters for spillovers from foreign direct investment and technology sourcing', *Cambridge Journal of Economics*, 30, pp. 277–291.

Disdier, A.C. & Head, K. (2008) 'The puzzling persistence of the distance effect on bilateral trade', *The Review of Economics and Statistics*, 90, pp. 37–48.

Dörrenbächer, C. & Gammelgaard, J. (2010) 'Multinational corporations, inter-organizational networks and subsidiary charter removals', *Journal of World Business*, 45, pp. 206–216.

Drazin, R. & Van de Ven, A.H. (1985) 'Alternate forms of fit in contingency theory', *Administrative Science Quarterly*, 30, pp. 514–539.

Dunning, J. (2009) 'Location and the multinational enterprise: John Dunning's thoughts on receiving the *Journal of International Business Studies* 2008 Decade Award', *Journal of International Business Studies*, 40, pp. 20–34.

Eden, L. & Miller, S.R. (2004) 'Distance matters: Liability of foreignness, institutional distance and ownership strategy', in Hitt, M.A. & Cheng, J.L.C. (Eds.), *Theories of the Multinational Enterprise: Diversity, Complexity and Relevance (Advances in International Management, Volume 16)*. Bingley, UK: Emerald Group Publishing Limited, pp. 187–221.

Egelhoff, W.G. (2010) 'How the parent headquarters adds value to an MNC', *Management International Review*, 50, pp. 413–431.

Forsgren, M. (2004) 'The use of network theory in the MNC research', in Mahnke, V. & Pedersen, T. (Eds.), *Knowledge Flows, Governance and the Multinational Enterprise: Frontiers in International Management Research*. Basingstoke, UK: Palgrave Macmillan, pp. 18–37.

Forsgren, M., Holm, U. & Johanson, J. (2007) *Managing the Embedded Multinational: A Business Network View*. Cheltenham, UK: Edward Elgar.

Gammelgaard, J., McDonald, F., Stephan, A., Tüselmann, H. & Dörrenbächer, C. (2012) 'The impact of increases in subsidiary autonomy and network relationships on performance', *International Business Review*, 21, pp. 1158–1172.

Gaur, A.S. & Kumar, V. (2009) 'International diversification, business group affiliation and firm performance: Empirical evidence from India', *British Journal of Management*, 20, pp. 172–186.

Ghemawat, P. (2001) 'Distance still matters', *Harvard Business Review*, 79, pp. 137–147.

Goerzen, A., Asmussen, C.G. & Nielsen, B.B. (2013) 'Global cities and multinational enterprise location strategy', *Journal of International Business Studies*, 44, pp. 427–450.

Hymer, S. (1972) 'The multinational corporation and the law of uneven development', in Bhagwati, J. (Ed.), *Economics and World Order from the 1970s to the 1990s*. London: Collier-Macmillan, pp. 113–140.

Jiang, G.F., Holburn, G.L.F & Beamish, P.W. (2016) 'The spatial structure of foreign subsidiaries and MNE expansion strategy', *Journal of World Business*, 51, pp. 438–450.

Johanson, J. & Vahlne, J.E. (2009) 'The Uppsala internationalization process model revisited: From liability of foreignness to liability of outsidership', *Journal of International Business Studies*, 40, pp. 1411–1431.

Jones, A. (2005) 'Truly global corporations? Theorizing "organizational globalization" in advanced business-services', *Journal of Economic Geography*, 5, pp. 177–200.

Knickerbocker, F.T. (1973) *Oligopolistic Reaction and the Multinational Enterprise*. Cambridge, MA: Harvard University Press.

Kogut, B. & Zander, U. (1992) 'Knowledge of the firm and the replication of technology', *Organization Science*, 3, pp. 383–397.

Lu, J.W. & Beamish, P.W. (2004) 'International diversification and firm performance: The S-curve hypothesis', *Academy of Management Journal*, 47, pp. 598–609.

Majocchi, A. & Presutti, M. (2009) 'Industrial clusters, entrepreneurial culture and the social environment: The effects on FDI distribution', *International Business Review*, 18, pp. 76–88.

McCann, P., Arita, T. & Gordon, I.R. (2002) 'Industrial clusters, transactions costs and the institutional determinants of MNE location behaviour', *International Business Review*, 11, pp. 647–663.

McCann, P. & Mudambi, R. (2004) 'The location and behavior of the multinational enterprise: Some analytical issues', *Growth and Change*, 35, pp. 491–524.

Meyer, K.E., Mudambi, R. & Narula, R. (2011) 'Multinational enterprises and local contexts: The opportunities and challenges of multiple embeddedness', *Journal of Management Studies*, 48, pp. 235–252.

Meyer, K.E. & Nguyen, H.V. (2005) 'Foreign investment strategies and sub-national institutions in emerging markets: Evidence from Vietnam', *Journal of Management Studies*, 42, pp. 63–93.

Morgan, G. (2001) 'Transnational communities and business systems', *Global Networks*, 1, pp. 113–130.

Nachum, L. (2000) 'Economic Geography and the location of TNCs: Financial and professional service FDI to the USA', *Journal of International Business Studies*, 31, pp. 367–385.

Nohria, N. & Ghoshal, S. (1997) *The Differentiated Network: Organizing Multinational Corporations for Value Creation*. San Francisco, CA: Jossey-Bass Publishers.

Pearce, R. (2001) 'Multinationals and industrialisation: The bases of "inward investment" policy', *International Journal of the Economics of Business*, 8, pp. 51–73.

Rugman, A.M. (1981) *Inside the Multinationals: The Economics of Internal Markets*. New York: Columbia University Press.

Rugman, A.M. (2005) *The Regional Multinationals: MNEs and "global" strategic management*, Cambridge, UK: Cambridge University Press.

Rugman, A.M. (2014) 'Regional performance, multiple embeddedness and sustainability', *Multinational Business Review*, 22, pp. 1–3.

Rugman, A.M. & Verbeke, A. (2001) 'Subsidiary-specific advantages in multinational enterprises', *Strategic Management Journal*, 22, pp. 237–250.

Rugman, A.M. & Verbeke, A. (2003) 'Extending the theory of the multinational enterprise: Internalization and strategic management perspectives', *Journal of International Business Studies*, 34, pp. 125–137.

Taylor, M. & Asheim, B. (2001) 'The concept of the firm in Economic Geography', *Economic Geography*, 77, pp. 315–328.

Teece, D.J. (1977) 'Technology transfer by multinational firms: The resource cost of transferring technological know-how', *The Economic Journal*, 87, pp. 242–261.

Vernon, R. (1979) 'The product cycle hypothesis in a new international environment', *Oxford Bulletin of Economics and Statistics*, 41, pp. 255–267.

Yeung, H.W.C. (2005) 'The firm as social networks: An organisational perspective', *Growth and Change*, 36, pp. 307–328.

PART IV

Key research at the interface of International Business and Economic Geography

18
CORPORATE LEARNING AND KNOWLEDGE FLOWS
From glass pipelines to dark pools

Philip Cooke

Introduction

This chapter focuses on the Economic Geography of corporate learning and knowledge flows. The chapter presents accounts of the sometimes convergent and sometimes divergent knowledge and learning pathways that informed the evolution of business knowledge and organisational learning in the corporate space economy until today. It will conclude by referencing three major trends. First, the emergence of "postsocial" knowledge and learning that begins to supersede human cognition. Second, it traces the growth of the quaternary economy and its implications for economic growth, profitability and innovation. Here new models of "recombinant" or "crossover" exploitation of knowledge are explored. Third, the quaternary industries benefit from enormous wealth generation for a few the "elites" of populist discourse and emerge as a developmental model for rivalrous learner firms and countries.

In the first section, the chapter identifies some milestones of corporate and regional learning. While in the second, knowledge flows are in focus, drawing upon key instances of research on both geographical and business literature. Here, perhaps Economic Geography and regional development economics were at the forefront. There then follows a section which acts as a transition point in the historical transition whereby corporate control of knowledge flows was "learned" by small and medium-sized enterprises (SMEs) that have, through "outsourcing", "global innovation networks" and "open innovation", taken over from large firms, who nevertheless control finance and often exert significant influence over design. In the fourth section the global shift of value chains and production networks towards global *innovation* networks of supplier platforms in many industries is briefly explored. In the fifth section the chapter moves to an understanding of the consolidation of SME supplier networks comparing and contrasting two key types of SME sub-system that have become "associative" institutions in the management of corporate buyer-supplier relations, namely regional innovation systems and entrepreneurial ecosystems.

Following this, in the sixth main section there is a brief exegesis of the deeper structure of economic learning and knowledge flow management emphasising – importantly as the chapter clearly implies – the important shift in the nature of *innovation* to corporate and SME supplier interactions. In this, the form of innovation in the corporate sphere ceased being mainly linear and evolved interactively in a realisation that much innovative potential is exploitable through "crossover" or "transversal" knowledge exchange among diverse industries and services. Pipeline connections designed to be secretive are now "glass pipelines", while agglomeration "buzz" has become more encrypted in "dark pools" on the "dark web". Military knowledge underpins the cyberforensics industry as aerospace informs automotives, hydrological algorithms inform structured finance and fine chemistry informs cuisine. No single corporate actor can control this but, without it, advanced economy capital accumulation is significantly arrested.

Corporate and regional learning

It is noteworthy that it was only in the last quarter of the twentieth century that either of the characteristics of corporate and regional learning in International Business analysis really became prominent (Easterby-Smith, Burgoyne & Araujo, 1999). Among the pioneers focusing on this from business studies include authors such as Kenneth Boulding, Chris Argyris and Donald Schön (the last-named being a spatial planner). Boulding (1956, 1981) was an evolutionary economic sociologist and co-founder of General Systems Theory (he, too, was planning and urban policy inflected). For Boulding and other evolutionary economists, they sought to understand how the disequilibrium processes that transform economies emerge from actions of diverse agents with "bounded rationality" (Simon, 1955), who can learn from experience and interactions and whose differences contribute to the change. Argyris and Schön (1978, 1996) articulated their approach in evolutionary systems language beyond that of Cyert and March (1963) who described how organisations learn by changing practice short-term or long-term according to specific or general feedback rules respectively. In Argyris and Schön's (1978) notion, single-loop feedback is repetitive while what they described as double-loop learning was based on organisational learning. The example of a thermostat is single loop action, while changing thermostat performance involves learning. This also involves changing "mental models" as Boulding advocated and as later did writers like Weick (1995). One normative pathway from this "post-military" single-loop organisational rubric led to the huge business consultancy field of "corporate culture change" (Kotter, 1996). In Argyris and Schön (1996) more is made of the importance for organisational learning of distinguishing mere information transmission from value-adding knowledge within and about corporate management communication and learning.

Other corporate learning pioneers from a later generation include Arie de Geus (1988) who evolved the concept of the "learning organisation" and the mantra that "planning is learning" while at Shell. Peter Senge designed management methodology in five steps for the "learning organisation" (Senge, 1990), which Easterby-Smith Burgoyne and Arauio, (1999) slightly misstate as the founding date. Etienne Wenger (Lave & Wenger, 1991; Wenger, 1998) coined "communities of practice", and Karl Weick (1995) introduced key concepts such as "loose coupling", "sensemaking" and "mindfulness" to analyse the dialectic between the subjective "frame" of the corporation and the objective reality as it evolves. SMEs have advanced such learning from their experiences in contracting to MNCs while the latter's sensemaking is often criticised for insensitivities of various kinds, e.g. treatment of suppliers by supermarkets and customers by Facebook and Google confronted with "hate mail". Many of these discursive elements are familiar to evolutionary and institutional economic geographers.

Fewer economic geographers wrote in the focused, if often normative, way that business scholars had with regard to "corporate learning". The literature is relatively brief and wedded substantially to the economic geographer's interest in geographical variety as represented in the concept of the region. A key collection on this can be found in Roel Rutten and Frans Boekema (2007) whose edited volume contains the earliest formulations by inter alia economic geographers Michael Storper, Richard Florida, Bjorn Asheim, Kevin Morgan and Robert Hassink. The interest in "learning" at regional level is different from "corporate learning" because it treats the corporation as just another actor among an institutional fabric. This exists in what is known as a regional "regime" of network governance among SMEs, start-ups, incubators, patent lawyers, training agencies, management consultants, corporate branch-management, universities, colleges and risk investors. It is held that regions have economic and even socio-cultural specificities that condition their evolutionary trajectories. These may be composed of a socio-technical "paradigm" as in dominated single-industry regions or others expressing variety across, say, engineering, agro-food or pharmaceuticals (as with New Jersey's historic appellation as the "Medicine Chest of the World"). Changing institutional learning trajectories through policies to re-track economic development, Florida (1995) observed, is especially difficult in "rustbelt regions" like the Great Lakes region of the US Midwest, northern England or Germany's Ruhrgebiet. It normally takes "paradigm shift", as with biotechnology that has undermined the "Big Pharma" corporate culture of New Jersey in favour of Boston, San Francisco and San Diego, home to the next-generation medical "genetic" paradigms.

Somewhere like Pittsburgh, which lost its "over-specialised" steel industry amidst that great metal-mechanical region, thus found it hard to adapt. It is recognised that the presence of Carnegie Mellon University could be expected to help transform the region's knowledge flows post-steel, but it seldom seems to happen. Most recently, cyber fibre has been seen as boosting economic attractiveness in the creative arts, where Pittsburgh has promoted "Pop des Fleurs" comprising public art installations of winter *flower* gardens made from *fibre* art materials. More prosaically, Pittsburgh made an agreement with Uber in 2016 to establish an experimental network of public autonomous vehicles. So "learning" from Silicon Valley can occur regarding future-oriented infrastructure, especially where cyber-entrepreneurs envision profitability from public services markets. This in itself represents a new learning curve for embattled public administrations in times of budget austerity.

Contrariwise, Morozov (2011) sees such "smart city" initiatives rather cynically as euphemisms for "privatisation" signalling the loss to public services of democratic control. Michael Storper analysed such regime variety usefully in his notion of "worlds of production" denoting standardised, specialised and dedicated production paradigms. As in most other "learning region" programmes, there are injunctions for less accomplished regions to learn from "success stories" like Silicon Valley, or fashionable and dynamic European small-firm regions like "the Rhine economies" of Germany or the Po Delta regions (from conservative Veneto to leftist Emilia-Romagna) of Italy. Here are found networks of dynamic and competitive SMEs that could usefully be emulated either as "developmental models" or as actual quests for foreign direct investment (FDI). This has been critiqued as one of the problems of learning regions which is that by definition they are already behind the leaders, have a cultural transformation challenge to change working practices and to re-invent life trajectories, while relying heavily on an increasingly vulnerable public sector to lead the project. Recently, "cluster policy" has been a favourite vehicle for "start-up regional economies". Today, this is superseded in multi-level governance jurisdictions (like the EU and OECD) inducing ambitious "smart specialisation" from regions often lacking the power or available finance to match such "global controller" policy aspirations. Accordingly, the originating lesson that regional variety is path dependent tends to be assumed away for those "who have seen the future, and it works", as the Soviet Union was once described.

From a business management point of view, a high priority is nowadays given to the questionable notion of "smartness" as capturing many of the organisational and service innovations many deploy or promote. Among these, some to be enlarged upon later, can be included knowledge flow management tools embodied in the so-called "Internet of Things" and more recently the "Internet of Everything". These purportedly enable domestic appliances to exchange information with users and each other. Another great challenge is corporate responsibility for privacy issues and even democratic processes involving exploitation of "Big Data" including access to prodigiously large databases like public health or electoral data. "Data analytics" enable learning by corporations of consumer profiles from trivial indicators such as "likes" clicked on Facebook. These, in turn, are subsequently transformed into social media advertising or propaganda shots monetised and distributed as so-called "click-bait" to consumers, healthcare patients and election voters (Patterson, 2012).

Knowledge flows

Knowledge flows were first conceptualised by urban sociologist and academic spatial planner Manuel Castells (1989, 1994, 1996, 1998), although the passive category "information" rather than the active "knowledge" was to the forefront. The author of *Flow: The Psychology of Optimal Experience*, Mihály Csikszentmihályi (1990), conceived flow as a single-minded immersion – popularly known as "in the zone", which expresses ultimate emotional control in the service of performing and learning. Knowledge is differentiated from information by its semantic "meaning" content. Dunning (2000) wrote early about the "knowledge-based economy" with timely and useful case material on global knowledge flows among, for example, Indian software firms in Bangalore, the US and Europe. Elsewhere, a brief debate occurred on whether a knowledge-"based" terminology was warranted when so much outside the scope of economics was also increasingly formalised in advanced learning and knowledge appropriation. Hence, Cooke (2002) and others preferred a more pervasive "knowledge economy" as the stronger, active form of Castells' "information economy" notion. This Economic Geography perspective, already "framed" by the second chapter, entitled "An evolutionary approach to learning, clusters and economic development" was a statement of intent. This offered the double advantage of highlighting the qualities of "evolutionary Economic Geography" (EEG; see later, for example, Boschma & Martin, 2010) and the emergent influence of agglomeration on both themes of this chapter: corporate learning and knowledge flows. Both were increasingly becoming dominated by the prodigious growth of innovation and entrepreneurship in new technology – often new, high growth-business firms. Chesbrough's (2003) US National Science Foundation data on the burgeoning small and medium-sized R&D sector heralded his specification of "open innovation" (OI) as the new, more efficient and effective "interactive model" of *innovation* that had risen to prominence as *the* competitive advantage of the late twentieth-century global corporation. This had overtaken the now by-passed former advantage a "linear model" of *production* by multinational corporations (MNCs) whose interest in location was stimulated by the quest for the cheapest labour component of that "international division of labour" framing. It is worth indicating here that the field of "agglomeration" and "cluster" studies, embodied equally in the work of both business management and regional Economic Geography, depended for a time on philosopher Michael Polanyi's distinction between "tacit" and "codified" knowledge. Thus "clusters" gained advantage from SME proximities allowing for the exchange of otherwise inaccessible "tacit" or "implicit" knowledge that was hard to learn or understand from books. Contrariwise, for a time it was thought that "codification" of knowledge made inter-firm or inter-agent relations mean the "death of distance" from a business perspective. Nowadays, it is widely accepted that complex instructions can be absorbed by supplier firms located a continent away from both the originator and final customer through codification. However, where this is not possible and where digital access to critical information exchange hubs is required, proximity or "co-location" near or even in data centres is a major asset in, for example, financial services (MacKenzie, 2008)

Knowledge outsourcing and open innovation

As Cohen and Levinthal (1989, 1990) had noticed, the heightened demand for advanced knowledge by often cumbersome MNCs was a danger to their "absorptive capacity" in the face of more nimble, flexible and innovative SMEs. The latter were increasingly "in the zone" for both basic R&D and downstream commercialisation of new knowledge. This was especially pronounced in pharmaceuticals where "Big Pharma" was regularly to be seen trailing smaller, cheaper, more innovative biotechnology firms centred in globally significant clusters like Boston, San Francisco and San Diego with European outliers like Cambridge (UK). But it was also true of knowledge flow directionality to MNCs from ICT clusters like the prodigious Silicon Valley and lesser agglomerations. In a foretaste of Owen-Smith and Powell's (2004) account of biotechnology entrepreneurs "leaking", in principle, proprietary knowledge among their ecosystem, the time economies of proximity became clear. This had been less pronounced within distant, corporate controlled knowledge "pipelines". But latterly the notion of "glass pipelines" through "open innovation" moderated the power of legal contracts over, for example, encryption. This is also the fashion in localised ecosystem biotechnology interactions where significant future value is anticipated from discoveries (e.g. university "disclosure agreements" on academic discoveries).

Of course, as always, such encryption moves are historically prone to decryption or "hacking". A celebrated case of this was the success of Israeli cybersecurity subsidiary Cellebrite in cracking Apple's password code which the Federal Bureau of Investigation (FBI) sought in order to access the mobile records of two deceased ISIS terrorists in San Bernardino, California. When acquired in 2007 by Japan's Sun Corporation, Cellebrite's speciality was mobile data transfer. Sun acquired this asset in the hope of enhancing its iPhone gambling capability. When that move failed, Cellebrite activated its cybersecurity expertise in "mobile forensics". This initiative was led by an alumnus of the Israeli Defence Force's Unit 8200 "cyberwarfare" division, an enterprise ecosystem of cybersecurity start-up firms nowadays incubated from a customised Advanced Technology Centre in Be'er Sheva, centred in Israel's Negev desert. The "hack" solved the legal battle between Apple and the FBI over password security in the US Constitution's Second Amendment.

It is empirically instructive, first, that only such a small cybersecurity firm could achieve the successful decrypt when no large enterprise could. Second, Cellebrite's "ecosystem" consisted of entrepreneurial ex-army signals intelligence (SIGINT) firms and intermediaries (including systems design, computer science and academic mathematicians). Finally, in theoretical terms, "crossover knowledge flows" as proposed in EEG of "recombinant innovation" and "preadaptation" from "evolutionary complexity theory" (ECT) explains the complex knowledge transfer flows involved (Kauffman, 2008). Preadaptation, also known as "exaptation" occurs when existing knowledge gains in value from a wholly novel application or adaptation. In ECT such "revealed related variety" (Neffke, Svensson-Henning & Boschma, 2011) is known as "strange attractors". Hence "crossover" innovation became increasingly commonplace whether in markets for "fusion" food, software "Windows for Mac or Linux", automotives' "sports utility vehicle (SUV) on a car platform", and so on.

International outsourcing had also agglomerated in specific advanced and less developed economies like Turkey where Konya and Bursa had emerged to a scale if not a sophistication of the Ontario automotive cluster that had now almost outgrown that of Detroit whose "Big Three" it once served. The global apparel industry had similarly trans-located into North African, Asian and Latin American agglomerations (see for the global apparel industry, Gereffi, 1996).

Finally, back in the global corporate metropolitan centres like Wall Street and the City of London, international banks and other financial services continued to surround themselves with outsourced expertise, as they had always done, with growth now typified in the post-crash era after 2009 by the rise of "fintech" (financial technology) and, for example, "high frequency trading" (Cooke, 2016). An indicator of the prodigious growth of "fintech" is that global investment in "fintech" increased from $930 million in 2008 to more than $12 billion in 2014 (*The Economist*, 2015).

Global shift to global innovation networks

For Economic Geography, such knowledge flows were of especial interest in understanding the changing nature of the global division of labour. This perspective had been dominated by the work of Peter Dicken (1986) who wrote carefully focused studies on the phenomenon of what he called "global shift" especially but not exclusively on the sectoral expansionism of the industries in the vanguard: namely automotive, ICT, pharmaceuticals and apparel amongst them. The strength of this analysis and its regular updating in successive editions meant it crossed boundaries from Economic Geography to business studies and beyond for researchers and as an original textbook of note. As the analysis progressed over the amended and extended editions, its perspective modernised with attention to the flows of knowledge as well as linear authority and/or MNC power interactions. This recognised the "relational turn" in MNC positioning towards states as well as congeries of small as well as – nowadays – massive on-shore systems-integrators like Taiwan's Foxconn. This huge firm, employing more than a million workers in China, is pivotal to the "global flagship" firms in ICT. These have included Dell and Hewlett-Packard, but market shift means the "flagships" are now Apple and Samsung who dominate the "smartphones" industry.

Operating from China, a small "Asian tiger" economy like Taiwan has been associated not just with "global production chains and networks" but emergent "global *innovation* networks". This occurred through the aspects of the global value chain for ICT that they dominate – as with flat screen technology – now colonised by Korea's hegemons Samsung and LG and "chipsets" for which Taiwan's Mediatek has been a leader. Judicious national innovation system (NIS) actors like the innovation agency ITRI have been key intermediaries between Taiwanese suppliers and global corporations, even facilitating FDI acquisitions (e.g. from IBM) amongst other actions. Such firms integrate system knowledge emanating overwhelmingly from Cambridge (UK) software and systems design firms – so-called "fabless" design requiring no domestic "chip" or semiconductor manufacturing in-house. Even a putative leader in such systems design, Apple's neighbour in Silicon Valley, Intel buys its "fab" designs from ARM (Advanced RISC Microprocessors) while the latter outsources the fabrication ("fab") to a specialised manufacturer called a semiconductor "foundry". Such foundries are typically, but not exclusively, located in China and Taiwan.

One of ARM's attractions to its 2016 acquirer, Japan's SoftBank, is that it has evolved the design of low energy chips that are crucial in computers, tablets and smartphones that suffer short-life battery capacity. SoftBank's attraction for ARM is limitless research investment for next generation designs (e.g. "Internet of Everything"). ARM thus followed its neighbour Cambridge Silicon Radio (CSR), a specialist Bluetooth chip designer ("InternetofEverything" and automated vehicles, especially) into foreign ownership in 2015, on this occasion acquired by Qualcomm, the San Diego mobile communication company. In passing, other recent

Cambridge acquisition targets have included *Datanomic*, a leading provider of customer risk and compliance data screening acquired in 2011 by Oracle for just $80 million. Then, later that year data-mining software flagship Autonomy was purchased for $10 *billion* by Hewlett Packard (HP) and seen as an indicator of HP's then policy of seeking to develop as a software and systems services firm. In 2016 UK firm MicroFocus of Newbury, Berkshire in the M4 corridor then acquired the enterprise software assets of the former Autonomy, now called Hewlett Packard Enterprise, in an $8 billion-plus deal. Other UK knowledge businesses recently acquired by US buyers have included artificial intelligence firm DeepMind, acquired by Google for $600 million, Tweetdeck a customer data analyst for $40 million by Twitter, and SwiftKey a keyboard software designer bought by Microsoft for $250 million. The "knowledge flow" conveyor belts inter-connecting these agglomeration platforms are a notable feature of contemporary globalisation.

So much has changed – as ably tracked by Dicken's monitoring of global economic geographies – that relatively few competitor texts exist. Richard Whitley performed comparably important studies and texts mapping the emergence and change in comparative global business systems (Whitley, 2007). However numerous articles and more recently some volumes on the Economic Geography of knowledge flows can be found in the literature. These include studies of knowledge flows in a variety of contemporary industries (Gertler & Levitte, 2005 – on the global biotechnology industry; Cooke, 2007 – also in biotechnology; Martin & Moodysson, 2011 – on creative animation; Cuadrado-Roura, 2013 – on services innovation; van Egeraat, Kogler & Cooke, 2014 – especially ICT and renewable energy). Perhaps inevitably these books and articles investigate challenging and complex new kinds of knowledge flow. These flows are iterative, negotiated and transactional, thus very different from the blueprints, instructions and authority flowing in the past from MNC to captive supplier firms. The latter have in many industries upgraded their knowledge and taken responsibility for functions hitherto managed by the MNC. Even in traditional, globalised industries, like apparel, responsibility for quality, reliability, turnaround time and maintenance or supply-network problem-solving are often delegated to agents or suppliers in distant continents. It is argued by some entrepreneurship business scholars that entrepreneurial firms in some settings behave like members of "entrepreneurial ecosystems". This may be an effort to emulate the successful analysis of regional innovation as a systemic phenomenon, but, in any case, it is rather a "leap of faith" from the classic connotations of entrepreneurship as "imitative", "profit-driven" and "individualistic" to characterising them as collaborative or co-operative as implied in the accepted meaning of "ecosystem". Nevertheless, it is valuable to analyse critical status claims made that may conceive of new knowledge flows being articulated among, for example, "apps communities" involving the aforementioned Facebook and Google phenomena (Scholten & Scholten, 2012).

Learning new knowledge flows: enterprise ecosystems and regional innovation systems

The ICT sector has become dominated by "flagship" firms, such as Amazon, Facebook and Google. These firms command prodigious profits, which they use, among other things, to pay for preferred supplier contracts and to support an ecosystem of entrepreneurial firms. These entrepreneurial firms are coordinated in a modularised system by global intermediary "aggregators". Despite the dominance of the flagship firms, so much has the wheel turned to favour research-based SMEs especially in ICT, the context for which is nowadays, smartphones, social media and cloud computing, that such "flagships" have long been "hollowed-out" as manufacturers. The flagships have thus become "design brands". Echoing this, a new research take on the phenomenon that purports to bring to entrepreneurship studies a first approximation of a more collective, less individualistic profit-seeking motivation, is known as the "entrepreneurial ecosystem", also known as less individualistically as the "enterprise ecosystem". As with the older and distinctive regional innovation system RIS model, it finally recognises that enterprise is a profoundly social not individual practice. Enterprise depends on social welfare investments (notably skills) made in the past and activated today through institutional and intermediary set-ups between public and private organisations. Firms recognise these characteristics in their valuation of interactive learning and social interaction on problem-solving and knowledge-sharing. One of the ways it has entered policy and practice consciousness is through "open innovation" (OI). Typically, policy began envisioning OI as "free innovation" displaying their poor grasp of the fundamental entrepreneurial vitamin, namely "greed". More recently, with study, the notion that OI is opposed not to profit but to closure (as in "closed innovation") has begun to be seriously discussed. We may trace the origins of today's "gig" or "sharing economy" to this knowledge-outsourcing innovation.

However, it is important to distinguish enterprise (or entrepreneurship) ecosystems from RIS on three key grounds. First, as innovation scholars since Schumpeter (1934) recognised, entrepreneurship is "imitative" whereas the commercialisation of novelty is "innovative". Thus they are highly distinctive skill-sets. Entrepreneurship involves optimising market sentiment for pure profit (as will be shown) to the point of fraudulence in numerous instances. Innovation is intended to be commercialised on markets but frequently fails to do so. Accordingly, entrepreneurs often doggedly pursue a profitable idea beyond the point at which an innovator would not. Why? Because while the entrepreneur may have a single idea that is adhered to and believed in until it eventually sells, an innovator has many ideas that can be preadapted for original or modified applications. Second, this means the collective "bonding" among entrepreneurs is often based on a single customer platform (Gawer & Henderson, 2007) or as a supplier of a highly specialist type of "imitative" service that may be equivalently customised (for example, high frequency traders (HFT) serving investment banks in stock markets). Finally, entrepreneurship is fundamentally competitive, individualistic and non-solidaristic, whereas "open innovation" was born from the tradition of "open science" and the collegiate tradition of research. Entrepreneurial ecosystems practise more closure than RIS set-ups. Thus as with other inhibitions on knowledge flow, closure can mean club-like practices of differentiating meaningful social relations. For each distinct category of social relations, members erect a boundary. They mark the boundary by means of names and practices and establish a set of distinctive understandings that operate within that boundary and designate certain sorts of economic transactions as appropriate and others not. This is a description by Zelizer (2012) of the entrepreneurial ecosystem for HFT, but it could equally refer to "restrictive practices" in, for example, the historical printing industry, real estate law, medical consultants or funeral directors and other "conspiracies against the layman" Adam Smith's celebrated admonition asserted. It expresses a critique of one of the favourite epithets of economic sociology and geography, corporate cultural studies and knowledgeable "communities of practice", namely "embeddedness". This is because it roots social relations in an immutable category (or independent variable) – "the economy" – which is treated as if it were unaffected by social relations and social creativity. It is sadly one of the keys to understanding gender, ethnic and homophobic discrimination in workplaces.

While not necessarily praising innovation practice overly as against entrepreneurship, there are three important characteristics differentiating them. First, innovation, by definition, aspires to create new knowledge and artifacts even if pieces of such knowledge already exist in different forms that can be stimulated to "flow" innovatively and with commercial purpose. Actually, much traditional corporate laboratory research was in the past subject to criticism (not least by shareholders) for its apparent purposelessness. Second, because it involves recombination of different knowledges, innovation is fundamentally co-operative and collaborative. Finally, it is not specifically profit-seeking for its own sake. Many innovations have been the subject of altruistic behaviour. Hence "embeddedness" exists but of a much more flexible kind in the innovation workspace, more like cultural than economic embeddedness. It is important to recognise that many of these insights arose from, particularly, Schumpeter's (1934) industrial political economy. The Neo-Schumpeterian school of innovation studies (notably Lundvall, 1992; Lundvall & Johnson, 1994) was also instrumental in analysing International Business systems from an "innovation systems" perspective. In EEG, the influential *regional* innovation systems school was largely sui generis although subsequently quite supportively interactive.

"Postsocial" knowledge flows: cybersecurity and HFT

Two brief vignettes of the "knowledge power flow" from entrepreneurial ecosystems conforming to the imitative, individualistic but not entirely atomised variants of enterprise ecosystems are provided, ultimately at corporate and governmental behest and involving cybersecurity and HFT. In 2015 the Israeli government delivered the promise that Be'er Sheva was destined to become "the cybercenter of the Western hemisphere" (Cooke, 2016). This included the world-renowned 8200 unit of the Israeli Defence Forces to have a planned location at the perimeter of the new Advanced Technology Park in Be'er Sheva beginning in 2020. Once again, SMEs monopolise much innovative cyberwarfare knowledge, and International Business learns at corporate scale how to exploit it, as the following list shows: tenants of the Advanced Technology Park already include *Deutsche Telekom, IBM, Oracle, Lockheed Martin, EMC* and *PayPal* – with Beer Sheva's Ben-Gurion University and its Cyber Security Research Center in attendance (Cooke, 2017).

Turning to advanced business innovation in structured finance promoted by global investment banks, the "dark pools" in the sub-title here, there are hidden deposits of enormous investments by global investment banks, pension funds and hedge funds also occupying parts of the "dark web". Such dark *pools* are inaccessible even to investors whose investments are directed to them by their chosen financial institution. Like pilot fish accompanying the bow-wave of the shark swimming in the ocean, the ecosystem of broker intermediaries is large in number (about 540 in the US) but small in scale. The obvious reason for "dark pools" is privacy, but for whom? Actually, it is especially for the investment banks and what Michael Lewis (2015, p. 179) called:

> [t]he hidden passages and trapdoors that riddled the (stock) exchanges (meant) . . . the world's financial markets were designed to maximize the number of collisions between ordinary investors, and for the benefit of high-frequency traders, exchanges, Wall Street banks, and online brokerage firms. Around these collisions an entire ecosystem had arisen.

An irony of this International Business ecosystem is that it evolved as a low-trust zone of individualism and predatory exploitation of tiny margins, "front-running" property, in effect, stolen from investor accounts. Where these are hidden in "dark pools" obscured from investors, HFTs pay enormous up-front fees to the nine banks responsible for designing the dark pools and controlling 70% of Wall Street stock market orders (Patterson, 2012). These were, by 2011 market share, Credit Suisse, Morgan Stanley, Bank of America, Merrill Lynch, Goldman Sachs, JPMorgan, UBS, Citi and Deutsche Bank. The banks also have their own HFTs, which are in competition with the rest of the ecosystem. To these can be added a variety of hedge funds with their favoured or captive HFTs. Characteristically, HFTs are populated by engineering and technology doctoral recruits who subsequently move on to found or consult for smaller HFT firms. It is estimated that within the larger Wall Street "entrepreneurial ecosystem", the technical "kingpin" elite of HFT innovators number no more than 25 experts, many of them Russian mathematicians. Thus we conclude on this timely reprise of the reversed relationship of monopoly corporate learning from top-down to bottom-up contingent on the advanced accumulation and processing of knowledge that biases the financial cash nexus in financial services further towards the banks and their ecosystems and against the ordinary investor who – through her or his mutual or pension fund – is represented by you and me. This kind of business knowledge, embodying "artificial intelligence" (AI) among automated trading systems (ATS) whose algorithms sense and anticipate stock market investor intentions, is more studied in "postsocial" economic sociology than Economic Geography (Knorr Cetina & Bruegger, 2002a, 2002b; Zelizer, 2012; MacKenzie, 2014, 2015). This "Geography of Everything" has resonated little as yet despite the role of geographers in designing "geographical information systems" on which such AI postsocial interactions rely.

In the research literature, relatively sophisticated questions about whether providing (selling) a new technology to secondary developers stimulates innovation is central to public policy and firm strategies in many high-tech industries (Boudreau, 2007). However, there is, so far, scant systematic evidence on this situation, wherein a kind of platform for open innovation or supplier innovation exists (Chesbrough, 2003; Lyons et al., 2012). Today, numerous articles exist that open up research findings on the policy and substance aspects of innovation policy and recognise the "platform-like" nature of contemporary "crossover" innovation practices by firms and other knowledge or policy agencies (Visser & Boschma, 2004; Harmaakorpi & Melkas, 2005; Harmaakorpi, 2006; Cooke, 2012). Platforms provide architectures to combine internal and external innovations in ways that create value throughout the chain of activities that deliver useful technology to the market (Chesbrough, 2003). In addition, within the networked "world of flows" (Castells, 1996), firms also recognise the power of the internet as a platform that can co-create value with customers (Sawhney, Verona & Prandelli, 2005).

As shown, many high-tech industries offer products or services that can be described as systems of interdependent components built around or on top of "platforms" (Gawer & Henderson, 2007). These writers show how, for example, Intel operates a platform of diversified suppliers that act like an ecosystem, as do numerous other social media, ICT and most automotive supply networks. Because of this, the behaviour of platform owners towards other firms in the ecosystem has been subject to some scrutiny. Here we may begin to differentiate the business *technology* platform from the type more typically noted in Economic Geography research. There are two fundamentally distinct approaches to the opening of a business *technology* platform and the different kinds of impact they have on innovation (Boudreau, 2010). One kind of impact is granting access to a platform, thereby opening up markets for complementary components around the platform. The other is giving up control over the platform. When a technological system continues to innovate after it has been opened, a new trade-off, which might be referred to as "diversity versus control", will occur (West, 2003). Indeed, drawing on external knowledge has been one of the more persuasive arguments to opening up innovation to the outside (Chesbrough, 2003; von Hippel, 2005).

Conclusion

So a key reason for this discussion to introduce recent corporate and regional learning and knowledge flows observations is the apparent inversion of directionality from linear "productivist" corporate "global controllers" (Beinhocker, 2006; Kauffman, 2008) downward to hitherto supplicant SME suppliers. Innovative knowledge flows have increasingly been inverted, moving interactively and non-linearly from suppliers to "controllers" who nowadays mainly manage finance and possibly design. This is most pronounced in pharmaceuticals where "Big Pharma" has been divesting research laboratories and medical divisions because of their own "drying pipelines". Until now, most efforts to capture this picture of loss of status by MNCs to innovative knowledge suppliers has been led by the "innovation systems" school of researchers, in the context of this chapter meaning "regional innovation systems" (RIS) analysts. But interest in collaborative regional entrepreneurship practice has now come into focus as an emerging literature on "entrepreneurial ecosystems". This also connects to a "platform" metaphor noted earlier, but while entrepreneurial ecosystems imitate, specialise and are pure profit-seekers, RIS work heralds path-*interdependence* ("strange attractors") among elements of regional paradigms that exploit Schumpeterian knowledge recombination in conducting innovation which can include "social innovation", e.g. in healthcare.

As is well-known, such Google and Facebook platforms are losing profitability because their knowledge has run away from them through reliance on AI algorithms that match advertisements with hate mail and terrorist websites. The evidence today is that these behemoths are actually slow learners, something complexity theory predicted in its infancy (Simon, 1962). Studies of smartphone App Store platforms have also been reviewed and researched. Application distribution platforms or App stores, such as Google Play or Apple's App Store, allow developers and users to submit feedback to downloaded applications in the form of ratings and reviews. An earlier study investigated how and when users provide feedback, inspected the feedback content, and analysed its impact on the user community by analysing over one million reviews from Apple's App Store (Pagano & Maalej, 2013). Software vendors usually lack the perspective to develop software within a software ecosystem. The inability to function in a software ecosystem has already led to the demise of many software vendors, leading to loss of competition, intellectual property and, eventually, jobs in the software industry (Janssen, Finkelstein & Brinkkemper, 2009). Mobile application stores have revolutionised software and content delivery in that these stores focus on applications, building around them an ecosystem of developers and consumers (Cuadrado & Dueñas, 2012). This is reminiscent of the early "knowledge entrepreneurs" that formed a "household hygiene" enterprise ecosystem around Procter & Gamble (P&G) (Chesbrough, 2003). This evolved once P&G had reinvented itself from a corporate decision "silo system" to a quasi-franchise OI set-up. Before that, for instance, demoralised by corporate knowledge barriers and "global control" of key decisions in Cincinnati, P&G junior brand manager Steve Case eventually innovated America Online (AOL) (Isaacson, 2014).

As noted earlier, the Apple App Store *disallows* platform customisability, and applications that overlap with existing functions are rejected. At the other end of the spectrum are the Android store-based platform functions (as used by Google, e.g. keyboard authentication) that can be replaced by market applications. Recent years have witnessed prodigious popularity and adoption of smartphones and mobile devices, accompanied by a massive amount and a wide variety of feature-rich smartphone applications (Zhou et al., 2012). For example, a number of third-party alternative marketplaces have also been created to host thousands of apps (e.g. to meet regional or localisation needs). Even though some portion of the mobile app explosion can be understood by software reuse in the Android mobile app market along two dimensions – reuse by inheritance and class reuse – a more significant portion comes directly from the platform attribute (Ruiz et al., 2012).

To conclude, there is a good deal of nonsense associated with the entrepreneurial ecosystems literature. The basic proposition of the approach has been stylised by Stam as a tautology:

"Entrepreneurial ecosystems are systems that produce successful entrepreneurship and where there is a lot of successful entrepreneurship there is apparently a good entrepreneurial ecosystem" (Stam, 2015, p. 1764; Cooke, 2016). In this variant of the approach, it is even becoming common to talk about innovation "systems" as "ecosystems" (Mazzucato, 2015). This may be unintentionally "sizeist" because ecosystems seem small, like entrepreneurial firms, or it may be a sign of a creeping neoliberal term that "marketises" innovation by emphasising its purely commodified – compared to social innovation – connotations. Both gain support from the following definition, which focuses only on the "small-firm flotilla" controlled by "a focal firm or platform" (e.g. Apple, Intel, etc.). Thus, Autio and Thomas (2014) define an innovation ecosystem as a network of interconnected organisations, connected to a focal firm or platform, which incorporates both production and use of side participants to create and appropriate new value (i.e. profit) through innovation. This version is of a "locked-in" relationship that may be a highly imperfect analogy for any evolving ecosystem as such, especially where innovation is widely understood as "promiscuous" in its free-ranging, crossover, "sociology of translations" (Latour, 2005).

So, finally, in monitoring the evolution of International Business and Economic Geography, it is evident that three features of modern economic and, especially, corporate life have come to the fore. First, business knowledge flows are becoming increasingly "postsocial" inasmuch as for key areas of profitability in fields such as financial analysis or "fintech", humans are in thrall to other, absent human designers of algorithms that massively outperform human reaction capabilities. This has, on more than one occasion caused "flash crashes" in which a trillion dollars can disappear in ten seconds or less. Learning to control such complexity is a lesson still waiting to be learned about "loose coupling" and system decentralisation (MacKenzie, 2014).

Second, geography of economics shows "globalisation" is becoming "thinner" than it was predicted to be. Research such as Krippner's (2005) impressive long-cycle data for the US economy showed how prodigiously dependent the US became, even by 2001, on "financialisation". Some 45% of US profitability already came from FIRE business (finance, insurance and real estate) by 2001 since when it had increased by a third to 2012. FIRE, alongside knowledge intensive technology businesses and services firms (biotechnology, software and systems design, data analytics and the FANG social media (Facebook, Amazon, Netflix and Google) won excessive growth through profitability. Harvard development theorist Dani Rodrik (2011) calls this "The Quaternary" economy, which has by-passed manufacturing and low order services typical of what he calls "thick globalisation" and posited a new post-IMF and World Bank model of development to the likes of China, Vietnam and other ambitious learning economies.

Third, the innovative knowledge through which such corporate learning has been energised in the quaternary sectors is mainly coming through leading edge (R1) research conducted in increasingly "privatised" universities and its exploitation by SME ecosystems who sell successful commercial innovations to "flagship" FIRE and FANG firms often co-located in a few prestigious "global controller" places where regulation is light, taxation is not too cumbersome and prodigious wealth can be earned, consumed and displayed.

References

Argyris, C. & Schön, D. (1978) *Organizational Learning: A Theory of Action Perspective*. Reading, MA: Addison Wesley.

Argyris, C. & Schön, D. (1996) *Organizational Learning II: Theory, Method and Practice*. Reading, MA: Addison Wesley.

Asheim, B. (2007) 'Industrial districts as "learning regions": A condition for prosperity', in Rutten, R. & Boekema, F. (Eds.), *The Learning Region: Foundations, State of the Art, Future*. Cheltenham, UK: Edward Elgar, pp. 71–100.

Autio, E. & Thomas, L.D.W. (2014) 'Innovation ecosystems: Implications for innovation management', in Dodgson, M., Gann, D.M. & Phillips, N. (Eds.), *The Oxford Handbook of Innovation Management*. Oxford, UK: Oxford University Press, pp. 204–288.

Beinhocker, E. (2006) *The Origin of Wealth: Evolution, Complexity and the Radical Remaking of Economics*. Boston, MA: Harvard Business Press.

Boschma, R. & Martin, R. (Eds.) (2010) *The Handbook of Evolutionary Economic Geography*. Cheltenham, UK: Edward Elgar.

Boudreau, K. (2007) *Does Opening a Platform Stimulate Innovation? The Effect on Systemic and Modular Innovations*. Boston, MA: MIT Sloan Research Paper.

Boudreau, K. (2010) 'Open platform strategies and innovation: Granting access vs. devolving control', *Management Science*, 56, pp. 1849–1872.

Boulding, K. (1956) *The Image: Knowledge in Life and Society*. Ann Arbor, MI: University of Michigan Press.

Boulding, K. (1981) *Evolutionary Economics*. London: Sage.

Castells, M. (1989) *The Informational City: Information Technology, Economic Restructuring, and the Urban–Regional Process*. Oxford, UK: Blackwell.

Castells, M. (1994) 'European cities, the informational society and the global economy', *New Left Review*, 204, pp. 18–32.

Castells, M. (1996) *The Information Age: Economy, Society and Culture. Vol. I: The Rise of the Network Society*. Oxford, UK: Blackwell.

Castells, M. (1998) *The Information Age: Economy, Society and Culture. Vol. III: End of Millennium*. Oxford, UK: Blackwell.

Chesbrough, H. (2003) *Open Innovation*. Boston, MA: Harvard Business School Press.

Cohen, W.M. & Levinthal, D.A. (1989) 'Innovation and learning: The two faces of R&D', *The Economic Journal*, 99, pp. 569–596.

Cohen, W.M. & Levinthal, D.A. (1990) 'Absorptive capacity: A new perspective on learning and innovation', *Administrative Sciences Quarterly*, 35, pp. 128–152.

Cooke, P. (2002/2006) *Knowledge Economies: Clusters, Learning and Co-operative Advantage*. London: Routledge.

Cooke, P. (2007) *Growth Cultures: The Global Bioeconomy & Its Bioregions*. London: Routledge.

Cooke, P. (2012) *Complex Adaptive Innovation Systems*. London: Routledge.

Cooke, P. (2016) 'Dark and light: Entrepreneurship and innovation in new technology spaces', *Investigaciones Regionales/Journal of Regional Research*, 36, pp. 151–168.

Cooke, P. (2017) '"Digital tech" and the public sector: What new role after public funding?' *European Planning Studies*, 25, pp. 1–16.

Csikszentmihályi, M. (1990) *Flow: The Psychology of Optimal Experience*. New York: Harper & Row.

Cuadrado, F. & Dueñas, J. (2012) 'Mobile application stores: Success factors, existing approaches, and future developments', *Communications Magazine, IEEE*, 50, pp. 160–167.

Cuadrado-Roura, J. (Ed.) (2013) *Service Industries and Regions: Growth, Location and Regional Effects*. Berlin: Springer.

Cyert, R. & March, J. (1963) *A Behavioral Theory of the Firm*. Upper Saddle River, NJ: Prentice-Hall.

De Geus, A. (1988) 'Planning as learning', *Harvard Business Review*, March-April, pp. 70–74.

Dicken, P. (1986) *Global Shift: Industrial Change in a Turbulent World*. London: Harper & Row.

Dunning, J. (Ed.) (2000) *Regions, Globalization and the Knowledge-Based Economy*. Oxford, UK: Oxford University Press.

Easterby-Smith, M., Burgoyne, J. & Araujo, L. (Eds.) (1999) *Organizational Learning and the Learning Organization*. London: Sage.

The Economist (2015) 'The fintech revolution', *The Economist*, March 9, p. 10.

Florida, R. (1995) 'Toward the learning region', *Futures*, 27, pp. 527–536.

Florida, R. (2007) 'Toward the learning region', in Rutten, R. & Boekema, F. (Eds.), *The Learning Region: Foundations, State of the Art, Future*. Cheltenham, UK: Edward Elgar.

Gawer, A. & Henderson, R. (2007) 'Platform owner entry and innovation in complementary markets: Evidence from Intel', *Journal of Economics & Management Strategy*, 16, pp. 1–34.

Gereffi, G. (1996) 'Commodity chains and regional divisions of labour in East Asia', *Journal of Asian Business*, 12, pp. 75–112.

Gertler, M. & Levitte, G. (2005) 'Local nodes in global networks: The geography of knowledge flows in biotechnology innovation', *Industry & Innovation*, 12, pp. 487–507.

Harmaakorpi, V. (2006) 'Regional development platform method as a tool for regional innovation policy', *European Planning Studies*, 14, pp. 1093–1112.

Harmaakorpi, V. & Melkas, H. (2005) 'Knowledge management in regional innovation networks', *European Planning Studies*, 13, pp. 641–660.
Hassink, R. (2007) 'The learning region: A constructive critique', in Rutten, R. & Boekema, F. (Eds.), *The Learning Region: Foundations, State of the Art, Future*. Cheltenham, UK: Edward Elgar, pp. 252–274.
Isaacson, W. (2014) *The Innovators*. New York: Simon & Schuster.
Janssen, S., Finkelstein, A. & Brinkkemper, S. (2009) 'A sense of community: A research agenda for software ecosystems', in *Software engineering-companion volume, 2009. ICSE-Companion 2009*. 31st International Conference. Vancouver, BC: IEEE.
Kauffman, S. (2008) *Reinventing the Sacred*. New York: Basic Books.
Knorr Cetina, K. & Bruegger, U. (2002a) 'Global microstructures: The virtual societies of financial markets', *American Journal of Sociology*, 107, pp. 905–951.
Knorr Cetina, K. & Bruegger, U. (2002b) 'Traders' engagement with markets: A postsocial relationship', *Theory, Culture and Society*, 19, pp. 161–185.
Kotter, J. (1996) *Leading Change*. Boston, MA: Harvard Business School Press.
Krippner, G. (2005) 'The financialization of the American economy', *Socio-Economic Review*, 3, pp. 173–208.
Latour, B. (2005) *Reassembling the Social: An Introduction to Actor-Network-Theory*. Oxford, UK: Oxford University Press.
Lave, J. & Wenger, E. (1991) *Situated Learning: Legitimate Peripheral Participation*. Cambridge, UK: Cambridge University Press.
Lewis, M. (2015) *The Flash Boys: Cracking the Money Code*. London: Penguin.
Lundvall, B. (1992) *National Systems of Innovation*. London: Frances Pinter.
Lundvall, B. & Johnson, B. (1994) 'The learning economy', *Journal of Industry Studies*, 1, pp. 23–42.
Lyons, A., Coronado Mondragon, A., Piller, F. & Poler, R. (2012) *Customer-driven Supply Chains: From Glass Pipelines to Open Innovation Networks*. London: Springer Verlag.
MacKenzie, D. (2008) *An Engine Not a Camera: How Financial Markets Shape Markets*. Cambridge, MA: MIT Press.
MacKenzie, D. (2014) 'At Cermak', *London Review of Books*, 36, p. 25.
MacKenzie, D. (2015) 'Dark markets', *London Review of Books*, 37, pp. 29–32.
Martin, R. & Moodysson, J. (2011) 'Innovation in symbolic industries: The geography and organization of knowledge sourcing', *European Planning Studies*, 19, pp. 1183–1203.
Mazzucato, M. (2015) *The Entrepreneurial State: Debunking Public vs. Private Sector Myths*. London: Anthem Press.
Morgan, K. (2007) 'The learning region: Institutions, innovation and regional renewal', in Rutten, R. & Boekema, F. (Eds.), *The Learning Region: Foundations, State of the Art, Future*. Cheltenham, UK: Edward Elgar, pp. 101–126.
Morozov, E. (2011) *The Net Delusion: The Dark Side of Internet*. London: Freedom.
Neffke, F., Svensson-Henning, M. & Boschma, R. (2011) 'How do regions diversify over time? Industry relatedness and the development of new growth paths in regions', *Economic Geography*, 87, pp. 237–265.
Owen-Smith, J. & Powell, W. (2004) 'Knowledge networks as channels and conduits: The effects of spillovers in the Boston biotechnology community', *Organization Science*, 15, pp. 5–21.
Pagano, D. & Maalej, W. (2013) 'User feedback in the AppStore: An empirical study', in *Proceedings of the 21st International Conference on Requirements Engineering*. Rio de Janeiro, Brasil: IEEE.
Patterson, S. (2012) *Dark Pools: High-speed Traders, A.I. Bandits and the Threat to the Global Financial System*. New York, NY: Random House.
Rodrik, D. (2011) 'The future of economic convergence', *NBER Working Papers 17400*, National Bureau of Economic Research; Proceedings – Economic Policy Symposium – Jackson Hole, Federal Reserve Bank of Kansas City, pp. 13–52.
Ruiz, I., Nagappan, M., Adams, B. & Hassan, A. (2012) 'Understanding reuse in the Android market', in *Program Comprehension (ICPC), 2012 IEEE 20th International Conference*. Passau, Germany: IEEE.
Rutten, R. & Boekema, F. (Eds.) (2007) *The Learning Region: Foundations, State of the Art, Future*. Cheltenham, UK: Edward Elgar.
Sawhney, M., Verona, G. & Prandelli, E. (2005) 'Collaborating to create: The internet as a platform for customer engagement in product innovation', *Journal of Interactive Marketing*, 19, pp. 4–17.
Scholten, S. & Scholten, U. (2012) 'Platform-based innovation management: Directing external innovational efforts in platform ecosystems', *Journal of the Knowledge Economy*, 3, 164–184.
Schumpeter, J. (1934) *The Theory of Economic Development*. Piscataway, NJ: Transaction Books.

Senge, P. (1990) *The Fifth Discipline: The Art and Practice of the Learning Organization*. New York: Doubleday.

Simon, H. (1955) 'A behavioral model of rational choice', *The Quarterly Journal of Economics*, 69, pp. 99–118.

Simon, H. (1962) 'The architecture of complexity', *Proceedings of the American Philosophical Society*, 106, pp. 467–482.

Stam, E. (2015) 'Entrepreneurial ecosystems and regional policy: A sympathetic critique', *European Planning Studies*, 23, pp. 1759–1769.

Storper, M. (2007) 'Regional "worlds" of production: Learning and innovation in the technology districts of France, Italy and the USA', in Rutten, R. & Boekema, F. (Eds.), *The Learning Region: Foundations, State of the Art, Future*. Cheltenham, UK: Edward Elgar, pp. 15–57.

Van Egeraat, C, Kogler, D. & Cooke, P. (Eds.) (2014) *Global and Regional Dynamics in Knowledge Flows and Innovation*. London: Routledge.

Visser, E. & Boschma, R. (2004) 'Learning in districts. Novelty and lock-in in a regional context', *European Planning Studies*, 12, pp. 793–808.

Von Hippel, E. (2005) 'Democratizing innovation: The evolving phenomenon of user innovation', *Journal für Betriebswirtschaft*, 55, pp. 63–78.

Weick, K. (1995) *Sensemaking in Organizations*. London: Sage.

Wenger, E. (1998) *Communities of Practice: Learning, Meaning and Identity*. Cambridge, UK: Cambridge University Press.

West, J. (2003) 'How open is open enough? Melding proprietary and open source platform strategies', *Research Policy*, 32, pp. 1259–1285.

Whitley, R. (2007) *Business Systems and Organizational Capabilities: The Institutional Structuring of Competitive Competences*. Oxford, UK: Oxford University Press.

Zelizer, V. (2012) 'How I became a relational economic sociologist and what does that mean?' *Politics & Society*, 40, pp. 145–174.

Zhou, W., Zhou, Y., Jiang, X. & Ning, P. (2012) 'Detecting repackaged smartphone applications in third-party android marketplaces', in *Proceedings of the Second ACM Conference on Data and Application Security and Privacy, CODASPY*. New York: ACM, pp. 317–326.

19

INTERNATIONAL KNOWLEDGE TRANSFER

Yan Wu and Yong Yang

Introduction

The traditional literature on multinational corporations (MNCs) emphasises that the parent company is regarded as the prime source of technological capability and know-how that its subsidiaries can exploit when operating in foreign markets (Vernon, 1966; Dunning, 1988). In this literature, knowledge and technology are transferred primarily from the parent company to its overseas subsidiaries.

Increasingly, there are both theoretical and empirical emphases that each foreign subsidiary in a given country has its own strategic task (Gupta & Govindarajan, 1991, 1994; Cantwell, 1995; Birkinshaw, 1997; Rugman & Verbeke, 2001; Harzing & Noorderhaven, 2006), and because of these different strategic roles, there exist significant differences in terms of knowledge flow patterns (Ambos, Ambos & Schlegelmilch, 2006; Driffield, Love & Menghinello, 2010), as well as corporate control (Driffield, Love & Yang, 2016) and knowledge transfer mechanisms or channels (Grant, 1996; Peltokorpi & Vaara, 2014) between the parent company and its subsidiaries, or between the subsidiary and its peer subsidiary. Implicit in this literature is that intra-MNCs' knowledge flows are not transferred only, or even primarily, from the parent company to its dispersed subsidiaries in overseas markets. As Cantwell (1995) argued and evidenced, MNCs have a high degree of international dispersal of innovation and technology activities outside of the home country.

In the current globalised economy, knowledge is regarded as the most crucial resource in MNCs, and the ability of a firm to leverage its dispersed knowledge leads to competitiveness and superior performance in the global market. Notably, a growing literature shows not only that a foreign subsidiary can develop its own innovation capability as well as learn knowledge from other foreign firms or domestic multinationals in a given country (Cantwell, 1995; Frost, 2001; Narula, 2002; Driffield, Love & Yang, 2014; Mudambi & Swift, 2014), but also that accumulated knowledge in the subsidiary can be transferred back to its parent company (Ambos, Ambos & Schlegelmilch, 2006; Driffield, Love & Yang, 2016).

Notwithstanding the fact that there are benefits associated with an increase in overseas investments, the returns from overseas investment are determined by the innovation capability and marketing abilities of the firm (Morck & Yeung, 1991; Contractor, Yang & Gaur, 2013). Driffield, Love and Menghinello (2010) illustrate not only that a foreign subsidiary can be established in a given country for exploiting parent company knowledge, sourcing external knowledge or a combination of both, but also that the direction of the knowledge flows is influenced by subsidiary research intensity and innovation capability. In the network of MNCs, there are competence-exploiting subsidiaries that utilise home-based proprietary advantages and competence-creating subsidiaries that explore new technological capabilities (Cantwell & Mudambi, 2005).

This chapter reviews literature on international knowledge transfer. The next section reviews the literature on knowledge of the firm, followed by a review of conventional and reverse knowledge transfers. Thereafter, the importance of competence-creating subsidiaries is reviewed. Then an overview of the importance of absorptive capacity, location choices and language in international knowledge flows is provided and, finally, a conclusion is given.

Knowledge

As a corollary, resources are treated as the basis for a firm to maintain its competitiveness if these resources are rare, valuable, inimitable, and non-substitutable (Wernerfelt, 1984; Barney, 1991). It has been noted that multinational enterprises possess a bundle of resources (Barney, 1991). Among these resources, it is almost axiomatic among economists and business scholars that their knowledge is generally regarded as the most crucial resource to be utilised in competing with rivals in the global context, wherein technological capability and firm efficiency are the keys for differentiating products and hence increasing competitive advantages (Gupta & Govindarajan, 2000; Rugman & Verbeke, 2001; Melitz, 2003; Helpman, Melitz & Stephen, 2004; Tallman & Phene, 2007; Driffield, Love & Yang, 2014, 2016).

Knowledge of the firm, as proposed by Kogut and Zander (1992), consists of information and know-how. Information, such as who knows what or what something means, is characterised as declarative and less tacit knowledge, in contrast to know-how that is a tacit, procedural type of knowledge which is learned and accumulated by the firm. Know-how embedding within the organisation allows firms to know how to operate efficiently and to solve problems smoothly. Notwithstanding the fact that knowledge resides at the individual level (Grant, 1996), an important task for a firm is to integrate and coordinate knowledge at different levels, including personal, group, organisation, and social networks (Kogut & Zander, 1992). This definition, and the literature (Kogut & Zander, 1993; Grant, 1996; Bresman, Birkinshaw & Nobel, 1999) that follows it, is recognised as a challenge to the transaction cost theory of the firm. According to knowledge-based theory, the firm is treated as an institution for integrating and coordinating knowledge that is a fundamental resource for maintaining the sustainable competitiveness advantages in the global setting (Kogut & Zander, 1992; Grant, 1996; Ambos, Ambos & Schlegelmilch, 2006). This differs from the transaction cost theory of the firm, which essentially highlights the need to share and transfer knowledge when intermediate goods in overseas markets are missing (Williamson, 1975).

In Gupta and Govindarajan (1991, 1994), the MNC is recognised as a network of capital, product, and knowledge transactions among differentiated subsidiaries across different foreign countries. Considering different knowledge flows patterns between a focal subsidiary and the rest of the MNC, Gupta and Govindarajan (1991, 1994) define four generic subsidiary roles, including global innovator, integrated player, local innovator, and implementer. In global innovator and integrated player roles, knowledge flows from subsidiaries to parent companies or peer subsidiaries are high. In contrast, there is a big extent of knowledge flows from parent companies to their subsidiaries acting in the roles of local innovator or implementer. Consequently, within MNCs, the direction and extent of knowledge flows depends on the role of the subsidiary in the network of the MNC's knowledge. Some subsidiaries that have integrated player or global innovator mandates are likely to source and upgrade their knowledge more than those subsidiaries that are local innovators or implementers (Ambos, Ambos & Schlegelmilch, 2006).

In Simonin's (2004) framework of knowledge transfer in strategic alliances, the extent of knowledge transfer and learning is largely determined by two theoretical constructs: the motivation to learn as a driver and knowledge ambiguity as an impediment. While sourcing knowledge externally has now gradually used a strategy to upgrade firm knowledge and improve efficiency, the existing knowledge of the firm, in most cases, is path dependent, which hinders inter-firm knowledge transfer. Song et al. (2003) bolster this argument through examining the impact of hiring engineers from other firms on the extent of inter-firm knowledge transfer, and they find that once external engineers are hired, path-dependence of firm knowledge will attenuate the knowledge transfer and learning from the engineers, especially when the knowledge of the hired engineers closely matches the firm's existing core technology trajectory. While the acquired subsidiary can allow the parent company to gain access to knowledge that is not available in the MNC network, compared with greenfield subsidiaries, acquired subsidiaries have lower internal legitimacy as a whole and, thus, require more effort in engaging in reverse knowledge transfer exercises in order to better connect to the parent company network (Mudambi, Piscitello & Rabbiosi, 2014).

Tacitness is another important characteristic of knowledge that influence the success of knowledge flows within MNCs. In order to sustain subsidiary competence in the long run, the subsidiary needs to incorporate and develop knowledge that is tacit and difficult to imitate or codify (Rugman & Verbeke, 2001). When comparing the transfer of technological know-how with the transfer of patents between acquiring and acquired firms, Bresman, Birkinshaw and Nobel (1999) found that as patents are codified and relatively articulable, the transfer of this type of knowledge, i.e. in the form of a patent, is positively influenced by the articulability of knowledge, whereas technological know-how is tacit knowledge, and transferring this kind of knowledge depends to a large extent on communications and integrations in the post-acquisition period. Given that distinctive competencies are typically embedded in organisations, and path-dependent, inter-firm knowledge transfer between strategic alliance partner firms is higher in joint venture alliances relative to alliances without any equity arrangement, this is to some extent because joint venture partners will find it is easier to understand those tacit – and perhaps complicated – types of knowledge, compared to other forms of alliances such as licensing (Mowery, Oxley & Silverman, 1996). Ambos, Ambos and Schlegelmilch (2006) also found that organisational differences between parent company and its subsidiaries in terms of structure, process, and values attenuate the extent of benefits that the parent company can derive from the reverse knowledge transfer.

The ability of a firm to identify and transfer the best practice within the firm is crucial for sustaining the competitiveness in the global context (Szulanski, 1996). It is axiomatic that transferring internal knowledge has fewer concerns regarding confidentiality and legal issues relative to acquiring knowledge externally. Nevertheless, the best practices or distinctive competencies, the way the tangible assets and firm specific assets are deployed effectively in value chain production, might not easily be transferred within the firm. The difficulty of effectively transferring those best practices internally, denoted internal stickiness of knowledge in Szulanski (1996), largely comes from the weak absorptive capability of the recipients, the causal ambiguity due to the lack of perfect understanding of idiosyncratic characteristics of incoming best practices, and the arduous relationship between the subsidiary and parent company because of ineffective communication.

In the conceptual framework of knowledge ambiguity and knowledge transfer, Simonin (1999) find that tacitness, complexity, cultural distance, and organisational distance increase the level of knowledge ambiguity. Prior experience, however, is positively associated with firm's familiarity and comfort with the content of the knowledge transferred, thereby lessening causal ambiguity. On this basis, with greater collaborative experience, partners can overcome new, unfamiliar situations during the alliance. Over time, partners in the strategic alliance have a better understanding of each other's best practices. Simonin (1999), for instance, finds that the duration of an alliance alleviates the issues of knowledge complexity, thereby enhancing knowledge sharing and learning in strategic alliances. As Szulanski, Ringov and Jensen (2016) propose, the timing of the knowledge transfer method can overcome the stickiness or the difficulty in the knowledge transfer. A high level of knowledge exchange between the source and recipient is needed during the initial phase of the knowledge transfer process when the causal ambiguity of incoming knowledge is high, whereas more support for knowledge exchange during the implementation phase is particularly useful for the recipient that is in an arduous relationship with the source.

International knowledge transfer within MNCs

While knowledge sourced from external markets is more open, intra-organisation knowledge is relatively easily understood and assimilated by the receiving units that are foreign subsidiaries, or multinational headquarters in reverse knowledge transfer.

There has been a large and burgeoning literature on the benefits of internationalisation (Contractor, Kundu & Hsu, 2003; Contractor, 2007; Yang, Martins & Driffield, 2013), and much of this multinational-performance literature has been built on internalisation theory, that is, by internalising knowledge and resources within the firm, parent companies are more effective in reducing transaction costs, particularly when the intermediate market is missing in the foreign market wherein knowledge is difficult to find or is non-tradeable. In the International Business literature, it has been a core assumption that multinational enterprises have advantages through internalising their firm specific intangible assets within the firm across different borders, and hence improving their competitiveness in the global market (Morck & Yeung, 1991; Rugman & Verbeke, 2001; Yang & Driffield, 2012). This internalisation theory, initially advocated by Hymer (1976), highlights that intra-MNE knowledge flows within the firm could be more efficiently integrated than knowledge acquired through external markets (Buckley & Casson, 1976). In the traditional model of MNCs or conventional knowledge transfer, parent companies are recognised as important sources of knowledge, and they possess abundant intangible assets and superior capabilities (Hymer, 1976; Vernon, 1966) that are transferred to their subsidiaries in foreign markets, and then followed by possible externalities, e.g. workforce mobility or technology spillover, from foreign subsidiaries to local firms (Driffield, Love & Yang, 2014).

Within the network of MNCs, some subsidiaries are given mandates or responsibilities for innovating or pursuing new technical capability initiatives (Birkinshaw, 1997). And these high value-added activities increase the likelihood that these subsidiaries become the centres of excellence in the MNC (Frost, Birkinshaw & Ensign, 2002). Over the past few decades, there has been an increasing emphasis on reverse knowledge transfer from foreign subsidiary to parent company (Bresman, Birkinshaw & Nobel, 1999; Ambos, Ambos & Schlegelmilch, 2006; Driffield, Love & Menghinello, 2010; Driffield, Love & Yang, 2016). Bresman et al. (1999) found that knowledge transfer was imposed from acquiring to acquired firms at an early stage in the post-acquisition period, while over time firms made efforts at integrating knowledge via effective communications, and that this led to two-way knowledge transfer, i.e. reciprocal knowledge transfer.

A firm can derive the benefits from 'the exploration of new knowledge and the exploitation of old certainties' (March, 1991, p. 71). Specifically, on the one hand, the firm maintains exploitative research and development to sustain its advantages of existing knowledge, and on the other, the firm increases its investment in exploratory research and development to develop its new innovations. As a result, a substantial increase in research and development is treated as an indication of transition from knowledge exploitation to exploration, which allows the firm to make the leap from both direction and process, leading to superior technological capabilities and firm performance (Mudambi & Swift, 2014). Driffield, Love and Yang (2014) provide evidence of reverse knowledge spillovers from domestic firms to foreign subsidiaries such that technological capability of domestic firms in host countries enhances productivity of foreign subsidiaries. They also find that MNCs can derive more productivity spillovers from the host country when they invest within the region, because not only is the firm likely to benefit more from the network of peer subsidiaries within the region (Rugman & Verbeke, 2004), but also they face a lower extent of liabilities of foreignness stemming from the distance between home and host country (Zaheer, 1995; Zaheer & Mosakowski, 1997).

The extent of reverse knowledge transfer differs between 'knowledge exploitation' and 'knowledge exploration' subsidiaries (March, 1991). For subsidiaries aiming at knowledge augmentation or creation through improving parent company production efficiency as a whole, or accessing local technological capabilities or know-how, the extent of reverse knowledge transfer is greater than in subsidiaries that exploit parent firm specific assets in local markets (Yang, Mudambi & Meyer, 2008). Knowledge relevance between receiving and sending units is another important aspect that influences knowledge flows. Knowledge relevance between parent firms and overseas subsidiaries, as evidenced in Yang et al. (2008), increases the extent of reverse knowledge transfer, as a high level of overlap or similarity of knowledge helps parent companies understand and assimilate subsidiary knowledge. Similarly, knowledge congruity is expected to be high when subsidiary knowledge has a large number of sources from the parent company or other MNCs (Asmussen, Foss & Pedersen, 2013). Within MNCs, organisation knowledge in general not only finds a use in one specific market but also retains its value in a wider set of markets, which is defined as fungibility (Teece, 1982). A focal subsidiary might have a stock of information and know-how stemming from internal or external sources, or a combination of both. Knowledge stocks in the subsidiary, with a good mix of internal and external sources, are more fungible and congruous and, thus, create more reverse knowledge transfers (Asmussen, Foss & Pedersen, 2013). Although there is the existence of different strategic motivations in alliances, partners that focus on sharing and upgrading technology and firm efficiency tend to have a bigger overlap of knowledge relative to other alliance motives such as market access (Mowery, Oxley & Silverman, 1996). By adopting the resource-based view of the firm, Mowery et al. (1996) propose that the overlap of knowledge and technological capability promotes inter-firm knowledge transfer between the firm and its strategic alliance partners, and, over time, the extent of technological knowledge overlapped in joint venture partners is greater in the post-collaboration period than before the equity alliance.

Competence-creating subsidiaries

Within the network of MNCs, an increase in the number of competence-creating subsidiaries shows a high level of corporate diversity and learning, and this leads to a desirable balance between knowledge exploitation and knowledge exploration in the firm (Cantwell & Mudambi, 2005). In addition, subsidiary initiatives are recognised as entrepreneurship activities that aim to advance a new approach for expanding firm capabilities or using resources in a more efficient way, which can promote the subsidiary's ability in local responsiveness, global integration, and learning (Birkinshaw, 1997). Within different types of parent-subsidiary linkages, subsidiaries are different in terms of not only their strategic roles in the MNC network, but also their capabilities to create competencies, and this will influence knowledge flows in MNCs. Analysing the impact of technological development of the affiliate, Driffield, Love and Menghinello (2010) found that the directionality of intra-knowledge flows within MNCs is contingent on the level of subsidiary research intensity and the investment in capital-embodied technology. And they found that the level of research intensity and firm-specific assets in the subsidiary increases the likelihood of knowledge transfer from the subsidiary to its parent company. Driffield, Love and Yang (2016) concurred with their findings: they found that the extent to which subsidiary technological capability actually enhances its parent company productivity is biggest for the subsidiary that only engages in research and development activities, as compared to other types of subsidiary.

In addition, the innovation capabilities of the subsidiary influence the origins of information and knowledge that are derived by the subsidiary. Frost (2001), for example, elucidates that the subsidiary that has a limited innovation scale has a lack of legitimacy and visibility in the host country, and in turn it relies on knowledge and information originating from the parent company rather than the local market. In contrast, Frost (2001) found that the subsidiary with a greater innovation scale is more likely to source information and ideas originating from the local market. Equally important, the type and characteristics of subsidiary knowledge and competences influence knowledge flows and learning. When subsidiary knowledge is non-duplicative and has great relevance to parent knowledge, the parent company will perceive the knowledge of the subsidiary as more valuable (Gupta & Govindarajan, 2000). Apart from technology relevance, it is also crucial for subsidiaries to develop knowledge that is unique, tacit, path-dependent, and non-locationally bound, which not only sustains subsidiary firm specific advantages but also attracts parent company attention and resources (Rugman & Verbeke, 2001). Specifically, those subsidiaries that are viewed as centres of excellence in MNCs typically have mandates or responsibilities for certain products or businesses for MNCs as a whole (Frost, Birkinshaw & Ensign, 2002).

Knowledge creation by a foreign subsidiary depends to a large extent on the level of its own research intensity as a whole, and acquiring subsidiaries that are motivated by strategic asset seeking are more likely associated with a great deal of knowledge production (Mudambi & Navarra, 2004). Given the potential usefulness of knowledge in acquired subsidiaries, Cantwell and Mudambi (2005) found that the parent company tends to increase its investment in research and development in an acquired subsidiary with a competence-creating mandate. While innovation capability is important for subsidiaries to differentiate their products from their rivals and to increase its strategic position in the value chain of MNCs, some subsidiaries, realistically, are more efficient and creative than others. Subsidiaries with a lesser innovative capability have a low ability to engage in an effective reverse knowledge transfer, and this is in contrast to subsidiaries with greater innovative capability that are more willing to engage in their own competence creation rather than reverse knowledge transfer exercises (Mudambi, Piscitello & Rabbiosi, 2014).

Such knowledge intensity will influence subsidiary bargaining power within MNCs. The more value-adding activities a subsidiary undertakes, the more internal bargaining power the subsidiary has. Foreign subsidiaries tend to exploit this power to bargain for more internal resources and to gain more attention from the multinational's headquarters (Bouquet & Birkinshaw, 2008). In the global context, subsidiaries engage in different levels of innovation that influence not only the ability to transfer knowledge back to the parent company but also its bargaining power with the parent company. The importance of a subsidiary in the MNC network depends to a large extent on its control over firm-specific assets of the MNC. The more the control with firm-specific assets the subsidiary has, the greater its bargaining power in the parent-subsidiary relationship (Mudambi & Navarra, 2004).

In the literature, there are two competing arguments about the benefits of subsidiary autonomy. On the one hand, autonomy of the subsidiary promotes its ability to identify and develop new capabilities in the local market without a great deal of intervention, or even without permission, from the parent company. This enhances the likelihood that the subsidiary contains a centre of excellence from which the parent company derives more learning benefits (Birkinshaw, 1997). As Cantwell and Mudambi (2005) argued, strategic autonomy or independence allows the subsidiary with a competence-creating mandate to invest in a high level of research and development, and this tends to reinforce its mandate and provide more benefits to MNCs as a whole. On the other hand, however, strategic autonomy or independence do not increase the research intensity of the subsidiary with competence-exploiting mandates. Though a certain degree of strategic independence encourages a subsidiary to develop know-how and upgrade its technological capability, Mudambi and Navarra (2004) found that the managers of value-adding subsidiaries tend to exploit the subsidiary's internal bargaining power to appropriate a great deal of rents for its subsidiary's own use. A similar finding emerged in a recent international rent-sharing study by Martins and Yang (2015) which documents that as the bargaining power of a foreign subsidiary increases, the parent company tends to pay higher wages to its overseas workers, and this bargaining power is higher for related subsidiaries that are part of a parent company network of value adding activities, relative to those unrelated subsidiaries. As evidenced in Driffield, Love and Yang (2016), the effect of reverse knowledge transfer on parent productivity is higher when the parent company has a higher equity control over its subsidiary.

Absorptive capacity

As noted by Gupta and Govindarajan (2000), while MNCs embrace a bundle of resources, and the existence of the firm primarily relies on knowledge flows within the firm, intra-organisation knowledge transfer, realistically, does not necessarily take place on a routine basis. The extent of knowledge flows from parent companies to their subsidiaries is significantly influenced by the absorptive capability of the receiving unit.

The absorptive capability of a foreign subsidiary to understand, assimilate, and implement knowledge transferred internally is conceptualised as some combination of both employee ability and their motivation to contribute to organisation efficiency (Cohen & Levinthal, 1990; Minbaeva et al., 2014a). The ability of employees is different in terms of their educational background and previous job-related experience, and employee motivation could be stimulated by various human resource management practices including performance-based pay incentives, fast-track promotion, merit-based appraisal, and internal communications (Minbaeva et al., 2014a).

The capacity to absorb the incoming knowledge is treated as an important barrier or facilitator for international transfer within the firm. The more the subsidiary is familiar with the incoming knowledge, or the higher the homophily between the subsidiary and the rest of the MNC, the greater the absorptive capability of the subsidiary (Gupta & Govindarajan, 2000). When the managers of the parent company have a better understanding of incoming knowledge from its overseas subsidiaries, the parent company can derive more benefits from reverse knowledge transfer (Ambos, Ambos & Schlegelmilch, 2006). The extent of the firm's ability to understand

and absorb knowledge outside the boundaries of the firm in the pre-alliance period accelerates knowledge sharing and learning during strategic alliances (Mowery, Oxley & Silverman, 1996).

Compared to acquired subsidiaries, greenfield subsidiaries are more likely to have duplicative knowledge vis-à-vis their parent company, which results in a greater overlap of knowledge and capability, and consequently an increase in knowledge transfer (Gupta & Govindarajan, 2000). Given the fact that, relative to local nationals, expatriates have much stronger social ties with parent company, Gupta and Govindarajan (2000) found that the greater the ratio of the number of expatriates within the subsidiary management team, the higher the absorptive capability. The learning capability of a firm in knowledge transfer is relevant to, but different from, absorptive capability, and it is conceptualised as firm assets and resources that can be deployed to drive the learning process (Simonin, 2004). By deploying greater resources in knowledge transfer, a firm dealing with causally ambiguous competencies can increase its absorptive capability and accelerate its learning speed, which to a large extent help to cope with cultural and organisation distance, and eventually the firm lowers the negative effect of ambiguity on knowledge transfer (Simonin, 1999).

Location choices

Although knowledge flow is geographically bounded (Driffield, Love & Yang, 2016), the innovative capabilities of the sending unit offer a useful signal to the receiving unit about the potential usefulness of incoming knowledge, and thus, in the context of lacking proximity, the receiving unit is more likely to deem important and accept the incoming knowledge, which increases the likelihood of knowledge flows between different countries or different clusters (Tallman & Phene, 2007). This section specifically reviews the importance of location choice in knowledge flows within MNCs.

The location choices in foreign direct investment are crucial for the success of investment (Dunning, 1988, 1998; Pantzalis, 2001; Berry, 2006; Yang & Martins, 2011; Driffield, Love & Yang, 2016). This links to another rich literature surrounding the returns to multinationality, discussed for example in Contractor, Kundu and Hsu (2003) and Yang and Driffield (2012). Within the corporate network of the MNC, the specialised role of each subsidiary is in accordance with the host country's market characteristics in terms of innovation capabilities, production costs, factor endowments, and customer preferences (Cantwell, 1995; Frost, 2001; Yang, Martins & Driffield, 2013). Frost (2001), for example, argued that regardless of whether a subsidiary receives mandates to expand international markets or to upgrade its technological capabilities, if the local market has specialised knowledge in fields of subsidiary innovations, the subsidiary will pay more attention to knowledge sources and ideas originating from the local market, rather than from sources and ideas from the home country.

More importantly, the ability of the firm to transfer, assimilate, and coordinate knowledge across dispersed and disparate subsidiaries explains the reason why some MNCs display superior performances, as reflected by higher firm efficiency and larger market shares, as well as greater profits. The existence of MNCs, as stated in Kogut and Zander (1993, p. 1), 'arise not out of the failure of markets for buying and selling knowledge, but out of its superior efficiency as organisation vehicle by which to transfer this knowledge across border[s]'.

In the literature, it demonstrates that the economic development of a host country influences not only the success of investment but also international knowledge flows within MNCs. In contrast to developing countries, developed countries on average are closer to the frontier of technology and possess valuable know-how (Martins & Yang, 2009; Yang & Mallick, 2010), and this significantly influences the extent of knowledge learning. In Gupta and Govindarajan's

(2000) work, it has been theoretically argued and empirically evidenced that a high level of economic development in the host country relative to the home country increases the extent of reverse knowledge transfer, as the parent company may view the knowledge stock of the subsidiary established in the advanced economy as more valuable than the subsidiary located in a less advanced economy. Advanced countries are more likely to be associated with sophisticated resources and technology (Porter, 1990), which shows a high level of competitiveness in a given country. In addition, historically, innovation and technology activities of MNCs are placed in specialised industry clusters (Cantwell, 1995), and thus the parent company is inclined to regard as potentially useful incoming knowledge that is transferred from advanced countries. Advantages of industry diamonds in a host country wherein the subsidiary resides provide a great opportunity for the subsidiary to become a centre of excellence, i.e. high value-added sources from which the parent company can derive more learning benefits from a host country location (Birkinshaw, 1997). Some subsequent empirical work finds similar results. Ambos, Ambos and Schlegelmilch (2006), for example, provided the evidence that a parent company can derive more benefits from knowledge that is transferred from subsidiaries located in a highly developed economy. As Driffield, Love and Yang (2016) found, firms are more willing to locate their core knowledge in a country with a high level of economic development, technological development, and intellectual property protection, and this in turn will enhance the extent of knowledge transfer from the subsidiary to its parent company.

The distance between the parent company and its subsidiary has been a crucial International Business topic. There is a rich and burgeoning literature that not only measures the distance between home and host country, but examines the impact of distance on the success of business as well (Ghemawat, 2001; Berry, Guillén & Zhou, 2010). The success of investment depends to a large extent on the factors stemming from the distance between the parent and its subsidiary in a given country, which not only augment the coordination cost within the MNCs (Driffield, Love & Yang, 2016), but also give rise to the liabilities of foreignness (Hymer, 1976; Zaheer, 1995). Specifically, Driffield et al. (2016) found that the differences between home and host country in terms of not only institutional environment but also economic development more generally attenuate reverse knowledge transfer from the subsidiary to its parent company.

Language

Apart from the differences in economic development and technological capabilities between home and host country, it has been widely accepted that common language and communication play an important role in integration and coordination within the firm, as effective verbal communication is crucial not only for understanding rules and directives, but also solving problems and making decisions (Grant, 1996).

Bresman, Birkinshaw and Nobel (1999) examine the importance of communications and interaction between acquirers and acquiring firms in international knowledge transfer, and they found that face-to-face discussion, as well as frequent visits and regular meetings, facilitate knowledge flows in the post-acquisition period. Good language skills are associated with superior ability to communicate with colleagues, form social networks, develop international proposals, and reduce the hierarchies through effectively and efficiently interacting with other colleagues in the parent company and the rest of the MNC (Peltokorpi & Vaara, 2014). Language can formulate a social network in which individuals interact with each other, and this language-based social network not only acts as a precursor of knowledge transfer, but can reconfigure the message as well; therefore language could be treated as a 'reconfiguration agent' in the international knowledge transfer process (Welch & Welch, 2008).

As Yang and Kwong (2013) evidenced, a subsidiary is more likely to develop its competence-creating when home and host country share the same language. With the focus on the multifaceted role of language on reverse knowledge transfer, Peltokorpi and Vaara (2014) elucidate that language-sensitive recruits can both promote and hinder the reverse knowledge transfer, that is, good language skills can enhance employees' ability to recognise and understand, and this increases reverse knowledge transfer up to a point beyond which increasing language skills will eventually hinder knowledge transfer as employees with extensive language skills will have less attachment to the organisation and show less commitment in knowledge transfer. The language and cultural background of employees also facilitates the extent of inter-firm knowledge flows across borders. A recent study by Liu et al. (2015) elucidates that bilingual and bicultural backgrounds of highly skilled migrants stemming from the country of origin and the country in which they reside are regarded as important sources for identifying key contacts and establishing the substantial relationship, thereby acting as a bridge in the knowledge exchange between the firms across borders.

Conclusion

Notwithstanding the fact that some firms concentrate their research and development activities at home, seeking knowledge in overseas markets is important, inter alia when radical innovation is needed or knowledge is externally generated (Narula, 2002). Knowledge is regarded as the critical resource for the firm to sustain its competitiveness (Wernerfelt, 1984; Barney, 1991), and MNCs are regarded as institutions for integrating and coordinating knowledge (Kogut & Zander, 1992; Grant, 1996; Ambos, Ambos & Schlegelmilch, 2006). It has now been accepted that the ability of a firm to leverage its dispersed knowledge is a core competence for maintaining its competitive advantages in the global market (Gupta & Govindarajan, 2000; Rugman & Verbeke, 2001; Helpman, Melitz & Stephen, 2004; Driffield, Love & Yang, 2014, 2016). As noted in Cantwell, Dunning and Lundan (2010), MNCs can co-evolve with institutional environments. On the one hand, MNCs can introduce best practices that are developed locally by its foreign subsidiary and then transferred to the parent company. On the other, the parent company can transfer some home country institutional practices to its dispersed foreign subsidiaries. A firm is likely to achieve superior performance and maintain competitiveness in the global setting if it allocates firm resources for both knowledge exploitation and knowledge exploration, and keeps a good balance between both directions and processes, instead of specifically focusing on one direction but exclusively overlooking the other direction (March, 1991; Driffield, Love & Menghinello, 2010; Mudambi & Swift, 2014).

The extent of knowledge flows from parent company to subsidiary, in an overarching knowledge transfer framework proposed by Gupta and Govindarajan (2000), is augmented by the value of the source unit's knowledge, motivational disposition to share knowledge, motivational disposition to acquire knowledge, richness of transmission channels or mechanism, and the absorptive capability of the receiving units (Cohen & Levinthal, 1990; Mudambi & Navarra, 2004; Welch & Welch, 2008; Yang & Kwong, 2013; Minbaeva et al., 2014b). In the retrospective summary of absorptive capability and MNC knowledge transfer, Minbaeva et al. (2014a) emphasise the importance of interaction between employee ability and motivation, and elucidate that with strong motivation, employees' ability to engage in inter- and intra-organisation knowledge transfer will be reinforced. In the International Business literature, the ability to transfer knowledge is conceptually different from the willingness to engage in knowledge transfer, and this ability-willingness dichotomy is to a large extent due to the innovative capability of the subsidiary (Mudambi, Piscitello & Rabbiosi, 2014). In addition, the extent of knowledge transfer is influenced by different characteristics of knowledge such as tacitness (Bresman, Birkinshaw & Nobel, 1999), path-dependence (Song et al., 2003), and complexity (Simonin, 1999).

Historically, it has been noted that measuring the effect of international knowledge transfer on technological capability and other firm competence is complicated in the empirical literature (Mowery, Oxley & Silverman, 1996). Despite widespread interest in knowledge flows within MNCs from academics, there are relatively few empirical studies looking specifically into the effect of knowledge flows on firm productivity, in large part because of a lack of availability of relevant data (Contractor, Yang & Gaur, 2013; Driffield, Love & Yang, 2016). Recently, there has been an increasing emphasis on the effect of knowledge flows on firm productivity (Driffield, Love & Yang, 2014, 2016). Driffield et al. (2016), for example, found not only that reverse knowledge transfer from the affiliate to the parent company exists, but also that the extent to which affiliate technological capability actually upgrades parent efficiency depends not merely on the research intensity of the subsidiary, but also on the subsidiary's geographical location, strategic position in the parent company's value chain, and the embeddedness of the subsidiary in the MNC's hierarchy.

References

Ambos, T.C., Ambos, B. & Schlegelmilch, B.B. (2006) 'Learning from foreign subsidiaries: An empirical investigation of headquarters' benefits from reverse knowledge transfers', *International Business Review*, 15, pp. 294–312.

Asmussen, C.G., Foss, N.J. & Pedersen, T. (2013) 'Knowledge transfer and accommodation effects in multinational corporations: Evidence from European subsidiaries', *Journal of Management*, 39, pp. 1397–1429.

Barney, J. (1991) 'Firm resources and sustained competitive advantage', *Journal of Management*, 17, pp. 99–120.

Berry, H. (2006) 'Shareholder valuation of foreign investment and expansion', *Strategic Management Journal*, 27, pp. 1123–1140.

Berry, H., Guillén, M.F. & Zhou, N. (2010) 'An institutional approach to cross-national distance', *Journal of International Business Studies*, 41, pp. 1460–1480.

Birkinshaw, J. (1997) 'Entrepreneurship in multinational corporations: The characteristics of subsidiary initiatives', *Strategic Management Journal*, 18, pp. 207–229.

Bouquet, C. & Birkinshaw, J. (2008) 'Weight versus voice: How foreign subsidiaries gain attention from corporate headquarters', *Academy of Management Journal*, 51, pp. 577–601.

Bresman, H., Birkinshaw, J. & Nobel, R. (1999) 'Knowledge transfer in international acquisitions', *Journal of International Business Studies*, 30, pp. 439–462.

Buckley, P.J., & Casson, M. (1976) *The Future of the Multinational Enterprise.* New York: Springer.

Cantwell, J. (1995) 'The globalisation of technology: What remains of the product cycle model?' *Cambridge Journal of Economics*, 19, pp. 155–174.

Cantwell, J., Dunning, J.H. & Lundan, S.M. (2010) 'An evolutionary approach to understanding International Business activity: The co-evolution of MNEs and the institutional environment', *Journal of International Business Studies*, 41, pp. 567–586.

Cantwell, J. & Mudambi, R. (2005) 'MNE competence-creating subsidiary mandates', *Strategic Management Journal*, 26, pp. 1109–1128.

Cohen, W.M. & Levinthal, D.A. (1990) 'Absorptive capacity: A new perspective on learning and innovation', *Administrative Science Quarterly*, 35, pp. 128–152.

Contractor, F.J. (2007) 'Is International Business good for companies? The evolutionary or multi-stage theory of internationalization vs. the transaction cost perspective', *Management International Review*, 47, pp. 453–475.

Contractor, F.J., Kundu, S.K. & Hsu, C.C. (2003) 'A three-stage theory of international expansion: The link between multinationality and performance in the service sector', *Journal of International Business Studies*, 34, pp. 5–18.

Contractor, F.J., Yang, Y. & Gaur, A. S. (2013) 'Firm-specific intangible assets and subsidiary profitability: The moderating role of distance', in *Academy of Management Proceedings*.

Driffield, N., Love, J.H. & Menghinello, S. (2010) 'The multinational enterprise as a source of international knowledge flows: Direct evidence from Italy', *Journal of International Business Studies*, 41, pp. 350–359.

Driffield, N., Love, J.H. & Yang, Y. (2014) 'Technology sourcing and reverse productivity spillovers in the multinational enterprise: Global or regional phenomenon?' *British Journal of Management*, 25, pp. S24–S41.

Driffield, N., Love, J.H. & Yang, Y. (2016) 'Reverse international knowledge transfer in the MNE: (Where) does affiliate performance boost parent performance?' *Research Policy*, 45, pp. 491–506.

Dunning, J.H. (1988) 'The theory of international production', *The International Trade Journal*, 3, pp. 21–66.

Dunning, J.H. (1998) 'Location and the multinational enterprise: A neglected factor?' *Journal of International Business Studies*, 29, pp. 45–66.

Frost, T.S. (2001) 'The geographic sources of foreign subsidiaries' innovations', *Strategic Management Journal*, 22, pp. 101–123.

Frost, T.S., Birkinshaw, J.M. & Ensign, P. C. (2002) 'Centers of excellence in multinational corporations', *Strategic Management Journal*, 23, pp. 997–1018.

Ghemawat, P. (2001) 'Distance still matters', *Harvard Business Review*, 79, pp. 137–147.

Grant, R.M. (1996) 'Toward a knowledge-based theory of the firm', *Strategic Management Journal*, 17, pp. 109–122.

Gupta, A.K. & Govindarajan, V. (1991) 'Knowledge flows and the structure of control within multinational corporations', *Academy of Management Review*, 16, pp. 768–792.

Gupta, A.K. & Govindarajan, V. (1994) 'Organizing for knowledge flows within MNCs', *International Business Review*, 3, pp. 443–457.

Gupta, A.K. & Govindarajan, V. (2000) 'Knowledge flows within multinational corporations', *Strategic Management Journal*, 21, pp. 473–496.

Harzing, A.W. & Noorderhaven, N. (2006) 'Knowledge flows in MNCs: An empirical test and extension of Gupta and Govindarajan's typology of subsidiary roles', *International Business Review*, 15, pp. 195–214.

Helpman, E., Melitz, M.J. & Stephen, R.Y. (2004) 'Exports versus FDI with heterogenous firms', *American Economic Review*, 94, pp. 300–316.

Hymer, S. (1976) *The International Operations of National Firms: A Study of Direct Foreign Investment*. Cambridge, MA: MIT Press.

Kogut, B. & Zander, U. (1992) 'Knowledge of the firm, combinative capabilities, and the replication of technology', *Organization Science*, 3, pp. 383–397.

Kogut, B. & Zander, U. (1993) 'Knowledge of the firm and the evolutionary theory of the multinational corporation', *Journal of International Business Studies*, 24, pp. 625–645.

Liu, X., Gao, L., Lu, J. & Wei, Y. (2015) 'The role of highly skilled migrants in the process of inter-firm knowledge transfer across borders', *Journal of World Business*, 50, pp. 56–68.

March, J.G. (1991) 'Exploration and exploitation in organizational learning', *Organization Science*, 2, pp. 71–87.

Martins, P.S. & Yang, Y. (2009) 'The impact of exporting on firm productivity: A meta-analysis of the learning-by-exporting hypothesis', *Review of World Economics*, 145, pp. 431–445.

Martins, P.S. & Yang, Y. (2015) 'Globalized labour markets? International rent sharing across 47 countries', *British Journal of Industrial Relations*, 53, pp. 664–691.

Melitz, M. (2003) 'The impact of trade on aggregate industry productivity and intra-industry reallocations', *Econometrica*, 71, pp. 1695–1725.

Minbaeva, D.B., Pedersen, T., Björkman, I. & Fey, C.F. (2014a) 'A retrospective on: MNC knowledge transfer, subsidiary absorptive capacity, and HRM', *Journal of International Business Studies*, 45, pp. 52–62.

Minbaeva, D.B., Pedersen, T., Björkman, I., Fey, C.F. & Park, H.J. (2014b) 'MNC knowledge transfer, subsidiary absorptive capacity and HRM', *Journal of International Business Studies*, 45, pp. 38–51.

Morck, R. & Yeung, B. (1991) 'Why investors value multinationality', *Journal of Business*, 43, pp. 165–187.

Mowery, D.C., Oxley, J.E. & Silverman, B.S. (1996) 'Strategic alliances and interfirm knowledge transfer', *Strategic Management Journal*, 17(S2), pp. 77–91.

Mudambi, R. & Navarra, P. (2004) 'Is knowledge power? Knowledge flows, subsidiary power and rent-seeking within MNCs', *Journal of International Business Studies*, 35, pp. 385–406.

Mudambi, R., Piscitello, L. & Rabbiosi, L. (2014) 'Reverse knowledge transfer in MNEs: Subsidiary innovativeness and entry modes', *Long Range Planning*, 47, pp. 49–63.

Mudambi, R. & Swift, T. (2014) 'Knowing when to leap: Transitioning between exploitative and explorative R&D', *Strategic Management Journal*, 35, pp. 126–145.

Narula, R. (2002) 'Innovation systems and "inertia" in R&D location: Norwegian firms and the role of systemic lock-in', *Research Policy*, 31, pp. 795–816.

Pantzalis, C. (2001) 'Does location matter? An empirical analysis of geographic scope and MNC market valuation', *Journal of International Business Studies*, 32, pp. 133–155.

Peltokorpi, V. & Vaara, E. (2014) 'Knowledge transfer in multinational corporations: Productive and counterproductive effects of language-sensitive recruitment', *Journal of International Business Studies*, 45, pp. 600–622.

Porter, M.E. (1990) 'The competitive advantage of nations', *Harvard Business Review*, 68, pp. 73–93.

Rugman, A.M. & Verbeke, A. (2001) 'Subsidiary-specific advantages in multinational enterprises', *Strategic Management Journal*, 22, pp. 237–250.

Rugman, A.M. & Verbeke, A. (2004) 'A perspective on regional and global strategies of multinational enterprises', *Journal of International Business Studies*, 35, pp. 3–18.

Simonin, B.L. (1999) 'Ambiguity and the process of knowledge transfer in strategic alliances', *Strategic Management Journal*, 20, pp. 595–623.

Simonin, B.L. (2004) 'An empirical investigation of the process of knowledge transfer in international strategic alliances', *Journal of International Business Studies*, 35, pp. 407–427.

Song, J., Almeida, P. & Wu, G. (2003) 'Learning–by–hiring: When is mobility more likely to facilitate interfirm knowledge transfer?' *Management Science*, 49, pp. 351–365.

Szulanski, G. (1996) 'Exploring internal stickiness: Impediments to the transfer of best practice within the firm', *Strategic Management Journal*, 17(S2), pp. 27–43.

Szulanski, G., Ringov, D. & Jensen, R.J. (2016) 'Overcoming stickiness: How the timing of knowledge transfer methods affects transfer difficulty', *Organization Science*, 27, pp. 304–322.

Tallman, S. & Phene, A. (2007) 'Leveraging knowledge across geographic boundaries', *Organization Science*, 18, pp. 252–260.

Teece, D.J. (1982) 'Towards an economic theory of the multiproduct firm', *Journal of Economic Behavior & Organization*, 3, pp. 39–63.

Vernon, R. (1966) 'International investment and international trade in the product cycle', *The Quarterly Journal of Economics*, 80, pp. 190–207.

Welch, D.E. & Welch, L.S. (2008) 'The importance of language in international knowledge transfer', *Management International Review*, 48, pp. 339–360.

Wernerfelt, B. (1984) 'A resource-based view of the firm', *Strategic Management Journal*, 5, pp. 171–180.

Williamson, O.E. (1975) *Markets and Hierarchies*. New York: Free Press.

Yang, Q., Mudambi, R. & Meyer, K. E. (2008) 'Conventional and reverse knowledge flows in multinational corporations', *Journal of Management*, 34, pp. 882–902.

Yang, Y. & Driffield, N. (2012) 'Multinationality-performance relationship', *Management International Review*, 52, pp. 23–47.

Yang, Y. & Kwong, C.C. (2013) 'The role of language on affiliates' competence creation: Evidence from the MNE linkage across 45 countries', in Cook, G. & Johns, J. (Eds.), *The Changing Geography of International Business*. Basingstoke, UK: Palgrave Macmillan, pp. 114–135.

Yang, Y. & Mallick, S. (2010) 'Export premium, self-selection and learning-by-exporting: Evidence from Chinese matched firms', *The World Economy*, 33, pp. 1218–1240.

Yang, Y. & Martins, P.S. (2011) 'Multinational performance and intellectual property rights: Evidence from 46 countries', in Berrill, J., Hutson, E. & Sinkovics, R. (Eds.), *Firm-Level Internationalization, Regionalism and Globalization*. Basingstoke, UK: Palgrave Macmillan, pp. 96–112.

Yang, Y., Martins, P.S. & Driffield, N. (2013) 'Multinational performance and the geography of FDI', *Management International Review*, 53, pp. 763–794.

Zaheer, S. (1995) 'Overcoming the liability of foreignness', *Academy of Management Journal*, 38, pp. 341–363.

Zaheer, S. & Mosakowski, E. (1997) 'The dynamics of the liability of foreignness: A global study of survival in financial services', *Strategic Management Journal*, 18, pp. 439–463.

20

CAPITAL PROJECTS AND INFRASTRUCTURE IN URBAN AND ECONOMIC DEVELOPMENT

Phillip O'Neill

Introduction

One of the most discussed public campaigns in urban affairs is the battle between New York urbanist Jane Jacobs and New York infrastructure tsar Robert Moses. In her book *Death and Life of Great American Cities* (1961) Jacobs holds up the road transportation projects of Robert Moses as the enemy of a loveable city, and her argument makes much sense. Yet at the same time, the book is blind to the extraordinary vehicle created by Moses and his colleagues, namely the Port Authority of New York and New Jersey (PANYNJ) (Doig, 2001). No explanation of the longstanding success of the New York city-state economy is possible without understanding the role of this authority in building the vital internal connections and flows which underpin the city. Unfortunately, we know little about these processes of city building. This is what this chapter is mainly about.

Central to our understanding of the delivery of urban infrastructure is the role of the state in infrastructure commissioning, financing and operation. Perhaps Robert Moses' greatest achievement was his assembly of a giant public sector utility responsible for multi-disciplinary transport provision for the urban economies of northeast America. Similar utilities were constructed across the developed world in the post-war period, and I suspect the PANYNJ was a model. Yet few of these utilities remain. Indeed, their dismantling is so advanced that once-noisy claims about the merits of holding large-scale infrastructure assets in state hands have become muted. There is a level of acceptance about the condition of the infrastructure sector as having become a mix of private and public capital and operators. That said, longstanding debates continue about the choice of infrastructure to be built, its design characteristics, and how it intersects with the urban fabric of a city. This chapter explores the parameters of these debates. This first section sketches the issues which seem to defy resolution in the infrastructure debate. The second section presents a brief history of the take-up of responsibility for major capital works in our cities, which is followed by an overview of a theoretical settlement in economics about what infrastructure has become. In the third section, however, we explore the absence of the urban circumstances of infrastructure in this theory and point to the vital economic role capital works perform. The fourth section explains the politics of funding and financing that pervade the infrastructure sector – largely because of its socio-spatial (rather than its stylised economic) qualities. The fifth section then reflects on the range of historical settlements to these politics with a view to identifying opportunities for constructive development of better infrastructure provisioning. Then the final section suggests an integrating framework for ongoing research and policy development.

A technical note needs to be made at this point. The focus of this chapter is on those capital works and infrastructure which are directly involved in enabling the physical and energy flows of a city. So the chapter discusses urban infrastructures that enable the transportation of people and freight, the supply of water and energy and the operation of telecommunications. Other vital urban infrastructures including health and education (sometimes called 'soft infrastructure') and green infrastructure are beyond the scope of the chapter.

History

The provision of infrastructure and capital works has never been an agreed-on field of activity with systematic, historically recorded debate over selection and design, finance and funding, and operation and governance. In the late 18th century in *The Wealth of Nations*, the father of classical economics Adam Smith assigned responsibility for infrastructure to 'the sovereign', which was a very privileged assignment given Smith had only two other duties for the sovereign on his list: the defence of the realm and the protection of private property (Smith, 1976, pp. 687–688). There is an interesting literature which seeks to understand why Smith saw infrastructure as different from other economic goods. A consensus (see West, 1977; Petkantchin, 2006) sees Smith wrestling with the rise of modernisation in Western Europe and the need for new types of political, institutional and spatial order. Accommodating these new demands involved 'constitution making', especially around joint ventures and activities such as banks and corporations. Important to these ventures was the determination of property titles, capital rights and liability protections, and these were also central features in the operation of public works. Smith's thinking, then, was not simply about who should undertake the construction of roads, railways and bridges, but who should have responsibility for the creation and preservation of the passageways and thoroughfares, and then for their capitalisation and maintenance through time. Smith was recognising the central role of legal frameworks and property rights in building larger-scale economies as capitalism sought new ways of securing physical passage to more distant territories to access labour and resources, distribute product, secure profits, and limit what might be devastating liabilities should there be physical failure of assets involving major land works, water storage and the like.

Smith's thinking, therefore, was very much a political economy of infrastructure provision. It is somewhat surprising, then, that classical economics has by-and-large stripped Smith's political economy explanation from its exposition of a theory of infrastructure and capital works. Let's begin with the foundational category for infrastructure in economics: the public good. In economics a public good is something that is consumed collectively. The idea is most often sourced to economist Paul A. Samuelson who explained that when anyone consumes a public good, say by driving on a road, this 'leads to no subtractions from any other individual's consumption of that good' (1954, p. 387). In our example, the road is still there for the next motorist to drive on it. Economists call this the non-rivalry characteristic of a public good. A second important characteristic is seen to be that of non-excludability, although this condition is not as clear as non-rivalry. Non-excludability refers to the difficulty of limiting the benefits of a public good to an exclusive group. Most of our infrastructure system uses road and street corridors for their rollout (water pipes, electricity wires, telecommunications cables, sewerage), meaning every householder has access to them, and that an additional user can be added to the system at minimal cost. Nevertheless, there are ways of limiting access to a public good, especially by user charges, making the non-excludability characteristic less than clear cut.

In economic theory, non-excludability comes very much from the scale of operation. Spring water from a deep well on a private property can be sold readily as an exclusive private good, while a catchment-wide storage and treatment system becomes by definition a public good. It is easily understood that this type of system also has natural monopoly characteristics such that an additional rival producer would undermine the benefits of there being only one catchment-wide operator. Moreover, the large scale which comes from the monopoly supply of a public good across a city throws up enormous cost advantages, the most important of which is that once operational the cost of servicing each extra consumer is virtually zero.

One more feature from economics concerning public goods is the presence of positive externalities. Because public goods are more or less non-excludable and, as monopolies, they deliver services across wider areas, they also generate additional material benefits unable to be captured easily by commodification. Some examples are the public health benefits shared widely as a result of a quality sewerage system, the reduced surface road congestion and improved air quality in inner city neighbourhoods arising from the establishment of a light rail train service, and the economic activity generated in the vicinity of an airport. Of course, large-scale infrastructure items are also capable of generating negative externalities such as the noise from a railway line, motorway or airport, and the loss of natural wetlands and river habitats that usually accompany large water storage facilities.

Clearly, economics has spawned both a useful language for talking about infrastructure and a way of analysing its efficiencies, with important differences identified between public infrastructure and privately bought and consumed goods and services. What economics has lacked, however, is a worthwhile contribution to understanding the processes of infrastructure assembly, including its financing and funding, and its intersection with the socio-spatial nature of urban economy and urban life more generally. This deficiency should be surprising given the substance of Adam Smith's original observations about public works, and of the nagging reminders over seven decades of the 20th century from Ronald H. Coase, the Nobel laureate, of the need for close consideration of the politics of infrastructure provision. Coase had a particular interest in the nature of public and monopoly goods, writing observations about the rise of a broadcasting service (1947) and a national electricity grid (1950), the tense relationships between national regulators and utility operators (1939), the justifications for monopoly provision of national postal services (1961), the rationale for price setting in public utilities (1970) and, famously, the complexities of assigning costs and apportioning benefits in the provision of lighthouse services to coastal shipping and ports operators (1974). On the other hand, the deficiency is to be expected given the persistent absence of geography in economic thought. The frustrating element here is that urban infrastructure is so blatantly a geographic event. Throughout its life course it is impossible to separate an infrastructure asset from its urban location and context. We look at this presence next.

The role of infrastructure in urban and economic development

It is important to separate the use of the term 'public good' from the popular expression 'the public good'. As we have seen, *a* public good is a particular category of economic transaction distinguishable, say, from a private consumption good; while *the* public good refers to a normative image of a state of collective betterment, and not necessarily in a monetised sense. The language and politics of infrastructure gets mixed messily between these two meanings. In this section we set out the ways infrastructure produces benefits of many types. Hopefully this dissection helps define both the word infrastructure and the categories where its meaning is played out (see Lakoff, 1987).

The first benefit of infrastructure comes from the city's primary role as an economic entity, indeed as the cornerstone of contemporary capitalism (Harvey, 1985). As discussed earlier, infrastructure is the central device for the assembly of labour and raw materials at production sites and then for the dissemination of finished products. Infrastructure provision generates all sorts of efficiencies for producers such that virtuous economic cycles are installed: the city as a drawing card for production and consumption → the city as a place which generates infrastructure investment → the infrastructure-enabled city where the aspiration for growth is realised → and so it goes on.

Benefits for the reproduction of labour follow accordingly. In many ways the reproduction of labour is an old-fashioned expression common in Marxist studies to refer to the social processes unfunded by producers but nonetheless necessary for the replenishment of labour, be it for work the next day or for the production of a newly skilled cohort of workers a generation later. It is immediately obvious that the transport, energy, water and telecommunications systems that enable successful capitalist processes at sites of production and consumption also contribute enormously to the daily health and longer-term stabilisation of a city's resident labour force. Here the marginal cost efficiencies of monopoly infrastructure suppliers come to the fore, as householders can be added as consumers of infrastructure services at very low cost, the high sunk costs of infrastructure investment having already been justified if not amortised by the presence of major infrastructure consumers in the production and commercial sectors.

But there is much more to infrastructure's fomenting power than the generation of scale and process events in firms (micro-economies) and in market relations (externalities), although these are major matters. Infrastructure plays the major role in the processes that give a city its structure and shape and then its daily flows and rhythms. Thereafter, infrastructure is directly responsible for the material networks that link the transacting city to outside spatial entities, especially to other cities but also to nations and other forms of economic territories. Here we attempt to give substance to what Brenner and Schmid (2015) describe as 'a territorial conceptualization [of a city] that includes the large scale operational landscapes of extended urbanization' (http://urbantheorylab.net/); and foreground the socio-technical equipment of a city as a key determinant of its social, economic and environmental conditions. Note, though, that we seek not so much a bland account of a city as wired materially by its physical infrastructure assets, but an exposition of the interplay between a city's material assets and its non-material plays. Intriguingly, such interplay is investigated at larger scales through concepts like 'infrastructural Europeanism' (Schipper & Schot, 2011) which exposes the role played by trans-European infrastructure networks, especially in telecommunications (Laborie, 2011) and electricity (Lagendijk, 2011; see also Hughes, 1983), in the rollout of a continental political grid that overlays Europe's, enabling inventions and innovations in infrastructure sectors.

For the scale of the city, such interplay should be readily evident, yet the links are not well made in the literature to date. Certainly, there is awareness of the importance of systematic, repeated movements of a city. Prominent here is the discussion by Amin and Thrift (2002, pp. 17ff) of a city's 'repetition and regularities', although Amin and Thrift look to soft technologies like public transport timetables and the rhythms of more-than-human habitations of a city across its daylight and night time hours rather than the obvious role played by large-scale infrastructure as a rhythm-generating device. More recently, however, Scott and Storper (2015) advance a view of the city wherein infrastructure as a generative space – alongside production spaces and special spaces – is named as one of three essential sources for the generation of a city's urban-land relations and its agglomeration processes. Importantly, Scott and Storper have a broad conceptualisation of the city as a vehicle for holding together the otherwise 'complex congeries of human activities' (2015, p. 6). Hence, rather than being dismissed as a piece of socio-technical equipment, or sidelined by an overconcentration on the soft technologies of a city (see Amin & Thrift, 2002, especially chapter 4), Scott and Storper (2015, p. 7) give first-order importance to infrastructure because of its ordering and agglomeration-assisting functions, seeing the city:

> [a]s a concrete, localized, scalar articulation within the space economy as a whole, identifiable by reason of its polarization, its specialized land uses, its relatively dense networks of interaction (including its daily and weekly rhythms of life), and the ways in which it shapes not just economic processes (such as the formation of land, housing and labour prices) but also socialization dynamics, mentalities and cultures.

Some simple theoretical claims can be made at this point. The first is that there is a socio-technical and spatial process involving the grouping of common urban living needs into manageable entities so that infrastructure services can be delivered efficiently. Buildings are aligned to streets, for example, so that they intersect with transport, energy, water and sewerage services, and their owners are compelled to pay for the operation of these services. Commuters who live along these streets are effectively 'assigned' each morning to train carriages by spacing themselves roughly equally along on a local railway platform. Motorways 'organise' the movement of cars in common directions over many kilometres having intervened at specific junctions to redirect them after their very disordered first few kilometres of local travel from their drivers' places of residence. And so on.

A second insight is that infrastructure, through its organisational functions, inserts persistent rhythms into urban movements via the thick sets of hard and soft regulatory devices that always accompany infrastructure services provision. This means that urban flows are patterned and sequenced into hourly, daily, weekly even seasonal time slots. As a consequence, a city takes on a readable logic giving order to the daily activities of a household – imagine the coordinated schedules, for example, of a family comprising a construction worker, an office worker, a toddler in child care, a school-aged child and an older person in care – to be undertaken without too much angst.

A third claim is that because infrastructure, once built, narrows the options available for urban functioning by shutting down some flows and investing heavily in others, it determines a city's structured and sequenced flows through time and across space. So the timetables of local buses, for example, are dictated by the timetables and direction of higher order flows, especially commuter journeys, to ensure the efficient movement of passengers within the constraint of a fixed set of capital stock. So bus operators are forced to focus on morning and evening peak flows with other flows, such as the journey-to-school, relegated to next-available time slots. School operating times are very much pre-determined as a consequence.

A fourth is that infrastructure propagates the flows that forge and order the spatial networks that connect cities; for example, through the prioritisation of signalling along major roads, the rationalisation of air traffic through hub and spoke operations, the speeds available for digital information movements according to capital qualities of a telecommunications network, the degree of access to an electricity grid according to generation source, and so on.

Put together, we can see the power of infrastructure as a planning force in our cities, creating in the first instance the social and economic spaces for urban life, especially for the flows of people, materials, energy, information and waste, and thereafter defining what is possible in the future. In effect, it is the entity of the city that takes on the classic characteristic of the monopoly infrastructure asset: that it is forced to bear huge sunk costs in infrastructure's establishment phases but thereafter is able to operate at astonishing levels of efficiency so long as there is little or no change in substance.

Explanation of the politics of infrastructure

Our discussion so far shows the impossibility of urban life without the city being infrastructure-equipped. Aspirations for economic prosperity, urban liveability and environmental sustainability depend on the presence of infrastructure. Yet this presence is not easily achieved. Infrastructure assets are usually massive material entities requiring careful planning and siting even though they carry considerable social legitimacy, at least at a general level. At the neighbourhood level there is reluctance to host major transport, energy, and water and waste corridors. Because corridors usually transverse discrete and unitised allotments of privately owned property, their assembly requires exceptional powers of land acquisition and zoning, and then expensive and time-consuming transactional processes to enable the corridors' capitalisation such as by laying railway tracks, constructing road surfaces or installing power or telecommunications cables. Then there are the major costs of acquisitions and investments and the need for large amounts of finance. Even though returns on investment are usually modest, they are typically stable over very long time periods, as we discuss later.

As Adam Smith anticipated, only the state has the legal and organisational powers to successfully transact major infrastructure investments. Yet wielding these powers on a recurring basis requires that the state has legitimacy – with both capital and labour – to impose the conditions for substantial flows of people, materials and energy across an urban landscape and to fund, either through taxation or user fees, the capital and operational costs involved. Claus Offe's insights (see, for example, Offe, 1985; for a review see O'Neill, 1996) into the role of the state in mediating the tensions between a post-war capitalism hungry for rapid growth and the political demands of the citizenry for better distributional outcomes might be usefully applied to the analysis of urban infrastructure provision. Important in assembling legitimacy as an infrastructure builder and operator is the way the state re-asserts its autonomy by never acting exclusively on behalf of vested interests be they commercial or community. In effect the state becomes as much the site for dispute, negotiation and settlement over infrastructure as it is the decision maker, for rarely do commercial and community groups agree on the selection of infrastructure projects, their design and their funding. Capital will seek to minimise its contribution to the costs of infrastructure provision and the minimisation of negative externalities while acting to maximise investment in infrastructure which raises factor productivity and enlarges markets. On the other hand, communities will lobby for infrastructure which improves liveability, local amenity and environmental sustainability. Thus the state inevitably holds contradictory positions (which, according to Offe, have no pure resolution) as it seeks to advance economic growth and profitability while pursing legitimisation and urban amenity goals. The tensions that arise in infrastructure decision making are thus impossible to resolve consistently, such is the heaviness of the politics in play (drawing on Offe, 1985).

The intensity of these politics is played out in three major ways. One is through the determination of which projects will be undertaken. So fraught is the selection process, with the presence of limited resources within the state apparatus to expend on the time and cost involved, governments have always had a tendency to delegate the commissioning process to quasi-external agencies. In the post-war 20th-century period, these were state-owned enterprises and utilities which acted at arm's length from governments. With growing privatisation of the sector it is increasingly common for governments to establish seemingly independent infrastructure management entities such as Infrastructure UK, Infrastructure Australia, Infrastructure Canada, and France's Commission Nationale du Débat.

A second political terrain is formed around funding. Here we need to distinguish between infrastructure financing and infrastructure funding (see Kim, 2016). Financing refers to the process of supplying capital to build and initiate an infrastructure asset. Financing might be delivered as equity (with the rewards of ownership and control over the asset) or as debt (with repayment and interest benefits), with each class of finance generating significant contractual obligations. Funding is different from financing and refers to the revenue stream available to meet the cost of financing; a distinction that has become increasingly important with finance now rarely provided by governments as direct non-repayable grants. Funding usually takes one of two forms: taxation or user charges. Obviously, then, how to fund infrastructure is a vexed question requiring complex political negotiations. At times of prolonged economic growth, such as occurred in the decades following the Second World War, the politics of funding infrastructure via taxation might be relatively inert given the costs of infrastructure construction might be easily covered by rising revenues from the taxpaying public. During stagnant economic periods, however, increased taxes are not popular even though the reason they are levied might be sound. User charges require different though no less fractious political negotiations. Infrastructure users – commuters, energy and water consumers, and business operators – are usually hostile to the high infrastructure user charges needed to generate the revenues to fund expensive construction and operation. In conjunction, user fees invariably have undesirable distributive consequences with poorer households denied the level of access to essential urban services compared to better-off households. Graham and Marvin (2001) capture the consequences of this inequity through the vivid metaphor 'splintering urbanism'.

Graham and Marvin's work extends our analysis to the third political contention of infrastructure, which is that of design, with all its complexities. The design of an infrastructure asset needs to consider its basic engineering precepts, its location and field of operation, how it connects with other infrastructure assets and networks, and the positive and negative externalities that are designed in and designed out. Clearly some will benefit more than others from these design outcomes, and there may well be net losers. Design of infrastructure, then, becomes a major political concern.

Historical resolutions to the politics of infrastructure

As we have seen, infrastructure was not magically invented in the 20th century by governments deploying Keynesian fiscal strategies. The need for an infrastructure base proceeded hand-in-glove with 18th and 19th century-industrialisation and economic modernisation with roads, railways, bridges and canals delivered by both state and private means. Infrastructure assets and their transformative passages and corridors through urban and rural territories were essential to early capitalism, as we have seen, for the assembly of labour and other factors of production and for the distribution of products to markets. Infrastructure enabled larger numbers of people to live in towns and cities. Supply chains could reach further into the countryside, and the growth of markets enabled the specialisations and divisions of labour that fuelled the growth of profits and the accumulation of capital.

Yet there *was* something intrinsically Keynesian about infrastructure investments in the decades following the Great Depression and the Second World War. Keynesian policies legitimised the commitment of government spending to infrastructure. The support of private enterprise flowed because of the commercial benefits, as did the backing of a wider electorate keen to see urban and suburban amenity enhanced as cities grew upwards and outwards. In addition, the Keynesian model readily embraced technological advancements and the need for investment in electricity grids, urban transit systems, telecommunications and broadcasting systems, and air routes. Infrastructure's very large economic multiplier benefits were a bonus.

Importantly, just as we have seen in the case of 'infrastructural Europeanism' earlier, infrastructure investment in the post-war period also created and expanded nation-state capacities. These included the development of urban planning, a government ministry essential to the rollout of post-war suburbanisation with infrastructure spending delivering value uplift to land subdivisions and related property developments. Also important was the creation of a new entity, the utility, an ownership and organisational vehicle that became the commonsense way that infrastructure was delivered. Here civic society, such as through its representation on the boards of utilities, gained a direct say in infrastructure design and rollout. This presence boosted public acceptance of the utilities' claim on monopoly power and their independence from formal politics, even though they relied heavily on finance flows funded from public balance sheets (Beasley, 1988).

By the late 1960s, there was near enough to universal acceptance of the importance of public investment in the passageways and conduits that enabled efficient flows of people, goods, water, energy and information in cities. Two things were important here (see O'Neill, 2014). First, infrastructure became a subsumed political process. Infrastructure was funded off the public sector balance sheet without political contestation. Then its procurement and provisioning were handled by state utilities with a corps of planners and engineers who, by and large, operated autonomously in evaluating urban infrastructure needs and finding technical and financial solutions. Importantly, within this apparatus of infrastructural venture, the risk of failure was accepted within the wider ambit of the state.

Second, infrastructure became a subsumed socio-spatial process as each new infrastructure item was bundled, synchronised and sequenced with pre-existing items. Sometimes this integration was planned for; but it also occurred as a matter of course, embedded in the daily work practices of the state apparatus: its utilities, government departments and ministries. Crucially, political endorsement flowed, reinforced by the norm of universal access; by the complementarities and externalities generated by the infrastructure rollout; by income and employment multiplier effects from construction; and from productivity improvements across the economy. In turn, enhanced economic growth rates yielded restorative public revenues.

It is a paradox that so effective was the state's design of the utility as a creator and distributor of infrastructure value that the task of infrastructure privatisation was a relatively easy one in later decades. From around the 1980s, forces in favour of infrastructure privatisation coalesced around issues of declining sovereignty in the face of globalisation, slowing economic growth rates, constraints on states' fiscal capacities, and a loss of confidence in the effectiveness of the state apparatus to supply essential public services. A common response was to source resuscitation programmes from the handbooks of neoliberalism based around the deployment of private capital in market-controlled systems of production and distribution. Agreement about infrastructure's commissioning, design, funding, ownership and operation, and about its use as a device in planning and building cities, and in aiding commerce, became confused at first and then vigorously contested. The shift to private procurement, financing and operation took about three decades in most advanced nations, such was the deeply entrenched nature of the utilities and state-owned enterprises in the urban infrastructure sector. In these decades there were many failed experiments in the commissioning and operation of private infrastructure assets alongside numerous instances when the transfer of public assets to private hands occurred without the state maximising commercial value or devising appropriate regulatory structures to minimise practices such as price gouging in circumstances where little or no supply choice existed. There were also bold experiments in heavily geared investment structures and synthetic financial products, many of which collapsed during the financial crisis, as did similar experiments in other investment classes. Yet despite market failure, and the recklessness and dishonesty that exaggerated the intensity of the financial crisis in the infrastructure sector, there is now an established presence in urban infrastructure of private financing, procurement, construction, operation, perhaps even regulation. A discussion of the nature of this maturing presence follows in the next section.

New modes of infrastructure financing

Within the general argument about the (potentially conflicting) roles and responsibilities of the public and private sectors in a modern economy, there is an ongoing public consternation about private ownership and private investment practices in urban infrastructure. On the one hand, as we have seen, the development and operation of infrastructure creates an integrated urban platform for collective use by a city's businesses and householders. This ensemble of activity enhances urban infrastructure's public good characteristics. On the other hand, infrastructure assets are being plucked from bundled utilities to operate as discrete private assets with their own revenue streams and independent managers that seek to maximise returns on private investment (O'Neill, 2009). Not surprisingly, these new arrangements come with new political tensions. There is a continuing project within a city's polity and its technocracy that sees infrastructure as needing to be planned and operated such that the functions and parts of a city are integrated, efficient and sustainable. At the same time, however, interest among private asset managers in wider urban management questions elevates attention to those matters bearing on the profitability of the asset for which they are responsible. We return to this issue later.

As we have seen, infrastructure has a number of characteristics which have enabled its transformation from entities designed to enable the flows of things in and around cities to entities capable of extracting private earnings from the monetisation of these flows. That said, it should be understood that infrastructure as an investment class has expanded beyond the textbook definition of infrastructure as a public good or natural monopoly. Infrastructure as an investment class includes more market-sensitive (and potentially competitive) assets like ports, airports and telecommunications installations; organisational entities that own infrastructure operating rights like an infrastructure services corporation; packages of urban services and amenities – quasi-infrastructure assets – that are demand-inelastic like parking meters and funeral service providers; and debt contracts and securities with rights over revenue streams from infrastructure user tolls. As investment items within their own asset class, then, the value of infrastructure assets to their owners involves a new set of qualities, ones related as much to financial measures like liquidity, risk and yield than to contributions to urban efficiency and amenity. Similarly, the performance of an infrastructure asset under for-profit arrangements is maximised by having exclusive rights over the urban thoroughfares where the flows of people, materials, energy and information are assigned and therefore to the revenues collected from users of these flows. Finally, there is a concomitant search for ways to privatise infrastructure's positive externalities, such as by securing property rights and value uplift in an area to be serviced, say, by a new metro line.

The general direction, then, is for a transformation of infrastructure assets from publicly provided entities that enable a city's economic and social functioning into the hands of commercial providers of services to markets where consumption is pretty much inelastic, meaning cash returns are generated on a regular, predictable basis over a very long time period. Certainly, exotic financial products and ownership structures were wrapped around these flows in the

1990s and early-mid 2000s. But the global financial crisis stripped much of these away leaving an asset class backed by genuine and observable value to a private investor. Moreover, infrastructure assets as investment products come with fairly simple metrics – traffic counts, usage rates, daily toll earnings – capable of being understood and verified through desktop checks by remote fund managers. The visibility of stable, long-term yields has made infrastructure products a natural fit for financing from superannuation and pension funds that carry the long-term responsibility to protect and moderately enhance the value of members' retirement savings or employers' paid-up obligations thereof.

The rise of the infrastructure investment sector has also generated a new set of institutional players in infrastructure provision and operation. First there are those companies spawned by the privatisation of major utilities in the 1980s and 1990s, chiefly in the electricity and telecommunications sectors in the UK and Western Europe. Many of these companies have subsequently grown through mergers and acquisitions into truly global corporations. The next group are the major banks, especially the large banks from North America, Europe and East Asia. These banks take multiple positions in infrastructure investing. In their role as capital aggregators, they contribute both debt and equity capital in major infrastructure deals. They are also key advisers to both investors and governments in transacting new and brownfield infrastructure investments, and they also operate independent investment funds. Major competitors to the banks are the savings aggregators, including the major pension funds, insurance companies and trusts, and some of the larger sovereign wealth funds. A key recent feature of investment practices among this group is a desire for direct investment, control and management of infrastructure assets in order to avoid the substantial fees that are payable to other agencies when these roles are outsourced, say to managed funds (Clark & Monk, 2013). There are also the multidisciplinary corporations, typically large, listed, former construction companies which have witnessed the gains available from taking equity positions in large infrastructure projects, alongside direct roles in construction contracts and project finance initiation. There are the specialist funds as well, in many ways a legacy group from the first wave of private infrastructure investing; but because of their control over many key assets sold in early wave privatisations, they maintain a major market presence often due to the strategic nature of their asset portfolios. And, finally, there is China which is keenly exploring a global role in infrastructure financing and provision, using a mix of the modes listed above. At times China operates as a direct investor, such as in resources infrastructure in Africa. It also operates as a direct lender and as a contributor to open and closed specialist funds, some based in Hong Kong, that undertake their own direct investment infrastructure projects. China also takes offshore infrastructure investment positions through its state-owned enterprises where it has powerful entities operating across all infrastructure platforms including energy, water, ports, airports and transport.

The replacement of the vertically integrated public utilities by portfolios of commercial, tradeable assets also requires the full kit of soft technologies, stabilised practices and industry service providers. At initiation, there is intense activity by professional services firms bringing public utilities and assets to market. Engineering firms conduct detailed appraisals of public infrastructure assets to ascertain the competence and life span of the material assets. Legal firms design new organisational structures, many with complex trustee, general partner and limited partner roles, to provide vehicles capable of controlling and dispersing revenues over long time periods. Financial services firms and merchant banks construct capital and refinancing structures to match the peculiar financing requirements of infrastructure assets over the investment life-cycle to appetites of infrastructure investors. A consequence of the intense participation of the finance sector's professional firms has been the inculcation of the infrastructure sector with established sets of calculative practices (see, for example, Mackenzie, 2006; Mitchell, 2007), and reasonably well-proven organisational and capital structures which enable, simultaneously, operation by professional managers, monitoring by government agencies (especially treasury officials) and investment activity by funds and savings aggregators. Moreover, because infrastructure investing post-dates the refinement of modern debt-driven financial practices, the monetisation of infrastructure assets and the sector's acceptance as a discrete class of investment assets (alongside, say, equities, property and private wealth) has reached maturity very quickly with infrastructure investors now concerned at the limited number of proven brownfield assets coming to market. This speed of acceptance has generated a mature investment landscape where the aspirations of 1990s policy makers for public gains from competitive practices and private sector operational efficiencies appear largely to have been disappointed.

Finally, a new regulatory regime for the infrastructure sector has been generated, although one characterised by opportunism and narrow, privately negotiated obligations and constraints rather than by transparent, institutionalised rules. Certainly there are various state experiments in the formal regulation of private infrastructure investing involving, for example, templated public-private partnership initiatives in Canada (Siemiatycki, n.d.), and across the UK more generally. Yet these practices have progressed little beyond their domestic territories with evidence of only modest international learning and no moves as yet towards transnational standardisation. Yet, as we have seen, infrastructure investing is so instilled with legal rights and protections that the prescription of powers and duties cannot be avoided. Here we can use the insights of Helm and Tindall (2009) who demonstrate the role of legal contracts as proxy regulatory devices with each side of an investment relationship (in this case in the infrastructure sector) having a substantial interest in the strength of these contracts. For the state, there is the need to ensure an asset delivers expected infrastructure services over its life course and that charges to consumers are fair and acceptable given the prevalence of monopoly positions for the new infrastructure owners and operators. For the investor, there is the need for adequate returns to cover operating costs and to ensure fixed costs are recoverable at a reasonable rate over the life of the asset. There is also the need for ownership assurance, seen by the investor as a primary way of managing risk given the high level of uncertainty surrounding a large urban infrastructure asset through lengthy time periods (see also Stern, 2012). Yet given the peculiar nature of the infrastructure sector, and therefore the unlikelihood of being able to import pre-existing regulatory devices and processes from other sectors or jurisdictions, infrastructure contracts between governments and investors have invariably been constructed on an ad hoc basis. Typically, the content of such contracts includes the functions of monitoring and control as well as prescriptions as to ownership rights, including property rights, market conditions, protection from competition, and so on and so forth. Helm and Tindall (2009, p. 149) conclude that, 'Because of this complex interplay of political and economic factors, each privatisation [has] had its own unique characteristics and, not surprisingly, the outcome of the privatisation programme as a whole [has been] a messy one'. Clearly, analysis of the role of privatised regulation in the infrastructure sector is a topic needing major research. Guidance as to its direction comes specifically from Cutler (2010) but also from the regulatory capitalism literature including Braithwaite (2008), Braithwaite and Drahos (2000) and David Levi-Faur (e.g. 2012; Levi-Faur & Gilad, 2004). Application of this literature to the development of the privatised and financialised infrastructure sector is urgently needed.

Conclusion

The infrastructure sector is too important to the quality of life in our cities to be free to evolve as a relatively unregulated new economic venture. The privatisation and financialisation of the sector introduces a conundrum: how is it possible in infrastructure management to prioritise actions to generate long-term financial returns from infrastructure investment and at the same time generate the raft of services and their externalities expected by a city's economic community and the wider public. The direction beckoned by privatised and financialised infrastructure now seems likely to be dominated by assets which are owned and managed privately; organised into discrete functional and organisational entities; have monetised costs and returns; have known and apportioned financial and operational risks; and to be controlled by bespoke regulatory arrangements where the financial viability of the asset could well be prioritised ahead of the functioning efficiency of its host city.

The problem with this direction, however, is that the absence of collective interest in the general condition of a city – economically, socially and environmentally – invariably undermines its economic and social health and thereby the profitability of any infrastructure asset. So a broader public interest must always take priority over the interests of the operators of any individual asset, which means there is a need for principles to guide infrastructure platforms for 21st-century cities that are just, prosperous and sustainable. The principles of universality, bundling, accessibility and being generative of positive externalities are four worthy of retention.

Yet adopting these principles in today's diverse, continually changing cities requires new approaches. A return to vertically integrated utility structures is impossible, and probably undesirable in a 21st-century hybrid economic setting. The point is that contributing to the public good by the urban infrastructure platform is essential, but it is not necessary that this be done by the public sector. Of course, only the public sector can provide the regulatory power to ensure infrastructure provision in cities; and surely the public sector is the organisational place for insistence on wider benefits beyond financial returns both for infrastructure assets and for infrastructure-in-aggregate. The state has the primary role to play as regulator and organiser. Then, in such a context, the dynamic efficiencies of private for-profit ventures might best drive successful 21st-century cities.

References

Amin, A. & Thrift, N. (2002) *Cities: Reimagining the Urban*. Cambridge, UK: Polity Press.

Beasley, M. (1988) *The Sweat of their Brows*. Sydney: Sydney Water Board.

Braithwaite, J. (2008) *Regulatory Capitalism: How It Works, Ideas for Making It Work Better*. Cheltenham, UK: Edward Elgar Publishing.

Braithwaite, J. & Drahos, P. (2000) *Global Business Regulation*. Melbourne: Cambridge University Press.

Brenner, N. & Schmid, C. (2015) 'Towards a new epistemology of the urban?' *City*, 19, pp. 151–182.

Clark, G.L. & Monk, A.H.B. (2013) 'The scope of financial institutions: In-sourcing, outsourcing and off-shoring', *Journal of Economic Geography*, 13, pp. 279–298.

Coase, R.H. (1939) 'Review', *The Economic Journal*, 49, pp. 757–758.

Coase, R.H. (1947) 'The origin of the monopoly of broadcasting in Great Britain', *Economica*, New Series, 14, pp. 189–210.

Coase, R.H. (1950) 'The nationalization of electricity supply in Great Britain', *Land Economics*, 26, pp. 1–16.

Coase, R.H. (1961) 'The British Post Office and the messenger companies', *The Journal of Law & Economics*, 4, pp. 12–65.

Coase, R.H. (1970) 'The theory of public utility pricing and its application', *The Bell Journal of Economics and Management Science*, 1, pp. 113–128.

Coase, R.H. (1974) 'The lighthouse in economics', *Journal of Law and Economics*, 17, pp. 357–376.

Cutler, A.C. (2010) 'The legitimacy of private transnational governance: Experts and the transnational market for force', *Socio-Economic Review*, 8, pp. 157–185.

Doig, J.W. (2001) *Empire on the Hudson: Entrepreneurial Vision and Political Power at the Port of New York Authority*. New York: Columbia University Press.

Graham, S. & Marvin, S. (2001) *Splintering Urbanism: Networked Infrastructures, Technological Mobilities, and the Urban Condition.* London: Routledge.

Harvey, D. (1985) *The Urbanization of Capital: Studies in the History and Theory of Capitalist Urbanization.* Baltimore, MD: Johns Hopkins University Press.

Helm, D. & Tindall, T. (2009) 'The evolution of infrastructure and utility ownership and its implications', *Oxford Review of Economic Policy*, 25, pp. 411–434.

Hughes, T.P. (1983) *Networks of Power: Electrification in Western Society, 1880–1930.* Baltimore, MD: Johns Hopkins Press.

Jacobs, J. (1961) *The Death and Life of Great American Cities.* New York: Random House.

Kim, J. (2016) *Handbook on Urban Infrastructure Finance.* New Cities Foundation, online at www.newcitiesfoundation.org.

Laborie, L. (2011) 'Fragile links, frozen identities: The governance of telecommunications networks and Europe', *History and Technology*, 27, pp. 311–330.

Lagendijk, V. (2011) '"An experience forgotten today": Examining two rounds of electricity liberalization', *History and Technology*, 27, pp. 291–310.

Lakoff, G. (1987) *Women, Fire and Dangerous Things: What Categories Reveal about the Mind.* Chicago, IL: University of Chicago Press.

Levi-Faur, D. (Ed.) (2012) *The Oxford Handbook of Governance.* Oxford, UK: Oxford University Press.

Levi-Faur, D. & Gilad, S. (2004) 'Review: The rise of the British regulatory state – Transcending the privatization debate', *Comparative Politics*, 37, pp. 105–124.

MacKenzie, D. (2006) *An Engine, Not a Camera: How Financial Models Shape Markets.* Cambridge MA: MIT Press.

Mitchell, T. (2007) 'The properties of markets', in MacKenzie, D.A., Muniesa, F. & Siu, L. (Eds.), *Do Economists Make Markets? On the Performativity of Economics.* Princeton, NJ: Princeton University Press, pp. 244–275.

Offe, C. (1985) *Contradictions of the Welfare State.* Cambridge, MA: MIT Press.

O'Neill, P.M. (1996) 'In what sense a region's problem? The place of redistribution in Australia's internationalisation strategy', *Regional Studies*, 30, pp. 405–415.

O'Neill, P.M. (2009) 'Infrastructure investment and the management of risk', in Clark, G.L., Dixon A.D. and Monk A.H.B. (Eds.), *Managing Financial Risks: From Global to Local.* Oxford, UK: Oxford University Press, pp. 163–188.

O'Neill, P.M. (2014) 'How infrastructure became a structured investment vehicle', in Roche, M., Mansvelt, J., Prince, R. & Gallagher, A. (Eds.), *Engaging Geographies: Landscapes Life Courses, and Mobilities.* Newcastle, UK: Cambridge Scholars Press, pp. 29–44.

Petkantchin, V. (2006) 'Is *The Wealth of Nations*' third duty of the sovereign compatible with laissez faire?' *Journal of Libertarian Studies*, 20, pp. 3–15.

Samuelson, P.A. (1954) 'The pure theory of public expenditure', *Review of Economics and Statistics*, 36, pp. 387–389.

Schipper, F. & Schot, J. (2011) 'Infrastructural Europeanism, or the project of building Europe on infrastructures: An introduction', *History and Technology*, 27, pp. 245–265.

Scott, A.J. & Storper, M. (2015) 'The nature of cities: The scope and limits of urban theory', *International Journal of Urban and Regional Research*, 39, pp. 1–15.

Siemiatycki, M. (n.d.) *Is There a Distinctive Canadian PPP Model? Reflections on Twenty Years of Practice*, mimeo. Department of Geography and Program in Planning, University of Toronto

Smith, A. (1976 [1776]) *An Inquiry into the Nature and Causes of the Wealth of Nations.* 2 volumes. Campbell, R.H. Skinner A.S. & Todd W.B. (Eds.). Oxford, UK: Oxford University Press.

Stern, J. (2012) 'The relationship between regulation and contracts in infrastructure industries: Regulation as ordered renegotiation', *Regulation & Governance*, 6, pp. 474–498.

West, E.G. (1977) 'Adam Smith's public economics: A re-evaluation', *Canadian Journal of Economics*, 10, pp. 1–18.

21

STEPPING OUT OF THE COMFORT ZONE?

An examination of regional orientation in emerging-economy MNEs' cross-border M&As

Yoo Jung Ha, Yingqi Wei and Yaoan Wu

Introduction

The geographic orientation of multinational enterprises (MNEs) has long attracted scholarly attention. Rugman and colleagues have argued that MNEs are regionally rather than globally oriented, and that such geographic orientation has a positive performance impact (Rugman, 2003, 2005; Rugman & Verbeke, 2004, 2005; Lee & Rugman, 2012; Rugman, Oh & Lim, 2012). In a parallel work, Ghemawat argues that today's environment should be characterised as "semi-globalisation", because empirical evidence on cross-border integration, including product-market integration (trade flows, foreign direct investment (FDI) and price) and factor-market integration (capital, labour and knowledge), shows that most measures still fall far short of "perfect integration" as envisaged by economic theory (Ghemawat, 2003, 2007). Studies have shown that large MNEs from developed economies (DMNEs) focus on their home region in the triad as this strategy can minimise costs of doing business across subsidiaries operating in nearby countries (Rugman & Verbeke, 2005). Examining data on the activities of the 500 largest MNEs from triad economies, Rugman and Verbeke (2004) find evidence of home-region bias. This research supports regional MNE theory (Rugman, 2005; Rugman & Verbeke, 2005; Lee & Rugman, 2012; Oh & Li, 2015) by proposing that regional distribution of MNEs' international activities focuses on leveraging home-region-specific assets. However, the empirical evidence so far is based on DMNEs. What could be expected of regional orientation of emerging-economy MNEs (EMNEs)?

EMNEs, relative to DMNEs, are at an early stage of their lifecycle, and their firm-specific assets are likely to be home-based and location-bound. It can thus be argued that in terms of regional orientation, EMNEs are not different from DMNEs and can be subject to home-region bias. However, this argument overlooks the fact that EMNEs often have different motives from DMNEs. While DMNEs often venture abroad to exploit existing firm-specific assets, EMNEs employ cross-border M&As (CBMAs) to acquire strategic assets possessed by developed economy firms so as to overcome latecomer disadvantages and to address competitive weakness in international markets (Buckley et al., 2007; Lu, Liu & Wang, 2011; Kedia, Gaffney & Clampit, 2012;

Buckley, Elia & Kafouros, 2014). For strategic asset-seeking EMNEs, they could find valuable strategic assets in a host region with more favourable institutional environments than the home region (Luo & Tung, 2007). Therefore, their strategic intent in geographic orientation could be to counter home-region bias and favour the non-home region as host location (Makino, Lau & Yeh, 2002; Sethi et al., 2003; Crescenzi, Pietrobelli & Rabellotti, 2016).

To the best of our knowledge, there has been a lack of research about factors driving EMNEs' departure from the home region (Jormanainen & Koveshnikov, 2012; Oh & Li, 2015). This study fills this research gap by focusing on EMNEs' CBMAs in developed economies and investigating factors influencing EMNEs' regional decisions for conducting CBMAs inside or outside of the home region.

We adopt institutional theory which has been noted as offering key explanations of DMNEs' CBMAs in emerging economies (Lebedev et al., 2015; Wei & Wu, 2015), but has rarely been considered in the studies of CBMAs by EMNEs in developed economies. In MNEs' regional strategy, both the selection of a regional and that of a host country to be an entry platform into the region matter (Rugman & Verbeke, 2004; Flores & Aguilera, 2007). Institutional homogeneity validates a region as a cluster of associated countries and it is therefore a relevant level of analysis of MNEs' geographic orientation. Hence, we focus on the level of institutional development of the host region relative to the home region and that of the platform country relative to the region to which it belongs. Further, we explore the mimetic effects due to peer EMNEs' agglomeration effects in the host location as a moderator.

For the empirical analysis, we obtained firm-level data from the Thomson Financial Security Data Corporation (SDC) Platinum Database and the Lexi-Nexis Academic Universe Database. Based on useable cases we focus on 530 CBMA deals made by 401 EMNEs from 34 emerging economies in 22 OECDE countries during 2000–2010. Using World Economic Forum (WEF) data, we developed country and regional institutional scores.

This study contributes to the existing CBMA literature in a few ways. Theoretically, grounded in institutional theory, we propose a conceptual framework of EMNEs' nested regional location decision that involves both regional- and country-level dimensions. More specifically, we explore the impact of the institutional development of a target region and that of an entry-platform country simultaneously. This research complements existing CBMA studies that often analyse country-level factors from resource-based or transaction-cost-minimising perspectives in the fields of accountancy, finance, economics and general management (Shimizu et al., 2004; Bauer & Matzler, 2014).

Empirically, we use a unique dataset combining a firm's CBMA location decision and institutional factors, providing new insights into EMNE internationalisation in general and EMNEs' geographical orientation in particular. The home-region bias that is currently found to be the case for DMNEs needs attention in the EMNE context. Our findings suggest that regional institutions matter to EMNEs' geographic orientation.

In the following sections, we first provide a literature review and introduce the theoretical background. We then derive our hypothesis, which is followed by sections on data and methodology and empirical results, respectively. The final section offers discussions and a conclusion.

Literature review and theoretical background

EMNEs' geographic orientation and non-home region

EMNEs refer to companies which originate from emerging economies (EEs) and are involved in outward FDI in one or more foreign countries. EMNEs have some unique features. First, most EMNEs are successful in the domestic market but are less competitive internationally (Child & Rodrigues, 2005). Hence, many EMNEs engage in CBMAs to gain access to foreign strategic assets to improve their global competitiveness. Second, EMNEs are likely to be backed by governments or are state-owned (Bekaert & Harvey, 2002; Buckley et al., 2007). With home-country institutional supports such as government underwriting and funding, it is expected that EMNEs can not only enhance their leading positions at home, but also seek opportunities in foreign markets (Luo & Tung, 2007; Ramasamy, Yeung, & Laforet, 2012).

This research focuses particularly on CBMAs conducted as part of an EMNE strategy to augment cross-regionally fungible firm-specific assets. Firm-specific assets bestow competitive advantage on a firm and can be acquired through several channels including internal R&D, cumulative experience, licensing, strategic alliance and CBMA. There are reasons why CBMA is a preferred mode for strategic asset-seeking EMNEs (Sun et al., 2012). For instance, with other modes more likely to be subject to market failure and high transaction costs, CBMAs overcome market failure and promote organisational learning by offering closer contacts and interactions between EMNEs and firms in developed economies, which is much needed if EMNEs are to fully benefit from the acquired strategic assets (Rabbiosi, Elia & Bertoni, 2012).

In recent decades, EMNEs have increasingly employed CBMAs to venture abroad (see Appendix 21.A). However, CBMAs by EMNEs have received little attention in academic research until recently, and existing studies tend to focus on their expansion into developing countries (Jormanainen & Koveshnikov, 2012). There is limited in-depth analysis of geographical orientation in EMNEs' internationalisation strategy (Ramasamy, Yeung & Laforet, 2012; Crescenzi, Pietrobelli & Rabellotti, 2016). This research focuses on EMNEs' regional decision in conducting CBMAs in developed economies.

In regional MNE theory, an MNE's competitiveness is linked to regional- as well as country-level strategies. This is because firm-specific assets can be fungible within a region due to intra-regional institutional homogeneity, but the assets' value could decline in a non-home region due to the liabilities of inter-regional foreignness (Rugman & Verbeke, 2004; Rugman, Oh & Lim, 2012). Hence, the region is a relevant unit of analysis in MNEs' locational decisions, which thus have a nested structure – the regional decision about whether to go beyond the home region to acquire cross-regional assets and a nested decision to select a host country which can provide an entry platform for the region (Arregle et al., 2013).

We argue that EMNEs conduct CBMAs in non-home regions in order to acquire host region-based strategic assets that are unavailable in the home region. When liabilities of inter-regional foreignness are high and a firm's assets are home-based, asset fungibility is suppressed and firms incur high costs in cross-regional expansion (Lee & Rugman, 2012). By contrast, the ownership of non-location-bound or host-location-based assets will allow an EMNE to enjoy cross-regional fungibility and expedite international diversification. Thus, EMNEs use CBMA to acquire host region-based assets and quickly augment cross-regional fungibility in firm-specific assets. We consider the role of both a region and a specific country's relative position in a region in determining an EMNE's decision to select a non-home region for CBMA activities. More specifically, we focus on an institutional perspective, highlighting the influence of institutional factors.

Institutional environment and CBMAs

The institutional context provides a foundation for firm activities and business transactions (Trevino, Thomas & Cullen, 2008). Institutions set the rules of the game that organisations have to follow to gain legitimacy and recognition from local stakeholders (North, 1990; Kostova & Zaheer, 1999; Eden & Miller, 2004). Institutions offer incentives and constraints which structure the characteristics, behaviours and managerial actions of firms (Schoenberg, 2006; Trevino, Thomas & Cullen, 2008; Meyer & Sinani, 2009). Moreover, institutions affect firm strategy through influencing the efficiency and effectiveness of business activities, resource allocations and incentives for business activities (Peng, Wang & Jiang, 2008). Therefore, an MNE's strategy, including its location strategy for CBMAs, is expected to be influenced by the broader institutional context, in addition to firm-specific resources. Though increasingly the role of institutions in EMNEs' CBMAs is recognised in the literature, studies remain limited (Lin et al., 2009; Zhang, Zhou & Ebbers, 2011; Stucchi, 2012; Lebedev et al., 2015; Wei & Wu, 2015). This research therefore contributes to this emerging strand of the literature by examining institutional factors in influencing an EMNE's location decision when conducting CBMAs in developed countries.

Legal and regulative institutions, such as laws, government policies and administrative institutions, determine the formal structure of rights in transactions and exchanges, and also determine the costs of making such transactions and exchanges (Dikova, Sahib & van Witteloostuijn, 2010). Acquirer firms are affected by both host country formal institutions, such as regulatory scrutiny of CBMA deals, and the home country formal institutions, such as policies governing outward FDI (Bittlingmayer & Hazlett, 2000). This complexity in the formal institutional context increases CBMA costs. Additionally, firms' operations are deeply affected by a location's normative and cognitive institutional factors (Dikova, Sahib & van Witteloostuijn, 2010). In the case of CBMAs, a key challenge is to work out how the resources of the acquirer firm and those of the acquired firm can be combined and put to most productive use through informal and formal governance mechanisms (Abdi & Aulakh, 2012). This is a process of change and is bound to be affected by normative and cognitive institutions.

Overall, an EMNE's regional orientation for CBMAs is likely to depend on whether the overall regional institutional environment is suitable for the EMNE. A region's attractiveness is also influenced by whether it includes an entry-platform country with an institutional environment that can support an EMNE's initial acquisition of regional strategic assets and consecutive penetration across countries in the region. Combining insights from both regional MNE theory and institutional theory, the following section will develop specific hypotheses concerning the influence of institutions at different levels on the regional distribution of EMNEs' CBMAs.

Hypotheses

Regional institution

Concerning geographical orientation, whether a firm favours a host country with better or similar institutional environments for FDI compared to its home country has gained scholarly attention (Liu et al., 1997; Kim & Aguilera, 2015). Quality of the host country institution determines the effectiveness and proper functioning of local markets. A host country with advanced institutional environments in the form of, for example, well-functioning factor markets, few government interventions and an effective mechanism for contract enforcement, is attractive to MNEs undertaking FDI in general and CBMAs in particular (Dunning & Lundan, 2008; Holmes et al., 2013).

Taking a regional perspective, this research explores the role of regional institutions in EMNEs' CBMA location decisions. We argue that EMNEs compare the quality of institutional environments of all countries in a specific region with their home region. Different from DMNEs which are attracted to similar institutional environments to their home country, EMNEs have shown inclinations towards host countries with better institutional environments than their home country (Di Giovanni, 2005; Malhotra, Sivakumar & Zhu, 2009; Hyun & Kim, 2010; Luo, Xue & Han, 2010; Kim & Aguilera, 2015). Thus, it is plausible to argue that EMNEs can be attracted by favourable institutions in developed economies for region-based strategic asset-seeking (Luo & Tung, 2007).

If countries in a host region collectively have better institutions than the home region, it is likely that the EMNEs can generate returns from acquired regional assets within the host region. In other words, the expected fungibility of host region-based assets could be high. A well-developed regional institution will support intra-regional reliable market information, efficient intermediary organisations, predictable government actions and an efficient intra-regional bureaucracy (Khanna & Palepu, 1997; Chan, Isobe & Makino, 2008). In contrast, when the overall institutional quality of the host region is low relative to the home region, acquired assets by EMNEs cannot be competitive enough to go beyond the target host country within the region; in other words, the expected fungibility of host region-based assets will be low. Thus, we formulate the following hypothesis:

> **Hypothesis 1:** *The likelihood of EMNEs conducting CBMAs outside their home region is positively related to the level of institutional development of the host region relative to that of the home region.*

Regional platform's institutions

A regional locational decision can be influenced by relative country factors. This is because nested in the regional decision is a country in the region that is used as an entry platform to that region (Arregle et al., 2013). On the one hand, differences in the regional institutional context from an EMNE's home region represent opportunities from the target asset's predicted fungibility within a non-home region which complements the EMNE's home-bound assets with limited cross-regional fungibility. On the other hand, institutional differences in the host country where EMNEs conduct initial CBMAs to acquire regional assets present a challenge to establishing an entry platform for a regional strategy, if that is linked to an EMNE's unfamiliarity with local institutions. The question therefore is to what extent the institutions of the host country (an entry platform for an EMNE's regional strategy) influence the EMNE's regional orientation?

Institutional development in a host country indicates a level of familiarity for EMNEs and thus concerns operational challenges in seeking strategic assets that are fungible in the non-home region. Unfamiliarity and failure to comply with a country's institutions may cause loss of legitimacy, resulting in some degree of difficulty or sluggishness in asset acquisition and integration processes (Arregle et al., 2016). If a host country selected as an entry platform into the region has advanced institutional frameworks and is thereby too dissimilar to home, EMNEs face increased hazards and costs. Unfamiliar institutional frameworks could impede effective inter-firm formal contractual and informal relational mechanisms in the utilisation of acquired assets (Abdi & Aulakh, 2012). Furthermore, the institutional context influences business costs in operating in an unfamiliar environment after asset acquisition (Gaur & Lu, 2007). Inexperience with different institutions and problems in managing relationships at a distance could lead to the "liability of foreignness" and additional costs, for example costs of monitoring and negotiating, dispute settlement, opportunistic behaviour of acquired firms and lack of trust (Sun et al., 2012). Thus to achieve a balance between dealing with the challenging institutional environment of a host country and acquiring strategic assets, EMNEs are likely to scan all countries in a region and compare the institutions of a platform country relative to the regional institutions. We argue:

> **Hypothesis 2:** *An EMNE is more likely to conduct CBMA outside its home region when the level of institutions of a platform country is low relative to the target region's overall institutional development.*

Mimetic effects

Despite the potential benefits for EMNEs operating in developed economies in non-home regions, they have to deal with difficulties in accessing information, recognising cause-effect relationships and predicting the full range of possible outcomes. To overcome uncertainty and ambiguity in an unfamiliar institutional context, EMNEs are likely to be receptive to information implicit in the actions of other economic agents and imitate them (namely mimetic isomorphism) (DiMaggio & Powell, 1983; Lu, 2002).

For an EMNE, mimetic effects can be observed in two ways. First, a subsidiary may mimic other subsidiaries in the same MNE. Such intra-organisational mimetic effects explain how a firm's previous foreign-entry experience influences the likelihood of subsequent foreign entry and operation. However, many EMNEs are at an early stage of internationalisation and therefore do not have much experience to transfer across subsidiaries. As a result, intra-firm mimetic effects are limited. Second, a mimetic effect can be observed between independent firms originating from a similar context (Lu, 2002). Thus EMNEs from the same home country tend to gravitate towards the same location, either a region or a specific country (Yang & Hyland, 2012). In other words, an EMNE which has entered a location previously can influence the entry decisions of other EMNEs from the same home country. By locating proximately, EMNEs can benefit from imitation so as to gain a better understanding of such matters as local consumer preferences, local distribution channels, and develop managerial methods, marketing techniques and organisational forms congruent with the local institutional context (Collins et al., 2009). Empirical evidence supports inter-organisational mimetic behaviour amongst EMNEs from the same home country (Crescenzi, Pietrobelli & Rabellotti, 2016). Thus, we propose:

> **Hypothesis 3:** *The likelihood of EMNEs conducting CBMAs outside their home region is positively related to the agglomeration of EMNEs from the same home country within the target region or in the platform country.*

Data and methodology

Firm-level data were gathered from the SDC Platinum Database and the Lexi-Nexis Academic Universe Database. The SDC reports CBMA data completed by EMNEs. Lexi-Nexis records financial information of acquired firms, such as return on assets and earnings per share. To operationalise EMNEs' decisions to conduct CBMAs inside vs. outside their home region, we first identified emerging economies and home regions. The emerging economies under consideration are shown in Appendix 21.B. Eight countries (Chile, Czech Republic, Estonia, Hungary, Mexico, Poland, Slovakia and Turkey) considered as emerging economies became members of the OECD during the sampling period. Given our research interests, they were retained in the emerging-economy category. We define a region as supra-national in geographic terms, following the World Bank's definition. This means we identify a region in terms of a cluster of countries that are geographically close, following the regional MNE literature (Arregle et al., 2013). Appendix 21.C lists the countries by region in our sample.

To further specify CBMAs for strategic asset-seeking in developed economies, we narrowed the sample down to CBMAs conducted by EMNEs in OECD countries. As a result, we identified a sample containing 694 completed CBMA transactions by EMNEs from 37 emerging economies in 24 OECD countries during the period 2000–2010 (see Appendix 21.B[1]). As a result of careful screening of data, deleting observations with missing data and collating information from other sources such as company websites and reports, the final sample contains 530 completed CBMA deals by 401 EMNEs from 34 emerging economies in 22 OECD countries.

To operationalise institutional frameworks at the regional and national levels, we gathered data from WEF. The WEF publishes a *Global Competitiveness Report* every year, covering all countries in the world. It includes survey scores from executive opinion surveys about dimensions in institutional frameworks, with scores ranging from one (not desirable) to seven (desirable). The Report also includes other scores not based on the survey but from various secondary databases, such as the World Bank, which we excluded. We focus on the years 2010–2015, when the questionnaire is largely consistent. Institutional variables were created by taking a six-year average of annual scores. A detailed explanation of variable construction is presented below.

Dependent and key independent variables

The dependent variable (*Non-home Region*) is binary. We assign 1 if an EMNE's CBMA is conducted outside its home region and 0 otherwise.

This study considers two institution variables – regional institutional distance between the home and the host regions (*Regional institutions*) and a specific platform country's institutional development relative to the region to which it belongs (*Platform's institutions*). To capture them, country-specific institutional scores are generated in the first instance and then we develop matching measures for the variables.

Country-specific institutional scores are generated as a composite measure. We first extract from the WEF's database 16 survey items representing the legal and regulatory institutional environment of a country (see Appendix 21.D). Concerning normative and cognitive institutional environments, we extract five survey items based on Chao and Kumar (2010). We additionally incorporate four items capturing a country's corporate-governance quality, given the importance of corporate governance in the acquisition process (Abdi & Aulakh, 2012). The 25 scores are six-year averages of annual scores across 2010–2015. Following Holmes et al. (2013), a principal component analysis (PCA) was conducted. The test uses the above 25 institutional scores to capture a country's regulatory, normative and cognitive institutional dimensions. The PCA produces a single factor, which we confirmed based on Kaiser's Criterion and Scree test.

In order to measure *Regional institutions*, we first generate a region's weighted institutional scores, which capture overall institutional quality in the region (Arregle et al., 2013). This is measured as the weighted average of the institutional score of all countries in a region. The weight is based on a country's share of regional GDP (i.e. the country's GDP/sum of all countries' GDP in the region). We then compare the home and the host region's institutional scores.

Concerning *Platform's institutions*, i.e. institutional development in a platform country where the target firm is located, and which is considered an entry platform for the region, a region-relative institutional score is calculated (Arregle et al., 2013). Thus, *Platform's institutions* captures the host or platform country's institutional environment in comparison to all other countries in that region. More specifically, it is a country's institutional score relative to the region's weighted institutional score.

The mimetic effect is related to the agglomeration of other EMNEs from the same host country in the location. We measure mimetic effects at two levels – regional and specific-country levels. At the country level, *Country mimetic* is measured as the count of CBMA deals in the target country by other firms from the same home country. At the specific-region level, *Regional mimetic* is measured by the count of CBMA deals in the target region by other firms from the same home country.

Control variables

We include a few control variables. *Total asset* is a target firm's asset size. *Diversification* captures whether CBMA was conducted as a result of an EMNE's diversification strategy. If the acquirer's industry is different from the acquired firm (target)'s industry, 1 is assigned, or 0 otherwise. *Host country's RTA* is the count of regional trade agreements in the host country. *After 2008* is whether a CBMA was completed by 2008; it was expected that EMNE decisions regarding CBMAs may have been affected by restructuring in major developed economies following the financial crisis. If the deal was completed by 2008, 1 is assigned, or 0 if later. All continuous variables were log-transformed. All variables are mean-centred.

Empirical results

The correlation matrix and descriptive statistics are presented in Table 21.1. As the dependent variable concerning the choice of home vs. non-home region selection is binary, we conducted the logistic regressions with respect to key independent variables. Table 21.2 presents regression results.

Model 1 is a baseline model including control variables only. The coefficients of Total asset and Host country's RTA show that the size of target firm involved in the CBMA deal and the host country's trade openness have positive effects on non-home-region selection. Thus, our baseline model is consistent with predictions made in general CBMA literature and EMNE locational decision literature.

First, Hypothesis 1 suggests a positive effect from a host region's institutional development relative to that of an EMNE's home region. Model 2 reports a positive coefficient on *Regional institutions* ($b = 25.63$, $p<0.001$), which enables us to accept Hypothesis 1.

Hypothesis 2 concerns a positive effect of institutional development in the target country relative to the host region. In Model 3 we find a negative, but statistically insignificant, coefficient on *Platform's institutions*. Thus, we cannot accept Hypothesis 2.

Hypothesis 3 addresses the positive influence of mimetic effects which result from an agglomeration of EMNEs from the same country/region of origin. As explained earlier, we measure mimetic effects in two ways – based on firms from the same home country within a specific platform country or within a supra-national region. The results in Models 4 and 5 show coefficients of *Country mimetic* and *Regional mimetic* are statistically insignificant. While the stand-alone effects do not support Hypothesis 3, further analysis reports a positive coefficient for the interaction term *Regional institutions x Country mimetic* ($b = 10.60$, $p<0.05$). In other words, country-level mimetic effects can be revealed under the condition that the overall institutional quality of host regions increases relative to an EMNE's home region.

Table 21.1 Correlation matrix and descriptive statistics

		1	*2*	*3*	*4*	*5*	*6*	*7*	*8*	*9*
1	Non-home region	1.0000								
2	Total asset	0.1230**	1.0000							
3	After 2008	−0.0428	0.1256**	1.0000						
4	Host country's RTA	0.0941*	0.1474****	−0.0376	1.0000					
5	Diversification	−0.0091	−0.0523	0.0397	0.0019	1.0000				
6	Regional institutions	0.3837***	0.0301	−0.0095	−0.4429***	0.0388	1.0000			
7	Platform's institutions	−0.2652***	−0.0750+	0.0089	0.0534	0.0619	−0.4134***	1.0000		
8	Country mimetic	0.0523	−0.1582***	−0.1009*	−0.2739***	0.0081	0.2317***	0.0359	1.0000	
9	Regional mimetic	−0.0185	−0.0564	−0.0591	0.0692	−0.0283	0.0512	0.1196**	0.6643***	1.0000
	Mean	0.7434	0.0000	0.5151	−0.0700	0.8698	−0.0049	0.0359	0.0330	−0.0450
	Standard deviation	0.4372	0.1498	0.5002	0.5994	0.3368	0.4234	0.5831	1.1603	1.0091

+ *p<0.10*

* p<0.05

** p<0.01

*** p<0.001

Table 21.2 Empirical results (dependent variable: non-home region selection)

	1	*2*	*3*	*4*	*5*	*6*	*7*
Total asset	1.878**	0.799	0.801	1.012	0.760	0.964	0.832
	(0.644)	(0.847)	(0.865)	(0.867)	(0.853)	(0.856)	(0.833)
After 2008	−0.256	−0.264	−0.262	−0.226	−0.284	−0.168	−0.290
	(0.204)	(0.238)	(0.239)	(0.239)	(0.241)	(0.242)	(0.242)
Host country's RTA	0.294+	1.173***	1.128***	1.218***	1.147***	1.349***	1.100***
	(0.174)	(0.211)	(0.209)	(0.238)	(0.202)	(0.253)	(0.198)
Diversification	−0.0243	−0.163	−0.105	−0.0898	−0.123	−0.0747	−0.138
	(0.302)	(0.324)	(0.327)	(0.332)	(0.325)	(0.329)	(0.330)
Regional institutions		25.63***	25.23***	25.80**	24.16**	30.86***	21.93**
		(7.743)	(7.490)	(8.096)	(7.695)	(7.527)	(7.136)
Platform's institutions			−0.347	−0.381+	−0.314	−0.300	−0.316
			(0.228)	(0.226)	(0.229)	(0.232)	(0.217)
Country mimetic				0.166		3.130*	
				(0.110)		(1.398)	
Regional mimetic					−0.0976		−2.046
					(0.132)		(1.970)
Regional Institutions x Country mimetic						10.60*	
						(4.978)	
Platform's institutions x Country mimetic						0.0649	
						(0.212)	
Regional institutions x Regional mimetic							−6.826
							(7.192)
Platform's institutions x Regional mimetic							0.0714
							(0.233)
Constant	1.269***	7.931***	7.851***	7.998***	7.568***	9.343***	6.932***
	(0.303)	(2.177)	(2.100)	(2.260)	(2.153)	(2.124)	(2.005)
Wald chi^2	11.64***	40.23***	51.02***	48.16***	57.95***	52.02***	56.62***
df	4	5	6	7	7	9	9
Pseudo R^2	0.0214	0.279	0.283	0.288	0.285	0.292	0.289
N	530	530	530	530	530	530	530

Note: Robust standard errors in parentheses.

+ p<0.10

* p<0.05

** p<0.01

*** p<0.001

Discussion and conclusion

This research analyses the determinants of an EMNE's location decision for conducting CBMAs in developed economies by taking a regional perspective. It helps improve our understanding of EMNEs' regional orientation. Past studies have explored EMNEs' locational decisions in internationalisation, but paid limited attention to the conditions under which they go beyond their home region. Given the large number of CBMA deals being made outside home regions, we attempt to address the research gap by describing EMNEs' locational decisions as nested decisions involving both regional- and country-specific considerations, thereby overcoming limitations in existing literature. Theoretically we develop hypotheses by introducing regional MNE theory into an examination of EMNE's CBMA location decision. The previous CBMA literature has focused on technological asset-seeking as a motivation. Yet resource fungibility and regional bounds of assets have not been considered. Based on institutional theory, we have identified that both regional- and country-institutional factors could influence EMNEs' regional orientation, a decision that goes beyond the home region.

Our findings show the significance of regional institutions on an EMNE's decision to go beyond its home region to conduct CBMAs. More specifically, we find that an EMNE is likely to go beyond its home region when it can identify foreign assets that allow access to a region where the overall institutional level is higher than in its home region. This finding is consistent with our discussion that an EMNE's strategic intent is likely to be regional and to seek out host region-based and non-location-bound assets.

We could not find evidence supporting the significance of a platform country's institutional development relative to the region. We explain the rejection of our hypothesis based on the so-called bootstrapping hypothesis: when the acquirer's corporate governance quality is poorer than the target's, the acquirer voluntarily bootstraps the target's superior governance standard (Martynova & Renneboog, 2008).

Our findings also show that inter-firm mimetic forces within a platform country complement regional institutional effects. An EMNE's pursuit of foreign assets in an institutionally advanced region is even stronger when other EMNEs from the same country are clustered in a specific platform country within the region. Such a positive mimetic effect applies to EMNEs trying to enter regions with significant institutional differences from their home region. However, the mimetic effects do not compensate for unfamiliar institutional environments. This is perhaps because when EMNEs are clustered together, the agglomeration may result in negative congestion effects, cancelling out positive mimetic effects and rendering the overall interaction effects insignificant (Crescenzi, Pietrobelli & Rabellotti, 2016).

This research has some managerial implications. As we find many EMNEs seek strategic assets in non-home regions offering favourable institutional environments, high competition amongst EMNEs within regional markets can be expected. Thus, an EMNE may assess their peers' foreign-entry patterns by region and design a cross-regional competition strategy and formulate CBMA strategy. As we find significance in country-level mimetic effects, it is recommended that an EMNE considers any potential negative congestion effects caused by increased convergence in an EMNE's locational choice. The target firm in a developed economy may analyse the regional approach of strategic asset-seeking EMNEs and their mimetic behaviours in order to predict the inflow of firms pursuing M&A deals.

We conclude the chapter by acknowledging a few limitations. We use the World Bank definition of geographic region. There could be a robustness analysis based on alternative definitions of region. While we discuss the generation of host-based and cross-regional fungible assets as a background motive for EMNEs' regional decisions, our data cannot identify the quality and characteristics of acquired assets. Our institutional variables are based on a composite index. There could be some analysis showing how different institutional dimensions affect a firm's locational decisions. As for control variables, there could be more micro-level variables about a deal's characteristics and EMNE characteristics so as to capture the intricate interactions between exogenous institutional factors and firm-level factors. These are suggested as possible future research agendas.

Appendix 21.A The pattern of EMNEs' CBMAs in developed economies

Year	*Total FDI inflows*	*Number of CBMAs*			*Volume of CBMAs*		
	World (US$ m)	*World*	*Emerging economies*	*Share (%)*	*World (US$ m)*	*Emerging economies*	*Share (%)*
1991	154,072.7	1,582	101	6.38	21,094	2,254	10.69
1992	165,880.8	2,132	144	6.75	48,106	7,453	15.49
1993	223,316.3	2,179	222	10.19	43,623	6,397	14.66
1994	255,999.9	2,774	293	10.56	91,769	9,946	10.84
1995	342,798.6	3,404	286	8.40	112,527	6,350	5.64
1996	390,899.5	3,650	412	11.29	142,557	14,371	10.08
1997	487,853.5	4,132	414	10.02	180,751	13,564	7.50
1998	706,265.9	4,942	325	6.58	406,427	12,691	3.12
1999	1,091,438.7	5,549	311	5.60	630,807	11,569	1.83
2000	1,400,540.6	6,280	531	8.46	905,214	57,599	6.36
2001	827,617.3	4,368	371	8.49	429,374	28,019	6.53
2002	627,974.8	3,114	426	13.68	248,446	29,711	11.96
2003	586,956.4	3,004	418	13.91	182,874	16,059	8.78
2004	744,329.2	3,683	523	14.20	227,221	25,934	11.41
2005	980,727.1	5,004	765	15.29	462,253	68,680	14.86
2006	1,463,351	5,747	839	14.60	625,320	114,922	18.38
2007	1,975,537	7,018	1,047	14.92	1,022,725	144,830	14.16
2008	1,790,706	6,425	1,011	15.74	706,543	105,849	14.98
2009	1,197,824	4,239	746	17.60	249,732	73,975	29.62
2010	1,309,001	5,484	1,084	19.77	344,029	98,149	28.53

Source: World Investment Report (various issues) and authors' own calculations.

Appendix 21.B The number of EMNEs' CBMAs by acquirer countries and target countries, 2000–2010

Acquirer country	*Number of EMNEs' CBMAs*	*Target country*	*Number of EMNEs' CBMAs*
Argentina	6	Australia	107
Bahrain	9	Austria	7
Brazil	31	Belgium	6
Bulgaria	2	Canada	48
Chile	7	Denmark	8
China	95	Finland	9
Colombia	4	France	32
Czech Republic	2	Germany	47
Egypt	4	Greece	4

(continued)

Appendix 21.B (continued)

Acquirer country	*Number of EMNEs' CBMAs*	*Target country*	*Number of EMNEs' CBMAs*
Estonia	5	Ireland	1
Hungary	4	Israel	6
India	130	Italy	13
Indonesia	6	Japan	9
Jordan	1	Luxembourg	1
Kuwait	9	Netherlands	17
Latvia	2	New Zealand	3
Lithuania	4	Norway	12
Malaysia	44	Portugal	11
Mauritius	2	South Korea	12
Mexico	39	Spain	33
Morocco	1	Sweden	7
Nigeria	2	Switzerland	7
Oman	4	United Kingdom	133
Peru	2	United States	161
Philippines	7		
Poland	14		
Qatar	17		
Russian Federation	74		
Saudi Arabia	8		
Slovakia	6		
South Africa	76		
Thailand	4		
Turkey	7		
Ukraine	2		
United Arab Emirates	59		
Venezuela	2		
Vietnam	3		

Source: Authors' calculations of data from the SDC Platinum Database.

Appendix 21.C Countries by region

1 **East Asia and Pacific**

Australia	South Korea	Philippines
China	Malaysia	Thailand
Indonesia	New Zealand	Vietnam
Japan		

2 **Europe and Central Asia**

Austria	Hungary	Romania
Belgium	Ireland	Russian Federation
Bulgaria	Italy	Slovakia
Czech Republic	Latvia	Spain
Denmark	Lithuania	Sweden
Estonia	Luxembourg	Switzerland
Finland	Netherlands	Turkey
France	Norway	United Kingdom
Germany	Poland	Ukraine
Greece	Portugal	

3 **Latin America and the Caribbean**		
Argentina	Colombia	Venezuela
Brazil	Mexico	Peru
Chile		
4 **Middle East and North Africa**		
Bahrain	Kuwait	Qatar
Egypt	Morocco	Saudi Arabia
Israel	Oman	United Arab Emirates
Jordan		
5 **North America**		
Canada	United States	
6 **South Asia**		
India		
7 **Sub-Saharan Africa**		
Mauritius	Nigeria	South Africa

Source: http://data.worldbank.org/about/country-and-lending-groups.

Appendix 21.D Institutional dimensions

Item category	*Details of 25 items*
Public institution	Numerical averages of the below items' annual scores in 2010–2015: 1.01 Property rights, 1–7 (best) 1.02 Intellectual property protection, 1–7 (best) 1.03 Diversion of public funds, 1–7 (best) 1.04 Public trust in politicians, 1–7 (best) 1.05 Irregular payments and bribes, 1–7 (best) 1.06 Judicial independence, 1–7 (best) 1.07 Favouritism in decisions of government officials, 1–7 (best) 1.08 Wastefulness of government spending, 1–7 (best) 1.09 Burden of government regulation, 1–7 (best) 1.10 Efficiency of legal framework in settling disputes, 1–7 (best) 1.11 Efficiency of legal framework in challenging regulations, 1–7 (best) 1.12 Transparency of government policymaking, 1–7 (best) 1.13 Business costs of terrorism, 1–7 (best) 1.14 Business costs of crime and violence, 1–7 (best) 1.15 Organised crime, 1–7 (best) 1.16 Reliability of police services, 1–7 (best)
Norms and cognitions	Numerical averages of the below items' annual scores in 2010–2015: 6.15 Customer orientation, 1–7 (best) 5.08 Extent of staff training, 1–7 (best) 11.09 Willingness to delegate, 1–7 (best) 7.06 Performance-related pay, 1–7 (best) 7.07 Reliance on professional management, 1–7 (best)
Corporate governance quality	Numerical averages of the below items' annual scores in 2010–2015: 1.17 Ethical behaviour of firms, 1–7 (best) 1.18 Strength of auditing and reporting standards, 1–7 (best) 1.19 Efficacy of corporate boards, 1–7 (best) 1.20 Protection of minority shareholders' interests, 1–7 (best)

Source: World Economic Forum's *Global Competitiveness Report*, 2010–2015.

Note

1 There is no agreed definition on the term "emerging economy". Different lists for emerging economies are compiled by the IMF, the Emerging Market Global Players project at Columbia University, the FTSE Group, MSCI Barra, Standard and Poor's, Dow Jones, BBVA Research, MasterCard and *The Economist*. Putting together these lists, this chapter considers that more than 50 fast-developing countries in Asia, Latin America, Africa and the Middle East can be classified as "emerging economies".

References

Abdi, M. & Aulakh, P.S. (2012) 'Do country-level institutional frameworks and interfirm governance arrangements substitute or complement in International Business relationships?' *Journal of International Business Studies*, 43, pp. 477–497.

Arregle, J.-L., Miller, T.L., Hitt, M.A. & Beamish, P.W. (2013) 'Do regions matter? An integrated institutional and semiglobalization perspective on the internationalization of MNEs', *Strategic Management Journal*, 34, pp. 910–934.

Arregle, J.-L., Miller, T.L., Hitt, M.A. & Beamish, P.W. (2016) 'How does regional institutional complexity affect MNE internationalization?' *Journal of International Business Studies*, 47, pp. 697–722.

Bauer, F. & Matzler, K. (2014) 'Antecedents of M&A success: The role of strategic complementarity, cultural fit and degree and speed of integration', *Strategic Management Journal*, 35, pp. 269–291.

Bekaert, G. & Harvey, C.R. (2002) 'Research in emerging markets finance: Looking to the future', *Emerging Markets Review*, 3, pp. 429–448.

Bittlingmayer, G. & Hazlett, T.W. (2000) 'Has antitrust action against Microsoft created value in the computer industry?' *Journal of Financial Economics*, 55, pp. 329–359.

Buckley, P.J., Clegg, L.J., Cross, A.R., Liu, X., Voss, H. & Zheng, P. (2007) 'The determinants of Chinese outward foreign direct investment', *Journal of International Business Studies*, 38, pp. 499–518.

Buckley, P.J., Elia, S. & Kafouros, M. (2014) 'Acquisitions by emerging market multinationals: Implications for firm performance', *Journal of World Business*, 49, pp. 611–632.

Chan, C.M., Isobe, T. & Makino, S. (2008) 'Which country matters? Institutional development and foreign affiliate performance', *Strategic Management Journal*, 29, pp. 1179–1205.

Chao, M.C.-H. & Kumar, V. (2010) 'The impact of institutional distance on the international diversity–performance relationship', *Journal of World Business*, 45, pp. 93–103.

Child, J. & Rodrigues, S.B. (2005) 'The internationalization of Chinese firms: A case for theoretical extension?' *Management and Organization Review*, 1, pp. 381–410.

Collins, J.D., Holcomb, T.R., Certo, S.T., Hitt, M.A. & Lester, R.H. (2009) 'Learning by doing: Cross-border mergers and acquisitions', *Journal of Business Research*, 62, pp. 1329–1334.

Crescenzi, R., Pietrobelli, C. & Rabellotti, R. (2016) 'Regional strategic assets and the location strategies of emerging countries' multinationals in Europe', *European Planning Studies*, 24, pp. 645–667.

Di Giovanni, J. (2005) 'What drives capital flows? The case of cross-border M&A activity and financial deepening', *Journal of International Economics*, 65, pp. 127–149.

Dikova, D., Sahib, P.R. & van Witteloostuijn, A. (2010) 'Cross-border acquisition abandonment and completion: The effect of institutional differences and organizational learning in the International Business service industry, 1981–2001', *Journal of International Business Studies*, 41, pp. 223–245.

DiMaggio, P.J. & Powell, W.W. (1983) 'The iron cage revisited: Institutional isomorphism and collective rationality in organizational fields', *American Sociological Review*, 48, pp. 147–160.

Dunning, J.H. & Lundan, S.M. (2008) *Multinational Enterprises and the Global Economy*. 2nd Edition. Cheltenham, UK: Edward Elgar.

Eden, L. & Miller, S.R. (2004) 'Distance matters: Liability of foreignness, institutional distance and ownership strategy', in Devinney, T., Pedersen, T. & Tihanyi, L. (Eds.), *The Evolving Theory of the Multinational Firm: Diversity, Complexity and Relevance (Advances in International Management, Volume 16)*. Amsterdam: Emerald Group Publishing Limited, pp. 187–221.

Flores, G.R. & Aguilera, V.R. (2007) 'Globalization and location choice: An analysis of US multinational firms in 1980 and 2000', *Journal of International Business Studies*, 38, pp. 1187–1210.

Gaur, A.S. & Lu, J.W. (2007) 'Ownership strategies and survival of foreign subsidiaries: Impacts of institutional distance and experience', *Journal of Management*, 33, pp. 84–110.

Ghemawat, P. (2003) 'Semiglobalization and International Business strategy', *Journal of International Business Studies*, 34, pp. 138–152.

Ghemawat, P. (2007) *Redefining Global Strategy: Crossing Borders in a World Where Differences Still Matter.* Cambridge, MA: Harvard Business School Press.

Holmes, R.M., Miller, T., Hitt, M.A. & Salmador, M.P. (2013) 'The interrelationships among informal institutions, formal institutions, and inward foreign direct investment', *Journal of Management*, 39, pp. 531–566.

Hyun, H.J. & Kim, H.H. (2010) 'The determinants of cross-border M&As: The role of institutions and financial development in the gravity model', *World Economy*, 33, pp. 292–310.

Jormanainen, I. & Koveshnikov, A. (2012) 'International activities of emerging market firms: A critical assessment of research in top international management journals', *Management International Review*, 52, pp. 691–725.

Kedia, B., Gaffney, N. & Clampit, J. (2012) 'EMNEs and knowledge-seeking FDI', *Management International Review*, 52, pp. 155–173.

Khanna, T. & Palepu, K. (1997) 'Why focused strategies may be wrong for emerging markets', *Harvard Business Review*, 75, pp. 41–51.

Kim, J.U. & Aguilera, R.V. (2015) 'Foreign location choice: review and extensions', *International Journal of Management Reviews*, 18, pp. 133–159.

Kostova, T. & Zaheer, S. (1999) 'Organizational legitimacy under conditions of complexity: The case of the multinational enterprise', *Academy of Management Review*, 24, pp. 64–81.

Lebedev, S., Peng, M.W., Xie, E. & Stevens, C.E. (2015) 'Mergers and acquisitions in and out of emerging economies', *Journal of World Business*, 50, pp. 651–662.

Lee, I.H. & Rugman, A.M. (2012) 'Firm-specific advantages, inward FDI origins, and performance of multinational enterprises', *Journal of International Management*, 18, pp. 132–146.

Lin, Z., Peng, M.W., Yang, H. & Sunny Li, S. (2009) 'How do networks and learning drive M&As? An institutional comparison between China and the United States', *Strategic Management Journal*, 30, pp. 1113–1132.

Liu, X., Song, H., Wei, Y. & Romilly, P. (1997) 'Country characteristics and foreign direct investment in China: A panel data analysis', *Weltwirtschaftliches Archiv*, 133, pp. 313–329.

Lu, J., Liu, X. & Wang, H. (2011) 'Motives for outward FDI of Chinese private firms: Firm resources, industry dynamics, and government policies', *Management and Organization Review*, 7, pp. 223–248.

Lu, J.W. (2002) 'Intra- and inter-organizational imitative behavior: Institutional influences on Japanese firms' entry mode choice', *Journal of International Business Studies*, 33, pp. 19–37.

Luo, Y. & Tung, R. (2007) 'International expansion of emerging market enterprises: A springboard perspective', *Journal of International Business Studies*, 38, pp. 481–498.

Luo, Y., Xue, Q. & Han, B. (2010) 'How emerging market governments promote outward FDI: Experience from China', *Journal of World Business*, 45, pp. 68–79.

Makino, S., Lau, C.-M. & Yeh, R.-S. (2002) 'Asset-exploitation versus asset-seeking: Implications for location choice of foreign direct investment from newly industrialized economies', *Journal of International Business Studies*, 33, pp. 403–421.

Malhotra, S., Sivakumar, K. & Zhu, P. (2009) 'Distance factors and target market selection: The moderating effect of market potential', *International Marketing Review*, 26, pp. 651–673.

Martynova, M. & Renneboog, L. (2008) 'Spillover of corporate governance standards in cross-border mergers and acquisitions', *Journal of Corporate Finance*, 14, pp. 200–223.

Meyer, K. & Sinani, E. (2009) 'When and where does foreign direct investment generate positive spillovers? A meta-analysis', *Journal of International Business Studies*, 40, pp. 1075–1094.

North, D.C. (1990) *Institutions, Institutional Change and Economic Performance.* Cambridge, MA: Cambridge University Press.

Oh, C.H. & Li, J. (2015) 'Commentary: Alan Rugman and the theory of the regional multinationals', *Journal of World Business*, 50, pp. 631–633.

Peng, M.W., Wang, D.Y. & Jiang, Y. (2008) 'An institution-based view of International Business strategy: A focus on emerging economies', *Journal of International Business Studies*, 39, pp. 920–936.

Rabbiosi, L., Elia, S. & Bertoni, F. (2012) 'Acquisitions by EMNCs in developed markets', *Management International Review*, 52, pp. 193–212.

Ramasamy, B., Yeung, M. & Laforet, S. (2012) 'China's outward foreign direct investment: Location choice and firm ownership', *Journal of World Business*, 47, pp. 17–25.

Rugman, A.M. (2003) 'Regional strategy and the demise of globalization', *Journal of International Management*, 9, pp. 409–417.

Rugman, A.M. (2005) *The Regional Multinationals: MNEs and 'Global' Strategic Management.* Cambridge, UK: Cambridge University Press.

Rugman, A.M., Oh, C.H. & Lim, D.S. (2012) 'The regional and global competitiveness of multinational firms', *Journal of the Academy of Marketing Science*, 40, pp. 218–235.

Rugman, A.M. & Verbeke, A. (2004) 'A perspective on regional and global strategies of multinational enterprises', *Journal of International Business Studies*, 35, pp. 3–18.

Rugman, A.M. & Verbeke, A. (2005) 'Towards a theory of regional multinationals: A transaction cost economics approach', *Management International Review*, 45, pp. 5–17.

Schoenberg, R. (2006) 'Measuring the performance of corporate acquisitions: An empirical comparison of alternative metrics', *British Journal of Management*, 17, pp. 361–370.

Sethi, D., Guisinger, E.S., Phelan, E.S. & Berg, M.D. (2003) 'Trends in foreign direct investment flows: A theoretical and empirical analysis', *Journal of International Business Studies*, 34, pp. 315–326.

Shimizu, K., Hitt, M.A., Vaidyanath, D. & Pisano, V. (2004) 'Theoretical foundations of cross-border mergers and acquisitions: A review of current research and recommendations for the future', *Journal of International Management*, 10, pp. 307–353.

Stucchi, T. (2012) 'Emerging market firms' acquisitions in advanced markets: Matching strategy with resource-, institution- and industry-based antecedents', *European Management Journal*, 30, pp. 278–289.

Sun, S.L., Peng, M.W., Ren, B. & Yan, D. (2012) 'A comparative ownership advantage framework for cross-border M&As: The rise of Chinese and Indian MNEs', *Journal of World Business*, 47, pp. 4–16.

Trevino, L.J., Thomas, D.E. & Cullen, J. (2008) 'The three pillars of institutional theory and FDI in Latin America: An institutionalization process', *International Business Review*, 17, pp. 118–133.

Wei, Y. & Wu, Y. (2015) 'How institutional distance matters to cross-border mergers and acquisitions by multinational enterprises from emerging economies in OECD countries', in Demirbag, M. & Yaprak, A. (Eds.), *Handbook of Emerging Market Multinational Corporations*. Cheltenham, UK: Edward Elgar, pp. 111–136.

Yang, M. & Hyland, M.A. (2012) 'Similarity in cross-border mergers and acquisitions: Imitation, uncertainty and experience among Chinese firms, 1985–2006', *Journal of International Management*, 18, pp. 352–365.

Zhang, J., Zhou, C. & Ebbers, H. (2011) 'Completion of Chinese overseas acquisitions: Institutional perspectives and evidence', *International Business Review*, 20, pp. 226–238.

22
THE EFFECT OF LOCATION ON ENTREPRENEURSHIP

Tarun Kanti Bose, Pavlos Dimitratos and Frank McDonald

Introduction

Historically the location of firms is to be considered a very important phenomenon to investigate. As time goes by and business becomes more competitive, large firms and successful firms tend to make the choice of locations a strategic issue and place an enormous amount of importance on this. The choice of location nowadays is as important as selecting destinations of target markets. The link between international performance and location is described within three main theoretical streams in modern business and management research. These are the structure-conduct-performance paradigm, the relational paradigm and the resource-based view of the firm.

The first stream, the structure-conduct-performance paradigm, asserts that the performance of firms depends significantly on the industry in which they operate (Cavusgil & Zou, 1994; Zou & Cavusgil, 2002; Ruppenthal, 2009). This means that the most important success factor is the market potential in the industry. Therefore, success mainly depends on selecting appropriate industries and also introducing products or services in the marketplace. The second theoretical stream is the relational paradigm that focuses on building and sustaining relationships with different parties such as customers or suppliers (Styles, Patterson & Ahmed, 2008; Matanda & Freeman, 2009; Ural, 2009). This stream points out that the success of firms in terms of business expansion depends on their ability to find and sustain key relationships with important parties. Thus, this stream is putting more importance on factors such as networking or relationship building and enhancement.

The third stream is the resource-based view. This stream is currently gaining huge attention in different streams of International Business research. This view mainly highlights the development of a few key resources and capabilities for business success. This stream is increasingly placing importance on having different strategic resources and capabilities, particularly for International Business. The resource-based view asserts that in order to be successful in domestic and international markets, firms need to have diversified resources. These resources also need to possess a few key attributes. These essential attributes are that resources must have some important value and possess the potential to minimize external and sudden threats from the market place. Also, these resources should not be common among firms and need to be considered core competencies that competitors do not have and would find very hard to access within a short period of time. In addition, the resources should be difficult for competitors to copy and be immensely hard to substitute (Barney, 1991; Zou & Stan, 1998; Wolff & Pett, 2000; Barney, Wright & Ketchen, 2001; Westhead et al., 2002; Morgan, Kaleka & Katsikeas, 2004; Ray, Barney & Muhanna, 2004; Akhter & Robels, 2006). Therefore, acquiring and utilizing diversified resources is very critical. Location is included in the list of critical resources covered by this stream of theories and practice over the years, but has not been central to the paradigm. Thus, evaluating how location is an important resource and how it plays a pivotal role in business success demands further elaboration.

In order to address the impact of location on performance and internationalization, this chapter includes three sections. The first section looks at the importance of location; empirical research papers in this field of study; important factors and forces arising from location (competition, networking, infrastructure); and a description of the differences between urban and rural firms. The next section reviews the different relevant theories which relate location to performance and internationalization. These theories mainly include two types of theories: relevant regional development theories (orthodox regional development theory and regional competitiveness theory) and relevant International Business theories (the stage model and network theory of internationalization). The third section includes a discussion about other important factors and issues regarding location and its impact on different outcomes. Those issues are: the eagerness of entrepreneurs to operating in familiar places; the benefits of 'staying long'; the liability of outsidership; regional embeddedness and opportunity identification; gaining experiences through chain operation in allocation; resource acquisition and mobilization; and location and institutional framework. The final section comprises an overall synopsis of the entire chapter and a brief conclusion of the outcomes.

The impact of location on performance and internationalization

Location as an important resource

The resource-based view is more relevant to the impact of location on business and entrepreneurial activities, and other strategic and operational aspects such as internationalization or exporting. In the past, a significant number of researchers in the field of the resource-based view have developed a number of factors that make firms capable of operating effectively and beyond domestic territories. In addition, a significant number of authors have also listed factors which particularly affect the exporting and internationalization capabilities of entrepreneurial firms. The list of those factors contains important issues under the major categories of physical, human, organizational and financial resources (Barney, 1991; Morgan & Hunt, 1999; Morgan, Kaleka & Katsikeas, 2004; Haber & Reichel, 2007). Physical resources are more or less tangible ones including the technological and operational equipment of firms, whereas human resources comprise the workforce available to the organization. Organizational resources are planning and coordinating as well as controlling expertise of firms, and financial resources are capital and other financial backing that are essential expertise in every sphere of operation. The resource-based view places an emphasis on capturing these resources to achieve better operations; however, a few recent research works have assigned more importance to combining resources in addition to acquiring resources. This is significant considering the fact that the acquisition of resources is challenging, but it is even more challenging to find the best combination of effective resources. The country and environmental contexts may also be profound reasons behind such relationships (Morgan & Hunt, 1999; Ibeh, 2003; Morgan, Kaleka & Katsikeas, 2004; Doole, Grimes & Demack, 2006; Sapienza et al., 2006).

It is evident that firms need diversified resources and need to find a suitable and appropriate combination of these. But location in a specific place always tends to exert a strong influence on their ability to capture these resources. This is because firms located in an isolated place will always find it difficult to acquire and combine all types of resources. It is clearly evident that firms in urban places will face different challenges in comparison to sub-urban and rural firms as to their acquisition and combination of resources. Therefore, it is very clear that the impact of location on performance is evident and such impact is also diverse. Over the years, many researchers have carried out empirical research to identify various impacts of location on performance and internationalization. This research has identified some interesting outcomes.

Empirical research on location, performance and internationalization

Only a few research articles have placed a strong emphasis on investigating the moderating role of locations between entrepreneurship and business performance (Vatne, 1995; Larsson, Hedelin & Garling, 2003). Some papers have also described that the trade-off between regional and urban locations of different types of firms has the potential to function as an important player in between firms' operations and performance (Zhao and Zou, 2002; Katsikeas et al., 2005). In spite of this, the importance of location and sites in different places within a country is still an area which is particularly under-researched and requires further attention (Mittelstaedt et al., 2006).

In their study on Australian SMEs in different locations, Freeman, Styles and Meredith (2012) have investigated the impact of situating in different locations on the export performances of entrepreneurial SMEs. The outcome of their study suggests that locations have an important effect on the firm's performance. This impact tends to take place in different aspects of business operations, including access to networking, infrastructure and other important services. This implies that SMEs existing in urban areas gain more advantages than rural SMEs simply because they have more access to networks, infrastructure and also important and relevant services, which are critical not only for domestic but also for international operations. Moreover, this study also points to the fact that SMEs, particularly exporting SMEs of Australia, which are located in regional rural areas, were finding themselves in a disadvantaged position because they did not have access to critical aspects of operations. That is also in line with the previous findings of the aforementioned studies. The lesson of the study clearly points towards the fact that belonging to particular locations (i.e. situating in urban areas) poses certain advantages and disadvantages. While urban firms are likely to get more facilities and resources compared to rural firms, the former are also more likely to find it easier to expand their operations in critical areas, for example, into the international marketplace.

The research work of Freeman, Styles and Meredith (2012) has used the resource-based view and theory for investigating the importance of location. Traditionally, the resource-based view accentuates acquisitions of different resources and their importance for business, including internationalization. Therefore, firm location can be used as an access to resources, and locating in key strategic places has the potential to contribute to this effect. Anchoring on the resource-based view, the study of Freeman et al. (2012) set hypotheses for their empirical research that locations matter, and the outcome of the hypotheses testing supported that presumption.

Empirical research on SMEs over the years suggests that the regional impact on SMEs is significant and plays a pivotal role in their operational aspects, i.e. entrepreneurship and internationalization. As mentioned earlier, these impacts are robust and multifaceted

(Lages, 2000; MacGregor & Varazalic, 2005; Meccheri & Pelloni, 2006). Few studies have specifically highlighted the fact that because of locating in a regional and remote area, SMEs tend to suffer from difficulties in attracting investment and accessing finance, recruiting and retaining skilled staff, dealing with government policies and programmes, and establishing and maintaining adequate infrastructure (Smallbone, Baldock & North, 2003; Costa Campi, Blasco & Marsal, 2004). Some studies indicate that in large cities, firms tend to gain big advantages on important operational aspects, particularly in International Business. Those advantages are in the areas of specialized infrastructure, information, networks of suppliers, specialized labour and knowledge, and concentration of existing exporters (Chevassus-Lozza & Galliano, 2003; Westhead, Wright & Ucbasaran, 2004). The influence of geographic location on shaping operations is increasingly being considered as one important aspect, and researchers acknowledge the fact that firms in a particular location (i.e. in cities) will always gain more advantages than disadvantages than firms in remote areas; and that these advantages will dictate the path to being entrepreneurial and international (Zhao & Zou, 2002; Chevassus-Lozza & Galliano, 2003; Capello & Faggian, 2005).

Important factors and forces arising from location

In spite of the increasing significance of the location effect on business performance (especially International Business performance), this field of research still remains an under-researched area. Still, there are a few studies that have empirically identified the different dimensions and areas of impact, which ultimately dictate the success of firms in their operations. Prior research works have largely pointed to the fact that the impact of location on International Business performance never takes place in isolation. Rather, there are a few factors which occur as a result of location differences, and the impacts of those factors are different between locations. These are: competition, networking, infrastructure, institutions, supplies, technologies and information (Kirat & Lung, 1999; Boschma, 2005). We elaborate on the main ones in this section.

Competition

The famous Diamond model of Michael Porter outlined strong competition and rivalry for developing one particular business in a country or location. In recent research the same importance of competition is also evident. Hence, competition between firms is always important not only for domestic businesses but also for international ones. Firms that are located in a certain place will always experience different degrees of competition than firms of a different place or country. Within a country, this scenario can also be the same, because in most countries more competition is observed in urban than in rural areas (Westhead, Wright & Ucbasaran, 2001; Bennett & Smith, 2002). Therefore, locations determine competition and competition intensity determines (along with other factors) internationalization performance and strategies (Zahra, Neubaum & Huse, 1997; Zhao & Zou, 2002).

In a significant study, Chevassus-Lozza and Galliano (2003) found that being sited near urban areas always has a greater impact and propensity towards exporting for SMEs. There is a static effect and a dynamic effect. The static one is within the country and the region. This means strong rivalry and competition will make firms work harder and go for more innovation and creative operations. That will automatically increase their quality of products and services and, through this process, will also make them capable of operating globally. The dynamic effect is that strong competition within the domestic set-up will speed up innovation, but at the same time will motivate firms to search for new markets. This is because they will find it difficult to retain momentum and keep growing within the domestic market. Searching for new markets will induce internationalization. This scenario emerged in many European firms over the years as they sought expansion and internationalization in emerging economies in particular (Phelps, Fallon & Williams, 2001; Chevassus-Lozza & Galliano, 2003; Westhead, Wright & Ucbasaran, 2004; Capello & Faggian, 2005; Belso-Martinez, 2006). While competition is different across locations, tools for fighting such competition are also varied across locations. One such modern tool of fighting with competition and utilizing it positively is networking.

Networking

The importance of networks for modern business has been addressed in a number of research studies. Networks of different types help firms in various ways. While networking is very important, access to proper networks is an even more significant prerequisite for acquiring the maximum benefits from networking. All kinds of modern firms including SMEs form networks not only with other firms but sometimes with government organizations and several other parties. These networks are often made with firms already existing in the value chain and also with people and institutions that have direct and indirect influence on operations. According to Westhead, Wright and Ucbasaran (2004), business organizations form networks with customers, suppliers, government institutions, clients, etc. Literature suggests that the firm's locations play a critical and pivotal role in forming these alliances. Locating in a metropolitan area opens up access to more fruitful networks than locating in a remote rural area. In this way, location dictates the terms of forming networks and, through this, further plays an important role in the internationalization or exporting decision making of firms.

It has been policy in many countries to form industrial clusters and regions which were developed as export processing zones, and some firms located there to gain location-specific advantages. These policies are now common in important emerging economies like India and China, and these countries ensure huge benefits by forming export processing zones and industrial clusters. Within these zones and clusters, firms access different benefits like tax advantages, full-time power supply at reduced rates, important linkage roads, weights and standard measurement tools, heavy and important machineries, etc. This is a very traditional yet significant domestic mechanism to induce International Business to a particular location, as it puts considerable focus on that location and its impact on exporting or internationalization. This also supports the notion that location matters (Raub & Weesie, 1990; Vatne, 1995; Capello & Faggian, 2005; Mittelstaedt et al., 2006).

The important role played by domestic location towards internationalization is also supported by a few other empirical research papers across the world. In their study on firms in New Zealand, Chevassus-Lozza and Galliano (2003) identified that extensive domestic networking in important aspects of the value chain such as distribution plays a critical role in the firm's ambition towards exporting and internationalization. Access to networks ensures the sharing of critical information and so enhances knowledge development and contributes towards strong International Business performance. Such access to networks is only possible, or at least is much easier, if a firm locates in the correct place (De Toni & Nassimbeni, 2001; Dyer & Hatch, 2006; Grimes et al., 2007).

Networks help in minimizing the impact of resource deficiency and also in strengthening competencies. Further, it also assists a lot towards mitigating the negative aspects of a location that often come from infrastructure, which is another very significant dimension of location.

Infrastructure

Infrastructure is another very important aspect of modern business. It is of huge significance not only for International Business but also all kinds of operations. Proper infrastructure makes business easier for firms as it significantly assists them to cut costs and also improve operations. Through this process they find themselves in strong positions vis-à-vis competition and thus they operate in better ways. These competitive advantages give them stability and growth in operations. From this perspective, firms can go for significant expansion into the international market and operate for a long period of time. One important aspect of this discussion is that all these advantages, and the internationalization of firms resulting from such advantages, can only occur if a firm is locating itself in a proper area where suitable infrastructure is available.

Studies on location, infrastructure and business performance including International Business performance have identified a number of issues. In the study by Mittelstaedt et al. (2006), they identified that cities are better locations for firms as far as infrastructure is concerned. This is because location in cities helps firms to reduce the costs of operation as well as transportation. In addition, a variety of services are available. In addition, a more skilled labour force is available in cities compared to rural areas. In a similar yet more elaborative research work, Albaum et al. (2005) and Leonidou (2004) identified that firms locating in cities are found to be more reliable exporters. The reason behind this is that these locations make it easier for firms to make deliveries on time and, more generally, simplifies logistics, e.g. through access to adequate warehousing. These findings are very important as far as exporting variables are concerned. In a number of studies, it has been mentioned that transportation, storage, delivery and insurance are important challenges for exporters and always play a critical role in the success of exporting. Therefore, locating in a suitable area gives firms competitive advantages and makes them more capable to withstand such exporting challenges (Aaby & Slater, 1989; Morgan & Katsikeas, 1997; Hart & McGuinness, 2003).

These challenges, which mainly arise from infrastructure, vary from location to location. The differences are even more significant if locations are more diverse and distinct. Such immense differences only arise if locations are vastly divergent from one another and are common between urban and rural firms.

Urban and rural firms

The advantages of urban location towards exporting are discussed in the research by Katsikeas, Leonidou and Morgan (2000) and Mittelstaedt et al. (2006). This is also supported by other research evidence (Keeble, 1997; Westhead, Ucbasaran & Binks, 2004; Fuller-Love et al., 2006) which identifies that urban areas ensure favourable supply side conditions, access to financial institutions, technology partners, specialized labour and export-related infrastructure, and thus help exporters in numerous ways. The empirical research of Bennett and Smith (2002) explained that government and institutional assistances of various forms are more accessible and available in urban areas and thus create a favourable atmosphere for exporting and internationalization, along with domestic business venturing.

Most of the studies on the impact of location on internationalization have highlighted the fact that urban firms enjoy more advantages than rural SMEs and also explain how and why such advantages are significant. Likewise, some studies have explained the relatively disadvantageous positions occupied by relative rural firms just because of their location. Atherton and Hannon (2006) explained that it is difficult to undertake any development activities including business development in remote and regional areas because of geographic location and the relatively lower skilled labour force. In addition, many rural firms, including SMEs, are relatively likely to be less creative and innovative due to less access to technology and information. As a result, these rural firms will be lagging behind in important strategic and operational fronts and will be less competitive in the international marketplace (North & Smallbone, 2000).

The previous discussion about location and its impact on firms' performance and internationalization have identified different empirical research works that have discussed the relationship between location and performance from various angles. The next section comprises different relevant theories of this field.

Theories which relate location to performance and internationalization

Relevant regional development theories

The regional development theories comprise two theories, namely orthodox regional development theory and regional competitiveness theory.

Orthodox regional development theory

The orthodox regional development theory suggests that, due to better supply side conditions, the development process for urban firms is much easier than that of rural firms (Keeble, 1997). Two main concepts of economics are added to the theory of orthodox regional development for describing why such enormous advantages are enjoyed by urban firms. Those two concepts are agglomeration economies and spatial externalities. Agglomeration economies are the advantages firms experience from situating close to one another in a cluster or in a special zone. Such clusters normally exist in urban areas and firms tend to be closer to one another. In contrast, rural firms stay in isolation and seldom get the advantages of agglomeration economies. The second aspect of spatial externalities are a combination of various important factors which are vital for business operations and also for developing a strong base of domestic activity for initiating the opportunities for international operations. Those factors are suppliers, labour, knowledge, information, technology, distribution, institution, etc. (Malmberg, Malmberg & Lundequist, 2000; Parr, 2002). In a significant study on location, performance and exporting, Chevassus-Lozza and Galliano (2003) pointed out that urban firms are more likely to secure greater advantages of agglomeration economies and as a result are more inclined towards internationalized operations than rural firms. This is an important addition to orthodox theory of regional development, which tends to be limited to only location, development and domestic business performance.

Regional competitiveness theory

The regional competiveness theory draws attention to the competitive and environmental pressures that dictate the operations of business organizations. Due to these pressures and desires to become more competitive, firms continually strive to acquire more resources. In line with the resource-based view, regional development theory also proposes location as a key resource that actually contributes significantly towards obtaining other resources (Keeble, 1997). Thus the process is complex yet very significant to understand. In the first phase, a location where many firms operate tends to enhance and uphold healthy competition among those firms. As a result, in order to stay well ahead in the race, firms recognize the need to acquire key strategic and operational resources that will provide them with competitive advantages. Those resources make them innovative and creative and, when the adoption of better knowledge and operations is compatible with international standards, firms tend to go for exporting or other forms of internationalization. Thus, location has a big influence over the operational processes of firms and considerably dictates their future path.

Relevant International Business theories

The second domain of theories comprises International Business theories, which mainly include two theories, namely the stage model and the network theory of internationalization.

The stage model

In the classic research work of Johanson and Vahlne (1990), the internationalization or exporting process of firms has been viewed as a sequential process comprising many stages. The process is a continuous one and throughout the process, firms are engaged in the development of knowledge and also in the acquisition of critical resources. Major critics of the stage-based model question the main tenet of the theory in its later stages. Their argument is that few firms can traditionally initiate at home and then go abroad, but in modern times there are firms that are initiated to operate globally. The latter firms are defined as 'born global' firms (Frosgren, 2002). Making an important addition to stage theory, O'Farrell and Wood (1998) have suggested that a wide range of supply and demand side factors significantly influences the exporting or internationalization process of firms. This notion of demand and supply side factors draws attention to important key issues from both perspectives that have a direct and indirect impact on the internationalization process.

Demand and supply from the perspective of firms depend on various factors. One of those factors is location. Demand for the firm's products and supply of the firm's different resources such as raw materials will never be the same across different locations. A few previous studies have suggested that firms in relatively crowded and large cities will most likely have larger market potential to capture than those in isolated rural areas. The question may arise as to whether rural firms can sell their product to urban areas as well, but that would cost them more in transportation and, as a result, they will likely lose their entire advantage.

Network theory of internationalization

The network theory of internationalization of firms has accentuated forming networks towards gaining different resources and competencies. This theory suggests that in order to internationalize, many firms need different sorts of domestic as well as international networking access to minimize their deficiencies. One important aspect of this theory is consistent with the location perspective. Firms in urban areas will always have the privilege of accessing more networks than rural ones. However, rural firms can mitigate a lot of their deficiencies though accessing membership of important networks. Gaining membership in an important network also paves the way for further membership, since many of the other participants of the network will have relationships with other firms. Research suggests that such networking will have a positive impact on exporting, as many firms in the network will have direct and indirect relationships with foreign firms (Phelps, Fallon & Williams, 2001; Andersson, 2002).

Other important issues regarding location

The following section will discuss other, different issues regarding location, which play important roles in business performance and operational aspects. These aspects include factors such as the benefits of staying in a familiar place, staying longer in the same place, obtaining regional embeddedness, overcoming the problem of foreignness, dealing with institutional frameworks, obtaining and mobilizing resources, identifying and exploiting opportunities, and also gaining experience through value-chain operations. Discussion of these issues will elaborate more on the importance and roles played by location, which ultimately influence the internationalization as well as overall performance of different firms.

The fondness for known places

The impact of geographic locations on the performance and behaviour of entrepreneurs is supported by ample streams of literature. In traditional as well as modern theories on entrepreneurship, entrepreneurs always tend to be explained as individuals who possess different traits and characteristics in comparison to typical people (Chmielewski & Paladino, 2007). In spite of having a diverse set of unique traits, entrepreneurs greatly appreciate home bonding as far as choosing their initial locations is concerned. Most of the traditional as well as modern entrepreneurs historically tend to prefer operating in their well-known territories. These well-known territories include places like their birth places, places where they have lived for a long period of time and also places which are very convenient and suitable for their individual operations (Michelacci & Silva, 2007; Dahl & Sorenson, 2009). There are multiple reasons behind why entrepreneurs prefer to select operations in known places than in unknown destinations. These factors include deep social capital, geographic comfort, proximity to family and friends, and regional embeddedness (Chevassus-Lozza & Galliano, 2003).

Empirical research (Cusumano & Takeishi, 1991; Costa Campi, Blasco & Marsal, 2004; Crick & Spence, 2005) on location, entrepreneurship and internationalization has outlined that entrepreneurial ventures could perform well in international start-ups if they were able to locate themselves in well-known territories. This is simply because, if they are situated in places that are familiar, they operate more independently and comfortably. This is because of a richer access to regionally socially embedded capital. In some research works, contrasting outcomes have also been investigated. This literature has highlighted the fact that when entrepreneurs locate in a known territory, they may also find little time for business and entrepreneurial decision making, due to the abundance of family and friends. This can cause what sociologists termed "over social embeddedness" (Kalnins & Chung, 2006; Kosova & Lafontaine, 2010).

It has been found that when entrepreneurial firms are located in known places, they live longer, obtain more profit and expand in domestic and international areas. In many cases entrepreneurs tend to open their businesses in a familiar territory rather than in unknown places even though the familiar place offers fewer economic and location benefits (Donthu & Kim, 1994). This opens up the debate about whether being in a known territory is always advantageous and offers stronger benefits. Scholars of Economic Geography (Ellis & Pecotich, 2001; Grimes et al., 2007) often stress multiple considerations before selecting the location for doing business. These include institutional, political, social, economic, operational and other factors. It is known that every location is very unlikely to be advantageous in all those aspects, and, therefore, entrepreneurs tend to make a trade-off and undertake a cost-benefit analysis before selecting one (Huang, Soutar & Brown, 2002; Hart & McGuinness, 2003; Haber & Reichel, 2007). The case becomes more important for international entrepreneurs because they need to consider even more issues. Analytically, research suggests that being in the home territory offers better chances of becoming successful both in domestic and international markets in spite of having fewer economic benefits (Larsson, Hedelin & Garling, 2003; Lages, Jap & Griffith, 2008). This indicates that all those location difficulties may be overcome by entrepreneurs through the utilization of other factors such as strong social capital and local networking (Sorenson & Audia, 2000; Figueiredo, Guimaraes & Woodward, 2002).

Some research findings have provided empirical evidences in support of this notion (Andersson, Gabrielsson & Wictor, 2004; Akhter & Robels, 2006; Belso-Martinez, 2006). It is highly likely that advantageous destinations, irrespective of local or international location, are more likely to be more competitive and therefore require distinct advantages to generate and sustain significant successes. Therefore, entrepreneurs who have the inherent trait of thinking outside the box tend to think differently and choose locations close to them to facilitate rapid success. Many scholars (Chevassus-Lozza & Galliano, 2003; Capello & Faggian, 2005) in entrepreneurship and International Business agree upon the fact that the initial days are the hardest days for all entrepreneurs, whether they be domestic or international entrepreneurs. If they survive the initial hardships, then success is more likely to come. Therefore, choosing a known place, surrounded by family and friends, and also deriving benefits from the rich social capital provide initial advantages for the entrepreneurs, which then work as a pivotal point for them and provide success in future years (Gimeno et al., 1997; Dahl & Sorenson, 2009).

Staying in home or known places provides diversified advantages for entrepreneurs. There are some negative sides to this as well. While staying at home means operating within their comfort zone, location in known places can mean having limited resources and not enough diversification. It appears then that location is a very important issue for operating efficiently, and if one operates in known places one can deal with any difficulties but operate with limited resources. Besides, only operating in one's comfort zone will not ensure the availability of all types of resources. Such resource shortages can be mitigated with social capital gained from the home area. As discussed, there are mostly positive aspects to staying and operating in a known place and the average entrepreneur also tends to prefer to stay in their familiar territory. There are a few disadvantages, too, which can be overcome in other ways.

The benefits of staying longer

Empirical studies (Wolff & Pett, 2000; Zhao et al., 2002; Zou, Fang & Zhao, 2003) suggest that entrepreneurs who stay in a place for long periods of time benefit significantly as they perform well in international and domestic marketplaces. This has two dimensions: first, staying long after starting operations and second, staying in a place for a prolonged period of time before starting operations. Entrepreneurs who stay in a location for a long time gains benefits from home advantage and also from endowment of social capital, as indicated in the earlier discussion (Westhead, Wright & Ucbasaran, 2004). This makes them more suited and accustomed to the environment and creates synergies for further expansion into different places including international ones. Apart from this, sometimes staying near friends and family energizes them more and that results in high business performance, while ignoring the negative sides of social embeddedness. Staying for a long time in the same location after starting the business also provides similar kinds of benefits and assists enormously in accelerating business expansion and operating internationally. Research in this field (Gimeno et al., 1997; Dahl & Sorenson, 2009) suggests that the number of years an entrepreneur lives and does business in a place is positively correlated to internationalization and business performance. This simply indicates that the longer an entrepreneur stays in the same place, the higher the chances of doing better in both the domestic and international marketplaces (Figueiredo, Guimaraes & Woodward, 2002; Cuervo-Cazurra, Maloney & Manrakhan, 2007; Dahl & Sorenson, 2010).

The study of Dahl and Sorenson (2010) has identified that entrepreneurs who stayed an average of seven years in a location performed significantly better internationally as well as domestically. Performance in terms of both growth and profit is significantly greater for firms that stay longer, when compared to newcomers, and this is significant for a number of reasons. Entrepreneurial venturing, and particularly international entrepreneurial venturing, is highly correlated with innovation and creativity and requires diversified operations (Westhead, Ucbasaran & Binks, 2004). Staying for a long time in a single place may inhibit the development of innovation and quality as it limits the process of assimilation and learning from one another. However, research (Andersson, Gabrielsson & Wictor, 2004; Akhter & Robels, 2006; Belso-Martinez, 2006) shows that such limitations on innovation and diversification can be negated by rich endowment, social capital and strong networking, which a firm normally enjoys if it stays in a place for longer periods of time.

The liability of outsidership

There is always a liability of foreignness in International Business. This is an important factor or barrier which each and every international entrepreneur faces when starting their International Business. This factor mainly arises due to location disadvantages, and literature suggests that it creates numerous problems, yet can be overcome using different strategies (Johanson & Vahlne, 2006). The liability of outsidership occurs mainly because International Businesses initiated by international entrepreneurs face numerous barriers such as restrictions, customs, rules, laws, taxes, language, customer differences amongst others (Johanson & Vahlne, 2006). These factors trigger further debate and discussion about domestic and main locations of the firm and its impact on international entrepreneurial venturing. If a firm remains only in a well-known location, then it might enjoy several benefits as discussed earlier. At the same time, the firm or entrepreneur will suffer enormously as a result of the liability of outsidership and foreignness (Cuervo-Cazurra, Maloney & Manrakhan, 2007).

The fields of International Business and international entrepreneurship have prescribed different solutions for eliminating the so-called liability of outsidership (Johanson & Vahlne, 2006). One such solution is popularly acknowledged as networking. In different literature on networking and International Business, it is suggested that networking is a viable solution for reducing the impact of outsidership and gaining insidership through networking successfully in international markets (Johanson & Vahlne, 2006; Cuervo-Cazurra, Maloney & Manrakhan, 2007; Dahl and Sorenson, 2010). For that purpose, it is important to have access and membership of important international networks that might be personal or business networks. While such networking will minimize many problems of internal operations, gaining entry or membership and finding a suitable and trustworthy network will always be a problem for every international entrepreneur. But entrepreneurs can overcome this because they presume to possess the inherent and required qualities of dealing with several challenges associated with international markets (Zaheer, 1995; Styles, 1998; Sorenson & Stuart, 2001; Ruef et al., 2003).

Therefore, locations have an important impact on international entrepreneurship performance particularly in terms of the foreignness factor. Firms that have direct and physical operations in the international market will normally enjoy more advantages (Cuervo-Cazurra, Maloney & Manrakhan, 2007; Dahl & Sorenson, 2010). Furthermore, firms which are only located in the domestic market will face more challenges, but such challenges can be overcome through networking.

Gaining experience through networking and chain operations

The literature on International Business and entrepreneurship suggests that, historically, entrepreneurs used to start their international entrepreneurial venturing by exporting. This situation changed over time as technology improved. This has resulted in new modes such as joint ventures, franchising (and) FDI in place of traditional exporting. In spite of this, many firms from emerging economies still participate in International Business mainly through direct exporting (Murray, 2006; Sorenson & Waguespack, 2006). In exporting, firms establish networks with buyers and other parties such as middlemen to acquire important information and get rid of the liabilities of outsidership. Along with exporting, other forms of International Business and entrepreneurship such as franchising or joint ventures also get accelerated by networking and establishing good rapport and communications (Cuervo-Cazurra, Maloney & Manrakhan, 2007; Dahl & Sorenson, 2010).

Locating in a domestic place and staying far away from the market is always a big challenge for firms. Ensuring networks and communication particularly with foreign parties is difficult (Ingram & Baum, 1997; Kalnins & Mayer, 2004). Therefore, it is important to gain experience and knowledge about different markets prior to the commencement of operations as well as during operations. Gaining such knowledge and information can be done through establishing franchising and other networks with foreign or even local firms within the country. As a result, firms can oust the location disadvantages they normally suffer when they are located in a common and well-known place (Ingram & Baum, 1997; Kalnins & Mayer, 2004).

Location, regional embeddedness, opportunity identification and impact on international entrepreneurship

Location always has played an important part in dictating all the essential operational and strategic aspects of international as well as domestic entrepreneurial venturing (Bennett & Smith, 2002; Bosworth, 2009). By locating in a particular area of a country, a firm both benefits and is simultaneously penalized due to so-called regional embeddedness. Regional embeddedness entails various surrounding factors and forces that shape the firm's operations internally and externally, and dictate the way it will expand (i.e. internationally) or shrink (i.e. revert to becoming domestic from international operators). Regional embeddedness also means a relationship that covers all the possible aspects of an association that can happen between an entrepreneur and the place or location in which he/she is situated (Gorton, 1999; Katsikeas, Leonidou & Morgan, 2000). Therefore, the right chemistry between place and people is important. Even if we consider the normal residence preference of an individual or family, we will be able to see such relationships being affected by several economic and social factors (Ingram & Baum, 1997; Kalnins & Mayer, 2004).

There will hardly be any location in the world which ticks all the boxes that an entrepreneur likes. This means in one particular location there may be an abundance of cheap labour, but it might also be technologically outdated at the same time. As a result, it will receive top marks for labour force and very low grades for technological quality. So, what is the next course of action for the entrepreneur to ensure an absolute gem of a location that is highly embedded with personal and business traits? Entrepreneurs often conduct the old-fashioned "marginal analysis", meaning they carry out a cost-benefit analysis to measure which location will ensure what benefits and costs and what sacrifices they will have to make if they choose that location. Such marginal analysis involves detecting each and every important criterion of business locations and scoring each against the alternative locations.

As suggested in numerous empirical articles (Katsikeas, Leonidou & Morgan, 2000; Knight, 2000; Mariotti & Piscitello, 2001; Mittelstaedt et al., 2006), this regional embeddedness assists entrepreneurial start-ups as well as existing firms to operate in better ways and expand internationally. Regional embeddedness means fruitful associations of an individual with the location. This may enable the entrepreneurs to find and satisfy unmet demand of customers in the area. Additionally, introducing a product, different promotional and other campaigns are essential for embeddedness within the local area. Regional embeddedness further ensures critical access to scarce resources and critical linkages with suppliers, and makes operation much easier. Regional embeddedness also ensures that the entrepreneur has a good understanding of the institutional framework of the region and does not get penalized for not understanding it properly (Michelacci & Silva, 2007; Dahl & Sorenson, 2009). From this discussion it is evident that location is enormously important as through it an entrepreneur can find proper regional embeddedness and derive maximum benefits from it.

Strong local and domestic performance obtained through regional embeddedness resulting from selecting an appropriate location paves the way for sound international entrepreneurship opportunities (Morgan & Katsikeas, 1997; Phelps, Fallon & Williams, 2001; Wennberg & Lindqvist, 2010). However, there are different challenges a firm must face in international markets. The firm of the home country will enjoy the benefits of regional embeddedness and will make things more difficult for the overseas firms trying to locate in the same area. Therefore, as suggested in the network theory and literatures of International Business and international entrepreneurship, entrepreneurs have to find linkages and networks with local firms for overcoming such barriers. If they are in these networks, then they will get the benefits of regional embeddedness which are obtained by the local firms though their knowledge and endowment of social capital (Zaheer, 1995; Kalnins & Mayer, 2004).

Location-resource acquisition and mobilization, and links to international performance

Entrepreneurs who locate in a particular destination will find it easier to acquire key strategic and operational resources if the firm is regionally embedded (Michelacci & Silva 2007; Dahl & Sorenson, 2009). This means if the location has a good match with the entrepreneur's capabilities then it will certainly be easier for them to capture resources. Along with regional embeddedness, the location also needs to be enriched with different resources that can be acquired. The best location is the one which comprises ample resources and is highly embedded with the entrepreneur. Research on capacity development of entrepreneurial venturing suggests that an entrepreneur must be able to capture, assemble and mobilize important resources such as financial capital, employees, supplies, energy and power, information and knowledge (Amit, Glosten & Muller, 1990; Camerer & Lovallo, 1999).

Location is important in resource acquisition, but empirical evidence suggests that how entrepreneurs use the location as a resource will dictate how effectively he/she will be able to take maximum benefits from the location (Breschi & Malerba, 2001; Folta, Cooper & Baik, 2006). This is simply because in every location there will be different positive and negative sides. There will also be fierce rivalry among different operators in the same business and different business for scarce resources. Therefore, it virtually depends on the ability of the entrepreneurs to make the best use of the locations and take maximum benefits as far as resource acquisitions are concerned. This will ensure maximum benefits for them and ultimately also help towards their ambition of international expansion (Kosova & Lafontaine, 2010).

Relationship and good bonding with the location are important also because of several factors which affect the resource acquisition process. First, if entrepreneurs want to recruit employees from any agency or obtain funding from banks or government institutions, then important factors such as networking, personal relationship, track records, trustworthiness, etc. will be taken into account (Raub & Weesie, 1990; Greif, 1993; Sorenson & Stuart, 2001). Consequently, if the entrepreneur has strong personal relationships and a good track record in the area, then it will be easier to capture employees and secure significant loans at the appropriate times. Thus, the relationship between location and performance will also be highly moderated by entrepreneurial skills such as identifying opportunities, building networks, maintaining relationships, finding new ways to communicate and making the best use of any situation (Zajonc, 1998; Sorenson & Waguespack, 2006).

This is an important addition to the resource-based view, which articulates the importance of having critical resources. The resource-based view posits that in order to be successful in domestic and international markets, firms need to have different types of idiosyncratic resources. Location ensures resource acquisition and mobilization. However, firms have to operate under certain institutional frameworks. Therefore, the institutional framework shapes the resource acquisition and mobilization process.

Location, institutional framework and international entrepreneurship performance

As suggested by the work of Kostova (1997), the institutional framework consists of regulatory, normative and cognitive dimensions. Regulatory dimensions consist of the rules, laws, regulations and other procedures that exist in the administrative and functioning system governed by the sovereign authority of a country, and every firm must follow and obey these in order to do business. Normative means the general standard of acceptable and moral behaviour within which a firm operates. The cognitive dimension of institutional framework covers the general attitude and perception of individuals of a country towards business, particularly entrepreneurial business venturing and beliefs about the nature of the world and the way the world works.

These institutional frameworks covering different dimensions have dissimilar degrees of presence as well as influences across different places even within a country. This degree of difference is even larger if a country is big in terms of population, such as India or China. For example, in India, the degree of administrative corruption is huge in the east part of the country whereas in the south it is virtually zero. Such differences also exist in normative and cognitive dimensions (Carlton, 1993; Dean, Meyer & DeCastro, 1993; Feldman, 2001). Even in western countries people and places do not have similar perceptions about entrepreneurs and do not possess the same degree of knowledge as far as various social, political or economic issues are concerned. These factors make locations hugely diversified in terms of different key aspects and the impact on international entrepreneurship (Staber, 1998; Rocha, 2004).

There are important implications from this. First, people of a country are unique in nature even though their identity or religion might be the same. Second, the institutional framework of a country in different regions is diverse as this is eventually affected by the people. From those people, some can be corrupt and inefficient. Third, these differences make the impact of location on business performance (i.e. International Business performance) more relevant and acute in nature. Finally, selecting an appropriate location is important as it will determine whether a firm will gain benefits or be penalized as a result of preferring one location over another.

Conclusion

Location is a very important factor for domestic as well as international entrepreneurship activities. In empirical qualitative as well as quantitative research, location is seen as a crucial force that dictates many terms of International Business activities. Location has a vital role to play in the process of international entrepreneurship activities by influencing the roles of a few important forces and factors such as competition, networking and infrastructure. Urban and rural firms and their differences because of location are prime examples of how and in what way location can play a critical role. There are different theories that have directly and indirectly described the influential roles played by locations. Those are the orthodox regional development theory, regional competitiveness theory, the stage model, and network theory of internationalization. These theories explained important aspects of the firm's operations and linked those aspects with the location from different prominent perspectives such as the resource-based view or network theories. Research on location and entrepreneurship also explains how people derive benefits from operating in a known place and stay in a single place for long periods of time. But, this also can result in outsidership and "liability of foreignness" problems when they seek International Business. This can be overcome by gaining experiences through networking and chain operation. The location of a firm also results in the creation of regional embeddedness and facilitates the exploration and exploitation of opportunities. Location is also likely to assist in resource acquisition and reduce the negative roles of institutional frameworks if it has been selected properly. Therefore, the decision on location is vital for all kinds of business activities, including international entrepreneurship activities.

References

Aaby, N. & Slater, S. (1989) 'Management influences on export performance: A review of the empirical literature 1978–88', *International Marketing Review*, 6, pp. 7–27.

Akhter, S. & Robels, F. (2006) 'Leveraging internal competency and managing environmental uncertainty', *International Marketing Review*, 23, pp. 98–115.

Albaum, G., Duerr, E. & Strandskov, J. (2005) *International Marketing and Export Management*. 5th Edition. London: Prentice Hall.

Amit, R., Glosten, L. & Muller, E. (1990) 'Entrepreneurial ability, venture investments, and risk sharing', *Management Science*, 36, pp. 1232–1245.

Andersson, P. (2002) 'Connected internationalization process: The case of internationalizing channel intermediaries', *International Business Review*, 11, pp. 365–383.

Andersson, S., Gabrielsson, J. & Wictor, I. (2004) 'International activities in small firms: Examining factors influencing the internationalization and export growth of small firms', *Canadian Journal of Administrative Sciences*, 21, pp. 22–34.

Atherton, A. & Hannon, P. (2006) 'Localised strategies for supporting incubation', *Journal of Small Business and Enterprise Development*, 13, pp. 48–61.

Barney, J.B. (1991) 'Firm resources and sustained competitive advantage', *Journal of Management*, 17, pp. 99–120.

Barney, J.B., Wright, M. & Ketchen, D. (2001) 'The resource-based view of the firm: Ten years after 1991', *Journal of Management*, 27, pp. 625–641.

Belso-Martinez, J.A. (2006) 'Do industrial districts influence export performance and export intensity? Evidence for Spanish SMEs' internationalization process', *European Planning Studies*, 14, pp. 791–810.

Bennett, R. & Smith, C. (2002) 'Competitive conditions, competitive advantage and the location of SMEs', *Journal of Small Business and Enterprise Development*, 9, pp. 73–86.

Boschma, R. (2005) 'Proximity and innovation: A critical assessment', *Regional Studies*, 39, pp. 61–74.

Bosworth, D. (2009) 'Education, mobility and rural business development', *Journal of Small Business and Enterprise Development*, 16, pp. 660–677.

Breschi, S. & Malerba, F. (2001) 'The geography of innovation and economic clustering: Some introductory notes', *Industrial and Corporate Change*, 10, pp. 817–833.

Camerer, C. & Lovallo, D. (1999) 'Overconfidence and excess entry: An experimental approach', *American Economic Review*, 89, pp. 306–318.
Capello, R. & Faggian, A. (2005) 'Collective learning and relational capital in local innovation processes', *Regional Studies*, 39, pp. 75–87.
Carlton, W.D. (1993) 'The location choice and employment choices of new firms: An econometric model with discrete and continuous endogenous variables', *Review of Economics and Statistics*, 65, pp. 440–449.
Cavusgil, S. & Zou, S. (1994) 'Marketing strategy-performance relationship: An investigation of the empirical link in export market ventures', *Journal of Marketing*, 58, pp. 1–21.
Chevassus-Lozza, E. & Galliano, D. (2003) 'Local spillovers, firm organization and export behavior: Evidence from the French Food Industry', *Regional Studies*, 32, pp. 147–158.
Chmielewski, D. & Paladino, A. (2007) 'Driving a resource orientation: Reviewing the role of resource and capability characteristics', *Management Decision*, 45, pp. 462–483.
Costa Campi, M., Blasco, A. & Marsal, E. (2004) 'The location of new firms and the life cycle of industries', *Small Business Economics*, 22, pp. 265–281.
Crick, D. & Spence, M. (2005) 'The internationalisation of "high performing" UK high-tech SMEs: A study of planned and unplanned strategies', *International Business Review*, 14, pp. 167–185.
Cuervo-Cazurra, A., Maloney, M.M. & Manrakhan, S. (2007) 'Causes of the difficulties in internationalization', *Journal of International Business Studies*, 38, pp. 709–725.
Cusumano, M. & Takeishi, A. (1991) 'Supplier relations and management: A survey of Japanese, Japanese-transplant, and US auto plants', *Strategic Management Journal*, 12, pp. 563–588.
Dahl, M.S. & Sorenson, O. (2009) 'The embedded entrepreneur', *European Management Review*, 6, pp. 172–181.
Dahl, M.S. & Sorenson, O. (2010) 'The social attachment to place', *Social Forces*, 89, pp. 633–658.
Dean, T.J., Meyer, G.D. & DeCastro, J. (1993) 'Determinants of new-firm formations in manufacturing industries: Industry dynamics, entry barriers, and organizational inertia', *Entrepreneurship: Theory & Practice*, 17, pp. 49–60.
De Toni, A. & Nassimbeni, G. (2001) 'The export propensity of small firms: A comparison of organisational and operational management levers in exporting and non-exporting firms', *International Journal of Entrepreneurial Behaviour & Research*, 7, pp. 132–147.
Donthu, N. & Kim, S. (1994) 'Implications of firm controllable factors on export growth', *Journal of Global Marketing*, 7, pp. 47–63.
Doole, I., Grimes, T. & Demack, S. (2006) 'An exploration of the management practices and processes most closely associated with high levels of export capability in SMEs', *Marketing Intelligence & Planning*, 24, pp. 632–647.
Dyer, J. & Hatch, N. (2006) 'Relation-specific capabilities and barriers to knowledge transfers: Creating advantage through network relationships', *Strategic Management Journal*, 27, pp. 701–719.
Ellis, P. & Pecotich, A. (2001) 'Social factors influencing export initiation in small and medium-sized enterprises', *Journal of Marketing Research*, 38, pp. 119–130.
Feldman, M.P. (2001) 'The entrepreneurial event revisited: Firm formation in a regional context', *Industrial and Corporate Change*, 10, pp. 861–891.
Figueiredo, O., Guimaraes, P. & Woodward, D. (2002) 'Home-field advantage: Location decisions of Portuguese entrepreneurs', *Journal of Urban Economics*, 52, pp. 341–361.
Folta, B.T., Cooper, A.C. & Baik, Y. (2006) 'Geographic cluster size and firm performance', *Journal of Business Venturing*, 21, pp. 217–242.
Forsgren, M. (2002) 'The concept of learning in the Uppsala internationalization process model: A critical review', *International Business Review*, 11, pp. 257–277.
Freeman, J., Styles, C. & Meredith, L. (2012) 'Does firm location make a difference to the export performance of SMEs?' *International Marketing Review*, 29, pp. 88–113.
Fuller-Love, N., Midmore, P. & Thomas, D. (2006) 'Entrepreneurship and rural economic development: A scenario analysis approach', *International Journal of Entrepreneurial Behaviour & Research*, 12, pp. 289–305.
Gimeno, J., Folta, T.B., Cooper, A.C. & Woo, C.Y. (1997) 'Survival of the fittest? Entrepreneurial human capital and the persistence of underperforming firms', *Administrative Science Quarterly*, 42, pp. 750–783.
Gorton, M. (1999) 'Spatial variations in markets served by UK-based small and medium-sized enterprises (SMEs)', *Entrepreneurship and Regional Development*, 11, pp. 39–55.
Greif, A. (1993) 'Contract enforceability and economic institutions in early trade: The Maghribi traders' coalition', *American Economic Review*, 83, pp. 525–548.

Grimes, A., Doole, I. & Kitchen, P. (2007) 'Profiling the capabilities of SMEs to compete internationally', *Journal of Small Business and Enterprise Development*, 13, pp. 64–80.

Haber, S. & Reichel, A. (2007) 'The cumulative nature of the entrepreneurial process: The contribution of human capital, planning and environment resources to small venture performance', *Journal of Business Venturing*, 22, pp. 119–145.

Hart, M. & McGuinness, S. (2003) 'Small firm growth in the UK regions 1994–1997: Towards an explanatory framework', *Regional Studies*, 37, pp. 109–122.

Huang, X., Soutar, G. & Brown, A. (2002) 'New product development processes in small and medium-sized enterprises: Some Australian evidence', *Journal of Small Business Management*, 40, pp. 27–42.

Ibeh, K. (2003) 'Towards a contingency framework of export entrepreneurship: Conceptualisations and empirical evidence', *Small Business Economics*, 20, pp. 49–68.

Ingram, P. & Baum, J.A.C. (1997) 'Opportunity and constraint: Organizations' learning from the operating and competitive experience of industries', *Strategic Management Journal*, 18, pp. 75–98.

Johanson, J. & Vahlne, J.-E. (1990) 'The mechanism of internationalization', *International Marketing Review*, 7, pp. 11–24.

Johanson, J. & Vahlne, J.-E. (2006) 'Commitment and opportunity development in the internationalization process: A note on the Uppsala internationalization process model', *Management International Review*, 46, pp. 1–14.

Kalnins, A. & Chung, W. (2006) 'Social capital, geography, and survival: Gujarati immigrant entrepreneurs in the U.S. lodging industry', *Management Science*, 52, pp. 233–247.

Kalnins, A. & Mayer, K.J. (2004) 'Franchising, ownership and experience: A study of pizza restaurant survival', *Management Science*, 50, pp. 1716–1728.

Katsikeas, C., Leonidou, L. & Morgan, N. (2000) 'Firm-level export performance assessment: Review, evaluation, and development', *Journal of the Academy of Marketing Science*, 28, pp. 493–511.

Katsikeas, E., Theodosiou, M., Morgan, R. & Papavassiliou, N. (2005) 'Export market expansion strategies of direct-selling small and medium-sized firms: Implications for export sales management activities', *Journal of International Marketing*, 13, pp. 57–92.

Keeble, D. (1997) 'Small firms, innovation and regional development in Britain in the 1990s', *Regional Studies*, 31, pp. 281–293.

Kirat, T. & Lung, Y. (1999) 'Innovation and proximity: Territories as loci of collective learning processes', *European Urban and Regional Studies*, 6, pp. 27–38.

Knight, G. (2000) 'Entrepreneurship and marketing strategy: The SME under globalization', *Journal of International Marketing*, 28, pp. 12–32.

Kosova, R. & Lafontaine, F. (2010) 'Survival and growth in retail and service industries: Evidence from franchised chains', *Journal of Industrial Economics*, 58, pp. 542–578.

Kostova, T. (1997) 'Country institutional profiles: Concept and measurement', *Academy of Management Best Paper Proceedings*, pp. 180–189.

Lages, L. (2000) 'A conceptual framework of the determinants of export performance: Reorganizing key variables and shifting contingencies in export marketing', *Journal of Global Marketing*, 13, pp. 29–51.

Lages, L., Jap, S. & Griffith, D. (2008) 'The role of past performance in export ventures: A short-term reactive approach', *Journal of International Business Studies*, 39, pp. 304–325.

Larsson, E., Hedelin, L. & Garling, T. (2003) 'Influence of expert advice on expansion goals of small businesses in rural Sweden', *Journal of Small Business Management*, 41, pp. 205–221.

Leonidou, L. (2004) 'An analysis of the barriers hindering small business export development', *Journal of Small Business Management*, 42, pp. 279–303.

MacGregor, R. & Varazalic, L. (2005) 'A basic model of electronic commerce adoption barriers: A study of regional small businesses in Sweden and Australia', *Journal of Small Business and Enterprise Development*, 12, pp. 510–527.

Malmberg, A., Malmberg, B. & Lundequist, P. (2000) 'Agglomeration and firm performance: Economics of scale, localization, and urbanization among Swedish export firms', *Environment and Planning A*, 32, pp. 305–321.

Mariotti, S. & Piscitello, L. (2001) 'Localized capabilities and the internationalization of manufacturing activities by SMEs', *Entrepreneurship & Regional Development*, 13, pp. 65–80.

Matanda, J. & Freeman, S. (2009) 'Effect of perceived environmental uncertainty on exporter importer inter-organisational relationships and export performance improvement', *International Business Review*, 18, pp. 89–107.

Meccheri, N. & Pelloni, G. (2006) 'Rural entrepreneurs and institutional assistance: An empirical study from mountainous Italy', *Entrepreneurship & Regional Development*, 18, pp. 371–392.
Michelacci, C. & Silva, O. (2007) 'Why so many local entrepreneurs?' *Review of Economics and Statistics*, 89, pp. 615–633.
Mittelstaedt, J., Ward, W. & Nowlin, E. (2006) 'Location, industrial concentration and the propensity of small US firms to export', *International Marketing Review*, 23, pp. 486–503.
Morgan, N., Kaleka, A. & Katsikeas, C. (2004) 'Antecedents of export venture performance: A theoretical model and empirical assessment', *Journal of Marketing*, 68, pp. 90–108.
Morgan, R. & Hunt, S. (1999) 'Relationship-based competitive advantage: The role of relationship marketing in marketing strategy', *Journal of Business Research*, 46, pp. 281–290.
Morgan, R. & Katsikeas, C. (1997) 'Obstacles to export initiation and expansion', *International Journal of Management Science*, 25, pp. 677–690.
Murray, M.P. (2006) 'Avoiding invalid instruments and coping with weak instruments', *Journal of Economic Perspectives*, 20, pp. 111–132.
North, D. & Smallbone, D. (2000) 'The innovativeness and growth of rural SMEs during the 1990s', *Regional Studies*, 34, pp. 145–157.
O'Farrell, P.N. & Wood, P.A. (1998) 'Internationalization by business service firms: Towards a new regionally based conceptual framework', *Environment and Planning A*, 30, pp. 109–128.
Parr, J.B. (2002) 'Agglomeration economics: Ambiguities and confusion', *Environment and Planning A*, 34, pp. 717–731.
Phelps, N., Fallon, R. & Williams, C. (2001) 'Small firms, borrowed size and the urban-rural shift', *Regional Studies*, 35, pp. 613–624.
Raub, W. & Weesie, J. (1990) 'Reputation and efficiency in social interactions: An example of network effects', *American Journal of Sociology*, 96, pp. 626–654.
Ray, G., Barney, J. and Muhanna, W. (2004) 'Capabilities, business processes, and competitive advantage: Choosing the dependent variable in empirical tests of the resource-based view', *Strategic Management Journal*, 25, pp. 23–37.
Rocha, O.H. (2004) 'Entrepreneurship and development: The role of clusters', *Small Business Economics*, 23, pp. 363–400.
Ruef, M., Aldrich, H.E. & Carter, N.M. (2003) 'The structure of founding teams: Homophily, strong ties and isolation among U.S. entrepreneurs', *American Sociological Review*, 68, pp. 195–222.
Ruppenthal, T. (2009) 'Research on export performance over the past 10 years: A narrative review', *European Journal of Management*, 3, pp. 328–364.
Sapienza, H., Autio, E., George, G. & Zahra, S. (2006) 'A capabilities perspective on the effects of early internationalization on firm survival and growth', *Academy of Management Journal*, 31, pp. 914–922.
Smallbone, D., Baldock, R. & North, D. (2003) 'Policy support for small firms in rural areas: The English experience', *Environment and Planning C – Government and Policy*, 21, pp. 825–841.
Sorenson, O. & Audia, P.G. (2000) 'The social structure of entrepreneurial activity: Geographic concentration of footwear production in the United States, 1940–1989', *American Journal of Sociology*, 106, pp. 424–462.
Sorenson, O. & Stuart, T.E. (2001) 'Syndication networks and the spatial distribution of venture capital investments', *American Journal of Sociology*, 106, pp. 1546–1588.
Sorenson, O. & Waguespack, D.M. (2006) 'Social structure and exchange: Self confirming dynamics in Hollywood', *Administrative Science Quarterly*, 51, pp. 560–589.
Staber, U. (1998) 'Inter-firm co-operation and competition in industrial districts', *Organization Studies*, 19, pp. 701–724.
Styles, C. (1998) 'Export performance measures in Australia and the United Kingdom', *Journal of International Marketing*, 6, pp. 12–36.
Styles, C., Patterson, P. & Ahmed, F. (2008) 'A relational model of export performance', *Journal of International Business Studies*, 39, pp. 880–900.
Ural, T. (2009) 'The effects of relationships quality on export performance', *European Journal of Marketing*, 43, pp. 139–168.
Vatne, E. (1995) 'Local resource mobilisation and internationalisation strategies in small and medium sized enterprises', *Environment and Planning A*, 27, pp. 63–80.
Wennberg, K. & Lindqvist, G. (2010) 'The effect of clusters on the survival and performance of new firms', *Small Business Economics*, 34, pp. 221–241.

Westhead, P., Binks, M., Ucbasaran, D. & Wright, M. (2002) 'Internationalization of SMEs: A research note', *Journal of Small Business and Enterprise Development*, 9, pp. 38–48.
Westhead, P., Ucbasaran, D. & Binks, M. (2004) 'Internationalization strategies selected by established rural and urban SMEs', *Journal of Small Business and Enterprise Development*, 11, pp. 8–22.
Westhead, P., Wright, M. & Ucbasaran, D. (2001) 'The internationalization of new and small firms: A resource-based view', *Journal of Business Venturing*, 16, pp. 333–358.
Westhead, P., Wright, M. & Ucbasaran, D. (2004) 'Internationalization of private firms: Environmental turbulence and organizational strategies and resources', *Entrepreneurship & Regional Development*, 16, pp. 501–522.
Wolff, J. & Pett, T. (2000) 'Internationalization of small firms: An examination of export competitive patterns, firm size, and export performance', *Journal of Small Business Management*, 38, pp. 34–47.
Zaheer, S. (1995) 'Overcoming the liability of foreignness', *Academy of Management Journal*, 38, pp. 341–363.
Zahra, S., Neubaum, D. & Huse, M. (1997) 'The effect of the environment on export performance among telecommunications new ventures', *Entrepreneurship Theory and Practice*, 22, pp. 25–47.
Zajonc, R.B. (1998) 'Attitudinal effects of mere exposure', *Journal of Personality and Social Psychology, Monographs*, 9, pp. 1–27.
Zhao, H., Luo, Y. & Zou, S. (2002) 'Product diversification, ownership structure and subsidiary performance in China's dynamic market', *Management International Review*, 3, pp. 27–48.
Zhao, H. & Zou, S. (2002) 'The impact of industry concentration and firm location on export propensity and intensity: An empirical analysis of Chinese manufacturing firms', *Journal of International Marketing*, 10, pp. 52–71.
Zou, S. & Cavusgil, S. (2002) 'The GMS: A broad conceptualization of global marketing strategy and its effect on firm performance', *Journal of Marketing*, 66, pp. 40–56.
Zou, S., Fang, E. & Zhao, S. (2003) 'The effect of export marketing capabilities on export performance: An investigation of Chinese exporters', *Journal of International Marketing*, 11, pp. 32–55.
Zou, S. & Stan, S. (1998) 'The determinants of export performance: A review of the empirical literature between 1987 and 1997', *International Marketing Review*, 15, pp. 333–356.

23

LANGUAGE AND THE DEVELOPMENT OF TRADE NETWORKS IN EARLY MODERN EUROPE

Modern reflexes, unexpected consequences

Sierk Horn and Nigel Holden

Introduction

That there exists some kind of correlation between human language behaviour and the creation, extension and consolidation of business networks seems intuitively to be true. But demonstrating this as a fact is exceptionally difficult. Faced with this challenge, we are taking the unusual step of probing a distinct historical period for insights into the nature of the language of business as an occupation-specific form of language in its own right. This might seem at first glance to be both irrelevant and self-indulgent. It follows that an explicit motivation for this chapter is to refute that proposition.

We argue that an exclusive reliance on contemporary developments actually handicaps our efforts to better understand why corporations make use of language the way they do today. However imperfect, data from the past are worth our attention, for they can serve as an extensive sounding board of current corporate behaviour. Our study will also show that the factors that shaped business in the past are not so irrelevant as they are currently thought to be. Adopting a comparative analysis of economic histories of language and regions – a business history approach – allows us to probe language behaviour 'then', especially the context-specific communication of merchants in their connected geographies. This will help us to put into perspective the role of language in business 'now'.

The period of interest is Early Modern Europe, which is held by most historians to span the years from the end of the 14th century to the end of the 18th century, the French Revolution of 1789 being regarded as its terminus. As we shall see, these four centuries bear witness to a general transformation not only of European life and thinking in every sphere but also of the continent's linguistic landscape. One factor that is crucial in this transformation of life in general and this linguistic landscape is the role of cities, which is very important from our point of view. In Early Modern Europe cities are not only major generators of business networks but incubators of *new* linguistic proficiencies. Our special focus of interest is on German merchants in that era.

In a study of language behaviour in ancient Mediterranean civilisations, which embraced several great empires (Assyrian, Egyptian, Greek, Roman) from *c.*3000 BC to AD 250, Holden concluded that throughout that long era business language 'was variously accommodating, evasive, high-flown and ever geared to the promotion of one's absolutely trustworthy self' (Holden, 2016a, p. 308). It did not matter whether that language was Latin, Greek, Punic or Assyrian or some ad hoc linguistic confection, nor where under the sun the merchants showed their wares, haggled, made their promises and – very importantly – socialised. This marked histrionic aspect of business language use remains an incontestable feature of language behaviour and business development in Early Modern Europe and today.

However, between that era and the long-lost Mediterranean civilisations, there are a number of significant contextual transformations. For example, in Early Modern Europe, as we shall see, the merchant houses invested considerable time and money in making their members – often as part of an apprenticeship – proficient in one or more European languages. But that in itself is only one facet of the bigger picture. We are dealing with the era in which Latin began its relative decline against the emergence of the new, thrusting European vernaculars. Let us put that briefly into context.

Our cursory reading of an admittedly small number of historical works in both German and English concerned with Early Modern Europe suggests that it was the combined endeavours of religious figures – most notably Martin Luther, of course – perpetuating the break with Rome, humanistic intellectuals (most notably Erasmus) and ground-breaking literati such as Dante, Shakespeare, Racine or Cervantes who facilitated the emergence of the vernaculars and precipitated the decline of Latin and with that the authority of the Roman Catholic Church. However, it appears to be the case that historians may be underestimating the considerable impact of merchants as a pan-European class on the transformation of the continent's linguistic landscape. Quite possibly they assume that this particular species of humanity could not conceivably exercise a real influence over anything beyond the confines of the economy. This chapter will advance the case for reassessing the role and importance of merchants in this regard.

Against these considerations this chapter seeks answers to three thematic questions:

- What were the motivations of merchants for engaging in second language learning?
- How and to what extent did these endeavours shape Europe's Early Modern linguistic landscape?
- How can we specify the relationship between language and business network development?

The chapter will proceed with a short overview of Early Modern Europe. The next section will outline the main linguistic developments associated with the period. We then proceed to consider the role of cities in European trade development, highlighting Frankfurt. This will set the scene for a discussion on merchants and the language of business. Special attention will be paid to Germany and the status of German and other languages with reference to the geographical position of trade routes (a) linking Italy and the Mediterranean and the great commercial cities of Northern Europe and (b) the trading cities of Central and Eastern Europe. At this point, we introduce the greatest of all merchant houses in Early Modern Europe, that of the Augsburg-based Fuggers. We then return to two other language topics, first the Mediterranean *lingua franca* and second the language of inland trade and trade routes. Having by now covered all our mean themes, we address in our discussion section the three thematic questions. In the conclusion, we draw attention to the importance of our topic to our understanding of the modern business world, which has to deal with its own multilingual realities.

Early Modern Europe

The term Early Modern Europe refers to the period of history from the end of the 14th century to the end of the 18th century. However much the expression 'Early Modern' raises objections (one being that it would be meaningless to people at the time), and however much we may challenge that geo-cultural designation 'Europe', it cannot be denied that it was in this era that 'the comforting cocoon of a world and universe with known limits, of rural religious uniformity, suddenly burst' (Collins and Taylor, 2006, p. 9).

It was a period in which the Reformation challenged the authority of the Catholic Church, the spread of printing created new cultural norms through the mass production of non-religious tracts and dissemination of new ideas, and the great voyages of discovery revealed new continents and initiated a process which today is called globalisation. But there was one thing about Early Modern Europe which had remained firmly embedded in human experience for centuries: 'trade, war and diplomacy [were] inextricably linked' (Moore and Lewis, 1999, p. 89).

Whereas in previous eras these activities occurred in defined geographical zones (such as, for example, the Roman Empire), the new age introduced a new dimension. War, trade and diplomacy were now being pursued on an intercontinental basis. It was the Portuguese who let the genie out of the bottle:

> Supremacy at sea, their technological expertise in fortress building, navigation, cartography and gunnery, their naval mobility and ability to co-ordinate operations over vast maritime spaces, the tenacity and continuity of their efforts – an investment over decades in shipbuilding, knowledge acquisition and human resources – these facilitated a new form of long-range sea-borne empire, able to control trade and resources across enormous distances. It gave the Portuguese ambitions with a global dimension.
>
> *(Crowley, 2015, pp. 310–311)*

The very novelty of new perspectives brought resistance from 'the possessing classes' whose tendency was to preserve 'the exclusive nature of their rights and privileges, while the dispossessed responded by resorting to violence in any one of its multifarious forms' (Elliott, 1980, p. 389). From the end of the 14th century to the end of the 18th century we witness the foundations of modern forms of government, the emergence of new sciences such as modern chemistry and meteorology, the dawn of industry and associated new developments in artefacts ranging from scientific instruments to iron bridges, from false teeth to roller-skates. One artefact more than any other symbolises what many historians take to be the closing event of Early Modern Europe, namely the French Revolution of 1789, the artefact in question being the guillotine.

Early Modern Europe: the linguistic context

The linguistic context of Early Modern Europe is exceptionally complex, and a detailed description would fill many volumes. Yet, if we stand back and examine what we might call the macro-sociolinguistic context over the four centuries in question, it is possible to discern striking shifts and developments, which we may summarise as follows:

1) The demise of Latin
2) The creation of the modern vernacular European languages and the development of literature

3) The European encounter with languages of Asia, Africa, Oceania and North America, which had no connection with Latin, Greek or Hebrew
4) The start of the transfer of European languages – notably Portuguese, Spanish, French, English and Dutch – beyond Europe as languages of international trade and administration
5) The emergence of French as the language of diplomacy
6) The impact of printing for disseminating new knowledge and new ideas beyond the control of the Catholic Church
7) The quest for a language of science and even a universal language
8) The decline of the lingua franca, the trade language linking Mediterranean ports

None of the developments should be taken as absolute, as several took hundreds of years to come to fruition. One immediately thinks of the demise of Latin, a process which is by no means near completion, such is the power of Ancient Rome over the minds of modern Europeans. By contrast, the quest in the 17th century for a universal language – one that 'would be unambiguous and describe things *as they truly are*' (Holden, 2002, p. 238; original emphasis) – proved to be a chimera. The emergence of the vernacular language was long and complicated in all European countries to the extent that several European states today recognise more than one national language. Think of Finland, Switzerland or Belgium. Then several European countries remain 'containers' of languages spoken by a relatively few number of speakers with respect to the national population, such as Basque in Spain, Gaelic in Scotland or Sorbian in Germany. Other languages are associated with large regional groupings, such as Catalan in Spain or Hungarian in Romania.

The point about these macro-sociolinguistic developments is that the merchant classes throughout Europe in the Early Modern period were strongly influenced by them. For example, not only did printing lead to commercial advertising, it also led to a new mode of communication, namely the formal business letter. But, more to the point, as we shall argue here, merchants had a far greater influence over the broad sociolinguistic context than is generally appreciated.

Cities

There can be no understanding of the development of business in Early Modern Europe without appreciating the significance of cities, which from the 15th century onwards were major drivers of economic change. Cities, though relatively few in number, were located throughout the European landmass on 'favoured land axes', along which 'there was an incessant and continuously increasing movement of men, goods, and livestock, together with one of experience, knowledge and culture' (Grohmann, 2007, p. 207).

All cities of economic importance established their own commercial quarters which were:

> [k]ey sites for the acquisition of information and new forms of knowledge, for linguistic exchange, and for dealing with money, credit, and expensive consumer goods . . . They were focal points in the cities, contributing to their identity and to their political and social life.
>
> *(Calabi & Keene, 2007, p. 286)*

It has been pointed out that the intellectual élites of the cities 'had far more in common with their similar groups from other cities' than with 'the illiterate majority in the cities themselves' (Padgen, 2002, p. 39). But a similar point can be made about the merchants: at least those of the greatest merchant houses in any European city you care to name. Was not this border-spanning kinship a motivation in its own right? Let us use the case of Frankfurt to illustrate and expand upon these points.

Frankfurt am Main was a prominent centre for interregional trade and exchange of goods in Early Modern Europe. Favourable geographic conditions, political history and their interplay are important conditions for Frankfurt's role in Europe-wide trade. In terms of geography, Frankfurt was linked via the Main to the Rhine (e.g., Koch, 1991). This main axis of Europe's North-South trade connected the two major economic areas of Upper Germany (spanning from the pre-Alps or Alpenvorland to the central uplands) and the North German Hanseatic League. Major land routes also met in the Frankfurt region. These provided direct links to the German Northeast (e.g., Lower Saxony, Leipzig), German Southwest, Northern Italy and, by extension, the Balkans.

The conversion from a local farm market ('Kornmarkt'), where agricultural surplus was traded, to trade fairs of supra-regional stature in the 14th century was flanked by (i) the successive decline in importance of trading fairs in the Champagne and Brie regions ('Champagne Messen'), (ii) the establishment of annual trade cycles with two two-week fairs, (iii) trade fair monopoly in the Rhein-Main region, and (iv) the opening up of Eastern European markets that subsequently imposed docking to upper and lower German trade routes (Schneidmüller, 1991). Within this context, Frankfurt emerged as a European centre for commercial activities, which were increasingly organised by craft cooperatives (especially cloth makers) and later by large trading companies with on-site firm bases (Schwind, 1984). Documentary evidence suggests that, at its height of influence as continental Europe's commercial hub, the trade fair's catchment area ranged from Flanders, Brabant and the Baltic Sea region, Poland to Austria, Hungary, Italy and France. By the mid-14th to mid-15th-centuries, merchants traded high-quality mass items and luxury goods from geographically disperse European regions.

However, this does not imply that merchants from foreign countries were regular visitors to Frankfurt's fairs. Evidence suggests that Italian and Oriental goods were imported by Upper German merchants, fabrics from London were sold by Cologne or Dutch merchants, Russian fur and wax were brought to Frankfurt by members of the Hanseatic League (Schneidmüller, 1991). As a consequence, Frankfurt trade fairs were international in the sense of goods on offer, but, not so much in terms of intercultural exchange.

The dominant use of German must, however, not be viewed as an expression of nationalism, but, rather as an adaptation to the prevailing conditions at the time. The need for understanding local customs also included comparative information on German trade practices, including money, weights and measures. Frankfurt obtained the right to measure merchant goods (*Wiegerecht*), which ensured standardised weights for the sale of all goods in the city. Language, thus, was only part of the intercultural exchange. Measures for trade were local (with the local Frankfurt language designation) and needed to be learned by the travelling merchants (Rothmann, 1991).

Dedicated living quarters provide evidence of social and linguistic separation. Next to ghettoisation (e.g., 'Judengasse') as a visible form of segregation (e.g. Backhaus, Gross & Kößling, 2016), we find that many cities had their own representative buildings in Frankfurt. The Nürnberger Hof combined the functions of trade, warehouse and restricted living quarters for merchants from Nuremberg. Merchants from Nuremberg used the Frankfurt trade fairs as a base for extending their trade networks from Italy to Eastern Europe (Hack, 1995).

If business, language and customs in Early Modern Europe were local (perhaps more so than we can fathom from today's perspective), quite separated from the 'foreignness' of speakers and their cultures, the question becomes, what effort did merchants invest in developing intercultural and linguistic skills that would support business activities?

Merchants and the language of business: the mediaeval heritage

In order to understand the nature of Early Modern Europe with reference to merchants, their international activities and associated language behaviour, it can be very instructive to take a brief look at the relevant sociolinguistic contexts in the 14th and 15th centuries. A study of the late Middle Ages reveals that sociolinguistic practices in that era are not only perpetuated in a more or less untrammelled way into the later era but took on new forms as a response to the impact of the factors mentioned earlier. An important study by Gerhard Fouquet (2006) on the theme of merchants and their travels highlights just how seriously the merchants of Europe took the issue of language in their intercultural dealings. Fouquet (2006) points out that French was the courtly language of Europe and as such enjoyed high prestige, but never evolved as a pan-European language of trade. Rather, merchants – at least the better educated in their number – chose to combine Latin with their native language, whereby it was possible to talk to merchants using pidgin-Latin. It is of course quite impossible to determine the extent of this practice.

Nevertheless, in those merchant houses in which apprentices were taught foreign languages, Latin was on the curriculum, it being recognised that a knowledge of Latin suggested an educated, civilised individual – a desirable attribute in a professional class very keen to promote its social respectability. It is striking that an aspiration of the trading houses was that merchants were bilingual, and provision was made for this by appointing in-house tutors or facilitating stays in the great cities of other countries. The main languages were Provençal, French, Italian and English. Foreign language instruction might even by accompanied by the study of rhetoric, which was seen to be important for the formulating of business letters (Fouquet, 2006).

With respect to business letters and records of accounts and inventories, these were already extensively used throughout Europe. In the case of England, they could be a mixture of idiosyncratic English and Latin. This 'mediaeval mixed-language business writing' was not so easy to denigrate because it appears that 'due to [the] scribal ignorance of Latin, [it] was actually the product of "considerable skill" and a high level of competence in Mediaeval Latin' (Wright, 2002, p. 473). It is worth emphasising this point for one important reason: first, written business language has *for centuries* played a far more significant part in business communication than seems to be generally recognised. Hence Wright is quite right to argue that these mixed written forms are 'a distinct variety' of language. But, more than that, they constitute forms of linguistic innovation for the sake of facilitating business transactions.

We have to remind ourselves that to the mediaeval mind a foreign language was not just a tool for doing business, but, represented something alien. It was an entry into a wholly mysterious thought-world. Instruction was often tailor-made with an emphasis on how to become courteous in another tongue whilst receiving the necessary commercial vocabulary: 'money and coinage, weights and measures' (Fouquet, 2006, p. 485). Merchants are known to have compiled their own bilingual and even multilingual glossaries. As an example of the former, Fouquet refers to a Latin-Persian glossary. As for the latter, he cites one such glossary stemming from the end of the 15th century which listed items – including greetings and words for good or bad – in Greek, Albanian, Arabic, Hebrew, Hungarian and Turkish.

Fouquet suggests that the great emphasis on 'bilingualism for business' (our expression, not Fouquet's), is citing the existence of pidgins based on Latin, French, Italian and Low German and characterising mediaeval international commercial language behaviour as 'a semi-communication strategy' (Fouquet, 2006, p. 471). There is a problem with this formulation. It implies that 'semi-speakers' (Wright, 2002, p. 483) are incompetent, seeing that they must perforce contribute to intercultural confusions, misunderstandings and breakdowns because one partner or the other has an imperfect knowledge of a particular language.

Such a view, so easily formed and music to the ears of foreign language teachers, misses two key points. First, there is a general one: that so-called semi-speakers 'are better at understanding than they are at producing' a given language. Second, an intercultural business interaction will involve people who as semi-speakers will make every effort to balance out this mismatch of comprehension and production in order to explore and possibly secure mutually advantageous agreement. 'Twas ever thus, as the saying goes.

The Fugger merchant house

Earlier we noted that we cannot really understand the development of business in Early Modern Europe without appreciating the significance of cities. In turn, we cannot understand cities without an appreciation of the role of merchants without saying a word about merchant houses. Accordingly, we introduce here a few lines about one of the greatest of European merchant houses, whose activities span the late mediaeval period and the first 150 years or so of Early Modern Europe.

It was Jakob Fugger (1459–1525) who built up the family business in Augsburg in textiles and banking into a massive commercial empire which, by the time of his death, had helped finance the territorial ambitions of the Habsburgs, becoming bankers to the Austro-Hungarian Empire; controlled vital commodities such as silver from Austria and copper from Hungary; helped finance a Portuguese scheme to relocate the pepper and spice trade to Lisbon; and had become major bankers to the Vatican (*Economist*, 2015). In 1505 the company financed Portuguese ships on their voyages to Goa. Thus, Fuggers were among the first of Europe's great trading houses to expand their business operations into Asia. So powerful had the house of Fugger become that the mid-1550s were spoken of as 'the age of the Fugger' (Elliott, 1980, p. 43). In the year of his death, the company was involved in mercury and silver mining in Spain and shortly after that engaged in more mining activities in Norway and Sweden. Jakob's nephew Anton involved the company in the transatlantic slave trade and through its Spanish connections established business activities with Latin America. The Fugger business empire dominated business in Europe and beyond until the mid-17th century.

What this brief overview reveals, is that the Fuggers were great believers in timely and accurate business information. This, along with the commercial advantage it bestowed, was one of Jakob's great legacies to his successors. According to a recent biographer, he had a thirst for information about trade and commerce that led him to create a network of couriers whose reports to Augsburg were printed and distributed to clients in the form of a primitive newspaper. 'Fugger had invented the world's first news service' (*Economist*, 2015). Indeed, during the 16th century and beyond, the Habsburgs found it indispensable to 'rely on the Fugger newsletter (an early equivalent of Reuters)' (Wilson, 2010, p. 243). At the same time, the company grew owing to its skills in making itself indispensable to all manner of potentates, who needed the Fuggers' banking skills.

Thus, in order to create one of the world's commercial empires in its day, the Fugger merchant house in Augsburg 'simultaneously moved in diverse economic, social and political spheres' (Häberlein, 2006, p. 204). At the human level we are dealing with a company that did not look upon remote countries and at the time unknown parts of the world as menacing; its leaders knew all too well that the greatest profits sprang from long-distance trade. It follows that the house of Fugger must have been adept at handling foreign languages in the pragmatic way that typified merchants in their era, about which there will be much to say later.

The lingua franca

In Early Modern Europe business activities and the language use associated with them were concentrated into two distinct, though partially overlapping geographical distinct regions: the littoral of the Mediterranean and its ports, where the *lingua franca* was the principal vehicle of intercultural communication, and continental Europe proper, which was crisscrossed with major trade routes and where vernacular languages dominated the operations of business people (see Holden, 2016b). This distinction, rarely observed, is important because it suggests that European merchants, macro-sociolinguistically speaking, used two markedly different forms of language *for geographical reasons*. But, as we shall see, this is not the only distinction of language types which our survey will uncover.

The one form, known as the *lingua franca*, was linked to the Mediterranean littoral; the other form, which lacks a precise designation, is associated with the inland cities and trade routes, and is associated with languages connected with regions, whereby some of those languages such as Italian and Low Middle German (*Niedermitteldeutsch*) are used beyond their nominal region and on occasion combine with other languages to form hybrid languages for business purposes. Let us consider first the case of the *lingua franca*.

This was a rough-and-ready maritime patois based on Italian, its use confined to Mediterranean ports; it did not even enjoy mutual intelligibility from one port to another, seeing that there existed for example, 'higher barriers between the Latin-based languages and the Arabic or Turkish of Muslim Lands' (Abulafia, 2011, p. 486). Commercially speaking, its main use was to facilitate haggling, in which endeavour the cross-cultural projection of an absolutely trustworthy self was as crucial as a fast, arithmetical brain for the calculation – and comparison – of prices, weights and measures in all their dizzying variations and cultural specificities.

The *lingua franca* was unwritten; as such it was predestined not to develop into a language of self-sustaining authority. It was not a language of international correspondence; it did not inspire bilingual glossaries or manuals for eager learners. Indeed, it died out in the 18th century as an ergonomic and economic failure. In a sense it was a victim of geography, seeing that it failed to penetrate much beyond the Mediterranean seashore, or establish itself as a working language of the great European land-based trade networks, the merchant houses and the dominant trading cities. Linguistic scholars who see in the *lingua franca* a prototype of English as the business language of modern Europe are attributing to it a real vigour and transnational reach that it never had (Holden, 2016b), whilst forgetting the crucial matter that it had no written form.

The language of inland cities and trade routes

On the continent, the relationship between trade and languages was startlingly different. If by the end of the 18th century the *lingua franca* was on its last legs, the new European vernaculars had established themselves as fully fledged languages replete with literatures, supported by dictionaries and serving the needs of societies which were breaking away from the constraints of religion and creating new *Weltanschauungen*, which the discoveries of science – and of new continents – were opening up.

Before considering the role of the emerging vernaculars, let us reflect on the status of Latin in Early Modern Europe. Latin was, in the final analysis, the province of a small number of clerics, scholars and intellectuals and, until the Reformation, was the closest thing Europe had to a common general language. For some time after the Reformation – until say the end of the 16th century – Latin was used in commercial documents and by merchants, for whom it was the only serviceable spoken language of business in specific encounters. In other words, Latin at least for a time complemented this or that local language. But, it cannot be considered for one moment to be a general European business language. On the other hand, Latin retained an important part of mixed-language written business communication until an emerging vernacular made Latin largely, but not completely, redundant. The staying power of Latin was directly due to its unassailable position as a source of legal terminology.

We may be assured that relatively few merchants spoke Latin very well. In their case, this refers to the extent to which they could use it to skilfully convey not only trustworthiness but also the de rigueur instrumental bonhomie, especially in discussions in sombre chambers of the business houses or in a tavern over a well-stocked table. This is not to say that they did not sprinkle their formal discourse and their banter of hospitality with bits of Latin. But, we may safely say that the formality of Latin only suited the intellectual elite, in whose professional interactions there was perhaps not the equivalent need for banter and bonhomie, whilst words needed by the merchants for the new products of the age and technical processes did not exist in Latin.

On the continent, the role of the emerging vernaculars differed in remarkable respects from that of the lingua franca, not least because the former played a crucial role in Europe-wide trade development as written media, as languages of commercial instruction and as creators of the major international trade routes. If the *lingua franca* was a victim of geography, the vernaculars were, in a manner of speaking, its beneficiaries and in ways that are not immediately obvious. We can cite three examples to support this contention.

The *lingua franca*, being an unwritten, uncultivated trade patois of random intelligibility, never became a systematically taught language of trade, whereas 'as of the 16th century there developed a lively demand for knowledge of living foreign languages' and not only with respect to the nobility, officialdom and military leaders, but also to the merchant classes (*Kaufmannschaft*) (Häberlein, 2015, p. 10). This, in turn, created a new professional class of language teachers. As these teachers (many were refugees escaping religious persecution and foreign conquest) were well-educated, they developed a side-line in imparting skills of writing 'commercial letters, bonds and receipts' (Budziak in Häberlein, 2015, p. 66). We should note that the emphasis on foreign-language learning was a direct continuation of late mediaeval practices.

A second significant geographically influenced contrast between the *lingua franca* and the vernaculars concerned the evolution of trade networks. The *lingua franca* was, as we have seen, confined to the Mediterranean littoral, whereas the vernaculars helped to expand the great trade routes of Early Modern Europe which linked the great cities together – from Zaragoza in the West to Novgorod and Lemberg (Lviv) in the East. But, more than that, the vernaculars also helped those cities not only to flourish as prominent trading cities but as great centres of culture and learning. The role of the *lingua franca* was puny by contrast.

Third, the invention of printing and the resultant expansion of lay education required merchants to take professional advantage of these developments. A striking example of this concerns the lure of Italy. It became both 'fashion and snobbery' for wealthy families of resident immigrants to send their sons to Padua to learn Italian, the language of 'the ruling families who governed trade and politics' (Braudel, 1981, p. 132). More specifically, the great German merchant families sent their sons to Italy not merely to learn Italian for everyday commercial purposes, but to acquire advanced Italian commercial know-how concerning bookkeeping and finance. To exaggerate the point, Italy was in a manner of speaking the Harvard Business School of its day. This observation brings with it a curious, if not ironic fact: that the self-same Italian which – admittedly rapidly shorn of its inflexions – became the basis of the *lingua franca*, also arose as the first great European language of commercial instruction. This was a function that Latin was incapable of fulfilling.

Another curious fact is that the *lingua franca* as a maritime patois never supplanted the vernaculars, but merely fused them in haphazard ways to its Italian base. By contrast not only was there nothing remotely like a *lingua franca* of the great European trade routes, but also no one vernacular emerged – as English has today – as a general continent-wide language of business. There was no rivalry between languages, as we understand it today. Hence, the businessman of Early Modern Europe was expected to be fluent in one or more languages as a most necessary competence, and the merchant houses made provision for this. For example, the sons of merchants in Germany might be sent at the age of fifteen to Zaragoza to learn Spanish for two or three years; after that might come a spell in Italy to learn Italian. A few would have made their way to London to learn English in order to take part in the wool trade.

Neither were the languages just taught to be spoken. It was most desirable to be able to write well in a foreign language in order to conduct the voluminous correspondence of the merchant houses (Origo, 1959). Furthermore, those with foreign language skills, together with expert knowledge of art, a wide range of connections and competence in financial matters, could find preferment with persons of high standing, provided of course that they shared the same political convictions (Häberlein, 2006). Thus, Hans Jakob Fugger (1516–1575), a scion of the formidable Augsburg-based trading dynasty, conducted the Italian correspondence of Duke Albrecht of Bavaria for some years, a very influential position which led to court and diplomatic appointments (Häberlein, 2006). In other words, foreign language competence – even in ancient languages, incidentally – was not seen as a mere business tool but as a worthy social accomplishment: the mark of an all-round educated person in tune with the times.

Discussion

Clearly, locality mattered very much in Early Modern Europe, and there is nothing unusual in the Frankfurt context we studied. In spite of the city's encouragement to participate in international trade (most notably for reasons of commercial growth), foreign merchants found it difficult to gain a local foothold. As it was increasingly possible for businesses to trade goods everywhere, merchants recognised that language was a means of dealing with these challenges. At the most fundamental level, language, then as now, facilitates knowledge transfer, blending and integration of information and even the management of linguistic capital.

The merchants in Early Modern Europe plainly saw advantages in learning foreign languages to support these endeavours; which brings us to the first of our thematic questions: What were the motivations of merchants for engaging in second language learning?

In a word, we find subtle and not so subtle differences as to what motivated merchants 'then' to acquire knowledge in a language other than Latin and their mother tongue (as opposed to the businessman 'now'). In Early Modern Europe language training was (next to mathematics) seen as a central building block of business education in the German-speaking regions. No wonder that, by extension, the ability to produce and to comprehend a 'foreign' language, was seen as a further indispensable skill of a merchant. Although time-consuming and costly, trading families invested substantial effort and money into the modern language learning of their offspring: male offspring that is. But, they were prepared to do it because communication was attached to future business potential.

The importance of language learning even extended to the acute awareness of language variants and dialects. Language learning abroad was highly professionalised if not standardised. Such training was often combined with an apprenticeship in the target country that introduced budding merchants into the customs and 'secrets' of the trade (e.g. double-entry bookkeeping was seen as a superior business technique). The 'now' of business education, of course, is very different. From a modern perspective, language learning is not an important part of business education. Language, if at all, only plays a minor role in the disciplinary contents of business studies. Contrast this to the common understanding 'then': 'If we do business in Estonia, we've got to understand Estonian'. Both the understanding and the use of language with respect to the demands of doing cross-cultural business were not seen in isolation.

Although language learning was primarily associated with pragmatic, utilitarian benefits of proficiency, we find that integrative considerations also provided an important terrain for language learning. Next to the main objective of developing the ability to communicate with foreign business partners orally and verbally, training abroad also introduced young merchants into local customs and techniques. The willingness to work in a foreign country for a prolonged period as well as the preparedness to learn the language and customs of the target country indicate relatively high degrees of intrinsic motivation. Evidence suggests that training was also intended to stimulate intellectual curiosity (art/culture) and to establish a social relationship with the local community.

Despite the absence of an overarching business language comparable with English today, these intercultural exchanges almost certainly helped to build and extend a pan-European merchant identity and led to the modern European national identities (Götz, 2016). For example, Italian merchants when travelling to upper Germany did not need to learn any German. The local business elite was already highly skilled in the Italian language (see Glück, Häberlein & Schröder, 2013). The combination of professional and integrative motives encompassed all elements of business transactions. These essential skills are not so different from modern business education requirements.

It is worth noting that a concomitant of this 'systematisation of foreign language learning' was the creation of a new *European* class of 'well educated and highly mobile workers', who not only taught foreign languages, but developed grammars and learning materials and manuals and in some cases compiled bilingual dictionaries (Glück, Häberlein & Schröder, 2013, pp. 341–347). These teachers provided their clients with the 'virtues of urbanity, courtesy and augmented social distinction' (Glück et al., 2013, p. 341). In short, foreign language education was equipping aspiring merchants with sophisticated social know-how for operating in International Business networks. Ironically, today, we would call that highly valued skill-set by one of the limpest words in the entire management lexicon: effectiveness.

We now consider our second thematic question: How and to what extent did merchants shape Europe's Early Modern linguistic landscape?

First, what emerges very clearly from our discussion of language and international trade in late mediaeval and Early Modern Europe is the importance of written business communication and its manifestation as a mixed-language form with Latin until the dominance of vernaculars in the 17th century. This mixed-language written business communication, which embraced letters, accounts and inventories, had two important consequences. First, it reinforced the distinction between speech and writing in business communication, which had emerged in the Ancient World (Holden, 2016a); and second, as a corollary of that, paved the way for the stilted and formal business letter across scores of languages.

Second, it is striking to what extent the business classes of several centuries ago, regardless of mother tongue, all considered that a good knowledge of an important language for trading purposes was decidedly advantageous. But, the motivation was not entirely commercial. Knowledge of a foreign language raised one's standing; it was a mark of professionalism, whereby the speaker or learner showed a willingness to break into the *Weltanschauungen* of others in an age when foreigners were all too readily seen as suspicious in some way. Hence, the foreign-language aspirations of the merchant classes set them apart from the churchmen and scholars who were still tied to the classical languages, seeing in them the true and only source of wisdom. In their own way, the merchants upstaged them.

Third, the distinction between the *lingua franca* and the inland languages of business was based on the different products they were dealing with. By and large, the sea-borne trade handled commodities, whereas the inland was dealing increasingly in more and more sophisticated products such as household articles, fashion items and even books. At the same time, new kinds of business methods were being created, of which an outstanding example was the joint-stock company. All of these innovations led to the creation of new words in many languages. Thus the inland languages became productive, whilst the *lingua franca* remained unproductive and uninfluential.

Fourth, it has emerged from the writing of this chapter that the geography-based distinction between the *lingua franca* of the Mediterranean littoral and the in-land languages of business throws up in turn yet another important distinction. What we have shown very clearly is that trade was conducted using the main working written as well as spoken language or languages of the merchant house (for example, Italian side by side with Latin), whilst business was transacted to a large extent, and possibly with the assistance of translators, in the local vernacular (which might be one of several regional variations of German). In short, we have a not too dissimilar situation today regarding the relationship between corporate languages and local languages. Then, as now, it is a question of getting the balance right for the practical purpose of conducting business.

Table 23.1 provides a comparative view of integrative and instrumental learning efforts, and how these, when combined, provided a social fabric for interlocking the International Business community. We have clustered factors under the following headings: (a) international posture, (b) utilitarian value, (c) attitudes, (d) friendship, travel and knowledge, (e) learning about other cultures, (f) integration in the host culture and (g) parental encouragement.

And now to our third thematic question: How can we specify the relationship between language and business network development?

In popular parlance a network is a set of business contacts of greater or lesser significance distributed across geographies (as far as International Business is concerned), these days inhabiting indeterminate space on the internet and accessed as electronic impulses via lap-tops, smart phones and other hand-held devices. This allusion to the modern information technologies might appear to sweep away the business realities and the multilingual linguistic context of Early Modern Europe as utterly insignificant. But, no: what our study has shown is that the merchant houses clearly viewed networks *as pathways to resources* – whether in the form of money (and credit), customers, privy information, political – even pontifical – influence, intelligence about new markets or rather 'market accessibility intelligence' (Moore & Lewis, 1999, p. 187).

Cities were the key hubs, the radiating networks were constantly groomed, languages passed along them bringing with them in the clear (as they say in the intelligence community) or in imperfect interpretation that most precious of commodities, namely news. As Braudel (1981, p. 365) has memorably characterised it, news as 'a luxury commodity was worth more than its weight in gold'. It was often passed on in confidence: 'political news, military news, news of the harvest or about expected merchandise' (Braudel, 1993, p. 409). It may not look like it, but these observations tell us a great deal about the purposes to which business people put language then *and* now.

First, the quest for reliable, up-to-date information suggests the frequent use of language as an instrument of enquiry to interrogate informants and verify their utterances. The point here is that the merchants had to be very good at listening comprehension as distinct from 'mere' speaking proficiency in their own language, a foreign language or even a *lingua franca*. Second,

Table 23.1 Summary of findings

<table>
<tr><td>International posture</td><td>Initial language training at home<ul><li>German and Latin</li><li>Practical reading, writing and numeracy</li><li>This was followed by training in countries with frequent trade relations, predominantly Italy (or, as alternatives, France or the Netherlands) at the age of fifteen</li><li>Modern language skills as prerequisite for social advancement</li><li>Two to three years of language training was considered sufficient (in some cases, a ten-week 'crash course')</li></ul></td></tr>
<tr><td>Utilitarian value</td><td>Training abroad as standard programme of vocation<ul><li>Language learning in the home of a native speaker</li><li>Combined with a visit to a school for accounting</li><li>Skill development not only for family company but also as springboard to prestigious trading houses</li><li>Language skills apparently relatively advanced</li><li>Written correspondence in Italian</li><li>Ability to translate legal documents</li></ul></td></tr>
<tr><td>Attitudes</td><td>Acquisition of modern language skills as prerequisite to carry out profession
Training abroad as integral part of career planning
Learning multiple languages not uncommon<ul><li>Italian as key language, due to commercial importance and trade linkages</li><li>Training in Venice/Genoa complemented by stays in France and Spain</li></ul>Apprenticeship abroad associated with high costs
Importance of language skills<ul><li>Italian indispensable as language of trade</li><li>Learning Italian as part of merchant socialisation</li></ul>Learning of modern languages also 'at home': Antwerp schoolmaster guild received the privilege to offer courses in Latin, French, German, Spanish and Italian</td></tr>
<tr><td>Friendship, travel and knowledge</td><td>Limited integrative motivation of learning about foreign culture<ul><li>Focus on practically usable knowledge: language and mercantile customs</li><li>But to some extent also intended to stimulate intellectual curiosity (art/culture)</li><li>Consolidation of merchant 'global virtues': honest, pious, god-fearing, obedient, assiduous, frugal, modest, displaying humility</li><li>Large 'expat' communities of German speakers</li><li>Integration into kinship groups</li><li>Building of local networks</li></ul></td></tr>
<tr><td>Learning about other cultures</td><td>Language (in combination with vocational) learning main purpose of travel<ul><li>Main objective: oral understanding</li><li>Later also reading and writing</li></ul>Some merchants made use of their modern language skills in translating literary and theological works</td></tr>
<tr><td>Integration into host culture</td><td>Limited assimilation</td></tr>
<tr><td>Parental encouragement</td><td>Initiative came primarily from household head
Trips were well prepared
Great care in selecting the 'right' family</td></tr>
</table>

Source: See Glück et al., (2013).

Table 23.2 Language as network enabler

	Network sustaining	*Network enabling*
Tactical use of language	Linguistic skills for negotiation (including instant calculation and gesticulation)	Linguistic proficiency used for constant enquiry and generation of information 'database'
Strategic use of language	Linguistic skills as pathways to resources	Linguistic proficiency used for strategic inputs (revision of plans and assessments)

Source: See Glück et al., (2013).

updates of news – which went from language to language – forced business people to revise their plans and assessments. This in turn suggests an explicit connection between corporate linguistic proficiency and strategic inputs – seemingly an interrelationship that the abundant literature on strategy has yet to explore. In other words, it was the role of the networks to *update* the city-dwelling merchants with such vitally important news. The greater the linguistic proficiency available to a merchant house, the greater the chances – in principle – of not misunderstanding key messages – and their implications – flowing through their international networks.

By way of summary of the multiplicity of discussion points raised in this chapter, we insert here a schematic chart (Table 23.2) of German merchants' perspectives on language learning.

Conclusion

If, as has been said many times, management scholars at large pay little attention to the role and function of language, then it is inevitably because the topic of mercantile language use in pre-modern eras is virtually off the radar of modern scholarship, including sociolinguistics (Wright, 2016). Yet, the relationship between language, commerce and network development in Early Modern Europe is not only a fascinating topic in its own right, but it also resonates with themes of direct relevance to the conduct of modern business. Exactly as their modern counterparts, the merchants of that era operated in an era-specific multilingual space, in which diverse interests, skills and resources had to be organised to best corporate advantage (Brannen, Piekkari & Tietze, 2014). Our historical journey has accordingly tapped into a modern theme of management thinking about the influence of language on the migration of firms and their human and non-human assets across geographies, language and cultures on a global scale (Piekkari, Welch & Welch, 2015).

We conclude by arguing why this very short historical study has relevance for today's business world. We advance four propositions. First, our study makes plain that the nature of language use for business purposes in multilingual economic space was and still is not only complicated, but unexpectedly so. Second, it is evident that written language played and continues to play a crucial role in general economic development. In other words, the written word complemented the spoken word in any language or in mixed-language interactions. Today, the position is more complicated owing to the plethora, reach *and* multilingual adaptability of modern communication technologies, not to mention the fact that email is a written language with speech characteristics. Third, merchant houses were prepared to invest heavily in foreign-language learning for their staff, the scale of which may, relatively speaking, may possibly astound us today. Lastly, there are important lessons to learn from the interplay of 'language' and 'geography' as based on our historical exploration. Then, as now, geographical facts inform how languages are used in business. We should not fall into the trap that geography plays no role today owing to the dominance of the English language.

Translations

Both authors are responsible for the translations from German.

Acknowledgement

The authors warmly acknowledge the assistance of Professor Dr Mark Häberlein, Professor of Early Modern History, University of Bamberg, and Dr Roman Fischer, Old Archives of the Institute for City History, Frankfurt, for their cooperation in helping the authors frame their topic.

References

Abulafia, D. (2011) *The Great Sea: A Human History of the Mediterranean*. Oxford, UK: Oxford University Press.

Backhaus, F., Gross, R. & Kößling, S. (2016) *Die Frankfurter Judengasse*. Geschichte, Politik, Kultur. Munich: C.H. Beck Verlag

Brannen, M.Y., Piekkari, R. & Tietze, S. (2014) 'The multifacetted role of language in International Business', *Journal of International Business Studies*, 45, pp. 495–507.

Braudel, F. (1993) *The Wheels of Commerce*. Berkeley, CA: University of California Press.

Braudel, F. (1981) *The Mediterranean and the Mediterranean World in the Age of Philip II*. London: Fontana/Collins.

Budziak, R. (2015) 'Sprachlehrer im frühneuzeitlichen Polen: Herkunft, Qualifikation und soziale Lage', in Häberlein, M. (Ed.), *Sprachmeister: Sozial- und kulturgeschichte eines prekären Berufsstands*. Bamberg, Germany: University of Bamberg Press, pp. 61–69.

Calabi, D. & Keene, D. (2007) 'Exchanges and cultural transfer in European cities', in Calabi, D. & Christensen, S.T. (Eds.), *Cultural Exchanges in Early Modern Europe. II. Cities and Cultural Exchange in Europe 1400–1700*. Cambridge, UK: Cambridge University Press, pp. 286–314.

Collins, J.B. & Taylor, K.L. (2006) *Early Modern Europe: Issues and Interpretations*. Oxford, UK: Blackwell.

Crowley, R. (2015) *Conquerors: How Portugal Seized the Indian Ocean and Forged the First Global Empire*. London: Faber and Faber.

The Economist (2015) *Goldenballs*. Review of Steinmetz, G. *The Richest Man Who Ever Lived: The Life and Times of Jacob Fugger*. Simon and Schuster. 1 August.

Elliott, J.H. (1980) *Europe Divided 1559–1598*. London: Fontana.

Fouquet, G. (2006) 'Kaufleute auf Reisen: Sprachliche Verständigung im Europa des 14. und 15, Jahrhunderts, in Schwinges, R.C., Hesse, C. & Moraw, P. (Eds.), *Europa im späten Mittelalter: Politik, Gesellschaft, Kultur*. Munich: R. Oldenbourg Verlag.

Glück, H., Häberlein, M. & Schröder, K. (2013) 'Die kaufmännische Auslandslehre', in Glück, H. & Schröder, K. (Eds.), *Fremdsprachen in Geschichte und Gegenwart*. Wiesebaden, Germany: Harrasowitz, pp. 55–92.

Götz, I. (2016) *Sprache und Diskriminierung: Die sollen erst mal anständig Deutsch lernen*! [Language and discrimination: They should learn proper German first!]. In *Spiegel* Online. www.spiegel.de/politik/deutschland/sprache-und-diskriminierung-gastbeitrag-von-irene-goetz-a-1098835.html.

Grohmann, A. (2007) 'Fairs as sites of economic and cultural exchange', in Calabi, D. & Christensen, S.T. (Eds.), *Cultural Exchanges in Early Modern Europe. II. Cities and Cultural Exchange in Europe 1400–1700*. Cambridge, UK: Cambridge University Press, pp. 207–226.

Häberlein, M. (2006) *Die Fugger: Geschichte einer Augsburger Familie (1367–1650)*. Stuttgart, Germany: Verlag W. Kohlkammer.

Häberlein, M. (Ed.) (2015) *Sprachmeister: Sozial- und kulturgeschichte eines prekären Berufsstands*. Bamberg, Germany: University of Bamberg Press.

Hack, N. (1995) *Der Gewürzhandel in Nürnberg des 14–16. Jahrhunderts*. Hamburg: Diplomarbeitagentur.
Holden, N.J. (2002) *Cross-Cultural Management: A Knowledge Management Perspective*. Harlow, UK: Pearson Education.
Holden, N.J. (2016a) 'Economic exchange and business language in the Ancient World: An exploratory review', in Ginsburgh, V. & Weber, S. (Eds.), *The Palgrave Handbook of Economics and Language*. London: Palgrave Macmillan, pp. 290–311.
Holden, N.J. (2016b) 'English in multilingual European economic space', in Linn, A. (Ed.), *Investigating English in Europe: Contexts and Agendas*. Berlin: De Gruyter, pp. 40–50.
Koch, R. (1991) 'Frankfurt am Main – Handlesdrehscheibe Europas', in Stahl, P. (Ed.), *Brücke zwischen den Völkern*. Frankfurt-am-Main, Germany: Historisches Museum, pp. 30–31.
Moore, K. & Lewis, D. (1999) *Birth of the Multinational: 2000 Years of Ancient Business History – From Ashur to Augustus*. Copenhagen: Copenhagen Business School Press.
Origo, I. (1959) *The Merchant of Prato: Francesco di Marco Dantini*. Oxford, UK: Alden Press for the Reprint Society London.
Padgen, A. (2002) *The Idea of Europe: From Antiquity to the European Union*. Cambridge, UK: Cambridge University Press.
Piekkari, R., Welch, D.E. & Welch, L. (2015) *Language in International Business: The Multilingual Reality of Global Business Expansion*. Cheltenham, UK: Edward Elgar.
Rothmann, M. (1991) 'Titelbild des "Handbuchs fuer den deutschen Kaufmann"', in Stahl, P. (Ed.), *Bruecke zwischen den Voelkern*. Frankfurt-am-Main, Germany: Historisches Museum, p. 43.
Schneidmüller, B. (1991) 'Die Frankfurter Messen des Mittelalters', in Pohl, H. (Ed.), *Frankfurt im Messenetz Europas*. Frankfurt-am-Main, Germany: Historisches Museum, pp. 67–84.
Schwind, F. (1984) 'Frankfurt vom frühen Mittelalter bis zur Mitte des 17. Jahrhunderts', in Schwind, F. (Ed.), *Geschichtlicher Atlas von Hessen*. Marburg, Germany: Hessisches Landeamt für geschichtliche Landeskunde, pp. 232–241.
Wilson, P.H. (2010) *Europe's Tragedy: A New History of the Seven Years War*. London: Penguin.
Wright, L. (2002) 'Code-intermediate phenomena in mediaeval mixed-language business texts', *Language Sciences*, 24, pp. 471–489.
Wright, S. (2016) 'Language choices: Political and economic factors in three European states', in Ginsburgh, V. & Weber, S. (Eds.), *The Palgrave Handbook of Economics and Language*. London: Palgrave Macmillan, pp. 447–488.

24

FOREIGN DIRECT INVESTMENT MOTIVATED BY INSTITUTION SHOPPING

Mike W. Peng and Young H. Jung[1]

Introduction

Why do multinational enterprises (MNEs) undertake foreign direct investment (FDI)? The number of MNEs that undertake FDI is increasing. The number of MNEs worldwide was approximately 7,000 in 1970, and increased to approximately 82,000 in 2009 (UNCTAD, 2009). The number of countries that receive FDI flow was 121 in 1970 and 201 in 2014 (UNCTAD, 2015). Since the 1970s, the world economy has witnessed the participation of the developing countries in East Asia, the transition economies in Central and Eastern Europe, and the emerging economies such as Brazil, Russia, India, and China (BRIC). These countries have not only become major recipients of FDI, but have also become breeding grounds for new multinationals that undertake significant outward FDI.

Conventional FDI research focuses on MNEs from developed economies (DMNEs) that already hold competitive advantages in their capabilities and exert such capabilities in foreign venues by seeking new markets or low-cost factors (Dunning, 1988, 1993). In short, these motives can be summarized as asset-based. However, the increase of participants as well as the spatial expansion of the world economy has brought gradual but dramatic changes to the landscape of FDI. First, MNEs from emerging economies (EMNEs), equipped with fewer competitive advantages than DMNEs, have increasingly undertaken FDI in developed economies as well as developing economies (Mathews, 2006; Peng, 2012; Xia, Ma, Lu & Yiu, 2014). Second, also surging is FDI toward destination countries with neither natural resources nor capable labor forces but lower corporate tax rates (Hines, 2010). These destination countries are often known as tax havens. Figure 24.1 illustrates that tax havens hold 22% of total FDI flows of the world, reaching $322 billion in 2013 (UNCTAD, 2015). These two phenomena have not been sufficiently addressed by the conventional asset-based motives of FDI, given that EMNEs may not be competitive undertakers of FDI and low-tax countries may not be attractive FDI destinations in view of asset-based perspectives.

Focusing on EMNEs, the recent literature on FDI posits that EMNEs are leveraging FDI in order to obtain competitive advantages with respect to technology or innovation, and that EMNEs are mitigating competitive disadvantages by escaping from non-transparent institutions of home countries (Luo & Tung, 2007; Witt & Lewin, 2007). As is shown in Figure 24.2, this FDI research shows significant theoretical development by providing a new category of motives in accordance with the institution-based view (Peng, Wang & Jiang, 2008; Peng, Sun, Pinkham & Chen, 2009).

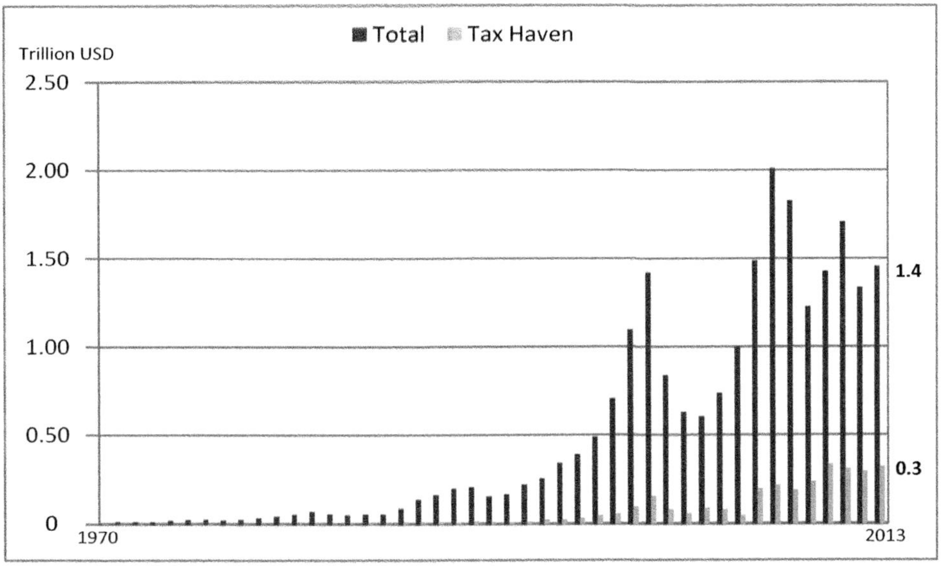

Figure 24.1 FDI in tax havens
Source: Authors' construction from UNCTAD (2015).

This new category of institution-based motives is different from traditional, asset-based motives. In spite of such progress, however, the literature does not fully address the MNEs' motive of FDI to seek specific institutions that offer benefits or mitigate costs of MNEs such as lower tax.

As depicted in Figure 24.2, we offer a complementary institution-based perspective on FDI and extend the existing frameworks, based on the analysis of costs and benefits provided

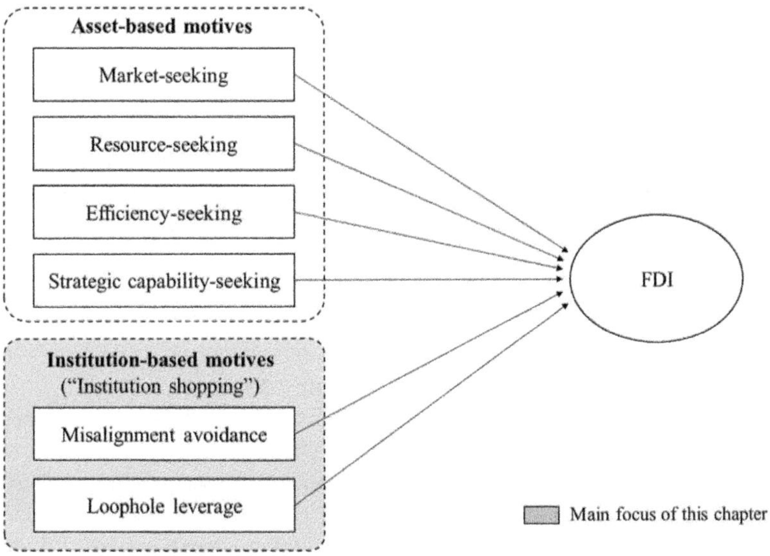

Figure 24.2 Conceptual framework of FDI
Source: Authors' construction.

by institutions. First, we define institutional benefits as the sum of the positive effects from a country's institutional factors that enhance firms' competitive advantages, whereas institutional costs are the sum of the negative effects from a country's institutional factors that diminish firms' competitive advantages or increase disadvantages. Second, we posit that, other conditions including resources being equal, MNEs may endeavor to maximize their net institutional benefits overall. Third, we argue that MNEs "shop around the world" to look for specific institutions that enhance firms' overall net institutional benefits. In short, they engage in "institution shopping". Finally, we probe two behaviors of shopping for institutions: (1) avoiding misaligned institutions that incur institutional costs, and (2) leveraging loopholes in the entanglement of institutions that provide institutional benefits.

We endeavor to make three contributions. First, we probe the costs and benefits of institutions, furthering the analysis on MNEs' choice of institutions beyond developed or underdeveloped institutions. Second, we shed new light on the countries attracting FDI inflows by offering institution-based benefits in spite of little asset-based appeal to MNEs. Third, we explore the active engagement of MNEs in order to maximize the benefits from the entangled institutions in the global setting of MNEs' business. Overall, we would advance our contributions to the FDI literature by extending conventional motives of FDI toward a comprehensive framework that may provide an overarching explanation on the FDI of both DMNEs and EMNEs that seek institutional benefits.

Conventional FDI motives

Asset-based perspectives on FDI

Why do firms undertake FDI? Constellations of literature have endeavored to answer this long-standing question in International Business (IB). Although their perspectives may not be identical, one of the common assumptions of the FDI literature would be that MNEs undertake FDI when the benefits from FDI exceed the costs. DMNEs may be the first group that took the initiative of such benefits from cross-country operations, and the eclectic paradigm of Dunning (1988, 1993) would be one of the principal theories that explain why and how DMNEs undertake FDI.

The eclectic paradigm, popularized as the ownership-location-internalization (OLI) framework, provides a theoretical framework on FDI with three analytical lenses: ownership (O), location (L), and internalization (I). The O-specific assets refer to MNEs' exclusive possession of intangible assets that may be transferred within the cross-border value-added activities of MNEs. The L-specific assets indicate the economic, political, and social benefits proffered by host countries. The I-specific assets are MNEs' capabilities of adding value to the O- and L-specific assets with their organizational efficiency (Dunning, 1988, 1993; Denisia, 2010). The advantages stipulated in the OLI framework are competitive advantages of MNEs from the comparison of firms' privileged intangible assets, proffered benefits from host countries, and firms' value-added organizational efficiencies that may not be held by competitor firms.

The OLI framework explains FDI based on asset-seeking motives. MNEs undertake FDI in order (1) to explore new market opportunities in different countries, (2) to procure natural resources that are not obtainable in their home countries, (3) to secure efficiency—with lower acquisition costs than those in the home country, and/or (4) to pursue strategic imperatives of international competitiveness (Dunning, 1993; Peng, 2014a). In other words, the OLI framework assumes that MNEs undertaking FDI retain competitive advantages such as the O-specific and I-specific assets that create advantages with L-specific assets provided by the destination of FDI.

Then, what about FDI undertaken by MNEs with no such asset-based competitive advantages? Recent trends in global FDI witness the expansion of EMNEs that lack their own O-specific assets such as technological advantages or managerial capabilities compared with DMNEs (Makino, Lau & Yeh, 2002; Barnard, 2010; Gammeltoft, Barnard & Madhok, 2010; Peng, 2012). Scholars suggest that EMNEs go abroad, *not* because they have and hold competitive advantages of O-specific assets, *but* because they attempt to obtain the competitive advantages of O-specific assets (Mathews, 2006; Peng, 2012; Xia et al., 2014).

In complementing the OLI framework that does not offer theoretical explanation of EMNEs' pursuit of O-specific assets, Mathews (2006) proposes an alternative framework of linkage-leverage-learning (LLL). Linkage refers to the relationship-building orientation of EMNEs in order to acquire assets (Peng & Luo, 2000). Leverage refers to the capabilities of EMNEs to link or ally foreign business entities in order to leverage assets owned by such foreign entities (Sun et al., 2012). Learning refers to the process of repeated linkage and leverage by EMNEs that enables them to obtain targeted O-specific assets such as technology, managerial know-how, or innovation (Zahra, Ireland & Hitt, 2000). In sum, the LLL framework complements the OLI framework with respect to the FDI of EMNEs that endeavor to source O-specific assets (Peng, 2014a). However, the LLL framework is also based on asset-based motives in the same way as the OLI framework.

Emergence of an institution-based perspective on FDI

The asset-based perspectives such as the OLI and the LLL frameworks share the assumption that MNEs undertake FDI in order to seek and obtain tangible and intangible assets to enhance competitive advantage. However, there exists some FDI that may not be explained by asset-based perspectives. Why do many US MNEs establish headquarters in a small island country that scarcely has any resources? How do many DMNEs pay minimal tax to local governments in spite of the substantial amount of sales in the country? Suppose a country maintains the social institutions of labor that are so inflexible that the institutions do not permit the termination of employment contracts at the employer's will. If an MNE decides to leave the country and undertakes FDI to operate in another country that maintains flexible labor institutions, such FDI undertaking may not be the case of asset-seeking, but rather that of institution-seeking.

This hypothetical anecdote would be explained using the institution-based view, one of the principal lenses to analyze IB (Peng, 2014a). Institutions would influence and determine the scope of the operation of MNEs, particularly when it comes to the influence from the link of institutions between home and host countries (Peng, Lee & Wang, 2005; Peng, Wang & Jiang, 2008). The influence from institutions of a country may incur institutional costs that diminish firms' competitive advantages or institutional benefits that enhance their competitive advantages. Thus, when institutions of home and host countries are linked, institutional costs and benefits would also be linked, and MNEs may endeavor to maximize net institutional benefits from overall cross-country operations (Hill & Hoskisson, 1987; Stevens, Xie & Peng, 2016). Therefore, MNEs may avoid institutions that are not aligned with the needs of MNEs, or seek institutions that provide the opportunity to leverage regulatory loopholes between different countries.

The literature exploring institution-based motives of FDI has focused on the avoidance of institutional misalignment by EMNEs in their home countries, especially emerging economies, based on the assumption that the institutional development of emerging economies is not as advanced as that of developed economies (Luo & Tung, 2007; Witt & Lewin, 2007). Such literature does not shed light on the similar behavior of DMNEs that also escape from advanced but unfriendly institutions of their home countries, i.e., developed economies. To begin filling such a gap found in the current research of institution-based motives of FDI, we probe the institution-seeking behavior of MNEs toward a comprehensive understanding of the institution-based motives of MNEs, with the introduction of "institution shopping" below.

Institution shopping: toward a comprehensive perspective

Drawing from the "shopping" metaphor, institution shopping refers to the aggressive institution-seeking behavior of MNEs to search and reach a specific set of institutions that enhances institutional benefits or mitigates institutional costs. We argue that institution shopping may be derived from (1) the motive to escape from the misaligned institutions that diminish competitive advantages, or (2) the motive to leverage loopholes in the institutions that enhance competitive advantages.

Misalignment avoidance

Some MNEs undertake FDI in order to escape from institutional hurdles in their home country (Boddewyn & Brewer, 1994). In other words, MNEs would escape their home countries when the institutional costs from the home countries' institutions that diminish firms' competitive advantages exceed institutional benefits that enhance firms' competitive advantages (Luo & Tung, 2007; Witt & Lewin, 2007). Such avoidance would be referred to as misalignment avoidance. Misalignment would be found in the institutions of emerging economies that often accompany institutional voids and hazards and, accordingly, erode the competitiveness of firms (De Soto, 2000; Sun et al., 2015). The underdeveloped institutions of the home country, departing from global standards, may compel MNEs to escape the home country in order to avoid the competitive disadvantages. In this respect, the institutions of developed or advanced economies are considered more business friendly than the institutions of emerging economies (De Soto, 2000; Peng et al., 2008). However, underdeveloped institutions would not be the sole catalyst of institutional misalignment. Misalignment may also be found in advanced institutions when firms in such an institutional environment regard the given institutions as business unfriendly. In this situation, firms may reckon that the institutional costs resulting from the unfriendliness toward business would exceed the benefits from the institutions. Thus, they may endeavor to avoid certain home-country-based institutions by undertaking FDI (Fung, Yau & Zhang, 2011; Hoskisson et al., 2013).

An example of misalignment in the advanced institutions of developed economies may be corporate tax. Corporate tax is a typical example of firms' institutional costs, levied by the tax regime of the country where the firm operates. Tax is the final line in assessing firms' net income and, accordingly, exerts a direct influence on profitability. Thus, firms endeavor to maximize tax efficiency—in other words, to maximize the after-tax cash flow (Scholes et al., 2002). Going forward, tax is one of the primary determinants of firms' capital structure (Heider & Ljungqvist, 2015). When firms have greater pre-tax income, they would be more inclined than other firms with smaller pre-tax income to undertake tax planning (Mills, Erickson & Maydew, 1998; Phillips, 2003). Specifically, MNEs that harvest profits from overseas markets may need to repatriate such foreign profits to their home countries. However, additional tax imposed by the home country tax regime on repatriated foreign profits may encourage these MNEs to look for ways to save such additional tax, by investing in lower tax locations.

DMNEs may be more concerned with tax than EMNEs, given that corporate tax rates of developed economies are generally higher than those of emerging economies.[2] However, EMNEs may also be concerned with tax if a jurisdiction offers lower tax than the home country

Table 24.1 List of tax havens

1 Andorra	19 Guernsey	37 Nauru
2 Anguilla	20 Hong Kong	38 Netherlands Antilles
3 Antigua and Barbuda	21 Ireland	39 Niue
4 Aruba	22 Isle of Man	40 Panama
5 Bahamas	23 Jersey	41 Samoa
6 Bahrain	24 Jordan	42 San Marino
7 Barbados	25 Lebanon	43 Seychelles
8 Belize	26 Liberia	44 Singapore
9 Bermuda	27 Liechtenstein	45 St. Kitts and Nevis
10 British Virgin Islands	28 Luxembourg	46 St. Lucia
11 Cayman Islands	29 Macao	47 St. Martin
12 Cook Islands	30 Maldives	48 St. Vincent and the Grenadines
13 Costa Rica	31 Malta	49 Switzerland
14 Cyprus	32 Marshall Islands	50 Tonga
15 Djibouti	33 Mauritius	51 Turks and Caicos Islands
16 Dominica	34 Micronesia	52 Vanuatu
17 Gibraltar	35 Monaco	
18 Grenada	36 Montserrat	

Source: Hines (2010, p. 104).

of EMNEs. Accordingly, many DMNEs and EMNEs engage in institution shopping by taking advantage of low-tax institutions offered by countries around the world, especially tax havens—jurisdictions that offer lower tax to firms that have business domicile there (Desai, Foley & Hines, 2006). According to Hines (2010), more than 50 countries and territories are commonly considered to be tax havens (see Table 24.1).

While some low-tax jurisdictions with poor governance structures may not attract FDI, tax havens tend to be relatively small and affluent countries that also have good governance structures (Dharmapala & Hines, 2009). Those friendly tax and corporate laws of tax havens may present strategic value to MNEs with respect to performance enhancement, because shareholders and managers usually prefer the reduction of tax payments in order to maximize the after-tax cash flow (Cary, 1974; Scholes et al., 2002).

As a result, MNEs have increased their FDI into tax havens. While the economic size of tax havens is minimal in the world economy,[3] the FDI into tax havens is significant. As shown in Table 24.2, tax havens hold approximately 20% of total FDI flows in the world, reaching approximately $300 billion (UNCTAD, 2015). This scale of tax havens in worldwide FDI supports empirical studies hypothesizing and finding that US firms operating in at least one tax haven carry less worldwide tax burden than firms with no operations in tax havens (Graham & Tucker, 2006; Dyreng & Lindsey, 2009).

Table 24.2 Recent five-year trend of FDI in tax havens (billion USD)

Year	*2009*	*2010*	*2011*	*2012*	*2013*
Worldwide FDI	1,222	1,422	1,700	1,330	1,452
FDI in tax havens	237	333	307	294	322
% FDI in tax havens	19%	23%	18%	22%	22%

Source: Authors' construction from UNCTAD (2015).

To mitigate institutional costs, tax havens have become satisfactory destinations for institution shoppers interested in lower taxes. Now many developed economies stipulate a black list of tax havens and strictly regulate the native MNEs of developed economies so as not to circumvent the higher corporate tax rates of home countries. However, MNEs keep on endeavoring to find legitimate ways to avoid tax in order to mitigate their institutional costs.

A typical example to leverage a tax haven would be tax inversion, a corporate practice to acquire a foreign firm and place the headquarters in the home country of the acquired foreign firm in order to avoid tax (Voget, 2011). However, tax inversion among US firms has occurred only twice between 1983 and 1994, the next decade (1994 to 2004) witnessed 27 incidents, and the latest decade (2004 to 2014) found 44 cases of corporate inversion (*Washington Post*, 2014). Although the US Treasury Department promulgated regulations in order to "stamp out the practice", America's tax policy imposing one of the highest corporate tax rates in the developed economies would not completely remove US MNEs' interest in tax inversion (*Economist*, 2015a). Earlier cases of tax inversion were involved with tax havens, and recent tax inversions have occurred in some low-tax countries, even developed economies such as Canada, that are not typically considered as a tax haven but which offers lower tax than the home country.

Case: Endo Health Solutions and Medtronic. In 2013, a US-based pharmaceutical firm Endo Health Solutions acquired a Canada-based pharmaceutic company Paladin Labs for $1.6 billion. In so doing, Endo Health Solutions created a holding company in Ireland as its new corporate headquarters. In 2014, the world's largest stand-alone medical device company Medtronic acquired an Irish health care producer Covidien for $42.9 billion. Upon the completion of the acquisition, Medtronic moved its headquarters from the US to Ireland in order to enjoy the 10% corporate tax rate offered by Ireland to domestic manufacturers.

The commonality in the acquisition cases related to both Endo Health Solutions and Medtronic is that the new venue of the headquarters was Ireland. As a member of the OECD, Ireland maintains a legal infrastructure that is similar to that of the UK and the US, and has endeavored to lure global high-tech and pharmaceuticals, in order to serve as a biotech hub (*Financial Times*, 2014). In this regard, Ireland offers a 10% corporate tax rate to the manufacturers legally domiciled in this country. Such a low tax rate is enjoyed by companies that are tax residents of Ireland, including Endo Health Solutions and Medtronic. Furthermore, such companies frequently engage in high royalty payments from Irish headquarters to subsidiaries located in other tax havens with lower tax rates, and thus minimize tax payments in Ireland as well as in their home countries by not repatriating any profits (Fuest et al., 2013).

Case: Burger King. Burger King, a US-based fast-food chain, acquired Tim Hortons, a Canadian coffee-and-doughnuts franchise, for $11.4 billion in December 2014. This acquisition boosted Burger King to become the world's third largest chain in the fast food industry. However, the alleged hidden motive of Burger King with respect to this acquisition might include avoidance of US taxes by removing its post-merger headquarters to Canada.[4] As a result, Burger King's acquisition of Tim Hortons is regarded as a tax inversion move. By making the move, Burger King successfully circumvented regulatory enforcement of heavier tax burden of the United States. That is, by the acquisition, shareholders of Burger King may opt for either stock of the resulting company or units of the newly-formed limited partnership in Canada. When a shareholder chooses to receive stock of the partnership, capital gains from such stock are out of the scope of US Treasury rule (Holtzblatt, Jermakowicz & Epstein, 2015).

Loophole leverage

The global operations of MNEs involve multiple institutions, including home and host countries (Stevens, Xie & Peng, 2016). The entanglement of institutions of countries frequently creates loopholes in regulating the operations of MNEs, because institutions are heterogeneous across countries. MNEs would shop institutions that create such loopholes and provide opportunities to leverage the loopholes—in other words, opportunities of effective use, enjoyment, and disposal of the MNEs' own tangible or intangible assets. Overall, MNEs undertake FDI for institutional benefits because such benefits may not be available in their home country or principal venue of business. Among various FDI for the sake of loophole leverage, we want to focus on transfer pricing and capital round-tripping.

Transfer pricing. Transfer pricing refers to "the pricing of cross-border intrafirm transactions between related parties" (Eden, 2001, p. 591). In other words, transfer pricing is moving profit around the world by pricing goods or services in the inter-subsidiary transactions to minimize profits in higher-taxed subsidiaries and to maximize profits in lower-taxed ones. Transfer pricing has critical strategic value for MNEs with evidence of positive relations with better performance of MNEs (Cravens, 1997). By engaging in transfer pricing, MNEs exploit arbitrage in different tax rates across countries.[5]

Such arbitrage usually results in a redistribution of tax revenues among countries and may curtail legitimate tax revenues from countries with higher tax rates (Borkowski, 1997; Slemrod & Kopczuk, 2002). Thus, on the one hand, countries including OECD members are cooperating to prevent transfer pricing practices (OECD Observer, 2011). However, on the other hand, countries also compete to "bid for firms" by levying lower tax in order to attract inward FDI (Black & Hoyt, 1989; Wilson, 1999). Such tax competition is the competition among countries for more supportive tax rates for the purposes of tax base enlargement (Edwards & Keen, 1996). Tax competition may be an effective strategy for a country to attract inward FDI as long as the revenue increase from the enlargement of the tax base from inward FDI outweighs the revenue decrease from tax cuts. In particular, smaller economies with a smaller tax base may enjoy the net increase in tax revenue from the enlarged tax base contributed by attracting foreign capital at the expense of the decrease in the cut in tax rates (Dehejia & Genschel, 1999). Thus, some developing countries may have stronger incentives to attract inward FDI through tax cuts than developed economies (McGee, 2010). Furthermore, developing countries with a smaller economy may resist the tax cooperation to ward off transfer pricing in their economic community.

Accordingly, tax competition may depart from the risk of a tax-cutting war among countries (Mendoza & Tesar, 2005). Going forward, heterogeneous interest across developing and developed countries may permit tax competition without the self-defeat of tax-cutting jurisdictions. Supportive evidence finds that the effective corporate tax rates of 16 countries in the European Union (EU) and G7 have decreased in the 1980s and the 1990s. But tax revenues have not decreased over the same period and have even increased in some small countries (Devereux, Griffith & Klemm, 2002).

This inconsistency in the corporate taxation policy across countries creates loopholes—structural ineffectiveness in regulating transfer pricing. These loopholes motivate MNEs to continue their shopping of institutions and leverage such regulatory loopholes by FDI (*Economist*, 2015b). That is, MNEs may undertake FDI in high- or low-tax jurisdictions, and transfer profits back and forth between subsidiaries with high- and low-tax jurisdictions.

Case: US MNEs in the UK. Starbucks UK officially recorded its sales of $640 million in 2012, but did not pay any tax to the UK tax authority. No tax payment with such a huge size of revenue could be attributed to, among others, the inter-subsidiary transactions with sister subsidiaries such as the royalty payment to Starbucks Netherlands and the payment for the purchase of coffee beans from Starbucks Switzerland. In a similar vein, in 2011, Amazon UK paid just \$3 million in taxes with sales of \$5.36 billion and Google UK paid only \$9.6 million with \$632 million sales (*BBC News Magazine*, 2013).

Capital round-tripping. Capital round-tripping means investing abroad and re-investing back into the home country (Fung, Yau & Zhang, 2011). This phenomenon is frequently involved with capital flight from and its return to emerging economies, because many emerging economies, in an effort to attract inward FDI, provide more preferential treatments for foreign firms than for domestic firms, such as tax incentives (Huang, 2003; Peng, 2012; Borga, 2016). Such preferential treatments for foreign firms often encourage domestic firms to obtain the status of "foreign firms" by investing abroad and becoming foreign firms (Luo & Tung, 2007; Peng, 2012). The round-tripped capital is legally treated as foreign investment, even though the origin of such capital is the original home country of such originally domestic (and now foreign) firms. Thus, MNEs from such emerging economies are likely to leverage the loophole for the purposes of obtaining preferential treatments that may not be available to other domestic firms staying in the home country without the round-tripping of capital.

Case: Outward and inward FDI of BRIC. Capital round-tripping is extensively found in FDI from and to BRIC. First, the largest recipient countries of the FDI from Brazil, Russia, India, and China are, respectively, the British Virgin Islands (BVI), Cyprus, Mauritius, and Hong Kong[6] (Peng, 2014b; Peng, Sun & Blevins, 2011). Given that the BVI, Cyprus, Mauritius, and Hong Kong are categorized as tax havens, the outward FDI from BRIC to these four recipients seems to be motivated, at least in part, by considerations for minimizing corporate tax. Second, what is also interesting is that the BVI, Cyprus, Mauritius, and Hong Kong[7] are also, respectively, the largest originating countries of the inward FDI to Brazil, Russia, India, and China[8] (Peng, Sun & Blevins, 2011; Peng, 2014b). It seems plausible that many BRIC-based firms have engaged in capital round-tripping, not only for the purposes of maximizing the institutional benefits offered by tax havens, but also attaining the status of "foreign firms" back home in an effort to circumvent the unfriendly institutions of home countries.

Discussion

FDI is one of the most extensively researched topics in IB. But its motives are not entirely explored, particularly when it comes to the participant increase and the spatial expansion of FDI (UNCTAD, 2009, 2015). FDI researchers have introduced asset-based and institution-based perspectives in explaining the motives of FDI (Dunning, 1988, 1993; Mathews, 2006; Luo & Tung, 2007; Witt & Lewin, 2007). However, the literature sheds less light on MNEs' motives for FDI to seek specific institutions that offer benefits or mitigate costs of MNEs—a move that we characterize as institution shopping.

In endeavoring to start filling this research void, we make important contributions along at least two facets of the conceptual approach to FDI by introducing the construct of institution shopping. First, we move beyond EMNEs, which are the principal focus of the existing literature on institution-based motives of FDI, by positing that both types of MNEs—EMNEs and DMNEs—may endeavor to maximize their institutional benefits by engaging in institution shopping. Second, as for FDI destinations, we extend the FDI literature into a novel consideration from the institution-based view that institutions may be a "selling point" for a country that could overcome its asset-wise deficiencies by inviting FDI in order to enhance its national wealth (Wilson, 1999). Combining those two, we extend the current discussion of whether specific institutions are developed or underdeveloped. That is, we contend that theoretically more important is whether the institutions provide institutional benefits or costs to MNEs. No matter how developed the institutions are in a country, MNEs may avoid the country when the institutions of that country do not provide institutional benefits. In this vein, we stipulate that there exists a global market of institutions where MNEs buy and FDI destinations sell MNE-friendly institutions that would maximize the net institutional benefits of MNEs. Overall, this chapter extends earlier institution-based research (Meyer & Peng, 2016; Peng, 2012, 2014b; Peng et al., 2005, 2008, 2009) with a sharper focus on institution shopping as an institution-based rationale behind FDI.

An avenue to future research can be found from the assumption of a global market of institutions. First, competition for friendly institutions may occur among countries that desperately need FDI (World Bank, 2015). As we see tax competition toward lower tax among some developing countries for the sake of inward FDI (Devereux, Griffith & Klemm, 2002), we may expect institutional competition among countries to increase with a bigger scale and wider scope, when more countries come out of isolation, integrate themselves into the global economy, and endeavor to overcome their late-mover disadvantages by institutional change (Peng, 2003). The institutional change by developing countries may provide MNEs with larger loopholes for regulatory arbitrage such as transfer pricing. In response to the loopholes, developed economies such as the OECD member countries would depart from bilateral negotiation to persuade emerging economies out of their loophole-creating institutions. Instead, developed economies may endeavor to build global institutions through not only transnational organizations such as the United Nations, but also supranational markets or states such as the EU in order to control the expected loophole-leveraging behavior of MNEs (Djelic & Quack, 2003).

Second, we probed whether MNEs may actively endeavor to shape the institutions. The traditional literature on institutions in an IB context has focused on the influence of institutions on MNEs (Peng et al., 2008; Greenwood et al., 2011; Meyer & Peng, 2016). But it has not paid close attention to MNEs that "purposely and strategically shape their institutional environment to enhance their competitive advantage" (Marquis & Raynard, 2015). Such active engagement of MNEs in shaping institutions may be worth investigating, given that MNEs may actively explore the likelihood of institutional benefits from the loopholes in the heterogeneous institutions. As a result, such active MNEs may bring changes to existing institutions or may create new institutions by leveraging resources (DiMaggio, 1988; see Battilana, Leca & Boxenbaum, 2009 for a review). Recent research has developed insights on building institutional infrastructure that purports to be business activities, but is currently inadequate or missing (Mair & Marti, 2009; Marquis & Raynard, 2015). We find this research may be extended further, particularly with respect to informal institutions such as corporate social responsibility (Peng et al., 2009).

Conclusion

Why do MNEs undertake FDI? In addition to the asset-based reasoning captured in the conventional FDI literature, we suggest an alternative answer: some MNEs may sometimes be shopping for business-friendly institutions around the world. In the case of tax inversion, the Obama administration has accused this practice of being "unpatriotic" (*Economist*, 2015a). Such criticisms reflect a fundamental lack of understanding of the institution-based rationale behind FDI. Institutions matter when transactions become costly (North, 1990). When operating in a country becomes costly, firms would look for another country in which operations are less costly. In conclusion, readers of this chapter—as well as ignorant officials from the Obama administration—can benefit from a quote from Adam Smith (1776/1991, p. 520):

> The proprietor of stock is properly a citizen of the world, and is not necessarily attached to any particular country. He would be apt to abandon the country in which he was exposed to a vexatious inquisition . . . and would remove his stock to some other country where he could either carry on his business, or enjoy his fortune more at his ease.

Notes

1 We thank Gary Cook for clear guidance, and Xiaoou Bai, Hanlin Chi, Jihyun Eun, Ayenda Kemp, Dong Shin Kim, Kyun Kim, Ziyuan Liu, Charlotte Reypens, Jason Shay, and Joyce Wang for helpful comments. This research was supported in part by the Jindal Chair and the Jindal School of Management Ph.D. Research Fellowship.

2 The average corporate tax rate (GDP-weighted) of G7 countries is 33.9% and the OECD member countries show an average rate of 31.6% (OECD, 2015). In contrast, the average rate of the emerging economies such as BRIC and South Africa is 27.3% (Pomerleau, 2015).

3 The total GDP of tax havens listed in Table 24.1 amounts to approximately $1.1 trillion (1.7% of world GDP) in 2010, which is comparable to that of New York State (Hines, 2010).

4 Burger King reportedly saved approximately $275 million of US corporate tax the company would have had to pay if they had been US domiciled (Reuters, 2014).

5 Transfer pricing differs from seeking low-tax jurisdiction. Seeking low-tax jurisdiction assumes the permanent change of firm's principal domicile in order to have a low corporate tax rate, while transfer pricing is moving profit from a low-tax jurisdiction to a high-tax one in order to reduce the overall tax incurred in both low-tax and high-tax jurisdictions.

6 If Hong Kong is regarded as part of China, then the largest *foreign* recipient of Chinese outward FDI is the BVI (Peng, Sun & Blevins, 2011).

7 In terms of outward FDI from China, the largest foreign originating country of Chinese inward FDI is also the BVI (Peng, Sun & Blevins, 2011).

8 Of course, not all inward FDI (IFDI) into China is driven by institutional shopping. There is substantial IFDI from DMNEs of the Western world, whose behavior can be mostly captured by existing theories such as the OLI framework. As a result, such IFDI is not our focus. Instead, we concentrate on interesting aspects of IFDI that have not been adequately addressed in the existing literature.

References

Barnard, H. (2010) 'Overcoming the liability of foreignness without strong firm capabilities: The value of market-based resources', *Journal of International Management*, 16, pp. 165–176.

Battilana, J., Leca, B. & Boxenbaum, E. (2009) 'How actors change institutions: Towards a theory of institutional entrepreneurship', *Academy of Management Annals*, 3, pp. 65–107.

BBC News Magazine (2013) *Google, Amazon, Starbucks: The rise of 'tax shaming'*. May 21. www.bbc.com/news/magazine-20560359.

Black, D.A. & Hoyt, W.H. (1989). 'Bidding for firms', *American Economic Review*, 79, pp. 1249–1256.

Boddewyn, J.J. & Brewer, T.L. (1994) 'International-business political behavior: New theoretical directions', *Academy of Management Review*, 19, pp. 119–143.

Borga, M. (2016) 'Not all foreign direct investment is foreign: The extent of round-tripping', in Sauvant, K.P. (Ed.), *Columbia FDI Perspectives*, no. 172. New York: Vale Columbia Center on Sustainable International Investment.

Borkowski, S.C. (1997) 'The transfer pricing concerns of developed and developing countries', *International Journal of Accounting*, 32, pp. 321–336.

Cary, W.L. (1974) 'Federalism and corporate law: Reflections upon Delaware', *Yale Law Journal*, 83, pp. 663–705.

Cravens, K.S. (1997) 'Examining the role of transfer pricing as a strategy for multinational firms', *International Business Review*, 6, pp. 127–145.
Dehejia, V.H. & Genschel, P. (1999) 'Tax competition in the European Union', *Politics & Society*, 27, pp. 403–430.
Denisia, V. (2010) 'Foreign direct investment theories: An overview of the main FDI theories', *European Journal of Interdisciplinary Studies*, 2, pp. 104–110.
Desai, M.A., Foley, C. & Hines, J.R. (2006) 'The demand for tax haven operations', *Journal of Public Economics*, 90, pp. 513–531.
De Soto, H. (2000) *The Mystery of Capital: Why Capitalism Triumphs in the West and Fails Everywhere Else*. New York: Basic Books.
Devereux, M.P., Griffith, R. & Klemm, A. (2002) 'Corporate income tax reforms and international tax competition', *Economic Policy*, 17, pp. 449–495.
Dharmapala, D. & Hines, J.R. (2009) 'Which countries become tax havens?' *Journal of Public Economics*, 93, pp. 1058–1068.
DiMaggio, P.J. (1988) 'Interest and agency in institutional theory', in Zucker, L. (Ed.), *Institutional Patterns and Organizations*. Cambridge, MA: Ballinger, pp. 3–22.
Djelic, M.L. & Quack, S. (Eds.) (2003) *Globalization and Institutions: Redefining the Rules of the Economic Game*. Cheltenham, UK: Edward Elgar.
Dunning, J.H. (1988) 'The eclectic paradigm of international production: A restatement and some possible extensions', *Journal of International Business Studies*, 19, pp. 1–31.
Dunning, J.H. (1993) *Multinational Enterprises and the Global Economy*. Basingstoke, UK: Addison Wesley.
Dyreng, S.D. & Lindsey, B.P. (2009) 'Using financial accounting data to examine the effect of foreign operations located in tax havens and other countries on US multinational firms' tax rates', *Journal of Accounting Research*, 47, pp. 1283–1316.
The Economist (2015a) *Inverted Logic*. August 15. www.economist.com/node/21660978/print.
The Economist (2015b) *New Rules, Same Old Paradigm*. October 10. www.economist.com/node/21672207/print.
Eden, L. (2001) 'Taxes, transfer pricing, and the multinational enterprise', in Rugman, A. (Ed.), *The Oxford Handbook of International Business*. Oxford, UK: Oxford University Press, pp. 591–619.
Edwards, J. & Keen, M. (1996) 'Tax competition and Leviathan', *European Economic Review*, 40, pp. 113–134.
Financial Times (2014) *Tax Avoidance: The Irish Inversion*. April 29. www.ft.com/intl/cms/s/2/d9b4fd34-ca3f-11e3-8a31-00144feabdc0.html.
Fuest, C., Spengel, C., Finke, K., Heckemeyer, J.H. & Nusser, H. (2013) 'Profit shifting and "aggressive" tax planning by multinational firms: Issues and options for reform', *World Tax Journal*, 4, pp. 307–324.
Fung, H.G., Yau, J. & Zhang, G. (2011) 'Reported trade figure discrepancy, regulatory arbitrage, and round-tripping: Evidence from the China–Hong Kong trade data', *Journal of International Business Studies*, 42, pp. 152–176.
Gammeltoft, P., Barnard, H. & Madhok, A. (2010) 'Emerging multinationals, emerging theory: Macro-and micro-level perspectives', *Journal of International Management*, 16, pp. 95–101.
Graham, J.R. & Tucker, A.L. (2006) 'Tax shelters and corporate debt policy', *Journal of Financial Economics*, 81, pp. 563–594.
Greenwood, R., Raynard, M., Kodeih, F., Micelotta, E.R. & Lounsbury, M. (2011) 'Institutional complexity and organizational responses', *Academy of Management Annals*, 5, pp. 317–371.
Heider, F. & Ljungqvist, A. (2015) 'As certain as debt and taxes: Estimating the tax sensitivity of leverage from state tax changes', *Journal of Financial Economics*, 118, pp. 684–712.
Hill, C.W. & Hoskisson, R.E. (1987) 'Strategy and structure in the multiproduct firm', *Academy of Management Review*, 12, pp. 331–341.
Hines, J.R. (2010) 'Treasure islands', *Journal of Economic Perspectives*, 24, pp. 103–126.
Holtzblatt, M., Jermakowicz, E.K. & Epstein, B.J. (2015) 'Tax heavens: Methods and tactics for corporate profit shifting', *International Tax Journal*, 41, pp. 33–44.
Hoskisson, R.E., Wright, M., Filatotchev, I. & Peng, M.W. (2013) 'Emerging multinationals from mid-range economies: The influence of institutions and factor markets', *Journal of Management Studies*, 50, pp. 1295–1321.
Huang, Y. (2003) *Selling China*. New York: Cambridge University Press.

Luo, Y. & Tung, R.L. (2007) 'International expansion of emerging market enterprises: A springboard perspective', *Journal of International Business Studies*, 38, pp. 481–498.

Mair, J. & Marti, I. (2009) 'Entrepreneurship in and around institutional voids: A case study from Bangladesh', *Journal of Business Venturing*, 24, pp. 419–435.

Makino, S., Lau, C.M. & Yeh, R.S. (2002) 'Asset-exploitation versus asset-seeking: Implications for location choice of foreign direct investment from newly industrialized economies', *Journal of International Business Studies*, 33, pp. 403–421.

Marquis, C. & Raynard, M. (2015) 'Institutional strategies in emerging markets', *Academy of Management Annals*, 9, pp. 291–335.

Mathews, J.A. (2006) 'Dragon multinationals: New players in 21st century globalization', *Asia Pacific Journal of Management*, 23, pp. 5–27.

McGee, R.W. (2010) 'Ethical issues in transfer pricing', *Manchester Journal of International Economic Law*, 7, pp. 24–41.

Mendoza, E.G. & Tesar, L.L. (2005) 'Why hasn't tax competition triggered a race to the bottom? Some quantitative lessons from the EU', *Journal of Monetary Economics*, 52, pp. 163–204.

Meyer, K.E. & Peng, M.W. (2016) 'Theoretical foundations of emerging economy business research', *Journal of International Business Studies*, 47, pp. 3–22.

Mills, L., Erickson, M.M. & Maydew, E.L. (1998) 'Investments in tax planning', *Journal of the American Taxation Association*, 20, pp. 1–20.

North, D.C. (1990) *Institutions, Institutional Change and Economic Performance*. New York: Cambridge University Press.

OECD (2015) *Revenue Statistics 2015*. Paris: Organization for Economic Cooperation and Development.

OECD Observer (2011) *Multinational Enterprises: Better Guidelines for Better Lives*. July 28. www.oecdobserver.org/news/fullstory.php/aid/3553/Multinational_enterprises:_Better_guidelines_for_better_lives.html.

Peng, M.W. (2003) 'Institutional transitions and strategic choices', *Academy of Management Review*, 28, pp. 275–296.

Peng, M.W. (2012) 'The global strategy of emerging multinationals from China', *Global Strategy Journal*, 2, pp. 97–107.

Peng, M.W. (2014a) *Global Business*. 3rd edition. Cincinnati, OH: Cengage Learning.

Peng, M.W. (2014b) 'New directions in the institution-based view', in Boddewyn, J. (Ed.), *International Business Essays by AIB Fellows*. Bingley, UK: Emerald, pp. 59–78.

Peng, M.W., Lee, S.-H. & Wang, D.Y. (2005) 'What determines the scope of the firm over time? A focus on institutional relatedness', *Academy of Management Review*, 30, pp. 622–633.

Peng, M.W. & Luo, Y. (2000) 'Managerial ties and firm performance in a transition economy: The nature of a micro-macro link', *Academy of Management Journal*, 43, pp. 486–501.

Peng, M.W., Sun, S.L. & Blevins, D.P. (2011) 'The social responsibility of International Business scholars', *Multinational Business Review*, 19, pp. 106–119.

Peng, M.W., Sun, S.L., Pinkham, B. & Chen, H. (2009) 'The institution-based view as a third leg for a strategy tripod', *Academy of Management Perspectives*, 23, pp. 63–81.

Peng, M.W., Wang, D.Y. & Jiang, Y. (2008) 'An institution-based view of International Business strategy: A focus on emerging economies', *Journal of International Business Studies*, 39, pp. 920–936.

Phillips, J.D. (2003) 'Corporate tax-planning effectiveness: The role of compensation-based incentives', *Accounting Review*, 78, pp. 847–874.

Pomerleau, K. (2015) 'Corporate income tax rates around the world, 2015', in Tax Foundation (Ed.), *Fiscal Fact*, no. 483. Washington, DC: Tax Foundation.

Reuters (2014) *Burger King to Save Millions in U.S. Taxes in 'Inversion': Study*. December 11. www.reuters.com/article/2014/12/11/us-usa-tax-burgerking-idUSKBN0JP0CI20141211.

Scholes, M., Wolfson, M., Erickson, M., Maydew, E. & Shevlin, T. (2002) *Taxes and Business Strategy: A Planning Approach*. 3rd Edition. Upper Saddle River, NJ: Prentice Hall.

Slemrod, J. & Kopczuk, W. (2002) 'The optimal elasticity of taxable income', *Journal of Public Economics*, 84, pp. 91–112.

Smith, A. (1776/1991) *The Wealth of Nations*. New York: Prometheus Books.

Stevens, C., Xie, E. & Peng, M.W. (2016) 'Toward a legitimacy-based view of political risk: The case of Google and Yahoo in China', *Strategic Management Journal*, 37, pp. 945–963.

Sun, S.L., Peng, M.W., Lee, R.P. & Tan, W. (2015) 'Institutional open access at home and outward internationalization', *Journal of World Business*, 50, pp. 234–246.

Sun, S.L., Peng, M.W., Ren, B. & Yan, D. (2012) 'A comparative ownership advantage framework for cross-border M&As: The rise of Chinese and Indian MNEs', *Journal of World Business*, 47, pp. 4–16.

UNCTAD (2009) *World Investment Report: Transnational Corporations, Agricultural Production and Development*. New York and Gueneva: United Nations. http://unctad.org/en/docs/wir2009_en.pdf.

UNCTAD (2015) *FDI Inflows, by Region and Economy, 1990–2014*. New York and Gueneva: United Nations. http://unctad.org/en/Pages/DIAE/World%20Investment%20Report/Annex-Tables.aspx.

Voget, J. (2011) 'Relocation of headquarters and international taxation', *Journal of Public Economics*, 95, pp. 1067–1081.

Washington Post (2014) *These Are the Companies Abandoning the U.S. to Dodge Taxes*. August 6. www.washingtonpost.com/news/wonkblog/wp/2014/08/06/these-are-the-companies-abandoning-the-u-s-to-dodge-taxes/.

Wilson, J.D. (1999) 'Theory of tax competition', *National Tax Journal*, 52, pp. 269–304.

Witt, M.A. & Lewin, A.Y. (2007) 'Outward foreign direct investment as escape response to home country institutional constraints', *Journal of Studies*, 38, pp. 579–594.

World Bank (2015) *Doing Business 2016: Measuring Regulatory Quality and Efficiency*. Washington, DC: World Bank. www.doingbusiness.org/~/media/GIAWB/Doing%20Business/Documents/Annual-Reports/English/DB16-Full-Report.pdf.

Xia, J., Ma, X., Lu, J.W. & Yiu, D.W. (2014) 'Outward foreign direct investment by emerging market firms: A resource dependence logic', *Strategic Management Journal*, 35, pp. 1343–1363.

Zahra, S.A., Ireland, R.D. & Hitt, M.A. (2000) 'International expansion by new venture firms: International diversity, mode of market entry, technological learning, and performance', *Academy of Management Journal*, 43, pp. 925–950.

PART V

Location and competitiveness

25

MULTINATIONAL PERFORMANCE AND THE GEOGRAPHY OF FDI

Issues of embeddedness, strategic fit and the dimensions of distance

Ioana R. Bedreaga, Raquel Ortega Argilés and Philip McCann

Introduction

This chapter examines the ideas and insights emerging from the Economic Geography and International Business literatures on the strategic fit and embeddedness of multinationals, their subsidiaries and their affiliates in host economies. While the core material is mainly evident in the International Business and Economic Geography, the relevant literature also spans various different disciplines and draws insights from quite different fields, including sociology, political science, management science, urban studies, strategy and economics. However, the locational setting of the multinational subsidiary turns out to be the context in which many different influences and dimensions are drawn together in a manner which heavily shapes corporate decision-making. These issues are discussed here from various perspectives, with a central organising framework of Economic Geography underpinning each. The rest of the chapter is organised as follows: the next section reviews the concepts and definitions linking the multinational to its location or place; then we examine the empirical evidence on embeddedness and strategic fit, followed by a discussion on the dimensions of distance, as they pertain to the Economic Geography of multinational investment decisions. The final section provides some brief conclusions.

Concepts and definitions linking the multinational to its location and place

Many scholars have tried to understand the development of internationalisation patterns, particularly in terms of foreign direct investment as they assume great additional costs, financial risk and strategic impact (Hymer, 1976). Theoretical mechanisms mainly imply a positive relationship between internationalisation strategies and performance based on economies of scale and scope (Kogut, 1985; Ghoshal, 1987), location-specific advantages (Dunning, 1980), new opportunities for learning and value creation (Barkema & Vermeulen, 1998) as well as the spread of risks and costs over larger markets (Contractor, Kundu & Hsu, 2003). Indeed, on almost every indicator of internationalisation, multinational activities and investments tend to out-perform their domestic equivalents (Iammarino & McCann, 2013). At the same time, however, at an empirical level, the cost-benefit trade-off of internationalisation has yielded mixed and often contradictory results (Bausch & Krist, 2007), suggesting that the relationship between internationalisation and performance is neither unidirectional nor monotonic, but instead appears also to be heavily moderated by contextual factors that can produce differential performance effects. These contextual factors can operate at the national, regional or local scales, depending on the issues in question. Importantly, geography moderates and shapes the impacts and performance of multinational activities in different ways and over different spatial scales, pervading all aspects of multinationalisation.

In general, operational performance has been theorised to depend on the interplay between the internal resources that are under the 'direct, real time control of the manager' and the environmental variables that 'are not subject to direct or positive real time control' (Luthans & Stewart, 1978, pp. 686–687) and thus, 'the best way to organize depends on the nature of the environment to which the organization relates' (Scott, 1992, p. 89). These ideas borrow from the schema first proposed by Alchian (1950), and imply that successful internationalisation depends heavily on the extent to which firms are able to adjust their operational behaviour to the exogenous characteristics of the foreign environments in which they operate. This extent to which the firm's actions and activities are adjusted to the firm's environment is often discussed in terms of the 'strategic fit' or the quality and degree of 'embeddedness' between the firm and its local environment. At the micro level these ideas underpin questions regarding the firm strategy, while at the meso or macro levels these ideas underpin the relationships between Economic Geography and multinational activities. In particular, there is now a growing awareness of the role played by systems of cities, and in particular key global cities, in reflecting, mediating and shaping the geography of multinationalism and globalisation. Taking their early analytical arguments to their logical conclusions led both Hymer (1972) and Vernon (1966) to originally conclude that there will be a close match between the international urban hierarchy and the international corporate hierarchy, with the observed long-run distribution of multinational activities and investments closely mirroring spatial structures. Part of the argument here relates exactly to the goodness of fit concept, in that the returns to global investments are likely to be maximised where the strategic fit between the specific investment and its local host environment is optimised. Different countries and cities offer different sets of resources, opportunities, challenges and complexities, and multinational investments which most appropriately reflect and build on these particular dimensions are those which are most likely to earn maximum returns.

The concepts of 'strategic fit' and 'embeddedness' which exist in the economic sociology and business strategy literatures are particularly relevant for understanding how multinational firms may increase the performance of their investments. Generically, these concepts are both based on the idea that organisational behaviour and performance cannot be understood as being independent of the social and institutional contexts surrounding the firm. Embeddedness relates to the scale, variety and depth of the firm's knowledge, monetary and institutional linkages with its host context and also that these tend to be related to the longevity of the firm in the context. Moreover, these linkages are likely to be two-way, implying mutual commitments both on the part of the foreign investor as well as the host country or region. Meanwhile, the closely related concept of strategic fit relates to the efficacy and efficiency of the matching and dovetailing which takes place between the points of contact on the part of the foreign investor and the host region. These two concepts are interrelated, in the sense that embeddedness acts as a mechanism to obtain strategic fit in various settings while, conversely, strategic fit acts so as to deepen and enrich a firm's embeddedness in its environment. In these two literatures, organisational performance is therefore understood to be dependent on the opportunities of the firms to better embed themselves in the socio-political environments of the host countries, and to develop two-way flows of knowledge and technology (Cantwell & Iammarino, 2003). As each individual host country carries different potential for embedding their foreign affiliates, it is expected that organisational performance will also vary depending on the idiosyncrasies of the local environments in which the firms operate.

The concept of 'embeddedness' has attracted extensive academic attention in a variety of fields. Economic sociologists originally developed the concept to capture the inherent dynamics between market structures and the surrounding environment, both in terms of the social interactions across business actors and also in terms of political, regulatory and institutional mechanisms (Krippner & Alvarez, 2007). Polanyi (1944) first introduced the concept of embeddedness to demonstrate that economic exchanges do not occur in isolation as the principles of market self-regulation prevailed at that time, but instead are entangled in economic and non-economic institutional settings, which in turn are entangled in the market relations. Later researchers changed the direction of the interpretation and suggested that economic action is effectively embedded into broader institutional and social frameworks. The turning point in the embeddedness literature was Granovetter's (1985) analysis, which shifted the analytical focus of transactions away from general market economies towards more specific scales of actors and relational networks defined by interpersonal relationships (Uzzi, 1997). In essence, the concept of embeddedness has broadly captured the integration of the economic action into the broader social and institutional environment, yet up to this point its applications have been flexible and spanned across multiple levels of analysis depending on the purpose of the study. Theoretical frameworks have ranged from social, cultural and institutional embeddedness (Granovetter, 1985; DiMaggio & Zukin, 1990), to geographic, spatial and also temporal forms of embeddedness (Halinen & Tornroos, 1998; Henderson et al., 2002), and multiple other variations exist along the embeddedness spectrum, depending on the academic sub-fields in which the concept has proliferated (Krippner & Alvarez, 2007). Arguments about 'network embeddedness' originally captured only inter-firm relationships with partners involved in the business processes, although some authors extended a firm's networks to its non-business partners and other institutional representatives such as governmental and non-governmental organisations as well as to broader themes of space and geography (Johannisson & Ramirez-Pasillas, 2002).

Embeddedness is therefore a multifaceted concept that captures the dynamics between various relational and institutional factors. At the same time, however, this multifaceted concept is also used in different fields in different ways, and despite the plethora of theoretical developments, little overall consensus currently exists as to its exact conceptualisation. Embeddedness still remains a somewhat fuzzy concept (Oinas, 1997; Markusen, 1999), with different meanings in different contexts, and capturing its complexity within a single approach is rather challenging.

Yet, understanding these different conceptualisations and understandings of embeddedness is important because more recently scholars have also adopted, adapted and applied the concept to spatial issues. Embeddedness is one of the key concepts which has helped to fuse together many strands of the International Business and economy geography literatures. In particular, scholars have used embeddedness as a lens through which they can better observe the locational strategies of multinational firms.

For our purposes, in the context of Economic Geography the phenomena of internationalisation and the emergence of the multinational firm, defined as a company which 'engages in foreign direct investment . . . and owns or controls value-adding activities in more than one country' (Dunning, 1993, p. 3), has turned the idea of 'embeddedness' into a largely spatial concept (Hess, 2004, p. 165). For instance, Economic Geography scholars have used the notion of embeddedness to investigate how foreign direct investment affects local development through additional employment and technological spillovers (Phelps et al., 2003), while in the business literature the focus has been on the multinational relocation of different corporate activities in different national or regional contexts (Heidenreich, 2012). In Economic Geography more generally, the idea of embeddedness has tended to be used in the sense of the depth, variety, strength and longevity of the linkages between a firm or establishment and its local context, and these ideas have also been reflected in the regional policy literature (McCann & Ortega-Argilés, 2015). As such, in terms of conceptions of space, the central idea behind the concept of embeddedness, at least as it is articulated within the setting of geography, relates to the nature and scale of the different forms of ties that position and bind the firm or establishment to its local and regional context.

In the case of the International Business literature focusing on multinational investments, the emphasis has been on the embeddedness of the foreign affiliates within business networks (Cantwell & Iammarino, 2003). For many years, the analysis of multinational firms and their foreign direct investments tended to be examined via the lens of the vertical or horizontal integration of activities (Caves, 1982) within the overall eclectic schema of Dunning's (1979) OLI paradigm of Ownership, Location and Internalisation (Beugelsdijk, McCann & Mudambi, 2010). However, the logic of these analytical approaches was inherently top-down in nature, reflecting the largely top-down architecture of the multinational corporate structures of the first half of the twentieth century, and failed to reflect many of the subsequently emerging features of multinationals. In particular, as multinationals evolved in the post-war era, increasingly they created value by establishing technological relationships with local business partners and qualified employees that helped to facilitate two-way organisational learning and the creation of new knowledge (Cantwell & Iammarino 2003; Cantwell & Mudambi, 2005; Iammarino & McCann, 2013) in which affiliates and subsidiaries increasingly played a critical learning and knowledge-generating role. And here again, there are differences of interpretation and understanding. For instance, Forsgren, Holm and Johanson (2005) attributed the concept of embeddedness only to those multinationals whose subsidiaries operate in dense and strong networks of local business relationships. Similarly, for Andersson, Forsgren and Holm (2002), firms' embeddedness refers to the co-evolution of technical products and production processes across business partners, as well as to the relationships with suppliers and customers.

In order to better capture these themes in an explicitly geographic or regional setting Halinen and Tornroos (1998) used the term 'spatial embeddedness' to emphasise the importance of location and geography in business networks and highlighted the dissimilarities of the various types of networks in which actors are engaged based on different spatial levels – be they international, national, regional or local territories. Generally, these ideas are also captured by the notion of 'territorial embeddedness', which 'considers the extent to which an actor is anchored in particular territories and places' (Hess, 2004, p. 178) and is largely moderated by the economic systems and social dynamics prevailing in those places. Specifically, it relates to local inter-firm relations, designated in particular by linkages with local suppliers (Henderson et al., 2002) and has been particularly relevant in Economic Geography and regional development studies (Turok, 1993; McCann, 1997; Phelps & Fuller, 2000; Phelps et al., 2003). Broadly, embeddedness is generally assumed to be beneficial both for the host regions, as local firms access new technological knowledge, create additional employment and promote economic growth, and also for the investors, as multinationals gain access to knowledge of local market conditions as well as to new and complementary resources that would enhance their overall performance (Henderson et al., 2002). In this sense, network embeddedness can be regarded as being a key factor in regional economic growth and in capturing global opportunities (Henderson et al., 2002). At the same time, however, the arguments underpinning the concept of 'strategic fit' also suggest that the extent to which organisations can exploit these benefits depends on their internal organisational trajectory or what Halinen and Tornroos defined as 'temporal embeddedness':

> [c]ompanies are bound to past, present and future modes of time . . . they have their own histories during which they have evolved; they are also in the midst of their own present, and have objectives and expectations about the future which affect their present decisions and actions.
>
> *(1998, p. 195)*

Further refinements or extensions to the idea of multinational embeddedness in geography also concern questions of the nature, quality and roles of the local institutional settings and networks (Beckert, 2003, 2007; Heidenreich 2012). Institutions encompass both formal frameworks, such as the regulatory, political and economic systems that establish market principles and dictate the interaction between economic actors and non-market societal institutions (DiMaggio & Zukin, 1990; Liu, 2000), as well as the informal mechanisms motivated and mediated by cognition and culture (DiMaggio & Zukin, 1990; Nooteboom, 2000). Meanwhile, Andersson, Forsgren and Holm (2002), Holm, Malmberg and Solvell (2003), and Forsgren, Holm and Johanson (2005) perceived network embeddedness as a strategic resource that increases a firm's expected performance via improving the scale, variety, intensity and speed of knowledge flows into and out of the firm. Similar views building upon the network theory paradigm are also employed by authors such as Ghoshal and Bartlett (1990), Hakansson and Snehota (1995), Dyer and Singh (1998), Ahuja (2000), Gulati, Nohria and Zaheer (2000) and Gilsing et al. (2008), and, as such, the related constructs of 'spatial embeddedness', 'societal embeddedness' (Hess, 2004) and 'network embeddedness' all heavily overlap. This is important, because the Economic Geography of the multinational affiliate represents one of the most sharply delineated contexts in which these overlapping dimensions critically determine the economic performance of the establishment (Cantwell & Iammarino, 2003; Iammarino & McCann, 2013). In general, the different notions of embeddedness come together when we discuss the nature, role and behaviour of the multinational subsidiary in an explicitly geographical or regional setting, and these settings also provide possibilities for extending empirical research on the topic.

Empirical research on embeddedness and strategic fit

Intuitively, embeddedness and strategic fit in their various forms have been assumed to affect organisational performance, although the empirical evidence on these issues is rather scarce. In part this may be due to measurement difficulties, due to either a lack of clear definitions or a 'confusing variety of meanings' (Hess, 2004, p. 176) that has prevented researchers from operationalising these concepts on a standard generally agreed basis amenable to empirical testing. Nevertheless, some empirical evidence is available, and Uzzi (1997) was the first to empirically study and operationalise embeddedness, restricting his research to the relational dimension of the concept. Uzzi (1997) identified three main aspects that underlined the quality of structural embeddedness, namely: trust, fine-grained information transfer and joint problem-solving arrangements that in conjunction promoted economies of time, integrative agreements, allocative efficiency and complex adaptation. These dimensions closely reflect the modern understandings of the key knowledge-based roles played by multinational subsidiaries and affiliates in helping to drive the overall performance of multinational firms (Cantwell & Iammarino, 2003;

Iammarino & McCann, 2013). They also link closely to other empirical work in this arena such as that by Andersson, Forsgren and Holm (2002), who gathered survey-based data to operationalise the embeddedness of subsidiaries by their relationships with suppliers, customers and competitors, and explicitly excluded larger institutional structures and non-business partners from their analysis. Taking the multinational and multi-plant subsidiary as the unit of analysis, Andersson, Forsgren and Holm (2002) demonstrated that the higher the degree to which a subsidiary is engaged in external business networks, the higher its own market performance and the higher its contribution to the overall development of the multinational's technological competencies (Forsgren, Holm & Johanson, 2005; Nell & Ambos, 2013). In a comparable manner, Johannisson and Ramirez-Passilas (2002) used a survey-based methodology to operationalise embeddedness in terms of an actor's relationships both with related business partners and with more general non-economic, institutional and political constituents and proved its 'leverage for business creation'. The authors particularly stressed the benefits of institutional elements as 'without institutions the embeddedness of the business community is incomplete since a considerable number of business persons remain disconnected, i.e. they are not directly related' (Johannisson & Ramirez-Passilas, 2002, p. 304). Other researchers have also considered the impact of cultural or institutional factors on business strategy – particularly the choice of entry modes – and more rarely on organisational performance (Halkos & Tzeremes, 2008).

One last stream of empirical studies which uses case study and qualitative research approaches has shifted the focus of analysis away from the corporate towards the mechanisms of regional development through 'territorial embeddedness'. Hardy, Currie and Ye (2005) employed a case-study approach in their evaluation of embeddedness, yet unlike previous studies that concentrated specifically on firm network embeddedness, the authors shifted the emphasis onto cultural and political embeddedness and evaluated how dissimilar political and cultural contexts convey different choices of strategic fit. Meanwhile Phelps et al. (2003) used five indicators to operationalise embeddedness: (1) corporate status and functions; (2) research, development and design activity; (3) supply chain and local purchases; (4) skills and training demands; and (5) repeated investment. By employing a case-study survey-based methodology, they found little evidence of foreign firms' embeddedness. In a comparable manner, White (2004) applied a case-study methodology to investigate the local embeddedness of the foreign software sector in Ireland and its impact on local development. This research suggested that embeddedness is moderated by the 'conditionalities of space' (White, 2004), which reflect the local conditions not directly related to inter-firm or institutional relations, such as growing spatial concentration of employment in an industry. Many other studies have also indirectly built upon the rationale of territorial embeddedness and evaluated whether foreign firms have an impact on regional development by establishing links with local suppliers and customers, but their findings have tended to be rather inconsistent (McCann, 1997; Javorcik, 2004; Crespo & Fontoura, 2007; Barrios, Gorg & Strobl, 2011; Giroud, Jindra & Marek, 2012). In part, this may be due to the fact that the geographical and regional contexts differ so much, but it may also be due to the fact that the concept itself is still somewhat broadly defined.

Yet, while each of these literatures has so far emphasised the positive aspect of embeddedness and strategic fit in the regional context, there is also a somewhat smaller literature that highlights the potentially negative aspects of these phenomena. Indeed, Uzzi (1997) also acknowledged the risks of 'over-embeddedness', underlying the potentially adverse 'lock-in' (David, 1985) effects and hysteresis which can frustrate performance 'if the social aspects of exchange supersede the economic imperatives' (Uzzi, 1997, p. 59). The dangers of adverse lock-in are well-known in the literatures on technology and science policy as well as in political science and economics, and the enhancement of local embeddedness is therefore not without its risks. Subsequent studies also highlighted the costs of embeddedness which might arise from over-reliance on a limited number of business partners, persistence of redundant ties and continuous exchange of homogenous information (Gargiulo & Benassi, 2000; Rowley, Behrens & Krackhardt, 2000; Masciarelli, Laursen & Prencipe, 2009). However, arguments from agency theory suggest that embeddedness reflects a dynamic (Hess, 2004; Heidenreich, 2012) two-way process because firms can adjust to and influence the institutional environment in which they operate: 'firms have an important agency role . . . they must make sense of, manipulate, negotiate, and partially construct their institutional environments' (Kostova, Roth & Dacin, 2008 p. 1001). The extent to which the embedded agency of organisations allows them to strategically involve themselves in local business networks and to effectively adapt to the institutional settings of their host countries is an important determinant in their success. This view puts into perspective embeddedness as a strategic alternative that multinationals can exploit, rather than a taken-for-granted situation. Multinationals opt for embedded strategies in their global undertakings depending on the degree of strategic fit between the firms' needs and business purposes and their regional conditions (Teece, 2006; Mattes, 2010).

Thus, insights from the agency theory underlie the potential of embeddedness as a contingent factor in explaining organisational performance, which also permits the overcoming of problems of lock-in. In this respect, embeddedness and strategic fit underlie the importance of multinationals to gain and retain legitimacy (Suchman, 1995) in the markets in which they are operating. When firms enter new foreign markets, they have to overcome the 'liability of foreignness' that stems from unfamiliarity with the local environment and comprises informational disadvantage, higher transactional uncertainty and lack of connections with local agents that lead to higher managerial costs and decreased subsidiary performance (Zaheer, 1995; Zaheer & Mosakowski, 1997). Foreign affiliates of multinationals need to adjust to a complex set of rules and values that dictate local behavioural norms and business routines (Johanson & Vahlne, 1977; Kostova & Roth, 2002) in order to embed them in the new socio-institutional context and minimise the costs born out of the liability of foreignness. If firms fail to adapt their organisational structures to be consistent with the isomorphic pressures from the local environment, they cannot earn the operational legitimacy necessary to integrate and succeed in the new context (Meyer & Rowan, 1977). Taken together, the basic expectation of these various arguments is therefore that the higher levels of embeddedness and the better the strategic fit of the multinational subsidiary in the host region and host country, generally leads to a higher level of performance of the multinational subsidiary, and therefore higher overall corporate performance.

There remains, however, one further key notion linking strategic fit to embeddedness, and this is the notion of distance. One might expect that, in general, a greater geographical distance might make it more difficult to achieve a good strategic fit between a multinational corporation's goals and the performance of its subsidiaries, primarily because distance may make management coordination processes more challenging. Yet, when it comes to international investment activities, geographical distance is only one relevant notion of distance. The performance of multinational affiliate investments also depends on other notions or dimensions of distance which mediate, enhance or attenuate the effects of geographical distance. These dimensions of distance are institutional distance, relational distance, and cultural or cognitive distance, and individually or together they can heavily shape the relationships between geographical distance, strategic fit and embeddedness.

Multinational investment and the dimensions of distance

Countries and regions vary enormously in terms of their levels of economic development and the nature and quality of their institutional systems. Moreover, as well as enormous differences between countries and regions in the global south and the global north, these differences also exist even within integrated trade areas such as the European Union or NAFTA (Hoskisson et al., 2000; Meyer & Peng, 2005). Operating in unfamiliar institutional settings raises transaction costs, increases uncertainty and limits the ability of multinational affiliates from engaging in complex operations (Meyer, 2001), so institutional proximity (Kostova, 1999; Xu & Shenkar, 2002) between the parent country or parent region and the host country or region, tends to facilitate engagement with more complex activities, while greater differences tend to delay or limit such activities. In contrast, institutional distance tends to reinforce liabilities of foreignness and decrease performance (Gaur & Lu, 2007; Dow & Larimo, 2009). In particular, because the foreign subsidiary is subject to an 'institutional dualism' (Kostova & Roth, 2002), it has to accommodate internal pressures imposed by the parent firm, as well as external pressures from the local environment. This implies that subsidiaries must implement business practices that often differ from those of the local organisations, and the mismatch in organisational behaviour becomes more evident as large institutional distance effectively inhibits the foreign subsidiaries from understanding and applying the formal institutional guidelines of the host country (Kostova & Zaheer, 1999). As a consequence, institutional distance can constrain the interaction of the subsidiaries with the local business partners and affects their pursuit for legitimacy in the host environment. In this respect, organisations must develop managerial and commercial practices that suit the variations in institutions, and the higher the variation, the more difficult the adaptation (Luo, 2001; Meyer, 2001; Xu & Shenkar, 2002). Institutional proximity tends to enhance both institutional embeddedness and local strategic fit in the foreign environment, and thereby increases the chances that subsidiaries align their business operations to the foreign institutional environment and, ultimately, implement the most efficient profit-maximisation strategies. In particular, multinational subsidiaries that are highly embedded in their local environments can more easily exploit localisation advantages (Jensen & Pedersen, 2011; Rugman, Verbeke & Yuan, 2011) and enhance their task-specific knowledge by accessing unique resources (Figueiredo, 2011) by more effectively building on local knowledge, social capital and networks (Granovetter, 1985; Uzzi, 1997; Dyer & Singh, 1998; Lin & Wan, 2008).

These social and network dimensions are critical because for multinational subsidiaries and foreign affiliates trust is at the core of social interaction and network embeddedness with local actors. Operating in high trust societies is of particular benefit in lowering uncertainty of doing business in unknown environments, as trust enhances the formation of social links which can carry valuable information about market characteristics, production technologies and potential trade partners. Trust also facilitates and encourages risk taking, which is essential in the context of business transactions between new foreign subsidiaries and local partners (Nahapiet & Ghoshal, 1998). Trust is indispensable for ensuring cooperation among strangers and individuals that encounter each other irregularly (LaPorta et al., 1996). In high-trust societies people develop generalised expectations about the trustworthiness of other people and engage in trust-based social interactions regardless of the level of familiarity between actors (Rotter, 1971). This is a vital benefit for foreign entrants in new markets, as they are lacking market legitimacy, and it provides the primary means to gain recognition from local actors and pursue business goals with unfamiliar customers and suppliers.

Cooperation and coordination with multinational subsidiaries and host regions in culturally distant countries are much more difficult as their perception and understanding of how organisational processes should unfold is different (Kostova & Roth, 2002). Thus, cultural-cognitive distance increases operational difficulties as firms often fail to understand the norms and values that afford social exchange and, therefore, their ability to operate effectively in the host market decreases (Hennart & Larimo, 1998). In addition, managing interaction across distinct cultures implies higher transaction costs in terms of training, monitoring and control, so it is expected that performance will decrease in culturally distant environments. In general, institutional environments with higher levels of trust and closer cultural and relational proximity between the parent and host regions make information exchanges between local actors easier, facilitate the establishment of denser local business networks, ensure an easier adaptation to the host regional environments and encourage more cooperative behaviour between local firms. This is because the critical cultural and cognitive knowledge for subsidiary and management and operations is often tacit and difficult to comprehend, and parent headquarter functions generally exert an overwhelming pressure on the ability of foreign subsidiaries to gain local legitimacy (Oliver, 1991; Boyacigiller, Goodman & Philips, 2004). Therefore, cultural distance, expressed in terms of cultural dissimilarities between countries (Kogut & Singh, 1988), can be a critical factor in moderating subsidiary embeddedness and implementing profit-maximisation strategies in the host environment. When subsidiaries are established in foreign countries, they need to be calibrated to different national cultures, which creates complexities both at a firm and at an individual level (Barkema, Bell & Pennings, 1996).

As mentioned earlier, for multinational investment patterns, each of these institutional, relational and cognitive dimensions of distance heavily moderate the shape of the effects of pure geographic distance on innovation performance (Boschma, 2007) and the levels of embeddedness and strategic fit of the multinational's affiliates and subsidiaries (Deadorff, 1998; Ghemawat, 2001; Ragozzino, 2009). Intuitively, a larger geographic distance inevitably assumes increasing costs in transportation, communication and coordination due to the more complex principal-agent problems inherent in managing across larger geographical distances with reduced face-to-face interactions between subsidiary managers and higher level corporate decision-makers (Zaheer, 1995; Dow, 2000; Hinds & Bailey, 2003). These distance-related difficulties are especially challenging when multinational firms are entering a new market, as they incur high knowledge-related transaction costs when first setting up new establishments and developing new business networks (Zaheer, 1995). However, accumulation of experience can serve as an accelerator for the foreign firm to acquire knowledge and understand the dynamics in the new markets they are entering, leading to better performance and higher success (Johanson & Vahlne, 1977; Delios & Beamish, 2001). Over time, and with experience, firms advance along the learning curve and become more comfortable with the new context, therefore reducing the effects of distance (Shenkar, 2001). In addition, the more foreign firms operate in the host environment, the more they start interacting and building ties with local external parties such as customers, suppliers and regulators so that they gradually become accepted as legitimate actors (Zaheer & Mosakowski, 1997; Li, Poppo & Zhou, 2010). As foreign firms accumulate greater local knowledge and gain legitimacy, the uncertainty induced by institutional and cultural distances reduces, giving them the opportunity to find and implement the most efficient profit-maximising strategies (Salomon and Wu, 2012). The more experienced a firm becomes in a foreign market, the more it learns to do business there and higher profitability is expected (Johanson & Vahlne, 1977). Importantly, geographical proximity has traditionally also been associated with longstanding FDI experience, and today, the role of proximity in facilitating FDI appears to be greater than ever, in spite of the advent of new information and communications technologies (Iammarino & McCann, 2013). A wide array of evidence suggests that over recent decades, geographic proximity has actually become even more associated with relational, institutional and cognitive proximity than in earlier periods, and therefore taken together, each of these dimensions of distance tends to favour strong geographic regionalisation patterns of foreign direct investment (Rugman, 2000, 2005; Rugman & Verbeke, 2004, 2005).

Conclusion

The Economic Geography of the multinational is the context in which spatial embeddedness, societal embeddedness and network embeddedness all interact and overlap in a critical manner. In general, greater embeddedness and strategic fit generate improved corporate performance, such that the goodness of fit associated with corporate investment decisions, and therefore the success of multinational strategies, are heavily shaped by these different embeddedness dimensions. However, there are also conditions under which high levels of local embeddedness can lead to challenges. Therefore, in order to identify the strengths and weaknesses as well as the opportunities and challenges associated with embeddedness and strategic fit, it is important to develop a detailed understanding of the different dimensions of distance as they impact on multinationals. Obviously geographical distance heavily influences the performance of corporate affiliates and subsidiaries, because geographical distance impacts on a firm's ability to align the goals and behaviour of the affiliate with that of the overall corporation. On the other hand, greater geographical distance is not necessarily indicative of reduced performance. This is because other notions of distance also shape the relationships between geographical distance and subsidiary performance by influencing the links between strategic fit and embeddedness. These additional notions of distance include institutional distance, cultural distance, cognitive distance and relational distance. These additional notions of distance also tend to favour geographical proximity, but they also imply some major discontinuities in these patterns. In general, the interactions between strategic fit, embeddedness and the different notions of distance tend to favour international proximity, but this is not always the case. Greater global regionalisation rather than globalisation per se, appears to be the key to modern corporate success, but these patterns are also seen to differ in different contexts, depending on the various dimensions of distance. If greater protectionism emerges in the global economy in the coming years, it remains to be seen how the various relationships described in this chapter will be affected.

References

Ahuja, G. (2000) 'Collaboration networks, structural holes, and innovation: A longitudinal study', *Administrative Science Quarterly*, 45, pp. 425–455.

Alchian, A.A. (1950) 'Uncertainty, Evolution and Economic Theory', *Journal of Political Economy*, 58, pp. 211–221.

Andersson, U., Forsgren, M. & Holm, U. (2002) 'The strategic impact of external networks: Subsidiary performance and competence development in the multinational corporation', *Strategic Management Journal*, 23, pp. 979–996.

Barkema, H., Bell, H. & Pennings, M. (1996) 'Foreign entry, cultural barriers, and learning', *Strategic Management Journal*, 17, pp. 151–166.

Barkema, H. & Vermeulen, F. (1998) 'International expansion through start-up or acquisition: A learning perspective', *Academy of Management Journal*, 41, pp. 7–26.

Barrios, S., Gorg, H. & Strobl, E. (2011) 'Spillovers through backward linkages from multinationals: Measurement matters', *European Economic Review*, 55, pp. 862–875.

Bausch, A. & Krist, M. (2007) 'The effect of context-related moderators on the internationalization-performance relationship: Evidence from meta-analysis', *Management International Review*, 47, pp. 319–347.

Beckert, J. (2003) 'Economic sociology and embeddedness: How shall we conceptualize economic action?' *Journal of Economic Issues*, 37, pp. 769–787.

Beckert, J. (2007) 'The great transformation of embeddedness: Karl Polanyi and the New Economic Sociology', Max Planck Institute for the Study of Societies Discussion Paper 07/1. *Available online at* www.mpifg.de/pu/mpifg_dp/dp07-1.pdf.

Beugelsdijk, S., McCann, M. & Mudambi, R. (2010) 'Place, space and organisation: Economic Geography and the multinational enterprise', *Journal of Economic Geography*, 10, pp. 485–493.

Boschma, R. (2007) 'Proximity and innovation: A critical assessment', *Regional Studies*, 39, pp. 61–74.

Boyacigiller, N., Goodman, A. & Phillips, M. (Eds.) (2004) *Crossing Cultures: Insights from Master Teachers*. New York: Routledge.

Cantwell, J. & Iammarino, S. (2003) *Multinational Corporations and European Regional Systems of Innovation*. London: Routledge.

Cantwell, J. & Mudambi, R. (2005) 'MNE competence-creating subsidiary mandates', *Strategic Management Journal*, 26, pp. 1109–1128.

Caves, R. (1982) *Multinational Enterprise and Economic Analysis*. Cambridge, UK: Cambridge University Press.

Contractor, F., Kundu, S. & Hsu, C. (2003) 'A three-stage theory of international expansion: The link between multinationality and performance in the service sector', *Journal of International Business Studies*, 34, pp. 5–18.

Crespo, N. & Fontoura, M. (2007) 'Determinant factors of FDI spillovers: What do we really know?' *World Development*, 35, pp. 410–425.

David, P.A. (1985) 'Clio and the Economics of QWERTY', *American Economic Review: Papers and Proceedings*, 75, pp. 332–337.

Deadorff, A. (1998) 'Determinants of bilateral trade: Does gravity work in a neoclassical world?' in Frankel, J.A. (Ed.), *The Regionalization of the World Economy*. Chicago, IL: The University of Chicago Press, pp. 7–31.

Delios, A. & Beamish, P. (2001) 'Survival and profitability: The roles of experience and intangible assets in foreign subsidiary performance', *Academy of Management Journal*, 44, pp. 1028–1038.

DiMaggio, P. & Zukin S. (Eds.) (1990) *The Structures of Capital: The Social Organisation of the Economy*. Cambridge, UK: Cambridge University Press.

Dow, D. (2000) 'A note on psychological distance and export market selection', *Journal of International Marketing*, 8, pp. 51–64.

Dow, D. & Larimo, J. (2009) 'Challenging the conceptualization and measurement of distance and international experience in entry mode choice research', *Journal of International Marketing*, 17, pp. 74–98.

Dunning, J. (1979) 'Explaining changing patterns of international production: In defence of the eclectic theory', *Oxford Bulletin of Economics and Statistics*, 41, pp. 269–295.

Dunning, J. (1980) 'Toward an eclectic theory of international production: Some empirical tests', *Journal of International Business Studies*, 11, pp. 9–31.

Dunning, J. (1993) *Multinational Enterprises and the Global Economy*. Wokingham, UK: Addison-Wesley.

Dyer, J. & Singh, H. (1998) 'The relational view: Cooperative strategy and sources of interorganizational competitive advantage', *The Academy of Management Review*, 23, pp. 660–679.

Figueiredo, P. (2011) 'The role of dual embeddedness in the innovative performance of MNE subsidiaries: evidence from Brazil', *Journal of Management Studies*, 48, pp. 417–440.

Forsgren, M., Holm, U. & Johanson, J. (2005) *Managing the Embedded Multinational: A Business Network View*. Cheltenham, UK: Edward Elgar.

Gargiulo, M. & Benassi, M. (2000) 'Trapped in your own net? Network cohesion, structural holes, and the adaptation of social capital', *Organization Science*, 11, pp. 183–196.

Gaur, A. & Lu, J. (2007) 'Ownership strategies and survival of foreign subsidiaries: Impacts of institutional distance and experience', *Journal of Management*, 33, pp. 84–110.

Ghemawat, P. (2001) 'Distance still matters: The hard reality of global expansion', *Harvard Business Review*, 36, pp. 137–147.

Ghoshal, S. (1987) 'Global strategy: An organizing framework', *Strategic Management Journal*, 8, pp. 425–440.

Ghoshal, S. & Bartlett, A. (1990) 'The multinational corporation as an interorganizational network', *The Academy of Management Review*, 15, pp. 603–625.

Gilsing, V., Nooteboom, B., Vanhaverbeke, W., Duysters, G. & van den Oord, A. (2008) 'Network embeddedness and the exploration of novel technologies: Technological distance, betweenness centrality and density', *Research Policy*, 37, pp. 1717–1731.

Giroud, A., Jindra, B. & Marek, P. (2012) 'Heterogeneous FDI in transition economies: A novel approach to assess the developmental impact of backward linkages', *World Development*, 40, pp. 2206–2220.

Granovetter, M. (1985) 'Economic action and economic structure: The problem of embeddedness', *American Journal of Sociology*, 91, pp. 481–510.

Gulati, R., Nohria, N. & Zaheer, A. (2000) 'Strategic networks', *Strategic Management Journal, Special Issue*, 21, pp. 203–215.

Hakansson, H. & Snehota, I. (1995) *Developing Relationships in Business Networks*. Routledge: London.

Halinen, A. & Tornroos, J. (1998) 'The role of embeddedness in the evolution of business networks', *Scandinavian Journal of Management*, 14, pp. 187–205.

Halkos, G. & Tzeremes, N. (2008) 'National culture and multinational performance', MPRA Paper 23763, University Library of Munich, Germany. Available at http://mpra.ub.uni-muenchen.de/23763/1/MPRA_paper_23763.pdf.

Hardy, J., Currie, F. & Ye, Z. (2005) 'Cultural and political embeddedness, foreign investment and locality in transforming economies: The case of ABB in Poland and China', *Competition and Change*, 9, pp. 277–297.

Heidenreich, M. (2012) 'State of the art: The social embeddedness of multinational companies. A literature review', *Socio-Economic Review*, 10, pp. 549–579.

Henderson, J., Dicken, P., Hess, M., Coe, N. & Yeung, H.W-C. (2002) 'Global production networks and the analysis of economic development', *Review of International Political Economy*, 9, pp. 436–464.

Hennart, J. & Larimo, J. (1998) 'The impact of culture on the strategy of multinational enterprises: Does national origin affect ownership decisions?' *Journal of International Business Studies*, 29, pp. 515–538.

Hess, M. (2004) '"Spatial" relationships? Towards a re-conceptualisation of embeddedness', *Progress in Human Geography*, 28, pp. 165–186.

Hinds, P. & Bailey, D. (2003) 'Out of sight, out of sync: Understanding conflict in distributed teams', *Organization Science*, 14, pp. 615–632.

Holm, U., Malmberg, A. & Solvell, O. (2003) 'Subsidiary impact on host-country economies: The case of foreign-owned subsidiaries attracting investment into Sweden', *Journal of Economic Geography*, 3, pp. 389–408.

Hoskisson, R., Eden, L., Lau, C. & Wright, M. (2000) 'Strategy in emerging economies', *Academy of Management Journal*, 43, pp. 249–267.

Hymer, S. (1972) 'The multinational corporation and the law of uneven development', in Bhagwati, J.N. (Ed.), *Economics and World Order: From the 1970s to the 1990s*. New York: Free Press.

Hymer, S. (1976) *The International Operations of National Firms: A Study of Direct Foreign Investment*. Cambridge, MA: MIT Press.

Iammarino, S. & McCann, P. (2013) *Multinationals and Economic Geography: Location, Technology and Innovation*. Cheltenham, UK: Edward Elgar.

Javorcik, B. (2004) 'Does foreign direct investment increase the productivity of domestic firms? In search of spillovers through backward linkages', *The American Economic Review*, 94, pp. 605–627.

Jensen, P. & Pedersen, T. (2011) 'The Economic Geography of offshoring: The fit between activities and local context', *Journal of Management Studies*, 48, pp. 352–372.

Johannisson, B. & Ramirez-Pasillas, M. (2002) 'The institutional embeddedness of local inter-firm networks: A leverage for business creation', *Entrepreneurship and Regional Development*, 14, 297–315.

Johanson, J. & Vahlne, J. (1977) 'The internationalization process of the firm: A model of knowledge development and increasing foreign market commitments', *Journal of International Business Studies*, 8, pp. 23–32.

Kogut, B. (1985) 'Designing global strategies: Profiting from operational flexibility', *Sloan Management Review*, 27, pp. 27–38.

Kogut, B. & Singh, H. (1988) 'The effect of national culture on the choice of entry mode', *Journal of International Business Studies*, 19, pp. 411–432.

Kostova, T. (1999) 'Transnational transfer of strategic organizational practices: A contextual perspective', *Academy of Management Review*, 24, pp. 308–324.

Kostova, T. & Roth, K. (2002) 'Adoption of an organizational practice by subsidiaries of multinational corporations: Institutional and relational effects', *Academy of Management Journal*, 45, pp. 215–233.

Kostova, T., Roth, K. & Dacin, M.T. (2008) 'Institutional theory in the study of multinational corporations: A critique and new directions', *Academy of Management Review*, 33, pp. 994–1006.

Kostova, T. & Zaheer, S. (1999) 'Organizational legitimacy under conditions of complexity: The case of the multinational enterprise', *Academy of Management Review*, 24, pp. 64–81.

Krippner, G. & Alvarez, A. (2007) 'Embeddedness and the intellectual projects of economic sociology', *Annual Review of Sociology*, 33, pp. 219–240.

LaPorta, R., Lopez-de-Silanes, F., Shleifer, A. & Vishny, R. (1996) 'Trust in large organizations', National Bureau of Economic Research (NBER) Working Papers Series, Working Paper 5864.

Li, J., Poppo, L. & Zhou, K. (2010) 'Relational mechanisms, formal contracts, and local knowledge acquisition by international subsidiaries', *Strategic Management Journal*, 31, pp. 349–370.

Lin, B. & Wan, T. (2008) 'Social capital and partnership opportunities: Management implication in integrated healthcare networks', in Klein, L.A. & Neumann, E.L. (Eds.), *Integrated Health Care Delivery*. Hauppauge, NY: Nova Publishers, pp. 49–66.

Liu, W. (2000) Geography of China's auto industry: Globalisation and embeddedness. Unpublished PhD Thesis, Dept. of Geography, University of Hong Kong.

Luo, Y. (2001) 'Determinants of entry in an emerging economy: A multilevel approach', *Journal of Management Studies*, 38, pp. 443–472.

Luthans, F. & Stewart, T. (1978) 'The reality or illusion of a general contingency theory of management: A response to the Longenecker and Pringle critique', *Academy of Management Review*, July, pp. 683–687.

Markusen, A. (1999) 'Fuzzy concepts, scanty evidence, policy distance: The case for rigour and policy relevance in critical regional studies', *Regional Studies*, 33, pp. 869–884.

Masciarelli, F., Laursen, K. & Prencipe, A. (April 2009) 'Trapped by over-embeddedness: The effects of regional social capital on internationalization', *DASTA Working Paper Series, No. 18*. Available at http://dipartimenti.unich.it/dec/arc/wpapers/2009/2009-018.pdf.

Mattes, J. (2010) *Innovation in Multinational Companies: Organisational, International and Regional Dilemmas*. Bern: Peter Lang International Academic Publishers.

McCann, P. (1997) 'How deeply embedded is Silicon Glen? A cautionary note', *Regional Studies*, 31, pp. 697–705.

McCann, P. & Ortega-Argilés, R. (2015) 'Smart specialization, regional growth and applications to EU cohesion policy', *Regional Studies*, 49, pp. 1291–1302.

Meyer, J. & Rowan, B. (1977) 'Institutionalized organizations: Formal structure as myth and ceremony', *American Journal of Sociology*, 83, pp. 340–363.

Meyer, K. (2001) 'Institutions, transaction costs, and entry mode choice in Eastern Europe', *Journal of International Business Studies*, 32, pp. 357–367.

Meyer, K. & Peng, M. (2005) 'Probing theoretically into Central and Eastern Europe: Transactions, resources, and institutions', *Journal of International Business Studies*, 35, pp. 600–621.

Nahapiet, J. & Ghoshal, S. (1998) 'Social capital, intellectual capital, and the organizational advantage', *The Academy of Management Review*, 23, pp. 242–266.

Nell, P. & Ambos, B. (2013) 'Parenting advantage in the MNC: An embeddedness perspective on the value added by headquarters', *Strategic Management Journal*, 34, pp. 1086–1103.

Nooteboom, B. (2000) 'Learning by interaction: Absorptive capacity, cognitive distance and governance', *Journal of Management and Governance*, 4, pp. 69–92.

Oinas, P. (1997) 'On the socio-spatial embeddedness of business firms', *Erdkunde*, 51, pp. 23–32.

Oliver, C. (1991) 'Strategic responses to institutional processes', *Academy of Management Review*, 16, pp. 145–179.

Phelps, N. & Fuller, C. (2000) 'Multinational, intra-corporate competition and regional development', *Economic Geography*, 76, pp. 224–243.

Phelps, N., Mackinnon, D., Stone, I. & Braidford, P. (2003) 'Embedding the multinationals? Institutions and the development of overseas manufacturing affiliates in Wales and North East England', *Regional Studies*, 37, pp. 27–40.

Polanyi, K. (1944) *The Great Transformation. The Political and Economic Origins of Our Time*. Boston, MA: Beacon Press.

Ragozzino, R. (2009) 'The effects of geographic distance on the foreign acquisition activity of U.S', *Management International Review*, 49, pp. 509–535.

Rotter, J. (1971) 'Generalized expectancies for interpersonal trust', *American Psychology Journal*, 26, pp. 443–452.

Rowley, T., Behrens, D. & Krackhardt, D. (2000) 'Redundant governance structures: An analysis of structural and relational embeddedness in the steel and semiconductor industries', *Strategic Management Journal*, 21, pp. 369–386.

Rugman, A. (2000) *The End of Globalisation*. London: Random House.

Rugman, A. (2005) *The Regional Multinationals: MNEs and Global Strategic Management*. Cambridge, UK: Cambridge University Press.

Rugman, A. & Verbeke, A. (2004) 'A perspective on regional and global strategies of multinational enterprises', *Journal of International Business Studies*, 35, pp. 3–18.

Rugman, A. & Verbeke, A. (2005) 'Toward a theory of regional multinationals: A transaction cost economics approach', *Management International Review*, 45, pp. 5–17.

Rugman, A., Verbeke, A. & Yuan, W. (2011) 'Re-conceptualizing Bartlett and Ghoshal's classification of national subsidiary roles in the multinational enterprise', *Journal of Management Studies*, 48, pp. 253–277.
Salomon, R. & Wu, Z. (2012) 'Institutional distance and local isomorphism strategy', *Journal of International Business Studies*, 43, pp. 343–367.
Scott, W. (1992) *Organizations: Rational, Natural, and Open Systems*. Englewood Cliffs, NJ: Prentice-Hall.
Shenkar, O. (2001) 'Cultural distance revisited: Towards a more rigorous conceptualization and measurement of cultural differences', *Journal of International Business Studies*, 32, pp. 519–535.
Suchman, M. (1995) 'Managing legitimacy: Strategic and institutional approaches', *Academy of Management Review*, 20, pp. 571–610.
Teece, D. (2006) 'Reflections on the Hymer thesis and the multinational enterprise', *International Business Review*, 15, pp. 124–139.
Turok, I. (1993) 'Inward investment and local linkages: How deeply embedded is "Silicon Glen?"' *Regional Studies*, 27, pp. 401–417.
Uzzi, B. (1997) 'Social structure and competition in interfirm networks: the paradox of embeddedness', *Administrative Science Quarterly*, 42, pp. 35–67.
Vernon, R. (1966) 'International investment and international trade in the product cycle', *Quarterly Journal of Economics*, 80, pp. 190–207.
White, M. (2004) 'Inward investment, firm embeddedness and place: An assessment of Ireland's multinational software sector', *European Urban and Regional Studies*, 11, pp. 243–260.
Xu, D. & Shenkar, O. (2002) 'Institutional distance and the multinational enterprise', *Academy of Management Review*, 27, pp. 608–618.
Zaheer, S. (1995) 'Overcoming the liability of foreignness', *Academy of Management Journal*, 38, pp. 341–363.
Zaheer, S. & Mosakowski, E. (1997) 'The dynamics of the liability of foreignness: A global study of survival in financial services', *Strategic Management Journal*, 18, pp. 439–463.

26
THE COMPETITIVENESS OF LOCATION IN INTERNATIONAL BUSINESS AND ECONOMIC GEOGRAPHY

Philippe Gugler

Introduction

The World Economic Forum (WEF) defines competitiveness as "the set of institutions, policies, and factors that determine the level of productivity of a country" (WEF, 2015, p. 4). A competitive location offers efficient opportunities and assets, allowing firms to achieve a high level of productivity (Porter, 2008, p. 176). The higher the competitiveness of a location, the more attractive it is as a business location. The attractiveness of a specific location will induce a concentration of enterprises and therefore economic activities within its boundaries. Domestic firms will grow, new firms will be created, and foreign firms will invest in the location. This phenomenon has raised the interest of scholars from several disciplines, particularly Economic Geography and International Business (IB) (Beugelsdijk, McCann & Mudambi, 2010, p. 485). From the establishment of these two fields until recently, theoretical and empirical studies had mainly been conducted in parallel (Dunning, 1998; Gertler, 2003). As stated by Beugelsdijk et al. (2010, p. 486), the scientific connections between them were very limited until the end of the 1990s. On the one side:

> [i]n terms of locational analysis, one of the obvious shortcomings of the traditional Economic Geography and regional science approaches was that the complex spatial behaviour of multiplant and multinational establishment was largely ignored, and where such issues were discussed, the analysis rarely ventured beyond being largely descriptive.

On the other side, the IB literature neglected the role of location for many years (Dunning, 1998, p. 49; Cantwell, 2009, p. 35; Iammarino & McCann, 2013, p. 33). Since the end of the 1990s, the competitive advantages of locations—as territorial capital attracting firms, particularly MNEs—have benefited from an increased interest in both schools. One of the convergent approaches of the two "schools" is to consider and to demonstrate that globalization has not reduced the importance and differences of local specificities (Venables, 2005, p. 1; Porter, 2008, pp. 252–253; Meyer, Mudambi & Narula, 2011, p. 235).

This chapter focuses on the competitiveness of location in the fields of IB and Economic Geography by investigating four interlinked features, highlighting the theoretical and empirical developments of both schools on this matter: (1) MNEs and the competitiveness of the host country location as an attractiveness factor; (2) MNEs and the competitiveness of the home country location as an enhancer of competitive advantages; (3) MNEs' internal and external networks, implying interconnection between the assets of host and home countries; and (4) the spillover effects of MNEs on the competitiveness of their host and home countries. This "artificial" division of these four issues reflects the different specific academic contributions dedicated to each of them.

MNEs and the competitiveness of the host country location

Roots regarding a host country's features in the IB literature were mainly identified in the late 1940s, but the first foundations of a theory of MNEs and features of their location did not appear until the 1960s (Dunning & Lundan, 2008, p. 82). Raymond Vernon's work on product life cycles had already considered the relationship between the comparative advantages of the host country and the home country as a driver of trade and FDI (Vernon, 1966). Referring to Chandler, Hymer is one of the pioneers in analyzing the "spatial dimension" of FDI (Hymer, 1972, pp. 122–125; see also Iammarino & McCann, 2013, p. 39). More specifically, he considered the concentration of MNEs in specific locations, such as cities (Hymer, 1972, p. 124). The seminal contribution of Hymer to the role of MNEs' location has been further developed by other scholars, particularly by Dunning (1981).

The role of location in IB observed new momentum in the "Ownership-Location-Internalization" (OLI) paradigm, which was proposed by Dunning in the late 1970s (Dunning, 1981). Dunning highlighted the role of location (in a host country) as one of the three legs explaining why firms operate value-added activities across national borders (Dunning, 1998, p. 45). The L-advantages reflect the "assets" offered by the recipient country, explaining why a specific firm decides to invest in a specific host location. The development of the OLI paradigm proposes a new theoretical angle to explain the role of a specific location in attracting FDI. Whereas the role of location was mainly considered from the macroeconomic point of view, despite the works of Vernon and Hymer (Iammarino & McCann, 2013, p. 62), Dunning focused on the microeconomic features of locations to understand MNEs' strategies.

During the two decades following the presentation of the OLI paradigm, scholars concentrated most of their studies on the O advantages (why MNEs) and I advantages (how MNEs) rather than on the L advantages (Cantwell, 2009, p. 36; Iammarino & McCann, 2013, p. 63). In 1998, Dunning highlighted this "loophole" in a paper that marked a significant "turn" in the IB literature (Dunning, 1998). This paper received an award for the most prominent research paper published in the *Journal of International Business Studies* over a ten-year period and was re-edited in 2009 (Dunning, 2009). One of the major questions was "Why do firms locate their activities in one country rather than another?" (Dunning & Lundan, 2008, p. 80). The question raises the feature of a location's competitiveness: "The spatial distribution of L-bound resources, capabilities and institutions is assumed to be uneven and, hence, will confer a competitive advantage on the countries possessing them over those that do not" (Dunning & Lundan, 2008, p. 100). "Local contexts vary in particular on two dimensions: institutional frameworks and resource endowments" (Meyer, Mudambi & Narula, 2011, p. 237). In this context, Dunning and Lundan (2008) have emphasized specific types of L advantages, such as L advantages reflecting the role of formal and informal institutions in the attraction of specific countries.

The specific assets of locations explaining the spatial allocation of firms have also been the core of Economic Geography, whose aim is to identify the inherited and created assets "shaping the geography of the firms" (Audretsch, 2000, p. 333; Storper, 2000, p. 147).

The role of competitiveness of locations has been considered in relation to the four main motivations to invest abroad: market-seeking investment, resource-seeking investment, efficient-seeking investment, and strategic asset-seeking investment (Dunning, 1998, p. 50; 2009, p. 8). This choice establishes an important link between the IB field and the field of Economic Geography (Shatz & Venables, 2000, pp. 129–133; Feldman, 2000, p. 388; Hanson, 2000, p. 485). On the Economic Geography side, the literature offers several models and approaches, such as the "Weber Location-Production Model" (Weber, 1909; model developed in Iammarino & McCann, 2013, pp. 71–90) as well as recent theoretical and empirical developments inspired by Michael Porter (1990, 2008).

Indeed, an important topic developed by Economic Geography is the "spatial allocation of economic activity" (Clark, Feldman & Gertler, 2000, p. 11), which includes the drivers of geographic location, the concentration of specific economic activities, and, in particular, a location's features that attract firms such as MNEs (Hanson, 2000, pp. 477–478). One of the major issues of Economic Geography is "the difference, differentiation, and heterogeneity . . . [that] characterize the economic landscape" (Clark et al., 2000, p. 4). These different comparative advantages, being based inter alia on human capital and technological capabilities, impact the location activities of firms (Audretsch, 2000, p. 336; Storper, 2000, p. 147). These differences are at the root of a location's comparative advantages reflected in Dunning's OLI paradigm.

Greater attention has been given to the role of location (location competitiveness) in the changing context of globalization that has impacted the motivations of MNEs to invest abroad. The increasing trend of asset-augmenting investments since the early 2000s has given new momentum to the importance of location. Strategic asset-seeking motivations drive the firms to choose a specific location where they can acquire a host country's assets and develop new assets because of their activities in the specific host country. As MNEs have become more knowledge intensive, strategic asset-seeking investment and therefore the competitive attraction of host places has gained a new impetus: "MNEs are increasingly seeking locations which offer the best economic and institutional facilities for their core competencies to be efficiently utilized" (Dunning, 2009, p. 9). More specifically, the increased flows of strategic asset-seeking investment since the 1990s has led researchers to more deeply scrutinize the interaction between L advantages and O advantages: "Such mostly intangible L advantages are highly localized and concentrated within specific locations, and contribute to enhancing firm-specific O advantages, which in turn strengthen those of the home and host location at the same time" (Iammarino & McCann, 2013, p. 63; see also Rugman & Verbeke, 1992, p. 762; Dicken, 2000, p. 280; Dunning & Lundan, 2008, pp. 72–74). Bartlett and Ghoshal (1989, pp. 116–121) studied the links between the role of MNE subsidiaries and the importance of the local environment of the recipient country. According to Dunning (2009, p. 6), the role of location is increasingly important, particularly when one considers the activities of "knowledge-intensive" MNEs: "the geography of International Business activity is not independent of its entry modes; nor, indeed, of the competitive advantage of the investing firms".

These trends may explain the development of common interests between the geography and IB scholars since the late 2000s (Dunning, 2009, p. 8). A more micro-economic approach to location competitiveness—developed inter alia by Porter (1990)—has been explored within the IB community. Referring to Michael Porter's work, Dunning and Lundan (2008, p. 190) note: "it is the availability and quality of L-bound institutions, resources and capabilities which MNEs need to complement their own O-specific advantages which are increasingly determining their global competitiveness". The competitiveness of locations is understood as a crucial parameter explaining not only the competitiveness of firms (Porter, 1990) but also their mode of entry and of expansion abroad (Dunning, 2009, p. 6). Michael Porter's framework based on the interactions of firms' competitiveness and location competitiveness (synthesized as the "diamond of competitive advantage") has been meaningful for further theoretical developments within the IB community on the role of recipient countries location: "I believe more attention needs to be given to the importance of location per se as a variable affecting the global competitiveness of firms" (Dunning, 2009, p. 16). From an exogenous variable, location features have been considered endogenous parameters, opening the door to geographic economics in the field of IB (Jensen & Pederson, 2011, p. 355). As highlighted by Meyer, Mudambi and Narula (2011, p. 237): "Local contexts have a central role in International Business research". Porter's approach towards the crucial role of localization had a major influence on Dunning's article published in 1998 and reproduced in 2009 (see Cantwell, 2009, p. 37).

Therefore, IB scholars have investigated the microeconomic assets offered by locations to understand the location choices of MNEs as well as their modes of entry and of operation. In this respect, the agglomeration of theoretical insights from Marshall to Porter has raised an increased interest in the IB literature:

> [t]he ease at which MNEs can transfer intangible assets across national boundaries is being constrained by the fact that the location of the creation and use of these assets is becoming increasingly influenced by the presence of immobile clusters of complementary value-added activities.
>
> *(Dunning, 2009, pp. 7–10; see also Cantwell, 2009, p. 37)*

The role of clusters as drivers of economic agglomeration of domestic as well as of foreign firms is an important common feature of both Economic Geography and IB. Indeed, clusters—particularly innovation networks—play an important role as premium locations for MNEs, generating productivity benefits (Asheim, 2000, p. 415; Clark, Feldman & Gertler, 2000, p. 8; Feldman, 2000, p. 374; Hanson, 2000, p. 479; Porter, 2000, p. 267; Venables, 2005, p. 8; Karna, Täube & Sonderegger, 2013, p. 211; Jacobs, Koster & van Oort, 2014, p. 445). Clusters offer assets that are "non-transferable across geographic space" (Audretsch, 2000, p. 333), the so-called location-bound assets (Rugman & Verbeke, 2001; Rugman, 2008). As stated by Krugman (2000, p. 50): "So economists believe that companies agglomerate because of agglomeration economies".

MNEs and the competitiveness of the home country location

The first developments of the IB literature focused mainly on the role of host countries' comparative advantages in explaining why firms may internalize some of their value-added activities in a specific foreign location. The role of home assets has attracted less attention (Rugman & Nguyen, 2014, p. 54). Nevertheless, the first attempts to explain trade and FDI in the 1960s started with the features of home countries' comparative advantages as an explanatory variable. According to Vernon (1966), U.S. firms' competitiveness was determined by the markets, institutions, and factor endowments of home countries. Links between the home and host countries' comparative advantages, first developed by Vernon, are at the core of the "investment development path" (IDP) proposed by Dunning (Dunning, 1981; Dunning & Narula, 1996). The IDP comprises five stages characterized by specific development of trade (imports and exports) and of FDI (inward and outward FDI) (Dunning & Lundan, 2008, p. 330). At each stage, trade and FDI are driven by specific competitive advantages or disadvantages of the home country and host countries (Dunning, Kim & Park, 2008, p. 164). The IDP highlights the interactions between the O advantages of firms and the L assets of home and host countries.

In the late 2000s, the IB community paid closer attention to the role of home countries' comparative advantages in the international expansion of MNEs (Peng, Wang & Jiang, 2008, p. 920; Cuervo-Cazurra, 2012, p. 154; Sun et al., 2012, pp. 5–6; Rugman & Nguyen, 2014, p. 54). As noted by Meyer et al. (2011, p. 239): "First, firms are shaped by the home context from which they originate . . . At the same time, MNEs' embeddedness in their home contexts may act as either inducements or constraints on some types of overseas business activities".

According to Dunning, the ownership-specific (O-specific) advantages of firms are impacted by home-based assets (Dunning, 1981, p. 34). Eminent IB scholars have acknowledged the work inter alia of Michael Porter regarding the quality of the local business environment as a driver of firms' competitiveness (O advantages) and therefore of their ability to expand abroad (Porter, 1990, pp. 69–70; Rugman & Verbeke, 2004, p. 12; Dunning, 2009, p. 16). Are the O advantages of MNEs based mainly on their own specific corporate's competitiveness and/or on their home countries' assets (Cuervo-Cazurra, 2011; Buckley, 2017)? This question has been dealt with wisely by Rugman (2008). Rugman proposes a matrix explaining firms' ability to compete and invest abroad according to the specificities of their home country's specific advantages (CSAs) and of their firm's specific advantages (FSAs). The FSAs reflect the unique assets and capabilities of a firm (Rugman, 2008, p. 12): "It may be built on product or process technology, marketing or distribution skills, or managerial know-how". The CSAs "are exogenous location factors in a country that represent economic and institutional environments (including geographic location, factor endowments, government policies, national culture, institutional framework, and industrial clusters)" (Rugman & Nguyen, 2014, p. 53). In this context, the tremendous role of the local environment is at the forefront of the foundation of IB theory (Rugman & Li, 2007, p. 335). According to Rugman, a firm's competitiveness and strategy in international markets depend on its home CSAs and on its FSAs, the roles of which may vary depending upon their respective strengths or weaknesses as drivers of competitiveness. Rugman proposes a matrix that expresses four scenarios according to the strengths or weaknesses of FSAs and of the home CSAs (Rugman & Li, 2007, p. 335; Rugman, 2008, p. 13).

The importance of home CSAs has been highlighted recently due to the increasing role of emerging country MNEs (EMNEs) (Gugler & Vanoli, 2015; Gugler, 2017). Most studies on the FDI of EMNEs in the 1990s and 2000s show that EMNEs' competitive advantages are mostly based on strong home CSAs rather than on their FSAs (Nelson & Pack, 1999, pp. 432–433; Debrah, McGovern & Budhwar, 2000, p. 319; Luo & Tung, 2007, p. 482; Dunning, Kim & Park, 2008, p. 174–177; Ramamurti, 2008, p. 7; Rugman, 2008, pp. 96–97). The impact of the comparative advantages of the home country on the capabilities of domestic enterprises to invest in foreign countries may change over time according to the stage of the investment development paths (Narula, 2012, p. 188).

The specific case of EMNEs shows that the evolution of the home CSAs has impacted the development of EMNEs' FSAs: "The nature of the CSA components in EMNEs' O-advantages has changed over time due to the increased integration of emerging countries in the world market and the inherent changes related to their institutional, structural and regulatory patterns" (Gugler, 2017). Some studies have also highlighted—inter alia in the case of EMNEs—the fact that upgrading the quality of home-based comparative advantages has a positive impact on domestic FSAs and therefore on firms' ability to expand abroad (Yiu, Lau & Bruton, 2007, pp. 520–526; Brandl & Mudambi, 2014, pp. 135–145; Zhang, Jiang & Cantwell, 2015, p. 228).

MNEs and home/host countries' competitiveness

The two previous sections investigated separately the interaction among MNEs' strategies and (i) the host countries' competitive advantages and (ii) the home countries' competitive advantages. This choice between host and home reflects the separate trends of some IB scholars focusing more exclusively on host countries' features and others focusing more on home countries' features. Studies concentrating on the strategies and organization of MNEs have uncovered the evidence that MNEs organize their activities according to the competitive assets of their home countries and of their different host countries. MNEs organize their internal and external networks, and therefore their global value chain, according to their own competitive advantages and disadvantages related to the comparative advantages of the location of their activities (Sölvell, 2002, p. 3; Ketels, 2008, p. 124; Mudambi, 2008; Porter, 2008, p. 315; Cuervo-Cazurra, 2013; Buckley, 2017; Gugler, 2017). As noted by Gugler, Keller and Tinguely (2015, p. 324; see also Mudambi & Swift, 2011, p. 1):

> As a result of their ability to supersede the market and internalize the benefits of the geographic distribution of their activities, multinational enterprises (MNEs) have distributed their value chain around the world and implemented a global network of subsidiaries that allow them to take advantage of the specific profile of different environments.

Studies on developed economy MNEs as well as on EMNEs report that companies' portfolios of activities are closely related to the configuration and the management of assets that are developed and sourced in different locations (Luo & Wang, 2012, p. 244; Tinguely, 2013; Gugler, Keller & Tinguely, 2015; Gugler & Vanoli, 2015). FSAs are impacted by the ability of the firm to take advantage of the assets that are related to the CSAs of home and host countries (Verbeke, 2009, p. 187; Buckley, Forsans & Munjal, 2012; Buckley, 2017). Multiple national diamonds are at work. As noted by Lessard (2014, p. 116) firms may create "a virtual diamond" based on the competitive assets offered by their different locations. The "network" approach analyzing the internal and external linkages of MNEs highlights not only the tremendous importance of the competitiveness of location but also the agglomeration of specific activities of the value chain in particular locations. This phenomenon has recently been explored in the case of EMNEs (De Beule & Duanmu, 2012; Estrin & Meyer, 2013; Deng & Yang, 2015). Here again, it is important to distinguish the different types of FSAs and CSAs, in particular the "location-bound FSAs" and the "non-location-bound FSAs" (Rugman, 1981; Rugman & Verbeke, 1992). The "location-bound FSAs" depend upon the CSA features of the home and host countries (Rugman & Verbeke, 2001). As noted by Gugler, Keller and Tinguely (2015, p. 328) "firms can take advantages of clusters as CSAs in their home country (home-CSA-cluster) and in their host locations (host-CSAs-cluster) and develop FSAs at the headquarter level (FSA-headquarter) and at the affiliate level (FSA-affiliate)".

As already stressed earlier, clusters are important drivers of location competitiveness explaining the agglomeration of activities and capabilities in specific locations: "What we can say is that the global economy is made up of intricately interconnected localized clusters of economic activity which are embedded in various ways into different forms of corporate network" (Dicken, 2000, p. 284). The role of clusters is crucial for strategic-assets seeking investment and may explain the concentration of R&D subsidiaries abroad within knowledge-intensive clusters (Dunning, 1998, p. 50; Gugler, Keller & Tinguely, 2015, p. 325). These developments highlight the impact of the agglomeration of specific activities of the value chain such as R&D activities.

IB scholars' research on innovative activities and the capabilities of firms has emphasized the positive impact of the agglomeration of economic activities on innovation (Jaffe, Trajtenberg & Henderson, 1993; Audretsch & Feldman, 1996; Feldman, 2000; Iammarino & McCann, 2013; Tinguely, 2013). MNEs increase their competiveness through the internationalization of the specific CSAs offered by various locations (Gugler, Keller & Tinguely, 2015, p. 329).

MNE spillovers on host and home countries' competitiveness

The assessment of MNE spillovers on host and home countries' competitiveness offers another field of the IB literature that has a direct link with Economic Geography patterns. This issue has been developed within the broad question related to the overall impact of MNEs (Dunning & Lundan, 2008, p. 295). Major attention has been dedicated to the impact of MNEs on host countries. Indeed, MNE affiliates may have an important impact on the quality of the business environment of the recipient region/country in terms of the factor conditions, the type of rivalry, the supporting and related industries, and the demand conditions (Porter's Diamond). Theoretical and empirical studies have also investigated the so-called "reverse spillovers" or in other words, the impact of MNEs on their home country's assets. This issue has attracted increased attention in light of the development of emerging countries' FDI, such as Chinese FDI.

From a theoretical point of view, the assumption that MNEs may create positive spillovers in the host economies relies inter alia on the "positive gap" between foreign affiliates and local firms (Gugler & Brunner, 2007, p. 272). As asserted by the OLI paradigm, MNEs decide to invest abroad if they possess O advantages over domestic firms (Dunning, 1993). The impact of MNEs on their host country's competitiveness is particularly relevant when one considers the spillovers on innovation, productivity, and therefore wealth creation within the recipient country/regions (Dunning & Gugler, 1994, p. 173). As stated by Blomström and Kokko (1998, p. 249), spillovers occur when "the entry or presence of MNC affiliates lead to productivity or efficiency benefits in the host country's local firms and the MNCs are not able to internalize the full value of these benefits". The spillover effects affect the L advantages of a recipient country (Dunning & Lundan, 2008, p. 323) characterized, either by the "environment/systems/policy (ESP) framework" (Koopmans & Montias, 1971) or the Diamond of Michael Porter (Porter, 1990).

The literature distinguishes two main spillover effects: the impact on competition and the impact on knowledge and technology. According to Ben Hamida and Gugler (2009, pp. 494–495):

> The competitive effects, or rather the incentives for competition, operate through either a more efficient use of existing technology and resources or an assimilation of foreign technologies. While knowledge transfer effects may result from the introduction of new know-how to local firms, by among other things, demonstrating new technologies and training workers who later work for local firms.

Because innovation is one of the major drivers of a location's competitiveness, the IB literature on technological spillovers is of particular interest. (Blomström & Kokko, 1998, pp. 247–248; Markusen & Venables, 1999, p. 336; Hubert & Pain, 2001, p. 136). The results of the studies devoted to this question are mixed (Görg & Strobl, 2001; Gugler & Brunner, 2007, pp. 273–276; Ben Hamida & Gugler, 2009, p. 497). The impact depends inter alia on the technological absorptive capacities of local firms and of the overall configuration of the diamond of the host location (Gugler & Brunner, 2007, p. 273). The main studies identifying positive spillovers focus on FDI in developed economies where the technological gaps between home and host economies are lower than in the case of FDI and developing countries (Rugman & Verbeke, 2001). The quality of the host country's business environment also plays an important role in the potential positive impact of technological spillovers on the local economy. For example, Smeets and de Vaal (2016) show that countries with strong intellectual property protection benefit more from technological spillovers created by foreign affiliates.

In that respect, the role of clusters in leveraging context to maximize the technological spillovers of MNE affiliates is particularly relevant. The agglomeration of economic and technological capacities plays an important role in benefiting from the efficiency and technology knowledge of foreign affiliates (Gugler & Brunner, 2007, p. 271; Franco & Kozovska, 2011, p. 131). The potential positive spillovers of MNEs on host countries are driven not only through transfer of know-how, knowledge, and technologies within existing clusters but also through their impulse toward the creation of new clusters and the development of embryonic clusters (Birkinshaw, 2000, pp. 99–103; Enright, 2000, p. 130; Porter, 2008, p. 247). In that respect, MNEs may contribute to strengthening the specialization and agglomeration of economics activities abroad, and therefore, the MNEs' impact is an important factor of the drivers of economic agglomeration trends studied by economic geographers.

The economic literature focuses also on the transfer of knowledge and capacities from the MNEs' foreign subsidiaries to the home country headquarters' business units. These so-called "reverse spillovers", quite neglected for many years, have observed increased interest among the IB and regional economics scholars (see, for example, Dunning & Lundan, 2008, pp. 406–408). Ambos, Ambos and Schlegelmilch (2006, p. 298) positively tested the following hypothesis: "headquarters' benefits from reverse knowledge transfers will be positively related to the competitive strength of the host country". Using patent citations, Tinguely (2013) clearly identified spillovers on both sides of Swiss pharmaceutical MNEs, i.e., within the home-based business and foreign affiliates. Tinguely's study highlights the role of clusters in this respect. In the case of Swiss pharmaceutical firms, the major R&D affiliates are located in specific clusters abroad and in the home country (Switzerland). These results confirm that the agglomeration of economic activities within clusters contributes to benefits not only from the spillover of foreign affiliates but also from the reverse spillovers from the home MNEs' affiliates located abroad (Tinguely, 2013; Gugler, Keller & Tinguely, 2015). The increase of the interest regarding reverse spillovers and their effects on the home country's competitiveness has taken on new impetus with the increasing trend of emerging country MNEs investing abroad—inter alia through mergers and acquisition—to acquire knowledge capabilities abroad that will profit home country parent firms lacking FSAs (e.g., in the case of Chinese firms: Bhaumik, Driffield & Zhou, 2016). Nair, Dermibag and Mellahi (2016) investigated the reverse knowledge transfer of Indian MNEs to their home parents. According to their study, the main transfer occurs when parent firms benefit from knowledge capabilities thanks inter alia to their FSAs developed through adequate domestic research and development infrastructures. Many factors influence the intensity of technological reverse spillovers. For example, as shown by Mudambi, Piscitello and Rabbiosi (2014, p. 60), the importance of reverse technology transfers depends inter alia upon the mode of entry into foreign countries: greenfield subsidiaries generate higher reverse transfers than acquisitions. Among all features influencing these patterns, it is important to highlight the role of the CSAs of the home and host countries, particularly when those CSAs are shaped by the presence of innovative clusters. MNEs located in a home-based cluster may benefit from stronger technological FSAs, allowing them to benefit from higher externalities when they locate their subsidiaries in foreign clusters. The increased capabilities acquired abroad will also strengthen the importance of technological reverse spillovers in their home country. These are potentially more important when home-based parent firms are themselves located in home clusters.

Conclusion

The competitiveness of location—as territorial, capital-attracting, value-added activities—has gained increased interest among the scientific community, particularly in the fields of Economic Geography and IB. Our review of the literature reflects four different, but interrelated, research orientations dedicated to the interconnection between the competitiveness of a specific location and MNEs' choice of where to spread their value-added activities. The first approach considers the comparative advantages of a specific recipient location as one important criterion for explaining why, where, and how firms invest abroad. The OLI paradigm, developed by Dunning, perfectly reflects the interdependence between the location advantages of a specific recipient area, the ownership advantages of the firm, and its internalization of advantages. The second approach investigates the role of the competitive assets of home countries as an enhancer of domestic firms' competitiveness and therefore as an enhancer of their ability to invest abroad. One of the major contributions in this field was offered by Alan Rugman, who considered CSAs on the one side and FSAs on the other to explain the international expansion strategies of firms. The third approach starts to consider the internal and external networks of MNEs. MNEs internalize the major assets, particularly the competitive location-bound assets, of their home and of their multiple host countries. Finally, the fourth approach studies MNEs' spillover on their recipient countries as well as the reverse spillovers on their home countries. These spillovers affect the competitive advantages of their locations (through labor, research and development, competition effects, etc.).

These four approaches find their roots and results in major issues developed by economic geographers, such as the role of clusters, in explaining the competitiveness of home and host countries, and therefore the geographical expansion of MNEs.

References

Ambos, T.C., Ambos, B. & Schlegelmich, B.B. (2006) 'Learning from foreign subsidiaries: An empirical investigation of headquarters' benefits from reverse knowledge transfers', *International Business Review*, 15, pp. 294–312.

Asheim, B.T. (2000) 'Industrial districts: The contributions of Marshall and beyond', in Clark, G.L., Feldman, M.P. & Gertler, M.S. (Eds.), *The Oxford Handbook of Economic Geography*. Oxford, UK: Oxford University Press, pp. 413–431.

Audretsch, D.B. (2000) 'Corporate form and spatial form', in Clark, G.L., Feldman, M.P. & Gertler, M.S. (Eds.), *The Oxford Handbook of Economic Geography*. Oxford, UK: Oxford University Press, pp. 333–347.

Audretsch, D.B. & Feldman, M.P. (1996) 'Knowledge spillovers and the geography of innovation and production', *American Economic Review*, 86, pp. 630–640.

Bartlett, C.A. & Ghoshal, S. (1989) *Managing Across Borders: The Transnational Solution*. Boston, MA: Harvard Business School Press.

Ben Hamida, L. & Gugler, P. (2009) 'Are there demonstration-related spillovers from FDI? Evidence from Switzerland', *International Business Review*, 18, pp. 494–508.

Beugelsdijk, S., McCann, P. & Mudambi, R. (2010) 'Introduction: Place, space and organization Economic Geography and the multinational enterprise', *Journal of Economic Geography*, 10, pp. 485–493.

Bhaumik, S.K., Driffield, N. & Zhou, Y. (2016) 'Country specific advantage, firm specific advantage and multinationality', *International Business Review*, 25, pp. 165–176.

Birkinshaw, J. (2000) 'Upgrading of industry clusters and foreign investment', *International Studies of Management & Organization*, 30, pp. 93–113.
Blomström, M. & Kokko, A. (1998) 'Technology transfer and spillovers: Does local participation with multinationals matter?' *NBER Working Paper 6816*. Cambridge, MA.
Brandl, K. & Mudambi, R. (2014) 'EMNCs and catch-up processes: The case of four Indian industries', in Cuervo-Cazurra, A. & Ramamurti, R. (Eds.), *Understanding Multinationals from Emerging Markets*. Cambridge, UK: Cambridge University Press, pp. 129–152.
Buckley, P.J. (2017) 'The competitiveness of emerging country multinational enterprise. Does it derive from CSAs or FSAs?' *Competitiveness Review*, forthcoming.
Buckley, P.J., Forsans, N. & Munjal, S. (2012) 'Host-home country linkages and host-home country specific advantages as determinants of foreign acquisitions by Indian firms', *International Business Review*, 21, pp. 878–890.
Cantwell, J. (2009) 'Location and the multinational enterprise', *Journal of International Business Studies*, 40, pp. 35–41.
Clark, G.L., Feldman, M.P. & Gertler, M.S. (2000) 'Economic Geography transition and growth', in Clark, G.L., Feldman, M.P. & Gertler, M.S. (Eds.), *The Oxford Handbook of Economic Geography*. Oxford, UK: Oxford University Press, pp. 4–17.
Cuervo-Cazurra, A. (2011) 'Global strategy and global business environment: The direct and indirect influences of the home country on a firm's global strategy', *Global Strategy Journal*, 1, pp. 382–386.
Cuervo-Cazurra, A. (2012) 'Extending theory by analysing developing country multinational companies: Solving the goldilocks debate', *Global Strategy Journal*, 2, pp. 153–167.
Cuervo-Cazurra, A. (2013) 'How emerging market multinational enterprises upgrade capabilities using value-chain configuration in advanced economies', in Williamson, P.J., Ramamurti, R., Fleury, A. & Fleury, M.T.L. (Eds.), *The Competitive Advantage of Emerging Market Multinationals*. Cambridge, MA: Cambridge University Press, pp. 174–179.
De Beule, F. & Duanmu, J.-L. (2012) 'Locational determinants of internationalization: A firm-level analysis of Chinese and Indian acquisitions', *European Management Journal*, 30, pp. 264–277.
Debrah, Y.A., McGovern, I. & Budhwar, P. (2000) 'Complementarity or competition: The development of human resources in a South-East Asian growth triangle: Indonesia, Malaysia and Singapore', *International Journal of Human Resource Management*, 11, pp. 314–335.
Deng, P. & Yang, M. (2015) 'Cross-border mergers and acquisitions by emerging market firms: A comparative investigation', *International Business Review*, 24, pp. 157–172.
Dicken, P. (2000) 'Places and flows: Situating international investment', in Clark, G.L., Feldman, M.P. & Gertler, M.S. (Eds), *The Oxford Handbook of Economic Geography*. Oxford, UK: Oxford University Press, pp. 275–291.
Dunning, J.H. (1981) *International Production and the Multinational Enterprise*. London: Allen & Unwin.
Dunning, J.H. (1993) *Multinational Enterprises and the Global Economy*. Wokingham, UK and Reading, MA: Addison Wesley.
Dunning, J.H. (1998) 'Location and the multinational enterprise: A neglected factor?', *Journal of International Business Studies*, 29, pp. 45–66.
Dunning, J.H. (2009) 'Location and the multinational enterprise: A neglected factor?' *Journal of International Business Studies*, 40, pp. 5–19.
Dunning, J.H. & Gugler, P. (1994) 'Technology based cross-border alliances', in David, J.J. (Ed.), *Technology Transfer and Business Enterprise*. Cheltenham, UK: Edward Elgar, pp. 173–220.
Dunning, J.H., Kim, C. & Park, D. (2008) 'Old wine in new bottles: A comparison of emerging-market TNCs today and developed-country TNCs thirty years ago', in Sauvant, K. (Ed.), *The Rise of Transnational Corporations from Emerging Markets*. Cheltenham, UK: Edward Elgar Publishing, pp. 158–182.
Dunning, J.H. & Lundan, S. (2008) *Multinational Enterprises and the Global Economy*. Cheltenham, UK: Edward Elgar Publishing.
Dunning, J.H. & Narula, R. (1996) *Foreign Direct Investment and Governments*. London: Routledge.
Enright, M.J. (2000) 'The globalisation of competition and the location of competitive advantage: Policies towards regional clustering', in Hood, N. & Young, S. (Eds.), *The Globalisation of Multinational Enterprise Activity and Economic Development*. London: MacMillan, pp. 303–331.

Estrin, S. & Meyer, K. (2013) *How Different are Emerging Economy MNEs? A Comparative Study of Location Choice*. LSE mimeo, [online]. Available at: http://personal.lse.ac.uk/estrin/Publication%20PDF's/How%20Different%20are%20Emerging%20Economy%20MNEs_20130122km.pdf.

Feldman, M.P. (2000) 'Location and innovation: The new Economic Geography of innovation spillovers, and agglomeration', in Clark, G.L., Feldman, M.P. & Gertler, M.S. (Eds.), *The Oxford Handbook of Economic Geography*. Oxford, UK: Oxford University Press, pp. 373–394.

Franco, C. & Kozovska, K. (2011) 'Mutual productivity spillovers and regional clusters in Eastern Europe: Some empirical evidence', in Rugraff, E. & Hansen, M.W. (Eds.), *Multinational Corporations and Local Firms in Emerging Economies*. Amsterdam: Amsterdam University Press, pp. 123–151.

Gertler, M. (2003) 'Tacit knowledge and the Economic Geography of context, or the undefinable tacitness of being (there)', *Journal of Economic Geography*, 3, pp. 75–99.

Görg, H. & Strobl, E. (2001) 'Multinational companies and productivity spillovers: A meta-analysis', *Economic Journal*, 111, pp. 723–739.

Gugler, P. (2017) 'Emerging countries' country specific advantages (CSAs) and the competitiveness of emerging market multinational enterprises (EMNEs): Where do we stand?' *Competitiveness Review*, 27, pp. 194–207.

Gugler, P. & Brunner, S. (2007) 'FDI effects on national competitiveness: A cluster approach', *International Advance in Economic Research*, 13, pp. 268–284.

Gugler, P., Keller, M. & Tinguely, X. (2015) 'The role of clusters in the global innovation strategy of MNEs', *Competitiveness Review*, 25, pp. 324–340.

Gugler, P. & Vanoli, L. (2015) 'Technology-sourcing investment abroad as an enhancer of Chinese MNEs' innovative capabilities', *International Journal of Emerging Markets*, 10, pp. 243–271.

Hanson, G.H. (2000) 'Firms, workers, and the geography concentration of economic activity', in Clark, G.L., Feldman, M.P. & Gertler, M.S. (Eds.), *The Oxford Handbook of Economic Geography*. Oxford, UK: Oxford University Press, pp. 477–494.

Hubert, F. & Pain, N. (2001) 'Inward investment and technical progress in the United Kingdom manufacturing sector', *Scottish Journal of Political Economy*, 48, pp. 134–147.

Hymer, S.H. (1972) 'The multinational corporation and the law of uneven development', in Bhagwati, J.N. (Ed.), *Economics and World Order: From the 1970 to the 1990s*. New York: The Free Press, pp. 113–140.

Iammarino, S. & McCann, P. (2013) *Multinationals and Economic Geography: Location, Technology and Innovation*. Cheltenham, UK and Reading, MA: Edward Elgar.

Jacobs, W., Koster, H.R. & van Oort, F. (2014) 'Co-agglomeration of knowledge-intensive business services and multinational enterprises', *Journal of Economic Geography*, 14, pp. 443–475.

Jaffe, A.B., Trajtenberg, M. & Henderson, R. (1993) 'Geographic localization of knowledge spillovers as evidenced by patent citations', *The Quarterly Journal of Economics*, 108, pp. 577–598.

Jensen, P.D.O. & Pedersen, T. (2011) 'The Economic Geography of offshoring: The fit between activities and local context', *Journal of Management Studies*, 48, pp. 253–372.

Karna, A., Täube, F. & Sonderegger, P. (2013) 'Evolution of innovation networks across geographical and organizational boundaries: A study of R&D subsidiaries in the Bangalore IT cluster', *European Management Review*, 10, pp. 211–226.

Ketels, C. (2008) 'Microeconomic determinants of location competitiveness for MNEs', in Dunning, J.H. & Gugler, P. (Eds.), *Foreign Direct Investment, Location and Competitiveness*. Oxford, UK: Elsevier, pp. 111–131.

Koopmans, K. & Montias, J.M. (1971) 'On the description and comparison of economic systems', in Eckstein, A. (Ed.), *Comparison of Economic Systems: Theoretical and Methodological Approaches*. Berkeley, CA: University of California Press, pp. 27–78.

Krugman, P. (2000) 'Where in the world is the 'New Economic Geography?' in Clark, G.L., Feldman, M.P. & Gertler, M.S. (Eds.), *The Oxford Handbook of Economic Geography*. Oxford, UK: Oxford University Press, pp. 49–60.

Lessard, D. (2014) 'The evolution of EMNCs and EMNC thinking: A capabilities perspective', in Cuervo-Cazurra, A. & Ramamurti, R. (Eds.), *Understanding Multinationals from Emerging Markets*. Cambridge, UK: Cambridge University Press, pp. 108–128.

Luo, Y. & Tung, R.L. (2007) 'International expansion of emerging market enterprises: A springboard perspective', *Journal of International Business Studies*, 38, pp. 481–498.

Luo, Y. & Wang, S.L. (2012) 'Foreign direct investment strategies by developing country multinationals: A diagnostic model for home country effects', *Global Strategy Journal*, 2, pp. 244–261.
Markusen, J.M. & Venables, A.J. (1999) 'Foreign direct investment as a catalyst for industrial development', *European Economic Review*, 43, pp. 335–356.
Meyer, K.E., Mudambi, R. & Narula, R. (2011) 'Multinational enterprises and local contexts: The opportunities and challenges of multiple embeddedness', *Journal of Management Studies*, 48, pp. 235–252.
Mudambi, R. (2008) 'Location, control, and innovation in knowledge-intensive industries', *Journal of Economic Geography*, 8, pp. 699–725.
Mudambi, R., Piscitello, L. & Rabbiosi, L. (2014) 'Reverse knowledge transfer in MNEs: Subsidiary innovativeness and entry modes', *Long Range Planning*, 47, pp. 49–63.
Mudambi, R. & Swift, T. (2011) 'Leveraging knowledge and competencies across space: The next frontier in International Business', *Journal of International Management*, 17, pp. 186–189.
Nair, S.R., Dermibag, M. & Mellahi, K. (2016) 'Reverse knowledge transfer in emerging market multinationals: The Indian context', *International Business Review*, 25, pp. 152–164.
Narula, R. (2012) 'Do we need different frameworks to explain infant MNEs from developing countries?' *Global Strategy Journal*, 2, pp. 188–204.
Nelson, R.R. & Pack, H. (1999) 'The Asian miracle of modern growth theory', *The Economic Journal*, 109, pp. 416–436.
Peng, M.W., Wang, D.Y.-L. & Jiang, Y. (2008) 'An institution-based view of International Business strategy: A focus on emerging economies', *Journal of International Business Studies*, 39, pp. 920–936.
Porter, M.E. (1990) *The Competitive Advantage of Nations*. New York: Free Press.
Porter, M.E. (2000) 'Locations, clusters, and company strategy', in Clark, G.L., Feldman, M.P. & Gertler, M.S. (Eds.), *The Oxford Handbook of Economic Geography*. Oxford, UK: Oxford University Press, pp. 253–274.
Porter, M.E. (2008) *On Competition*. Cambridge, MA: Harvard Business Press.
Ramamurti, R. (2008) 'What have we learned about emerging-market MNEs?' in *Conference on Emerging Multinationals: Outward FDI from Emerging and Developing Economies*. Copenhagen: Copenhagen Business School.
Rugman, A.M. (1981) *Inside the Multinationals*. New York: Columbia University Press.
Rugman, A.M. (2008) 'How global are TNCs from emerging countries?' in Sauvant, K.P. (Ed.), *The Rise of Transnational Corporations from Emerging Markets: Threats or Opportunity?* Cheltenham, UK: Edward Elgar, pp. 86–106.
Rugman, A.M. & Li, J. (2007) 'Will China's multinationals succeed globally or regionally?' *European Management Journal*, 25, pp. 333–343.
Rugman, A.M. & Nguyen, Q.T.K. (2014) 'Modern International Business theory and emerging market multinational companies', in Cuervo-Cazurra, A. & Ramamurti, R. (Eds.), *Understanding Multinationals from Emerging Markets*. Cambridge, UK: Cambridge University Press, pp. 53–80.
Rugman, A.M. & Verbeke, A. (1992) 'A note on the transactional solution and the transaction cost theory of multinational strategic management', *Journal of International Business Studies*, 23, pp. 761–771.
Rugman, A.M. & Verbeke, A. (2001) 'Subsidiary-specific advantages in multinational enterprises', *Strategic Management Journal*, 22, pp. 237–250.
Rugman, A.M. & Verbeke, A. (2004) 'A perspective on regional and global strategies of multinational enterprises', *Journal of International Business Studies*, 35, pp. 3–18.
Shatz, H.J. & Venables, A.J. (2000) 'The geography of international investment', in Clark, G.L., Feldman, M.P. & Gertler, M.S. (Eds.), *The Oxford Handbook of Economic Geography*. Oxford, UK: Oxford University Press, pp. 126–145.
Smeets, R. & de Vaal, A. (2016) 'Intellectual property rights and the productivity effects of MNE affiliates on host-country firms', *International Business Review*, 25, pp. 419–434.
Sölvell, O. (2002) 'The multi-home based multinational: Combining global competitiveness and local innovativeness', in Symposium in honor of John Stopford, London.
Storper, M. (2000) 'Globalization, localization, and trade', in Clark, G.L., Feldman, M.P. & Gertler, M.S. (Eds.), *The Oxford Handbook of Economic Geography*. Oxford, UK: Oxford University Press, pp. 146–165.
Sun, S.L., Peng, M.W., Ren, B. & Yan, D. (2012) 'A comparative ownership advantage framework for cross-border M&As: The rise of Chinese and Indian MNEs', *Journal of World Business*, 47, pp. 4–16.

Tinguely, X. (2013) *The New Geography of Innovation: Clusters, Competitiveness and Theory*. Basingstoke, UK: Palgrave Macmillan.

Venables, A.J. (2005) *New Economic Geography*. Mimeo, London School of Economics and CEPR.

Verbeke, A. (2009) *International Business Strategy*. Cambridge, UK: Cambridge University Press.

Vernon, R. (1966) 'International investment and international trade in the product cycle', *Quarterly Journal of Economics*, 80, pp. 190–207.

Weber, A. (1909) *Theory of the Location of Industries*. Chicago, IL: The University of Chicago Press.

World Economic Forum (WEF) (2015) *Global Competitiveness Report 2015–2016*. Geneva: WEF.

Yiu, D.W., Lau, C. & Bruton, G.D. (2007) 'International venturing by emerging economy firms: The effects of firm capabilities, home country networks, and corporate entrepreneurship', *Journal of International Business Studies*, 38, pp. 519–540.

Zhang, F., Jiang, G. & Cantwell, J.A. (2015) 'Subsidiary exploration and innovative performance of large multinational corporations', *International Business Review*, 24, pp. 224–234.

27

THE CHANGING GEOGRAPHY OF INNOVATION AND THE MULTINATIONAL ENTERPRISE

Davide Castellani

Introduction[1]

The Economic Geography literature largely recognises that there are benefits from localised interactions and exchanges of knowledge which generate what Storper and Venables (2004) characterise as the 'local buzz' that tends to lead to an ever-increasing geographical concentration of innovation activity in a few regions. However, it may be both unrealistic and undesirable for economic regions to rely only on 'local buzz' for developing their knowledge base, and successful clusters need to combine knowledge internal and external to the cluster. To this end, 'global pipelines' need to be established in order to allow external knowledge to flow into the clusters (Bathelt, Malmberg & Maskell, 2004; Owen-Smith & Powell, 2004). The International Business literature has long established that multinational enterprises (MNEs) – that can be conceptualised as global orchestrators of knowledge – are in a privileged position to build these pipelines by tapping into diverse knowledge clusters and thanks to their ability to de-contextualise tacit knowledge and transfer it within the MNE and across space (Castellani & Zanfei, 2006; Meyer, Mudambi & Narula, 2011; Cano-Kollmann et al., 2016).

Based on this conceptual map, this chapter provides descriptive evidence of the changing geography of inventive activity and the role of MNEs in international research and development (R&D), with quite an extensive geographical coverage. On the one hand, OECD REGPAT data on 1,482 regions in 39 countries allow us to describe the changing patterns in patenting activity over 32 years, from 1980 until 2011. On the other, fDi Markets data on over 110,000 investment projects referring to the period 2003–2014, in more than 10,000 cities in 184 different countries, allow us to characterise the geographical concentration of MNEs activities, with special reference to their international R&D.

The rest of the chapter is organised as follows. The next section briefly articulates the conceptual map described earlier. Then we describe the data used in the analysis, and the following section presents the empirical evidence. The final section concludes.

'Local buzz', 'global pipelines' and the role of MNEs in global innovation

The role of 'local buzz' and 'global pipelines' in the changing geography of innovation

Recent research in the geography of innovation has established several stylised and commonly accepted facts including: (i) innovation is spatially concentrated, and (ii) knowledge spillovers are geographically localised (Feldman & Kogler, 2010). The literature has emphasised that while effective knowledge transfer requires a combination of cognitive, organisational, social and institutional proximity (Boschma, 2005; Balland, Boschma & Frenken, 2015), 'the high level of embeddedness of local firms in a very thick network of knowledge sharing, which is supported by close social interactions and by institutions building trust and encouraging informal relations among actors' (Breschi & Malerba, 2001, p. 819) boosts the success of local knowledge production and circulation processes. Technological spillovers are held to be easier in compact spaces for a number of reasons. As Marshall (1927) himself pointed out, information is likely to flow more easily because of the natural tendency of people in the same trade to share ideas and discuss and demonstrate improvements. Experimentation is also easier; it is easier to try out new ideas because there is rapid feedback (from demanding customers), and firms are more likely to be able to find the complementary knowledge, resources and assets they need in order to bring their ideas to fruition. Storper and Venables (2004) characterise this localised flow of specialised, highly tacit knowledge as the 'buzz' that distinguishes economically dynamic centres of innovation. In their view, 'local buzz', refers to the 'information and communication ecology created by face-to-face contacts, co-presence and co-location of people and firms within the same industry and place or region' (Bathelt, Malmberg & Maskell, 2004, p. 38). Actors continuously contribute to and benefit from the diffusion of information, gossip and news by just 'being there' (Gertler, 2003). 'Local buzz' generates opportunities for the transmission of sticky, non-articulated, tacit forms of knowledge between firms located there, and leads to innovation becoming more clustered over time.

However, it may be both unrealistic and undesirable for economic regions to rely only on 'local buzz' for developing their knowledge base. Indeed, few, if any, local economies are likely to be completely self-sufficient in terms of the knowledge base from which they draw (Gertler, 2008). Knowledge internal to the cluster eventually needs to be integrated with knowledge external to the cluster. Following Owen-Smith and Powell (2004), Bathelt, Malmberg and Maskell (2004) address these non-local knowledge flows through the concept of global pipelines, which refer to channels of communication used in the interaction between firms in different knowledge-producing centres located at a distance from one another. They argue that 'global pipelines' can 'pump' information about markets and technologies into the cluster, making the 'buzz' more dynamic, by providing access to a more variegated set of knowledge pools from which to draw.

But how (and how much) knowledge is transferred in these global pipelines? How can the obstacles of 'not being there' be overcome? (Gertler, 2003, 2008). The Economic Geography literature has not reached a well-developed understanding of how knowledge is supposed to flow across long distances via global pipelines, or under what circumstances this is more – or less – likely to be the case.

At the most basic level, pipelines can be created by firms and organisations, or through personal networks. Lorenzen and Mudambi (2013) examine the role of migrant diasporas in facilitating the creation of such pipelines, with reference to the cases of the movie and IT clusters of Bollywood and Bangalore in India. Maskell, Bathelt and Malmberg (2006) point out the role of temporary clusters, emerging from the participation in trade fairs, exhibition, conventions congresses and conferences. Gertler (2008) discusses how communities of practices, which are defined as groups of workers informally bound together by shared experience, expertise and commitment to a joint enterprise, can be vehicles for supporting learning at a distance. These communities mediate in the joint production and diffusion/transmission of knowledge within and between organisations. Furthermore, they allow some degree of relational proximity, which facilitates knowledge flows across regional and national boundaries. As Gertler (2008) notes, the formation of communities of practice can be encouraged in large MNEs with 'distributed' knowledge bases and multiple sites of innovation, and supported by advanced means of electronically mediated communication, to overcome the friction of geographical separation. Indeed, as the next section will argue, the view of the MNEs as global orchestrators of geographically dispersed knowledge have long been established in the International Business literature.

MNE as global orchestrators of knowledge

There has been a long-standing literature which has identified MNEs as being important actors who transfer technology across international borders (Dunning & Lundan, 2008). Initially, the emphasis in the literature was on the role of foreign direct investment (FDI) as a means whereby firms with an advantage in technology could exploit that advantage in overseas markets. The existence of significant market failures in markets for technology creates a bias in favour of internalisation (Buckley & Casson, 1976).

This view of the MNE is confirmed by the fact that MNEs are key actors in global R&D expenditures, and the bulk of R&D is concentrated in the home country of the MNE (Belderbos, Leten & Suzuki, 2013). However, a discernible trend has emerged going back at least to the 1980s, but accelerating in recent years, for MNEs to disperse their R&D activity geographically (Dunning & Lundan, 2009). This internationalisation of R&D has been driven by demand and supply factors. On the one hand, there are often locational advantages for MNEs to establish overseas R&D operations to tailoring the firm's product or service more closely to local tastes (Narula & Zanfei, 2005). On the other, the increasing importance of knowledge-based assets as a source of competitive advantage (Hitt, Hoskisson & Him, 1997) has seen an increased focus on location in particularly fertile regions, which are leading centres of knowledge generation and innovation (Cantwell & Iammarino, 2003; Cantwell, 2017). This has been reflected in the increased use of competence-creating mandates to MNE subsidiaries and an increased emphasis on balancing greater autonomy for subsidiaries with the smooth coordination of activities in increasingly complex MNE networks (Cantwell & Mudambi, 2005). Tapping into localised sources of innovation requires conscious effort by MNEs to build suitable business relationships, rather than simply relying on some passive process of osmosis. Cantwell argues that MNEs create portfolios of locational assets which bear a complementary and synergistic relation to each other (Cantwell, 2009).

MNEs are thus becoming global orchestrators of knowledge. By tapping into diverse knowledge clusters, and thanks to their ability to de-contextualise tacit knowledge and transfer it within the MNE and across space (Cantwell & Santangelo, 1999; Castellani & Zanfei, 2006; Meyer, Mudambi & Narula, 2011), they create institutional proximity that allows connections between knowledge sources and to share tacit knowledge across locations despite geographical distance (Almeida, Song & Grant, 2002; Cano-Kollmann et al., 2016; Hannigan, Perri & Scalera, 2016). In other words, MNE are privileged actors to connect clusters (Iammarino & McCann, 2013) and build global pipelines between them.

But, in order to act as conduits of knowledge between clusters, MNEs need to locate R&D in dispersed locations. Despite the fact that the world is increasingly inter-connected, national borders and distance still matter (Ghemawat, 2016). This begs the question of 'How far are MNEs willing to go with their R&D in order to be close to the knowledge cluster?' Castellani, Jimenez and Zanfei (2013) address this question, and argue that on the one hand, concentration of knowledge in few geographically concentrated clusters reduces the set of possible available locations where specific bits of knowledge can be sourced. This may leave the MNE no choice but to locate R&D in a relatively remote location. On the other, the relative unimportance of transport costs in the case of knowledge inputs and outputs, combined with the fact that MNEs have developed routines and organisational structures that enable them to codify, process and transfer (codified and tacit) knowledge across national boundaries and within their internal networks (Gupta & Govindarajan, 1991; Kogut & Zander, 1992; Cantwell & Santangelo, 1999; Zanfei, 2000; Almeida, Song & Grant, 2002; Ambos & Ambos, 2009; Alcácer & Zhao, 2012), makes it more likely that MNEs set up R&D labs in relatively more remote locations. Using data on R&D and manufacturing investments of 6,320 firms in 59 countries, Castellani, Jimenez and Zanfei (2013) find that geographic distance has a lower negative impact on the probability of setting up R&D than manufacturing plants. Furthermore, once having accounted for measures of institutional proximity (such as, belonging to the same trade area or sharing similar religious attitudes and language), MNEs are equally likely to set up R&D labs in nearby or in more remote locations.

Data

Later in this chapter we will highlight some patterns in the geography of inventive activity for the regions of the world from the OECD Regional Innovation Dataset and of the R&D activities of MNEs based on cross-border investment project from the fDi Markets database. Below are brief descriptions of the two sources.

OECD Regional Innovation Dataset (REGPAT)

Data on the inventive activity of regions is drawn from REGPAT, which is part of the OECD Regional Innovation Dataset, and can be retrieved from http://stats.oecd.org.[2] REGPAT covers 34 OECD countries, plus 10 non-OECD member countries (Brazil, Colombia, Costa Rica, China, India, Indonesia, Latvia, Lithuania, Russia and South Africa). For the purpose of this analysis, data on Costa Rica, Greece, Indonesia and Slovenia could not be used.

The OECD has classified two levels of subnational units. This classification has been officially established and is relatively stable in all member countries, and is used by many countries as a framework for implementing regional policies. The more aggregate level is Territorial Level 2 (TL2), which covers the first administrative tier of subnational government, while a more fine-grained geographical disaggregation is available at Territorial Level 3 (TL3). The OECD regional typology is primarily based on a criterion which identifies rural communities according to population density. A community is defined as rural if its population density is below 150 inhabitants per km^2 (500 inhabitants for Japan and Korea to account for the fact that the national population density exceeds 300 inhabitants per km^2). Thus, each TL3 region has been classified as: Predominantly Urban (PU), Intermediate (IN), Predominantly Rural (PR). The vast majority of the latter group of regions are also classified as to whether they are close to a city, or are relatively remote. For these regions, REGPAT allows the tracking of the patent applications. For the purposes of this analysis, we use information from 1980 to 2011 on: Patent Cooperation

Table 27.1 Basic information on the sample of regions

		# Regions (%)	# Patents (%)	# Patents (median)	Population (median)	Patents per million inhabitants (median)
TL2		13.3%	7.9%	4	2,621,091	1
TL3 – intermediate		27.2%	23.7%	10	511,840	22
TL3 – rural		3.5%	0.1%	2	144,751	17
TL3 – close to a city		22.5%	11.4%	8	392,842	20
TL3 – remote		10.6%	1.4%	3	180,787	19
TL3 – urban		22.9%	55.4%	22	841,717	32
Total		100.0% (1,482)	100.0% (2,124,022)	9	503,407	19
Top 10 countries						
USA	TL3	12.1%	35.4%	17	668,486	24
JPN	TL3	3.2%	14.7%	29	1,723,006	17
DEU	TL3	6.5%	12.5%	29	615,003	44
GBR	TL3	9.3%	4.9%	10	298,243	34
FRA	TL3	6.5%	4.7%	9	495,900	21
KOR	TL3	1.1%	3.3%	36	1,855,040	17
CHN	TL2	2.1%	3.1%	9	34,911,028	0.2
SWE	TL3	1.4%	2.5%	28	260,197	102
NLD	TL3	0.8%	2.4%	25	1,041,552	43
ITA	TL3	7.4%	2.0%	5	355,929	13

Source: Author's elaboration on OECD Regional Innovation Database (stats.oecd.org).

Treaty (PCT) applications (fractional count by inventor and priority year), number of patents with more than one co-inventor, and the share of co-inventors within the same region, the same country, or foreign. Data on patents have been complemented with information on population. Since data on regional population are not available on the OECD regional dataset prior to the year 2000, we extrapolated regional population using country-wide data, based on the share of each region in a country's population in the latest available year. For Germany, since data was not available from http://stats.oced.org on population at the same level of disaggregation as for patents, we retrieved data from national sources for 2015 and used the share of regions in national population in that year to extrapolate regional population based on country-wide population for the period 1980–2011.[3]

Table 27.1 shows that we have a total of 1,482 regions, of which 86.7% are TL3. For eight countries (Brazil, Canada, China, India, Israel, Portugal, Russia and South Africa) data is available at TL2. Among TL3 regions, 22.9% are urban, 22.5% are rural but close to a city, and the remaining 54.6% are either intermediate or rural-remote. Despite being obviously larger (the median population is over 2.5 million), TL2 are not necessarily patenting more. They account for less than 8% of overall patents, and the median region has only 4 patents per year. On the contrary, patenting activity is overwhelmingly concentrated in urban areas (55.4% of all patents and a median of 22 patents). TL3 regions classified as intermediate, or close to a city, account for 34.1% of overall patents, and have median patents of 10 and 8 respectively.

fDi Markets

fDi Markets is a database produced by fDi Intelligence, a division of the Financial Times Ltd, which tracks cross-border greenfield investments across different industries and countries worldwide. According to the Financial Times Ltd, the information about cross-border investment projects is collected through a variety of sources, such as thousands of media sources, over 2,000 industry organisations and investment agencies, and data purchased from market research and publication companies (more details at www.fdimarkets.com/). fDi Markets is now a widely used source of information for activities of MNEs around the world, both by international organisation such as the UN (UNCTAD, 2016) and academic researchers (D'Agostino, Laursen & Santangelo, 2012; Castellani & Pieri, 2013, 2016; Crescenzi, Pietrobelli & Rabellotti, 2013; Belderbos et al., 2016; Castellani & Lavoratori, 2017; Castellani & Santangelo, 2017; Crescenzi & Iammarino, 2017; Damioli & Vertesy, 2017, among others).

We have access to a database containing 111,310 investment projects referring to the period 2003–2014, in 184 different countries. For each one of these projects fDi Markets reports information about the investing company name (and its parent), home country and city of the parent company, the industry and the business activity involved in the project, as well as the location of project destination (host country and city). The database contains projects in 17 different types of business activity which, for the purposes of our analysis, we grouped into 5 categories: Coordination activities, R&D-related activities, Production activities, Support services and Advanced services.

The bulk of investments are in Advanced services (including Business services and Sales and Marketing) and production activities, 47.8% and 30.0% respectively. Support services activities account for about 10% of the projects, while R&D-related activities account for 7% and investments aimed to establish global, country or regional headquarters are 5.4% of all investments.

Results

'Local buzz' and the geographic concentration of inventive activity

Using REGPAT data we are able to provide a quite detailed picture of the changing geography of inventive activity. In Figures 27.1 and 27.2 we offer a first glance into this evolution, by showing that the number of regions with at least one patent has increased threefold in the period 1980–2011, from fewer than 500 in 1980 to about 1,500 in 2010. The average number of patents per patenting region in each year has increased exponentially over the same period, from a handful in the 1980s to well over 100 after the year 2000. The geographical concentration of the patenting activity is enormous.

The lower panel of Table 21.1 shows the figures for ten largest countries in terms of overall patenting activity, revealing that these countries account for roughly 90% of worldwide patents (with the top three countries, the US, Japan and Germany accounting for over 60%). But countrywide data hide an even higher concentration in a few locations in each country. Figure 27.3 shows that in the first five years of this analysis, the top 100 patenting regions (out of approximately 800, that is roughly 12% of all the patenting regions) accounted for about 70% of the world's patents. To appreciate the magnitude of this concentration, consider that these top 100 regions accounted for about 10% of the world's population in the same period. In last period of this analysis (2006–2011), Figure 27.4 reveals that the top 100 regions still account for 70% of patenting but, on the one hand, the number of patenting regions has increased to almost 1,500 thus pointing to a higher concentration. On the other, the top 100 regions in terms of patenting account for 20% of the world's population, that is twice as much than in the 1980s. This suggests looking at the distribution of patenting per million population, to control for the effect of the increase in the size of regions on their patenting activity.

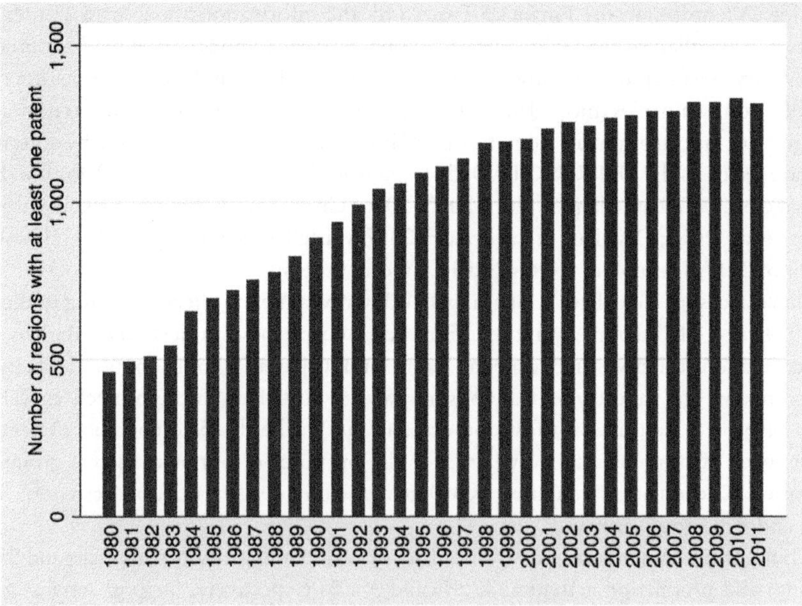

Figure 27.1 Number of regions with a least one patent, 1980–2011

Source: Author's elaboration on OECD Regional Innovation Database (stats.oecd.org).

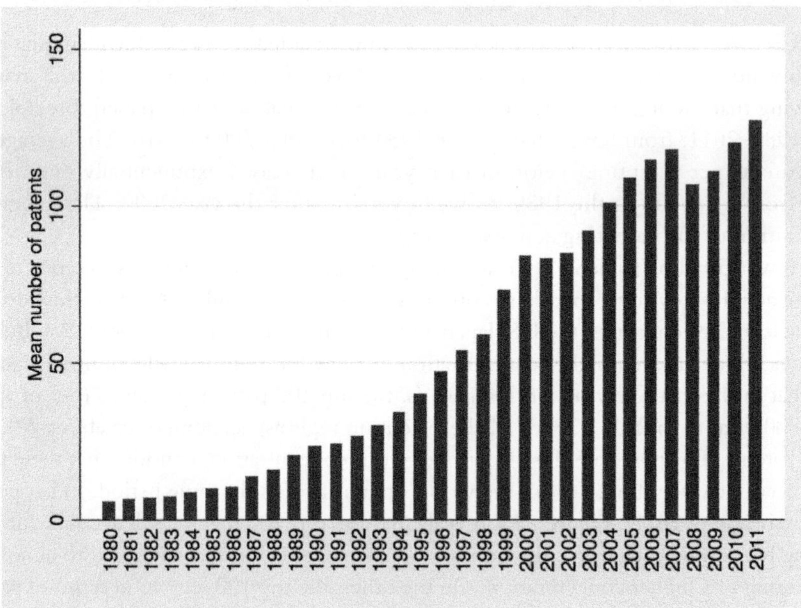

Figure 27.2 Average number of patents per region, 1980–2011

Source: Author's elaboration on OECD Regional Innovation Database (stats.oecd.org).

In Figure 27.5 we show that behind the increase in average patenting per region shown in Figure 27.2, there is a great regional heterogeneity. In fact, the median number of patents per region slightly increases over time, but does not exhibit an exponential growth, standing well

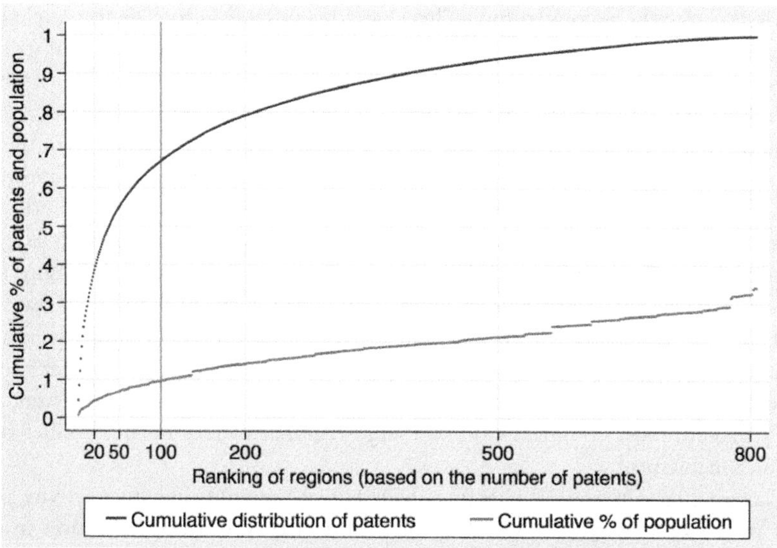

Figure 27.3 Regional concentration of patents, 1980–1984

Source: Author's elaboration on OECD Regional Innovation Database (stats.oecd.org).

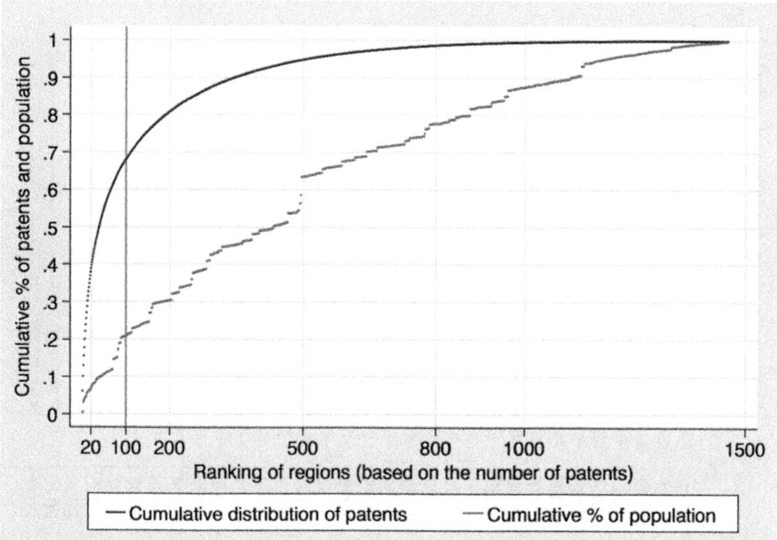

Figure 27.4 Regional concentration of patents, 2006–2011

Source: Author's elaboration on OECD Regional Innovation Database (stats.oecd.org).

below 50 even at the end of the period. Instead, the 75th percentile and the extreme values of the distribution reach close to 100 and over 200, respectively. In other words, few regions appear to have increased their patenting activity dramatically, thus leading to an apparent increase in overall patenting activity, which instead has been very much concentrated in a few locations.

In Figure 27.6 we provide further evidence of the changing distribution of regional patent activity (per million population). The chart depicts the kernel density[4] of patent per million inhabitants in six different five-year periods. Interestingly, while the distribution in 1980–1984 appears quite symmetrical and relatively shifted to the left, in 1985–1989 we can observe a slight shift to the right (suggesting an increase in average patenting per region), but also an increase in the variance and a thickening left tail. From the beginning of the 1990s, a singular pattern merges: the left tail of the distribution – that is regions with approximately fewer than 2.5 patents per population[5] – does not seem to change over time, but the distribution becomes ever more skewed to the right and with increased variance. This suggests that, over time, some regions with more significant patenting activity keep increasing their rate of inventive activity, while others lag behind. This is consistent with the idea that inventive activity benefits from the 'local buzz' stemming from clustering: the more regions engage in innovative activities, the more they create positive externalities for further innovation. Interestingly, a large regional heterogeneity in patenting activity is not a feature of a few countries. Indeed, most countries exhibit a large regional variety in the number of patents per million inhabitants.[6]

The changing distribution of patenting suggests that previous inventive activity is a major predictor of future activity. We test this conjecture first by showing transition matrices[7] of regions according to their quintile of the patents per million inhabitants, and then with slightly more rigorous regression analyses.

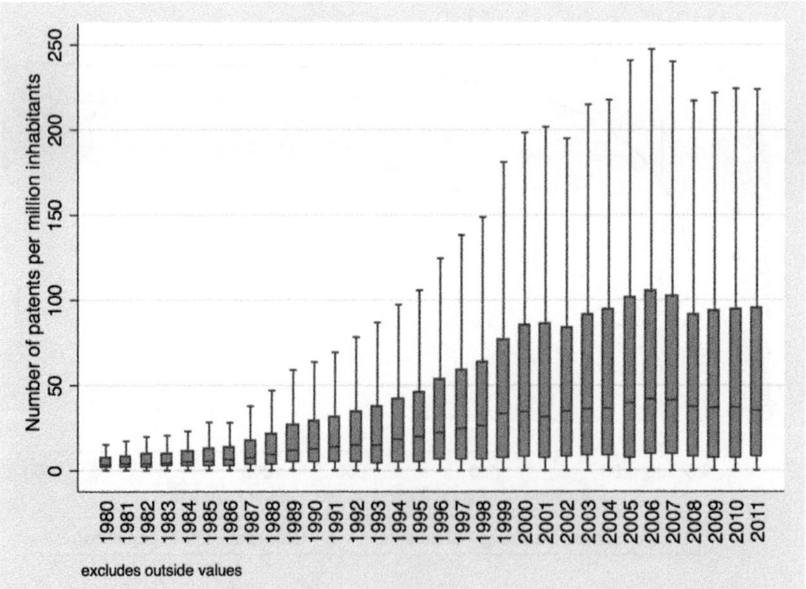

Figure 27.5 Box-plot of number of patents per million inhabitants per region, 1980–2011
Source: Author's elaboration on OECD Regional Innovation Database (stats.oecd.org).

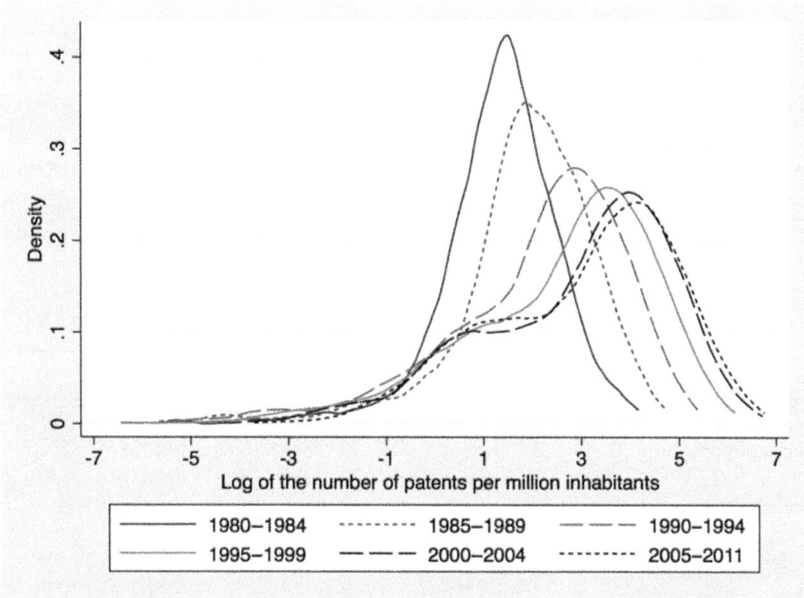

Figure 27.6 Kernel density of the regional distribution of patents per million inhabitants, 1980–2011 (five-year intervals)

Source: Author's elaboration on OECD Regional Innovation Database (stats.oecd.org).

Table 27.2 tabulates regions according to the quintiles of the distribution in patents per million inhabitants they are in year $t-1$ and in year t, where t denotes a five-year interval during 1980–1984. Results reveal that regions are extremely likely to remain in the same quintile: percentages along the diagonal of the transition matrix range from 60.89% to 80.8%. However, the probability of moving upwards or downwards is not negligible. For example, regions in the 4th quintile in $t-1$ have a 21.4% probability of falling to the third quintiles in the next five-year period, and a 16.7% probability of moving to the top percentile. Table 27.3 provides more evidence consistent with this result, this time using yearly data and controlling for other sources of regional heterogeneity. We estimate the following regression:

Table 27.2 Transition matrix of regions, by quintiles of number of patents per million inhabitants, 1980–2011 (five-year periods)

		Quintiles of the number of patents per million inhabitants at time t (five-year period)					
		1st	*2nd*	*3rd*	*4th*	*5th*	*Total*
Quintiles of the number of patents per million inhabitants at time t−1 (five-year period)	**1st**	69.58	20.87	6.48	2.10	0.98	100
	2nd	22.42	65.50	11.88	0.21	0.00	100
	3rd	1.86	13.23	63.45	20.03	1.43	100
	4th	0.48	0.54	21.40	60.87	16.71	100
	5th	0.34	0.07	1.70	17.13	80.76	100

Source: Author's elaboration on OECD Regional Innovation Database (stats.oecd.org).

$$p_{it} = \alpha + \beta p_{i,t-1} + \delta x_{it} + \mu_j + \theta_t + \varepsilon_{it} \tag{1}$$

where p_{it} denotes the log of 1 + number of patents with inventors from region i at time t, x_{it} denotes regional population, μ_j and θ_t denote country and time fixed effects respectively.

This regression provides some information on the degree of persistence of regional patenting activity, or the extent to which regional patents are explained by previous patenting activity, once controlled for the size of a region and country characteristics. We estimate equation (1) with OLS and present results in column (2) of Table 27.3. In column (4) we estimate the

Table 27.3 Regressions of the number of patents by region, 1980–2011 (five-year periods)

Dep. Var.: log(# patents + 1)$_t$	*(1)*	*(2)*	*(3)*	*(4)*
Estimation method	OLS	OLS	OLS	WG
Log of regional population $_{t-1}$		0.868***	0.123***	−0.301***
		(0.004)	(0.003)	(0.034)
log(# patents + 1) $_{t-1}$			0.885***	0.748***
			(0.002)	(0.003)
Country dummies (AUS is the baseline)				
AUT	0.212***	0.345***	0.082***	
BEL	1.272***	0.043	−0.088**	
BRA	−0.846***	−3.535***	−0.478***	
CAN	0.606***	−0.357***	−0.022	
CHE	1.041***	1.206***	0.181***	
CHL	−1.486***	−1.748***	−0.231***	
CHN	−0.160**	−4.504***	−0.556***	
CZE	−0.578***	−1.699***	−0.198***	
DEU	1.541***	0.438***	0.089***	
DNK	1.765***	1.125***	0.144***	
ESP	−0.575***	−1.284***	−0.146***	
EST	−1.059***	−1.345***	−0.167***	
FIN	0.762***	0.753***	0.113***	
FRA	0.578***	-0.185***	0.001	
GBR	0.611***	0.184***	0.035**	
HUN	−0.564***	−1.338***	−0.175***	
IND	−0.685***	−4.263***	−0.555***	
IRL	0.357***	−0.326***	−0.004	
ISL	−1.003***	0.728***	0.117***	
ISR	1.739***	0.487***	0.131***	
ITA	−0.260***	−0.871***	−0.088***	
JPN	1.666***	−0.334***	−0.026	
KOR	0.773***	−1.277***	−0.094***	
LTU	−1.717***	−2.327***	−0.249***	
LUX	1.016***	0.380**	0.104	
LVA	−1.617***	−2.097***	−0.243***	
MEX	−1.428***	−2.185***	−0.300***	
NLD	1.702***	0.316***	0.072**	
NOR	0.555***	0.502***	0.080***	
NZL	−0.255***	−0.163**	0.003	
POL	−1.175***	−2.131***	−0.274***	
PRT	−1.101***	−1.817***	−0.235***	
RUS	−1.036***	−2.743***	−0.363***	
SVK	−0.839***	−1.943***	−0.242***	
SWE	1.761***	1.380***	0.162***	

TUR	−1.384***	−2.325***	−0.315***	
USA	1.189***	0.002	0.005	
ZAF	−0.102	−2.673***	−0.344***	
Time dummies	Yes	Yes	Yes	Yes
Constant	0.284***	−9.820***	−1.413***	4.674***
Number of observations	47,160	45,678	45,678	45,678

Source: Author's elaboration on OECD Regional Innovation Database (stats.oecd.org).

same equation using region fixed effects (within-group estimator). While we cannot interpret such estimates as strictly causal, due to endogeneity issues, it is generally accepted that true coefficients will be in the range of values between OLS, which will tend to yield slightly upward biased estimates, and the within-group, which will tend to return downward biased estimates. Table 27.3 suggests that persistence is quite high, and comprised between 0.885 and 0.748. Figure 27.7 and Figure 27.8 are based on estimates retrieved from the variants of equation (1). In particular, we allow the persistence effect to change over time, by interacting past patents with year dummies, using OLS and within-group estimators respectively (equation (2)).

$$p_{it} = \alpha + \Sigma^{L}_{i=1} \gamma_i (p_{it-1} \times D_i) + \delta x_{it} + \mu_j + \theta_t + \varepsilon_{it} \quad (2)$$

Results suggest that persistence has increased quite rapidly over the 1980s and remained relatively stable thereafter. This implies that the importance of clustering of innovation has been consistently high for more than two decades now, suggesting that, conditional on size, country and even other unobserved regional characteristics, current patenting strongly depends on previous inventive activity.

In sum, the analysis of global inventive activity over three decades suggests that the number of regions that participate in the global production of innovation has substantially increased, but the bulk of these activities remains very concentrated in a few locations, which are not necessarily the largest. This is consistent with the idea that innovation benefits from the 'local buzz' stemming from clustering of innovators, and this favours a persistence of innovation in a few locations.

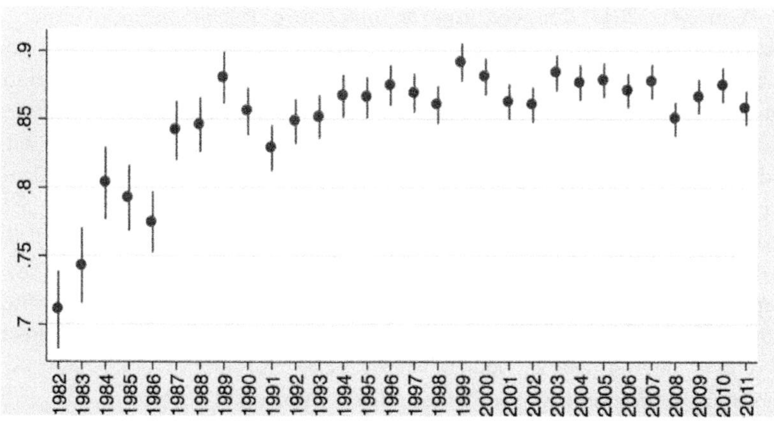

Figure 27.7 Time varying coefficients of the persistence in regional patenting activity, OLS estimates (with country fixed effects)

Source: Author's elaboration on OECD Regional Innovation Database (stats.oecd.org).

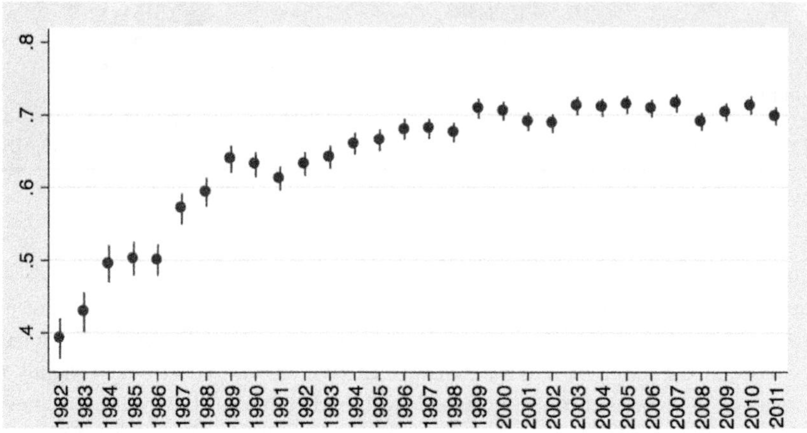

Figure 27.8 Time varying coefficients of the persistence in regional patenting activity, within-group estimates

Source: Author's elaboration on OECD Regional Innovation Database (stats.oecd.org).

'Global pipelines' and the increasing need to collaborate with distant partners in inventive activity

While the 'local buzz' argument predicts that innovation would tend to be concentrated in few locations that persistently produce more innovative output than others, the 'global pipelines' argument suggests that clusters need to favour the influx of external knowledge, in order to further enrich the local knowledge base. We try to provide some evidence of this mechanism by looking at the dynamics of co-inventions. In particular, we exploit the information available in REGPAT on the share of co-invented regional patents with co-inventors located within the region, within the country (but outside the region) or abroad. Figure 27.9 shows that in each of the five-year periods from 1980 until 2011, the co-invention with partners located within the region is by far the highest. The median value ranges from close to 60% in 1980–1984 to roughly 50% in 2005–2011. This confirms the importance of 'being there' (Gertler, 2003). In order to exchange knowledge, geographical proximity is vital. However, it is quite interesting to notice that international collaboration in inventive activity has increased substantially over time. Figure 27.9 reveals that the median share of such long-distance co-inventing activities remained close to zero for the best part of the 1980s, and then consistently increased to about 8% over the 2000s. Most notably, a significant heterogeneity across regions is evidenced, with the 75th percentile reaching over 15% of international collaboration in patenting activity and extreme values over 35%. This is confirmed by Figure 27.10, showing the kernel densities of the share of co-patenting with foreign inventors over time. It is quite evident that the right tail has become constantly fatter. Therefore, more than showing a trend of increasing international collaboration, data suggest that some regions have increased their degree of co-patenting with foreign inventors. Interestingly, substantial heterogeneity exists in most countries (to save space, data are not shown, but they are available from the authors upon request).

In sum, data on co-invention confirm the importance of proximity for exchanging knowledge, but also reveal that some regions are increasingly setting up global pipelines. These results are consistent with other evidence from the UK, showing that geographical proximity is only weakly linked to collaboration among inventors (Crescenzi, Nathan & Rodríguez-Pose, 2016).

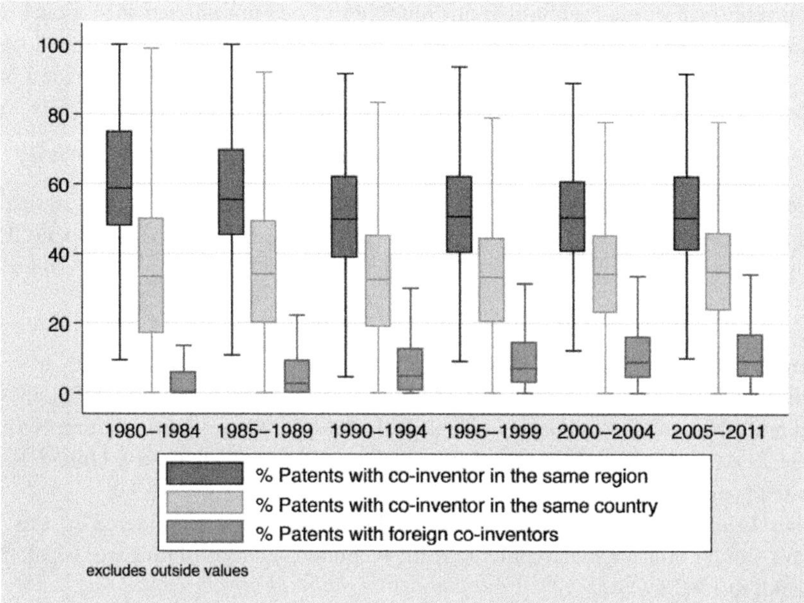

Figure 27.9 Box-plot of the propensity to co-patent, by location of the co-inventor, 1980–2011 (five-year periods)

Source: Author's elaboration on OECD Regional Innovation Database (stats.oecd.org).

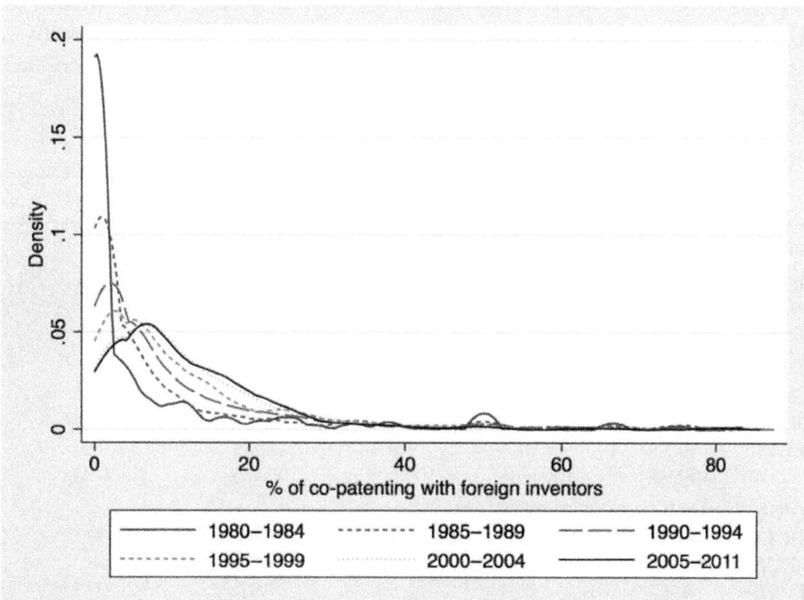

Figure 27.10 Kernel density of the regional propensity to co-patent with foreign co-inventors, 1980–2011 (five-year intervals)

Source: Author's elaboration on OECD Regional Innovation Database (stats.oecd.org).

At the current stage of the analysis it is not possible to ascertain whether such global pipelines are established by the top performing regions where 'global pipelines' complement 'local buzz', or rather by laggard locations that use 'global pipelines' to substitute for limited 'local buzz'.

Emerging economies and the regional patterns of inventive activity

In this section, we uncover some evidence on the role of emerging economies in shaping the regional patterns of inventive activity. Given that the sample is largely based on OECD countries plus some emerging and transition economies, we have decided to group countries as to whether they are:

a Core OECD countries that joined the OECD prior to 1980. This group of countries includes the traditionally advanced economies, such as Australia, Austria, Belgium, Canada, Denmark, Finland, France, Germany, Iceland, Ireland, Italy, Japan, Luxembourg, Netherlands, New Zealand, Norway, Portugal, Spain, Sweden, Switzerland, Turkey, United Kingdom, United States.
b Other OECD countries that joined OECD in the period considered in this analysis (1980–2011), and include Chile, Czech Republic, Estonia, Hungary, Israel, Mexico, Poland, Korea, Slovakia.
c Non-OECD countries, which include Brazil, China, India, Latvia (that joined OECD only in 2016), Lithuania, Russia, South Africa.

Table 27.4 provides some descriptive statistics on the patterns of inventive activities in these groups of countries. First, it shows the dynamics of the number of patenting regions. While the number of patenting regions has increased across the board, emerging regions involved in patenting activity increased approximately ten-fold (from 29 to 239 'Other OECD' and from 16 to 178 'Non-OECD' regions). Second, this increased participation in inventive activity is mirrored in a substantial share of patents in more recent decades. In the second half of the

Table 27.4 Patenting activity, by groups of countries and five-year periods, 1980–2011

	1980–1984	*1985–1989*	*1990–1994*	*1995–1999*	*2000–2004*	*2005–2011*
Number of patenting regions						
Core OECD	762	880	954	986	1,017	1,042
Other OECD	29	50	112	170	194	239
Non-OECD	16	36	120	143	162	178
Percentage in total number of patents						
Core OECD	97.7%	98.6%	97.3%	95.6%	92.6%	85.5%
Other OECD	1.9%	1.1%	1.4%	2.6%	4.4%	6.8%
Non-OECD	0.5%	0.4%	1.3%	1.8%	3.0%	7.7%
	100.0%	100.0%	100.0%	100.0%	100.0%	100.0%
Average number of patents per patenting region						
Core OECD	5.39	12.3	28.18	61.05	100.39	123.31
Other OECD	2.70	2.38	3.56	9.53	24.98	42.94
Non-OECD	1.17	1.09	2.90	7.97	20.09	65.06
Mean number of patents per million inhabitants per region						
Core OECD	7.05	14.08	27.54	52.84	79.14	91.42
Other OECD	3.10	2.49	3.42	7.99	14.15	19.24
Non-OECD	0.16	0.14	0.69	1.32	2.47	3.98

Coefficient of variation in the number of patents per million inhabitants per region						
Core OECD	1.20	1.12	1.11	1.16	1.20	1.20
Other OECD	1.35	1.46	2.01	3.11	3.06	3.20
Non-OECD	1.13	1.14	1.49	2.12	1.85	2.14
Average share of co-inventions with foreign partners per region						
Core OECD	6.05	7.24	8.67	10.08	11.01	11.21
Other OECD	13.31	22.27	15.45	14.14	17.21	18.33
Non-OECD	44.24	32.22	15.18	14.20	13.66	11.25

Source: Author's construction.

Notes:

Core OECD are countries that joined OECD before 1980: Australia, Austria, Belgium, Canada, Denmark, Finland, France, Germany, Iceland, Ireland, Italy, Japan, Luxembourg, Netherlands, New Zealand, Norway, Portugal, Spain, Sweden, Switzerland, Turkey, United Kingdom, United States.

Other OECD countries joined OECD between 1980–2011: Chile, Czech Republic, Estonia, Hungary, Israel, Mexico, Poland, Korea, Slovakia.

Non-OECD countries: Brazil, China, India, Latvia (joined OECD in 2016), Lithuania, Russia, South Africa.

The latter two groups may be considered emerging or recently industrialised economies.

2000s the share of patents in core OECD regions dropped to 85.5%, as compared to 98% in the 1980s. Similarly, by the end of the period under consideration, the number of patents per patenting region in the core OECD regions is twice the corresponding figure in non-OECD countries in the sample, while in the 1980s they were between five and ten times larger. Third, these figures partly reflect the dramatic increase in population in some of these emerging countries. When the number of patents is normalised by population, the gap between the core OECD countries and the non-OECD group remains fairly large. Despite an increase that brought the average number of patents per population from below 1 until the early 1990s to close to 4 by the end of the 2000s, still the more advanced countries have more than 20 times more patents per million inhabitants. Fourth, the increase in patenting activity in emerging economies appears to be very heterogeneous across regions: the coefficient of variation, that is the standard deviation as a proportion of the mean, is above 3 in 'Other OECD' countries and around 2 for 'Non-OECD' countries, from the 1990s onwards. This suggests that in emerging countries the variability in regional patenting activity is substantially larger than in more advanced economies. This is consistent with a higher disparity in economic development across regions within the former group of countries. Fifth, the propensity to engage in international co-inventions reveals opposite dynamics over time for different groups of countries. On the one hand, the core OECD regions exhibit a consistent increase in the importance of co-patenting with foreign inventors. On the other, emerging economies exhibit generally a higher share of international co-patenting, with a somewhat decreasing, although volatile, trend. This suggests that global pipelines may be necessary both in late coming clusters in emerging economies to provide an initial boost to local knowledge creation that eventually spurs the 'local buzz' effect, and in established clusters in advanced economies to provide external knowledge to complement knowledge internal to the cluster.

MNEs and the location of international R&D activities

The empirical analysis so far has highlighted the fact that few locations in the world account for a disproportionate amount of global inventive activity, and that regions increasingly engage in long-distance collaborations for innovation. The data do not allow us to ascertain to what extent such international collaborations are in fact driven by MNEs locating in a certain region. In fact, it is quite possible that the presence of a subsidiary of an MNE spurs co-invention with local firms, and the inventors' team also includes some researcher engaged in the other labs within the MNE (in the home country or elsewhere). Indeed, earlier we argued that MNEs are privileged actors for establishing global pipelines linking different local clusters. In this section, we will provide some evidence broadly consistent with this view. The analysis will rely on data on cross-border R&D-related investments from the fDi Markets database. Figure 27.11 provides some evidence matching the extreme geographical concentration of patenting activity. Likewise, activities of MNEs are extremely concentrated. fDi Markets does not provide directly information on TL2 and TL3 regions, so we use cities as the geographical unit of analysis here. Business services are the most geographically concentrated activity, but R&D is also

Table 27.5 Cross-border investment projects and average distance, by main business activity, 2003–2014

	No. of cross-border investment projects		*Average distance between home and host city (in km)*
Headquarters	6,026	5.4%	7,316
R&D-related (R&D, Design, Development and Testing)	7,788	7.0%	7,771
Production (Manufacturing, Construction, Extraction)	33,346	30.0%	5,707
Support svcs. (Technical/Customer svcs, Logistics, Maintenance)	10,980	9.9%	6,033
Advanced svcs. (Business svcs, Sales and Marketing)	53,170	47.8%	6,489
Total	111,310	100.0%	6,347

Source: Author's elaboration on fDi Markets.

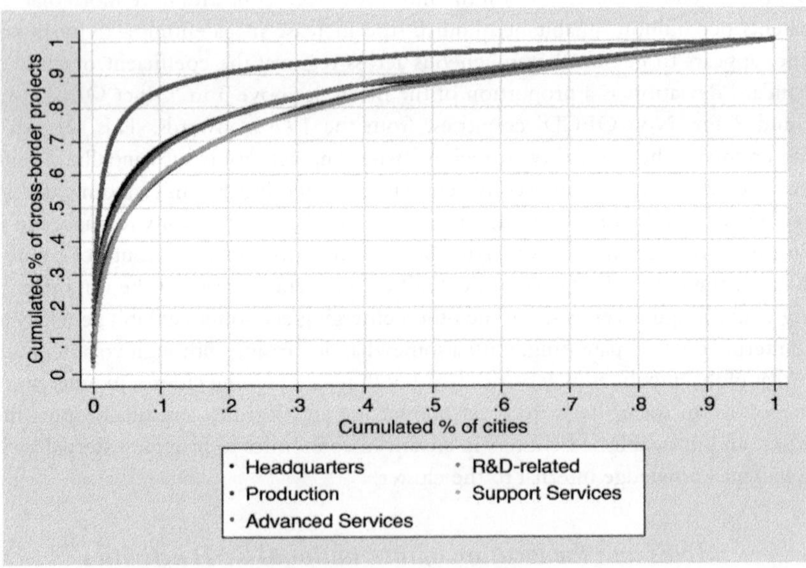

Figure 27.11 Concentration of cross-border investment projects by city, 2003–2014

Source: Author's elaboration on fDi Markets.

quite concentrated in a few locations. For example, 5% of about 1,600 cities attracting at least one investment in R&D and Design, Development & Testing over the period 2003–2014 (that is roughly 80 cities), received 60% of all R&D-related centres established in the period. This degree of concentration is not dissimilar from the concentration of patenting activity, although unfortunately at this stage we are not able to match the cities to TL2 and TL3 regions, so we cannot ascertain the degree of overlap between the geographical distribution of patents and cross-border R&D investments.

However, the evidence is consistent with the idea that MNEs may be locating their R&D in order to tap into clusters providing specific and advanced sources of knowledge. According to the theoretical arguments laid out earlier, MNEs may need to travel long distances to tap into such clusters. Consistent with this argument, Table 27.5 shows that the distance between the home and host city is the largest when MNEs locate R&D activities abroad: 7,771 km vs an average distance of 6,347 km (22.4% higher) and 5,707 km in the case of production-related investments (36% higher). More robust evidence along these lines is provided in Castellani, Jimenez and Zanfei (2013).

Concluding remarks

Building on a sketched conceptual framework that links Economic Geography and International Business literature, this chapter has highlighted that the geography of innovation is shaped by forces leading to increasing geographical concentration of innovative activities, benefiting from localised interactions and exchanges of knowledge (the 'local buzz' argument). However, successful clusters need to combine knowledge internal and external to the cluster. To this end, 'global pipelines' need to be established to allow external knowledge to flow into the clusters. Such pipelines can be the result of links between both individuals and institutions. International collaboration in patenting activity and MNEs can play a key role in building these pipelines. In particular, MNEs can be conceptualised as global orchestrators of knowledge. By tapping into diverse knowledge clusters and thanks to their ability to de-contextualise tacit knowledge and transfer it within the MNE and across space, they create institutional proximity that allows connections between knowledge sources and to share tacit knowledge across locations despite geographical distance. But, in order to act as conduits of knowledge between clusters, MNEs need to locate R&D in dispersed locations.

Using this conceptual map, we have provided descriptive evidence of the changing geography of inventive activity and the role of MNEs' international R&D activities, with quite an extensive geographical coverage. On the one hand, OECD REGPAT data on 1,482 regions in 39 countries allowed us to describe the changing patterns in patenting activity over 32 years, from 1980 until 2011. On the other, fDi Markets data on 111,310 investment projects referring to the period 2003–2014, in more than 10,000 cities in 184 different countries, allow us to characterise the geographical concentration of MNEs' activities, with special reference to their international R&D.

Results confirm the widely established fact that innovation is geographically concentrated, but highlight some important nuanced findings. First, the number of regions involved in patenting has increased threefold since the 1980s. This increase is largely due to innovative activity starting in emerging countries, but even in core-OECD countries the number of regions with some inventive activity has increased by more than 35% over the past three decades. Second, despite this increase in the number of regions' patenting, 70% of inventions come from the top 100 regions. While large emerging regions have become more important in overall patenting, advanced economies still overwhelmingly dominate in terms of patents per inhabitant. Third, although the hierarchy of the top patenting regions is not immobile, the propensity to patent is quite dependent on previous innovation. This leads to an increasingly fat-tailed distribution of patenting and high heterogeneity in patenting activity. Not surprisingly, this geographical diversity in patterns of innovation is markedly more evident in emerging countries, but it is a feature of most advanced countries as well. Fourth, international collaboration in patenting has been steadily on the rise over the last three decades. This seems to be the result of a combination of the higher incidence of innovation from emerging countries, where co-invention with foreign partners is systematically higher (although on a downward trend), and a non-negligible increase in the importance of co-inventions across national borders in core-OECD regions (which almost doubled over time). Fifth, international R&D investments of MNEs are indeed also very concentrated in a few locations, which can also be quite distant from the MNEs' headquarters' location.

Overall, the findings are consistent with our conceptual map, and, in particular, they highlight that 'local buzz' is crucial for the development of knowledge in local economies, and it leads to persistence in innovative activities. However, 'global pipelines' are also becoming a crucial element for the successful development of local knowledge, by 'pumping' information about markets and technologies into the cluster, making the 'buzz' more dynamic, and providing access to a more variegated set of knowledge pools from which to draw. This is evidenced by the increased role of cross-border co-invention which, interestingly, seems to characterise both clusters in emerging economies that may use such 'global pipelines' to catch-up, and by clusters in advanced economies, which may use them to revive their knowledge base and keep up with increased competition for innovation. Finally, the evidence suggests that MNEs can play a key role in bridging knowledge across clusters, and they indeed locate their R&D labs in few centres of excellence, and in doing this, they overcome the cost of managing activities quite dispersed in geographic space.

Much needs to be done in the area of research, and in particular, we believe that this chapter could spur further analyses on the factors underlying the engagement of regions in cross-border inventions, or more generally, the establishment of 'global pipelines'. Key questions to be addressed are: Are the most innovative regions also engaging in international collaboration to further their lead in knowledge production? Or instead, to what extent are global pipelines a means to catch-up? Furthermore, by combining data on R&D investments by MNEs and patenting activity at the same local level, one could assess the extent to which MNEs are attracted to innovative regions, and/or contribute to it. In this respect, a key question to be addressed is about the role of MNEs in establishing such long-distance collaboration in patenting: Are these truly collaborations across borders, or are they mediated by the presence of subsidiaries of foreign MNEs in the local economies?

Notes

1 The author is extremely grateful to Gary Cook for his editorial role and for precious suggestions that helped shape this manuscript.

2 REGPAT has been extensively used for geographical analysis of patenting activity, but, to the best of our knowledge, very few studies use it to describe worldwide patterns of inventive activity. Examples in this direction are Usai (2011) for a truly worldwide analysis similar to the one carried out in this work; Crescenzi, Rodríguez-Pose and Storper (2007, 2012) provide pairwise comparisons of large countries and economic areas such as the US and Europe and China and India.

3 I am thankful to Bjorn Jindra for providing these data.

4 Kernel densities are a non-parametric way to estimate the probability density function of a random variable. In a nutshell, kernel density estimation is a way to smooth observed frequencies of a variable,

to provide an indication of the density in a population based on a finite data sample. Each point of a kernel density can be interpreted as the probability to observe a certain value of a variable x (on the horizontal axis).

5 Values on the horizontal axis of Figure 27.6 are natural logarithms of the number of patents per million inhabitants, therefore a value of 1 corresponds to approximately 2.5 patents per million inhabitants.

6 To save space, data are not shown, but they are available from the authors upon request.

7 A transition matrix provides information on the probability that individuals move from one state to another over time. In this case, the matrix is based on the five quintiles of the regional distribution of patents by five-year periods, and indicates the probability that a region that is a certain quintile of the distribution in one period, is the same or another quintile in the next period.

References

Alcácer, J. & Zhao, M. (2012) 'Local R&D strategies and multilocation firms: The role of internal linkages', *Management Science*, 58, pp. 734–753.

Almeida, P., Song, J. & Grant, R.M. (2002) 'Are firms superior to alliances and markets? An empirical test of cross-border knowledge building', *Organization Science*, 13, pp. 147–161.

Ambos, T.C. & Ambos, B. (2009) 'The impact of distance on knowledge transfer effectiveness in multinational corporations', *Journal of International Management*, 15, pp. 1–14.

Balland, P.A., Boschma, R. & Frenken, K. (2015) 'Proximity and innovation: From statics to dynamics', *Regional Studies*, 49, pp. 907–920.

Bathelt, H., Malmberg, A. & Maskell, P. (2004) 'Clusters and knowledge: Local buzz, global pipelines and the process of knowledge creation', *Progress in Human Geography*, 28, pp. 31–56.

Belderbos, R., Leten, B. & Suzuki, S. (2013) 'How global is R&D? Firm-level determinants of home-country bias in R&D', *Journal of International Business Studies*, 44, pp. 765–786.

Belderbos, R., Sleuwaegen, L., Somers, D. & De Backer, K. (2016) 'Where to locate innovative activities in global value chains', *OECD Science, Technology and Industry Policy Papers, No. 30*. Paris: OECD.

Boschma, R. (2005) 'Proximity and innovation: A critical assessment', *Regional Studies*, 39, pp. 61–74.

Breschi, S. & Malerba, F. (2001) 'The geography of innovation and economic clustering: Some introductory notes', *Industrial and Corporate Change*, 10, pp. 817–833.

Buckley, P.J. & Casson, M. (1976) *The Future of the Multinational Enterprise*. New York: Springer.

Cano-Kollmann, M., Cantwell, J., Hannigan, T.J., Mudambi, R. & Song, J. (2016) 'Knowledge connectivity: An agenda for innovation research in International Business', *Journal of International Business Studies*, 47, pp. 255–262.

Cantwell, J. (2009) 'Location and the multinational enterprise', *Journal of International Business Studies*, 40, pp. 35–41.

Cantwell, J. (2017) 'Innovation and International Business', *Industry and Innovation*, 24, 41–60.

Cantwell, J. & Iammarino, S. (2003) *Multinational Corporations and European Regional Systems of Innovation*. London: Routledge.

Cantwell, J. & Mudambi, R. (2005) 'MNE competence-creating subsidiary mandates', *Strategic Management Journal*, 26, pp. 1109–1128.

Cantwell, J. & Santangelo, G.D. (1999) 'The frontier of international technology networks: Sourcing abroad the most highly tacit capabilities', *Information Economics and Policy*, 11, pp. 101–123.

Castellani, D., Jimenez, A. & Zanfei, A. (2013) 'How remote are R&D labs? Distance factors and international innovative activities', *Journal of International Business Studies*, 44, pp. 649–675.

Castellani, D. & Lavoratori, K. (2017) 'The lab and the plant. Offshore R&D and co-location with production activities'. Paper presented at the 2017 R&D Management Conference, Leuven 1–5 July 2017.

Castellani, D. & Pieri, F. (2013) 'R&D offshoring and the productivity growth of European regions', *Research Policy*, 42, pp. 1581–1594.

Castellani, D. & Pieri, F. (2016) 'Outward investments and productivity: Evidence from European regions', *Regional Studies*, 50, pp. 1945–1964.

Castellani, D. & Santangelo, G. (2017) 'Quo Vadis? Cities and the location of MNEs activities along the value chain', Paper presented at the 44th AIB-UK&I Conference and 6th Reading Conference, Reading, 6–8 April 2017.

Castellani, D. & Zanfei, A. (2006) *Multinational Firms, Innovation and Productivity*. Cheltenham, UK: Edward Elgar.

Crescenzi, R. & Iammarino, S. (2017) 'Global investments and regional development trajectories: The missing links', *Regional Studies*, 51, pp. 97–115.

Crescenzi, R., Nathan, M. & Rodríguez-Pose, A. (2016) 'Do inventors talk to strangers? On proximity and collaborative knowledge creation', *Research Policy*, 45, pp. 177–194.

Crescenzi, R., Pietrobelli, C. & Rabellotti, R. (2013) 'Innovation drivers, value chains and the geography of multinational corporations in Europe', *Journal of Economic Geography*, 14, pp. 1053–1086.

Crescenzi, R., Rodríguez-Pose, A. & Storper, M. (2007) 'The territorial dynamics of innovation: A Europe–United States comparative analysis', *Journal of Economic Geography*, 7, pp. 673–709.

Crescenzi, R., Rodríguez-Pose, A. & Storper, M. (2012) 'The territorial dynamics of innovation in China and India', *Journal of Economic Geography*, 12, pp. 1055–1085.

D'Agostino, L.M., Laursen, K. & Santangelo, G.D. (2012) 'The impact of R&D offshoring on the home knowledge production of OECD investing regions', *Journal of Economic Geography*, 13, pp. 145–175.

Damioli, G. & Vertesy, D. (2017) 'The seductive power of Irish rain. Location determinants of foreign R&D investments in European regions'. Paper presented at the 2017 R&D Management Conference, Leuven 1–5 July 2017.

Dunning, J.H. & Lundan, S. (2008) *Multinational Enterprises and the Global Economy*. Cheltenham, UK: Edward Elgar.

Dunning, J.H. & Lundan, S. (2009) 'The internationalization of corporate R&D: A review of the evidence and some policy implications for home countries', *Review of Policy Research*, 26, pp. 13–33.

Feldman, M.P. & Kogler, D. (2010) 'Stylized facts in the geography of innovation', in Hall, B. & Rosenberg, N. (Eds.), *Handbook of the Economics of Innovation*. Volume 1. Amsterdam: Elsevier, pp. 381–410.

Gertler, M. (2003) 'Tacit knowledge and the Economic Geography of context, or the undefinable tacitness of being (there)', *Journal of Economic Geography*, 3, pp. 75–99.

Gertler, M. (2008) 'Buzz without being there? Communities of practice in context', in Amin, A. & Roberts, J. (Eds.), *Community, Economic Creativity, and Organization*. Oxford, UK: Oxford University Press, pp. 203–226.

Ghemawat, P. (2016) *The Laws of Globalization and Business Applications*. Cambridge, UK: Cambridge University Press.

Gupta, A.K. & Govindarajan, V. (1991) 'Knowledge flows and the structure of control within multinational corporations', *Academy of Management Review*, 16, pp. 768–792.

Hannigan, T.J., Perri, A. & Scalera, V.G. (2016) *The Dispersed Multinational: Does Connectedness Across Spatial Dimensions Lead to Broader Technological Search?* Working paper No. 11. Department of Management, Università Ca'Foscari Venezia.

Hitt, M.A., Hoskisson, R.E. & Him, H. (1997) 'International diversification: Effects on innovation and firm performance in product diversified firms', *Academy of Management Journal*, 40, pp. 767–798.

Iammarino, S. & McCann, P. (2013) *Multinationals and Economic Geography: Location, Technology and Innovation*. Cheltenham, UK: Edward Elgar.

Kogut, B. & Zander, U. (1992) 'Knowledge of the firm, combinative capabilities, and the replication of technology', *Organization Science*, 3, pp. 383–397.

Lorenzen, M. & Mudambi, R. (2013) 'Clusters, connectivity and catch-up: Bollywood and Bangalore in the global economy', *Journal of Economic Geography*, 13, pp. 501–534.

Marshall, A. (1927) *Industry and Trade*. London: Macmillan.

Maskell, P., Bathelt, H. & Malmberg, A. (2006) 'Building global knowledge pipelines: The role of temporary clusters', *European Planning Studies*, 14, pp. 997–1013.

Meyer, K.E., Mudambi, R. & Narula, R. (2011) 'Multinational enterprises and local contexts: The opportunities and challenges of multiple embeddedness', *Journal of Management Studies*, 48, pp. 235–252.

Narula, R. & Zanfei, A. (2005) 'Globalisation of innovation', in Fagerberg, J., Mowery, D. & Nelson, R.R. (Eds.), *Handbook of Innovation*. Oxford, UK: Oxford University Press, pp. 318–345.

Owen-Smith, J. & Powell, W.W. (2004) 'Knowledge networks as channels and conduits: The effects of spillovers in the Boston biotechnology community', *Organization Science*, 15, 5–21.

Storper, M. & Venables, A.J. (2004) 'Buzz: Face-to-face contact and the urban economy', *Journal of Economic Geography*, 4, pp. 351–370.

UNCTAD (2016) *World Investment Report 2016. Investor Nationality: Policy Challenges*. New York and Geneva: UNCTAD.

Usai, S. (2011) 'The geography of inventive activity in OECD regions', *Regional Studies*, 45, pp. 711–731.

Zanfei, A. (2000) 'Transnational firms and changing organisation of innovative activities', *Cambridge Journal of Economics*, 24, pp. 515–554.

PART VI

Services, International Business and Economic Geography

28

AN ECONOMIC GEOGRAPHY OF GLOBALIZING RETAIL

Emergence, characteristics, contribution

Neil Wrigley and Steve Wood

Introduction

By the end of the first decade of the 21st century – more than fifteen years after Gereffi's (1994) identification of retailer buyer-driven global supply chains, and the subsequent engagement of economic geographers with the transformational impacts of multinational retailers within emerging economies (Coe & Wrigley, 2007), Hamilton, Senauer and Petrovic (2011, p. 3) summarized the increasing consensus that large retailers had become 'the key organizers of the global economy'. But what have been the contributions of International Business studies (IB) and Economic Geography to this consensus? In this chapter, we provide an assessment of these contributions in order to understand how Economic Geography has been able to make a distinct and strategically important impact despite its modest scale compared to the critical mass of IB studies.

Our characterization is one which begins with the acceptance that IB is undoubtedly one of the crown jewels of the business management discipline, alongside marketing, strategy, entrepreneurship, organizational behaviour, and finance and accounting studies. Inevitably this has implied that retail internationalization has been viewed through the lens of the dominant frameworks of IB. However, our view is that while this was a considerable strength, it left gaps that needed to be filled by other social science disciplines if the centrality and dynamism of retailing within the global economy was to be fully understood.

In this chapter we position the contribution of Economic Geography as a necessary – albeit small – critical influence which has the potential and to enrich the dialogue between IB and mainstream social science. We begin with a necessarily simplistic summary of the manner in which IB has dealt with the burgeoning force of retail internationalization since the mid-1990s – asking to what extent its dominant conceptualizations proved sufficiently flexible to incorporate the sheer dynamism of these developments. We then characterize our view of what Economic Geography was able to bring to these debates – providing in the body of the chapter an in-depth assessment of four dimensions of that contribution. Our aim in the chapter is not to privilege one discipline over another, but rather to demonstrate and understand why some IB scholars (e.g. Cantwell, Mudambi, Buckley) have increasingly taken the view that Economic Geography has a contribution to make within IB.

IB's engagement with the globalization of retailing

IB scholars have been far from silent regarding the role of location, place and geography in affecting the growth of (retail) firms – a tendency that has become increasingly evident (Buckley & Ghauri, 2004). An important contribution was the debunking of attempts to promote an overarching retail globalization thesis. Rugman and Girod (2003, p. 24) noted that, in common with their findings concerning manufacturing firms, 'retail MNEs are not global but regional, especially if we consider the term "global" in its two different meanings: a global sales presence on the one hand, and a global strategy on the other hand'. Indeed, this tendency towards 'semi-globalization' (Rugman & Verbeke, 2004, p. 17) appeared to be more pronounced for multinational service firms compared to manufacturing firms (Rugman & Verbeke, 2008) – in turn, suggesting the variegated nature of Economic Geography and the need for sensitivity to location, place and space.

There have also been attempts to 'import' IB theory, based predominantly on FDI and the manufacturing sector, in order to explain trends becoming evident within a global *retail* context. However, geographer-turned-management scholar, John Dawson (1994), urged caution in this regard. He noted that cross-border retail expansion is notably distinct from FDI in manufacturing in a number of respects. These dimensions include: the balance between centralized and decentralized decision-making; the relative value of stock and the importance of sourcing; the degree of spatial dispersion typical of retail store and distribution portfolios; the cash flow characteristics of retail operations; and the relative importance of organizational-scale versus establishment-scale economies. Nevertheless, many of the insights emanating from IB offer relevance for framing an understanding of international retailing. Three models have been particularly influential and warrant brief consideration.

First, the well-known eclectic paradigm of Dunning (2000, 2009) which proposes that three advantages influence FDI: (i) ownership (O) advantages; (ii) location (L) advantages; and (iii) internalization (I) advantages. Although the concept has been employed to explain international retail entry modes (e.g. Park & Sternquist, 2008), it struggles to integrate country and firm-level interactions (Rugman, Verbeke & Nguyen, 2011). In particular, given that location decisions are also organizational and informational decisions, the (retail) MNC in reality 'has to make organizational decisions *in tandem* with location decisions' (McCann & Mudambi, 2004, p. 494, emphasis in original).

Second, Bartlett and Ghoshal's (1989) Integration-Responsiveness Framework, which suggests four broadly defined strategies related to the pressure for global integration and efficiency versus pressure for local responsiveness within host markets, has frequently been employed to provide explanatory insights regarding the challenges of international retail expansion (e.g. Salmon & Tordjman, 1989; Swoboda, Elsner & Morschett, 2014; Wood, Coe & Wrigley, 2016). Such work speaks to related work within the social sciences that discusses the importance of 'glocalization' more widely (e.g. Robertson, 1995) as well as the need for 'flexible replication' of business models (Jonsson & Foss, 2011).

Third, the so-called Uppsala internationalization model (Johanson & Vahlne, 1977) which seeks to explain international expansion as a path-dependent process in which a firm's expansion develops in an incremental manner in terms of the nature of its commitment and its geographical scope. This is a conceptualization which has a long history of application to the retail internationalization process. 'Distance' is seen as central to these activities and defines the degree to which a firm is uncertain of the characteristics of a new market. The model suggests that countries with what is termed close 'psychic distance' will be entered first given their likely geographic, cultural and institutional proximity, followed by subsequent expansion to psychically more distant markets. In the specific context of international retail expansion, O'Grady and Lane (1996) suggested a 'psychic distance paradox' whereby operations in psychically close countries are not necessarily easier to manage, largely because assumptions of similarity can prevent executives from learning about critical differences. The implication is that divestment may occur more frequently than expected in countries that were initially perceived as psychically close as executives underestimate the degree of cultural difference.

More recent research has seen IB scholars adopt a resource-bundling perspective, viewing MNEs as operating a portfolio of interdependent subsidiaries that command sets of internal and external resources that they can access within specific locations (Bartlett & Ghoshal, 1986; Rugman, Verbeke & Yuan, 2011). Within this resource-based view (RBV) of the firm, the (retail) MNC is tasked with (re)combining a set of firm specific advantages (FSAs) with country specific advantages (CSAs) (Rugman, 1981). Subsequent work has contended that while FSAs can be generated anywhere within the MNE network, they can also be location-bound (LB) or non-location bound (NLB) (Rugman, Verbeke & Yuan, 2011). This places importance on an ability to successfully deploy the (retail) MNE's advantages given the nature and characteristics of particular regions or countries. Rugman and Verbeke (2001) argued that subsidiaries within host countries may develop their own subsidiary-specific advantages (SSAs) as a result of their autonomous activities – something beyond simply enhancing home-based NLB FSAs with necessary local strengths. Such perspectives view the (retail) MNE increasingly as a network where knowledge and competencies can be passed between head office and subsidiaries across host markets in both a conventional 'top-down' and reverse ('bottom-up') manner (Gupta & Govindarajan, 1991; Yang, Mudambi & Meyer, 2008). The challenge of realizing successful international (retail) expansion is thus focused on recombining extant resources with resources located in host countries (Hennart, 2009), and doing so requires sensitivity to the spatially variegated demands of places where 'cultural, economic, and institutional elements can play equally strong roles' (Verbeke & Asmussen, 2016, p. 1056). However, it is noted that identifying and combining relevant resources is a considerable challenge given the bounded nature of rationality and the limitations of being a 'foreigner' within host markets (Johanson & Vahlne, 2009).

It is clear from these brief summaries, therefore, that there is an increasing geographical sensitivity within IB. However, many IB scholars still highlight a tendency within the subject to conceptualize geography and location in a way that goes little beyond acknowledging that national boundaries and nation states matter 'without providing any . . . nuanced examination of locational features' (Beugelsdijk, McCann & Mudambi, 2010, p. 487; see also Beugelsdijk & Mudambi, 2013). In particular, in IB all too often: 'MNEs are still basically portrayed in geographical space as independent units agglomerating in certain locations, leaving the nature of the interaction between places and space as a black box' (Beugelsdijk, McCann & Mudambi, 2010, p. 488).

This view echoes the opinions expressed by McCann and Mudambi (2004, 2005) five years earlier when they drew attention to the limited attempts to conceptualize the complexity of firm strategy at a sub-national scale within IB compared to Economic Geography. In contrast, as we will argue later, geographers take a more complex view in which a multi-scalar, contextual and culturally variegated view of place is adopted which is underpinned by networked relations between actors of varying degrees of power, which is sensitive to governance effects across space, and which encourages an awareness of the interactions and mutual constitution of all spatial scales from local to global (cf. Wood, Coe & Wrigley, 2016 from a retail context).

Nevertheless, taken as whole, in recent years within IB we note a trend towards increased richness in both uncovering the complexity of *local* geographies and appreciating the implications this can have for (retail) MNE development (Cantwell, 2009). This is important – as *place* suggests a sensitivity to location-related (sub-national) aspects, while *space* emphasizes distance and network characteristics (McCann, 2011). Two illustrations of these trends would be, first, Gamble's research papers exploring multinational retail development in China, which have underlined the differing perspectives of consumers with regard to retail multinationals which exist *between* Chinese cities (Chaney & Gamble, 2008), and which have analysed the necessarily 'hybridized' nature of organizational practices required for appropriate anchoring of retail MNEs within China (Gamble, 2010). Second, is Meyer, Mudambi and Narula's (2011) paper, which is notable in arguing that MNEs must manage 'multiple embeddedness' across heterogeneous contexts at two levels: first, at the MNE level by organizing their networks to exploit similarities and differences of their multiple host locations; and second, at the subsidiary level, where they need to balance 'internal' embeddedness within the MNE network with their 'external' embeddedness in the host market. Meyer, Mudambi and Narula (2011) take the view that this balancing of the subsidiary's strategic role within the wider MNE and its local identity and domestic linkages represents a challenging trade off.

Having outlined the nature of IB's contributions to the understanding of global retailing, we now turn to the approaches Economic Geography has injected into the study of this phenomena.

Economic Geography's engagement with the globalization of retailing

In common with IB, Economic Geography was relatively slow to interrogate the nature of the internationalization of retail distribution. With the exception of the work of Dawson (1994) which was noted earlier and targeted at a business studies/management audience, it was not until Wrigley's (2000a) contribution which highlighted the 'myopic neglect of distribution systems and industries' in the burgeoning literature on economic globalization that the scale, characteristics and growth of the leading retail MNCs began to engage the attention of economic geographers. That contribution was important in several ways. First, in identifying the rapid shift in power and leverage of retail capital and the emergence of retailers as 'market makers' and key drivers of global supply chains (themes taken up a decade later by Hamilton, Senauer & Petrovic, 2011). Second, in charting new ways of exploring retail change, which built on earlier contributions relating to the conceptualization of a 'new' retail geography (Wrigley & Lowe, 1996). From Wrigley's viewpoint, the processes of retail internationalization exposed a set of richly geographical issues, including challenges relating to the innovation, operation and localization of store networks, the difficulties of achieving global scale and maintaining corporate control across large dispersed operations, and the nature and transformative impacts of local sourcing networks and supply chains. It also raised the challenges of conceptualizing the retail structure of different host markets, the demands of identifying and spreading 'know-how' and best practice between the home market and retail subsidiaries in host markets, and was notable for its foregrounding of financial dimensions of these processes, alongside the management of human/capital resources.

Building on this initial contribution, Coe (2004) then used relational and network concepts to extend and enrich Wrigley's perspectives on retail globalization. In the process he noted that a point of difference provided by the adoption of Economic Geography approaches included a departure from 'firm-centric models in which retailers are . . . distanced from the political-economic contexts in which they are embedded' (p. 1586). He further contended:

> [n]etworks both constitute and are reconstituted by the economic, social, and political arrangements of the places in which they are embedded . . . They are also influenced by a range of institutions – for example, supranational organisations, government agencies, trade unions, employer associations, nongovernmental organisations (NGOs), and consumer groups – that shape firm activities in those places.
>
> *(Coe, 2004, p. 1572)*

There then followed two significant papers (Wrigley, Coe & Currah, 2005; Coe & Wrigley, 2007) which more fully articulated that relational and networked view of retail globalization. It was a conceptualization in which 'necessarily embedded and essentially networked' retail multinationals were viewed as key agents in the global economy struggling with the challenges of establishing embeddedness within host markets and with managing a complex range of intra-, inter- and extra-firm relations with consumers, suppliers, local partners, regulators and finance providers. From this perspective, retail multinationals could not be viewed as capable of simply imposing their will on the host economies/societies they entered. Instead, they faced continuous consumer-based, competitive and regulatory responses, and had little alternative other than to seek to contribute actively to influencing institutional change in those host economies (Durand & Wrigley, 2009). It was a perspective in which power was viewed as very much contextual and situational (Yeung, 2009) and where geography was not merely a locational backcloth but provided a lens on the nature and effects of retail capital, which in turn was seen as increasingly sensitive to the challenges of establishing embeddedness within the host markets entered.

In this way, Economic Geography began to inject a number of important thematic contributions into the conceptualization of retail globalization processes, practices and effects. We now consider in greater detail four of those contributions before moving onto an assessment of what they might offer to, and in turn what additionally might be needed in order to, generate a creative conversation between IB and Economic Geography on this topic.

Four dimensions of the contribution of Economic Geography to the conceptualization of retail globalization processes, practices and effects

A necessarily embedded and essentially networked process

A networked/relational perspective views retail MNCs as having to become necessarily embedded within their host markets to succeed and to be essentially networked in order to achieve that (Wrigley, Coe & Currah, 2005). More specifically, building on the work of Hess (2004), it suggests a multidimensional view of embeddedness which draws attention in particular to three crucial dimensions (see Table 28.1).

First, is the need for retail firms to realize high levels of *territorial embeddedness* across local cultures of consumption, real estate/land-use planning systems, and supply chains and logistics networks (see Figure 28.1) in order to achieve 'organizational legitimacy' in the host markets they have entered (Bianchi & Arnold, 2004). Second, is the *societal embeddedness* of those firms – namely the 'genetic code' that the firms carry with them from the cultural, institutional and

Table 28.1 Embeddedness in retail MNC expansion

Territorial embeddedness	How the retail MNC is *anchored* in different places. Requires the acceptance across markets and cultures of consumption, planning and property systems, and logistical and supply chain operations.
Societal embeddedness	Underlines how the cultural, institutional and historical *origins* of the retail MNC affect how it operates in new markets. This may relate to industrial relations systems, business practices and prevailing corporate cultures in the firm's home market.
Network embeddedness	Refers to the *composition and structure of network relations* of the retail MNC within and beyond the firm, e.g. with (joint venture) partners, suppliers, competitors, special interest groups and customers.

Sources: Hess (2004); Wrigley, Coe & Currah (2005); Wood & Reynolds (2014).

regulatory context of their home markets. Third, is their *network embeddedness* – that is to say, 'the web of inter- and extra-firm relationships with suppliers, customers, competitors, and other organizations that provide those firms with access to products, markets, technologies, information, and influence in the markets in which they enter and operate' (Lowe & Wrigley, 2010, p. 384). The challenge both conceptually and managerially is to understand how successful retailers who are likely to be well embedded in their home markets can achieve similar positions in new and often culturally and organizationally distinct host markets as they expand (Burt, Johansson & Dawson, 2016).

Crucially, achieving territorial embeddedness requires retail MNCs to develop high levels of sensitivity to and understanding of the cultures and institutions of the host markets they enter. Levels which are sufficient not least to gauge the degree of adaptation – particularly of customer-facing elements of the retail offer – necessary to succeed. For food retailers, local sourcing and supply networks are especially important elements within the embeddedness process. In contrast to apparel retailers – firms that are widely known to have benefited from global supply chains to exploit low labour costs (albeit moderated by considerations relating to delivery timelines, e.g. Tokatli & Kızılgün, 2010) – fresh food is perishable and therefore requires the development of more localized in-country networks of suppliers and associated logistics networks which require deepening as a retail MNC's store portfolio expands (Coe & Hess, 2005). This represents a delicate balance. Bloom and Hinrichs (2017), for example, examine how Walmart's efforts at realizing lean, centralized management and distribution systems, its practices of cutting out intermediaries, and its emphasis on standardization have frequently presented barriers to establishing necessarily embedded supply networks. Indeed, appropriate forms of embeddedness involve identification of the characteristics of the retailer's preferred business model that it can replicate within a host market – something that is likely to vary significantly between host market contexts, retail sectors and individual business models (Burt, Johansson & Dawson, 2016, 2017). Elements of the retail business model that tend to be more transferable

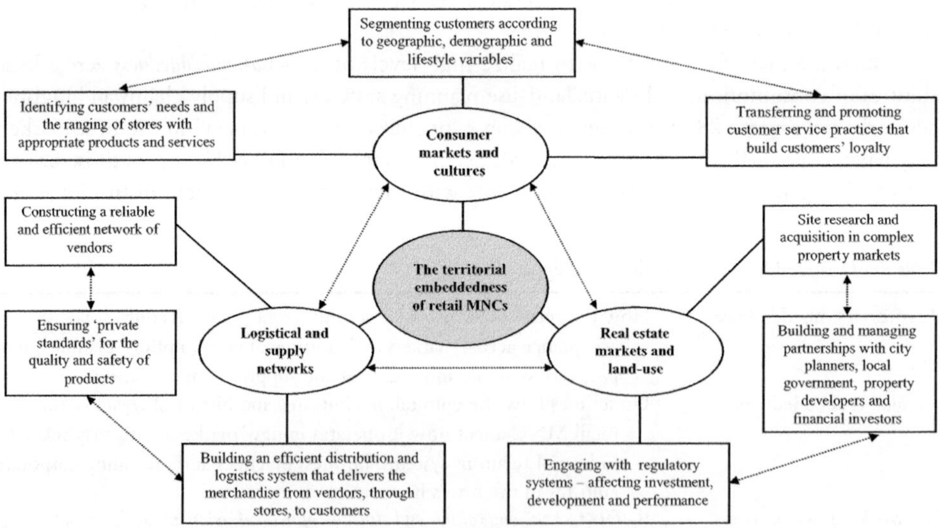

Figure 28.1 Dimensions of the territorial embeddedness of retail MNCs
Source: Amended from Tacconelli & Wrigley (2009).

across geographies include an array of 'back office' functions such as IT systems, as well as loyalty schemes, product ranging expertise, logistics and distribution capabilities, human resources policies, etc. (Wood, Coe & Wrigley, 2016).

Aoyama (2007) considers the decision between standardization and localization to be inherently paradoxical, with the latter moving against the rationale for efficiency and cost reduction. In many senses therefore, concerns with embeddedness and 'strategic localization' resonate to some degree with imperatives discussed in the IB literature relating to the pressures for global integration and local responsiveness (e.g. Bartlett & Ghoshal, 1989; Salmon & Tordjman, 1989). However, what an embeddedness conceptualization highlights is the need for a more richly structured and geographically informed understanding of the numerous dimensions of achieving acceptance within international markets and the relationships within and beyond the retail firm that are required to achieve this.

Lowe, George and Alexy (2012) note that attempts to achieve territorial and network embeddedness in practice in a new host market may lead to three processes: 'transference', 'splicing' and 'enhanced imitation'. They argue that *transference* relates to the unmodified replication of the retailer's existing capabilities in a new market, *splicing* relates to an apparent hybridization with the creation of novel capabilities in the new market via the reconfiguration of existing competencies drawn from other parts of the firm's operations, and *enhanced imitation* refers to the creation of new capabilities in that market through the emulation and active adaptation of the best practices of industry rivals (see also Lowe & Wrigley, 2010). The latter two categories appear to have much in common with subsidiary-specific advantages as detailed in the IB literature (see Rugman & Verbeke, 2001). Indeed, more broadly, they signify a need for retail multinationals to pursue a 'hybridized' approach to pursuing embeddedness within their expansion (Morgan, 2001; Gamble & Huang, 2009; Siebers, 2017).

The realization of embeddedness is clearly more than a one-off initial adjustment at the point of market entry, but is instead 'a dynamic and contested series of processes that unfold over time' (Coe & Lee, 2013, p. 332). This was particularly evident in Coe and Lee's contributions (2006, 2013) exploring the longitudinal evolution of Tesco's recently divested operations in South Korea through format innovation, deepening and reshaping supply networks and expanding its product offer to include new retail services. In addition to the temporal dimensions, spatial scale is important to the realization of such embeddedness. Wood, Coe and Wrigley (2016) in their study of food retailer entry in China note the requirement for a multi-scalar approach to strategic localization given the geographical variation in consumer cultures, climate and retail structure – simply focusing at the scale of the nation state is insufficient.

One of the key aspects of territorial embeddedness includes the importance of retail MNCs engaging with regulatory systems within host markets. Regulatory variability between and within markets is known to affect investment, development and performance – something which economic geographers have explored and to which we now turn.

A critically regulatory constrained and institutionally contextualized process

Arguably, by adopting the relational/networked perspective discussed earlier, economic geographers have been able to provide a greater sensitivity to the regulatory constrained and institutionally contextualized nature of the retail globalization process. Retail regulation has been viewed not simply as a set of market rules that are simplistically followed, but more as prescriptions that are affected by differential power relations and resources between retail firms and the host market state authorities responsible for enforcement. Regulations thus require interpretation in specific contexts and often at different spatial scales (Wood & Alexander, 2016), and as such they are affected by the wider political climate with judgements liable to change over time (Buckland-Wright, 2016).

This concern with the regulation of retail globalization processes first came to prominence within Economic Geography in the late 1990s as the authors of this chapter separately (and jointly) explored the rapid transformation of the US retail system at that time. In the food retail sector, rapid consolidation was ongoing driven by new indigenous competitive forces entering the market (e.g. the emergence of Walmart as a food retailer), by the pressure of international retail MNC entry and expansion, by the unwinding of the financial engineering of the late 1980s/early 1990s, and by continuous re-interpretation of market rules by the Federal Trade Commission (FTC) (Wrigley, 1992, 1997, 1999; Wood, 2013). In the department store sector, Wood (2001) demonstrated the manner in which retailers were not just 'rule takers' but active agents factoring in the likely responses of government regulators when contemplating merger and acquisition activity.

Taken together, the contributions on these two sectors highlighted the need to engage seriously with regulation within studies of the wider retail globalization process. One of the chief ways in which that has operated is through the nation state controlling access to – as well as governing the nature, scale and location – of retailing within host markets. The deregulation and 'opening up' of retail markets to retail FDI through the 1990s and 2000s was pivotal in facilitating a wave of retailers, chiefly emanating from Western Europe and North America, entering developing economies, particularly across Asia and Eastern Europe (Coe & Wrigley, 2007). However, the role of host market regulation on retail MNCs has more profound effects than simply limiting or permitting access to new markets – it can also moderate the freedom to operate alongside domestic operators. Wrigley and Lowe (2010) note the manner in which the host markets may, for example, restrict the registration of land ownership for companies with a significant percentage of foreign ownership, with retail MNCs prohibited from purchasing particular types of commercial property; while competition laws which seek to control unfair trade practices can be interpreted in a way that produces an anti-competitive assessment of multinational retail expansion on business competition in the host economy. Furthermore, there may be restrictions on the proportion of a firm's capital that can be owned by a retail MNC, which limits the degree of control afforded to a multinational and significantly affects the possible entry methods it might pursue. Other forms of regulation may specifically and differentially impact international retailers through land-use zoning, building and outlet size codes, hours of operation restrictions, environmental impact assessment requirement, and so on.

The introduction of large retail multinationals has often had considerable effects on the retail structure of host countries. Frequently, this has seen sudden shifts in the share of trade channelled through 'developed' retail formats such as hypermarkets with associated rapid market share gains for newly entered retail MNCs (Reardon & Hopkins, 2006; Nguyen, Wood & Wrigley, 2013). We earlier noted Durand and Wrigley's (2009) notion of international retailers being 'institution makers' as well as 'takers'. Consequently, there are occasions where not only are retail MNCs impacted by the institutional/regulatory environment they enter, but where, reciprocally, they actively seek to re-make that institutional environment. As a result, the prospering of large format international retailers has led to forms of resistance and lobbying within host markets as their presence has been linked with detrimental effects on traditional domestic retailers operating small, traditional stores and adversely affected power relations between retailers and suppliers (e.g. Franz, 2010):

> Due to a combination of the scale economies enjoyed by the transnational retailers and their expertise and sophistication in the retail segment, downward pressure has been placed on the profit and cost structure throughout the existing local retail trade, making it particularly difficult for small, independent merchants who have traditionally served the region's urban neighbourhoods to survive and thrive.
>
> *(Mutebi & Ansari, 2008, p. 2710)*

This has led to (re)regulation pressures, particularly against large format retail multinationals and in favour of traditional, smaller domestic players. Mutebi (2007) provides one of the few accounts of how this has played out in SE Asia, noting the restrictions that are applicable generally, and those which are specifically targeted at international retailers. Such restrictions have material effects on the performance of multinational retailers. For example, constraints introduced in South Korea, which included the necessity for large supermarket chains to close their stores every other Sunday, was linked to the operating margin of Tesco-owned stores in the country falling from 5.1 per cent to 2 per cent in the space of three years (*Financial Times*, 2015).

Economic geographers are in the early stages of exploring the evolution of regulatory systems within host countries exposed to international retail capital and the subsequent effects on domestic retail competition. One exception is the study by Buckland-Wright (2016) who tracks regulatory changes within Thailand and Malaysia over a decade-long period of development. She conceptualizes national retail markets as dynamic, path dependent and contested multi-actor sectoral systems that are continually shaped by the institutional and political landscapes within which they are embedded. Her analysis explores the strategies of resistance and competition by domestic market actors and the responses of national governments via sectoral regulation. The work uncovers the intense negotiations that occur between these actors and charts the divergent approaches of regulation that emerge between the two countries.

Networked relations with regulators at the level of the nation state have clearly therefore been an important theme in Economic Geography's engagement with the globalization of retailing. Similarly important have been relationships with the finance community – issues to which we now turn.

A process which highlights the role of financial market relations

Accounts of the globalization of economic activity within Economic Geography have increasingly taken the role of finance seriously (Coe et al., 2014). This is especially the case with regards to exploring the critical role that financial market relations play in facilitating, moderating and constraining the nature of international retail expansion. The surge of retail FDI through the late 1990s was driven in part by free cash flow generated by the retail multinationals from their core markets, but also by the ease of access of those firms to low cost debt or equity capital (Coe & Wrigley, 2007). Alongside that access, however, came investor and capital market scrutiny and pressure plus requirements for public disclosure – although there are several privately held retail MNCs (e.g. Aldi), these tend to be the exception rather than the rule (Okeahalam & Wood, 2009).

The nature of the funding of the leading retail multinational firms has led to economic geographers developing a keen awareness of the role of so-called 'financialization' and thus 'the growing influence of capital markets, their intermediaries, and processes in contemporary economic and political life' (Pike & Pollard, 2010, p. 30). In particular, there is an acceptance of the need 'to understand firm finances as integral to our understandings of firm behaviour, governance and strategy' (Pollard, 2003, p. 422). Given that share prices and shareholder value remain extremely important objectives for active management, and given that most borrowing is based on credit ratings derived from share price performance (Christopherson et al., 2013), pressures to improve the share price can significantly affect corporate behaviour and, as a result, retaining the faith of the capital markets is essential.

Economic geographers have become keenly aware of the implications for international retail development when the faith of the capital markets evaporates. Wrigley and Currah (2003) explored the implications for Dutch food retailer, Royal Ahold, which had funded its largely acquisitive international expansion in the late 1990s and early 2000s by successive equity placements and high levels of debt. However, when views concerning the emerging markets of Latin America and East Asia which Ahold had entered turned negative, the retailer found its pipeline of equity funding effectively closed:

> What had once been an important competitive advantage in a rapidly globalizing and consolidating industry – namely Ahold's high tolerance for financial leverage – suddenly became an important competitive disadvantage as it was forced to 'tear up the script' of its previous corporate strategy and adopt a new strategy of organic 'capital-efficient' growth.
> *(Wrigley & Currah, 2003, p. 236)*

However, it is not only changing conditions within the host markets that might lead to a loss of faith from the investment community. In addition, if performance in the retailer's home market deteriorates, analysts become increasingly sensitive to international market returns and the associated toll on senior management time. Such burdens particularly affected UK food retailer Sainsbury's, and led to the investment community demanding a shift towards 'core market focus' just as the retailer was expanding within the US through its Shaw's business, which was subsequently sold in 2004 (Wrigley, 2000b).

The reactive nature of financial markets make it increasingly important that financialized retail MNCs actively seek to *manage* capital market network relations. Wood, Wrigley and Coe (2017) explore how UK-based Tesco acquired a reputation for strong capital discipline within the investment community through the late 1990s and early 2000s despite aggressively expanding internationally. They also examine the subsequent unravelling of this reputation for prudence following a number of profligate international ventures, particularly within the US and China. The research highlights the importance of the retailer actively managing relationships with influential equity analysts by providing good access to senior executives and offering guided tours of its international operations, distribution facilities and even competitor stores. Nevertheless, acute balance sheet pressures and failed international entries led to uncompromising negative sentiment from the capital markets and a necessary recasting of the retailer's international strategy to one focused on limited capital expenditure and the diverting of investment back to the core, home market (Coe, Lee & Wood, 2017). These pressures are by no means unique. Dawson and Mukoyama (2014) note more widely evidence of a decrease in so-called 'flag planting' expansion involving a presence in many host markets to one increasingly involving representation in fewer markets with a priority on developing market leadership and profitable scale.

A process which highlights selective capability transfer and learning within the retail MNCs

The relational and networked views characteristic of Economic Geography's perspective on retail globalization have additionally been employed to explore the manner in which knowledge, culture and capabilities are transferred throughout the international retail firm. To some extent, there are parallels with many of the debates within IB and broader management studies relating to knowledge management (e.g. Alavi & Leidner, 2001) as well as a distinct strand of literature concerning these issues within Economic Geography (e.g. Amin & Cohendet, 2004; Faulconbridge, 2006; Vallance, 2011).

Part of the challenge of retailing across international borders is not only about transferring competencies and knowledge – equally it concerns developing appropriate corporate cultures for retail subsidiaries in host markets. Shackleton (1998) explored this issue with regards to Sainsbury's Shaw's food retail business in the US, noting the dominance of the UK parent firm and, in large part, the imposition of its culture and wider working practices on the US operation. However, a systematic top-down approach to the management of knowledge and practice within international retailing is known to often be inappropriate and insensitive to heterogeneous economic, institutional and cultural contexts (Wood, Coe & Wrigley, 2016). Instead, Currah and Wrigley (2004) explore the necessary balancing act between 'bottom-up' learning and 'top-down' coordination. More specifically, they assess the challenge of capturing and protecting innovations from extra-firm/firm-place networks and then spreading that knowledge within intra-firm networks. This 'bottom-up' learning, they argue, emanates from 'communities of practice' (cf. Wenger, 1998) situated across numerous spatial scales from the individual retail store, up through regional head offices and to the central headquarters. The role of 'virtual' communities further facilitates these processes which would otherwise be more challenging given distance. Meanwhile, Wood and Reynolds (2012, 2013) explore how intra-firm communities of practice located at different spatial scales within the retail organization inform and influence decisions relating to store expansion. In particular, there are challenges relating to the mediation between tacit and codified knowledge as well as accounting for differential power relations between different stakeholders in the decision-making process. Making use of insights and analysis to affect practice within international retail businesses is demanding and depends partly on the 'absorptive capacity' of the organization.

These 'bottom-up' processes must be balanced by more 'top-down' activities of co-ordination which involve the diffusion of best practice and 'transferable learning'. Wood, Coe and Wrigley (2016) specifically explore these issues, noting how successful international expansion may be supported by a retailer's organizational structure to underpin knowledge and capability flows from the centre to the subsidiaries. They note how the presence of an international support office may provide guidance across a range of retail operational competencies such as marketing, HR, retail skills, finance and sourcing. Such top-down processes may themselves be balanced with local expertise via shared learning groups at all levels of the organization. The development of these channels for sharing capabilities means that there is the potential for learning to pass between retail subsidiaries themselves and back to the retailer's home market, as well as the conventional direction from the home market to the subsidiaries (Jonsson, 2008).

Discussion and conclusion

It is not our intention in this chapter to attempt to privilege the contribution of one discipline over the other – we value tremendously the interest displayed in Economic Geography by the IB community, and we wish to encourage and promote that. However, as this chapter demonstrates, this has to be an engaged debate whereby the disciplines mutually enhance one another. We wholeheartedly agree with John Cantwell's (2014) aim of promoting a greater conversation between those interested in the topic of location from different backgrounds and starting points. However, that must be a serious conversation which reflects more than a decade of the rising importance of Economic Geography within social science debates (Monk & Monk, 2007), as the discipline captured the zeitgeist of the period and produced work of the highest quality. One of the keys is to understand that economic geographers hold a complex view of location which is characterized by a contextual view of space and place, which lends itself in quantitative terms to multi-level modelling approaches (Jones, 1991) and in qualitative terms to an increasingly deep and subtle appreciation of the nature of why 'geography matters' (Massey, 1994). This view is relational, networked, multi-scalar and sensitive to differential power relations. Moreover, we believe that Cantwell (2014, p. 2) goes a considerable way towards identifying key themes in a future creative conversation between the disciplines when he identifies a 'marked increase in scholarly interest in international knowledge linkages between locations' and, in particular, highlights the key topics of foreign direct investment (FDI) flows, innovation and knowledge spillovers, the role of analysis of location beyond the nation state, the role of local clusters in International Business and the complexity of the relationships between firms and International Business (Johns, 2016).

In this context, we note that it is now approaching 20 years since Erica Schoenberger (1999) characterized that complex relationship in terms of what she called the 'firm in the region' and the 'region in the firm'. That tradition has continued to inform the engagement of Economic Geography with the multinational firm, and in particular characterizes the approach that we advocate to the study of retail globalization. In this chapter we have examined themes which resonate with those identified by Cantwell. These have included a specific focus on how retail firms must become necessarily embedded and essentially networked within their host markets, how global retailing is a critically regulatory-constrained and institutionally contextualized process, how it is affected by relations with the finance community, and how it relies on the selective transfer of capabilities and learning within, and between, host markets.

Despite its modest scale compared to the critical mass of International Business studies, we suggest there is accumulating evidence that over a 15-year period Economic Geography has been able to make a distinct and strategically important impact relating to the way processes of retail globalization and the effects of those processes are understood and conceptualized across the many academic disciplines now drawn into engagement with retailers as the 'key organizers of the global economy'. In particular, as Bloom and Hinrichs (2017) argue, the firm embeddedness approach articulated by economic geographers offers an attractive theoretical framework for analysing how retailers develop strategies and business models determined by their home country context, but also adapted to new places, consumers and networks, and it is an approach that has gained considerable traction

Our intention in this chapter is therefore simply to encourage the deepening of that engagement in a creative way. We believe that the importance of retail globalization cannot be underestimated not least because of the unique positioning of retailing between production and consumption (Wrigley & Lowe, 1996). Continuing to explore this phenomenon is essential, for as Hamilton and Petrovic (2011, p. 3) noted, retail globalization represents a:

> [f]undamental transformation in the organization of the overall global economy, [a] transformation that continues to change not only the world of retailing, or even the relative power of retailers and their suppliers, but also the shape of international trade, economic development, product worlds, and consumption practices.

References

Alavi, M. & Leidner, D. (2001) 'Review: Knowledge management and knowledge management systems: conceptual foundations and research issues', *MIS Quarterly*, 25, pp. 107–136.

Amin, A. & Cohendet, P. (2004) *Architectures of Knowledge. Firms, Capabilities, and Communities*. Oxford, UK: Oxford University Press.

Aoyama, Y. (2007) 'Oligopoly and the structural paradox of retail TNCs: An assessment of Carrefour and Wal-Mart in Japan', *Journal of Economic Geography*, 7, pp. 471–490.
Bartlett, C.A. & Ghoshal, S. (1986) 'Tap your subsidiaries for global reach', *Harvard Business Review*, 64, pp. 87–94.
Bartlett, C.A. & Ghoshal, S. (1989) *Managing across Borders*. Boston, MA: Harvard University Press.
Beugelsdijk, S., McCann, P. & Mudambi, R. (2010) 'Introduction: Place, space and organization – Economic Geography and the multinational enterprise', *Journal of Economic Geography*, 10, pp. 485–493.
Beugelsdijk, S. & Mudambi, R. (2013) 'MNEs as border-crossing multi-location enterprises: The role of discontinuities in geographic space', *Journal of International Business Studies*, 44, pp. 413–426.
Bianchi, C.C. & Arnold, S.J. (2004) 'An institutional perspective on retail internationalization success: Home Depot in Chile', *The International Review of Retail, Distribution and Consumer Research*, 14, pp. 149–169.
Bloom, J.D. & Hinrichs, C.C. (2017) 'The long reach of lean retailing: Firm embeddedness and Wal-Mart's implementation of local produce sourcing in the US', *Environment and Planning A*, 49, pp. 168–185.
Buckland-Wright, A. (2016) Transnational retail in Southeast Asia: Transformation and regulation in the national markets of Malaysia and Thailand. Unpublished PhD thesis, Faculty of Humanities, University of Manchester, UK.
Buckley, P.J. & Ghauri, P.N. (2004) 'Globalisation, Economic Geography and the strategy of multinational enterprises', *Journal of International Business Studies*, 35, pp. 81–98.
Burt, S., Johansson, U. & Dawson, J. (2016) 'International retailing as embedded business models', *Journal of Economic Geography*, 16, pp. 715–747.
Burt, S., Johansson, U. & Dawson, J. (2017) 'Dissecting embeddedness in international retailing', *Journal of Economic Geography*, doi:10.1093/jeg/lbw045.
Cantwell, J. (2009) 'Location and the multinational enterprise', *Journal of International Business Studies*, 40, pp. 35–41.
Cantwell, J. (Ed.) (2014) *Location of International Business Activities: Integrating Ideas from Research in International Business, Strategic Management and Economic Geography*. Basingstoke, UK: Palgrave Macmillan.
Chaney, I. & Gamble, J. (2008) 'Retail store ownership influences on Chinese consumers', *International Business Review*, 17, pp. 170–183.
Christopherson, S., Martin, R. & Pollard, J. (2013) 'Financialisation: Roots and repercussions', *Cambridge Journal of Regions, Economy and Society*, 6, pp. 351–357.
Coe, N.M. (2004) 'The internationalisation/globalisation of retailing: Towards an economic – Geographical research agenda', *Environment and Planning A*, 36, pp. 1571–1594.
Coe, N.M. & Hess, M. (2005) 'The internationalization of retailing: Implications for supply network restructuring in East Asia and Eastern Europe', *Journal of Economic Geography*, 5, pp. 449–473.
Coe, N.M., Lai, K. & Wójcik, D. (2014) 'Integrating finance into Global Production Networks', *Regional Studies*, 48, pp. 761–777.
Coe, N.M. & Lee, Y.S. (2006) 'The strategic localization of transnational retailers: The case of Samsung–Tesco in South Korea', *Economic Geography*, 82, pp. 61–88.
Coe, N., Lee, Y-S. & Wood, S. (2017) 'Conceptualising contemporary retail divestment: Tesco's departure from South Korea', *Environment and Planning A*, 49, pp. 2739– 2742.
Coe, N.M. & Lee, Y.S. (2013) '"We've learnt how to be local": The deepening territorial embeddedness of Samsung–Tesco in South Korea', *Journal of Economic Geography*, 13, pp. 327–356.
Coe, N.M. & Wrigley, N. (2007) 'Host economy impacts of transnational retail: The research agenda', *Journal of Economic Geography*, 7, pp. 341–371.
Currah, A. & Wrigley, N. (2004) 'Networks of organizational learning and adaptation in retail TNCs', *Global Networks*, 4, pp. 1–23.
Dawson, J. (1994) 'Internationalization of retailing operations', *Journal of Marketing Management*, 10, pp. 267–82.
Dawson, J. & Mukoyama, M. (Eds.). (2014) *Global Strategies in Retailing: Asian and European Experiences*. London: Routledge.
Dunning, J.H. (2000) 'The eclectic paradigm as an envelope for economic and business theories of MNE activity', *International Business Review*, 9, pp. 163–190.
Dunning, J.H. (2009) 'The key literature on IB activities: 1960–2006', in Rugman, A.M. (Ed.), *The Oxford Handbook of International Business*. 2nd Edition. Oxford, UK: Oxford University Press, pp. 37–71.
Durand, C. & Wrigley, N. (2009) 'Institutional and economic determinants of transnational retailer expansion and performance: A comparative analysis of Wal-Mart and Carrefour', *Environment and Planning A*, 41, pp. 1534–1555.

Faulconbridge, J.R. (2006) 'Stretching tacit knowledge beyond a local fix? Global spaces of learning in advertising professional service firms', *Journal of Economic Geography*, 6, pp. 517–540.

Financial Times. (2015) 'Tesco set to close door on South Korean success story', September 6, 2015.

Franz, M. (2010) 'The role of resistance in a retail production network: Protests against supermarkets in India', *Singapore Journal of Tropical Geography*, 31, pp. 317–329.

Gamble, J. (2010) 'Transferring organizational practices and the dynamics of hybridization: Japanese retail multinationals in China', *Journal of Management Studies*, 47, pp. 705–732

Gamble, J. & Huang, Q. (2009) 'The transfer of organizational practices: A diachronic perspective from China', *The International Journal of Human Resource Management*, 20, pp. 1683–1703.

Gereffi, G. (1994) 'The organization of buyer-driven global commodity chains: How U.S. retailers shape overseas production networks', in Gereffi, G. & Korzeniewicz, M. (Eds.), *Commodity Chains and Global Capitalism*. Westport, CT: Praeger, pp. 95–122.

Gupta, A.K. & Govindarajan, V. (1991) 'Knowledge flows and the structure of control within multinational corporations', *Academy of Management Review*, 16, pp. 768–792.

Hamilton, G.G. & Petrovic, M. (2011) 'Introduction', in Hamilton, G., Petrovic, M. & Senauer, B. (Eds.), *The Market Makers: How Retailers are Reshaping the Global Economy*. Oxford, UK: Oxford University Press, pp. 1–28.

Hamilton, G.G., Senauer, B. and Petrovic, M. (2011) *The Market Makers: How Retailers are Reshaping the Global Economy*. Oxford, UK: Oxford University Press.

Hennart, J.F. (2009) 'Down with MNE-centric theories! Market entry and expansion as the bundling of MNE and local assets', *Journal of International Business Studies*, 40, pp. 1432–1454.

Hess, M. (2004) '"Spatial" relationships? Towards a reconceptualization of embeddedness', *Progress in Human Geography*, 28, pp. 165–186.

Jones, K. (1991) 'Specifying and estimating multi-level models for geographical research', *Transactions of the Institute of British Geographers*, 16, pp. 148–159.

Johanson, J. & Vahlne, J.E. (1977) 'The internationalization process of the firm: A model of knowledge development and increasing foreign market commitments', *Journal of International Business Studies*, 8, pp. 23–32.

Johanson, J. & Vahlne, J.E. (2009) 'The Uppsala internationalization process model revisited: From liability of foreignness to liability of outsidership', *Journal of International Business Studies*, 40, pp. 1411–1431.

Johns, J. (2016) 'Location of International Business activities: Integrating ideas from research in International Business, strategic management and Economic Geography', *Journal of Economic Geography*, 16, pp. 267–270.

Jonsson, A. (2008) 'A transnational perspective on knowledge sharing: Lessons learned from IKEA's entry into Russia, China and Japan', *International Review of Retail, Distribution & Consumer Research*, 18, pp. 17–44.

Jonsson, A. & Foss, N.J. (2011) 'International expansion through flexible replication: Learning from the internationalization experience of IKEA', *Journal of International Business Studies*, 42, pp. 1079–1102.

Lowe, M., George, G. & Alexy, O. (2012) 'Organizational identity and capability development in internationalization: Transference, splicing and enhanced imitation in Tesco's US market entry', *Journal of Economic Geography*, 12, pp. 1021–1054.

Lowe, M. & Wrigley, N. (2010) 'The "continuously morphing" retail TNC during market entry: Interpreting Tesco's expansion into the United States', *Economic Geography*, 86, pp. 381–408.

Massey, D. (1994) *Space, Place and Gender*. Cambridge, UK: Polity Press.

McCann, P. (2011) 'International Business and Economic Geography: Knowledge, time and transactions costs', *Journal of Economic Geography*, 11, pp. 309–317.

McCann, P. & Mudambi, R. (2004) 'The location behavior of the multinational enterprise: Some analytical issues', *Growth and Change*, 35, pp. 491–524.

McCann, P. & Mudambi, R. (2005) 'Analytical differences in the economics of geography: The case of the multinational firm', *Environment and Planning A*, 37, pp. 1857–1876.

Meyer, K.E., Mudambi, R. & Narula, R. (2011) 'Multinational enterprises and local contexts: The opportunities and challenges of multiple embeddedness', *Journal of Management Studies*, 48, pp. 235–252.

Monk, A.H.B. & Monk, C.S. (2007) 'Economic Geography: The rising star of the social sciences', *Oxonomics*, 2, pp. 16–20.

Morgan, G. (2001) 'Transnational communities and business systems', *Global Networks*, 1, pp. 113–130.

Mutebi, A.M. (2007) 'Regulatory responses to large-format transnational retail in south-east Asian cities', *Urban Studies*, 44, pp. 357–379.

Mutebi, A.M. & Ansari, R. (2008) 'Small independent merchants and transnational retail encounters on main street: Some insights from Bangkok', *Urban Studies*, 45, pp. 2689–2714.
Nguyen, N.T.H., Wood, S. & Wrigley, N. (2013) 'The emerging food retail structure of Vietnam: Phases of expansion in a post-socialist environment', *International Journal of Retail & Distribution Management*, 41, pp. 596–626.
O'Grady, S. & Lane, H.W. (1996) 'The psychic distance paradox', *Journal of International Business Studies*, 27, pp. 309–333.
Okeahalam, C.C. & Wood, S. (2009) 'Financing internationalisation: A case study of an African retail transnational corporation', *Journal of Economic Geography*, 9, pp. 511–537.
Park, Y. & Sternquist, B. (2008) 'The global retailer's strategic proposition and choice of entry mode', *International Journal of Retail & Distribution Management*, 36, pp. 281–299.
Pike, A. & Pollard, J. (2010) 'Economic geographies of financialization', *Journal of Economic Geography*, 86, pp. 29–51.
Pollard, J.S. (2003) 'Small firm finance and Economic Geography', *Journal of Economic Geography*, 3, pp. 429–452.
Reardon, T. & Hopkins, R. (2006) 'The supermarket revolution in developing countries: Policies to address emerging tensions among supermarkets, suppliers and traditional retailers', *The European Journal of Development Research*, 18, pp. 522–545.
Robertson, R. (1995) 'Glocalization: Time-space and homogeneity-heterogeneity', in Featherstone, M., Lash, S. & Robertson, R. (Eds.), *Global Modernities, Theory, Culture & Society*. London: Sage, pp. 25–44.
Rugman, A.M. (1981) *Inside the Multinationals: The Economics of Internal Markets*. New York: Columbia University Press.
Rugman, A.M. & Girod, S. (2003) 'Retail multinationals and globalization: The evidence is regional', *European Management Journal*, 21, pp. 24–37.
Rugman, A.M. & Verbeke, A. (2001) 'Subsidiary-specific advantages in multinational enterprises', *Strategic Management Journal*, 22, pp. 237–250.
Rugman, A.M. & Verbeke, A. (2004) 'A perspective on regional and global strategies of multinational enterprises', *Journal of International Business Studies*, 35, pp. 3–18.
Rugman, A.M. & Verbeke, A. (2008) 'A new perspective on the regional and global strategies of multinational services firms', *Management International Review*, 48, pp. 397–411.
Rugman, A.M., Verbeke, A. & Nguyen, P.C.Q.T. (2011) 'Fifty years of International Business theory and beyond', *Management International Review*, 51, pp. 755–786.
Rugman, A.M., Verbeke, A. & Yuan, W. (2011) 'Re-conceptualizing Bartlett and Ghoshal's classification of national subsidiary roles in the multinational enterprise', *Journal of Management Studies*, 48, pp. 253–277.
Salmon, W. & Tordjman, A. (1989) 'The internationalisation of retailing', *International Journal of Retailing*, 4, pp. 3–16.
Schoenberger, E. (1999) 'The firm in the region and the region in the firm', in Barnes, T. & Gertler, M.S. (Eds.), *The New Industrial Geography: Regions, Regulation and Institutions*. London: Routledge, pp. 204–225.
Shackleton, R. (1998) 'Exploring corporate culture and strategy: Sainsbury at home and abroad during the early to mid 1990s', *Environment and Planning A*, 30, pp. 921–940.
Siebers, L.Q. (2017) 'Hybridization practices as organizational responses to institutional demands: The development of Western retail TNCs in China', *Journal of Economic Geography*, 7, pp. 1–29.
Swoboda, B., Elsner, S. & Morschett, D. (2014) 'Preferences and performance of international strategies in retail sectors: An empirical study', *Long Range Planning*, 47, pp. 319–336.
Tacconelli, W. & Wrigley, N. (2009) 'Organizational challenges and strategic responses of retail TNCs in post-WTO-entry China', *Economic Geography*, 85, pp. 49–73.
Tokatli, N. & Kızılgün, Ö. (2010) 'Coping with the changing rules of the game in the global textiles and apparel industries: Evidence from Turkey and Morocco', *Journal of Economic Geography*, 10, pp. 209–229.
Vallance, P. (2011) 'Relational and dialectical spaces of knowing: Knowledge, practice, and work in Economic Geography', *Environment and Planning A*, 43, pp. 1098–1117.
Verbeke, A. & Asmussen, C.G. (2016) 'Global, local, or regional? The locus of MNE strategies', *Journal of Management Studies*, 53, pp. 1051–1075.
Wenger, E. (1998) *Communities of Practice: Learning, Meaning, and Identity*. Cambridge, UK: Cambridge University Press.

Wood, S. (2001) 'Regulatory constrained portfolio restructuring: The US department store industry in the 1990s', *Environment and Planning A*, 33, pp. 1279–1304.

Wood, S. (2013) 'Revisiting the US food retail consolidation wave: Regulation, market power and spatial outcomes', *Journal of Economic Geography*, 13, pp. 299–326.

Wood, S. & Alexander, A. (2016) 'Regulation in practice: Power, resources and context at the local scale in UK food retailing', *Environment and Planning A*, 48, pp. 1848–1863.

Wood, S., Coe, N.M. & Wrigley, N. (2016) 'Multi-scalar localization and capability transference: Exploring embeddedness in the Asian retail expansion of Tesco', *Regional Studies*, 50, pp. 475–495.

Wood, S. & Reynolds, J. (2012) 'Managing communities and managing knowledge: Strategic decision making and store network investment within retail multinationals', *Journal of Economic Geography*, 12, pp. 539–565.

Wood, S. & Reynolds, J. (2013) 'Knowledge management, organisational learning and memory in UK retail network planning', *The Service Industries Journal*, 33, pp. 150–170.

Wood, S. & Reynolds, J. (2014) 'Establishing territorial embeddedness within retail transnational corporation (TNC) expansion: The contribution of store development departments', *Regional Studies*, 48, pp. 1371–1390.

Wood, S., Wrigley, N. & Coe, N. M. (2017) 'Capital discipline and financial market relations in retail globalization: Insights from the case of Tesco plc', *Journal of Economic Geography*, 17, pp. 31–57.

Wrigley, N. (1992) 'Antitrust regulation and the restructuring of grocery retailing in Britain and the USA', *Environment and Planning A*, 24, pp. 727–749.

Wrigley, N. (1997) 'Foreign retail capital on the battlefields of Connecticut: Competition regulation at the local scale and its implications', *Environment and Planning A*, 29, pp. 1141–1152.

Wrigley, N. (1999) 'Market rules and spatial outcomes: Insights from the corporate restructuring of US food retailing', *Geographical Analysis*, 31, pp. 288–309.

Wrigley, N. (2000a) 'The globalization of retail capital: themes for Economic Geography', in Clark, G.L., Feldman, M.P. & Gertler, M.S. (Eds.), *The Oxford Handbook of Economic Geography*. Oxford, UK: Oxford University Press, pp. 292–313.

Wrigley, N. (2000b) 'Strategic market behaviour in the internationalization of food retailing: Interpreting the third wave of Sainsbury's US diversification', *European Journal of Marketing*, 34, pp. 891–919.

Wrigley, N., Coe, N.M. & Currah, A. (2005) 'Globalizing retail: Conceptualizing the distribution-based transnational corporation (TNC)', *Progress in Human Geography*, 29, pp. 437–457.

Wrigley, N. & Currah, A. (2003) 'The stresses of retail internationalization: Lessons from Royal Ahold's experience in Latin America', *The International Review of Retail, Distribution and Consumer Research*, 13, pp. 221–243.

Wrigley, N. & Lowe, M. (Eds.) (1996) *Retailing, Consumption and Capital: Towards the New Retail Geography*. Basingstoke, UK: Longman.

Wrigley, N. & Lowe, M. (2010) *The Globalization of Trade in Retail Services*. Report commissioned by the OECD Trade Policy Linkages and Services Division for the OECD Experts Meeting on Distribution Services, Paris 17 November 2010.

Yang, Q., Mudambi, R. & Meyer, K.E. (2008) 'Conventional and reverse knowledge flows in multinational corporations', *Journal of Management*, 34, pp. 882–902.

Yeung, H.W.-C. (2009) 'Transnational corporations, global production networks, and urban and regional development: A geographer's perspective on multinational enterprises and the global economy', *Growth and Change*, 40, pp. 197–226.

29

INNOVATION, MARKET SEGMENTATION AND ENTREPRENEURSHIP IN SERVICES

The case of the hotel industry

Jeremy Howells and Michelle Lowe

Introduction

Although services are now the dominant form of economic activity and change in advanced economies, researchers are still grappling with the 'peculiarities of services' (Barras, 1986), which makes their analysis challenging and different (Miles, 2005; Preissl, 2000). Thus services often come in intangible forms, have simultaneous production and consumption (which leads to the inability to store service products) frequently with the direct involvement of the customer (Howells, 2010, p. 70). The distinctive nature of these peculiarities in particular can be seen when considering services in relation to economic change and development, leading to different approaches towards conceptualisation and change. Many of those leading such developments in these fields have come from Economic Geography backgrounds in both International Business (see, for example, Enderwick, 1987; Roberts, 1999; Buckley & Ghauri, 2004; McCann, 2011) and innovation (see, for example, Daniels, 1983; Howells & Green, 1986; Moulaert & Gallouj, 1993; Tether, 2005; Love, Roper & Hewitt-Dundas, 2010; Bryson, Daniels & Warf, 2013; Meliciani & Savona, 2015; Freel, 2016)

Despite being considered a low tech sector (Hertog, den Gallouj & Segers, 2011), the hotel industry represents a highly dynamic and competitive market that continues to grow steadily as disposable incomes and consumer mobility have risen worldwide. The expansion of international hotel chains has been part of this trend (Peters & Frehse, 2005), together with more recent merger and acquisition activity. Market liberalisation and deregulation have led to more opportunities for international expansion, as well as increased competition, and have often resulted in ever more homogenous service packaging in the hotel industry.

Set against this trend of commodification and homogeneity, *existing* hotel chains (in contrast to new entrants; see later) have sought differentiation strategies by offering new experiences or levels of service. Thus, for example, Frehse (2006) provides a detailed account of the growth of 'spa and health facilities' in such large chains and how this is linked to both competitive and innovative processes. This type of innovative practice can be characterised as Schumpeterian

Mode II type innovation and competitive practices (Schumpeter, 1943), reflecting how established players seek to control and grow in a market. This kind of activity is significant in most industries and for the hotel sector still remains the dominant form of change; as well as in innovative activity, at least in terms of incremental innovation.

Equally though, as a way of avoiding such increasingly commodified and cost-driven markets, entrepreneurs as *new entrants* have sought to create hotels and hotel formats which offer unique characteristics (Hinterhuber, 2001), which contrast with standard hotel formats. These Mode I types of Schumpeterian innovation, associated with the creation and formation of new types of entrant (as well as the decline and eventual closure of others), have the potential of introducing more radical and disruptive innovation in the sectors and markets in which they emerge (Metcalfe, 1998). Such new niche types of hotel are disruptive forms of innovation in the context of the hotel industry by creating differentiation and hence new segmentation within the hotel market. This, in turn, makes it harder for direct competition through difficulty of imitation, thereby allowing monopolistic rents to be generated, at least on a partial basis. Moreover, this is not only about innovation in terms of a new and differentiated product but also is linked to new 'ways of doing' in terms of delivering a different type of operational and organisational form and how this is then spread and diffused internationally.

In the context of a volume which focuses on exploring the potential of the 'boundary space' between Economic Geography and International Business, this chapter on the hotel industry has four objectives. First, to position service industries and the conceptualisation of innovation and entrepreneurial activity in the service sector as issues of central concern within that 'boundary space', albeit acknowledging that they are currently significantly under-researched (Miles, 2005; Howells, 2010; Hertog, den Gallouj & Segers, 2011; Carlborg, Kindström & Kowalkowski, 2014). Second, to explore the emergence of new hotel forms in the sector, conceptualising those developments in terms of the disruptive and emergent forms of innovation (Bower & Christensen, 1995; Christensen, 1997) typical of Mode I Schumpeterian innovation. Third, the study connects the creation of a new hotel form with wider social network relationships and trajectories associated with the emergence of a 'diaspora' of entrepreneurial innovators (Lowe et al., 2012; Sørensen & Fuglsang, 2014). Lastly, the findings of this study are then related back to inform the theoretical development and conceptualisation of service innovation and internationalisation more widely. The first two elements of the objectives form the main part of the analysis, although the third element is crucial in the development of our wider analysis of innovation in the service economy as well as to its theorisation at the boundary between Economic Geography and International Business (see, for example, McCann, 2011).

Hotel innovation: differentiation and segmentation

Innovation types within the hotel sector

Although the hotel industry is seen as being a low technology dependent, low innovation sector, innovation is still important in the way the industry competes, for its continued growth and in its role as a major employer in both developed and developing economies. Given its size and significance, the hotel sector is also an important consumer and co-developer of new technology and digital media. In the context of services, there are three broad types of innovation: development of new products, development of new processes and development of new organisational design (Howells & Tether, 2004; Miles, 2005). However, it is accepted that all three can be highly inter-related in the context of services, where intangibility levels and blurring between inputs and effects are high.

In relation to hotels specifically, and tourism in general, it is suggested here that there are four main arenas of interest where innovation research has been focused in relation to the sector. These relate to:

1) A comprehensive overview of innovation in the hotel and tourism sector, more recently acknowledging the role of a holistic perspective and ambidexterity in the innovation process.
2) The effect of information technology, back-office operations and e-markets in the hotel sector.
3) The role of skills, training and their impact on productivity in relation to the industry.
4) Innovation and its relationship with user interaction, new product development, product differentiation and market segmentation.

Within this wider context of service innovation, hospitality and tourism studies have started to highlight and analyse innovative activity from a set of different perspectives and foci. Thus, a number of these have taken a more high-level approach seeking to cover innovative practices right across the industry, focusing on more high-level strategy and performance within the industry (Ottenbacher, Vivienne & Lockwood, 2006), but also to seek to understand the nature and profile of innovation in the industry (Pikkemaat & Peters, 2006) and how this may differ from other services sectors. Tsai (2015), for example, has recently explored the inter-related nature of innovation dimensions in five star hotels and linked this customer experience and customer loyalty within a framework of holistic innovation. Similarly, a study by Grissemann et al. (2013) suggested that innovative activity in hotels' service and IT areas was influenced by four closely inter-related innovation dimensions, namely employee engagement, customer participation, innovation management and information technologies. This group of studies has implications for the development of how we understand the process of service innovation both within the industry but also more generally.

A second set of studies has focused on the role of information technology (IT) and the rise of the internet. This can be seen in work analysing back office and automated booking functions (see, for example, Sheldon, 1983; Bilgihan et al., 2011; Sirirak, Islam & Ba Khang, 2011), but also the impact of the internet on the industry more generally. In particular, these approaches have sought to examine how information technology, automation and more recently the internet, especially in relation to sales and marketing, have affected the industry, its productivity and levels of service. Yelkur and Nêveda DaCosta (2001), for example, explored the role of the web on differential pricing in various segments of the hotel sector (see later). Related to this, but important in its effects, were the indirect effects of disintermediation in the tourism, hotel and hospitality sectors (see, for example, Stamboulis & Skayannis, 2003; Buhalis & Law, 2008).

A third set of work has focused on the specific hotel operations and staff skills, training and productivity. There is a close connection between training and changes in technology in services (Howells & Tether, 2004), whilst significant technological change is usually accompanied by a need to upgrade and adapt the skills of the service organisations (Evangelista & Savona, 2003). In this respect, the hospitality and tourism industries appear no different (Chang, Gong & Shum, 2011; Dhar, 2015). Hoque (2013, p. 9) emphasises that human resource management (HRM) is a key strategic lever within the industry and is closely associated with all aspects of the innovation process and more particularly its successful application. In addition, hospitality services often have high levels of intangibility, and production and consumption are simultaneous. Hospitality services, therefore, depend heavily on the skills and experiences of the employees that deliver them (Ottenbacher, Vivienne & Lockwood, 2006, p. 126).

Lastly, a group of studies has centred on creativity and innovation focusing on user experiences and consumer interaction in terms of new product development, market provision and segmentation (see, for example, Peters & Frehse, 2005; Frehse, 2006). Tourism is an industry very close to the customer; however, paradoxically, all too often most innovations in the industry are through 'technology push' rather than through 'user pull'. In this way innovation in hotels is often too technology-driven and not customer-friendly in their outputs (Bieger, Beritelli & Laesser, 2009). Nonetheless, generating a differentiated product or service through new and innovative practices and organisational design is a means to avoid direct competition and to gain monopolistic rents, at least for a period until new entrants appear in the market or market segment (Grant, 1991, p. 124).

Product innovation, differentiation, segmentation and new business models

This chapter, and the associated case study it draws upon, seeks to focus on this latter aspect of innovation in the hotel industry. This is notwithstanding the fact that all aspects of the innovation process within the hotel interact with each other; for example, improved training may be part of enhancing the customer experience. As noted earlier, the market drivers also affecting innovation decisions may be considered through the competitive strategy. The crucial factor for innovation is still the intensity of competition in the market (Preissl, 2000). Frehse (2006, p. 130) in reviewing the key competitive challenges for international hotel chains identified three core challenges that they face in terms of:

1) taking account of continuously changing trends in the market and their resulting planning process requirements;
2) finding new ways and methods to attract guests with innovative offerings as well as increase their quality of life experience during their hotel stay; and,
3) creating instruments that differentiate them from their competitors.

Effectively, a firm's strategic decision to differentiate itself from competitors will affect its productive resources, the services it offers, the organisation and management of the operations, and, therefore, its innovation decisions (Sundbo & Gallouj, 2000). Baum and Haveman (1997) indicate that in the hotel industry, a differentiation strategy may be the most effective. They show that travellers decide to book tourist accommodation based on its price, on the quality of its service, on the services offered and on the image of hotel establishments. Consequently, an establishment may implement a competitive strategy that differentiates its service offerings from those of its closest competitors (adjusting it to the demand) or in the provision process (improving its productive efficiency). Furthermore, Canina, Enz and Harrison (2005) indicate that there are strong incentives for what they term 'lodging firms' to pursue strategies that differentiate them from competitors in their local market. A key element, therefore, for hotels as they face greater competitive pressure from globalisation and the trend towards ever greater customisation, is the need to meet customer demand for unique and memorable experiences (Gilmore & Pine, 2002; Chathoth et al., 2013) and to provide quality service to customers effectively (Wang, Chen & Chen, 2012). To survive in the industry, a hotel needs to respond to the explicit requests provided by customers regarding service improvement and create new services to satisfy potential customer needs.

These issues reflect the wider challenges faced by all hoteliers, aside from simple cost reduction and efficiency improvements. In particular, the industry seeks novelty and differentiation within a crowded market, something that will make their hotel or hotel chain stand out from other hotels and create a 'new' experience. In turn, 'non-imitability' – making it difficult for rival businesses to copy the new product offering at least over the short and medium term – becomes a key to success. This process of differentiation is also associated with and, in a sense culminates in, the segmentation of the industry.

In summary, new hotels help lead this process of innovation and experimentation in the industry, but over time they then come under pressures of imitation and standardisation by new and existing hotels and hotel chains entering the market segment. In this sense, Schumpeterian Mode I patterns of innovation, with more radical Darwinian creation, experimentation and all too often decline and death, are then succeeded by Mode II incremental change often copied by established players, consisting of existing hotel chains and successful Mode I firms that have managed to survive and prosper. This more established, second phase leads eventually to a new definable segment in the market being created.

The link between differentiation and innovativeness seems, therefore, to be unusually important in this sector. For example, Pikkemaat and Peters' (2006) study of innovation processes amongst small and medium-sized hotels highlights the linkage, finding that entrepreneurs who focus on clearly defined target markets seem to be more innovative and in the long run more successful (Pikkemaat & Peters, 2006, p. 108). Moreover, results pertaining to the introduction of additional services have been shown to have a positive effect on all innovation types. Hence quality-based strategies adding value to the customer stay (Medina-Múñoz et al., 2003) have been found to prompt innovation in other dimensions of hotel activity (Orfila-Sintes & Mattsson, 2009, p. 389). That is to say, the emergence and development of a new type of hotel segment is not only associated with a process of new product development and differentiation, but is also linked with the formation of new business models (Teece, 2010) and ways of running a hotel. Souto (2015), for example, notes that the rise of new business models within the industry is a form of a non-technological innovation, but also one that effectively combines both technological and (other) non-technological innovations. Although this is usually not associated with radically new types of business model in hotel and leisure, there are exceptions; Airbnb, part of the 'shared economy' (Grinevich et al., 2015) on the fringes of the hotel sector, for example, has this disruptive potential. It is also evident in the rise of digital intermediaries in hotel search and booking functions; in new customer service practices; and in the greening of the supply chain (in turn, associated localism and environmental strategies).

New innovative formats in the hotel industry

Background and methodology

This case study explores the role of segmentation, innovation and the evolving trajectory of entrepreneurial social networks in the hotel industry. The study focuses on the rise of the 'Shabby Chic Hotel' (SCH) from an earlier sub-market creation, the Boutique Hotel (BH) in the UK, and the innovative dimensions of its emergence through experimentation, creativity and enterprise. SCHs can be defined by the following characteristics: a traditional British country house hotel set up in the refined yet less formal style associated with the relaxed US West Coast retro look (see Gudis, 2013). The 'chic' element signals the exclusive and fashionable luxury combined with the high design aspect of the style. SCHs additionally emphasise luxury local foods grown, reared or produced in a sustainable way, combining the new British food movement with the slow food movement. Well-kept country gardens (including kitchen gardens) imitating those found in traditional country houses in Britain and Ireland are a feature.

In the UK, Country House Hotels (CHHs) began to emerge in the late nineteenth century (McGuffie, 1987) with the rise of the railways (Simmons, 1984) followed by the rise of the motorcar in the 1920s and 1930s (Pope, 2000). As car ownership spread amongst the affluent upper classes, new patterns of tourism consumption associated with cultural change and the search for authenticity emerged (Urry, 1990). Access to country houses in previously inaccessible rural areas (Jeremiah, 2010) became possible, while on the supply-side availability of suitable houses was boosted as high inheritance tax levels ('death duty') took their toll, particularly in the inter-war and immediate post-war periods. Although often regarded as quintessentially British, CCHs from their initial emergence incorporated important European influences ranging from French and Italian house and garden styles through to more recent adoptions such as of Italian 'slow movement' characteristics in cooking and localism in food. But most important is the link between the SCH segment and the earlier emergence of the 'boutique' hotel movement in the UK (Aggett, 2007) and elsewhere (Rogerson, 2010), a predominately urban phenomenon.

Figure 29.1 captures in diagrammatic form some of this evolution of the SCH as a distinctive form and market segment, positioning it within the wider industry trajectory, which includes the CHH and BH forms.

The case study draws on that contextualisation and offers insights from an ongoing in-depth investigation into the growth and innovative development of the hotel industry. It explores the role of segmentation, innovation and the evolving trajectory of entrepreneurial social networks in the hotel industry. The case study involves arguably one of the most disruptive and leading sub-markets in the UK, which in turn has evolved out of earlier differentiation and segmentation strategies of key entrepreneurs and their peers. The research is by its nature exploratory, but

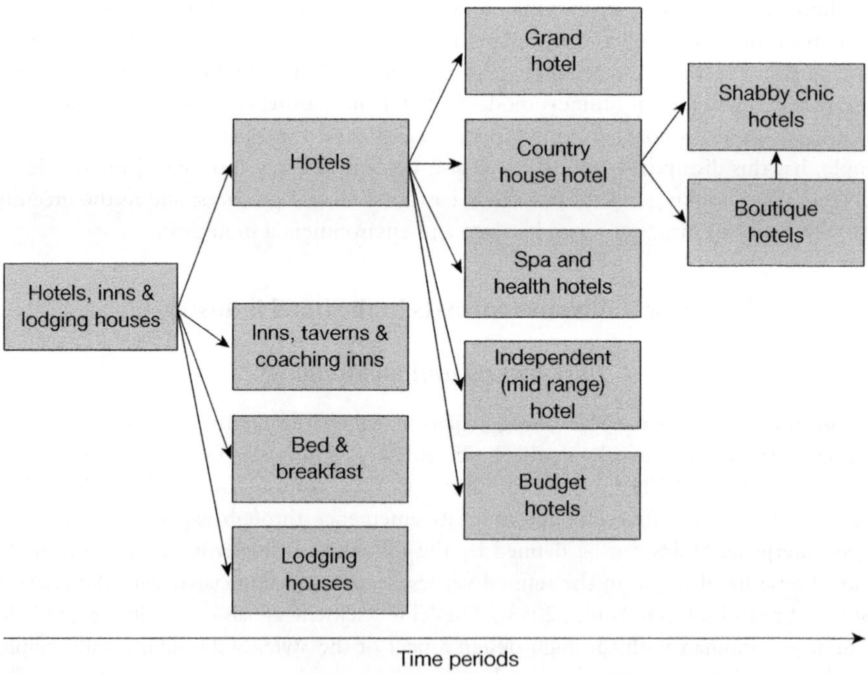

Figure 29.1 Innovation trajectory of differentiation and segmentation in the hotel industry
Source: Authors' construction.

does seek to provide generalisability, counter-example and validity. It has used multiple methods of triangulation, including several methods of data collection (interviews, archival research, participant observation) and multiple cross-relating information sources which help to capture the numerous, complex and interwoven perspectives which exist relating to the history of the new SCH hotel sub-market. The study is therefore built on 'a participative form of research' (Van de Ven, 2007) in which the founders and managers of the case study firm were engaged, as well as obtaining perspectives of other key stakeholders, including the original suppliers of private equity finance and other entrepreneurs in the network. Accessing the views of these stakeholders involved in-depth semi-structured interviews, obtained via a 'snowballing' technique and conducted in a 'close dialogue'. The method involved complex relationships between interviewers and interviewees (Schoenberger, 1991) and, despite its many virtues in allowing insight into corporate decision-making, has clear limitations to which the researcher must remain sensitive. Additionally, there were issues relating to building generality in a systematic way from the insights the researcher obtains, and also to validating the research. The research also undertook extensive 'triangulation' of our interview material with information drawn from archival sources. Analysis of the interviews was undertaken to identify key themes discussed in the literature and to organise these into nodes (or codes), which were then referenced against a timeline capturing the history of the firms. These nodes were then structured and classified to focus the analytical work and explore the themes in more depth, linking the nodes across each interview transcript. This was particularly useful for analysing interviews, which converged on many topics, but which involved contrasting individual perspectives, namely interviewees whose opinion and recall offered varying levels of detail on important events.

Differentiation and segmentation

It is well established that differentiation delivering perceived superiority and enhanced customer value can lead to competitive advantage in the market place (see Day & Wensley, 2002, pp. 91–92). The case study reinforces that by highlighting how differentiation and subsequent segmentation are linked to innovation and enterprise and how these strategies and activities are intertwined. In particular, Table 29.1 shows how our case study respondents perceive the segmentation and taxonomy of the hotel industry in the UK to have developed over time. This trajectory of development will clearly be different in other national hotel systems, reflecting the continuing strength of cultural influences (Tajeddini & Trueman, 2012), but over time will start to converge with other national hotel markets as international chains spread and develop and therefore more rapidly diffuse differentiation strategies and models. Equally, new hotel formats are now more likely to be established early in overseas markets as global barriers continue to fall.

New product types, over time, develop into definable market segments with their own sub-markets and competitive and price profiles. New hotel types have the advantage of being able to gain some monopolistic advantage and therefore price protection, although over time this will erode as new competitors enter the market. Nonetheless, this temporary monopoly power can last for a significant time period (even in the highly competitive personal computer market of the 1980s; Bresnahan, Stern & Trajtenberg, 1996), whilst the hotelier can then build brand and loyalty from customers who have experienced the new differentiated service product.

Some of these have been well charted, others less so or more confined, to begin with, in certain national settings. Thus, Frehse's (2006) study explores the emergence of a new form of hotel type or segment, the spa or health hotel, as part of its adoption and (new product) development by hotel chains. The point here is that individual spa hotels have long been in existence right across Europe (Nagy, 2014) and beyond as early as the eighteenth century, with people

Table 29.1 New hotel formats, differentiation, segmentation and innovation

Price range	*Period*				
	Up to 1900	*1900–1945*	*1946–1979*	*1980–2010*	*2010–*
High					
Ultra-luxury	Grand hotel	Grand hotel	Grand hotel	Grand hotel	Grand hotel
			Foreign exclusive	Foreign exclusive	Foreign exclusive
Luxury		Country house hotel	Country house hotel	Country house hotel	Country house hotel
					Shabby chic hotel
				Boutique hotel	Boutique hotel
	Spa hotel	Spa hotel	Spa hotel	Spa hotel	Spa hotel
Mid-range			Mid-range hotel chain	Mid-range hotel chain	Mid-range hotel chain
	Seaside hotel	Seaside hotel	Seaside hotel	Seaside hotel	Seaside hotel
			Motel	Motel	
Economy				Budget hotel	Budget hotel
	Inn, tavern & pub	Inn, tavern & pub	Inn, tavern & pub	Inn, tavern & pub	Inn, tavern & pub
		Bed & breakfast	Bed & breakfast	Bed & breakfast	Bed & breakfast
Low	Lodging house	Lodging house	Lodging house	–	–

Source: Authors' construction.

wishing to stay in comfortable surroundings and enjoy the health benefits of the spa. However, their adoption by hotel chains has been much more recent and has involved combining them with scaleable versions of the spa experience, without the actual historic spa being present, and combining it with swimming pools and gyms taking up the increased health concerns of individuals from the 1970s and 1980s onwards.

Entrepreneurial networking and the role of the diaspora

Under conditions of Mode 1 Schumpeterian innovation, which the formation of new hotel forms and differentiation is about, innovation is closely linked with entrepreneurialism. This is in turn associated with leadership and vision, two qualities Schumpeter (1934) associated strongly with entrepreneurship (Fagerberg et al., 2012). Under these conditions, innovation is the outcome of the continuous struggle in historical times by key individual entrepreneurs advocating novel solutions to particular problems. This is not to suggest that all innovations develop under these conditions, but knowing the entrepreneur *and* the circles or networks they reside in and build is important in understanding how new innovative forms, such as new hotel types, are formed and developed. What is important here is that innovation and entrepreneurship are about knowing the individual *and* their network contexts. It is not just about the lone individual or just about the network; it is understanding them in combination. Understanding the former is important in the context of understanding the role of leadership and strategy, noted earlier. Understanding the latter is important because personal and inter-organisational network processes are where the exchanges of knowledge and experiences take place (Pechlaner, Fischer & Hammann, 2006, p. 52), which are important for how individual entrepreneurs gain wider cooperative support for their innovative experiments.

Novelli, Schmitz and Spencer (2006) found that networking and cooperation is a great advantage in developing new products and fostering innovation. This is supported by Grissemann, Pikkemaat and Weger (2013) who found that innovation behaviour is influenced by the innovation networks in which individuals and organisations are found. Innovation tends to increase when it is implemented together with external partners and collaborators. Thus, enterprises that engage in cooperation tend to have a significantly higher degree of innovation than those not engaged in cooperation. For hotels and tourism, the entrepreneur tends to be naturally bound up in a range of networks, associated with social, employment and supply chain relations. To achieve long-term competitiveness, various forms of synergistic cooperation are essential among the traditionally fragmented tourism providers. Cooperation not only helps to improve existing services but also benefits the creation of completely new synergistic innovative service experiences. As such, entrepreneurs have to recognise that the creation of new services and innovation is easier in cooperation or in a network with partners (Grissemann, Pikkemaat & Weger, 2013 p. 20). The formation and the maintenance of networks in tourism destinations is a challenge, but is important to achieve a competitive advantage in mature markets. Equally, those hotels and tourism ventures in weak networks and local innovation systems will find it difficult to develop new forms of innovative practices (Carson et al., 2014).

In this context Lowe et al. (2012, p. 1117) in a previous study use the term 'knowledgeable' individuals who are at the heart of self-organising networks and draw upon Baker et al.'s (2003) argument that entrepreneurial competencies are embedded in networks. Recent work by Nieves and Segarra-Ciprés (2015, p. 56) suggests it is the combination of both internal knowledge capacities of individuals within the firm, the hotel, and collaboration with external agents that enhance the likelihood of introducing new management innovation in the firm. In particular, the external social relationships of managers were found to be an important determinant on innovation (Nieves, Quintana & Osorio, 2014, p. 70). Sørensen (2007), however, in an interesting study of Malaga in southern Spain, found that social networks were both weak and ineffective as transmitters of new innovative practice.

The role of entrepreneurs in networks has been less well explored or acknowledged. The exception here is the actor-network research by Paget, Dimanche and Mounet (2010) of the Alpine ski resort, which highlights the role of the 'leader translator' (Paget et al., 2010, p. 840) in stimulating innovation in the resort area. However, there are few other studies of this enterprise-innovation nexus within the hotel and tourism sector. Certainly entrepreneurs starting up businesses characteristically 'introduce innovative practices an+d new technology that challenge incumbents' performance' (Blake, Sinclair & Soria, 2006, p. 1104), whether in the start-up stages or subsequent business spin-offs. These ideas have particular application to small hotels where resource constraints can be major obstacles to innovation (Lee-Ross, 1998; Enz, Canina & Walsh, 2006; Morrison and Conway, 2007).

The importance of this study is therefore highlighting the role of entrepreneurs, and in particular within the context of serial innovator-entrepreneur and social networks, the 'diasporic' network of original suppliers of private equity finance and entrepreneurs. In relation to both BHs and SCHs in the UK (Figure 29.2), the key founders had close personal links, and many had early-stage career experience of the industry through working in a single hotel, Chewton Glen (Gerard Bassett, Robin Hutson and Mike Warren) and, for many, in the subsequent Hotel du Vin (Ashley Levett, Gerard Bassett, Peter Chittock, Robin Cook, Robin Hutson, Vincent Gasnier) founded by Robert Hutson and Gerard Bassett in 1994.

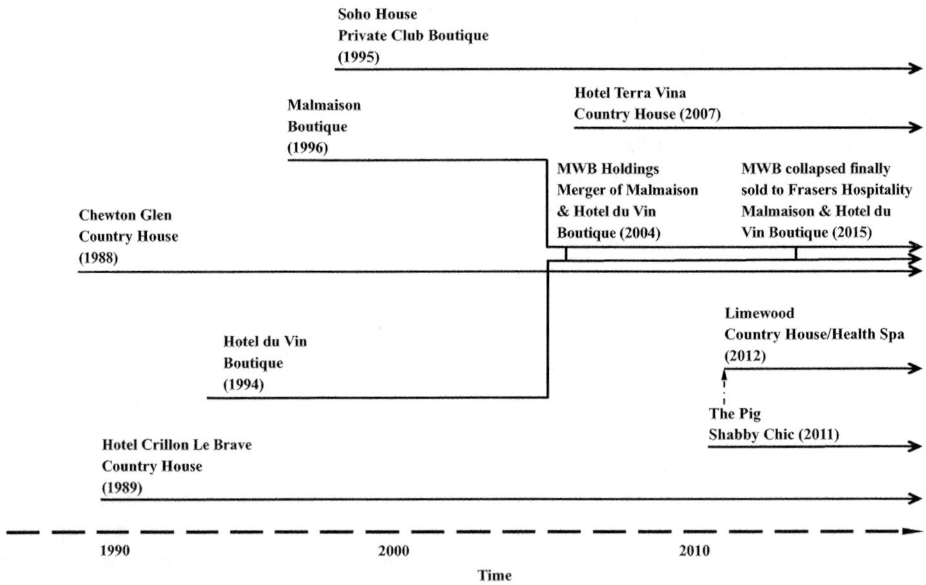

Figure 29.2 Innovation trajectories of UK boutique and shabby chic hotel diaspora

Source: Authors' construction.

A key 'animateur' in this whole network was the role of serial entrepreneur Robin Hutson, who worked initially at Chewton Glen and then went on to found the iconic boutique hotel chain, Hotel du Vin. Robin Huston subsequently sold Hotel du Vin, before going on to found The Pig in 2011 and having a stake in, and becoming the chairman of, The Limewood Hotel (part of the Lime Wood Group) established in 2012. There are now five Pig hotels as part of the Home Grown Hotels chain. The Malmaison chain, of which Robert Cook and Mike Warren were in senior management positions there (founded by Ken McCullough in Leigh also in 1994), merged with Hotel du Vin in 2004 when they became part of the MWB Group. Gerard Bassett then went on to create TerraVina Hotel in 2007. Peter Chittick set up his own hotel, Hotel Crillon Le Brave in Anjou, France in 1989, as well as becoming a shareholder and partner in Soho House. Vincent Gasnier also had links with Soho House as a wine consultant. Soho House & Company is somewhat an exception here in that it was founded by Nick Jones in 1995 as a boutique-led private members' club in London aimed at professionals working in the creative industries. It has subsequently expanded to cover clubs, restaurants, hotels and spas across the UK and overseas.

All seven of these key individuals played a major role in shaping the evolving country house, boutique and shabby chic hotel forms and sub-segments in the UK and internationally. Their 'teacher'/'student' relationships with each other, their entrepreneurship and financing of new hotel forms and their links in multiple forms across these chains all played an important part in the shaping of this innovative and lucrative hotel sub-market.

International diffusion of new service forms

The above has stressed the strong creative rush to develop these new hotel formats, but how should this be seen in an international context? As has been noted earlier, the earliest appearance of boutique and latterly shabby chic hotels has been in the United States and Europe and more particularly the west coast of the United States, the UK and certain Scandinavian countries.

This spread quite rapidly to other parts of the world including South Africa and parts of Asia (Rogerson, 2010). This international spread, however, has been largely driven through the experimentation, copying and imitation of individual hotel owners in specific countries. This is not surprising that both BHs and SCHs embody independent and unique ambiances that are difficult to replicate in an authentic way (and the inter-organisational diffusion of such models is therefore limited; Greenhalgh et al., 2004). This individual creative establishment and copying of these new service formats in separate national markets can be classed as a 'Type A' model of international new service diffusion.

Those BHs and SCHs that have in turn developed into burgeoning chains have naturally begun this process within their own domestic country realms, but have over time set up hotels in geographically or culturally adjacent countries. This is not an uncommon process in service oriented foreign direct investment (FDI) and multinational enterprise (MNE) strategic models (Dunning, 1989) and in this context relates more specifically to 'location bound' services that seek expansion through innovation-based comparative advantage (Enderwick, 2013). Thus, overseas expansion by these chains has therefore been gradual and exploratory moving into proximate markets either geographically or culturally or both. 'Reproduction' of such new organisational forms within multi-unit organisations (see Van der Aa & Elfring, 2002) remains challenging and even harder when it is overseas. Thus, Soho House has now established private clubs in seventeen locations in North America and Europe, but began such expansion in the UK and then the west coast of the United States. The model of international expansion in new service formats is therefore what might be termed a 'Type B' model of international new service diffusion.

It is, however, notable that large, multinational chains, by contrast, have found it difficult to move into this rapidly expanding hotel sector and have, at best, been laggards in its development. Thus, the Intercontinental Hotel Group (IHG), for example, established the Hotel Indigo chain in 2004 to provide quirky boutique and spa type offerings to compete in this market segment. In other cases, it is via more commonplace international acquisition strategies that lead boutique hotels to frequently end up as part of larger chains (Mun Lim & Endean, 2009). In the case of the Malmaison and Hotel du Vin chains, this was via poor husbandry as part of the MWB Group, and they fell into receivership in 2012. The group was finally bought out by Frasers Hospitality Group based in Singapore in 2015. This international, inter-organisational spread of new formats through being acquired by larger service MNEs can be defined as a 'Type C' model of international service format diffusion.

Either way, because of the tacit knowledge dimension of these innovative service market and group formats (Leonard & Sensiper, 1998; Howells, 2002), it makes them difficult to replicate and copy between different competitors as it so innately bound up with individual knowledge bases and behaviours (Vona & Consoli, 2015). The training of staff and the flexible HRM that allow creative, flexible, responsive and authentic interactions of staff with hotel clients is extremely difficult to instil and embody. This problem is true even within the new entrepreneurial chains themselves. This is because BH and SCH hotels try to create unique and original offerings that also stress authenticity. Chains or groups of hotels seeking to consistently recreate this format are therefore almost an anathema to the whole concept. This may explain why international growth of these formats has been so fragmentary.

Conclusion

This chapter seeks to make a contribution in three areas of research in service innovation and development, which cover the extant and overlapping realms of International Business and Economic Geography. First, existing literature surrounding the emergence of new service innovations has neglected issues around emergence and the formation of new niche markets and their international market trajectories. The hotel industry is an example of both the dynamics and trajectory of the sector being shaped by new market entrants and the development of new niche market forms led by entrepreneurs. However, this phenomenon has been largely neglected in the research literature (see Ioannides, 2006) as it has been lost in the gap between the interstices of two major research fields, innovation and entrepreneurship, which still largely remain separate (Metcalfe & Ramlogan, 2008; Autio et al., 2014). Moreover, these innovation formats and concepts sit uneasily between product-oriented service innovations and business model innovation and have been a neglected field of research (Howells, 2010). Nonetheless, this is now changing with a shift towards tourism in Economic Geography focusing on the role of innovation and evolution (Hassink & Ma, 2017) reflecting the wider impact of novelty and co-evolution in Economic Geography (see, for example, Martin & Sunley, 2007, 2010).

Second, it has been shown that the role of serial entrepreneurs and the community of entrepreneurs can have a profound impact in delivering new innovative service offerings and crucially shaping new markets. In the context of new hotel service offerings, the innovation process cannot be understood without understanding the process of entrepreneurial learning and diffusion. Within these entrepreneurial communities, the 'diaspora' (Lowe et al., 2012), both teacher and student entrepreneurs can help test new formats and also receive advice and financial support in setting up these new ventures (Rusanen, Halinen & Jaakkola, 2014; Sørensen & Fuglsang, 2014; Stam, Arzlanian & Elfring, 2014). Although over time, this dissipates as teachers learn from their students, and there is a close and ongoing interaction between them which can re-engage when new opportunities arise. Moreover, as has been shown, these evolving and innovative entrepreneurial networks can have a profound impact on developing new niches, which then become important markets and sub-markets over time.

Lastly, the spread of these new service concepts overseas has been outlined and explored through three different types of international diffusion models that have some similarities with wider service-led FDI models (see Davies & Guillin, 2014; Baena & Cerviño, 2015). However, the very process of creativity, uniqueness and authenticity of new hotel formats evident in BHs and SCHs make diffusion and overseas development of such concepts so difficult to replicate even through select social networks and diasporas (Ye, 2016). The difficult and tacit nature of the introduction and diffusion of such new forms makes their worth even more desirable and valued.

References

Aggett, M. (2007) 'What as influenced growth in the UK's boutique hotel sector?' *International Journal of Contemporary Hospitality Management*, 19, pp. 169–177.

Autio, E., Kenney, M., Mustar, P., Siegel, D. & Wright, M. (2014) 'Entrepreneurial innovation: The importance of context', *Research Policy*, 43, pp. 1097–1108.

Baena, V. & Cerviño, J. (2015) 'New criteria to select foreign entry mode choice of global franchise chains into emerging markets', *Procedia-Social and Behavioral Sciences*, 175, pp. 260–267.

Baker, T., Miner, A. & Eesley, D. (2003) 'Improvising firms: Bricolage, account giving and improvisational competencies in the founding process', *Research Policy*, 32, pp. 255–276.

Barras, R. (1986) 'Towards a theory of innovation in services', *Research Policy*, 15, pp. 161–173.

Baum, J.A.C. & Haveman, H.A. (1997) 'Love the neighbour? Differentiation and agglomeration in the Manhattan hotel industry', *Administrative Science Quarterly*, 42, pp. 304–338.

Bieger, T., Beritelli, P. & Laesser, C. (2009) 'Size matters! Increasing DMO effectiveness and extending tourist destination boundaries', *Turizam: Znanstveno-Stru ni Casopis*, 57, pp. 309–327.

Bilgihan, A., Okumus, F., Nusair, K. & Kwun, D. (2011) 'Information technology applications and competitive advantage in hotel companies', *Journal of Hospitality and Tourism Technology*, 2, pp. 139–153.

Blake, A., Sinclair, M.T. & Soria, J.A.C. (2006) 'Tourism productivity: Evidence from the UK', *Annals of Tourism Research*, 33, pp. 1099–1120.

Bower, J.L. & Christensen, C.M. (1995) 'Disruptive technologies: Catching the wave', *Harvard Business Review*, January-February, pp. 43–53.

Bresnahan, T.F., Stern, S. & Trajtenberg, M. (1996) 'Market segmentation and the sources of rents from innovation: Personal computers in the late 1980's', *RAND Journal of Economics*, 28, pp. S17–S44.

Bryson, J., Daniels, P. & Warf, B. (2013) *Service Worlds: People, Organisations, Technologies*. London: Routledge.

Buckley, P.J. & Ghauri, P.N. (2004) 'Globalisation, Economic Geography and the strategy of multinational enterprises', *Journal of International Business Studies*, 35, pp. 81–98.

Buhalis, D. & Law, R. (2008) 'Progress in information technology and tourism management: 20 years on and 10 years after the Internet – The state of e-tourism research', *Tourism Management*, 29, pp. 609–623.

Canina, L., Enz, C.A. & Harrison, J.S. (2005) 'Agglomeration effects and strategic orientations: Evidence from the U.S. lodging industry', *Academy of Management Journal*, 48, pp. 565–581.

Carlborg, P., Kindström, D. & Kowalkowski, C. (2014) 'The evolution of service innovation research: A critical review and synthesis', *The Service Industries Journal*, 34, pp. 373–398.

Carson, D.A., Carson, D.B. & Hodge, H. (2014) 'Understanding local innovation systems in peripheral tourism destinations', *Tourism Geographies*, 16, pp. 457–473.

Chang, S., Gong, Y. & Shum, C. (2011) 'Promoting innovation in hospitality companies through human resource management practices', *International Journal of Hospitality Management*, 30, pp. 812–818.

Chathoth, P., Altinay, L., Harrington, R.J., Okumus, F. & Chan, E.S. (2013) 'Co-production versus co-creation: A process based continuum in the hotel service context', *International Journal of Hospitality Management*, 32, pp. 11–20.

Christensen, C.M. (1997) *The Innovator's Dilemma*. New York: Collins.

Daniels, P.W. (1983) 'Service industries: Supporting role or centre stage?' *Area*, pp. 301–309.

Davies, R.B. & Guillin, A. (2014) 'How far away is an intangible? Services FDI and distance', *The World Economy*, 37, pp. 1731–1750.

Day, G.S. & Wensley, R. (2002) 'Market strategies and theories of the firm', in Weitz, B. & Wensley, R. (Eds.), *Handbook of Marketing*. London: Sage, pp. 85–105.

Dhar, R.L. (2015) 'The effects of high performance human resource practices on service innovative behaviour', *International Journal of Hospitality Management*, 51, pp. 67–75.

Dunning, J.H. (1989) 'Multinational enterprises and the growth of services: Some conceptual and theoretical issues', *Service Industries Journal*, 9, pp. 5–39.

Enderwick, P. (1987) 'The strategy and structure of service-sector multinationals: Implications for potential host regions', *Regional Studies*, 21, pp. 215–223.

Enderwick, P. (2013) 'Some economics of service-sector multinational enterprises', in Enderwick, P. (Ed.), *Multinational Service Firms*. London: Routledge, pp. 3–34.

Enz, C.A. Canina, L. & Walsh, K. (2006) *Intellectual Capital: A Key Driver of Hotel Performance*. Report by the Centre for Hospitality Research, Cornell University. Ithaca, NY: Cornell University.

Evangelista, R. & Savona, M. (2003) 'Innovation, employment and skills in services: Firm and sectoral evidence', *Structural Change and Economic Dynamics*, 14, pp. 449–474.

Fagerberg, J., Fosaas, M. & Sapprasert, K. (2012) 'Innovation: Exploring the knowledge base', *Research Policy*, 41, pp. 1132–1153.

Freel, M. (2016) *Knowledge-Intensive Business Services: Geography and Innovation*. London: Routledge.

Frehse, J. (2006) 'Innovative product development in hotel operations', *Journal of Quality Assurance in Hospitality & Tourism*, 6, pp. 129–146.

Gilmore, J.H. & Pine, B.J. (2002) 'Differentiating hospitality operations via experiences: Why selling services is not enough', *The Cornell Hotel and Restaurant Administration Quarterly*, 43, pp. 87–96.

Grant, R.M. (1991) 'The resource-based theory of competitive advantage: Implications for strategy formulation', *California Management Review*, 33, pp. 114–135.

Greenhalgh, T., Robert, G., Macfarlane, F., Bate, P. & Kyriakidou, O. (2004) 'Diffusion of innovations in service organizations: Systematic review and recommendations', *Milbank Quarterly*, 82, pp. 581–629.

Grinevich, V., Huber, F., Baines, L. & Eder, M. (2015). *Upscaling in the Sharing Economy: Insights from the UK*. Report by Centre for Excellence for Innovation and Enterprise, University of Southampton and Privatuniversitat Schloss Seeburg, Salzburg: University of Seeburg.

Grissemann, U.S., Pikkemaat, B. & Weger, C. (2013) 'Antecedents of innovation activities in tourism: An empirical investigation of the Alpine hospitality industry', *Turizam*, 61, pp. 7–27.

Gudis, C. (2013) 'I thought California would be different: Defining California through visual culture', in Deverell, W. & Igler, D. (Eds.), *A Companion to California History*. Chichester, UK: Wiley Blackwell, pp. 40–74.

Hassink, R. & Ma, M. (2017) 'Tourism area research and Economic Geography theories: Investigating the notions of co-evolution and regional innovation systems', in Brouder, P., Anton Clave, S., Gill, A. & Ioannides, D. (Eds.), *Tourism Destination Evolution*. London: Routledge, pp. 65–80.

Hertog, P., den Gallouj, F. & Segers, J. (2011) 'Measuring innovation in a "low-tech" service industry: The case of the Dutch hospitality industry', *The Service Industries Journal*, 31, pp. 1429–1449.

Hinterhuber, H. H. (2001) 'Wie fuhre ich mein Hotel in die Einzigartigkeit?' in Weiemair, K., Peters, M. and Reiger, E. (Eds.), *Vom Alten Zum Neuen Tourismus*. Innsbruck, Austria: Studiea, pp. 102–107.

Hoque, K. (2013) *Human Resource Management in the Hotel Industry: Strategy, Innovation and Performance*. London: Routledge.

Howells, J. (2002) 'Tacit knowledge, innovation and Economic Geography', *Urban Studies*, 39, pp. 871–884.

Howells, J. (2010) 'Services and innovation and service innovation: New theoretical directions', in Gallouj, F. & Djellal, F. (Eds.), *Handbook of Service Innovation*. Cheltenham, UK: Edward Elgar, pp. 69–83.

Howells, J. & Green, A.E. (1986) 'Location, technology and industrial organisation in UK services', *Progress in Planning*, 26, pp. 83–183.

Howells, J. & Tether, B. (2004) *Innovation in Services: Issues at Stake and Trends*. Final Report, Commission of the European Communities, Brussels.

Ioannides, D. (2006) 'The Economic Geography of the tourist industry: Ten years of progress in research and an agenda for the future', *Tourism Geographies*, 8, pp. 76–86.

Jeremiah, D. (2010) 'Motoring and the British countryside', *Rural History*, 21, pp. 233–250.

Lee-Ross, D. (1998) 'Comment: Australia and the small to medium-sized hotel sector', *International Journal of Contemporary Hospitality Management*, 10, pp. 177–179.

Leonard, D. & Sensiper, S. (1998) 'The role of tacit knowledge in group innovation', *California Management Review*, 40, pp. 12–132.

Love, J.H., Roper, S. & Hewitt-Dundas, N. (2010) 'Service innovation, embeddedness and business performance: Evidence from Northern Ireland', *Regional Studies*, 44, pp. 983–1004.

Lowe, M.S., Williams, A.M., Shaw, G. & Cudworth, K. (2012) 'Self-organizing innovation networks, mobile knowledge carriers and diasporas: Insights from a pioneering boutique hotel chain', *Journal of Economic Geography*, 12, pp. 1113–1138.

Martin, R. & Sunley, P. (2007) 'Complexity thinking and evolutionary Economic Geography', *Journal of Economic Geography*, 7, pp. 573–602.

Martin, R. & Sunley, P. (2010) 'The place of path dependence in an evolutionary perspective on the economic landscape', in Boschma, R. & Martin, R. (Eds.), *Handbook of Evolutionary Economic Geography*. Cheltenham, UK: Edward Elgar, pp. 62–92.

McCann, P. (2011) 'International Business and Economic Geography: Knowledge, time and transactions costs', *Journal of Economic Geography*, 11, pp. 309–317.

McGuffie, J. (1987) 'UK hotel industry: Revival for the chains at home and abroad', *Travel & Tourism Analyst*, (September), pp. 15–31.

Medina-Múñoz, R.D., Medina-Múñoz, D.R. & García-Falcón, J.M. (2003) 'Understanding European tour operators' control on accommodation companies: Empirical evidence', *Tourism Management*, 24, pp. 135–147.

Meliciani, V. & Savona, M. (2015) 'The determinants of regional specialisation in business services: Agglomeration economies, vertical linkages and innovation', *Journal of Economic Geography*, 15, pp. 387–416.

Metcalfe, J.S. (1998) *Evolutionary Economics and Creative Destruction*. London: Routledge.

Metcalfe, J.S. & Ramlogan, R. (2008) 'Innovation systems and the competitive process in developing economies', *Quarterly Review of Economics*, 48, pp. 433–446.

Miles, I. (2005) 'Innovation in services', in Fagerberg, J., Mowery, D. & Nelson, R.R. (Eds.), *The Oxford Handbook of Innovation*. Oxford, UK: Oxford University Press, pp. 433–458.

Morrison, A. & Conway, F. (2007) 'The status of the small hotel firm', *The Service Industries Journal*, 27, pp. 7–58.

Moulaert, F. & Gallouj, C. (1993) 'The locational geography of advanced producer service firms: The limits of economies of agglomeration', *Service Industries Journal*, 13, pp. 91–106.

Mun Lim, W. & Endean, M. (2009) 'Elucidating the aesthetic and operational characteristics of UK boutique hotels', *International Journal of Contemporary Hospitality Management*, 21, pp. 38–51.

Nagy, A. (2014) 'The orientation towards innovation of spa hotel management: The case of Romanian spa industry', *Procedia: Social and Behavioral Sciences*, 124, pp. 425–431.

Nieves, J., Quintana, A. & Osorio, J. (2014) 'Knowledge-based resources and innovation in the hotel industry', *International Journal of Hospitality Management*, 38, pp. 65–73.

Nieves, J. & Segarra-Ciprés, M. (2015) 'Management innovation in the hotel industry', *Tourism Management*, 46, pp. 51–58.

Novelli, M., Schmitz, B. & Spencer, T. (2006) 'Networks, clusters and innovation in tourism: A UK experience', *Tourism Management*, 26, pp. 1141–1152.

Orfila-Sintes, F. & Mattsson, J. (2009) 'Innovation behavior in the hotel industry', *Omega*, 37, pp. 380–394.

Ottenbacher, M., Vivienne, S. & Lockwood, A. (2006) 'An investigation of the factors affecting innovation performance in chain and independent hotels', *Journal of Quality Assurance in Hospitality & Tourism*, 6, pp. 113–128.

Paget, E., Dimanche, F. & Mounet, J.P. (2010) 'A tourism innovation case: An actor-network approach', *Annals of Tourism Research*, 37, pp. 828–847.

Pechlaner, H., Fischer, E. & Hammann, E-M. (2006) 'Leadership and innovation processes: Development of products and services based on core competencies', *Journal of Quality Assurance in Hospitality & Tourism*, 6, pp. 31–57.

Peters, M. & Frehse, J. (2005) 'The internationalization of the European hotel industry in the light of competition theories', *Tourism*, 53, pp. 55–65.

Pikkemaat, B. & Peters, M. (2006) 'Towards the measurement of innovation: A pilot study in the small and medium sized hotel industry', *Journal of Quality Assurance in Hospitality & Tourism*, 6, pp. 89–112.

Pope, R. (2000) 'A consumer service in interwar Britain: The hotel trade, 1924–1938', *Business History Review*, 74, pp. 657–682.

Preissl, B. (2000) 'Service innovation: What makes it different? Empirical evidence from Germany', in Metcalfe, J.S. & Miles, I. (Eds.), *Innovations Systems in the Service Economy*. Boston, MA: Kluwer Academic Publishers, pp. 125–148.

Roberts, J. (1999) 'The internationalisation of business service firms: A stages approach', *Service Industries Journal*, 19, pp. 68–88.

Rogerson, J.M. (2010) 'The boutique hotel industry in South Africa: Definition, scope, and organization', *Urban Forum*, 21, pp. 425–439.

Rusanen, H., Halinen, A. & Jaakkola, E. (2014) 'Accessing resources for service innovation: The critical role of network relationships', *Journal of Service Management*, 25, pp. 2–29.

Schoenberger, E. (1991) 'The corporate interview as a research method in Economic Geography', *The Professional Geographer*, 43, pp. 180–189.

Schumpeter, J.A. (1934) *The Theory of Economic Development: An Inquiry into Profits, Capital, Credit, Interest and the Business Cycle*. Cambridge, MA: Harvard University Press.

Schumpeter, J.A. (1943) *Capitalism, Socialism and Democracy*. New York: Harper and Brothers.

Sheldon, P.J. (1983) 'The impact of technology on the hotel industry', *Tourism Management*, 4, pp. 269–278.

Simmons, J. (1984) 'Railways, hotels and tourism in Great Britain 1839–1914', *Journal of Contemporary History*, 19, pp. 201–222.

Sirirak, S., Islam, N. & Ba Khang, D. (2011) 'Does ICT adoption enhance hotel performance?' *Journal of Hospitality and Tourism Technology*, 2, pp. 34–49.

Sørensen, F. (2007) 'The geographies of social networks and innovation in tourism', *Tourism Geographies*, 9, pp. 22–48.

Sørensen, F. & Fuglsang, L. (2014) 'Social network dynamics and innovation in small tourism companies', in McLeod, M. & Vaughan, R. (Eds.), *Knowledge Networks and Tourism*. London: Routledge, pp. 28–45.

Souto, J.E. (2015) 'Business model innovation and business concept innovation as the context of incremental innovation and radical innovation', *Tourism Management*, 51, pp. 142–155.

Stam, W., Arzlanian, S. & Elfring, T. (2014) 'Social capital of entrepreneurs and small firm performance: A meta-analysis of contextual and methodological moderators', *Journal of Business Venturing*, 29, pp. 152–173.

Stamboulis, Y. & Skayannis, P. (2003) 'Innovation strategies and technology for experience-based tourism', *Tourism Management*, 24, pp. 35–43.

Sundbo, J. & Gallouj, F. (2000) 'Innovation as a loosely coupled system in services', *International Journal of Service Technologies and Management*, 1, pp. 15–36.

Tajeddini, K. & Trueman, M. (2012) 'Managing Swiss hospitality: How cultural antecedents of innovation and customer-oriented values systems can influence performance in the hotel industry', *International Journal of Hospitality Management*, 11, pp. 1119–1129.

Teece, D.J. (2010) 'Business models, business strategy and innovation', *Long Range Planning*, 43, pp. 172–194.

Tether, B.S. (2005) 'Do services innovate (differently)? Insights from the European innobarometer survey', *Industry & Innovation*, 12, pp. 153–184.

Tsai, S.P. (2015) 'Driving holistic innovation to heighten hotel customer loyalty', *Current Issues in Tourism*, 20, pp. 1604–1619.

Urry, J. (1990) *The Tourist Gaze: Leisure and Travel in Contemporary Societies*. London: Sage.

Van der Aa, W. & Elfring, T. (2002) 'Realizing innovation in services', *Scandinavian Journal of Management*, 18, pp. 155–171.

Van de Ven, A. (2007) *Engaged Scholarship*. Oxford, UK: Oxford University Press.

Vona, F. & Consoli, D. (2015) 'Innovation and skill dynamics: A life-cycle approach', *Industrial and Corporate Change*, 24, pp. 1393–1415.

Wang, D., Chen, K.Y. & Chen, S.C. (2012) 'Total quality management, market orientation and hotel performance: The moderating effects of external environmental factors', *International Journal of Hospitality*, 31, pp. 119–129.

Ye, M. (2016) 'Utility and conditions of diffusion by diasporas: Examining foreign direct investment liberalization in China and India', *Journal of East Asian Studies*, 16, pp. 261–280.

Yelkur, R. & Nêveda DaCosta, M.M. (2001) 'Differential pricing and segmentation on the Internet: The case of hotels', *Management Decision*, 39, pp. 252–262.

30

THE INTERNATIONALIZATION OF PRODUCER SERVICES

Sharmistha Bagchi-Sen and Torsten Schunder

Introduction

Theoretical and empirical research explaining international transaction behavior of multinational enterprises (MNEs) continues to enhance our understanding of International Business. While mostly applied to manufacturing, an increasing body of literature explores foreign direct investment (FDI) in services, and especially cross-border investments in producer services as this specific subset of services is enabling other businesses to operate more successfully by supplying them with expertise. Advanced producer and professional service firms include financial, business, and ICT services and are facilitators of business, International Business, and globalization as they enable clients to expand, optimize, and work in global environments, and are a key measure of the importance and power of cities around the globe. Given this important key function in the global economy, we focus on this subset of the service industry in this chapter. Producer services distinguish themselves from other services by mainly serving the intermediate demand of producers rather than meeting the final demand of consumers. Financial and legal services, advertising, accounting, and insurance services are seen traditionally as part of this subgroup but now other creative services (e.g., including R&D services) supplying knowledge to other corporations are increasingly seen as part of this subgroup.

The service sector accounted for over 50% of GDP in high-income and middle-income nations in 2014. The share is increasing substantially in developing economies (World Bank, 2015) and constitutes a big part of global cross-border investments (UNCTAD, 2004). The formation of major trading blocs (i.e., NAFTA, EU) and increasing globalization have supported the growth of multinational firms in producer services (PS). Since 1995, cross-border mergers and acquisitions (M&As) in the service industry, except in 2011, have been responsible for more than 50% of the total global M&As. The PS sector comprises the majority of those service M&As (including financial, business, and ICT services). PS firms seem to be susceptible to economic downturns with a significant decline in their performance in the following periods: recession in the early 1990s, dot.com bust in 2002, and the 2007/2008 financial crisis.

In this chapter, we will explore what PS are, how they emerge in contextual relationship to manufacturing, and how they internationalize. In regards of internationalization, we explore the internationalization process, the motivation and entry modes of PS, the role of culture for PS internationalization, and how institutions affect PS. Additionally, we will examine the activities of PS in emerging/transitional economies, as well as the internationalization of PS from emerging/transitional economies.

Definition of PS

In contrast to manufacturing, services are characterized by intangibility, perishability, inseparability, and heterogeneity. Services are categorized into private (marketed) and public (nonmarketed) sectors (Enderwick, 1989). The private service sector contains profit-oriented business operations whereas the public service sector is nonprofit oriented. The marketed services are usually categorized as consumer (final demand) and producer (intermediate) services; however, these categories are not necessarily mutually exclusive, and a firm can fulfill intermediate and final demand. PS firms provide services to other business and government organizations (Beyers & Lindahl, 1996; Faulconbridge, Hall & Beaverstock, 2008). They have the expertise and experience to adapt to customer needs and are thus focused on flexible economies of scope (Enderwick, 1989). This constitutes the major difference within the service sector, meaning that companies have to adapt to the preferences and needs of different customer groups.

A variety of definitions of advanced producer exists in the literature. The OECD (2000) defines advanced PS/professional services (OECD) as all activities contained in the following International Standard Industrial Classification (ISIC) sub-groups: business and professional services, financial services, insurance services, and real estate services. The North American Industry Classification Systems (NAICS) classifies PS with the NAICS Codes 51, 52, and 54 (Table 30.1) (Thompson, 2004). All are characterized by mainly addressing intermediate demand serving businesses/producers rather than final demand.

Table 30.1 NAICS definitions

NAICS Code	*Description*	*Services*
51	Information	Telecommunications
		Internet service providers
		Web search portals
		Data processing services
		Broadcasters
		Motion picture and sound recording industries
		Publishers
52	Financial and insurance	Banks and financing
		Securities
		Commodity contracts
		Insurance carriers and related activities
		Funds and trusts
54	Professional, scientific, and technical services	Legal services
		Accounting
		Architecture
		Engineering
		Design services
		Computer systems design
		Management
		Scientific and technical consulting
		Advertising

Source: Based on Thompson (2004).

Other definitions seek to separate services based on their characteristics. Boddewyn, Halbrich and Perry (1986) distinguish services based upon locational mobility into three groups: (1) foreign tradeable services which generate products separable from the production process and are thus exportable (e.g., music and software); (2) location-bound services which are tied to the production process (e.g., hotel accommodation, retailing services, business and professional services, and commercial banking); and (3) combination services which are partially tradeable while other parts are location bound (e.g., in remote data-processing information from the customer is sent to the producer to be processed while input and delivery are location bound). Erramilli (1991) divides internationally traded services into hard and soft services where hard services are characterized by production that is separable from consumption, and soft services are simultaneously produced and consumed which has implications for the facilities needed to create and deliver services. For hard services, service production and delivery are not bound to a specific location, whereas soft services require the compresence of producer and consumer. Others (Contractor, Kundu & Hsu, 2003; Sanchez-Peinado, Pla-Barber & Hébert, 2007) divide services into knowledge-intensive services and capital-intense services, where capital intensity represents the volume of investment in fixed assets that are necessary to begin production and operations in a given industry (Erramilli & Rao, 1993). Capital intensive services require substantial equipment investments resulting in internationalization patterns similar to patterns found in manufacturing. Knowledge-intensive firms do not require substantial equipment investment in the host country, and thus traditional variables influencing international trade patterns might be not applicable.

A subgroup of knowledge-intensive services are Knowledge-Intensive Business Services (KIBS) containing a range of services from ICT and software services to R&D services. Definitions are based on the share of non-routine tasks, formal education, and patent activity in an industry (Zieba, 2013) (see Table 30.2).

Table 30.2 Definitions of knowledge-intensive business services (KIBS)

Author	*KIBS definition*	*KIBS characteristics*
Miles et al. (1995)	"services that involved economic activities which are intended to result in the creation, accumulation or dissemination of knowledge"	– They rely on professional knowledge to a great extent – They either are themselves primary sources of information/knowledge or they use knowledge to produce intermediate services for their clients' production processes – They are of competitive importance and supplied primarily to business
Den Hertog (2000)		– Private companies/organizations – They rely on knowledge or expertise related to a specific (technical) discipline or (technical) functional domain – They supply intermediate products and services that are knowledge based

(continued)

Table 30.2 (continued)

Author	*KIBS definition*	*KIBS characteristics*
Toivonen (2004)	"those services provided by businesses to other businesses or to the public sector in which expertise plays an especially important role"	– They have numerous and versatile contacts with different stakeholders – They form a node in a system of customers, cooperation partners, public institutions, and R&D establishments
Pardos, Gomex-Loscos and Rubiera-Morollon (2007)	"personalized services that offer a relatively diversified range with high quality provision"	– They imply an important connection with information, new technologies, new management, new production/sales techniques to new markets
Koch and Strotmann (2008)	"highly application-oriented services (in which) tacit knowledge plays an important role"	– They require specialized knowledge and cumulative learning processes
Consoli and Elche-Hortelano (2010)	"intermediary firms which specialize in knowledge screening, assessment and evaluation, and trade professional consultancy services"	– Intermediary firms – Specialize in knowledge screening, assessment and evaluation – Trade their service in the form of consultancy – Integrate knowledge, particularly tacit knowledge into a tradable output

Source: Zieba 2013, p. 5.

It must be noted that the industries included in the above definitions vary considerably. This relates to the degree of standardization of products, which is for example relatively higher in accounting than in consulting. Business interactions differ as well as the length of service delivery. Whereas law and accounting firms often have continuous relationships with clients, other companies such as those in engineering consulting, often are project-based (Ball, Lindsay & Rose, 2008; Abecassis-Moedas et al., 2012; Faulconbridge & Jones, 2012). The output of services also differs considerably resulting in different degrees of exportability – whereas blueprints and digital media can be easily transported, contextual information can be effectively communicated mostly in an interactive face-to-face environment (Ball, Lindsay & Rose, 2008; Rugman & Verbeke, 2008), thus encouraging FDI. These differences result in different internationalization pathways and modes as well as how different types of producer services enter and engage with international markets. The heterogeneity of the service sector and the increasing complexity of its clients make it difficult to apply a single theory or conceptual framework to explain the patterns of internationalization in the past twenty years.

Growth of producer services

Traditionally, the growth of a producer service complex in a country is seen as a function of linkages between manufacturing and producer services. Guerrieri and Meliciani (2005) investigate the relationship between industrial specialization and international competitiveness of PS (e.g., financial, communication, and business services) using country-level data. ICT usage, labor cost, and the use of services as intermediary inputs in manufacturing and services are discussed as determinants of competitiveness. They use country-level data from OECD and Eurostat including ICT expenditures (i.e., the GDP share of information and communication gross fixed capital formation), intermediate use of services within manufacturing specialization captured by calculating specialization in manufacturing weighted by the use of services by manufacturing industries and services, and labor cost (i.e., costs measured as the share of labor costs in total production costs). They find that a country's PS sector competitiveness depends on a specialized manufacturing sector using PS. Countries with specialized manufacturing industries relying heavily on PS have advantages reinforcing growth and competitiveness in PS. On the other hand, Dicken (2007) shows that more than 50% of the output from service industries is sold to other service industries, indicating that service firms are significant contributors to the growth of the overall service sector and these consumers are driving the demand (Beyers, Alvine & Johnson, 1985; Goe, 1990; Bagchi-Sen & Sen, 1997; Sako, 2015). However, in emerging markets, the strong relationship between industries and services might remain a major factor in the development of the producer/professional service industry.

Demand for producer/professional services is driven by changes in production inputs, composition, and changes in regulations in a country (Thompson, 2004; Faulconbridge, Hall & Beaverstock, 2008; Xinya, Jie & Ye, 2011). Also, technological developments (e.g., mobility, communication, ICT) fostering global trade and the expansion of multinational corporations have influenced the growth in PS (Sassen, 2001; Guerrieri & Meliciani, 2005; Dicken, 2007). The development of ICT has allowed service firms to separate tasks such as routine or standardized back-office functions and specialized or front office functions (Zaheer & Manrakhan, 2001; Roberts, 2002; Ball, Lindsay & Rose, 2008); back office functions have often moved offshore.

As companies become more specialized to fulfill a growing market for differentiated products, business functions are also externalized to reduce cost, increase efficiency, and gain access to specialized knowledge (Noyelle & Stanback, 1984; Piore, 1986; Thompson, 2004). This process of externalization has continued to influence the growth of PS. While organizational structures change and organizational complexity increases in a global economy, the need for (internationalized) professional services goes up (Bagchi-Sen & Sen, 1997; Roberts, 2002):

> The demand-side factors include the increasing differentiation of goods and services, emphasis on how diverse goods and services are being produced, the complex international and national business environment, government intervention and regulation, the growing internal complexity of the firm, cost considerations, flexibility, risk reduction, and the need for specialized expertise driving the share of indirect labor involved in production. The supply-side factors have been associated with advances in telecommunications, information, and computer technology and the capability of PSF [Producer Service Firms] to recognize business opportunities, changing buyer needs, changes in government regulations, and in input costs.
>
> *(Bagchi-Sen & Sen, 1997, p. 1155)*

While a strong focus on FDI from developed economies exists, Gammeltoft (2008) showed by analyzing outward FDI from the BRIC and related nations that India invests in ICT and broadcasting, China in trade and services, South Africa in finance, and Brazil in all types of services. Nevertheless, market expansion of the service sector has been predominantly local (Beyers, Alvine & Johnson, 1985; Rugman & Verbeke, 2008). The degree of internationalization of service MNEs compared to manufacturing is complex given the need for local adaptation (Rugman & Verbeke, 2008). Thus, service firms are more likely to remain local or engage in their home market due to low cultural and institutional distance. The nonlocal market expansion is driven by specific considerations. In developed economies changes in industrial organization, changes in household structure, growth in income, the income elasticity of demand, and labor productivity in services are important factors for growth in the PS sector (Bagchi-Sen & Sen, 1997). In the context of emerging economies, growth in PS is driven by manufacturing industries and the absolute market size but also by the demand of developed nations for outsourcing to access skilled professionals at relatively lower wages compared to their home markets (Tuan & Ng, 2003; Outreville, 2008).

Explanations of internationalization of producer services

Theories of FDI by MNEs explain why business enterprises invest in other countries instead of trading in goods and services (Kindleberger, 1969; Buckley & Casson, 1976; Hymer, 1976; Dunning, 1979, 1993; Rugman, 1981; Caves, 1996; Bagchi-Sen & Sen, 1997; Coffey, 2000; Faulconbridge, Hall & Beaverstock, 2008; Taylor et al., 2014). Key elements explaining the emergence of MNEs, such as firm-specific or ownership-specific advantages, location-specific advantages, and internalization advantages have been identified and combined by Dunning (1989, 1993) in his eclectic paradigm (referred to as the OLI concept). A combination of those advantages and sectoral specificities 'determine the pattern, extent, and growth of MNE activities' (Bagchi-Sen & Sen, 1997, p. 1157).

The OLI concept combines firm-specific or ownership-specific advantages, location-specific advantages, and internalization advantages. Ownership-specific advantages are a product of the home market environment – imperfect markets favor those with competitive advantages such as patented technology, unpatented, secret know-how, large capital requirements, economies of large-scale production, and expertise in differentiating products. These firms are often fierce competitors in the host country and can offset the cost of involvement in a foreign market. In this concept, large firms erect barriers to entry for smaller firms, and internationalization decisions are often based on competitors following to protect market share and to minimize risks (Bagchi-Sen & Sen, 1997). Nachum (2003a) argues that not all firms in a home country can exploit specific advantages; firm characteristics determine competitiveness based on how firms can actively shape advantages to facilitate national and international operations.

Firm-specific or ownership-specific advantages alone cannot explain the decision to engage in FDI. Firms engage in FDI if internalization of operations (e.g., production activities) or knowledge provides the firm with advantages in exploiting a firm-specific advantage by either protecting knowledge, ensuring quality, facilitating the flow of intermediaries, or reducing opportunistic behavior by high degrees of control (Rugman, 1981; Caves, 1996; Buckley & Casson, 2009; Hennart, 2010). Industries relying on strong customer interaction are considered more likely to engage in FDI (Oldenski, 2012). Oldenski (2012) expands the proximity-concentration trade-off literature exploring the decision between FDI and export by evaluating the cost of communicating complex information using a two-level OLS estimator on inward US FDI in manufacturing and services from the Bureau of Economic Analysis and secondary data about exports derived from the U.S. Census (BEA survey). While communication intensity is related to FDI, complex information activities (non-routine) are more likely to be sold via export. This might represent the comparative advantage of the US regarding human capital. The author concludes that FDI has a hidden cost in the form of communication cost of complex information adding to traditional transportation cost and transaction cost. The effect is stronger than GDP, distance, tax rates, wages, institutions, or education variables.

Location-specific factors such as policies (e.g., trade barriers), market size, input costs, and factor productivity affect FDI decisions. The existence of trade barriers, for example, favors the establishment of local subsidiaries. Producers, especially professional services, are known as key elements of command

Table 30.3 Global cities

Global cities
Functionally comprehensive global cities
(1) Leading duo: London and New York (2) Smaller contribution and with cultural bias: Los Angeles, Paris, and San Francisco (3) Incipient global cities: Amsterdam, Boston, Chicago, Madrid, Milan, Moscow, and Toronto
Global niche cities – specialized global contributions
(1) Economic: Hong Kong, Singapore, and Tokyo (2) Political and social: Brussels, Geneva, and Washington, DC
World cities sub-net articulator cities
(1) Cultural: Berlin, Copenhagen, Melbourne, Munich, Oslo, Rome, and Stockholm (2) Political: Bangkok, Beijing, and Vienna (3) Social: Manila, Nairobi, and Ottawa
World-wide leading cities
(1) Primarily economic global contributions: Frankfurt, Miami, Munich, Osaka, Singapore, Sydney, and Zurich (2) Primarily non-economic global contributions: Abidjan, Addis Ababa, Atlanta, Basle, Barcelona, Cairo, Denver, Harare, Lyon, Manila, Mexico City, Mumbai, New Delhi, and Shanghai

Source: Taylor, 2005, p. 1606.

and control functions within the global world city hierarchy (Sassen, 2001; Taylor, 2004). Taylor (2005) examines a dataset of 446 MNEs from the Fortune 500 and creates a taxonomy of global cities (Table 30.3). Frankfurt, Chicago, Tokyo, New York, and London are at the top of the hierarchy, but there are considerable differences across service sectors, and thus no global service geography exists (Taylor, 2004, 2005). Service patterns are thus products of distinctive origins and uneven opportunities.

The applicability of FDI theories derived from manufacturing examples to services is contested (Brouthers & Brouthers, 2003; Tuan & Ng, 2003; Ramasamy & Yeung, 2010). While Ramasamy and Yeung (2010) concluded that the determinants for both manufacturing and service sectors are similar and that established FDI theories can be applied to the service sector, others argue that both sectors differ considerably. Characteristics of services (e.g., intangibility, perishability, inseparability, and heterogeneity) require special attention in the application of established FDI theories limiting their explanatory power. Furthermore, service MNEs differ from manufacturing MNEs regarding size (e.g., service MNEs being smaller) and scope of activities. Based on transaction cost theory, Brouthers and Brouthers (2003) argue that manufacturing and service industries differ regarding their reaction to transaction costs. Analyzing 227 cases of German, Dutch, and British service and manufacturing companies involved in Central and East European countries, Brouthers and Brouthers (2003) find that the entry mode choice of manufacturing is strongly influenced by risk propensity and environmental uncertainty due to their capital intensive nature, while service firms are influenced by trust propensity and asset specificity due to their reliance on people and interaction.

Rugman and Verbeke (2008) analyzed the flexibility of value chains of manufacturing and service MNEs and concluded that manufacturing MNEs have greater flexibility in separating their up and downstream activities, while in service MNEs upstream and downstream activities are closely linked together in a complex system requiring local adaptation. Regulation and liability of foreignness constitute high barriers to entry leading to a lower degree of internationalization of service MNEs, and the authors conclude that the degree of globalization of service MNEs is low preferring investments in spaces culturally and institutional close to the country of origin.

While differences between services and manufacturing are widely discussed, it must be noted that interdependencies between those sectors exist given that the manufacturing industry is a major client of producer services. Analyzing the determinants of inward FDI in business services across European regions, Castellani, Meliciani and Mirra (2016) find that at the regional level, adjusting for spatial effects and including country dummy variables, only market size measured using GDP and the existence of manufacturing industries are significant explanatory variables explaining the location of business service FDI. They acknowledge that variables differ across spatial scales and while traditional determinants work at the country level, the location within a country is ultimately driven by demand.

Tuan and Ng (2003) analyze the impact of agglomerations on manufacturing and service FDI flows in China based on Krugman's core-periphery model. The analysis of a joint venture dataset of firms (e.g., 15.5% are service joint ventures) who invested in Guangdong shows that the location of FDI in manufacturing and services is highly correlated. In contrast, Jones and Wren (2016) find that service and manufacturing FDI in the UK have distinct patterns with no evidence that the location of FDI in services converges with the location of manufacturing FDI over time. Trade and investment data of FDI inflows from 1996–2005 are obtained from the UK government agencies for the above study.

A capability approach and a network approach based on organizational learning and organizational resources, and embeddedness in institutional and relational contexts, supplement the framework focused on firm-specific advantages (Nachum, 2003b; Reihlen & Apel, 2007). The capabilities approach emphasizes intra-organizational dynamic learning enhancing the capabilities (managerial or organizational) via experiential knowledge, defined as 'knowledge that firms accumulate by being active in foreign markets' (Blomstermo et al., 2004, p. 356). Thus firms become more experienced and exposed to new knowledge by acquiring assets such as human talent or local knowledge in foreign locations. Tacit knowledge is an important driver of internationalization, and building tacit firm capabilities via internationalization supports subsequent internationalization enhancing capabilities iteratively as Scott-Kennel and von Batenburg (2012) show by exploring the importance of knowledge and learning in internationalization, studying a weather forecast service firm. Based on a constructivist perspective, learning in producer service firms is a result of local socio-cultural embeddedness and interaction, and the establishment of networks (Reihlen & Apel, 2007).

Networking enables firms to establish relationships, actively seek clients, and learn from partners (O'Farrell, Wood & Zheng, 1998). The production of services requires 'multiple simultaneous inputs and feedbacks' (Sassen, 2001, p. 71) making embeddedness in networks with immediate access to experts/assets a competitive advantage (Sassen, 2001; Ball, Lindsay & Rose, 2008) – these networks require trust and reciprocity to be functional (Glückler & Armbrüster, 2003; Hanlon, 2004). Face-to-face communication with colleagues, clients, competitors, and other agents is the main mode of knowledge transfer (Beaverstock, 2004; Kipping and Clark, 2012) and is additionally relevant in building trust, quality control, and acquiring clients. Markets are characterized by institutional and transactional uncertainty, and networks based on trust and reputation allow clients to reduce uncertainty. Networks increase competitive advantages in internationalization, determining access to information/clients and local knowledge, and often reduce uncertainty by providing access to customers from the home country who are also engaged in the same host region targeted by the internationalized PS firm (Jung, 2004; Ball et al., 2008; Freeman & Sandwell, 2008; Faulconbridge & Jones, 2012). Guler and Guillén (2010) find that the higher the network centrality of a firm, a representation of its social status and brokerage relationships measured by co-investments, the greater the likelihood of foreign market entry. Those results are reinforced by Spies (2010) who finds that common borders, local demand, as well as existing firm networks, determine the location of foreign companies in Germany.

The topic of supply chains in producer services is not widely addressed (Ellram, Tate & Billington, 2004; Baltacioglu et al., 2007). In contrast to manufacturing industries, service MNEs face a sector-specific complex relationship between closely linked upstream and downstream activities requiring local adaptation for both value chains. Thus both upstream and downstream value chains are subject to market regulations (e.g., banking) and liability of foreignness, resulting in lower degrees of internationalization of service firms and an investment concentration in the home region facilitated by low cultural and institutional distance. However, the separability of service tasks is enhanced by technological progress enabling the internationalization of advanced PS (Zaheer & Manrakhan, 2001; Roberts, 2002; Ball, Lindsay & Rose, 2008). Knowledge-intensive services with a high degree of heterogeneity cannot easily separate activities of the value chain – a highly integrated service supply chain adapted to the specificities of an industry sector has to consider information flow, capacity and skill management, relationship management with suppliers and customers, cash flow, delivery, as well as technology and information management as they consider internationalization (Ellram, Tate & Billington, 2004; Baltacioglu et al., 2007).

The internationalization process

The internationalization process of producer services is characterized by the decision to enter a foreign market, market selection, and the choice of entry mode, product, and market diversification strategies (Coffey, 2000). Historically, empirical research on the internationalization process of service firms focused mostly on banking and finance and on professional and business services, but increasingly specialized studies of subgroups of PS have been conducted showing the variability and differences between divergent service industries and their varying internationalization strategies. A variety of studies continues to assess specific service sectors outlining the determinants and pathways to internationalization within sub-groups (Sanchez-Peinado, Pla-Barber & Hébert, 2007; Castellani, Meliciani & Mirra, 2016): design, executive staffing, and engineering consultancy, real estate, banking, and insurance (Wu & Strange, 2000; Lai & Fischer, 2007; Faulconbridge, Hall & Beaverstock, 2008; Outreville, 2008; Abecassis-Moedas et al., 2012).

Key resources in internationalization vary across firms and sectors. Abecassis-Moedas et al. (2012) analyzed interviews with 11 European design consultancies, which is an example of KIBS, to identify key resources in their internationalization process. They identified three distinctive categories of firms and resource sets to be relevant. Star-based creative KIBS (e.g., architecture) rely on the reputation/talent of a specific designer establishing contact with customers via popularity/competitions and international exhibitions. Process-based creative KIBS rely on organizational capital mainly represented as formalized creative collective processes and methods which are exported to their customers via human capital or import of clients. Glocality-based creative KIBS rely on physical capital (field offices) and organizational capital maintaining direct relationships with their clients while better understanding their needs via localized market research and expanding their services to other clients with similar needs in the host market.

Human capital, that is, professionals embodying knowledge, skills, practice, and trustworthiness, is a major factor in advertising and marketing services. Thus, employee talent, reputation, and experience have a significant impact on the firm's reputation (Beaverstock, 2004;

Hitt et al., 2006; Abecassis-Moedas et al., 2012). Hitt et al. (2006) highlight the role of resources in the internationalization of professional business firms by analyzing the performance of 72 law firms. Resources are defined as human capital resources in the form of partner education and experience, client relational capital in the form of the number of top 250 US firms a company has a relationship with, and relational capital with foreign government based on lawsuits represented. They show that human capital and client relational capital interact and affect internationalization positively. Corporate client relational capital, along with high levels of human capital advantages, are effective in enhancing performance. Human capital positively affects firm performance in the context of internationalization (measured as the ratio of worldwide net income to total firm revenue), and a similar effect can be found for client relational capital. Government client relational capital is associated with lower levels of performance. While the interaction term of human capital and internationalization positively affects performance, interaction terms of internationalization and relational capital (corporate and government) show no moderating influence on firm performance.

Motivating factors

The literature identifies diverse not mutually exclusive motivations and strategical considerations for the internationalization of producer service firms. Internationalization decision and entry modes for knowledge-intensive services are driven by strategic considerations of global markets and exploitation, whereas strategic considerations are, except for client following, less important for capital intensive services (Sanchez-Peinado, Pla-Barber & Hébert, 2007). Resource-oriented approaches are only feasible for highly standardized elements of the service production, while relocation of specific aspects of the value chain in services (e.g., KIBS) relying heavily on face-to-face contact, trust, and tacit knowledge, are market oriented (Roberts, 2002). Motivations for internationalization can be active or passive (Ball, Lindsay & Rose, 2008). Passive forms include following clients, which is driven by internationally operating clients of a firm and the necessity to provide services abroad to prevent the loss of business to foreign or other domestic competitors. Following domestic competitors is a protective form of internationalization driven by the interest to protect overall market share. Active forms of internationalization are driven by strategic considerations of market exploitation, customer/market seeking, and asset acquisition, whereas the latter relates to human capital, knowledge, location, prestige, or network access (Jung, 2004, Faulconbridge & Jones, 2012). Other factors influencing the internationalization decision and motivation are the risk propensity, attitude, and experience of a company's management as well as the personal disposition of decision makers (Herrmann & Datta, 2006).

Producer service firms internationalize to increase their global influence, gather intelligence for innovation, gain market knowledge, and improve connectedness of markets (Faulconbridge, Hall & Beaverstock, 2008; Sassen, 2011; Taylor et al., 2014). Specific locations provide innovative advantages due to their specific resource endowment. While New York, London, and Hong Kong foster financial innovation (Lai, 2012), Palo Alto fosters innovation in deal making, start-up advisory, venture capital access, and M&A activities (Reiffenstein, 2009; Taylor et al., 2014). While acquiring new knowledge helps these firms diversify with new knowledge-intensive products, new markets are characterized by uncertainty. These realities motivate firms to develop specialized market knowledge and can be seen as an asset-seeking strategy with regards to specific resources.

Consumer perception of quality and reputation are important factors for the success of professional service firms and essential in acquiring clients. To ensure high levels of quality, PSFs tend to internalize processes leading to the establishment of subsidiaries to exert control

(Coffey, 2000; Hennart, 2010). PS firms require high degrees of customization and interaction with clients thus requiring intensive contact and exchange of ideas in intra- and inter-organizational communication – therefore, the need for proximity leads to internationalization.

Client following is an important motivation and protective form of internationalization. Firms internationalize to follow clients preventing the loss of business to foreign or domestic competitors. This not only fulfills the demand of the internationalized client but also reduces the risk of internationalization for the service firm by providing initial customers in the new market (Ball, Lindsay & Rose, 2008). US accounting firms, for example, started following their clients in the 1950s (Bagchi-Sen & Sen, 1997).

Changing institutional environments provides opportunities attracting PSFs, and changes are accommodated by an increasing presence of foreign firms taking advantage of economic integration and deregulation. PSFs tend to enter those countries to exploit arising opportunities or in anticipation of change. For example, after China became a WTO member, multinational banks become more involved (Xiaogang, Skully & Brown, 2005). The case of the Chinese real estate industry shows that international companies entered the market in anticipation of change. With developments in ICT, PSFs are increasingly able to separate tasks of the value chain allowing them to pursue an international division of labor, thereby profiting from wage differentials and professional labor pools. This affects standardized functions like accounting and software which are outsourced/offshored to India, while data processing relocates to the Philippines and the Caribbean (Sanderson et al., 2015). Non-routine tasks and front office functions are not outsourced.

Increasing market presence is another motivation. Large PSFs tend to establish a presence in major cities globally to establish and project their reputation and can be found in accounting (big four), financial institutions, and staffing agencies (Beaverstock, 1996; Coe, Johns & Ward, 2007; Wójcik, 2011). First- mover advantages can be observed for the advertisement industry – firms with previous international experience can exploit them indicating that firms with a vast subsidiary network develop competitive advantages through international experience, and although such advantages cannot universally be observed among PSFs, in certain cases it might motivate expansion (Magnusson, Westjohn & Boggs, 2009).

Entry mode

Multinational producer service firms' entry modes in overseas markets depend on the regulatory constraints as well as the institutional and cultural distance of the host country (Faulconbridge, Hall & Beaverstock, 2008). Depending on firm strategy, entry modes may include fully owned offices (e.g., traditional FDI, greenfield, or acquisition), joint ventures/cooperation with a local partner, licensing, or export market development (Ball, Lindsay & Rose, 2008). These entry modes coincide with literature related to the overall service sector, although the analysis of the overall service sector still emphasizes producer services (Grönroos, 1999). The transaction costs associated with each mode decrease with higher resource commitment, hence opportunism is reduced with higher levels of control (Hennart, 2010). In the context of advanced producer and professional services, a high interaction intensity with clients is assumed requiring frequent face-to-face contact with clients, thus favoring permanent foreign facilities. This view is challenged by Ball, Lindsay and Rose (2008), who claim that advanced services have less resource-intensive ways of entering foreign markets. While elements of the service delivery process requiring customer interaction are either exported or located in a host country, other unrelated parts of the service delivery process (e.g., data processing and analysis) can be located at different locations given a sufficient ICT infrastructure. ICT facilitates the separation of tasks in the value chain and thereby reduces the need for resource-intensive involvement.

Different entry modes across a company's portfolio are not mutually exclusive, and companies might follow different strategies in different markets depending on its global expansion strategy (McQuillan & Scott, 2015). Faulconbridge, Hall and Beaverstock (2008) show, for example, that firms might maintain full subsidiaries only in strategic places (e.g., Frankfurt, London, and New York) while use less resource intense entry modes in less strategic places. Determining factors for entry mode choice are (perceived) risk (economic, political) and transaction cost considerations, and especially in the context of advanced services, human capital, market size, and market potential (Tuan & Ng, 2003; Outreville, 2008; Njegomir & Stojic, 2012). Firm size is an important determinant in entry mode decision (Tuan & Ng, 2003). Large firms have considerable resources and managerial capabilities favoring fully owned subsidiaries; smaller companies often lack the resources to establish resource intensive operations in foreign markets, thus relying on export markets or collaborations to mitigate risk and reduce the cost of involvement. Firm experience and strategy influence the choice as well as the individual experience of decision makers (Herrmann & Datta, 2006; Abecassis-Moedas et al., 2012; Muzychenko & Liesch, 2015). Increasing international experience endows firms with tacit knowledge enhancing the possibilities of gaining from further internationalization. Strategies and motives are also associated with entry modes. Global business approaches, asset exploitation motives, and experience with previous full control modes, for example, are associated with a preference for full control modes. Firms with previous experience in shared control modes are more prone to shared control modes if they have explorative or offensive/aggressive strategies (Sanchez-Peinado, Pla-Barber & Hébert, 2007).

The characteristics of individuals in a firm can have a significant impact on internationalization and entry mode choice. CEOs have substantial influence and act based on experience (e.g., tenure, age, internationalization). Studying internationalization events, Herrmann and Datta (2006) find that age and experience are associated with the use of joint ventures and a lower risk propensity, whereas CEOs with increasing international experience tend to prefer high control modes favoring greenfield investments over acquisitions. CEOs with a background in operations and finance tend to prefer acquisitions over other entry modes given their increased experience with financial tools. In smaller firms, entrepreneurs have a substantial impact on internationalization due to their ability to realize opportunities and use these based on perceived risk (Muzychenko & Liesch, 2015). Additionally, individual factors like a desire for cross-cultural encounters support opportunity identification from relationship-building experiences. Business models can be built around the talent and reputation of a single individual and can be found in creative industries such as architecture. In this case, contact with customers is established via popularity/competitions, invitations, and international exhibitions, thus making the internationalization highly dependent on the contacts and reputation of a single person (Abecassis-Moedas et al., 2012; McQuillan & Scott, 2015).

Cultural distance

Cultural distance, predominantly measured by the Hofstede Index or five dimensions, is a recurring decisive factor for market selection and an important determinant for intrafirm communication, whereas large distances are disadvantages causing friction (Capar & Kotabe, 2003; Nachum, 2003a; Boussebaa, 2009). Services delivered in a host country need to be adapted to the local specific demand requiring adaptation to cultural and linguistic differences thereby increasing transaction cost (liability of foreignness) (Capar & Kotabe, 2003). Liability of foreignness applies to services and represents all tacit and social costs of getting involved in foreign markets that are not incurred by local companies (Zaheer, 1995; Zaheer & Mosakowski, 1997) and is decreasing over time with increased adaptation and local acceptance. Cultural proximity encourages FDI, while with increasing distance other modes become more likely. Jung (2004) specifically analyzed the impact of cultural distance on the decision between joint ventures and wholly owned subsidiaries, finding that with increasing cultural distance joint ventures with local partners are sought to minimize risk and rely on local networks to access local knowledge and acquire customers. Networking with clients and adaptation (services and routines) can help offset these costs as Freeman and Sandwell (2008) show using three case studies of professional service firms from Australia entering emerging markets. Firms rely on social networks to overcome entry barriers (e.g., face-to-face communication, language, cultural, work practices, and government regulations) using local contacts to overcome the liability of foreignness. Collaborative entry or client following reduces cost allowing a reputation to be gained while already serving established clients from the home country (Ball, Lindsay & Rose, 2008). Nachum (2003b) questions the general existence of liability of foreignness showing that London shows no signs of liability of foreignness, which is either a result of superior firm-specific advantages compensating for disadvantages or a limited importance of home country effects in this highly integrated place. Additionally, firm characteristics strongly impact the effects of the liability of foreignness on firm operations. Thus, Nachum suggests that a reconceptualization of the liability of foreignness concept is necessary.

Cultural distance can also become an intra-organizational problem. Advanced producer services are individualized contextual services favoring an autonomous governance mode for subsidiaries to adapt to the local context. Based on case studies of four polycentric global professional firms located in London, Boussebaa (2009) identifies a common misalignment between center and subsidiary regarding quality standards and staff quality (language), which leads to problems with global clients expecting the highest service standard of the center and causing reputational damage if subsidiaries underperform. Cultural differences reinforce tension, especially for US-centric firms with a belief in a global set of values, thereby alienating subsidiaries. Additionally, intra-organizational friction arises in cross-country projects if compensation mechanisms for the host country subsidiary are lacking, encouraging subsidiaries to focus high-level resources on local client acquisition, thereby reducing the quality of cross-country projects. Because clients expect global quality and access to knowledge on a global scale (Beaverstock, 2004), managing intra-organizational friction is important.

Institutions

While trade liberalization in the wake of the WTO 2000 service negotiations reduced tariff barriers, non-tariff entry barriers remain an important determining factor for FDI in services (Roberts, 2001). Regulatory barriers have a strong sector-specific impact on producer service firms. Common issues related to regulation are the protection of firm-specific assets including property rights and knowledge and intangible assets, but also access to markets or professions (e.g., standards, certifications) (Roberts, 2001; Falkenbach, 2009; Sako, 2015). Furthermore, regulations can force specific entry modes requiring the involvement of local parties or imposing regulations on specific occupations (Sako, 2015). Deregulation of professions and markets is beneficial for firms, hence it allows them to separate work processes and outsource/offshore tasks to non- or semi-professionals. By doing so, they can focus on high-value tasks demanding the attention of professionals and allowing firms to utilize advantages of different markets via outsourcing or offshoring (Sako, 2015).

Barattieri, Borchert and Mattoo (2014) evaluate the role of policy and inter-sectoral linkages in M&As in the service sector, which is an understudied field. Using the Thompson Reuters

Platinum Database, the authors acquired a comprehensive dataset of global M&As (firm level) from 2003–2009 and collected policy data from the Services Trade Restrictions Database at the country level. The analysis using probit models show that trade barriers reduce M&A inflows although the negative effect of trade barriers can be mitigated if the GDP of a country has certain structural characteristics (e.g., high manufacturing share). Falkenbach (2009) analyzes market selection determinants for international real estate investments. The study uses descriptive statistics based on questionnaire data from real estate investors who made investments in Europe. A total of 22 complete samples from mostly northern European investors is used. Most important factors commonly identified are the safety of property rights and the expected return on investment. Institutional factors are of importance as well as the maturity of markets. The presence of professional services and indirect investment opportunities are only identified by a part of the sample, indicating that management strategies might also be an important factor in market selection.

Hurmelinna-Laukkanen and Ritala (2012) argue that appropriability regimes are important drivers of service firm internationalization. While intellectual property rights (IPR) protection is identified as an external market condition, the authors argue that firms can actively construct their appropriability regimes thus making it an internal factor. The authors identified 762 individual Finnish firms with more than 100 employees. A questionnaire survey yielded 209 responses, which are separated into service- and product-oriented firms based on the share of sales derived from products/services. Using logistic regression, the authors show that the development of formal and informal means of IPR protection are important factors for internationalization for both groups, while internationalizing service industries have strong appropriability mechanisms in place. Limitations of the study are the small cross-sectional sample.

Emerging markets and transitional economies

Emerging markets are becoming increasingly important actors providing a pool of well-educated human capital at comparatively lower prices, investing in developing countries with market seeking intentions, and investing in developed economies to acquire assets. Emerging markets have the highest growth rates of knowledge-intensive business services and:

> [k]nowledge-based services have emerged as important engines for economic growth in emerging markets that are evolving into knowledge economies. Emerging markets in KIBS sectors are gaining prominence and achieving equal status with partners that are based in advanced economies.
>
> *(Javalgi et al., 2011)*

The quality and knowledge intensity of services offshored to emerging markets increases over time with R&D decentralization (Massini & Miozzo, 2012). Due to agglomeration and cluster effects, offshore destinations, mainly India but also China, have emerged as an important source of innovation. Transitional economies have a rising demand for PS and are characterized by institutional changes increasing economic integration and reducing regulation (Keren & Ofer, 2002; Roberts, 2002; Faulconbridge, Hall & Beaverstock, 2008). For example, after China became a WTO member, multinational banks wanted to become more involved in FDI in China (Xiaogang, Skully & Brown, 2005), but central planning does result in high barriers of entry (regulation) making immediate utilization of those markets difficult (Keren & Ofer, 2002).

Firms entering emerging markets from developed economies have to cope with differences in language, cultural, work practices, and government regulations (Freeman & Sandwell, 2008). In this context, social networks and personal contacts are actively used to enter emerging markets and overcome communication and governmental barriers as well as to acquire market knowledge influencing the strategic entry decision. Foreign network actors are valuable assets with a strong influence on the entry decision, process, and mode. Investments from emerging countries in services have been growing since 1995 (Gammeltoft, 2008). While investments into resource extraction are common, in several countries the service sector has become an important destination for FDI. For example, Indian outward FDI has increased substantially since 1995 (Pradhan, 2003). During 1996–2001, a substantial share was directed towards professional services – 56.17% of service outward FDI have been made in IT, communication and software, followed by 33.65% in media, broadcasting, and publishing. Other sectors are financial services (2.62), civil, contracting, and engineering services (0.64), consulting (0.30), trading and marketing (0.25), transportation (1.69), and other professional services (1.96). Main investment destinations were Western Europe (39.68%, of which the UK is 90.65%), North America (32.65%), and developing countries (27.1%). Buckley et al. (2014) research the impact on the performance of developed market service and manufacturing firms which have been acquired by emerging market MNEs. They use the Thompson Reuter One database to develop a panel data set from 1999–2008 based on 79 deals measuring firm performance before and after acquisition, yielding 570 observations (note: the share of service MNEs is low). The nature of the acquiring emerging market MNE is undisclosed. Using a lagged performance variable in a panel regression, the authors find that the impact of the previous experience of the MNEs is limited to specific conditions. Experience is only beneficial if similar endeavors are undertaken (e.g., acquisition in a developed country followed by another acquisition in a developed country), whereas negative impacts on performance are observed if new forms of engagement are used. The findings suggest that intangible resources of emerging market MNEs are insignificant in determining success, supporting a view that these MNEs are mainly sourcing assets through FDI.

Conclusion

Producer and professional services are a heterogeneous group with varying definitions. This variety makes comparisons among studies difficult and might hamper the theoretical development in the field. While studies explore the specific subfield of advanced producer services, they serve to highlight the specifics of the observed industry. It remains in general unclear how, except for the sector specific variables, the observed industry sets itself apart from general services or producer services. Defining what sets producer services apart from consumer services and how that relates to different internationalization pathways from consumer services seems to require more attention as the general service sector encompasses an even wider variety of firms ranging from retail to legal services.

The heterogeneity of PS regarding key factors and resources is widely analyzed. Additionally, it seems to be necessary to evaluate how those differences in key resources and determinants affect internationalization pathways. The different requirements of firms and key factors for success strongly impact the internationalization decision as well as the mode of entry together with the resource endowment of the firm. The behavior of architecture companies to follow prestigious competitions to generate reputational value differs greatly, for example, from the internationalization pathways of accounting firms motivated initially by client internationalization. While studies identify this for single industries, overall comparisons are lacking. Questions remain if those differences would allow us to characterize a unified sector of (advanced) producer services and how conclusions about the overall sector can be drawn from all the existing case studies. This also affects other aspects of the discussed elements. For example, is cultural distance important for all types of producer services or only for specific types (e.g., technological consulting versus business services)? In the context of emerging markets, a rise of producer services in their domestic markets with international spillovers can be observed. But it remains unclear if these corporations face additional obstacles based on their origin (e.g., India, Indonesia) or just from a competitive perspective (e.g., resource or knowledge base).

This chapter draws upon selected literature to discuss the internationalization of PSFs. The studies focus on the drivers of internationalization, but data limitations make it difficult to understand the evolution of the development of those investments (e.g., ownership advantages) over time (Puck, Holtbrügge & Mohr, 2009). Furthermore, the world city hierarchy of producer services shows that a global theory of service geography is not easy to develop given the inherent heterogeneity of advanced producer services. A related issue is the transferability of theories of FDI by MNEs in manufacturing to the service sector. The inclusion of strategic considerations does show the importance of human and relational capital, as well as the experience of the CEO. One other complicating factor is the involvement of small- and medium-sized firms who are born globals. Factors that are noted as significant in deepening the internationalization process include the reduction of transaction cost with the acquisition of local knowledge, adaptation, and increased experience. Whether reduced transaction costs encourage conversion of joint ventures into wholly owned subsidiaries has not been established for service companies. Therefore, much-needed research is required to understand the life cycle of the producer service firms once they enter a foreign market.

References

Abecassis-Moedas, C., Ben Mahmoud-Jouini, S., Dell'Era, C., Manceau, D. & Verganti, R. (2012) 'Key resources and internationalization modes of creative knowledge-intensive business services: The case of design consultancies', *Creativity and Innovation Management*, 21, pp. 315–331.

Bagchi-Sen, S. & Sen, J. (1997) 'The current state of knowledge in International Business in producer services', *Environment and Planning A*, 29, pp. 1153–1174.

Ball, D.A., Lindsay, V.J. & Rose, E.L. (2008) 'Rethinking the paradigm of service internationalisation: Less resource-intensive market entry modes for information-intensive soft services', *Management International Review*, 48, pp. 413–431.

Baltacioglu, T., Ada, E., Kaplan, M.D., Yurt And, O. & Cem Kaplan, Y. (2007) 'A new framework for service supply chains', *The Service Industries Journal*, 27, pp. 105–124.

Barattieri, A., Borchert, I. & Mattoo, A. (2014) 'Cross-border mergers and acquisitions in services: The role of policy and industrial structure', *World Bank Policy Research Working Paper* 6905.

Beaverstock, J.V. (1996) 'Migration, knowledge and social interaction: Expatriate labour within investment banks', *Area*, 28, pp. 459–470.

Beaverstock, J.V. (2004) '"Managing across borders": Knowledge management and expatriation in professional service legal firms', *Journal of Economic Geography*, 4, pp. 157–179.

Beyers, W.B., Alvine, M.J. & Johnson, E.G. (1985) 'The service sector: A growing force in the regional export base', *Economic Development Commentary*, 9, pp. 3–7.

Beyers, W.B. & Lindahl, D.P. (1996) 'Lone eagles and high fliers in rural producer services', *Rural Development Perspectives*, 11, pp. 2–10.

Blomstermo, A., Eriksson, K., Lindstrand, A. & Sharma, D.D. (2004) 'The perceived usefulness of network experiential knowledge in the internationalizing firm', *Journal of International Management*, 10, pp. 355–373.

Boddewyn, J.J., Halbrich, M.B. & Perry, A. (1986) 'Service multinationals: Conceptualization, measurement and theory', *Journal of International Business Studies*, 17, pp. 41–57.

Boussebaa, M. (2009) 'Struggling to organize across national borders: The case of global resource management in professional service firms', *Human Relations*, 62, pp. 829–850.

Brouthers, K.D. & Brouthers, L.E. (2003) 'Why service and manufacturing entry mode choices differ: The influence of transaction cost factors, risk and trust', *Journal of Management Studies*, 40, pp. 1179–1204.

Buckley, P.J. & Casson, M.C. (1976) *The Future of the Multinational Enterprise* (Vol. 1). London: Macmillan.

Buckley, P.J. & Casson, M.C. (2009) 'The internalisation theory of the multinational enterprise: A review of the progress of a research agenda after 30 years', *Journal of International Business Studies*, 40, pp. 1563–1580.
Buckley, P.J., Elia, S. & Kafouros, M. (2014) 'Acquisitions by emerging market multinationals: Implications for firm performance', *Journal of World Business*, 49, pp. 611–632.
Capar, N. & Kotabe, M. (2003) 'The relationship between international diversification and performance in service firms', *Journal of International Business Studies*, 34, pp. 345–355.
Castellani, D., Meliciani, V. & Mirra, L. (2016) 'The determinants of inward foreign direct investment in business services across European regions', *Regional Studies*, 50, pp. 671–691.
Caves, R.E. (1996) *Multinational Enterprise and Economic Analysis*. Cambridge, UK: Cambridge University Press.
Coe, N.M., Johns, J. & Ward, K. (2007) 'Mapping the globalization of the temporary staffing industry', *The Professional Geographer*, 59, pp. 503–520.
Coffey, W.J. (2000) 'The geographies of producer services', *Urban Geography*, 21, pp. 170–183.
Consoli, D. & Elche-Hortelano, D. (2010) 'Variety in the knowledge base of knowledge intensive business services', *Research Policy*, 39, pp. 1303–1310.
Contractor, F.J., Kundu, S.K. & Hsu, C.C. (2003) 'A three-stage theory of international expansion: The link between multinationality and performance in the service sector', *Journal of International Business Studies*, 33, pp. 48–60.
Den Hertog, P. (2000) 'Knowledge-intensive business services as co-producers of innovation', *International Journal of Innovation Management*, 4, pp. 491–552.
Dicken, P. (2007) *Global Shift: Mapping the Changing Contours of the World Economy*. 6th Edition. London: Paul Chapman Publishing.
Dunning, J.H. (1979) 'Explaining changing patterns of international production: In defence of the eclectic theory', *Oxford Bulletin of Economics and Statistics*, 41, pp. 269–295.
Dunning, J.H. (1989) 'Trade and foreign-owned production in services: Some conceptual and theoretical issues', in Giersch, H. (Ed.), *Services in World Economic Growth: Symposium*. Boulder, CO: Westview Press, pp. 108–151.
Dunning, J.H. (1993) 'Trade, location of economic activity and the multinational enterprise: A search for an eclectic approach', *The Theory of Transnational Corporations*, 1, pp. 183–218.
Ellram, L.M., Tate, W.L. & Billington, C. (2004) 'Understanding and managing the services supply chain', *Journal of Supply Chain Management*, 40, pp. 17–32.
Enderwick, P. (1989) *Multinational Service Firms*. London: Routledge.
Erramilli, M.K. (1991) 'The experience factor in foreign market entry behavior of service firms', *Journal of International Business Studies*, 22, pp. 479–501.
Erramilli, M.K. & Rao, C.P. (1993) 'Service firms' international entry-mode choice: A modified transaction-cost analysis approach', *The Journal of Marketing*, 57, pp. 19–38.
Falkenbach, H. (2009) 'Market selection for international real estate investments', *International Journal of Strategic Property Management*, 13, pp. 299–308.
Faulconbridge, J.R., Hall, S.J. & Beaverstock, J.V. (2008) 'New insights into the internationalization of producer services: Organizational strategies and spatial economies for global headhunting firms', *Environment and Planning A*, 40, pp. 210–234.
Faulconbridge, J. & Jones, A. (2012) 'The geographies of management consultancy firms', in Kipping, M. & Clark, T. (Eds.), *The Oxford Handbook of Management Consulting*. Oxford, UK: Oxford University Press, pp. 225–246.
Freeman, S. & Sandwell, M. (2008) 'Professional service firms entering emerging markets: The role of network relationships', *Journal of Services Marketing*, 22, pp. 198–212.
Gammeltoft, P. (2008) 'Emerging multinationals: Outward FDI from the BRICS countries', *International Journal of Technology and Globalisation*, 4, pp. 5–22.
Glückler, J. & Armbrüster, T. (2003) 'Bridging uncertainty in management consulting: The mechanisms of trust and networked reputation', *Organization Studies*, 24, pp. 269–297.
Goe, W.R. (1990) 'Producer services, trade and the social division of labour', *Regional Studies*, 24, pp. 327–342.
Grönroos, C. (1999) 'Internationalization strategies for services', *Journal of Services Marketing*, 13, pp. 290–297.
Guerrieri, P. & Meliciani, V. (2005) 'Technology and international competitiveness: The interdependence between manufacturing and PSs', *Structural Change and Economic Dynamics*, 16, pp. 489–502.

Guler, I. & Guillén, M.F. (2010) 'Home country networks and foreign expansion: Evidence from the venture capital industry', *Academy of Management Journal*, 53, pp. 390–410.

Hanlon, G. (2004) 'Institutional forms and organizational structures: Homology, trust and reputational capital in professional service firms', *Organization*, 11, pp. 186–210.

Hennart, J.F. (2010) 'Transaction cost theory and International Business', *Journal of Retailing*, 86, pp. 257–269.

Herrmann, P. & Datta, D.K. (2006) 'CEO experiences: Effects on the choice of FDI entry mode', *Journal of Management Studies*, 43, pp. 755–778.

Hitt, M.A., Bierman, L., Uhlenbruck, K. & Shimizu, K. (2006) 'The importance of resources in the internationalization of professional service firms: The good, the bad, and the ugly', *Academy of Management Journal*, 49, pp. 1137–1157.

Hurmelinna-Laukkanen, P. & Ritala, P. (2012) 'Appropriability as the driver of internationalization of service-oriented firms', *The Service Industries Journal*, 32, pp. 1039–1056.

Hymer, S.H. (1976) *The International Operations of National Firms: A Study of Direct Foreign Investment*. Cambridge, MA: MIT Press.

Javalgi, R.R.G., Gross, A.C., Benoy Joseph, W. & Granot, E. (2011) 'Assessing competitive advantage of emerging markets in knowledge intensive business services', *Journal of Business & Industrial Marketing*, 26, pp. 171–180.

Jones, J. & Wren, C. (2016) 'Does service FDI locate differently to manufacturing FDI? A regional analysis for Great Britain', *Regional Studies*, 50, pp. 1980–1994.

Jung, J. (2004) 'Acquisitions or joint ventures: Foreign market entry strategy of US advertising agencies', *The Journal of Media Economics*, 17, pp. 35–50.

Keren, M., & Ofer, G. (2002) 'The role of FDI in trade and financial services in transition: What distinguishes transition economies from developing economies?' *Comparative Economic Studies*, 44, pp. 15–45.

Kindleberger, C.P. (1969) 'American business abroad', *Thunderbird International Business Review*, 11, pp. 11–12.

Kipping, M. & Clark, T. (2012) *The Oxford Handbook of Management Consulting*. Oxford, UK: Oxford University Press.

Koch, A. & Strotmann, H. (2008) 'Absorptive capacity and innovation in the knowledge-intensive business service sector', *Economics of Innovation and New Technology*, 17, pp. 511–531.

Lai, K. (2012) 'Differentiated markets: Shanghai, Beijing and Hong Kong in China's financial centre network', *Urban Studies*, 49, pp. 1275–1296.

Lai, P.-Y. & Fischer, D. (2007) 'The determinants of foreign real estate investment in Taiwan', *Pacific Rim Property Research Journal*, 13, pp. 263–279.

Magnusson, P., Westjohn, S.A. & Boggs, D.J. (2009) 'Order-of-entry effects for service firms in developing markets: An examination of multinational advertising agencies', *Journal of International Marketing*, 17, pp. 23–41.

Massini, S. & Miozzo, M. (2012) 'Outsourcing and offshoring of business services: Challenges to theory, management and geography of innovation', *Regional Studies*, 46, pp. 1219–1242.

McQuillan, D. & Scott, P.S. (2015) 'Models of internationalization: A business model approach to professional service firm internationalization', in Baden-Fuller, C. & Mangematin, V. (Eds.), *Business Models and Modelling*. Bingley, UK: Emerald Group Publishing Limited, pp. 309–345.

Miles, I., Kastrinos, N., Flanagan, K., Bilderbeek, R., Den Hertog, P., Hutink, W. & Bouman, M. (1995) *Knowledge Intensive Business Services: Their Roles As Users, Carriers and Sources of Innovation*. PREST, Manchester: University of Manchester, *mimeo*.

Muzychenko, O. & Liesch, P.W. (2015) 'International opportunity identification in the internationalisation of the firm', *Journal of World Business*, 50, pp. 704–717.

Nachum, L. (2003a) 'Does nationality of ownership make any difference and, if so, under what circumstances? Professional service MNEs in global competition', *Journal of International Management*, 9, pp. 1–32.

Nachum, L. (2003b) 'Liability of foreignness in global competition? Financial service affiliates in the city of London', *Strategic Management Journal*, 24, pp. 1187–1208.

Njegomir, V. & Stojic, D. (2012) 'Determinants of non-life insurance market attractiveness for foreign investments: Eastern European evidence', *Economic Research*, 25, pp. 297–310.

Noyelle, T.J. & Stanback Jr., T.M. (1984) *The Economic Transformation of American Cities*. Lanham, ML: Rowman & Littlefield Publishing Incorporated.

OECD (2000) *OECD Employment Outlook*, June. Paris: OECD.

O'Farrell, P.N., Wood, P.A. & Zheng, J. (1998) 'Regional influences on foreign market development by business service companies: Elements of a strategic context explanation', *Regional Studies*, 32, pp. 31–48.

Oldenski, L. (2012) 'Export versus FDI and the communication of complex information', *Journal of International Economics*, 87, pp. 312–322.

Outreville, J.F. (2008) 'Foreign affiliates of the largest insurance groups: Location-specific advantages', *Journal of Risk and Insurance*, 75, pp. 463–491.

Pardos, E., Gomex-Loscos, A. & Rubiera-Morollon, F. (2007) '"Do versus buy" decisions in the demand for knowledge intensive business services', *The Service Industries Journal*, 27, pp. 233–249.

Piore, M.J. (1986) 'Perspectives on labor market flexibility', *Industrial Relations: A Journal of Economy and Society*, 25, pp. 146–166.

Pradhan, J.P. (2003) 'Rise of service sector outward foreign direct investment from Indian economy: Trends, patterns, and determinants', *GITAM Journal of Management*, 4, pp. 70–97.

Puck, J.F., Holtbrügge, D. & Mohr, A.T. (2009) 'Beyond entry mode choice: Explaining the conversion of joint ventures into wholly owned subsidiaries in the People's Republic of China', *Journal of International Business Studies*, 40, pp. 388–404.

Ramasamy, B. & Yeung, M. (2010) 'The determinants of foreign direct investment in services', *The World Economy*, 33, pp. 573–596.

Reiffenstein, T. (2009) 'Specialization, centralization, and the distribution of patent intermediaries in the USA and Japan', *Regional Studies*, 43, pp. 571–588.

Reihlen, M. & Apel, A.B. (2007) 'Internationalization of professional service firms as learning: A constructivist approach', *International Journal of Service Industry Management*, 18, pp. 140–151.

Roberts, J. (2001) 'Challenges facing service enterprises in a global knowledge-based economy: Lessons from the business services sector', *International Journal of Services Technology and Management*, 2, pp. 402–433.

Roberts, J. (2002) 'From markets to resource-oriented overseas expansion: Re-examining a study of the internationalization of UK business service firms', in Miozzo, M. & Miles, I. (Eds.), *Internationalization, Technology and Services*. Cheltenham, UK: Edward Elgar, pp. 161–183.

Rugman, A.M. (1981) *Inside the Multinationals: The Economics of Internal Markets*. New York: Columbia University Press.

Rugman, A.M. & Verbeke, A. (2008) 'A new perspective on the regional and global strategies of multinational services firms', *Management International Review*, 48, pp. 397–411.

Sako, M. (2015) 'Outsourcing and offshoring of professional services', in Empson, L., Muzio, D., Broschak, D, & Hinings, B. (Eds.), *The Oxford Handbook of Professional Service Firms*. Oxford, UK: Oxford University Press, pp. 327–347.

Sanchez-Peinado, E., Pla-Barber, J. & Hébert, L. (2007) 'Strategic variables that influence entry mode choice in service firms', *Journal of International Marketing*, 15, pp. 67–91.

Sanderson, M.R., Derudder, B., Timberlake, M. & Witlox, F. (2015) 'Are world cities also world immigrant cities? An international, cross-city analysis of global centrality and immigration', *International Journal of Comparative Sociology*, 56, pp. 173–197.

Sassen, S. (2001) *The Global City: New York, London, Tokyo*. Princeton, NJ: Princeton University Press.

Sassen, S. (2011) *Cities in a World Economy*. Thousand Oaks, CA: Sage Publications.

Scott-Kennel, J. & von Batenburg, Z. (2012) 'The role of knowledge and learning in the internationalisation of professional service firms', *The Service Industries Journal*, 32, pp. 1667–1690.

Spies, J. (2010) 'Network and border effects: Where do foreign multinationals locate in Germany?' *Regional Science and Urban Economics*, 40, pp. 20–32.

Taylor, P.J. (2004) 'The new geography of global civil society: NGOs in the world city network', *Globalizations*, 1, pp. 265–277.

Taylor, P.J. (2005) 'Leading world cities: Empirical evaluations of urban nodes in multiple networks', *Urban Studies*, 42, pp. 1593–1608.

Taylor, P.J., Derudder, B., Faulconbridge, J., Hoyler, M. & Ni, P. (2014) 'Advanced producer service firms as strategic networks, global cities as strategic places', *Economic Geography*, 90, pp. 267–291.

Thompson, E.C. (2004) 'Producer services', in *Kentucky Annual Economic Report*. Lexington, KY: Centre for Business and Economic Research, University of Kentucky, pp. 19–23.

Toivonen, M. (2004) 'Foresight in services: Possibilities and special challenges', *The Service Industries Journal*, 24, pp. 79–98.

Tuan, C. & Ng, L.F. (2003) 'FDI facilitated by agglomeration economies: Evidence from manufacturing and services joint ventures in China', *Journal of Asian Economics*, 13, pp. 749–765.

UNCTAD (2004) *World Investment Report 2004. The Shift Towards Services*. New York and Geneva: United Nations.

Wójcik, D. (2011) 'Securitization and its footprint: The rise of the US securities industry centres 1998–2007', *Journal of Economic Geography*, 11, pp. 925–947.

World Bank (2015) *World Development Indicators*. Retrieved from: http://data.worldbank.org.

Wu, X. & Strange, R. (2000) 'The location of foreign insurance companies in China', *International Business Review*, 9, pp. 383–398.

Xiaogang, C., Skully, M. & Brown, K. (2005) 'Banking efficiency in China: Application of DEA to pre-and post-deregulation eras: 1993–2000', *China Economic Review*, 16, pp. 229–245.

Xinya, G., Jie, L. & Ye, Z. (2011) 'Study progress of producer services', in *International Conference on Management and Service Science (MASS)*. Wuhan, China: IEEE, pp. 1–4.

Zaheer, S. (1995) 'Overcoming the liability of foreignness', *Academy of Management Journal*, 38, pp. 341–363.

Zaheer, S. & Manrakhan, S. (2001) 'Concentration and dispersion in global industries: Remote electronic access and the location of economic activities', *Journal of International Business Studies*, 32, pp. 667–686.

Zaheer, S. & Mosakowski, E. (1997) 'The dynamics of the liability of foreignness: A global study of survival in financial services', *Strategic Management Journal*, 18, pp. 439–463.

Zieba, M. (2013) 'Knowledge-intensive business services (KIBS) and their role in the knowledge-based economy', in Janiunaite, B. & Petraite, M. (Eds.), *Proceedings of the 14th European Conference on Knowledge Management*. Kaunas, Lithuania: Kaunas University of Technology, pp. 785–792.

31

DESIGNED HERE, RE-DESIGNED THERE BUT MADE SOMEWHERE ELSE

Geography, translocal business and the exploitation of difference

John R. Bryson

From local to translocal business

This chapter explores the ways in which goods are designed and redesigned by International Businesses to meet the needs of many local consumer cultures. The onset of international trade is associated with the development of international logistics, but with structures and systems that are intended to facilitate product localisation, which is the development of products to meet the needs of localised consumer cultures or a process that modifies existing products for sale in many different national settings. There are products that can be sold in many different localities and the only alterations will be related to marketing and packaging. Other products must be altered to meet local consumer expectations. This is a complex process that involves two elements. First, local design expertise must exist that informs the development of products for local markets. Second, companies must develop structures or mechanisms that enable them to localise their designs. This takes many different forms. It involves the establishment of local design centres that can be owned by translocal firms or be provided by specialist independent providers of design expertise. This chapter begins with an overview of research on International Business and geography to identify some of the key characteristics of International Business activity and to explain the focus on design, business and professional services and the distribution of production-related tasks. The focus on distribution highlights that the selection of a location for a task is the consequence of a deliberative process that is designed to provide a firm with some form of strategic advantage.

The characteristics of International Business have now been explored for over a century by economic geographers, economists, management and International Business and strategy academics, business historians, economic sociologists and organisational theorists (Rugman & Collinson, 2005; Iammarino & McCann, 2013; Bryson, 2015). Many different approaches to understanding International Businesses have emerged, but with few attempts to develop an integrated cross-disciplinary approach to understanding the international dimensions of business activities. Each academic tradition applies different methodologies, theories and even definitions to International Business (Yeung, 2009). Nevertheless, three key questions or issues have been explored across the social sciences. First, a concern with understanding why international businesses develop or exist combined with a focus on understanding the geography of International Business including the location of offices or plants (Yamin, 2000). Second, there has been a focus on understanding the impacts of International Business. This literature explores the positive and negative impacts of foreign direct investment (FDI) on localities, but also the benefits that accrue to a firm from international activity as well as the complexities of engaging in International Business. The third set of issues reflects a concern with understanding linkages between places and firms. This literature highlights the emergence, operation and characteristics of what have been described as global commodity chains (GCC) or global production networks (GPN).

There have been two attempts to develop an integrated or unified theory of International Business. First, John Dunning developed the eclectic paradigm as an attempt to integrate different strands of research on International Business that had emerged in the field of management and strategy (Dunning, 2001, 2003). His organisation, location and internalisation (OLI) framework made an important contribution to understanding why International Business occurs and some elements of their geography, but it failed to appreciate management and organisational complexity involved in running International Businesses. Second, the chain-based approaches of GCCs or global value chains (GVC) (Gereffi et al., 2005, 2008) and GPNs (Coe et al., 2004, 2008; Coe & Yeung, 2015) have attempted to develop a unified theory. Dunning continued to develop and alter the OLI in response to criticisms and also to developments in the International Business literature (Dunning, 2003). The chain-based approaches and, in particular, the GPN approach continue to evolve to try to embrace all aspects of International Business. Within Economic Geography the GPN approach has become the dominant approach (Weller, 2008). There is no attempt to develop an alternative, and the current focus is on the application of a network metaphor to understanding International Business and one in which the global nature of business activities is considered to be more important than local drivers.

One could argue that the attempt to develop an integrated or unified theory has foundered or been displaced by a focus on chain-based metaphors. This is unfortunate; what is required is the development of a conceptual approach to International Business that includes micro, meso and macro aspects of the organisation, geography and management of International Business (Rusten & Bryson, 2010b), but also an approach that includes economic history or an appreciation of the evolution of International Business activities over time. Understanding the evolution of the international aspects of a business is important as this reveals the decisions that are made at particular times that contribute to the long-term emergence of an International Business. Such decisions produce sunk costs that are embedded in particular locations and lead to path dependencies (Bryson & Ronayne, 2014). In a detailed study of the economic history of Smiths, a UK global engineering company, Nye notes that the history of this firm is bound up with a wide variety of twentieth-century consumer products and with less visible products developed for specialist professionals, but the twentieth-century Smiths is remarkably different from the twenty-first-century Smiths (Nye, 2014). This difference reflects an approach in which there is a lean UK corporate headquarters and 'management is devolved overseas to the local level', but the corporate strategy is based on:

> [t]he continued pursuit of the full potential of each business, achieved in a wide variety of ways – whether through an emphasis on lean production, or the use of benchmarking methods to enhance performance, or the deployment of secure and effective mechanisms of knowledge management and transfer.
>
> *(Nye, 2014, p. 324)*

This reflects the importance of adapting to changing market conditions.

It is perhaps unsurprising that the study of International Business is a multidisciplinary endeavour; the geography, organisation and management of International Businesses is a multifaceted and multidisciplinary phenomenon (Vanchan et al., 2015). It would be possible to argue that an International Business is in no way different to any other type of business. For example, Dunning's OLI could be applied to firms that have no direct International Business activities, and a GPN or GCC approach could be applied in the form of understanding local production networks (LPNs) or local commodity chains (LCC). Perhaps there has been too much focus on geography without an appreciation that an International Business is just a business. In this regard it is worth noting that social scientists still have much to learn about businesses in general before adding in the complexity of international or global business and the difference that local culture adds to business activity. Nevertheless, it may be the case that any attempt to develop an integrated theory of International Business is like chasing a mirage. The explanation lies in the changing nature of business activities that includes alterations in the organisation and geography of economic activity in response to the emergence of new technologies, new forms of consumer behaviour and lifestyles, and new approaches to management and organisation. On the one hand, the fundamentals of business remain the same – the development of a revenue appropriation mechanism that covers the cost of finance with sufficient profit to reflect the risk reward ratio. On the other, all firms are in a continual process of becoming – a process of adaptation, change and innovation.

A key issue to consider is the definition of International Business. The social science literature on International Business uses three terms: International Business, multinational corporations (MNCs) or multinational enterprises (MNEs), and transnational corporations (TNCs). International Business is the most generic and value neutral as it highlights economic activity that occurs beyond the confines of a single nation state, or more correctly between different national settings. The term MNE draws attention to firms that own, control or co-ordinate activities in many different national settings. In contrast the term TNC emphasises relationships across national boundaries. Terms are important as they contain embedded metaphors that can enable and constrain understanding. In many respects, the best term is International Business, with the emphasis placed on relationships between nations. There is an alternative term – translocal enterprises (TLE) or translocal business (TLB). This term provides a more precise account of the geographical aspects of International Business. Thus, a GPN approach highlights and arguably overemphasises the global nature of production, while an MNC or TNC approach stresses relationships between business activities located in different national settings. Nevertheless, business activities that cross national boundaries have very precise geographies. The decision to engage in a foreign activity involves a decision regarding a country and the wider framework conditions that exist nationally (taxation, employment law, etc.) combined with a decision about the actual location in a place. The term translocal thus highlights that all International Business activity involves relationships between localities or places. There are thus three issues for a company to consider: (i) the characteristics of the national setting, (ii) the advantages of a particular location within a national setting and (iii) the connectivity or relationship between a location and other locations that are important for the business activity. This includes access to skilled labour, land and other localised factor inputs, for example product design and marketing expertise, as well as the ability for the site to engage with other sites within the international firm.

Change and adapting to change are critical aspects of business and reflect the definition of business used in this chapter – a business is in a continual process of becoming. Firms try to change through learning, innovation and the development of processes of adaptation. Such adaptation includes effective cost control and the management of the procurement process to spread risk and also to reduce dependency on any one supplier. Adaptive firms will procure components and raw materials from a number of different suppliers and will play suppliers off against each other. Adaptive firms try to ensure that their products (goods and services) are designed and developed to meet the requirements of local markets. Products may be designed in one place for the global market, but there are very few truly global products as consumer culture is localised and culturally embedded. Products must meet the requirements set by national governments in terms of health and safety and other local regulations. This means that products tend to be designed in one place, often in many places, manufactured in other places and marketed in targeted locations. Understanding the geography of International Business is critical as place-based differentials lie behind flows of goods, materials, services, ideas, innovations and people. These place-based differentials may reflect physical geography in terms of the availability of raw materials and connectivity, the accumulation of many decisions made by people, firms and governments that transform places providing them with differentiation, and also differences in lifestyles that create distinctive consumer cultures. This builds upon the emphasis placed in Economic Geography in which relative advantage or disadvantage may reflect decisions made in the past that produce path dependency (Bryson & Ronayne, 2014).

Creativity and expertise are critical for corporate and national competitiveness. Design is a key strategic creative business process and plays an important role in the competitiveness of firms, regions and nations (Rusten & Bryson, 2010a; Bryson & Rusten, 2011) and in International Business strategy. This separation between design and manufacturing is highlighted in many products that acknowledge that the thing was designed in one place and manufactured in another. Thus, Apple's iPod proudly proclaims that it is 'Designed in California, Made in China', and a Microsoft computer mouse is labelled 'Designed in Redmond, WA USA, Made in China'; it is interesting to note that this product's US association is printed in a large font with added bold whilst the Chinese connection is in a small font with no highlighting. The Italian design-intensive conglomerate, Tonino Lamborghini, creates products that take place-based associations one step further by differentiating between design and place, and fabrication and place. The Tonino Lamborghini electric hedge cutters are advertised as 'Italian design and outstanding "made in Germany quality"'. The separation of the design task from the place of manufacture highlights the continued development of the international division of labour as tasks are distributed in different places, but linked by cables, satellites, boats and planes.

Products are developed to meet the needs of consumers, but there is no such thing as the representative consumer. Consumption varies by place, age, class and gender, and there are many other influences on consumer motivations, expectations and taste. Products were initially developed to meet the needs of local consumers. This was a period before trading relationships were established. The onset of trading relationships between regions and subsequently nations led to the spread of products and altered consumer expectations. Nevertheless, the difference that place makes is still critical for forming consumer expectations and developing localised taste communities. Internationalisation and globalisation have eroded some place-based consumer differences, but there are still important nationally articulated consumer cultures. Companies can produce products to service local markets. They can also decide to export products to foreign markets. Exported goods may have to be altered to meet the needs of localised consumer cultures (Gertler, 1995, 2004).

The design process operates at the interface between production and consumption. It is the key process involved in mediating this relationship. Design alters products but also consumer behaviour – design and the work of named designers can shape or influence consumer demand. This is a complex process involving the role of celebrity designers, fashion or style magazines, telephone, product placement and celebrity product endorsement. The study of design, the processes that are used to shape the relationship between production and consumption, must be central to all social sciences interested in exploring wealth creation through the production and sale of products and identity construction through consumption. The relationship between design, marketing and the development of consumer cultures requires further detailed research (Bryson et al., 2004). The development of fashions and styles needs to be explored in the context of design-intensive production. Fashion develops in one place and spreads from place to place and becomes localised or adapted to place-based circumstances (Vinodrai, 2006, 2010; Lewis et al., 2008). The adoption and adaption of fashions that were initially developed in one place is an inherently geographical process that is facilitated by the media, celebrities and various forms of technology (television, the internet, etc.). This relationship between fashion and place is reflected in the fashion magazines. Such magazines are global brands, but a single global edition of a magazine is not produced; the European version of a US fashion magazine will be edited out of Europe. The European magazine must have content that meets the needs of local readers, but also content that supports local advertising and localised consumer cultures.

Fashions spread from place to place – a product, fashion or design is created in one place and spreads to another. Fashion and product localisation are two distinct but related processes. Product localisation involves minor or major alterations to products. It can also involve alteration to a product's name, packaging, embedded or supporting services, and marketing strategy. Product localisation might involve very minor alterations, for example, translating user instructions into a local language, or translating a software package into a local language. It can involve fundamental design alterations that are only intended to meet the needs of a specific market. These needs may reflect actual or perceived differences in consumer expectations, or they may reflect pricing that is driven by local competition. The latter might force a company to reduce a product's production costs and this might result in a product's redesign.

Placing international products: place-based consumer cultures

The relationship between design, local conditions and consumer expectations is extremely important. Volkswagen, the German automotive company, has developed cars for the Indian market. They built a manufacturing plant at Chakan near Pune, and began production of their first made-in-India car in December 2009. The localisation of design and production was extremely important. Initially, 50 per cent of the Indian version of the VW Polo was made in India and this was increased to 80 per cent. The Polo stands for first-class German engineering and state-of-the-art technology, but VW has had to redesign the car to align the Indian model systematically with local customers' expectations. Part of the redesign has involved reducing the cost of the car so that it can compete aggressively in the small car Indian market. The relationship between regionalised production and consumption cultures determines consumer expectations, behaviour and culture. It plays an important role in the design and development of products, both products developed for local markets and 'global' products.

There is a danger in over-emphasising the importance of consumption in the relationship between place and product. Consumption is critical in this relationship, but consumer behaviour is influenced and even determined by production decisions that have been made in the past. Production and consumption must never be separated; both are integral to the ways in which products (goods and services) are created and consumed. Consumers' create demand, but producers engage in activities to make or create markets for existing products, new products or modified products. Product characteristics are determined by local regulations and existing local technologies and infrastructure. There are very few truly global products; products that are designed, manufactured and marketed in the same way in all markets. The difficulty in developing global products highlights the importance of localised material cultures. Such cultures have their origins in the historical evolution of the relationship between community, place and production, and material culture. Localised consumer and production cultures, or material cultures, are the product of a complex set of processes involving tradition, consumer expectation, path dependency or product inertia and regulation. A good example is the development of a country's electrical system. National differences in electrical sockets, plugs and voltages are based on decisions made in the past. These decisions are enshrined in existing capital investments, regulations and consumer behaviour. The development of regional systems, infrastructures, technologies and consumer cultures reflects the historic evolution between place and technology, but also corporate strategies to segment the global economy. Product segmentation by place may be founded on local consumer cultures and local circumstances, but it also reflects strategies to maximise revenue or the relationship between intellectual property rights, product and place. On the one hand, products may be modified for local circumstances or different nationally articulated product regulations may prevent a product produced in one place from being sold in another. On the other, a product's intellectual property rights are often distributed between different producers targeting different national markets via licensing agreements or through the localised sale of patent rights or copyrights.

From the eighteenth century, capitalism reshaped space and time by undermining the relationship between product and place through trade and FDI, enabled by breakthroughs in transportation technologies. This process of time space compression (Harvey, 1989) had the potential to simplify the mass production of products leading to the creation of mass global consumption. This process was partially successful. Place still matters; differences embedded in place-based regulations, production and consumer expectations, production and consumer cultures and traditions distort some of the consequences of time space compression. These distortions provide opportunities for businesses to exploit place-based differences, but they increase the complexity of developing products (goods and services) that are going to be distributed across different national markets. Regulation, international standards and trade agreements play an important role in this process by attempting to remove some of the differentials or distortions that exist between national economies, but they are only partially successful. The European Union's ongoing project to create a single market comes with the implementation of a set of European regulations intended to remove barriers to trade in goods and services. Many of these barriers are non-tariff barriers related to local regulations (safety, accreditation, professional qualifications), but also consumer cultures. The European Union's foreign trading partners have been forced to incorporate many aspects of European regulations into their own legal systems. To facilitate trade with Europe, for example, China has had to adopt regulations developed by the European Union.

Local and translocal industrial design

The production process for services and physical products incorporates the exploitation and use of various forms of tacit and explicit knowledge during pre-production, production and post-production (Nonaka & Takeuchi, 1995; Nonaka & Teece, 2001; Bryson, et al., 2004). All three stages involve a complex interplay between internal and external knowledge and expertise. The substantial literature on external knowledge and the knowledge (or information) society stresses the contribution made by business and professional services (BPS) to the activities of clients. The BPS literature represents a concern with knowledge-intensive business services (KIBS) or producer services (Bryson et al., 2004). The term business services covers a broad spectrum of activities that provide intermediate inputs into the activities of private and public sector organisations. BPS firms have made an important contribution in facilitating the internationalisation of business activity. BPS firms make two contributions to gross domestic product (GDP); they create GDP in their own right, but also enhance value creation within client companies. Two types of business services exist. First, goods-related services directly support clients' operational activities (cleaning services) and, second, KIBS provide expertise-intensive and often strategic inputs into client companies. Goods-related services tend to be provided by large companies, and they have relatively high barriers to entry. BPS firms have a bipolar distribution with many very small firms and few large firms. The growth of business services reflects a range of cost- and non-cost drivers related to issues such as transaction costs, flexibility and the growing complexity of business. Successful BPS entrepreneurs possess three important attributes: professional expertise, an established reputation and a network of client contacts. Traditionally, BPS firms were produced and consumed locally, but ICT and new business models have led to the development of a second global shift in which service functions can be delivered from lower cost locations (Bryson, 2007b).

BPS firms have grown dramatically both in the numbers of firms and in employees over the last 25 years. They are considered to form an essential element of the knowledge economy and, in many respects, should be considered as part of the so-called 'creative' economy (Peck, 2005; Bryson, 2007a). Much of the BPS literature has been largely concerned with analysing the production (and consumption) of intangibles (Clark, 1995; Robertson & Swan, 1998; Wood, 2002) and this has diverted attention from those service functions that are directly involved with the development of new physical products or the modification and transformation of existing products. The emphasis on services that are intangible, cannot be stored and must be consumed simultaneously was a reaction against manufacturing-dominated accounts of the economy. During the 1970s a number of pioneering scholars began to question the neglect of services in contemporary Economic Geography (see Bryson et al., 2004); the concern with 'pure' services that followed appears to have cast a shadow over the manufacturing part of the economy and especially those service functions that contribute directly to the production of physical products. Amongst the most important of these are those individuals and firms that are directly or indirectly engaged in the design of physical products as well as the creation of outputs associated with service activities (such as graphic design). Design is an important BPS that is fundamental to the production system of advanced capitalism and the on-going evolution of translocal business. Unlike many BPS activities, designers produce tangible products; products that can be directly tested via market research and ultimately through sales.

Individuals experience the world through a visual environment that is largely the result of a multifaceted and evolving interrelationship between a set of design processes and manufacturing systems; in other words an intermingling of service and manufacturing expertise in some type of production process. Design expertise contributes to the development and modification of production processes as well as products. Design is a complex activity that involves innovation, change, invention and creativity, and these elements combine together to contribute to the development of new products or the modification of existing products.

Design consultancy firms are key sources of external knowledge, expertise and innovation in post-industrial economies, but their contribution has largely been overlooked in the academic literature on the new knowledge economy (Bryson et al., 2004; Rusten & Bryson, 2007, Rusten et al., 2007). Recent research on BPS has identified an important relationship between BPS firms and place-based or place-formed expertise (Rusten et al., 2005; MacPherson & Vanchan, 2010). Business service firms connect client firms located in a particular place with expertise that may have been developed in other regional contexts. This means that one important role performed by business service firms is to link different scales of business activity together – from the local to the global. Expertise, as well as processes (production-based and management systems, for example), developed in one context are transferred by business service professionals from place to place as part of a complex evolving spatial division of expertise. The quality of expertise consumed by clients is more important than its location. Expertise located in non-global cities/regions may be extremely specialist and of high quality, as local firms and the branch offices of major business service firms develop local specialisms constructed around the needs of the local market in which they are embedded (Rusten et al., 2005). This is an important point and is one which is determined by the relationship that exists between the production and consumption of expertise. Local demand will encourage the development of local specialisations within knowledge intensive services. Local firms and branch offices can become so specialised that they are transformed into national and international centres of excellence. This means that expertise which is developed to mirror the needs of a region's economic structure may become so important that the regional branch begins to provide sector and sometime functional expertise to other offices.

BPS expertise is developed locally, regionally and nationally to support the needs of clients. This means BPS expertise is geographically differentiated as it is formed around local client need. Particular regions will develop local concentrations of BPS firms that have formed around the requirements of local clients. In a series of papers, MacPherson and Vanchan explore the economic geographies of industrial design firms in the United States (Vanchan & MacPherson, 2008a, 2008b; MacPherson & Vanchan, 2009, 2010). They found that most US design firms are less than 20 years old and that most firms in the industry serve clients in a single sector and tend not to venture beyond their core markets. The US industrial design sector is concentrated in a small number of states; the top ten states account for over 70 per cent of total employment in the sector (MacPherson & Vanchan, 2010, p. 82). Like most BPS firms, design consultancy firms tend to be small; on average, US firms had 6.4 employees. The size of design firms varied little by state, but Michigan is the exception as the mean employment size was 13.6 employees. The size of the Michigan design firms reflects the fact that this state is the centre of America's automotive and machine tools industries. In the United States, there is 'a noticeable geography of design service specialization across the nation. Specifically, the types of services offered in any given metropolitan centre tend to mirror the structure of local production (i.e. prominent or dominant sectors)' (MacPherson & Vanchan, 2010, p. 84). The geographies of design expertise have developed in response to the needs of local clients. Centres of design excellence have been created that can be accessed by client companies located anywhere.

The majority of industrial design firms are small and have been established to provide services to local clients (Rusten & Bryson, 2007; MacPherson & Vanchan, 2010; Vanchan & Bryson, 2015). Some industrial design firms have established offices in other countries, and this has led to the emergence of a small number of transnational or more correctly translocal design firms. In 1969, Hartmut Esslinger established a design company in a small garden shed at his home in Altensteig in the German Black Forest. Early in his career Esslinger won a student design competition. Subsequently, the German electronics company, Wega, invited him to design a new television and this led to Esslinger designing over 100 products for this company. Wega was acquired by Sony and Esslinger began working for Sony. Esslinger changed the name of his company from Esslinger Design to 'frogdesign' and eventually in 1998 the company was renamed 'Frog'. In 1981 Steve Jobs of Apple Computers was 'searching for the elusive magic that would give his computer company Apple a market edge' (Sweet, 1999, p. 11). Jobs was looking for a strategy-focused design company that he could work with to differentiate Apple's products from those of his competitors and that would transform a computer into a cult object. When Esslinger met Jobs in California in 1981, Frog was on its way to becoming a global design player. Its work with Sony had opened it to clients located in Asia, and Apple would enable Frog to develop a major presence in the US market. Steve Jobs invited eight mainly European design companies to enter into a competition to design a new computer and the Esslinger design won by a large margin (Bürdek, 1999, p. 29). Jobs offered Esslinger a multi-million-dollar contract, and Frog established an office in California and worked with Jobs to complete the design of the Macintosh computer.

The company's presence in Silicon Valley enhanced Frog's reputation, and the firm's list of high-profile clients grew. Frog shifted its headquarters to San Francisco and, by 2010, had established design studios at locations in Amsterdam, Austin, Milan, Munich, New York, Seattle and Shanghai. By 2010, the company employed over 450 designers, strategists and technologists and worked hand-in-hand to find product solutions for major companies. Frog's distributed design operations enable the firm to design products for firms based in its core local markets, but also to establish a transnational/local design team for clients that includes designers located in key target consumer markets. A product may be designed for the US market using designers based in New York or Seattle, but equally a product might be developed for the US and European markets by assembling a design team that includes US as well as European designers.

The development of transnational design firms provides clients with the opportunities to access distributed design expertise that reflects consumer behaviour and expectations in core markets. The emphasis is on expertise located in core markets rather than on global expertise. None of the major transnational design firms has design centres located in all possible markets, and all focus their resources on North America, Europe and Asia Pacific.

Distributed design and design localisation

Changing business practices and enhanced competition have been important drivers behind the growth of business services. Changing business practices as an explanation is, of course, related to the process of externalisation if only because strategic downsizing and cost-cutting especially by large client companies meant that many firms no longer had sufficient staff to internalise business service functions. The result was the creation of large numbers of new independent business service firms (Bryson, 1997; Bryson et al., 2004). Much of the research into the drivers behind the growth of business services has revealed that cost-driven externalisation was not a major factor behind the growth of business service firms (Bryson, 1997). The most important factor was demand for specialised technical expertise combined with myriad non-cost and cost-driven factors.

The precise process of design is infinitely varied and complex. It can be expressed through the efforts of one person, for example Philippe Starck's 'juicy lemon squeezer', or as the outcome of the efforts of a creative design team (the Aeron© Chair) whether exclusively in-house or as a combination of in-house and external expertise. Much design expertise in large corporations is deemed to be highly confidential, as a company's primary competitive advantage may be vested in the resulting proprietary knowledge. Excessive reliance on in-house expertise may, however, limit innovation. To overcome this problem, translocal enterprises develop global centres of design expertise but try not to isolate them from highly localised sources of design knowledge. Local designers are used, for example, to modify products so that they become integrated into local consumer cultures. Transnational companies that rely on internal design expertise will still employ external designers, as they realise they must be open to new forms of knowledge, new experiences that have been formed outside a large corporate environment and new ways of looking at the world.

Independent design firms with studios distributed in core markets provide expertise to local clients as well as for clients trying to develop products that will be sold in more than one country. Large client firms have also developed significant internal design expertise to support the development and design of their own products. The literature on business and professional service firms highlights the importance of a process known as externalisation. Externalisation describes the tendency for firms to externalise or outsource functions and activities previously produced in-house (internalised). This process has been one of the best-known hypotheses used to explain the rapid relative growth of business services (Beyers & Lindahl, 1996; Bryson et al., 2004, pp. 83–84). It has its origins in research on the importance of complementarity and economies of scale for decisions by firms about whether to externalise or internalise service functions. The problem facing all firms, irrespective of sector, is whether to 'make' or to 'buy' specified service inputs. Few firms can avoid making these decisions, because the inputs provided by business services can improve organisational efficiency and add value to a good or a service at different stages in the production chain. The more advanced or complicated the production process, the more significant the decisions about business service inputs. By choosing to 'buy', usually on a contractual basis negotiated in advance, the firm is likely to be able to command the services of an expert employed by a firm specialising in a particular activity such as advertising, website construction and maintenance, or advanced computer software installation and configuration for firm-specific tasks.

For large firms, design has become a distributed task that is informed by blending different types of expertise together. This expertise can be culturally embedded or be technical expertise. The designer's role is to ensure that products are developed to meet consumer needs; such needs may reflect the requirements of people with different abilities or localised consumer expectations. Designers must experience different cultures and be aware of different design traditions and consumer lifestyles and related identities. All transnational firms have to access design expertise located in their core markets. This is to differentiate between products that are designed and developed for all markets and products that have been created for specific local, regional or national markets.

Electrolux, the Swedish manufacturer of home and professional appliances, has grown by acquisition linked to the development of strong brands and modern localised designs. The company manufactures the majority of its products in low cost locations, but still manufactures difficult to transport products close to market. The internal elements of Electrolux products tend to be the same, but the design is altered to meet the needs of local consumer cultures. Electrolux has developed a series of global product platforms that blend the advantages that come from standardisation with product localisation. Design is an integral part of the firm's strategy based on consumer insights. Consumers are interviewed and also observed during home visits using conventional ethnographic techniques. Consumers are filmed using Electrolux products and the tapes are analysed by professional ethnographers. Consumer insight is combined with 'foresight' that is identified by 'trend' managers who travel and search for new trends and fashions that reflect lifestyle alterations. In 2010 Electrolux launched a new range of dishwashers in Europe – the RealLife range. This product was based on thousands of hours of consumer observation and interviews across Europe. The product is quieter than other machines; research identified that consumers tend to dine and socialise in their kitchens and the machines use less water and energy, but also have greater capacity.

Electrolux employs 150 designers distributed in 7 countries across 4 continents. The company's design hub is located in Stockholm, and there are design centres located in North America, Brazil, Italy, Singapore, Australia (Sydney) and China (Shanghai). The regional design centres work with local independent design studios. The design centres focus on trying to understand consumers and their lifestyles and to create new products or modify existing products to meet local needs. The company's strategy is based on creating products that can be sold worldwide on the basis of common global needs as well as products that are designed to meet the requirements of local consumer cultures. Electrolux tries to balance the development of products that are designed to meet the needs of local consumers with the benefits that come from economies of scale; mass production is facilitated by localised customisation.

Design localisation involves employing designers located in core target markets. This involves distributing design tasks in core markets and in ensuring that designers located at a central headquarters experience different consumer cultures and lifestyles. This is a complex process involving a close dialogue between designers and consumers. Companies develop and design products by observing everyday human behaviour. Large companies often send their designers on lengthy sabbaticals to foreign countries. They can be encouraged to complete a postgraduate qualification in another country or to work in the area and then report back to headquarters on local developments in design, styling and fashion. Short, intensive research trips overseas are encouraged. Such trips are considered a valuable way of engaging with local cultures and identifying local design idioms and consumer behaviour.

Design provides companies with competitive advantage. It is important that companies design and develop products that meet the expectations and cultures of particular place-based consumer communities. Companies can try to develop global products, but for the majority of products some form of design localisation must occur. This may involve alterations to a product's name, packaging, marketing strategy and even specification. Companies have been established in low-cost economies to provide manufacturing capacity for established Western brands. Companies with established brands may have transformed themselves into virtual manufacturing firms. Such firms are no longer directly involved in the manufacturing process, but rather design and develop products that are fabricated by contract manufacturers. Virtual manufacturers compete through the creation of a strong brand, designer products, the orchestration of many contractual relationships with manufacturers and via the development and implementation of effective marketing strategies. To the consumer the contract manufacturer is invisible; such firms are anonymous companies who compete on price rather than design and brand. There is a real danger that contract manufacturers located in low cost economies transform themselves from anonymous companies into heavily branded design-intensive firms. For US and European companies, the real danger will be the emergence of strong Chinese design-intensive brands.

Conclusion

This chapter began with a review of the on-going debate on International Business across the social sciences. It was noted that no unified or integrated theory of International Business exists. The eclectic paradigm provides some useful insights to explain why firms internationalise, but is weaker in explaining the evolution of International Business. The chain-based approaches tend to adopt more of a macro-approach to International Business, neglecting the everyday activities that are required to organise and manage International Business. On the one hand, one could argue that a single integrated theory of International Business is not required. On the other, an International Business is a single integrated organisation – or is it? – and as such requires the explanatory power of a single integrated conceptual framework or theory. This chapter has made two assumptions. First, that an International Business is in a continual process of becoming – it never becomes. In other words, an International Business is an on-going process involving resources, assets, people, routines, practices, motivations, sunk costs and previous decisions that provide path dependency. Second, an International Business involves the management of a set of tasks that may be distributed across many places or localities. Some of these distributed tasks are perhaps more critical and place-dependent than others. The use of the word distribution highlights that this is a process of decision-making for some long-term objective. At the core of this chapter is an appreciation that products (goods and services) are critical for the success of an International Business and that understanding innovation, design and creativity in the development of products for international markets should form a critical part of the on-going literature on International Business.

Products are developed through blending different types of expertise together, and in many instances these different forms of knowing are located in different places or in different communities of understanding. Products are developed to meet the needs of specific markets, and this means that design localisation is an important part of the design process. Products can be created for specific markets and then modified to meet the needs of consumers located in other places. Design localisation involves design expertise located in core markets, and this has resulted in the development of distributed design capacity and capability – distributed across design centres located in core markets. Distributed design processes have been facilitated by developments in ICT and in specialist design software that enables designers located in many different places to be involved in the co-design of products in real time. Many products are designed, manufactured and marketed using facilities and expertise located in core markets. A product may be designed by a transnational design team and be manufactured in facilities distributed in core consumer markets; design localisation can go hand in hand with production localisation. Products can also be designed by a transnational team and manufactured in low cost locations.

Products are created through interactive processes that blend expertise, capacities and capabilities located in different places. There are many different types of product design and production strategy. On the one hand, some companies compete on the basis of products that are designed and manufactured in one country. Such companies are competing by developing non-price-based associations between design, product, brand and place. On the other, companies can compete by developing products using distributed design expertise and production facilities. Both types of company will develop products by using a complex system of sources, brokers and distributers. Central to this process are money, people and business strategy. Money is required to support the design and development process, and this can come directly from the sale of products or be borrowed from banks and venture capitalists or obtained from the stock market or from government loans or subsidiaries. People play a central role in providing the expertise, imagination and creativity required to develop products. People must also be co-ordinated, led and controlled. The management of project teams, especially complex teams composed of many geographically distributed tasks, poses special problems and requires further research. Design has become an important part of many companies' business strategies and will continue to be a core source of competitive advantage. The importance of design for corporate competitiveness provides another way in which geography or place matters. Design is a place-based process involving the creation of products that reflect national design identities. The distributed design localisation process enables firms to adapt products to meet the needs of local customers, but at the same time to benefit from economies of scale; localised design is blended with translocal production capabilities and this may enhance a company's resilience. Product ideas developed in one place can be transferred and modified to meet the needs of other national markets. Distributed design localisation ensures that firms balance the benefits that accrue from global manufacturing against customer demands for localised products. Design is a key service function that plays an important role at the interface between production and consumption and is a critical service process.

References

Beyers, W.B. & Lindahl, D.P. (1996) 'Explaining the demand for producer services', *Papers in Regional Science*, 75, pp. 351–74.

Bryson, J.R. (1997) 'Business service firms, service space and the management of change', *Entrepreneurship and Regional Development*, 9, pp. 93–111.

Bryson, J.R. (2007a) 'Arts, dance, cultural infrastructure and city regeneration: Knowledge, audience development, networks and conventions and the relocation of a royal ballet company from London to Birmingham', *The Norwegian Journal of Geography*, 61, pp. 98–110.

Bryson, J.R. (2007b) 'A "second" global shift? The offshoring or global sourcing of corporate services and the rise of distanciated emotional labour', *Geografiska Annaler*, 89B, pp. 31–43.

Bryson, J.R. (2015) 'Geography of entrepreneurship', in '*The International Encyclopaedia of the Social and Behavioural Sciences*. 2nd Edition. Oxford, UK: Elsevier.

Bryson, J.R., Daniels, P.W. & Warf, B. (2004) *Service Worlds: People, Organisations, Technologies*. Routledge: London.

Bryson, J.R. & Ronayne, M. (2014) 'Manufacturing carpets and technical textiles: Routines, resources, capabilities, adaptation, innovation and the evolution of the British textile industry', *Cambridge Journal of Regions, Society and Economy*, 7, pp. 471–488.

Bryson, J.R. & Rusten, G. (2011) *Design Economies and the Changing World Economy: Innovation, Production and Competitiveness*. London: Routledge Studies in Human Geography.

Bürdek, B.R. (1999) *Design Classics: The Apple Macintosh*. Frankfurt: Verlag.

Clark, T. (1995) *Managing Consultants*. Milton Keynes, UK: Open University Press.

Coe, N.M., Dicken, P. & Hess, M. (2008) 'Global production networks: Realizing the potential', *Journal of Economic Geography*, 8, pp. 271–195.

Coe, N.M., Hess, M., Yeung, H.W., Dicken, P. & Henderson, J. (2004) '"Globalising" regional development: A global production networks perspective', *Transactions of the Institute of British Geographers, NS29*, pp. 468–484.

Coe, N.M. & Yeung, H.W. (2015) *Global Production Networks: Theorizing Economic Development in an Interconnected World*. Oxford, UK: Oxford University Press.

Dunning, J. (2001) 'The eclectic (OLI) paradigm of international production: Past, present and future', *International Journal of Economics and Business*, 8, pp. 173–190.

Dunning, J. (2003) 'The key literature on IB activities: 1960–2000', in Rugman, A.M. & Brewer, T. (Eds.), *The Oxford Handbook of International Business*. Oxford, UK: Oxford University Press.

Gereffi, G., Humphrey, J. & Sturgeon, T. (2005) 'The governance of global value chains', *Review of International Political Economy*, 12, pp. 78–104.

Gereffi, G., Wadhwa, V., Rissing, B. & Ong R. (2008) 'Getting the numbers right: International engineering education in the United States, China, and India', *Journal of Engineering Education*, 97, pp. 13–25.

Gertler, M.S. (1995) '"Being there": Proximity, organisation, and culture in the development and adoption of advanced manufacturing technologies', *Economic Geography*, 71, pp. 1–26.

Gertler, M.S. (2004) *Manufacturing Culture: The Institutional Geography of Industrial Practice*. Oxford, UK: Oxford University Press.

Harvey, D. (1989) *The Condition of Postmodernity: An Enquiry into the Origins of Cultural Change*. Oxford, UK: Blackwell.

Iammarino, S. & McCann, P. (2013) *Multinational and Economic Geography: Location, Technology and Innovation*. Cheltenham, UK: Edward Elgar.

Lewis, N., Larner, W. & Le Heron, R. (2008) 'The New Zealand designer fashion industry: Making industries and co-constituting political projects', *Transactions of the Institute of British Geographers*, NS 33, pp. 42–59.

MacPherson, A.D. & Vanchan, V. (2009) 'The outsourcing of industrial design by large US manufacturing companies: an exploratory study', *International Regional Science Review*, 33, pp. 3–30.

MacPherson, A.D. & Vanchan, V. (2010) 'Locational patterns and competitive characteristics of industrial design firms in the United States', in Rusten, G. & Bryson, J.R. (Eds.), *Industrial Design, Competition and Globalization*. Basingstoke, UK: Palgrave Macmillan, pp. 81–92.

Nonaka, I. & Takeuchi, H. (1995) *The Knowledge-Creating Company: How Japanese Companies Create the Dynamics of Innovation*. Oxford, UK: Oxford University Press.

Nonaka, I. & Teece, D.J. (Eds.) (2001) *Managing Industrial Knowledge*. London: Sage.

Nye, J. (2014) *A Long Time in Making: The History of Smiths*. Oxford, UK: Oxford University Press.

Peck, J. (2005) 'Struggling with the creative class', *International Journal of Urban and Regional Research*, 29, pp. 740–770.

Robertson, M. & Swan, J. (1998) 'Modes of organizing in an expert consultancy', *Organization*, 5, pp. 543–564.

Rugman, A.M. & Collinson, S. (2005) *International Business*. Upper Saddle River, NJ: Prentice Hall.

Rusten, G. & Bryson, J.R. (2007) 'The production and consumption of industrial design expertise by small and medium-sized firms: Some evidence from Norway', *Geografiska Annaler*, 89, pp. 75–87.

Rusten, G. & Bryson, J.R. (Eds.) (2010a) *Industrial Design, Competition and Globalization*. Basingstoke, UK: Palgrave Macmillan.

Rusten, G. & Bryson, J.R. (2010b) 'Placing and spacing services: Towards a balanced Economic Geography of firms, clusters, social networks, contracts and the geographies of enterprise', *Tidschrift voor Economische en Sociale Geografie*, 101, pp. 248–261.

Rusten, G., Bryson, J.R. & Aarflot, U. (2007) 'Places through product and products through places: Industrial design and spatial symbols as sources of competitiveness', *Norwegian Journal of Geography*, 61, pp. 133–144.

Rusten, G., Bryson, J.R. & Gammelsæter, H. (2005) 'Dislocated versus local business service expertise and knowledge and the acquisition of external management consultancy expertise by small and medium-sized enterprises in Norway', *Geoforum*, 36, pp. 525–539.

Sweet, F. (1999) *Frog: Form Follows Emotion*. New York: Watson-Guptill.

Vanchan, V. & Bryson, J.R. (2015) 'Design and manufacturing: The competitiveness of American, European and Chinese industrial design companies', in Bryson J.R., Clark, J. & Vanchan, V. (Eds.), *Handbook of Manufacturing in the World Economy*. Cheltenham, UK: Edward Elgar, pp. 147–162.

Vanchan, V., Bryson, J.R. & Clark, J. (2015) 'Manufacturing matters: Space, place, time and production', in Bryson J.R., Clark, J. & Vanchan, V. (Eds.), *Handbook of Manufacturing in the World Economy*. Cheltenham, UK: Edward Elgar, pp. 3–16.

Vanchan, V. & MacPherson, A. (2008a) 'The competitive characteristics of U.S. firms in the industrial design sector: Evidence from a national survey', *Competition and Change*, 12, pp. 262–280.

Vanchan, V. & MacPherson, A. (2008b) 'The recent growth performance of US firms in the industrial design sector: An exploratory study', *Industry and Innovation*, 15, pp. 11–17.

Vinodrai, T. (2006) 'Reproducing Toronto's design ecology: Career paths, intermediaries, and local labor markets', *Economic Geography*, 82, pp. 237–264.

Vinodrai, T. (2010) 'Designed here, made there? Project-based design work in Toronto, Canada', in Rusten, G. & Bryson, J.R. (Eds.), *Industrial Design, Competition and Globalization*. Basingstoke, UK: Palgrave Macmillan, pp. 117–140.

Weller, S. (2008) 'Beyond "global production networks": Australian Fashion Week's trans-sectoral synergies', *Growth and Change*, 39, pp. 104–122.

Yamin, M. (2000) 'A critical re-evaluation of Hymer's contribution to the theory of the transnational corporation', in C.N. Pitelis & R. Sugden (Eds.), *The Nature of the Transnational Firm*, 2nd Edition. London: Routledge.

Yeung, H.W. (2009) 'Transnationalizing entrepreneurship: A critical agenda for Economic Geography', *Progress in Human Geography*, 33, pp. 201–235.

Wood, P. (2002) *Consultancy and Innovation*. London: Routledge.

32
THE CULTURE OF FINANCE

Gordon L. Clark

Introduction

The culture of finance is the stuff of books, plays and films, as in Belfort's (2007) *The Wolf of Wall Street* and Lewis's (2011) *The Big Short*. The concept is used to represent Wall Street and the City of London after deregulation and during the global financial crisis, wherein long-term relationships and trust in other market participants apparently gave way to uninhibited self-seeking behaviour. Luyendijk's (2015) anthropological take on the City of London after the global financial crisis has reinforced perceptions of an industry out of control. Yet he does something different and important: while providing evidence of a pervasive culture of amorality in major financial institutions, he also indicates that these types of organisations seem to lack the appetite or the capacity to manage the behaviour of their employees.

The culture of finance is also on the academic agenda (Zingales, 2015; Lo, 2016). The erosion of the values held integral to relationships reliant upon mutual benefit and reciprocity is believed to be evident in the costs to the 'real' economy of financial instability (Haldane, 2014). Critics of finance also suggest that the industry is something of a pariah in promoting a form of amorality not found in wider society (Morris & Vines, 2015). Those sharing this opinion tend to be advocates of re-invigorated notions of ethical norms that appeal to a 'golden-rule' for behaviour that discounts self-interest in favour of society (Clark, 2014a). Is finance so different from other segments of society? Some ethical theorists believe that the erosion of virtue is endemic to modern society, and is the result of locating morality with individuals rather than society (MacIntyre, 1981).

Here, it is argued that focus upon the individual sidesteps the fact that the vast majority of participants in the industry are the employees of companies (e.g. asset managers) and institutions (e.g. asset owner) (Stambaugh, 2014; Axelson & Bond, 2015). It is suggested that the proper focus of any study of the culture of finance is on the relationships between institutions and between employees and their employers rather than just individuals. Whereas it has been convenient for some to label those employees found to have violated community norms as 'rogues', thereby discounting any suggestion that their behaviour is representative of their employers or the industry (Clark, 1997), I do not share the assumption evident in much of the literature that institutional investors are fundamentally different and/or more effective than individual traders (see Shleifer & Summers, 1990; Scheinkman, 2014). My focus is upon why aberrant behaviour is rewarded in some segments of the global financial services industry but not in others.

The chapter proceeds in the following manner. First, an analytical model is presented so as to better understand the co-existence of different kinds of financial agents and organisations in the industry. Initially, the model is conceived without reference to time (risk and uncertainty) or space (being co-located or not with a global financial centre). This allows for an elaboration of Hart and Moore's (2008) model of the firm, where compensation depends upon internal factors related to task and performance, and external factors including fairness with respect to similarly placed individuals in other organisations. Thereafter, time and space re-enter the analysis, demonstrating that the costs and consequences of being embedded is specific to the ecology of finance; see generally Taylor and Asheim (2001) and Maskell (2015). Second, the argument of the chapter is developed by reference to the fact that individual and organisational performance is only known *ex post*, notwithstanding *ex ante* commitment. Third, it is shown that location matters: the 'power' of norms and conventions depend upon the local instantiation of the industry and its relationship with global financial centres located near and far from their home site (Clark, 2016).

Befitting a volume on Economic Geography and International Business, this chapter is a mapping exercise that seeks to situate the culture of finance in the ecology and morphology of finance. In terms of exposition, the chapter is designed to be conceptual, eschewing the details of specific cases and places in the interests of presenting an analytical framework through which to understand industry behaviour. In doing so, I refer to the relevant literature inside and outside of Economic Geography. Given the importance of the global financial services industry, I also 'place' the industry in the evolving landscape of national and international financial centres, referencing the tension between the virtues of jurisdictional arbitrage and embeddedness. In the following section, I locate my analysis on the theoretical side of academic practice, but note that my approach is grounded in fieldwork and case studies; a mode of inquiry and exposition familiar to Economic Geography and International Business.

The life of organisations

The chapter proceeds via principles and ideal-types rather than reporting on the findings from fieldwork and ethnographic studies of organisational behaviour (compare Jarzabkowski, Bednarek & Spee, 2015). In part, this reflects the evident value of conceptualising the organisational ecology of the financial services industry (Haldane & May, 2011). There are many insightful and empirically founded studies of the industry, including those that provide information on sector-specific employment practices (Beaverstock, 2004; Faulconbridge, 2009) and their spatial manifestations (Dörry, 2015). At the same time, analytical progress has not always kept pace with commentary in economics and finance on the status of finance in modern societies as well as the political debate over income inequality (Piketty & Goldhammer, 2014). It would seem the legitimacy of the academic discipline of finance is in play (Zingales, 2015), along with the capacity of the discipline to translate models of markets, organisations and behaviour into the world at large (Lo, 2016). There is a symbiotic relationship between empirical research and theory-building (see Beugelsdijk, McCann & Mudambi, 2010).

Here, inside knowledge of financial institutions is used to provide an analytical framework through which to understand the nature and scope of the culture of finance. By 'inside knowledge' I mean the information and knowledge gleaned from field work, active participation in the organisations and institutions of the industry, and recognition of the responsibilities and predicaments faced by senior managers when seeking to realise the goals and objectives of their organisations.

Closely related to my 'inside' perspective is the use of key concepts and assumptions that underpin the analytical perspective used to understand the culture of finance in the investment management industry. In doing so, I defer to Davis's (2015) argument about the importance of realism and doing the hard work of understanding how organisations and institutions function in industry and the economy (local and global). I am also conscious of Rodrik's (2015) argument that being explicit about the 'critical assumptions' underpinning the analysis allows the analyst to transcend popular stories about what has happened and will happen. This approach is also to be found in management studies and in the economics literature (see Baker, Gibbons & Murphy, 2001, 2002), and is the lifeblood of Economic Geography (Clark, 1998).[1]

Any inside perspective must be sensitive to how the industry manages itself. There are various ways of representing industry governance practices. Given my interest in organisations and behavior, in this chapter the issue of 'culture' is framed, in part, by reference to industry norms and conventions, where 'norms' refer to expectations as to the nature and scope of acceptable behaviour and 'conventions' refer to the practices of the industry (Brennan et al., 2014, pp. 17, 20–21, 100–102).[2] My approach 'grounds' the idea of a shared culture in the financial services industry even if government regulators have found it problematic when attempting to define, measure and enforce codes of practice in the financial industry. Too often industry culture is defined by reference to undesirable outcomes rather than organising principles. Witness the announcement in December 2015 that the UK Financial Conduct Authority (FCA) had abandoned its inquiry into the culture of UK financial institutions. It appears the FCA had found it difficult to frame a work-programme on the issue.

In any event, it is suggested here that the behaviour of one type of person (traders) in a specific type of organisation (broker and/or investment bank) is too often used to represent all financial agents and organisations. The ecology of finance is truncated, whereas analysts should also consider the diversity of organisations and their employment practices across the industry and across markets. Different sorts of financial agents (by task and function) and different types of organisations (by purpose and legal form) coexist with one another. In some instances, 'difference' is subsumed by complementarity (Clark, 2002). In other cases, 'difference' cuts against the generality of industry norms and conventions. It is also observed that some financial agents and organisations deliberately locate themselves outside of the norms and conventions of the industry, fostering internal standards of behaviour so as to trump industry standards of behaviour.

Building blocks

To analyse the structure and performance of the finance industry, we begin with the key concepts that underpin the global financial services industry and set it apart from other service-sector industries. Three issues are emphasised: the organisations of the industry, the process whereby investment returns are produced, and the environment in which the industry functions and organisations flourish (or not). The industry is shown to be distinctive if not unique.

Organisations

The financial industry is based upon three types of organisation. The first is asset holders, including those organisations that represent beneficiaries and have a legal entitlement to assets under management (for example, pension funds and sovereign wealth funds) as well as those organisations that provide investment services (for example, asset management companies) (Davis & Steil, 2001). These organisations are joined together in the pursuit of risk-adjusted rates of return on assets under management (Clark & Monk, 2017). These organisations can have different legal forms and status depending upon their 'home' jurisdictions.

The second type of organisation is the financial market (or markets). Financial markets can be public and private. In public markets, entry and exit are limited only by the capacity of an organisation to meet the formal and informal conditions required for transacting in these markets. In private markets, however, entry and exit are determined by organisations that have the power to set terms and conditions as regards the placement of assets, any entitlements that come with those placements, and any commitments or obligations to the lead organisations and/or partner organisations. In one sense, financial markets are owned, being limited in number and in their locations (Wójcik, 2010, 2011). In another sense, financial markets are continuous and virtually unbounded that when linked together trading can take place almost every minute of every day across the world (O'Brien, 1992).

The third type of organisation underpinning the global financial services industry is government. As indicated earlier, different types of asset holders have certain legal privileges and obligations. How they go about realising their objectives (risk-adjusted rates of return on assets under management) is also subject to government regulation, including standards of behaviour such as fiduciary duty. This is also true of financial markets. In the past, governments required asset holders to invest in certain types of securities and, in some cases, according to fixed proportions. These types of regulations were largely discarded through the 1980s and 1990s. Nonetheless, the map of government regulation affecting asset holders and financial markets is highly differentiated as are the modes of regulation (La Porta, Lopez-de-Silanes & Shleifer, 1998; Wainwright, 2011).

Skill and expertise

Fundamental to the production of risk-adjusted rates of return are the skills and expertise of employees and the employees of service providers that either operate with or collaborate with investment organisations (Axelson & Bond, 2015). Skills and expertise are domain-specific, such that the overlap between asset classes and styles of investment may be relatively limited or, more likely, come at a price (under-performance). Whereas it was once possible to talk about 'reading the market', via networks of informants, analytical and quantitative skills have become essential in framing and executing investment strategies. Likewise, expertise – judgement and experience – is a crucial element in sustaining investment performance in the context of market risk and uncertainty (Clark, 2014b). This means, of course, successful employees can exact high rents on their skills and expertise.

For many years, outsourcing was the conventional way in which asset owners managed the production process. Asset owners relied upon the market for financial services and for the component parts of the production process. In many cases, asset owners used consultants to assemble and coordinate external providers towards realising their return objectives. However, large asset owners have begun to in-source production so as to reap the benefits of scale and the benefits of employment contracts, as opposed to service contracts. Disintermediation and selected re-intermediation are responses to the costs of the culture of finance (Clark & Monk, 2017).

Time and space

The production of investment returns is set to targets to be realised at some time in the future. Given a track record, it is possible to anticipate the risks associated with setting a rate of return target over a specific period. Asset holders do not control the immediate environment in which the production process takes place, neither do they control public and private financial markets (although they might seek to do so). These markets are subject to the unanticipated behaviour of other market participants and exogenous shocks that disturb the market expectations of all participants. In this respect, asset holders commit resources to a planned rate of return target (*ex ante*) knowing that realisation of that rate of return target (*ex post*) is subject to risk and uncertainty (Litterman, 2004).

Asset holders can be co-located with the financial markets through which they invest; for example, being located in London alongside the London Stock Exchange and the many public and private opportunities for investment offered by London-based investment organisations. Alternatively, asset holders can be located at some distance from the financial markets through which they invest (Dixon & Monk, 2014). In these circumstances, asset holders rely upon the communication and electronic networks that link their sites with those markets. This may be unproblematic, but may be difficult if market information is expensive to obtain. Market pricing need not reflect the available information, and can be systematically skewed in unobserved ways due to the existence of other financial agents and/or organisations able to realise their interests over others. In many cases, being geographically close to the market is advantageous (Alevy, Haigh & List, 2007), notwithstanding the effects of overlapping expectations and portfolio construction (Pool, Stoffman & Yonker, 2015).

Ecology of finance

One way of understanding the structure and performance of any industry is through an appreciation of the genesis, nature and diversity of their constituent organisations (Padgett & Powell, 2012). Early on, Hannan and Freeman (1989) were critical of analysts who treated organisations as self-contained entities without regard to their internal and external relationships. Hannan and Freeman's approach to the study of organisations relied upon work by March and Simon (1958), Cyert and March (1963), and others who have followed this same line of inquiry. In this chapter, the focus is less about the emergence of the financial services industry (see Clark, 2000), than it is upon the organisational diversity of the industry and the strategic response of market agents to the costs and consequences of their location in the industry pecking-order.

Organisational diversity

In the previous section, it was suggested that there are two types of asset holders (owners and managers), and that organisations can be differentiated from one another according to size (assets under management). It was also noted that these organisations are subject to government regulation – it is often the case that asset holders have a 'national' identity, although they may well operate across the globe (Huberman, 2001). It is notable that the largest asset owners operate from a home base, but may do so through offshore offices and intermediaries. The largest asset managers have extensive operations around the world. A number of asset owners are outside of major financial centres and operate through spatially extensive networks (Dixon & Monk, 2014).

The asset management industry is dominated by a handful of very large companies (Bongini, Nieri & Pelagatti, 2015). These are full-service organisations that provide a broad spectrum of investment services, asset classes and styles of investment. These companies are often global, bringing together clients from around the world with investment services in public and private markets. There are also mid-sized investment companies that are important providers of investment services even if their scope, in terms of services and geographical reach, is more limited and often based upon national and macro-regions (for example, Europe and the Middle East, North America and East Asia). Finally, there are many small asset management companies offering specialised investment options inside and outside public markets. The share of assets under management of small asset management companies is far smaller than might be expected, relative to the number of those smaller companies (Clark, 2016).

Relationships and market position

Given the importance of size and jurisdiction for these organisations, they could be treated as separate and different. To do so would underestimate the ways in which these organisations relate to one another and the ways in which these relationships are fostered in specific financial centres. Large and small asset holders complement, compete and, in some cases, collaborate with one another. It is not uncommon for small asset managers to pick up clients that large asset managers are either not willing or are unable to provide with a level of service demanded by clients. Large asset managers tend to be weak in terms of innovation, and pass on clients that seek services that fall outside conventional ways of producing investment returns. Small asset managers thrive in those areas of the market in which large asset managers are unwilling or unable to effectively operate.

At another level, all asset holders compete with one another in the production of their rates of return. In a rising market, this competition need not be a zero-sum game: asset owners and asset managers alike can benefit from asset appreciation. In a falling market, however, successful asset managers may be able to attract disenchanted asset owners from those providers unable to stem losses and/or meet target rates of return. In betting on the expected path of financial markets, asset managers offer potential clients the option to switch, so as to realise 'out-performance'. Given scale economies, inflows of assets sustain the scope and price-competitiveness of well-managed asset managers. Equally, outflows of assets undercut the scope and performance of poorly managed asset managers. Few asset owners are subject to the short-term rewards and penalties of (relative) performance that drive competition amongst asset managers.

Hierarchies as pecking orders

Implicit in our discussion of the ecology of the global financial services industry is the existence of hierarchies – referencing the size of organisations, the nature and scope of offered services, the skills and expertise of investment managers, and the relationships between financial organisations. Williamson (1975), Hannan and Freeman (1989), and Rajan and Zingales (2001) amongst others note that senior managers typically rely upon a hierarchical distribution of powers and resources within their organisations so as to control activities and functions. Hierarchies in the global financial services industry should also be understood as pecking orders – the opportunities that accrue to high-order organisations over low-order or less endowed organisations.

Once established, pecking orders reduce conflict and, at the limit, privilege those organisations that have the best chance of success. Organisations that observe the industry pecking order may also be able to form alliances. In these ways, stability and mutual benefit (if not equal benefit) dampen competition and are the basis for co-dependence and cooperation. Related reasoning is found in microeconomics (Bowles, 2005), corporate finance (Myers & Majluf, 1984) and Economic Geography (Glückler, 2010; Schamp, 2010). While the concept is meaningful in terms of the hierarchical order of organisations in the global financial services industry, in the next section it is suggested that the adaptive capacity of organisations is not necessarily limited by their place in the industry pecking order. Senior managers may well situate their organisations outside of dominant norms and conventions so as to enhance their strategic capacity.

To illustrate the significance of pecking orders in the finance industry, consider the following.

- Large asset owners typically have greater degrees of freedom in terms of framing and implementing investment strategies than small asset owners. Large asset owners have the option to insource the production of investment returns – small asset owners do not.
- Large asset managers are able to provide a wide range of services, thereby capturing the full range of asset owners (clients) and sustaining growth in assets under management – small asset managers must specialise, relying upon a narrow range of clients and thereby limiting growth potential.
- Large asset owners and asset managers are able to marshall capabilities and resources consistent with dampening volatility in performance in relation to target rates of return – small asset owners and asset managers have limited capabilities and resources, and are vulnerable to the volatility of financial markets.
- Large asset owners and asset managers are able to invest in the capabilities and resources of their organisations, including infrastructure, the skills and expertise of managers, and risk control functions – small asset owners and asset managers are resource-constrained, prompting reliance upon the services offered by other organisations and/or the purchase of generic services over services tailored to their investment strategies.
- Large asset owners are better able to govern their relationships with asset managers – small asset owners are so reliant upon service providers that any leverage in these relationships falls to asset managers rather than asset owners.
- Large asset owners have the skills and expertise to develop collaborative partnerships, and the power and authority to choose partners – small asset owners seeking partnerships with larger asset owners must simply take what is offered.
- Large asset owners have the resources to compete in the market for skills and expertise, and may be able to insource production – small asset owners lack comparable resources and must outsource production.
- Large asset owners and large asset managers can become complex and unwieldy organisations due to their size and scope – small asset owners and managers may be more flexible and fleet-of-foot, but lack the capabilities and resources to fully capitalise on this advantage.
- Large asset owners and large asset managers may be able to compensate for their complexity by forming units of innovation (in the sense of being more adaptive to changing market conditions) just inside or outside the formal boundaries of their organisations – small asset owners and managers may be innovative, but lack the resources to make good on this advantage over the long term.

Earlier, large organisations were juxtaposed with small organisations; nonetheless, the hierarchy in each case should be understood as a continuum from largest to smallest. In each case, the pecking order is based upon relative size and resources (Helfat & Peteraf, 2009). This is reflected in the strategic relationships between large and small asset managers, wherein the former may acquire the latter for their skills and expertise in areas not easily developed or managed within large organisations. Large asset managers can also spin-out certain functions and services given the inertia of these organisations. Ultimately, the stock and flow of assets under management determines the pecking order within the global financial services industry.

Morphology of finance

Research on the ecology of organisations is self-conscious of the debt owed to biology and evolutionary science, especially in the use of concepts such as diversity and path dependence in explaining observed variations in organisational form (Hannan & Freeman, 1989). Just as important are persistent variations in organisational form and functions across space (Boschma & Martin, 2010). The morphology of finance is intimately connected to the ecology of finance. Here, we focus upon spatial scale (global, national and local) and nodal points (financial centres) so as to locate global finance and thereby explain apparent variations in organisational form and functions across jurisdictions (Clark, 2005).

Financial flows

It is widely recognised that capital flows around the world on a 24/7 basis at a rate that far exceeds trade-based commodity exchange. In part, the flow of capital takes place between regions that have a surplus of financial assets and regions that have a deficit. Surplus regions are often well-endowed but face countervailing forces: for example, the export of resources to the developed and developing economies of the world produces earnings which flow back to the exporting countries, and then are turned around to flow back to global financial centres located in developed economies. Commodity markets are also financial markets; the expected price of resources tends to drive resource extraction, export and earnings. In good times, these markets attract investors seeking a risk premium over and above that found in conventional stock markets.

At the other end of the spatial hierarchy, local insurance companies, pension funds and banks collect contributions and deposits from individuals and companies, pooling these separate and often small financial flows into common funds that, in turn, enable these organisations to discount the costs of collection, management and investment. In federated countries, these entities often have a presence at the local and state (provincial) levels. The flow of funds from the local level are normally channelled through financial companies and organisations to entities located at the national level. Given the economies of scale in the financial services industry, pooling financial assets in organisations located in large financial centres benefits contributors and depositors alike, just as it benefits the companies that manage and invest those assets. Mergers and acquisitions between local, provincial and national banks have accelerated the collection and channelling process, thereby centralising the holding and management of financial assets.

Financial centralisation and decentralisation

The rise of financial centres in many developed countries is an expression of the scale economies apparent in pooling and coordinating the flow of financial assets. Historically, the process of centralisation was facilitated through banking systems, wherein taking deposits and lending locally was transformed by regional banks taking deposits at the local level and, through the pooling process, investing those assets in economic and financial opportunities regardless of origin (national and international). Over the second half of the 20th century, banks and related deposit-taking institutions were transformed into financial institutions and organisations. In some countries, the geographical centralisation and financialisation of banking was so thorough that by the start of the 21st century, just one financial centre dominated the nation-state (e.g. Amsterdam in The Netherlands, Stockholm in Sweden, London in the UK, Paris in France, etc.).

Notwithstanding the claims made about the 'end of geography' in financial markets, there remains a premium on being at, or adjacent to, financial centres that encompass major financial markets. The premium on co-location varies, however, by the transparency or otherwise of relevant financial products. For example, opaque financial products that require information and knowledge not readily accessible through existing channels of information (e.g. Bloomberg) are best assessed and priced through networks of information that are geographically and functionally specific (Clark & O'Connor, 1997; Storper & Venables, 2004). By contrast, transparent financial products may be well-priced in the market, such that there is no privileged location (geographically based information asymmetries). Trading from remote locations may be just as effective as trading from central locations, assuming that electronic and communications technologies are universal in terms of their efficiency and effectiveness (Wójcik, 2010, 2011).

Financial centres

The asset management industry is highly concentrated, both in terms of the share of financial assets held by the largest asset managers and in terms of their sites of operation – major financial centres. As noted earlier, large asset managers have many advantages over small asset managers. By offering a broad range of financial products and instruments, large asset managers are often able to function as 'one-stop shops' that retain clients rather than having to compete, as much smaller entities must compete, for individual mandates. These managers are also able to bring together clients nationally and internationally through sites of operation and management linking together global financial centres and markets (Clark, 2002).

More often than not, asset owners search for, or receive presentations from, service providers whose principal sites of operation are in national financial centres. Both sides of the market benefit from the spatial morphology of the industry: product providers locate in national financial centres so as to reap the benefits of being close to the market. Financial centres therefore embody two types of overlapping and intersecting markets: markets through which to place financial assets and reap investment returns, and markets for services across a broad range of functions and providers. As Grossman and Helpman (2004, 2005) observe when discussing the benefits of large urban centres in developing economies for service providers, co-location facilitates the search process on both sides of the market.

There is also a spatial hierarchy of financial centres. New York dominates Chicago and Chicago dominates the West Coast, just as London dominates Edinburgh and all other European financial centres. One explanation for this is to be found in the significance of their related public and private financial markets. This much is obvious. However, just as important is the fact that the largest financial centres embody a broad range of financial intermediaries (by type) and a large number of intermediaries (by function) than is the case for smaller, albeit significant financial centres. Indeed, in the largest financial centres, intermediaries can afford to specialise in terms of the nature and scope of the functions that they offer because of the scope of the market for financial services. European financial institutions go to London not only for investment opportunities but also for access to specialised service providers that cannot survive in Amsterdam, Frankfurt or Stockholm. To the extent that these types of specialised services exist in smaller markets, these are primarily located in large multipurpose banks and related organisations. Client access to these services is through the purchase of related products.

Norms and conventions

In this section, we take a first cut at the 'culture of finance', drawing upon the previous discussion concerning the ecology and morphology of finance. From the outset, it is assumed that the culture of finance embodies norms – shared expectations about how people should behave – and conventions – how people behave in certain circumstances. It is assumed that the culture of finance has a normative and a positive element, the former being more problematic than the latter, since shared expectations can reinforce aberrant behaviour (Barberis, 2013). Social conventions can also be quite damaging in that, in certain circumstances, people may act in ways that can be thought to reinforce system-wide instability (Haldane & May, 2011).

Service contracts

Consider the contractual relationships between asset owners (e.g. pension funds and sovereign wealth funds) and asset managers (e.g. Blackrock, JPMorgan, etc.). At one level, these relationships are formally codified and underwritten by the law of contract. The global financial services industry has a strong preference for the laws of England and Wales and its progeny, as found in North America and Australasia (Riles, 2011). This type of contract law is preferred because it is founded upon private property rights, due deference to the interests and actions of the parties to contracts, and a presumption in favour of *Pareto optimality* – that is, the parties to contracts freely enter into enforceable agreements expecting to benefit (or at least not lose) from such relationships (Bolton & Dewatripont, 2005). This type of contract law is also preferred because of the perceived expertise and independence of the Anglo-American judiciary (Clark & Monk, 2017).

Most service contracts are based upon templates that are widely accepted across the global investment management industry. These templates are written in the shadow of contract law, and are best understood as conventions – they represent standard practice across the industry, albeit subject to modification in those jurisdictions that require variations in accordance with statute and case law. Templates can be justified on three grounds. First, they allow parties to contracts to economise on the process whereby contracts are written. Second, templates provide a framework for negotiation on specific issues without having to negotiate the whole agreement. Third, templates tend to reduce the risks associated with negotiating 'new' contracts, recognising that, having stood the test of time, the likelihood of being contested in court is low (Gilson, Sabel & Scott, 2013).

These contracts represent 'standard' rather than 'best' practice. To illustrate, Figure 32.1 represents the contractual relationships between asset managers (large and small) and asset owners (large and small). For the moment, this typology takes no account of jurisdiction, size of financial centre or the skill and expertise of investment managers. Contractual relationships are deemed symmetrical (SYM) when both parties have well-founded expectations as to the equitable nature of such agreements. By contrast, contractual relationships are deemed asymmetrical (ASM) when one party dominates the other (including veiled threats of domination). Assume that both parties come to the negotiation table with the relevant industry template. Also assume that size represents the capabilities and resources of the organisation and, more often than not, the place of the organisation in the industry pecking order.

Where a small asset owner contracts with a small asset manager, it is symmetrical in the sense that neither party can do more than suggest minor modifications to the relevant template. For different reasons, both parties are likely to desire such a relationship, legitimated by the widespread belief that the template represents standard practice in the industry. As noted previously, relatively small asset managers operate in the shadow of larger asset managers unless they are highly specialised and operate in a segment of the market that larger groups find difficult to penetrate. Small asset owners can find themselves effectively excluded from participation with larger investment management groups unless their status provides large groups with a reputational benefit. Where a large asset owner contracts with a large asset manager, the contract is likely symmetrical because both parties have the capabilities and resources to vary

		Asset managers	
		Small	Large
Asset owners	Small	SYM	ASM
	Large	ASM	SYM

Figure 32.1 Contractual relationships between asset owners and asset managers

Source: Author.

the industry template. In fact, the deal struck in these cases may be quite different from industry conventions underwriting, for example, long-term relationships based on shared benefits.

The case where a small asset owner contracts with a large asset manager is asymmetrical because any agreement to provide investment services is based upon the industry template and is offered by the latter on a take-it-or-leave-it basis. In fact, a small asset owner could be placed in a queue to gain access to the manager, rank-ordered in terms of volume of assets. The case where a large asset owner contracts with a small asset manager is asymmetrical because the former could dominate the latter by virtue of the need of the latter for inflows of assets under management. The deals struck, in these situations, could be quite exacting, with variations on the industry template provided by lawyers representing the asset owner. This may suit a small asset manager in the early stages of its development seeking to capitalise on its skills and expertise as well as a market niche that hitherto has been relatively ignored or not exploited. However, the deal and the relationship with the large asset owner could subsequently become a significant constraint on its development.

There are two points of complication. First, if both parties are located in a national rather than a global financial centre, asymmetries in relationships can be dampened by a mutual interest in a close relationship (thereby discounting the costs of searching for partners in a global financial centre). Second, if small asset managers are able to rise in the pecking order by virtue of their distinctive skills and expertise, a queue may form behind their investment programme. They may be able to negotiate variations on the industry template that enhance their powers and compensation. In their heyday, successful (small) hedge funds located in London and New York were able to enforce asymmetrical contracts for services.

Employment contracts

In some European countries, employment contracts and compensation remain contentious issues where governments, unions and industry associations promote norms aimed at limiting the dispersion in salaries between the lowest and highest paid workers. In some cases, governments have sought to cap the salaries of workers in banks and related financial institutions, whether directly owned or underwritten by national governments. By contrast, in the Anglo-American world, it is widely recognised that employment conditions including compensation vary significantly between industries and especially within the financial services industry. Industry-wide employment contracts have been discounted in favour of individual contracts, in part reflecting the dismantling of collective bargaining and, in part, reflecting relatively tight labour markets over the last twenty-five years. As a consequence, there is a spatial pecking order across Europe in relation to London regarding compensation in the financial services industry.

Even so, as theorists of the firm have noted (Hart & Moore, 2008), employment contracts and related compensation practices are typically subject to industry norms and conventions (embedded in the ecology and the morphology of finance). By convention, asset owners and asset managers reward employees with favourable employment conditions and compensation in accordance with the importance of their functions and performance relative to the mission of the organisation. Since asset management companies compete with other companies for investment mandates and, overall, the stock of assets under management, it is not surprising that these companies tend to privilege portfolio managers over other types of employees. In investment companies, there is a hierarchy in terms of the significance attributed to different types of employees in relation to the overall mission of the organisation. By convention, the highest-paid employees also face considerable uncertainty as to their job tenure – performance-based pay implies an upside (bonuses) and a downside (termination) not shared by those in lower-tier functions (Clark, 2016).

The privileging of those responsible for investment performance over those engaged with other, more routine tasks and functions is characteristic of the industry, and can also be found in many asset owners. However, there are some significant, albeit subtle, differences that deserve recognition. One key difference is to be found in the relevance of organisation-wide performance as opposed to fund-specific and portfolio-specific performance. Asset owners are judged, in part, in relation to their overall investment performance, even if the measure of performance is rather abstract and need not reflect the interests of all beneficiaries and/or sponsors. By contrast, asset managers are rarely judged in relation to the *overall* performance of their organisation. More often than not, they are evaluated in terms of the growth in assets under management, profitability and shareholder value. While the retention of clients and increasing market share depend upon being able to demonstrate superior investment performance, clients are most concerned with their mandate-specific performance not the overall performance of the investment company. Both sides of the market accept that investment performance by asset class and organisation are subject to stochastic shocks.

In Figure 32.2 we are concerned with two (interacting) aspects of the competition for talent in the industry. We distinguish between situations where the reference point for determining whether an employment contract is 'fair', whether internal or external to the organisation. Here, we are more concerned with norms than with conventions in that employees expect to be treated in accordance with their market value. Given the overarching objectives of asset owners, their reference point is internal in the sense that the value of an investment professional is assessed against his or her contribution to realising the organisation's goals and objectives. By contrast, asset managers are more concerned with recruiting and retaining high performing investment professionals than they are concerned with fitting those individuals within an employment contract governing the entire organisation.

On the other side of the matrix is market density. This refers to the number and range of financial intermediaries in the local marketplace – a market characterised by high density is a market with a large number of financial organisations covering a wide range of activities (single function and multifunction organisations). By contrast, a market characterised by low density is a market with a relatively small number of financial organisations and more limited

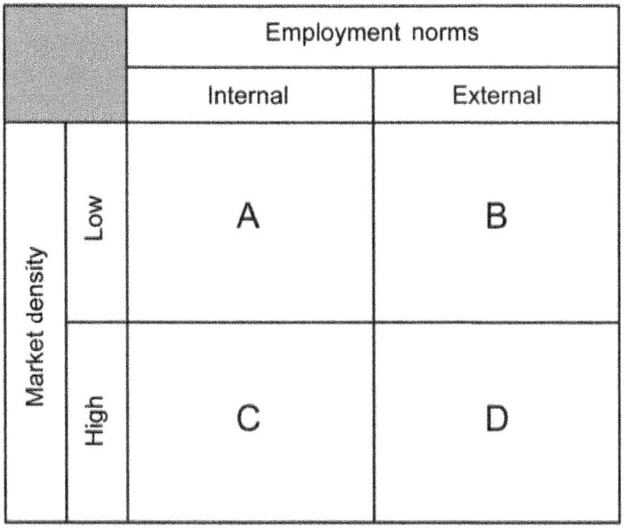

Figure 32.2 Competition for talent in the investment management industry
Source: Author.

range of activities. London is a large market for both financial services and labour, within which there are a remarkable number and range of financial organisations. Amsterdam and Stockholm have a relatively small number of financial organisations and a limited range of financial services available therein. In these centres, it is arguable that the markets for financial services and labour have been internalised by large multifunction financial institutions.

In Figure 32.2, instance A is a situation where low market density prompts employees and employers to assess the fairness or otherwise of employment contracts in relation to internal, rather than external norms. Indeed, it is arguable that the relevant external norms are not found locally, but rather in London and New York. For asset owners and asset managers alike, salary compression is the most likely result. The dominance of internal norms is likely to influence employment conditions and compensation for the most talented investment professionals. Salary compression may prompt the flight of investment professionals from asset owners to asset managers. But given the lack of opportunities (relative to London), the market for switching is likely to be episodic rather than continuous. By contrast, Instance D is a situation where high market density prompts employees and employers alike to assess the fairness or otherwise of employment contracts in relation to external norms rather than internal norms. The market for switching is highly developed, sustaining the flow of talented investment professionals from asset owners to asset managers and from relatively small asset managers to relatively large asset managers.

By this logic, Instance B and Instance C simply don't exist. However, Instance B is representative of the predicament facing large investment institutions headquartered in Amsterdam and Stockholm. Employers judge the fairness of proffered employment contracts against internal norms, while the most talented professionals judge the fairness of these contracts against external norms (as found in London). In this situation, the geographical extent of the market for financial services is much smaller than the geographical extent of the market for financial professionals. Instance C is rarer still. Notwithstanding high market density, the relevant norms are internal to asset owners and asset managers. This is possible if there is a high degree of intermediation, such that financial companies specialise in a particular part of the value chain that makes up the production of investment returns. In this world, companies specialise and complement one another with different functions along with different employment norms.

The culture of finance

The global financial services industry has an ecology and morphology in which organisations are distinguished by type, size, place in the pecking order and location. As such, the ecology and morphology of finance cuts against claims of there being *a* single culture of finance (Lambert, 2014). Nonetheless, it is also shown that the largest asset managers located in the most important financial centres affect the norms and conventions that underpin contractual relationships – service and employment – across the industry. As a consequence, the compensation packages claimed by successful investment professionals can influence industry compensation practices, whatever the notional differences between organisations.

Senior managers across the industry are, quite obviously, aware of the costs and consequences of following the contractual norms and conventions of the dominant investment managers. In response, a set of strategies has been developed by asset owners and certain types of asset managers so as to discount the culture of finance. By considering these strategies, we follow the lead of Hannan and Freeman (1989) who indicated that when applying ecological principles to organisations, social scientists should allow for strategic adaptation. They reject approaches to the study of organisational behaviour that suppose agents are able to optimise the 'fit' between organisational form and function with the competitive environment. Nonetheless, deliberation is a key ingredient in organisational innovation (Birkinshaw et al., 2008). Here, we identify a series of initiatives taken by asset owners and some types of asset managers to sustain their *own* organisational cultures.

Insourcing

Recognising the costs and consequences of the 'star trader' culture, some of the larger asset owners have sought to take control of the process whereby risk-adjusted rates of return are produced. For many years, it was customary practice to outsource the production of returns via investment mandates allocated to competing asset managers who are governed by at-will service contracts. As noted earlier, more often than not, these types of contractual relationships tended to benefit one party at the expense of the other. Clients rarely confronted the costs involved, thereby legitimating industry norms and conventions on compensation practices and charges. Whereas it was believed that segmenting the investment process by allocating mandates to competing managers enhanced the power of asset owners, this strategy added significant costs to the coordination of fund-specific investment strategies. Insourcing is an opportunity to directly manage costs, maintain an integrated investment strategy and serve the goals and objectives of the organisation rather than industry norms and conventions.

Re-intermediation

As suggested in the previous section, larger asset owners can forge long-term relationships with smaller, specialised service providers to mutual benefit. This involves discounting industry norms and conventions as regards service contracts in favour of bespoke agreements that provide mechanisms for governing longer-term relationships. Re-intermediation is made possible by having on staff, or close-at-hand, legal teams whose own incentives and compensation are consistent with the goals and objectives of the asset owner. One approach has been to bring in-house requisite legal skills and expertise. Another is to tie small, specialised law firms to the financial institution. Either way, a deal is made with two types of providers: those that are able to design and implement agreements that withstand scrutiny across the market for financial services and those that are willing to accept agreements for long-term rewards rather than for the short-term benefits typical of the industry.

Alliances

Whereas re-intermediation is controlled by a dominant asset owner, alliances can be formed between asset owners and groups of service providers such that overlapping relationships become subsystems of the global financial services industry with their own norms and conventions. In these arrangements, alliances are relationship-intensive rather than transaction-intensive (Bathelt & Glückler, 2011). More often than not, successful alliances are geographically framed, if not geographically embedded (Grabher, 1994). The incentives used to foster continuity of relationships within such alliances are typically transparent to the parties involved *and* sufficiently different from those of the industry so as to dampen the temptation to defect. Reinforcing these relationships can be done in a variety of ways, including formalising alliances into organisations. In some cases, asset owners have placed senior managers onto the governing boards of the entities charged with responsibility for governing these alliances (Clark & Monk, 2017).

In situ segmentation

Insourcing, re-intermediation and alliances are designed to gain control over the framing and implementation of investment strategy. These strategies are relevant to asset owners, but have also been taken up by some types of asset managers who rely upon the market for financial services for the provision of complementary tasks and functions. For example, as hedge funds and private equity investors have grown in terms of assets under management, they have sought greater control over the service providers that hitherto provided services on a take-it-or-leave-it basis. But integration can come with costs, including the costs of complexity and coordination. These issues are widely recognised in the industry and in the academic literature concerned with the issue of make-or-buy (see Coase, 1937; Baker, Gibbons & Murphy, 2001, 2002). *In situ* segmentation is one way of coping with the costs of integration, and coping with external incentive structures and compensation packages that cannot be reconciled with internal norms and conventions.

Spatial segmentation

The success of *in situ* segmentation strategies depend upon the sophistication of potential partners – domain-specific skills and expertise are more important to investors than simply providing the relevant tasks and functions. The success of such a strategy also depends upon the efficacy of lock-in devices – mechanisms that ensure continuity of commitment without exploiting either side of the relationship. And success depends upon the timeliness of oversight, whether direct by designated relationship managers or indirect via board members and representatives. Most importantly, success depends upon the density of the local market for financial services (the range of services available, the number of service providers, and the diversity of skills and expertise). Meeting these conditions for success is quite difficult in national and regional financial centres compared to the handful of global financial centres. As a consequence, *in situ* segmentation is often complemented by spatial segmentation.

Offshoring

In many respects, offshoring is synonymous with outsourcing, even if cast in terms of establishing an offshore office so as to take advantage of the nature and scope of investment opportunities and potential partners in global financial centres. This strategy involves taking advantage of the scope of an offshore market for financial services to advantage the home organisation without ceding control of those opportunities to the offshore unit. This problem may be accentuated by differences in the financial cultures of the home-base relative to the offshore financial centre. These differences may be expressed in terms of language, norms and conventions, and the presence in offshore financial centres of global investment management organisations that prioritise transactions over relationships. In these circumstances, it can be meaningful to talk of national differences in financial culture. These differences may be the 'opportunities' sought by asset owners and asset managers unable or unwilling to realise opportunities at home.

Offshoring with control

There are three management 'problems' associated with offshoring. The first problem is entirely obvious: the need to control the offshore unit in ways consistent with the goals and objectives of the 'home' organisation. Control can be expressed in a variety of ways, including management oversight and accountability, the placement of executives from the home organisation with the offshore unit, the recruitment and retention of employees in the offshore unit, and the nature of the mandate provided to the offshore unit in terms of its goals and objectives in relation to the home organisation. The second problem is no less obvious: the need to hold the offshore unit at arm's length from the 'home' organisation, so as to ensure some balance in terms of mediating the costs of control in relation to the opportunities occasioned by discretion. The third management problem is perhaps less obvious: the 'home' organisation may need insulation from the offshore unit so that differences in service and employment contracts do not flow back to the home organisation.

Governments may also recognise the need for barriers between the offshore and home-grown cultures of finance. This can be accomplished in a number of ways, including restrictions on the nature and scope of the activities of global financial companies when seeking to establish offices in the local jurisdiction. Likewise, governments can require much higher levels of reporting and transparency of those activities they believe to be associated with the culture of finance. If they permit home-based financial organisations to make related commitments and investments in offshore global financial centres, these governments may, in effect, outsource and offshore the burden associated with being an effective regulator of the norms and conventions associated with the culture of finance.

Implications and conclusion

Media commentators concerned with the probity of the global financial services industry pounce upon every instance where a 'rogue trader' takes advantage of his or her employer to reap personal gain. These actions, and the obvious weaknesses of the companies concerned, are used to suggest that the finance industry is not to be trusted. Looking back, Jaffer, Morris and Vines (2015) argue that, prior to the deregulation of the UK financial services industry in the 1980s, it was reasonable to suppose that relationships mattered and trust was sufficient to bind together the buy side with the supply side of the market. If plausible, it is shown in this chapter that contracts dominate the industry by framing the relationships between the buyers and sellers of financial services, the relationships between intermediaries in the production of investment returns and the relationships between employers and employees. In many respects, contracts for services are asymmetrical in that the providers of services are able to offer products on a (contractual) take-it-or-leave-it basis.

Commentators often accuse the large, integrated financial service providers of privileging 'sales' over 'relationships' (Jaffer et al., 2015, p. 9). This issue was considered in relation to the apparent scale economies that dominate the industry – the volume of assets under management is the litmus test of market position in the industry as it enhances company profitability and underwrites compensation practices. At the same time, it was suggested that the skills and expertise of investment professionals is a key ingredient in sustaining the investment performance of these organisations. Not surprisingly, large financial service companies are able to pay a premium to attract high performing professionals (measured in terms of past performance). These large companies also have the resources to buy out poor performing professionals (measured in terms of current performance), thereby creating a revolving door of hiring and firing, switching people between companies and driving an ever-changing compensation frontier.

It is arguable that payment-for-performance is at once arbitrary (unexpected market volatility can significantly affect traders' performance) and self-defeating (contributing to the revolving door syndrome). It is also arguable that this type of compensation regime attracts, at the margin, those with an unusual appetite for risk and a willingness to stake their reputations on highly advantageous one-off results. Noe and Young (2015) argue that incentive contracts contribute to the culture of finance. While we would agree, it is also the case that it has proven difficult to articulate a rationale or purpose for large financial service companies that is anything more than the joint maximisation of individual welfare. Shareholder value is a rather abstract idea when the production of financial returns depends upon human capital orchestrated by self-interested managers. In theory, at least, financial intermediation is a necessary ingredient in the long-term creation of economic growth and social welfare (Mayer & Vives, 1995). But, given the short-term nature of the industry, and the compensation culture that dominates the largest financial service organisations, it is difficult to argue that these organisations have a higher purpose other than their (separate) immediate benefit.

Three implications follow from our mapping of the industry. First, different types of financial organisations have diverse goals and objectives. This is especially the case for asset owners, although it is also suggested that investment groups lower down in the sell-side pecking order are conceived and organised in ways quite apart from the large investment houses. Second, the relationships between the component parts of the industry matter a great deal, notwithstanding the fact that these relationships are framed in the shadow of contract law. Just as there are obvious asymmetries in these relationships, there are instances where relationships are symmetrical and mutually beneficial. Indeed, these relationships may be deliberately framed as such, recognising the costs and consequences of the default position. Third, it is apparent that there is value to be had lower down in the pecking order. It is arguable that asset owners have not invested sufficient resources in the search for alternatives.

Most importantly, it was argued that contractual templates, in a sense, privilege the sell-side over the buy-side, thereby framing contractual relationships between service providers and clients. Too often, the cost advantages of using contractual templates trump a deeper interest in framing and implementing service agreements that meet the goals and objectives of the buy-side of the market. This is because many clients lack the capabilities and resources to be discriminating consumers of financial services. A virtue has been made of organisational shallowness, assuming that industry templates across a broad range of services are mutually beneficial. Reinforcing this presumption is the fact that many clients contract out advisory services, legal services and accounting services – these service providers, like the largest financial houses, benefit from accumulating clients and minimising costs by providing generic rather than bespoke advice. In many cases, the very idea of making a contract as opposed to using a template is dismissed out-of-hand.

Employment contracts are equally problematic. Absent a compelling organisational mandate that identifies the goals and objectives with which employees are required to align themselves, it is not surprising that external employment norms and conventions tend to trump internal norms. In these circumstances, external norms and conventions are invoked to justify employment terms and conditions that benefit individual employees or a class of employees, but which may not benefit the organisation. For investment managers, the reference point is the employment packages offered by the largest financial houses. Where the senior managers of an organisation are unwilling or unable to represent the mission of their organisation, the default position is either the industry average, or, more likely, the upper-tier of the pecking order. For these reasons, *the* culture of finance can cascade down the pecking order and across to other segments of the market, notwithstanding very different organisational forms and functions (see, generally, Alevy, Haigh & List, 2007).

The culture of finance is perceived by many organisations in the global financial services industry to be pernicious and a threat to their functional effectiveness. In this respect, strategies have been framed, implemented and designed to circumvent the culture of finance, whether at home or in offshore financial centres. The list of strategies is partial and a snapshot of a deliberate process of differentiation – these strategies represent a form of adaptation to a mode of organisation which is self-defeating. At issue is the capacity to adapt; the largest investment groups may have little capacity to change inherited practices. Entrenchment and path dependence may be sufficient to drive that segment of the market to irrelevance or worse.

Acknowledgements

The research programme on the global asset management industry at Oxford has been made possible by a series of engagements with university and industry partners including Allianz Global Investors and Stanford University's Global Projects Center. The author also benefited from involvement in the AP Fund Review (Sweden), Kay Review (UK) and the Fraser Review (Australia), all of which considered, in part, the barriers to long-term investment. The author has been involved with the investment of Oxford's endowment assets, the investment of pension fund assets through the Oxford Staff Pension Scheme, and advice on these matters through Kalytix LLC. None of the above has a direct or material interest in the findings of this chapter. Preparation of the chapter was enabled by Alice Chautard, Seth Collins and Angela Sidaway. Helpful comments on previous drafts of the chapter were received from Harald Bathelt, Christine Brown, Jennifer Johns, Ashby Monk and Phil O'Neill. None of the above should be held responsible for any errors or omissions in the chapter or the views and opinions expressed herein.

Notes

1 Rodrik (2015, pp. 43–44) scorns description for description's sake. But Davis (2015) is concerned that the premium on theory in management studies threatens the relevance of the discipline to a world that is rapidly changing. For Economic Geography, the logic espoused by Davis is heartening. What is concerning, however, is the use of stories in the media of egregious instances of the culture of finance to stand in the stead of analysis of causes and consequences.

2 Dodd (2015, p. 272) makes a similar move when he acknowledges that 'defining culture is, of course, not easy' and then suggests a "baseline" definition which is 'shared meanings, and our representation of them'. This is consistent with norms and conventions, albeit based upon a constructivist notion of the formation of rules.

References

Alevy, J., Haigh, M.S. & List, J.A. (2007) 'Information cascades: Evidence from a field experiment with financial market professionals', *Journal of Finance*, 62, pp. 151–180.

Axelson, U. & Bond, P. (2015) 'Wall Street occupations', *Journal of Finance*, 70, pp. 1949–1996.

Baker, G., Gibbons, R. & Murphy, K.J. (2001) 'Bringing the market inside the firm', *American Economic Review*, 91, pp. 212–218.

Baker, G., Gibbons, R. & Murphy, K.J. (2002) 'Relational contracts and the theory of the firm', *Quarterly Journal of Economics*, 117, pp. 39–84.

Barberis, N.C. (2013) 'Psychology and the financial crisis of 2007–2008', in Haliassos, M. (Ed.), *Financial Innovation: Too Much or Too Little?* Cambridge, MA: MIT Press, pp. 15–28.

Bathelt, H. & Glückler, J. (2011) *The Relational Economy: Geographies of Knowing and Learning*. Oxford, UK: Oxford University Press.

Beaverstock, J. (2004) '"Managing across borders": Knowledge management and expatriation in professional service legal firms', *Journal of Economic Geography*, 4, pp. 157–179.

Belfort, J. (2007) *The Wolf of Wall Street*. New York: Random House.

Beugelsdijk, S., McCann, P. & Mudambi, R. (2010) 'Introduction: Place, space and organisation – Economic Geography and the multinational enterprise', *Journal of Economic Geography*, 10, pp. 485–493.

Birkinshaw, J., Hamel, G. & Mol, M.J. (2008) 'Management innovation', *Academy of Management Review*, 33, pp. 825–845.

Bolton, P. & Dewatripont, M. (2005) *Contract Theory*. Cambridge, MA: MIT Press.

Bongini, P., Nieri, L. & Pelagatti, M. (2015) 'The importance of being systemically important financial institutions', *Journal of Banking and Finance*, 50, pp. 562–574.

Boschma, R. & Martin, R. (2010) 'The aims and scope of evolutionary Economic Geography', in Boschma, R. & Martin, R. (Eds.), *The Handbook of Evolutionary Economic Geography*. Cheltenham, UK: Edward Elgar Publishing, pp. 3–39.

Bowles, S. (2005) *Microeconomics: Behavior, Evolution and Institutions*. Princeton NJ: Princeton University Press.

Brennan, G., Eriksson, L., Goodin, R.E. & Southwood, N. (2014) *Explaining Norms*. Cambridge, UK: Cambridge University Press.

Clark, G.L. (1997) 'Rogues and regulation in global finance: Maxwell, Leeson and the City of London', *Regional Studies*, 31, pp. 219–234.

Clark, G.L. (1998) 'Stylized facts and close dialog: Methodology in Economic Geography', *Annals of the Association of American Geographers*, 88, pp. 73–87.

Clark, G.L. (2000) *Pension Fund Capitalism*. Oxford, UK: Oxford University Press.

Clark, G.L. (2002) 'London in the European financial services industry: Locational advantage and product complementarities', *Journal of Economic Geography*, 2, pp. 433–453.

Clark, G.L. (2005) 'Money flows like mercury: The geography of global finance', *Geografiska Annaler B*, 87, pp. 99–112.

Clark, G.L. (2014a) 'Fiduciary duty and the search for a shared conception of sustainable investment', in Hawley, J.P., Hoepner, A.G.F., Johnson, K.L., Sandberg, J., and Waitzer, E.J. (Eds.), *Institutional Investment and Fiduciary Duty*. Cambridge, UK: Cambridge University Press, pp. 265–276.

Clark, G.L. (2014b) 'Information, knowledge, and investing in offshore financial markets', *Journal of Sustainable Finance and Investment*, 4, pp. 299–320.

Clark, G.L. (2016) 'The components of talent: Company size and financial centres in the European investment management industry', *Regional Studies*, 50, pp. 168–181.

Clark, G.L. & Monk, A.H.B. (2017) *Institutional Investors in Global Markets*. Oxford, UK: Oxford University Press.

Clark, G.L. & O'Connor, K. (1997) 'The informational content of financial products and the spatial structure of the global finance industry', in Cox, K. (Ed.), *Spaces of Globalisation*. New York: Guilford, pp. 89–114.

Coase, R.H. (1937) 'The nature of the firm', *Economica*, 4, pp. 386–405.

Cyert, R. & March, J. (1963) *Behavioral Theory of the Firm*. Englewood Cliffs, NJ: Prentice Hall.

Davis, E.P. & Steil, B. (2001) *Institutional Investors*. Cambridge, MA: MIT Press.

Davis, G.F. (2015) 'Editorial essay: What is organizational research for?' *Administrative Science Quarterly*, 60, pp. 179–188.

Dixon, A.D. & Monk, A.H.B. (2014) 'Frontier finance', *Annals, Association of American Geographers*, 104, pp. 852–868.

Dodd, N. (2015) *The Social Life of Money*. Princeton, NJ: Princeton University Press.

Dörry, S. (2015) 'Strategic nodes in investment fund global production networks: The example of the Luxembourg financial center', *Journal of Economic Geography*, 15, pp. 797–814.

Faulconbridge, J. (2009) 'Managing the transnational law firm: A relational analysis of professional systems, embedded actors and time-space sensitive governance', *Economic Geography*, 84, pp. 185–210.

Gilson, R., Sabel, C. & Scott, R.E. (2013) 'Contract and innovation: The limited role of generalist courts in the evolution of novel contractual forms', *New York University Law Review*, 88, pp. 128–169.

Glückler, J. (2010) 'The evolution of a strategic alliance network: Exploring the case of stock photography', in Boschma, R. & Martin, R. (Eds.), *The Handbook of Evolutionary Economic Geography*. Cheltenham, UK: Edward Elgar Publishing, pp. 298–315.

Grahber, G. (Ed.) (1994) *The Embedded Firm: On the Socioeconomics of Industrial Networks*. London: Routledge.

Grossman, G.M. & Helpman, E. (2004) 'Managerial incentives and the international organisation of production', *Journal of International Economics*, 63, pp. 237–262.

Grossman, G.M. & Helpman, E. (2005) 'Outsourcing in a global economy', *Review of Economic Studies*, 72, pp. 135–159.

Haldane, A. (2014) 'Macroprudential policy in prospect', in Akerlof, G., Blanchard, O., Romer, D. & Stiglitz, J. (Eds.), *What Have We Learned? Macroeconomic Policy After the Crisis*. Cambridge, MA: MIT Press, pp. 65–70.

Haldane, A. & May, R. (2011) 'Systemic risk in banking systems', *Nature*, 469, pp. 351–355.

Hannan, M.T. & Freeman, J. (1989) *Organizational Ecology*. Cambridge, MA: Harvard University Press.

Hart, O. & Moore, J. (2008) 'Contracts as reference points', *Quarterly Journal of Economics*, 123, pp. 1–48.

Helfat, C. & Peteraf, M. (2009) 'Understanding dynamic capabilities: Progress along a developmental path', *Strategic Organization*, 7, pp. 91–102.

Huberman, G. (2001) 'Familiarity breeds investment', *The Review of Financial Studies*, 14, pp. 659–680.

Jaffer, S., Morris, N. & Vines, D. (2015) 'Why trustworthiness is important', in Morris, N. & Vines, D. (Eds.), *Capital Failure: Rebuilding Trust In Financial Services*. Oxford, UK: Oxford University Press, pp. 3–31.

Jarzabkowski, P., Bednarek, R. & Spee, P. (2015) *Making a Market for Acts of God: The Practice of Risk-Trading in The Global Reinsurance Industry*. Oxford, UK: Oxford University Press.

Lambert, R. (2014) *Culture and Banking Standards*. HM Government, House of Commons, London, 14 May 2014.

La Porta, R., Lopez-de-Silanes, F. & Shleifer, A. (1998) 'Law and finance', *Journal of Political Economy*, 106, pp. 1113–1155.

Lewis, M. (2011) *The Big Short: Inside the Doomsday Machine*. New York: Penguin.

Litterman, B. (2004) *Modern Investment Management*. New York: Wiley.

Lo, A.W. (2016) 'The Gordon Gekko effect: The role of culture in the financial industry'. *Draft paper, Sloan School of Management, Massachusetts Institute of Technology*.

Luyendijk, J. (2015) *Swimming with Sharks: My Journey into the World of the Bankers*. London: Guardian Faber.

MacIntyre, A. (1981) *After Virtue*. London: Duckworth.

March, J. & Simon, H. (1958) *Organizations*. New York: Wiley.

Maskell, P. (2015) 'Accessing remote knowledge: The roles of trade fairs, pipelines, crowd-sourcing and listening posts', in Bathelt, H. & Zeng, G. (Eds.), *Temporary Knowledge Ecologies: The Rise of Trade Fairs in the Asia-Pacific Region*. Cheltenham, UK: Edward Elgar Publishing, pp. 19–41.

Mayer, C. & Vives, X. (Eds.) (1995) *Capital Markets and Financial Intermediation*. Cambridge, UK: Cambridge University Press.

Morris, N. & Vines, D. (Eds.) (2015) *Capital Failure: Rebuilding Trust in Financial Services*. Oxford, UK: Oxford University Press.

Myers, S.C. & Majluf, N.S. (1984) 'Corporate financing and investment decisions when firms have information that investors do not have', *Journal of Financial Economics*, 13, pp. 187–221.

Noe, T. & Peyton Young, H. (2015) 'The limits to compensation in the financial sector', in Morris, N. & Vines, D. (Eds.), *Capital Failure: Rebuilding Trust in Financial Services*. Oxford, UK: Oxford University Press, pp. 65–78.

O'Brien, R. (1992) *Global Financial Integration: The End of Geography*. London: Chatham House.

Padgett, J.F. & Powell, W.W. (2012) *The Emergence of Organisations and Markets*. Princeton, NJ: Princeton University Press.

Piketty, T. & Goldhammer, A. (2014) *Capital in the Twenty-First Century*. Cambridge, MA: The Belknap Press of Harvard University Press.

Pool, V.K., Stoffman, N. & Yonker, S.E. (2015) 'The people in your neighbourhood: Social interaction and mutual fund portfolios', *Journal of Finance*, 70, pp. 2679–2732.

Rajan, R. & Zingales, L. (2001) 'The firm as a dedicated hierarchy: A theory of the origins and growth of firms', *Quarterly Journal of Economics*, 116, pp. 805–851.

Riles, A. (2011) *Collateral Knowledge*. Chicago, IL: University of Chicago Press.

Rodrik, D. (2015) *Economics Rules*. Oxford, UK: Oxford University Press.

Schamp, E.W. (2010) 'On the notion of co-evolution in Economic Geography', in Boschma, R. & Martin, R. (Eds.), *The Handbook of Evolutionary Economic Geography*. Cheltenham, UK: Edward Elgar, pp. 432–449.

Scheinkman, J.A. (2014) 'Speculation, trading and bubbles'. Kenneth J Arrow Lecture Series with K.J. Arrow, P. Bolton, S.J. Grossman, and J.E. Stiglitz. New York: Columbia University Press, pp. 7–80.

Shleifer, A. & Summers, L.H. (1990) 'The noise trader approach to finance', *Journal of Economic Perspectives*, 4, pp. 19–33.

Stambaugh, R.F. (2014) 'Presidential address: Investment noise and trends', *Journal of Finance*, 69, pp. 1415–1453.

Storper, M. & Venables, A. (2004) 'Buzz: Face-to-face contact and the urban economy', *Journal of Economic Geography*, 4, pp. 351–370.

Taylor, M.J. & Asheim, B. (2001) 'The concept of the firm in Economic Geography', *Economic Geography*, 77, pp. 315–328.

Wainwright, T. (2011) 'Tax doesn't have to be taxing: London's "on shore" finance industry and the fiscal spaces of a global crisis', *Environment and Planning A*, 43, pp. 1287–1304.

Williamson, O. (1975) *Markets and Hierarchies*. New York: Free Press.

Wójcik, D. (2010) *Revolution in the Stock Exchange Industry: Two-sided Platforms, Battle for Liquidity, and Financial Centres*. Available at SSRN: http://ssrn.com/abstract=1653827. or http://dx.doi.org/10.2139/ssrn.1653827.

Wójcik, D. (2011) *The Global Stock Market: Investors and Intermediaries in an Uneven World*. Oxford, UK: Oxford University Press.

Zingales, L. (2015) 'Presidential address: Does finance benefit society?' *Journal of Finance*, 70, pp. 1327–1363.

33

THE INTERNATIONALIZATION AND LOCALIZATION OF PROFESSIONAL SERVICES

The case of executive search firms in Australia

Jonathan Beaverstock and William S. Harvey

Introduction

There is now an established literature on the internationalization of global professional service firms (PSFs) (e.g. Aharoni, 1993; Brock, Powell & Hinings, 1999; Jones, 2005; Morgan & Quack, 2006; Faulconbridge, Hall & Beaverstock, 2008; Segal-Horn & Dean, 2011; Boussebaa, Morgan & Sturdy, 2012; Brock, 2012; Muzio & Faulconbridge, 2013). Yet, within these literatures, there remains a knowledge deficit and a lack of evidence-based understandings of internationalization outside of North America and Europe, although there are notable exceptions within the field of Economic Geography (e.g. Morshidi, 2000; O'Connor & Daniels, 2001; Beaverstock, 2004; Hutton, 2004; Daniels, 2012). Few scholars of International Business have focused on global PSFs (except notably, Dunning, 1993). The aim of this chapter is to advance knowledge on the internationalization of global PSFs through an analysis of the retained executive search industry in Australia. We focus on retained executive search firms in Australia because the industry has been well-established since the 1970s. Although the sector is relatively invisible in certain academic disciplines, it is highly influential for assessing, placing and developing leaders in a variety of economic sectors.

The remainder of the chapter focuses on the internationalization of global retained executive search firms in Australia and primarily Sydney. The chapter is structured in four major parts. In the next part, the discussion focuses specifically on the internationalization of executive search. Second and third, drawing on our primary and secondary data analysis, we present our research findings on the internationalization and localization of the executive search industry in Asia-Pacific and Australia, respectively. Finally, we report several contributions from our study which raises many implications for future work.

The research cited in the chapter has been obtained from four major sources. The first was data collected from two separate face-to-face interview surveys undertaken in 2009 (9 interviews) and 2013 (13 interviews – including 5 of those interviewed in 2009 and 1 senior member of an association representing the executive search sector) with the managing or senior partners of leading global retained firms in Sydney (see Tables 33.1 and 33.4). The second and third types

Table 33.1 Leading retained executive search firms in Australia, 2009–2013

Firm	*Opened*	*Network*	*World offices*		*Australian*	*Australian consultants*		*Assignments per year*	
			2009	*2013*	*offices*	*2009*	*2013*	*2009*	*2013*
Asia Pacific Management	1990	Taplow	49	N.A.	North Balwyn	3	N.A.	36*	N.A.
Alexander Hughes	N.A.	Alexander Hughes	N.A.	37	Sydney	N.A.	1	N.A.	12*
Boyden International	1966	Integrated	63	64	Sydney	6	3	30	30
Cordiner King[1]	1985	Amrop Hever	60	85	Sydney Melbourne	7	5	84*	60*
Cornerstone Sydney	1989[2]	Cornernstone International	87	87	Chatsworth	1	1	12*	12*
Crown & Marks	2001	Signium International	40	41	Sydney Melbourne Perth	7	5	84*	60*
De Jager & Associates	1990	IIC Group	60	N.A.	Sydney Melbourne	5	N.A.	45	N.A.
Douglas Walker International	1980	World Search Group	31	N.A.	Melbourne	2	N.A.	12	N.A.
Egon Zehnder Int. PTY LTD	1973	Integrated	62	64	Sydney Melbourne Perth	10	10	120*	120*
EMA Partners Australia/Slade	1988	EMA Partners International	50	N.A.	Melbourne	21	N.A.	108	N.A.
Geddes Parker & Partners	1989	IESF	14	N.A.	Sydney	6	N.A.	36*	N.A.
Harvey Nash	N.A.	Integrated	N.A.	40	Sydney	N.A.	3	N.A.	36*
Heidrick & Struggles	1989	Integrated	63	56	Sydney Melbourne	22	15	264*	180*

(continued)

Table 33.1 (continued)

Firm	*Opened*	*Network*	*World offices*		*Australian*	*Australian consultants*		*Assignments per year*	
			2009	*2013*	*offices*	*2009*	*2013*	*2009*	*2013*
Horton International	1992	Horton International	40	38	Melbourne	2	8	24*	96*
Jo Fisher	N.A.	IMD International	N.A.	25	Melbourne Sydney	N.A.	9	N.A.	108*
Korn/Ferry	1979	Integrated	73	64	Sydney Melbourne	13	N.A.	156*	N.A.
Mode HR PTY LTD	2005	INAC Worldwide	48	N.A.	Sydney	1	N.A.	12*	N.A.
Odgers Berndston	1976	Integrated	57	42	Sydney Canberra	7	7	84*	84*
Russell Reynolds	1984	Integrated	37	40	Sydney Melbourne	9	5	54*	54*
Search International	N.A.	IESF Group	N.A.	N.A.	Sydney	N.A.	N.A.	N.A.	N.A.
Spencer Stuart	1970	Integrated	50	29	Melbourne Sydney	7	5	84*	60*
Stanton Chase	1986	Stanton Chase	68	70	Sydney	5	5	60*	60*
Strategic Executive Search	1986	Alexander Hughes	8	N.A.	Sydney	1	N.A.	12*	N.A.
Walford Partnership	1993[2]	World Search Group	31	N.A.	Sydney	3	N.A.	32	N.A.
Watermark Search	N.A.	Transearch	55	N.A.	Sydney	1	N.A.	12*	N.A.

Sources: Firm websites; The Executive Grapevine (2009, 2012).

Notes:

1 Included in the 2013 survey, renamed as Amrop Cordiner King (Amrop Group)

2 Approximate date of establishment

N.A. Information not available

* Estimated at 12 searches/year/consultant (after, Garrison-Jenn, 2005)

of data were derived from published and unpublished secondary sources on retained executive search (e.g. Baird, 1985; Byrne, 1986; Jones, 1989; Watson et al., 1990; Garrison-Jenn, 1993, 2005; and The Executive Grapevine's 2009 and 2012 *International Directories of Executive Search Firms and Consultants*). The fourth data source was derived from the firm's individual websites including information for the leading Australian firms, the global firms and network structures.

Internationalization and the birth of a 'mature market' for executive search in the Asia-Pacific

Since the late 1980s, there has emerged a rich body of research from across Economic Geography, and to a lesser extent business and management, which has investigated the intrinsic knowledge-intensive characteristics, internationalization and local adaptation of professional services (referred to as producer services in Economic Geography), and the emergence of the global PSF. Many of the key authors in these debates have already been cited in the introduction, but others include Marshall et al. (1988), Dunning (1993), Bagchi-Sen and Sen (1997), Morris and Empson (1998), Hanlon (1999), Aharoni and Nachum (2000), Lowendahl (2000) and Sassen (2013). The key organizational structures and localizing governance attributes of internationalizing PSFs in new market locations or jurisdictions have been discussed at length through firm case studies in North America and Europe, mainly through scholars in organization studies and focused on the legal profession (see Muzio & Faulconbridge, 2013). It is not our intention to rehearse these issues again, but what is of significance in taking these agendas forward is to look closely at the internationalization of PSFs emerging in another mature market, Australia, which is increasingly influenced by closer ties to the Asia-Pacific.

Executive search firms are elite labor market intermediaries, 'agents', in a three-pronged firm-client-candidate relationship, employed by 'clients' (who wish to seek elite labor) to search the labor market for suitable 'candidates' (Garrison-Jenn, 1993, 2005; Gurney, 2000; Finlay & Coverdill, 2002). Executive search firms are knowledge-intensive, professional services who rely on the deep bespoke knowledge, experience and intelligence of their managing partners and search consultants, to manage the relationships between client and candidate, and ultimately fill the post (Byrne, 1986; Jones, 1989). Much of the published work on the executive search industry has emanated from an Anglo-American perspective, absorbed with, first, the rise and internationalization of the 'headhunting business' from the USA in the 1940s to its rollout and indigenous growth throughout Europe; second, the 'Europeanization' of executive search and the localization strategies of firms through the region's world cities; third, the 'art' of executive search and selection, and the tripartite 'agent' relationship between firm, client and candidate; and fourth, how to use them in the market, for both clients and candidates (Byrne, 1986; Jones, 1989; Watson et al., 1990; Garrison-Jenn, 1993, 2005; Boyle et al., 1996; Britton, Doherty & Ball, 1997; Gurney, 2000; Finlay & Coverdill, 2002). From the late 2000s, Beaverstock, Faulconbridge and Hall (2015) have provided fresh understandings of the globalization of leading retained global firms in a context of rapidly changing information technology and management systems, and the 'openness' of China and India.

Faulconbridge, Hall and Beaverstock (2008) identified four major factors that prompted the internationalization of the global retained executive search industry across specific 'Western' or advanced capitalist regional markets from the 1960s, including the Asia-Pacific. First, client-led internationalization. The rapid internationalization of primary, manufacturing and service transnational firms, particularly in banking, financial and business services, created unprecedented demand for the retained firms search and selection services in new foreign markets. Clients expected their executive search firms to supply bespoke services in situ directly in the market, particularly in the key world and capital cities of the Asia-Pacific. Like most other PSFs who deliver knowledge-intensive services, executive search firms had to be physically located in the market through an office or subsidiary structure. Second, executive search firms sought new international office locations to be in proximity to pools of highly skilled labor, across the spectrum of levels of seniority, occupations and industrial sectors. 'Old-boy networks' could no longer be trusted as an efficient mechanism to recruit the ideal candidate, particularly outside of North America, Europe and, particularly, the United Kingdom. Third, the retained firms internationalized their office networks to new foreign markets to overcome the so-called, 'off-limits' problem (Watson et al., 1990; Boyle et al., 1996). Thus, internationalization reduced 'blockages' in particular labor markets as a firm's recent past client can be the source of a potential candidate for another client if the search is orchestrated from a different jurisdiction (i.e. another international office). Fourth, executive search firms need to be physically located in the market place for both clients and candidates to undertake their function of a labor market intermediary.

Moreover, drawing on Dunning's (1993) Ownership-Location-Internalization (OLI) paradigm, Faulconbridge, Hall and Beaverstock (2008) provided the first significant theoretical analysis of the internationalization of the executive search industry (also see Dunning & Norman, 1987). This resource-based view of the internationalization of retained executive search is shown in Table 33.2, where each of the three major competitive advantages for internationalization (the OLI) are benchmarked with the major organizational forms of the internationalization taken by the firms, through wholly-owned offices, membership of networks of independent firms who retain their own local identity or membership structures of independent firms who take the global 'brand' in the local market, the so-called 'hybrid' approach (Watson et al., 1990; Garrison-Jenn, 2005). Localization is a key competitive advantage for executive search because it provides bespoke personalization for clients through relationship building without losing the benefits of global reach and expertise.

Table 33.2 The OLI paradigm applied to the internationalization of retained global executive search firms

Ownership (competitive advantages)	*Location (configuration advantages)*	*Internalization (coordinating advantages)*	*Organizational form*
(O1) Access to transnational clients (O2) Reputation (O3) Headhunting practices that can be reproduced and promoted overseas to create new market demand	(L1) Access to existing overseas markets (L2) Face-to-face contact with local representatives of existing transnational clients (L3) Adaptation to local labor laws (L4) The ability to market and promote services to new clients and develop demand in the marketplace (L5) Reduction in 'off-limits blockages' by creating 'Chinese' walls between spatially separated offices	(I1) Protection of client-databases from outsiders' eyes (I2) Quality control easily maintained (I3) The ability to develop globally uniform standards and systems, ultimately bringing economies of scale through integration	(F1) Wholly owned transnational when advantages O3, L4 and L5 can be gained from opening overseas offices (F2) Network transnational when O3, L4 and L5 advantages are unlikely to be gained immediately (F3) Hybrid when O3, L4 and L5 advantages exist but with some locally contingent influences

Source: Faulconbridge, Hall & Beaverstock, (2008), adapted from Dunning (1993).

Turning specifically to executive firm market entry, the cities of Hong Kong, Singapore, Sydney, Melbourne and Tokyo became the new international battleground for the retained industry from the 1960s. The US firm Boyden International opened the first office in Tokyo in 1962, followed by Sydney and Melbourne in 1966/67.[1] Both Spencer Stuart and Korn Ferry opened in Sydney, Tokyo, Singapore and Hong Kong in the 1970s.[2] By 1985, the top 15 global leading executive search firms had between them 39 offices in the region (15% of the world total), and almost three-quarters of those offices (29 offices) were concentrated in Sydney (8 firm offices), and Singapore, Hong Kong and Tokyo (each with 7 firm offices) (Baird, 1985). Between 1985 and 2012, there was an absolute growth of more than 138 offices (+358%) in the region, which placed the Asia-Pacific almost on a par with North America in terms of share of the total number of offices worldwide (at 21% or 177 offices) (Baird, 1985; The Executive Grapevine, 2012). Through the 1990s and early 2000s, firm entry into the region was not only by the establishment of new wholly owned offices. Many of the leading global firms acquired local independent retained firms, who had primarily formed after partners had 'split' from the US and European early entrants. For example, Heidrick & Struggles entered markets in Seoul, Taipei, Singapore and Shanghai after the merger with the TAO Group in 2000 (Heidrick & Struggles International, 2000). Also, those firms in global partnership arrangements entered the region through network relationships with well-established local independent firms (again, mainly those who had been established by partners who had 'split' from the leading US and European firms). For example, the IIC Partners Executive Search Worldwide Group grew its presence in the region by adding these local independents to its network: De Jager and Associates (1991 in Sydney and Melbourne); PCI Executive Search (1991 in Beijing, Shanghai and Taipei); Stones International (Hong Kong); KTA Associates (1995 in Mumbai); GKR Daulet-Singh (1995 in New Delhi); You and Partners Inc (2003 in Seoul); Porath Executive Search (1997 in Auckland); Executive Talent (Singapore); and, RGC Executive (1987 in Bangkok).[3]

Internationalization and Australia's retained executive search industry

The history of the Australian, and specifically Sydney and Melbourne's, global retained executive search industry can be traced back to the establishment of the US-owned Boyden International office in Sydney in 1966, followed by Spencer Stuart and Associates (1970) and Korn Ferry International (1979). The first European firm, Egon Zehnder, entered Australia in 1973 and the first UK owned firm, Odgers Berndtson, arrived in 1976. The two other US-owned global leading firms established offices in 1984 (Russell Reynolds) and 1989 (Heidrick & Struggles International) (see Table 33.3). In almost all cases, these leading global retained executive search firms entered Australia through the establishment of new wholly owned offices, which paralleled the temporal and organizational mode of similar early office growth in Hong Kong, Singapore and Tokyo (Garrison-Jenn, 1993, 2005; Faulconbridge, Hall & Beaverstock, 2008; Beaverstock, Faulconbridge & Hall, 2015). A notable exception was Korn Ferry International which entered Australia after acquiring a local firm, Guy Pease, in 1979 (and later Amrop in 2000) (Garrison-Jenn, 2005). By 1984/5, the Australian retained executive search industry was dominated by the operations of the global US and European owned firms.

During the period of internationalization of the leading global firms into Australia in the 1970s and 1980s, the country's own indigenous retained executive search industry was developing in Melbourne and Sydney. There is a dearth of available firm data on the profiles of these small and medium-sized enterprises (SMEs), but an examination of The Executive Grapevine for selected years indicated the growth of trailblazing 'local' firms like Cordiner King (established 1985),

Table 33.3 World leading retained executive search firms in Australia, 1984/5

Firm	*Established*	*Head Office*	*Opened in Australia*	*Structure*	*Member firm*	*World offices*	*Australian offices*	*Asia-pacific offices*
Amrop International	1977	Brussels	N.A.	Network	Brauer Gault & Co.	20[1]	Melbourne Sydney	Singapore[2]
Boyden International	1946	New York	1966	Owned		34	Melbourne Sydney	Bangkok Hong Kong Singapore Taipei Tokyo
Christopher Tilly & Associates[3]	1971	London	N.A.	Network	Graham Smith Partners	16[4]	Melbourne Sydney	None
DPSC International	1969	London	N.A.	Hybrid	DPSC International	7[5]	Sydney	None
Egon Zehnder International	1964	Zurich	1973[6]	Owned		21	Melbourne Sydney	Singapore Tokyo
Korn Ferry International	1967	Los Angeles	1979	Owned		34	Melbourne Sydney	Hong Kong Kuala Lumpur Singapore Tokyo
Odgers & Company LTD	1970	London	1976	Owned		9	Sydney	None
Russell Reynolds	1969	New York	1984	Owned		17	Sydney	Hong Kong Singapore
Spencer Stuart & Associates	1969	New York	1984	Owned		28	Melbourne Sydney	Hong Kong Singapore
Transearch International	1981	Paris	N.A.	Network	J.E.G Raggett & Associates	13[7]	Adelaide	Tokyo[8] Hong Kong[9] Singapore[10]

Source: Baird (1985).

Notes:

1 Number of member firm offices of Amrop International.
2 Tan Soo Jin Consultants Pte Limited, Singapore.
3 Christopher Tilly and Associates is associated with Ward Howell International.
4 Number of member firm offices of Christopher Tilly and Associates.
5 Member firm offices of DPSC International.
6 Personal communication with CEO of the Sydney office.
7 Number of member firm offices of Transearch International.
8 The Cambridge Corporation.

De Jager and Associates (1990), Douglas Walker (1980), Geddes Parker and Partners (1989) and Strategic Executive Search (1986) (Table 33.3). It is highly debatable as to which were the first SMEs to offer retained executive search in Australia as organizations like Brauer Gault, DPSC International, Graham Smith Partners and J.E.G. Raggatt and Associates were established pre-1985. By the late 2000s, there were several well-established independent retained executive search firms in Australia and many had offices in Sydney and Melbourne (e.g. EMA Partners/Slade (established 1988); Cornerstone Sydney (established c. 1989); Crown and Marks, Reddin Partners, and Fish and Nankivell (all established in 2001) (see Table 33.3).

Another internationalization process in which Australia's sector has become transnational has been through the membership of local SMEs in worldwide networks and/or strategic alliances of independent firms, often referred to as networks or hybrids (Garrison-Jenn, 2005). During 1984/5, the three largest worldwide network groups of retained executive search firms, Amrop International, Christopher Tilly and Associates (with Ward Howell International) and Transearch International had a direct presence in Australia through the membership of local, independent firms, respectively: Brauer Gault and Co; Graham Smith Partners; and J.E.G. Raggett and Associates. By 2009, almost all the leading global network and hybrid groups – Amrop Hever, Signium International, IIC Group, World search group, INAC Worldwide, for example – had a direct presence in Australia, with independent and hybrid Sydney, Melbourne and Perth SMEs included in their Asia-Pacific geographical regions (Table 33.3).

From the late 2000s and up to 2013, paralleling the two periods of the interview-based surveys (see Table 33.4), five distinctive features characterized the industry's structure in Australia.

Table 33.4 List of interviewees

2009:
1 Partner, boutique firm
2 Partner, international network firm
3 Partner, international network firm
4 Managing Partner, international network firm
5 Managing Partner, international network firm
6 Managing Partner, boutique firm
7 Partner, boutique firm
8 Partner, boutique firm
9 Director, global firm
2013:
10 Senior Manager, association of executive search firms
11 Partner, international network firm
12 Managing Partner, global firm
13 Managing Partner, international network firm
14 Managing Partner, boutique firm
15 Partner, global firm
16 Managing Partner, boutique firm
17 Managing Partner, boutique firm
18 Managing Partner, international network firm
19 Managing Partner, international network firm
20 Managing Partner, boutique firm
21 Managing Partner, boutique firm
22 Director, global firm

First, all the leading global wholly owned firms continue to have offices in Australia and they are US or European owned. Second, Australian SMEs enhance their international presence by seeking membership of worldwide networks and alliances of independent member firms under the umbrella of US and European organizations like Amrop, Signium International and the I.I.C. Partners. Third, although the retained sector market (for both candidates and clients) is dominated by the wholly owned global firms and leading Australian members of worldwide networks, our findings suggest that there is a competitive retained 'boutique' SME sector which is highly specialized in either practice specific industries (e.g. financial services, energy, not-for-profit) or function of search (e.g. CEO, general management to mid-tier levels). Fourth, the retained industry is clustered in Sydney and Melbourne, but given the energy and resources 'boom' in Western Australia, firms have increasingly explored the viability of establishing offices in Perth, like Crown and Marks. Fifth, as the executive search industry across Australia is unregulated and, therefore, barriers to entry are low, there is a constellation of SMEs (including sole proprietors) whose existence in the market is somewhat precarious and ephemeral according to the performance of the general business cycle, which is particularly evident in the 'contingency' sector of the market (where SMEs continually pitch for searches and present short-listed candidates, without the guarantee of being appointed to conduct the actual search).

Internationalization, localization and coordinating across borders

An important issue for PSFs is identifying whether clients value having local access to firms, clients and suppliers, particularly in an era of mass online business communication. Interviewees were divided in whether geographic proximity to clients was important. One managing partner, for instance, said that because executive search involves low volume, it is important to build strong relationships through face-to-face interaction:

> We've always tended to be in the low-volume end of the market and it is those client relationships that get the repeat business and the referrals. Being close to clients is important, but understanding the client culture and getting the chemistry right with the individual in the client culture is really important.
>
> *(Interviewee #1, Partner of boutique firm, 2009)*

Another managing director said that clients valued having executive search companies nearby and being located at the 'right end of town':

> Clients and candidates can come down here and nobody has to go very far. If you're dealing with the top end that's what they want to do. We're in the right end of town . . . We meet and interview shortlisted candidates here. We go to see clients.
>
> *(Interviewee #3, Partner of international network firm, 2009)*

Many interviewees hinted at the importance of the transfer of trusted information through informal face-to-face conversations, which is what clients 'want to do'. This raises the importance for firms to provide a local and tailored service to clients and candidates. In sum, many interviewees in 2009 and 2013 recognized the value of localization where, 'face-to-face contact is vital in senior tier work' (Interviewee #22, Director of global firm, 2013). But, some interviewees suggested in 2009 that it can be an advantage in certain contexts to not being local, 'in reality, it isn't critical to be located close to the client. [We] benefit from being outside of

Canberra for government work as the government like to do business with a Sydney based firm' (Interviewee #2, partner of international network firm, 2009). Indeed, it was felt that using a local executive search firm in some smaller cities may be perceived as only recruiting local talent, as one managing partner noted, 'a number of our Brisbane clients come to us because they don't want a firm in Brisbane, simply recycling Brisbane talent' (Interviewee #19, Managing Partner of international network firm, 2013). Another managing partner argued that the location of an office depended on the sector:

> [i]n banking and financial services a lot of work can be done over coffee and face-to-face contact is important to sustain the relationships. For candidates, it is important to have an office in the CBD, for accessibility and building relationships.
>
> *(Interviewee #6, Managing Partner of boutique firm, 2009)*

With respect to internationalization, many interviewees recognized that they needed to increase their business engagements internationally. In the words of one managing partner in 2009, 'tapping Australian talent pools offshore is very important for seeking candidates for Australian placements or other international financial centres' (Interviewee #6, Managing Partner of boutique firm, 2009). This is particularly the case because of the opportunity of online recruitment websites such as LinkedIn to source clients and candidates across international borders. This indicates the significance of being both globally connected to build business in new markets as well as locally rooted to maintain existing client and candidate relationships. Another managing partner also commented on how his firm had joined a global network of executive search firms with a view to garnering more business from the Asia-Pacific, but this has not proved particularly successful:

> The attraction of [. . . network partnership] is its affiliation to other independent members . . . It's a loose affiliation. We have a close relationship with [. . . network partnership] . . . it's resulted in some referrals, but it hasn't resulted in a lot of work in terms of cross-border assignments. There are other members in the Asia-Pacific region, but not Australia.
>
> *(Interviewee #1, Partner of boutique firm, 2009)*

Interviewees in 2009 emphasized that there was cooperation between partners in other geographic regions, particularly within the Asia-Pacific, for work rather than coordination:

> It is cooperation in most part. Each office in the Asia-Pacific will team up on global assignments if clients want an Asian wide search, but it is very independent most often with our internal relationships rather than being corporate.
>
> *(Interviewee #1, Partner of boutique firm, 2009)*

The partner quoted above stresses that the level of cooperation between partners will depend upon the demands of the client, but in most cases the partnership is usually based on particular individuals working together rather than a strategic coordinated search operating at an organizational level:

> We certainly don't compete. We cooperate and work with them and we do refer clients to each other. It's very much a cooperative relationship and from an external client's perspective our objective is to look the same as the major integrated firms.
>
> *(Interviewee #4, Managing Partner of an international network firm, 2009)*

The above managing partner stresses that he is not in competition, but in partnership with other organizations within the global network membership with the goal of referring more work to one another and as an external signalling device to potential clients that they have the capacity, status and reputation to conduct high-level global searches. But, in one instance, a managing partner said that he had decided to cease his firm's membership of a global network of executive search firms because, 'they wanted to put a lot of pins on maps and they weren't very involved in what we were doing' (Interviewee #3, Partner of international network firm, 2009).

A major shift in 2013, driven by the financial crisis, was the greater emphasis on the needs of the client. Whereas in 2009, executive search firms had greater autonomy in how they conducted searches, by 2013 there was greater input from clients in terms of their expectations. As one senior associate shows:

> I think that . . . the clients always want the best candidate . . . So, I think, from our perspective, it's always good that we have lots of experience of bringing people across geographies. In terms of the functional expertise, it depends what the local market actually has in terms of, you know, what the role requires. It depends I guess, in terms of the client's business, in terms of what they're trying to achieve with this appointment.
>
> *(Interviewee #14, Managing Partner of boutique firm, 2013)*

Another trend identified in 2013 was a greater blurring of the global and the local in internationalization processes. One partner emphasized how geography was becoming less important as executive search firms organized themselves less by geography and more by industry expertise:

> The way it works is, if there's a need for a CEO of a specific industry, a client could be in Melbourne, but the capability on the search side may be in Sydney. It doesn't matter where you are anymore, physically, to do executive search. So, we're organized by practices – Energy, Industrial, Metals and Mining, Financial Services, Consumer, the whole gamut, and we're also organized by functional background – board of directors, chairmen, CEOs, CFOs, CMOs, CTOs, CHROs.
>
> *(Interviewee #15, Partner of global firm, 2013)*

In another context, global executive firms may seek the support of a partner firm in Australia to help with a local search, as one managing partner explains:

> The reality is that most of the work that one does tends to be local, so the relationships with our other offices tend to be around the relationships with the client, rather than in the actual execution of an individual search. So, an office in the U.S. has, for example, recently referred two assignments to us, where they have a client headquartered in the U.S., has a need to find a country manager and a senior finance person here in Australia for their business here in Australia. So, you know, they refer it to us, they help manage that relationship in the U.S., in the head office, but the execution happens here. So, we go out and look in the local market for people who can fill those particular roles. And that can happen the other way around as well.
>
> *(Interviewee #13, Managing Partner of international network firm, 2013)*

The above quotation highlights the importance of coupling localization for managing client relationships with internationalization for operationalizing the search. Another internationalization trend between 2009 and 2013 has been the erosion of the importance of sourcing talent from the Asia-Pacific region and an increasing emphasis on a truly global search, as one managing partner highlights:

> It's global, it's not even A-Pac, and again it depends on the sector. You know, working with financial services organizations, yes, they'll want to look at A-Pac, but they'll want to look in Europe and the UK and the US and Canada . . . they'll want to look globally for senior roles, and so it's more what does the global talent pool look like rather than what does the A-Pac talent pool look like.
>
> *(Interviewee #12, Managing Partner of global firm, 2013)*

The implication then is that not only are searches going beyond the Asia-Pacific, but that major Australian cities are no longer considered as the hubs for business as other major Asian cities have grown. This is also shown through a growing demand for board members of Australian companies being sourced from outside of Australia, as one managing partner describes:

> The one thing we're seeing a lot more of is Australian-listed entities putting international board directors onto their boards, and that's not always A-Pac, but it's a fair amount, so Chinese-based directors onto listed boards here, Hong Kong-based, Singapore-based, but then also . . . US-based . . . European-based, depending on the business strategy of the entity.
>
> *(Interviewee #12, Managing Partner of global firm, 2013)*

Again, this new trend shows a blending of the local and the global with clients seeking searches from outside of the local region and Australia and beyond the Asia-Pacific region. From an Economic Geography perspective, internationalization processes are not only collapsing space-time dimensions between firms, clients and candidates, but are also reaffirming the notion that organizations compete in a truly global labor market for scarce resources.

Concluding comments

In this chapter, we have undertaken the first systematic analysis of the internationalization of retained executive search in Australia. We have started to fill the dearth of knowledge on the internationalization of global PSFs outside of the North American-European research fields. We have drawn on the literatures that cross business and management as well as Economic Geography, to discuss the internationalization and localization of global PSFs in Sydney. Empirically, we have charted the internationalization of the large US and European global retained firms into Australia and the wider Asian-Pacific. Increasingly, this region of the globe, including China, will become a significant market for such PSFs, geographically fixed to the region's world cities. The internationalization of these firms into Australia mimic Faulconbridge, Hall and Beaverstock's (2008) findings and benchmark neatly Dunning's (1993) OLI framework pertaining to the globalization of business services.

We also found that executive search firms were divided on the value of being networked with other offices as part of an international partnership. Many partners whose organizations were part of an international network of executive search firms were at best ambivalent and at worst highly sceptical about the benefits. This is a surprising finding given the strong emphasis of being embedded within a global network in this sector (as corroborated by Garrison-Jenn, 2005). In terms of localization and internationalization, we found that it was not an either/or but a coupling of localization for managing client relationships with internationalization for operationalizing the search.

Although the term Asia-Pacific was a well-recognized term within executive search, partners almost exclusively remarked that there was little if any value with focusing on this region alone. Typically, if their business with clients or candidates went outside of Australia then partners argued that it was just as likely if not more likely to extend to Europe and North America as it was to the Asia-Pacific. Finally, it is the contribution of economic geographers who have championed research on the globalization of profession services outside Europe and North America. This is not a surprise given that research in this field in business and management is more prevalent in organization studies (e.g. Morgan & Boussebaa, 2015) rather than International Business. We think that now is timely for the International Business community to more actively engage with knowledge-intensive and professional service firms such as executive search in their empirical research.

Acknowledgements

Jonathan Beaverstock would like to thank the University of Western Sydney and Professor Phillip O'Neill for hosting his visit at the Urban Research Centre, Parramatta during the English cricket Ashes winning summer of July and August 2009. William Harvey would like to acknowledge the financial support of the University of Sydney Business School in 2013. Both authors are highly grateful for the time and support of all the interviewees.

Notes

1 www.boyden.com/offices__associates/.
2 www.kornferryasia.com/about_history.asp.
3 The Executive Grapevine (2012) and http://iicpartners.com/global-offices/.

References

Aharoni, Y. (1993) *Coalitions and Competition: The Globalization of Professional Business Services*. London: Routledge.

Aharoni, Y. & Nachum, L. (Eds.) (2000) *The Globalization of Services: Some Implications for Theory and Practice*. Routledge: London.

Bagchi-Sen, S. & Sen, J. (1997) 'The current state of knowledge in International Business in producer services', *Environment and Planning A*, 29, pp. 1153–1174.

Baird, R.B. (1985) *The Executive Grapevine*. 4th Edition. Suffolk, UK: Halesworth Press.

Beaverstock, J.V. (2004) '"Managing across borders": Knowledge management and expatriation in professional legal service firms', *Journal of Economic Geography*, 4, pp. 157–179.

Beaverstock, J.V., Faulconbridge, J.R. & Hall, S.J.E. (2015) *The Globalization of Executive Search. Professional Services Strategy and Dynamics in the Contemporary World*. London: Routledge.

Boussebaa, M., Morgan, G. & Sturdy, A. (2012) 'Constructing global firms? National, transnational and neo-colonial effects in international management consultancies', *Organization Studies*, 33, pp. 465–486.

Boyle, M., Findlay, A., Lelievre, E. & Paddison, R. (1996) 'World cities and the limits to global control: A case study of executive search firms in Europe's leading cities', *International Journal of Urban and Regional Research*, 20, pp. 498–517.

Britton, L., Doherty, C. & Ball, D. (1997) 'Executive search and selection in France, Germany and the UK', *Zeitschrift Fur Betriebswirtschaft*, 67, pp. 219–232.

Brock, D.M. (2012) 'Building global capabilities: A study of globalizing professional service firms', *The Service Industries Journal*, 32, pp. 1593–1607.

Brock, D.M., Powell, M. & Hinings, C.R. (Eds.) (1999) *Restructuring the Professional Organisation. Accounting, Healthcare and Law*. London: Routledge.

Byrne, J. (1986) *The Headhunters*. New York: Macmillan Publishing.

Daniels, P.W. (2012) 'Changing landscapes of services and restructuring in Asian cities', in Daniels, P.W., Ho, K.C. & Hutton, T.A. (Eds.), *New Economic Spaces in Asian Cities: From Industrial Restructuring to the Cultural Turn*. London: Routledge, pp. 17–30.
Dunning, J. (1993) *The Globalization of Business*. London: Routledge.
Dunning, J. & Norman, G. (1987) 'The location choices of offices of international companies', *Environment and Planning A*, 19, pp. 613–631.
The Executive Grapevine (2009) *Directory of Executive Recruitment International Edition 2009*. St. Albans, UK: The Executive Grapevine Ltd.
The Executive Grapevine (2012) *Global Directory of Executive Recruitment Consultants 2012/13*. St Albans, UK: The Executive Grapevine Ltd.
Faulconbridge, J.R., Hall, S. & Beaverstock, J.V. (2008) 'New insights into the internationalization of producer services: Organizational strategies and spatial economies for global headhunting firms', *Environment and Planning A*, 40, pp. 210–234.
Finlay, W. & Coverdill, J.E. (2002) *Headhunters. Matchmaking in the Labor Market*. Ithaca, NY: Cornell University Press.
Garrison-Jenn, N. (1993) *Executive Search in Europe*. London: The Economist Intelligence Unit.
Garrison-Jenn, N. (2005) *Headhunters and How to Use Them*. London: The Economist and Profile Books.
Gurney, D. (2000) *Headhunters Revealed! Career Secrets for Choosing and Using Professional Recruiters*. New York: Hunters Arts Publishing.
Hanlon, G. (1999) *Lawyers, the State and the Market. Professionalism Revisited*. Basingstoke, UK: Macmillan.
Heidrick & Struggles International (2000) *Annual Report*. Available from: www.heidrick.com/About/Investor-Relations.
Hutton, T.A. (2004) 'Service industries, globalization and urban restructuring within the Asia-Pacific: New Development trajectories and planning responses', *Progress in Planning*, 61, pp. 1–74.
Jones, A. (2005) 'Truly global corporations? Theorising organizational globalization in advanced business services', *Journal of Economic Geography*, 5, pp. 177–200.
Jones, S. (1989) *The Headhunting Business*. Basingstoke: Macmillan.
Lowendahl, B. (2000) *Strategic Management of Professional Service Firms*. 2nd Edition. Copenhagen: Copenhagen Business School.
Marshall, J.N., Wood, P., Daniels, P.W., McKinnon, A., Bachtler, J., Damesick, P., Thrift, N., Gillespie, A., Green, A. & Leyshon, A. (1988) *Service Development and Uneven Development*. Oxford, UK: Oxford University Press.
Morgan, G. & Boussebaa, M. (2015) 'Internationalization of professional service firms', in Empson, L., Hinings, R., Muzio, D. & Broschak, J. (Eds.), *Oxford Handbook of Professional Service Firms*. Oxford, UK: Oxford University Press, pp. 71–91.
Morgan, G. & Quack, S. (2006) 'Institutional legacies and firm dynamics: The growth and globalization of UK and German law firms', *Organization Studies*, 26, pp. 1765–1785.
Morris, T. & Empson, L. (1998) 'Organisation and expertise: An exploration of knowledge bases and the management and consulting firms', *Accounting Organizations and Society*, 23, pp. 609–624.
Morshidi, S. (2000) 'Globalising Kuala Lumpur and the strategic role of the producer service sector', *Urban Studies*, 37, pp. 2217–2240.
Muzio, D. & Faulconbridge, J.R. (2013) 'The global professional service firm: "One firm" models versus (Italian) distance institutionalised practices', *Organization Studies*, 34, pp. 897–925.
O'Connor, K. & Daniels, P.W. (2001) 'The geography of international trade in services: Australia and the APEC region', *Environment and Planning A*, 33, pp. 281–296.
Sassen, S. (2013) *Cities in a World Economy*. 4th Edition. London: Sage.
Segal-Horn, S. & Dean, A. (2011) 'The rise of super-elite law firms: Towards global strategies', *The Service Industries Journal*, 31, pp. 195–213.
Watson, H., Ball, D., Britton, L.C. & Clark, T. (1990) *Executive Search and the European Recruitment Market*. London: The Economist Publications.

PART VII

Epilogue

34
EPILOGUE

Gary Cook

I write this epilogue towards the end of a long editorial process. It is time to face the obvious question: was it worth it? The structure of the epilogue is to return to the challenges set out in the introduction, both by the editors and by Henry Yeung at the 2012 Academy of International Business UK & Ireland conference. It will end with a short section on "what next?", which will outline some practical measures to encourage dialogue and joint working, as well as sketching some key research themes and questions.

Establishing the common ground

Both Economic Geography and International Business have been alert in identifying that there has been a profound change taking place over the past 30 years or so, and which is still continuing, in the nature of firm strategies and the structure of the global economic system. That change is characterised by the radical vertical disintegration and geographical dispersion of production, part of which has gone alongside more extensive reliance on third parties. Several chapters in this volume, some contributed from geographers, some from International Business scholars, probe this phenomenon, particularly the chapters by Coe, Strange and Magnani, Glaister, and Sinkovics et al. As argued by Coe, there are some distinctive contributions which Economic Geographers have made to the study of this phenomenon, such as the more careful analysis of how power relations constitute the value chains/production networks and how the particular institutional context of the "hub" multinational orchestrating a chain or network influences the particular form of that network. They have also given more attention to the political economy of the international and national regulatory regimes which both constrain and enable firm strategies, as do the activities of various stakeholder groups such as trade unions and consumer groups. As ever, Geographers have a greater interest in the implications of such networks for processes of uneven development, International Business scholars in how they can enhance and sustain the competitive advantage of firms, although Geographers acknowledge that those regions which attract such activity must be able to offer strategic advantages to firms. Moreover, as Coe shows, current developments in the theory of global production networks conceptualise them as lead-firm-based configurations, rather than as stylised industry patterns. They are also placing greater emphasis on the multiple strategies firms pursue to place themselves as best they can within a complex and pressured economic environment. These developments clearly bring the two disciplines closer together. Glaister reveals the magnitude and diversity of the literature on alliances in International Business, which incorporates insights from a range of disciplinary fields. As he argues, greater understanding of this corpus of work will enhance the analysis of relations and networks within Economic Geography. Likewise, Strange and Magnani show how the literature on the "global factory" in International Business can complement the literature on global production networks.

Economic Geography and International Business share a common interest in the sub-national region as a crucial arena in which economic activity takes place. As Fuller clearly shows in his chapter, the two perspectives do have some fundamental differences, perhaps the critical one being that geographers do not associate regions with administrative boundaries, but with the operation of a particular set of institutional processes. It is also true that International Business has developed its interest in the sub-national scale much later than Economic Geography. Both disciplines have a common interest in agglomeration and recognise the same fundamental sources: Marshallian economies based on within-industry effects; Jacobs externalities based on cross-industry effects, scale, competition and external connectivity. Strangely, International Business gives less attention to Jacobs' externalities, peculiar given their international dimension and the emphasis on the process of competition. The nature and extent of a region's extra-regional connections are integral to how geographers conceive of regions and the economic processes that take place within them. Geographers are also more interested in connections between regions than is the case in International Business. Economic Geographers and International Business scholars both recognise that the degree of embeddedness of the firm within a region is a fundamental influence on the ability of the firm to build competitive advantage based on the tangible and intangible assets within that region. Again, it is fair to say that geographers have been more careful in their conceptualisation of embeddedness than International Business. Both disciplines have a strong interest in what drives the location choices of MNEs, what drives the particular arrangements firms make in each location (e.g. what activities to site there, what supplier linkages to make) and the impact inward investment has on the host region. As Fuller points out, Economic Geographers are more alert to the fact particular "clusters" are far from being homogeneous and that the particular nature of the cluster will condition what it is possible to achieve by locating there. There is also a tension between the emphasis on knowledge spillovers and the palpable fact that firms typically strive to keep core knowledge proprietary.

In Chapter 7 Barnes and Sheppard identify core research areas within Economic Geography, which have had influence outside the discipline, specifically industrial districts, spatial labour markets, innovation milieus, global production networks and commodity chains. These are all clearly within the domain of International Business, as is the broader agenda of Economic Geography identified by Barnes and Sheppard, examining the places and spaces in which economic activities are carried out and circulate. Industrial districts (or, to use another shorthand, clusters) feature prominently in many of the chapters in this Companion contributed by International Business scholars, such as the chapters by Gugler, Cook and Pandit, and Goerzen et al. Likewise, global production networks and commodity chains, commented on at greater length by Coe and Yeung, which feature in the contributions from Strange and Magnani and Sinkovics et al., although the latter add a sobering note of qualification regarding the extent to which ideas from Economic Geography have penetrated into the International Business mainstream. There is a very active literature in International Business and in Economic Geography examining the linkages between location and innovation, highlighted in the chapter by Castellani. There is common interest in the rapid economic development of emerging economies and their implications for both established and emerging economy multinationals.

Barnes and Sheppard outline some of the key "hot topics" in Economic Geography research, some of which have clear relevance for International Business. Economic Geography is taking a closer interest in how firms make decisions and how this is influenced by spatial factors. This is also a priority area for International Business. Likewise, how markets form is a fundamental question, as is the relationship between cultural factors and firm strategies in shaping consumer preferences. The area of the interplay between labour markets and the changing geography of production, powerfully influenced by MNE strategies, is a relatively neglected area within International Business. Both disciplines have developed a keen interest in how economic activity is regulated, at international, national and local levels, and how this affects the economic dynamism of particular places. Geographers have placed more attention on services, and above all the internationalisation of the financial services industry and how this interacts with the changing internationalisation of other forms of economic activity.

Both Economic Geography and International Business have an intense interest in knowledge flows and their link with innovation and the strategic creation of competitive advantage by firms. The chapters by Cooke (Economic Geography) and Wu and Yang (International Business) focus in particular on this issue. Cooke notes that early writing on learning in the business literature (not specifically International Business) was framed by evolutionary thinking, a paradigm which has recently gained significant traction in Economic Geography, as the chapter by Rigby details. Again, as Cooke notes, the literature in Economic Geography has placed less emphasis on corporate or organisational learning compared to the business and management fields. Economic Geographers have been more interested in learning within regions, which speaks more closely to their interest in regional development and regimes of uneven development. The chapter by Castellani is significant in this regard, as he shows how MNEs are key actors linking regions in innovation and that, despite strong persistence in the location of innovation activity, some regions have prospered disproportionately, and this concentration is particularly marked where MNEs are involved in collaborative innovation.

The melding of powerful complementary, but incomplete, perspectives on International Business, the phenomenon

An initial observation is in order at the start of this section. It is telling that there is far more reflection in the contributions to this Companion by Economic Geographers regarding how their discipline can strengthen International Business than the other way around. One can speculate as to the reasons for this. It may be that, on the whole, geographers are better informed about the other field than in the converse case. I have no real evidence on the extent to which that is true. There is more evidence that geographers do see it as odd that an inherently spatial field like International Business has not thought more deeply about the conceptualisation of space.

One of the key areas, possibly the most important area, where Economic Geography can complement International Business is in terms of the conceptualisation of space, which is more sophisticated in Economic Geography, despite the fact that International Business is inherently a spatial concept. In terms of a richer conceptualisation of space, Yeung makes a distinction between physical space, which can be measured in terms of the physical location of an MNEs operations, and organisational space, which is fundamentally relational in character. Clearly there will be internal relationships between the various parts of the MNE. It is also clear that in each location where the MNE operates, there will be influences at a range of spatial scales on the institutional and economic context in which the subsidiary or HQ operates. These relationships and contexts also change over time, partly as a direct result of the actions the MNE takes, and those actions in turn are influenced by both the particular contexts in which individual units operate and by the totality of the MNEs' international scope. The interaction between the MNEs' strategy and actions and network relationships in which they are situated is influenced by what Yeung terms strategic coupling, which he defines in this Companion as "a process of multiple actors taking advantage of their mutual complementarities in networks".

Despite the "obvious" connections which appear between the two disciplines, given their common interest in the same phenomenon, the connections between the literatures in the two disciplines in this area have been quite small to date, as noted by both Coe, from the geography perspective, and Sinkovics et al. from the International Business perspective. Coe argues International Business will be enriched by making networks the unit of analysis, rather than the firm, and by considering in greater depth how networks are governed and how knowledge flows within networks. What International Business can contribute is powerful insights into the creation and enhancement of superior resources and capabilities and theoretical analysis and evidence relating to the make-or-buy (internalisation) decisions which are central to whether, and under what circumstances, the firm will outsource or not. Gammelgaard and McDonald suggest that failing to appreciate the increasing importance of location as a means to enhance competitive advantage is a weakness in the treatment of firm networks in Economic Geography, which can be addressed by drawing on International Business. They also argue that International Business casts light on the importance of spatial transaction costs and the dangers of spreading operations over too wide a span of countries. International Business also has much to contribute to Economic Geography in terms of the analysis of the internal governance of multinational firms and the types of governance structures they set up to manage alliance relationships of various sorts. The chapter by Glaister gives an excellent overview of the issues involved in establishing and managing alliances. Those by Nguyen and Verbeke and Yuan probe the internal governance issues within multinationals. Other points of common interest concern how learning is structured within networks and how firms strategise to capture value.

Wrigley and Wood in Chapter 28 acknowledge the importance (but note some limitations) of some fundamental frameworks in International Business that may be of service to geographers, namely Dunning's eclectic OLI framework, Bartlett and Ghoshal's Integration-Responsiveness framework and the Uppsala "stages" model of internationalisation. These frameworks have been the subject of critical debate within International Business, but they have also, to varying degrees, stood the test of time. Others should be added to the list. Internalisation theory brings powerful insights into the make-or-buy decision, which is fundamental in any explanation of the organisation of industry, as famously argued by Coase (1972), albeit in a somewhat constrained sense of the division of economic coordination between firm and market. The Resource-Based View (RBV) has also become central in probing the ways in which firms establish and maintain competitive advantage, duly acknowledged by Wrigley and Wood with reference to Rugman and Verbeke's Country Specific Advantage and Subsidiary Specific Advantage framework. The RBV has important relatives in the Knowledge-Based View and the dynamic capabilities framework. The International New Venture framework of Oviatt and McDougall (1994) is an important qualifier to the Uppsala stages model. One might note the increasing importance of the Institutional View (Peng & Khoury, 2009); however, this is less relevant to this epilogue, given that Economic Geography is thoroughly imbued with the institutional perspective and, indeed, has much to teach International Business about its application to both theorisation and applied work. The chapter by Bagchi-Sen and Schunder provides an important analysis of the extent to which a broad range of frameworks from IB can be of service in geographically based analyses of the internationalisation strategies of advanced producer services. At the same time, they sound notes of caution about the extent to which they can be applied in services in the same way they do to manufacturing firms. Likewise, Bryson, who also highlights the relationship between advanced producer services and manufacture in his chapter, makes a strong case for the need for genuinely inter-disciplinary work, rather than attempting to construct one "grand theory" of International Business (the phenomenon).

The stronger emphasis on cities and the relationship between cities within Economic Geography has been shown to be important in several chapters in this volume, notably those by Cook and Pandit, Derudder et al. and Beaverstock and Harvey. Geographers have a much stronger grip on what it is that makes a city more or less central in the global economic system, as demonstrated in the chapter by Derudder et al. The chapter by Holden and Horn is particularly interesting as it traces the importance of cities and relationships between cities to International Business back to the Early Modern era in Europe. It is not a new phenomenon. The chapter also makes a contribution to undermining the "geography is dead" thesis, by showing the central role of cities, and the International Business facilitated and coordinated through them, in shaping which languages were used in International Business and how they were used. The world has not become flat, just because English is used as the most common International Business language. This has an important connection with the insights which Economic Geography provides on the importance of the relationship between places, exemplified in the relational perspective, clearly articulated in the chapter by Murphy. The International Business community is catching on to the importance of cities and this is evident in the chapters by Cook and Pandit, Castellani, and Goerzen et al. By the same token, Geographers recognise the importance of the agency of firms and of firm strategies in constructing the nature of cities and the relationship between them. A revealing spotlight is placed on this issue in the chapter by O'Neill, which looks at the importance of infrastructure investment in underpinning both the economic dynamism of cities and also a high level, and fair distribution, of amenity to citizens. This issue is thrown into sharp relief in the present age, where the private sector is assuming more responsibility for planning and funding infrastructure development in cities. This poses important challenges in terms of the balance between economic efficiency and fairness.

Economic Geographers have much to learn from International Business scholars about the intricacies of strategy and strategic competition, as well as the thorny issues posed regarding the relationship between HQs and subsidiaries and among subsidiaries within corporate networks, as shown in the chapters by Gammelgaard and McDonald, Nguyen, Verbeke and Yuan, and Strange and Magnani. One could broaden the scope by referring to frameworks from Economics, of which International Business scholars are more fully aware, such as Transaction Cost Economics, the economic analysis of property rights, the economics of internal organisation and principal-agent theory. These provide important insights into the links between strategy and the internal structure of the firm and also to the types of contractual and non-contractual governance which firms employ, both internally and externally with third parties. There is much still to do and more will be accomplished if there is serious interpenetration between Economic Geography and International Business and more joint working between scholars in these fields.

Economic Geographers have given more prominence to the internationalisation of professional service firms than have International Business scholars and this is evidenced by the chapters by Wrigley and Wood, Howells and Lowe, Bagchi-Sen and Schunder, Clark, and Beaverstock and Harvey. Beaverstock and Harvey's chapter also underscores the importance of global labour markets in underpinning the strategies and competitive advantage of MNEs, a topic which deserves fuller treatment within International Business. Both topics provide fertile ground for research within International Business.

Economic Geographers have become more interested in the actions of firms as economic agents, as detailed in the chapters by Fuller, Coe, and Yeung. Actor-network theory is now well established as a framework in Economic Geography, which does recognise the agency of firms, yet which comes at it from a different perspective, that of power relations. This is a dimension which is under-explored in International Business, which does recognise market power in the economic sense, and indeed the understanding of market power within International Business can enrich the conceptualisation of power in Economic Geography. Having a much closer affiliation with Industrial Organisation, International Business has benefitted from the vastly more sophisticated theorisation and empirical evidence regarding the creation, maintenance and exercise of market power. The chapter by Verbeke and Yuan gives a compelling framework for analysing subsidiary roles, appealing to the insights of Edith Penrose. They also show how the literature within International Business provides a sophisticated framework for analysing the nature and evolution of subsidiary roles and the circumstances under which these will be strongly related to national institutions and changes in the degree of (triad) regional integration.

International Business has moved closer to Economic Geography in recognising that there is a complex relationship between subsidiaries, subsidiaries and HQ, and, crucially, between the mandates and strategic assets subsidiaries accumulate and the particular places in which they are sited. The contributions of both Gammelgaard and McDonald, and Fuller highlight the view of the MNE as a differentiated network as exemplifying theorising which has moved the two disciplines closer together. It remains the case that geographers have a richer conceptualisation and empirical literature on the idiosyncrasies of subsidiary location and the types of action subsidiaries take and the capabilities they possess. This is rooted in the relational perspective, which is concerned with how the different places in which an MNE operates are connected, rather than viewing the location decision regarding individual operating units within a firm as being isolated, which International Business is more prone to do, at least implicitly. Both recognise that these things are not static, although temporal aspects tend to be given greater prominence in Economic Geography.

As has featured in many of the chapters in the book, and as articulated with clarity by Murphy in Chapter 10, the relational perspective has become a core assumption for many geographers, although there is clearly debate within the discipline about the status and conceptualisation of rationality. It is important to recognise this assumption, which, as Murphy explains, seeks to bridge the gap between atomistic views of agents, who, in some approaches are seen to operate autonomously with free will and freedom of choice, and strongly structural perspectives, which assert that human cognition and behaviour are determined (or at least strongly influenced) by social processes and social institutions. The full structure-agency debate is well beyond the scope of this volume and also goes well beyond the field of Economic Geography. Nevertheless, the importance of social institutions in conditioning the way people (managers) perceive the world and both enabling and constraining which actions are feasible (and desirable) is central to much of modern thought in Economic Geography. What is more, geographers have a highly developed sense of the ways in which these institutions that shape behaviour are rooted in particular places and the relationships between places. International Business, in as much as it has increasingly espoused the Institutional View, has become more cognisant of the importance of social structures in framing behaviour, not just of firms, but also of customers, labour, and regulators and politicians. The chapter by Peng and Jung is important in this regard, as it places emphasis on the role of institutions in shaping the location choices of MNEs. The chapter by Gugler also argues that the quality of institutions is a fundamental influence on the attractiveness of a location to MNEs. International Business scholars have not come as far, however, in analysing the complex geographies of the processes which give rise to particular institutions in particular places. Murphy points out the influence of Granovetter's (1985) writing on embeddedness and the importance of recognising that networks of personal relationships can give rise to norms of trust and reciprocity, which mean that either pure market or pure hierarchy (in the Williamsonian sense) may be less efficient than some hybrid governance structure in between the two. This thought resonates with Dunning's (1995) writing on the transformations being ushered in by what he termed the "era of alliance capitalism". More generally, the importance of social capital is well recognised by International Business scholars, including those at the "harder" economic and quantitative end of the discipline.

Murphy explicates some other features of the geographer's perspective, which do not find such strong counterparts in International Business, which partly reflects the different questions researchers in the two fields are most interested in. Relational geography is very concerned with micro-social processes. Economic agents need to establish a shared understanding of the situation with other agents, in order to act effectively; however, they are able to imagine futures which are different from the present or the past, therefore they can bring about institutional change. This leads to the third leg of the relational approach, which Murphy terms the socio-material base of the economic order. Here the two influential bodies of thought are Giddens' structuration theory, which emphasises the mutual dependency of agency and structure (agency creates and recreates structure but structure both enables and constrains agency), and actor-network theory. Actor-network theory is poststructuralist and sees the economic order as arising from the messy interplay of economic actors. Although the economic order can be stable for extended periods, it is also seen as shifting and capable of being rapidly changed (one thinks of the tumultuous consequences of the fall of the "iron curtain").

Murphy goes on to argue that two particular aspects of the relational approach hold a lot of promise for International Business scholars seeking to understand the organisation, management and performance of firms, markets and value chains. The first is to expand on ideas about why physical proximity matters by recognising the importance of relational proximity. This asserts that a "cluster" or region that is isolated may become prone to lock-in and ossification and that linkages to other territories outside the region can enable a flow of fresh ideas, which sustain dynamism. This idea is very close to those of Jane Jacobs, who strongly emphasised the role of external connections in fostering innovation. Relational proximity is needed to foster trust and mutual understanding at a distance, just as these things underpin positive externalities within the region. Multinational firms are powerful agents who can create such relational proximity through their internal and external relationships. Relational proximity is a critical concept in understanding how MNEs are able to operate geographically dispersed operations and act effectively at distance both in their internal working and their interactions with external agents. The second key concept is socio-spatial practice. This is concerned, putting it a little simplistically, with how firms go about their everyday business, which entails how they interpret and make sense of the world within which they act and also take actions in pursuit of their business. A primary question for geographers is to analyse the circumstances in which the actual practice of firms leads to superior performance. Underperformance, of course, can lead to changes in practice.

Understanding the key assumptions each side is making

Barnes and Sheppard provide an excellent guide to the research agenda and research paradigms in Economic Geography, which will give the uninitiated a sound platform on which to build as they immerse themselves in the Economic Geography literature. They also point out some of the distinctive features of Economic Geography, which highlight some key areas where thinking in International Business can be enriched by engagement with that discipline. First, the fact that the geography of economic activities co-evolves with the economy itself. Here the activities of MNEs are very important. Second, that economic processes are strongly influenced by political and cultural processes, an idea which has gained increasing traction within International Business as the Institutional View has become influential. Third, Economic Geographers challenge the notion that free market capitalism is either inevitable or desirable. Fourth, that Economic Geography is very pluralist in both theory and methodology. These last two features provide more of a challenge to International Business scholars, but awareness of them will make them reflect more on the assumptions they are making and, perhaps, remind them that there are alternative perspectives on the phenomena they study. Cook and Pandit caution that there are some fundamental differences in epistemology and theoretical assumptions, which mean it is not straightforward to meld the two disciplines. Put crudely, Economic Geography is at the idiographic end of the spectrum, emphasising difference and uniqueness, whereas International Business has largely been at the nomothetic end of the spectrum, looking for general principles and laws. The contributions of Barnes and Sheppard, and Fuller point out that it is misleading not to recognise that there is significant pluralism in Economic Geography. International Business is also not monolithic, either in methodology or epistemology. Nevertheless, as a crude generalisation, International Business remains much more closely wedded to Popperian falsificationism, whereas Economic Geography is more imbued with critical realism and post structuralism. This makes it difficult for International Business scholars who venture into the Economic Geography literature, as these epistemological frameworks are alien and key terms are not understood. The converse is less true, as Economic Geographers have typically thought about positivism and falsificationism and explicitly rejected them.

Yeung makes some sharp observations about the fact that the importance of time and space, as part of the fundamental analytical frameworks of geographers, attested to in many other chapters, is not at all central to much work in the business and management area. International Business research is fundamentally concerned with space, yet to the eyes of a geographer the conception of space appears impoverished and simplistic. He does duly acknowledge that International Business scholars have become aware of the extent to which location and geography are relatively poorly understood. International Business has a lot to say about the motives behind particular location decisions, but has much less to say about how the locations it operates in will in turn shape the way it behaves and the strategy it formulates. This coevolution of firms and territories is a key area in which Economic Geography can enrich analysis in International Business. It is naïve to think that strategy is formulated in some ivory tower in corporate HQ in the home country, bereft of any influence of the home country context, and then optimal locations are chosen as if in some maximisation algorithm and then smoothly implemented exactly as envisaged in the master plan. Surely no International Business scholar worthy of the name actually believes such a thing consciously, and there is abundant evidence in the extant International Business literature that they believe something very different. Yet, Yeung has a point that something akin to this is often implicitly assumed and that there is little explicit theorising of the reverse linkages between the places in which a firm operates and the actions it takes and the strategies it formulates.

The chapter by Rigby outlines the nature and progress of evolutionary approaches within Economic Geography. Its impact within the field has been real, but somewhat limited, partly due to the lack of coherence within Evolutionary Economics and evolutionary approaches more generally. Nevertheless, the case is made that evolutionary approaches do have value to add when examining the dynamics of regional development. Evolutionary Economics has had an even more limited impact within International Business, yet it has clearly been identified as having promise for an understanding of the co-evolution of firms and the institutional environments within which they operate (Cantwell, Dunning & Lundan, 2010). Rigby identifies that one aspect of the evolutionary approach is under-researched and that is the formation of self-organising networks. He specifically links this to the issue that there is considerable variation in how "linked-in" firms are within networks in clusters and points out that emerging findings indicate that firms with greater centrality in networks are able to extract greater benefits from cluster location. This seems like a glimpse of the blindingly obvious, but why then is the strongly differentiated ability of firms to benefit from cluster location often absent from discussions regarding the nature and attractiveness of clusters, beyond typically vague remarks about the importance of embeddedness?

Evidence that the missing elements matter

Bedreaga, Argilés and McCann show in their chapter that geography and processes operating at a variety of spatial scales, from the local to the international, moderate the internationalisation-performance relationship. The proposition that proper adaptation to the host country environment will influence the performance of a subsidiary is not controversial within International Business and their key concepts of "strategic fit" and "embeddedness" are well recognised. Likewise, the idea that embeddedness becomes more problematic as institutional distance, broadly understood, increases, would be broadly accepted. As the authors note, Hymer himself recognised that there would be a hierarchy of overseas investments which mirrored the hierarchy of world cities – see also the chapter by Derudder et al. in this Companion. Embededdness will specifically increase the likelihood that firms benefit from information flows and mutually beneficial cooperation, although the authors note a potential risk of "over-embeddedness" where social relations outweigh economic imperatives. Bedreaga, Argilés and McCann argue that, as far as the study of MNEs is concerned, there has been a focus on embeddedness in both the Economic Geography and International Business literatures, albeit that the former has been more concerned with implications for the host region and the latter with implications for firm performance.

The chapters by Coe, Yeung, and Bedreaga, Argilés and McCann review a considerable body of evidence relating to the nature and importance of global production networks and the institutional and relational processes which underpin them. From the IB side, the chapters by Glaister, Strange and Magnani, and Nguyen survey a vast corpus of empirical evidence in IB that shows the importance of standard economic and strategy frameworks in IB for understanding the nature of the networks and alliances firm form, the constraints on how truly global firms are, and can be, and the important interplay between the scale and scope of firms' global and (triad) regional strategies and the internal organisation of the firm.

Clark's contribution on the Culture of Finance (Chapter 32) is very instructive, as it takes first a standard economic framework and then shows how being embedded (or not) in a particular place materially affects the behaviour of economic agents. This exemplifies how important it is to recognise that culture matters, and that culture has a particular geography, which goes beyond standard frameworks in International Business. His emphasis on clear and rigorous theory building to provide a framework for analysis sits well with best practice in International Business. The chapter is also of great contemporary interest as it explicates why the behaviour of individuals can be hard for organisations to control. Howells and Lowe's chapter melds geographic and business perspectives to explore the origins of innovation in the hotel industry and the various modes of internationalisation which diffuse those innovations internationally. Here the pressure of competition and the social networks of entrepreneurs, including international diasporas, emerge as being highly important.

Wrigley and Wood's chapter, summarising evidence from empirical studies on retailing, identifies four key contributions made by Economic Geography, which could enrich International

Business in important ways. First, a sophisticated view of embeddedness, recognising territorial embeddedness (necessary to achieve legitimacy by conforming to formal and informal institutions relevant to a full range of stakeholders in the host economy); societal embeddedness, which concerns the imprint MNEs bring from their home institutional context; and network embeddedness, which concerns the relationships the MNE constructs both internally and with a wide range of external stakeholders to gain access to markets, resources, information and influence. Establishing and maintaining embeddedness is a process which plays out over time and across different spatial scales, from the very local to the international. Second, recognising the influence of regulatory constraints and the informal institutional context. Third, highlighting the fundamental importance of relationships with financial markets and suppliers of financial services (which one might extend to include other providers of professional services, as other chapters in the Companion highlight). This relates to a broader concern in Economic Geography with the process of "financialisation" whereby capital markets and financial intermediaries exercise increasing influence over economic agents and the functioning of the economic system. Fourth, analysis of the selective transfer of knowledge, capabilities and culture from the home context to the host context. Retail is particularly instructive in this regard, given the number of high profile instances of retailers making expensive failed forays into overseas markets, despite their considerable strength in their home market, in some cases making elementary mistakes regarding what is acceptable to the consumer in the target market.

The place for critical perspectives in International Business research

The issue of critical perspectives poses some challenges for Economic Geographers working with International Business scholars. Whilst International Business is not overtly managerialist – much of the research in the field is "positive" in the sense that it seeks to understand what is there, rather than to further the agenda of corporations at the expense of its internal or external stakeholders – critical perspectives do not constitute part of the core research programme. This creates a sharp problem of incentives, since the top-ranked International Business journals do not include critical perspectives within their aims and scope. Such work is not "off limits", rather there is no particular interest in it, with the obvious exception of the recently founded journal *Critical Perspectives in International Business*. There are some avenues open, however, within the top tier journals. Issues regarding governance, corporate social responsibility and sustainability are within scope. There is also interest in the link between the scale and scope of MNE operations and the economic development of the regions in which they are situated, and this interest is long standing. Moreover, the interest of International Business scholars in where MNEs will choose to locate, the scale of their commitment and the scope of the mandate given to particular subsidiaries in particular places is germane to the central issue of uneven development for Economic Geographers, stated clearly in the chapter by Yeung. Yeung highlights the particular issue of "bypassed places", to coin a telling phrase from Jane Jacobs, regions and countries which do not attract much inward direct investment. Here there is a clear research agenda which would be of interest to International Business scholars regarding policy options for national or regional governments which might encourage more inward direct investment, and their accumulated expertise regarding the influences on the location choices of MNEs will be of good service. Indeed, in a much quoted paper, Buckley and Ghauri (2004) explicitly call for this link between MNE activity and economic development to be the subject of more research. Nevertheless, there is little evidence that critical perspectives will become central to the mainstream in International Business.

Summary

What lessons do the contributions in this Companion make to the challenges laid down by Henry Yeung at the Academy of International Business UK & Ireland 2012 conference?

1 To explain the critical links between regions and the global economy, particularly through the lens of firms and their production networks.

The literatures in Economic Geography on global production networks, the internationalisation of professional service firms and on the hierarchy of world cities and relationships between them speak powerfully to this theme. Of these literatures, that on global production networks has had the most impact on thinking in International Business. As this Companion has shown, there is a lot further to go. Within International Business, the literature on the global factory also speaks to this theme, and here there is real scope for fruitful interchange between the two disciplines. International Business is beginning to become alert to the importance of cities, picking up threads Hymer laid down over 40 years ago. There is a literature concerned with service industries and service firms in International Business, and here again there is scope for fruitful interchange.

2 To use a transdisciplinary perspective to understand flows and relations across space and their significance, moving beyond the agency(firm)-centric views of International Business and Economics.

This issue is perhaps the crux of how and why joint work between Economic Geography and International Business is important to progress. To summarise crudely, Economic Geography provides powerful insights into relations across space and to the institutional influence on the behaviour of economic actors; International Business speaks powerfully to the agency of firms and has much to say about the strategies firms employ to create, sustain and exploit competitive advantage. As noted several times, the penetration of the Institutional View into the mainstream of International Business and the growing interest in Economic Geography to take firms seriously as economic actors give grounds for optimism.

3 To transform knowledge in International Business through engagement and connectivity.

This is already happening. There is joint work going on between geographers and International Business scholars. The composition of the editorial team for this Companion, and their shared history of joint working, is living proof, and but is the tip of the iceberg. Many of the chapters in this Companion exemplify the insights gained by the interpenetration of the two disciplines, and many papers are cited which have bridged the gap. The success of the fairly recently founded *Journal of Economic Geography* also bears witness. The interest in the special sessions on the boundaries between Economic Geography and International Business at the 2012 and 2014 Academy of International Business UK & Ireland Conferences also give tangible proof of the receptivity of scholars in both disciplines. These things are, perhaps, little more than a beginning, but a promising beginning.

What next?

As noted in the introduction, the editors of this volume were motivated to embark on the project by their lived experience that dialogue and inter-disciplinary work between Economic Geography and International Business are both intellectually stimulating and help to get a more complete grasp on the phenomena being studied. It is clear that this belief is shared by many of the contributors to this volume and in the work cited which has, to one degree or another, explored the interface between these two academic fields. We hope that this Companion will both stimulate others to put their toe in the water and make it easier for them to immerse themselves more fully. Wrigley and Wood, in the conclusion to Chapter 28, welcome the opening of dialogue but insist there must be a serious conversation. This Companion is one small contribution, among many others, seeking to open up that conversation, based on mutual respect, mature constructive criticism, rigorous debate and a spirit of open-mindedness.

As Fuller argues, the primary need for dialogue is to meld the insights of International Business into the internal dynamics and organisational attributes of MNEs with the insights of Economic Geographers into the dynamics and attributes of regions. Here proper account needs to be taken that the particular attributes of regions are socially constructed and can only be understood by recognising the geographical relations that give rise to them. This will require a reassessment of the extent to which locational advantages within particular clusters can be thought of as depending on local processes, and researchers will need to be more cognisant of the fact that "local" cluster advantages depend on relationships with other places. More research is needed into the relationship between embeddeness and firm performance and the relationship with regional development. As Bedreaga, Argilés and McCann argue, this will need to be more precise regarding the exact definition of embeddedness, which is a multidimensional concept ranging from the scale, depth and strength of linkages a subsidiary forms with local business networks, to the broader embedding of a foreign affiliate in the social and cultural fabric of the host economy. As Fuller points out in his chapter, we know comparatively little about how institutional change occurs as regions become recipients of inward direct investment and as they develop new and/or deeper connections with other regions. Peng and Jung, in their chapter, make the case for more research on the role of institutions in the location strategies of MNEs.

As has been noted in the introduction, prior sections in this epilogue and several of the chapters, Economic Geography works within epistemological frameworks which are unfamiliar and alien to International Business scholars (whereas the converse is less true). This is a tough nut to crack, as it does require effort to inform oneself about epistemological issues. This is simply part of the price one has to pay to gain access to insights of geographers and it is a fairly ubiquitous challenge in inter-disciplinary work. There is scope here for understanding to be fostered by workshops, special tracks and plenary sessions at conferences and non-technical review articles being published in IB journals. This Companion, we hope, also goes some way to helping bridge this gap – and also convincing some that the benefits are worth it.

There is a significant gap to be filled in enhancing understanding of the creation and maintenance of competitive advantage in service industries and the internationalisation process by which those advantages are exploited in overseas markets. Argument and evidence appear in the chapters by Howells and Lowe, Wrigley and Wood, Bryson, Bagchi-Sen and Schunder, and Beaverstock and Harvey.

There appears to be promise in exploiting more fully evolutionary approaches, both within Economic Geography and International Business. This applies both to the analysis of the dynamics of firm performance and to the evolution of the global economic system as a complex system. The core issues in the evolutionary analysis of variety and selection are especially apposite in the current era where variety, in the shape of the rapid economic development of emerging economies and the rapid internationalisation of some firms from those countries, is presenting both opportunities and threats to MNEs from developed countries. Evolutionary Economics in particular sits well within International Business, which does not style firms as omniscient economic agents, optimising on the basis of flawless calculation, and which recognises, often implicitly, that strategy does emerge in something of a trial and error fashion, as firms experiment and adapt to their changing competitive environment. More specifically, the challenge laid down by Klepper (1996; Klepper & Sleeper, 2005) in his evolutionary approach to clusters, asserting that the propagation of superior routines from the best firms, rather than externalities, is the true source of cluster dynamism, seems well suited to the research agenda in International Business, which has strongly espoused the Resource-Based View of the firm, which asserts that the greater part of differences in firm performance are due to idiosyncratic features of the firm itself.

Both Economic Geography and International Business are somewhat lacking in their understanding of the dynamics of institutional change. Again, given the complex evolution of the global economic system and the increase in the heterogeneity of the institutional environments which are now critical to MNEs and, indeed, the institutional backgrounds from which MNEs emerge, this lacuna warrants serious attention. Basic questions are: how will the institutional environments in emerging economies alter as a result of (i) the rapid internationalisation of some of their indigenous firms and (ii) the rapid increase of the activities of developed economy MNEs within them. Both sets of MNEs have to cope with the "institutional voids" within emerging economies (Khanna & Palepu, 2006). As the chapter by Jung, Wei and Wu demonstrates, emerging economy MNEs are attracted by high quality institutional environments oversees, as they expand into developed economies, partly in order to upgrade their competitive strengths. Both Economic Geography and International Business have paid limited attention to the selection mechanism, whereby some firms die as others prosper. Given the growing intensity of international competition, this again appears as a research gap to be filled.

As Rigby notes, it is a moot point whether the pluralisation of Economic Geography and its multiplicity of "turns" has improved its substantive grip on the key questions which are core to its research. This begs the question of whether trying to leverage insights from International Business will really improve matters from the geographer's perspective, or whether yet another turn will serve only to weary people and muddy the waters? Rigby identifies three areas where the combined efforts of (Evolutionary) Economic Geography and International Business may yield valuable fruit: understanding the co-evolution of firms and their institutional environments; building better data to understand the changing geographic patterning of economic activity; and understanding the complex geography of knowledge production, management by firms and transmission to create competitive advantage.

Yeung calls for an incorporation of spatial strategy into the framework of corporate strategy in International Business. This creates a research agenda in terms of the conceptualisation of strategy and also an empirical agenda in terms of understanding the extent to which MNEs have a spatial strategy and how they come to formulate and implement it. This leads to a second research agenda suggested by Yeung, to probe how actors in business organisations actually think about space.

In summary, there is an exciting research agenda in view, which invites joint working. Practical actions to encourage it include more special sessions in conferences and special issues of leading journals in each field, a joint workshop series and cooperative ventures such as this Companion. To the list might be added more jointly authored papers, joint bids for research funds and joint supervision of PhD students. Others, with more imagination, can surely think of additional things.

References

Buckley, P.J. & Ghauri, P. (2004) 'Globalisation, Economic Geography and the strategy of multinational enterprises', *Journal of International Business Studies*, 35, pp. 81–98.

Cantwell, J., Dunning, J.H. & Lundan, S.M. (2010) 'An evolutionary approach to understanding International Business activity: The co-evolution of MNEs and their institutional environment', *Journal of International Business Studies*, 41, pp. 567–586.

Coase, R.H. (1972) 'Industrial Organization: A proposal for research', in Fuchs, V.R. (Ed.), *Economic Research: Retrospect and Prospect, volume 3, Policy Issues and Research Opportunities in Industrial Organization.* Cambridge, MA: National Bureau for Economic Research, pp. 59–73.

Dunning, J.H. (1995) 'Reappraising the Eclectic Paradigm in an age of alliance capital', *Journal of International Business Studies*, 26, pp. 461–491.

Granovetter, M. (1985) 'Economic action and social structure: The problem of embeddedness', *American Journal of Sociology*, 91, 481–510.

Khanna, T. & Palepu, K.G. (2006) 'Emerging giants: Building world-class companies in developing countries', *Harvard Business Review*, October, pp. 60–69.

Klepper, S. (1996) 'Entry, exit, growth and innovation over the product life cycle', *American Economic Review*, 86, pp. 562–583.

Klepper, S. & Sleeper, S. (2005) 'Entry by spinoffs', *Management Science*, 51, pp. 1291–1306.

Oviatt, B.M. & McDougall, P.P. (1994) 'Toward a theory of international new ventures', *Journal of International Business Studies*, 25, pp. 45–64.

Peng, M.W. & Khoury, T.A. (2009) 'Unbundling the institution-based view of International Business strategy', in Rugman, A.M. (Ed.), *The Oxford Handbook of International Business.* 2nd Edition. Oxford, UK: Oxford University Press, pp. 256–268.

INDEX

Please note the following – page numbers in *italic* refer to figures/illustrations; page numbers in **bold** refer to tables.

Abecassis-Moedas, C. *et al.* (2012) 517
absorptive capacity 338–339, 487
Academy of International Business UK & Ireland 3–4, 5, 581, 591
accountancy firms 243, 512, 519, 523
accounting standards 80, 82
actor-network theory (ANT) 164–165, 222, 501, 585–586, 587, 591; evolutionary Economic Geography (EEG) 150, 153
adapting strategies 50, 531–532
additive manufacturing (3D printing) 61, 72
advanced countries 34, 340
advanced producer services (APS) 14, 20, 21, 459, 584–585, 591; cities and city regions 233, 234; definition of 509, **510**, **511–512**; growth of 512–514; internationalization of 514, **515**, 516–524; strategic cities 242, 243–244, **247**, 253, 254, 255; *see also* executive search firms
Advanced RISC Microprocessors (ARM) 322
Advanced Technology Park (Be'er Sheva) 325
agency theory 4, 5, 585, 586, 587, 591; cities and city regions 235; Economic Geography 184; foreign direct investment (FDI) 433; networks and alliances (N&As) 47–48; relationality 161, 163–164, 168
agglomeration economies 1, 4, 157, 190, 368, 582; cities and city regions 228, 230, 231–232, 234, 235, 236; cluster dynamics 444, 446–447, 448; Economic Geography 120, 122, 181; evolutionary Economic Geography (EEG) 133, 135, 136; knowledge-based view 318, 320, 321; location **192**, 195, 200, 201, *203*, 206, 207; relationality 165, 170; spatiality 39, 41; urban/rural enterprises 381
aggregation strategies 98
Aguilera, R.V. 204 *et al.* (2007) 80; *see also* Flores, R. *et al.* (2013)
Airbnb 497
Albaum, G. *et al.* (2005) 380
Albertoni, F. *et al.* (2015) 63
Alcácer, J. 201
Alchian, A.A. 428
Aldrich, H. *et al.* (2008) 131
Alexy, O. 483
Alford, M. *et al.* (2017) 8
Allen, J. 222, 233
alliance capitalism 10, 228, 587
alliances *see* networks and alliances (N&As)
Almeida, P. 219; *see also* Song, J. *et al.* (2003)
Aman, B. 88
Amazon 323, 418
Ambos, B. 87–88, 334, 340
Ambos, T.C. 334, 340
America Online (AOL) 327
Amin, A. 1, 167, 348
Amrop Hever 571
Amrop International 571, 572
Amsterdam 555
Andersson, U. 430, 431, 432
Android store-based platform functions 327
Annual Respondents Database (ARD) (United Kingdom) 66
Ansari, R. 485
Aoyama, Y. 483
apparel industries 61, 66, 322, 323, 482, 532–533
Apple 321, 322, 327, 532, 536–537
application distribution platforms (App stores) 327
appropriability regime 157

Araujo, L. 318
arbitrage strategies 98, 417, 419
Argentina 287
Argyris, Chris 318
ARM *see* Advanced RISC Microprocessors
Arregle, J.-L. 80; *see also* Marano, V. *et al.* (2016)
Arrow, K. 195
Arvidsson, N. 301
ASEAN *see* Association of Southeast Asian Nations
Asheim, Bjorn 319
Asia Pacific 197, 377, 521, 552; executive search firms 567, **568**, 569, 572–573, 575, 576; leading executive research firms in Australia **565–566**; regional economic development 79, 80, 87, 88; world leading retained executive search firms in Australia **570**, **571**
Asian tiger economies 322
Asmussen, C.G. 6, 82, 200, 203, 227, 231
asset management industry 545–548, 549, 551, 557, 559; contract law 552, *553*, 554, *555*, 556
asset-based perspective 443, 446, 518; foreign direct investment (FDI) 410, 412–413, 418, 419
Association of Southeast Asian Nations (ASEAN) 101, 102, 103
asymmetric power relationships 65
asymmetrical (ASM) contracts 552, 553
Atherton, A. 380–381
Aulakh, P.S. 51–52
Australia 377, 521, 552; executive search firms 567, **568**, 569, 572; leading executive research firms **565–566**; world leading retained executive search firms **570**, **571**
Autio, E. 328
automated trading systems (ATS) 326
automobiles and automobile components 61, 79, 97, 156, 533; global value chains (GVCs) 286, 287, 288; knowledge-based view 321, 322
Autonomy 323
Azmeh, S. 286

backward linkages 34, *35*, 36, 37
Bagchi-Sen, S. 243, 513
Baker, L.T. 70
Baldwin, Richard 27, 120
Balkanization 119
Ball, D.A. 519
Balland, R. 133, 134, 138
Banalieva, E.R. 82, 83, 287
Bangalore 287
banking and financial services 79
Barabasi, A. *see* Hidalgo, C. *et al.* (2007)
Barattieri, A. 521–522
Bardhan, P. 67, **68**
bargaining power 215, 337, 338
Barnes, T. 132
Barney, J. 138
Bartlett, C.A. 11, 50–51, 300, 443, 478, 584; regional economic development 83, 86, 96, 108
Basic Survey of Commercial and Manufacturing Structure and Activity (Japanese Ministry of International Trade & Industry) 66
'basin of attraction' 38
Bathelt, H. 167, 201, 455, 456
Baum, J.A.C. 496
Bayard, K. 66
BEA *see* Bureau of Economic Analysis
Beamish, P.W. 46, 48, 80, 83
Beaverstock, J.V. 233, 520, 567, **568**, 575; *see also* Faulconbridge, J.R. *et al.* (2008)
Beijing 253
Beinhocker, E. 131, 137
Belfort, J. 543
Ben Hamida, L. 447
Ben Mahmoud-Jouini, S. *see* Abecassis-Moedas, C. *et al.* (2012)
Bennett, R. 380
Benoy Joseph, W. *see* Javalgi, R.R.G. *et al.* (2011)
Bergmann, L. 137
Bernard, A.B. 65, 66; *et al.* (2015) 28, *29*
Beugelsdijk, S. 157, 182, 213, 221, 233
Beugelsdijk, S. *et al.* (2010) 441
bi-regional firms 81
Bierman, L. *see* Hitt, M.A. *et al.* (2006)
Big Data 320
Big Pharma 319, 321, 327
The Big Short (Lewis) 543
bilingualism *see* language
Binks, M. 379
biotechnology industries 321
Birch, K. *see* MacKinnon, D. *et al.* (2009)
Bird, A. 82
Birkinshaw, J.M. 220, 301, 334, 340; regional economic development 104, 105, 107; *see also* Bresman, H. et al. (1999)
Björkman, I. *see* Minbaeva, D.B. *et al.* (2014a)
black box econometrics 1
Black, D.A. 200
black holes 84
Blank, S. 100
Bleackley, M. 103, 104
Blinder, A.S. 63
Blomström, M. 447
Bloom, J.D. 482, 488
Boddenwyn, J.J. 511; *see also* Picard, J. *et al.* (1998)
Boekema, Frans 318–319
Boggs, J.S. 165–166, 235
bootstrapping hypothesis 368
Borchert, I. 521–522
Borgatti, S.P. 44

Boschma, R. 132, 133, 134, 135, 136, 137–8
Boulding, Kenneth 318
bounded rationality/reliability 85, 86, 130, 318, 479
Boussebaa, M. 521
Boutique Hotel (BH) 497, 498, 501, *502*, 503, 504
Boyden International 569
BPS *see* business and professional services
Braidford, P. *see* Phelps, N. *et al.* (2003)
Braithwaite, J. 355
Brakman, S. *et al.* (2016) 39
branch interdependence 201
branch plant syndrome 216
brands 84
Brandt, L. 156
Braudel, F. 405
Brauer Gault and Co 571
break point 38, *39*
Brenner, N. 348
Breschi, S. 137
Bresman, H. 334, 340; *et al.* (1999) 335
BRIC countries 418, 513
Brisbane 573
Broekel, T. 137
Brouthers, K.D. and L.E. 515
Brown, W. 136
brownfield assets 354, 355
Brunei 36, 37
Buckland-Wright, A. 485
Buckley, P.J. 1, 138, 194, 260, 303, 590; *et al.* (2003) 95; *et al.* (2014) 523; global production networks (GPNs) 155, 289; International Business theory (IB) 180, 185; offshoring/outsourcing 61, **62**; *see also* Johns, J. *et al.* (2015)
Bureau of Economic Analysis (BEA) (United States) 45, 514
Burger King 416, 420n4
Burgoyne, J. 318
business letters 397, 399, 402, 404
business and professional services (BPS) 534–535, 536, 537, 538
business services and networking events 166, 231
business technology platform 326
buyer-driven chains 262
bypassed places 590
Byrne, D. 66

Cairns, G. 260, 264, 288
Calas, M. *see* Jack, G. *et al.* (2008)
Cambodia 37
Cambridge Silicon Radio (CSR) 322
Cambridge (United Kingdom) 322–323
Campling, L. *see* Johns, J. *et al.* (2015)
Canada 37, 201, 416; multinational enterprise (MNE) subsidiaries 100, 101, 103; strategic cities 251, 255
Canina, L. 496
Cantner, U. 137–138
Cantwell, J.A. 97, 456, 487, 488; knowledge transfer 332, 337, 338, 341
capacity development 387
capital markets 61, 486
capital per worker 29
capital projects 345, 350
capital round-tripping 418
capital-intense services 511
capitalism 10, 150, 214, 535, 587, 588; Economic Geography 115–116, 123, 124, 125, 162, 178; evolutionary Economic Geography (EEG) 131, 134; infrastructure 346, 350, 351; regional economic development 223, 228
capture 150
Caribbean 519
Carlier, A. *see* Tenev, S. *et al.* (2003)
Cassi, L. 138
Casson, M. 195, 260
Castellani, D. 457, 471, 516
Castells, Manuel 233, 320
CBMAs *see* cross-border mergers and acquisitions
Cellebrite 321
central place theory 120–121, 299
centralization 15, 85, 299–300; differentiated networks 304, 305, 306, 307, 308, 310–311; financial markets 550–551
CEOs *see* chief executive officers
Chandler, Alfred 64, 301
Chao, M.C.-H. 364
Chaudry, O. *see* Tenev, S. *et al.* (2003)
Chen, C.I. 204
Chen, S. 289
Cheng, J.L.C. 106
Chesbrough, H. 320
Chevassus-Lozza, E. 378, 379, 381
Chewton Glen (hotel) 501, 502
Chicago **515**, 551
chief executive officers (CEOs) 520, 524, 574
China 125, 156, 178, 322, 354, 575; advanced producer services (APS) 519, 522, 567; cities and city regions 236, 251; differentiated networks 286, 288; foreign direct investment (FDI) 420n6–8, 516; location 197, 200, 201, 204, 379, 388; retail industry 480, 483, 486; space 34, 36, 37, 39, 41; spillover effects 447; translocalism 532, 534, 539
Chisholm, George 116
Christopher Tilly and Associates 571
Chung, W. 201
Ciabuschi, F. 220
cities and city regions 13–14, 16, 17, 585, 589, 591; advanced producer services (APS) **515**, 519; Economic Geography (EG) 227, 228–231, 232–235, 238; executive search firms 569, 571, 572, 573, 575; financial centres 544,

550, 551, 557, 573; foreign direct investment (FDI) 191, 196, 200, 201, 428; infrastructure 345, 346, 348, 349, 353, 356; International Business theory (IB) 227–231, 233, 235, 238; language 397–8, 401–403, 405, 407; location 6–7, 378, 380, 382; urban economics (UB) 227, 228–230, 235, 236–238; *see also* regional economic development; strategic cities
Clegg, J. *see* Buckley, P.J. *et al.* (2003)
click-bait 320
client relational capital 518
cluster dynamics 2, 3, 9, 582, 587, 589, 592–593; advanced producer services (APS) 243–244; cities and city regions 228, 230; differentiated networks 301, 302, 304; emerging-economy multinational enterprises (EMNEs) 359, 368; evolutionary Economic Geography (EEG) 135, 137, 181; executive search firms 572; global production networks (GPNs) 148, 287; International Business theory (IB) 214, 220; knowledge transfer 339–340, 454–455, 456–457, 466, 469, 471; knowledge-based view 319, 320, 321; location 191, 195–6, 201, 379, 381, 444, 446, 448; regional economic development 214, 220; relationality 161, 165, 166, 167, 168; retail industry 488; spatiality 39, 41
co-location 8, 166–167, 195, 196, 321, 551
Coase, Ronald H. 347, 584
Cochrane, A. 222
Coe, N.M. 215–216, 223, 288, 581; *et al.* (2008) 235; networks and alliances (N&As) 52, 53–54, 55, 56; retail industry 480, 483, 486, 487
Coeurderoy, R. 204
cognitive lock-in (common worldview) 136
Cohen, W.M. 321
Cohendet, P. 167
collaboration *see* networks and alliances (N&As)
Collinson, S. 79, 85
commercial geography 116–117, 119
Commodity Chains and Global Capitalism (Gereffi and Korceniewiecz) 148
commodity production/chains 148, 550, 582; Economic Geography 115, 117, 123, 124
communications *see* information and communication technology
communities of practice 318
competencies: multinational enterprise (MNE) subsidiaries 98, 103–104, 219, 333, 336–338
competition and competitive advantage 581–582, 583–584, 585, 589, 592, 593; advanced producer services (APS) 513, 514, 518; cities and city regions 229; differentiated networks 299, 300, *305*, 309, 310; emerging-economy multinational enterprises (EMNEs) 360, 368; executive search firms 568; financial markets 548, 554, *555*; foreign direct investment (FDI) 410, 412, 413, 414, 417, 419; global production networks (GPNs) 152, 216; host/home location 441–449; hotel and tourism industry 501; imperfect competition 38, 64, 194; innovation 496; knowledge transfer 332, 333, 335, 341, 456; location 18–19, 194, 195, 200, 207, 378–379, 384, 389; networks and alliances (N&As) 43, 46–47, 48, 49, 54; offshoring/outsourcing 65, 70; ownership 443–444, 445; regional economic development 135, 220; retail industry 484; selection 136–137, 138; service values matrix 245–6; spatiality 29; translocalism 532, 537, 539, 540; transnational corporations (TNCs) 179, 181, 183
The Competitive Advantage of Nations (Porter) 9, 227
competitive subsidiary dynamics 102
complementarity 47, 157, 538, 584
complex systems 157, 342, 355, 549, 557, 586; differentiated networks 299, 300, 302, *305*, 307, 308; evolutionary Economic Geography (EEG) 131, 137
computer hardware industries 66
connectivity/connectedness 235, 301
construction industries 156
consumption and consumerism 54, 83, 97, 493, 559–560, 583; advanced producer services (APS) 518–519, 521; global production networks (GPNs) 152, 155; infrastructure 348; translocalism 532, 533–534, 538, 539
contract law 552, *553*, 554, *555*, 556, 558–560
Contractor, F.J. 287, 339; *et al.* (2010) 155
contributors 84, 108
Cook, G. *see* Johns, J. *et al.* (2015)
Cooke, P. 320
cooperation 501; executive search firms 573, 574; networks and alliances (N&As) 43, 44; subsidiary dynamics 102, 103
coordination 52, 557, 572–576
Cordiner King 569
CORE database 45
'core' model of geographical economics 28, 38
Cornerstone Sydney 571
corporate culture change 318
corporate inversion (taxation) 416, 419
corporate learning 15, 487, 516, 583; foreign direct investment (FDI) 427, 430; knowledge flows 317, 318–320
corporate strategy 156, 181, 186, 206
corporate tax 414
Corredoira, R.A. 287
cosmetics industry 79
cost-capability ratios 152
Country House Hotels (CHHs) 497–498
country specific assets (CSA) 15, 479, 584; differentiated networks 303–304, *305*; location 445, 446, 448–449

Covidien 416
Cowan, R. 137
The Creative Class (Florida) 235
creative destruction model 130
Critical Perspectives in International Business 5, 590
critical realism 119, 213, 214, 545, 588
Croatia 37
cross-border mergers and acquisitions (CBMAs) 16–17, 45, 64, 178, 493, 550; advanced producer services (APS) 509, 522; differentiated networks 302, 310; innovation 459–460, **470**; emerging-economy multinational enterprises (EMNEs) 358–359, 360-365, **366–367**, 368, **369–371**
crossover knowledge flows 321
Crown and Marks 571, 572
CSA *see* country specific assets
Csikszentmihályi, Mihály 320
Cudworth, K. *see* Lowe, M.S. *et al.* (2012)
cultural distance 434–435, 558, 589; advanced producer services (APS) 513, 516, 519, 520–521, 523–524; differentiated networks 297, 307, 310; regional economic development 96, 97, 100
Cumbers, A. *see* MacKinnon, D. *et al.* (2009); Pike, A. *et al.* (2016)
Currah, A. 486, 487
Currie, F. 432
Cutler, A.C. 355
cybersecurity 321, 325–326
Cyert, R. 138, 318, 547
Czaban, L., *see also* Sinkovics, N. *et al.* (2015)

Dahl, M.S. 385
Dalsace, F. **67**
dark pools 325–326
Darwinian model of evolution 130–131
Das, T.K. 44
data analytics 320
'data reduction' methodology 246
Datanomic 323
Datta, D.K. 520
Davis, G.F. 545
Dawley, S. *see* Pike, A. *et al.* (2016)
Dawson, John 478, 480, 486
DDC *see* direct domestic contribution
De Geus, Arie 318
De Jager and Associates 569, 571
De Marchi, V. 155, 157, 259
de Vaal, A. 448
De Vaan, M. 138
Death and Life of Great American Cities (Jacobs) 345
decentralization 45, 120, 184, 328, 522; financial markets 550–551
decision-making models 206, 218
decoupling 154
Dedrick, J. 157
deep integration schemes 97
DeepMind 323
deindustrialization 121
Deleuze thinking 217
Delios, A. 83, 197
delivery times 63
Dell 322
Dell'Era, C. *see* Abecassis-Moedas, C. *et al.* (2012)
Dellestrand, H. 220
Denicolai, S. 65
Denmark 303
department stores 484
Desai, M.A. 45
design localisation/distribution 529, 532–533, 535, 537–540
developed economy multinational enterprises (DMNEs) 7, 124, 339, 550, 592; advanced producer services 513, 514, 522, 523; cross-border mergers and acquisitions (CBMAs) 358, 360, 362, 364, **369**; foreign direct investment (FDI) 410, 412–414, **415**, 417, 418, 419; International Business theory (IB) 262–263; location 191, 195
developing economies 7, 72, 339, 360, 448; financial markets 550, 551; foreign direct investment (FDI) 410, 417; global production networks (GPNs) 156, 261
Dhanaraj, C. 82, 83
Di Guardo, M.C. 52
Di Maria, E. 155, 157, 259
Diamond model 9, 287, 378, 444, 447–448
Díaz-Mora, C. 66, **69**, 70
Dicken, Peter 7–8, 9, 227, 288, 513; International Business theory (IB) 178, 185, 214; knowledge-based view 322, 323; networks and alliances (N&As) 52, 53–54, 55; *see also* Coe, N.M. *et al.* (2008)
differentiated networks 15, 586; Economic Geography and 297–304, *305*, 306, *307*, 308–310; global value chains (GVCs) 310–11; hotel industry 493–497, *498*, 499, **500**, 501, *502*
DiMaggio, P. 5
Dimanche, F. 501
direct domestic contribution (DDC) 35
direct ownership 178
disintermediation 546
disruptive subsidiary dynamics 102, 103
distance 11, 222, 297, 302, 320, 478–479; embeddedness 427, 433–436; innovation 466, *467*, 468; regional economic development 96, 97, 100
distributed design processes 540
distribution networks 302, 307–308
diverse economies 115, 125
diversification 133, 365

DMNEs *see* developed economy multinational enterprises
Dollimore, D. 130, 138
domestic markets 29, 30, 35, 36
domestic sales 82
double-loop learning 318
Douglas, S.P. 82–83
Douglas Walker 571
Dow Jones Index 165
Doz, Y.L. 83
Drahos, P. 355
Drazin, R. 300
Driffield, N. 332–333, 336, 337, 338, 339, 340, 342
dual headquarter strategy 253
Duerr, E. *see* Albaum, G. *et al.* (2005)
Dunning, J.H. 8, 15, 320, 341, 479; alliance capitalism 10, 228, 587; *et al.* (2007) 80, 194–195, 218, 221; *see also* Eclectic Paradigm
Durand, C. 484
Duranton, G. 136
Dyer, J.H. 46, 52
dynamic capabilities approach 105, 516, 549, 584
dynamism 122, 123

East Asia 41, 185, **370**
Easterby-Smith, M. 318
Eclectic Paradigm 1, 6, 9, 13, 20, 584; advanced producer services (APS) 243, 514, **568**, 575; cities and city regions 227, 230, 243; competition 442–443, 444, 445, 447, 449; foreign direct investment (FDI) 194, 412, 413, 430; innovation 465; International Business theory (IB) 180, 181, 182, 185, 287; regional economic development 218, 220, 221; retail industry 478; translocalism 530, 531, 539; *see also* Dunning, J.H.
economic activity 3, 352, 583; diversity of practice 124, 125; unequal spatial distribution 27
economic development 124–125
economic distance 97, 166, 302, 307, 310
Economic Geography (EG) 35–9, 147, 383, 430, 545; cities and city regions 227, 228–231, 232–235, 238; commercial and regional geography 116–117; competition and competitive advantage 441, 443; current research programme 115–116, 120–125, 587–588; differentiated networks 297–304, *305*, 306, *307*, 308–310; International Business theory (IB) and 221–223, 581, 582, 583; key schools of thought 11–12; knowledge-based view 317; methodological diversity 119; regional economic development 213–217; relationality 165–166; retail industry 480–481, *482*, 483–488; spatial science and 117–119
Economic Geography (Finch and Whitbeck) 117
Economic Geography (journal) 8
economic restructuring 61
economic sociology 121
economic theory 346–347
economies of scale 38, 83
ECT *see* evolutionary complexity theory
Eddleston, K.A. 83
Edinburgh 551
EEG *see* evolutionary Economic Geography
Egelhoff, W.G. 86–87, 301
Egon Zehnder 569
Elango, B. 83
Electrolux 538–539
electronics and electrical industries 83, 95, 179, 287, 538–539; offshoring/outsourcing 60, 61, 66
Elia, S. *see* Albertoni, F. *et al.* (2015); Buckley, P.J. *et al.* (2014)
embeddedness 3, 7, 18; advanced producer services (APS) 516; differentiated networks 301, 302, 303, 304, 309; distance and 432, 433–436; financial markets 544; global production networks (GPNs) 54, 150, 154, 157, 214; International Business theory (IB) 177, 185, 582, 586–587, 589, 590, 592; knowledge transfer 333, 334, 342, 455; knowledge-based view 324–325; location and 197, 383, 384–385, 386–387, 389, 427–433; regional economic development 88, 219, 220, 222, 223, 386–387; relationality 161, 162–163, 166, 167, 170; retail industry 480, **481**, *482*, 483, 488; translocalism 532, 534, 536, 538
emerging-economy multinational enterprises (EMNEs) 3, 4, 5, 582, 592, 593; advanced producer services (APS) 513, 514, 521, 522–523, 524; cities and city regions 235, 238; foreign direct investment (FDI) 17–18, 410, 412, 413–414, **415**, 418; geographic orientation/non-home region 16, 358–360, 368, **369–371**, 372n1; global production networks (GPNs) 156, 261; innovation **468–469**, 471, 472; institutional environment 359, 360–365, **366–367**; International Business theory (IB) 287, 289; location 379, 445, 446; patents **468–469**
Emirbayer, M. 163
EMNEs *see* emerging-economy multinational enterprises (EMNEs)
employment contracts: financial markets 553–554, *555*, 556
The End of Capitalism (As We Knew It) (Gibson-Graham) 125
The End of Globalization: Why Global Strategy is a Myth and How to Profit from the Realities of Regional Markets (Rugman) 79
Enderwick, P. 63
Endo Health Solutions 416

endogenous growth theory 230
Eng, T.-Y. 286
EngineCo 108
enhanced imitation 483
enhancement 150
Enright, M.J. 88
Ensign, P.C. 220
enterprise ecosystems 317, 323–325
enterprise of management 106–107, 108
entrepreneurship 17, 51, 122, 161, 520, 589; hotel and tourism industry 494, 500–501, *502*, 504; knowledge transfer 336–337; knowledge-based view 317, 319, 320–321, 323–324, 326, 327–328; location 377, 378, 383, 384–385, 386–388, 389; regional economic development 87, 88, 103, 105–106, 107, 223; translocalism 535
entry modes 20, 515, 519–520, 523
Environment and Planning A (journal) 8
environmental issues 55–56
Enz, C.A. 496
Eriksson, R. 137
Ernst, D. 288
Erramilli, M.K. 511
Essletzbichler, J. 133, 136, 137
Esslinger, Hartmut 536–537
ethics: financial markets 543–544, 558
Europe 41, 88, **370**, 539; advanced producer services (APS) 522, 523; executive search firms 567, 569, 572, 576; infrastructure 348, 352; multinational enterprise (MNE) subsidiaries 98, 101, 107
European Union (EU) 33, 417, 534; regional economic development 95, 97, 100, 104
Eurostat 513
evolutionary complexity theory (ECT) 321
evolutionary Economic Geography (EEG) 12, 139, 588–589, 592–593; cities and city regions 235–236; Economic Geography 120, 162, 166, 217; evolutionary analysis 131–132; global production networks (GPNs) 152–153; key perspectives 129–131; knowledge-based view 320; path dependence/lock-in 135–136; production and destruction of variety 132–135; self-organization in networks 137–138; silence of selection 136–137
evolutionary economics (EE) 129–131
evolutionary game theory 131
The Executive Grapevine 569–570
executive search firms 21, 564, 567, **568**, 569; internationalization/localization/coordination 572–576; leading executive research firms in Australia **565–566**; world leading retained executive search firms in Australia **570**, **571**; *see also* advanced producer services (APS); labour
Executive Talent 569
exploitation strategies 50
exporting firms 232, 512, 532; location 376, 379, 382, 386; spatality 28, *29*, 30–31; value 31, *32*, 139
'external' embeddedness 480
externalisation theory 261, 262, 537–538, 582
extra-firm networks 150, 165, 184, 216, 481, 487; bargaining **153**, 154

'fabless' design 322
face-to-face interaction 166
Facebook 323, 327
factoryless goods producers (FGPs) 10, 61, 65–66, 70, 72n9
Falkenbach, H. 522
falsificationism 229, 588
fashion 532–533
Faulconbridge, J.R. 167–168, 520, 567, **568**, 575; *et al.* (2008) 243, 244
FCA *see* Financial Conduct Authority (United Kingdom)
FDI *see* foreign direct investment
fDi Markets database (fDi Intelligence) 19, 454, 458–459, *470*, 471
feminist Economic Geography 118, 121, 125, 166
Ferrett, B. 206
Fey, C.F. *see* Minbaeva, D.B. *et al.* (2014a)
FGPs *see* factoryless goods producers
film industry 455–456
final products 38
finance, insurance and real estate business (FIRE) 328
financial capital 56, 351
Financial Conduct Authority (FCA) (United Kingdom) 545
financial markets 123, 152, 354, 589, 590; advanced producer services (APS) 519, 522; culture of 543–544, 556–560; dark pools 325–326; deregulation 61; ecology of 544, 545, 547–549, 556; key concepts 545–547; life of organisations 544–545; morphology of 544, 550–551, 556; norms/conventions 551–552, *553*, 554, *555*, 556, 560; relationality 165, 166; retail industry 485–486; strategic cities 243, 252, 253, 322, 557
financial reporting and disclosure 80–81
financial technology (fintech) 322, 328
Financial Times Ltd 459–460
financialization 152, 262, 590
Finch, Vernor 117
Finland 303, 522
FIRE *see* finance, insurance and real estate business
firm-specific advantages (FSAs): advanced producer services (APS) 514, 516, 521; competition 445, 446, 448, 449; differentiated networks 304, *305*, 306, 308, 309, 310, 311;

locations 190–191, 203, 204, 206, 207, 304; regional economic development 84–85, 86, 96, 102, 218; retail industry 479
firm-specific assets 65, 337, 338, 358, 360, 521
firm-territory nexus 8–9
firms *see* multinational enterprises (MNE)
Fish and Nankivell 571
'flag planting' expansion 486
flagship firms 184, 322, 323, 328
Flamm, K. 61, **62**
Flores, R.G. 204; *et al.* (2013) 80; *see also* Aguilera, R.V. *et al.* (2007)
Florida, R. 234, 235, 319
Flow: The Psychology of Optimal Experience (Csikszentmihályi) 320
flows 550, 583, 584, 589; knowledge-based view 320–1, 323–328, 333–334, 339, 341, 342
Flyer, F. 201
Foley, C.F. Jr. 45
'fondness for known places' 383–384
food and beverage industry 79, 102, 416, 420n4; retail industry 482, 484, 485, 486, 487
footwear industries 61, 63, 66
Ford UK 236
Fordism 118, 121, 122
foreign direct investment (FDI) 4, 18, 354, 361, 530, 534; advanced producer services (APS) 509, 513–514, 516, 520–521, 523, 524; competition 442, 443; conventional motives 412–414; differentiated networks 297, 301–302, 304; embeddedness 427, 429–430, 433–435; firm-specific factors 201, **202**, 203; hotel and tourism industry 503, 504; infrastructure 354, 355; institution-shopping 410, *411*, 412, 413–414, **415**, 416–420, 420n8; interaction of macro-locational/micro-locational/firm-specific factors *203*, 204, **205**, 206–207; International Business theory (IB) 180, 181, 182, 261, 287, 289; knowledge transfer 319, 332–333, 339; location choice 190–1, **192–3**, 194–7, 386, 389, 444–445, 448; micro-location factors 197, **198–199**, 200–201; multinational enterprises (MNE) 79, 80; networks and alliances (N&As) 45, 46; offshoring/outsourcing 60, 61, 62, 71; regional economic development 95, 97, 218; retail industry 478, 485, 488
foreign sales 82, 86, 87
foreign subsidiaries *see* multinational enterprise (MNE) subsidiaries
foreign value-added trade (FVA) 34
foreignness and outsidership 7, 62, 85, 231, 479, 515; differentiated networks 302, 307, 308, 398; embeddedness 433, 434; emerging-economy multinational enterprises (EMNEs) 360, 362; foreign direct investment (FDI) 194, 196, 197, 200, 204; knowledge transfer 336, 340; liability of country foreignness/regional foreignness (LCF/LRF) 85; location and 385
formalization 15, 299, 300, 310–311; differentiated networks 301, 304, 305, 306, 307, 308
Forsans, N. *see* Buckley, P.J. *et al.* (2003)
Forsgren, M. 301, 430, 431, 432
Fort, T.C. 65, 66
Fortune Global 500 rankings 79, 81, 87
forward linkages *35*, 36, 37
Foster, P.C. 44
Fouquet, Gerhard 399
Fourth Industrial Revolution 72
Fowler, C. 137
Foxconn 322
fragmentation 262
France 88
franchising 386, 416
Frankfurt 398, 403, **515**
Frasers Hospitality Group 503
Fratocchi, L. *see* Albertoni, F. *et al.* (2015)
Frederick, S. 286
free trade agreements 85, 95–96, 100, 124
Free Trade Zones 122
Freeman, J. 377, 547, 548, 556
Freeman, S. 521
Frehse, J. 493, 496, 499
French regulation theory 122
Frenken, K. 133, 135, 137
Fried, Y. 183
Friedman, J. 232–233
Friedman, Thomas 78
Frog (electronics company) 536–537
Frost, T.S. 220, 337, 339
FSAs *see* firm-specific advantages
Fugger, Hans Jakob 403
Fugger, Jakob (merchant) 400
Fujita, M. 181; *see also* Dunning, J.H. *et al.* (2007)
Fuller, C. 108, 217
functional lock-in (inter-firm relations) 136
fungibility 336, 360, 362, 368
FVA *see* foreign value-added trade

GAAP FASB 131 Disclosures about Segments of an Enterprise and Related Information (1997) 80
Gabrielsson, M. *see* Vapola, T.J. *et al.* (2010)
Galliano, D. 378, 379, 381
Gamble, J. 480
Gammeltoft, P. 513
Gao, L. *see* Liu, X. *et al.* (2015)
garment industries *see* apparel industries
Garretsen, H. *see* Brakman, S. *et al.* (2016)
GATT *see* General Agreement on Tariffs and Trade
GCCs *see* global commodity chains
GDP *see* gross domestic product
Geddes Parker and Partners 571

General Agreement on Tariffs and Trade (GATT) 97
General Systems Theory 318
Generalized Darwinism 131, 132, 137
geographic economics 38, *39*, 115, 119, 303
geographical distance 87, 436; differentiated networks 297, 302, 304, 305, 307, 310
geographical information systems 326
'geography is dead' thesis 585
George, G. 483
Gereffi, G. 148, 155, 262, 263; International Business theory (IB) 286, 287, 288; outsourcing/offshoring 61, **62**; retail industry 477
Germany 17, 36, 37, 319, 458, 515; integrative and instrumental language learning **406–407**; language 394, 395, 398, 402, 403, 404–405; translocalism 532, 533, 536
Gertler, M. 134, 456
Ghauri, P.N. 61, **62**, 185, 303, 590; *see also* Piekkari, R. *et al.* (2010)
Ghemawat, P. 96, 358
Ghoshal, S. 11, 50–51, 180, 443, 584; differentiated networks 298, 299, 300–301; regional economic development 83, 86, 96, 108
Gibbons, M. 133
Gibson-Graham, J.K. 118, 125
Giddens, A. 164, 587
Gilbert, D.U. 83
Gilley, K.M. 70
Girma, S. 66, **67**
Girod, S. 478
Giroud, A. 286
Giuliani, E. 259, 286, 288
GKR Daulet-Singh 569
Glaeser, E.L. 237
The Global City (Sassen) 233, 242, 253, 254, 255
global city theory 231, 244, 591; foreign direct investment (FDI) 196, 200, *203*, 206
global commodity chains (GCCs) 8, 52; global production networks (GPNs) 148, **149**, 150–151; translocalism 530, 531, 539
Global Competitiveness Report (World Economic Forum (WEF)) 364, **371**
global corporations/firms *see* multinational corporations
global factory 10, 260–261, 289, 582; outsourcing/offshoring 61, **62**, 70
global pipelines 167, 223, 318, 321, 327; innovation 454–457, 466, *467*, 468, 471, 472
global productions networks (GPNs) 2, 6, 10, 12, 20, 147; cities and city regions 235; defining/driving 151–152; dependency 154–155; developing **153**, 154; Economic Geography 8, 118, 581, 582, 591; global commodity chains (GCCs) and 148, **149**, 150–151; networks and alliances (N&As) 52–56, 309, 589; productive points of exchange 155–158; regional economic development 214, 215, 216, 221; relationality 161, 166, 168, 170; strategic coupling 184, 185, 215; translocalism 530, 531, 539
global regions: World Bank 38, **39**
'global shift' 178, 322
Global Shift: Industrial Change in a Turbulent World (Dicken) 7–8, 9
global value chains (GVCs) 4, 6, 7, 179, 581; advanced producer services (APS) 517, 519; differentiated networks 298–299, 301, 304, 306, 308, 310–11; global production networks (GPNs) 148, **149**, 155; knowledge-based view 322, 337, 342; location 203, 207, 446; offshoring/outsourcing 60, 61, 62, 66, 71; offshoring/outsourcing 52–53, 54, 56, 60, 63–65, 72n3; regional economic development 81, 109, 219
'Globalisation and World Cities' (GaWC) 233–234
globalization 11, 138, 242, 328, 396, 532; Economic Geography 121, 124–125, 126, 179; extensive/intensive **246–7**, 248; innovation 496; location 441, 443; multinational enterprises (MNE) 78–84, 89, 97–98; retail industry 478–480, **481**, *482*, 483–488
glocalization 478
Glückler, J. 53, 137, 138
Godfrey, A.B. 63
Goerzen, A. 6, 200, 203, 227, 231
Goffman, Erving 163
Gomez-Lievano, A. *see* Muneepeerakul, R. *et al.* (2013)
goods-related services 535
Google 323, 327, 418
Görg, H. 66, **67**
governance and regulation 122–123, 364, 521–522, 584, 585, 590; financial markets 546, 556–558; global production networks (GPNs) 148, 155, 156, 258; global value chains (GVCs) 7, 262, 263, 264, 286, 288, 289; networks and alliances (N&As) 46, 50, 52, 56; outsourcing/offshoring **62**, 71; regional economic development 85, 217, 218; retail industry 483–485; small and medium-sized enterprises (SMEs) 319
government client relational capital 518
Govindarajan, V. 78, 333, 338, 339–340, 341
Grabher, G. 136, 137, 162
Graf, H. 137–138
Graham, S. 351
Graham Smith Partners 571
Granot, E. *see* Javalgi, R.R.G. *et al.* (2011)
Granovetter, Mark 162, 214, 429, 586–587
The Great Transformation (Polanyi) 162

greenfield subsidiaries 201, 448, 458, 519, 520; knowledge transfer 334, 339
Grissemann, U.S. *et al.* (2013) 495, 501
Gross, A.C. *see* Javalgi, R.R.G. *et al.* (2011)
gross domestic product (GDP) 33, 535
gross exports 34, 36
gross trade flows 33, 34
Grosse, R. *see* Picard, J. *et al.* (1998)
Grossman, G.M. 65, 551
groupthink 196
growth theory 101–102, 220, 230, 231–232
Grunwald, J. 61, **62**
Guerrieri, P. 512
Gugler, P. 446, 447
Guillén, M.F. 516–517
Guler, I. 516–517
Gupta, A. 78
Gupta, A.K. 333, 338, 339–340, 341
GVC/GPN literature 14–15, 258–264, *285*, 287–289, *290*, 291; International Business theory (IB) **265–284**, **286**
GVCs *see* global value chains

Haar, J. 100
Hagedoorn, J. 45, 46, 48
Halbrich, M.B. 511
Halinen, A. 430, 431
Hall, P. 232
Hall, S.J. 520, 567, **568**, 575; *see also* Faulconbridge, J.R. *et al.* (2008)
Hamilton, G.G. 477, 488
Handbook of Commercial Geography (Chisholm) 116
Hannan, M.T. 547, 548, 556
Hannon, P. 380–381
Hardy, J. 432
Harrigan, K.R. 52
Harrison, J.S. 496
Hart, O. 544
Hartshorne, Richard 117
Harvey, David 118, 123, 124, 131
Hassink, Robert 136, 319
Hatani, F. 289
Hatch, N.W. 52
Hausmann, R. *see* Hidalgo, C. *et al.* (2007)
Haveman, H.A. 496
Haworth, N. 286
Hayek, Friedrich 131
headquarters-based (HQ) approach 585, 586; cities and city regions 234, 237; differentiated networks 299, 302, 309; foreign direct investment (FDI) 200, 220; regional economic development 85, 86, 87–88, 100, 103
Hebert, L. 80
Heidrick & Struggles 569
Heinecke, P. 83
Helm, D. 355
Helpman, E. 65, 551
Henderson, J.V. 237
Henderson, R. *see* Jaffe, A. *et al.* (1993)
Henning, M. 133, 136
Hercules Powder Company 106
Herrmann, P. 520
Hess, M. 52, 53–54, 55, 56, 288, 481; *see also* Coe, N.M. *et al.* (2008); Johns, J. *et al.* (2015)
heterogeneity 46, 88; evolutionary Economic Geography (EEG) 132, 133; location 201, 203, 206; space 28, *29*, *30*
Hewlett-Packard (HP) 322, 323
Hidalgo, C. *et al.* (2007) 133
hierarchies: financial markets 548–549, 553, 554, 556, 559, 560
high frequency traders (HFT) 324, 325–326
high income workers 122
high-tech industries 184, 253–254, 326
Hikmet, T.K. 63
Hines, J.R. 45, 415
Hinrichs, C.C. 482, 488
Hitt, M.A. *et al.* (2006) 518; *see also* Holmes, R.M. *et al.* (2013); Marano, V. *et al.* (2016)
Hodgson, G. 130, 131, 137, 138; *see also* Aldrich, H. *et al.* (2008)
Hoenen, A. 88
Hoffmann, W.H. 49–50, 51
Hofstede Index 520
Hogenbirk, A.E. 95
Holden, N.J. 395
Holl, A. 66, **69**, 70
Holm, U. 301, 430, 431, 432
Holmes, R.M. *et al.* (2013) 364
Home Grown Hotels 502
home-region-oriented firms 81, 82, 83, 84, 89, 215; competition and location 441–449; emerging-economy multinational enterprises (EMNEs) 358, 359, 360, 362, 363, 368; 'home origin' 178, 179
Honeywell Home 101, 103
Hong, J. 201
Hong Kong 253, 420n6, 569
Hood, N. 100, 104
Hoque, K. 495
Hoque, S.F. *see* Alford, M. *et al.* (2017); Sinkovics, N. *et al.* (2015)
horizontal agglomeration 195–196
horizontal s-shaped relationships 307
Horner, R. 170
hospitality sector *see* hotel and tourism industry
host-region-oriented firms 81, 194, 196, 441–449
Hotel Crillon Le Brave 502
Hotel du Vin 501, 502, 503
Hotel Indigo (hotel chain) 503
hotel and tourism industry 20, 589; innovation 493–497, *498*, 499, **500**, 501, *502*; international diffusion of new service forms 502–504

household hygiene products 299, 327
Hoyt, W.H. 200
Hsu, C.C. 339
Huang, H. 197, 200
Hull, D. *see* Aldrich, H. *et al.* (2008)
human capital *see* labour
human resource management (HRM) 495
Humphrey, J. 148, 262, 286, 288
Huntington, Ellsworth 116
Hurmelinna-Laukkanen, P. 522
hybrid approach 243–244, 568
Hymer, S.H. 261, 335, 428, 442, 591; cities and city regions 227, 233

Iammarino, S. 133
IB *see* International Business theory
IBM Scotland 107
IDC *see* indirect domestic contribution
IDP *see* investment development path
IE *see* International Economics
IFRS8-Operating Segments (2006) 80
IIC Group/Partners Executive Search Worldwide Group 569, 571, 572
IKEA 81
IMF *see* International Monetary Fund
imperfect competition 38, 64, 194
implementers 84, 108
imports *32*, 37, 139, 228, 232
improvement schemes 125
in situ segmentation 557
INAC Worldwide 571
incremental subsidiary dynamics 102
India 37, 170, 320, 448, 456, 533; advanced producer services (APS) 519, 522, 523, 567; entrepreneurship 379, 388
indirect domestic contribution (IDC) 35
industrial design 534–537
information and communication technology 540; advanced producer services (APS) 513, 519; costs 62, 513; financial markets 547; financialization 123; hotel and tourism industry 495, 496, 497; infrastructure 287, 346, 348, 350, 354; knowledge-based view 322–324; new technologies 27, 61, 63, 82, 234
information economy 320
information processing theories 86
infrastructure 16, 345–347, 356, 380, 389, 585; new modes of financing 353–355; politics of 350–353; role in urban/economic development 347–350
innovation 19, 157, 549, 582, 583, 587, 589; advanced producer services (APS) 518, 522; cities and city regions 231, 234, 235, 236, 237; cross-border investment 457, **458**, 459, *460*, *461*, *462*, *463*, **464**, *465*, *466*; differentiated networks 299, 302, 306; Economic Geography 120, 122, 287; emerging-economy multinational enterprises (EMNEs) **468–469**, 471, 472; hotel industry 493–497, *498*, 499, **500**, 501, *502*; knowledge transfer 332, 337–338, 341; knowledge-based view 317–318, 320, 321–322, 324–325, 326; 'local buzz'/'global pipelines' 454–457, 459, *460–462*, 463, 465, *466*; location 194, 196, 378, 382, 488; patents 457, 458, 459, *466*, *467*, 471–472; regional economic development 65, 105, 214, 219; relationality 161, 162, 166–167, 168, 170; research and development (R&D) 454, 469, ***470***, 471–472; strategic cities 252, 253
input-output linkages/structures 39, 148
insourcing 556
Institute of British Geographers 3, 8
institution-shopping: foreign direct investment (FDI) 412, 413–414, 417, 419; tax havens 410, *411*, **415**, 416, 418, 420n8
institutional distance 158, 191, 222, 364, 435; advanced producer services (APS) 516, 519; differentiated networks 302, 307, 310
institutional governance 122–123
institutions and institutional theory 5, 9, 13; advanced producer services (APS) 513, 521–522; critical perspectives 590, 591, 592, 593; embeddedness 162–163, 166, 431; emerging-economy multinational enterprises (EMNEs) 359, 360–365, **366–367**, **371**; evolutionary Economic Geography (EEG) 134–136, 139; foreign direct investment (FDI) 190; global production networks (GPNs) 151, 287; governance and regulation 483–485; International Business theory (IB) 584, 586, 587; location 190, **192**, 196–197, *203*, 388, 389; regional economic development 215, 221, 354; sub-national institutions 197, *198–199*, 200
integration 64, 83, 88
Integration–Responsiveness (I–R) framework 50–51, 478, 584
Intel 322, 326
intellectual property rights (IPR) 10, 45, 448, 522, 543; outsourcing/offshoring 61, 63, 65
inter-firm networks 150, 177, 184, 216, 481; control/partnership **153**, 154; relationality 166–167, 168, 170, 171
inter-regional flows 39, *40*, 41
inter-subjective scale 167
Intercontinental Hotel Group (IHG) 503
interlocking network model 244–245
intermediate products 38
'internal' embeddedness 480
internal stickiness: knowledge-based view 334
internalization theory 180, 194, 204, 218, 584; International Business theory (IB) 260, 261, 262, 287, 289

International Business theory (IB) 3–9, 413, 581, 582, 583–587; cities and city regions 227–231, 233, 235, 238; emerging-economy multinational enterprises (EMNEs) 287, 289; evolution of 138, 260–261; geographical foundations 177, 178–182, 186; global production networks (GPNs) 155, 156, 158; GVC/GPN literature 261–264, **265–284**, *285*, **286**, 287–289, *290*, 291; location 190–191, 206, 382, 443, 444–445, 446; multinational enterprise (MNE) subsidiaries 219, 220, 221, 223; regional economic development 177, 179, 213, 218–223; relationality 166, 170, 171; retail industry 478–480; spatiality 177, 183–185, 298; translocalism 529–530, 531, 539–540
International Economics (IE) 229
International Monetary Fund (IMF) 165
International New Venture framework 584
International Standard Industrial Classification (ISIC) 510
international trade theory 27
internationalization 11, 17, 41, 84, 259, 532; advanced producer services (APS) 514, **515**, 516–524; differentiated networks 298, 306, *307*, 308, 309, 310, 311; embeddedness 427–428, 429; emerging-economy multinational enterprises (EMNEs) 360, 363, 368; executive search firms 569, **570**, **571**, 572–576; impact of location 376–381, 383, 384, 389; knowledge transfer 335; strategic cities 243, 244; Uppsala 'stages' model 382, 389, 478, 584
Internet of Things/Everything 320, 322, 326, 495
interorganizational learning 47
intra-country institutions 197
intra-firm networks **153**, 177, 182, 216, 481, 487; relationality 165, 166–167, 168
intra-regional flows 39, *40*, 41
investment *see* foreign direct investment (FDI)
investment development path (IDP) 444–445
'invisible hand' concept 131
inward direct investment *see* foreign direct investment (FDI)
Ireland, R.D. 70
Ireland, Republic of 416, 432
ISIC *see* International Standard Industrial Classification
isolating mechanisms 65
isomorphism framework 5, 197, 363, 433
Israel 321, 325
Istanbul 200
IT industries *see* information and communication technology; software and systems design firms
Italianate industrial districts 165
Italy 98, 133, 319, 532; networks and alliances (N&As) 402, 403, 404, 405
ITRI 322

Jack, G. *et al.* (2008) 138
Jacobs, Jane 9, 13, 135, 196, 345; cities and city regions 228, 230, 231–232, 236, 238; externalities 582, 587, 590
Jaffe, A. *et al.* (1993) 137
Jaffer, S. 558
Japan 41, 66, 178, 197, 215–216; knowledge-based view 321, 322; multinational enterprises (MNE) 87, 88, 99, 101
Japanese Ministry of International Trade & Industry (MITI) 66
Jaussaud, J. 88
Javalgi, R.R.G. *et al.* (2011) 522
J.E.G. Raggett and Associates 571
Jensen, J.B. *see* Bernard, A.B. *et al.* (2015)
Jensen, R.J. 335
Jessop, B. 222
Jiang, X. 47
Jimenez, A. 457, 471
Jobs, Steve 536–537
Johannisson, B. 431
Johanson, J. 301, 382, 430, 431
Johns, J. *et al.* (2015) 5, 8, 259
Joines, J.A. 63
joint ventures 346, 386; advanced producer services (APS) 519, 520, 521; knowledge transfer 334, 336; networks and alliances (N&As) 44, 45, 46, 47, 48
joint-stock companies 405
Jonard, R. 137
Jones, A. 168–169
Jones, J. 516
Jones, M. 222
Jonsson, S. 104
Journal of Economic Geography 8, 119, 165–166, 182, 591
Journal of International Business Studies 442
Jung, J. 521

Kafouros, M. *see* Buckley, P.J. *et al.* (2014)
Kale, P. 48–49
Katsikeas, C. 380
Keller, M. 446
Kemeny, T. 133
kernel densities 472–473n4
Kesner, I.F. 106
Ketchen, D.J. Jr. 70
Khan, Z. 286
Khoury, T. *see* Qian, G. *et al.* (2010)
KIBS *see* knowledge-intensive business services
Kilicaslan, Y. **68**, 70
Kim, L. 288
Kimura, F. 66, **67**, 287–288
Kinkel, S. 63
Kirman, A. 131
Klepper, S. 135
Klinger, A. *see* Hidalgo, C. *et al.* (2007)

Knickerbocker, F.T. 194
knowledge coherence 133
knowledge creation 337
knowledge flows 15, 16, 583, 584, 589; corporate learning 320–1, 323–328; knowledge transfer 333–334, 339, 341, 342
knowledge transfer 16, 335, 486–487, 516, 590; absorptive capacity 338–339, 341; foreign direct investment (FDI) 431, 434; knowledge flows 333–334, 339, 341, 342; language 340–341, 403; location 339–340, 448; multinational enterprise (MNE) subsidiaries 332, 336–338; multinational enterprises (MNEs) 335–336
knowledge workers 122
knowledge-based view 15, 64, 219, 427, 513, 582; cities and city regions 228, 230; corporate learning 317, 318–320, 430; differentiated networks 301; evolutionary Economic Geography 134, 138, 139; executive search firms 572–573; global innovation networks 322–323, 454, 455, 456–7, 471; global production networks (GPNs) 150, 155, 287; hotel and tourism industry 501; language and 397, 400, 405, 407; location 195, 386; networks and alliances (N&As) 47, 48; outsourcing and open innovation 317, 321–322; regional economic development 84, 103, 219, 220–221, 223; retail industry 480; spatial proximity 166; translocalism 534, 535
knowledge-capital model 195
knowledge-intensive business services (KIBS) 20, **511–512**, 517, 518, 522, 534; executive search firms 567, 568, 576
Knudsen, T. 131, 137; *see also* Aldrich, H. *et al.* (2008)
Kogler, D. 133
Kogut, B. 299, 333, 339
Koka, B.R. 51
Kokko, A. 447
Kolko, J. 237
Kone 88
Kong, X.X. 286
Koput, K. *see* Powell, W. *et al.* (2005)
Kor, Y.Y. 105
Korea 322
Korn/Ferry 244, 255, 569
Korzeniewicz, M. 148
Kostova, T. 388
Kraemer, K.L. 157
Krajewski, S. 95
Krippner, G. 328
Krueger, A.B. 63
Krugman, Paul 9, 10, 287, 444, 516; Economic Geography 115, 119; spatiality 28, 38
KTA Associates 569
Kudina, A. 83
Kumar, V. 364; *see also* Contractor, F.J. *et al.* (2010)
Kumaraswamy, A. *et al.* (2012) 289
Kundu, S.K. 339; *see also* Contractor, F.J. *et al.* (2010)
Kwong, C.C. 340

Laamanen, T. 231
labour 56, 166, 263, 303, 583, 585; advanced producer services (APS) 517–518, 519, 522; cities and city regions 228, 231, 232, 234–235, 236, 237, 238; Economic Geography 116, 118, 121–122, 482; employment contracts 544, 553–554, *555*, 556, 558–559, 560; foreign direct investment (FDI) 413; infrastructure 348, 354; job mobility 137–138; knowledge-based view 320, 322; location 204, 376, 380, 386, 388; offshoring/outsourcing 63, 65, 70, 72; skill/expertise 546, 557, 559; translocalism 531, 540; *see also* executive search firms
Lahiri, S. 71
Lai, K. 253
Lane, H.W. 479
Langlois, Richard 64, 71
language 17, 340–341, 394–395; *lingua franca* in Early Modern Europe 397, 401–403, 405; linguistic context of Early Modern Europe 396–401, 404, **406–407**, 408
Lassere, P. 87
Latin (language) 395, 396, 397, 399, 400, 401–403
law firms 253–254, 354, 512, 518, 557
Law, J. 164
LCCs *see* local commodity chains
lead firms 54, 55, 178, 184; definition and delimitation/driving of global production networks (GPNs) 151–153; global production networks (GPNs) 147, 150, 155, 156, 157, 158; location 200; offshoring 60, 62–63; outsourcing 60, 64, 65, 66, 70, 71, 72n2;8; regionalization 214, 215, 216
learning organisation/regions 214, 318
Lee, J. 263, 358
Lee, Y.S. 483
Leiblein, M. **67**
Lengyel, B. 137
Lenzi, C. 137
Leonidou, L. 380
Lessard, D. 446
Levi-Faur, David 355
Levinthal, D.A. 321
Levitt, T. 82–83
Lew, Y.K. 286
Lewis, Michael 325, 543
Lexi-Nexis Academic Universe Database 359, 363
LG 322
Li, G.H. 88
Li, L. 83, 85

Li, P.F. 200, 201
Li, P.P. 289
Li, Y. 47
Li, Y.S. 286
licensing 334
Lim, D.S. 358
Lin, S. 67, **68**
Linden, G. 157
Lindsay, V.J. 519
lingua franca (Early Modern Europe) 17, 397, 401–403, 405
'Linkage, Learning and Leverage' (LLL) model 289, 413, 428, 430
Lissoni, F. 137
Liu, X. et al. (2015) 341
LLL *see* linkage-leverage-learning (LLL)
Lobo, J. *see* Muneepeerakul, R. *et al.* (2013)
'local buzz': innovation 454–457, 466, *467*, 468, 471, 472
local commodity chains (LCCs) 531
local production networks (LPNs) 531
localization 39, 104, 120, 529–533, 550; evolutionary Economic Geography (EEG) 134, 135; executive search firms 568, 572–576
location 5–6, 9, 11, 13; advanced producer services (APS) 511, 514, 515; as-dots approach 184; cities and city regions 231, 233–234; competitiveness 18–19; differentiated networks 297, 298, 301–305, 306, 310–311; emerging-economy multinational enterprises (EMNEs) 361, 362, 363, 368; executive search firms **568**, 574; financial markets 551–552, *553*, 554, *555*, 556; firm-specific factors 201, **202**, 203; foreign direct investment (FDI) 190–1, **192–3**, 194–7; global factory **62**; global production networks (GPNs) 147; host/home location competitiveness 441–449; impact on performance/internationalization 375, 376–381, 387–388; interaction of macro-/micro-locational and firm-specific factors *203*, 204, **205**, 206–207; International Business theory (IB) 180, 181, 182, 184, 185, 230–231; knowledge transfer 339–340; micro-location factors 197, **198–199**, 200–201; multinational enterprises (MNEs) 582, 583, 586, 588, 590, 592; regional economic development 216, 217, 218, 219; relationality 166; retail industry 478, 479, 488; translocalism 532, 540
location-boundness (LB) 11, 84, 301, 358, 464, 511; competitiveness 444, 449; regional economic development 98, 100, 102
lock-in 15, 135–136, 328, 557, 587; differentiated networks 305, 306; embeddedness 432, 433; relationality 162, 167
logistics industries 201
Lomi, A. 182
London, City of 14, 230–231, 322; advanced producer services (APS) **515**, 518, 521; financial markets 543, 547, 551, 553, 555; strategic cities 248, 251, 252–253
London School of Economics 119
loophole leverage: foreign direct investment (FDI) 412, 417–418, 419
loose coupling 328
Lorenzen, M. 455–456
Love, J.H. 332–333, 336, 337, 338, 340, 342
low-paid workers 122
Lowe, M.S. 483, 484; *et al.* (2012) 501
LPNs *see* local production networks
Lu, J. *see* Liu, X. *et al.* (2015)
Lundan, S.M. 181, 185, 218, 221, 341; ownership 442–443, 443–444
Lupton, N.C. 46, 48
Luxembourg 36
Luyendijk, J. 543

Ma, X. 197
McCann, M. *see* Beugelsdijk, S. *et al.* (2010)
McCann, P. 182, 213, 218, 220, 221, 479
Macchi, C. 259
McDermott, G.A. 287
McDougall, P.P. 584
McGaughey, S.L. 289
machine tool industries 156
MacKinnon, D. 54, 55, 215; *et al.* (2009) 132, 134, 135; *see also* Phelps, N. *et al.* (2003); Pike, A. *et al.* (2016)
McMaster, R. *see* MacKinnon, D. *et al.* (2009); Pike, A. *et al.* (2016)
MacPherson, A.D. 536
Madhok, A. 51–52
Mahdian, A. *see* Flores, R. *et al.* (2013)
Mahoney, J.T. 105
'make or buy' decision 156
Malaysia 485
Malmaison (hotel chain) 502, 503
Malmberg, A. 8, 135, 167, 431, 455, 456
management: enterprise/competence 106–107, 165, 170, 540
Manceau, D. *see* Abecassis-Moedas, C. *et al.* (2012)
manufacturing firms 97, 201; advanced producer services (APS) 513, 515; offshoring/outsourcing 60–61, **62**, 63–66, **67–69**, 70–71, 72n1;4–5; spatiality 28, 29, 30; translocalism 532, 535, 539
Marano, V. *et al.* (2016) 32
March, J. 138, 318, 547
marginal analysis 386
market density 554–556
market imperative 155–156
market segmentation, hotel industry 493–497, *498*, 499, **500**, 501, *502*

marketing strategies 65, 82, 102–103, 121, 186
marketization 115, 121, 161, 166, liberalization/ deregulation 61, 493; imperfect competition 194; regionalization 96, 97, 170
Marshall, A. 9, 13, 165, cities and city regions 228, 230, 236, 238, 455, 582; evolutionary Economic Geography (EEG) 130, 135; location 190, 195, 196, 444
Martín, O. 220
Martin, R. 9, 132, 135, 136
Martínez-Mora, C. 63
Martins, P.S. 338
Marvin, S. 351
Marxism 118, 123, 125, 229, 348
Maskell, P. 135, 167, 455, 456
Massey, Doreen 118, 131, 216
material resources 115, 123–124
Mathews, J.A. 261, 289
Mattoo, A. 521–522
Mediatek 322
Medtronic 416
Melbourne 569, 571, 572
Meliciani, V. 512, 516
Menghinello, S. 332–333, 337
merchandizing industries 79
merchants (Early Modern Europe) 17, 394, 395, 397–8, 404–405; language 396–397, 399–400, 401–403
Meredith, L. 377
mergers and acquisitions *see* cross-border mergers and acquisitions (CBMAs)
Merino, F. 63
MERIT-CATI database 45
Metcalfe, J. 131, 133
methodological nationalism 182
METI *see* Ministry of Economy, Trade & Industry (Japan)
Mexico City 98, 254–255
Meyer, K. E. 444, 445, 480; *see also* Yang, Q. *et al.* (2008)
Michigan (United States) 536
micro-social agencies 163–164
MicroFocus 323
Microsoft 323, 532
middle income countries 34
migrants 122, 236
Miller, T. *see* Holmes, R.M. *et al.* (2013)
mimetic isomorphism 17, 363, 365, 368
Minbaeva, D.B. *et al.* (2014a) 341
Ministry of Economy, Trade & Industry (METI) (Japan) 66
Mirra, L. 516
Mirza, H. 286
misalignment avoidance: foreign direct investment (FDI) 412, 414, **415**, 416
Mische, A. 163
Mithas, S. 67, **68**
MITI *see* Japanese Ministry of International Trade & Industry
Mittelstaedt, J. *et al.* (2006) 380
Mode I Schumpeterian innovation 493–494, 497
Mokyr, J. *see* Aldrich, H. *et al.* (2008)
monopolistic competition 38
Moore, J. 544
Morgan, Kevin 319
Morgan, N. 380
Morikawa, M. 66
Morozov, E. 319
Morris, N. 558
Morrison, A. 137, 138
Moses, Robert 345
Mounet, J.P. 501
Mowery, D.C. *et al.* (1996) 336
Mudambi, Ram 3, 4, 182, 204, 233, 289; knowledge transfer 337, 338, 455–456; location 444, 445, 448, 479, 480; networks and alliances (N&As) 60, 157; regional economic development 213, 218, 220, 221; *see also* Beugelsdijk, S. *et al.* (2010); Kumaraswamy, A. *et al.* (2012); Yang, Q. *et al.* (2008)
Mukoyama, M. 486
multi-alliance management 49–50
multinational corporations *see* multinational enterprises (MNEs)
multinational enterprise (MNE) subsidiaries 11, 94, 200, 431, 434, 586; differentiated networks 299, 300, 302–303, 308; International Business theory (IB) 219, 220, 221, 223; knowledge transfer 332, 334, 335, 336–338, 341; mimetic isomorphism 363; Penrosean perspective 104–106, *107*, 108, 109; regional economic development 83, 84, 85, 86, 88; regional integration and 95, **96**, 97–98, 99, 100; role dynamics *99*, 100–103, 108; subsidiary competences 98, 103–104
Multinational Enterprises and the Global Economy (Dunning and Lundan) 181
multinational enterprises (MNEs) 11, 138–139, 213, 259, 260, 261; cities and city regions 227, 228–229, 231, 232, 233, 238; differentiated networks 297–304, *305*, 306, *307*, 308–310; International Business theory (IB) 178, 181, 182, 289, 291; knowledge transfer 335–336; location 191, 194–197, 200, 201–204, 206–207; offshoring/outsourcing 60, 61, **62**; regional economic development 78–88, 214, 215, 216, 217, 218, 219, 220, 223; space and 27, 30, *31*, *32*, 33, 34, 39, 41; uneven development 125
multiple embeddedness 480
Muneepeerakul, R. *et al.* (2013) 133
Murdoch, J. 164–165
Murphy, J.T. 167, 168–169, 170

Murray, G. 204
Mutebi, A.M. 485

Nachum, L. 201, 203, 514, 521
Nadvi, K. 286
NAFTA *see* North American Free Trade Agreement
NAICS *see* North American Industry Classification Systems
Narula, R. 444, 445, 480
national responsiveness 83, 84
National Science Foundation 320
national subsidiaries 88, 100
Navarra, P. 338
Neffke, F. 133, 136
negative externalities 347
Nell, P. 88; *see also* Piekkari, R. *et al.* (2010)
Nelson, R. 130, 138
neo-classical trade theory 191, 194
neo-Darwinism 130
neoclassical economics 130, 229
neoliberalism 121, 122, 124, 165, 328, 352
Nestlé 98, 101, 102, 103
Netherlands 95, 486, 515, 555
network embeddedness 54, 162–163, 223, 590; foreign direct investment (FDI) 428, 429, 430–431, 433, 436
network theory of internationalization 17, 382, 389
networks and alliances (N&As) 7, 10, 14, 43–44, 584, 587, 589; advanced producer services (APS) 516, 521, 522–523, 568; alliance portfolios 48–52; data availability and trends 45–46; definitions 44–5; executive search firms 571, 575; financial markets 549, 557; global production networks (GPNs) 52–56, 148, **149**, 150, 151, 157; hotel and tourism industry 494, 500–501, *502*; International Business theory (IB) 261, 263, 287; knowledge transfer 336; language 397, 396, 398, 401–403, 404, 405, 407; location 379, 384, 385, 386, 389, 446; regional economic development 214, 219, 221; retail industry 481, *482*, 483, 488; self-organization 137–138; strategic/global connectivity **250–251**; theoretical perspectives 46–48; 'webs without spiders' 184
Nêveda DaCosta, M.M. 495
new Economic Geography (NEG) 9, 115, 119; International Business theory (IB) 181, 182; spatiality 38, *39*
new institutionalism 134
new internalization theory 84
new regionalism 214
New York 14, 322, 345; advanced producer services (APS) **515**, 518; financial markets 551, 553, 555; strategic cities 248, 251, 252–253
New Zealand 379
Newton, J. 261
Ng, L.F. 516
Nguyen, Q.T.K. 79–80, 83, 84, 85; *see also* Tenev, S. *et al.* (2003)
Nielsen, B.B. 6, 200, 203, 227, 231
Nieves, J. 501
Nigeria 124
Nkomo, S. *see* Jack, G. *et al.* (2008)
Nobel, R. 334, 340; *see also* Bresman, H. *et al.* (1999)
nodes (networks) 44, 550–551
Noe, T. 559
Nohria, N. 298, 299, 300–301
non-excludability 346–247
non-exporting firms 29
non-firm actors 154
non-imitability 497
non-location-boundness (NLB) 11, 84, 301, 337; competition and competitive advantage 446, 479; regional economic development 100, 360, 368
Norman, G. 243
normative integration 299–300, 304–305, 306, 307, 308, 309
North America 88, 103, 523, 552, 569, 576
North American Free Trade Agreement (NAFTA) 95, 97, 104, 255
North American Industry Classification Systems (NAICS) **510**
North, D. 134
North, Douglass 221
Norway 303
Noteboom, B. 133
Novelli, M. 501
Nowlin, E. *see* Mittelstaedt, J. *et al.* (2006)
nursery cities model 136, 237
Nye, J. 530

Ó Huallacháin, B. 201
Odgers Berndtson 569
OECD *see* Organisation for Economic Co-operation and Development
OECD-WTO trade in value-added database 34, 36, 37
OEM-ODM-OBM differentiation 289
The End of Capitalism (As We Knew It) (Gibson-Graham) 118
O'Farrell, P.N. 382
Offe, Claus 350
offshoring 5, 10, 72n4–5, 354, 521; financial markets 558; global factory 60, 61, **62**, 63, 70, 71, 73; global production networks (GPNs) 152, 155
O'Grady, S. 479
Oh, C.H. 79, 81, 82, 358
Ohmae, K. 80
oil exporting nations 36

old-boy networks 568
Ono, Y. 237
open innovation (OI) 320, 324, 326, 327
operating segments 81
operational efficiency 103–104
opportunity identification 386–387
optimal cognitive distance 133
Oracle 323
Organisation for Economic Co-operation and Development (OECD); advanced producer services (APS) 510, 513; innovation 19, 454, 457, **458**, 466, 468, 471
organisational learning 318
organizational and management structures 544–546; diversity 547–548; regionalization 85–88, 216
organizational routines 52
organizational space 183
orthodox regional development theory 381, 389
Osborn, R.N. 48
Osegowitsch, T. 81–82
Oum, S. 287–288
out-performance 548
outsidership *see* foreignness and outsidership
outsourcing 5, 10, 60, 63, 72n1; advanced producer services (APS) 519, 521; determinants of 66, **67–69**, 70, 71; financial markets 546, 549, 556; global factory 61, **62**, 70; global production networks (GPNs) 152, 155; knowledge-based view 317, 321–322; rationale for 64–65
over social embeddedness 383, 432
Oviatt, B.M. 584
Owen-Smith, J. 321, 455; *see also* Powell, W. *et al.* (2005)
ownership 355, 514, 531, **568**, 575; networks and alliances (N&As) **62**, 64
Ownership Location Internalization (OLI) *see* Eclectic Paradigm
Oxley, J.E. *see* Mowery, D.C. *et al.* (1996)

Pacific 41
Paget, E. 501
Pakistan 286
Paladin Labs 416
Palo Alto 251, 253–254, 518
Pananond, P. 286, 287
Panitz, R. 138
PANYNJ *see* Port Authority of New York and New Jersey
parallel markets 253
Pardo, R. **69**, 70
Pareto optimality 552
Parkhe, A. 43, 52
Parmigiani, A. 44
Parnreiter, C. 254
part-timeism 122
partnerships 549; executive search firms 569, 573, 574, 575; global production networks (GPNs) **153**, 154; networks and alliances (N&As) 44, 45, 48, 51
patents 19, 334, 448, 534; emerging-economy multinational enterprises (EMNEs) **468–469**; innovation 457, 458, 459, *466*, *467*, 471–472; regional economic development *460–463*, **464**, 465
path dependence 12, 135–136, 179, 204, 235, 560; knowledge-based view 319, 327, 334, 337, 342; retail industry 478, 485; translocalism 532, 539
Paukku, M. *see* Vapola, T.J. *et al.* (2010)
payment-for-performance 559
PCI Executive Search 569
Pearce, R. 302–303, 305
Peck, J. 134
pecking orders 548–549, 553, 554, 556, 559, 560
Pedersen, T. *see* Contractor, F.J. *et al.* (2010); Minbaeva, D.B. *et al.* (2014a)
Peltokorpi, V. 340
Peltonen, T. *see* Jack, G. *et al.* (2008)
Peng, M.W. *see* Qian, G. *et al.* (2010)
Penrose, E.T. 11, 104–106, *107*, 108, 109, 586
Pentecost, E. 206
perfect integration 358
performance 51, 64, 70, 170, 338, 587; embeddedness 429, 435, 592; financial markets 554, 559; impact of location 375, 376–381, 384, 387–388; regional economic development 83–84, 86
performative agency 168
Perry, A. 511
Perry, M. *see* Yeung, H.W. *et al.* (2001)
Perth 571, 572
Peters, M. 497
Petrofina 104
Petrovic, M. 477, 488
Peyton Young, H. 559
pharmaceuticals 79, 170, 416, 448; knowledge-based view 319, 321, 322, 327; offshoring/outsourcing 61, 66; regional economic development 97, 100
Phelps, N.A. 108, 217; *et al.* (2003) 432
Phene, A. 219
Philippines 519
Picard, J. *et al.* (1998) 87
Piekkari, R. *et al.* (2010) 88
Pietrobelli, C. 286, 288
The Pig (hotel) 502
Pike, A. *et al.* (2016) 132; *see also* MacKinnon, D. *et al.* (2009)
Pikkemaat, B. 497, 501; *see also* Grissemann, U.S. *et al.* (2013)
Pisano, G. *see* Teece, D. *et al.* (1997)
Piscitello, L. 448; *see also* Albertoni, F. *et al.* (2015)

Pittsburgh (United States) 319
place *see* location
place-based consumer cultures 533–534
place-dependency 135
Platinum Database (Thomson Financial Security Data Corporation (SDC)) 359, 363
Plummer, P. 137
Poland 197
Polanyi, K. 162, 429
Polanyi, Michael 320
political economy 118, 126, 214, 223, 231; evolutionary Economic Geography (EEG) 131, 132; global productions networks (GPNs) 152, 154; infrastructure 346
political lock-in 136
Ponte, S. 155, 157, 259
Poon, J. *see* Yeung, H.W. *et al.* (2001)
populations: selection 136–137
Porath Executive Search 569
Port Authority of New York and New Jersey (PANYNJ) 345
Porter, Michael 9, 227; competitiveness 443, 445; Diamond model 287, 378, 444, 447–448; International Business theory (IB) 178–179, 181
portfolio alliance management 44, 48, 49, 50–51, 52
positivism 117, 119, 588, 590
'postsocial' knowledge flows 317, 325–326
poststructuralism 118, 121, 125, 166, 588; regional economic development 213–214, 217
Potter, A. 135
Powell, W.W. 5, 321, 455; *et al.* (2005) 137
power relations 3, 10, 55, 150, 298, 586; International Business theory (IB) 260, 261; outsourcing/offshoring 65, 71; regional economic development 215, 216
practice-oriented thinking 168, **169**, 170–171
Prahalad, C.K. 83
preadaptation 321
Prescott, J.E. 51
principal component analysis (PCA) 364
private service sector 510
privatisation 352–354, 355–356
proactiveness 52
Procter & Gamble (P&G) 108, 327
producer services *see* advanced producer services (APS)
producer-consumer services 243
producer-driven chains 262
product localisation 532–533
product mandate subsidiaries (PM) 303
production costs 65
productivity 29, 30, 302, 352, 441; cities and city regions 236–237, 238; knowledge transfer 336, 338, 342
products and production systems 45, 95, 181, 229, 288, 320; differentiation 201, 203; labour and 121–12; life cycle 194, 236; networks and alliances (N&As) 53–54, 55, 147, 150, 303; space and 27, 33, 34; translocalism 532–533, 540; variety 133
professional service firms (PSFs) *see* advanced producer services (APS); executive search firms
property rights 346, 353
protectionism 95, 436
proximity (geographic/spatial/relational) 53, 321, 363, 521, 587; differentiated networks 302, 304, 306, 307, 311; foreign direct investment (FDI) 434, 435; innovation 456, 466
proximity-concentration hypothesis 195, 201, 220
psychic distance paradox 478–479
public good 346–347, 353
public service sector 510
public-private partnership 355
Puga, D. 136
purchasing 186

Qian, G. 85; *et al.* (2010) 83
Qian, Z. *see* Qian, G. *et al.* (2010)
Qualcomm 322
quality control 63
quantitative/qualitative methodology 117, 119
quaternary economy 15, 317, 328
Quatraro, F. 133
Qubbaj, M. *see* Muneepeerakul, R. *et al.* (2013)
The Quest for Global Dominance (Govindarajan and Gupta) 78

Rabbiosi, L. 448
Rabellotti, R. 286, 288
Radbone, I. 200
radical Economic Geography 121
Ragozzino, R. 47–48
Rajan, R. 548
Ralston, D.A. 43, 52
Rama, R. **69**, 70
Ramasamy, B. 515
Ramirez-Pasillas, M. 431
Ramu, S.C. 286
Rantisi, N.M. 165–166, 235
Rasciute, S. 206
Rasheed, A. 70
Rasiah, R. 287–288
rationalization programs 100, 101, 103, 586
rationalized product subsidiary (RPS) 303, 308
Rauch, J.E. 237
RBV *see* resource-based view (RBV)
re-imported domestic value-added content of exports (RIM) 35
re-intermediation 546, 556–557

real estate investments 522
recession 32
reciprocal knowledge transfer 335
Reckwitz, A. 168
recombinant innovation 15, 321
recontracting 64
recoupling 154
Reddin Partners 571
Redding, S.J. *see* Bernard, A.B. *et al.* (2015)
regional competitiveness theory 381–382
regional economic development 13, 16, 17, 135; differentiated networks 302, 306, 309, 310; Economic Geography 213–217, 488; financial markets 550; foreign direct investment (FDI) 194; global production networks (GPNs) 154; International Business theory (IB) 582, 583, 586, 590, 592, 213, 218–223; knowledge-based view 317, 319; location and 381–382, 386–387, 389; networks and alliances (N&As) 54; patents *460–463*, ***465***; relationality 161, 165, 166, 167, 170; spatiality 177, 179; *see also* cities and city regions
regional Economic Geography 116–117
regional headquarters (RHQs) 87–88
Regional Innovation Dataset (REGPAT) (Organisation for Economic Co-operation and Development (OECD)) 19, 454, 457, **458**, 466, 468, 471
regional innovation systems (RIS) 214, 317, 323–325, 327
regional integration schemes 85; multinational enterprise (MNE) subsidiaries 94, 95, **96**, 97–98, 99, 100, 109
regional management centres (RMCs) 88
regional resilience 123
regional specific advantage (RSA) 304, *305*
The Regional World (Storper) 234
regionalization: emerging-economy multinational enterprises (EMNEs) 359–360, 362–363, 368, **369–371**; evolutionary Economic Geography 120; multinational enterprises (MNE) 78–88, 436
REGPAT *see* Regional Innovation Dataset
regulation *see* governance and regulation
Reid, N. 201
Reiffenstein, T. 253–254
Reilly, K.T. *see* Buckley, P.J. *et al.* (2003)
related party trade 30, 32, 33
relational capital/assets 234, 518
relational proximity 12, 166–168, 170, 288, 435, 456
relationality 2, 12–13, 17, 133, 585, 586, 587; cities and city regions 235–236; institutional and network embeddedness 161, 162–163, 166; knowledge-based view 322; location 375; micro-social agencies 163–164; socio-material bases of economic order 164–165; socio-spatial practice 168, *169*, 170–171; spatiality 183–184; 'turn' in Economic Geography 165–166, 170
relationship Economic Geography 309–310, 311
replica plants 95, 101
research and development (R&D) 97, 201, 230, 522; innovation 454, 456, 457, 469, ***470***, 471–472; knowledge transfer 336, 337; partnerships 45; transferability 88
reshoring 63, 72n8
resource-based view (RBV) 7, 9, 17, 229, 584, 593; advanced producer services (APS) 518, 520; emerging-economy multinational enterprises (EMNEs) 359, 368; executive search firms 568; foreign direct investment (FDI) 201, *203*, 434; knowledge transfer 333, 336; location 195, 375–376, 377, 381, 382, 384, 387–388, 389; networks and alliances (N&As) 46–47, 303–304; retail industry 479; social capital 162–163
resource-endowment 50, 53, 178, 297, 523
retail geography 480
retail industry 19, 79, 121, 154, 155, 589–590; Economic Geography (EG) 477, 480–481, *482*, 483–488; International Business theory (IB) 477, 478–480
retention 130, 132, 135–136
Reuer, J.J. 47–48, **67**
reverse knowledge transfer 334, 335, 336, 337, 338, 340–2
reverse spillovers 447, 448, 449
Review of International Political Economy 288
Reynolds, J. 487
RGC Executive 569
Rigby, D. 132, 133, 134, 136, 137
Ringov, D. 335
The Rise of the Network Society (Castells) 233
'rising power' 261
risk 62, 152, 216
Ritala, P. 522
Rivera-Santos, M. 44
RMCs *see* regional management centres
robotics 61, 72
Rodrik, Dani 328, 545
role dynamics: multinational enterprise (MNE) subsidiaries *99*, 100–103, 108
Romer, P.M. 195
Ronen, S. 80
Rose, E.L. 519
Rousseau, D.M. 183
Royal Ahold 486
Royal Geographical Society 3, 8
RPS *see* rationalized product subsidiary
Rugman, A.M. 11, 100, 515–516, 584; differentiated networks 301, 304, 305; location 445, 449; organizational structures 79, 80, 81, 82, 83, 84–87, 89; regional economic development 219, 358; retail industry 478, 479

rural enterprises 377, 378, 380–381, 382, 389, 457
Russell Reynolds 569
Russia 36, 37
Rutten, Roel 318–319

Sack, Bob 180
Safarzynska, K. 131
Sainsbury's 486, 487
Saiz, A. 237
Sako, M. 156, 157, 158n3
Salmador, M.P. *see* Holmes, R.M. *et al.* (2013)
Sammartino, A. 81–82
Samsung 322
Samuelson, Paul A. 346
Sandwell, M. 521
Saranga, H. *see* Kumaraswamy, A. *et al.* (2012)
Sarathy, R. 287
Sarkar, M.B. 51–52
Sassen, S.: cities and city regions 231, 233; strategic cities 242, 244, 252, 253, 254, 255
Saudi Arabia 36, 37
savings aggregators 354, 355
Saviotti, P. 133
SBUs *see* strategic business units
scale (spatial) 589, 590; cities and city regions 228; differentiated networks 297, 298, 301, 305, 306, 310–311; global production networks (GPNs) 150, 157; infrastructure 347, 348; International Business theory (IB) 177, 182, 184, 186; relationality 161, 167, 170
Schaaper, J. 88
Schatzki, T.R. 168
Schilling, M.A. 44
Schlegelmilch, B.B. 87, 334, 340
Schmid, C. 348
Schmitt, A. 288
Schmitz, B. 501
Schmitz, H. 286, 288
Schoenberger, Erica 183, 488
Schön, Donald 318
Schott, P.K. *see* Bernard, A.B. *et al.* (2015)
Schumpeter, J. 130; hotel and tourism industry 493–494, 497, 500; knowledge-based view 324, 325, 327
Scotland 107
Scott, A.J. 5, 227, 234, 235, 348–349
Scott-Kennel, J. 516
SDC database 45
second unbundling 27, 38, 41
sector fixed effects 29
Seetoo, D.H. 88
Segarra-Ciprés, M. 501
segment reporting/disclosure 80–81
selection 130, 132, 133, 135, 136–137
selective capability transfer 486–487
semi-globalisation 358, 478
semiconductor industries 66, 286
Sen, J. 243, 513
Senauer, B. 477
Senge, Peter 318
sensemaking 318
SEPI Foundation 67
service contracts: financial centres 552, *553*, 556, 559–560
service industries 19–20, 79, 122, 551, 592; innovation 493–497, *498*, 499, **500**, 501, *502*
service values matrix 245–246
Services Trade Restrictions Database 522
'Shabby Chic Hotel' (SCH) 497, 498, 501, *502*, 503, 504
Shackleton, R. 487
Shanghai 253
shaping strategies 50
shared economy 497
shared ownership 45
shared values 301
shareholder value 152, 485–486, 559
Shaver, J.M. 201
Shaw, G. *see* Lowe, M.S. *et al.* (2012)
Shaw's (food retailer) 486, 487
Shenkar, O. 80
Sheppard, E. 132, 137
Shi, Y. 201
Shimizu, K. *see* Hitt, M.A. *et al.* (2006)
shipments 28, *29*
Shuen, A. *see* Teece, D. *et al.* (1997)
Shutters, S. *see* Muneepeerakul, R. *et al.* (2013)
signals intelligence (SIGINT) firms 321
Signium International 571, 572
Silicon Valley 1, 253–254, 319, 321, 537
Silverman, B.S. *see* Mowery, D.C. *et al.* (1996)
Simon, H. 547
Simonin, B.L. 334–335
Simula, T. 231
Singapore 87, 102, 569
Singh, H. 46, 48
single-loop feedback 318
Sinkovics, N. *et al.* (2015) 288; *see also* Alford, M. *et al.* (2017)
Sinkovics, R.R. 286; *see also* Johns, J. *et al.* (2015); Sinkovics, N. *et al.* (2015)
skill per worker 29
skill relatedness 133
slack 105–106
Sliwa, M. 260, 264
small and medium-sized enterprises (SMEs): executive search firms 569, 571, 572; knowledge-based view 317, 318, 319, 321, 323, 325, 327–328; location 377, 378, 379, 380, 381
'smartphone/mobile devices' industries 322, 327
SMEA 66
Smeets, R. 448

SMEs *see* small and medium-sized enterprises
smile of value creation 289
Smith, Adam 131, 324, 346, 347, 350, 420
Smith, C. 380
Smith, D. 66
Smith, R.G. 233, 252
Smiths (engineering company) 530
social capital: cities and city regions 233, 235; location 383, 384, 385; relationality 162–163, 166–167
social media 323, 327, 328
social network theories 47
social upgrading 263
social/spatial proximity 137–138, 166–168, *169*, 170, 222
socialization 300, 310–311
societal embeddedness 54, 436, **481**, 590
socio-spatial practice 161, 166, 168, **169**, 170, 587
socioeconomic order 164–165, 229
SoftBank 322
software and systems design firms 320, 322–323, 327, 432, 456, 540
Soho House (hotel) 502, 503
Solvell, O. 431
Sonderegger, P. 287
Song, J. *et al.* (2003) 334
Sony 60, 536, 537
Sørensen, F. 501
Sorenson, O. 385
South Asia 41, 80, 288, 485
South Korea 483, 485
Souto, J.E. 497
spa and health facilities 493–494, 499, 500
Spadafora, E. *see* Marano, V. *et al.* (2016)
Spain 63
Spanish Industrial Companies Survey 70
Spanish Survey on Business Strategies (SEPI Foundation) 67
'spatial allocation of economic activity' 443
spatial embeddedness 430, 436
spatial equilibrium concept 236
spatial externalities 381
spatial segmentation 557
spatiality 352, 455, 494, 583, 588, 591; cities and city regions 228–229, 230, 233, 234, 235; concept of 3–6, 7, 9, 12, 15; Economic Geography 117, 118, 119, 120, 123, 126; financial markets 5, 46–5, 47, 550–551; firm heterogeneity and 28, *29*, *30*; geography and economics 38, *39*; global production networks (GPNs) 34, *35*, *36*, *37*, 38, 157; International Business theory (IB) 180, 181, 182, 183–185, 186, 583; location 204–205; multinational enterprises (MNEs) 27–8, 30, *31*, *32*, 33; production and destruction of variety 132–135; proximity 137–138, 166–168, *169*, 170; regional economic development 218, 222; relationality 137–138, 166–168, *169*, 170; retail industry 478, 479–480; trade flows 32, *33*, 39, ***40***, 41; trade in value-added 28, *33*, 34; translocalism 532, 534, 535, 540; uneven spatial distribution 27, 125, 129
Spencer Stuart 569
Spencer, T. 501
Spickett-Jones, J.G. 286
Spies, J. 517
spillover effects 1, 4, 185, 488, 524, 582; cities and city regions 228, 230; foreign direct investment (FDI) 194, 196; International Business theory (IB) 217, 223; knowledge transfer 335, 336, 455; location 447–449
spinoff model of cluster formation 135, 232, 237
splicing 483
'splintering urbanism' 351
spontaneous order concept 131
SSAs *see* subsidiary-specific advantages
stabilizing strategies 50, 222
'stages' model *see* Uppsala 'stages' model of internationalization
stakeholder-based approach 260, 264, 291
Stam, E. 327–328
Starbucks 417–418
Starck, Philippe 537
state-owned enterprises and utilities 39, 350–351, 354
statistical modelling and analysis 117
Stevens, M.J. 82
stochastic actor-oriented model 138
Stockholm 555
Stone, I. *see* Phelps, N. *et al.* (2003)
Stones International 569
Storper, M. 133, 319, 348–349; cities and city regions 234, 235; innovation 454, 455
Strandskov, J. *see* Albaum, G. *et al.* (2005)
Strange, R. **62**, 65, 155, 261
strategic business units (SBUs) 88
strategic cities 18, 242–243, 322, advanced producer services (APS) 242, 243–244, 247, 254, 255; city-dyad comparisons 251–255; extensive/intensive globalization **246–7**, 248; identification of 248, **249**; interlocking network model 244–245; service values matrix 245–246; strategic/global network connectivity **250–251**; *see also* cities and city regions
strategic coupling: global production networks (GPNs) 150–151, 154, 185, 215–216, 222, 584
Strategic Executive Search 571
strategic fit 427–436, 589
strategic leaders 84, 108
strategic localization 483
strategic management 82
strategic outsourcing 64
strategic presence approach 243, 244, 255

structuration theory 161, 164–165, 587
structure-conduct-performance paradigm 17, 375
Sturgeon, T. 148, 262, 288
Styles, C. 377
sub-national regions 213, 221; institutions 197, *198–199*, 200; locations 190–191, 206, 207n1, 304
Sub-Sahara Africa 41
subcontracting 261
subjective scale 167
subnational spatial heterogeneity 157
subsidiaries *see* multinational enterprise (MNE) subsidiaries
subsidiary evolution 104–106, *107*, 108
subsidiary-specific advantages (SSAs) 479, 483, 584
subunit portfolio perspective 48
Sukpanich, N. 83, 84
Sun Corporation 321
Sun, Q. 204
Sunley, P. 9, 132
superstar firms 31
supply chains 9–10, 317, 351, 353, 382, 517; offshoring/outsourcing 63, 64–65, 71; retail industry 477, 480; spatiality 34, *36*, *37*, 38, 41
sustain point 38, *39*
sustainability 104
Sweden 81, 133, 301, 538, 555
SwiftKey 323
Switzerland 448
Sydney 569, 571, 572, 573, 575
symmetrical (SYM) contracts 552
Szulanski, G. 334, 335

tacit knowledge 487, 503, 534; advanced producer services (APS) 516, 520; innovation 454, 455, 456, 457, 471; knowledge transfer 334, 337, 342
Taiwan 87, 88, 215–216, 322
TAO Group 569
Täube, F. 287
tax havens 410, *411*, **415**, 416, 418, 420n8
taxation 45, 197, 351, 379; foreign direct investment (FDI) 413, 414, 417
Taylor, P.J. 233, 244–245, 515
Taymaz, E. **68**, 70
technological relatedness 133
technology 322; dynamism 300; evolution of 157; transfer of 45, 84, 88, 286, 456
Teece, D. *et al.* (1997) 138, 157
temporality 483, 534, 546–547, 569, 586, 588; Economic Geography 183, 213; embeddedness 429, 431; location 204, 206, 207; outsourcing/offshoring 60, 70; relationality 163, 169
Tenev, S. *et al.* (2003) 197
Teng, B.-S. 44
Ter Wal, A. 138
TerraVina Hotel 502
territorial embeddedness 54, 430, 432; retail industry **481**, 482, 483, 590
territoriality 148, 217
Tesco 483, 485, 486
Thailand 101, 485
Theodore, N. 134
Theory of the Growth of the Firm (Penrose) 105
thick globalisation 328
'third world' countries 251
Thisse, J-F. 181
Thomas, L.D.W. 328
Thompson, E.C. **510**
Thompson Reuter One database 523
Thompson Reuters Platinum Database 521–522
Thomson Financial Security Data Corporation (SDC) 359, 363
'three pillars' theory 5
3M 101, 102, 103
Thrift, N. 1, 348
Thun, E. 156
Tim Hortons (franchise) 416
time space compression 534, 588
time-to-market 152
Tindall, T. 355
Tinguely, X. 446, 448
TMR *see* truncated miniature replicate
TNCs *see* transnational corporations
Tokyo **515**, 569
Tomahawk diagram 38, *39*
Tomiura, E. 66, **68**, 70
Tong, W. 204
Tonino Lamborghini 532
'topological' approach: regional economic development 222, 223
Tornroos, J. 430, 431
Torstila, S. 231
total factor productivity 29
Total Global Strategy: Managing for Worldwide Competitive Advantage (Yip) 78
toy industries 61
Toyota 97–98
tractable scale economies 38
trade fairs 398
trade routes (Early Modern Europe) 397, 396, 398, 401–403, 404, 405
trade and trade agreements 304, 434; barriers 27; fairs 166; flows 32, *33*, 39, ***40***, 41; linkages 34, *35*, 36; tariffs 97, 100, 303, 308, 521, 534; theories 195; in value-added *33*, 34
traders: financial markets 545, 556
Trajtenberg, M. *see* Jaffe, A. *et al.* (1993)
transaction cost economics (TCE) 4, 5, 7, 535, 584, 585; advanced producer services (APS) 514, 515, 519, 520, 524; cities and city regions 229–230; differentiated networks 298, 302, 304, 309; Economic Geography (EG)

178, 181; emerging-economy multinational enterprises (EMNEs) 359, 360; foreign direct investment (FDI) 194, 200, 435; knowledge transfer 333, 335; networks and alliances (N&As) 46, 65, 287; regional economic development 219, 220
Transearch International 571
transfer pricing 417–418, 419
transferability: knowledge-based view 84, 88, 302, 431
transference 483
transition economies 410, 522–523
transition matrix 473n7
translation 164–165, 533
translocalism 20, 529–531; design localisation/ distribution 532–533, 535, 537–540; industrial design 534–537; place-based consumer cultures 533–534
transnational corporations (TNCs) 53, 531; global production networks (GPNs) 147, 155, 158; relationality 167, 168; spatiality 178, 179, 180–182, 183, 184, 185, 186
transnationalism 86
transportation 9, 200, 229, 380, 457, 514; differentiated networks 302, 307–308; infrastructure 346, 348, 349, 350, 352; offshoring/outsourcing 61, 62, 63; spatiality 27, 38
Triguero-Cano, A. 66, **69**
Tripathy, A. *see* Kumaraswamy, A. *et al.* (2012)
Trommetter, M. 133
truncated miniature replicate (TMR) 303, 308
trust 455, 572, 586–587; foreign direct investment (FDI) 434, 435; relationality 166, 167, 170
Tsai, S.P. 495
Tuan, C. 516
Tucker, I. 133
Turkey 70, 321
Tweetdeck 323
Twitter 323

u-shaped relationships 306
Uber 319
ubiquitous presence approach 243, 244, 255
Ucbasaran, D. 379
Uhlenbruck, K. *see* Hitt, M.A. *et al.* (2006)
Uluskan, M. 63
unbundling 27, 38, 41
UNCTAD 61, 147
uneven spatial distribution 27, 124, 170, 229, 583, 590; evolutionary Economic Geography (EEG) 129, 134, 135; International Business theory (IB) 178, 179
Unilever 299
United Kingdom (UK) 97, 322–323, 417–418, 486; advanced producer services (APS) 515, 523; executive search firms 569; financial markets 543, 545, 547, 551, 553, 555; hotel and tourism industry 497–498, 499, 501, 502; spatiality 36, 37
United States (US) 45, 178, 251, 319, 328, 555; advanced producer services (APS) 514, 518, 519, 521; executive search firms 569, 572, 574; foreign direct investment (FDI) 416, 417–418; hotel and tourism industry 502; location 197, 201, 204; offshoring/outsourcing 63, 66, 98; regionalization 87, 100, 101, 103, 216; retail industry 484, 486, 487; space 28, *29*, 33, 36, 37; translocalism 530–531, 536, 537, 539
untraded interdependencies 234
unused productive resources 105–106, 107, 108
upgrading: global value chains (GVCs) 148, 150; International Business theory (IB) 262, 263, 264, 286, 287, 288, 289
Uppsala 'stages' model of internationalization 10, 17, 382, 389, 478, 584
urban economics (UB) 13–14, 135, 206, 297; cities and city regions 227, 228–230, 235, 236–238; foreign direct investment (FDI) 190, 191, 195; location 377, 378, 380, 382, 389
user charges 351
utilities 348, 349, 350, 352, 354–355, 356, 534
Uzzi, B. 431, 432

Vaaler, P.M. *see* Aguilera, R.V. *et al.* (2007); Flores, R. *et al.* (2013)
Vaara, E. 340
Vahlne, J.-E. 382
value capture 154, 156–157
value chains *see* global value chains (GVCs)
value creation 150, 151, 157, 289
value-added trade 29, 28, *33*, 34, *35*, 139
van Biesebroeck, J. 288
Van de Ven, A.H. 300
van den Bergh, J. 131
van Essen, M. *see* Marano, V. *et al.* (2016)
van Kranenburg, H.L. 95
van Oort, F. 133
Vanberg, V. *see* Aldrich, H. *et al.* (2008)
Vanchan, V. 536
vanishing hand hypothesis 64
Vapola, T.J. *et al.* (2010) 50, 51
variety 130, 132–135, 136, 228
Veblen, T. 130, 134
Venables, A.J. 237, 454, 455
Venzin, M. 60
Verbeke, A. 515–516, 584; differentiated networks 301, 305; organizational structures 79, 80, 81, 82, 83, 84–87, 89; regional economic development 219, 358; subsidiary dynamics 100
Verburg, T. 133

Verganti, R. *see* Abecassis-Moedas, C. *et al.* (2012)
Vernon, Raymond 180, 236, 237, 428, 442, 444
vertical agglomeration 196
vertical integration 63–64, 70, 259, 262
vertical specialization 179
Vietnam 197, 236
Vines, D. 558
Visible Hand (Chandler) 64
Vizir 108
Volkswagen 533
von Batenburg, Z. 516

wages 29, 38, 66, 204
Wales 108
Wall Street 165, 252, 322, 325, 326, 543
Wallerstein, Immanuel 124, 148
Walmart 482, 484
Ward Howell International 571
Ward, W. *see* Mittelstaedt, J. *et al.* (2006)
Wasserman, S. 43, 50, 52
Wassmer, U. 48
Watts, H. 135
Watts, Michael 124
The Wealth of Nations (Smith) 346
Webber, M. 132
Weber Location-Production Model 443
WEF *see* World Economic Forum
Wega (electronics company) 536
Weger, C. 501; *see also* Grissemann, U.S. *et al.* (2013)
Wei, Y. *see* Liu, X. *et al.* (2015)
Wei, Y.D. 197, 200
Weick, Karl 318
Wenger, Etienne 169, 318
Wernerfelt, B. 138
Westhead, P. 379
Westney, D.E. 180
Whitaker, J. 67, **68**
Whitbeck, Ray 117
White, D. *see* Powell, W. *et al.* (2005)
White, M. 432
Whitley, Richard 8, 323
Williams, A.M. *see* Lowe, M.S. *et al.* (2012)
Williamson, O.E. 134, 287, 548
Williamson, P. 103, 104
Wilson, D. 131
Wind, Y. 82–83
Winter, S. 130, 138
WIOD *see* World Input-Output Data (WIOD) database (EU-Groningen)
within-firm transactions 30
Wójcik, D. 252
Wolf, J. 86
The Wolf of Wall Street (Belfort) 543
women 122
Wood, P.A. 382
Wood, S. 483, 484, 486, 487
workers: migration 38, *39*
workers of colour 122
workforce *see* labour
working class 121
World Bank 39, **40**, 165, 364, 368
world cities 2, 7, 232–234, 237, 589, 591
The World Cities (Hall) 232
'world cities hypothesis' (Friedman) 232–233
world city network analysis 242, 244–245, 254, 255
World Economic Forum (WEF) 359, 364, **371**, 441
world factory 155
World Input-Output Data (WIOD) database (EU-Groningen) 33
World Investment Report 2013 (UNCTAD) 147
The World is Flat: A History of the Twenty-First Century (Friedman) 78
World search group 571
world systems theory 124, 148
World Trade Organization (WTO): advanced producer services (APS) 519, 521, 522; spatiality 33, 34, *35*, *36*, *37*, 39
World of Yesterday/Today 4
worlds of production 319
Wren, C. 516
Wright, L. 399
Wrigley, N. 480, 483, 484, 486, 487
WTO *see* World Trade Organization
Wu, G. *see* Song, J. *et al.* (2003)
Wu, J. 200
Wymbs, C. 201, 203

Yakova, N. *see* Dunning, J.H. *et al.* (2007)
Yamin, M. 261
Yang, D.Y. 215–216
Yang, Q. *et al.* (2008) 336
Yang, Y. 336, 337, 338, 339, 340, 342
Ye, Z. 432
Yeh, C.H. 204
Yelkur, R. 495
Yeung, Henry 3–4, 5, 215, 223, 581, 591, 593; *et al.* (2001) 87; networks and alliances (N&As) 52, 53, 54, 55, 56
Yeung, M. 515
Yip, George 78, 83
You and Partners Inc 569
Young, S. 100
Yu, C.M. 88
Yu, Q. 204
Yuan, W. 100, 219

Zander, U. 299, 333
Zanfei, A. 457, 471
Zelizer, V. 324

Zhang, L. 200
Zhang, M. 286
Zhao, S.X. 200
Zhao, Z. *see* Brakman, S. *et al.* (2016)
Zieba, M. **511–512**
Zimmerman, Erich 123
Zimmerman, J. 137
Zingales, L. 548
Zucchella, A. 65
Zylberberg, E. 156, 157, 158n3